CONTEMPORARY LEGAL DEBATES

EMERGING TRENDS

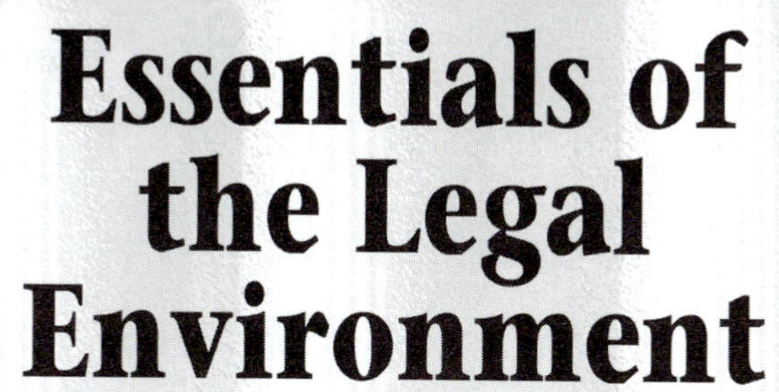

Essentials of the Legal Environment

Roger LeRoy Miller
Institute for University Studies
Arlington, Texas

Frank B. Cross
Herbert D. Kelleher
Centennial Professor in Business Law
University of Texas at Austin

Gaylord A. Jentz
Herbert D. Kelleher
Emeritus Professor in Business Law
University of Texas at Austin

THOMSON
™
SOUTH-WESTERN
WEST

Australia · Canada · Mexico · Singapore · Spain · United Kingdom · United States

WEST

Essentials of the Legal Environment

Roger LeRoy Miller
Institute for University Studies
Arlington, Texas

Frank B. Cross
Herbert D. Kelleher
Centennial Professor in Business Law
University of Texas at Austin

Gaylord A. Jentz
Herbert D. Kelleher
Emeritus Professor in Business Law
University of Texas at Austin

Vice President and Editorial Director:
Jack Calhoun

Vice President and Editor-in-Chief:
George Werthman

Sr. Acquisitions Editor:
Rob Dewey

Sr. Developmental Editor:
Jan Lamar

Marketing Manager:
Steve Silverstein

Production Manager:
Bill Stryker

Media Developmental Editor:
Christine A. Wittmer

Media Production Editor:
Amy Wilson

Manufacturing Coordinator:
Rhonda Utley

Compositor:
Parkwood Composition
New Richmond, WI

Printer:
Transcontinental Printing inc.

Sr. Design Project Manager:
Michelle Kunkler

Internal Designer:
Bill Stryker

Cover Designer:
Paul Neff Design

Printed in Canada
2 3 4 5 07 06 05

For more information contact South-Western, 5191 Natorp Boulevard, Mason, Ohio 45040. Or you can visit our Internet site at:

http://www.westbuslaw.com

Library of Congress Control Number: 2003114096

ISBN 0-324-20365-9

Contents in Brief

Contents

UNIT ONE 1
The Foundations

Preface to the Instructor

The legal environment of business has universal applicability. A student entering virtually any field of business must have at least a passing understanding of the legal environment in order to function in the real world. Additionally, students preparing for a career in accounting, government and political science, economics, and even medicine can fruitfully use much of the information they learn in a legal environment course.

Key Areas of Emphasis

To make sure that instructors and students alike can rely on the coverage, accuracy, and applicability of *Essentials of the Legal Environment,* we emphasize the following elements throughout the text.

E-Commerce

In the last several years, cyberspace has become a normal part of the business environment. For that reason, instead of treating cyberlaw in a separate chapter, we have integrated coverage of Internet law throughout the text. Students will learn how existing laws are being adapted to the online environment with respect to specific topics. They will also be introduced to new legislation that has been necessary to address some of the unique issues posed by e-commerce. In addition, we have included an entire section on e-contracts (in Chapter 11) that focuses on contracting in the electronic environment.

Access to Technology

Just as the content of *Essentials of the Legal Environment* is up to date, so, too, is the manner in which additional resources can be accessed. Every chapter ends with a feature entitled *Law on the Web,* in which students are directed to useful online resources as well as Internet activities that they can perform to explore specific legal sources on the Web. Also, every *Focus on Legal Reasoning* and *Emerging Trends* feature (described below) presented in this text concludes with a brief section that refers students to relevant Web sites.

To facilitate online research efforts by students, every new copy of *Essentials of the Legal Environment* is packaged with a booklet entitled *Online Legal Research Guide.* Additionally, as will be discussed later in this preface, Westlaw® Campus is now available to students using West Legal Studies in Business texts. Qualified adopters of this book also have free access to ten hours on Westlaw®.

Finally, extensive online legal resources keyed to the text are found at the *Essentials of the Legal Environment* Web site at **http://ele.westbuslaw.com** (discussed below).

Ethics and Corporate Accountability

In addition to an extensive discussion of ethics and business decision making in Chapter 4, every unit ends with a *Focus on Ethics*. The *Focus on Ethics* concluding the first unit explores the concept of corporate social responsibility. In subsequent features, we present a number of examples of the interrelationship between ethics and business law. Throughout these features, we emphasize the importance of ethics in business decision making. Additionally, each chapter includes *A Question of Ethics and Social Responsibility* at the end of the *Questions and Case Problems* section.

We have also included special features called *Ethical Issues*. These features, which are closely integrated with the text, open with a question addressing an ethical dimension of the topic being discussed.

The Sarbanes-Oxley Act of 2002. In this text, we include references to the Sarbanes-Oxley Act of 2002 and the corporate scandals that led to the passage of that legislation. For example, Chapter 4, which focuses on ethics and business decision making, contains an entire section examining the deceptive accounting practices of Enron Corporation and the requirements of the Sarbanes-Oxley Act relating to confidential reporting systems. In Chapter 18, we discuss this act in the context of securities law and present an exhibit (Exhibit 18–1) containing some of the key provisions of the act relating to corporate accountability with respect to securities transactions.

Enron Web Project. Available to users of this text, at an additional cost, is a special Web project, entitled *Inside Look,* focusing on Enron. This project can be accessed on the Web at **http://insidelook.westbuslaw.com**. There you will find in-depth articles and expert analysis concerning the events leading to Enron's collapse and the continuing investigation of that company. *Inside Look* provides analysis from all angles by using an interdisciplinary approach emphasizing accounting, business law, and management disciplines.

Critical Thinking and Legal Reasoning

Your students' critical-thinking and legal-reasoning skills will be increased as they work through the numerous pedagogical devices within the book. Questions concluding the *Emerging Trends* and *Focus on Ethics* sections encourage critical thinking about the topics covered in those features.

We have also included a feature, titled *Contemporary Legal Debates,* that is specifically designed to elicit critical thought and discussion concerning controversial issues in today's legal arena. Additionally, the *Focus on Legal Reasoning* features at the end of each unit will help your students develop skills in the areas of legal reasoning and analysis, as well as critical thinking. **Suggested answers to all critical-thinking questions can be found in both the *Instructor's Manual* and the *Answers Manual* that accompany this text.**

International and Comparative Law

Chapter 8 ("International and Comparative Law") helps your students gain a background in the international and comparative aspects of the law, an increasingly important subject. We have also included in selected chapters a section dealing with the international dimensions of the area of law covered in the chapter.

Essentials of the Legal Environment on the Web

When you visit our Web site at **http://ele.westbuslaw.com**, you will find a broad array of teaching/learning resources, including the following:

- Links to selected statutes that have been referenced in the text.
- A continually updated set of new cases, specifically keyed to each chapter in the text.
- A sample answer for each *Case Problem with Sample Answer* (the answers are located in the "Interactive Study Center" on the text's Web site).
- A set of Internet exercises, including at least two exercises for every chapter in the text (located in the "Interactive Study Center").
- Interactive quizzes for every chapter in the text.
- URLs that you and your students can use to access information on topics discussed in *Emerging Trends* features throughout the text (located in the "Interactive Study Center").
- A "Talk to the Authors" feature that allows you and your students to e-mail your questions about *Essentials of the Legal Environment* to the authors.
- Links to other legal resources that are available for free on the Web.

An Effective Case Format

To ensure that *Essentials of the Legal Environment* meets the needs of instructors and students alike, we have devoted significant efforts to finding cases that not only provide on-point illustrations of the principles of law discussed in the text but also are of high interest to students. Our selection includes some classic, landmark cases as well as numerous cases from the early 2000s to provide modern examples of business law.

Basic Case Format

Each case in *Essentials of the Legal Environment* is presented in the following basic format:

- The case title and full case citation (including all parallel citations) are presented at the beginning of each case. When available, a URL for a Web site that includes the case is given.
- An introductory section contains a summary, in the authors' own words, of the events leading up to the lawsuit.
- Following the summary of the background of the case, an excerpt from the actual court opinion is presented—in a contrasting typeface to differentiate it from the surrounding textual material. Whenever the court opinion contains a term or phrase that may be difficult for the student to understand, we provide a brief explanation of the term in brackets. When important phrases and sentences are italicized, bracketed notes clearly indicate that the emphasis was added by the authors, not by the court.

- A concluding section summarizes, in the authors' own words, the outcome of the case.
- Three critical-thinking questions are presented at the end of each case.

Featured Cases

In each of the five units of this text, we present a *Featured Case* that does not include the usual pedagogy—the case background section and the concluding section summarizing the outcome of the case. Instead, only the words of the court are given, including a dissenting opinion. The words of the court are followed by a series of five questions in a section titled "Test Your Comprehension: Case Details."

Other Special Features of This Text

We have included in *Essentials of the Legal Environment* a number of additional pedagogical devices and special features, including those discussed here.

Emerging Trends

Presented throughout this text are several features entitled *Emerging Trends.* These features examine new developments in the legal environment and their potential effect on businesspersons. Here are some examples of these features:

- Mandatory Arbitration in the Employment Context (Chapter 3).
- Employment Issues in the Virtual Workplace (Chapter 14).
- Narrowing the Definition of "Disability" (Chapter 15).

Contemporary Legal Debates

Essentials of the Legal Environment also includes a feature called *Contemporary Legal Debates.* Each feature introduces the student to a controversial issue that is currently being debated within the legal community. A *Where Do You Stand?* section concluding each feature asks the student to identify his or her position on the issue. Some examples of these features are:

- International Jurisdiction and the Internet (Chapter 2).
- Copyright Law versus Free Speech (Chapter 13).
- Environmental Takings (Chapter 16).

Concept Summaries

Whenever key areas of the law need additional emphasis, we provide a *Concept Summary.* These summaries include the following:

- Schools of Jurisprudential Thought (Chapter 1).
- Types of Crimes (Chapter 7).
- Intentional Torts (Chapter 12).

Exhibits

When appropriate, we have illustrated important aspects of the law in graphic or summary form in exhibits. The exhibits featured in *Essentials of the Legal Environment* include the following:

- Civil and Criminal Law Compared (Exhibit 7–1).
- Forms of Intellectual Property (Exhibit 13–1).
- Some Key Provisions of the Sarbanes-Oxley Act of 2002 Relating to Corporate Accountability (Exhibit 18–1).

Questions and Case Problems

Every chapter in this text ends with nine or ten questions and case problems. Normally, the first three to five of these are hypothetical questions. The remainder are actual case problems, many of which are from the early 2000s.

For those instructors who would like students to have sample answers available for some of the case problems, we have included in *Essentials of the Legal Environment* a problem in each chapter entitled *Case Problem with Sample Answer.* This problem directs the student to the "Interactive Study Center" on the text's accompanying Web site (at **http://ele.westbuslaw.com**) for a sample answer to the problem.

Concluding each *Questions and Case Problems* section is a problem entitled *In Your Court.* This problem poses a hypothetical situation and then asks a series of questions that requires the student to engage in legal reasoning and analysis. *A Question of Ethics and Social Responsibility* is also included at the end of the *Questions and Case Problems* section, followed by a *For Critical Analysis* question. **Complete answers for all questions and case problems in the text are given in the *Answers Manual* accompanying this text.**

Special Unit-Ending Materials

Each of the five units in this text concludes with the following special features:

- *Focus on Legal Reasoning*—Just after the final chapter in each unit, we present an extended case study entitled *Focus on Legal Reasoning.* The subtitle of each *Focus* gives the full case title of the case being studied. The feature opens with *Introduction* and *Case Background* sections, which are followed by excerpts from the court's majority and dissenting opinions (including legal sources cited by the court). A series of questions then asks students to perform tasks involving legal research, legal analysis, critical thinking, and case briefing. The feature concludes with a *Going Online* section, in which students are referred to a series of Web sites for further study of the case or the issue it addresses. **Three questions for each *Focus on Legal Reasoning* are included in the *Test Bank.***
- *Focus on Ethics*—Following the *Focus on Legal Reasoning* is a *Focus on Ethics.* This section addresses ethical aspects of the law discussed in the preceding unit. Each section is designed to elicit comments and discussion on ethical issues from the student-readers. For this reason, each *Focus* ends with a set of discussion questions. **Three questions for each *Focus on Ethics* are included in the *Test Bank.***

Appendices

Essentials of the Legal Environment includes the appendices listed below.

A The Constitution of the United States.
B URLs for Selected Statutes Referenced in the Text.

The Supplements Package

Essentials of the Legal Environment is accompanied by a number of teaching and learning supplements. We have already mentioned the supplemental resources available on the *Essentials of the Legal Environment* Web site at **http://ele.westbuslaw.com**, as well as the Enron Web project (*Inside Look*), at **http://insidelook.westbuslaw.com**. In addition, there are other supplements, including those listed below, that make up the complete teaching/learning package. For further information on the *Essentials of the Legal Environment* teaching/learning package, contact your local West sales representative. An additional source of information is our *Essentials of the Legal Environment* Web site.

Printed Supplements

- *Online Legal Research Guide* (packaged with every new copy of the text).
- *Instructor's Manual,* including sections entitled "Additional Cases Addressing This Issue" at the end of selected case synopses.
- A comprehensive *Test Bank,* co-written by text author Roger LeRoy Miller—contains approximately 600 multiple-choice questions with answers, over 600 true-false questions with answers, two or more short essay questions per chapter, two multiple-choice questions for every *Emerging Trends* and *Contemporary Legal Debates* feature, and three multiple-choice questions for each *Focus on Legal Reasoning* and *Focus on Ethics* section.
- *Answers to Questions and Case Problems*—This *Answers Manual* includes answers to all questions presented in the text.

Software and Multimedia Supplements

- ExamView Testing Software.
- Westlaw® (ten free hours on Westlaw available to qualified adopters).
- Video Library (including *Court TV*®, the *Drama of the Law* videos, and West's Digital Video Library). For further information on video supplements, go to **http://videos.westbuslaw.com**.

Westlaw® Campus

Westlaw® Campus is now available to students using West Legal Studies in Business texts. Westlaw Campus is derived from Westlaw, the preferred computer-assisted legal research database of legal professionals. It can be bundled with your text, at an outstanding discount, to every student through a passcode. (Students who buy used books may purchase access to Westlaw Campus at **http://campus.westbuslaw.com**.)

In addition to primary legal materials (federal and state cases, statutes and administrative law), Westlaw Campus offers secondary resources, such as *American Law Reports (ALR), American Jurisprudence 2d (Am.Jur.2d),* and law reviews. These materials can greatly enhance research assignments, critical-thinking exercises, and term papers.

Acknowledgments

We owe a debt of extreme gratitude to the numerous individuals who worked directly with us or at West/South-Western. We especially wish to thank Lavina Leed Miller for her management of the entire project, as well as for the application of her superb editorial skills. William Eric Hollowell, who also coauthored the *Instructor's Manual* and *Test Bank,* helped with much of the research. We were fortunate to have the copyediting services of Suzie Franklin DeFazio. Literally dozens of individuals helped proofread the galleys and pages of this edition. They include Lavina Leed Miller, William Eric Hollowell, Katherine Silsbee, Pat Lewis, and Roxanna Lee. In addition, we thank Suzanne Jasin of K&M Consulting for her many special efforts on this project.

We were the fortunate recipients of an incredibly skilled and dedicated editorial, production, and printing and manufacturing team at West. In particular, we wish to thank Rob Dewey and Jan Lamar for their helpful advice and guidance during all of the stages of this project. Jan Lamar also was instrumental in ensuring that the supplements came out on time. Christine Wittmer and Amy Wilson deserve a special note of appreciation for their incredibly masterful work on the *Essentials of the Legal Environment* home page and just about everything else relating to technology for this text. We are also indebted to Steve Silverstein for his marketing talents.

Our textbook designer and production manager at West, Bill Stryker, provided us with a visually stunning edition and an error-free printing. His ability to turn around our materials quickly amazes us. We appreciate his efforts more than he can ever imagine.

If you wish to comment on this text, please contact us. We welcome all comments and promise to respond promptly. By incorporating your ideas, we can continue to write a legal environment text that is best for you and best for your students.

R. L.M.
F. B.C.
G.A. J.

DEDICATION

To Olivier Privat,
Meeting you was a wonderful event.
Knowing you continues to be eventful.
Stay healthy.
Your friend,
R.L.M.

To my parents and sisters,
F.B.C.

To my wife, JoAnn; my children, Kathy,
Gary, Lori, and Rory; and my grandchildren,
Erin, Megan, Eric, Emily, Michelle, Javier,
Carmen, and Steve.
G.A.J.

Preface to the Student

To fully understand the law with respect to the legal environment of business, you must be able to read and understand court decisions. To make this task easier, you can use a method of case analysis that is called *briefing*. In the first part of this preface, we examine this method and provide you with an example of a briefed sample court case.

Part of the study of the legal environment usually involves analyzing case problems, such as those included in this text at the end of each chapter. Following the discussion of case briefing, we provide instructions and a method of legal analysis and reasoning that you can employ when analyzing a case problem.

Briefing Cases

There is a fairly standard procedure that you can follow when you "brief" any court case. You must first read the case opinion carefully. When you feel you understand the case, you can prepare a brief of it.

Although the format of the brief may vary, typically it will present the essentials of the case under headings such as those listed below.

1. **Citation.** Give the full citation for the case, including the name of the case, the date it was decided, and the court that decided it.
2. **Facts.** Briefly indicate (a) the reasons for the lawsuit; (b) the identity and arguments of the plaintiff(s) and defendant(s), respectively; and (c) the lower court's decision—if appropriate.
3. **Issue.** Concisely phrase, in the form of a question, the essential issue before the court. (If more than one issue is involved, you may have two—or even more—questions here.)
4. **Decision.** Indicate here—with a "yes" or "no," if possible—the court's answer to the question (or questions) in the *Issue* section above.
5. **Reason.** Summarize as briefly as possible the reasons given by the court for its decision (or decisions) and the case or statutory law relied on by the court in arriving at its decision.

An Example of a Briefed Sample Court Case

As an example of the format used in briefing cases, we present here a briefed version of the sample court case that is presented in the appendix following Chapter 1 in Exhibit 1A–3.

WILLIAMS v. DOMINION TECHNOLOGY PARTNERS, L.L.C.
Virginia Supreme Court, 2003.
576 S.E.2d 752.

FACTS Dominion Technology Partners, L.L.C., is an employment firm. When Stihl, Inc., a power-tool manufacturing company, sought a computer consultant to oversee the installation of a new software package on computer systems at Stihl's facilities in Virginia, Dominion recruited Donald Williams as a candidate. Dominion offered Williams an at-will employment contract, which he accepted. In January 1999, Stihl contracted with Dominion to employ Williams for three months. After the installation was complete, Stihl retained Williams in a support and maintenance role for an indefinite period on a monthly basis. More than a year later, Williams indicated that he would prefer to work under a direct agreement with Stihl. In March 2000, Williams resigned as Dominion's employee. In May, Dominion learned that Williams had continued working at Stihl. Dominion filed a suit in a Virginia state court against Williams, alleging breach of fiduciary duty, among other things. The court entered a judgment in Dominion's favor. Williams appealed to the Virginia Supreme Court.

ISSUE Did Williams breach a duty of loyalty to Dominion?

DECISION No. The Virginia Supreme Court reversed the judgment of the lower court and entered a judgment in Williams's favor. The state supreme court held that "an employee has the right to make arrangements during his employment to compete with his employer after resigning his post" unless there is a contract stating otherwise.

REASON The court recognized that an employee "owes a fiduciary duty of loyalty to his employer during his employment. Subsumed within this general duty of loyalty is the more specific duty that the employee not compete with his employer during his employment." The court explained, however, "[T]hat particular conduct of an employee caused harm to his employer does not establish that the conduct breached any duty to the employer. This is so because the law will not provide relief to every disgruntled player in the rough-and-tumble world comprising the competitive marketplace." Without a contract limiting Williams's actions, "it cannot be said that Williams's conduct to safeguard his own interests was either disloyal or unfair to Dominion. * * * [B]y providing reasonable notice of his intent to resign his post * * *, Williams allowed Dominion to receive all the benefits for which it had bargained."

Review of Sample Court Case

Here we provide a review of the briefed version to indicate the kind of information that is contained in each section.

CITATION The name of the case is *Williams v. Dominion Technology Partners, L.L.C.* Williams is the petitioner (in this case, the party appealing the lower court's decision); Dominion is the respondent (in this case, the party responding to the appeal). The Virginia Supreme Court decided this case in 2003. The citation states that this case can be found in volume 576 of the *South Eastern Reporter, Second Series,* on page 752. (An explanation of how to read case citations is provided in the appendix following Chapter 1.)

FACTS The *Facts* section identifies the petitioner and the respondent, describes the events leading up to this suit, the allegations made by the respondent in the initial suit, and (because this case is an appellate court decision) the lower courts' rulings and the party appealing those rulings. The appellant's contention on appeal is also sometimes included here.

ISSUE The *Issue* section presents the central issue (or issues) decided by the court. In this case, the Virginia Supreme Court reviewed the lower court's conclusion that an employee breached a duty of loyalty to an employer. The relevant law includes principles of both contract law (see Chapter 10) and employment law (discussed in Chapter 14).

DECISION The *Decision* section includes the court's decision on the issue before it. The decision reflects the opinion of the majority of the judges or justices hearing the case. Decisions by appellate courts are frequently phrased in reference to the lower court's decision; that is, the appellate court may "affirm" the lower court's ruling or "reverse" it. Here, the state supreme court determined that in the absence of a contract to the contrary, an employee can arrange during employment to compete with his or her employer after resigning. The court reversed the lower court's judgment on this point and entered a judgment in the petitioner's favor.

REASON The *Reason* section includes references to the relevant laws and legal principles that were applied in coming to a conclusion in the case before the court. The relevant law here consisted of contract and employment law principles relating to an employee's duty of loyalty to an employer. This section also explains the court's application of the law to the facts in the case.

Analyzing Case Problems

For each case problem in this book, we provide the relevant background and facts of the lawsuit and the issue before the court. When you are assigned one of these problems, your job will be to determine how the court should decide the issue, and why. In other words, you will need to engage in legal analysis and reasoning. Here we offer some suggestions on how to make this task less daunting. We begin by presenting a sample problem:

> While Janet Lawson, a famous pianist, was shopping in Quality Market, she slipped and fell on a wet floor in one of the aisles. The floor had recently been mopped by one of the store's employees, but there were no signs warning customers that the floor in that area was wet. As a result of the fall, Lawson injured her right arm and was unable to perform piano concerts for the next six months. Had she been able to perform the scheduled concerts, she would have earned approximately $60,000 over that period of time. Lawson sued Quality Market for this amount, plus another $10,000 in medical expenses. She claimed that the store's failure to warn customers of the wet floor constituted negligence and therefore the market was liable for her injuries. Will the court agree with Lawson? Discuss.

Understand the Facts

This may sound obvious, but before you can analyze or apply the relevant law to a specific set of facts, you must clearly understand those facts. In other words, you should read through the case problem carefully and more than once, if necessary, to make sure you understand the identity of the *plaintiff* (the party initiating the suit) and the *defendant* (the party against whom the suit is brought) in the case and the progression of events that led to the lawsuit.

In the sample case just given, the identity of the parties is fairly obvious. Janet Lawson is the one bringing the suit; therefore, she is the plaintiff. Quality Market, against whom she is bringing the suit, is the defendant. Some of the case problems you work on may have multiple plaintiffs or defendants. Often, it is helpful to use abbreviations for the parties. To indicate a reference to a plaintiff, for example, the *pi* symbol—π—is often used, and a defendant is denoted by a *delta*—Δ—a triangle.

The events leading to the lawsuit are also fairly straightforward. Lawson slipped and fell on a wet floor, and she contends that Quality Market should be liable for her injuries because it was negligent in not posting a sign warning customers of the wet floor.

When you are working on case problems, realize that the facts should be accepted as they are given. For example, in our sample problem, it should be accepted that the floor was wet and that there was no sign. In other words, avoid making conjectures, such as "Maybe the floor wasn't too wet," or "Maybe an employee was getting a sign to put up," or "Maybe someone stole the sign." Questioning the facts as they are presented only adds confusion to your analysis.

Legal Analysis and Reasoning

Once you understand the facts given in the case problem, you can begin to analyze the case. In Chapter 1, you will read that the IRAC method is a helpful tool to use in the legal analysis and reasoning process. IRAC is an acronym for *I*ssue, *R*ule, *A*pplication, *C*onclusion. Applying this method to our sample problem would involve the following steps:

1. First, you need to decide what legal **issue** is involved in the case. In our sample case, the basic issue is whether Quality Market's failure to warn customers of the wet floor constituted *negligence.* As discussed in Chapter 12, negligence is a *tort*—a civil wrong. In a tort lawsuit, the plaintiff seeks to be compensated for another's wrongful act. A defendant will be deemed negligent if he or she breached a duty of care owed to the plaintiff and the breach of that duty caused the plaintiff to suffer harm.
2. Once you have identified the issue, the next step is to determine what **rule of law** applies to the issue. To make this determination, you will want to review carefully the text of the chapter in which the problem appears to find the relevant rule of law. Our sample case involves the tort of negligence, covered in Chapter 12. The applicable rule of law is the tort law principle that business owners owe a duty to exercise reasonable care to protect their customers ("business invitees"). Reasonable care, in this context, includes either removing—or warning customers of—*foreseeable* risks about which the owner *knew* or *should have known.* Business owners need not warn customers of "open and obvious" risks, however. If a business owner breaches this duty of care (fails to exercise the appropriate degree of care toward customers), and the breach of duty causes a customer to be injured, the business owner will be liable to the customer for the customer's injuries.
3. The next—and usually the most difficult—step in analyzing case problems is the **application** of the relevant rule of law to the specific facts

of the case you are studying. In our sample problem, applying the tort law principle just discussed presents few difficulties. An employee of the store had mopped the floor in the aisle where Lawson slipped and fell, but no sign was present indicating that the floor was wet. That a customer might fall on a wet floor is clearly a foreseeable risk. Therefore, the failure to warn customers about the wet floor was a breach of the duty of care owed by the business owner to the store's customers.

4. Once you have completed step 3 in the IRAC method, you should be ready to draw your **conclusion.** In our sample case, Quality Market is liable to Lawson for her injuries, because the market's breach of its duty of care caused Lawson's injuries.

The fact patterns in the case problems presented in this text are not always as simple as those demonstrated in our sample problem. Often, for example, as already mentioned, there may be more than one plaintiff or defendant. There also may be more than one issue involved in a case and more than one applicable rule of law. Furthermore, in some case problems the facts may indicate that the general rule of law should not apply. For example, suppose that a store employee advised Lawson not to walk on the floor in the aisle because it was wet, but Lawson decided to walk on it anyway. This fact could alter the outcome of the case because the store could then raise the defense of assumption of risk (see Chapter 12). Nonetheless, a careful review of the chapter should always provide you with the knowledge you need to analyze a problem thoroughly and arrive at accurate conclusions.

UNIT ONE

The Foundations

CHAPTER 1

Business and Its Legal Environment

CONTENTS

CHAPTER OBJECTIVES

After reading this chapter, you should be able to answer the following questions:

1. What is the common law tradition?
2. What is a precedent? When might a court depart from precedent?
3. What is the difference between remedies at law and remedies in equity?
4. What is the Uniform Commercial Code?
5. What are some important differences between civil law and criminal law?

One of the important functions of law in any society is to provide stability, predictability, and continuity so that people can be sure of how to order their affairs. If any society is to survive, its citizens must be able to determine what is legally right and legally wrong. They must know what sanctions will be imposed on them if they commit wrongful acts. If they suffer harm as a result of others' wrongful acts, they need to know how they can seek redress. By setting forth the rights, obligations, and privileges of citizens, the law enables individuals to go about their business with confidence and a certain degree of predictability. The stability and predictability created by the law provide an essential framework for all civilized activities, including business activities.

WHAT IS LAW?

What do we mean when we speak of "the law"? Although this term has had, and will continue to have, different definitions, they are all based on a general observation: at a minimum, **law** consists of *enforceable rules governing relationships among individuals and between individuals and their society.* These "enforceable rules" may consist of unwritten principles of behavior established by a nomadic tribe. They may be set forth in a law code, such as the Code of Hammurabi in ancient Babylon (c. 1780 B.C.E.) or the law code of one of today's European nations. They may consist of written laws and court decisions created by modern legislative and judicial bodies, as in the United States. Regardless of how such rules are created, they all have one thing in common: they establish rights, duties, and privileges that are consistent with the values and beliefs of their society or its ruling group.

Law • A body of enforceable rules governing relationships among individuals and between individuals and their society.

Those who embark on a study of law will find that these broad statements leave unanswered some important questions concerning the nature of law. Part of the study of law, often referred to as **jurisprudence,** involves learning about different schools of jurisprudential thought and discovering how the approaches to law characteristic of each school can affect judicial decision making. We open this introductory chapter with an examination of that topic. We then look at an important question for any student reading this text: How does the legal environment affect business decision making? We

Jurisprudence • The science or philosophy of law.

next describe the basic sources of American law, the common law tradition, and some general classifications of law.

SCHOOLS OF JURISPRUDENTIAL THOUGHT

You may think that legal philosophy is far removed from the practical study of business law and the legal environment. In fact, it is not. As you will learn in the chapters of this text, how judges apply the law to specific disputes, including disputes relating to the business world, depends in part on their philosophical approaches to law.

Clearly, judges are not free to decide cases solely on the basis of their personal philosophical views or their opinions on the issues before the court. A judge's function is not to *make* the laws—that is the function of the legislative branch of government—but to interpret and apply them. From a practical point of view, however, the courts play a significant role in defining what the law is. This is because laws enacted by legislative bodies tend to be expressed in general terms. Judges thus have some flexibility in interpreting and applying the law. It is because of this flexibility that different courts can, and often do, arrive at different conclusions in cases that involve nearly identical issues, facts, and applicable laws. This flexibility also means that each judge's unique personality, legal philosophy, set of values, and intellectual attributes necessarily frame the judicial decision-making process to some extent.

We look now at some of the significant schools of legal, or jurisprudential, thought that have evolved over time.

The Natural Law School

An age-old question about the nature of law has to do with the finality of a nation's laws, such as the laws of the United States at the present time. For example, what if a particular law is deemed to be a "bad" law by a substantial number of that nation's citizens? Must a citizen obey the law if it goes against his or her conscience to do so? Is there a higher or universal law to which individuals can appeal? One who adheres to the natural law tradition would answer this question in the affirmative. **Natural law** denotes a system of moral and ethical principles that are inherent in human nature and that people can discover through the use of their natural intelligence, or reason.

Natural law • The belief that there are universal moral and ethical principles that are inherent in human nature. The natural law school is the oldest and one of the most significant schools of legal thought.

The natural law tradition is one of the oldest and most significant schools of jurisprudence. It dates back to the days of the Greek philosopher Aristotle (384–322 B.C.E.), who distinguished between natural law and the laws governing a particular nation. According to Aristotle, natural law applies universally to all humankind.

The notion that people have "natural rights" stems from the natural law tradition. Those who claim that a specific foreign government is depriving certain citizens of their human rights implicitly are appealing to a higher law that has universal applicability. The question of the universality of basic human rights also comes into play in the context of international business operations. Should rights extended to workers in the United States, such as the right to be free of discrimination in the workplace, be extended to workers employed by a U.S. firm doing business in another country that does not provide for such rights? This question is rooted implicitly in a concept of universal rights that has its origins in the natural law tradition.

The Positivist School

In contrast, **positive law,** or national law (the written law of a given society at a particular point in time), applies only to the citizens of that nation or society. Those who adhere to the **positivist school** believe that there can be no higher law than a nation's positive law. According to the positivist school, there are no "natural rights." Rather, human rights exist solely because of laws. If the laws are not enforced, anarchy will result. Thus, whether a law is "bad" or "good" is irrelevant. The law is the law and must be obeyed until it is changed—in an orderly manner through a legitimate lawmaking process. A judge with positivist leanings probably would be more inclined to defer to an existing law than would a judge who adheres to the natural law tradition.

Positive law • The body of conventional, or written, law of a particular society at a particular point in time.

Positivist school • A school of legal thought whose adherents believe that there can be no higher law than a nation's positive law—the body of conventional, or written, law of a particular society at a particular time.

The Historical School

The **historical school** of legal thought emphasizes the evolutionary process of law by concentrating on the origin and history of the legal system. Thus, this school looks to the past to discover what the principles of contemporary law should be. The legal doctrines that have withstood the passage of time—those that have worked in the past—are deemed best suited for shaping present laws. Hence, law derives its legitimacy and authority from adhering to the standards that historical development has shown to be workable. Adherents of the historical school are more likely than those of other schools to strictly follow decisions made in past cases.

Historical school • A school of legal thought that emphasizes the evolutionary process of law and that looks to the past to discover what the principles of contemporary law should be.

Legal Realism

In the 1920s and 1930s, a number of jurists and scholars, known as legal realists, rebelled against the historical approach to law. **Legal realism** is based on the idea that law is just one of many institutions in society and that it is shaped by social forces and needs. The law is a human enterprise, and judges should take social and economic realities into account when deciding cases. Legal realists also believe that the law can never be applied with total uniformity. Given that judges are human beings with unique personalities, value systems, and intellects, obviously different judges will bring different reasoning processes to the same case.

Legal realism left a lasting imprint on American jurisprudence. It also strongly influenced the growth of what is sometimes called the **sociological school** of jurisprudence. This school views law as a tool for promoting justice in society. In the 1960s, for example, the justices of the United States Supreme Court played a leading role in the civil rights movement by upholding long-neglected laws calling for equal treatment for all Americans, including African Americans and other minorities. Generally, jurists who adhere to this philosophy of law are more likely to depart from past decisions than are those jurists who adhere to the other schools of legal thought.

Legal realism • A school of legal thought that was popular in the 1920s and 1930s and that challenged many existing jurisprudential assumptions, particularly the assumption that subjective elements and social forces play no part in judicial reasoning.

Sociological school • A school of legal thought that views the law as a tool for promoting justice in society.

Concept Summary 1.1
Schools of Jurisprudential Thought

School of Thought	Description
The Natural Law School	One of the oldest and most significant schools of legal thought. Those who believe in natural law hold that there is a universal law applicable to all human beings. This law is discoverable through reason and is of a higher order than positive (national) law.
The Positivist School	A school of legal thought centered on the assumption that there is no law higher than the laws created by the government. Laws must be obeyed, even if they are unjust, to prevent anarchy.
The Historical School	A school of legal thought that stresses the evolutionary nature of law and that looks to doctrines that have withstood the passage of time for guidance in shaping present laws.
Legal Realism	A school of legal thought, popular during the 1920s and 1930s, that left a lasting imprint on American jurisprudence. Legal realists generally advocated a less abstract and more realistic and pragmatic approach to the law, an approach that would take into account customary practices and the circumstances in which transactions take place. Legal realism strongly influenced the growth of the *sociological school* of jurisprudence, which views law as a tool for promoting social justice.

Business Activities and the Legal Environment

As those entering the world of business will learn, laws and government regulations affect virtually all business activities—from hiring and firing decisions, to workplace safety, to the manufacturing and marketing of products, to business financing, and so on. To make good business decisions, a basic knowledge of the laws and regulations governing these activities is beneficial, if not essential. Realize also that in today's world a knowledge of "black-letter" law is not enough. Businesspersons are also pressured to make ethical decisions. Thus, the study of business law necessarily involves an ethical dimension.

Many Different Laws May Affect a Single Business Transaction

As you will note, each chapter in this text covers a specific area of the law and shows how the legal rules in that area affect business activities. Although compartmentalizing the law in this fashion promotes conceptual clarity, it does not indicate the extent to which a number of different laws may apply to just one transaction.

Consider an example. Suppose that you are the president of NetSys, Inc., a company that creates and maintains computer network systems for its clients, including business firms. NetSys also markets software for customers who need an internal computer network but cannot afford an individually designed intranet. One day, Janet, an operations officer for Southwest Distribution Corporation (SDC), contacts you by e-mail about a possible contract concerning SDC's computer network. In deciding whether to enter into a contract with SDC, you need to consider, among other things, the legal requirements for an enforceable contract. Are there different requirements for a contract for services and a contract for products? What are your options if SDC **breaches** (breaks, or fails to perform) the contract? The answers to these questions are part of contract law and sales law.

Breach • To violate a law, by an act or an omission, or to break a legal obligation that one owes to another person or to society.

Other questions might concern the rights to NetSys's software, or there may be a question of liability if the software is defective. There may also be an issue as to whether you and Janet have the authority to make the deal in the first place. Resolutions of these questions may be found in areas of the law that relate to intellectual property, e-commerce, torts, product liability, agency, or business organizations.

Finally, how will you settle any disputes that arise under your contract? Should you include provisions that require any dispute to be resolved through mediation or arbitration proceedings, to avoid the expense of having a court decide the issue? If you do not specify any method of alternative dispute resolution in your contract, then the rules concerning courts and court procedures spell out the steps of a lawsuit. Exhibit 1–1 illustrates the various areas of law covered in this text that may influence business decision making.

EXHIBIT 1–1 • AREAS OF THE LAW THAT MAY AFFECT BUSINESS DECISION MAKING

Ethics and Business Decision Making

Merely knowing the areas of law that may affect a business decision is not sufficient in today's business world. Businesspersons must also take ethics into account. As you will learn in Chapter 4, *ethics* is generally defined as the study of what constitutes right or wrong behavior. In today's world, business decision makers need to consider not just whether a decision is profitable and legal, but also whether it is ethical.

Throughout this text, you will learn about the relationship between the law and ethics, as well as about some of the types of ethical questions that may arise in the business context. For example, the unit-ending *Focus on Ethics* features in this text are devoted solely to the exploration of ethical dimensions of selected topics treated within the unit. Additionally, Chapter 4 offers a detailed look at the importance of ethical considerations in business decision making. Finally, various other elements in this text, such as the ethical question that concludes each chapter, are designed to introduce you to ethical aspects of specific cases involving real-life situations.

SOURCES OF AMERICAN LAW

There are numerous sources of American law. *Primary sources of law,* or sources that establish the law, include the following:

1. The U.S. Constitution and the constitutions of the various states.
2. Statutory law—including laws passed by Congress, state legislatures, or local governing bodies.
3. Regulations created by administrative agencies, such as the Food and Drug Administration.
4. Case law and common law doctrines.

We describe each of these important sources of law in the following pages.

Secondary sources of law are books and articles that summarize and clarify the primary sources of law. Examples include legal encyclopedias, treatises, articles in law reviews, and compilations of law, such as the *Restatements of the Law* (which will be discussed shortly). Courts often refer to secondary sources of law for guidance in interpreting and applying the primary sources of law discussed here.

Constitutional Law

The federal government and the states have separate written constitutions that set forth the general organization, powers, and limits of their respective governments. **Constitutional law** is the law as expressed in these constitutions.

Constitutional law • Law that is based on the U.S. Constitution and the constitutions of the various states.

According to Article VI of the U.S. Constitution, the Constitution is the supreme law of the land. As such, it is the basis of all law in the United States. A law in violation of the Constitution, if challenged, will be declared unconstitutional and will not be enforced, no matter what its source. Because of its importance in the American legal system, we present the complete text of the U.S. Constitution in Appendix A.

The Tenth Amendment to the U.S. Constitution reserves to the states all powers not granted to the federal government. Each state in the union has its own constitution. Unless it conflicts with the U.S. Constitution or a federal law, a state constitution is supreme within the state's borders.

Statutory Law

Laws enacted by legislative bodies at any level of government, such as the statutes passed by Congress or by state legislatures, make up the body of law generally referred to as **statutory law.** When a legislature passes a statute, that statute ultimately is included in the federal code of laws or the relevant state code of laws (these codes are discussed in the appendix following this chapter).

Statutory law • The body of law enacted by legislative bodies (as opposed to constitutional law, administrative law, or case law).

Statutory law also includes local **ordinances**—statutes (laws, rules, or orders) passed by municipal or county governing units to govern matters not covered by federal or state law. Ordinances commonly have to do with city or county land use (zoning ordinances), building and safety codes, and other matters affecting the local unit.

Ordinance • A law passed by a local governing unit, such as a municipality or a county.

A federal statute, of course, applies to all states. A state statute, in contrast, applies only within the state's borders. State laws thus may vary from state to state. No federal statute may violate the U.S. Constitution, and no state statute or local ordinance may violate the U.S. Constitution or the relevant state constitution.

Uniform Laws. The differences among state laws were particularly notable in the 1800s, when conflicting state statutes frequently made trade and commerce among the states very difficult. To counter these problems, in 1892 a group of legal scholars and lawyers formed the National Conference of Commissioners on Uniform State Laws (NCCUSL) to draft **uniform laws,** or model laws, for the states to consider adopting. The NCCUSL still exists today and continues to issue uniform laws.

Uniform law • A model law created by the National Conference of Commissioners on Uniform State Laws and/or the American Law Institute for the states to consider adopting. If the state adopts the law, it becomes statutory law in that state. Each state has the option of adopting or rejecting all or part of a uniform law.

Each state has the option of adopting or rejecting a uniform law. *Only if a state legislature adopts a uniform law does that law become part of the statutory law of that state.* Note that a state legislature may adopt all or part of a uniform law as it is written, or the legislature may rewrite the law however the legislature wishes. Hence, even when a uniform law is said to have been adopted in many states, those states' laws may not be entirely "uniform."

The earliest uniform law, the Uniform Negotiable Instruments Law, was completed by 1896 and adopted in every state by the early 1920s (although not all states used exactly the same wording). Over the following decades, other acts were drawn up in a similar manner. In all, over two hundred uniform acts have been issued by the NCCUSL since its inception. The most ambitious uniform act of all, however, was the Uniform Commercial Code.

The Uniform Commercial Code. The Uniform Commercial Code (UCC), which was created through the joint efforts of the NCCUSL and the American Law Institute,[1] was first issued in 1952. All fifty states, the District of Columbia, and the Virgin Islands have adopted the UCC.[2] It facilitates commerce among the states by providing a uniform, yet flexible, set of rules governing commercial transactions. The UCC assures businesspersons that their contracts, if validly entered into, normally will be enforced.

To read the text of Article 2 of the Uniform Commercial Code, go to the "Statutes" page of our Web site at **http://ele.westbuslaw.com**

1. This institute was formed in the 1920s and consists of practicing attorneys, legal scholars, and judges.
2. Louisiana has not adopted Articles 2 and 2A (covering contracts for the sale and lease of goods), however.

As you will read in later chapters, from time to time the NCCUSL revises the articles contained in the UCC and submits the revised versions to the states for adoption. During the 1990s, for example, four articles (Articles 3, 4, 5, and 9) were revised, and two new articles (Articles 2A and 4A) were added. In 2003, amendments to Articles 2 and 2A were issued. Because of its importance in the area of commercial law, we cite the UCC frequently in Chapter 11.

Administrative Law

Administrative law • The body of law created by administrative agencies (in the form of rules, regulations, orders, and decisions) in order to carry out their duties and responsibilities.

Administrative agency • A federal, state, or local government agency established to perform a specific function. Administrative agencies are authorized by legislative acts to make and enforce rules to administer and enforce the acts.

Executive agency • An administrative agency within the executive branch of government. At the federal level, executive agencies are those within the cabinet departments.

Independent regulatory agency • An administrative agency that is not considered part of the government's executive branch. Independent agency officials cannot be removed without cause.

An important source of American law is **administrative law,** which consists of the rules, orders, and decisions of administrative agencies. An **administrative agency** is a federal, state, or local government agency established to perform a specific function. Administrative law and procedures, which will be examined in detail in Chapter 6, constitute a dominant element in the regulatory environment of business. As discussed earlier, rules issued by various administrative agencies now affect virtually every aspect of a business's operations.

At the national level, numerous **executive agencies** exist within the cabinet departments of the executive branch. For example, the Food and Drug Administration is an agency within the Department of Health and Human Services. Executive agencies are subject to the authority of the president, who has the power to appoint and remove officers of federal agencies. There are also major **independent regulatory agencies** at the federal level, such as the Federal Trade Commission, the Securities and Exchange Commission, and the Federal Communications Commission. The president's power is less pronounced in regard to independent agencies, whose officers serve for fixed terms and cannot be removed without just cause.

There are administrative agencies at the state and local levels as well. Commonly, a state agency (such as a state pollution-control agency) is created as a parallel to a federal agency (such as the Environmental Protection Agency). Just as federal statutes take precedence over conflicting state statutes, so federal agency regulations take precedence over conflicting state regulations.

ETHICAL ISSUE

Do administrative agencies exercise too much authority? Administrative agencies, such as the Federal Trade Commission, combine functions normally divided among the three branches of government into a single governmental entity. The broad range of authority that agencies exercise sometimes engenders questions of fairness. After all, agencies create rules that are as legally binding as the laws passed by Congress—the only federal government institution authorized by the Constitution to make laws. To be sure, arbitrary rulemaking by agencies is checked by the procedural requirements set forth in the Administrative Procedure Act (APA), as well as by the courts, to which agency decisions may be appealed. Yet some people claim that these checks are not enough.

Consider that in addition to *legislative rules,* which are subject to the procedural requirements of the APA, agencies also create *interpretive rules*—rules that specify how the agency will interpret and apply its regulations. The APA does not apply to interpretive rulemaking. Additionally, although a firm that challenges an agency's rule may be able to appeal the agency's decision in the matter to a court, the policy of the courts is generally to defer to agency rules, including interpretative rules, and to agency decisions.

Case Law and Common Law Doctrines

The rules of law announced in court decisions constitute another basic source of American law. These rules of law include interpretations of constitutional provisions, of statutes enacted by legislatures, and of regulations created by administrative agencies. Today, this body of judge-made law is referred to as **case law,** or the common law. Because of the importance of the common law in our legal system, we look at the origins and characteristics of the common law tradition in some detail in the pages that follow.

Case law • The rules of law announced in court decisions. Case law includes the aggregate of reported cases that interpret statutes, regulations, and constitutional provisions.

The Common Law Tradition

Because of our colonial heritage, much of American law is based on the English legal system, which originated in medieval England and continued to evolve in the following centuries. A knowledge of this system is necessary to an understanding of the American legal system today.

Early English Courts

The origins of the English legal system—and thus the U.S. legal system as well—date back to 1066, when the Normans conquered England. William the Conqueror and his successors began the process of unifying the country under

Concept Summary 1.2
Sources of American Law

Source	Description
Constitutional Law	The law as expressed in the U.S. Constitution and the state constitutions. The U.S. Constitution is the supreme law of the land. State constitutions are supreme within state borders to the extent that they do not violate a clause of the U.S. Constitution or a federal law.
Statutory Law	Laws (statutes and ordinances) created by federal, state, and local legislatures and governing bodies. None of these laws may violate the U.S. Constitution or the relevant state constitution. Uniform statutes, when adopted by a state, become statutory law in that state.
Administrative Law	The rules, orders, and decisions of federal, state, or local government administrative agencies.
Case Law and Common Law Doctrines	Judge-made law, including interpretations of constitutional provisions, of statutes enacted by legislatures, and of regulations created by administrative agencies.

their rule. One of the means they used to do this was the establishment of the king's courts, or *curiae regis*. Before the Norman Conquest, disputes had been settled according to the local legal customs and traditions in various regions of the country. The king's courts sought to establish a uniform set of customs for the country as a whole. What evolved in these courts was the beginning of the **common law**—a body of general rules that applied throughout the entire English realm. Eventually, the common law tradition became part of the heritage of all nations that were once British colonies, including the United States.

Common law • That body of law developed from custom or judicial decisions in English and U.S. courts, not attributable to a legislature.

Courts of Law and Remedies at Law. The early English king's courts could grant only very limited kinds of **remedies** (the legal means to recover a right or redress a wrong). If one person wronged another in some way, the king's courts could award as compensation one or more of the following: (1) land, (2) items of value, or (3) money. The courts that awarded this compensation became known as **courts of law,** and the three remedies were called **remedies at law.** (Today, the remedy at law normally takes the form of money **damages**—money given to a party whose legal interests have been injured.) Even though the system introduced uniformity in the settling of disputes, when a complaining party wanted a remedy other than economic compensation, the courts of law could do nothing, so "no remedy, no right."

Remedy • The relief given to an innocent party to enforce a right or compensate for the violation of a right.

Court of law • A court in which the only remedies that could be granted were things of value, such as money damages. In the early English king's courts, courts of law were distinct from courts of equity.

Remedy at law • A remedy available in a court of law. Money damages are awarded as a remedy at law.

Damages • Money given to a party whose legal interests have been injured.

Courts of Equity and Remedies in Equity. Equity is a branch of law, founded on what might be described as notions of justice and fair dealing, that seeks to supply a remedy when no adequate remedy at law is available. When individuals could not obtain an adequate remedy in a court of law because of strict technicalities, they petitioned the king for relief. Most of these petitions were decided by an adviser to the king, called a **chancellor,** who was said to be the "keeper of the king's conscience." When the chancellor thought that the claims were fair, new and unique remedies were granted. Eventually, formal chancery courts, or **courts of equity,** were established.

Chancellor • An adviser to the king at the time of the early king's courts of England. Individuals petitioned the king for relief when they could not obtain an adequate remedy in a court of law, and these petitions were decided by the chancellor.

Court of equity • A court that decides controversies and administers justice according to principles of equity.

Remedy in equity • A remedy allowed by courts in situations in which remedies at law are not appropriate. Remedies in equity include injunction, specific performance, and rescission.

The remedies granted by the equity courts became known as **remedies in equity,** or equitable remedies. These remedies include *specific performance* (ordering a party to perform an agreement as promised), an *injunction* (ordering a party to cease engaging in a specific activity or to undo some wrong or injury), and *rescission* (the cancellation of a contractual obligation). We discuss these and other equitable remedies in more detail at appropriate points in the chapters that follow.

As a general rule, today's courts, like the early English courts, will not grant equitable remedies unless the remedy at law—money damages—is inadequate. For example, suppose that you form a contract (a legally binding agreement—see Chapter 10) to purchase a parcel of land that you think will be just perfect for your future country home. Further suppose that the seller breaches this agreement. You could sue the seller for the return of any deposits or down payment you might have made on the land, but this is not the remedy you really seek. What you want is to have the court order the seller to go through with the deal. In other words, you want the court to grant the equitable remedy of specific performance because money damages are inadequate in this situation.

Equitable maxim • A general proposition or principle of law that has to do with fairness (equity).

Equitable Maxims. In fashioning appropriate remedies, judges often were (and continue to be) guided by so-called **equitable maxims**—propositions or general statements of equitable rules. Exhibit 1–2 lists some important

EXHIBIT 1–2 • EQUITABLE MAXIMS

1. *Whoever seeks equity must do equity.* (Anyone who wishes to be treated fairly must treat others fairly.)
2. *Where there is equal equity, the law must prevail.* (The law will determine the outcome of a controversy in which the merits of both sides are equal.)
3. *One seeking the aid of an equity court must come to the court with clean hands.* (Plaintiffs must have acted fairly and honestly.)
4. *Equity will not suffer a wrong to be without a remedy.* (Equitable relief will be awarded when there is a right to relief and there is no adequate remedy at law.)
5. *Equity regards substance rather than form.* (Equity is more concerned with fairness and justice than with legal technicalities.)
6. *Equity aids the vigilant, not those who rest on their rights.* (Equity will not help those who neglect their rights for an unreasonable period of time.)

equitable maxims. The last maxim listed in that exhibit—"Equity aids the vigilant, not those who rest on their rights"—merits special attention. It has become known as the equitable doctrine of **laches** (a term derived from the Latin *laxus,* meaning "lax" or "negligent"), and it can be used as a defense. A **defense** is an argument raised by the **defendant** (the party being sued) indicating why the **plaintiff** (the suing party) should not obtain the remedy sought. (Note that in equity proceedings, the party bringing a lawsuit is called the **petitioner,** and the party being sued is referred to as the **respondent.**)

The doctrine of laches arose to encourage people to bring lawsuits while the evidence was fresh. What constitutes a reasonable time, of course, varies according to the circumstances of the case. Time periods for different types of cases are now usually fixed by **statutes of limitations.** After the time allowed under a statute of limitations has expired, no action can be brought, no matter how strong the case was originally.

Laches • The equitable doctrine that bars a party's right to legal action if the party has neglected for an unreasonable length of time to act on his or her rights.

Defense • That which a defendant offers and alleges in an action or suit as a reason why the plaintiff should not recover or establish what he or she seeks.

Defendant • One against whom a lawsuit is brought; the accused person in a criminal proceeding.

Plaintiff • One who initiates a lawsuit.

Petitioner • In equity practice, a party that initiates a lawsuit.

Respondent • In equity practice, the party against whom an action is taken.

Statute of limitations • A federal or state statute setting the maximum time period during which a certain action can be brought or certain rights enforced.

Legal and Equitable Remedies Today

The establishment of courts of equity in medieval England resulted in two distinct court systems: courts of law and courts of equity. The systems had different sets of judges and granted different types of remedies. Parties who sought legal remedies, or remedies at law, would bring their claims before courts of law. Parties seeking equitable relief, or remedies in equity, would bring their claims before courts of equity. During the nineteenth century, however, most states in the United States adopted rules of procedure that resulted in combined courts of law and equity, and today, few, if any, states still retain the distinction. A party now may request both legal and equitable remedies in the same action, and the trial court judge may grant either or both forms of relief.

The distinction between legal and equitable remedies remains relevant to students of business law, however, because these remedies differ. To seek the proper remedy for a wrong, one must know what remedies are available. Additionally, certain vestiges of the procedures used when there were separate courts of law and equity still exist. For example, a party has the right to demand a jury trial in an action at law, but not in an action in equity. In the old courts of equity, the chancellor heard both sides of an issue and decided what should be done. Juries were considered inappropriate. In actions at law, however, juries participated in determining the outcome of cases, including the amount of damages to be awarded. Exhibit 1–3 summarizes the procedural differences (applicable in most states) between an action at law and an action in equity.

The Doctrine of *Stare Decisis*

One of the unique features of the common law is that it is judge-made law. The body of principles and doctrines that form the common law emerged over time as judges decided actual legal controversies.

Case Precedents and Case Reporters. When possible, judges attempted to be consistent and to base their decisions on the principles suggested by earlier cases. They sought to decide similar cases in a similar way and considered new cases with care because they knew that their decisions would make new law. Each interpretation became part of the law on the subject and served as a legal **precedent**—that is, a decision that furnished an example or authority for deciding subsequent cases involving similar legal principles or facts.

Precedent • A court decision that furnishes an example or authority for deciding subsequent cases involving identical or similar facts.

By the early fourteenth century, portions of the most important decisions of each year were being gathered together and recorded in *Year Books,* which became useful references for lawyers and judges. In the sixteenth century, the *Year Books* were discontinued, and other forms of case publication became available. Today, cases are published, or "reported," in volumes called **reporters,** or *reports.* We describe today's case reporting system in detail in the appendix that follows this chapter.

Reporter • A publication in which court cases are published, or reported.

Stare Decisis* and the Common Law Tradition.** The practice of deciding new cases with reference to former decisions, or precedents, became a cornerstone of the English and American judicial systems. The practice forms a doctrine called ***stare decisis[3] (a Latin phrase meaning "to stand on decided cases"). Under this doctrine, judges are obligated to follow the precedents established within their jurisdictions. The term *jurisdiction* refers to an area in which a court or courts have the power to apply the law—see Chapter 2.

Stare decisis • A common law doctrine under which judges are obligated to follow the precedents established in prior decisions within their jurisdictions.

For example, suppose that the lower state courts in California have reached conflicting conclusions on whether drivers are liable for accidents they cause

3. Prononunced *ster*-ay dih-*si*-ses.

EXHIBIT 1–3 • PROCEDURAL DIFFERENCES BETWEEN AN ACTION AT LAW AND AN ACTION IN EQUITY

PROCEDURE	ACTION AT LAW	ACTION IN EQUITY
Initiation of lawsuit	By filing a complaint	By filing a petition
Parties	Plaintiff and defendant	Petitioner and respondent
Decision	By jury or judge	By judge (no jury)
Result	Judgment	Decree
Remedy	Monetary damages	Injunction, specific performance, or rescission

while merging into freeway traffic. Some courts have held drivers liable even though the drivers looked and did not see any oncoming traffic and even though witnesses (passengers in their cars) testified to that effect. To settle the law on this issue, the California Supreme Court decides to review a case involving this fact pattern. The court rules that in such a situation, the driver who is merging into traffic is liable for any accidents caused by the driver's failure to yield to freeway traffic—even if the driver looked carefully and did not see an approaching vehicle.

The California Supreme Court's decision on this matter is a **binding authority**—a case precedent or statute that must be followed. (Nonbinding legal authorities on which judges may rely for guidance, such as precedents established in other jurisdictions, are referred to as *persuasive authorities.*) In other words, the California Supreme Court's decision will influence the outcome of all future cases on this issue brought before the California state courts. Similarly, a decision on a given question by the United States Supreme Court (the nation's highest court) is binding on all courts.

Binding authority • Any source of law that a court must follow when deciding a case. Binding authorities include constitutions, statutes, and regulations that govern the issue being decided, as well as court decisions that are controlling precedents within the jurisdiction.

The doctrine of *stare decisis* helps the courts to be more efficient, because if other courts have carefully analyzed a similar case, their legal reasoning and opinions can serve as guides. *Stare decisis* also makes the law more stable and predictable. If the law on a given subject is well settled, someone bringing a case to court can usually rely on the court to make a decision based on what the law has been in the past.

Departures from Precedent. Although courts are obligated to follow precedents, sometimes a court will depart from the rule of precedent if it decides that the precedent should no longer be followed. If a court decides that a ruling precedent is simply incorrect or that technological or social changes have rendered the precedent inapplicable, the court might rule contrary to the precedent. Cases that overturn precedent often receive a great deal of publicity.[4]

Note that judges have some flexibility in applying precedents. For example, a trial court may avoid applying a Supreme Court precedent by arguing that the facts of the case before the court are distinguishable from the facts in the Supreme Court case and that, therefore, the Supreme Court's ruling on the issue does not apply to the case before the court.

When There Is No Precedent. Occasionally, the courts must decide cases for which no precedents exist. Such cases, called *cases of first impression,* often result when new practices or technological developments in society create new types of legal disputes. In the last several years, for example, the courts have had to deal with disputes involving transactions conducted via the Internet. When existing laws governing free speech, pornography, fraud, jurisdiction, and other areas were drafted, cyberspace did not exist. Although

4. For example, when the United States Supreme Court held in the 1950s that racial segregation in the public schools was unconstitutional, it expressly overturned a Supreme Court precedent upholding the constitutionality of "separate-but-equal" segregation. The Supreme Court's departure from precedent received a tremendous amount of publicity as people began to realize the ramifications of this change in the law. See *Brown v. Board of Education of Topeka,* 347 U.S. 483, 74 S.Ct. 686, 98 L.Ed. 873 (1954). (Legal citations are explained in the appendix at the end of this chapter.)

new laws are being created to govern such disputes, in the meantime the courts have to decide, on a case-by-case basis, what rules should be applied.

Generally, in deciding cases of first impression, courts may consider a number of factors, including persuasive authorities (such as cases from other jurisdictions, if there are any), legal principles and policies underlying previous court decisions or existing statutes, fairness, social values and customs, **public policy** (a government policy based on widely held societal values), and data and concepts drawn from the social sciences. Which of these sources is chosen or receives the greatest emphasis depends on the nature of the case being considered and the particular judge or judges hearing the case. As mentioned previously, judges are not free to decide cases on the basis of their own personal views. In cases of first impression, as in all cases, judges must have legal reasons for ruling as they do on particular issues. When a court issues a written opinion on a case (we discuss court opinions in the appendix following this chapter), the opinion normally contains a carefully reasoned argument justifying the decision.

Public policy • A government policy based on widely held societal values and (usually) expressed or implied in laws or regulations.

Stare Decisis and Legal Reasoning

Legal reasoning is the reasoning process used by judges in deciding what law applies to a given dispute and then applying that law to the specific facts or circumstances of the case. Through the use of legal reasoning, judges harmonize their decisions with those that have been made before, as the doctrine of *stare decisis* requires.

Legal reasoning • The process of reasoning by which a judge harmonizes his or her decision with the judicial decisions of previous cases.

Students of business law and the legal environment also engage in legal reasoning. For example, you may be asked to provide answers for some of the case problems that appear at the end of every chapter in this text. Each problem describes the facts of a particular dispute and the legal question at issue. If you are assigned a case problem, you will be asked to determine how a court would answer that question, and why. In other words, you will need to give legal reasons for whatever conclusion you reach.[5] We look here at the basic steps involved in legal reasoning and then describe some forms of reasoning commonly used by the courts in making their decisions.

Basic Steps in Legal Reasoning. At times, the legal arguments set forth in court opinions are relatively simple and brief. At other times, the arguments are complex and lengthy. Regardless of the length of a legal argument, however, the basic steps of the legal reasoning process remain the same. These steps, which you also can follow when analyzing cases and case problems, form what is commonly referred to as the *IRAC method* of legal reasoning. IRAC is an acronym formed from the first letters of the following words: Issue, Rule, Application, and Conclusion. To apply the IRAC method, you would ask the following questions:

1. *What are the key facts and issues?* For example, suppose that a plaintiff comes before the court claiming *assault* (a wrongful and intentional action, or tort, in which one person makes another fearful of immediate physical harm). The plaintiff claims that the defendant threatened her while she was sleeping. Although the plaintiff was unaware that she was

5. See the Preface to the Student at the beginning of this book for further instructions on how to analyze case problems.

being threatened, her roommate heard the defendant make the threat. The legal issue, or question, raised by these facts is whether the defendant's actions constitute the tort of assault, given that the plaintiff was not aware of those actions at the time they occurred.

2. *What rules of law apply to the case?* A rule of law may be a rule stated by the courts in previous decisions, a state or federal statute, or a state or federal administrative agency regulation. In our hypothetical case, the plaintiff **alleges** (claims) that the defendant committed a tort. Therefore, the applicable law is the common law of torts—specifically, tort law governing assault (see Chapter 12 for more detail on torts). Case precedents involving similar facts and issues thus would be relevant. Often, more than one rule of law will be applicable to a case.

Allege • To state, claim, assert, or charge.

3. *How do the rules of law apply to the particular facts and circumstances of this case?* This step is often the most difficult one because each case presents a unique set of facts, circumstances, and parties. Although cases may be similar, no two cases are ever identical in all respects. Normally, judges (and lawyers and law students) try to find **cases on point**—previously decided cases that are as similar as possible to the one under consideration. (Because of the difficulty—and importance—of this step in the legal reasoning process, we discuss it in more detail in the next subsection.)

Case on point • A previous case involving factual circumstances and issues that are as similar as possible to the case before the court.

4. *What conclusion should be drawn?* This step normally presents few problems. Usually, the conclusion is evident if the previous three steps have been followed carefully.

Forms of Legal Reasoning. Judges use many types of reasoning when following the third step of the legal reasoning process—applying the law to the facts of a particular case. Three common forms of reasoning are deductive reasoning, linear reasoning, and reasoning by analogy.

Deductive Reasoning. Deductive reasoning is sometimes called syllogistic reasoning because it employs a **syllogism**—a logical relationship involving a major premise, a minor premise, and a conclusion. For example, consider the hypothetical case presented earlier, in which the plaintiff alleged that the defendant committed assault by threatening her while she was sleeping. The judge might point out that "under the common law of torts, an individual must be *aware* of a threat of danger for the threat to constitute assault" (major premise); "the plaintiff in this case was unaware of the threat at the time it occurred" (minor premise); and "therefore, the circumstances do not amount to an assault" (conclusion).

Syllogism • A form of deductive reasoning consisting of a major premise, a minor premise, and a conclusion.

Linear Reasoning. A second important form of legal reasoning that is commonly employed might be thought of as "linear" reasoning because it proceeds from one point to another, with the final point being the conclusion. An analogy will help make this form of reasoning clear. Imagine a knotted rope, with each knot tying together separate pieces of rope to form a tight length. As a whole, the rope represents a linear progression of thought logically connecting various points, with the last point, or knot, representing the conclusion. For example, suppose that a tenant in an apartment building sues the landlord for damages for an injury resulting from an allegedly dimly lit stairway. The court may engage in a reasoning process involving the following "pieces of rope":

1. The landlord, who was on the premises the evening the injury occurred, testifies that none of the other nine tenants who used the stairway that night complained about the lights.
2. The fact that none of the tenants complained is the same as if they had said the lighting was sufficient.
3. That there were no complaints does not prove that the lighting was sufficient but does prove that the landlord had no reason to believe that it was not.
4. The landlord's belief was reasonable because no one complained.
5. Therefore, the landlord acted reasonably and was not negligent with respect to the lighting in the stairway.

On the basis of this reasoning, the court concludes that the tenant is not entitled to compensation on the basis of the stairway's allegedly insufficient lighting.

Analogy • In logical reasoning, an assumption that if two things are similar in some respects, they will be similar in other respects also.

Reasoning by Analogy. Another important type of reasoning that judges use in deciding cases is reasoning by *analogy.* To reason by **analogy** is to compare the facts in the case at hand to the facts in other cases and, to the extent that the patterns are similar, to apply the same rule of law to the present case. To the extent that the facts are unique, or "distinguishable," different rules may apply. For example, in case A, the court held that a driver who crossed a highway's center line was negligent. Case B involves a driver who crossed the line to avoid hitting a child. In determining whether case A's rule applies in case B, a judge would consider what the reasons were for the decision in A and whether B is sufficiently similar for those reasons to apply. If the judge holds that B's driver is not liable, that judge must indicate why case A's rule does not apply to the facts presented in case B.

There Is No One "Right" Answer

Many persons believe that there is one "right" answer to every legal question. In most situations involving a legal controversy, however, there is no single correct result. Good arguments can often be made to support either side of a legal controversy. Quite often, a case does not present the situation of a "good" person suing a "bad" person. In many cases, both parties have acted in good faith in some measure or have acted in bad faith to some degree.

Additionally, as already mentioned, each judge has her or his own personal beliefs and philosophy, which shape, at least to some extent, the process of legal reasoning. This means that the outcome of a particular lawsuit before a court can never be predicted with absolute certainty. In fact, in some cases, even though the weight of the law would seem to favor one party's position, judges, through creative legal reasoning, have found ways to rule in favor of the other party in the interests of preventing injustice.

The Common Law Today

Today, the common law continues to be applied throughout the United States. Common law doctrines and principles govern all areas *not* covered by statutory or administrative law. In a dispute concerning a particular employment practice, for example, if a statute regulates that practice, the statute will

CONCEPT SUMMARY 1.3
The Common Law Tradition

ASPECT	DESCRIPTION
Origins of the Common Law	The American legal system is based on the common law tradition, which originated in medieval England. Following the conquest of England in 1066 by William the Conqueror, king's courts were established throughout England, and the common law was developed in these courts.
Legal and Equitable Remedies	The distinction between remedies at law (money or items of value, such as land) and remedies in equity (including specific performance, injunction, and rescission of a contractual obligation) originated in the early English courts of law and courts of equity, respectively.
Case Precedents and the Doctrine of *Stare Decisis*	In the king's courts, judges attempted to make their decisions consistent with previous decisions, called precedents. This practice gave rise to the doctrine of *stare decisis*. This doctrine, which became a cornerstone of the common law tradition, obligates judges to abide by precedents established in their jurisdictions.
***Stare Decisis* and Legal Reasoning**	Legal reasoning refers to the reasoning process used by judges in applying the law to the facts and issues of specific cases. Legal reasoning involves becoming familiar with the key facts of a case, identifying the relevant legal rules, linking those rules to the facts, and drawing a conclusion. In linking the legal rules to the facts of a case, judges may use deductive reasoning, linear reasoning, or reasoning by analogy.

apply rather than the common law doctrine that applied prior to the enactment of the statute.

The Continuing Importance of the Common Law

Because the body of statutory law has expanded greatly since the beginning of this nation, thus narrowing the applicability of common law doctrines, it might seem that the common law has dwindled in importance. This is not true, however. For one thing, even in areas governed by statutory law, there is a significant interplay between statutory law and the common law. For example, many statutes essentially codify existing common law rules, and regulations issued by various administrative agencies usually are based, at least in part, on common law principles. Additionally, the courts, in interpreting statutory law, often rely on the common law as a guide to what the legislators intended.

Furthermore, how the courts interpret a particular statute determines how that statute will be applied. If you wanted to learn about the coverage and applicability of a particular statute, for example, you would, of course, need to locate the statute and study it. You would also need to see how the courts in your jurisdiction have interpreted and applied the statute. In other words, you would need to learn what precedents have been established in your jurisdiction with respect to that statute. Often, the applicability of a newly enacted statute does not become clear until a body of case law develops to clarify how, when, and to whom the statute applies.

Restatements of the Law

The American Law Institute (ALI) has drafted and published compilations of the common law called *Restatements of the Law,* which generally summarize the common law rules followed by most states. There are *Restatements of the Law* in the areas of contracts, torts, agency, trusts, property, restitution, security, judgments, and conflict of laws. The *Restatements,* like other secondary sources of law, do not in themselves have the force of law but are an important source of legal analysis and opinion on which judges often rely in making their decisions.

Many of the *Restatements* are now in their second or third editions. We refer to the *Restatements* frequently in subsequent chapters of this text, indicating in parentheses the edition to which we are referring. For example, we refer to the second edition of the *Restatement of the Law of Contracts* simply as the *Restatement (Second) of Contracts.*

Classifications of Law

Because the body of law is so large, one must break it down by some means of classification. A number of classification systems have been devised. For example, one classification system divides law into substantive law and procedural law. **Substantive law** consists of all laws that define, describe, regulate, and create legal rights and obligations. **Procedural law** consists of all laws that establish the methods of enforcing the rights established by substantive law. Other classification systems divide law into federal law and state law, private law (dealing with relationships between private entities) and public law (addressing the relationship between persons and their governments), national law and international law, and so on. Here we look at still another classification system, which divides law into civil law and criminal law, as well as at what is meant by the term *cyberlaw.*

Substantive law • Law that creates and defines legal rights and obligations.

Procedural law • Rules that define the manner in which the rights and duties established by substantive law may be enforced.

Civil Law and Criminal Law

Civil law is concerned with the duties that exist between persons or between citizens and their governments, *excluding* the duty not to commit crimes. Typically, in a civil case, a private party sues another private party (although the government can also sue a party for a civil law violation) to make that other party comply with a duty or pay for the damage caused by failure to comply with a duty. Much of the law that we discuss in this text is civil law. Contract law, for example, covered in Chapter 10, is civil law. The whole body of tort law (see Chapter 12) is civil law.

Civil law • The branch of law dealing with the duties that exist between persons or between citizens and their government, *excluding* the duty not to commit crimes.

Criminal law, in contrast, is concerned with wrongs committed *against society as a whole.* Criminal acts are defined and prohibited by local, state, or federal government statutes and prosecuted by public officials, such as a district attorney (D.A.), on behalf of the state, not by their victims or other private parties. (See Chapter 7 for a further discussion of the distinction between civil law and criminal law.)

Criminal law • Law that defines and governs actions that constitute crimes. Generally, criminal law has to do with wrongful actions committed against society as a whole for which society demands redress.

Cyberlaw

Over the last decade, the use of the Internet to conduct business transactions has led to new types of legal issues. In response, courts have had to adapt traditional laws to situations that are unique to our age. Additionally, legislatures have created laws to deal specifically with such issues. The growing body of law that deals specifically with issues raised by cyberspace transactions is often referred to as *cyberlaw.* Cyberlaw is not really a classification of law; rather, it is an informal term used to describe how traditional classifications of law, such as civil law and criminal law, are being applied to online activities.

Realize, too, that cyberlaw is not a new *type* of law. For the most part, it consists of traditional legal principles that have been modified and adapted to fit situations that are unique to the online world. Of course, in some areas new statutes have been enacted, at both the federal and state levels, to cover specific types of problems stemming from online communications.

Anyone preparing to enter today's business world will find it useful to know how old and new laws are being applied to activities conducted online, such as advertising, contracting, banking, filing documents with the courts or government agencies, employment relations, and a variety of other transactions. For that reason, many sections in this text are devoted to this topic.

KEY TERMS

administrative agency 10
administrative law 10
allege 17
analogy 18
binding authority 15
breach 7
case law 11
case on point 17
chancellor 12
civil law 20
common law 12
constitutional law 8
court of equity 12
court of law 12
criminal law 20
damages 12
defendant 13
defense 13
equitable maxims 12
executive agency 10
historical school 5
independent regulatory agency 10
jurisprudence 3
laches 13
law 3
legal realism 5
legal reasoning 16
natural law 4
opinion 32
ordinance 9
petitioner 13
plaintiff 13
positive law 5
positivist school 5
precedent 14
procedural law 20
public policy 16
remedy 12
remedy at law 12
remedy in equity 12
reporter 14
respondent 13
sociological school 5
***stare decisis* 14**
statute of limitations 13
statutory law 9
substantive law 20
syllogism 17
uniform law 9

FOR REVIEW

1. What is the common law tradition?
2. What is a precedent? When might a court depart from precedent?
3. What is the difference between remedies at law and remedies in equity?
4. What is the Uniform Commercial Code?
5. What are some important differences between civil law and criminal law?

QUESTIONS AND CASE PROBLEMS

1–1. After World War II, which ended in 1945, an international tribunal of judges convened at Nuremberg, Germany. The judges convicted several Nazis of "crimes against humanity." Assuming that the Nazi war criminals who were convicted had not disobeyed any law of their country and had merely been following their government's (Hitler's) orders, what law had they violated? Explain.

1–2. How does statutory law come into existence? How does it differ from the common law? If statutory law conflicts with the common law, which law will govern?

1–3. Assume that you want to read the entire court opinion in the case of *Kelly v. Arriba Soft Corp.*, 280 F.3d 934 (9th Cir. 2002). The case considers whether a photographer's images could be legally displayed on another person's Web site without the photographer's permission. First read the appendix to this chapter, and then explain specifically where you would find the court's opinion.

1–4. This chapter discussed a number of sources of American law. Which source of law takes priority in the following situations, and why?

(a) A federal statute conflicts with the U.S. Constitution.
(b) A federal statute conflicts with a state constitutional provision.
(c) A state statute conflicts with the common law of that state.
(d) A state constitutional amendment conflicts with the U.S. Constitution.

1–5. In the text of this chapter, we stated that the doctrine of *stare decisis* "became a cornerstone of the English and American judicial systems." What does *stare decisis* mean, and why has this doctrine been so fundamental to the development of our legal tradition?

1–6. Based on the discussion of case terminology in the appendix to this chapter, what is the difference between a concurring opinion and a majority opinion? Between a concurring opinion and a dissenting opinion? Why do judges and justices write concurring and dissenting opinions, given that these opinions will not affect the outcome of the case at hand, which has already been decided by majority vote?

1–7. Courts can overturn precedents and thus change the common law. Should judges have the same authority to overrule statutory law? Explain.

1–8. "The judge's role is not to make the law but to uphold and apply the law." Do you agree or disagree with this statement? Discuss fully the reasons for your answer.

1–9. IN YOUR COURT

Arthur Rabe is suing Xavier Sanchez for breaching a contract in which Sanchez promised to sell Rabe a Van Gogh painting for $150,000. Assume that you are the judge in the trial court hearing the case and answer the following questions:

(a) In this lawsuit, who is the plaintiff and who is the defendant?
(b) Rabe wants Sanchez to perform the contract as promised. What remedy should he seek?
(c) Suppose that Rabe wants to cancel the contract because Sanchez fraudulently misrepresented the painting as an original Van Gogh when in fact it is a copy. What remedy is Rabe seeking?
(d) Will the remedy Rabe seeks in either situation be a remedy at law or a remedy in equity?
(e) Suppose that you grant one of these remedies. Sanchez then appeals the decision to a higher court. Read the appendix following this chapter and then answer the following question: On appeal, which party will be the appellant (or petitioner), and which party will be the appellee (or respondent)?

1–10. A QUESTION OF ETHICS AND SOCIAL RESPONSIBILITY

On July 5, 1884, Dudley, Stephens, and Brooks—"all able-bodied English seamen"—and an English teenage boy were cast adrift in a lifeboat following a storm at sea. They had no water with them in the boat, and all they had for sustenance were two one-pound tins of turnips. On July 24, Dudley proposed that one of the four in the lifeboat be sacrificed to save the others. Stephens agreed with Dudley, but Brooks refused to consent—and the boy was never asked for his opinion. On July 25, Dudley killed the boy, and the three men then fed on the boy's body and blood. Four days later, the men were rescued by a passing vessel. They were taken to England and tried for the murder of the boy. If the men had not fed on the boy's body, they would probably have died of starvation within the four-day period. The boy, who was in a much weaker condition, would likely have died before the rest. [*Regina v. Dudley and Stephens*, 14 Q.B.D. (Queen's Bench Division, England) 273 (1884)]

(a) Should the survivors be subject to penalties under English criminal law, given the men's unusual circumstances? Why or why not?
(b) Should judges ever have the power to look beyond the written "letter of the law" in making their decisions? Explain.

1–11. FOR CRITICAL ANALYSIS

Courts of equity tend to follow general rules or maxims rather than common law precedents, as courts of law do. Some of these maxims were listed in Exhibit 1–2. Why would equity courts give credence to such general maxims rather than to a hard-and-fast body of law?

Today, business law and legal environment professors and students can go online to access information on virtually every topic covered in this text. A good point of departure for online legal research is the Web site for *Essentials of the Legal Environment,* which can be found at **http://ele.westbuslaw.com**. There you will find numerous materials relevant to this text and to business law generally, including links to various legal resources on the Web. Additionally, every chapter in this text ends with a *Law on the Web* feature that contains selected Web addresses.

You can access many of the sources of law discussed in Chapter 1 at the FindLaw Web site, which is probably the most comprehensive source of free legal information on the Internet. (FindLaw is now a part of West Group.) Go to

http://www.findlaw.com

The Legal Information Institute (LII) at Cornell Law School, which offers extensive information about U.S. law, is also a good starting point for legal research. The URL for this site is

http://www.law.cornell.edu

The Library of Congress offers extensive links to state and federal government resources at

http://www.loc.gov

The Virtual Law Library Index, created and maintained by the Indiana University School of Law, provides an index of legal sources categorized by subject at

http://www.law.indiana.edu/v-lib/index.html

LEGAL RESEARCH EXERCISES ON THE WEB

Go to **http://ele.westbuslaw.com**, the Web site that accompanies this text. Select "Interactive Study Center," and then click on "Chapter 1." There you will find the following Internet research exercises that you can perform to learn more about sources of law on the Web.

Activity 1–1: LEGAL PERSPECTIVE—Internet Sources of Law

Activity 1–2: MANAGEMENT PERSPECTIVE—Online Assistance from Government Agencies

BEFORE THE TEST

Go to **http://ele.westbuslaw.com**, the Web site that accompanies this text. Select "Interactive Quizzes." You will find at least twenty interactive questions relating to this chapter.

WESTLAW® CAMPUS

If your textbook provided for a subscription to Westlaw® Campus, or if you have otherwise purchased access to the Westlaw Campus database, you can access any of the cases cited in this chapter by using your Westlaw Campus account.

APPENDIX TO CHAPTER 1
FINDING AND ANALYZING THE LAW

This text includes numerous citations to primary sources of law—federal and state statutes, regulations issued by administrative agencies, and court cases. (A **citation** is a reference to a publication in which a legal authority—such as a statute or a court decision or other source—can be found.) In this appendix, we explain how you can use citations to find primary sources of law.

Citation • A reference to a publication in which a legal authority—such as a statute or a court decision—or other source can be found.

FINDING STATUTORY LAW

When Congress passes laws, they are collected in a publication titled *United States Statutes at Large*. When state legislatures pass laws, they are collected in similar state publications. Most frequently, however, laws are referred to in their codified form—that is, the form in which they appear in the federal and state codes.

In these codes, laws are compiled by subject. The *United States Code* (U.S.C.) arranges all existing federal laws of a public and permanent nature by subject. Each of the fifty subjects into which the U.S.C. arranges the laws is given a title and a title number. For example, laws relating to commerce and trade are collected in Title 15, "Commerce and Trade." Titles are subdivided by sections. A citation to the U.S.C. includes title and section numbers. Thus, a reference to "15 U.S.C. Section 1" means that the statute can be found in Section 1 of Title 15. ("Section" may also be designated by the symbol §, and "Sections," by §§.) Sometimes a citation includes the abbreviation *et seq.*, as in "15 U.S.C. Sections 1 *et seq.*" The term is an abbreviated form of *et sequitur*, which in Latin means "and the following"; when used in a citation, it refers to sections that concern the same subject as the numbered section and follow it in sequence.

State codes follow the U.S.C. pattern of arranging law by subject. They may be called codes, revisions, compilations, consolidations, general statutes, or statutes, depending on the preferences of the states. In some codes, subjects are designated by number. In others, they are designated by name. For example, "13 Pennsylvania Consolidated Statutes Section 1101" means that the statute can be found in Title 13, Section 1101, of the Pennsylvania code. "California Commercial Code Section 1101" means that the statute can be found under the subject heading "Commercial Code" of the California code in Section 1101. Abbreviations may be used. For example, "13 Pennsylvania Consolidated Statutes Section 1101" may often be abbreviated "13 Pa. C.S. §1101," and "California Commercial Code Section 1101" may be abbreviated "Cal. Com. Code §1101."

Commercial publications of these laws and regulations are available and are widely used. For example, West Group publishes the *United States Code Annotated* (U.S.C.A.). The U.S.C.A. contains the complete text of laws included in the U.S.C., plus notes on court decisions that interpret and apply specific sections of the statutes, as well as the text of presidential proclamations and executive orders. The U.S.C.A. also includes research aids, such as cross-references to related statutes, historical notes, and library references. A citation to the U.S.C.A. is similar to a citation to the U.S.C.: "15 U.S.C.A. Section 1."

FINDING ADMINISTRATIVE LAW

Rules and regulations adopted by federal administrative agencies are initially published in the *Federal Register,* a daily publication of the U.S. government. Later, they are incorporated into the *Code of Federal Regulations* (C.F.R.). Like the U.S.C., the C.F.R. is divided into fifty titles. Rules within each title are assigned section numbers. A full citation to the C.F.R. includes title and section numbers. For example, a reference to "17 C.F.R. Section 230.504" means that the rule can be found in Section 230.504 of Title 17.

FINDING CASE LAW

To understand how to read citations to court cases, we need first to look briefly at the court system. As will be discussed in Chapter 2, there are two types of courts in the United States, federal courts and state courts. Both the federal and state court systems consist of several levels, or tiers, of courts.

Trial courts, in which evidence is presented and testimony given, are on the bottom tier (which also includes lower courts handling specialized issues). Decisions from a trial court can be appealed to a higher court, commonly an intermediate *court of appeals,* or an *appellate court.* Decisions from these intermediate courts of appeals may be appealed to an even higher court, such as a state supreme court or the United States Supreme Court.

When reading the cases presented in this text, you will note that most of the state court cases are from state appellate courts. This is because most state trial court opinions are not published. Except in New York and a few other states that publish selected opinions of their trial courts, decisions from the state trial courts are merely filed in the office of the clerk of the court, where they are available for public inspection. Many of the federal trial (district) courts do publish their opinions, however, and you will find that several of the cases set forth in this book are from these courts, as well as the federal appellate courts.

State Court Decisions

Written decisions of the state appellate, or reviewing, courts are published and distributed in volumes called *Reports,* which are numbered consecutively.

Reporters Containing State Court Decisions. Decisions of the appellate courts of a particular state are usually found in the reporters of that state. A few states—including those with intermediate appellate courts, such as California, Illinois, and New York—have more than one reporter for opinions given by their courts.

Additionally, state court opinions appear in regional units of the National Reporter System, published by West Group. Most lawyers and libraries have the West reporters because they report cases more quickly, and are distributed more widely, than the state-published reporters. In fact, many states have eliminated their own reporters in favor of West's National Reporter System. The National Reporter System divides the states into the following geographic areas: *Atlantic* (A. or A.2d), *South Eastern* (S.E. or S.E.2d), *South Western* (S.W.,

S.W.2d, or S.W.3d), *North Western* (N.W. or N.W.2d), *North Eastern* (N.E. or N.E.2d), *Southern* (So. or So.2d), and *Pacific* (P., P.2d, or P.3d). (The *2d* and *3d* in the preceding abbreviations refer to *Second Series* and *Third Series,* respectively.) The states included in each of these regional divisions are indicated in Exhibit 1A–1.

Case Citations. After an appellate decision has been published, it is normally referred to (cited) by the name of the case (called the *style* of the case); the volume, name, and page of the state's official reporter (if different from West's National Reporter System); the volume, unit, and page number of the National Reporter; and the volume, name, and page number of any other selected reporter. (Citing a reporter by volume number, name, and page number, in that order, is common to all citations; often, as in this book, the year the decision was made will be included in parentheses, just after the citations to reporters.) When more than one reporter is cited for the same case, each reference is called a *parallel citation.*[1]

For example, consider the following case citation: *Davidson v. Microsoft Corp.,* 143 Md.App. 43, 792 A.2d 336 (2002). We see that the opinion in this case may be found in Volume 143 of the official *Maryland Appellate Reports,* on page 43. The parallel citation is to Volume 792 of the *Atlantic Reporter, Second Series,* page 336. In reprinting appellate opinions in this text, in addition to the reporter, we give the name of the court hearing the case and the year of the court's decision.

Sample citations to state court decisions are explained in Exhibit 1A–2, which begins on page 29.

Federal Court Decisions

Federal district (trial) court decisions are published unofficially in West's *Federal Supplement* (F.Supp. or F.Supp.2d), and opinions from the circuit courts of appeals are reported unofficially in West's *Federal Reporter* (F., F.2d, or F.3d). Cases concerning federal bankruptcy law are published unofficially in West's *Bankruptcy Reporter* (Bankr.).

The official edition of all decisions of the United States Supreme Court for which there are written opinions is the *United States Reports* (U.S.), which is published by the federal government. The series includes reports of Supreme Court cases dating from the August term of 1791, although many of the Supreme Court's decisions were not reported in the early volumes.

Unofficial editions of Supreme Court cases include West's *Supreme Court Reporter* (S.Ct.), which includes cases dating from the Court's term in October 1882; and the *Lawyers' Edition of the Supreme Court Reports* (L.Ed. or L.Ed.2d), published by the Lawyers Cooperative Publishing Company (now a part of West Group). The latter contains many of the decisions not reported in the early volumes of the *United States Reports.*

1. Note that Wisconsin has adopted a "public domain citation system" in which the format is somewhat different. For example, a Wisconsin Supreme Court decision might be designated "2003 WI 40," meaning that the case was decided in the year 2003 by the Wisconsin Supreme Court and was the fortieth decision issued by that court during that year. (Parallel citations to the *Wisconsin Reports* and West's *North Western Reporter* are still required when citing Wisconsin cases.)

EXHIBIT 1A-1 • NATIONAL REPORTER SYSTEM—REGIONAL/FEDERAL

Regional Reporters	Coverage Beginning	Coverage
Atlantic Reporter (A. or A.2d)	1885	Connecticut, Delaware, Maine, Maryland, New Hampshire, New Jersey, Pennsylvania, Rhode Island, Vermont, and District of Columbia.
North Eastern Reporter (N.E. or N.E.2d)	1885	Illinois, Indiana, Massachusetts, New York, and Ohio.
North Western Reporter (N.W. or N.W.2d)	1879	Iowa, Michigan, Minnesota, Nebraska, North Dakota, South Dakota, and Wisconsin.
Pacific Reporter (P., P.2d, or P.3d)	1883	Alaska, Arizona, California, Colorado, Hawaii, Idaho, Kansas, Montana, Nevada, New Mexico, Oklahoma, Oregon, Utah, Washington, and Wyoming.
South Eastern Reporter (S.E. or S.E.2d)	1887	Georgia, North Carolina, South Carolina, Virginia, and West Virginia.
South Western Reporter (S.W., S.W.2d, or S.W.3d)	1886	Arkansas, Kentucky, Missouri, Tennessee, and Texas.
Southern Reporter (So. or So.2d)	1887	Alabama, Florida, Louisiana, and Mississippi.
Federal Reporters		
Federal Reporter (F., F.2d, or F.3d)	1880	U.S. Circuit Court from 1880 to 1912; U.S. Commerce Court from 1911 to 1913; U.S. District Courts from 1880 to 1932; U.S. Court of Claims (now called U.S. Court of Federal Claims) from 1929 to 1932 and since 1960; U.S. Courts of Appeals since 1891; U.S. Court of Customs and Patent Appeals since 1929; U.S. Emergency Court of Appeals since 1943.
Federal Supplement (F.Supp. or F.Supp.2d)	1932	U.S. Court of Claims from 1932 to 1960; U.S. District Courts since 1932; and U.S. Customs Court since 1956.
Federal Rules Decisions (F.R.D.)	1939	U.S. District Courts involving the Federal Rules of Civil Procedure since 1939 and Federal Rules of Criminal Procedure since 1946.
Supreme Court Reporter (S.Ct.)	1882	U.S. Supreme Court since the October term of 1882.
Bankruptcy Reporter (Bankr.)	1980	Bankruptcy decisions of U.S. Bankruptcy Courts, U.S. District Courts, U.S. Courts of Appeals, and U.S. Supreme Court.
Military Justice Reporter (M.J.)	1978	U.S. Court of Military Appeals and Courts of Military Review for the Army, Navy, Air Force, and Coast Guard.

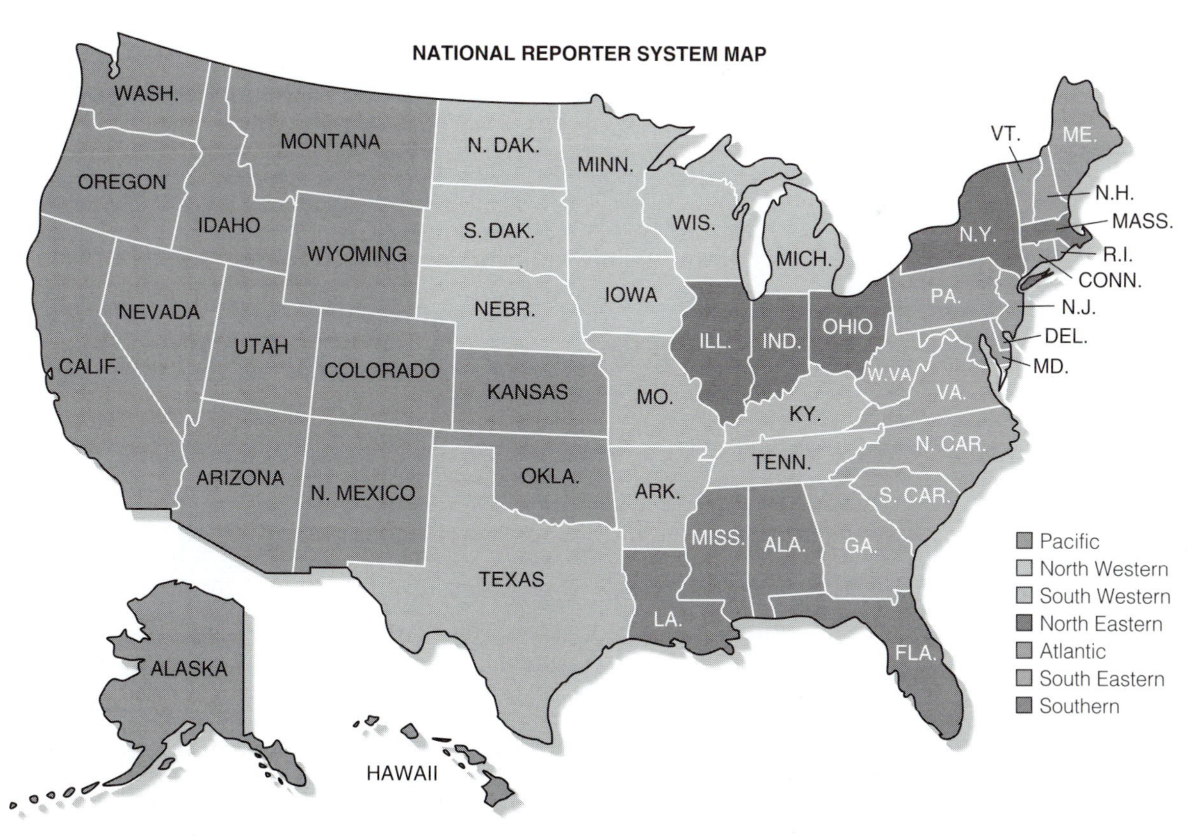

Sample citations for federal court decisions are also listed and explained in Exhibit 1A–2.

Old Case Law

On a few occasions, this text cites opinions from old, classic cases dating to the nineteenth century or earlier; some of these are from the English courts. The citations to these cases may not conform to the descriptions given above because the reporters in which they were published were often known by the name of the person who compiled the reporter and have since been replaced.

Case Digests and Legal Encyclopedias

The body of American case law consists of over five million decisions, to which more than forty thousand decisions are added each year. Because judicial decisions are published in chronological order, finding relevant precedents would be a Herculean task if it were not for secondary sources of law that classify decisions according to subject. Two important "finding tools" that are helpful when researching case law are case digests, such as West's *American Digest System;* and legal encyclopedias, such as *American Jurisprudence, Second Edition,* and *Corpus Juris Secundum,* both published by West Group.

How to Read and Understand Case Law

The decisions made by the courts establish the boundaries of the law as it applies to virtually all business relationships. It thus is essential that businesspersons know how to read and understand case law. The cases that we present in this text have been condensed from the full text of the courts' opinions and are presented in a special format. In each case, we have summarized the background and facts, as well as the court's decision and remedy, in our own words and have included only selected portions of the court's opinion. For those who wish to review court cases to perform research projects or to gain additional legal information, however, the following sections will provide useful insights into how to read and understand case law.

Case Titles

The title of a case, such as *Adams v. Jones,* indicates the names of the parties to the lawsuit. The *v.* in the case title stands for *versus,* which means "against." In the trial court, Adams was the plaintiff—the person who filed the suit. Jones was the defendant. If the case is appealed, however, the appellate court will sometimes place the name of the party appealing the decision first, so the case may be called *Jones v. Adams* if Jones is appealing. Because some appellate courts retain the trial court order of names, it is often impossible to distinguish the plaintiff from the defendant in the title of a reported appellate court decision. You must carefully read the facts of each case to identify the parties. Otherwise, the discussion by the appellate court may be difficult to comprehend.

EXHIBIT 1A-2 • HOW TO READ CITATIONS

State Courts

263 Neb. 881, 644 N.W.2d 128 (2002)[a]

N.W. is the abbreviation for West's publication of state court decisions rendered in the *North Western Reporter* of the National Reporter System. *2d* indicates that this case was included in the *Second Series* of that reporter. The number 644 refers to the volume number of the reporter; the number 128 refers to the page in that volume on which this case begins.

Neb. is an abbreviation for *Nebraska Reports,* Nebraska's official reports of the decisions of its highest court, the Nebraska Supreme Court.

98 Cal.App.4th 892, 120 Cal.Rptr.2d 576 (2002)

Cal.Rptr. is the abbreviation for West's unofficial reports—titled *California Reporter*—of the decisions of the California Supreme Court and California appellate courts.

97 N.Y.2d 463, 768 N.E.2d 1121, 742 N.Y.S.2d 182 (2002)

N.Y.S. is the abbreviation for West's unofficial reports—titled *New York Supplement*—of the decisions of New York courts.

N.Y. is the abbreviation for *New York Reports,* New York's official reports of the decisions of its court of appeals. The New York Court of Appeals is the state's highest court, analogous to other states' supreme courts. (In New York, a supreme court is a trial court.)

253 Ga.App. 639, 560 S.E.2d 40 (2002)

Ga.App. is the abbreviation for *Georgia Appeals Reports,* Georgia's official reports of the decisions of its court of appeals.

Federal Courts

534 U.S. 184, 122 S.Ct. 681, 151 L.Ed.2d 615 (2002)

L.Ed. is an abbreviation for *Lawyers' Edition of the Supreme Court Reports,* an unofficial edition of decisions of the United States Supreme Court.

S.Ct. is the abbreviation for West's unofficial reports—titled *Supreme Court Reporter*—of decisions of the United States Supreme Court.

U.S. is the abbreviation for *United States Reports,* the official edition of the decisions of the United States Supreme Court.

a. The case names have been deleted from these citations to emphasize the publications. It should be kept in mind, however, that the name of a case is as important as the specific numbers of the volumes in which it is found. If a citation is incorrect, the correct citation may be found in a publication's index of case names. The date of a case is also important because, in addition to providing a check on error in citations, the value of a recent case as an authority is likely to be greater than that of an earlier case.

EXHIBIT 1A–2 • HOW TO READ CITATIONS (CONTINUED)

Federal Courts (continued)

287 F.3d 122 (2d Cir. 2002)

2d Cir. is an abbreviation denoting that this case was decided in the United States Court of Appeals for the Second Circuit.

187 F.Supp.2d 1288 (D.Colo. 2002)

D.Colo. is an abbreviation indicating that the United States District Court for the District of Colorado decided this case.

English Courts

9 Exch. 341, 156 Eng.Rep. 145 (1854)

Eng.Rep. is an abbreviation for *English Reports, Full Reprint,* a series of reports containing selected decisions made in English courts between 1378 and 1865.

Exch. is an abbreviation for *English Exchequer Reports,* which included the original reports of cases decided in England's Court of Exchequer.

Statutory and Other Citations

18 U.S.C. Section 1961(1)(A)

U.S.C. denotes *United States Code,* the codification of *United States Statutes at Large.* The number 18 refers to the statute's U.S.C. title number and 1961 to its section number within that title. The number 1 refers to a subsection within the section and the letter A to a subdivision within the subsection.

UCC 2–206(1)(b)

UCC is an abbreviation for *Uniform Commercial Code.* The first number 2 is a reference to an article of the UCC and 206 to a section within that article. The number 1 refers to a subsection within the section and the letter b to a subdivision within the subsection.

Restatement (Second) of Contracts, Section 162

Restatement (Second) of Contracts refers to the second edition of the American Law Institute's *Restatement of the Law of Contracts.* The number 162 refers to a specific section.

17 C.F.R. Section 230.505

C.F.R. is an abbreviation for *Code of Federal Regulations,* a compilation of federal administrative regulations. The number 17 designates the regulation's title number, and 230.505 designates a specific section within that title.

EXHIBIT 1A-2 • HOW TO READ CITATIONS (CONTINUED)

Westlaw® Citations[b]

2005 WL 10238

WL is an abbreviation for Westlaw®. The number 2005 is the year of the document that can be found with this citation in the Westlaw® database. The number 10238 is a number assigned to a specific document. A higher number indicates that a document was added to the Westlaw® database later in the year.

Uniform Resource Locators (URLs)

http://www.westlaw.com[c]

The suffix *com* is the top level domain (TLD) for this Web site. The TLD *com* is an abbreviation for "commercial," which means that normally a for-profit entity hosts (maintains or supports) this Web site.

westlaw is the host name—the part of the domain name selected by the organization that registered the name. In this case, West Group registered the name. This Internet site is the Westlaw database on the Web.

www is an abbreviation for "World Wide Web." The Web is a system of Internet servers that support documents formatted in *HTML* (hypertext markup language). HTML supports links to text, graphics, and audio and video files.

http://www.uscourts.gov

This is "The Federal Judiciary Home Page." The host is the Administrative Office of the U.S. Courts. The TLD *gov* is an abbreviation for "government." This Web site includes information and links to, and about, the federal courts.

http://www.law.cornell.edu/index.html

This part of a URL points to a Web page or file at a specific location within the host's domain. This page is a menu with links to documents within the domain and to other Internet resources.

This is the host name for a Web site that contains the Internet publications of the Legal Information Institute (LII), which is a part of Cornell Law School. The LII site includes a variety of legal materials and links to other legal resources on the Internet. The TLD *edu* is an abbreviation for "educational institution" (a school or a university).

http://www.ipl.org/ref

ref is an abbreviation for "Internet Public Library Reference Center," which is a map of the topics into which the links at this Web site have been categorized.

ipl is an abbreviation for Internet Public Library, which is an online service that provides reference resources and links to other information services on the Web. The IPL is supported chiefly by the School of Information at the University of Michigan. The TLD *org* is an abbreviation for "organization (normally nonprofit)."

b. Many court decisions that are not yet published or that are not intended for publication can be accessed through Westlaw®, an online legal database.
c. The basic form for a URL is "service://hostname/path." The Internet service for all of the URLs in this text is *http* (hypertext transfer protocol). Most Web browsers will add this prefix automatically when a user enters a host name or a hostname/path.

Terminology

The following terms, phrases, and abbreviations are frequently encountered in court opinions and legal publications. Because it is important to understand what is meant by these terms, phrases, and abbreviations, we define and discuss them here.

Parties to Lawsuits. As mentioned in Chapter 1, the party initiating a lawsuit is referred to as the *plaintiff* or *petitioner,* depending on the nature of the action. The party against whom a lawsuit is brought is the *defendant* or *respondent.* Lawsuits frequently involve more than one plaintiff and/or defendant. When a case is appealed from the original court or jurisdiction to another court or jurisdiction, the party appealing the case is called the **appellant.** The **appellee** is the party against whom the appeal is taken. (In some appellate courts, the party appealing a case is referred to as the petitioner, and the party against whom the suit is brought or appealed is called the respondent.)

Appellant • The party who takes an appeal from one court to another.

Appellee • The party against whom an appeal is taken—that is, the party who opposes setting aside or reversing the judgment.

Judges and Justices. The terms *judge* and *justice* are usually synonymous and represent two designations given to judges in various courts. All members of the United States Supreme Court, for example, are referred to as justices, and justice is the formal title usually given to judges of appellate courts, although this is not always the case. In New York, a justice is a judge of the trial court (which is called the Supreme Court), and a member of the Court of Appeals (the state's highest court) is called a judge. The term *justice* is commonly abbreviated to J., and *justices,* to JJ. A Supreme Court case might refer to Justice Kennedy as Kennedy, J., or to Chief Justice Rehnquist as Rehnquist, C.J.

Decisions and Opinions. Most decisions reached by reviewing, or appellate, courts are explained in written **opinions.** The opinion contains the court's reasons for its decision, the rules of law that apply, and the judgment.

Opinion • A statement by the court expressing the reasons for its decision in a case.

Unanimous, Concurring, and Dissenting Opinions. When all judges or justices unanimously agree on an opinion, the opinion is written for the entire court and can be deemed a *unanimous opinion.* When there is not a unanimous opinion, a *majority opinion* is written; the majority opinion outlines the view supported by the majority of the judges or justices deciding the case. If a judge agrees, or concurs, with the majority's decision, but for different reasons, that judge may write a *concurring opinion.* A *dissenting opinion* presents the views of one or more judges who disagree with the majority's decision. The dissenting opinion is important because it may form the basis of the arguments used years later in overruling the precedential majority opinion.

Other Types of Opinions. Occasionally, a court issues a *per curiam* opinion. *Per curiam* is a Latin phrase meaning "of the court." In *per curiam* opinions, there is no indication of which judge or justice authored the opinion. This term may also be used for an announcement of a court's disposition of a case that is not accompanied by a written opinion. Some of the cases presented in this text are *en banc* decisions. When an appellate court reviews a case *en banc,* which is a French term (derived from a Latin term) for "in the bench," generally all of the judges sitting on the bench of that court review the case.

A Sample Court Case

To illustrate the various elements contained in a court opinion, we present an annotated court opinion in Exhibit 1A–3, which begins on the next page. The opinion is from an actual Virginia Supreme Court case decided in 2003.

Backgound of the Case. Dominion Technology Partners, L.L.C.,[2] initiated a suit against Donald Williams, claiming in part that Williams breached a duty of loyalty that he owed to Dominion as its employee. The court ruled in Dominion's favor on this claim, and Williams appealed. The question before the Virginia Supreme Court was whether the trial court erred in its conclusion that Williams had breached a duty of loyalty to Dominion.

Editorial Practices. You will note that triple asterisks (* * *) and quadruple asterisks (* * * *) frequently appear in the opinion. The triple asterisks indicate that we have deleted a few words or sentences from the opinion for the sake of readability or brevity. Quadruple asterisks mean that an entire paragraph (or more) has been omitted. Additionally, when the opinion cites another case or legal source, the citation to the case or other source has been omitted to save space and to improve the flow of the text. These editorial practices are continued in the other court opinions presented in this text.[3] In addition, whenever we present a court opinion that includes a term or phrase that may not be readily understandable, a bracketed definition or paraphrase has been added.

Briefing Cases. Knowing how to read and understand court opinions and the legal reasoning used by the courts is an essential step in undertaking accurate legal research. Yet a further step is "briefing," or summarizing, the case. Legal researchers routinely brief cases by reducing the texts of the opinions to their essential elements. Generally, when you brief a case, you first summarize the background and facts of the case, as the authors have done for the cases presented within this text. You then indicate the issue (or issues) before the court. An important element in the case brief is, of course, the court's decision on the issue and the legal reasoning used by the court in reaching that decision. Detailed instructions on how to brief a case are given in the Preface to the Student, which also includes a briefed version of the sample court case presented in Exhibit 1A–3.

---

2. *L.L.C.* is an abbreviation for *limited liability company,* which is a particular form of business enterprise that limits the liability of its owners for the firm's debts and other obligations. See Chapter 9.
3. We make an exception in the unit-ending *Focus on Legal Reasoning* sections, however, in which we retain the courts' citations to facilitate student research.

EXHIBIT 1A-3 • A SAMPLE COURT CASE

WILLIAMS v. DOMINION TECHNOLOGY PARTNERS, L.L.C.

Virginia Supreme Court, 2003.
576 S.E.2d 752.

> This line gives the name of the judge who authored the opinion of the court.

LAWRENCE L. KOONTZ, JR., Justice.

* * * *

> The court divides the opinion into three parts. The first part of the opinion summarizes the factual background of the case.

BACKGROUND

* * * *

Dominion Technology Partners, L.L.C. * * * is an employment firm specializing in recruiting qualified computer consultants and placing them * * * on a temporary basis with various companies. Sometime in late 1998 or early 1999, Dominion learned that Stihl, Inc. (Stihl), a power tool manufacturing firm, was seeking a computer consultant to oversee the installation of a new software package on computer systems at Stihl's facilities in Virginia Beach.

> Employment at will is a common law doctrine under which an employer or an employee may terminate their relationship at any time for any reason, unless a contract specifies otherwise.

Dominion recruited Donald Williams as a possible candidate to fill the position at Stihl. * * * Dominion offered to employ Williams as an **at-will employee,** paying Williams $80 per hour. * * * Williams [agreed].

> An agreement that can be enforced in court; formed by two or more parties, each of whom agrees to perform, or to refrain from performing, some act now or in the future.

* * * On January 22, 1999, Stihl entered into a **contract** * * * to employ Williams for an initial period of three months. * * *

* * * *

* * * Williams was responsible for the installation of a new software package related to Stihl's computer word processing, production and materials planning, and customer shipment functions. * * * The installation was completed on time, and Stihl decided to **retain** Williams in "a support and maintenance role" for an indeterminate period * * * on "a monthly basis * * * ."

> To keep; to engage the services of a party.

* * * *

[More than a year later, when] Stihl was considering a further software upgrade to its computer systems * * * , Williams indicated that he would prefer to continue working at Stihl under a direct agreement * * * .

* * * *

EXHIBIT 1A–3 • A SAMPLE COURT CASE (CONTINUED)

Unconditionally offered to perform an act (in this case, to quit employment).

* * * In a letter dated March 4, 2000, Williams formally **tendered** his resignation as an at-will employee of Dominion to be effective April 14, 2000. * * *

* * * In May 2000, Dominion learned that Williams had continued working at Stihl * * * [for which he was] paid $115 per hour * * * .

A duty, imposed on a party by virtue of his or her position, to act primarily for another's benefit.

On July 11, 2000, Dominion filed a [suit in a Virginia state court] against Williams alleging * * * breach of **fiduciary duty** [among other things].

* * * *

Final order or decision.

* * * [T]he trial court entered **judgment** [in favor of Dominion.] * * * [W]e awarded Williams this appeal.

The second major section of the opinion analyzes the issue before the court.

DISCUSSION

* * * *

We have long recognized that under the common law an employee, including an employee at will, owes a fiduciary duty of loyalty to his employer during his employment. Subsumed within this general duty of loyalty is the more specific duty that the employee not compete with his employer during his employment. Nonetheless, in the absence of a contract restriction regarding this duty of loyalty, an employee has the right to make arrangements during his employment to compete with his employer after resigning his post. * * *

* * * *

Allegations; declarations; statements claimed to be true.

* * * [T]he essence of Dominion's **assertions** against Williams * * * is that Williams, * * * while still an employee of Dominion, arranged [to continue working for Stihl] effective upon his resignation from Dominion.

A question as to which a final answer will resolve a controversy.

The **dispositive question** * * * is whether this conduct * * * was sufficient to constitute a breach of Williams's fiduciary duty of loyalty to Dominion. * * *

* * * [T]hat particular conduct of an employee caused harm to his employer does not establish that the conduct breached any duty to the employer. This is so because the law will not provide **relief** to every disgruntled player in the rough-and-tumble world comprising the competitive marketplace,

A general designation of the remedy that a complainant seeks from a court.

EXHIBIT 1A–3 • A SAMPLE COURT CASE (CONTINUED)

A loss or injury of any kind to any person resulting from any cause. Courts do not grant relief for all harms.

A contractual promise to refrain from competing with another party for a certain period of time and within a reasonable geographic area. Also called a covenant not to compete.

To be added as increase or profit.

Information; knowledge of the existence of a fact.

Design, resolve, or determination; the state of mind with which an act is done or omitted. Intent should not be confused with *motive,* which is what prompts a person to act, or fail to act.

The final section of the opinion, in which the court gives its order.

especially where, through more prudent business practices, the **harm** complained of could easily have been avoided.

* * * *

* * * Dominion had not sought a **noncompete agreement** from Williams * * * . In such circumstances, it cannot be said that Williams's conduct to safeguard his own interests was either disloyal or unfair to Dominion. Rather, we are of opinion that Dominion's contracts provided it with nothing more than a subjective belief or hope that the business relationships would continue and merely a possibility that future economic benefit would **accrue** to it.

* * * [B]y providing reasonable **notice** of his **intent** to resign his post * * * , Williams allowed Dominion to receive all the benefits for which it had bargained. Dominion's disappointment that its hopes did not bear the expected additional benefit it might have obtained under a different contractual agreement * * * does not translate into a breach of any fiduciary duty Williams owed to Dominion.

CONCLUSION

* * * Accordingly, we will reverse the judgment in favor of Dominion, and enter final judgment for Williams.

CHAPTER 2

The Court System

CONTENTS

CHAPTER OBJECTIVES

After reading this chapter, you should be able to answer the following questions:

1. What is judicial review? How and when was the power of judicial review established?

2. Before a court can hear a case, it must have jurisdiction. Over what must it have jurisdiction? In what circumstances does a federal court have jurisdiction?

3. What is the difference between a trial court and an appellate court?

4. In a lawsuit, what are the pleadings? What is discovery?

5. What are the steps involved in an appeal?

Today, in the United States, there are fifty-two court systems—one for each of the fifty states, one for the District of Columbia, and a federal system. Keep in mind that the federal courts are not superior to the state courts; they are simply an independent system of courts, which derives its authority from Article III, Section 2, of the U.S. Constitution. By the power given to it under Article I of the U.S. Constitution, Congress has extended the federal court system beyond the boundaries of the United States to U.S. territories such as Guam, the Virgin Islands, and Puerto Rico.[1] As we shall see, the United States Supreme Court is the final controlling voice over all of these fifty-two systems, at least when questions of federal law are involved.

Every businessperson will likely face a lawsuit at some time in his or her career. It is thus important for anyone involved in business to have an understanding of the American court systems, as well as the various methods of dispute resolution that can be pursued outside the courts. In this chapter, after examining the judiciary's general role in the American governmental scheme, we discuss some basic requirements that must be met before a party may bring a lawsuit before a particular court. We then look at the court systems and judicial procedures of the United States in some detail. We examine alternative methods of settling disputes, including online dispute resolution, in Chapter 3.

THE JUDICIARY'S ROLE IN AMERICAN GOVERNMENT

As you learned in Chapter 1, the body of American law includes the federal and state constitutions, statutes passed by legislative bodies, administrative law, and the case decisions and legal principles that form the common law. These laws would be meaningless, however, without the courts to interpret and apply them. This is the essential role of the judiciary—the courts—in the

1. In Guam and the Virgin Islands, territorial courts serve as both federal courts and state courts; in Puerto Rico, they serve only as federal courts.

American governmental system: to interpret the laws and apply them to specific situations.

As the branch of government entrusted with interpreting the laws, the judiciary can decide, among other things, whether the laws or actions of the other two branches are constitutional. The process for making such a determination is known as **judicial review.** The power of judicial review enables the judicial branch to act as a check on the other two branches of government, in line with the checks and balances system established by the U.S. Constitution.[2]

Judicial review • The process by which courts decide on the constitutionality of legislative enactments and actions of the executive branch.

The power of judicial review is not mentioned in the Constitution (although many constitutional scholars conclude that the founders intended the judiciary to have this power). Rather, this power was explicitly established by the United States Supreme Court in 1803 by its decision in *Marbury v. Madison,*[3] in which the Supreme Court stated, "It is emphatically the province and duty of the Judicial Department to say what the law is. . . . If two laws conflict with each other, the courts must decide on the operation of each. . . . So if the law be in opposition to the Constitution . . . [t]he Court must determine which of these conflicting rules governs the case. This is the very essence of judicial duty." Since the *Marbury v. Madison* decision, the power of judicial review has remained unchallenged. Today, this power is exercised by both federal and state courts.

Basic Judicial Requirements

Before a lawsuit can be brought before a court, certain requirements must be met. These requirements relate to jurisdiction, venue, and standing to sue. We examine each of these important concepts here.

Jurisdiction

In Latin, *juris* means "law," and *diction* means "to speak." Thus, "the power to speak the law" is the literal meaning of the term **jurisdiction.** Before any court can hear a case, it must have jurisdiction over the person against whom the suit is brought or jurisdiction over the property involved in the lawsuit. The court must also have jurisdiction over the subject matter.

Jurisdiction • The authority of a court to hear and decide a specific action.

Jurisdiction over Persons. Generally, a particular court can exercise ***in personam* jurisdiction** (personal jurisdiction) over residents of a certain geographic area. A state trial court, for example, normally has jurisdictional authority over residents of a particular area of the state, such as a county or district. A state's highest court (often called the state supreme court)[4] has jurisdictional authority over all residents within the state. Keep in mind throughout this discussion of personal jurisdiction that we are talking about jurisdiction over the *defendant* in a lawsuit.

***In personam* jurisdiction** • Court jurisdiction over the "person" involved in a legal action; personal jurisdiction.

2. In a broad sense, judicial review occurs whenever a court "reviews" a case or legal proceeding—as when an appellate court reviews a lower court's decision. When referring to the judiciary's role in American government, however, the term *judicial review* is used to indicate the power of the judiciary to decide whether the actions of the other two branches of government do or do not violate the Constitution.
3. 5 U.S. (1 Cranch) 137, 2 L.Ed. 60 (1803).
4. As will be discussed shortly, a state's highest court is often referred to as the state supreme court, but there are exceptions. For example, in New York the supreme court is a trial court.

Long arm statute • A state statute that permits a state to obtain personal jurisdiction over nonresident defendants. A defendant must have "minimum contacts" with that state for the statute to apply.

In some cases, under the authority of a state **long arm statute,** a court can exercise personal jurisdiction over out-of-state defendants as well. Before a court can exercise jurisdiction over an out-of-state defendant under a long arm statute, though, it must be demonstrated that the defendant had sufficient contacts, or *minimum contacts,* with the state to justify the jurisdiction.[5] For example, if an individual has committed a wrong within the state, such as injuring someone in an automobile accident or selling defective goods, a court can usually exercise jurisdiction even if the person causing the harm is located in another state. Similarly, a state may exercise personal jurisdiction over a nonresident defendant who is sued for breaching a contract that was formed within the state.

In regard to corporations,[6] the minimum-contacts requirement is usually met if the corporation does business within the state, advertises or sells its products within the state, or places its goods into the "stream of commerce" with the intent that the goods be sold in the state. Suppose that a business incorporated under the laws of Maine and headquartered in that state has a branch office or manufacturing plant in Georgia. Does this facility constitute sufficient contacts with the state of Georgia to allow a Georgia court to exercise jurisdiction over the corporation? Yes, it does. If the Maine corporation advertises and sells its products in Georgia, or places goods within the stream of commerce with the expectation that the goods will be purchased by Georgia residents, those activities may also suffice to meet the minimum-contacts requirement. In the following case, the issue was whether phone calls and letters constituted sufficient minimum contacts to give a court jurisdiction over a nonresident defendant.

5. The minimum-contacts standard was established in *International Shoe Co. v. State of Washington,* 326 U.S. 310, 66 S.Ct. 154, 90 L.Ed. 95 (1945).

6. In the eyes of the law, corporations are "legal persons"—entities that can sue and be sued. See Chapter 9.

CASE 2.1

United States Court of Appeals, Sixth Circuit, 1998. 133 F.3d 433. **http://www.law.emory.edu/6circuit/jan98/index.html**[a]

COLE v. MILETI

Nick Mileti, a resident of California, co-produced a movie called Streamers *and organized a corporation, Streamers International Distributors, Inc., to distribute the film. Joseph Cole, a resident of Ohio, bought two hundred shares of Streamers stock. Cole also lent the firm $475,000, which he borrowed from Equitable Bank of Baltimore. The film was unsuccessful. Mileti agreed to repay Cole's loan in a contract arranged through phone calls and correspondence between California and Ohio. When Mileti did not repay the loan, the bank sued Cole, who in turn filed a suit against Mileti in a federal district court in Ohio. The court entered a judgment against Mileti. He appealed to the U.S. Court of Appeals for the Sixth Circuit, arguing in part that the district court's exercise of jurisdiction over him was unfair.*[b]

a. This page, which is part of the Web site of the Emory University School of Law, lists the published opinions of the U.S. Court of Appeals for the Sixth Circuit for January 1998. Scroll down the list of cases to the *Cole* case. To access the opinion, click on the case name.

b. As will be discussed shortly, federal courts can exercise jurisdiction over disputes between parties living in different states. This is called *diversity-of-citizenship* jurisdiction. When a federal court exercises diversity jurisdiction, the court normally applies the law of the state in which the court sits—in this case, the law of Ohio.

MERRITT, J.[c]

[There is] a three-part test to determine whether specific jurisdiction exists over a nonresident defendant like Mileti. First, the defendant must purposefully avail himself of the privilege of conducting activities within the forum state [the state in which the lawsuit is initiated]; second, the cause of action must arise from the defendant's activities there; and third, the acts of the defendant or consequences caused by the defendant must have a substantial enough connection with the forum state to make its exercise of jurisdiction over the defendant fundamentally fair.

If, as here, a nonresident defendant transacts business by negotiating and executing a contract via telephone calls and letters to an Ohio resident, then the defendant has purposefully availed himself of the forum by creating a continuing obligation in Ohio. Furthermore, if the cause of action is for breach of that contract, as it is here, then the cause of action naturally arises from the defendant's activities in Ohio. Finally, when we find that a defendant like Mileti purposefully availed himself of the forum and that the cause of action arose directly from that contact, we presume the specific assertion of personal jurisdiction was proper.

The U.S. Court of Appeals for the Sixth Circuit held that the district court could exercise personal jurisdiction over Mileti. The appellate court reasoned that a federal district court in Ohio can exercise personal jurisdiction over a resident of California who does business in Ohio via phone calls and letters.

QUESTIONS

1. Why did Mileti argue on appeal that the district court's exercise of jurisdiction over him was unfair?
2. Why did the U.S. Court of Appeals for the Sixth Circuit hold that the district court could exercise jurisdiction over Mileti?
3. Why might a defendant prefer to be sued in one state rather than in another?

c. "J." is an abbreviation for *judge*. As explained in the Appendix to Chapter 1, an individual who presides in a court may be designated *judge* or *justice*, depending on the jurisdiction. In either case, the title is abbreviated "J." The title "chief judge" or "chief justice" is shortened to "C.J." We will use these abbreviations throughout this book.

Jurisdiction over Property. A court can also exercise jurisdiction over property that is located within its boundaries. This kind of jurisdiction is known as ***in rem* jurisdiction,** or "jurisdiction over the thing." For example, suppose a dispute arises over the ownership of a boat in dry dock in Fort Lauderdale, Florida. The boat is owned by an Ohio resident, over whom a Florida court normally cannot exercise personal jurisdiction. The other party to the dispute is a resident of Nebraska. In this situation, a lawsuit concerning the boat could be brought in a Florida state court on the basis of the court's *in rem* jurisdiction.

***In rem* jurisdiction** • Court jurisdiction over a defendant's property.

Jurisdiction over Subject Matter. Jurisdiction over subject matter is a limitation on the types of cases a court can hear. In both the federal and state court systems, there are courts of *general* (unlimited) *jurisdiction* and courts of *limited jurisdiction*. A court of general jurisdiction can decide cases involving a broad array of issues. An example of a court of general jurisdiction is a state

Probate court • A state court of limited jurisdiction that conducts proceedings relating to the settlement of a deceased person's estate.

Bankruptcy court • A federal court of limited jurisdiction that handles only bankruptcy proceedings. Bankruptcy proceedings are governed by federal bankruptcy law.

trial court or a federal district court. An example of a state court of limited jurisdiction is a probate court. **Probate courts** are state courts that handle only matters relating to the transfer of a person's assets and obligations after that person's death, including issues relating to the custody and guardianship of children. An example of a federal court of limited subject-matter jurisdiction is a bankruptcy court. **Bankruptcy courts** handle only bankruptcy proceedings, which are governed by federal bankruptcy law.

A court's jurisdiction over subject matter is usually defined in the statute or constitution creating the court. In both the federal and state court systems, a court's subject-matter jurisdiction can be limited not only by the subject of the lawsuit but also by how much money is in controversy, whether the case is a felony (a more serious type of crime) or a misdemeanor (a less serious type of crime), or whether the proceeding is a trial or an appeal.

Original and Appellate Jurisdiction. The distinction between courts of original jurisdiction and courts of appellate jurisdiction normally lies in whether the case is being heard for the first time. Courts having original jurisdiction are courts of the first instance, or trial courts—that is, courts in which lawsuits begin, trials take place, and evidence is presented. In the federal court system, the *district courts* are trial courts. In the various state court systems, the trial courts are known by different names, as will be discussed shortly.

The key point here is that, normally, any court having original jurisdiction is known as a trial court. Courts having appellate jurisdiction act as reviewing courts, or appellate courts. In general, cases can be brought before appellate courts only on appeal from an order or a judgment of a trial court or other lower court.

Federal question • A question that pertains to the U.S. Constitution, acts of Congress, or treaties. A federal question provides a basis for federal jurisdiction.

Diversity of citizenship • Under Article III, Section 2, of the Constitution, a basis for federal court jurisdiction over a lawsuit between (1) citizens of different states, (2) a foreign country and citizens of a state or of different states, or (3) citizens of a state and citizens or subjects of a foreign country. The amount in controversy must be more than $75,000 before a federal court can take jurisdiction in such cases.

Jurisdiction of the Federal Courts. Because the federal government is a government of limited powers, the jurisdiction of the federal courts is limited. Article III of the U.S. Constitution establishes the boundaries of federal judicial power. Section 2 of Article III states that "[t]he judicial Power shall extend to all Cases, in Law and Equity, arising under this Constitution, the Laws of the United States, and Treaties made, or which shall be made, under their Authority." In effect, this clause means that whenever a plaintiff's cause of action is based—at least in part—on the U.S. Constitution, a treaty, or a federal law, a **federal question** arises. Any lawsuit involving a federal question comes under the judicial authority of the federal courts and can originate in a federal court. People who claim that their constitutional rights have been violated, for example, can begin their suits in a federal court.

Federal district courts can also exercise original jurisdiction over cases involving **diversity of citizenship.** This term applies whenever a federal court has jurisdiction over a case that does not involve a question of federal law. The most common type of diversity jurisdiction has two requirements:[7] (1) the plaintiff and defendant must be residents of different states, and (2) the dollar amount in controversy must exceed $75,000. For purposes of

7. Diversity jurisdiction also exists in cases between (1) a foreign country and citizens of a state or of different states and (2) citizens of a state and citizens or subjects of a foreign country. These bases for diversity jurisdiction are less commonly used.

diversity jurisdiction, a corporation is a citizen of both the state in which it is incorporated and the state in which its principal place of business is located. A case involving diversity of citizenship can be filed in the appropriate federal district court. If the case starts in a state court, it can sometimes be transferred, or "removed," to a federal court. A large percentage of the cases filed in federal courts each year are based on diversity of citizenship.

Note that in a case based on a federal question, a federal court will apply federal law. In a case based on diversity of citizenship, however, a federal court will apply the relevant state law (which is often the law of the state in which the court sits).

Exclusive versus Concurrent Jurisdiction. When both federal and state courts have the power to hear a case, as is true in suits involving diversity of citizenship, **concurrent jurisdiction** exists. When cases can be tried only in federal courts or only in state courts, **exclusive jurisdiction** exists. Federal courts have exclusive jurisdiction in cases involving federal crimes, bankruptcy, patents, and copyrights; in suits against the United States; and in some areas of admiralty law (law governing transportation on the seas and ocean waters). State courts also have exclusive jurisdiction over certain subject matters—for example, divorce and adoption.

Concurrent jurisdiction • Jurisdiction that exists when two different courts have the power to hear a case. For example, some cases can be heard in either a federal or a state court.

Exclusive jurisdiction • Jurisdiction that exists when a case can be heard only in a particular court or type of court, such as a federal court or a state court.

When concurrent jurisdiction exists, a party has a choice of whether to bring a suit in a federal or a state court. The party's lawyer will consider several factors in counseling the party as to which choice is preferable. The lawyer may prefer to litigate the case in a state court because she or he is more familiar with the state court's procedures, or perhaps the attorney believes that the state's judge or jury would be more sympathetic to the client's case. Alternatively, the lawyer may advise the client to sue in federal court. Perhaps the state court's **docket** (the court's schedule listing the cases to be heard) is crowded, and the case could be brought to trial sooner in a federal court. Perhaps some feature of federal practice or procedure could offer an advantage in the client's case. Other important considerations include the law in an available jurisdiction, how that law has been applied in the jurisdiction's courts, and what the results in similar cases have been in that jurisdiction.

Docket • The list of cases entered on a court's calendar and thus scheduled to be heard by the court.

Jurisdiction in Cyberspace

The Internet's capacity to bypass political and geographic boundaries undercuts the traditional basis for a court to assert personal jurisdiction. This basis includes a party's contacts with a court's geographic jurisdiction. As already discussed, for a court to compel a defendant to come before it, there must be at least minimum contacts—the presence of a salesperson within the state, for example. Are there sufficient minimum contacts if the only connection to a jurisdiction is an ad on a Web site originating from a remote location?

The "Sliding-Scale" Standard. Gradually, the courts are developing a standard—called a "sliding-scale" standard—for determining when the exercise of jurisdiction over an out-of-state defendant is proper. In developing this standard, the courts have identified three types of Internet business contacts: (1) substantial business conducted over the Internet (with contracts, sales, and so on); (2) some interactivity through a Web site; and (3) passive advertising.

Jurisdiction is proper for the first category, improper for the third, and may or may not be appropriate for the second.[8]

In the following case, the court considered whether jurisdiction could be exercised over defendants whose only contacts with the jurisdiction were through their Web site.

8. For a leading case on this issue, see *Zippo Manufacturing Co. v. Zippo Dot Com, Inc.*, 952 F.Supp. 1119 (W.D.Pa. 1997).

CASE 2.2

United States Court of Appeals, Sixth Circuit, 2002. 289 F.3d 865. **http://pacer.ca6.uscourts.gov/opinions/main.php**[a]

BIRD v. PARSONS

Darrell Bird, a citizen of Ohio, has operated Financia, Inc., a national computer software business, since 1983. Financia, Inc., owns the domain name financia.com. Dotster, Inc., a domain name registrar incorporated in Washington, operates its registry at ***http://www.dotster.com***.[b] *Dotster allows registrants who lack an Internet server to which a name can be assigned to park their names on Dotster's "Futurehome" page. Marshall Parsons registered the name efinancia.com on Dotster's site in 2000 and parked the name on the Futurehome page with the address* ***http://www.efinancia.com***. *George DeCarlo and Steven Vincent, on behalf of Dotster, activated Parsons's site. The name efinancia.com was soon offered for sale at* ***http://www.afternic.com***, *an auction site for the sale of domain names. Bird filed a suit against Dotster and others in a federal district court, alleging, in part, trademark infringement, copyright infringement, and cybersquatting.*[c] *Dotster, DeCarlo, and Vincent (the "Dotster defendants") asked the court to dismiss the complaint against them for, among other reasons, lack of personal jurisdiction. The court dismissed the suit. Alleging that Dotster sold 4,666 registrations to Ohio residents, Bird appealed to the U.S. Court of Appeals for the Sixth Circuit.*

GILMAN, J.

[J]urisdiction over the Dotster defendants is permissible only if their contacts with Ohio satisfy [a] three-part test * * *:

> First, the defendant must purposefully avail himself of the privilege of acting in the forum state [the state in which the lawsuit is initiated] or causing a consequence in the forum state. Second, the cause of action must arise from the defendant's activities there. Finally, the acts of the defendant or consequences caused by the defendant must have a substantial enough connection with the forum state to make the exercise of jurisdiction over the defendant reasonable.

a. This is a page within the Web site of the U.S. Court of Appeals for the Sixth Circuit. In the left-hand column, click on "Opinions Search." In the "Short Title contains" box, type "Parsons" and click on "Submit Query." In the "Opinion" box corresponding to the name of the case, click on the number to access the opinion.

b. Dotster's registration process is in conjunction with the Domain Registration of Internet Assigned Names and Numbers, which is maintained by Network Solutions, Inc. (owned by VeriSign), and regulated by the Internet Corporation for Assigned Names and Numbers (ICANN). Dotster is an ICANN–accredited registrar.

c. *Cybersquatting* is registering another person's trademark as a domain name and offering it for sale. This is a violation of the Anticybersquatting Consumer Protection Act of 1999. Cybersquatting and trademark and copyright infringement are discussed in more detail in Chapter 13.

* * * We conclude that by maintaining a website on which Ohio residents can register domain names and by allegedly accepting the business of 4,666 Ohio residents, the Dotster defendants have satisfied the *purposeful-availment requirement.* * * * [Emphasis added.]

The second requirement * * * involves an analysis of whether Bird's claims arise from the Dotster defendants' contacts with Ohio. * * *

The operative facts in the present case include Bird's allegation that the Dotster defendants committed copyright and trademark law violations by registering Parsons's domain name efinancia.com. Both the Dotster defendants' contacts with Ohio and Bird's claim of copyright and trademark violations stem from these defendants' operation of the Dotster website. As a result, the operative facts are at least marginally related to the alleged contacts between the Dotster defendants and Ohio. * * *

The final requirement * * * is that the exercise of jurisdiction be reasonable in light of the connection that allegedly exists between the Dotster defendants and Ohio. * * *

Although the Dotster defendants might face a burden in having to defend a lawsuit in Ohio, they cannot reasonably object to this burden given that Dotster has allegedly transacted business with 4,666 Ohio residents. Ohio has a legitimate interest in protecting the business interests of its citizens, *even though all of Bird's claims involve federal law.* Bird has an obvious interest in obtaining relief, and *Ohio might be the only forum where jurisdiction would exist over all of the defendants.* Although the state of Washington also has an interest in this dispute, because the claim involves its citizens, this interest does not override the other factors suggesting that personal jurisdiction in Ohio is reasonable. [Emphasis added.]

The U.S. Court of Appeals for the Sixth Circuit concluded that the lower court erred in granting the Dotster defendants' motion to dismiss for lack of personal jurisdiction. Bird had established that the court's exercise of jurisdiction over the Dotster defendants was proper.

QUESTIONS

1. Why did Bird allege on appeal that Dotster sold 4,666 domain name registrations to Ohio residents?
2. What reasons did the U.S. Court of Appeals for the Sixth Circuit use to conclude that the district court erred when it dismissed this suit?
3. Is the U.S. Court of Appeals for the Sixth Circuit applying traditional jurisdictional rules to cyberspace or creating new rules?

International Jurisdictional Issues. Because the Internet is international in scope, international jurisdictional issues understandably have come to the fore. We discuss some of these issues in this chapter's *Contemporary Legal Debates* feature on the following page. The world's courts seem to be developing a standard that echoes the requirement of "minimum contacts" applied by the U.S. courts. Most courts are indicating that minimum contacts—doing business within the jurisdiction, for example—are enough to exercise jurisdiction over a defendant. The effect of this standard is that a business firm may have to comply with the laws in any jurisdiction in which it actively targets customers for its products.

CONTEMPORARY LEGAL DEBATES

International Jurisdiction and the Internet

As you read elsewhere, *jurisdiction* is an important legal concept that relates to the authority of a court to hear and decide a case. Within the United States, there is a federal court system, which has jurisdiction over specific types of cases. There are also fifty state court systems, each having jurisdiction over certain types of cases. In today's interconnected world, the issue of jurisdiction has become critical. Specifically, businesses using the Internet can reach individuals in any part of the world. Does that mean that every court everywhere has jurisdiction over, say, an Internet company based in Chicago? This is one of today's legal debates.

THE MINIMUM-CONTACTS REQUIREMENT

Domestically, jurisdiction over individuals and businesses is based on the requirement of minimum contacts as outlined in *International Shoe Co. v. State of Washington.*[a] Essentially, this requirement means that a business must have a minimum level of contacts with residents of a particular state for that state's courts to exercise jurisdiction over the firm. In the context of the Internet, most courts have *not* viewed the mere existence of a *passive* Web site as sufficient minimum contacts to exercise jurisdiction over a person or entity located out of state. Rather, a site must offer some degree of interactivity (such as allowing a person to order goods from the site) to meet the minimum-contacts requirement.

Internationally, other countries' courts are applying the requirement of minimum contacts as developed by the U.S. courts. As a result, a business in the United States offering products for sale via its Web site must comply with the laws of any jurisdiction in which it targets customers for its products. Nonetheless, a major debate continues surrounding other aspects of international jurisdiction with respect to the Internet. Consider a French court's judgment against the U.S.–based Internet company Yahoo! Inc.

THE FRENCH CASE AGAINST YAHOO

Yahoo operates an online auction site on which Nazi memorabilia have been offered for sale. In France, the display of any objects representing symbols of Nazi ideology subjects the person or entity displaying such objects to both criminal and civil liability. The International League against Racism and Anti-Semitism filed suit in Paris against Yahoo for displaying Nazi memorabilia and offering them for sale via its Web site. The French court in which the suit was filed asserted jurisdiction over the U.S.–based company on the ground that the materials on the company's U.S.–based servers could be viewed on a Web site accessible in France. The French court ordered Yahoo to eliminate all Internet access in France to the Nazi memorabilia offered for sale through its online auctions.

Yahoo took the case to a federal district court in the United States to resolve a much larger issue: Can a foreign court dictate what will or will not appear on a U.S. company's Web site? Or does such an order violate the U.S. constitutional right to free speech and expression under the First Amendment? The federal district court agreed with Yahoo's argument that the French court's order violated the First Amendment and was thus not enforceable in the United States. The court reasoned as follows: "It is preferable to permit the nonviolent expression of offensive viewpoints rather than impose viewpoint-based government regulation upon speech. The government and people of France have a different judgment based on their own experience."[b]

a. 326 U.S. 310, 66 S.Ct. 154, 90 L.Ed. 95 (1945).

b. *Yahoo! Inc. v. La Ligue Contre le Racisme et l'Antisemitisme,* 169 F.Supp.2d 1181 (N.D.Cal. 2001).

Venue

Venue • The geographical district in which an action is tried and from which the jury is selected.

Jurisdiction has to do with whether a court has authority to hear a case involving specific persons, property, or subject matter. **Venue**[9] is concerned with the most appropriate location for a trial. For example, two state courts

9. Pronounced *ven*-yoo.

CONTEMPORARY LEGAL DEBATES

International Jurisdiction and the Internet

In the world of business, the *Yahoo* case was important because it was the first time a U.S. court had decided whether to honor a foreign judgment in the context of the Internet. Had Yahoo lost in federal court, a potential alternative would have been to force Yahoo and anyone else who posts anything on the Internet to become answerable to the laws of any country in which the message might be received. Several other countries—including North Korea, Syria, the People's Republic of China, Cuba, Iran, Belarus, and Saudi Arabia—have even stricter restrictions on free speech than France. Had the U.S. court held otherwise in the case against Yahoo, those countries could have had a field day suing Internet companies for supposedly "politically undesirable" speech.

INTERNATIONAL JURISDICTIONAL PROBLEMS CONTINUE

Consider now the possibility of another nation's court ordering a U.S. business to pay damages for violating that nation's laws via the Internet. Dow Jones & Company, the U.S. publisher of the *Wall Street Journal,* found itself in just that situation. The *Wall Street Journal* has a Web site that contains articles written by its reporters. One such article had information about an American businessperson, Joseph Gutnick, living in Melbourne, Australia. Gutnick decided to sue the *Wall Street Journal* for defamation in an Australian court. (As you will read in Chapter 12, defamation is a tort, or civil wrong, that is committed when one makes a false statement that harms the good reputation of another.)

Dow Jones argued that the Australian court could not exercise jurisdiction over its U.S. servers, which were located in New Jersey, but the Australian judge rejected this argument. The judge claimed that the event (libel) had occurred in the place where the article was viewed or downloaded—in this case, of course, Australia. Therefore, the Australian court could exercise jurisdiction.[c] In its decision, the court was guided by an earlier British precedent. In that case, Britain's House of Lords had concluded that England was an appropriate forum for a defamation suit brought against U.S.-based *Forbes* magazine, even though *Forbes* sold only two thousand copies of its magazine in all of England and Wales.[d]

If the Australian decision is upheld on appeal, any U.S. company with an Internet presence could potentially become subject to worldwide jurisdiction for defamation and other alleged torts.

WHERE DO YOU STAND?

In general, no country wants to give up jurisdiction because domestic courts wish to protect their own citizens. Nonetheless, some contend that extending the jurisdiction of courts to include any company that uses the Internet—regardless of where that company is located—will have a "chilling" effect on the growth of Internet commerce, as well as on the dissemination of ideas. Others argue that national governments should have the right to enforce laws prohibiting certain forms of speech or certain types of product sales within their national borders in the interests of protecting the welfare of their citizenry. What is your position on this issue? Are there any situations in which jurisdiction should be extended internationally because the Internet was used?

c. *Gutnick v. Dow Jones & Co., Inc.,* VSC 305 (August 28, 2001).
d. *Berezousky v. Michaels,* 2 ALL E.H. 986 (2000).

(or two federal courts) may have the authority to exercise jurisdiction over a case, but it may be more appropriate or convenient to hear the case in one court than in the other.

Basically, the concept of venue reflects the policy that a court trying a suit should be in the geographic neighborhood (usually the county) where the incident leading to the lawsuit occurred or where the parties involved in the lawsuit reside. Pretrial publicity or other factors, though, may require a change of venue to another community, especially in criminal cases in which the defendant's right to a fair and impartial jury has been impaired.

Standing to Sue

Standing to sue • The requirement that an individual must have a sufficient stake in a controversy before he or she can bring a lawsuit. The plaintiff must demonstrate that he or she either has been injured or threatened with injury.

In order to bring a lawsuit before a court, a party must have **standing to sue,** or a sufficient "stake" in a matter to justify seeking relief through the court system. In other words, to have standing, a party must have a legally protected and tangible interest at stake in the litigation. The party bringing the lawsuit must have suffered a harm or been threatened with a harm by the action about which he or she has complained. In some circumstances, a person can have standing to sue on behalf of another person. For example, suppose that a child suffers serious injuries as a result of a defectively manufactured toy. Because the child is a minor, a lawsuit can be brought on her or his behalf by another person, such as the child's parent or legal guardian.

Justiciable controversy • A controversy that is not hypothetical or academic but real and substantial; a requirement that must be satisfied before a court will hear a case.

Standing to sue also requires that the controversy at issue be a **justiciable[10] controversy**—a controversy that is real and substantial, as opposed to hypothetical or academic. For instance, in the above example, the child's parent could not sue the toy manufacturer merely on the ground (legal basis) that the toy was defective. The issue would become justiciable only if the child had actually been injured due to the defect in the toy as marketed. In other words, the parent normally could not ask the court to determine what damages might be obtained if the child had been injured, because this would be merely a hypothetical question.

The State and Federal Court Systems

As mentioned earlier in this chapter, each state has its own court system. Additionally, there is a system of federal courts. Although no two state court systems are exactly the same, the right-hand side of Exhibit 2–1 on page 50 illustrates the basic organizational framework characteristic of the court systems in many states. The exhibit also shows how the federal court system is structured. We turn now to an examination of these court systems, beginning with the state courts.

State Court Systems

Typically, a state court system includes several levels, or tiers, of courts. As indicated in Exhibit 2–1, state courts may include (1) local trial courts of limited jurisdiction, (2) state trial courts of general jurisdiction, (3) state courts of appeals (intermediate appellate courts), and (4) the state's highest court (often called the state supreme court). Judges in the state court system are usually elected by the voters for specified terms.

Generally, any person who is a party to a lawsuit has the opportunity to plead the case before a trial court and then, if he or she loses, before at least one level of appellate court. Finally, if a federal statute or federal constitutional issue is involved in the decision of a state supreme court, that decision may be further appealed to the United States Supreme Court.

---

10. Pronounced jus-*tish*-a-bul.

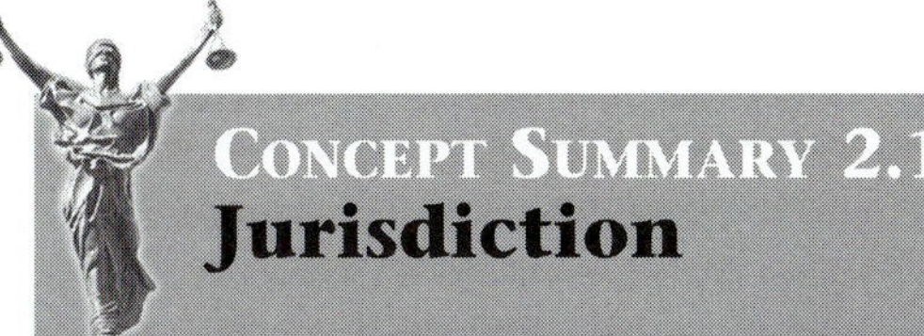

CONCEPT SUMMARY 2.1
Jurisdiction

TYPE OF JURISDICTION	DESCRIPTION
Personal/Property	Exists when a defendant or a defendant's property is located within the territorial boundaries within which a court has the right and power to decide cases. Jurisdiction may be exercised over out-of-state defendants under state long arm statutes.
Subject Matter	Limits the court's jurisdictional authority to particular types of cases. ① *Limited jurisdiction*—Exists when a court is limited to a specific subject matter, such as probate or divorce. ② *General jurisdiction*—Exists when a court can hear cases involving a broad array of issues.
Original	Exists with courts that have the authority to hear a case for the first time (trial courts).
Appellate	Exists with courts of appeal and review; generally, appellate courts do not have original jurisdiction.
Federal	Arises in the following situations: ① When a federal question is involved (when the plaintiff's cause of action is based at least in part on the U.S. Constitution, a treaty, or a federal law). ② In diversity-of-citizenship cases between citizens of different states when the amount in controversy exceeds $75,000. (Diversity jurisdiction also exists in cases between a foreign country and citizens of a state or of different states and in cases between citizens of a state and citizens or subjects of a foreign country.)
Concurrent	Exists when both federal and state courts have authority to hear the same case.
Exclusive	Exists when only state courts or only federal courts have authority to hear a case.
Jurisdiction in Cyberspace	Because the Internet does not have physical boundaries, traditional jurisdictional concepts have been difficult to apply in cases involving activities conducted via the Web. Gradually, the courts are developing standards to use in determining when jurisdiction over a Web site owner or operator in another state is proper. A significant legal challenge with respect to cyberspace transactions has to do with resolving jurisdictional disputes in the international context.

Trial Courts. Trial courts are exactly what their name implies—courts in which trials are held and testimony taken. State trial courts have either general or limited jurisdiction. Trial courts that have general jurisdiction as to subject matter may be called county, district, superior, or circuit courts.[11] State trial courts of general jurisdiction have jurisdiction over a wide variety of subjects, including both civil disputes and criminal prosecutions. In some states, trial courts of general jurisdiction may hear appeals from courts of limited jurisdiction.

11. The name in Ohio and Pennsylvania is Court of Common Pleas; the name in New York is Supreme Court, Trial Division.

EXHIBIT 2–1 • THE STATE AND FEDERAL COURT SYSTEMS

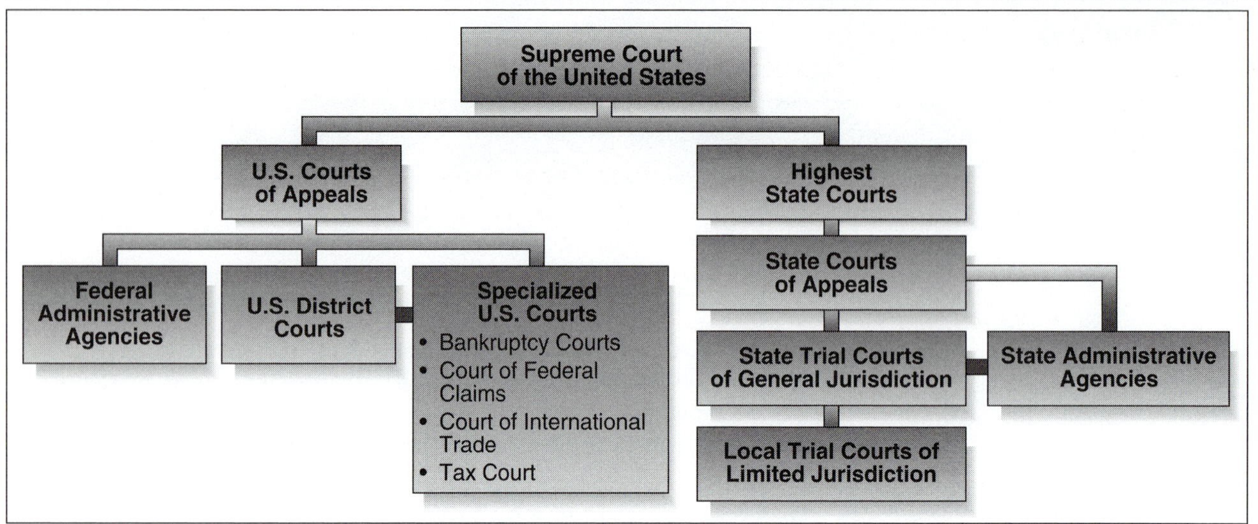

Small claims courts • Special courts in which parties may litigate small claims (usually, claims involving $5,000 or less). Attorneys are not required in small claims courts, and in many states attorneys are not allowed to represent the parties.

Courts of limited jurisdiction as to subject matter are often called special inferior trial courts or minor judiciary courts. **Small claims courts** are inferior trial courts that hear only civil cases involving claims of less than a certain amount, such as $5,000 (the amount varies from state to state). Suits brought in small claims courts are generally conducted informally, and lawyers are not required. In a minority of states, lawyers are not even allowed to represent people in small claims courts for most purposes. Decisions of small claims courts may be appealed to a state trial court of general jurisdiction.

Other courts of limited jurisdiction include domestic relations courts, which handle only divorce actions and child-custody cases; local municipal courts, which mainly handle traffic cases; and probate courts, as mentioned earlier.

Appellate Courts. Every state has at least one appellate court (court of appeals, or reviewing court). An appellate court may be an intermediate appellate court or the state's highest court. About three-fourths of the states have intermediate appellate courts. Generally, courts of appeals do not conduct new trials, in which evidence is submitted to the court and witnesses are examined. Rather, an appellate court panel of three or more judges reviews the record of the case on appeal, which includes a transcript of the trial proceedings, and then determines whether the trial court committed an error. In addition to reviewing decisions by courts within their jurisdictions, appellate courts may also review decisions made by administrative agencies.

Question of fact • In a lawsuit, an issue involving a factual dispute that is decided by a trial court judge (or, in a jury trial, a jury).

Question of law • In a lawsuit, an issue involving the application or interpretation of a law; therefore, the judge, and not the jury, decides the issue.

Appellate courts look at questions of law and procedure. Usually, they are concerned with questions of law, not questions of fact. A **question of fact** deals with what really happened in regard to the dispute being tried—such as whether a party actually burned a flag. A **question of law** concerns the application or interpretation of the law—such as whether flag-burning is a form of speech protected by the First Amendment to the Constitution. Questions of fact are decided by a trial judge (in a nonjury trial) or by a jury (in a jury trial) based on the evidence presented. Questions of law can be decided only by a judge, not a jury. Normally, an appellate court will defer to the trial court's judgment on questions of fact because the trial court judge and jury were in a better position to evaluate testimony. They directly observed witnesses' gestures, demeanor, and other nonverbal behavior during the trial. At the appellate level, the judges review the written transcript of the trial, which does not include these nonverbal elements.

An appellate court will tamper with a trial court's finding of fact only when the finding is clearly erroneous (that is, when it is contrary to the evidence presented at trial) or when there is no evidence to support the finding. For example, if at trial a jury concluded that a manufacturer's product had harmed the plaintiff but no evidence was submitted to the court to support that conclusion, the appellate court would hold that the trial court's decision was erroneous.

State Supreme (Highest Appellate) Courts. The highest state courts usually are called simply supreme courts, but they may be designated by other names. For example, in both New York and Maryland, the highest state court is called the Court of Appeals. In Maine and Massachusetts, the highest court is labeled the Supreme Judicial Court. In West Virginia, the highest state court is the Supreme Court of Appeals.

The decisions of each state's highest court on all questions of state law are final. Only when issues of federal law are involved can a decision made by a state's highest court be overruled by the United States Supreme Court. For example, suppose that a city ordinance prohibits citizens from engaging in door-to-door advocacy without first registering with the mayor's office and receiving a permit. Further suppose that a religious group sues the city, arguing that the law violates the freedoms of speech and religion guaranteed by the First Amendment. If the state supreme court upholds the law, the group could appeal the decision to the United States Supreme Court—because a constitutional (federal) issue is involved.

The Federal Court System

The federal court system is basically a three-tiered model consisting of (1) U.S. district courts (trial courts of general jurisdiction) and various courts of limited jurisdiction, (2) U.S. courts of appeals (intermediate courts of appeals), and (3) the United States Supreme Court.

Unlike state court judges, who are usually elected, federal court judges—including the justices of the Supreme Court—are appointed by the president of the United States, subject to confirmation by the U.S. Senate. Article III of the Constitution states that federal judges "hold their offices during good Behaviour." In effect, this means that federal judges have lifetime appointments. Although they can be impeached (removed from office) for misconduct, this is rarely done. In the entire history of the United States, only seven federal judges have been removed from office through impeachment proceedings.

U.S. District Courts. At the federal level, the equivalent of a state trial court of general jurisdiction is the district court. U.S. district courts have original jurisdiction in federal matters, and federal cases typically originate in district courts. There are other federal courts with original, but special (or limited), jurisdiction, such as the federal bankruptcy courts and others shown earlier in Exhibit 2–1.

There is at least one federal district court in every state. The number of judicial districts can vary over time, primarily owing to population changes and corresponding changes in case loads. Currently, there are ninety-four federal judicial districts. Exhibit 2–2 shows the boundaries of the U.S. district courts, as well as the boundaries of U.S. courts of appeals (discussed next).

U.S. Courts of Appeals. In the federal court system, there are thirteen U.S. courts of appeals—referred to as U.S. circuit courts of appeals. Twelve of the federal courts of appeals (including the Court of Appeals for the D.C. Circuit) hear appeals from the federal district courts located within their respective judicial "circuits," or geographic boundaries (shown in Exhibit 2–2). The court of appeals for the thirteenth circuit, called the Federal Circuit, has national appellate jurisdiction over certain types of cases, such as cases involving patent law and cases in which the U.S. government is a defendant. The decisions of a circuit court of appeals are binding on all courts within the circuit court's jurisdiction and are final in most cases, but appeal to the United States Supreme Court is possible.

United States Supreme Court. At the highest level in the three-tiered federal court system is the United States Supreme Court. According to the language of Article III of the U.S. Constitution, there is only one national Supreme Court. All other courts in the federal system are considered "inferior." Congress is empowered to create other inferior courts as it deems necessary. The inferior courts that Congress has created include the second tier in our model—the U.S. circuit courts of appeals—as well as the district courts and the various federal courts of limited, or specialized, jurisdiction.

The United States Supreme Court consists of nine justices. Although the Supreme Court has original, or trial, jurisdiction in rare instances (set forth in Article III, Section 2), most of its work is as an appeals court. The Supreme Court can review any case decided by any of the federal courts of appeals, and it also has appellate authority over cases involving federal questions that have been decided in the state courts. The Supreme Court is the final arbiter of the U.S. Constitution and federal law.

How Cases Reach the Supreme Court. In order to bring a case before the Supreme Court, a party requests the Court to issue a writ of *certiorari.* A **writ of *certiorari***[12] is an order issued by the Supreme Court to a lower court requiring the latter to send it the record of the case for review. The Court will not issue a writ unless at least four of the nine justices approve of it. This is called the **rule of four.**

Writ of *certiorari* • A writ from a higher court asking the lower court for the record of a case.

Rule of four • A rule of the United States Supreme Court under which the Court will not issue a writ of *certiorari* unless at least four justices approve of the decision to issue the writ.

Whether the Court will issue a writ of *certiorari* is entirely within its discretion. The Court is not required to issue one, and most petitions for writs are denied. (Thousands of cases are filed with the Supreme Court each year, yet it hears, on average, less than one hundred of these cases.)[13] A denial is not a decision on the merits of a case, nor does it indicate agreement with the lower

12. Pronounced sur-shee-uh-*rah*-ree.

13. From the mid-1950s through the early 1990s, the Supreme Court reviewed more cases per year than it has since then. In the Court's 1982–1983 term, for example, the Court issued written opinions in 151 cases. In contrast, during the Court's 2001–2002 term, the Court issued written opinions in only 79 cases.

EXHIBIT 2–2 • GEOGRAPHICAL BOUNDARIES OF THE U.S. DISTRICT COURTS AND COURTS OF APPEALS

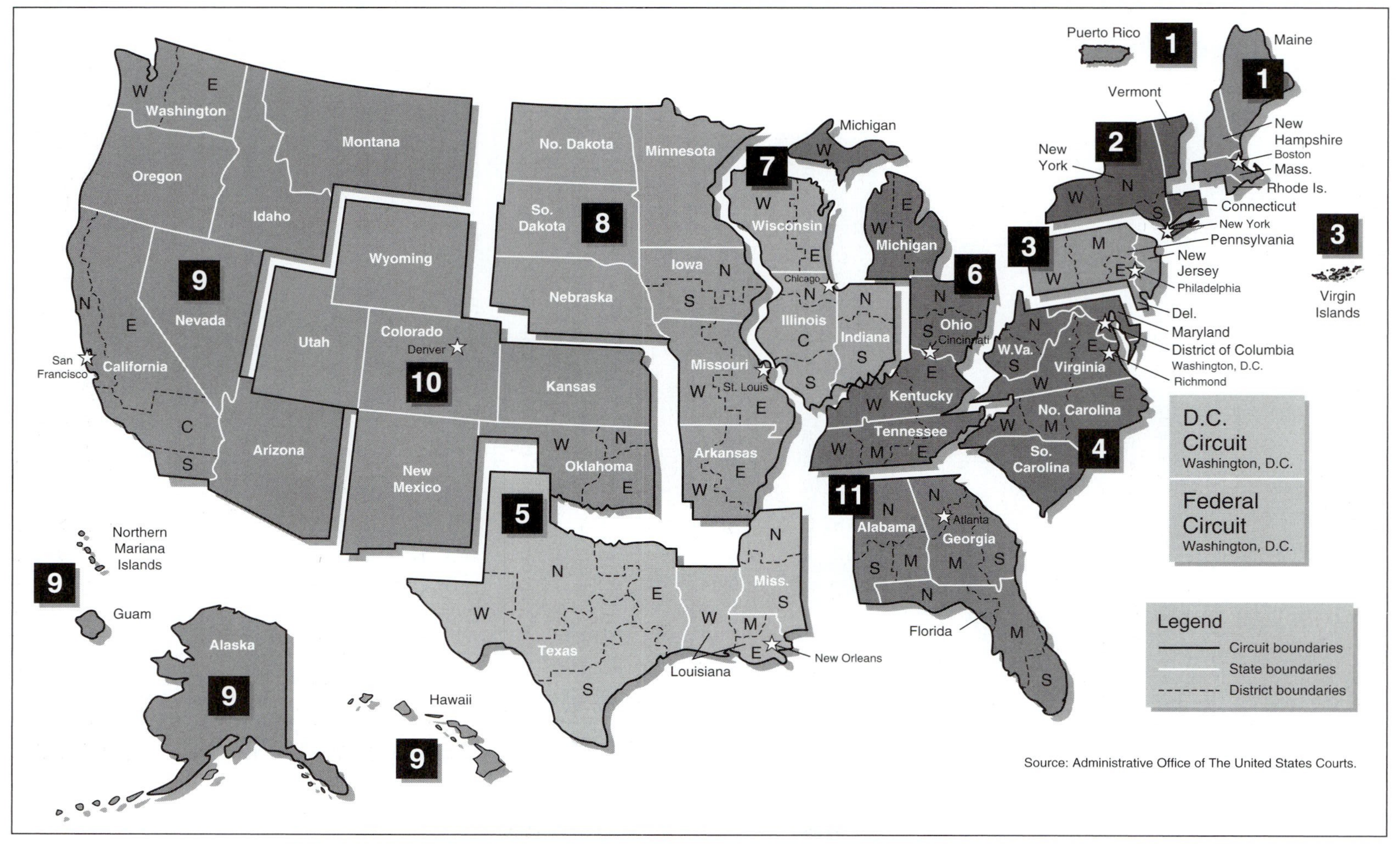

Source: Administrative Office of The United States Courts.

CONCEPT SUMMARY 2.2
Types of Courts

COURT	DESCRIPTION
Trial Courts	Trial courts are courts of original jurisdiction in which actions are initiated. ① *State courts*—Courts of general jurisdiction can hear any case that has not been specifically designated for another court; courts of limited jurisdiction include domestic relations courts, probate courts, municipal courts, small claims courts, and others. ② *Federal courts*—The federal district court is the equivalent of the state trial court. Federal courts of limited jurisdiction include the bankruptcy court and others shown in Exhibit 2–1 on page 50.
Intermediate Appellate Courts	Courts of appeals are reviewing courts; generally, appellate courts do not have original jurisdiction. About three-fourths of the states have intermediate appellate courts. In the federal court system, the U.S. circuit courts of appeals are the intermediate appellate courts.
Supreme Court	The highest state court is that state's supreme court, although it may be called by some other name. Appeal from state supreme courts to the United States Supreme Court is possible only if a federal question is involved. The United States Supreme Court is the highest court in the federal court system and the final arbiter of the U.S. Constitution and federal law.

court's (usually, a federal appellate court's) opinion. Furthermore, denial of the writ has no value as a precedent. A denial of the writ simply means that the decision of the lower court remains the law within that court's jurisdiction.

Typically, the petitions granted by the Court involve cases that raise important constitutional questions or cases that conflict with other state or federal court decisions. The Court can then render a definitive opinion on the matter, thus clarifying the law for the lower courts. For example, after the 2000 presidential elections, the Supreme Court decided to review the Florida Supreme Court's decision that the votes in selected Florida counties could be manually recounted. The Court concluded that the case raised an important constitutional question—whether manually counting votes in some counties but not others violated the equal protection clause of the U.S. Constitution. The Court thus reviewed (and overturned) the Florida court's decision.[14]

JUDICIAL PROCEDURES: FOLLOWING A CASE THROUGH THE COURT SYSTEM

American and English courts follow the *adversarial system of justice*. Although clients are allowed to represent themselves in court (called *pro se* representation),[15] most parties to lawsuits hire attorneys to represent them. Each lawyer

14. *Bush v. Gore,* 531 U.S. 98, 121 S.Ct. 525, 148 L.Ed.2d 388 (2000).
15. This right was definitively established in *Faretta v. California,* 422 U.S. 806, 95 S.Ct. 2525, 45 L.Ed.2d 562 (1975).

acts as his or her client's advocate, presenting the client's version of the facts in such a way as to convince the judge (or the jury, in a jury trial) that this version is correct.

Most of the judicial procedures that you will read about in the following pages are rooted in the adversarial framework of the American legal system. In this section, after a brief overview of judicial procedures, we illustrate the steps involved in a lawsuit with a hypothetical civil case (criminal procedures will be discussed in Chapter 7).

Procedural Rules

The parties to a lawsuit must comply with the procedural rules of the court in which the lawsuit is filed. These rules specify what must be done at each stage of the litigation process. All civil trials held in federal district courts are governed by the **Federal Rules of Civil Procedure (FRCP).**[16] Each state also has rules of civil procedure that apply to all courts within that state. In addition, each court has its own local rules of procedure that supplement the federal or state rules.

Federal Rules of Civil Procedure (FRCP) • The rules controlling procedural matters in civil trials brought before the federal district courts.

Broadly speaking, the litigation process has three phases: pretrial, trial, and posttrial. Each phase involves specific procedures. Although civil lawsuits may vary greatly in terms of complexity, cost, and detail, they typically progress through the specific stages charted in Exhibit 2–3 on the next page.

We now turn to our hypothetical civil case. The case arose from an automobile accident, which occurred when a car driven by Antonio Carvello, a resident of New Jersey, collided with a car driven by Jill Kirby, a resident of New York. The accident took place at an intersection in New York City. Kirby suffered personal injuries, which caused her to incur medical and hospital expenses as well as lost wages for four months. In all, she calculated that the cost to her of the accident was $100,000.[17] Carvello and Kirby have been unable to agree on a settlement, and Kirby now must decide whether to sue Carvello for the $100,000 compensation she feels she deserves.

Consulting with an Attorney

The first step taken by virtually anyone contemplating a lawsuit is to obtain the advice of a qualified attorney. In the hypothetical Kirby-Carvello case, Kirby may consult with an attorney, who will advise her as to what she can expect to gain from a lawsuit, her probability of success if she sues, what procedures will be involved, and how long it may take to resolve the issue through the judicial process. Depending on the court hearing the case, the time costs of the litigation may be significant. Personal-injury cases may take two to three years to resolve, so this is an important factor for Kirby to consider.

Legal Fees. Another crucial factor that Kirby must consider is, of course, the cost of the attorney's time—the legal fees that she will have to pay to collect damages from the defendant, Carvello. Attorneys base their fees on such factors as the difficulty of a matter, the amount of time involved, the experience and skill of the attorney in the particular area of the law, and the cost of doing

16. The United States Supreme Court's authority to promulgate these rules is set forth in 28 U.S.C. Sections 2071–2077.

17. In this example, we are ignoring damages for pain and suffering or for permanent disabilities. Often, plaintiffs in personal-injury cases seek such damages.

EXHIBIT 2–3 • STAGES IN A TYPICAL LAWSUIT

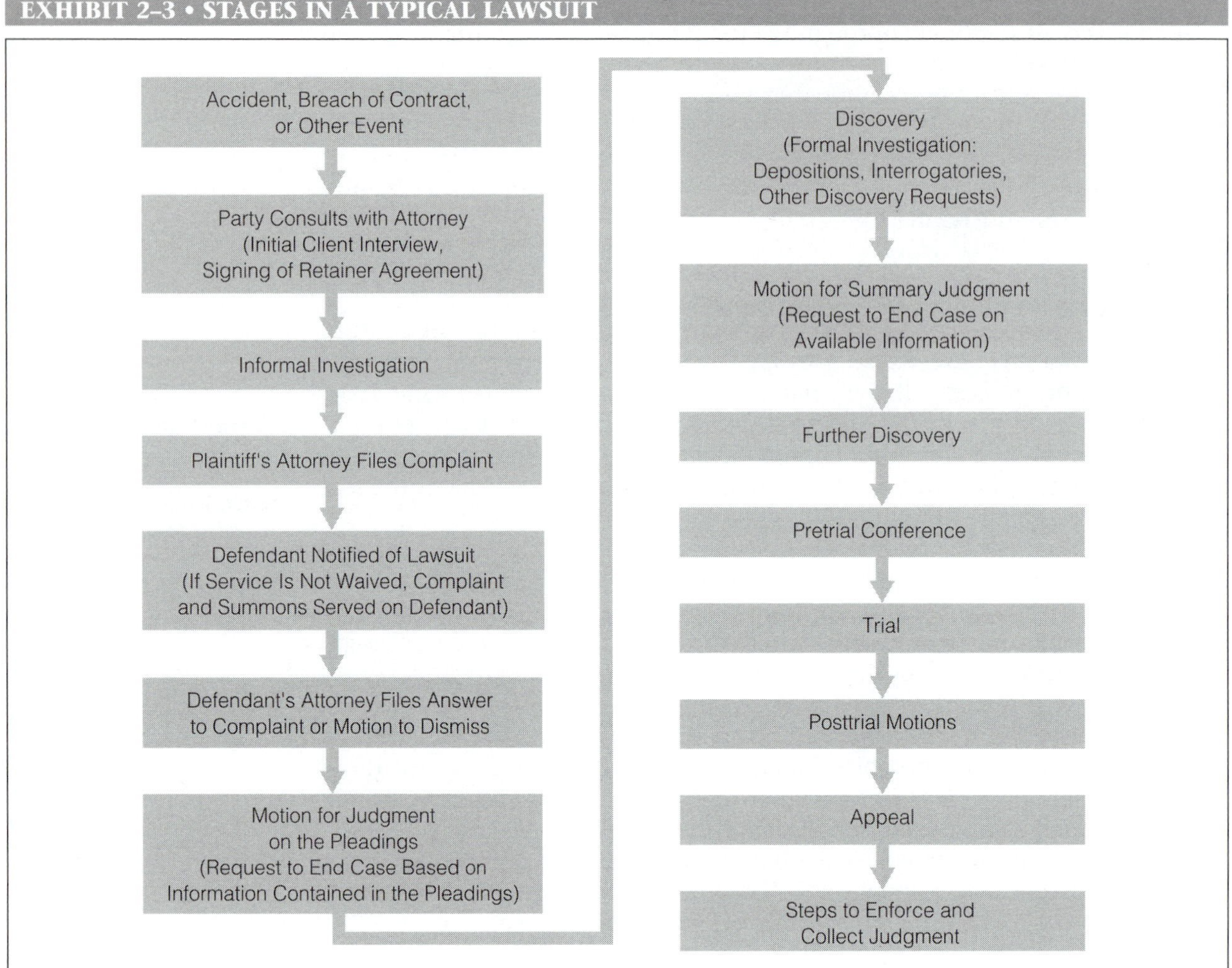

business. In the United States, legal fees range from $75 to $500 per hour or even higher (the average fee per hour is between $150 and $175). In addition to paying these fees, the client must also reimburse the attorney for various expenses relating to the case, often called "out-of-pocket" costs, that the attorney pays on the client's behalf. These costs include court filing fees, travel expenses, the cost of expert witnesses and investigators, and so on.

For a particular legal matter, an attorney may charge one type of fee or a combination of several types. *Fixed fees* may be charged for the performance of such services as drafting a simple will. *Hourly fees* may be computed for matters that will involve an indeterminate period of time. Any case brought to trial, for example, may involve an expenditure of time that cannot be precisely estimated in advance. *Contingency fees* are fixed as a percentage (usually between 25 and 40 percent) of a client's recovery in certain types of lawsuits, such as a personal-injury lawsuit. If the lawsuit is unsuccessful, the attorney receives no fee. If Kirby retains an attorney on a contingency-fee basis, she normally will not have to pay any fees unless she wins the case. (She will, however, have to pay the court fees and any other expenses incurred by the attorney on her behalf.)

Many state and federal statutes allow for an award of attorneys' fees in certain legal actions, such as probate matters. In these cases, a judge sets the amount of the fee, based on such factors as the results obtained by the attorney and the fee customarily charged for similar services. In some situations, a client may receive an award of attorneys' fees as part of her or his recovery.

Settlement Considerations. Frequently, the extent to which an attorney will pursue a resolution of a legal problem is determined largely by how much time and money the client wishes to invest in the process. If the client decides that he or she can afford a lengthy trial and one or more appeals, the attorney may pursue those actions. Often, however, once a client learns the costs involved in litigation, he or she may decide to settle the claim for a lower amount by using one of the methods of alternative dispute resolution that we will discuss in Chapter 3, such as negotiation or mediation.

Another important factor in deciding whether to pursue litigation is the defendant's ability to pay the damages sought. Even if Kirby is awarded damages, it may be difficult to enforce the court's judgment. (We will discuss the problems involved in enforcing a judgment later in this chapter.)

ETHICAL ISSUE

Are confidential settlement agreements contrary to the public interest? One of the major advantages of a settlement agreement, aside from avoiding litigation costs, is confidentiality. A defendant manufacturer, for example, might place a high value on keeping allegations that its product is defective from reaching the public or other potential plaintiffs. In the past, the courts tended to approve settlement agreements, including confidentiality provisions, with few objections. This tradition is now changing. Increasingly, "sunshine-in-government" or "sunshine-in-litigation" laws and court rules are imposing requirements on the courts that make it difficult for parties to obtain a court's consent to a confidentiality agreement. This is particularly true when the agreement relates to disputes concerning products or practices that may be harmful to the public. Clearly, shielding the public from knowledge of harmful products or services by means of confidentiality agreements may not be in the public interest. Yet limiting the availability of confidentiality agreements may not be in the public interest either, because it makes settlements less attractive for many litigants. As a result, more cases will go to trial and an already strained court system will be even more heavily burdened.

Pretrial Procedures

The pretrial litigation process involves the filing of the *pleadings,* the gathering of evidence (called *discovery*), and possibly other procedures, such as a pretrial conference and jury selection.

Pleadings • Statements made by the plaintiff and the defendant in a lawsuit that detail the facts, charges, and defenses involved in the litigation; the complaint and answer are part of the pleadings.

The Pleadings. The *complaint* and *answer* (and other documents discussed next), taken together, are known as the **pleadings.** The pleadings notify each party of the claims of the other and specify the issues (disputed questions) involved in the case. Pleadings remove the element of surprise from a case.

They allow lawyers to gather the most persuasive evidence and to prepare better arguments, thus increasing the probability that a just and true result will be forthcoming from the trial. The basic pleadings are the complaint and answer.

Complaint • The pleading made by a plaintiff alleging wrongdoing on the part of the defendant; the document that, when filed with a court, initiates a lawsuit.

The Plaintiff's Complaint. Kirby's action against Carvello will commence when her lawyer files a **complaint**[18] with the clerk of the trial court in the appropriate geographic area—the proper venue. (Typically, the lawyer or her or his assistant delivers the complaint in person to the trial court clerk. Increasingly, however, courts are experimenting with electronic filing.)

In most states, the court would be one having general jurisdiction; in others, it might be a court having special jurisdiction with regard to subject matter. The complaint will contain (1) a statement alleging, or asserting, the facts necessary for the court to take jurisdiction, (2) a short statement of the facts necessary to show that the plaintiff is entitled to a remedy, and (3) a statement of the remedy the plaintiff is seeking. A typical complaint is shown in Exhibit 2–4.

The complaint will state that Kirby was driving her car through a green light at the specified intersection, exercising good driving habits and reasonable care, when Carvello negligently drove his vehicle through a red light and into the intersection from a cross street, striking Kirby's car and causing serious personal injury and property damage. The complaint will go on to state that Kirby is seeking $100,000 in damages. (Note that in some state civil actions, the amount of damages sought is not specified.)

Service of process • The delivery of the complaint and summons to a defendant.

Summons • A document informing a defendant that a legal action has been commenced against him or her and that the defendant must appear in court on a certain date to answer the plaintiff's complaint. The document is delivered by a sheriff or any other person so authorized.

Default judgment • A judgment entered by a court against a defendant who has failed to appear in court to answer or defend against the plaintiff's claim.

Service of Process. Before the court can exercise jurisdiction over the defendant (Carvello)—in effect, before the lawsuit can begin—the court must have proof that the defendant was notified of the lawsuit. The process of notifying the defendant of a lawsuit is called **service of process.** Service of process involves serving the defendant with a summons and a copy of the complaint—that is, delivering these items to the defendant. The **summons** notifies defendant Carvello that he is required to prepare an answer to the complaint and to file a copy of his answer with both the court and the plaintiff's attorney within a specified time period (twenty days in the federal courts).

The summons also informs Carvello that if he fails to answer or respond to the plaintiff's complaint within the required time period (unless he can provide a convincing reason to the court why he could not do so), the result will be a default judgment for the plaintiff. A **default judgment** in Kirby's favor would mean that she would be awarded the damages alleged in her complaint. A typical summons is shown in Exhibit 2–5 on page 60.

How service of process occurs depends on the rules of the court or jurisdiction in which the lawsuit is brought. Under the Federal Rules of Civil Procedure (FRCP), service of process in federal court cases may be effected by anyone who is not a party to the lawsuit and who is at least eighteen years of age. In state courts, the process server is often a county sheriff. Usually, the server effects the service by handing the summons to the defendant personally or by leaving it at the defendant's residence or place of business. In a few

18. Sometimes, the document filed with the court is called a petition or a declaration instead of a complaint.

EXHIBIT 2–4 • A TYPICAL COMPLAINT

IN THE UNITED STATES DISTRICT COURT
FOR THE SOUTHERN DISTRICT OF NEW YORK

JILL KIRBY Plaintiff, vs. ANTONIO CARVELLO Defendant.	CIVIL NO. 5-1047 COMPLAINT

The plaintiff brings this cause of action against the defendant, alleging as follows:

1. This action is between the plaintiff, who is a resident of the State of New York, and the defendant, who is a resident of the State of New Jersey. There is diversity of citizenship between the parties.
2. The amount in controversy, exclusive of interest and costs, exceeds the sum of $75,000.
3. On September 10th, 2004, the plaintiff, Jill Kirby, was exercising good driving habits and reasonable care in driving her car through the intersection of Boardwalk and Pennsylvania Avenue, New York City, New York, when the defendant, Antonio Carvello, negligently drove his vehicle through a red light at the intersection and collided with the plaintiff's vehicle.
4. As a result of the collision, the plaintiff suffered severe physical injury, which prevented her from working, and property damage to her car.

WHEREFORE, the plaintiff demands judgment against the defendant for the sum of $100,000 plus interest at the maximum legal rate and the costs of this action.

By Joseph Roe
Joseph Roe
Attorney for Plaintiff
100 Main Street
New York, New York

1/2/05

EXHIBIT 2-5 • A TYPICAL SUMMONS

SUMMONS IN A CIVIL ACTION

United States District Court

FOR THE SOUTHERN **DISTRICT OF:** NEW YORK

CIVIL ACTION FILE NO. 5-1047

JILL KIRBY

Plaintiff,

vs.

ANTONIO CARVELLO

Defendant.

SUMMONS

To the above named Defendant:

You are hereby summoned and required to serve upon Joseph Roe

plaintiff's attorney, whose address is 100 Main Street New York, New York

an answer to the complaint which is herewith served upon you, within 20 days after service of this summons upon you, exclusive of the day of service. If you fail to do so, judgment by default will be taken against you for the relief demanded in the complaint.

Samuel Raeburn

Clerk of Court

Mary Doakes

Deputy Clerk

Date: 1/10/05

[Seal of Court]

NOTE:—This summons is issued pursuant to Rule 4 of the Federal Rules of Civil Procedure.

states, a summons can be served by mail if the defendant so agrees. When the defendant cannot be reached, special rules sometimes permit the summons to be served by leaving it with a designated person, such as the state's secretary of state.

In the following case, the issue was whether service of process could be accomplished via e-mail.

RIO PROPERTIES, INC. v. RIO INTERNATIONAL INTERLINK

CASE 2.3

United States Court of Appeals, Ninth Circuit, 2002. 284 F.3d 1007.

Rio Properties, Inc., owns the Rio All Suite Casino Resort in Las Vegas, Nevada. To protect its rights in the "Rio" name, Rio has registered numerous trademarks with the U.S. Patent and Trademark Office. When Rio sought to expand its presence onto the Internet, it registered the domain name playrio.com. At ***http://www.playrio.com****, Rio operates a Web site that informs prospective customers about its hotel and accepts reservations. Rio International Interlink (RII) is a Costa Rican entity that participates in an Internet sports gambling operation, doing business as Rio International Sportsbook, Rio Online Sportsbook, or Rio International Sports, at* ***http://www.riosports.com****. RII grosses an estimated $3 million annually. When Rio became aware of RII's operation, Rio demanded that RII stop infringing Rio's trademark. RII disabled the "riosports" site but soon activated* ***http://www.betrio.com*** *to host an identical operation. Rio filed a suit in a federal district court against RII, alleging trademark infringement. To effect service of process, Rio attempted to locate RII, but its U.S. address housed only its international courier, which was not authorized to accept service on RII's behalf, and RII did not have an address in Costa Rica. RII advertised that it preferred communication through its e-mail address,* ***email@betrio.com****. Unable to serve RII by traditional means, Rio filed a motion for alternative service of process, asking the court for permission to serve RII via its e-mail address. The court granted the motion. When RII later failed to comply with the court's orders for discovery (discovery is discussed later in this chapter), the court entered a default judgment against RII. RII appealed to the U.S. Court of Appeals for the Ninth Circuit, alleging in part that the service of process was insufficient.*

TROTT, J.

[W]e turn to the district court's order authorizing service of process on RII by email at *email@betrio.com*. We acknowledge that we tread upon untrodden ground. The parties cite no authority condoning service of process over the Internet or via e-mail, and our own investigation has unearthed no decisions by the United States Courts of Appeals dealing with service of process by e-mail * * * . Despite this dearth of authority, however, we do not labor long in reaching our decision. Considering the facts presented by this case, we conclude not only that service of process by e-mail was proper—that is, reasonably calculated to apprise [inform] RII of the * * * action and afford it an opportunity to respond—but in this case, it was the method of service most likely to reach RII.

To be sure, *the Constitution does not require any particular means of service of process, only that the method selected be reasonably calculated to provide notice and an opportunity to respond.* In proper circumstances, this broad constitutional principle unshackles the federal courts from anachronistic methods of service and permits them entry into the technological renaissance. * * * Electronic communication via satellite can and does provide instantaneous transmission of notice and information. No longer must process be mailed to a defendant's door when he can receive complete notice at an electronic terminal inside his very office, even when the door is steel and bolted shut. * * * [Emphasis added.]

Although communication via e-mail and over the Internet is comparatively new, such communication has been zealously embraced within the business community. RII particularly has embraced the modern e-business model and profited immensely from it. In fact, RII structured its business such that it could be contacted *only* via its e-mail address. RII listed no easily discoverable street address in the United States or in Costa Rica. Rather, on its website and print media, RII designated its e-mail address as its preferred contact information.

* * * In addition, email was the only court-ordered method of service aimed directly and instantly at RII * * * . Indeed, when faced with an international e-business scofflaw [habitual violator], playing hide-and-seek with the federal court, e-mail may be the only means of effecting service of process. Certainly in this case, it was a means reasonably calculated to apprise RII of * * * the lawsuit, and the Constitution requires nothing more.

The U.S. Court of Appeals for the Ninth Circuit upheld the lower court's order for service of process via e-mail. Because RII did not have an address in the United States or Costa Rica where service could be accomplished through traditional means, and RII advertised that it preferred contact through its e-mail address, service by e-mail was proper.

QUESTIONS

1. Why did RII allege on appeal that the service of process was insufficient?
2. On what basis did the U.S. Court of Appeals for the Ninth Circuit uphold the lower court's order for service of process via e-mail?
3. What are the advantages of effecting service of process via e-mail?

Serving Corporate Defendants. In cases involving corporate defendants, the summons and complaint may be served on an officer or *registered agent* (representative) of the corporation. The name of a corporation's registered agent can usually be obtained from the secretary of state's office in the state where the company incorporated its business (and, usually, from the secretary of state's office in any state where the corporation does business).

Waiver of Formal Service of Process. The FRCP allow formal service of process to be waived by defendants in federal cases, provided that certain procedures are followed. Kirby's attorney, for example, could mail to defendant Carvello a copy of the complaint, along with "Waiver of Service of Summons" forms for Carvello to sign. If Carvello signs and returns the forms within thirty days, formal service of process is waived. To encourage defendants to waive formal service of process, the FRCP provide that defendants who sign and return the waiver are not required to respond to the complaint for sixty days after the date on which the request for waiver of service was sent, instead of the twenty days allowed if formal service of process is undertaken.

The Defendant's Response to the Complaint. The defendant's response to the plaintiff's complaint may take the form of an **answer,** in which the defendant either admits the statements or allegations set out in the complaint or denies them and sets out any defenses that he or she may have. If Carvello admits to all of Kirby's allegations in his answer, a judgment will be entered for Kirby. If Carvello denies Kirby's allegations, the matter will proceed further.

Answer • Procedurally, a defendant's response to the plaintiff's complaint.

Carvello can also admit the truth of Kirby's complaint but raise new facts to show that he should not be held liable for Kirby's damages. This is called raising an **affirmative defense.** As will be discussed in subsequent chapters, affirmative defenses can be raised by defendants in both civil and criminal cases. For example, a defendant accused of physically harming another might claim that he or she acted in self-defense. A defendant charged with breach of contract might defend on the ground of mistake or the fact that the contract was oral when it was required by law to be in writing. In the Kirby-Carvello case, assume that Carvello has obtained evidence that Kirby was not exercising good driving habits at the time the accident occurred (she was looking at a child in the back of her car instead of watching the road). Carvello could assert Kirby's own negligence as a defense. In some states, a plaintiff's contributory negligence operates as a complete defense. In most states, however, the plaintiff's own negligence constitutes only a partial defense (see Chapter 12).

Affirmative defense • A response to a plaintiff's claim that does not deny the plaintiff's facts but attacks the plaintiff's legal right to bring an action.

Carvello could also deny Kirby's allegations and set forth his own claim that the accident occurred as a result of Kirby's negligence and that therefore Kirby owes Carvello money for damages to his car. This is appropriately called a **counterclaim.** If Carvello files a counterclaim, Kirby will have to submit an answer to the counterclaim.

Counterclaim • A claim made by a defendant in a civil lawsuit that in effect sues the plaintiff.

Dismissals and Judgments before Trial. Many actions for which pleadings have been filed never come to trial. The parties may, for example, negotiate a settlement of the dispute at any stage of the litigation process. There are also numerous procedural avenues for disposing of a case without a trial. Many of them involve one or the other party's attempts to get the case dismissed through the use of various motions.

A **motion** is a procedural request submitted to the court by an attorney on behalf of her or his client. When one party files a motion with the court, that party must also send to, or serve on, the opposing party a *notice of motion.* The notice of motion informs the opposing party that the motion has been filed. **Pretrial motions** include the motion to dismiss, the motion for judgment on the pleadings, and the motion for summary judgment.

Motion • A procedural request or application presented by an attorney to the court on behalf of a client.

Pretrial motion • A written or oral application to a court for a ruling or order, made before trial.

Motion to Dismiss. If the defendant challenges the sufficiency of the plaintiff's complaint, the defendant can present to the court a **motion to dismiss** for failure to state a claim for which relief (a remedy) can be granted, or a *demurrer.* (The rules of civil procedure in many states do not use the term *demurrer;* they use only *motion to dismiss.*) The motion to dismiss for failure to state a claim for which relief can be granted is an allegation that even if the facts presented in the complaint are true, their legal consequences are such that there is no reason to go further with the suit and no need for the defendant to present an answer. If, for example, Kirby's complaint had alleged facts that precluded the possibility of negligence on Carvello's part, Carvello could move to dismiss the case.

Motion to dismiss • A pleading in which a defendant asserts that the plaintiff's claim fails to state a cause of action (that is, has no basis in law) or that there are other grounds on which a suit should be dismissed.

Defendant Carvello could also file a motion to dismiss if he believed that he had not been properly served, that the complaint had been filed in the wrong court (for example, that the court lacked personal or subject-matter jurisdiction or that the venue was improper), or for other specific reasons.

Often, instead of filing an answer with the court, a defendant files a motion to dismiss. If the court denies the motion, the defendant generally is given an extension of time to file an answer (or further pleading). If the defendant fails to file the appropriate pleading, a judgment will normally be entered for the plaintiff. If the court grants the motion to dismiss, the defendant is not required to answer the complaint. The plaintiff generally is given time to file an amended complaint. If the plaintiff does not file this amended complaint, a judgment will be entered against the plaintiff solely on the basis of the pleadings, and the plaintiff will not be allowed to bring suit on the matter again.

If Kirby wishes to discontinue the suit because, for example, an out-of-court settlement has been reached, she can likewise move for dismissal. The court can also dismiss a case on its own motion.

Motion for judgment on the pleadings • A motion by either party to a lawsuit at the close of the pleadings requesting the court to decide the issue solely on the pleadings without proceeding to trial. The motion will be granted only if no facts are in dispute.

Motion for Judgment on the Pleadings. After the pleadings are closed—after the complaint, answer, and any other pleadings have been filed—either of the parties can file a **motion for judgment on the pleadings.** This motion may be filed when it appears from the pleadings that the plaintiff has failed to state a cause of action for which relief may be granted. The motion may also be filed when the pleadings indicate that no facts are in dispute and the only question is how the law applies to a set of agreed-on facts. For example, assume for a moment that in the Kirby-Carvello case, defendant Carvello admitted to all of Kirby's allegations in his answer and raised no affirmative defenses. In this situation, Kirby would file a motion for judgment on the pleadings in her favor.

The difference between this motion and a motion for summary judgment, discussed next, is that the party requesting the motion may support a motion for summary judgment with sworn statements and other materials that would be admissible as evidence at trial; on a motion for a judgment on the pleadings, however, a court may consider only what is contained in the pleadings.

Motion for summary judgment • A motion requesting the court to enter a judgment without proceeding to trial. The motion can be based on evidence outside the pleadings and will be granted only if no facts are in dispute.

Motion for Summary Judgment. A **motion for summary judgment** is similar to a motion for judgment on the pleadings in that the party filing the motion is asking the court to grant a judgment in that party's favor without a trial. As with a motion for judgment on the pleadings, a court will grant a motion for summary judgment only if it determines that no facts are in dispute and the only question is how the law applies to the facts.

Affidavit • A written or printed voluntary statement of facts, confirmed by the oath or affirmation of the party making it and made before a person having the authority to administer the oath or affirmation.

To support a motion for summary judgment, one party can submit, prior to trial, sworn evidence obtained at any point prior to trial (including during the discovery stage of litigation—to be discussed shortly) that refutes the other party's factual claim. The evidence may consist of **affidavits** (sworn statements by parties or witnesses), as well as documents, such as a contract. The evidence must be *admissible* evidence—that is, evidence that the court would allow to be presented during the trial. Hearsay, for example, normally would not be admissible. As mentioned, the use of this additional evidence is one of the features that distinguishes the motion for summary judgment from the motion to dismiss and the motion for judgment on the pleadings.

In the Kirby-Carvello accident, whether the light was red is a question of fact. Assume that during discovery, Carvello obtained indisputable evidence that the stoplight was not working when he drove through the intersection. Assume further that Carvello has evidence (a witness's testimony) that he was not exceeding the legal speed limit. Carvello could file a motion for summary judgment on the ground that there was no evidence in the record to support Kirby's claim. The court might grant Carvello's motion because there would be no genuine factual dispute and Carvello would be entitled to judgment as a matter of law.

A motion for summary judgment can be made before or during a trial, but it will be granted only if, when the evidence is viewed in the light most favorable to the other party, there clearly are no factual disputes in contention.

Discovery. Before a trial begins, the parties can use a number of procedural devices to obtain information and gather evidence about the case. Kirby, for example, will want to know how fast Carvello was driving, whether he had been drinking or was under the influence of any medication, whether he was wearing corrective lenses if he was required by law to do so while driving, and so on. The process of obtaining information from the opposing party or from witnesses prior to trial is known as **discovery.**

Discovery • A phase in the litigation process during which the opposing parties may obtain information from each other and from third parties prior to trial.

The Federal Rules of Civil Procedure and similar rules in the states set forth the guidelines for discovery activity. Discovery includes gaining access to witnesses, documents, records, and other types of evidence. Discovery prevents surprises by giving both parties access to evidence that might otherwise be hidden. This allows the litigants to learn as much as they can about what to expect at a trial before they reach the courtroom. Discovery also serves to narrow the issues so that trial time is spent on the main questions in the case.

The rules governing discovery are designed to make sure that a witness or a party is not unduly harassed, that privileged material is safeguarded, and that only information relevant to the case at hand—or likely to lead to the discovery of relevant information—is discoverable. The rules thus place limits on what a party can obtain as part of the discovery process. For example, a business firm in litigation with a competitor normally will not be given unrestricted access to the competitor's trade secrets, customer lists, and other confidential records. A court may order that only the firm's attorneys and certain experts can view such sensitive information.

Depositions and Interrogatories. At a minimum, discovery involves the use of depositions, interrogatories, or both. A **deposition** is sworn testimony by a party to the lawsuit or by any witness, recorded by an authorized court official. The person deposed gives testimony and answers questions asked by the attorneys from both sides. The questions and answers are recorded, sworn to, and signed. These answers, of course, will help the attorneys prepare their cases. Depositions also give attorneys the opportunity to evaluate how their witnesses will conduct themselves at trial. In addition, depositions can be employed in court to impeach (challenge the credibility of) a party or a witness who changes testimony at the trial. A deposition can also be used as testimony if the witness is not available at trial.

Deposition • The testimony of a party to a lawsuit or a witness taken under oath before a trial.

Interrogatories are written questions for which written answers are prepared and then signed under oath. Interrogatories are addressed only to parties directly involved in a lawsuit (plaintiffs or defendants), not to witnesses,

Interrogatories • A series of written questions for which written answers are prepared and then signed under oath by a party to a lawsuit, usually with the assistance of the party's attorney.

and the parties can prepare their answers with the aid of attorneys. Whereas depositions are useful for eliciting candid responses from a party and answers not prepared in advance, interrogatories are designed to obtain accurate information about specific topics, such as how many contracts were signed, the specific dates on which certain contracts were signed, and so on.

Requests for Admissions. One party can serve the other party with a written request for an admission of the truth of matters relating to the trial. Any fact admitted under such a request is conclusively established as true for the trial. For example, Kirby can ask Carvello to admit that his driver's license was suspended at the time of the accident. A request for admission shortens the trial because the parties will not have to spend time proving facts on which they already agree.

Requests for Documents, Objects, and Entry upon Land. A party can gain access to documents and other items not in her or his possession in order to inspect and examine them. Likewise, a party can gain "entry upon land" to inspect the premises. Carvello, for example, can gain permission to inspect and copy Kirby's repair bills.

Request for Examinations. When the physical or mental condition of one party is in question, the opposing party can ask the court to order a physical or mental examination by an independent examiner. If the court agrees to make the order, the opposing party can obtain the results of the examination. Note that the court will make such an order only when the need for the information outweighs the right to privacy of the person to be examined.

Costs. Under the Federal Rules of Civil Procedure, any relevant material may be the object of a discovery request, and generally the party responding must pay the expense of complying. A court can limit the scope of a request, however, if compliance would be too burdensome or the cost would be too great.

As individuals and businesses have increased their use of computers to create and store documents, make deals, and exchange e-mail, the universe of discoverable material has expanded exponentially. The more information there is to discover, however, the more expensive it is to discover all the relevant information.

Some courts have balanced these competing principles by shifting the cost of discovery to the requesting party. The point of contention has been when this "cost-shifting" should occur. In the following case, involving the discovery of electronic data, the court developed a new set of factors for determining when discovery costs should be shifted to the requester.

CASE 2.4

United States District Court, Southern District of New York, 2003. __ F.Supp.2d __.

ZUBULAKE v. UBS WARBURG, LLC

UBS Warburg, LLC, is an investment sales firm. Each UBS salesperson receives nearly two hundred e-mails each day. UBS maintains e-mail files in three forms: active user e-mail files, archived e-mails on optical disks, and back-up data stored on tapes. The active data is the most accessible: it is online data that resides on an active server and can be accessed immediately. The optical disk data is only slightly less accessible; the disks need to be located and read, but the system is configured to make searching sim-

ple and automated once they are located. E-mail stored on back-up tape is indexed, which makes finding a specific message relatively simple, but restoring a message stored on tape takes five days. UBS hired Laura Zubulake in August 1999 as a director and senior salesperson in a department managed by Dominic Vail. At the time, Zubulake was told that she would be considered for Vail's position if it became vacant. In December 2000, however, when the position opened, she was not considered—UBS hired Matthew Chapin instead. Less than eight months later, Zubulake filed a complaint with the Equal Employment Opportunity Commission, alleging that Chapin had, among other things, excluded her from work-related activities with male co-workers and clients.[a] *Less than eight weeks later, she was fired. She filed a suit in a federal district court against UBS, alleging violations of discrimination laws. As part of a discovery request, Zubulake asked UBS for "[a]ll documents concerning any communication by or between UBS employees concerning Plaintiff," including "without limitation, electronic or computerized data compilations." UBS produced one hundred pages of e-mail but refused to search further, claiming that the cost would be too high.*

SCHEINDLIN, J.

The world was a far different place in 1849, when Henry David Thoreau opined in admirably broader context that "[t]he process of discovery is very simple." That hopeful maxim has given way to rapid technological advances, requiring new solutions to old problems. The issue presented here is one such problem, recast in light of current technology: To what extent is inaccessible electronic data discoverable, and who should pay for its production?

* * * *

* * * Faced with similar [issues], courts generally engage in some sort of cost-shifting analysis * * * .

The first question, however, is whether cost-shifting must be considered in every case involving the discovery of electronic data, which—in today's world—includes virtually all cases. In light of the accepted principle * * * that electronic evidence is no less discoverable than paper evidence, the answer is, "No." * * * *[T]he presumption is that the responding party must bear the expense of complying with discovery requests* * * * . Any principled approach to electronic evidence must respect this presumption. [Emphasis added.]

* * * *

Thus, cost-shifting should be considered only *when electronic discovery imposes an undue burden or expense on the responding party.* The burden or expense of discovery is, in turn, undue when it outweighs its likely benefit, taking into account the needs of the case, the amount in controversy, the parties' resources, the importance of the issues at stake in the litigation, and the importance of the proposed discovery in resolving the issues. [Emphasis added.]

Many courts have automatically assumed that an undue burden or expense may arise simply because electronic evidence is involved. This makes no sense. Electronic evidence is frequently cheaper and easier to produce than paper evidence because it can be searched automatically, key words can be run for privilege checks, and the production can be made in electronic form obviating the need for mass photocopying.

In fact, whether production of documents is unduly burdensome or expensive turns primarily on whether it is kept in an *accessible* or *inaccessible* format

a. This allegation, and Zubulake's other charges, related to employment discrimination, which is discussed in detail in Chapter 15.

(a distinction that corresponds closely to the expense of production). In the world of paper documents, for example, a document is accessible if it is readily available in a usable format and reasonably indexed. Examples of inaccessible paper documents could include (a) documents in storage in a difficult to reach place; (b) documents converted to microfiche and not easily readable; or (c) documents kept haphazardly, with no indexing system, in quantities that make page-by-page searches impracticable. But in the world of electronic data, thanks to search engines, any data that is retained in a machine readable format is typically accessible.

* * * *

In summary, deciding disputes regarding the scope and cost of discovery of electronic data requires a three-step analysis:

First, it is necessary to thoroughly understand the responding party's computer system, both with respect to active and stored data. For data that is kept in an accessible format, the usual rules of discovery apply: the responding party should pay the costs of producing responsive data. A court should consider cost-shifting *only* when electronic data is relatively inaccessible, such as in backup tapes.

Second, because the cost-shifting analysis is so fact-intensive, it is necessary to determine what data may be found on the inaccessible media. Requiring the responding party to restore and produce responsive documents from a small sample of the requested backup tapes is a sensible approach in most cases.

Third, and finally, in conducting the cost-shifting analysis, the following factors should be considered, weighted more-or-less in the following order:

1. The extent to which the request is specifically tailored to discover relevant information;
2. The availability of such information from other sources;
3. The total cost of production, compared to the amount in controversy;
4. The total cost of production, compared to the resources available to each party;
5. The relative ability of each party to control costs and its incentive to do so;
6. The importance of the issues at stake in the litigation; and
7. The relative benefits to the parties of obtaining the information.

Accordingly, UBS is ordered to produce *all* responsive e-mails that exist on its optical disks or on its active servers * * * at its own expense. UBS is also ordered to produce, at its expense, responsive e-mails from any *five* backup tapes selected *by Zubulake.* UBS should then prepare an affidavit detailing the results of its search, as well as the time and money spent. After reviewing the contents of the backup tapes and UBS's [affidavit], the Court will conduct the appropriate cost-shifting analysis.

The court issued a new seven-factor test for determining when the cost of discovery of electronic data should be shifted to the requesting party. Based on this test, the court ordered UBS to retrieve all data from easily accessible media at its own expense. The court also ordered the defendant to retrieve, from a "relatively inaccessible" medium (the back-up tapes), certain sample data, the expense and content of which the court would review to decide whether the plaintiff should pay the cost to retrieve more.

QUESTIONS

1. Why did Zubulake ask UBS for "[a]ll documents concerning any communication by or between UBS employees concerning Plaintiff"?
2. On what did the court base its order to UBS to retrieve electronic data?
3. Should cost-shifting be considered in every case involving the discovery of electronic data?

Pretrial Conference. After discovery has taken place and before the trial begins, the attorneys may meet with the trial judge in a **pretrial conference.** The purpose of this conference is to clarify the issues that remain in dispute after discovery has taken place and to explore the possibility of settling the conflict without a trial. If a settlement is not possible at this time, the parties and the judge discuss the manner in which the trial will be conducted. In particular, the parties may attempt to establish ground rules to restrict such things as the number of expert witnesses or the admissibility of certain types of evidence. Once the pretrial conference concludes, both parties will have to turn their attention to the trial itself and, if the trial is to be a jury trial, to the selection of jurors who will hear the case.

Pretrial conference • A conference, scheduled before the trial begins, between the judge and the attorneys litigating the suit. The parties may settle the dispute, clarify the issues, and so on during the conference.

The Right to a Jury Trial. The Seventh Amendment to the U.S. Constitution guarantees the right to a jury trial for cases at law in federal courts when the amount in controversy exceeds $20. Most states have similar guarantees in their own constitutions, although many states set a higher minimum. For example, Iowa requires the dollar amount of damages to be at least $1,000 before there is a right to a jury trial. The right to a trial by jury does not have to be exercised, and many cases are tried without a jury. If there is no jury, the judge determines the truth of the facts alleged in the case. In most states and in federal courts, one of the parties must request a jury, or the right is presumed to be waived.

Jury Selection. Prior to the commencement of any jury trial, a panel of jurors must be assembled. The clerk of the court will usually notify local residents by mail that they have been selected for jury duty. These prospective jurors are chosen in various ways, but often the court clerk selects names at random from lists of registered voters or lists of persons to whom the state has issued driver's licenses. These persons then report to the courthouse on the date specified in the notice. There they are gathered into a single pool of jurors, and the process of selecting those jurors who will actually hear the case begins. Although some types of trials require twelve-person juries, most civil matters can be heard by six-person juries.

Voir Dire. The process by which the jury is selected is known as ***voir dire.***[19] In most jurisdictions, *voir dire* consists of oral questions that attorneys for the plaintiff and the defendant ask a group of prospective jurors to determine

Voir dire • Old French verbs meaning "to speak the truth." In jury trials, the phrase refers to the process in which the attorneys question prospective jurors to determine whether they are biased or have any connection with a party to the action or with a prospective witness.

19. Pronounced *vwahr deehr.*

whether a potential juror is biased or has any connection with a party to the action or with a prospective witness. Usually, jurors are questioned one at a time, although when large numbers of jurors are involved, the attorneys may direct their questions to groups of jurors instead to minimize the amount of time spent in jury selection. Sometimes, jurors are asked to fill out written questionnaires. Some trial attorneys use psychologists and other professionals to help them select jurors.

Challenges during Voir Dire. During *voir dire,* a party may challenge a certain number of prospective jurors *peremptorily*—that is, ask that these individuals not be sworn in as jurors without providing any reason for excluding them. The total number of peremptory challenges allowed each side is determined by statute or by the court. Furthermore, a party may challenge any juror *for cause*—that is, provide a reason why an individual should not be sworn in as a juror. If the judge grants the challenge, the individual is asked to step down. A prospective juror, however, may not be excluded by the use of discriminatory challenges, such as those based on racial criteria[20] or gender.[21] Of course, *proving* that a particular challenge is discriminatory can be difficult because an attorney may give another reason for the challenge even though the underlying reason may be discriminatory.

After both sides have completed their challenges, those jurors who have been excused will be permitted to leave. The remaining jurors—those who have been found acceptable by the attorneys for both sides—will be seated in the jury box.

Alternate Jurors. Because unforeseeable circumstances or illness may necessitate that one or more of the sitting jurors be dismissed, the court, depending on the rules of the particular jurisdiction and the expected length of the trial, may choose to have two or three alternate jurors present throughout the trial. If a juror has to be excused in the middle of the trial, then an alternate may take his or her place without disrupting the proceedings. Once the jury members are seated, the judge will swear in the jury members, and the trial itself can begin.

The Trial

Various rules and procedures govern the trial phase of the litigation process. There are rules governing what kind of evidence will or will not be admitted during the trial, as well as specific procedures that the participants in the lawsuit must follow.

Rules of evidence • Rules governing the admissibility of evidence in trial courts.

Rules of Evidence. Whether evidence will be admitted in court is determined by the **rules of evidence**—a series of rules that have been created by the courts to ensure that any evidence presented during a trial is fair and reliable. The Federal Rules of Evidence govern the admissibility of evidence in federal courts.

20. *Batson v. Kentucky,* 476 U.S. 79, 106 S.Ct. 1712, 90 L.Ed.2d 69 (1986).

21. *J.E.B. v. Alabama ex rel. T.B.,* 511 U.S. 127, 114 S.Ct. 1419, 128 L.Ed.2d 89 (1994)—see the *Question of Ethics and Social Responsibility* at the end of this chapter for a discussion of this case. (*Ex rel.* is an abbreviation of the Latin *ex relatione.* The phrase refers to an action brought on behalf of the state, by the attorney general, at the instigation of an individual who has a private interest in the matter.)

CONCEPT SUMMARY 2.3
Pretrial Procedures

PROCEDURE	DESCRIPTION
Pleadings	① *The plaintiff's complaint*—The plaintiff's statement of the cause of action and the parties involved, filed with the court by the plaintiff's attorney. After the filing, the defendant is notified of the suit through service of process. ② *The defendant's response*—The defendant's response to the plaintiff's complaint may take the form of an answer, in which the defendant may admit to or deny the plaintiff's allegations. The defendant may raise an affirmative defense and/or assert a counterclaim.
Pretrial Motions	① *Motion to dismiss*—A motion made by the defendant—often prior to filing an answer to the complaint—requesting the judge to dismiss the case for reasons that are provided in the motion (such as failure to state a claim for which relief can be granted). ② *Motion for judgment on the pleadings*—May be made by either party; will be granted if no facts are in dispute and only questions of law are at issue. ③ *Motion for summary judgment*—May be made by either party; will be granted if no facts are in dispute and only questions of law are at issue. Unlike the motion for judgment on the pleadings, the motion for summary judgment may be supported by evidence outside the pleadings, such as testimony and other evidence obtained during the discovery phase of litigation.
Discovery	The process of gathering evidence concerning the case; involves (1) *depositions* (sworn testimony by either party or any witness); (2) *interrogatories* (in which parties to the action write answers to questions with the aid of their attorneys); and (3) requests for admissions, documents, examinations, or other information relating to the case.
Pretrial Conference	A pretrial hearing, at the request of either party or the court, to identify the matters in dispute after discovery has taken place and to explore the possibility of settling the dispute without a trial. If no settlement is possible, the parties plan the course of the trial.
Jury Selection	In a jury trial, the selection of members of the jury from a pool of prospective jurors. During a process known as *voir dire,* the attorneys for both sides may challenge prospective jurors either for cause or peremptorily (for no cause).

Evidence will not be admitted in court unless it is relevant to the matter in question. **Relevant evidence** is evidence that tends to prove or disprove a fact in question or to establish the degree of probability of a fact or action. For example, evidence that a suspect's gun was in the home of another person when a victim was shot would be relevant—because it would tend to prove that the suspect did not shoot the victim.

Relevant evidence • Evidence tending to make a fact at issue in the case more or less probable than it would be without the evidence. Only relevant evidence is admissible in court.

Even relevant evidence may not be admitted in court if its reliability is questionable or if its probative (proving) value is substantially outweighed by other important considerations of the court. For example, a video or a photograph that shows in detail the severity of a victim's injuries would be relevant evidence, but the court might exclude this evidence on the ground that it would emotionally inflame the jurors.

Hearsay • An oral or written statement made out of court that is later offered in court by a witness (not the person who made the statement) to prove the truth of the matter asserted in the statement. Hearsay is generally inadmissible as evidence.

Generally, hearsay is not admissible as evidence. **Hearsay** is defined as any testimony given in court about a statement made by someone else. Literally, it is what someone heard someone else say. For example, if a witness in the Kirby-Carvello case testified in court concerning what he or she heard another observer say about the accident, that testimony would be hearsay—secondhand knowledge. Admitting hearsay into evidence carries many risks because, even though it may be relevant, there is no way to test its reliability.

Opening statement • A statement made to the jury at the beginning of a trial by a party's attorney, prior to the presentation of evidence. The attorney briefly outlines the evidence that will be offered and the legal theory that will be pursued.

Opening Statements. At the commencement of the trial, both attorneys are allowed to make **opening statements** concerning the facts that they expect to prove during the trial. The opening statement provides an opportunity for each lawyer to give a brief version of the facts and the supporting evidence that will be used during the trial.

Direct examination • The examination of a witness by the attorney who calls the witness to the stand to testify on behalf of the attorney's client.

Cross-examination • The questioning of an opposing witness during the trial.

Examination of Witnesses. Because Kirby is the plaintiff, she has the burden of proving that her claim is correct. Kirby's attorney begins the presentation of Kirby's case by calling the first witness for the plaintiff and examining (questioning) the witness. (For both attorneys, the types of questions and the manner of asking them are governed by the rules of evidence.) This questioning is called **direct examination.** After Kirby's attorney is finished, the witness is subject to **cross-examination** by Carvello's attorney. Then Kirby's attorney has another opportunity to question the witness in *redirect examination,* and Carvello's attorney may follow the redirect examination with a *recross-examination.* When both attorneys have finished with the first witness, Kirby's attorney calls the succeeding witnesses in the plaintiff's case, each of whom is subject to examination by the attorneys in the manner just described.

Motion for a directed verdict • In a jury trial, a motion for the judge to take the decision out of the hands of the jury and direct a verdict for the moving party on the ground that the other party has not produced sufficient evidence to support his or her claim; referred to as a motion for judgment as a matter of law in the federal courts.

Rebuttal • The refutation by the plaintiff's attorney of evidence introduced by the defendant's attorney.

Rejoinder • The defendant's answer to the plaintiff's rebuttal.

Closing argument • An argument made after the plaintiff and defendant have rested their cases. Closing arguments are made prior to the jury charges.

At the conclusion of the plaintiff's case, the defendant's attorney has the opportunity to ask the judge to direct a verdict for the defendant on the ground that the plaintiff has presented no evidence to support the plaintiff's claim. This is called a **motion for a directed verdict** (federal courts use the term *judgment as a matter of law* instead of *directed verdict*). In considering the motion, the judge looks at the evidence in the light most favorable to the plaintiff and grants the motion only if there is insufficient evidence to raise an issue of fact. (Motions for directed verdicts at this stage of a trial are seldom granted.)

The defendant's attorney then presents the evidence and witnesses for the defendant's case. Witnesses are called and examined by the defendant's attorney. The plaintiff's attorney has the right to cross-examine them, and there may be a redirect examination and possibly a recross-examination. At the end of the defendant's case, either attorney can move for a directed verdict, and the test again is whether the jury can, through any reasonable interpretation of the evidence, find for the party against whom the motion has been made. After the defendant's attorney has finished introducing evidence, the plaintiff's attorney can present a **rebuttal,** which includes additional evidence to refute the defendant's case. The defendant's attorney can, in turn, refute that evidence in a **rejoinder.**

Closing Arguments. After both sides have rested their cases, each attorney presents a closing argument. In the **closing argument,** each attorney summarizes the facts and evidence presented during the trial, indicates why the facts and evidence support the client's claim, reveals the shortcomings of the points made by the opposing party during the trial, and generally urges a verdict in favor of the client. Each attorney's comments must be relevant to the issues in dispute.

Jury Instructions. After the closing arguments, the judge instructs the jury (assuming it is a jury trial) in the law that applies to the case. The instructions to the jury are often called *charges*. A charge includes statements of the applicable laws, as well as a review of the facts as they were presented during the case. Because the jury's role is to serve as the fact finder, the factual account contained in the charge is not binding on the jurors. Indeed, they may disregard the facts as noted in the charge entirely. They are not free to ignore the statements of law, however. The charge will help to channel the jurors' deliberations.

The Jury's Verdict. After receiving the instructions, the jury retires to the jury room to deliberate the case. In a civil case, the standard of proof is a *preponderance of the evidence*. That is, the plaintiff (Kirby in our hypothetical case) need not provide indisputable proof that she is entitled to a judgment. She need only show that her factual claim is more likely to be true than the defendant's. (As you will read in Chapter 7, in a criminal trial the prosecution has a higher standard of proof to meet—it must prove its case *beyond a reasonable doubt.*)

Note that some civil claims must be proved by "clear and convincing evidence," meaning that the evidence must show that the truth of the party's claim is highly probable. This standard applies in suits involving charges of fraud, suits to establish the terms of a lost will, some suits relating to oral contracts, and other suits in which the circumstances are thought to present a particular danger of deception.

Once the jury has reached a decision, it may issue a **verdict** in favor of one party; the verdict specifies the jury's factual findings and the amount of damages to be paid by the losing party. After the announcement of the verdict, which marks the end of the trial itself, the jurors will be discharged.

Verdict • A formal decision made by a jury.

Posttrial Motions

After the jury has rendered its verdict, either party may make a posttrial motion. The prevailing party usually files a motion for a judgment in accordance with the verdict. The nonprevailing party frequently files one of the motions discussed next.

Motion for a New Trial. At the end of the trial, a motion can be made to set aside an adverse verdict and any judgment and to hold a new trial. The **motion for a new trial** will be granted only if the judge (1) is convinced, after looking at all the evidence, that the jury was in error but (2) does not feel it is appropriate to grant judgment for the other side. This will usually occur when the jury verdict is obviously the result of a misapplication of the law or a misunderstanding of the evidence presented at trial.

Motion for a new trial • A motion asserting that the trial was so fundamentally flawed (because of error, newly discovered evidence, prejudice, or other reason) that a new trial is necessary to prevent a miscarriage of justice.

A new trial can also be granted on the grounds of newly discovered evidence, misconduct by the participants (such as the attorneys, the judge, or the jury) during the trial, or error by the judge. If a motion for a new trial is

CONCEPT SUMMARY 2.4
Trial Procedures

PROCEDURE	DESCRIPTION
Opening Statements	Each party's attorney is allowed to present an opening statement indicating what the attorney will attempt to prove during the course of the trial.
Examination of Witnesses	① Plaintiff's introduction and direct examination of witnesses, cross-examination by defendant's attorney, possible redirect examination by plaintiff's attorney, and possible recross-examination by defendant's attorney. ② Defendant's introduction and direct examination of witnesses, cross-examination by plaintiff's attorney, possible redirect examination by defendant's attorney, and possible recross-examination by plaintiff's attorney. ③ Possible rebuttal of defendant's argument by plaintiff's attorney, who presents more evidence. ④ Possible rejoinder by defendant's attorney to meet that evidence.
Closing Arguments	Each party's attorney argues in favor of a verdict for his or her client.
Jury Instructions	The judge instructs the jury as to how the law applies to the issue.
Jury Verdict	The jury renders its verdict, thus bringing the trial to an end.

denied, the judge's denial may be appealed to a higher court. In the following case, the defendants filed a motion for a new trial based on the "improper and inflammatory" remarks made by the plaintiff's attorney.

CASE 2.5

Supreme Court of New Hampshire, 1997.
141 N.H. 579, 688 A.2d 556.
http://www.courts.state.nh.us/supreme/opinions/1997/94-198.htm[a]

LEBLANC v. AMERICAN HONDA MOTOR CO.

*While riding on a snowmobile, Thomas LeBlanc was injured when the snowmobile collided with an off-road vehicle manufactured by American Honda Motor Company (a subsidiary of a Japanese corporation). LeBlanc sued Honda and the driver in a New Hampshire state court. During the trial, LeBlanc's lawyer, Vincent Martina, asked Honda's expert witness if he had ever wondered why the Honda vehicle was "red, white, and blue, the colors of the American flag." During his closing argument, Martina told the jury that the case was not about "Pearl Harbor or the Japanese prime minister saying Americans are lazy and stupid. * * * What this case is about is not American xenophobia; it's about corporate greed." When the jury returned a verdict in favor of LeBlanc, Honda filed a motion for a new trial, which the court denied. Honda appealed to the Supreme Court of New Hampshire, arguing in part that Martina's remarks so tainted the proceedings as to deprive Honda of a fair trial.*

BROCK, C. J.

To justify a [new trial], remarks or * * * conduct must be more than merely inadmissible; they must constitute an irreparable injustice * * *.

a. This is a page within the collection of New Hampshire Supreme Court opinions available at the Web site of the New Hampshire state government.

* * * *

* * * [A] new trial may be warranted where counsel attempts to appeal to the sympathies, passions, and prejudices of jurors grounded in race or nationality, by reference to the opposing party's religious beliefs or lack thereof, or by reference to a party's social or economic condition or status. Such an appeal was attempted in this case.

* * * It is true that counsel's closing reference was brief. At the same time, when an elephant has passed through the courtroom one does not need a forceful reminder.

The Supreme Court of New Hampshire reversed the decision in favor of LeBlanc and remanded the case for a new trial. The court held that remarks made during a trial to cultivate in the jury a racial and national bias constitute sufficient grounds for a new trial.

QUESTIONS

1. What was the basis for Honda's argument on appeal that it was deprived of a fair trial?
2. Why did the Supreme Court of New Hampshire reverse the decision of the lower court?
3. If Martina, during his closing argument, had not mentioned Pearl Harbor and the Japanese prime minister's remark about American's being "lazy and stupid," would the outcome of the case have been different?

Motion for Judgment *N.O.V.* If Kirby wins, and if Carvello's attorney has previously moved for a directed verdict, Carvello's attorney can now make a **motion for judgment *n.o.v.***—from the Latin *non obstante veredicto,* meaning "notwithstanding the verdict." (As with a motion for a directed verdict, federal courts use the term *judgment as a matter of law* instead of judgment *n.o.v.*) The standards for granting a judgment *n.o.v.* often are the same as those for granting a motion to dismiss or a motion for a directed verdict. Carvello can state that even if the evidence is viewed in the light most favorable to Kirby, a reasonable jury should not have found in Kirby's favor. If the judge finds this contention to be correct or decides that the law requires the opposite result, the motion will be granted. If the motion is denied, Carvello may then appeal the case. (Kirby may also appeal the case, even though she won at trial. She might appeal, for example, if she received a smaller money award than she had sought.)

Motion for judgment *n.o.v.* • A motion requesting the court to grant judgment in favor of the party making the motion on the ground that the jury verdict against him or her was unreasonable and erroneous.

The Appeal

Either party may appeal not only the jury's verdict but also any pretrial or posttrial motion. Many of the appellate court cases that appear in this text involve appeals of motions to dismiss, motions for summary judgment, or other motions that were decided by trial court judges. Note that few trial court decisions are reversed on appeal. In most appealed cases (approximately 90 percent), the trial court's decision is affirmed and thus becomes final.

Filing the Appeal. If Carvello decides to appeal the verdict in Kirby's favor, then his attorney must file a *notice of appeal* with the clerk of the trial court within a prescribed period of time. Carvello then becomes the *appellant.* The clerk of the trial court sends to the reviewing court (usually an intermediate court of appeals) the *record on appeal,* which contains the following: (1) the pleadings, (2) a transcript of the trial testimony and copies of the exhibits, (3) the judge's rulings on motions made by the parties, (4) the arguments of counsel, (5) the instructions to the jury, (6) the verdict, (7) the posttrial motions, and (8) the judgment order from which the appeal is taken.

Brief • A formal legal document submitted by the attorney for the appellant—or the appellee (in answer to the appellant's brief)—to an appellate court when a case is appealed. The appellant's brief outlines the facts and issues of the case, the trial court's rulings that should be reversed or modified, the applicable law, and the arguments on the client's behalf.

Carvello's attorney will file a **brief** with the reviewing court. The brief contains (1) a short statement of the facts; (2) a statement of the issues; (3) the rulings by the trial court that Carvello contends are erroneous and prejudicial (biased in favor of one of the parties); (4) the grounds for reversal of the judgment; (5) a statement of the applicable law; and (6) arguments on Carvello's behalf, citing applicable statutes and relevant cases as precedents. The attorney for the *appellee* (Kirby, in our hypothetical case) usually files an answering brief. Carvello's attorney can file a reply, although it is not required. The reviewing court then considers the case.

Appellate Review. A court of appeals does not hear any evidence. Its decision concerning a case is based on the record on appeal and the briefs. The attorneys can present oral arguments, after which the case is taken under advisement. The court then issues a written opinion. In general, the appellate courts do not reverse findings of fact unless the findings are unsupported or contradicted by the evidence.

An appellate court has several options after reviewing a case: it can *affirm* the trial court's decision; it can *reverse* the trial court's judgment if it concludes that the trial court erred or that the jury did not receive proper instructions; or it can *remand* (send back) the case to the trial court for further proceedings consistent with its opinion on the matter. The court might also affirm or reverse a decision *in part.* For example, the court might affirm the jury's finding that Carvello was negligent but remand the case for further proceedings on another issue (such as the extent of Kirby's damages). An appellate court can also *modify* a lower court's decision. If the appellate court decides that the jury awarded an excessive amount in damages, for example, the court might reduce the award to a more appropriate, or fairer, amount.

Higher Appellate Courts. If the reviewing court is an intermediate appellate court, the court may allow the losing party to appeal the decision to the state supreme court. Such a petition corresponds to a petition for a writ of *certiorari* in the United States Supreme Court. If the petition is granted, new briefs must be filed before the state supreme court, and the attorneys may be allowed or requested to present oral arguments. Like the intermediate appellate courts, the supreme court may reverse or affirm the appellate court's decision or remand the case.

Unless it is remanded, the case has reached its end at this point unless a federal question is at issue—a question concerning a constitutional right, for example, or a question as to how a federal statute should be interpreted. If a federal question is involved, the losing party (or the winning party, if that party is dissatisfied with the relief obtained) may appeal the decision to the United States Supreme Court by petitioning the Court for a writ of *certiorari.* The Supreme Court may or may not grant the writ, depending on the significance of the issue in dispute.

Enforcing the Judgment

The uncertainties of the litigation process are compounded by the lack of guarantees that any judgment will be enforceable. Even if the jury awards Kirby the full amount of damages requested ($100,000), for example, she might not, in fact, "win" anything at all. Carvello's auto insurance coverage might have lapsed, in which event the company would not pay any of the damages. Alternatively, Carvello's insurance policy might be limited to $50,000, meaning that Carvello personally would have to pay the remaining $50,000.

If Carvello does not have that amount of money available, then Kirby will need to go back to court and request that the court issue a *writ of execution*—an order, usually issued by the clerk of the court, directing the sheriff to seize and sell Carvello's nonexempt assets (certain assets are exempted by law from creditors' actions). The proceeds of the sale would then be used to pay the damages owed to Kirby. Any excess proceeds of the sale would be returned to Carvello. Alternatively, the nonexempt property itself could be transferred to Kirby in lieu of an outright payment.

The problem of collecting a judgment is less pronounced, of course, when a party is seeking to satisfy a judgment against a defendant, such as a major corporation, that has substantial assets that can be easily located. Usually, one of the factors considered before a lawsuit is initiated is whether the defendant has sufficient assets to cover the amount of damages sought, should the plaintiff win the case.

Concept Summary 2.5
Posttrial Options

Procedure	Description
Posttrial Motions	① *Motion for a new trial*—If the judge is convinced that the jury was in error or the trial was fundamentally flawed due to newly discovered evidence, prejudice, or some other reason, the motion will be granted. ② *Motion for judgment n.o.v. ("notwithstanding the verdict")*—The party making the motion must have filed a motion for a directed verdict at the close of all the evidence during the trial; the motion will be granted if the judge is convinced that the jury was in error.
Appeal	Either party can appeal the trial court's judgment to an appropriate court of appeals. ① *Filing the appeal*—The appealing party must file a notice of appeal with the clerk of the trial court, who forwards to the appellate court the record on appeal. Attorneys' briefs are filed. ② *Appellate review*—The appellate court does not hear evidence but bases its opinion, which it issues in writing, on the record on appeal and the attorneys' briefs and oral arguments. The court may affirm or reverse all (or part) of the trial court's judgment and/or remand the case for further proceedings consistent with its opinion. Most decisions are affirmed on appeal. ③ In some cases, further review may be sought from a higher appellate court, such as a state supreme court. Ultimately, if a federal question is involved, the case may be appealed to the United States Supreme Court.

KEY TERMS

affidavit 64
affirmative defense 63
answer 63
bankruptcy court 42
brief 76
closing argument 72
complaint 58
concurrent jurisdiction 43
counterclaim 63
cross-examination 72
default judgment 58
deposition 65
direct examination 72
discovery 65
diversity of citizenship 42
docket 43
exclusive jurisdiction 43
federal question 42
Federal Rules of Civil Procedure (FRCP) 55
hearsay 72
***in personam* jurisdiction 39**
***in rem* jurisdiction 41**
interrogatories 65
judicial review 39
jurisdiction 39
justiciable controversy 48
long arm statute 40
motion 63
motion for a directed verdict 72
motion for a new trial 73
motion for judgment *n.o.v.* 75
motion for judgment on the pleadings 64
motion for summary judgment 64
motion to dismiss 63
opening statement 72
pleadings 57
pretrial conference 69
pretrial motion 63
probate court 42
question of fact 50
question of law 50
rebuttal 72
rejoinder 72
relevant evidence 71
rule of four 52
rules of evidence 70
service of process 58
small claims court 50
standing to sue 48
summons 58
venue 46
verdict 73
***voir dire* 69**
writ of *certiorari* 52

FOR REVIEW

1. What is judicial review? How and when was the power of judicial review established?
2. Before a court can hear a case, it must have jurisdiction. Over what must it have jurisdiction? In what circumstances does a federal court have jurisdiction?
3. What is the difference between a trial court and an appellate court?
4. In a lawsuit, what are the pleadings? What is discovery?
5. What are the steps involved in an appeal?

QUESTIONS AND CASE PROBLEMS

2–1. The defendant in a lawsuit is appealing the trial court's decision in favor of the plaintiff. On appeal, the defendant claims that the evidence presented at trial to support the plaintiff's claim was so scanty that no reasonable jury could have found for the plaintiff. Therefore, argues the defendant, the appellate court should reverse the trial court's decision. May an appellate court ever reverse a trial court's findings with respect to questions of fact? Discuss fully.

2–2. Appellate courts normally see only written transcripts of trial proceedings when they are reviewing cases. Today, in some states, videotapes are being used as the official trial reports. If the use of videotapes as official reports continues, will this alter the appellate process? Should it? Discuss fully.

2–3. Marya Callais, a citizen of Florida, was walking one day near a busy street in Tallahassee, Florida, when a large crate flew off a passing truck and hit her, resulting in numerous injuries. She incurred a great deal of pain and suffering, plus significant medical expenses, and she could not work for six months. She wants to sue the trucking firm for $300,000 in damages. The firm's headquarters are in Georgia, although the company does business in Florida. In what court might Callais bring suit—a Florida state court, a Georgia state court, or a federal court? What factors might influence her decision?

2–4. When and for what purpose is each of the following motions made? Which of them would be appropriate if a defendant claimed that the only issue between the parties was a question of law and that the law was favorable to the defendant's position?

(a) A motion for judgment on the pleadings.
(b) A motion for a directed verdict.
(c) A motion for summary judgment.
(d) A motion for judgment *n.o.v.*

2–5. During *voir dire,* the parties, through their attorneys, select those persons who will serve as jurors during the trial. The parties are prohibited, however, from excluding potential jurors on the basis of race or other discriminatory criteria. One issue concerns whether the prohibition against discrimination extends to potential jurors who have physical or mental disabilities. Federal law prohibits discrimination against an otherwise qualified person with a disability when that person could be accommodated without too much difficulty. Should this law also apply to the jury selection process? For example, should parties be prohibited from excluding blind persons, through either challenges for cause or peremptory challenges, from serving on juries? Discuss fully.

CASE PROBLEM WITH SAMPLE ANSWER

2–6. Motion for a New Trial. Washoe Medical Center, Inc., admitted Shirley Swisher for the treatment of a fractured pelvis. During her stay, Swisher suffered a fatal fall from her hospital bed. Gerald Parodi, the administrator of her estate, and others filed an action against Washoe seeking damages for the alleged lack of care in treating Swisher. During *voir dire,* when the plaintiffs' attorney returned a few minutes late from a break, the trial judge led the prospective jurors in a standing ovation. The judge joked with one of the prospective jurors, whom he had known in college, about his fitness to serve as a judge and personally endorsed another prospective juror's business. After the trial, the jury returned a verdict in favor of Washoe. The plaintiffs moved for a new trial, but the judge denied the motion. The plaintiffs then appealed, arguing that the tone set by the judge during *voir dire* prejudiced their right to a fair trial. Should the appellate court agree? Why or why not? [*Parodi v. Washoe Medical Center, Inc.,* 111 Nev. 365, 892 P.2d 588 (1995)]

➡ *To view a sample answer for this case problem, go to this book's Web site at* **http://ele.westbuslaw.com** *and click on "Interactive Study Center."*

2–7. Jury Selection. Ms. Thompson filed a suit in a federal district court against her employer, Altheimer & Gray, seeking damages for alleged racial discrimination in violation of federal law. During *voir dire,* the judge asked the prospective jurors, "[Is] there . . . something about this kind of lawsuit for money damages that would start any of you leaning for or against a particular party?" Ms. Leiter, one of the prospective jurors, raised her hand and explained that she had "been an owner of a couple of businesses and am currently an owner of a business, and I feel that as an employer and owner of a business that will definitely sway my judgment in this case." She explained, "I am constantly faced with people that want various benefits or different positions in the company or better contacts or, you know, a myriad of issues that employers face on a regular basis, and I have to decide whether or not that person should get them." Asked by Thompson's lawyer whether "you believe that people file lawsuits just because they don't get something they want," Leiter answered, "I believe there are some people that do." In answer to another question, she said, "I think I bring a lot of background to this case, and I can't say that it's not going to cloud my judgment. I can try to be as fair as I can, as I do every day." Thompson filed a motion to strike Leiter for cause. Should the judge grant the motion? Explain. [*Thompson v. Altheimer & Gray,* 248 F.3d 621 (7th Cir. 2001)]

2–8. Motion for a Directed Verdict. Gerald Adams worked as a cook for Uno Restaurants, Inc., at Warwick Pizzeria Uno Restaurant & Bar in Warwick, Rhode Island. One night, shortly after Adams's shift began, he noticed that the kitchen floor was saturated with a foul-smelling liquid coming from the drains and backing up water onto the floor. He complained of illness and went home, where he contacted the state health department. A department representative visited the restaurant and closed it for the night, leaving instructions to sanitize the kitchen and clear the drains. Two days later, in the restaurant, David Badot, the manager, shouted at Adams in the presence of other employees. When Adams shouted back, Badot fired Adams and had him arrested. Adams filed a suit in a Rhode Island state court against Uno, alleging that he had been unlawfully terminated for contacting the health department. Arguing that Adams had been fired for threatening Badot, Uno filed a motion for a directed verdict. What does a court weigh in considering whether to grant such a motion? Should the court grant the motion in this case? Why or why not? [*Adams v. Uno Restaurants, Inc.,* 794 A.2d 489 (R.I. 2002)]

2–9. E-Jurisdiction. American Business Financial Services, Inc. (ABFI), a Pennsylvania firm, sells and services loans to businesses and consumers. First Union National Bank, with its principal place of business in

North Carolina, provides banking services. Alan Boyer, an employee of First Union, lives in North Carolina and has never been to Pennsylvania. In the course of his employment, Boyer learned that the bank was going to extend a $150 million line of credit to ABFI. Boyer then attempted to manipulate the stock price of ABFI for personal gain by sending disparaging e-mails to ABFI's independent auditors in Pennsylvania. Boyer also posted negative statements about ABFI and its management on a Yahoo bulletin board. ABFI filed a suit in a Pennsylvania state court against Boyer, First Union, and others, alleging wrongful interference with a contractual relationship, among other things. Boyer filed a motion to dismiss the complaint for lack of personal jurisdiction. Could the court exercise jurisdiction over Boyer? Explain. [*American Business Financial Services, Inc. v. First Union National Bank,* __ A.2d __ (Pa.Comm.Pl. 2002)]

2–10. Jurisdiction. Kazaa BV was a company formed under the laws of the Netherlands. Kazaa distributed Kazaa Media Desktop (KMD) software that enabled users to exchange, via a peer-to-peer transfer network, digital media, including movies and music. Kazaa also operated the Kazaa.com Web site, through which it distributed the KMD software to millions of California residents and other users. Metro-Goldwyn-Mayer Studios, Inc., and other parties in the entertainment industries based in California filed a suit in a federal district court against Kazaa and others, alleging copyright infringement. Kazaa filed a counterclaim, but while legal action was pending, the firm passed its assets and its Web site to Sharman Networks, Ltd., a company organized under the laws of Vanuatu and doing business principally in Australia. Sharman explicitly disclaimed assumption of any of Kazaa's liabilities. When the plaintiffs added Sharman as a defendant, Sharman filed a motion to dismiss on the ground that the court did not have jurisdiction. Would it be fair to subject Sharman to suit in this case? Explain. [*Metro-Goldwyn-Mayer Studios, Inc. v. Grokster, Ltd.,* 243 F.Supp.2d 1073 (C.D.Cal. 2003)]

2–11. IN YOUR COURT

Aldo Uberti and Co., an Italian corporation, manufactures a six-shot, single-action revolver known as the Cattleman. Uberti sells its guns to a U.S. distributor for sale throughout the country. Henry Pacho, a resident of Arizona, bought one of the guns, wrapped it in a towel, and put it under the seat of his car. His two-year-old niece, Corrina, was helping to clean the car when the gun fell out of the towel, hit the pavement, and discharged. The bullet struck Corrina in the head and killed her. Corrina's parents filed a suit in an Arizona state court against Uberti, alleging that the company was liable for the "design, manufacture, sale, and distribution of a defective and unreasonably dangerous product." Uberti asked the court to dismiss the suit on the ground that the court did not have personal jurisdiction over Uberti. Assume that you are the Arizona state judge hearing this case and answer the following questions:

(a) Do Corrina's parents have "standing to sue" in this case? Explain.
(b) Can an Arizona state court exercise jurisdiction over the defendant in this case? Why or why not?
(c) Suppose that the defendant corporation was headquartered in New York instead of Italy. Would this change in the facts of the case affect your decision?

2–12. A QUESTION OF ETHICS AND SOCIAL RESPONSIBILITY

The state of Alabama, on behalf of a mother (T.B.), brought a paternity suit against the alleged father (J.E.B.) of T.B.'s child. During jury selection, the state, through peremptory challenges, removed nine of the ten prospective male jurors. J.E.B.'s attorney struck the final male from the jury pool. As a result of these peremptory strikes, the final jury consisted of twelve women. When the jury returned a verdict in favor of the mother, the father appealed. The father argued that eliminating men from the jury constituted gender discrimination and violated his rights to equal protection and due process (see Chapter 5). The father asked the court to extend the principle enunciated in *Batson v. Kentucky* (cited in footnote 20 of this chapter), which prohibited peremptory strikes based solely on race, to include gender-based strikes. The appellate court refused to do so. [*J.E.B. v. Alabama ex rel. T.B.,* 511 U.S. 127, 114 S.Ct. 1419, 128 L.Ed.2d 89 (1994)]

(a) Do you agree with J.E.B. that the state's exercise of its peremptory challenges violated his right to equal protection and due process? Why or why not?
(b) If you were the judge, how would you rule?
(c) The late Supreme Court Justice Thurgood Marshall urged, when the Court was reviewing the *Batson* case, that peremptory challenges be banned entirely. Do you agree with this proposal? Discuss.

2–13. FOR CRITICAL ANALYSIS

American courts are forums for adversarial justice, in which attorneys defend the interests of their respective clients before the court. This means that an attorney may end up claiming before a court that his or her client is innocent, even though the attorney knows that the client acted wrongfully. Is it ethical for attorneys to try to "deceive" the court in these situations? Can the adversarial system of justice really lead to "truth"?

For updated links to resources available on the Web, as well as a variety of other materials, visit this text's Web site at

http://ele.westbuslaw.com

If you are interested in learning more about the Federal Rules of Civil Procedure (FRCP) and the Federal Rules of Evidence (FRE), they can now be accessed via the Internet at the following Web site:

http://www.cornell.edu

On January 9, 2002, the state of Michigan launched the nation's first "cyber court." For information about this virtual court and how it is designed to operate, go to

http://www.michigancybercourt.net

For the decisions of the United States Supreme Court, as well as information about the Supreme Court, go to

http://supremecourtus.gov

The Web site for the federal courts offers information on the federal court system and links to all federal courts at

http://www.uscourts.gov

The National Center for State Courts (NCSC) offers links to the Web pages of all state courts. Go to

http://www.ncsconline.org

LEGAL RESEARCH EXERCISES ON THE WEB

Go to **http://ele.westbuslaw.com**, the Web site that accompanies this text. Select "Interactive Study Center," and then click on "Chapter 2." There you will find the following Internet research exercises that you can perform to learn more about topics covered in this chapter.

Activity 2–1: LEGAL PERSPECTIVE—Civil Procedure

Activity 2–2: TECHNOLOGICAL PERSPECTIVE—Virtual Courtrooms

Activity 2–3: HISTORICAL PERSPECTIVE—The Judiciary's Role in American Government

BEFORE THE TEST

Go to **http://ele.westbuslaw.com**, the Web site that accompanies this text. Select "Interactive Quizzes." You will find at least twenty interactive questions relating to this chapter.

WESTLAW® CAMPUS

If your textbook provided for a subscription to Westlaw® Campus, or if you have otherwise purchased access to the Westlaw Campus database, you can access any of the cases presented or cited in this chapter by using your Westlaw Campus account.

CHAPTER 3

Alternative and Online Dispute Resolution

CONTENTS

CHAPTER OBJECTIVES

After reading this chapter, you should be able to answer the following questions:

1. What is alternative dispute resolution?

2. How do the processes of negotiation and mediation differ?

3. What are the steps in the arbitration process?

4. What are the differences between court-annexed arbitration and voluntary arbitration?

5. How are online forums used to resolve disputes?

Trials are costly and time consuming. It has been said that this is the result of "too many lawyers, too many lawsuits, and too many laws." In fact, since 1960, the number of lawyers has tripled, the number of lawsuits has tripled, and the number of laws has multiplied, while the numbers of judges and courts have not kept pace.

Although it is true that the number of lawsuits filed has grown rapidly, only 5 to 10 percent of lawsuits filed actually go to trial. Most cases are settled or dismissed long before the parties enter a courtroom. Moreover, the number of cases that are litigated does not appear to be growing any faster than the population. When compared with the large number of transactions that occur in our highly complex society, the rate of litigation appears low to some.

Nevertheless, in any individual case, it may be months before a hearing can even be scheduled. Depending on the complexity of the case, the extent of discovery proceedings required, and whether the opposing party employs tactics to delay the proceeding, years may be spent in litigation. Even in the best of situations, the civil procedures discussed in Chapter 2 all require significant time and money costs. As the cost and complexity of litigation have grown, businesspersons and other individuals have asked, "Is there a more appropriate way to resolve disputes?"

The Search for Alternatives to Litigation

A number of solutions have been implemented, and others have been proposed, to reduce the congestion in our court system and to reduce the litigation costs facing all members of society. The enforcement of arbitration clauses, the use of court-referred arbitration and mediation, and the emergence of an increasing number of private forums for dispute resolution have all helped to reduce the caseload of the courts.

Another solution to the problem involves putting caps on damage awards, particularly for pain and suffering. Without the probability of obtaining multimillion-dollar judgments for pain and suffering, some potential litigants will be deterred from undertaking lawsuits to obtain damages. Another avenue of attack is to penalize those who bring frivolous lawsuits. Rule 11 of the Federal Rules of Civil Procedure allows for disciplinary sanctions against lawyers and litigants who bring frivolous lawsuits in federal courts.

Many courts require mediation or arbitration before a case goes to trial. There are proposals to further reduce delay and expenses in federal civil cases, and proposals are being considered by the states as well. Some of the proposals can be viewed as case-management plans. One proposal, for example, would require each federal district court to implement procedures for placing cases on different tracks, with simple cases being handled more quickly than complex ones.

Politics and Law

Because reforms of any system affect individuals and groups differently, they seldom are accomplished easily and quickly. Reform of the court system is a prime example. At the federal level, members of Congress long have been concerned with bringing court costs and delay under control. These concerns gave rise to the enactment of legislation in the early 1990s that required the federal courts to develop a plan to cut costs and reduce delay within the federal judicial system.

New Methods and Arrangements

The search for alternative means to resolve disputes has produced several distinct methods and arrangements. These range from neighbors sitting down over a cup of coffee to work out their differences to huge multinational corporations agreeing to resolve a dispute through a formal hearing before a panel of experts. All of these alternatives to traditional litigation make up what is broadly termed **alternative dispute resolution (ADR).**

Alternative dispute resolution (ADR) • The resolution of disputes in ways other than those involved in the traditional judicial process. Negotiation, mediation, and arbitration are forms of ADR.

ADR describes any procedure or method for resolving disputes outside the traditional judicial process. ADR is normally a less expensive and less time-consuming process than formal litigation. In some cases, it also has the advantage of being more private. Except in cases involving court-annexed arbitration (discussed later in this chapter), no public record of ADR proceedings is created; only the parties directly involved are privy to the information presented during the process. This is a particularly important consideration in many business disputes, because such cases may involve sensitive commercial information. As you will read later in this chapter, today ADR also includes online methods of resolving disputes.

NEGOTIATION AND MEDIATION

Alternative dispute resolution methods differ in the degree of formality involved and the extent to which third parties participate in the process. Generally, negotiation is the least formal method and traditionally involved no third parties. Mediation may be similarly informal but, by definition, does involve the participation of a third party.

Negotiation

Negotiation • In regard to dispute settlement, a process in which parties attempt to settle their dispute without going to court, with or without attorneys to represent them.

In the process of **negotiation,** the parties come together informally, with or without attorneys to represent them. Within this informal setting, the parties air their differences and try to reach a settlement or resolution without the involvement of independent third parties. Because no third parties are involved and because of the informal setting, negotiation is the simplest form of ADR. Even if a lawsuit has been initiated, the parties may continue to negotiate their differences at any time during the litigation process and attempt to resolve their dispute. Less than 10 percent of all corporate lawsuits, for example, end up in trial—the rest are settled beforehand.

Preparation for Negotiation. In spite of the informality of negotiation, each party must carefully prepare his or her side of the case. The elements of the dispute should be considered, and documents and other evidence should be collected. Negotiating from a well-prepared position improves the odds of obtaining a favorable result. Even if a dispute is not resolved through negotiation, preparation for negotiation will reduce the effort required to get ready for the next step in the dispute-resolution process.

Assisted Negotiation. To facilitate negotiation, various forms of what might be called "assisted negotiation" have emerged in recent years. Assisted negotiation, as the term implies, involves the assistance of a third party. Forms of ADR associated with the negotiation process include mini-trials, early neutral case evaluation, and conciliation. Another form of assisted negotiation—the summary jury trial—is discussed later in this chapter.

A **mini-trial** is a private proceeding in which each party's attorney briefly argues the party's case before the other party. Typically, a neutral third party, who acts as an adviser and an expert in the area being disputed, is also present. If the parties fail to reach an agreement, the adviser renders an opinion as to how a court would likely decide the issue. The proceeding assists the parties in determining whether they should negotiate a settlement of the dispute or take it to court.

Mini-trial • A private proceeding in which each party to a dispute argues its position before the other side and vice versa. A neutral third party may be present and act as an adviser if the parties fail to reach an agreement.

In **early neutral case evaluation,** the parties select a neutral third party (generally an expert in the subject matter of the dispute) to evaluate their respective positions. The parties explain their positions to the case evaluator however they wish. The evaluator then assesses the strengths and weaknesses of the parties' positions, and this evaluation forms the basis for negotiating a settlement.

Early neutral case evaluation • A form of alternative dispute resolution in which a neutral third party evaluates the strengths and weaknesses of the disputing parties' positions; the evaluator's opinion forms the basis for negotiating a settlement.

Disputes may also be resolved in a friendly, nonadversarial manner through **conciliation,** in which a third party assists parties to a dispute in reconciling their differences. The conciliator helps to schedule negotiating sessions and carries offers back and forth between the parties when they refuse to face each other in direct negotiations. Technically, conciliators are not to recommend solutions. In practice, however, they often do. In contrast, a mediator is expected to propose solutions.

Conciliation • A form of alternative dispute resolution in which the parties reach an agreement themselves with the help of a neutral third party, called a conciliator, who facilitates the negotiations.

Mediation

One of the oldest forms of ADR is mediation. In the **mediation** process, the parties themselves attempt to negotiate an agreement, but with the assistance of a neutral third party, called a *mediator.* The mediator need not be a lawyer. The mediator may be a single person, such as a paralegal, an attorney, or a volunteer from the community. Alternatively, a panel of mediators may be used.

Mediation • A method of settling disputes outside of court by using the services of a neutral third party, called a mediator. The mediator acts as a communicating agent between the parties and suggests ways in which the parties can resolve their dispute.

Mediation is essentially a form of assisted negotiation. We treat it separately here because traditionally it has been viewed as an alternative to negotiation. Additionally, a mediator usually plays a more active role than do neutral third parties in assisted negotiation.

Advantages of Mediation. Few procedural rules are involved in the mediation process—far fewer than in a courtroom setting. The proceedings can be tailored to fit the needs of the parties. For example, the mediator can be told to maintain a diplomatic role or be asked to express an opinion about the dispute, lawyers can be excluded from the proceedings, and the exchange of a few documents can replace the more expensive and time-consuming process of pretrial discovery. Disputes are often settled far more quickly in mediation than in formal litigation.[1]

There are other benefits. Because the parties reach agreement by mutual consent, the bitterness that often flows from the winner-take-all outcome of a formal trial decision is avoided. Hard feelings are also minimized by the less stressful environment provided by mediation; the absence of the formal rules and adversarial tone of courtroom proceedings lessens the hostility the parties may feel toward one another. Minimizing hard feelings can be very important when the parties have to continue working with one another while the controversy is being resolved or after it has been settled. This is frequently the case when two businesses—say, a supplier and a purchaser—have a long-standing, mutually beneficial relationship that they would like to preserve despite their controversy. Similarly, in the context of management and labor disputes, employee disciplinary matters and grievances are subjects that invite mediation as an alternative to formal litigation.

Another important benefit of mediation is that the mediator is selected by the parties. In litigation, the parties have no control over the selection of a judge. In mediation, the parties may select a mediator on the basis of expertise in a particular field as well as for fairness and impartiality. To the degree that the mediator has these attributes, he or she will more effectively aid the parties in reaching an agreement over their dispute.

Disadvantages of Mediation. Mediation is not without disadvantages. A mediator is likely to charge a fee. (This can be split between the parties, though, and would likely be far less than the parties would pay if they went to court.)

Informality and the absence of a third party referee can also be disadvantageous. (Remember that a mediator can only help the parties reach a decision, not make a decision for them.) Without a deadline hanging over the parties' heads, and without the threat of sanctions if they fail to negotiate in good faith, they may be less willing to make concessions or otherwise strive honestly and diligently to reach a settlement. This can slow the process or even cause it to fail.

ARBITRATION

A third method of dispute resolution combines the advantages of third party decision making—as provided by judges and juries in formal litigation—with the speed and flexibility offered by rules of procedure and evidence that are less rigid than those governing courtroom litigation. This is the process of **arbitration**—the settling of a dispute by an impartial third party (other than a court) who renders a decision. The third party who renders the deci-

Arbitration • The settling of a dispute by submitting it to a disinterested third party (other than a court), who renders a decision. The decision may or may not be legally binding.

1. In Florida alone, as many as fifty thousand disputes that might have ended up in court are instead resolved through mediation each year.

sion is called an *arbitrator.* The key difference between arbitration and the forms of ADR just discussed is that in arbitration, the third party's decision may be legally binding on the parties.

When a dispute arises, the parties can agree to settle their differences informally through arbitration rather than formally through the court system. Alternatively, the parties may agree ahead of time that, if a dispute should arise, they will submit to arbitration rather than bring a lawsuit. If the parties agree that the arbitrator's decision will be legally binding, they are obligated to abide by the arbitrator's decision regardless of whether or not they agree with it.

The federal government and many state governments favor arbitration over litigation. The federal policy favoring arbitration is embodied in the Federal Arbitration Act (FAA) of 1925.[2] The FAA requires that courts give deference to all voluntary arbitration agreements in cases governed by federal law. Virtually any dispute can be the subject of arbitration. A voluntary agreement to arbitrate a dispute normally will be enforced by the courts if the agreement does not compel an illegal act or contravene public policy.

The Federal Arbitration Act

The FAA does not establish a set arbitration procedure. The parties themselves must agree on the manner of resolving their dispute. The FAA provides the means for enforcing the arbitration procedure that the parties have established for themselves.

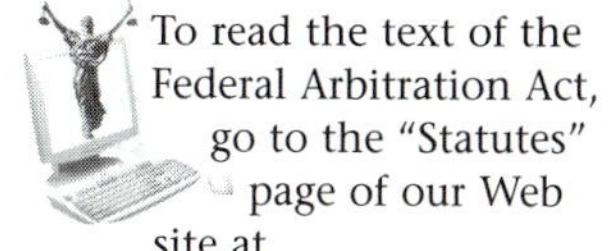

To read the text of the Federal Arbitration Act, go to the "Statutes" page of our Web site at

http://ele.westbuslaw.com

Section 4 of the FAA allows a party to petition a federal district court for an order compelling arbitration under an agreement to arbitrate a dispute. If the judge is "satisfied that the making of the agreement for arbitration or the failure to comply therewith is not in issue, the court shall make an order directing the parties to proceed with arbitration in accordance with the terms of the agreement."

Under Section 9 of the FAA, the parties to the arbitration may agree to have the arbitrator's decision confirmed in a federal district court. Through confirmation, one party obtains a court order directing another party to comply with the terms of the arbitrator's decision. Section 10 establishes the grounds by which the arbitrator's decision may be set aside (canceled). The grounds for setting aside a decision are limited to misconduct, fraud, corruption, or abuse of power in the arbitration process itself; a court will not review the merits of the dispute or the arbitrator's judgment.

The FAA covers any arbitration clause in a contract that involves interstate commerce. Business activities that have even remote connections to or minimal effects on commerce between two or more states are considered to be included. Thus, arbitration agreements involving transactions only slightly connected to the flow of interstate commerce may fall under the FAA, even if the parties, at the time of contracting, did not expect their arbitration agreement to involve interstate commerce.[3]

At issue in the early 2000s was whether the FAA applied to employment contracts. Some lower courts had claimed that when Congress passed the FAA it intended to exempt such contracts from coverage. In the following *Featured Case,* the United States Supreme Court addressed this issue.

2. 9 U.S.C. Sections 1–15.

3. *Allied-Bruce Terminix Cos., Inc. v. Dobson,* 513 U.S. 265, 115 S.Ct. 834, 130 L.Ed.2d 753 (1995).

FEATURED CASE

CASE 3.1

Supreme Court of the United States, 2001.
532 U.S. 105,
121 S.Ct. 1302,
149 L.Ed.2d 234.

CIRCUIT CITY STORES, INC. v. ADAMS

MAJORITY OPINION

KENNEDY, J.

Section 1 of the Federal Arbitration Act (FAA) excludes from the Act's coverage "contracts of employment of seamen, railroad employees, or any other class of workers engaged in foreign or interstate commerce." * * *

* * * *

I

In October 1995, respondent Saint Clair Adams applied for a job at petitioner Circuit City Stores, Inc., a national retailer of consumer electronics. Adams signed an employment application which included the following provision:

> I agree that I will settle any and all previously unasserted claims, disputes or controversies arising out of or relating to my application or candidacy for employment, employment and/or cessation of employment with Circuit City, *exclusively* by final and binding *arbitration* before a neutral Arbitrator. By way of example only, such claims include claims under federal, state, and local statutory or common law, such as the Age Discrimination in Employment Act, Title VII of the Civil Rights Act of 1964, as amended, including the amendments of the Civil Rights Act of 1991, the Americans with Disabilities Act, the law of contract and the law of tort. [Emphasis in original.]

Adams was hired as a sales counselor in Circuit City's store in Santa Rosa, California.

Two years later, Adams filed an employment discrimination lawsuit against Circuit City in state court, asserting claims under * * * California law. Circuit City filed suit in the United States District Court for the Northern District of California, seeking to enjoin the state-court action and to compel arbitration of respondent's claims pursuant to the FAA. The District Court entered the requested order. Respondent, the court concluded, was obligated by the arbitration agreement to submit his claims against the employer to binding arbitration. An appeal followed.

* * * [T]he Court of Appeals held the arbitration agreement between Adams and Circuit City was contained in a "contract of employment," and so was not subject to the FAA. Circuit City petitioned this Court * * * . We granted *certiorari* to resolve the issue.

II

A

* * * [T]he FAA compels judicial enforcement of a wide range of written arbitration agreements. * * *

* * * *

The instant case [the case now before the Court] * * * involves * * * the exemption from coverage under [Section] 1. * * * Most Courts of Appeals conclude the exclusion provision is limited to transportation workers, defined, for instance, as those workers "actually engaged in the movement of goods in interstate commerce." * * * [T]he Court of Appeals for the Ninth

Circuit takes a different view and interprets the [Section] 1 exception to exclude all contracts of employment from the reach of the FAA. * * *

B

* * * *

Respondent, endorsing the reasoning of the Court of Appeals for the Ninth Circuit that the provision excludes all employment contracts, relies on the asserted breadth of the words "contracts of employment of * * * any other class of workers engaged in * * * commerce." * * * [R]espondent contends [Section] 1's interpretation should have a like reach, thus exempting all employment contracts. The two provisions, it is argued, are coterminous [contained within the same boundaries]; under this view the "involving commerce" provision brings within the FAA's scope all contracts within the Congress's commerce power, and the "engaged in * * * commerce" language in [Section] 1 in turn exempts from the FAA all employment contracts falling within that authority.

This reading of [Section] 1, however, runs into an immediate and, in our view, insurmountable textual obstacle [a problem in interpreting the text of Section 1 of the FAA]. * * * [T]he words "any other class of workers engaged in * * * commerce" constitute a residual phrase, following, in the same sentence, explicit reference to "seamen" and "railroad employees." Construing the residual phrase to exclude all employment contracts fails to give independent effect to the statute's enumeration of the specific categories of workers which precedes it; there would be no need for Congress to use the phrases "seamen" and "railroad employees" if those same classes of workers were subsumed within the meaning of the "engaged in * * * commerce" residual clause. The wording of [Section] 1 calls for the application of * * * the statutory canon [rule for interpreting statutes] that *"[w]here general words follow specific words in a statutory enumeration, the general words are construed to embrace only objects similar in nature to those objects enumerated by the preceding specific words."* Under this rule of construction the residual clause should be read to give effect to the terms "seamen" and "railroad employees," and should itself be controlled and defined by reference to the enumerated categories of workers which are recited just before it; the interpretation of the clause pressed by respondent fails to produce these results. [Emphasis added.]

* * * [E]ven if the term "engaged in commerce" stood alone in [Section] 1, we would not construe the provision to exclude all contracts of employment from the FAA. Congress uses different modifiers to the word "commerce" in the design and enactment of its statutes. The phrase "affecting commerce" indicates Congress's intent to regulate to the outer limits of its authority under the Commerce Clause. The "involving commerce" phrase, the operative words for the reach of the basic coverage provision in [Section] 2, was at issue in [a previous Supreme Court case]. * * * Considering the usual meaning of the word "involving," and the pro-arbitration purposes of the FAA, [we] held the word "involving," like "affecting," signals an intent to exercise Congress's commerce power to the full. Unlike those phrases, however, the general words "in commerce" and the specific phrase "engaged in commerce" are understood to have a more limited reach. * * * [T]he words "in commerce" are often-found words of art that we have not read as expressing congressional intent to regulate to the outer limits of authority under the Commerce Clause.

* * * *

In sum, the text of the FAA forecloses the construction of [Section] 1 followed by the Court of Appeals in the case under review, a construction which would exclude all employment contracts from the FAA. * * *

* * * *

For the foregoing reasons, the judgment of the Court of Appeals for the Ninth Circuit is reversed, and the case is remanded for further proceedings consistent with this opinion.[a]

It is so ordered.

DISSENTING OPINION

STEVENS, J.

History amply supports the proposition that [the exclusion] was an uncontroversial provision that merely confirmed the fact that no one interested in the enactment of the FAA ever intended or expected that [Section] 2 would apply to employment contracts. * * *

The irony of the Court's reading of [Section] 2 to include contracts of employment is compounded by its cramped interpretation of the exclusion inserted into [Section] 1. As proposed and enacted, the exclusion fully responded to the concerns of the Seamen's Union and other labor organizations that [Section] 2 might encompass employment contracts by expressly exempting not only the labor agreements of "seamen" and "railroad employees," but also of "*any other class of workers* engaged in foreign or interstate commerce." Today, however, the Court fulfills the original—and originally unfounded—fears of organized labor by essentially rewriting the text of [Section] 1 to exclude the employment contracts solely of "seamen, railroad employees, or any other class of *transportation* workers engaged in foreign or interstate commerce." In contrast, whether one views the legislation before or after the amendment to [Section] 1, it is clear that it was not intended to apply to employment contracts at all. [Emphasis added.]

TEST YOUR COMPREHENSION: CASE DETAILS

1. What was Adams's primary complaint against Circuit City in the state court, and how did the case end up in the federal court system?
2. Did the U.S. Court of Appeals for the Ninth Circuit decide that Adams's employment contract was subject to the mandatory arbitration provisions of the FAA?
3. What reasons did the United States Supreme Court cite for reversing the Ninth Circuit Court of Appeal's decision?
4. How did the dissent evaluate the Court's use of the rules of statutory construction?
5. Did Adams end up having to arbitrate the case against Circuit City after all? Why or why not?

a. As discussed in this chapter's *Emerging Trends* feature, on remand the U.S. Court of Appeals for the Ninth Circuit nonetheless refused to enforce the agreement. The court held that under state law Circuit City's arbitration agreement was too unfair and one sided to be enforceable.

State Arbitration Statutes

Virtually all states follow the federal approach to voluntary arbitration. Most of the states and the District of Columbia have adopted the Uniform Arbitration Act, which was drafted by the National Conference of Commissioners on Uniform State Laws in 1955. Those states that have not adopted the uniform act nonetheless follow many of the practices specified in it.

Under the uniform act, the basic approach is to give full effect to voluntary agreements to arbitrate disputes between private parties. The act supplements private arbitration agreements by providing explicit procedures and remedies for enforcing arbitration agreements. The uniform act does not, however, dictate the terms of the agreement. Moreover, under both federal and state statutes, the parties are afforded considerable latitude in deciding the subject matter of the arbitration and the methods for conducting the arbitration process. In the absence of a controlling statute, the rights and duties of the parties are established and limited by their agreement.

The Arbitration Process

The arbitration process begins with a *submission,* which is the act of referring a dispute to an arbitrator. The next step is the *hearing,* in which evidence and arguments are presented to the arbitrator. The process culminates in an *award,* which is the decision of the arbitrator.

The right to appeal the award to a court is limited. If the award was made under a voluntary arbitration agreement, a court normally will not set it aside even if it was the result of an erroneous determination of fact or an incorrect interpretation of law by the arbitrator.

There are at least two reasons for this limitation. First, if an award is not treated as final, then, rather than speeding up the dispute-resolution process, arbitration would merely add one more layer to the process of litigation. Second, the basis of arbitration—the freedom of parties to agree among themselves how to settle a controversy—supports treating an award as final. Having had the opportunity to frame the issues and to set out the manner for resolving the dispute, one party should not complain if the result was not what that party had hoped it would be.

Submission. The parties may agree to submit questions of fact, questions of law, or both to the arbitrator. The parties may even agree to leave the interpretation of the arbitration agreement to the arbitrator. In the case of an existing agreement to arbitrate, the clause itself is the submission to arbitration.

The submission typically states the identities of the parties, the nature of the dispute to be resolved, the monetary amounts involved in the controversy, the place at which the arbitration is to take place, and the intention of the parties to be bound by the arbitrator's award. Exhibit 3–1 on the following page contains a sample submission form.

Most states require that an agreement to submit a dispute to arbitration be in writing. Moreover, because the goal of arbitration is speed and efficiency in resolving controversies, most states require that matters be submitted within a definite period of time, generally six months from the date on which the dispute arises.

EXHIBIT 3–1 • SAMPLE SUBMISSION FORM

American Arbitration Association

SUBMISSION TO DISPUTE RESOLUTION

Date: ________________

The named parties hereby submit the following dispute for resolution under the ______________ ____ Rules* of the American Arbitration Association:

Procedure Selected: ☐ Binding arbitration ☐ Mediation settlement
☐ Other ____
(Describe)

THE NATURE OF THE DISPUTE

THE CLAIM OR RELIEF SOUGHT (the Amount, if Any):

TYPE OF BUSINESS: Claimant ____________________ Respondent ____________________

PLACE OF HEARING: ____

We agree that, if binding arbitration is selected, we will abide by and perform any award rendered hereunder and that a judgment may be entered on the award.

To Be Completed by the Parties

Name of Party	Name of Party
Address	Address
City, State, and ZIP Code	City, State, and ZIP Code
( ) Telephone Fax	( ) Telephone Fax
Signature†	Signature†
Name of Representative for Party	Name of Representative for Party
Name of Firm (if Applicable)	Name of Firm (if Applicable)
Representative's Address	Representative's Address
City, State, and ZIP Code	City, State, and ZIP Code
( ) Telephone Fax	( ) Telephone Fax
Signature†	Signature†

Please file three copies with the AAA.

* *If you have a question as to which rules apply, please contact the AAA.*
† *Signatures of all parties are required for arbitration.*
1997-W

The Hearing. The parties must state in their arbitration agreement the issues that will be submitted for arbitration and the powers that the arbitrator will exercise. The arbitrator may be given power at the outset of the process to establish rules that will govern the proceedings. Typically, these rules are much less restrictive than those governing formal litigation. Regardless of who establishes the rules, the arbitrator will apply them during the course of the hearing.

Restrictions on the kind of evidence and the manner in which it is presented may be less rigid in arbitration than in a court proceeding, partly because the arbitrator is likely to be an expert in the subject matter involved in the controversy. Restrictions may also be less stringent because there is less fear that the arbitrator will be swayed by improper evidence. In contrast, evidence in a jury trial must sometimes be presented twice: once to the judge, outside the presence of the jury, to determine if the evidence may be heard by the jury, and—depending on the judge's ruling—again, to the jury.

In the typical hearing format, the parties begin as they would at trial by presenting opening arguments to the arbitrator and stating what remedies should or should not be granted. After the opening statements have been made, evidence is presented. Witnesses may be called and examined by both sides. After all of the evidence has been presented, the parties give their closing arguments. On completion of the closing arguments, the arbitrator ends the hearing.

The Award. After each side has had an opportunity to present evidence and to argue its case, the arbitrator reaches a decision. The final decision of the arbitrator is referred to as an **award,** even if no money is conferred on a party as a result of the proceedings. Under most statutes, the arbitrator must render an award within thirty days of the close of the hearing.

Award • In the context of arbitration, the arbitrator's decision.

In most states, the award need not state the arbitrator's findings regarding factual questions in the case. Nor must the award state the conclusions that the arbitrator reached on any questions of law that may have been presented. All that is required for the award to be valid is that it contain a ruling on the matter that completely resolves the controversy.

Most states do, however, require that the award be in writing, regardless of whether any conclusions of law or findings of fact are included. If the arbitrator does state his or her legal conclusions and factual findings, then a letter or an opinion will be drafted containing the basis for the award. Even when there is no statutory requirement that the arbitrator state the factual and legal basis for the award, the parties may impose the requirement in their submission or in their predispute agreement to arbitrate.

Enforcement of Agreements to Submit to Arbitration

The role of the courts in the arbitration process is limited. One important role is played at the prearbitration stage. A court may be called on to order one party to an arbitration agreement to submit to arbitration under the terms of the agreement. The court in this role is essentially interpreting a contract. The court must determine what the parties have committed themselves to before ordering that they submit to arbitration.

The Issue of Arbitrability. When a dispute arises as to whether the parties have agreed in an arbitration clause to submit a particular matter to arbitration, one party may file suit to compel arbitration. The court before which the suit is brought will not decide the basic controversy but must determine the issue of arbitrability—that is, whether the issue is one that must be resolved through arbitration. If the court finds that the subject matter in controversy is covered by the agreement to arbitrate, a party may be compelled to arbitrate the dispute involuntarily.

Although the parties may agree to submit the issue of arbitrability to an arbitrator, the agreement must be explicit; a court will never *infer* an agreement to arbitrate. Unless a court finds an *explicit* agreement to have the arbitrator decide whether a dispute is arbitrable, the court will decide the issue. This is an important initial determination, because no party will be ordered to submit to arbitration unless the court is convinced that the party has consented to do so.

Mandatory Arbitration in the Employment Context. A significant question in the last several years has concerned mandatory arbitration clauses in employment contracts. Are violations of rights granted to employees by employment statutes appropriate subjects for arbitration? For example, should a court order the arbitration of a claim involving an alleged violation of a federal statute protecting an employee from employment discrimination? Many claim that employees' rights are not sufficiently protected when they are forced, in order to be hired, to agree to arbitrate all disputes and thus to waive their rights under statutes specifically designed to protect employees.

Compulsory arbitration agreements often spell out the rules for a mandatory proceeding. For example, an agreement may address in detail the amount and payment of filing fees and other expenses. Some courts have overturned provisions in employment-related agreements that require the parties to split the costs on the basis of an individual worker's ability to pay. The court in the following case took this reasoning a step further. (For a more detailed discussion of this issue, see this chapter's *Emerging Trends* feature starting on page 97.)

CASE 3.2

United States Court of Appeals, Sixth Circuit, 2003. 317 F.3d 646. **http://pacer.ca6.uscourts.gov/opinions/main.php[a]**

MORRISON v. CIRCUIT CITY STORES, INC.

Lillian Morrison, an African American female with a bachelor's degree in engineering from the U.S. Air Force Academy and a master's degree in administration from Central Michigan University, applied for a managerial position at a Circuit City store in Cincinnati, Ohio. As part of the job application, Morrison was required to sign an agreement that mandated arbitration for any employment-related dispute. The employee was to pay one-half the costs of the arbitration, unless the arbitrator decided otherwise. An employee's share might be limited to either $500 or 3 percent of her most recent annual salary, but all charges were to be paid within ninety days of the issuance of an award. Morrison was hired in 1995, but two years later she was terminated. She filed a suit in an Ohio state court against Circuit City, alleging in part

a. This is a page within the Web site of the U.S. Court of Appeals for the Sixth Circuit. In the left-hand column, click on "Opinions Search." In the "Short Title contains" box, type "Morrison" and click "Submit Query." In the "Opinion" box corresponding to the name of the case, click on the number to access the opinion.

that the employer had discriminated against her on the basis of her race and gender.[b] *The case was moved to a federal district court, which ordered the parties to proceed to arbitration. Morrison appealed to the U.S. Court of Appeals for the Sixth Circuit, arguing in part that the cost-splitting provision was unenforceable. Meanwhile, the arbitration proceeded, and, as part of the award, the arbitrator did not require Morrison to pay any of the costs.*

MOORE, J.

We hold that *potential litigants must be given an opportunity, prior to arbitration on the merits, to demonstrate that the potential costs of arbitration are great enough to deter them and similarly situated individuals from seeking to vindicate their federal statutory rights in the arbitral forum.* * * * Thus, in order to protect the statutory rights at issue, the reviewing court must look to more than just the interests and conduct of a particular plaintiff. A particular plaintiff may be determined to pursue his or her claims, regardless of costs. But a court considering whether a cost-splitting provision is enforceable should consider similarly situated potential litigants, for whom costs will loom as a larger concern, because it is, in large part, their presence in the system that will deter discriminatory practices. * * * [Emphasis added.]

For this reason, *if the reviewing court finds that the cost-splitting provision would deter a substantial number of similarly situated potential litigants, it should refuse to enforce the cost-splitting provision in order to serve the underlying functions of the federal statute.* In conducting this analysis, the reviewing court should define the class of such similarly situated potential litigants by job description and socioeconomic background. It should take the actual plaintiff's income and resources as representative of this larger class's ability to shoulder the costs of arbitration. * * * [Emphasis added.]

Moreover, in addressing the effect of arbitration costs on a class, the reviewing court should look to average or typical arbitration costs, because that is the kind of information that potential litigants will take into account in deciding whether to bring their claims in the arbitral forum. In considering the decision-making process of the typical member of a class, it is proper to take into account the typical or average costs of arbitration.

* * *

This analysis will yield different results in different cases. It will find, in many cases, that high-level managerial employees and others with substantial means can afford the costs of arbitration, thus making cost-splitting provisions in such cases enforceable. In the case of other employees, however, this standard will render cost-splitting provisions unenforceable in many, if not most, cases.

* * *

* * * Circuit City argues that Morrison could have avoided having to pay half of the cost of the arbitration * * * if she could have arranged to pay the greater of $500 or three percent of her annual salary (in this case, three percent of $54,060, or $1,622) within ninety days of the arbitrator's award. * * *

In the abstract, this sum may not appear prohibitive, but it must be considered from the vantage point of the potential litigant in a case such as this.

b. Employment discrimination is discussed in detail in Chapter 15.

Recently terminated, the potential litigant must continue to pay for housing, utilities, transportation, food, and the other necessities of life in contemporary society despite losing her primary, and most likely only, source of income. Unless she is exceedingly fortunate, the potential litigant will experience at least a brief period of unemployment. Turning to the arbitration agreement with her employer, the potential litigant finds that * * * she will be obligated to pay half the costs of any arbitration which she initiates.

Minimal research will reveal that the potential costs of arbitrating the dispute easily reach thousands, if not tens of thousands, of dollars, far exceeding the costs that a plaintiff would incur in court. Courts charge plaintiffs initial filing fees, but they do not charge extra for in-person hearings, discovery requests, routine motions, or written decisions, costs that are all common in the world of private arbitrators. * * * Based on these considerations, along with the evidence that Morrison presented regarding her previous salary, we conclude that the default cost-splitting rule in the Circuit City arbitration agreement would deter a substantial percentage of potential litigants from bringing their claims in the arbitral forum.

The provision reducing the (former) employee's exposure to the greater of $500 or three percent of her annual compensation presents a closer issue. However, a potential litigant considering arbitration would still have to arrange to pay three percent of her most recent salary, in this case, $1,622, within a three-month period, or risk incurring her full half of the costs * * *. Faced with this choice—which really boils down to risking one's scarce resources in the hopes of an uncertain benefit—it appears to us that a substantial number of similarly situated persons would be deterred from seeking to vindicate their statutory rights under these circumstances.

Based on this reasoning, we hold that Morrison has satisfied her burden in the present case in demonstrating that * * * the cost-splitting provision in the agreement was unenforceable with respect to her claims.

The U.S. Court of Appeals for the Sixth Circuit held that the cost-splitting provision in Circuit City's mandatory arbitration agreement was unenforceable because, regardless of an individual employee's ability to pay those costs, the provision would deter "similarly situated individuals" from exercising their rights.[c]

QUESTIONS

1. On what argument did Morrison base her appeal of the court's order to arbitrate her employment discrimination claims?
2. Why did the U.S. Court of Appeals for the Sixth Circuit hold in Morrison's case that the arbitration agreement's cost-splitting provision was unenforceable?
3. Does the court's ruling in this case mean that cost-splitting provisions in compulsory arbitration agreements are always unenforceable?

---

c. The court also concluded that the provision could be severed from the agreement, which meant that the rest of the agreement could be enforced. Because the arbitration in this case had already occurred, and Morrison had not been required to pay any part of the costs, the court affirmed the lower court's order compelling arbitration, "on these different grounds."

EMERGING TRENDS

Mandatory Arbitration in the Employment Context

Arbitration is normally simpler, speedier, and less costly than litigation. For that reason, arbitration clauses are increasingly being included not only in commercial contracts but also in employment contracts. Over the past fifteen years, however, a number of employees and groups concerned with employees' rights have voiced objections to the enforcement of arbitration clauses in employment contracts.

These groups (and some courts) have concluded that forcing employees to agree to arbitration clauses as a condition of their employment is unfair and one sided. After all, the employees typically have little or no say in determining the specifics of the arbitration procedures that must be followed if a dispute arises. Rather, the arbitration clauses are drafted by the employers and presented to job candidates on a "take-it-or-leave-it" basis.

THE SUPREME COURT'S POSITION

The United States Supreme Court has consistently taken the position that because the Federal Arbitration Act favors the arbitration of disputes, arbitration clauses should generally be enforced. In a precedent-setting 1991 decision, the United States Supreme Court held that a claim brought under the Age Discrimination in Employment Act (ADEA) of 1967[a] could be subject to compulsory arbitration.

The plaintiff in the case, Robert Gilmer, had been discharged from his employment at the age of sixty-two. Gilmer sued his employer, claiming that he was a victim of age discrimination. The employer argued that Gilmer had to submit the dispute to arbitration because he had agreed, as part of a required registration application to be a securities representative with the New York Stock Exchange, to arbitrate "any dispute, claim, or controversy" relating to his employment. The Supreme Court held that Gilmer, by agreeing to arbitrate any dispute, had waived his right to sue.[b]

The *Gilmer* decision was controversial and generated much discussion during the 1990s. By the early 2000s, at issue was whether the Federal Arbitration Act (FAA) even applied to employment contracts. Some lower courts claimed that Congress, when passing the FAA, intended to exempt such contracts from coverage. The United States Supreme Court addressed this issue in *Circuit City Stores, Inc. v. Adams.*[c]

As noted elsewhere in this chapter, the Court held that the act applied to employment contracts generally and remanded the case to the U.S. Court of Appeals for the Ninth Circuit for further action consistent with that ruling.

UNFAIR OR ONE-SIDED ARBITRATION CLAUSES MAY NOT BE ENFORCED, HOWEVER

Although the Supreme Court has made it clear that employers may legally require employees to arbitrate employment disputes, courts are finding reasons not to enforce arbitration clauses in employment contracts in some situations. For example, when the Court of Appeals for the Ninth Circuit reviewed the *Circuit City* case on remand, that court refused to enforce the clause at issue on the ground that the agreement was unconscionable. (An unconscionable contract or clause is one that is so one sided and unfair that a court will refuse to enforce it—see Chapter 10.) According to the court, the agreement was so one sided and unfair as to be unenforceable under "ordinary principles of state contract law."

The court pointed out that the agreement was a standard form contract drafted by Circuit City (the party with superior bargaining power) and that the plaintiff had to sign it without any modification as a prerequisite to employment. Moreover, only the employees were required to arbitrate their disputes, while Circuit City remained free to litigate in court any claims it had against its employees. Also important was the fact that Circuit City's contract severely limited the relief that was available to employees, required employees to split the arbitrator's fee, and imposed a strict one-year statute

a. For a fuller discussion of the ADEA, see Chapter 15.

b. *Gilmer v. Interstate/Johnson Lane Corp.*, 500 U.S. 20, 111 S.Ct. 1647, 114 L.Ed.2d 26 (1991).

c. 532 U.S. 105, 121 S.Ct. 1302, 149 L.Ed.2d 234 (2001). This case was presented as a *Featured Case*—see Case 3.1.

Continued on next page

EMERGING TRENDS

Mandatory Arbitration in the Employment Context—Continued

of limitations on claims. For all of these reasons, the court held the entire arbitration agreement unenforceable. The court justified its decision by pointing out that Section 2 of the FAA provides that arbitration agreements should be considered valid, unless other grounds exist at law or in equity to revoke the contract.[d]

IMPLICATIONS FOR THE BUSINESSPERSON

1. The Supreme Court decisions discussed above mean that employers may generally take advantage of the benefits of arbitrating employment disputes rather than having to engage in costly litigation when disputes with employees arise.
2. Note, though, that employers should exercise caution when drafting arbitration clauses. It is especially important to make sure that the terms of the agreement are not so one sided that a court could declare the entire agreement unconscionable.

FOR CRITICAL ANALYSIS

1. Why would employees and groups concerned with employees' rights object to the mandatory arbitration of employment disputes?
2. Federal laws protecting employees' rights—to be free from discrimination in the workplace, for example—allow employees to sue their employers when these rights are violated.[e] In your opinion, has the Supreme Court given sufficient weight to these laws in its decisions regarding the enforceability of arbitration clauses in employment contracts?

RELEVANT WEB SITES

To locate information on the Web concerning the issues discussed in this feature, go to this text's Web site at **http://ele.westbuslaw.com** and click on "Interactive Study Center."

d. *Circuit City Stores, Inc. v. Adams*, 279 F.3d 889 (2002).

e. As you will read in Chapter 15, under these laws an employee who claims that he or she has suffered from discriminatory treatment normally must first file a claim with the Equal Employment Opportunity Commission (EEOC). This agency administers federal laws prohibiting discrimination in employment. If the EEOC decides not to take action against the employer, the employee is permitted to sue the employer directly.

Setting Aside an Arbitration Award

After the arbitration has been concluded, the losing party may appeal the arbitrator's award to a court, or the winning party may seek a court order compelling the other party to comply with the award. The scope of review in either situation is much more restricted than in an appellate court's review of a trial court's decision. The court does not look at the merits of the underlying dispute, and the court will not add to or subtract from the remedies provided by the award. The court's role is limited to determining whether there exists a valid reason to set aside the award. If not, the court will order the parties to comply with the terms. The general view is that because the parties were free to frame the issues and set the powers of the arbitrator at the outset, they cannot complain about the result.

Fact Findings and Legal Conclusions. The arbitrator's fact findings and legal conclusions are normally final. That the arbitrator may have erred in a ruling during the hearing or made an erroneous fact finding is normally no basis for setting aside an award: the parties agreed that the arbitrator would be the judge of the facts. Similarly, no matter how obviously the arbitrator was mistaken in a conclusion of law, the award is normally nonetheless binding: the parties agreed to accept the arbitrator's interpretation of the law. A court will not look at the merits of the dispute, the sufficiency of the evidence presented, or the arbitrator's reasoning in reaching a particular decision.

This approach is consistent with the underlying view of all voluntary arbitration—that its basis is really contract law. If the parties freely contract with one another, courts will not interfere simply because one side feels that it received a bad bargain. Any party challenging an award must face the presumption that a final award is valid. But is an award final or binding if the parties did not agree that it would be? That was the issue in the following case.

CASE 3.3

United States Court of Appeals, Third Circuit, 1996.
100 F.3d 296.

ORLANDO v. INTERSTATE CONTAINER CORP.

Joseph Orlando, an employee of Interstate Container Corporation, underwent heart bypass surgery. For several months, he did not work but collected disability benefits, in part as provided by a collective bargaining agreement.[a] *When his condition improved, he asked to return to work, but Interstate denied his request. He filed a complaint with the company, which, under the collective bargaining agreement, went to arbitration, culminating in an arbitrator's decision in Interstate's favor. The agreement did not state that the arbitrator's decision would be "final" or "binding," however. In Orlando's subsequent suit against Interstate, a federal district court ruled that the decision was not binding. Interstate appealed.*

WEIS, J.

[Interstate] argues that because the contract makes arbitration mandatory, it must necessarily be final as well. That argument finds support in the policy favoring arbitration as a means of resolving disputes, but fails to meet the requirement of authorization by agreement of the parties. * * *

* * * *

* * * *[W]e must give full credit to the language the parties have chosen to include—or not include—in their agreement.* [Emphasis added.]

Collective bargaining agreements almost invariably explain that arbitration proceedings will be "final," "binding," or "exclusive," or use other words to that effect. This agreement was drafted by parties well versed in labor matters and cognizant [aware] of that convention. The omission of any indication that arbitration proceedings should be final and binding leads us to conclude that, if we nevertheless declared them to be so, we would not be enforcing the will of the parties, as expressed in their agreement.

The U.S. Court of Appeals for the Third Circuit affirmed the lower court's decision. The award was not final or binding because the parties did not agree that it would be.

QUESTIONS

1. On Interstate's appeal of the district court's ruling that the arbitrator's decision was not binding, what was the reasoning underlying Interstate's argument?

---

a. A collective bargaining agreement is a contract negotiated by employees and their employer concerning the terms and conditions of employment.

2. Why did the U.S. Court of Appeals for the Third Circuit affirm the lower court's ruling that the arbitrator's award was not binding?
3. Would the court's decision have been different if the arbitration agreement had been drafted by parties who were *not* "well versed in labor matters"? Why or why not?

Public Policy and Illegality. In keeping with contract law principles, no award will be enforced if compliance with the award would result in the commission of a crime or would conflict with some greater social policy mandated by statute. A court will not overturn an award, however, simply because the arbitrator was called on to resolve a dispute involving a matter of significant public concern. For an award to be set aside, it must call for some action on the part of the parties that would conflict with or in some way undermine public policy.[4]

Defects in the Arbitration Process. There are some bases for setting aside an award when there is a defect in the arbitration process. These bases are typified by those set forth in the Federal Arbitration Act. Section 10 of the act provides four grounds on which an arbitration award may be set aside:

1. The award was the result of corruption, fraud, or other "undue means."
2. The arbitrator exhibited bias or corruption.
3. The arbitrator refused to postpone the hearing despite sufficient cause, refused to hear evidence pertinent and material to the dispute, or otherwise acted to substantially prejudice the rights of one of the parties.
4. The arbitrator exceeded his or her powers or failed to use them to make a mutual, final, and definite award.

The first three bases for setting aside the award include actions or decisions that are more than simply mistakes in judgment. Each requires some "bad faith" on the part of the arbitrator. Bad faith actions or decisions are ones that affect the integrity of the arbitration process. The honesty and impartiality, rather than the judgment, of the arbitrator are called into question.

Sometimes it is difficult to make the distinction between honest mistakes in judgment and actions or decisions made in bad faith. A bribe is clearly the kind of "undue means" included in the first basis for setting aside an award. Letting only one side argue its case is likewise a clear violation of the second basis.

Meetings between the arbitrator and one party outside the presence of the other party also taint the arbitration process. Although meetings might not involve the kind of corruption that results from taking a bribe, they do affect the integrity of the process; the third basis for setting aside an award is meant to protect against this.

Not every refusal by an arbitrator to admit certain evidence is grounds for setting aside an award under the third basis. As noted, to provide a basis for overturning an award, the arbitrator's decision must be more than an error in judgment, no matter how obviously incorrect that judgment might appear to another observer. The decision must be so obviously wrong or unfair as to imply bias or corruption. Otherwise, the decision normally cannot be a basis for setting aside an award.

---

4. See, for example, *Meehan v. Nassau Community College,* 647 N.Y.S.2d 865 (App.Div. 2 Dept. 1996).

The fourth basis for setting aside an award is that the arbitrator exceeded his or her powers in arbitrating the dispute. This issue involves the question of arbitrability. An arbitrator exceeds his or her powers and authority by attempting to resolve an issue that is not covered by the agreement to submit to arbitration.

In the following case, a party to an arbitration proceeding asked a court to set aside the award.

CASE 3.4

Supreme Court of the United States, 2001.
532 U.S. 1015,
121 S.Ct. 1724,
149 L.Ed.2d 740.
http://supct.law.cornell.edu/supct/cases/name.htm[a]

MAJOR LEAGUE BASEBALL PLAYERS ASSOCIATION v. GARVEY

In 1986, 1987, and 1988, the Major League Baseball Players Association complained that the Major League Baseball Clubs had engaged in collusion to underpay some of the players. The grievance was submitted to arbitration before a panel chaired by Thomas Roberts. During a hearing in 1986, Ballard Smith, the president of the San Diego Padres, testified that there had been no collusion. Roberts's panel rejected this testimony as false. The Association and the Clubs entered into a settlement agreement under which the Clubs set up a fund of $280 million to be distributed to players who suffered losses due to the collusion, and the Association established a framework for evaluating each player's claim. A player could challenge the Association's recommendation in binding arbitration. Steve Garvey, who had played for the Padres between 1983 and 1987 under a contract, filed a claim for damages, alleging that the Padres would have extended his contract for the 1988 and 1989 seasons but for the collusion. Roberts, the arbitrator in Garvey's case, denied the claim. Roberts cited Smith's testimony in the 1986 hearing that the Padres were not interested in extending Garvey's contract. Roberts refused to consider Smith's admission, in a 1996 letter, that he had not told the truth during those hearings and that he had made Garvey an offer that was withdrawn due to the collusion. Garvey filed a suit in a federal district court against Roberts and the Association (the defendants) to have the arbitrator's award set aside. The court ruled in the defendants' favor. Garvey appealed to the U.S. Court of Appeals for the Ninth Circuit, which reversed the ruling of the lower court and remanded the case with directions to set aside the arbitrator's award. The defendants appealed to the United States Supreme Court.

PER CURIAM [by the whole court].

Courts are not authorized to review the arbitrator's decision on the merits despite allegations that the decision rests on factual errors or misinterprets the parties' agreement. * * * [I]f an arbitrator is even arguably construing or applying the contract and acting within the scope of his authority, the fact that a court is convinced he committed serious error does not suffice to overturn his decision. It is only when the arbitrator strays from interpretation and application of the agreement and effectively dispenses his own brand of * * * justice that his decision may be unenforceable. * * *

* * * Even in the very rare instances when an arbitrator's procedural aberrations rise to the level of affirmative misconduct, as a rule the court must

a. In the "Search" box, type "Garvey." In the pull-down menu, select "all current and historic decisions," and click on "submit." In the result, click on the first item that includes the name of the case to access the opinion. The Legal Information Institute of Cornell Law School in Ithaca, New York, maintains this Web site.

not foreclose further proceedings by settling the merits according to its own judgment of the appropriate result. That step * * * would improperly substitute a judicial determination for the arbitrator's decision that the parties bargained for in their agreement. Instead, the court should simply vacate the award, thus leaving open the possibility of further proceedings if they are permitted under the terms of the agreement.

To be sure, the Court of Appeals here recited these principles, but its application of them is nothing short of baffling. The substance of the Court's discussion reveals that it overturned the arbitrator's decision because it disagreed with the arbitrator's factual findings, particularly those with respect to credibility. The Court of Appeals, it appears, would have credited Smith's 1996 letter, and found the arbitrator's refusal to do so at worst irrational and at best bizarre. But *even serious error on the arbitrator's part does not justify overturning his decision, where, as here, he is construing a contract and acting within the scope of his authority.* [Emphasis added.]

* * * [The court] both rejected the arbitrator's findings and went further, resolving the merits of the parties' dispute based on the court's assessment of the record before the arbitrator. For that reason, the court found further arbitration proceedings inappropriate. But again, established law ordinarily precludes a court from resolving the merits of the parties' dispute on the basis of its own factual determinations, no matter how erroneous the arbitrator's decision. Even when the arbitrator's award may properly be vacated, the appropriate remedy is to remand the case for further arbitration proceedings. * * * The Court of Appeals usurped the arbitrator's role by resolving the dispute and barring further proceedings.

The United States Supreme Court reversed the judgment of the lower court and remanded the case for further proceedings. The Court held that the appellate court "usurped the arbitrator's role" when the court rejected the arbitrator's findings and resolved the dispute on the basis of its own assessment of the record.

QUESTIONS

1. What was the likely basis for the defendants' position on appeal that the lower court's decision should be reversed?
2. On what ground did the United States Supreme Court reverse the judgment of the U.S. Court of Appeals for the Ninth Circuit in this case?
3. Should courts defer to arbitrators' findings of facts even if those findings are clearly mistaken?

Waiver. Although a defect in the arbitration process is sufficient grounds for setting aside an award, a party sometimes forfeits the right to challenge an award by failing to object to the defect in a timely manner. The party must object when he or she learns of the problem. After making the objection, the party can still proceed with the arbitration process and still challenge the award in court after the arbitration proceedings have concluded. If, however, a party makes no objection and proceeds with the arbitration process, then a later court challenge to the award may be denied on the ground that the party *waived* the right to challenge the award on the basis of the defect.

Frequently, this occurs when a party fails to object that an arbitrator is exceeding his or her powers in resolving a dispute because the subject matter is not arbitrable or because the party did not agree to arbitrate the dispute. The question of arbitrability is one for the courts to decide. If a party does not object on this issue at the first demand for arbitration, however, a court may consider the objection waived.

Conflicts of Law. Parties are afforded wide latitude in establishing the manner in which their disputes will be resolved. Nevertheless, an agreement to arbitrate may be governed by the Federal Arbitration Act (FAA) or one of the many state arbitration acts, even though the parties do not refer to a statute in their agreement. Recall that the FAA covers any arbitration clause in a contract that involves interstate commerce. Frequently, however, transactions involving interstate commerce also have substantial connections to particular states, which may in turn have their own arbitration acts. In such situations, unless the FAA and state arbitration law are nearly identical, the acts may conflict. How are these conflicts to be resolved?

As a general principle, the supremacy clause and the commerce clause of the U.S. Constitution are the bases for giving federal law preeminence; when there is a conflict, state law is preempted by federal law. Thus, in cases of arbitration, the strong federal policy favoring arbitration can override a state's laws that might be more favorable to litigation.

Choice of Law. Notwithstanding federal preemption of conflicting state laws, the Federal Arbitration Act has been interpreted as allowing the parties to choose a particular state law to govern their arbitration agreement. The parties may choose to have the laws of a specific state govern their agreement by including in the agreement a *choice-of-law clause.* The FAA does not mandate any particular set of rules that parties must follow in arbitration; the parties are free to agree on the manner best suited to their needs. Consistent with this view that arbitration is at heart a contractual matter between private parties, the United States Supreme Court has upheld arbitration agreements containing choice-of-law provisions.

Disadvantages of Arbitration

Arbitration has some disadvantages. The result in any particular dispute can be unpredictable, in part because arbitrators do not need to follow any previous cases in rendering their decisions. Unlike judges, arbitrators do not have to issue written opinions that facilitate a participant's appeal to a court. Arbitrators must decide disputes according to whatever rules have been provided by the parties, regardless of how unfair those rules may be. In some cases, arbitration can be nearly as expensive as litigation. In part, this is because both sides must prepare their cases for presentation before a third party decision maker, just as they would have to do to appear in court. Discovery is usually not available in arbitration, however, which means that during the hearing the parties must take the time to question witnesses whom, in a lawsuit, they would not need to call.

Concept Summary 3.1
Alternative Dispute Resolution (ADR)

Type of ADR	Description
Negotiation	The parties come together, with or without attorneys to represent them, and try to reach a settlement. Traditionally, no third party was involved in the process. Today, several forms of "assisted negotiation"—negotiation involving a neutral (unbiased) third party—are used, including mini-trials, early neutral case evaluation, and conciliation.
Mediation	The parties themselves reach an agreement with the help of a third party, called a mediator, who plays an active role in the dispute settlement. The mediator tries to discover and assess the real causes of the dispute (through discussions with the parties individually and jointly), assists the parties in evaluating their positions, and proposes possible solutions. Mediation is usually the preferred method of ADR in cases involving ongoing or long-term relationships.
Arbitration	In this more formal method of ADR, the parties submit their dispute to a neutral third party, the arbitrator, who renders a decision. The decision is normally binding unless the parties (or a court, in court-related arbitration) specify otherwise. Arbitration awards may be appealed to a court, but only in special circumstances (such as if the award is contrary to public policy) will a court set aside an arbitrator's award. If there is a question concerning the arbitrability of a certain type of claim, a court must decide the issue.

The Integration of ADR and Formal Court Procedures

Increasingly, courts are requiring that parties attempt to settle their differences through some form of ADR before proceeding to trial. For example, several federal district courts encourage nonbinding arbitration for cases involving amounts less than $100,000. Less than 10 percent of the cases referred for arbitration ever go to trial. Today, about half of all federal courts have adopted formal rules regarding the use of ADR, and many other courts without such rules use ADR procedures.

Most states have adopted programs that allow them to refer certain types of cases for negotiation, mediation, or arbitration. Typically—as in California and Hawaii—court systems have adopted mandatory mediation or nonbinding arbitration programs for certain types of disputes, usually involving less than a specified dollar amount. Only if the parties fail to reach an agreement, or if one of the parties disagrees with the decision of a third party mediating or arbitrating the dispute, will the case be heard by a court. South Carolina was the first state to institute a voluntary arbitration program at the appellate court level. In the South Carolina system, litigants must waive a court hearing when requesting arbitration. All decisions by the arbitrators are final and binding.

Court-Annexed Arbitration

Court-annexed arbitration, which is arbitration that is mandated by a court, differs significantly from the voluntary arbitration process discussed above. There are some disputes that courts will not allow to go to arbitration. Most states, for example, do not allow court-annexed arbitration in disputes involving title to real estate or in cases in which a court's equity powers are involved.

A Fundamental Difference. The fundamental difference between voluntary arbitration and court-annexed arbitration is the finality and reviewability of the award. With respect to court-annexed arbitration, either party may reject the award for any reason. In the event that one of the parties does reject the award, the case will proceed to trial, and the court will hear the case *de novo*—that is, the court will reconsider all the evidence and legal questions as though no arbitration had occurred.

Everyone who has a recognizable cause of action or against whom such an action is brought is entitled to have the issue decided in a court of law. Because court-annexed arbitration is not voluntary, there must be some safeguard against using it in a way that denies an individual his or her day in court. This safeguard is provided by permitting either side to reject the award regardless of the reason.

The party rejecting the award may be penalized, however. Many statutes providing for court-annexed arbitration impose court costs and fees on a party who rejects an arbitration award but does not improve his or her position by going to trial. Thus, for example, if a party rejects an arbitration award, and the award turns out to be more favorable to that party than the subsequent jury verdict, the party may be compelled to pay the costs of the arbitration or some fee for the costs of the trial.

In court-annexed arbitration, discovery of evidence occurs before the hearing. After the hearing has commenced, a party seeking to discover new evidence must usually secure approval from the court that mandated the arbitration. This is intended to prevent the parties from using arbitration as a means of previewing each other's cases and then rejecting the arbitrator's award.

The Role of the Arbitrator. Notwithstanding the differences between voluntary and court-annexed arbitration, the role of the arbitrator is essentially the same in both types of proceedings. The arbitrator determines issues of both fact and law. The arbitrator also makes all decisions concerning applications of the rules of procedure and evidence during the hearing.

Applicable Rules. Regarding the rules of evidence, there are differences among the states. Most states impose the same rules of evidence on an arbitration hearing as on a trial. Other states, such as New Jersey, allow all evidence relevant to the dispute regardless of whether the evidence would be admissible at trial. Still other jurisdictions, such as Washington, leave it to the arbitrator to decide what evidence is admissible.

Waiver. Once a court directs that a dispute is to be submitted to court-annexed arbitration, the parties must proceed to arbitration. As noted above, either side may reject the award that results from the arbitration for any reason. If a party fails to appear at or participate in the arbitration proceeding as directed by the court, however, that failure constitutes a waiver of the right to reject the award.

Court-Related Mediation

Mediation is proving to be more popular than arbitration as a court-related method of ADR, and mediation programs continue to increase in number in both federal and state courts. Today, more court systems offer or require mediation, rather than arbitration, as an alternative to litigation.

Mediation is often used in disputes relating to employment law, environmental law, product liability, and franchises. One of the most important business advantages of mediation is its lower cost, which can be 25 percent (or less) of the expense of litigation. Another advantage is the speed with which a dispute can go through mediation (possibly one or two days) compared with arbitration (possibly months) or litigation (possibly years).

Part of the popularity of mediation is that its goal, unlike that of litigation and some other forms of ADR, is for opponents to work out a resolution that benefits both sides. Generally, the rate of participants' satisfaction with the outcomes in mediated disputes is high.

At issue in the following case was whether a court has the authority to compel an unwilling party to participate in, and share the costs of, mediation.

CASE 3.5

United States Court of Appeals, First Circuit, 2002. 304 F.3d 135. **http://www.ca1.uscourts.gov/opinions/main.php**[b]

In re ATLANTIC PIPE CORP.[a]

In 1996, Thames-Dick Superaqueduct Partners entered into an agreement with the Puerto Rico Aqueduct and Sewer Authority (PRASA) to construct, operate, and maintain the North Coast Superaqueduct Project in Puerto Rico. Thames-Dick subcontracted much of the work to other companies, including Atlantic Pipe Corporation (APC), which agreed to fabricate the pipe. After the project was completed, a segment of pipe burst. Thames-Dick repaired the damage and sought to recover the cost from its subcontractors. As part of the ensuing litigation, investors in the agreement between Thames-Dick and PRASA filed a suit in a federal district court against Thames-Dick and others, which filed complaints against still others, including APC. Thames-Dick filed a motion to refer the case to mediation. The court ordered nonbinding mediation to proceed, with the parties to share the expense. APC appealed this order to the U.S. Court of Appeals for the First Circuit.

SELYA, J.

[Federal] district courts have substantial inherent power to manage and control their calendars. * * *

---

a. *In re* means "in the matter of" or "concerning." This is the usual method of entitling a case in which there are no adversaries but only a matter, such as bankruptcy, to be resolved through judicial proceedings.

b. This is a page within the Web site of the U.S. Court of Appeals for the First Circuit. In the left-hand column, click on "Search." On that page, in the "Opinion Number begins with" box, type "02-1339.01A" and click on "Submit Query." In the result, click on the number of the case to access the opinion.

* * * *

In some cases, a court may be warranted in believing that compulsory mediation could yield significant benefits even if one or more parties object. * * *

This is particularly true in complex cases involving multiple claims and parties. The fair and expeditious resolution of such cases often is helped along by creative solutions—solutions that simply are not available in the binary framework of traditional adversarial litigation. Mediation with the assistance of a skilled facilitator gives parties an opportunity to explore a much wider range of options * * * . Mindful of these potential advantages, we hold that *it is within a district court's inherent power to order non-consensual mediation in those cases in which that step seems reasonably likely to serve the interests of justice.* [Emphasis added.]

* * * *

[However,] any such order must be crafted in a manner that preserves procedural fairness and shields objecting parties from undue burdens. * * *

* * * [T]he complexity of this case militates in favor of ordering mediation. At last count, the suit involves twelve parties, asserting a welter of claims * * * predicated on a wide variety of theories. * * * Untangling the intricate web of relationships among the parties, along with the difficult and fact-intensive arguments made by each, will be time-consuming and will impose significant costs on the parties and the court. Against this backdrop, mediation holds out the dual prospect of advantaging the litigants and conserving scarce judicial resources.

* * * *

* * * [W]ithout default cost-sharing rules, the use of valuable ADR techniques (like mediation) becomes hostage to the parties' ability to agree on the concomitant [accompanying] financial arrangements. This means that the district court's inherent power to order private mediation in appropriate cases would be rendered nugatory [invalid] absent the corollary power to order the sharing of reasonable mediation costs. To avoid this pitfall, we hold that the district court, in an appropriate case, is empowered to order the sharing of reasonable costs and expenses associated with mandatory nonbinding mediation.

The U.S. Court of Appeals for the First Circuit ruled that the lower court's mediation order was valid, reasoning that it was justified by the goals of promoting flexibility and creative problem solving in the handling of litigation. The appellate court also held, however, that the lower court's failure to set reasonable limits on the duration of the mediation and on the mediator's fees "dooms the decree," and vacated and remanded the case for further proceedings (which could include mediation if limits were set).

QUESTIONS

1. What is a likely reason for APC's appeal of the lower court's order to proceed with nonbinding arbitration?
2. Why did the U.S. Court of Appeals for the First Circuit state that the lower court's order was "valid" but "doom[ed]"?
3. If all of the parties to this case had objected to participating in mediation, could the court still have ordered the parties to proceed to nonbinding mediation?

Summary Jury Trials

Summary jury trial • A method of settling disputes in which a trial is held, but the jury's verdict is not binding. The verdict acts only as a guide to both sides in reaching an agreement during negotiations following the trial.

Another means by which the courts have integrated alternative dispute resolution methods into the traditional court process is through the use of summary jury trials. A **summary jury trial** is a mock trial that occurs in a courtroom before a judge and jury. Evidence is presented in an abbreviated form, along with each side's major contentions. The jury then presents a verdict.

The fundamental difference between a traditional trial and a summary jury trial is that in the latter, the jury's verdict is only advisory. The goal of a summary jury trial is to give each side an idea of how it would fare in a full-blown jury trial with a more elaborate and detailed presentation of evidence and arguments. At the end of the summary jury trial, the presiding judge meets with the parties and may encourage them to settle their dispute without going through a standard jury trial.

ADR Forums and Services

Services facilitating dispute resolution outside the courtroom are provided by both government agencies and private organizations.

Nonprofit Organizations

The major source of private nonprofit arbitration services is the American Arbitration Association (AAA). Most of the largest law firms in the nation are members of this association. Founded in 1926, the AAA now settles more than 200,000 disputes a year and has offices in every state. Cases brought before the AAA are heard by an expert or a panel of experts—of whom usually about half are lawyers—in the area relating to the dispute. To cover its costs, this nonprofit organization charges a fee, paid by the party filing the claim. In addition, each party to the dispute pays a price for each hearing day, as well as a special additional fee in cases involving personal injuries or property loss.

In addition to the AAA, hundreds of other state and local nonprofit organizations provide arbitration services. For example, the Arbitration Association of Florida provides ADR services in that state. The Better Business Bureau offers ADR programs to aid in the resolution of certain types of disagreements. Many industries—including the insurance, automobile, and securities industries—also now have mediation or arbitration programs to facilitate timely and inexpensive settlement of claims.

For-Profit Organizations

Those who seek to settle their disputes quickly can turn to private, for-profit organizations to act as mediators or arbitrators. The leading firm in this private system of justice is JAMS/Endispute, which is based in Santa Ana, California. Hundreds of other private firms around the country offer for-profit dispute-resolution services.

Procedures in these private courts are fashioned to meet the desires of the clients seeking their services. For example, the parties might decide on the date of the hearing, the presiding judge, whether the judge's decision will be legally binding, and the site of the hearing—which could be a conference room, a law school office, or a leased courtroom complete with flag and Bible. The judges may follow procedures similar to those of the federal courts and use similar rules. Each party to the dispute may pay a filing fee and a designated fee for a half-day hearing session or a special, one-hour settlement conference.

Online Dispute Resolution

An increasing number of companies and organizations are offering dispute-resolution services using the Internet. The settlement of disputes in these online forums is known as **online dispute resolution (ODR).** To date, the disputes resolved in these forums have most commonly involved disagreements over the rights to domain names (Web site addresses—see Chapter 13) and disagreements over the quality of goods sold via the Internet, including goods sold through Internet auction sites.

Online dispute resolution (ODR) • The resolution of disputes with the assistance of organizations that offer dispute-resolution services via the Internet.

Currently, ODR may be best for resolving small- to medium-sized business liability claims, which may not be worth the expense of litigation or traditional methods of alternative dispute resolution. Rules being developed in online forums, however, may ultimately become a code of conduct for everyone who does business in cyberspace. Most online forums do not automatically apply the law of any specific jurisdiction. Instead, results are often based on general, more universal legal principles. As with offline methods of dispute resolution, any party may appeal to a court at any time.

Negotiation and Mediation Services

The online negotiation of a dispute is generally simpler and more practical than litigation. Typically, one party files a complaint, and the other party is notified by e-mail. Password-protected access is possible twenty-four hours a day, seven days a week. Fees are sometimes nominal and otherwise low (often 2 to 4 percent, or less, of the disputed amount).

CyberSettle.com, Inc., clickNsettle.com, U.S. Settlement Corporation (ussettle.com), and other Web-based firms offer online forums for negotiating monetary settlements. The parties to a dispute may agree to submit offers; if the offers fall within a previously agreed-on range, they will end the dispute, and the parties will split the difference. Special software keeps secret any offers that are not within the range. If there is no agreed-on range, typically an offer includes a deadline by which the other party must respond before the offer expires. The parties can drop the negotiations at any time.

Mediation providers are also resolving disputes online. SquareTrade, one of the mediation providers that has been used by eBay, the online auction site, mediates disputes involving $100 or more between eBay customers, currently for no charge. SquareTrade, which also resolves disputes among other parties, uses Web-based software that walks participants through a five-step resolution process. Negotiation between the parties occurs on a secure page within SquareTrade's Web site. If the parties prefer, they may consult a mediator. The entire process takes as little as ten to fourteen days, and there is no fee unless the parties use a mediator.

Arbitration Programs

A number of organizations and companies offer online arbitration programs. The Internet Corporation for Assigned Names and Numbers (ICANN), a nonprofit corporation that the federal government set up to oversee the distribution of domain names, has issued special rules for the resolution of domain name disputes.[5] ICANN has also authorized several organizations to arbitrate domain name disputes in accordance with its rules. Additionally, the American Arbitration Association now offers technology-based arbitration services as well.

Resolution Forum, Inc. (RFI), a nonprofit organization associated with the Center for Legal Responsibility at South Texas College of Law, offers arbitration services through its CAN-WIN conferencing system. Using standard browser software and an RFI password, the parties to a dispute access an online conference room. When multiple parties are involved, private communications and breakout sessions are possible via private messaging facilities. RFI also offers mediation services.

The Virtual Magistrate Project (VMAG) is affiliated with the American Arbitration Association, Chicago-Kent College of Law, Cyberspace Law Institute, National Center for Automated Information Research, and other organizations. VMAG offers arbitration for disputes involving users of online systems; victims of wrongful messages, postings, and filings; and system operators who are subject to complaints or similar demands. VMAG also arbitrates intellectual property, personal property, real property, and tort disputes related to online contracts. VMAG attempts to resolve a dispute within seventy-two hours. The proceedings occur in a password-protected online news group setting, and private e-mail among the participants is possible. A VMAG arbitrator's decision is issued in a written opinion. A party may appeal the outcome to a court.

INTERNATIONAL DISPUTE RESOLUTION

Businesspersons who engage in international business transactions normally take special precautions to protect themselves in the event that a party with whom they are dealing in another country breaches an agreement. Often, parties to international contracts include special clauses in their contracts providing for how any disputes arising under the contracts will be resolved.

Forum-Selection and Choice-of-Law Clauses

Parties to international contracts often include *forum-selection clauses*. These clauses designate the jurisdiction (court or country) in which any dispute arising under the contract will be litigated. Choice-of-law clauses, which were discussed earlier in this chapter, specify what nation's law will be applied and are also frequently included in international contracts. If no forum and choice-of-law clauses have been included in an international contract, however, legal proceedings will be more complex and attended by much more uncertainty. For example, litigation may take place in two or more countries, with each country applying its own national law to the particular transactions.

Furthermore, even if a plaintiff wins a favorable judgment in a lawsuit litigated in the plaintiff's country, there is no guarantee that the court's judgment will be enforced by judicial bodies in the defendant's country. As will be discussed in Chapter 8, for reasons of courtesy, the judgment may be enforced

5. ICANN's Rules for Uniform Domain Name Dispute Resolution Policy are online at **http://www.icann.org/udrp/udrp-rules-24oct99.htm**. Domain names will be discussed in more detail in Chapter 13, in the context of trademark law.

in the defendant's country, particularly if the defendant's country is the United States and the foreign court's decision is consistent with U.S. national law and policy. Other nations, however, may not be as accommodating as the United States, and the plaintiff may be left empty handed.

Arbitration Clauses

In an attempt to prevent such problems, parties to international contracts often include arbitration clauses in their contracts, requiring that any contract disputes be decided by a neutral third party. In international arbitration proceedings, the third party may be a neutral entity (such as the International Chamber of Commerce), a panel of individuals representing both parties' interests, or some other group or organization. The United Nations Convention on the Recognition and Enforcement of Foreign Arbitral Awards[6]—which has been implemented in more than fifty countries, including the United States—assists in the enforcement of arbitration clauses, as do provisions in specific treaties among nations. The American Arbitration Association provides arbitration services for international as well as domestic disputes.

6. June 10, 1958, 21 U.S.T. 2517, T.I.A.S. No. 6997 (the "New York Convention").

KEY TERMS

alternative dispute resolution (ADR) 84
arbitration 86
award 93
conciliation 85
early neutral case evaluation 85
mediation 85
mini-trial 85
negotiation 84
online dispute resolution (ODR) 109
summary jury trial 108

FOR REVIEW

1. What is alternative dispute resolution?
2. How do the processes of negotiation and mediation differ?
3. What are the steps in the arbitration process?
4. What are the differences between court-annexed arbitration and voluntary arbitration?
5. How are online forums used to resolve disputes?

QUESTIONS AND CASE PROBLEMS

3–1. In an arbitration proceeding, the arbitrator need not be a judge or even a lawyer. How, then, can the arbitrator's decision have the force of law and be binding on the parties involved?

3–2. Two private U.S. corporations enter into a joint-venture agreement to conduct mining operations in the newly formed Middle Eastern nation of Euphratia. As part of the agreement, the companies include an arbitration clause and a choice-of-law provision. The first states that any controversy arising out of the performance of the agreement will be settled by arbitration. The second states that the agreement is to be governed by the laws of the location of the venture, Euphratia. A dispute arises, and the parties discontinue operations. One of the parties claims sole ownership to the Euphratian mines and orders the other party to remove its equipment from the mines. The other party disputes the claim of sole ownership and seeks an order from a U.S. federal court compelling the parties to submit to arbitration over the ownership issue and alleged breaches of the joint-venture agreement. How should the court rule if the laws of Euphratia state that, whereas arbitration agreements are to be enforced generally, matters of ownership of natural resources can only be resolved in a Euphratian court of law? Does it matter that two U.S. companies engaged in international commerce would be governed by the Federal Arbitration Act?

3–3. Two brothers, both of whom are certified public accountants (CPAs), form a professional association to provide tax-accounting services to the public. They also agree, in writing, that any disputes that arise between them over matters concerning the association will be submitted to an independent arbitrator, whom they designate to be their father, who is also a CPA. A dispute arises, and the matter is submitted to the father for arbitration. During the course of arbitration, which occurs over several weeks, the father asks the older brother, who is visiting one evening, to explain a certain entry in the brothers' association accounts. The younger brother learns of the discussion at the next meeting for arbitration; he says nothing about it, however. The arbitration is concluded in favor of the older brother, who seeks a court order compelling the younger brother to comply with the award. The younger brother seeks to set aside the award, claiming that the arbitration process was tainted by bias because "Dad always liked my older brother best." The younger brother also seeks to have the award set aside on the basis of improper conduct in that matters subject to arbitration were discussed between the father and older brother without the younger brother's being present. Should a court confirm the award or set it aside? Why?

3–4. After resolving their dispute, the two brothers encountered in Problem 3–3 above decide to resume their tax-accounting practice according to the terms of their original agreement. Again a dispute arises, and again it is decided by the father (now retired except for numerous occasions on which he acts as an arbitrator) in favor of the older brother. The older brother files a petition to enforce the award. The younger brother seeks to set aside the award and offers evidence that the father, as arbitrator, made a gross error in calculating the accounts that were material to the dispute being arbitrated. If the court is convinced that the father erred in the calculations, should the award be set aside? Why or why not?

CASE PROBLEM WITH SAMPLE ANSWER

3–5. Compelling Arbitration. In 1981, AT&T laid off seventy-nine workers in the Chicago area, purportedly because of a slowdown in economic activity. The Communications Workers of America, a union representing some AT&T workers, argued that there was no lack of work and objected to the layoffs as violations of the terms of a collective bargaining agreement between the union and AT&T. The agreement provided that "differences arising with respect to the interpretation of this contract or the performance of any obligation" under the agreement would be resolved through arbitration. The agreement reserved to AT&T the right to freely exercise managerial functions such as hiring and firing employees. Although the agreement conditioned such decision making on compliance with the terms of the contract, it expressly excluded disputes over those decisions from arbitration. AT&T relied on this exclusion to avoid the union's demand for arbitration over the layoffs. The union sought a court order to compel arbitration. The court held that the issue of whether the dispute over the layoffs was subject to arbitration should be decided by the arbitrator and ordered the parties to submit the question to the arbitrator. An appellate court affirmed the holding, and AT&T appealed to the United States Supreme Court. How should the Court rule? Discuss fully. [*AT&T Technologies v. Communications Workers of America,* 475 U.S. 643, 106 S.Ct. 1415, 89 L.Ed.2d 648 (1990)]

➧ *To view a sample answer for this case problem, go to this book's Web site at* **http://ele.westbuslaw.com** *and click on "Interactive Study Center."*

3–6. Arbitration. New York State revised its New Car Lemon Law to allow consumers who complained of purchasing a "lemon" to have their disputes arbitrated before a professional arbitrator appointed by the New York attorney general. Before this revision, the Lemon Law allowed for arbitration of disputes, but the forum in which arbitration took place was sponsored by trade associations within the automobile industry, and consumers often complained of unfair awards. The revised law also provided that consumers could choose between two options: arbitration before a professional arbitrator and suing the manufacturer in court. Manufacturers, however, were compelled to arbitrate claims if a consumer chose to do so and could not resort to the courts. Trade associations representing automobile manufacturers and importers brought an action seeking a declaration that the alternative arbitration mechanism of the

Lemon Law was unconstitutional because it deprived them of their right to trial by jury. How will the court decide? Discuss. [*Motor Vehicle Manufacturers Association of the United States v. State,* 75 N.Y.2d 175, 550 N.E.2d 919, 551 N.Y.S.2d 470 (1990)]

3–7. Arbitration. Phillip Beaudry, who suffered from mental illness, worked in the Department of Income Maintenance for the state of Connecticut. Beaudry was fired from his job when it was learned that he had misappropriated approximately $1,640 in state funds. Beaudry filed a complaint with his union, Council 4 of the American Federation of State, County, and Municipal Employees (AFSCME), and eventually the dispute was submitted to an arbitrator. The arbitrator concluded that Beaudry had been dismissed without "just cause," because Beaudry's acts were caused by his mental illness and "were not willful or volitional or within his capacity to control." Because Beaudry was disabled, the employer was required, under state law, to transfer him to a position that he was competent to hold. The arbitrator awarded Beaudry reinstatement, back pay, seniority, and other benefits. The state appealed the decision to a court. What public policies must the court weigh in making its decision? How should the court rule? [*State v. Council 4, AFSCME,* 27 Conn.App. 635, 608 A.2d 718 (1992)]

3–8. Arbitration. Randall Fris worked as a seaman on an Exxon Shipping Co. oil tanker for eight years without incident. One night, he boarded the ship for duty while intoxicated, in violation of company policy. This policy also allowed Exxon to discharge employees who were intoxicated and thus unfit for work. Exxon discharged Fris. Under a contract with Fris's union, the discharge was submitted to arbitration. The arbitrators ordered Exxon to reinstate Fris on an oil tanker. Exxon filed a suit against the union, challenging the award as contrary to public policy, which opposes having intoxicated persons operate seagoing vessels. Can a court set aside an arbitration award on the ground that the award violates public policy? Should the court set aside the award in this case? Explain. [*Exxon Shipping Co. v. Exxon Seamen's Union,* 11 F.3d 1189 (3d Cir. 1993)]

3–9. Arbitration. Stephanie Prince was an employee of Coca-Cola Bottling Co. of New York, Inc. (CNY), and a member of the Soft Drink and Brewery Workers Union. An agreement between CNY and the Union set out a procedure to follow in the event of a dispute between an employee and CNY relating to "any matter whatsoever, including the meaning, interpretation, application or violation of this Agreement." In this context, the agreement mentioned some employment laws but did not mention federal discrimination laws. After the Union was notified, and if the grievance was not resolved within thirty days, the dispute was to be submitted to arbitration. Prince reported to the Union, which told CNY, that she was being sexually harassed by her supervisors, Michael Drake and Leonard Erlanger. When no action was taken and Prince was subject to retaliatory behavior by Drake and Erlanger, she filed a complaint with the Equal Employment Opportunity Commission. The supervisors retaliated again by ordering her to leave the workplace and "stay home." Prince filed a suit in a federal district court against CNY and the supervisors, alleging, among other things, violations of federal discrimination law. CNY responded that its agreement with the Union required Prince to submit her claim to arbitration. Is CNY right? In whose favor should the court rule? Why? [*Prince v. Coca-Cola Bottling Co. of New York, Inc.,* 37 F.Supp.2d 289 (S.D.N.Y. 1999)]

3–10. Arbitrator's Authority. In 1999, Michael Steinmetz agreed to buy espresso equipment and the training to use it from Malted Mousse, Inc. (MM), in Tacoma, Washington. Steinmetz gave MM a $5,000 deposit, but later, believing that MM misrepresented the condition of the equipment and the extent of the training, he stopped payment on the check. MM filed a suit in a Washington state court against Steinmetz to recover the amount of the deposit. Under the rules of the court, the parties submitted their dispute to arbitration. The arbitrator issued an award in favor of Steinmetz, who asked for attorneys' fees on the basis of a state statute that required their award in cases involving less than $10,000. The arbitrator declared that the statute was unconstitutional and denied Steinmetz's request. Steinmetz appealed this denial to the court, arguing that the arbitrator exceeded his authority. Should the court reverse the arbitrator's award on the issue of the fees? Explain. [*Malted Mousse, Inc. v. Steinmetz,* 113 Wash.App. 157, 52 P.3d 555 (Div. 2, 2002)]

3–11. Arbitration. Alexander Little worked for Auto Steigler, Inc., an automobile dealership in Los Angeles County, California; eventually, he became the service manager. While employed, Little signed an arbitration agreement that required the submission of all employment-related disputes to arbitration. The agreement also provided that any award over $50,000 could be appealed to a second arbitrator. Little was later demoted and terminated. Alleging that these actions were in retaliation for investigating and reporting warranty fraud and thus were in violation of public policy, Little filed a suit in a California state court against Auto Stiegler. The defendant filed a motion with the court to compel arbitration. Little responded that the arbitration agreement should not be enforced in part because the appeal provision was unfairly one sided. Is this provision enforceable? Should the court grant Auto Steigler's motion? Why or why not? [*Little v. Auto Steigler, Inc.*, 29 Cal.4th 1064, 63 P.3d 979, 130 Cal.Rptr.2d 892 (2003)]

3–12. IN YOUR COURT

Linda Bender, in her application for registration as a stockbroker with A. G. Edwards & Sons, Inc., agreed to submit any disputes with her employer to arbitration. Bender later sued her supervisor and employer (the defendants) for sexual harassment in violation of Title VII of the Civil Rights Act of 1964, which prohibits, among other things, employment discrimination based on gender. The defendants requested the court to compel arbitration. Assume that you are the judge hearing this case and answer the following questions:

(a) Does the right to a postarbitration judicial forum equate to the right to initial access to a judicial forum in employment disputes? Should you grant the defendants' request? Why or why not?
(b) Should the fact that reviewing courts rarely set aside arbitrators' awards have any bearing on the arbitrability of certain types of claims, such as those brought under Title VII?

3–13. A QUESTION OF ETHICS AND SOCIAL RESPONSIBILITY

Colorado's Mandatory Arbitration Act required that all civil lawsuits involving damages of less than $50,000 be arbitrated rather than tried in court. The statutory scheme, which was a pilot project, affected eight judicial districts in the state. It provided for a court trial for any party dissatisfied with an arbitrator's decision. It also provided that if the trial did not result in an improvement of more than 10 percent in the position of the party who demanded the trial, that party had to pay the costs of the arbitration proceeding. The constitutionality of the act was challenged by a plaintiff who maintained in part that it violated litigants' rights of access to the courts and to trial by jury. [*Firelock, Inc. v. District Court, 20th Judicial District,* 776 P.2d 1090 (Colo. 1989)]

(a) Would such a statute do anything to reduce the congestion in the courts if any dissatisfied party could challenge an arbitrator's decision?
(b) Does such a statute violate the rights of persons with legal claims to have access to the courts?

3–14. FOR CRITICAL ANALYSIS

Under the laws in some states, some businesses may be required to submit to arbitration, or another method of alternative dispute resolution (ADR), if a consumer with a claim opts for it. In that circumstance, the business may not be able to litigate the dispute. What policy judgments are reflected in a decision to require businesses to submit to ADR?

For updated links to resources available on the Web, as well as a variety of other materials, visit this text's Web site at

http://ele.westbuslaw.com

For information on alternative dispute resolution, go to the Web site of the American Arbitration Association at

http://www.adr.org

To learn more about online dispute resolution, go to the following Web sites:

http://clicknsettle.com

http://cybersettle.com

http://SquareTrade.com

LEGAL RESEARCH EXERCISES ON THE WEB

Go to **http://ele.westbuslaw.com**, the Web site that accompanies this text. Select "Interactive Study Center," and then click on "Chapter 3." There you will find the following Internet research exercises that you can perform to learn more about topics covered in this chapter.

Activity 3–1: LEGAL PERSPECTIVE—Alternative Dispute Resolution

Activity 3–2: MANAGEMENT PERSPECTIVE—Resolve a Dispute Online

BEFORE THE TEST

Go to **http://ele.westbuslaw.com**, the Web site that accompanies this text. Select "Interactive Quizzes." You will find at least twenty interactive questions relating to this chapter.

WESTLAW® CAMPUS

If your textbook provided for a subscription to Westlaw® Campus, or if you have otherwise purchased access to the Westlaw Campus database, you can access any of the cases presented or cited in this chapter by using your Westlaw Campus account.

CHAPTER 4

Ethics and Business Decision Making

CONTENTS

CHAPTER OBJECTIVES

After reading this chapter, you should be able to answer the following questions:

1. What is ethics? What is business ethics?
2. Why is business ethics important?
3. Why is ethical leadership important?
4. What is the relationship between business ethics and the law?
5. In what ways do duty-based ethical standards differ from outcome-based ethical standards?

Just because business ethics scandals have been in the news during the early part of the 2000s does not mean that the subject was unimportant before then. Nor does it mean that as soon as the current scandals subside, businesspersons can go back to "business as usual." Few today would doubt that ethically run businesses will survive in the long run, while companies whose officers and directors act with little regard for established ethical norms will fail.

Certainly, those responsible for grossly inflating the reported profits at WorldCom, Inc., ended up not only destroying shareholder value in a great company but also facing possible prison terms. Those officers and directors at Enron Corporation who utilized a system of complicated off-the-books transactions to inflate current earnings saw their company go bankrupt—one of the largest bankruptcies in U.S. history. They harmed not only their employees and shareholders but also the communities in which they worked—and themselves (some of them may be serving prison sentences when you read this). The officers and directors of Tyco International who used corporate funds to pay for lavish personal lifestyles also ended up in court. The shareholders of that company suffered dearly, too.

Ethical business decision making is not just theory. It is practical, useful, and essential. While a good understanding of business law and the legal environment is critical, it is not enough. Understanding how one should act in her or his business dealings is equally—if not more—important in today's business arena. How one should act in business is the focus of this chapter, which is business ethics.

BUSINESS ETHICS

Before we look at business ethics, we need to discuss what is meant by ethics generally. **Ethics** can be defined as the study of what constitutes right or wrong behavior. It is the branch of philosophy that focuses on morality and the way in which moral principles are derived or the way in which a given set of moral principles applies to one's conduct in daily life. Ethics has to do with questions relating to the fairness, justness, rightness, or wrongness of an

Ethics • Moral principles and values applied to social behavior.

action. What is fair? What is just? What is the right thing to do in this situation? These are essentially ethical questions.

What Is Business Ethics?

Business ethics • Ethics in a business context; a consensus of what constitutes right or wrong behavior in the world of business and the application of moral principles to situations that arise in a business setting.

Business ethics focuses on what constitutes right or wrong behavior in the business world and on how moral and ethical principles are applied by businesspersons to situations that arise in their daily activities in the workplace. Note that business ethics is not a separate *kind* of ethics. The ethical standards that guide our behavior as, say, mothers, fathers, or students apply equally well to our activities as businesspersons. Business decision makers, though, must often address more complex ethical issues and conflicts in the workplace than they face in their personal lives.

Why Is Business Ethics Important?

Why is business ethics important? The answer to this question is clear from this chapter's introduction. A keen and in-depth understanding of business ethics is important to the long-run viability of a corporation. A thorough knowledge of business ethics is also important to the well-being of the individual officers and directors of the corporation, as well as to the welfare of the firm's employees.

You will be exposed to a series of ethical issues at the end of every unit in this text. These special *Focus on Ethics* features offer practical examples of the interplay between business ethics and the law. Additionally, in the *Focus on Ethics* following this chapter, you will read about corporate social responsibility and the duties that a corporation owes to various "stakeholders" in the entity's well-being. Certainly, corporate decisions and activities can significantly affect not only those who own, operate, or work for the company but also such groups as suppliers, the community, and society as a whole. Some of these same concepts will be touched on in this chapter on business ethics.

Note that questions concerning ethical and responsible behavior are not confined to the corporate context. Business ethics applies to *all* businesses, regardless of their organizational forms. In a business partnership, for example, partners owe a fiduciary duty to each other and to their firm—that is, a duty to act primarily for another's benefit. This duty can sometimes conflict with what a partner sees as his or her own best interest. Partners who act solely in their own interests may violate their duties to the other partners and the firm, however. By violating this duty, they may end up paying steep penalties—as the following case illustrates.

CASE 4.1

Georgia Court of Appeals, 2002. 254 Ga.App. 598, 563 S.E.2d 178.

TIME WARNER ENTERTAINMENT CO. v. SIX FLAGS OVER GEORGIA, L.L.C.

The Six Flags Over Georgia theme park in Atlanta, Georgia, was developed in 1967 as a limited partnership known as Six Flags Over Georgia, L.L.C. (Flags). The sole limited partner was Six Flags Fund, Limited (Fund). The general partner was Six Flags Over Georgia, Inc. (SFOG). In 1991, Time Warner Entertainment Company (TWE) became the majority shareholder of SFOG. The next year, TWE secretly bought 13.7 acres of *land next to the park, limiting the park's expansion opportunities. Over the next couple of years, using confidential business information from the park, TWE began plans to develop a competing park. Meanwhile, TWE installed no major new attractions at the park, deferred basic maintenance, withheld financial information from Fund (the limited partner), and began signing future employment contracts with SFOG officers. TWE also charged Flags for unrelated expenses, including over $4 million for lunches in New York City and luxury automobiles for TWE officers. Flags and Fund filed a suit in a Georgia state court against TWE and SFOG, alleging, among other things, breach of fiduciary duty. A jury awarded the plaintiffs $197,296,000 in compensatory damages and $257,000,000 in punitive damages. TWE appealed to a state intermediate appellate court, alleging in part that the amount of the punitive damages award was excessive.*

ELLINGTON, J.

We begin our analysis by examining the degree of reprehensibility [wrongfulness] of appellants' conduct in this case. *In examining the degree of reprehensibility of a defendant's conduct, [there are] a number of aggravating factors [to consider], including whether the harm was more than purely economic in nature, and whether the defendant's behavior evinced indifference to or reckless disregard for the health and safety of others.* Here, although the harm to Flags and Fund was primarily economic, it was caused by conduct we find especially reprehensible. Appellants' intentional breach of its fiduciary duty revealed a callous indifference to the financial well-being of its limited partners and their individual investors. [Emphasis added.]

* * * [T]he evidence * * * supported the jury's conclusion that appellants acted in concert to breach SFOG's fiduciary duty to its business partners. * * * [T]his evidence clearly and convincingly supported an award of punitive damages * * * because the evidence showed that the appellants withheld vital business information from Fund and Flags, undertook to compete with them, took money belonging to them, and carried out a plan to depress the value of their investment, the Six Flags Over Georgia Park. Moreover, the jury found a specific intent to cause harm * * *.

Appellants' conduct toward its partners and those who invested in the limited partnership was part of a premeditated plan surreptitiously [secretly] executed over a period of years. Appellants' conduct was deceitful, self-serving, and financially damaging. More importantly, however, appellants' conduct was a breach of fiduciary duty, a violation of a confidential relationship of trust requiring the utmost in good faith. * * * Appellants' conduct was, in short, the kind of behavior we find deserving of reproof [disapproval], rebuke, or censure; blameworthy—the very definition of reprehensible. * * * *Trickery and deceit are reprehensible wrongs, especially when done intentionally through affirmative acts of misconduct.* * * * [Emphasis added.]

* * * *

In this case, the ratio of compensatory to punitive damages is 1 to 1.3. We see no shocking disparity inherent in this figure. Nor does it appear to approach that fuzzy line suggesting the bounds of constitutional impropriety. More importantly, however, given the amount of intentional economic damage inflicted by the appellants, corporate entities with collective assets measured in billions of dollars, we believe the award of punitive damages was reasonably calculated to punish them and to deter such conduct in the future.

The state intermediate appellate court affirmed the judgment of the lower court, finding that the award of punitive damages was not excessive, considering the defendants' financial status and "reprehensible" conduct toward the plaintiffs.

QUESTIONS

1. What factors indicate a degree of wrongful conduct sufficiently great to warrant imposing punitive damages, according to the court in this case?
2. On what did the state intermediate appellate court base its finding that the award of punitive damages was not excessive?
3. If TWE had proceeded with its plans to build a competing park but had not acted otherwise "reprehensibly" with regard to Flags and Fund, would the decision in this case likely have been different?

SETTING THE RIGHT ETHICAL TONE

Many unethical business decisions are made simply because they *can* be made. In other words, the decision makers not only have the opportunity to make such decisions but also are not too concerned about being seriously sanctioned for their unethical actions. Perhaps one of the most difficult challenges for business owners and upper-level managers today is to create the right "ethical tone" in their workplaces so as to deter unethical conduct.

The Importance of Ethical Leadership

Talking about ethical business decision making means nothing if management does not set standards. Moreover, managers must apply those standards to themselves as well as to the employees in the company.

Attitude of Top Management. One of the most important factors in creating and maintaining an ethical workplace is the attitude of top management. Managers who are not totally committed to maintaining an ethical workplace will rarely succeed in creating one. Surveys of business executives indicate that management's behavior, more than anything else, sets the ethical tone of a firm. In other words, employees take their cue from management. If a firm's managers adhere to obvious ethical norms in their business dealings, employees will likely follow their example. In contrast, if managers act unethically, employees will see no reason not to do so themselves. For example, if an employee observes a manager cheating on her expense account, the employee quickly understands that such behavior is acceptable.

Looking the Other Way. A manager who looks the other way when he knows about an employee's unethical behavior also sets an example—one indicating that ethical transgressions will be accepted. Managers must show that they will not tolerate unethical business behavior. Although this may seem harsh, managers have found that discharging even one employee for ethical reasons has a tremendous impact as a deterrent to unethical behavior in the workplace.

Creating Realistic Goals Helps. Managers can reduce the probability that employees will act unethically by setting realistic production or sales goals. If a sales quota, for example, can be met only through high-pressure, unethical sales tactics, employees trying to act "in the best interests of the firm" may think that management is implicitly asking them to behave unethically.

Periodic Evaluation. Some companies require their managers to meet individually with employees and to grade them on their ethical (or unethical) behavior. One company, for example, asks its employees to fill out ethical checklists each week and return them to their supervisors. This practice serves two purposes: First, it demonstrates to employees that ethics matters. Second, employees have an opportunity to reflect on how well they have measured up in terms of ethical performance.

Creating Ethical Codes of Conduct

One of the most effective ways of setting a tone of ethical behavior within an organization is to create an ethical code of conduct. A well-written code of ethics explicitly states a company's ethical priorities.

Costco—An Example. A code of ethics was created by Costco Wholesale Corporation, a large warehouse-club retailer with over 35 million "members." This code of conduct indicates Costco's commitment to legal compliance, as well as to the welfare of its members (those who purchase its goods), its employees, and its suppliers. The code also details some specific ways in which the interests and welfare of these different groups will be protected. In its code, Costco acknowledges that by protecting these groups' interests, it will realize its "ultimate goal"—rewarding its shareholders with maximum shareholder value.

Another Necessity—Clear Communication to Employees. For an ethical code to be effective, its provisions must be clearly communicated to employees. Most large companies have implemented ethics training programs, in which management discusses with employees on a face-to-face basis the firm's policies and the importance of ethical conduct. Some companies hold periodic ethics seminars during which employees can openly discuss any ethical problems that they may be experiencing and learn how the firm's ethical policies apply to those specific concerns.

Johnson & Johnson—An Example of Web-Based Ethics Training. Creating a code of conduct and implementing it are two different activities. In many companies, codes of conduct are simply documents that have very little relevance to day-to-day operations. When Johnson & Johnson wanted to do "better" than other companies with respect to ethical business decision making, it created a Center for Legal and Credo Awareness. (Its code of ethical conduct is called its *credo*.)

The center created a Web-based set of instructions designed to enhance the corporation's efforts to train employees in the importance of following its code of conduct. Given that Johnson & Johnson has over 120,000 employees throughout the world, reinforcing its code of conduct and following its values have not been easy, but Web-based training has helped. The company established a Web-based legal and compliance center, which consists of a set of interactive modules to train employees in areas of the law and ethics.

Corporate Compliance Programs

In large corporations, ethical codes of conduct are usually just one part of a comprehensive corporate compliance program. Other components of such a program, some of which were already mentioned, include a corporation's ethics committee, ethical training programs, and internal audits to monitor compliance with applicable laws and the company's standards of ethical conduct.

Requirements under the Sarbanes-Oxley Act. The Sarbanes-Oxley Act of 2002[1] requires that companies set up confidential systems so that employees and others may "raise red flags" about suspected illegal or unethical auditing and accounting practices. The act required publicly traded companies to have such systems in place by April 2003. At least one Web-based reporting system was implemented in 2002. Employees can click on an icon on their computer that anonymously links them with Ethicspoint, an organization based in Vancouver, Washington. Through Ethicspoint, employees may report suspicious accounting practices, sexual harassment, and other possibly unethical behavior. Ethicspoint, in turn, alerts management personnel or the audit committee at the designated company to the potential problem. Those who have used the system say that it is less intimidating than calling a company's 800 number.

Compliance Programs Must Be Integrated. To be effective, a compliance program must be integrated throughout the firm. For large corporations, such integration is essential. Ethical policies and programs need to be coordinated and monitored by a committee that is separate from various corporate departments. Otherwise, unethical behavior in one department can easily escape the attention of those in control of the corporation or the corporate officials responsible for implementing and monitoring the company's compliance program.

Conflicts and Trade-Offs

Management constantly faces ethical trade-offs, some of which may lead to legal problems. As mentioned earlier, firms have implied ethical (and legal) duties to a number of groups, including shareholders and employees.

When a company decides to reduce costs by downsizing and restructuring, the decision may benefit shareholders, but it will harm those employees who are laid off or fired. When downsizing occurs, which employees should be laid off first? Cost-cutting considerations might dictate firing the most senior employees, who generally have higher salaries, and retaining less senior employees, whose salaries are much lower. A company does not necessarily act illegally when it does so. Yet the decision to be made by management clearly involves an important ethical question: Which group's interests—

1. H.R. 3762. This act, which became effective on August 29, 2002, will be discussed in Chapter 18.

those of the shareholders or those of employees who have been loyal to the firm for a long period of time—should take priority in this situation?

Selling information can bolster a company's profits, which may satisfy the firm's obligation to its owners, but when the data is personal, its sale may violate an ethical or legal duty. In what circumstances might a party who sells information about someone else have a duty to that other party with respect to the sale of the information? This question arose in the following case.

REMSBURG v. DOCUSEARCH, INC.

New Hampshire Supreme Court, 2003.
816 A.2d 1001.
http://www.courts.state.nh.us/supreme/opinions/index.htm[a]

Docusearch, Inc., operates Docusearch.com, an Internet-based investigation and information service. In July 1999, Liam Youens, a resident of New Hampshire, contacted Docusearch through its Web site and requested information about Amy Boyer, another New Hampshire resident. Youens provided his name, address, and phone number, and paid Docusearch's fee by credit card. Docusearch provided Boyer's home address, birth date, and Social Security number. Youens also asked for Boyer's workplace address. To obtain this information, Michele Gambino, a Docusearch subcontractor, placed a "pretext" phone call to Boyer. Gambino lied about who she was and the purpose of her call. On October 15, Youens drove to Boyer's workplace and fatally shot her, and then shot and killed himself. The police discovered Youens's Web site, which referred to stalking and killing Boyer. Helen Remsburg, Boyer's mother, filed a suit in a federal district court against Docusearch and others, claiming that the defendants acted wrongfully. The court asked the New Hampshire Supreme Court whether, under the state's common law, a person who sells information about another has a duty to the other party with respect to the sale.

DALIANIS, J.

[T]he United States District Court for the District of New Hampshire certified to us the following [question] of law:

> * * * Under the common law of New Hampshire and in light of the undisputed facts presented by this case, does a private investigator or information broker who sells information to a client pertaining to a third party have a cognizable legal duty to that third party with respect to the sale of the information?

* * * *

All persons have a duty to exercise reasonable care not to subject others to an unreasonable risk of harm. Whether a defendant's conduct creates a risk of harm to others sufficiently foreseeable to charge the defendant with a duty to avoid such conduct is a question of law, because the existence of a duty does not arise solely from the relationship between the parties, but also from the need for protection against reasonably foreseeable harm. Thus, in some cases, a party's actions give rise to a duty. *Parties owe a duty to those third parties foreseeably endangered by their conduct with respect to those risks whose likelihood and magnitude make the conduct unreasonably dangerous.* [Emphasis added.]

---

a. Click on "February 2003." In the "February 18, 2003" section, click on the name of the case to access the opinion. This is a page within a Web site maintained by the Judicial Branch of the State of New Hampshire.

In situations in which the harm is caused by criminal misconduct, however, determining whether a duty exists is complicated by the competing rule that a private citizen has no general duty to protect others from the criminal attacks of third parties. This rule is grounded in the fundamental unfairness of holding private citizens responsible for the unanticipated criminal acts of third parties, because under all ordinary and normal circumstances, in the absence of any reason to expect the contrary, the actor may reasonably proceed upon the assumption that others will obey the law.

In certain limited circumstances, however, we have recognized that there are exceptions to the general rule where a duty to exercise reasonable care will arise. We have held that such a duty may arise because: (1) a special relationship exists; (2) special circumstances exist; or (3) the duty has been voluntarily assumed. The special circumstances exception includes situations where there is an especial temptation and opportunity for criminal misconduct brought about by the defendant. This exception follows from the rule that a party who realizes or should realize that his conduct has created a condition which involves an unreasonable risk of harm to another has a duty to exercise reasonable care to prevent the risk from occurring. The exact occurrence or precise injuries need not have been foreseeable. Rather, where the defendant's conduct has created an unreasonable risk of criminal misconduct, a duty is owed to those foreseeably endangered.

Thus, if a private investigator or information broker's * * * disclosure of information to a client creates a foreseeable risk of criminal misconduct against the third person whose information was disclosed, the investigator owes a duty to exercise reasonable care not to subject the third person to an unreasonable risk of harm. In determining whether the risk of criminal misconduct is foreseeable to an investigator, we examine two risks of information disclosure implicated by this case: stalking and identity theft.

It is undisputed that stalkers, in seeking to locate and track a victim, sometimes use an investigator to obtain personal information about the victims.

Public concern about stalking has compelled all fifty States to pass some form of legislation criminalizing stalking. Approximately one million women and 371,000 men are stalked annually in the United States. Stalking is a crime that causes serious psychological harm to the victims, and often results in the victim experiencing post-traumatic stress disorder, anxiety, sleeplessness, and sometimes, suicidal ideations. Not only is stalking itself a crime, but it can lead to more violent crimes, including assault, rape or homicide.

Identity theft, *i.e.,* the use of one person's identity by another, is an increasingly common risk associated with the disclosure of personal information, such as a [Social Security number, or SSN]. * * * Armed with one's SSN, an unscrupulous individual could obtain a person's welfare benefits or Social Security benefits, order new checks at a new address on that person's checking account, obtain credit cards, or even obtain the person's paycheck.

Like the consequences of stalking, the consequences of identity theft can be severe. The best estimates place the number of victims in excess of 100,000 per year and the dollar loss in excess of $2 billion per year. Victims of identity theft risk the destruction of their good credit histories. This often destroys a victim's ability to obtain credit from any source and may, in some cases, render the victim unemployable or even cause the victim to be incarcerated.

The threats posed by stalking and identity theft lead us to conclude that the risk of criminal misconduct is sufficiently foreseeable so that an investigator has a duty to exercise reasonable care in disclosing a third person's personal information to a client. And we so hold. This is especially true when, as in this case, the investigator does not know the client or the client's purpose in seeking the information. [Emphasis added.]

The New Hampshire Supreme Court held that an information broker who sells to a client information about a third person has a duty to exercise reasonable care in disclosing the information. The court reasoned that the risk of criminal misconduct is sufficiently foreseeable to impose this duty, in light of threats posed by stalking and identity theft.

QUESTIONS

1. How did the question in this case come before the New Hampshire Supreme Court?
2. According to the New Hampshire Supreme Court, why does a broker who sells information about a third party have a duty to exercise reasonable care in disclosing that information?
3. What might the defendants in this case have done to satisfy their legal and ethical duties?

DEFYING THE RULES: THE ENRON CASE

For years to come, the Enron debacle—one of the largest bankruptcies in the history of U.S. business—will remain a symbol of the cost of unethical behavior to management, employees, suppliers, shareholders, the community, society, and indeed the world. Shareholders lost $62 billion of value in a very short period of time in the early 2000s. This case study of "cooking the books," conflicts of interest, and deviation from accepted ethical standards of business has all of the trappings of an epic novel. For the thousands of employees who lost millions of dollars and for the millions of shareholders who lost billions of dollars, however, the Enron story was not fiction.

The Growth of Enron in a Nutshell

In the 1990s, two gas-pipeline companies, Houston Natural Gas Corporation and InterNorth, Inc., merged to create a very large energy trading company, Enron Corporation. It was a "first mover" in a deregulated electricity market and enjoyed impressive growth. By 1998, Enron was the largest energy trader in the world. Then it entered the online energy trading market. By December 2000, its shares were selling at $85. Most Enron employees had a large part or even all of their retirement packages tied up in the company's stock.

When competition in energy trading increased, Enron diversified into water, power plants in Brazil and India, and finally fiber optics and high-speed Internet transmission.

Accounting Issues

According to the rules of the Financial Accounting Standards Board, energy traders such as Enron could include in *current* earnings profits that they *anticipated* on energy contracts. Herein lay the beginning of a type of accounting "fudging" that increased over time as the company struggled to improve its reported current earnings. By 2000, 50 percent of Enron's $1.4 billion of reported pretax profits consisted of "anticipated" future earnings on energy contracts.

Because Enron's managers received bonuses based on whether they met earnings goals, they had an incentive to inflate the anticipated earnings on such contracts. Some of the contracts extended as long as twenty years into the future. In retrospect, the temptation to management was too great, and common norms of both ethical and legal business decision making were violated as managers overestimated future earnings in order to inflate current earnings.

Off-the-Books Transactions

To artificially maintain and even increase its reported earnings, Enron also created a complex network of subsidiaries that enabled it to move losses from the core company to the subsidiaries—companies that did not show up on Enron's books. When it created the subsidiaries, Enron transferred assets to them, assigning a value to the assets that was much greater than their actual market value. The effect was to increase Enron's apparent net worth. Consider one example: Enron sold its unused fiber-optic cable capacity to a subsidiary for $30 million in cash and a $70 million promissory note. This transaction added $53 million to Enron's reported earnings for just one quarter. The value of the unused fiber-optic cable would soon be negligible, however.

For several years, Enron transferred assets from its books, along with the accompanying debt, to partnerships outside the main corporation. Many of these transactions were carried out in the Cayman Islands, a haven for those seeking corporate secrecy as well as a means for avoiding federal income taxes.

Self-Dealing

Enron's chief executive officer (CEO) frequently did business with companies owned by his son and his daughter. The son created a company that was later bought by Enron. The son was then hired as an executive with a guaranteed pay package of $1 million over three years as well as 20,000 Enron stock options. The CEO's daughter owned a Houston travel agency that received over $10 million—50 percent of the agency's total revenues—from Enron during a three-year period.

The Corporate Culture

The many transgressions just described could not have happened without a corporate culture that fostered unethical and, in many instances, illegal business decision making. This case study of unethical behavior is sufficiently important that West Legal Studies in Business has created a project titled "Inside Look," accessible on the Web at **http://insidelook.westbuslaw.com**. There you will discover how, on numerous occasions, Enron management was apprised, both by insiders and outsiders, that a "house of cards" had been created. Nonetheless, upper management more often than not refused to investigate and reveal to the public (or to its shareholders and employees) the financial improprieties that had occurred over the previous three years.

BUSINESS ETHICS AND THE LAW

Today, legal compliance is regarded as a **moral minimum**—the minimum acceptable standard for ethical business behavior. Had Enron Corporation strictly complied with existing laws and generally accepted accounting practices, very likely the "Enron scandal" would never have happened. Simply obeying the law does not fulfill all business ethical obligations, however. In the interests of preserving personal freedom, as well as for practical reasons, the law does not—and cannot—codify all ethical requirements. No law says, for example, that it is illegal to lie to one's family, but it may be unethical to do so.

Moral minimum • The minimum degree of ethical behavior expected of a business firm, which is usually defined as compliance with the law.

It may seem that determining the legality of a given action should be simple. Either something is legal or it is not. In fact, one of the major challenges businesspersons face is that the legality of a particular action is not always clear. In part, this is because there are so many laws regulating business that a firm may violate one of them without realizing it. The law also contains numerous "gray areas," making it difficult to predict with certainty how a court will apply a given law to a particular action. This is particularly true when technological advances bring about new situations that have not yet been addressed by the courts.

Laws Regulating Business

Today's business firms are subject to extensive government regulation. As mentioned in Chapter 1, virtually every action a firm undertakes—from the initial act of going into business, to hiring and firing personnel, to selling products in the marketplace—is subject to statutory law and to numerous rules and regulations issued by administrative agencies. Furthermore, these rules and regulations are changed or supplemented frequently.

Determining whether a planned action is legal thus requires that decision makers keep abreast of the law. Normally, large business firms have attorneys on their staffs to assist them in making key decisions. Small firms must also seek legal advice before making important business decisions because the consequences of just one violation of a regulatory rule may be costly.

Ignorance of the law will not excuse a business owner or manager from liability for violating a statute or regulation. In one case, the court imposed criminal fines, as well as imprisonment, on a company's supervisory employee for violating a federal environmental act—even though the employee was completely unaware of what was required under the provisions of that act.[2]

"Gray Areas" in the Law

In many situations, business firms can predict with a fair amount of certainty whether a given action would be legal. For example, firing an employee solely because of that person's race or gender would clearly violate federal laws prohibiting employment discrimination. In some situations, though, the legality of a particular action may be less clear.

For example, suppose that a firm decides to launch a new advertising campaign. How far can the company go in making claims for its products or services? Federal and state laws prohibit firms from engaging in "deceptive advertising." At the federal level, the test for deceptive advertising normally

2. *United States v. Hanousek,* 176 F.3d 1116 (9th Cir. 1999). This case will be presented in Chapter 7 as Case 7.1.

ETHICAL ISSUE

Do firms have a duty to prevent criminal misuses of their products? Should pesticide manufacturers be held liable when their products are used to create bombs that cause destruction? Should service stations be held liable for selling gasoline to purchasers who then use the gas to set buildings on fire? Such questions have come before the courts on several occasions. In a Colorado case, for example, the plaintiff was injured when, after an argument with a man, the man went to a gas station, bought a cupful of gasoline, threw it on the plaintiff, and set her on fire. The plaintiff argued that the defendant gas station was negligent because it should have foreseen, based on the man's behavior and appearance, that selling him a cupful of gas could create a risk that he might harm someone with it. Routinely, the courts have held that such criminal uses of products are unforeseeable misuses for which the manufacturers of the products cannot be held liable. In the Colorado case, the state appellate court also reached this conclusion. The court stated that the risk that a purchaser of gasoline would intentionally throw it on a victim and set the victim on fire was not reasonably foreseeable.[a]

a. *Walcott v. Total Petroleum, Inc.*, 964 P.2d 609 (Colo.App. 1998).

used by the Federal Trade Commission is whether an advertising claim would deceive a "reasonable consumer." At what point, though, would a reasonable consumer be deceived by a particular ad?

Another gray area in the law has to do with product misuse. Product liability laws require manufacturers and sellers to warn consumers of the kinds of injuries that might result from the foreseeable misuse of their products (see Chapter 12). An exception to this rule is made when a risk associated with a product is "open and obvious." Sharp knives, for example, can obviously injure their users. Sometimes, though, a business has no way of predicting whether a court will decide that a particular risk is open and obvious or that consumers should be warned of the risk.

In short, business decision makers need to proceed with caution and evaluate an action and its consequences from an ethical perspective. Generally, if a company can demonstrate that it acted in good faith and responsibly in the circumstances, it has a better chance of successfully defending its action in court or before an administrative law judge.

Even courts often disagree on certain issues. In the following case, for example, the trial court and the appellate court arrived at different conclusions on whether a warning on an aerosol can of butane adequately alerted consumers to the danger of inhaling the contents of the can.

CASE 4.3

United States Court of Appeals, Third Circuit, 1998. 135 F.3d 876. **http://www.findlaw.com/casecode/courts/3rd.html**[a]

PAVLIK v. LANE LTD./TOBACCO EXPORTERS INTERNATIONAL

Butane is a fuel used in cigarette lighters. Zeus brand butane is distributed in small aerosol cans by Lane Limited/Tobacco Exporters International (Lane). On each can is the warning "DO NOT BREATHE SPRAY." Twenty-year-old Stephen Pavlik died from

a. In the "Browsing by date" section, select "1998" and "February" and click on "Search." When that page opens, scroll down the list to the *Pavlik* case name and click on it to access the opinion.

intentionally inhaling the contents of one of the cans. His father, George Pavlik, filed a suit in a federal district court against Lane and others, claiming in part that the statement on the can did not adequately warn users of the hazards of butane inhalation. The court issued a summary judgment in the defendants' favor, reasoning in part that Stephen must have been aware of the dangers of inhaling butane and that a more specific warning would not have affected his conduct. George Pavlik appealed to the U.S. Court of Appeals for the Third Circuit.

BECKER, C. J.

[A]n otherwise properly designed product may still be unreasonably dangerous (and therefore "defective") for strict liability purposes if the product is distributed without sufficient warnings to apprise the ultimate user of the latent dangers in the product.

* * * *

* * * [W]e have serious doubts that the Zeus warning sufficiently warns users of the potentially fatal consequences of butane inhalation, and we are not convinced of its adequacy * * * . More specifically, the "DO NOT BREATHE SPRAY" warning appears to give the user no notice of the serious nature of the danger posed by inhalation, intentional or otherwise, and no other language on the Zeus can does so. Yet, we similarly cannot find that such a directive is inadequate as a matter of law, and so we must leave the question for the jury.

The U.S. Court of Appeals for the Third Circuit held that it was not clear that Stephen was fully aware of the dangers of inhaling butane, based on the label on the Zeus can. The court reversed the judgment of the lower court and remanded the case for trial.

QUESTIONS

1. What was the basis for the lower court's decision in favor of the manufacturer and the other defendants?
2. On what ground did the U.S. Court of Appeals for the Third Circuit base its holding that the defendants might be liable for Stephen's death?
3. Would it have made any difference to the outcome of this case if Stephen's parents had warned him of the dangers of inhaling butane?

Technological Developments and Legal Uncertainties

Uncertainties concerning how particular laws may apply to specific factual situations have been compounded in the cyber age. As noted in earlier chapters, the widespread use of the Internet has given rise to situations never before faced by the courts.

The case presented next is illustrative. The case involved an airline pilot who claimed that defamatory, gender-based messages made by her co-workers in an online forum created a hostile working environment. Federal law prohibits harassment in the workplace, including "hostile-environment harassment," which occurs when an employee is subjected to sexual conduct or comments that he or she perceives as offensive (see Chapter 15). Generally, employers are expected to take immediate and appropriate corrective action in response to employees' complaints of sexual harassment or abusive behavior in the workplace. Otherwise, they may be held liable for the harassing actions of an employee's co-workers or supervisors. At issue in the case that follows was whether the online forum could be considered part of the "workplace" over which the employer had control.

CASE 4.4
New Jersey Supreme Court, 2000.
751 A.2d 538.
http://lawlibrary.rutgers.edu/search.shtml[a]

BLAKEY v. CONTINENTAL AIRLINES, INC.

CompuServe, Inc., a subsidiary of America Online, Inc., is the Internet service provider for Continental Airlines, Inc. CompuServe provides Continental's pilots and other crew members with online access to a "Crew Members Forum" for the exchange of ideas and information via messages and threads.[b] *Tammy Blakey, a pilot for Continental Airlines since 1984, was the airline's first female captain—and one of only five Continental pilots—to fly an Airbus, or A300, aircraft. Shortly after qualifying to be a captain on the A300, Blakey complained about pornographic photos and vulgar gender-based comments directed at her in her plane's cockpit and other work areas by her male co-employees. Blakey pursued claims against Continental with the Equal Employment Opportunity Commission, the federal agency that administers federal laws prohibiting employment discrimination, and in a federal district court.*[c] *Meanwhile, Continental pilots published a series of harassing, gender-based, defamatory messages about Blakey on the forum. When the court refused to consider these messages, Blakey filed a complaint against Continental and others in a New Jersey state court. She alleged, in part, gender-based harassment arising from a hostile work environment. Continental filed a motion for summary judgment on this claim, which the court granted. A state intermediate appellate court upheld the summary judgment, and Blakey appealed to the New Jersey Supreme Court.*

O'HERN, J.

When an employer knows or should know of the harassment and fails to take effective measures to stop it, the employer has joined with the harasser in making the working environment hostile. The employer, by failing to take action, sends the harassed employee the message that the harassment is acceptable and that the management supports the harasser. *"Effective" remedial measures are those reasonably calculated to end the harassment.* * * * [Emphasis added.]

* * * *

* * * Continental's liability [depends] on whether the Crew Members Forum was such an integral part of the workplace that harassment on the Crew Members Forum should be regarded as a continuation or extension of the pattern of harassment that existed in the Continental workplace.

---

a. This page includes a search box for a database of the recent opinions of the New Jersey state courts. In the box, type "Blakey" and click on the "Search" link. When the results appear, scroll down the list and click on the *Blakey* case name to access the opinion. This Web site is maintained by Rutgers School of Law in Camden, New Jersey.

b. A *thread* is a sequence of responses to an initial message posting. This enables a user to follow or join an individual discussion.

c. In 1997, the federal court ruled in favor of Blakey on a claim of gender-based harassment, awarding her a total of $495,000 in forgone pay and $250,000 for emotional distress, pain, and suffering. The court also found that Blakey had failed to mitigate damages (reduce her damages—by finding other work, for example) and subtracted $120,000 from her back pay award.

Our common experience tells us how important are the extensions of the workplace where the relations among employees are cemented or sometimes sundered [destroyed]. If an "old boys' network" continued, in an after-hours setting, the belittling conduct that edges over into harassment, what exactly is the outsider (whether black, Latino, or woman) to do? Keep swallowing the abuse or give up the chance to make the team? We believe that severe or pervasive harassment in a work-related setting that continues a pattern of harassment on the job is sufficiently related to the workplace that an informed employer who takes no effective measures to stop it, sends the harassed employee the message that the harassment is acceptable and that the management supports the harasser. * * *

* * * *

CompuServe's role may * * * be analogized to that of a company that builds an old-fashioned bulletin board. If the maker of an old-fashioned bulletin board provided a better bulletin board by setting aside space on it for employees to post messages, we would have little doubt that messages on the company bulletin board would be part of the workplace setting. Here, the Crew Members Forum is an added feature to the company bulletin board.

The New Jersey Supreme Court reversed the judgment of the lower court and remanded the case for further proceedings. The state supreme court indicated that the trial court was to determine, among other things, which messages were harassing, whether Continental had notice of those messages, and the severity or pervasiveness of the harassing conduct.

QUESTIONS

1. Why did Blakey file a second suit against Continental in a different court?
2. According to the New Jersey Supreme Court, why can harassment in an employees' online forum be regarded as an extension of harassment in the workplace?
3. Does the holding in the *Blakey* case mean that employers have a duty to monitor their employees' e-mail and other online communications?

APPROACHES TO ETHICAL REASONING

Each individual, when faced with a particular ethical dilemma, engages in **ethical reasoning**—that is, a reasoning process in which the individual examines the situation at hand in light of her or his moral convictions or ethical standards. Businesspersons do likewise when making decisions with ethical implications.

Ethical reasoning • A reasoning process in which an individual links her or his moral convictions or ethical standards to the particular situation at hand.

How do business decision makers decide whether a given action is the "right" one for their firms? What ethical standards should be applied? Broadly speaking, ethical reasoning relating to business traditionally has been characterized by two fundamental approaches. One approach defines ethical behavior in terms of duty, which also implies certain rights. The other approach determines what is ethical in terms of the consequences, or outcome, of any given action. We examine each of these approaches here.

Duty-Based Ethics

Duty-based ethical standards often are derived from revealed truths, such as religious precepts. They can also be derived through philosophical reasoning.

Religious Ethical Standards. In the Judeo-Christian tradition, which is the dominant religious tradition in the United States, the Ten Commandments of the Old Testament establish fundamental rules for moral action. Other religions have their own sources of revealed truth. Religious rules generally are absolute with respect to the behavior of their adherents. For example, the commandment "Thou shalt not steal" is an absolute mandate for a person, such as a Jew or a Christian, who believes that the Ten Commandments reflect revealed truth. Even a benevolent motive for stealing (such as Robin Hood's) cannot justify the act because the act itself is inherently immoral and thus wrong.

Ethical standards based on religious teachings also involve an element of *compassion*. Therefore, for example, even though it might be profitable for a firm to lay off a less productive employee, if that employee would find it difficult to find employment elsewhere and his or her family would suffer as a result, this potential suffering would be given substantial weight by the decision makers. Compassionate treatment of others is also mandated—to a certain extent, at least—by the Golden Rule of the ancients ("Do unto others as you would have them do unto you"), which has been adopted by most religions.

Kantian Ethics. Duty-based ethical standards may also be derived solely from philosophical reasoning. The German philosopher Immanuel Kant (1724–1804), for example, identified some general guiding principles for moral behavior based on what he believed to be the fundamental nature of human beings. Kant held that it is rational to assume that human beings are qualitatively different from other physical objects occupying space. Persons are endowed with moral integrity and the capacity to reason and conduct their affairs rationally. Therefore, their thoughts and actions should be respected. When human beings are treated merely as a means to an end, they are being regarded as the equivalent of objects and are being denied their basic humanity.

A central postulate in Kantian ethics is that individuals should evaluate their actions in light of the consequences that would follow if *everyone* in society acted in the same way. This **categorical imperative** can be applied to any action. For example, suppose that you are deciding whether to cheat on an examination. If you have adopted Kant's categorical imperative, you will decide not to cheat because if everyone cheated, the examination would be meaningless.

Categorical imperative • A concept developed by the philosopher Immanuel Kant as an ethical guideline for behavior. In deciding whether an action is right or wrong, or desirable or undesirable, a person should evaluate the action in terms of what would happen if everybody else in the same situation, or category, acted the same way.

The Principle of Rights. Because a duty cannot exist without a corresponding right, duty-based ethical standards imply that human beings have basic rights. For example, the commandment "Thou shalt not kill" implies that individuals have a right to live. Additionally, religious ethics may involve a rights component because of the belief—characteristic of some religions—that an individual is "made in the image of God." This belief confers on the individual great dignity as a person. For one who holds this belief, not to respect that dignity—and the rights and status that flow from it—would be morally wrong. Kantian ethics also implies fundamental rights based on the personal dignity of each individual. Just as individuals have a duty not to treat others as a means to an end, so individuals have a right to have their status and moral integrity as human beings treated with respect.

The principle that human beings have certain fundamental rights (to life, freedom, and the pursuit of happiness, for example) is deeply embedded in Western culture. As discussed in Chapter 1, the natural law tradition embraces the concept that certain actions (such as killing another person) are morally wrong because they are contrary to nature (the natural desire to continue living). Those who adhere to this **principle of rights,** or "rights theory," believe that a key factor in determining whether a business decision is ethical is how that decision affects the rights of others. These others include the firm's owners, its employees, the consumers of its products or services, its suppliers, the community in which it does business, and society as a whole.

Principle of rights • The principle that human beings have certain fundamental rights (to life, freedom, and the pursuit of happiness, for example). Those who adhere to this "rights theory" believe that a key factor in determining whether a business decision is ethical is how that decision affects the rights of others.

Which Rights Are Most Important? A potential dilemma for those who support a rights theory, however, is that they may disagree on which rights are most important. When considering all of those who may be affected by a business decision, for example, how much weight should be given to employees relative to shareholders, customers relative to the community, or employees relative to society as a whole?

In general, rights theorists believe that whichever right is stronger in a particular circumstance takes precedence. For example, suppose that a firm can either shut down a plant to avoid dumping pollutants in a river that would affect the health of thousands of people or save the jobs of the twelve workers in the plant. In this situation, a rights theorist can easily choose which group to favor. (Not all choices are so clear-cut, however.)

Outcome-Based Ethics: Utilitarianism

"Thou shalt act so as to generate the greatest good for the greatest number." This is a paraphrase of the major premise of the utilitarian approach to ethics. **Utilitarianism** is a philosophical theory developed by Jeremy Bentham (1748–1832) and then advanced, with some modifications, by John Stuart Mill (1806–1873)—both British philosophers. In contrast to duty-based ethics, utilitarianism is outcome oriented. It focuses on the consequences of an action, not on the nature of the action itself or on any set of preestablished moral values or religious beliefs.

Utilitarianism • An approach to ethical reasoning in which ethically correct behavior is not related to any absolute ethical or moral values but to an evaluation of the consequences of a given action on those who will be affected by it. In utilitarian reasoning, a "good" decision is one that results in the greatest good for the greatest number of people affected by the decision.

Under a utilitarian model of ethics, an action is morally correct, or "right," when, among the people it affects, it produces the greatest amount of good for the greatest number. When an action affects the majority adversely, it is morally wrong. Applying the utilitarian theory thus requires (1) a determination of which individuals will be affected by the action in question; (2) a **cost-benefit analysis,** which involves an assessment of the negative and positive effects of alternative actions on these individuals; and (3) a choice among alternative actions that will produce maximum societal utility (the greatest positive net benefits for the greatest number of individuals).

Cost-benefit analysis • A decision-making technique that involves weighing the costs of a given action against the benefits of the action.

The utilitarian approach to decision making commonly is employed by businesses, as well as by individuals. Weighing the consequences of a decision in terms of its costs and benefits for everyone affected by it is a useful analytical tool in the decision-making process. At the same time, utilitarianism is often criticized because its objective, calculated approach to problems tends to reduce the welfare of human beings to plus and minus signs on a cost-benefit worksheet and to "justify" human costs that many find totally unacceptable.

Business Ethics on a Global Level

Given the various cultures and religions throughout the world, one should not be surprised if frequent conflicts in ethics arise between foreign and U.S. businesspersons. For example, in certain countries the consumption of alcohol and specific foods is forbidden for religious reasons. Under such circumstances, it would be thoughtless and imprudent for a U.S. businessperson to invite a local business contact out for a drink.

The role played by women in other countries may also present some difficult ethical problems for firms doing business internationally. Equal employment opportunity is a fundamental public policy in the United States, and Title VII of the Civil Rights Act of 1964 prohibits discrimination against women in the employment context (see Chapter 15). Some other countries, however, offer little protection for women against gender discrimination in the workplace, including sexual harassment.

We look here at how laws governing workers in other countries, particularly developing countries, have created some especially difficult ethical problems for U.S. sellers of goods manufactured in foreign countries. We also examine some of the ethical ramifications of a U.S. law that prohibits U.S. businesspersons from bribing foreign officials to obtain favorable business contracts.

Monitoring the Employment Practices of Foreign Suppliers

Many U.S. businesses now contract with companies in developing nations to produce goods, such as shoes and clothing, because the wage rates in those nations are significantly lower than in the United States. Yet what if a foreign company exploits its workers—by hiring women and children at very low wage rates, for example, or by requiring its employees to work long hours in a workplace full of health hazards? What if the company's supervisors routinely engage in workplace conduct that is offensive to women?

Given today's global communications network, few companies can assume that their actions in other nations will go unnoticed by "corporate watch" groups that discover and publicize unethical corporate behavior. As a result, U.S. businesses today usually take steps to avoid such adverse publicity—either by refusing to deal with certain suppliers or by making arrangements to monitor their suppliers' workplaces to ensure that the workers are not being mistreated.

The Foreign Corrupt Practices Act

Another ethical problem in international business dealings has to do with the legitimacy of certain side payments to government officials. In the United States, the majority of contracts are formed within the private sector. In many foreign countries, however, decisions on most major construction and manufacturing contracts are made by government officials because of extensive government regulation and control over trade and industry. Side payments to government officials in exchange for favorable business contracts are not unusual in such nations, nor are they considered to be unethical. In the past, U.S. corporations doing business in these countries largely followed the dictum, "When in Rome, do as the Romans do."

In the 1970s, however, the U.S. press, and government officials as well, uncovered a number of business scandals involving large side payments by U.S. corporations—such as Lockheed Aircraft—to foreign representatives for the purpose of securing advantageous international trade contracts. In response to this unethical behavior, in 1977 Congress passed the Foreign Corrupt Practices Act (FCPA), which prohibits U.S. businesspersons from bribing foreign officials to secure advantageous contracts.

Prohibition against the Bribery of Foreign Officials. The first part of the FCPA applies to all U.S. companies and their directors, officers, shareholders, employees, and agents. This part prohibits the bribery of most officials of foreign governments if the purpose of the payment is to get the official to act in his or her official capacity to provide business opportunities.

The FCPA does not prohibit payment of substantial sums to minor officials whose duties are ministerial. These payments are often referred to as "grease," or facilitating payments. They are meant to accelerate the performance of administrative services that might otherwise be carried out at a slow pace. Thus, for example, if a firm makes a payment to a minor official to speed up an import licensing process, the firm has not violated the FCPA. Generally, the act, as amended, permits payments to foreign officials if such payments are lawful within the foreign country. The act also does not prohibit payments to private foreign companies or other third parties unless the U.S. firm knows that the payments will be passed on to a foreign government in violation of the FCPA.

Accounting Requirements. In the past, bribes were often concealed in corporate financial records. Thus, the second part of the FCPA is directed toward accountants. All companies must keep detailed records that "accurately and fairly" reflect the company's financial activities. In addition, all companies must have an accounting system that provides "reasonable assurance" that all transactions entered into by the company are accounted for and legal. These requirements assist in detecting illegal bribes. The FCPA further prohibits any person from making false statements to accountants or false entries in any record or account.

Penalties for Violations. In 1988, the FCPA was amended to provide that business firms that violate the act may be fined up to $2 million. Individual officers or directors who violate the FCPA may be fined up to $100,000 (the fine cannot be paid by the company) and may be imprisoned for up to five years.

Other Nations Denounce Bribery

For twenty years, the FCPA was the only law of its kind in the world, despite attempts by U.S. political leaders to convince other nations to pass similar legislation. That situation is now changing. In 1997, the Organization for

Economic Cooperation and Development, to which twenty-six of the world's leading industrialized nations belong, adopted a convention (treaty) that made the bribery of foreign public officials a serious crime. Each signatory is obligated to enact legislation within its nation in accordance with the treaty. The agreement may not only improve the ethical climate in international trade but may also level the playing field for U.S. businesspersons.

KEY TERMS

business ethics 118
categorical imperative 132
cost-benefit analysis 133
ethical reasoning 131
ethics 117
moral minimum 127
principle of rights 133
utilitarianism 133

FOR REVIEW

1. What is ethics? What is business ethics?
2. Why is business ethics important?
3. Why is ethical leadership important?
4. What is the relationship between business ethics and the law?
5. In what ways do duty-based ethical standards differ from outcome-based ethical standards?

QUESTIONS AND CASE PROBLEMS

4–1. Some business ethicists maintain that whereas personal ethics has to do with "right" or "wrong" behavior, business ethics is concerned with "appropriate" behavior. In other words, ethical behavior in business has less to do with moral principles than with what society deems to be appropriate behavior in the business context. Do you agree with this distinction? Do personal and business ethics ever overlap? Should personal ethics play any role in business ethical decision making?

4–2. Susan Whitehead serves on the city planning commission. The city is planning to build a new subway system, and Susan's brother-in-law, Jerry, who owns the Custom Transportation Co., has submitted the lowest bid for the system. Susan knows that Jerry could complete the job for the estimated amount, but she also knows that once Jerry completes this job, he will probably sell his company and quit working. Susan is concerned that Custom Transportation's subsequent management might not be as easy to work with if revisions need to be made on the subway system after its completion. She is torn as to whether she should tell the city about the potential changes in Custom Transportation's management. If the city knew about the instability of Custom Transportation, it might prefer to give the contract to one of Jerry's competitors, whose bid was only slightly higher than Jerry's. Does Susan have an ethical obligation to disclose the information about Jerry to the city planning commission? How would you apply duty-based ethical standards to this question? What might be the outcome of a utilitarian analysis? Discuss fully.

4–3. Assume that you are a high-level manager for a shoe manufacturer. You know that your firm could increase its profit margin by producing shoes in Indonesia, where you could hire women for $40 a month to assemble them. You also know, however, that human rights advocates recently accused a competing shoe manufacturer of engaging in exploitative labor practices because the manufacturer sold shoes made by Indonesian women working for similarly low wages. You personally do not believe that paying $40 a month to Indonesian women is unethical because you know that in that impoverished country, $40 a month is a better-than-average wage rate. Assuming that the decision is yours to make, should you have the shoes manufactured in Indonesia and make higher profits for your company? Or should you avoid the risk of negative publicity and the consequences of that publicity for the firm's reputation and subsequent profits? Are there other alternatives? Discuss fully.

4–4. Shokun Steel Co. owns many steel plants. One of its plants is much older than the others. Equipment at the old plant is outdated and inefficient, and the costs of production at that plant are now twice as high as at any of Shokun's other plants. Shokun cannot increase the price of its steel because of competition, both domestic and international. The plant is located in Twin Firs, Pennsylvania, which has a population of about 45,000, and currently employs over a thousand workers. Shokun is contemplating whether to close the plant. What factors should the firm consider in making its decision? Will the firm violate any ethical duties if it closes the plant? Analyze these questions from the two basic perspectives on ethical reasoning discussed in this chapter.

CASE PROBLEM WITH SAMPLE ANSWER

4–5. Consumer Welfare. Isuzu Motors America, Inc., does not warn its customers of the danger of riding unrestrained in the cargo beds of its pickup trucks. Seventeen-year-old Donald Josue was riding unrestrained in the bed of an Isuzu truck driven by Iaone Frias. When Frias lost control of the truck, it struck a concrete center divider. Josue was ejected and his consequent injuries rendered him a paraplegic. Josue filed a suit in a Hawaii state court against Isuzu, asserting a variety of legal claims based on its failure to warn of the danger of riding in the bed of the truck. Should Isuzu be held liable for Josue's injuries? Why or why not? [*Josue v. Isuzu Motors America, Inc.*, 87 Haw. 413, 958 P.2d 535 (1998)]

➧ *To view a sample answer for this case problem, go to this book's Web site at* **http://ele.westbuslaw.com** *and click on "Interactive Study Center."*

4–6. Ethical Conduct. Richard and Suzanne Weinstein owned Elm City Cheese Co. Elm City sold its products to three major customers that used the cheese as a "filler" to blend into their cheeses. In 1982, Mark Federico, a certified public accountant, became Elm City's accountant and the Weinsteins' personal accountant. The Weinsteins had known Federico since he was seven years old, and even before he became their accountant, he knew the details of Elm City's business. Federico's duties went beyond typical accounting work, and when the Weinsteins were absent, he was put in charge of operations. In 1992, Federico was made a vice president of the company, and a year later he was placed in charge of day-to-day operations. He also continued to serve as Elm City's accountant. The relationship between Federico and the Weinsteins deteriorated, and in 1995, he resigned as Elm City's employee and as its accountant. Less than two years later, Federico opened Lomar Foods, Inc., to make the same products as Elm City by the same process and to sell the products to the same customers. Federico located Lomar close to Elm City's suppliers. Elm City filed a suit in a Connecticut state court against Federico and Lomar, alleging, among other things, misappropriation of trade secrets. Elm City argued that it was entitled to punitive damages because Federico's conduct was "willful and malicious." Federico responded in part that he did not act willfully and maliciously because he did not know that Elm City's business details were trade secrets. Were Federico's actions "willful and malicious"? Were they ethical? Explain. [*Elm City Cheese Co. v. Federico,* 251 Conn. 59, 752 A.2d 1037 (1999)]

4–7. Ethical Conduct. Richard Fraser was an "exclusive career insurance agent" under a contract with Nationwide Mutual Insurance Co. Fraser leased computer hardware and software from Nationwide for his business. During a dispute between Nationwide and the Nationwide Insurance Independent Contractors Association, an organization representing Fraser and other exclusive career agents, Fraser prepared a letter to Nationwide's competitors asking whether they were interested in acquiring the represented agents' policyholders. Nationwide obtained a copy of the letter and searched its electronic file server for e-mail indicating that the letter had been sent. It found a stored e-mail that Fraser had sent to a co-worker indicating that the letter had been sent to at least one competitor. The e-mail was retrieved from the co-worker's file of already received and discarded messages stored on the server. When Nationwide canceled its contract with Fraser, he filed a suit in a federal district court against the firm, alleging, among other things, violations of various federal laws that prohibit the interception of electronic communications during transmission. In whose favor should the court rule, and why? In any event, did Nationwide act ethically in retrieving the e-mail? [*Fraser v. Nationwide Mutual Insurance Co.,* 135 F.Supp.2d 623 (E.D.Pa. 2001)]

4–8. IN YOUR COURT

Francis Rogowski fell asleep at the wheel of his Mazda pickup truck and collided head on with a large tree. To recover for the cost of his injuries, Rogowski sued the manufacturer of the pickup, Mazda Motor of America, Inc. Rogowski claimed, among other things, that Mazda should have warned him that the seat belts would not protect him from all injuries if he were in an accident. Assume that you are the judge in the trial court hearing this case and answer the following questions:

(a) The major issue before your court is whether the danger not warned of by Mazda (that the seat belts would not protect Rogowski from all injuries if he were in an accident) was open and obvious. If the danger was open and obvious, then Mazda had no duty to warn consumers of this danger under product liability laws. How will you rule on this issue? Why?

(b) Compare this case with Case 4.3 *(Pavlik v. Lane Ltd./Tobacco Exporters International)*, which involved a similar issue. What did the court decide in that case, and for what reasons? Does the court's decision in that case differ from your conclusion regarding Rogowski's claim? Explain.

4–9. A QUESTION OF ETHICS AND SOCIAL RESPONSIBILITY

Hazen Paper Co. manufactured paper and paperboard for use in such products as cosmetic wrap, lottery tickets, and pressure-sensitive items. Walter Biggins, a chemist hired by Hazen in 1977, developed a water-based paper coating that was both environmentally safe and of superior quality. By the mid-1980s, the company's sales had increased dramatically as a result of its extensive use of "Biggins Acrylic." Because of this, Biggins thought he deserved a substantial raise in salary, and from 1984 to 1986, Biggins's persistent requests for a raise became a bone of contention between him and his employers. Biggins ran a business on the side, which involved cleaning up hazardous wastes for various companies. Hazen told Biggins that unless he signed a "confidentiality agreement" promising to restrict his outside activities during the time he was employed by Hazen and for a limited period afterward, he would be fired. Biggins said he would sign the agreement only if Hazen raised his salary to $100,000. Hazen refused to do so, fired Biggins, and hired a younger man to replace him. At the time of his discharge in 1986, Biggins was sixty-two years old, had worked for the company nearly ten years, and was just a few weeks away from being entitled to pension rights worth about $93,000. In view of these circumstances, evaluate and answer the following questions. [*Hazen Paper Co. v. Biggins*, 507 U.S. 604, 113 S.Ct. 1701, 123 L.Ed.2d 338 (1993)]

(a) Did the company owe an ethical duty to Biggins to raise his salary, given the fact that its sales increased dramatically as a result of Biggins's efforts and ingenuity in developing the coating? If you were one of the company's executives, would you have increased Biggins's salary? Why or why not?

(b) Generally, what public policies come into conflict in cases involving employers who, for reasons of cost and efficiency of operations, fire older, higher-paid workers and replace them with younger, lower-paid workers? If you were an employer facing the need to cut back on personnel to save costs, what would you do, and on what ethical premises would you justify your decision?

4–10. FOR CRITICAL ANALYSIS

If a firm engages in "ethically responsible" behavior solely for the purpose of gaining profits from the goodwill it generates, the "ethical" behavior is essentially a means toward a self-serving end (profits and the accumulation of wealth). In this situation, is the firm acting unethically in any way? Should motive or conduct carry greater weight on the ethical scales in this situation?

For updated links to resources available on the Web, as well as a variety of other materials, visit this text's Web site at

http://ele.westbuslaw.com

As mentioned earlier in this chapter, West's Legal Studies in Business offers an "Inside Look" at Enron at

http://insidelook.westbuslaw.com

You can find articles on issues relating to shareholders and corporate accountability at the Corporate Governance Web site. Go to

http://www.corpgov.net

For an example of an online group that focuses on corporate activities from the perspective of corporate social responsibility, go to

http://www.corpwatch.org

Global Exchange offers information on global business activities, including some of the ethical issues stemming from those activities, at

http://www.globalexchange.org

LEGAL RESEARCH EXERCISES ON THE WEB

Go to **http://ele.westbuslaw.com,** the Web site that accompanies this text. Select "Interactive Study Center," and then click on "Chapter 4." There you will find the following Internet research exercises that you can perform to learn more about topics covered in this chapter.

Activity 4–1: LEGAL PERSPECTIVE—Ethics in Business

Activity 4–2: MANAGEMENT PERSPECTIVE—Environmental Self-Audits

BEFORE THE TEST

Go to **http://ele.westbuslaw.com,** the Web site that accompanies this text. Select "Interactive Quizzes." You will find at least twenty interactive questions relating to this chapter.

WESTLAW® CAMPUS

If your textbook provided for a subscription to Westlaw® Campus, or if you have otherwise purchased access to the Westlaw Campus database, you can access any of the cases presented or cited in this chapter by using your Westlaw Campus account.

FOCUS ON LEGAL REASONING
Pavlovich v. Superior Court

INTRODUCTION

Chapter 2 discusses jurisdiction. In this *Focus on Legal Reasoning,* we look at *Pavlovich v. Superior Court,*[1] a decision in which the court considered whether it could exercise jurisdiction over a nonresident defendant based solely on the individual's posting of information on a Web site.

CASE BACKGROUND

DVDs provide high-quality images digitally formatted on convenient five-inch media. Before the commercial release of DVDs containing movies, the Content Scrambling System (CSS) was developed to encrypt and protect copyrighted films on DVDs. The CSS prevents the playing and copying of movies on DVDs without the algorithms and keys to decrypt the data on the disc. DVD Copy Control Association, Inc. (DVD CCA), a nonprofit association based in California, controls and licenses the CSS.

Matthew Pavlovich studied computer engineering at Purdue University in Indiana, where he founded and led the LiVid video project. The project's Web site provided information but did not permit an interactive exchange of data or transact any business. LiVid's goal was "to improve video and DVD support for Linux" by enabling the decryption and copying of movie DVDs. In 1999, LiVid posted the code of a program called DeCSS, which allows users to circumvent the CSS. Currently, Pavlovich lives in Texas where he is the president of Media Driver, LLC.

DVD CCA filed a suit in a California state court against Pavlovich and others, alleging misappropriation of trade secrets (see Chapter 13). Pavlovich responded that California lacked jurisdiction over his person. The court rejected this contention. Pavlovich appealed to a state intermediate appellate court, which also concluded that the lower court's exercise of jurisdiction was reasonable. Pavlovich appealed to the California Supreme Court.

1. 29 Cal.4th 262, 58 P.3d 2, 127 Cal.Rptr.2d 329 (2002).

MAJORITY OPINION

BROWN, J.

Although we have never considered the scope of personal jurisdiction based solely on Internet use, other courts have considered this issue, and most have adopted *a sliding scale analysis.* * * * *[Under this analysis, a] passive Web site that does little more than make information available to those who are interested in it is not grounds for the exercise of personal jurisdiction.* * * * *Zippo Manufacturing Co. v. Zippo Dot Com, Inc.*, 952 F.Supp. 1119 (W.D.Pa. 1997). [Emphasis added.]

Here, LiVid's Web site merely posts information and has no interactive features. There is no evidence in the record suggesting that the site targeted California. Indeed, there is no evidence that any California resident ever visited, much less downloaded the DeCSS source code from, the LiVid Web site. Thus, Pavlovich's alleged conduct in * * * posting a passive Web site on the Internet is not, by itself, sufficient to subject him to jurisdiction in California. *Creating a site, like placing a product into the stream of commerce, may be felt nationwide—or even worldwide—but, without more, it is not an act purposefully directed toward the forum state.* Otherwise, personal jurisdiction in Internet-related cases would almost always be found in any forum in the country. Such a result would vitiate [render ineffective] long-held and inviolate [not violated] principles of personal jurisdiction. [Emphasis added.]

Nonetheless, DVD CCA contends * * * Pavlovich knew the posting would harm not only a licensing entity but also the motion picture, computer and consumer electronics industries centered in California. According to DVD CCA, this knowledge establishes that Pavlovich intentionally targeted California and is sufficient to confer jurisdiction * * * .

* * * *

* * * In most, if not all, intentional tort cases [*torts* are civil wrongs—see Chapter 12], the defendant is or should be aware of the industries that may be

affected by his tortious [legally wrongful under tort law] conduct. Consequently, any plaintiff connected to industries centered in California—i.e., the motion picture, computer, and consumer electronics industries—could sue an out-of-state defendant in California for intentional torts that *may* harm those industries. For example, any creator or purveyor of technology that enables copying of movies or computer software—including a student in Australia who develops a program for creating backup copies of software and distributes it to some of his classmates or a store owner in Africa who sells a device that makes digital copies of movies on videotape—would be subject to suit in California because they should have known their conduct may harm the motion picture or computer industries in California. Indeed, DVD CCA's interpretation would subject any defendant who commits an intentional tort affecting the motion picture, computer, or consumer electronics industries to jurisdiction in California even if the plaintiff was not a California resident. Under this logic, plaintiffs connected to the auto industry could sue any defendant in Michigan, plaintiffs connected to the financial industry could sue any defendant in New York, and plaintiffs connected to the potato industry could sue any defendant in Idaho. Because finding jurisdiction under the facts in this case would effectively subject all intentional tortfeasors whose conduct may harm industries in California to jurisdiction in California, we decline to do so.

* * * *

Accordingly, we reverse the judgment of the Court of Appeal and remand for further proceedings consistent with this opinion.

DISSENTING OPINION

BAXTER, J.

I respectfully dissent. That this case involves a powerful new medium of electronic communication, usable for good or ill, should not blind us to the essential facts and principles. The record indicates that, by intentionally posting an unlicensed decryption code for the Content Scrambling System (CSS) on their Internet Web sites, defendant and his network of "open source" associates sought to undermine and defeat the very purposes of the licensed CSS encryption technology, i.e., *copyright protection* for movies recorded on digital versatile discs (DVD's) and *limitation of playback* to operating systems licensed to unscramble the encryption code. The intended targets of this effort were not individual persons or businesses, but entire industries. Defendant knew at least two of the intended targets—the movie industry and the computer industry involved in producing the licensed playback systems—either were centered in California or maintained a particularly substantial presence here. Thus, the record amply supports the trial court's conclusion, for purposes of specific personal jurisdiction, that defendant's intentional act, even if committed outside California, was "expressly aimed" at California.

In the particular circumstances, it cannot matter that defendant may not have known or cared about the *exact identities* or *precise locations* of each individual target, or that he happened to employ a so-called passive Internet Web site, or whether any California resident visited the site. By acting with the broad intent to harm *industries he knew were centered or substantially present in this state,* defendant forged sufficient minimum contacts with *California* that he should reasonably anticipate being haled into court *here.* [Emphasis in original.]

* * * *

Accordingly, I conclude the Court of Appeal's judgment should be affirmed.

LEGAL REASONING AND ANALYSIS

1 Legal Analysis. The majority cites, in its opinion, *Zippo Manufacturing Co. v. Zippo Dot Com, Inc.,* 952 F.Supp. 1119 (W.D.Pa. 1997) (see the *Law on the Web* feature at the end of Chapter 2 for instructions on how to access federal court opinions). Compare the facts and issues in that case to those of the *Pavlovich* case. How are the legal principles expressed in the *Zippo* case applied to the facts and issues of the *Pavlovich* case?

2 Legal Reasoning. What reasons does the dissent give to support its assertion that the majority's opinion is incorrect?

3 Legal Application. If all other courts rule as the majority in the *Pavlovich* case did, what will be

FOCUS ON LEGAL REASONING

the likely result? If all other courts adopt the opinion of the dissent, what might be the effect?

❹ **Implications for the Business Owner.** Does the decision in this case mean that a business has no forum in which to file a complaint against a nonresident defendant based on conduct such as Pavlovich's?

❺ **Case Briefing Assignment.** Using the guidelines for briefing cases given in the "Preface to the Student" at the beginning of this text, brief the *Pavlovich* case.

GOING ONLINE

This text's Web site, at **http://ele.westbuslaw.com,** offers links to West's Court Case Updates, as well as to other online research sources. You can also locate court cases at the Web sites listed in the *Law on the Web* section at the end of Chapter 2.

A page within the Web site of the Legal Information Institute (LII), at **http://www.law.cornell.edu/topics/jurisdiction.html,** includes links to court decisions, federal and state statutes, and other resources on jurisdiction. The LII is part of Cornell Law School in Ithaca, New York.

UNIT ONE

FOCUS ON ETHICS

Ethics and the Legal Environment of Business

Recall from Chapter 4 that *ethics* can be defined as the study of what constitutes right or wrong behavior. *Business ethics,* as the term implies, focuses on what constitutes right or wrong behavior in the business world. Certainly, it is not wrong for a businessperson to try to increase his or her firm's profits. But there are limits, both ethical and legal, to how far businesspersons can go. In the early 2000s, for example, it was clear that such firms as Enron Corporation, WorldCom, Inc., and Arthur Andersen, LLP, had overreached these limits. The public was outraged when the deceptive accounting practices and stock-price manipulations of these firms came to light and pressured Congress to enact legislation requiring greater accountability. The consequences for the companies themselves included bankruptcy.

In preparing for a career in business, you will find that a background in business ethics and a commitment to ethical behavior are just as important as a knowledge of the specific laws that are covered in this text. Of course, no textbook can give an answer to each and every ethical question that arises in the business environment. Nor can it anticipate the types of ethical questions that will arise in the future, as technology continues to transform the workplace and business relationships.

The most we can do is examine the types of ethical issues that businesspersons have faced in the past and that they are confronting today. In Chapter 4, we looked at

the ethical standards that typically guide businesspersons when making decisions, as well as at other aspects of ethical business behavior. In the *Focus on Ethics* sections in this book, we provide examples of specific ethical issues that have arisen in various areas of business activity.

In this initial *Focus on Ethics,* we look first at various obstacles to ethical behavior in the business context. We then examine the concept of corporate social responsibility, which is a significant element of today's legal environment of business.

OBSTACLES TO ETHICAL BUSINESS BEHAVIOR

People sometimes behave unethically in the business context, just as they do in their private lives. Some businesspersons knowingly engage in unethical behavior because they think that they can "get away with it"—that no one will ever learn of their unethical actions.

Examples of this kind of unethical behavior include padding expense accounts, casting doubts on the integrity of a rival co-worker to gain a job promotion, stealing company supplies or equipment, and so on. Obviously, these acts are unethical, and many of them are illegal as well. In some situations, however, businesspersons who would choose to act ethically may be deterred from doing so because of situational circumstances or external pressures.

Ethics and the Corporate Environment

Individuals in their personal lives normally are free to decide ethical issues as they wish and to follow through on those decisions. In the business world, and particularly in the corporate environment, rarely is such a decision made by one person. If you are an officer or a manager of a large company, for example, you will find that the decision as to what is right or wrong for the company is not totally yours to make. Your input may weigh in the conclusion, but ultimately a corporate decision is a collective undertaking.

Additionally, collective decision making, because it places emphasis on consensus and unity of opinion, tends to hinder individual ethical assertiveness. For example, suppose that a director has ethical misgivings about a planned corporate venture that promises to be highly profitable. If the other directors have no such misgivings, the director who does may be swayed by the others' enthusiasm for the project and downplay her or his own criticisms.

Furthermore, just as no one person makes a collective decision, so no one person (normally) is held accountable for the decision. The corporate enterprise thus tends

FOCUS ON ETHICS

to shield corporate personnel from both personal exposure to the consequences of their decisions (such as direct experience with someone who suffers harm from a corporate product) and personal accountability for those decisions.

Ethics and Management

As you learned in Chapter 4, much unethical business behavior occurs simply because management does not always make clear what ethical standards and behaviors are expected of the firm's employees. Although most firms now issue ethical policies or codes of conduct, these policies and codes are not always effective in creating an ethical workplace. At times, this is because the firm's ethical policies are not communicated clearly to employees or do not bear on the real ethical issues confronting decision makers.

Additionally, particularly in a large corporation, unethical behavior in one corporate department may simply escape the attention of those in control of the corporation or the corporate officials responsible for implementing and monitoring the company's ethics program.

CORPORATE SOCIAL RESPONSIBILITY

At one time, businesses faced few ethical requirements other than complying with the law. Generally, if an action was legal, it was regarded as ethical. By the 1960s, however, this attitude had begun to change significantly. Groups concerned with civil rights, employee safety and welfare, consumer protection, environmental preservation, and other principles began to pressure corporate America to behave in a more responsible manner with respect to these principles. Thus was born the concept of *corporate social responsibility*—the idea that corporations can and should act ethically and be accountable to society for their actions.

Just what constitutes corporate social responsibility has been debated for some time. Clearly, though, corporations that go too far in an attempt to increase their profits at the expense of individuals and groups affected by their decisions ultimately may face public outrage and government remedial action—as Enron, WorldCom, and other companies learned in the early 2000s.

Generally, the debate over corporate social responsibility has to do less with whether corporations *should* be responsible than with *how* and *to whom* they should be responsible. Today, there are a number of views on this issue, including those discussed next.

Profit Maximization

Corporate directors and officers have a duty to act in the shareholders' interests. Because of the nature of the relationship between corporate directors and officers and the shareholder-owners, the law holds directors and officers to a high standard of care in business decision making (see Chapter 9). Traditionally, it was perceived that this duty to shareholders took precedence over all other corporate duties and that the primary goal of corporations should be profit maximization. Milton Friedman, the Nobel Prize–winning economist and a proponent of the profit-maximization view, saw "one and only one" social responsibility of a corporation: "to use its resources and engage in activities designed to increase its profits, so long as it stays within the rules of the game, which is to say, engages in open and free competition without deception and fraud."[1]

Those who accept this position argue that a firm can best contribute to society by generating profits. Society benefits because a firm realizes profits only when it markets products or services that are desired by society. These products and services enhance the standard of living, and the profits accumulated by successful businesses generate national wealth. Our laws and court decisions promoting trade and commerce reflect the public policy that the fruits of commerce (income and wealth) are desirable and good. Because our society regards income and wealth as ethical goals, corporations, by contributing to income and wealth, automatically are acting ethically.

The Stakeholder Approach

Another view of corporate social responsibility stresses that a corporation's duty to its shareholders should be weighed against its duties to other groups affected by corporate decisions. Corporate decision makers should consider not only the welfare of shareholders but also that of

1. Milton Friedman, "Does Business Have Social Responsibility?" *Bank Administration,* April 1971, pp. 13–14.

FOCUS ON ETHICS

stakeholders—employees, customers, suppliers, communities, and any group that has a stake in the corporation. The reasoning behind this "stakeholder view" of corporate social responsibility is that in some circumstances, one or more of these groups may have a greater stake in company decisions than the shareholders do.

Consider an example. A heavily indebted corporation is facing imminent bankruptcy. The shareholder-investors have little to lose in this situation because their stock is already next to worthless. The corporation's creditors will be first in line for any corporate assets remaining. Because in this situation it is the creditors who have the greatest "stake" in the corporation, under the stakeholder view, corporate directors and officers should give greater weight to the creditors' interests than to those of the shareholders.

Corporate Citizenship

Another theory of social responsibility argues that corporations should actively promote goals that society deems worthwhile and take positive steps toward solving social problems. Because so much of the wealth and power of this country is controlled by business, business in turn has a responsibility to society to use that wealth and power in socially beneficial ways. To be sure, since the nineteenth century and the emergence of large business enterprises in America, corporations have generally contributed some of their shareholders' wealth to meet social needs. Indeed, virtually all large corporations today have established nonprofit foundations for this purpose. Yet corporate citizenship requires more than just making donations to worthwhile causes. Under a corporate citizenship view of social responsibility, companies are also judged on how they conduct their affairs with respect to employment discrimination, human rights, environmental concerns, and so on.

Critics of this view believe that it is inappropriate to use the power of the corporate business world to fashion society's goals by promoting social causes. Determinations as to what exactly is in society's best interest involve questions that are essentially political; therefore, the public, through the political process, should have a say in making those determinations. The legislature—not the corporate board room—is thus the appropriate forum for such decisions.

It Pays to Be Ethical

Most corporations today have learned that it pays to be ethically responsible—even if it means less profit in the short run (and it often does). Today's corporations are subject to more intensive scrutiny—by both government agencies and the public—than corporations of the past. "Corporate watch" groups monitor the activities of U.S. corporations, including activities conducted in foreign countries. With the availability of the Internet, complaints about a corporation's practices can easily be published to a worldwide audience. Similarly, dissatisfied customers and employees can voice their complaints about corporate policies, products, or services in Internet chat rooms and other online forums. Thus, if a corporation fails to conduct its operations ethically or to respond quickly to an ethical crisis, its goodwill and reputation (and thus future profits) will likely suffer as a result.

There are other reasons as well for a corporation to behave ethically. For example, companies that demonstrate a commitment to ethical behavior—by implementing ethical programs, complying with environmental regulations, and promptly investigating product complaints, for example—often receive more lenient treatment from government agencies and the courts. Additionally, investors may shy away from a corporation's stock if the corporation is perceived to be socially irresponsible. Finally, unethical (and/or illegal) corporate behavior may result in government action—new laws imposing further requirements on corporate entities.

DISCUSSION QUESTIONS

❶ What might be some other deterrents to ethical behavior in the business context, besides those discussed in this *Focus?*

❷ Can you think of a situation in which a business firm may be acting ethically but not in a socially responsible manner? Explain.

❸ Why are consumers and the public generally more concerned with ethical and socially responsible business behavior today than they were, say, fifty years ago?

FOCUS ON ETHICS

❹ Perceptions of social responsibility differ among countries. Discuss some of the ethical implications of these differences for American firms that do business abroad.

❺ Suppose that an automobile manufacturing company has to choose between two alternatives: contributing $1 million annually to the United Way or reinvesting the $1 million in the company. In terms of ethics and social responsibility, which is the better choice?

UNIT TWO

The Public and International Environment

CHAPTER 5

Constitutional Law

CONTENTS

CHAPTER OBJECTIVES

After reading this chapter, you should be able to answer the following questions:

1. What is the basic structure of the U.S. government?

2. Which constitutional clause empowers the federal government to regulate commercial activities among the states?

3. Which constitutional clause gives laws enacted by the federal government priority over conflicting state laws?

4. What is the Bill of Rights, and which freedoms are guaranteed by the First Amendment?

5. Where in the Constitution can the due process clause be found?

The U.S. Constitution is the supreme law in this country.[1] As mentioned in Chapter 1, neither Congress nor any state may pass a law that conflicts with the Constitution. Laws that govern business have their origin in the lawmaking authority granted by this document.

In this chapter, we examine some basic constitutional concepts and clauses and their significance for businesspersons. We then look at certain freedoms guaranteed by the first ten amendments to the Constitution—the Bill of Rights—and discuss how these freedoms affect business activities.

THE CONSTITUTIONAL POWERS OF GOVERNMENT

Following the Revolutionary War, the states created a *confederal form* of government. The Articles of Confederation, which went into effect in 1781, established a confederation of independent states and a central government of very limited powers. The central government could handle only those matters of common concern expressly delegated to it by the member states, and the national congress had no authority to make laws directly applicable to individuals unless the member states explicitly supported such laws. In short, the *sovereign power*[2] to govern rested essentially with the states. The Articles of Confederation clearly reflected the central tenet of the American Revolution—that a national government should not have unlimited power.

The confederation, however, faced serious problems. For one thing, laws passed by the various states hampered national commerce and foreign trade by preventing the free movement of goods and services across state borders. By 1784, the nation faced a serious economic depression. Many who could not afford to pay their debts were thrown into "debtors' prisons." By 1786, a series of uprisings by farmer debtors were proving difficult to control because

1. See Appendix A for the full text of the U.S. Constitution.
2. Sovereign power refers to that supreme power to which no other authority is superior or equal.

the national government did not have the authority to raise revenues (by levying taxes, for example) to support a militia.

Amend • To change and improve through a formal procedure.

Because of these problems, a national convention was called to **amend** (change, alter) the Articles of Confederation. Instead of amending the Articles, however, the delegates to the convention, now called the Constitutional Convention, created the Constitution and a completely new type of government. Many of the provisions of the Constitution, including those discussed in the following pages, were shaped by the delegates' experiences during the confederal era (1781–1789).

A Federal Form of Government

Federal form of government • A system of government in which the states form a union and the sovereign power is divided between a central government and the member states.

The new government created by the Constitution reflected a series of compromises made by the convention delegates on various issues. Some delegates wanted sovereign power to remain with the states; others wanted the national government alone to exercise sovereign power. The end result was a compromise—a **federal form of government** in which the national government and the states *share* sovereign power.

The Constitution sets forth specific powers that can be exercised by the national government and provides that the national government has the implied power to undertake actions necessary to carry out its expressly designated powers. All other powers are retained by the states. According to the language of the Tenth Amendment to the Constitution, "The powers not delegated to the United States by the Constitution, nor prohibited by it to the States, are reserved to the States respectively, or to the people."

National versus State Powers—An Ongoing Debate. The broad language of the Constitution has left much room for debate over the specific nature and scope of the respective powers of the states and the national government. Generally, it has been the task of the courts to determine where the boundary line between state and national powers should lie—and that line changes over time. For most of the twentieth century, for example, the national government met little resistance from the courts when extending its regulatory authority over broad areas of social and economic life. Today, in contrast, the courts, and particularly the United States Supreme Court, are more willing to interpret the Constitution in such a way as to curb the national government's regulatory powers and bolster the rights of state governments.

Relations among the States. The Constitution also includes provisions concerning relations among the states in our federal system. Particularly important are the privileges and immunities clause and the full faith and credit clause.

Privileges and immunities clause • A provision found in Article IV, Section 2, of the Constitution that requires states not to discriminate against one another's citizens. A resident of one state cannot be treated as an alien when in another state; he or she may not be denied such privileges and immunities as legal protection, access to courts, travel rights, or property rights.

The Privileges and Immunities Clause. Article IV, Section 2, of the U.S. Constitution provides that the "Citizens of each State shall be entitled to all Privileges and Immunities of Citizens in the several States." This clause is often referred to as the interstate **privileges and immunities clause.**[3] When a citizen of one state engages in basic and essential activities in another

3. Interpretations of this clause commonly use the terms *privilege* and *immunity* synonymously. Generally, the terms refer to certain rights, benefits, or advantages enjoyed by individuals.

state (the "foreign state"), such as transferring property, seeking employment, or accessing the court system, the foreign state must have a *substantial reason* for treating the nonresident differently from its own residents. The foreign state must also establish that its reason for the discrimination is substantially related to the state's ultimate purpose in adopting the legislation or activity.[4]

Charging nonresidents $2,500 for a shrimp-fishing license, for example, when residents are charged only $25 for the same license, may be considered unconstitutional discrimination against nonresidents who are pursuing the essential activity of making a living.[5] Similarly, attempting to limit the practice of law to residents only (on the premise that it would help reduce the state's unemployment rate) may unconstitutionally restrict a nonresident's professional pursuit without substantial justification.[6]

The Fourteenth Amendment provides that "[n]o State shall make or enforce any law which shall abridge the privileges or immunities of citizens of the United States."[7]

The Full Faith and Credit Clause. Article IV, Section 1, of the Constitution provides that "Full Faith and Credit shall be given in each State to the public Acts, Records, and judicial Proceedings of every other State." This clause, which is referred to as the **full faith and credit clause,** applies only to civil matters. It ensures that rights established under deeds, wills, contracts, and the like in one state will be honored by other states. It also ensures that any judicial decision with respect to such property rights will be honored and enforced in all states.

Full faith and credit clause • A clause in Article IV, Section 1, of the Constitution that provides that rights established under deeds, wills, contracts, and the like in one state will be honored by the other states and that any judicial decision with respect to such property rights will be honored and enforced in all states.

The full faith and credit clause originally was included in the Articles of Confederation to promote mutual friendship among the people of the various states. In fact, it has contributed to the unity of American citizens because it protects their legal rights as they move about from state to state. It also protects the rights of those to whom they owe obligations, such as judgment creditors. This is extremely important for the conduct of business in a country with a very mobile citizenry.

The Separation of National Government Powers

To prevent the possibility that the national government might use its power arbitrarily, the Constitution provided for three branches of government. The legislative branch makes the laws, the executive branch enforces the laws, and the judicial branch interprets the laws. Each branch performs a separate function, and no branch may exercise the authority of another branch.

Each branch, however, has some power to limit the actions of the other two branches. Congress, for example, can enact legislation relating to spending and commerce, but the president can veto that legislation. The executive branch is responsible for foreign affairs, but treaties with foreign governments require the advice and consent of members of the Senate. Although Congress determines the jurisdiction of the federal courts, the federal courts have the power to hold acts of the other branches of the federal government

4. *Supreme Court of New Hampshire v. Piper,* 470 U.S. 274, 105 S.Ct. 1272, 84 L.Ed.2d 205 (1985).

5. *Toomer v. Witsell,* 334 U.S. 385, 68 S.Ct. 1156, 92 L.Ed. 1460 (1948).

6. *Hicklin v. Orbeck,* 437 U.S. 518, 98 S.Ct. 2482, 57 L.Ed.2d 397 (1978).

7. This clause protects all individuals, as citizens of the United States, from *state* action that might infringe on their privileges or immunities.

Checks and balances • The national government is composed of three separate branches: the executive, the legislative, and the judicial branches. Each branch of the government exercises a check on the actions of the others.

Commerce clause • The provision in Article I, Section 8, of the U.S. Constitution that gives Congress the power to regulate interstate commerce.

unconstitutional.[8] Thus, with this system of **checks and balances,** no one branch of government can accumulate too much power.

The Commerce Clause

To prevent states from establishing laws and regulations that would interfere with trade and commerce among the states, the Constitution expressly delegated to the national government the power to regulate interstate commerce. Article I, Section 8, of the U.S. Constitution expressly permits Congress "[t]o regulate Commerce with foreign Nations, and among the several States, and with the Indian Tribes." This clause, referred to as the **commerce clause,** has had a greater impact on business than any other provision in the Constitution. The commerce clause provides the basis for the national government's extensive regulation of state and even local affairs.

One of the early questions raised by the commerce clause was whether the word *among* in the phrase "among the several States" meant *between* the states or *between and within* the states. For some time, the national government's power under the commerce clause was interpreted to apply only to commerce between the states (*interstate* commerce) and not to commerce within the states (*intrastate* commerce). In 1824, however, in *Gibbons v. Ogden,*[9] the United States Supreme Court held that commerce within the states could also be regulated by the national government as long as the commerce *substantially affected* commerce involving more than one state.

The Expansion of National Powers under the Commerce Clause. As the nation grew and faced new kinds of problems, the commerce clause became a vehicle for the additional expansion of the national government's regulatory powers. Even activities that seemed purely local in nature came under the regulatory reach of the national government if those activities were deemed to substantially affect interstate commerce.

In a 1942 case, for example, the Supreme Court held that wheat production by an individual farmer intended wholly for consumption on his own farm was subject to federal regulation.[10] In *Heart of Atlanta Motel v. United States,*[11] a landmark case decided in 1964, the Supreme Court upheld the national government's authority to prohibit racial discrimination nationwide in public facilities, including local motels, based on its powers under the commerce clause. The Court noted that "if it is interstate commerce that feels the pinch, it does not matter how local the operation that applies the squeeze." In *McLain v. Real Estate Board of New Orleans, Inc.,*[12] a 1980 case, the Supreme Court acknowledged that the commerce clause had "long been interpreted to extend beyond activities actually in interstate commerce to reach other activities, while wholly local in nature, which nevertheless substantially affect interstate commerce."

---

8. As discussed in Chapter 2, the power of judicial review was established by the United States Supreme Court in *Marbury v. Madison,* 5 U.S. (1 Cranch) 137, 2 L.Ed. 60 (1803).

9. 22 U.S. (9 Wheat.) 1, 6 L.Ed. 23 (1824).

10. *Wickard v. Filburn,* 317 U.S. 111, 63 S.Ct. 82, 87 L.Ed. 122 (1942).

11. 379 U.S. 241, 85 S.Ct. 348, 13 L.Ed.2d 258 (1964).

12. 444 U.S. 232, 100 S.Ct. 502, 62 L.Ed.2d 441 (1980).

The Commerce Power Today. Today, at least theoretically, the power over commerce authorizes the national government to regulate all commercial enterprises in the United States. The breadth of the commerce clause permits the national government to legislate in areas in which Congress has not explicitly been granted power. In the last decade, however, the Supreme Court has begun to curb somewhat the national government's regulatory authority under the commerce clause. In 1995, the Court held—for the first time in sixty years—that Congress had exceeded its regulatory authority under the commerce clause. The Court stated that the Gun-Free School Zones Act of 1990, which banned the possession of guns within one thousand feet of any school, was unconstitutional because it attempted to regulate an area that had "nothing to do with commerce."[13]

Two years later, in 1997, the Court struck down portions of the Brady Handgun Violence Prevention Act of 1993, which obligated state and local law enforcement officers to do background checks on prospective handgun buyers until a national instant check system could be implemented. The Court stated that Congress lacked the power to "dragoon" state employees into federal service through an unfunded mandate of this kind.[14] In 2000, the Court invalidated key portions of the federal Violence Against Women Act of 1994, which allowed women to sue in federal court when they were victims of gender-motivated violence, such as rape. According to the Court, the commerce clause did not justify national regulation of noneconomic, criminal conduct.[15]

Nonetheless, the commerce clause continues to serve as the constitutional backbone for national laws regulating a broad number of activities, including activities that may jeopardize privacy rights. At issue in the following case was whether Congress had exceeded its constitutional authority when it passed the Driver's Privacy Protection Act (DPPA) of 1994.

13. *United States v. Lopez,* 514 U.S. 549, 115 S.Ct. 1624, 131 L.Ed.2d 626 (1995).
14. *Printz v. United States,* 521 U.S. 898, 117 S.Ct. 2365, 138 L.Ed.2d 914 (1997).
15. *United States v. Morrison,* 529 U.S. 598, 120 S.Ct. 1740, 146 L.Ed.2d 658 (2000).

RENO v. CONDON

CASE 5.1

Supreme Court of the United States, 2000.
528 U.S. 141,
120 S.Ct. 666,
145 L.Ed.2d 587.
http://supct.law.cornell.edu/supct/cases/name.htm[a]

Each state's Department of Motor Vehicles (DMV) requires drivers and automobile owners to provide personal information, including name, address, telephone number, and Social Security number, as a condition of obtaining a driver's license or registering an automobile. Many states sell this information to individuals and businesses. Wisconsin's DMV, for example, receives approximately $8 million each year from the sale of such data. Under the DPPA, before a state can sell this information, a driver must consent to its release. In other words, a person must choose to "opt in." There are exceptions for government use, motor vehicle recalls, and certain other purposes. In contrast to the federal DPPA, under South Carolina state law, information in DMV

a. This is the "Historic Supreme Court Decisions—by Party Name" page within the "Caselists" collection of Cornell University's Legal Information Institute. Click on the "R" link or scroll down the list of cases to the entry for the *Reno* case to access the opinion.

records is available to anyone who promises not to use it for telemarketing. Only if a South Carolina driver affirmatively "opts out" will the state of South Carolina refuse to release the information. Charles Condon, the attorney general of South Carolina, filed a suit in a federal district court against Janet Reno, then the attorney general of the United States, alleging that the DPPA violated the U.S. Constitution. The court granted an injunction to prevent the DPPA's enforcement, and the U.S. Court of Appeals for the Fourth Circuit upheld the order. Reno appealed to the United States Supreme Court.

REHNQUIST, C.J.

The United States asserts that the DPPA is a proper exercise of Congress's authority to regulate interstate commerce under the Commerce Clause. The United States bases its Commerce Clause argument on the fact that the personal, identifying information that the DPPA regulates is a "thin[g] in interstate commerce," and that the sale or release of that information in interstate commerce is therefore a proper subject of congressional regulation. We agree with the United States' contention. The motor vehicle information which the States have historically sold is used by insurers, manufacturers, direct marketers, and others engaged in interstate commerce to contact drivers with customized solicitations. The information is also used in the stream of interstate commerce by various public and private entities for matters related to interstate motoring. *Because drivers' information is, in this context, an article of commerce, its sale or release into the interstate stream of business is sufficient to support congressional regulation.* * * * [Emphasis added.]

But the fact that drivers' personal information is, in the context of this case, an article in interstate commerce does not conclusively resolve the constitutionality of the DPPA. In [other cases] we held federal statutes invalid * * * because those statutes violated the principles of federalism contained in the Tenth Amendment.[b] * * * While Congress has substantial powers to govern the Nation directly, including in areas of intimate concern to the States, *the Constitution has never been understood to confer upon Congress the ability to require the States to govern according to Congress's instructions.* [Emphasis added.]

* * * Congress cannot compel the States to enact or enforce a federal regulatory program. * * * Congress cannot circumvent that prohibition by conscripting the States' officers directly. The Federal Government may neither issue directives requiring the States to address particular problems, nor command the States' officers, or those of their political subdivisions, to administer or enforce a federal regulatory program.

* * * *

* * * [However, the] DPPA does not require the States in their sovereign capacity to regulate their own citizens. The DPPA regulates the States as the owners of databases. It does not require the South Carolina Legislature to enact any laws or regulations, and it does not require state officials to assist in the enforcement of federal statutes regulating private individuals. We

---

b. Under the Tenth Amendment to the U.S. Constitution, "[t]he powers not delegated to the United States by the Constitution, nor prohibited by it to the States, are reserved to the States respectively, or to the people."

accordingly conclude that the DPPA is consistent with the constitutional principles * * *.

The United States Supreme Court reversed the judgment of the U.S. Court of Appeals for the Fourth Circuit. The Supreme Court held that the DPPA was a proper exercise of Congress's power under the commerce clause and did not violate other constitutional provisions.

QUESTIONS

1. Who brought this case to court, and who was the opposing party?
2. According to the United States Supreme Court, is the DPPA a proper exercise of Congress's power under the commerce clause? Why or why not?
3. Are there ethical reasons for a state to keep private its drivers' personal information?

The Regulatory Powers of the States. As part of their inherent sovereignty, state governments have the authority to regulate affairs within their borders. This authority stems in part from the Tenth Amendment to the Constitution, which reserves all powers not delegated to the national government to the states, or to the people. State regulatory powers are often referred to as **police powers.** The term does not relate solely to criminal law enforcement but rather refers to the broad right of state governments to regulate private activities to protect or promote the public order, health, safety, morals, and general welfare. Fire and building codes, antidiscrimination laws, parking regulations, zoning restrictions, licensing requirements, and thousands of other state statutes covering virtually every aspect of life have been enacted pursuant to states' police powers. Local governments, including cities, also exercise police powers.[16]

Police powers • Powers possessed by states as part of their inherent sovereignty. These powers may be exercised to protect or promote the public order, health, safety, morals, and general welfare.

State Regulation and the "Dormant" Commerce Clause. The United States Supreme Court has interpreted the commerce clause to mean that the national government has the *exclusive* authority to regulate commerce that substantially affects trade and commerce among the states. This express grant of authority to the national government, which is often referred to as the "positive" aspect of the commerce clause, implies a negative aspect—that the states do *not* have the authority to regulate interstate commerce. This negative aspect of the commerce clause is often referred to as the "dormant" (implied) commerce clause.

The dormant commerce clause comes into play when state regulations impinge on interstate commerce. In this situation, the courts normally weigh the state's interest in regulating a certain matter against the burden that the state's regulation places on interstate commerce. For example, in one case, the United States Supreme Court invalidated state regulations that, in the interest of promoting traffic safety, limited the length of trucks traveling on the state's

---

16. Local governments derive their authority to regulate their communities from the state, because they are creatures of the state. In other words, they cannot come into existence unless authorized by the state to do so.

highways. The Court concluded that the regulations imposed a "substantial burden on interstate commerce" yet failed to "make more than the most speculative contribution to highway safety."[17] Because courts balance the interests involved, it is extremely difficult to predict the outcome in a particular case.

An emerging issue relates to state laws that regulate interstate commerce via the Internet. The court in the following case applied this balancing test to a state statute regulating unsolicited commercial e-mail, or spam. (For a discussion of how commerce clause principles are being applied in cases involving the sale of wine via the Internet, see this chapter's *Contemporary Legal Debates* feature on pages 158 and 159.)

17. *Raymond Motor Transportation, Inc. v. Rice,* 434 U.S. 429, 98 S.Ct. 787, 54 L.Ed.2d 664 (1978).

CASE 5.2

California Court of Appeal, First District, 2002. 94 Cal.App.4th 1255, 115 Cal.Rptr.2d 258.

FERGUSON v. FRIENDFINDERS, INC.

Friendfinders, Inc., and other businesses in Palo Alto, California, sent unsolicited e-mail ads to Mark Ferguson, a California resident. Contrary to the requirements of Section 17538.4 of the California Business and Professions Code, the subject lines of the e-mail ads did not begin with the characters "ADV," the first lines in the ads did not contain information about how recipients could have their e-mail addresses removed from future ad campaigns, the ads did not include valid return e-mail addresses to which the recipients could respond, and the ads' headers were altered to mask the senders' identities. Ferguson filed a suit in a California state court against Friendfinders and the others, alleging in part that the transmission of the ads was an unfair business practice because the ads were misleading and deceptive without the required information. Ferguson asked for damages and an injunction. The defendants responded that the state statute was an unconstitutional interference with interstate commerce, arguing that the Internet cannot be regulated by individual states because it is a national infrastructure without territorial boundaries. The court dismissed Ferguson's suit, holding that the statute violated the dormant commerce clause. Ferguson appealed to a state intermediate appellate court.

HAERLE, J.

[T]he costs created by UCE [unsolicited commercial e-mail] are substantial. Internet Service Providers (ISPs) incur significant business related costs accommodating bulk e-mail advertising and dealing with the problems it creates. ISPs attempt to defray those costs by charging higher fees to their customers. Individuals who receive UCE can experience increased Internet access fees because of the time required to sort, read, discard and attempt to prevent future sending of UCE. If the individual undertakes this process at work, his or her employer suffers the financial consequences of the wasted time.

The financial harms caused by the proliferation of UCE have been exacerbated by the use of deceptive tactics which are used to disguise the identity of the UCE sender and the nature of his or her message. * * *

* * * *

* * * *[P]rotecting a state's citizens from the economic damage caused by deceptive UCE constitutes a legitimate local purpose.* In addition, we find that deceptive UCE poses noneconomic dangers as well. * * * Studies indicate

that UCE often contains offensive subject matter, is a favored method for pursuing questionable if not fraudulent business schemes, and has been successfully used to spread harmful computer viruses. [Emphasis added.]

We find that California has a substantial legitimate interest in protecting its citizens from the harmful effects of deceptive UCE and that Section 17538.4 furthers that important interest. *By requiring disclosure of the advertising * * * nature of an unsolicited e-mail in the subject line, Section 17538.4 establishes a quick and simple way of identifying UCE without having to read it first.* By requiring establishment and disclosure of a legitimate procedure for responding to a UCE, Section 17538.4 holds UCE senders accountable for their actions. And, by requiring that senders of UCE honor requests that future mailings not be sent to recipients who do not want them, Section 17538.4 protects California residents from all of the potential harms associated with unwanted UCE. [Emphasis added.]

* * * *

To the extent that Section 17538.4 requires truthfulness in advertising, it does not burden interstate commerce at all but actually facilitates it by eliminating fraud and deception. Further, truthfulness requirements * * * make spamming unattractive to many fraudulent spammers, thereby reducing the volume of spam. Nor do the statute's affirmative disclosure requirements impose any appreciable burden on senders of UCE. * * * [T]he cost of placing particular letters in the subject line of the e-mail and including a valid return address in the message itself is appreciably zero in terms of time and expense. Finally, respondents do not identify any burden on interstate commerce arising from the requirement that an express request to be eliminated from a UCE sender's mailing list must be honored. Any conceivable burden clearly does not outweigh the local benefits of Section 17538.4.

The state intermediate appellate court held that the state statute regulating unsolicited e-mail ads did not violate the dormant commerce clause of the Constitution. The court reversed this part of the lower court's decision and remanded the case for further proceedings. The appellate court reasoned that the burdens the statute imposed on interstate commerce were minimal and did not outweigh the statute's benefits.

QUESTIONS

1. Why did Friendfinders, Inc., and the other defendants argue on appeal that the state statute was an unconstitutional interference with interstate commerce?
2. Why did the state intermediate appellate court reverse the lower court's dismissal of Ferguson's suit?
3. Why are some individuals and organizations attempting to inhibit the use of e-mail as an advertising tool?

Supremacy clause • The provision in Article VI of the Constitution that provides that the Constitution, laws, and treaties of the United States are "the supreme Law of the Land." Under this clause, state and local laws that directly conflict with federal laws will be rendered invalid.

The Supremacy Clause and Federal Preemption

Article VI of the Constitution provides that the Constitution, laws, and treaties of the United States are "the supreme Law of the Land." This article, commonly referred to as the **supremacy clause,** is important in the ordering of state and federal relationships. When there is a direct conflict between a federal law and

CONTEMPORARY LEGAL DEBATES

Internet Wine Sales and the Commerce Clause

In the past, most states barred direct consumer purchases of alcoholic beverages from out-of-state sellers. Because relatively few consumers purchased such goods from out-of-state suppliers, however, these laws were rarely challenged. Today, because the Internet has become a popular vehicle for such sales, the constitutionality of state laws prohibiting wine sales via the Internet has been at issue in a growing number of cases.

THE DORMANT COMMERCE CLAUSE

As mentioned elsewhere, the commerce clause implies a negative, or "dormant," aspect: the states do *not* have the authority to regulate interstate commerce. Does this mean that state statutes prohibiting consumers from purchasing wine directly from out-of-state sellers violate the dormant commerce clause? In one case addressing this issue, *Dickerson v. Bailey,*[a] the plaintiffs—Texas residents who wanted to receive wine shipments directly from out-of-state suppliers—claimed that a Texas statute prohibiting such purchases violated the dormant commerce clause. The statute prohibited Texans from importing for their personal use more than three gallons of wine without a permit unless the resident "personally accompan[ies] the wine or liquor as it enters the state." A federal district court held that the statute violated the dormant commerce clause. In effect, the law discriminated against interstate commerce by prohibiting out-of-state wineries from shipping wines to Texas residents while allowing local Texas wineries or retailers to do so.

In another case addressing this issue, *Bolick v. Roberts,*[b] the court reached a similar conclusion. The case involved a Virginia statute that prohibited out-of-state suppliers from selling wine directly to consumers in Virginia. A federal district court held that the Virginia statute violated the commerce clause and was thus invalid.

In the Texas case, and in some other cases involving this issue, one of the arguments made by state authorities is that their liquor regulations are justified by Section 2 of the Twenty-first Amendment.[c] That section reads, "The transportation or importation into any State, Territory, or possession of the United States for delivery or use therein of intoxicating liquors, *in violation of the laws thereof,* is hereby prohibited." (Emphasis added.)

a. 87 F.Supp.2d 691 (S.D.Tex. 2000).

b. 199 F.Supp.2d 397 (E.D.Va. 2002).

c. Section 1 of the Twenty-first Amendment (ratified in 1933) repealed the Eighteenth Amendment (ratified in 1919), which had made the manufacture, sale, or transportation of alcoholic beverages illegal. Section 2 of the Twenty-first Amendment effectively left the regulation of such activity up to the states.

a state law, the state law is rendered invalid. Because some powers are *concurrent* (shared by the federal government and the states), however, it is necessary to determine which law governs in a particular circumstance.

Preemption • A doctrine under which certain federal laws preempt, or take precedence over, conflicting state or local laws.

Federal Preemption. When Congress chooses to act exclusively in an area in which the federal government and the states have concurrent powers, it is said to have *preempted* the area. When federal **preemption** occurs, a valid federal statute or regulation will take precedence over a conflicting state or local law or regulation on the same general subject. For example, the federal Controlled Substances Act[18] of 1970 strictly prohibits the manufacture and distribution of marijuana. When California legalized the use of marijuana for

18. This is the popular name for the Comprehensive Drug Abuse Prevention and Control Act of 1970, 21 U.S.C. Sections 801 *et seq.*

CONTEMPORARY LEGAL DEBATES

Internet Wine Sales and the Commerce Clause—Continued

DOES THE TWENTY-FIRST AMENDMENT CREATE AN EXCEPTION TO THE DORMANT COMMERCE CLAUSE?

Does the Twenty-first Amendment create an exception to the normal operation of the commerce clause? The courts have reached different conclusions on this issue. In the Texas case, for example, the court held that the amendment did not create such an exception. The court did note that substantial deference is given to a state's power to regulate the sale and distribution of liquor within its boundaries when the goal of the regulation is "to combat the perceived evils of an unrestricted traffic in liquor." The court concluded, however, that no temperance goal was served by the Texas statute because residents of that state could "become as drunk on local wines" as they could on wines that were effectively "kept out of the state by the statute." Because the goal of the Texas law was primarily to protect the economic interests of in-state wine distributors and retailers, the law was not entitled to such deference and violated the commerce clause.

The first federal appellate court to rule on this issue reached a different conclusion. In *Bridenbaugh v. Freeman-Wilson,*[d] Indiana residents challenged the constitutionality of a state statute making it unlawful for persons in another state or country to ship alcoholic beverages directly to Indiana residents. The court concluded that the primary purpose of the Twenty-first Amendment was not necessarily to promote temperance; rather, it was designed to close a "loophole" created by the dormant commerce clause. This loophole allowed direct shipments from out-of-state sellers to consumers to "bypass state regulatory (and tax) systems." The Indiana statute did not involve any substantial discrimination against interstate commerce; it merely enabled the state "to collect its excise tax equally from in-state and out-of-state sellers."

WHERE DO YOU STAND?

By and large, the courts are applying traditional commerce clause analysis to attempts by the states to regulate the Internet. In other words, the courts tend to invalidate state laws that place too great a burden on interstate commerce or that openly discriminate against interstate commerce in favor of in-state economic activities. With respect to Internet sales of alcoholic beverages, however, at least one federal appellate court has upheld state regulation of such sales on the basis of the Twenty-first Amendment. In your opinion, should the Twenty-first Amendment be given more weight than the commerce clause?

d. 227 F.3d 848 (7th Cir. 2000).

medical purposes by a ballot initiative in 1996, the law was challenged as unconstitutional because it conflicted with the federal law. Ultimately, the United States Supreme Court ruled that the state law was preempted by the 1970 federal act.[19]

Whether the federal government has preempted a certain area can have important implications for businesspersons. For example, for some time it was not clear whether tobacco companies that complied with federal cigarette-labeling requirements could be sued under state laws requiring cigarette manufacturers to sufficiently warn consumers of the potential dangers associated with cigarette smoking. In a 1992 case, *Cipollone v. Liggett Group, Inc.,*[20] the

19. *United States v. Oakland Cannabis Buyers' Co-op,* 532 U.S. 483, 121 S.Ct. 1711, 149 L.Ed.2d 722 (2001).
20. 505 U.S. 504, 112 S.Ct. 2608, 120 L.Ed.2d 407 (1992).

United States Supreme Court held that the Federal Cigarette Labeling and Advertising Act of 1965, which requires specific warnings to be included on cigarette packages, preempted the state laws requiring warnings. The Court stated, however, that there was no indication that Congress had intended to preempt state laws that fall *outside* the scope of the federal law, such as laws governing fraudulent misrepresentation.

Determining Congressional Intent. In *Cipollone* and other cases involving preemption issues, the courts must decide whether Congress, when enacting a particular statute, *intended* to preempt the area and thus preclude plaintiffs from bringing claims under state law. In determining congressional intent, courts look at the wording of the statute itself, as well as at the legislative history of the statute (such as congressional committee reports on the topic).

For example, in *Tebbetts v. Ford Motor Co.,*[21] a plaintiff alleged that a 1988 Ford Escort was defectively designed because it did not contain an air bag on the driver's side. The defendant-manufacturer contended that it had complied with federal safety regulations authorized by the National Traffic and Motor Vehicle Safety Act (NTMVSA) of 1966 and that those regulations preempted recovery under state product-safety laws. The court interpreted House and Senate reports on the issue, as well as a clause included in the act itself, to mean that not all state law claims were preempted by the federal regulations. (The relevant clause stated that "[c]ompliance with any Federal motor vehicle safety standard issued under this [act] does not exempt any person from any liability under common law.") Thus, the plaintiff in *Tebbetts* was not precluded by the NTMVSA from suing Ford under state product liability laws (see Chapter 12).

Generally, it is difficult to predict whether a defendant will be subject to liability under state laws notwithstanding the defendant's compliance with federally mandated product-safety standards. Courts differ in their interpretations of congressional intent, and the outcomes in cases involving similar facts can thus also differ.

The Taxing and Spending Powers

Article I, Section 8, provides that Congress has the "Power to lay and collect Taxes, Duties, Imposts, and Excises." Section 8 further provides that "all Duties, Imposts and Excises shall be uniform throughout the United States." The requirement of uniformity refers to uniformity among the states, and thus Congress may not tax some states while exempting others.

Traditionally, if Congress attempted to regulate indirectly, by taxation, an area over which it had no authority, the tax would be invalidated by the courts. Today, however, if a tax measure is reasonable, it is generally held to be within the national taxing power. Moreover, the expansive interpretation of the commerce clause almost always provides a basis for sustaining a federal tax.

Under Article I, Section 8, Congress has the power "to pay the Debts and provide for the common Defence and general Welfare of the United States." Through the spending power, Congress disposes of the revenues accumulated from the taxing power. Congress can spend revenues not only to carry out its

21. 665 A.2d 345 (N.H. 1995).

expressed powers but also to promote any objective it deems worthwhile, so long as it does not violate the Bill of Rights. For example, Congress could not condition welfare payments on the recipients' agreement not to criticize government policies. The spending power necessarily involves policy choices, with which taxpayers may disagree.

BUSINESS AND THE BILL OF RIGHTS

The importance of a written declaration of the rights of individuals eventually caused the first Congress of the United States to submit twelve amendments to the Constitution to the states for approval. The first ten of these amendments, commonly known as the **Bill of Rights,** were adopted in 1791 and embody a series of protections for the individual against various types of interference by the federal government.[22] The protections guaranteed by these ten amendments are summarized in Exhibit 5–1.[23] Some of these constitutional protections apply to business entities as well. For example, corporations exist as separate legal entities, or *legal persons,* and enjoy many of the same rights and privileges as *natural persons* do.

Bill of Rights • The first ten amendments to the U.S. Constitution.

As originally intended, the Bill of Rights limited only the powers of the national government. Over time, however, the United States Supreme Court "incorporated" most of these rights into the protections against state actions afforded by the Fourteenth Amendment to the Constitution. That amendment, passed in 1868 after the Civil War, provides in part that "[n]o State shall . . .

22. Another of these proposed amendments was ratified 203 years later (in 1992) and became the Twenty-seventh Amendment to the Constitution. See Appendix A.
23. See the Constitution in Appendix A for the complete text of each amendment.

EXHIBIT 5–1 • PROTECTIONS GUARANTEED BY THE BILL OF RIGHTS

First Amendment: Guarantees the freedoms of religion, speech, and the press and the rights to assemble peaceably and to petition the government.	**Sixth Amendment:** Guarantees the accused in a criminal case the right to a speedy and public trial by an impartial jury and with counsel. The accused has the right to cross-examine witnesses against him or her and to solicit testimony from witnesses in his or her favor.
Second Amendment: States that the right of the people to keep and bear arms shall not be infringed.	**Seventh Amendment:** Guarantees the right to a trial by jury in a civil case involving at least twenty dollars.[a]
Third Amendment: Prohibits, in peacetime, the lodging of soldiers in any house without the owner's consent.	**Eighth Amendment:** Prohibits excessive bail and fines, as well as cruel and unusual punishment.
Fourth Amendment: Prohibits unreasonable searches and seizures of persons or property.	**Ninth Amendment:** Establishes that the people have rights in addition to those specified in the Constitution.
Fifth Amendment: Guarantees the rights to indictment by grand jury, to due process of law, and to fair payment when private property is taken for public use; prohibits compulsory self-incrimination and double jeopardy (being tried again for an alleged crime for which one has already stood trial).	**Tenth Amendment:** Establishes that those powers neither delegated to the federal government nor denied to the states are reserved to the states, and to the people.

a. Twenty dollars was forty days' pay for the average person when the Bill of Rights was written.

deprive any person of life, liberty, or property, without due process of law." Starting in 1925, the Supreme Court began to define various rights and liberties guaranteed in the national Constitution as constituting "due process of law," which was required of state governments under the Fourteenth Amendment. Today, most of the rights and liberties set forth in the Bill of Rights apply to state governments as well as the national government. In other words, neither the federal government nor state governments can deprive persons of those rights and liberties.

The rights secured by the Bill of Rights are not absolute. As you can see in Exhibit 5–1 on the previous page, many of the rights guaranteed by the first ten amendments are described in very general terms. For example, the Fourth Amendment prohibits *unreasonable* searches and seizures, but it does not define what constitutes an unreasonable search or seizure. Similarly, the Eighth Amendment prohibits *excessive* bail or fines, but no definition of *excessive* is contained in that amendment. Ultimately, it is the United States Supreme Court, as the final interpreter of the Constitution, that defines our rights and determines their boundaries.

Freedom of Speech

A democratic form of government cannot survive unless people can freely voice their political opinions and criticize government actions or policies. Freedom of speech, particularly political speech, is thus a prized right, and traditionally the courts have protected this right to the fullest extent possible.

Symbolic speech • Nonverbal conduct that expresses opinions or thoughts about a subject. Symbolic speech is protected under the First Amendment's guarantee of freedom of speech.

Symbolic speech—gestures, movements, articles of clothing, and other forms of expressive conduct—is also given substantial protection by the courts. For example, in a 1989 case, *Texas v. Johnson,*[24] the United States Supreme Court ruled that state laws that prohibited the burning of the American flag as part of a peaceful protest violated the freedom of expression protected by the First Amendment. Congress responded by passing the Flag Protection Act of 1989, which was ruled unconstitutional by the Supreme Court in 1990.[25] In a subsequent case, the Supreme Court ruled that a city statute banning bias-motivated disorderly conduct (including, in this case, the placing of a burning cross in another's front yard as a gesture of hate) was an unconstitutional restriction of speech.[26]

Governments can and do place restraints on free speech, of course, but such restraints are permissible only when they are necessary to protect other substantial interests and rights. It is up to the courts—and, ultimately, the United States Supreme Court—to determine the point at which laws restricting free speech can be justified by the need to protect other rights.

The court in the following case applied these principles to determine the constitutionality of a county ordinance that regulated video games based on their content—the ordinance applied only to "graphically violent" video games.

---

24. 491 U.S. 397, 109 S.Ct. 2533, 105 L.Ed.2d 342 (1989).
25. *United States v. Eichman,* 496 U.S. 310, 110 S.Ct. 2804, 110 L.Ed.2d 287 (1990).
26. *R.A.V. v. City of St. Paul, Minnesota,* 505 U.S. 377, 112 S.Ct. 2538, 120 L.Ed.2d 305 (1992).

CASE 5.3

United States Court of Appeals, Eighth Circuit, 2003. 329 F.3d 954.

INTERACTIVE DIGITAL SOFTWARE ASSOCIATION v. ST. LOUIS COUNTY, MISSOURI

St. Louis County, Missouri, passed an ordinance that made it unlawful for any person knowingly to sell, rent, or make available "graphically violent" video games to minors, or to "permit the free play of" such games by minors, without a parent or guardian's consent.[a] Interactive Digital Software Association and other firms that create or provide the public with video games and related software filed a suit against the county in a federal district court. The plaintiffs asserted that the ordinance violated the First Amendment and filed a motion for summary judgment. The court denied the motion and dismissed the case. The plaintiffs appealed to the U.S. Court of Appeals for the Eighth Circuit.

ARNOLD, J.

In rejecting the plaintiffs' constitutional challenge to the ordinance, the district court first concluded that video games were not a protected form of speech under the first amendment. The district court believed that, because video games are a new medium, they must "be designed to express or inform, and there has to be a likelihood that others will understand that there has been some type of expression" before they are entitled to constitutional protection. But the [United States] Supreme Court has long emphasized that the First Amendment protects entertainment, as well as political and ideological speech and that a particularized message is not required for speech to be constitutionally protected.

The record in this case includes scripts and story boards showing the storyline, character development, and dialogue of representative video games, as well as excerpts from four video games submitted by the County. If the First Amendment is versatile enough to shield the painting of Jackson Pollock, music of Arnold Schoenberg, or Jabberwocky verse of Lewis Carroll, we see no reason why the pictures, graphic design, concept art, sounds, music, stories, and narrative present in video games are not entitled to a similar protection. The mere fact that they appear in a novel medium is of no legal consequence. Our review of the record convinces us that these violent video games contain stories, imagery, age-old themes of literature, and messages, even an ideology, just as books and movies do. Indeed, we find it telling that the County seeks to restrict access to these video games precisely because their content purportedly affects the thought or behavior of those who play them.

We recognize that while children have in the past experienced age-old elemental violent themes by reading a fairy tale or an epic poem, or attending a Saturday matinee, the interactive play of a video game might present different difficulties. The County suggests in fact that with video games, the story lines are incidental and players may skip the expressive parts of the game and proceed straight to the player-controlled action. But the same could be said of action-packed movies like "The Matrix" or "Charlie's Angels"; any viewer with a videocassette or DVD player could simply skip to and isolate the action

a. St. Louis County Revised Ordinances Sections 602.425 through 602.460.

sequences. *The fact that modern technology has increased viewer control does not render movies unprotected by the First Amendment, and equivalent player control likewise should not automatically disqualify modern video games that are analytically indistinguishable from * * * protected media such as motion pictures.* [Emphasis added.]

We note, moreover, that *there is no justification for disqualifying video games as speech simply because they are constructed to be interactive;* indeed, literature is most successful when it draws the reader into the story, makes him identify with the characters, invites him to judge them and quarrel with them, to experience their joys and sufferings as the reader's own. In fact, some books, such as the pre-teen oriented "Choose Your Own Nightmare" series (in which the reader makes choices that determine the plot of the story, and which lead the reader to one of several endings, by following the instructions at the bottom of the page) can be every bit as interactive as video games. [Emphasis added.]

Whether we believe the advent of violent video games adds anything of value to society is irrelevant; *guided by the First Amendment, we are obliged to recognize that they are as much entitled to the protection of free speech as the best of literature.* * * * [Emphasis added.]

* * * *

The County's conclusion that there is a strong likelihood that minors who play violent video games will suffer a deleterious effect on their psychological health is simply unsupported in the record. It is true that a psychologist appearing on behalf of the County stated that a recent study that he conducted indicates that playing violent video games "does in fact lead to aggressive behavior in the immediate situation * * * that more aggressive thoughts are reported and there is frequently more aggressive behavior." But this vague generality falls far short of a showing that video games are psychologically deleterious. The County's remaining evidence included the conclusory comments of county council members; a small number of ambiguous, inconclusive, or irrelevant (conducted on adults, not minors) studies; and the testimony of a high school principal who admittedly had no information regarding any link between violent video games and psychological harm.

Before the County may constitutionally restrict the speech at issue here, the County must come forward with empirical support for its belief that violent video games cause psychological harm to minors. In this case, * * * the County has failed to present the substantial supporting evidence of harm that is required before an ordinance that threatens protected speech can be upheld. We note, moreover, contrary to the district court's suggestion, that the County may not simply surmise that it is serving a compelling state interest because "[s]ociety in general believes that continued exposure to violence can be harmful to children." Where First Amendment rights are at stake, the Government must present more than anecdote and supposition.

The U.S. Court of Appeals for the Eighth Circuit reversed the judgment of the lower court and remanded the case for the entry of an injunction against the county's enforcement of its ordinance. Video games are entitled to the same First Amendment protection as other types of speech, and the defendants failed to present the required evidence of harm to uphold a law threatening protected speech.

QUESTIONS

1. Who brought this case before the U.S. Court of Appeals for the Eighth Circuit, and why?
2. What was the ruling of the U.S. Court of Appeals for the Eighth Circuit, and what was the reasoning behind this decision?
3. In determining whether a medium of speech is entitled to constitutional protection, should a court consider the messages communicated by that medium? Why or why not?

Commercial Speech. Speech and communications—primarily advertising—made by business firms are called *commercial speech.* Although commercial speech is protected by the First Amendment, it is not protected as extensively as noncommercial speech. A state may restrict certain kinds of advertising, for example, in the interest of preventing consumers from being misled by the advertising practices. States also have a legitimate interest in the beautification of roadsides, and this interest allows states to place restraints on billboard advertising.

Generally, a restriction on commercial speech will be considered valid as long as it meets the following three criteria: (1) it must seek to implement a substantial government interest, (2) it must directly advance that interest, and (3) it must go no further than necessary to accomplish its objective. At issue in the following case was whether a government agency had unconstitutionally restricted commercial speech when it prohibited the inclusion of a certain illustration on beer labels.

BAD FROG BREWERY, INC. v. NEW YORK STATE LIQUOR AUTHORITY

CASE 5.4

United States Court of Appeals, Second Circuit, 1998.
134 F.3d 87.
http://www.tourolaw.edu/2ndCircuit/January98/97-79490.html[a]

Bad Frog Brewery, Inc., makes and sells alcoholic beverages. Some of the beverages feature labels that display a drawing of a frog making the gesture generally known as "giving the finger." Bad Frog's authorized New York distributor, Renaissance Beer Company, applied to the New York State Liquor Authority (NYSLA) for brand label approval, as required by state law before the beer could be sold in New York. The NYSLA denied the application, in part because "the label could appear in grocery and convenience stores, with obvious exposure on the shelf to children of tender age." Bad Frog filed a suit in a federal district court against the NYSLA, asking for, among other things, an injunction against the denial of the application. The court granted summary judgment in favor of the NYSLA. Bad Frog appealed to the U.S. Court of Appeals for the Second Circuit.

---

a. This page is part of a Web site maintained by the Touro College Jacob D. Fuchsberg Law Center in Huntington, New York.

NEWMAN, J.

[T]o support its asserted power to ban Bad Frog's labels [NYSLA advances] * * * the State's interest in "protecting children from vulgar and profane advertising" * * *.

[This interest is] substantial * * *. *States have a compelling interest in protecting the physical and psychological well-being of minors* * * *. [Emphasis added.]

* * * *

* * * NYSLA endeavors to advance the state interest in preventing exposure of children to vulgar displays by taking only the limited step of barring such displays from the labels of alcoholic beverages. *In view of the wide currency of vulgar displays throughout contemporary society, including comic books targeted directly at children, barring such displays from labels for alcoholic beverages cannot realistically be expected to reduce children's exposure to such displays to any significant degree.* [Emphasis added.]

* * * If New York decides to make a substantial effort to insulate children from vulgar displays in some significant sphere of activity, at least with respect to materials likely to be seen by children, NYSLA's label prohibition might well be found to make a justifiable contribution to the material advancement of such an effort, but its currently isolated response to the perceived problem, applicable only to labels on a product that children cannot purchase, does not suffice. * * * [A] state must demonstrate that its commercial speech limitation is part of a substantial effort to advance a valid state interest, not merely the removal of a few grains of offensive sand from a beach of vulgarity.

* * * *

* * * Even if we were to assume that the state materially advances its asserted interest by shielding children from viewing the Bad Frog labels, it is plainly excessive to prohibit the labels from all use, including placement on bottles displayed in bars and taverns where parental supervision of children is to be expected. Moreover, to whatever extent NYSLA is concerned that children will be harmfully exposed to the Bad Frog labels when wandering without parental supervision around grocery and convenience stores where beer is sold, that concern could be less intrusively dealt with by placing restrictions on the permissible locations where the appellant's products may be displayed within such stores.

The U.S. Court of Appeals for the Second Circuit reversed the judgment of the district court and remanded the case for the entry of a judgment in favor of Bad Frog. The NYSLA's ban on the use of the labels lacked a "reasonable fit" with the state's interest in shielding minors from vulgarity, and the NYSLA did not adequately consider alternatives to the ban.

QUESTIONS

1. Why did the U.S. Court of Appeals for the Second Circuit rule in favor of Bad Frog?
2. Whose interests are advanced by the banning of certain types of advertising?
3. If Bad Frog had sought to use the offensive label to market toys instead of beer, would the court's ruling likely have been the same?

Corporate Political Speech. Political speech that otherwise would fall within the protection of the First Amendment does not lose that protection simply because its source is a corporation. For example, in *First National Bank of Boston v. Bellotti,*[27] national banking associations and business corporations asked the United States Supreme Court to review a Massachusetts statute that prohibited corporations from making political contributions or expenditures that individuals were permitted to make. The Court ruled that the statute was unconstitutional because it violated the right of corporations to freedom of speech.

Similarly, the Supreme Court has held that a law forbidding a corporation from using bill inserts to express its views on controversial issues violates the First Amendment.[28] Although in 1990 a more conservative Supreme Court reversed this trend somewhat,[29] corporate political speech continues to be given significant protection under the First Amendment.

Unprotected Speech. The United States Supreme Court has made it clear that certain types of speech will not be protected under the First Amendment. Speech that harms the good reputation of another, or defamatory speech (see Chapter 12), is not protected under the First Amendment. Speech that violates criminal laws (threatening speech and pornography, for example) is not constitutionally protected. Other unprotected speech includes "fighting words" (speech that is likely to incite others to respond violently).

The Supreme Court has also held that obscene speech is not protected by the First Amendment. The Court has grappled from time to time with the problem of establishing an objective definition of obscene speech. In a 1973 case, *Miller v. California,*[30] the Supreme Court created a test for legal obscenity, including a set of requirements that must be met for material to be legally obscene. Under this test, material is obscene if (1) the average person finds that it violates contemporary community standards; (2) the work taken as a whole appeals to a prurient (arousing or obsessive) interest in sex; (3) the work shows patently offensive sexual conduct; and (4) the work lacks serious redeeming literary, artistic, political, or scientific merit.

Because community standards vary widely, the *Miller* test has had inconsistent applications, and obscenity remains a constitutionally unsettled issue. Numerous state and federal statutes make it a crime to disseminate obscene materials, however, and the Supreme Court has often upheld such laws, including laws prohibiting the sale and possession of child pornography.[31]

Online Obscenity. A significant problem facing the courts and lawmakers today is how to control the dissemination of obscenity and child pornography via the Internet. Congress first attempted to protect minors from pornographic materials on the Internet by passing the Communications Decency Act (CDA) of 1996. The CDA made it a crime to make available to minors

27. 435 U.S. 765, 98 S.Ct. 1407, 55 L.Ed.2d 707 (1978).
28. *Consolidated Edison Co. v. Public Service Commission,* 447 U.S. 530, 100 S.Ct. 2326, 65 L.Ed.2d 319 (1980).
29. See *Austin v. Michigan Chamber of Commerce,* 494 U.S. 652, 110 S.Ct. 1391, 108 L.Ed.2d 652 (1990), in which the Supreme Court upheld a state law prohibiting corporations from using general corporate funds for independent expenditures in state political campaigns.
30. 413 U.S. 15, 93 S.Ct. 2607, 37 L.Ed.2d 419 (1973).
31. For example, see *Osborne v. Ohio,* 495 U.S. 103, 110 S.Ct. 1691, 109 L.Ed.2d 98 (1990).

online any "obscene or indecent" message that "depicts or describes, in terms patently offensive as measured by contemporary community standards, sexual or excretory activities or organs."[32] The act was immediately challenged by civil rights groups as an unconstitutional restraint on speech, and ultimately the United States Supreme Court ruled that portions of the act were unconstitutional. The Court held that the terms *indecent* and *patently offensive* covered large amounts of nonpornographic material with serious educational or other value.

Subsequent Attempts to Regulate Online Obscenity. Subsequent attempts by Congress to curb pornography on the Internet have also encountered constitutional stumbling blocks. For example, the Child Pornography Prevention Act (CPPA)[33] of 1996 made it illegal to distribute or possess computer-generated images that appear to depict minors engaging in lewd and lascivious behavior. In 2002, the United States Supreme Court held that, because the CPPA's ban on virtual child pornography abridged the freedom to engage in a substantial amount of lawful speech, the act was overbroad and unconstitutional under the First Amendment.[34]

The Children's Online Privacy Protection Act (COPPA)[35] of 1998, which imposed criminal penalties on those who distribute material that is "harmful to minors" without using some kind of age-verification system to separate adult and minor users, has been tied up in the courts since its passage. The Child Online Protection Act (COPA)[36] of 1998 made it a crime to communicate material via the Internet that is "harmful to minors" according to "contemporary community standards." The constitutionality of this act was also challenged, in part because a "community standards test" would essentially require every Web communication to abide by the most restrictive community's standards. In 2002, however, the Supreme Court held that the COPA's reference to contemporary community standards in defining what was harmful to minors did not alone render the act unconstitutional.[37]

Filtering Software in Public Schools and Libraries. In 2000, Congress enacted the Children's Internet Protection Act,[38] which required public schools and libraries, as a condition of receiving federal funds, to block adult content from access by children through the installation of **filtering software.** Such software is designed to prevent persons from viewing certain Web sites at specific times by responding to a site's uniform resource locator (URL, or Internet address) or its **meta tags** (key words). In 2002, a federal district court held that the act was unconstitutional on the ground that it induced libraries to violate the First Amendment.[39] In 2003, however, the United States Supreme Court overturned this ruling and upheld the act, stating that any encroachment on

Filtering software • A computer program that includes a pattern through which data are passed. When designed to block access to certain Web sites, the pattern blocks the retrieval of a site whose URL or key words are on a list within the program.

Meta tags • Words inserted into a Web site's key words field to increase the site's appearance in search engine results.

32. 47 U.S.C. Section 223(a)(1)(B)(ii).
33. 18 U.S.C. Section 2256(8).
34. *Ashcroft v. Free Speech Coalition,* 535 U.S. 234, 122 S.Ct. 1389, 152 L.Ed.2d 403 (2002).
35. 13 U.S.C. Sections 1301–1308.
36. 15 U.S.C. Sections 6501–6506.
37. *Ashcroft v. American Civil Liberties Union,* 535 U.S. 564, 122 S.Ct. 1700, 152 L.Ed.2d 771 (2002).
38. 24 U.S.C. Sections 1701–1741.
39. *American Library Association, Inc. v. United States,* 201 F.Supp.2d 401 (E.D.Pa. 2002).

the free speech of adult library patrons could be eliminated by their ability to request that librarians remove the blocking software.[40]

Freedom of Religion

The First Amendment states that the government may neither establish any religion nor prohibit the free exercise of religious practices. The first part of this constitutional provision is referred to as the **establishment clause,** which has to do with the separation of church and state. The second part of the provision is known as the **free exercise clause.**

Establishment clause • The provision in the First Amendment to the U.S. Constitution that prohibits Congress from creating any law "respecting an establishment of religion."

Free exercise clause • The provision in the First Amendment to the U.S. Constitution that prohibits Congress from making any law "prohibiting the free exercise" of religion.

The Establishment Clause. The establishment clause prohibits the government from establishing a state-sponsored religion, as well as from passing laws that promote (aid or endorse) religion or that show a preference for one religion over another. Establishment clause issues often involve such matters as the legality of allowing or requiring school prayers, using state-issued school vouchers to pay for tuition at religious schools, the teaching of evolutionary versus creationist theory, and state and local government aid to religious organizations and schools.

Federal or state laws that do not promote or place a significant burden on religion are constitutional even if they have some impact on religion. "Sunday closing laws," for example, make the performance of some commercial activities on Sunday illegal. These statutes, also known as "blue laws" (from the color of the paper on which an early Sunday law was written), have been upheld on the ground that it is a legitimate function of government to provide a day of rest to promote the health and welfare of workers. Even though closing laws admittedly make it easier for Christians to attend religious services, the courts have viewed this effect as an incidental, not a primary, purpose of Sunday closing laws.

The First Amendment does not require a complete separation of church and state. On the contrary, it affirmatively mandates accommodation of all religions and forbids hostility toward any.[41] An ongoing challenge for the courts is determining the extent to which governments can accommodate a religion without appearing to promote that religion, which would violate the establishment clause.

ETHICAL ISSUE

Do religious displays on public property violate the establishment clause? The thorny issue of whether religious displays on public property violate the establishment clause often arises during the holiday season. Time and again, the courts have wrestled with this issue, but it has never been resolved in a way that satisfies everyone. In a 1984 case, the United States Supreme Court decided that a city's official Christmas display, which included a crèche (Nativity scene), did not violate the establishment clause because it was just one part of a larger holiday display that featured secular symbols, such as reindeer and candy canes.[42] In a later case, the Court held that the presence of a crèche

40. *United States v. American Library Association,* ___ U.S. ___, 123 S.Ct. 2297, 156 L.Ed.2d 221 (2003).

41. *Zorach v. Clauson,* 343 U.S. 306, 72 S.Ct. 679, 96 L.Ed. 954 (1952).

42. *Lynch v. Donnelly,* 465 U.S. 668, 104 S.Ct. 1355, 79 L.Ed.2d 604 (1984).

within a county courthouse violated the establishment clause because it was not in close proximity to nonreligious symbols, including a Christmas tree, which were located outside, on the building's steps. The presence of a menorah (a nine-branched candelabrum used in celebrating Chanukah) on the building's steps, however, did not violate the establishment clause because the menorah was situated in close proximity to the Christmas tree.[43] The courts continue to apply this reasoning in cases involving similar issues.

The Free Exercise Clause. The free exercise clause guarantees that no person can be compelled to do something that is contrary to his or her religious beliefs. For this reason, if a law or policy is contrary to a person's religious beliefs, exemptions are often made to accommodate those beliefs. When, however, religious practices work against public policy and the public welfare, the government can act. For example, regardless of a child's or parent's religious beliefs, the government can require certain types of vaccinations. Additionally, public school students can be required to study from textbooks chosen by school authorities.

For business firms, an important issue involves the accommodation that businesses must make for the religious beliefs of their employees. For example, if an employee's religion prohibits her or him from working on a certain day of the week or at a particular type of job, the employer must make a *reasonable* attempt to accommodate these religious requirements. Employers must reasonably accommodate an employee's religious belief even if the belief is not based on the tenets or dogma of a particular church, sect, or denomination. The only requirement is that the belief be religious in nature and sincerely held by the employee.[44] (See Chapter 15 for a further discussion of religious freedom in the employment context.)

Searches and Seizures

The Fourth Amendment protects the "right of the people to be secure in their persons, houses, papers, and effects." Before searching or seizing private property, law enforcement officers are required to obtain a **search warrant**—an order from a judge or other public official authorizing the search or seizure.

Search warrant • An order granted by a public authority, such as a judge, that authorizes law enforcement personnel to search particular premises or property.

Search Warrants and Probable Cause. To obtain a search warrant, law enforcement officers must convince a judge that they have reasonable grounds, or probable cause, to believe a search will reveal a specific illegality. To establish **probable cause,** the officers must have trustworthy evidence that would convince a reasonable person that the proposed search or seizure is more likely justified than not. Furthermore, the Fourth Amendment prohibits *general* warrants. It requires a particular description of whatever is to be searched or seized. General searches through a person's belongings are impermissible. The search cannot extend beyond what is described in the warrant.

Probable cause • Reasonable grounds to believe the existence of facts warranting certain actions, such as the search or arrest of a person.

The requirement for a search warrant has several exceptions. One exception applies when it is likely that the items sought will be removed before a warrant can be obtained. For example, if a police officer has probable cause to

43. See, for example, *County of Allegheny v. American Civil Liberties Union,* 492 U.S. 573, 109 S.Ct. 3086, 106 L.Ed.2d 472 (1989).

44. *Frazee v. Illinois Department of Employment Security,* 489 U.S. 829, 109 S.Ct. 1514, 103 L.Ed.2d 914 (1989).

believe that an automobile contains evidence of a crime and that the vehicle will likely be unavailable by the time a warrant is obtained, the officer can search the vehicle without a warrant.

Searches and Seizures in the Business Context. Constitutional protection against unreasonable searches and seizures is important to businesses and professionals. As federal and state regulation of commercial activities increased, frequent and unannounced government inspections were conducted to ensure compliance with the regulations. Such inspections were at times extremely disruptive. In *Marshall v. Barlow's, Inc.,*[45] the United States Supreme Court held that government inspectors do not have the right to enter business premises without a warrant, although the standard of probable cause is not the same as that required in nonbusiness contexts. The existence of a general and neutral enforcement plan will justify issuance of the warrant.

Lawyers and accountants frequently possess the business records of their clients, and inspecting these documents while they are out of the hands of their true owners also requires a warrant. A warrant is not required, however, for the seizure of spoiled or contaminated food. In addition, warrants are also not required for searches of businesses in such highly regulated industries as liquor, guns, and strip mining. General manufacturing is not considered to be one of these highly regulated industries, however.

Of increasing concern to many government employers is how to maintain a safe and efficient workplace without jeopardizing the Fourth Amendment rights of employees "to be secure in their persons." Requiring government employees to undergo random drug tests, for example, may be held to violate the Fourth Amendment. In Chapter 14, we will discuss Fourth Amendment issues in the employment context, as well as employee privacy rights in general, in greater detail.

Self-Incrimination

The Fifth Amendment guarantees that no person "shall be compelled in any criminal case to be a witness against himself." Thus, in any federal proceeding, an accused person cannot be compelled to give testimony that might subject him or her to any criminal prosecution. Nor can an accused person be forced to testify against himself or herself in state courts because the due process clause of the Fourteenth Amendment (to be discussed shortly) incorporates the Fifth Amendment's provision against self-incrimination.

The Fifth Amendment's guarantee against self-incrimination extends only to natural persons. Because a corporation is a legal entity and not a natural person, the privilege against self-incrimination does not apply to it. Similarly, the business records of a partnership do not receive Fifth Amendment protection.[46] When a partnership is required to produce these records, it must do so even if the information provided incriminates the persons who constitute the business entity. In contrast, sole proprietors and sole practitioners (those who fully own their businesses) who have not incorporated cannot be compelled to

---

45. 436 U.S. 307, 98 S.Ct. 1816, 56 L.Ed.2d 305 (1978).

46. The privilege has been applied to some small family partnerships. See *United States v. Slutsky,* 352 F.Supp. 1005 (S.D.N.Y. 1972).

produce their business records. These individuals have full protection against self-incrimination because they function in only one capacity; there is no separate business entity.

Due Process and Equal Protection

Other constitutional guarantees of great significance to Americans are mandated by the *due process clauses* of the Fifth and Fourteenth Amendments and the *equal protection clause* of the Fourteenth Amendment.

Due Process

Due process clause • The provisions of the Fifth and Fourteenth Amendments to the Constitution that guarantee that no person shall be deprived of life, liberty, or property without due process of law. Similar clauses are found in most state constitutions.

Both the Fifth and the Fourteenth Amendments provide that no person shall be deprived "of life, liberty, or property, without due process of law." The **due process clause** of these constitutional amendments has two aspects—procedural and substantive. Note that the due process clause applies to "legal persons" (that is, corporations), as well as to individuals.

Procedural Due Process. *Procedural* due process requires that any government decision to take life, liberty, or property must be made equitably. For example, fair procedures must be used in determining whether a person will be subjected to punishment or have some burden imposed on her or him. Fair procedure has been interpreted as requiring that the person have at least an opportunity to object to a proposed action before an impartial, neutral decision maker (which need not be a judge). Thus, for example, if a driver's license is construed as a property interest, some sort of opportunity to object to its suspension or termination by the state must be provided.

Substantive Due Process. *Substantive* due process focuses on the content, or substance, of legislation. If a law or other governmental action limits a *fundamental right,* it will be held to violate substantive due process unless it promotes a *compelling* or *overriding state interest.* Fundamental rights include interstate travel, privacy, voting, and all First Amendment rights. Compelling state interests could include, for example, the public's safety. Thus, even though laws designating speed limits affect interstate travel, they may be upheld if they are shown to reduce highway fatalities, because the state has a compelling interest in protecting the lives of its citizens.

In all other situations, a law or action does not violate substantive due process if it rationally relates to any legitimate government purpose. It is almost impossible for a law or action to fail this "rational basis" test. Under this test, virtually any business regulation will be upheld as reasonable—the United States Supreme Court has upheld insurance regulations, price and wage controls, banking controls, and controls of unfair competition and trade practices against substantive due process challenges.

Suppose that a state legislature enacted a law imposing a fifteen-year term of imprisonment without a trial on all businesspersons who appeared in their own television commercials. This law would be unconstitutional on both substantive and procedural grounds. Substantive review would invalidate the legislation because it abridges freedom of speech, a fundamental right. Procedurally, the law is constitutionally invalid because it imposes a penalty without giving the accused a chance to defend his or her actions.

Equal Protection

Under the Fourteenth Amendment, a state may not "deny to any person within its jurisdiction the equal protection of the laws." The United States Supreme Court has used the due process clause of the Fifth Amendment to make the **equal protection clause** applicable to the federal government. Equal protection means that the government must treat similarly situated individuals in a similar manner.

Equal protection clause • The provision in the Fourteenth Amendment to the Constitution that guarantees that no state will "deny to any person within its jurisdiction the equal protection of the laws." This clause mandates that state governments treat similarly situated individuals in a similar manner.

Both substantive due process and equal protection require review of the substance of the law or other governmental action rather than review of the procedures used. When a law or action limits the liberty of all persons to do something, it may violate substantive due process; when a law or action limits the liberty of some persons but not others, it may violate the equal protection clause. Thus, for example, if a law prohibits all persons from buying contraceptive devices, it raises a substantive due process question; if it prohibits only unmarried persons from buying the same devices, it raises an equal protection issue.

In an equal protection inquiry, when a law or action distinguishes between or among individuals, the basis for the distinction—that is, the classification—is examined by the courts. Depending on the classification, the courts may use one of three standards—strict scrutiny, intermediate scrutiny, or the "rational basis" test—to determine the constitutionality of the law or action.

Strict Scrutiny. If a law or action prohibits or inhibits some persons from exercising a fundamental right, the law or action will be subject to "strict scrutiny" by the courts. Under this standard, the classification must be necessary to promote a *compelling state interest.* Also, if the classification is based on a *suspect trait*—such as race, national origin, or citizenship status—the classification must be necessary to promote a compelling state interest. Compelling state interests include remedying past unconstitutional or illegal discrimination but do not include correcting the general effects of "society's" discrimination. Thus, for example, if a city gives preference to minority applicants in awarding construction contracts, the city normally must identify the past unconstitutional or illegal discrimination against minority construction firms that it is attempting to correct. Generally, few laws or actions survive strict-scrutiny analysis by the courts.

In the following *Featured Case,* the United States Supreme Court considered whether the use of race as a factor in student admissions by the University of Michigan Law School violated the equal protection clause under the strict-scrutiny standard.

GRUTTER v. BOLLINGER

Supreme Court of the United States, 2003. __ U.S. __, 123 S.Ct. 2325, 156 L.Ed.2d 304.

MAJORITY OPINION

O'CONNOR, J.

The [University of Michigan] Law School ranks among the Nation's top law schools. It receives more than 3,500 applications each year for a class of around 350 students. Seeking to "admit a group of students who individually and collectively are among the most capable," the Law School looks for individuals with "substantial promise for success in law school" and "a strong likelihood of succeeding in the practice of law and contributing in diverse ways to the well-being of others." More broadly, the Law School seeks "a mix of students with varying backgrounds and experiences who will respect and learn from each other." * * *

The hallmark of [the Law School's admissions] policy is its focus on academic ability coupled with a flexible assessment of applicants' talents, experiences, and potential "to contribute to the learning of those around them." The policy requires admissions officials to evaluate each applicant based on all the information available in the file, including a personal statement, letters of recommendation, and an essay describing the ways in which the applicant will contribute to the life and diversity of the Law School. In reviewing an applicant's file, admissions officials must consider the applicant's undergraduate grade point average (GPA) and Law School Admissions Test (LSAT) score because they are important (if imperfect) predictors of academic success in law school. * * *

* * * *

* * * The policy [also affirms] the Law School's longstanding commitment to "one particular type of diversity," that is, "racial and ethnic diversity with special reference to the inclusion of students from groups which have been historically discriminated against, like African Americans, Hispanics and Native Americans, who without this commitment might not be represented in our student body in meaningful numbers." * * *

* * * *

Petitioner Barbara Grutter is a white Michigan resident who applied to the Law School in 1996 with a 3.8 grade point average and 161 LSAT score. The Law School initially placed petitioner on a waiting list, but subsequently rejected her application. In December 1997, petitioner filed suit in the United States District Court for the Eastern District of Michigan against * * * Lee Bollinger (Dean of the Law School from 1987 to 1994, and President of the University of Michigan from 1996 to 2002) [and others]. Petitioner alleged that respondents discriminated against her on the basis of race in violation of the Fourteenth Amendment [and various federal statutes].

* * * *

In the end, the District Court concluded that the Law School's use of race as a factor in admissions decisions was unlawful. * * *

Sitting *en banc* [with all of the judges of the court on the bench], the [U.S.] Court of Appeals [for the Sixth Circuit] reversed the District Court's judgment * * *.

* * * *

We granted *certiorari* to resolve the disagreement * * * on a question of national importance: *Whether diversity is a compelling interest that can justify the narrowly tailored use of race in selecting applicants for admission to public universities.* [Emphasis added.]

* * * *

* * * *[A]ll racial classifications imposed by government must be analyzed by a reviewing court under strict scrutiny. This means that such classifications are constitutional only if they are narrowly tailored to further compelling governmental interests.* * * * [Emphasis added.]

* * * *

* * * [R]espondents assert only one justification for their use of race in the admissions process: obtaining "the educational benefits that flow from a

diverse student body." In other words, the Law School asks us to recognize, in the context of higher education, a compelling state interest in student body diversity.

* * * *[W]e hold that the Law School has a compelling interest in attaining a diverse student body.* [Emphasis added.]

* * * *

As part of its goal of "assembling a class that is both exceptionally academically qualified and broadly diverse," the Law School seeks to "enroll a 'critical mass' of minority students." The Law School's interest is not simply to assure within its student body some specified percentage of a particular group merely because of its race or ethnic origin. That would amount to outright racial balancing, which is patently unconstitutional. Rather, the Law School's concept of critical mass is defined by reference to the educational benefits that diversity is designed to produce.

These benefits are substantial. * * * [T]he Law School's admissions policy promotes cross-racial understanding, helps to break down racial stereotypes, and enables students to better understand persons of different races. * * *

* * * *

These benefits are not theoretical but real, as major American businesses have made clear that the skills needed in today's increasingly global marketplace can only be developed through exposure to widely diverse people, cultures, ideas, and viewpoints. * * *

* * * *

We find that the Law School's admissions program bears the hallmarks of a narrowly tailored plan. * * * [T]ruly individualized consideration demands that race be used in a flexible, nonmechanical way. * * * [U]niversities cannot establish quotas for members of certain racial groups or put members of those groups on separate admissions tracks. * * * Universities can, however, consider race or ethnicity more flexibly as a "plus" factor in the context of individualized consideration of each and every applicant. [Emphasis added.]

* * * *

Here, the Law School engages in a highly individualized, holistic review of each applicant's file, giving serious consideration to all the ways an applicant might contribute to a diverse educational environment. * * * [T]he Law School awards no mechanical, predetermined diversity "bonuses" based on race or ethnicity. * * *

* * * *

* * * The judgment of the Court of Appeals for the Sixth Circuit, accordingly, is affirmed.

DISSENTING OPINION

THOMAS, J.

Because I wish to see all students succeed whatever their color, I share, in some respect, the sympathies of those who sponsor the type of discrimination advanced by the University of Michigan Law School * * * . The Constitution does not, however, tolerate institutional devotion to the status quo in admissions policies when such devotion ripens into racial discrimination. Nor does the Constitution countenance the unprecedented deference the Court gives to the Law School, an approach inconsistent with the very concept of "strict scrutiny."

No one would argue that a university could set up a lower general admission standard and then impose heightened requirements only on black applicants. Similarly, a university may not maintain a high admission standard and grant exemptions to favored races. The Law School, of its own choosing, and for its own purposes, maintains an exclusionary admissions system that it knows produces racially disproportionate results. Racial discrimination is not a permissible solution to the self-inflicted wounds of this elitist admissions policy.

* * * *

The Constitution abhors classifications based on race, not only because those classifications can harm favored races or are based on illegitimate motives, but also because every time the government places citizens on racial registers and makes race relevant to the provision of burdens or benefits, it demeans us all. Purchased at the price of immeasurable human suffering, the equal protection principle reflects our Nation's understanding that such classifications ultimately have a destructive impact on the individual and our society.

TEST YOUR COMPREHENSION: CASE DETAILS

1. How and why did this suit concerning the use of race in the selection of applicants for admission to public universities come before the United States Supreme Court?
2. Did the Supreme Court rule that the law school's admissions policy violated the equal protection clause? Why or why not?
3. Which, if any, of the forms of legal reasoning described in Chapter 1 did the majority use to reach its conclusion?
4. Why did more than sixty major U.S. corporations submit briefs to the Court in support of the law school's admissions policy?
5. What arguments did the dissent make to support its assertion that the majority's conclusion was incorrect?

Intermediate Scrutiny. Another standard, that of "intermediate scrutiny," is applied in cases involving discrimination based on gender or legitimacy. Laws using these classifications must be *substantially related to important government objectives.*

For example, an important government objective is preventing illegitimate teenage pregnancies. Therefore, because males and females are not similarly situated in this regard—only females can become pregnant—a law that punishes men but not women for statutory rape will be upheld, even though it treats men and women unequally. A state law requiring illegitimate children to bring paternity suits within six years of their births, however, will be struck down if legitimate children are allowed to seek support from their parents at any time. An important objective behind statutes of limitations is to prevent persons from bringing stale or fraudulent claims, but distinguishing between support claims on the basis of legitimacy has no relation to this objective.

The "Rational Basis" Test. In matters of economic or social welfare, the classification will be considered valid if there is any conceivable *rational basis* on which the classification might relate to a legitimate government interest.

It is almost impossible for a law or action to fail the rational basis test. Thus, for example, a city ordinance that in effect prohibits all pushcart vendors, except a specific few, from operating in a particular area of the city will be upheld if the city provides a rational basis—perhaps regulation and reduction of traffic in the particular area—for the ordinance. In contrast, a law that provides unemployment benefits only to people over six feet tall would violate the guarantee of equal protection. There is no rational basis for distributing unemployment compensation on the basis of height. Such a distinction could not further any legitimate government objective.

PRIVACY RIGHTS

The U.S. Constitution does not explicitly mention a general right to privacy, and only relatively recently have the courts regarded the right to privacy as a constitutional right. In a 1928 Supreme Court case, *Olmstead v. United States,*[47] Justice Louis Brandeis stated in his dissent that the right to privacy is "the most comprehensive of rights and the right most valued by civilized men." The majority of the justices at that time did not agree, and it was not until the 1960s that a majority on the Supreme Court endorsed the view that the Constitution protects individual privacy rights. In a landmark 1965 case, *Griswold v. Connecticut,*[48] the Supreme Court held that a constitutional right to privacy was implied by the First, Third, Fourth, Fifth, and Ninth Amendments to the Constitution.

In the last several decades, Congress has enacted a number of statutes that protect the privacy of individuals in various areas of concern. In the 1960s, Americans were sufficiently alarmed by the accumulation of personal information in government files that they pressured Congress to pass laws permitting individuals to access their files. Congress responded in 1966 with the Freedom of Information Act, which allows any person to request copies of any information on her or him contained in federal government files. In 1974, Congress passed the Privacy Act, which also gives persons the right to access such information. Since then, Congress has passed a number of other laws protecting individuals' privacy rights with respect to financial transactions, electronic communications, health care, and other activities in which personal information may be gathered and stored by organizations.

State constitutions and statutes also protect individuals' privacy rights, often to a significant degree. Privacy rights are also protected under tort law (see Chapter 12). Additionally, the Federal Trade Commission has played an active role in protecting the privacy rights of online consumers. The protection of employees' privacy rights, particularly with respect to electronic monitoring practices, is an area of growing concern (see Chapter 14).

47. 277 U.S. 438, 48 S.Ct. 564, 72 L.Ed. 944 (1928).
48. 381 U.S. 479, 85 S.Ct. 1678, 14 L.Ed.2d 510 (1965).

KEY TERMS

amend 150
Bill of Rights 161
checks and balances 152
commerce clause 152
due process clause 172
equal protection clause 173
establishment clause 169
federal form of government 150

filtering software 168
free exercise clause 169
full faith and credit clause 151
meta tags 168
police powers 155
preemption 158
privileges and immunities clause 150
probable cause 170
search warrant 170
supremacy clause 157
symbolic speech 162

FOR REVIEW

❶ What is the basic structure of the U.S. government?

❷ Which constitutional clause empowers the federal government to regulate commercial activities among the states?

❸ Which constitutional clause gives laws enacted by the federal government priority over conflicting state laws?

❹ What is the Bill of Rights, and which freedoms are guaranteed by the First Amendment?

❺ Where in the Constitution can the due process clause be found?

QUESTIONS AND CASE PROBLEMS

5–1. A Georgia state law requires the use of contoured rear-fender mudguards on trucks and trailers operating within Georgia state lines. The statute further makes it illegal for trucks and trailers to use straight mudguards. In approximately thirty-five other states, straight mudguards are legal. Moreover, in Florida, straight mudguards are explicitly required by law. There is some evidence suggesting that contoured mudguards might be a little safer than straight mudguards. Discuss whether this Georgia statute violates any constitutional provisions.

5–2. A business has a backlog of orders, and to meet its deadlines, management decides to run the firm seven days a week, eight hours a day. One of the employees, Abe Placer, refuses to work on Saturday on religious grounds. His refusal to work means that the firm may not meet its production deadlines and may therefore suffer a loss of future business. The firm fires Placer and replaces him with an employee who is willing to work seven days a week. Placer claims that by terminating his employment, his employer has violated his constitutional right to the free exercise of his religion. Do you agree? Why or why not?

5–3. The framers of the Constitution feared the twin evils of tyranny and anarchy. Discuss how specific provisions of the Constitution and the Bill of Rights reflect these fears and protect against both of these extremes.

CASE PROBLEM WITH SAMPLE ANSWER

5–4. Freedom of Religion. Thomas worked in the nonmilitary operations of a large firm that produced both military and nonmilitary goods. When the company discontinued the production of nonmilitary goods, Thomas was transferred to a plant producing military equipment. Thomas left his job, claiming that it violated his religious principles to participate in the manufacture of goods to be used in destroying life. In effect, he argued, the transfer to the war-materials plant forced him to quit his job. He was denied unemployment compensation by the state because he had not been effectively "discharged" by the employer but had voluntarily terminated his employment. Did the state's denial of unemployment benefits to Thomas violate the free exercise clause of the First Amendment? Explain. [*Thomas v. Review Board of the Indiana Employment Security Division,* 450 U.S. 707, 101 S.Ct. 1425, 67 L.Ed.2d 624 (1981)]

➧ *To view a sample answer for this case problem, go to this book's Web site at* **http://ele.westbuslaw.com** *and click on "Interactive Study Center."*

5–5. Equal Protection. With the objectives of preventing crime, maintaining property values, and preserving the quality of urban life, New York City enacted an ordinance to regulate the locations of commercial establishments that featured adult entertainment. The ordinance expressly applied to female, but not male, topless entertainment. Adele Buzzetti owned the Cozy Cabin, a New York City cabaret, that featured female topless dancers. Buzzetti and an anonymous dancer filed a suit in a federal district court against the city, asking the court to block the enforcement of the ordinance. The plaintiffs argued in part that the ordinance violated the equal protection clause. Under the equal protection clause, what standard applies to the court's consideration of this ordinance? Under this test, how should the court rule? Why? [*Buzzetti v. City of New York,* 140 F.3d 134 (2d Cir. 1998)]

5–6. Freedom of Speech. The City of Tacoma, Washington, enacted an ordinance that prohibited the playing of car sound systems at a volume that would be "audible" at a distance greater than fifty feet. Dwight Holland was arrested and convicted for violating the ordinance. The conviction was later dismissed, but Holland filed a civil suit in a Washington state court against the city. He claimed in part that the ordinance violated his freedom of speech under the First Amendment. On what basis might the court conclude that this ordinance is constitutional? (Hint: In playing a sound system, was Holland actually expressing himself?) [*Holland v. City of Tacoma,* 90 Wash.App. 533, 954 P.2d 290 (1998)]

5–7. Freedom of Speech. The members of Greater New Orleans Broadcasting Association, Inc., operate radio and television stations in New Orleans. They wanted to broadcast ads for private, for-profit casinos that are legal in Louisiana. A federal statute banned casino advertising, but other federal statutes exempted ads for tribal, government, nonprofit, and "occasional and ancillary" commercial casinos. The association filed a suit in a federal district court against the federal government, asking the court to hold that the statute, as it applied to the Louisiana casinos' ads, violated the First Amendment. The government argued that the ban should be upheld because, "[u]nder appropriate conditions, some broadcast signals from Louisiana broadcasting stations may be heard in neighboring states including Texas and Arkansas," where private casino gambling is unlawful. What is the test for whether a regulation of commercial speech violates the First Amendment? How might it apply in this case? How should the court rule? [*Greater New Orleans Broadcasting Association, Inc. v. United States,* 527 U.S. 173, 119 S.Ct. 1923, 144 L.Ed.2d 161 (1999)]

5–8. Freedom of Speech. The Telephone Consumer Protection Act (TCPA) of 1991 made it unlawful for any person "to use any telephone facsimile machine, computer, or other device to send an unsolicited advertisement to a telephone facsimile machine." In enacting the TCPA, Congress did not consider any studies or empirical data estimating the cost of receiving a fax or the number of unsolicited fax ads that an average business receives in a day. American Blast Fax, Inc. (ABFI), provides fax ad services in Missouri. Between July 2000 and June 2001, the office of Jeremiah Nixon, the Missouri attorney general, received 229 unsolicited faxes, some of which were ads. Nixon filed a suit in a federal district court against ABFI and others, alleging in part violations of the TCPA. ABFI filed a motion to dismiss, asserting that the TCPA provision on unsolicited fax ads was unconstitutional. Nixon claimed that the ads shifted costs from advertisers to recipients and tied up recipients' fax machines, but he offered no evidence of the expense in money or time. What is the test for considering a restriction on commercial speech? Is the TCPA provision valid? Explain. [*Nixon v. American Blast Fax, Inc.,* 196 F.Supp.2d 920 (E.D.Mo. 2002)]

5–9. Freedom of Speech. Henry Mishkoff is a Web designer whose firm does business as "Webfeats." When Taubman Co. began building a mall called "The Shops at Willow Bend" near Mishkoff's home, Mishkoff registered the domain name "shopsatwillowbend.com" and created a Web site with that address. The site featured information about the mall, a disclaimer indicating that Mishkoff's site was unofficial, and a link to the mall's official site. Taubman discovered Mishkoff's site and filed a suit in a federal district court against him. Mishkoff then registered other names, including "taubmansucks.com," with links to a site documenting his battle with Taubman. (A Web name with "sucks.com" attached to it is known as a "complaint name," and the process of registering and using such names is known as "cybergriping.") Taubman asked the court to order Mishkoff to stop using all of these names. Should the court grant Taubman's request? On what basis might the court protect Mishkoff's use of the names? [*Taubman Co. v. Webfeats,* 319 F.3d 770 (6th Cir. 2003)]

5–10. IN YOUR COURT

A state legislature enacted a statute that required any motorcycle operator or passenger on the state's highways to wear a protective helmet. Jim Alderman, a licensed motorcycle operator, sued the state to block enforcement of the law. Alderman asserted, among other things, that the statute violated the equal protection clause because it placed requirements on motorcyclists that were not imposed on other motorists. Assume that you are the judge in the trial court hearing this case and answer the following questions:

(a) What type of government interest must be served in order to justify discriminatory classifications under each of the three standards of scrutiny, or "tests," discussed in this chapter?

(b) Which standard, or test, applies to this case? Why?

(c) Applying this standard, or test, is the helmet statute constitutional? Why or why not?

5–11. A QUESTION OF ETHICS AND SOCIAL RESPONSIBILITY

In 1999, in an effort to reduce smoking by children, the Massachusetts attorney general issued comprehensive regulations governing the advertising and sale of tobacco products. Among other things, the regulations banned cigarette advertisements within one thousand feet of any elementary school, secondary school, or public playground and required retailers to post any advertising in their stores at least five feet off the floor, out of the immediate sight of young children. A group of tobacco manufacturers and retailers filed suit against the state, claiming that the regulations were preempted by the federal Cigarette Labeling and Advertising Act of 1965, as amended. That act sets uniform labeling requirements and bans broadcast advertising for cigarettes. Ultimately, the case reached the United States Supreme Court, which held that the federal law on cigarette ads preempted the cigarette advertising restrictions adopted by Massachusetts. The only portion of the Massachusetts regulatory package to survive was the requirement that retailers had to place tobacco products in an area accessible only by the sales staff. In view of these facts, consider the following questions. [*Lorillard Tobacco Co. v. Reilly,* 533 U.S. 525, 121 S.Ct. 2404, 69 L.Ed.2d 532 (2001)]

(a) Some argue that having a national standard for tobacco regulation is more important than allowing states to set their own standards for tobacco regulation. Do you agree? Why or why not?

(b) According to the Court in this case, the federal law does not restrict the ability of state and local governments to adopt general zoning restrictions that apply to cigarettes, as long as those restrictions are "on equal terms with other products." How would you argue in support of this reasoning? How would you argue against it?

5–12. FOR CRITICAL ANALYSIS

In recent years, many people have criticized the film and entertainment industries for promoting violence by exposing the American public, and particularly American youth, to extremely violent films and song lyrics. Do you think that the right to free speech can (or should) be traded off to reduce violence in America?

For updated links to resources available on the Web, as well as a variety of other materials, visit this text's Web site at

http://ele.westbuslaw.com

For an online version of the Constitution that provides hypertext links to amendments and other changes, as well as the history of the document, go to

http://www.constitutioncenter.org

For discussions of current issues involving the rights and liberties contained in the Bill of Rights, go to the Web site of the American Civil Liberties Union at

http://www.aclu.org

LEGAL RESEARCH EXERCISES ON THE WEB

Go to **http://ele.westbuslaw.com**, the Web site that accompanies this text. Select "Interactive Study Center," and then click on "Chapter 5." There you will find the following Internet research exercises that you can perform to learn more about topics covered in this chapter.

Activity 5–1: LEGAL PERSPECTIVE—Commercial Speech

Activity 5–2: MANAGEMENT PERSPECTIVE—Privacy Rights in Cyberspace

BEFORE THE TEST

Go to **http://ele.westbuslaw.com**, the Web site that accompanies this text. Select "Interactive Quizzes." You will find at least twenty interactive questions relating to this chapter.

WESTLAW® CAMPUS

If your textbook provided for a subscription to Westlaw® Campus, or if you have otherwise purchased access to the Westlaw Campus database, you can access any of the cases presented or cited in this chapter by using your Westlaw Campus account.

CHAPTER 6

Administrative Law

CONTENTS

CHAPTER OBJECTIVES

After reading this chapter, you should be able to answer the following questions:

1

How are federal administrative agencies created?

2

What are the three basic functions of most administrative agencies?

3

What sequence of events must normally occur before an agency rule becomes law?

4

How do administrative agencies enforce their rules?

How do the three branches of government limit the power of administrative agencies?

Government agencies established to administer the law have a tremendous impact on the day-to-day operation of the government and the economy. In the early years of our nation, the relatively simple, nonindustrial economy required little regulation. Consequently, only a few administrative agencies were needed to create and enforce regulations. Today, however, administrative agencies have multiplied. They issue rules covering virtually every aspect of a business's operation.

At the federal level, the Securities and Exchange Commission regulates a firm's capital structure and financing, as well as its financial reporting. The National Labor Relations Board oversees relations between a firm and any unions with which it may deal. The Equal Employment Opportunity Commission also regulates employer-employee relationships. The Environmental Protection Agency and the Occupational Safety and Health Administration affect the way a firm manufactures its products. The Federal Trade Commission influences the way it markets these products.

Added to this layer of federal regulation is a second layer of state regulation that, when not preempted by federal legislation, may cover many of the same activities or regulate independently those activities not covered by federal regulation. Finally, agency regulations at the county or municipal level also affect certain types of business activities.

The rules, orders, and decisions of administrative agencies make up the body of *administrative law*. You were introduced briefly to some of the main principles of administrative law in Chapter 1. In the following pages, we look at these principles in much greater detail.

AGENCY CREATION AND POWERS

Because Congress cannot possibly oversee the actual implementation of all of the laws it enacts, it must delegate such tasks to others, particularly when highly technical areas, such as air and water pollution, are involved. By delegating some of its authority to make and implement laws to administrative agencies, Congress can monitor indirectly a particular area in which it has passed legislation without becoming bogged down in the details of enforcement—details that are often best left to specialists.

Enabling Legislation

Enabling legislation • A statute enacted by Congress that authorizes the creation of an administrative agency and specifies the name, composition, purpose, functions, and powers of the agency being created.

To read the text of the Federal Trade Commission Act of 1914, go to the "Statutes" page of our Web site at **http://ele.westbuslaw.com**

To create an administrative agency, Congress passes **enabling legislation,** which specifies the name, composition, purpose, functions, and powers of the agency being created. Federal administrative agencies may exercise only those powers that Congress has delegated to them in enabling legislation. Through similar enabling acts, state legislatures create state administrative agencies.

Consider the enabling legislation for the Federal Trade Commission (FTC). The enabling statute for this agency is the Federal Trade Commission Act of 1914.[1] The act prohibits unfair methods of competition and deceptive trade practices. It also describes the procedures that the FTC must follow to charge persons or organizations with violations of the act, and it provides for judicial review of agency orders. The act grants the FTC the power to do the following:

1. Create rules and regulations for the purpose of carrying out the act.
2. Conduct investigations of business practices.
3. Obtain reports from interstate corporations concerning their business practices.
4. Investigate possible violations of federal antitrust statutes.[2]
5. Publish findings of its investigations.
6. Recommend new legislation.
7. Hold trial-like hearings to resolve certain kinds of trade disputes that involve FTC regulations or federal antitrust laws.

Agency Organization and Structure

The FTC can also provide an example of the organization and structure of a federal administrative agency. The commission that heads the FTC is composed of five members; each is appointed by the president, with the advice and consent of the Senate, for a term of seven years. The president designates one of the commissioners to be chairperson. Various offices and bureaus within the FTC undertake different administrative activities for the agency. Exhibit 6–1 illustrates the organization of the FTC.

Types of Agencies

As discussed in Chapter 1, there are two basic types of administrative agencies: executive agencies and independent regulatory agencies. Federal *executive agencies* include the cabinet departments of the executive branch, which were formed to assist the president in carrying out executive functions, and the subagencies within the cabinet departments. The Occupational Safety and Health Administration, for example, is a subagency within the Department of Labor. Exhibit 6–2 on page 186 lists the cabinet departments and some of their most important subagencies.

All administrative agencies are part of the executive branch of government, but *independent regulatory agencies* are outside the major executive departments. The Federal Trade Commission and the Securities and Exchange Commission are examples of independent regulatory agencies. These and

1. 15 U.S.C. Sections 41–58.

2. The FTC shares enforcement of the Clayton Act with the Antitrust Division of the U.S. Department of Justice. (Antitrust law will be discussed in Chapter 17.)

EXHIBIT 6–1 • ORGANIZATION OF THE FEDERAL TRADE COMMISSION

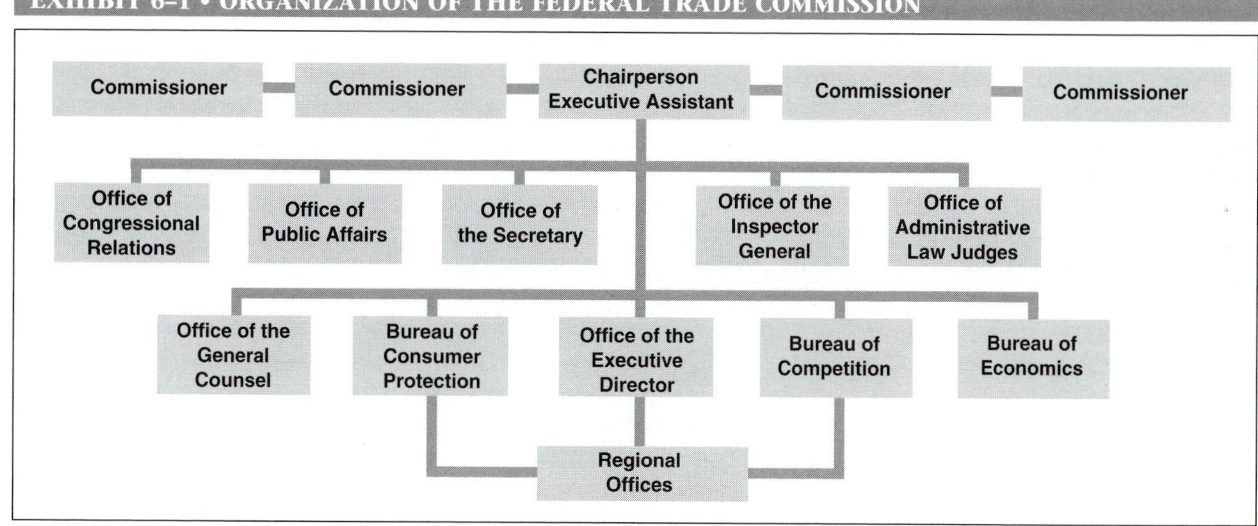

other selected independent regulatory agencies, as well as their principal functions, are listed in Exhibit 6–3 on page 187.

The accountability of the regulators is the most significant difference between the two types of agencies. Agencies that are considered part of the executive branch are subject to the authority of the president, who has the power to appoint and remove federal officers. In theory, this power is less pronounced in regard to independent agencies, whose officers serve for fixed terms and cannot be removed without just cause. In practice, however, the president's ability to exert influence over independent agencies is often considerable.

Agency Powers and the Constitution

Administrative agencies occupy an unusual niche in the U.S. legal scheme because they exercise powers that are normally divided among the three branches of government. Notice that in the FTC's enabling legislation, discussed earlier, the FTC's grant of power incorporates functions associated with the legislative branch (rulemaking), the executive branch (enforcement of the rules), and the courts (**adjudication,** or the formal resolution of disputes).

Adjudication • The process of adjudicating, or formally resolving, a dispute.

Legislative Rules. As you learned in Chapter 5, the constitutional principle of checks and balances allows each branch of government to act as a check on the actions of the other two branches. Furthermore, the U.S. Constitution authorizes only the legislative branch to create laws. Yet administrative agencies, to which the Constitution does not specifically refer, make **legislative rules,** or *substantive rules*, that are as legally binding as laws that Congress passes.

Legislative rule • An administrative agency rule that carries the same weight as a congressionally enacted statute.

The Delegation Doctrine. Courts generally hold that Article I of the U.S. Constitution authorizes delegating such powers to administrative agencies. In fact, courts generally hold that Article I is the basis for all administrative law. Section 1 of that article grants all legislative powers to Congress and requires Congress to oversee the implementation of all laws. Article I, Section 8, gives Congress the power to make all laws necessary for executing its specified powers. The courts interpret these passages, under what is referred to as the **delegation doctrine,** as granting Congress the power to

Delegation doctrine • A doctrine based on Article I, Sections 1 and 8, of the U.S. Constitution, which have been construed to allow Congress to delegate some of its power to make and implement laws to administrative agencies. The delegation is considered to be proper as long as Congress sets standards outlining the scope of the agency's authority.

EXHIBIT 6–2 • EXECUTIVE DEPARTMENTS AND SELECTED SUBAGENCIES

DEPARTMENT	DATE FORMED	SELECTED SUBAGENCIES
State	1789	Passport Office; Bureau of Diplomatic Security; Foreign Service; Bureau of Human Rights and Humanitarian Affairs; Bureau of Consular Affairs; Bureau of Intelligence and Research
Treasury	1789	Internal Revenue Service; U.S. Mint
Interior	1849	U.S. Fish and Wildlife Service; National Park Service; Bureau of Indian Affairs; Bureau of Land Management
Justice	1870[a]	Federal Bureau of Investigation; Drug Enforcement Administration; Bureau of Prisons; U.S. Marshals Service
Agriculture	1889	Soil Conservation Service; Agricultural Research Service; Food Safety and Inspection Service; Farmers Home Administration
Commerce	1913[b]	Bureau of the Census; Bureau of Economic Analysis; Minority Business Development Agency; U.S. Patent and Trademark Office; National Oceanic and Atmospheric Administration
Labor	1913[b]	Occupational Safety and Health Administration; Bureau of Labor Statistics; Employment Standards Administration; Office of Labor-Management Standards; Employment and Training Administration
Defense	1949[c]	National Security Agency; Joint Chiefs of Staff; Departments of the Air Force, Navy, and Army
Housing and Urban Development	1965	Assistant Secretary for Community Planning and Development; Government National Mortgage Association; Assistant Secretary for Fair Housing and Equal Opportunity
Transportation	1967	Federal Aviation Administration; Federal Highway Administration; National Highway Traffic Safety Administration; Federal Transit Administration
Energy	1977	Office of Civilian Radioactive Waste Management; Office of Nuclear Energy; Energy Information Administration
Health and Human Services	1980[d]	Food and Drug Administration; Health Care Financing Administration; Public Health Service
Education	1980[d]	Office of Special Education and Rehabilitation Services; Office of Elementary and Secondary Education; Office of Postsecondary Education; Office of Vocational and Adult Education
Veterans' Affairs	1989	Veterans Health Administration; Veterans Benefits Administration; National Cemetery System
Homeland Security	2002	Bureau of Citizenship and Immigration Services; U.S. Coast Guard; Federal Emergency Management Agency

a. Formed from the Office of the Attorney General (created in 1789).
b. Formed from the Department of Commerce and Labor (created in 1903).
c. Formed from the Department of War (created in 1789) and the Department of the Navy (created in 1798).
d. Formed from the Department of Health, Education, and Welfare (created in 1953).

establish administrative agencies that can create rules for implementing those laws.

The three branches of government exercise certain controls over agency powers and functions, as will be discussed later in this chapter, but in many

EXHIBIT 6–3 • SELECTED INDEPENDENT REGULATORY AGENCIES

NAME	DATE FORMED	PRINCIPAL DUTIES
Federal Reserve System Board of Governors (Fed)	1913	Determines policy with respect to interest rates, credit availability, and the money supply.
Federal Trade Commission (FTC)	1914	Prevents businesses from engaging in unfair trade practices; stops the formation of monopolies in the business sector; protects consumer rights.
Securities and Exchange Commission (SEC)	1934	Regulates the nation's stock exchanges, in which shares of stock are bought and sold; enforces the securities laws, which require full disclosure of the financial profiles of companies that wish to sell stock and bonds to the public.
Federal Communications Commission (FCC)	1934	Regulates all communications by telegraph, cable, telephone, radio, satellite, and television.
National Labor Relations Board (NLRB)	1935	Protects employees' rights to join unions and bargain collectively with employers; attempts to prevent unfair labor practices by both employers and unions.
Equal Employment Opportunity Commission (EEOC)	1964	Works to eliminate discrimination in employment based on religion, gender, race, color, disability, national origin, or age; investigates claims of discrimination.
Environmental Protection Agency (EPA)	1970	Undertakes programs aimed at reducing air and water pollution; works with state and local agencies to help fight environmental hazards.
Nuclear Regulatory Commission (NRC)	1975	Ensures that electricity-generating nuclear reactors in the United States are built and operated safely; regularly inspects operations of such reactors.

ways administrative agencies function independently. For this reason, administrative agencies, which constitute the **bureaucracy,** are sometimes referred to as the "fourth branch" of the U.S. government.

Bureaucracy • A large organization that is structured hierarchically to carry out specific functions.

Administrative Process

The three functions mentioned previously—rulemaking, enforcement, and adjudication—make up what is known as the **administrative process.** Administrative process involves the administration of law by administrative agencies, in contrast to **judicial process,** which comprises the administration of law by the courts.

Administrative process • The procedure used by administrative agencies in the administration of law.

Judicial process • The procedures relating to, or connected with, the administration of justice through the judicial system.

All federal agencies must follow specific procedural requirements in their rulemaking, adjudication, and other functions. Sometimes, Congress specifies certain procedural requirements in an agency's enabling legislation. In the absence of any directives from Congress concerning a particular agency procedure, the Administrative Procedure Act (APA) of 1946[3] applies. The APA is such an integral part of the administrative process that its application will be examined as we go through the basic functions carried out by administrative

3. 5 U.S.C. Sections 551–706.

To read the text of the Administrative Procedure Act of 1946, go to the "Statutes" page of our Web site at **http://ele.westbuslaw.com**

Rulemaking • The process undertaken by an administrative agency when formally adopting a new regulation or amending an old one. Rulemaking involves notifying the public of a proposed rule or change and receiving and considering the public's comments.

Notice-and-comment rulemaking • An administrative rulemaking procedure that involves the publication of a notice of a proposed rulemaking in the *Federal Register,* a comment period for interested parties to express their views on the proposed rule, and the publication of the agency's final rule in the *Federal Register.*

agencies. In addition, agency procedures are guided indirectly by the courts' interpretation of APA requirements.

Rulemaking

A major function of an administrative agency is **rulemaking**—the formulation of new regulations. In an agency's enabling legislation, Congress confers the agency's power to make legislative rules, as already mentioned. For example, the Occupational Safety and Health Act of 1970 authorized the Occupational Safety and Health Administration (OSHA) to develop and issue rules governing safety in the workplace. In formulating any new legislative rule, OSHA has to follow specific rulemaking procedures required under the APA.

In addition to making legislative rules, administrative agencies also make *interpretive rules.* These rules are not legally binding on the public but simply indicate how an agency plans to interpret and enforce its statutory authority. For example, the Equal Employment Opportunity Commission periodically issues interpretive rules, usually referred to as enforcement guidelines, indicating how it plans to interpret and apply a provision of a certain statute, such as the Americans with Disabilities Act. When making interpretive rules, an agency need not follow the requirements of the APA.

The most commonly used rulemaking procedure is called **notice-and-comment rulemaking.** This procedure involves three basic steps: notice of the proposed rulemaking, a comment period, and the final rule.

Notice of the Proposed Rulemaking. When a federal agency decides to create a new rule, the agency publishes a notice of the proposed rulemaking proceedings in the *Federal Register,* a daily publication of the executive branch that prints government orders, rules, and regulations. The notice states where and when the proceedings will be held, the agency's legal authority for making the rule (usually its enabling legislation), and the terms or subject matter of the proposed rule.

Comment Period. Following the publication of the notice of the proposed rulemaking proceedings, the agency must allow ample time for persons to comment in writing on the proposed rule. The purpose of this comment period is to give interested parties the opportunity to express their views on the proposed rule in an effort to influence agency policy. The comments may be in writing or, if a hearing is held, may be given orally.

The agency need not respond to all comments, but it must respond to any significant comments that bear directly on the proposed rule. The agency responds by either modifying its final rule or explaining, in a statement accompanying the final rule, why it did not make any changes. In some circumstances, particularly when the procedure being used in a specific instance is less formal, an agency may accept comments after the comment period is closed. The agency should summarize these *ex parte* (private, "off-the-record") comments in the record for possible review.

The Final Rule. After the agency reviews the comments, it drafts the final rule and publishes it in the *Federal Register.* The final rule is later compiled with the rules and regulations of other federal administrative agencies in the *Code of Federal Regulations* (C.F.R.). Final rules have binding legal effect unless the courts later overturn them.

In the following case, AT&T Corporation and other established local telephone service providers asked the United States Supreme Court to overturn a Federal Communications Commission (FCC) rule issued to implement part of the Telecommunications Act of 1996. The Court considered how the FCC interpreted certain terms in the act when it formulated its rule.

AT&T CORP. v. IOWA UTILITIES BOARD

CASE 6.1

Supreme Court of the United States, 1999.
525 U.S. 366,
119 S.Ct. 721,
142 L.Ed.2d 835.
http://supct.law.cornell.edu/supct/search/search.html[a]

Until the 1990s, local telephone service was thought to be a natural monopoly. States typically granted an exclusive franchise in each local service area to a local exchange carrier (LEC), which would own, among other things, the local loops (wires connecting telephones to switches), the switches (equipment directing calls to their destinations), and the transport trunks (wires carrying calls between switches) that constitute a local exchange network. When technological advances made competition among multiple providers of local service seem possible, however, Congress enacted the Telecommunications Act of 1996 to end the state-sanctioned monopolies. The Telecommunications Act required existing LECs to, among other things, share elements of their networks (loops, switches, and trunks) with their new competitors. The act ordered the Federal Communications Commission (FCC) to issue rules to implement this requirement. In deciding which elements to make available, the FCC was directed to consider whether access to each element was "necessary" and whether a lack of access would "impair" a competitor's ability to provide service. The FCC concluded that access was "necessary" even if a competitor could substitute an element from another source and that "impairment" occurred if a competitor experienced any increase in cost or decrease in quality when access was denied. The FCC issued Rule 319, requiring the LECs to give their new competitors access to seven specific network elements.[b] *The LECs, including AT&T Corporation, and others filed suits in courts across the United States to challenge the FCC's new rules, including Rule 319. The suits were combined into a single case in the U.S. Court of Appeals for the Eighth Circuit, which held, among other things, that the FCC's interpretations of "necessary" and "impair" were reasonable. The LECs appealed to the United States Supreme Court.*

SCALIA, J.

[T]he [Telecommunications] Act requires the FCC to apply some limiting standard, rationally related to the goals of the Act, which it has simply failed to do. * * * [I]t is hard to imagine when [an LEC's] failure to give access to the element[s] would *not* constitute an "impairment" under [the FCC's] standard. * * * [T]hat judgment allows [competitors], rather than the [FCC], to determine whether access to [the] elements is necessary, and whether the failure to obtain access to [the] elements would impair the ability to provide

a. This page is part of the database of United States Supreme Court opinions maintained by the Legal Information Institute of Cornell Law School. On this page, in the "Search for:" box, type in "Iowa Utilities Board" and select "All decisions." Click on the case title to access the opinion.
b. 47 C.F.R. Section 51.319. The seven elements included "the local loop, the network interface device, switching capability, interoffice transmission facilities, signaling networks and call-related databases, operations support systems functions, and operator services and directory assistance."

services. *The [FCC] cannot, consistent with the statute, [ignore] the availability of elements outside the [LEC's] network.* That failing alone would require [Rule 319] to be set aside. In addition, however, the [FCC's] assumption that any increase in cost (or decrease in quality) imposed by denial of a network element renders access to that element "necessary," and causes the failure to provide that element to "impair" the [competitor's] ability to furnish its desired services, is simply not in accord with the ordinary and fair meaning of those terms. [A competitor] whose anticipated annual profits from the proposed service are reduced [by only 1 percent] of [its] investment has perhaps been "impaired" in its ability to amass earnings, but has not * * * been "impair[ed] * * * in its ability to provide the services it seeks to offer"; and it cannot realistically be said that the network element enabling it to [increase] its profits [by 1 percent] is "necessary." In a world of perfect competition, in which all carriers are providing their service at marginal [incremental] cost, the [FCC's] total equating of increased cost (or decreased quality) with "necessity" and "impairment" might be reasonable; but it has not established the existence of such an ideal world. [Emphasis added.]

The United States Supreme Court concluded that the FCC did not interpret the terms of the Telecommunications Act in a "reasonable fashion" and vacated Rule 319. The Court indicated that the FCC should consider the availability, to competitors, of elements outside the LECs' networks.

QUESTIONS

1. Why did the LECs appeal this case to the United States Supreme Court?
2. Why did the Supreme Court disagree with the FCC's interpretation of the terms *necessary* and *impair*?
3. Why doesn't Congress always define specifically what an administrative agency is to consider when making rules?

Investigation

Administrative agencies conduct investigations of the entities that they regulate. One type of agency investigation occurs during the rulemaking process to obtain information about a certain individual, firm, or industry. The purpose of such an investigation is to ensure that the rule issued is based on a consideration of relevant factors and is not arbitrary and capricious. After final rules are issued, agencies conduct investigations to monitor compliance with those rules. A typical agency investigation of this kind might begin when a citizen reports a possible violation.

Inspections. Many agencies gather information through on-site inspections. Sometimes, inspecting an office, a factory, or some other business facility is the only way to obtain the evidence needed to prove a regulatory violation. Administrative inspections and tests cover a wide range of activities, including safety inspections of underground coal mines, safety tests of commercial equipment and automobiles, and environmental monitoring of factory emissions. An agency may also ask a firm or individual to submit certain documents or records to the agency for examination.

Normally, business firms comply with agency requests to inspect facilities or business records because it is in any firm's interest to maintain a good relationship with regulatory bodies. In some instances, however, such as when a firm thinks an agency's request is unreasonable and may be detrimental to the firm's interest, the firm may refuse to comply with the request. In such situations, an agency may resort to the use of a *subpoena* or a *search warrant.*

Subpoenas. There are two basic types of subpoenas. The subpoena *ad testificandum* ("to testify") is an ordinary subpoena. It is a writ, or order, compelling a witness to appear at an agency hearing. The subpoena *duces tecum*[4] ("bring it with you") compels an individual or organization to hand over books, papers, records, or documents to the agency. An administrative agency may use either type of subpoena during an investigation.

There are limits on the information an agency can demand. To determine whether an agency is abusing its discretion in its pursuit of information as part of an investigation, a court may consider such factors as the following:

1. *The purpose of the investigation.* An investigation must have a legitimate purpose. Harassment is an example of an improper purpose.
2. *The relevance of the information being sought.* Information is relevant if it reveals that the law is being violated or if it assures the agency that the law is not being violated.
3. *The specificity of the demand for testimony or documents.* A subpoena must, for example, adequately describe the material being sought.
4. *The burden of the demand on the party from whom the information is sought.* In responding to a request for information, a party must bear the costs of, for example, copying the documents that must be handed over; a business is generally protected from revealing such information as trade secrets, however.

In addition, a subpoena might not be enforced when the subject matter of an investigation is not within the authority of the agency to investigate. The issue in the following case was whether the subject matter of certain subpoenas issued by the Federal Trade Commission had exceeded the agency's statutory authority.

4. Pronounced *doo*-seez *tay*-kum.

FEDERAL TRADE COMMISSION v. KEN ROBERTS CO.

CASE 6.2

United States Court of Appeals, District of Columbia Circuit, 2001. 276 F.3d 583.

Ken Roberts Company, Ken Roberts Institute, Inc., United States Chart Company, and Ted Warren Corporation (collectively, Roberts) sell instructional materials that claim to teach would-be investors how to make money investing. In 1999, the Federal Trade Commission (FTC) began investigating whether a variety of online businesses were engaged in deceptive marketing practices in violation of the Federal Trade Commission Act. Aiming at high-risk, high-yield investment activity and suspicious Internet advertising, the FTC soon focused on Roberts. The FTC issued subpoenas that required Roberts to produce documents and answer written questions relating to the companies' business practices. Roberts refused to respond to most of the requests. The FTC asked a federal district court to enforce the subpoenas. When the court ordered Roberts to comply, Roberts appealed to the U.S. Court of Appeals for the District of Columbia Circuit. Roberts argued that the FTC's authority to investigate Roberts's practices was preempted by other federal statutes regulating investment advisers, including the Investment Advisers Act (IAA).

EDWARDS, J.

Subpoena enforcement power is not limitless * * * . *[A] subpoena is proper only where the inquiry is within the authority of the agency, the demand is not too indefinite, and the information sought is reasonably relevant.* Accordingly, there is no doubt that a court asked to enforce a subpoena will refuse to do so if the subpoena exceeds an express statutory limitation on the agency's investigative powers. Thus, a court must assure itself that the subject matter of the investigation is within the statutory jurisdiction of the subpoena-issuing agency. * * * [Emphasis added.]

* * * *

On its own terms, the FTC Act gives the FTC ample authority to investigate and, if deceptive practices are uncovered, to regulate appellants' advertising practices. Therefore, the FTC is entitled to have its subpoenas enforced unless some other source of law patently [clearly] undermines these broad powers. * * *

* * * *

[Appellants], whose businesses involve securities * * * , assert that the comprehensive scope of the Investment Advisers Act of 1940 preempts the FTC's jurisdiction to regulate the fraudulent practices of "investment advisers" such as themselves. * * *

* * * [T]he IAA contains no express exclusive jurisdiction provision. * * * [But] where intended by Congress, a precisely drawn, detailed statute preempts more general remedies. This can occur either where the two enactments are in irreconcilable conflict or where the latter was clearly meant to serve as a substitute for the former. Appellants contend that the antifraud provision of the IAA, which prohibits investment advisers from engaging "in any transaction, practice, or course of business which operates as a fraud or deceit upon any client or prospective client," stands as just such a specific remedy that displaces the more general coverage of the FTC Act.

* * * *

Because we live in an age of overlapping and concurring regulatory jurisdiction, a court must proceed with the utmost caution before concluding that one agency may not regulate merely because another may. In this case, while it may be true that the IAA and the FTC Act employ different verbal formulae to describe their antifraud standards, it hardly follows that they therefore impose conflicting or incompatible obligations. Undoubtedly, entities in appellants' position can—and of course should—refrain from engaging in both "unfair and deceptive acts or practices" *and* "any transaction, practice, or course of business which operates as a fraud or deceit upon a client or prospective client." The proscriptions of the IAA are not diminished or confused merely because investment advisers must also avoid that which the FTC Act proscribes. And, because these statutes are capable of co-existence, it becomes the *duty* of this court to regard each as effective—at least absent clear congressional intent to the contrary.

Appellants can point to nothing in the background or history of the IAA that demonstrates (or even hints at) a congressional intent to preempt the antifraud jurisdiction of the FTC over those covered by the new statute. Nor does the subsequent case law interpreting these statutes contain such declarations.

The U.S. Court of Appeals for the District of Columbia Circuit affirmed the lower court's decision. The appellate court held that the FTC was entitled to the enforcement of its subpoenas against Roberts. The Investment Advisers Act does not preempt the FTC's authority to investigate possibly deceptive advertising and marketing practices merely because those practices relate to the investment business.

QUESTIONS

1. On what did Roberts base its appeal of this case to the U.S. Court of Appeals for the District of Columbia Circuit?
2. Why did the U.S. Court of Appeals for the District of Columbia Circuit hold that the FTC was entitled to enforce its subpoenas against Roberts?
3. The FTC has never undertaken to adjudicate deceptive conduct in the sale and purchase of securities (stocks and bonds). Is this fact alone sufficient to indicate that the agency does not have that power?

Search Warrants. The Fourth Amendment protects against unreasonable searches and seizures by requiring that a search warrant be obtained prior to the search, at least in most instances. An agency's search warrant is an order directing law enforcement officials to search a specific place for a specific item and present it to the agency. Although it was once thought that administrative inspections were exempt from the warrant requirement, the United States Supreme Court held in *Marshall v. Barlow's, Inc.,*[5] that the requirement does apply to the administrative process.

Agencies can conduct warrantless searches in several situations. Warrants are not required to conduct searches in highly regulated industries. Firms that sell firearms or liquor, for example, are automatically subject to inspections without warrants. Sometimes, a statute permits warrantless searches of certain types of hazardous operations, such as coal mines. Also, a warrantless inspection in an emergency situation is normally considered reasonable.

Adjudication

After conducting an investigation of a suspected rule violation, an agency may begin to take administrative action against an individual or organization. Most administrative actions are resolved through negotiated settlements at their initial stages, without the need for formal adjudication.

Negotiated Settlements. Depending on the agency, negotiations may take the form of a simple conversation or a series of informal conferences. Whatever form the negotiations take, their purpose is to rectify the problem to the agency's satisfaction and eliminate the need for additional proceedings.

---

5. 436 U.S. 307, 98 S.Ct. 1816, 56 L.Ed.2d 305 (1978).

Settlement is an appealing option to firms for two reasons: to avoid appearing uncooperative and to avoid the expense involved in formal adjudication proceedings and in possible later appeals. Settlement is also an attractive option for agencies. To conserve their own resources and avoid formal actions, administrative agencies devote a great deal of effort to giving advice and negotiating solutions to problems.

Administrative law judge (ALJ) • One who presides over an administrative agency hearing and who has the power to administer oaths, take testimony, rule on questions of evidence, and make determinations of fact.

Formal Complaints. If a settlement cannot be reached, the agency may issue a formal complaint against the suspected violator. If the Environmental Protection Agency (EPA), for example, finds that a factory is polluting groundwater in violation of federal pollution laws, the EPA will issue a complaint against the violator in an effort to bring the plant into compliance with federal regulations. This complaint is a public document, and a press release may accompany it. The factory charged in the complaint will respond by filing an answer to the EPA's allegations. If the factory and the EPA cannot agree on a settlement, the case will be adjudicated. Agency adjudication may involve a trial-like procedure before an **administrative law judge (ALJ).** The adjudication process is described next and illustrated graphically in Exhibit 6–4.

EXHIBIT 6–4 • THE PROCESS OF FORMAL ADMINISTRATIVE ADJUDICATION

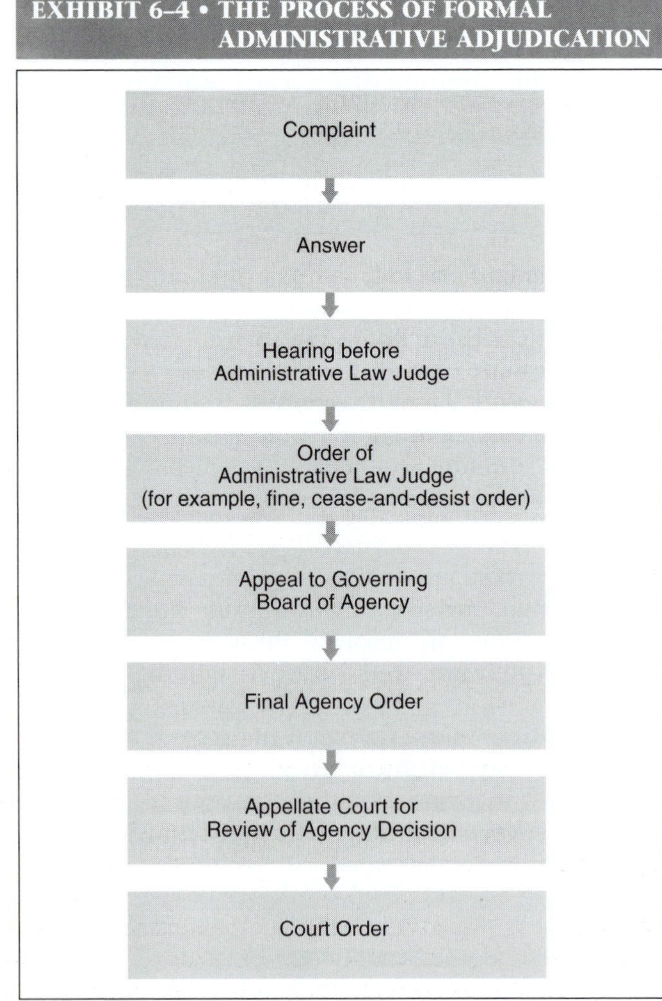

The Role of the Administrative Law Judge. The ALJ presides over the hearing and has the power to administer oaths, take testimony, rule on questions of evidence, and make determinations of fact. Although formally the ALJ works for the agency prosecuting the case (in our example, the EPA), the law requires an ALJ to be an unbiased adjudicator (judge).

Certain safeguards prevent bias on the part of the ALJ and promote fairness in the proceedings. For example, the Administrative Procedure Act (APA) requires that the ALJ be separate from an agency's investigative and prosecutorial staff. The APA also prohibits *ex parte* (private) communications between the ALJ and any party to an agency proceeding, such as the EPA or the factory in our example. Finally, provisions of the APA protect the ALJ from agency disciplinary actions unless the agency can show good cause for such an action.

Hearing Procedures. Hearing procedures vary widely from agency to agency. Administrative agencies generally exercise substantial discretion over the type of procedure that will be used. Frequently, disputes are resolved through informal adjudication proceedings. For example, the parties, their counsel, and the ALJ may simply meet at a table in a conference room to attempt to settle the dispute.

A formal adjudicatory hearing, in contrast, resembles a trial in many respects. Prior to the hearing, the parties are permitted to undertake extensive discovery (involving depositions, interrogatories, and requests for documents or other information, as described in Chapter 2). During the hearing, the parties may give testimony, present other evidence, and cross-examine adverse witnesses. A significant difference between a trial and an administrative agency hearing, though, is that normally much more information, including hearsay (secondhand information), can be introduced as evidence during an administrative hearing.

Agency Orders. Following a hearing, the ALJ renders an **initial order,** or decision, on the case. Either party can appeal the ALJ's decision to the board or commission that governs the agency. If the factory in the example given earlier is dissatisfied with the ALJ's decision, it can appeal the decision to the commission that governs the EPA. If the factory is dissatisfied with the commission's decision, it can appeal the decision to a federal court of appeals. If no party appeals the case, the ALJ's decision becomes the **final order** of the agency. The ALJ's decision also becomes final if a party appeals and the commission and the court decline to review the case. If a party appeals and the case is reviewed, the final order is the commission's decision or (if that decision is appealed to a federal appellate court) the court's decision.

Initial order • In the context of administrative law, an administrative law judge's order. The order becomes final unless it is appealed.

Final order • The final decision of an administrative agency on an issue. If no appeal is taken, or if the case is not reviewed or considered anew by the agency commission, the administrative law judge's initial order becomes the final order of the agency.

LIMITATIONS ON AGENCY POWERS

Combining the functions normally divided among the three branches of government into an administrative agency concentrates considerable power in a single organization. Because of this concentration of authority, one of the major policy objectives of the government is to control the risks of arbitrariness and overreaching by administrative agencies without hindering the effective use of agency power to deal with particular problem areas, as Congress intended.

The judicial branch of the government exercises control over agency powers through the courts' review of agency actions. The executive and legislative branches of government also exercise control over agency authority.

Judicial Controls

The Administrative Procedure Act provides for judicial review of most agency decisions, as already discussed. Agency actions are not automatically subject to judicial review, however.

The Ripeness Doctrine. Under what is known as the *ripeness doctrine,* a court will not review an administrative agency's decision until the case is "ripe for review." Generally, a case is ripe for review if the parties can demonstrate that they have met certain requirements. The party bringing the action must have *standing to sue* the agency (the party must have a direct stake in the outcome of the judicial proceeding), and there must be an *actual controversy* at issue. These are basic judicial requirements that must be met before any court will hear a case, as discussed in Chapter 2. With regard to agency decisions, however, the party must also have *exhausted all possible administrative remedies.* Each agency has its "chain of review," and the party must follow agency appeal procedures before a court will conclude that administrative remedies have been exhausted.

The rationale for this doctrine is to prevent courts from entangling themselves in abstract disagreements over administrative policies. The doctrine also protects agencies from judicial interference until an administrative decision has been formalized and its effects are clear. The court can then evaluate both the appropriateness of an issue for judicial decision and the hardship the decision will cause to the challenging party if the court refuses to consider the case.

Issues Considered When Reviewing Agency Decisions. Recall from Chapter 2 that appellate courts normally defer to the decisions of trial courts on questions of fact. In reviewing administrative actions, the courts show a similar deference to (reluctance to question) the factual findings of agencies.

In reviewing an administrative agency's decision, a court normally will consider the following types of issues:

1. Whether the agency has exceeded its authority under its enabling legislation.
2. Whether the agency has properly interpreted laws applicable to the agency action under review.
3. Whether the agency has violated any constitutional provisions.
4. Whether the agency has acted in accordance with procedural requirements of the law.
5. Whether the agency's actions were arbitrary, capricious, or an abuse of discretion.
6. Whether any conclusions drawn by the agency are not supported by substantial evidence.

The fifth element in the above list is often referred to as the "arbitrary and capricious" test. An agency action will be deemed arbitrary and capricious if it was taken willfully and unreasonably, and without considering the facts of the case.

In the case presented next, the Cellular Telecommunications & Internet Association and others asked a court to review an order of the Federal Communications Commission (FCC) relating to the enforcement of an FCC rule. The court considered how the FCC interpreted and applied a phrase in the Telecommunications Act of 1996 when the agency issued its order.

CASE 6.3

United States Court of Appeals, District of Columbia Circuit, 2003. 330 F.3d 502. **http://www.findlaw.com/casecode/courts/dc.html**[a]

CELLULAR TELECOMMUNICATIONS & INTERNET ASSOCIATION v. FEDERAL COMMUNICATIONS COMMISSION

*Congress enacted the Telecommunications Act of 1996 to "promote competition and reduce regulation in order to secure lower prices and higher quality services for American telecommunications consumers and encourage the rapid deployment of new telecommunications technologies." The act directs the Federal Communications Commission (FCC) to "forbear from applying any regulation * * * if the [FCC] determines that * * * enforcement * * * is not necessary for the protection of consumers."*[b] *At the time, a wireless telephone customer who wished to switch from one wireless service provider to another had to also change phone numbers. In 1996, the FCC issued rules that required wireless service providers to offer, by June 30, 1999, number portability.*[c] *In 1999, the FCC granted a request of the Cellular Telecommunications & Internet Association (CTIA) and others for a temporary forbearance from enforcing these rules and extended the deadline to November 24, 2002 (and later to November 24, 2003), partly because the industry needed more time to develop its technology. The FCC issued an order refusing to permanently forbear from enforcing the rules, however, on finding that consumers would otherwise be "forced to stay with carriers with whom they may be dissatisfied," due to price, service, or coverage, "because the cost of giving up their wireless phone number in order to move to another carrier is too high." The CTIA and others filed a suit against the FCC in the U.S. Court of Appeals for the District of Columbia Circuit for a review of this order. The plaintiffs argued, in part, that the FCC misinterpreted and misapplied the statutory phrase requiring the agency to forbear from enforcing its regulations if "enforcement * * * is not necessary for the protection of consumers."*

EDWARDS, J.

Petitioners' challenge to the Commission's [order] centers on the meaning of the statutory term "necessary." Petitioners contend that * * * the Commission erred in failing to construe "necessary" to mean "absolutely required," "indispensable," or "essential." Petitioners' position is that the Commission must forbear from enforcement of its wireless number portability rules if enforcement is not *absolutely required* to protect consumers. Petitioners argue that enforcement of the wireless number portability rules is not absolutely required to protect consumers, because, in petitioners' view, the rate of wireless consumers switching carriers is high even absent number portability.

Petitioners contend that this reasoning is compelled by the plain meaning of the adjective "necessary," which, they point out, often is defined as "absolutely required," "indispensable," or "essential." But dueling over dictionary definitions is pointless, for it fails to produce any plain meaning of the disputed word. If we focus on legal contexts, *Black's Law Dictionary* defines "necessary and proper" to mean "[b]eing appropriate and well adapted to fulfilling an objective." * * * Hence the word "necessary" does not always mean absolutely required or indispensable.

---

a. In the "By Date" section, select "2003" and "June," and then click on "search." In the list of results, click on "Cell Telecom v. FCC" to access the opinion.

b. 47 U.S.C. Section 160(a).

c. *Number portability* is the ability of consumers to keep their phone numbers when they switch carriers.

Indeed, there are many situations in which the use of the word "necessary," in context, means something that is done, regardless of whether it is indispensable, to achieve a particular end. For example, "necessary improvement" is defined as "an improvement to property that is made to prevent its deterioration" [in] *Webster's Third New International Dictionary of the English Language Unabridged.* * * *

* * * *

* * * [I]f a house foundation is weakening due to excess water on the property, and the goal of a home improvement project is to eliminate the water problem, viable solutions might include rebuilding the foundation to make it strong enough to withstand any water, digging around the house to divert water away from the house, or adding sump pumps to the house interior to expel water excesses. A solution is "required to achieve the desired goal," thus "necessary." None of the solutions is "indispensable" in the sense that it is absolutely required, because either of the other two might do as well to achieve the desired goal. But the selection of any one of the solutions is "necessary" to achieve the desired goal. Thus, the solution that is selected is necessary to achieve the desired goal.

Courts have frequently interpreted the word "necessary" to mean less than absolutely essential, and have explicitly found that a measure may be necessary even though acceptable alternatives have not been exhausted. Context is relevant to the interpretation of the term "necessary." The meaning varies with context, and a dictionary definition by no means tells us what "necessary" means in every statutory context.

* * * *

In the * * * forbearance context, *application of petitioners' definition of "necessary" would lead to an absurd result, because it is difficult to imagine a regulation whose enforcement is absolutely required or indispensable to protect consumers.* Indeed, when counsel for petitioners was questioned about this, he could not give a viable example of a "necessary" regulation. None. In the forbearance context, we think that it would defy common sense to adopt a construction of "necessary" that results in a criterion that can never be met. What would follow is that every regulation would, strictly speaking, be "not necessary for the protection of consumers." * * * The Commission always would be required to forbear from enforcement * * * . [Emphasis added.]

Adopting petitioners' rigid construction of "necessary" in the forbearance context would result in a further absurdity. Under petitioners' view, the FCC, which is permitted to promulgate regulations which are subject to limited review under an arbitrary and capricious standard, could be required, the very next day, to forbear from enforcement of the same regulations, because the unattainable criterion of "necessary" cannot be met. In fact, under petitioners' view of [the Telecommunications Act] the Commission must also forbear from enforcement of all *statutory provisions* (not only agency regulations) that are not "absolutely required" or "indispensable." We can find no evidence that this is what Congress intended when it enacted [the Telecommunications Act] especially when petitioners' definition of "necessary" admits of no obvious applications.

* * * *

* * * [W]e find the Commission's interpretation of "necessary" eminently reasonable. In the forbearance context, for the reasons already stated, it is reasonable to construe "necessary" as referring to the existence of a strong connection between what the agency has done by way of regulation

and what the agency permissibly sought to achieve with the disputed regulation. In other words, *the number portability rules are required to achieve the desired goal of consumer protection. That is essentially the definition of "necessary" that the Commission embraced and applied in its Order.* We therefore find that deference to the agency's reasonable interpretation * * * is appropriate. [Emphasis added.]

The U.S. Court of Appeals for the District of Columbia Circuit dismissed the plaintiffs' challenge to the FCC's decision not to forbear from enforcing its number portability rules. The court concluded that the FCC's interpretation of the term necessary *was reasonable. The FCC applied this interpretation to find that the number portability rules were required to achieve the goal of consumer protection.*

QUESTIONS

1. Who filed this suit in the U.S. Court of Appeals for the District of Columbia Circuit, and why?
2. Why did the U.S. Court of Appeals for the District of Columbia Circuit dismiss the plaintiffs' suit?
3. On what basis might an agency decide that a *temporary* forbearance from the enforcement of a rule is justified while a *permanent* forbearance is not?

Executive Controls

The executive branch of government exercises control over agencies both through the president's power to appoint federal officers and through the president's veto power. The president may veto enabling legislation presented by Congress or congressional attempts to modify an existing agency's authority.

Legislative Controls

Congress also exercises authority over agency powers. Through enabling legislation, Congress gives power to an agency. Of course, an agency may not exceed the power that Congress has delegated to it. Through subsequent legislation, Congress can take away that power or even abolish an agency altogether. Legislative authority is required to fund an agency, and enabling legislation usually sets certain time and monetary limits on the funding of particular programs. Congress can always revise these limits.

In addition to its power to create and fund agencies, Congress has the authority to investigate agencies and how they are implementing the laws. Individual legislators may also affect agency policy through their "casework" activities, which involve attempts to help their constituents deal with agencies.

Congress also has the power to "freeze" the enforcement of most federal regulations before the regulations take effect. Under the Small Business Regulatory Enforcement Fairness Act of 1996,[6] all federal agencies must submit final rules to Congress before the rules become effective. If, within sixty days, Congress passes a joint resolution of disapproval concerning a rule,

---

6. 5 U.S.C. Sections 801–808.

enforcement of the regulation is frozen while the rule is reviewed by congressional committees.

Another legislative check on agency actions is the Administrative Procedure Act, discussed earlier in this chapter. Additionally, the laws discussed in the next section provide certain checks on the actions of administrative agencies.

PUBLIC ACCOUNTABILITY

As a result of growing public concern over the powers exercised by administrative agencies, Congress passed several laws to make agencies more accountable through public scrutiny. We discuss here the most significant of these laws.

Freedom of Information Act

Enacted in 1966, the Freedom of Information Act (FOIA)[7] requires the federal government to disclose certain "records" to "any person" on request, even if no reason is given for the request. The FOIA exempts certain types of records. For other records, though, a request that complies with the FOIA procedures need only contain a reasonable description of the information sought (see Exhibit 6–5 for a sample FOIA request letter). An agency's failure to comply with a request may be challenged in a federal district court. The media, industry trade associations, public-interest groups, and even companies seeking information about competitors rely on these FOIA provisions to obtain information from government agencies.

Under a 1996 amendment to the FOIA, all federal government agencies now have to make their records available electronically—on the Internet, on computer disks, and in other electronic formats. As of November 1, 1996, any document created by an agency must be available on computer within a year after its creation. Agencies must also provide a clear index to all of their documents.

Government-in-the-Sunshine Act

Congress passed the Government-in-the-Sunshine Act,[8] or open meeting law, in 1976. It requires that "every portion of every meeting of an agency" be open to "public observation." The act also requires the establishment of procedures to ensure that the public is provided with adequate advance notice of scheduled meetings and agendas. Like the FOIA, the sunshine act contains certain exceptions. Closed meetings are permitted when (1) the subject of the meeting concerns accusing any person of a crime, (2) an open meeting would frustrate the implementation of agency actions, or (3) the subject of the meeting involves matters relating to future litigation or rulemaking. Courts interpret these exceptions to allow open access whenever possible.

Regulatory Flexibility Act

Concern over the effects of regulation on the efficiency of businesses, particularly smaller ones, led Congress to pass the Regulatory Flexibility Act in 1980.[9] Under this act, whenever a new regulation will have a "significant

7. 5 U.S.C. Section 552.
8. 5 U.S.C. Section 552b.
9. 5 U.S.C. Sections 601–612.

EXHIBIT 6–5 • A FREEDOM OF INFORMATION ACT REQUEST LETTER

Agency Head [or Freedom of Information Act Officer] Date ____________________
Name of Agency
Address of Agency
City, State, Zip Code

Re: Freedom of Information Act Request

Dear ______________ :

This is a request under the Freedom of Information Act.

I request that a copy of the following documents [or documents containing the following information] be provided to me: [identify the documents or information as specifically as possible].

In order to help to determine my status for purposes of determining the applicability of any fees, you should know that I am (insert a suitable description of the requester and the purpose of the request).

[Optional] I am willing to pay fees for this request up to a maximum of $XX. If you estimate that the fees will exceed this limit, please inform me first.

[Optional] I request a waiver of all fees for this request. Disclosure of the requested information to me is in the public interest because it is likely to contribute significantly to public understanding of the operations or activities of the government and is not primarily in my commercial interest. [Include specific details, including how the requested information will be disseminated by the requester for public benefit.]

[Optional] I request that the information I seek be provided in electronic format, and I would like to receive it on a personal computer disk [or a CD–ROM].

[Optional] I ask that my request receive expedited processing because XXXX. [Include specific details concerning your "compelling need," such as being someone "primarily engaged in disseminating information" and specifics concerning your "urgency to inform the public concerning actual or alleged Federal Government activity."]

[Optional] I also include a telephone number at which I can be contacted during the hours of XXXX, if necessary, to discuss any aspect of my request.

Thank you for your consideration of this request.

Sincerely,
[Signature]
Name
Address
City, State, Zip Code
Telephone number [Optional]

Source: U.S. Congress, House Committee on Government Reform, *A Citizen's Guide on How to Use the Freedom of Information Act and the Privacy Act Requesting Government Documents,* 106th Congress, 1st session, H.R. 106–50, 1999.

impact upon a substantial number of small entities," the agency must conduct a regulatory flexibility analysis. The analysis must measure the cost that the rule would impose on small businesses and must consider less burdensome alternatives. The act also contains provisions to alert small businesses—through advertising in trade journals, for example—about forthcoming regulations. The act reduces some record-keeping burdens for small businesses, especially with regard to hazardous waste management.

Small Business Regulatory Enforcement Fairness Act

The Small Business Regulatory Enforcement Fairness Act (SBREFA) of 1996 allows Congress to review new federal regulations for at least sixty days before they take effect. This period gives opponents of the rules time to present their arguments to Congress.

The SBREFA also authorizes the courts to enforce the Regulatory Flexibility Act. This helps to ensure that federal agencies, such as the Internal Revenue Service, will consider ways to reduce the economic impact of new regulations on small businesses. Federal agencies are required to prepare guides that explain in "plain English" how small businesses can comply with federal regulations.

The SBREFA also set up the National Enforcement Ombudsman at the Small Business Administration to receive comments from small businesses about their dealings with federal agencies. Based on these comments, Regional Small Business Fairness Boards rate the agencies and publicize their findings.

Finally, the SBREFA allows small businesses to recover their expenses and legal fees from the government when an agency makes demands for fines or penalties that a court considers excessive.

State Administrative Agencies

Although most of this chapter deals with federal administrative agencies, state agencies play a significant role in regulating activities within the states. Many of the factors that encouraged the proliferation of federal agencies also fostered the expanded presence of state agencies. For example, one reason for the growth of administrative agencies at all levels of government is the inability of Congress and state legislatures to oversee the implementation of their laws. Another is the greater technical competence of the agencies.

Parallel Agencies

Commonly, a state creates an agency as a parallel to a federal agency to provide similar services on a more localized basis. Such parallel agencies include the federal Social Security Administration and the state welfare agency, the Internal Revenue Service and the state revenue department, and the Environmental Protection Agency and the state pollution-control agency. Not all federal agencies have parallel state agencies, however. For example, the Federal Bureau of Investigation and the Nuclear Regulatory Commission have no parallel agencies at the state level.

Conflicts between Parallel Agencies

If the actions of parallel state and federal agencies conflict, the actions of the federal agency will prevail. Consider an example. If the Federal Aviation Administration specifies the hours during which airplanes may land at and depart from airports, a state or local government cannot issue inconsistent laws or regulations governing the same activities. The priority of federal laws over conflicting state laws is based on the supremacy clause of the U.S. Constitution. Remember from Chapter 5 that this clause, which is found in Article VI of the Constitution, states that the Constitution and "the Laws of the United States which shall be made in Pursuance thereof . . . shall be the supreme Law of the Land."

Judicial Review of State Agency Actions

Most state agency decisions are subject to judicial review by state courts, provided that the parties seeking that review first meet certain requirements. Once a petition for review is granted, state courts, like their federal counterparts, consider such issues as whether a state or local agency exceeded its authority.

The following case provides an example of a state supreme court's review of a state agency decision. The court was asked to determine whether the agency's decision in a certain case was "[a]rbitrary, capricious, an abuse of discretion or otherwise not in accordance with law."

SWIFT v. SUBLETTE COUNTY BOARD OF COUNTY COMMISSIONERS

CASE 6.4

Wyoming Supreme Court, 2002.
2002 WY 32,
40 P.3d 1235.

Joe's Concrete and Lumber, Inc., operates a gravel pit on agricultural land near Boulder, Wyoming, at the intersection of State Highway 187 and Sublette County Road 353. The Zoning and Development Regulations Resolutions of Sublette County allow gravel pits in agricultural districts under certain conditions. Gravel pits and "associated extraction activities" are permissible on issuance of a conditional use permit and compliance with specific development standards. In June 2000, Joe's applied for a conditional use permit to add a batch plant to its site.[a] *Adjacent landowners Sara Swift and Circle Nine Ranch, Inc., opposed the application. They objected to the increased traffic, noise, and dust associated with a batch plant. The Sublette County Board of County Commissioners approved the permit. Swift and Circle Nine petitioned for a review of this decision with a Wyoming state court, which certified the dispute to the Wyoming Supreme Court.*[b]

HILL, J.

[T]he crux of [this] dispute is over whether or not [a batch plant] is an "associated extraction" activity. The root of "associated" has several different meanings depending upon the context in which the word is used and whether it is used as an adjective, verb, or noun. The word is used in the Zoning Regulations as a modifier of "activity." In that context, the plain meaning of the word can easily be discerned [according to *Merriam-Webster's Collegiate Dictionary* (10th ed. 1998)]:

> **Associate—1:** closely connected (as in function or office) with another **2:** closely related esp. in the mind.

"Extraction" is the process of extracting something:

> **Extract—1** * * * **b:** to pull or take out forcibly * * * **2:** to withdraw (as a juice or fraction) by physical or chemical process; *also:* to treat with a solvent so as to remove a soluble substance **3:** to separate (a metal) from an ore.

Putting the plain meaning of the words together, the Zoning Regulations define gravel pit operations to include activities closely connected or related to the process of withdrawing the gravel from the ground. The question now is whether a concrete batch plant fits within that plain meaning.

* * * *There is nothing in the record to indicate that the batch plant bears any relation to the actual physical extraction of the gravel from the ground.* There is no indication that a batch plant refines or processes the gravel in a manner that removes or separates the gravel from other substances. The batch plant processes the gravel with other ingredients to create a product—concrete—it does not extract or assist in the extraction of the gravel from the ground. This conclusion is supported by reference to the Zoning Regulations where cement

---

a. A batch plant mixes gravel with sand, water, and cement to produce concrete.

b. *Certification* in this context is a procedure by which the lower court abstained from deciding the question in this dispute until the state supreme court had an opportunity to rule on it.

and concrete manufacturing is an authorized use in a heavy industrial district but is noticeably absent from the list of authorized uses for agricultural districts. This evidences intent on the part of the drafters of the Zoning Regulations to treat concrete manufacturing distinctly from gravel pit operations. There is no rational argument to support a finding that the batch plant is "closely connected or related to the process of withdrawing the gravel." [Emphasis added.]

The Wyoming Supreme Court reversed the decision of the local board granting a conditional use permit to Joe's. The court concluded that a batch plant is not an "associated extraction" activity that is closely connected to a gravel pit operation. The agency's interpretation of the phrase was inconsistent with the plain meaning of the words in the regulation.

QUESTIONS

1. What was the reasoning underlying the Wyoming Supreme Court's ruling in this case?
2. If the regulation in this case had not used the word *extraction* and had allowed permits for any "associated" activity, would the plaintiffs have been successful?
3. Should every agency action be subject to automatic judicial review? Why or why not?

KEY TERMS

adjudication 185
administrative law judge (ALJ) 194
administrative process 187
bureaucracy 187
delegation doctrine 185
enabling legislation 184
final order 195
initial order 195
judicial process 187
legislative rule 185
notice-and-comment rulemaking 188
rulemaking 188

FOR REVIEW

1. How are federal administrative agencies created?
2. What are the three basic functions of most administrative agencies?
3. What sequence of events must normally occur before an agency rule becomes law?
4. How do administrative agencies enforce their rules?
5. How do the three branches of government limit the power of administrative agencies?

QUESTIONS AND CASE PROBLEMS

6–1. Assume that the Food and Drug Administration (FDA), using proper procedures, adopts a rule describing its future investigations. This new rule covers all future circumstances in which the FDA wants to regulate food additives. Under the new rule, the FDA is not to regulate food additives without giving food companies an opportunity to cross-examine witnesses. Some time later, the FDA wants to regulate methylisocyanate, a food additive. The FDA undertakes an informal rulemaking procedure, without cross-examination, and regulates methylisocyanate. Producers protest, saying that the FDA promised them the opportunity for cross-examination. The

FDA responds that the Administrative Procedure Act does not require such cross-examination and that it is free to withdraw the promise made in its new rule. If the producers challenge the FDA in court, on what basis would the court rule in their favor?

6–2. For decades, the Federal Trade Commission (FTC) resolved fair trade and advertising disputes through individual adjudications. In the 1960s, the FTC began promulgating rules that defined fair and unfair trade practices. In cases involving violations of these rules, the due process rights of participants were more limited and did not include cross-examination. Although anyone found violating a rule would receive a full adjudication, the legitimacy of the rule itself could not be challenged in the adjudication. Any party charged with violating a rule was almost certain to lose the adjudication. Affected parties complained to a court, arguing that their rights before the FTC were unduly limited by the new rules. What will the court examine to determine whether to uphold the new rules?

CASE PROBLEM WITH SAMPLE ANSWER

6–3. Rulemaking Procedures. The Atomic Energy Commission (AEC) was engaged in rulemaking proceedings for nuclear reactor safety. An environmental group sued the commission, arguing that its proceedings were inadequate. The commission had carefully complied with all requirements of the Administrative Procedure Act. The environmentalists argued, however, that the very hazardous and technical nature of the reactor safety issue required elaborate procedures above and beyond those set forth in the act. A federal court of appeals agreed and overturned the AEC rules. The commission appealed the case to the United States Supreme Court. How should the Court rule? Discuss. [*Vermont Yankee Nuclear Power Corp. v. Natural Resources Defense Council, Inc.*, 435 U.S. 519, 98 S.Ct. 1197, 55 L.Ed.2d 460 (1978)]

To view a sample answer for this case problem, go to this book's Web site at **http://ele.westbuslaw.com** *and click on "Interactive Study Center."*

6–4. Agency Investigations. A state statute required vehicle dismantlers—persons whose business includes dismantling automobiles and selling the parts—to be licensed and to keep records regarding the vehicles and parts in their possession. The statute also authorized warrantless administrative inspections; that is, without first obtaining a warrant, agents of the state department of motor vehicles or police officers could inspect a vehicle dismantler's license and records, as well as vehicles on the premises. Pursuant to this statute, police officers entered an automobile junkyard and asked to see the owner's license and records. The owner replied that he did not have the documents. The officers inspected the premises and discovered stolen vehicles and parts. Charged with possession of stolen property and unregistered operation as a vehicle dismantler, the junkyard owner argued that the warrantless inspection statute was unconstitutional under the Fourth Amendment. The trial court disagreed, reasoning that the junkyard business was a highly regulated industry. On appeal, the highest state court concluded that the statute had no true administrative purpose and impermissibly authorized searches whose only purpose was to discover stolen property. The state appealed to the United States Supreme Court. Should the Court uphold the statute? Discuss. [*New York v. Burger*, 482 U.S. 691, 107 S.Ct. 2636, 96 L.Ed.2d 601 (1987)]

6–5. Arbitrary and Capricious Test. In 1977, the Department of Transportation (DOT) adopted a passive-restraint standard (known as Standard 208) that required new cars to have either air bags or automatic seat belts. By 1981, it had become clear that all of the major auto manufacturers would install automatic seat belts to comply with this rule. The DOT determined that most purchasers of cars would detach their automatic seat belts, rendering them ineffective. Consequently, the department repealed the regulation. State Farm Mutual Automobile Insurance Co. and other insurance companies sued in the District of Columbia Circuit Court of Appeals for a review of the DOT's repeal of the regulation. That court held that the repeal was arbitrary and capricious because the DOT had reversed its rule without sufficient support. The motor vehicle manufacturers, who initially had wanted to avoid the costs associated with implementing Standard 208, then appealed this decision to the United States Supreme Court. What will result? Discuss fully. [*Motor Vehicle Manufacturers Association v. State Farm Mutual Automobile Insurance Co.*, 463 U.S. 29, 103 S.Ct. 2856, 77 L.Ed.2d 443 (1983)]

6–6. Judicial Review. American Message Centers (AMC) provides answering services to retailers. Calls to a retailer are automatically forwarded to AMC, which pays for the calls. AMC obtains telephone service at a discount from major carriers, including Sprint. Sprint's tariff (a public document setting out rates and rules relating to Sprint's services) states that the "subscriber shall be responsible for the payment of all charges for service." When AMC learned that computer hackers had obtained the access code for its lines and had made nearly $160,000 in long-distance calls, it asked Sprint to absorb the cost. Sprint refused. AMC filed a complaint with the Federal Communications Commission (FCC), claiming in part that Sprint's tariff was vague and ambiguous, in violation of the Communications Act of 1934 and FCC rules. These laws require that a carrier's tariff "clearly and definitely" specify any "exceptions or conditions which in any way affect the rates named in the tariff." The FCC rejected AMC's complaint. AMC appealed the FCC's decision to a federal appellate court, claiming that the FCC's decision to reject AMC's complaint was arbitrary and capricious. What should the court decide? Discuss fully. [*American Message Centers v. Federal Communications Commission,* 50 F.3d 35 (D.C.Cir. 1995)]

6–7. Rulemaking. The Occupational Safety and Health Administration (OSHA) is part of the U.S. Department of Labor. OSHA issued a "Directive" under which each employer in selected industries was to be inspected unless it adopted a "Comprehensive Compliance Program (CCP)" —a safety and health program designed to meet standards that in some respects exceeded those otherwise required by law. The Chamber of Commerce of the United States objected to the Directive and filed a petition for review with the U.S. Court of Appeals for the District of Columbia Circuit. The Chamber claimed, in part, that OSHA did not use proper rulemaking procedures in issuing the Directive. OSHA argued that it was not required to follow those procedures because the Directive itself was a "rule of procedure." OSHA claimed that the rule did not "alter the rights or interests of parties, although it may alter the manner in which the parties present themselves or their viewpoints to the agency." What are the steps of the most commonly used rulemaking procedure? Which steps are missing in this case? In whose favor should the court rule? Why? [*Chamber of Commerce of the United States v. U.S. Department of Labor,* 174 F.3d 206 (D.C.Cir. 1999)]

6–8. Arbitrary and Capricious Test. Lion Raisins, Inc., is a family-owned, family-operated business that grows and markets raisins to private enterprises. In the 1990s, Lion also successfully bid on more than fifteen contracts awarded by the U.S. Department of Agriculture (USDA). In May 1999, a USDA investigation reported that Lion appeared to have falsified inspectors' signatures, given false moisture content, and changed the grade of raisins on three USDA raisin certificates issued between 1996 and 1998. Lion was subsequently awarded five more USDA contracts. Then, in November 2000, the company was the low bidder on two new USDA contracts for school lunch programs. In January 2001, however, the USDA awarded these contracts to other bidders and, on the basis of the May 1999 report, suspended Lion from participating in government contracts for one year. Lion filed a suit in the U.S. Court of Federal Claims against the USDA, seeking, in part, lost profits on the school lunch contracts on the ground that the USDA's suspension was arbitrary and capricious. On what reasoning might the court grant a summary judgment in Lion's favor? [*Lion Raisins Inc. v. United States,* 51 Fed.Cl. 238 (2001)]

6–9. Investigation. Maureen Droge began working for United Air Lines, Inc. (UAL), as a flight attendant in 1990. In 1995, she was assigned to Paris, France, where she became pregnant. Because UAL does not allow its flight attendants to fly during their third trimester of pregnancy, Droge was placed on involuntary leave. She applied for temporary disability benefits through the French social security system, but her request was denied because UAL does not contribute to the French system on behalf of its U.S.–based flight attendants. Droge filed a charge of discrimination with the U.S. Equal Employment Opportunity Commission (EEOC), alleging that UAL had discriminated against her and other Americans. The EEOC issued a subpoena, asking UAL to detail all benefits received by all UAL employees living outside the United States. UAL refused to provide the information in part on the grounds that it was irrelevant and compliance would be unduly burdensome. The EEOC filed a suit in a federal district court against UAL. Should the court enforce the subpoena? Why or why not? [*Equal Employment Opportunity Commission v. United Air Lines, Inc.,* 287 F.3d 643 (7th Cir. 2002)]

6–10. IN YOUR COURT

Assume that the Securities and Exchange Commission (SEC) has a rule that it will enforce statutory provisions prohibiting insider trading only when the insiders make monetary profits for themselves. Then the SEC makes a new rule, declaring that it has the statutory authority to bring an enforcement action against an individual even if she or he does not personally profit from the insider trading. In making the new rule, the SEC does not conduct a rulemaking proceeding but simply announces its new decision. A securities organization objects and says that the new rule was unlawfully developed without opportunity for public comment. The organization challenges the rule in an action that ultimately is reviewed by a federal appellate court. Assume that you are a judge on the appellate court reviewing this case and answer the following questions:

(a) Should the SEC's new rule be invalidated under the Administrative Procedure Act? Why or why not?
(b) Is the SEC's new rule a legislative rule or an interpretive rule? Why is this distinction important to the outcome of this case?

6–11. A QUESTION OF ETHICS AND SOCIAL RESPONSIBILITY

The Marine Mammal Protection Act was enacted in 1972 to reduce incidental killing and injury of marine mammals during commercial fishing operations. Under the act, commercial fishing vessels are required to allow an employee of the National Oceanic and Atmospheric Administration (NOAA) to accompany the vessels to conduct research and observe operations. In December 1986, after NOAA had adopted a new policy of recruiting female as well as male observers, NOAA notified Caribbean Marine Services Co. that female observers would be assigned to accompany two of the company's fishing vessels on their next voyages. The owners and crew members of the ships (the plaintiffs) moved for an injunction against the implementation of the NOAA directive. The plaintiffs contended that the presence of a female onboard a fishing vessel would be very awkward, because the female would have to share the crew's quarters, and crew members enjoyed little or no privacy with respect to bodily functions. Further, they alleged that the presence of a female would be disruptive to fishing operations, because some of the crew members were "crude" men with little formal education who might harass or sexually assault a female observer, and the officers would therefore have to devote time to protecting the female from the crew. Finally, the plaintiffs argued that the presence of a female observer could destroy morale and distract the crew, thus affecting the crew's efficiency and decreasing the vessel's profits. [*Caribbean Marine Services Co. v. Baldrige,* 844 F.2d 668 (9th Cir. 1988)]

(a) In general, do you think that the public policy of promoting equal employment opportunity should override the concerns of the vessel owners and crew? If you were the judge, would you grant the injunction? Why or why not?

(b) The plaintiffs pointed out that fishing voyages could last three months or longer. Would the length of a particular voyage affect your answer to the preceding question?

(c) The plaintiffs contended that even if the indignity of sharing bunk rooms and toilet facilities with a female observer could be overcome, the observer's very presence in the common areas of the vessel, such as the dining area, would unconstitutionally infringe on the crew members' right to privacy in these areas. Evaluate this claim.

6–12. FOR CRITICAL ANALYSIS

Does Congress delegate too much power to federal administrative agencies? Do the courts defer too much to Congress in its grant of power to those agencies? What are the alternatives to the agencies that we encounter in every facet of our lives?

For updated links to resources available on the Web, as well as a variety of other materials, visit this text's Web site at

http://ele.westbuslaw.com

To view the text of the Administrative Procedure Act of 1946, go to

http://www.archives.gov/federal_register/public_laws/acts.html

The Internet Law Library contains links to federal and state regulatory materials, including the *Code of Federal Regulations*. This page can be found at

http://www.lawguru.com/ilawlib

LEGAL RESEARCH EXERCISES ON THE WEB

Go to **http://ele.westbuslaw.com**, the Web site that accompanies this text. Select "Interactive Study Center," and then click on "Chapter 6." There you will find the following Internet research exercises that you can perform to learn more about topics covered in this chapter.

Activity 6–1: LEGAL PERSPECTIVE—The Freedom of Information Act

Activity 6–2: MANAGEMENT PERSPECTIVE—Agency Inspections

BEFORE THE TEST

Go to **http://ele.westbuslaw.com**, the Web site that accompanies this text. Select "Interactive Quizzes." You will find at least twenty interactive questions relating to this chapter.

WESTLAW® CAMPUS

If your textbook provided for a subscription to Westlaw® Campus, or if you have otherwise purchased access to the Westlaw Campus database, you can access any of the cases presented or cited in this chapter by using your Westlaw Campus account.

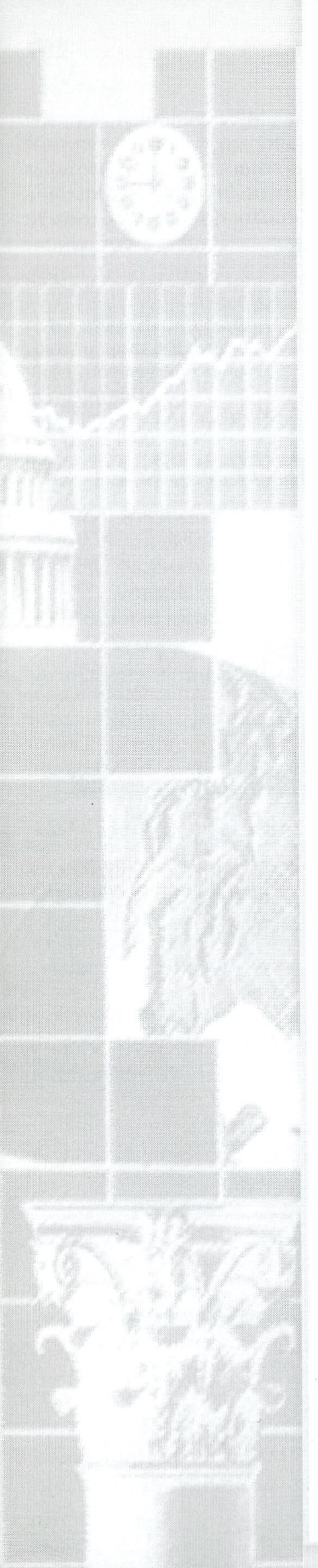

CHAPTER 7

Criminal Law and Cyber Crimes

CONTENTS

CHAPTER OBJECTIVES

After reading this chapter, you should be able to answer the following questions:

1

What two elements must exist before a person can be held liable for a crime? Can a corporation be liable for crimes?

2

What are the five broad categories of crimes? What is white-collar crime?

3

What defenses might be raised to avoid liability for criminal acts?

What constitutional safeguards protect persons accused of crimes? What are the basic steps in the criminal process?

What is cyber crime? How does cyber crime differ from traditional crime?

The law imposes various sanctions in attempting to ensure that individuals engaging in business in our society can compete and flourish. These sanctions include those imposed by civil law, such as damages for various types of tortious conduct (to be discussed in Chapter 12); damages for breach of contract (to be discussed in Chapter 10); and the equitable remedies discussed in Chapters 1 and 10. Additional sanctions are imposed under criminal law. Indeed, many statutes regulating business provide for criminal as well as civil penalties. Therefore, criminal law joins civil law as an important element in the legal environment of business.

In this chapter, after examining some essential differences between criminal law and civil law, we look at how crimes are classified, the basic requirements that must be met for criminal liability to be established, the various types of crimes that exist, and the defenses that can be raised to avoid criminal liability. We conclude the chapter with a discussion of crimes that occur in cyberspace, which are often referred to as **cyber crime.** Generally, cyber crime refers more to the way in which particular crimes are committed than to a new category of crimes.

Cyber crime • A crime that occurs online, in the virtual community of the Internet, as opposed to the physical world.

CIVIL LAW AND CRIMINAL LAW

Recall from Chapter 1 that *civil law* pertains to the duties that exist between persons or between citizens and their governments. Criminal law, in contrast, has to do with crime. A **crime** can be defined as a wrong against society proclaimed in a statute and punishable by a fine and/or imprisonment—or, in some cases, death. As mentioned in Chapter 1, because crimes are *offenses against society as a whole,* they are prosecuted by a public official, such as a district attorney (D.A.) or an attorney general (A.G.), not by victims.

Crime • A wrong against society proclaimed in a statute and, if committed, punishable by society through fines and/or imprisonment—and, in some cases, death.

Major Differences between Civil Law and Criminal Law

Because the state has extensive resources at its disposal when prosecuting criminal cases, there are numerous procedural safeguards to protect the rights of defendants. We look here at one of these safeguards—the higher standard of proof that applies in a criminal case—as well as at the harsher sanctions for criminal acts as compared to civil wrongs. Exhibit 7–1 summarizes these and other key differences between civil law and criminal law.

Burden of Proof. In a civil case, the plaintiff usually must prove his or her case by a *preponderance of the evidence.* Under this standard, the plaintiff must convince the court that, based on the evidence presented by both parties, it is more likely than not that the plaintiff's allegation is true.

Beyond a reasonable doubt • The standard used to determine the guilt or innocence of a person who has been charged with a crime. To be guilty of a crime, one must be proved guilty "beyond and to the exclusion of every reasonable doubt." A reasonable doubt is one that would cause a prudent person to hesitate before acting in matters important to him or her.

In a criminal case, in contrast, the state must prove its case **beyond a reasonable doubt.** If the jury views the evidence in the case as reasonably permitting either a guilty or a not guilty verdict, then the jury's verdict must be not guilty. In other words, unless the government (prosecutor) proves beyond a reasonable doubt that the defendant has committed every essential element of the offense with which she or he is charged, a juror must find the defendant not guilty. Note also that in a criminal case, the jury's verdict must be unanimous—agreed to by all members of the jury—to convict the defendant. (In a civil trial by jury, in contrast, only three-fourths of the jurors need to agree.)

The higher standard of proof in criminal cases reflects a fundamental social value—the belief that it is worse to convict an innocent individual than to let a guilty person go free. We will look at other safeguards later in the chapter, in the context of criminal procedure.

Criminal Sanctions. The sanctions imposed on criminal wrongdoers are also harsher than those that are applied in civil cases. As you will learn in Chapter 12, the primary purpose of tort law is to allow persons harmed by the wrongful acts of others to obtain compensation, or money damages, from the wrongdoer or to enjoin (prevent) a wrongdoer from undertaking or continuing a wrongful action. In contrast, criminal sanctions are designed to punish those who commit crimes and to deter others from committing similar acts in the future. Criminal sanctions include fines as well as the much harsher penalty of the loss of one's liberty by incarceration in a jail or prison. The harshest criminal sanction is, of course, the death penalty.

EXHIBIT 7–1 • CIVIL AND CRIMINAL LAW COMPARED

ISSUE	CIVIL LAW	CRIMINAL LAW
Area of concern	Rights and duties between individuals	Offenses against society as a whole
Wrongful act	Harm to a person or to a person's property	Violation of a statute that prohibits some type of activity
Party who brings suit	Person who suffered harm	The state
Standard of proof	Preponderance of the evidence	Beyond a reasonable doubt
Remedy	Damages to compensate for the harm or an equitable remedy to prevent further harm	Punishment (fine and/or imprisonment)

Civil Liability for Criminal Acts

Some torts, such as assault and battery, provide a basis for a criminal prosecution as well as a tort action. For example, Jonas is walking down the street, minding his own business, when a person attacks him. In the ensuing struggle, the attacker stabs Jonas several times, seriously injuring him. A police officer restrains and arrests the wrongdoer. In this situation, the attacker may be subject both to criminal prosecution by the state and to a tort lawsuit brought by Jonas to obtain compensation for his injuries. Exhibit 7–2 illustrates how the same wrongful act can result in both a civil action (for the tort of assault and battery—see Chapter 12) and a criminal action against the wrongdoer (for a violent crime—a type of crime discussed later in this chapter).

CLASSIFICATION OF CRIMES

Depending on their degree of seriousness, crimes are classified as felonies or misdemeanors.

EXHIBIT 7–2 • TORT LAWSUIT AND CRIMINAL PROSECUTION FOR THE SAME ACT

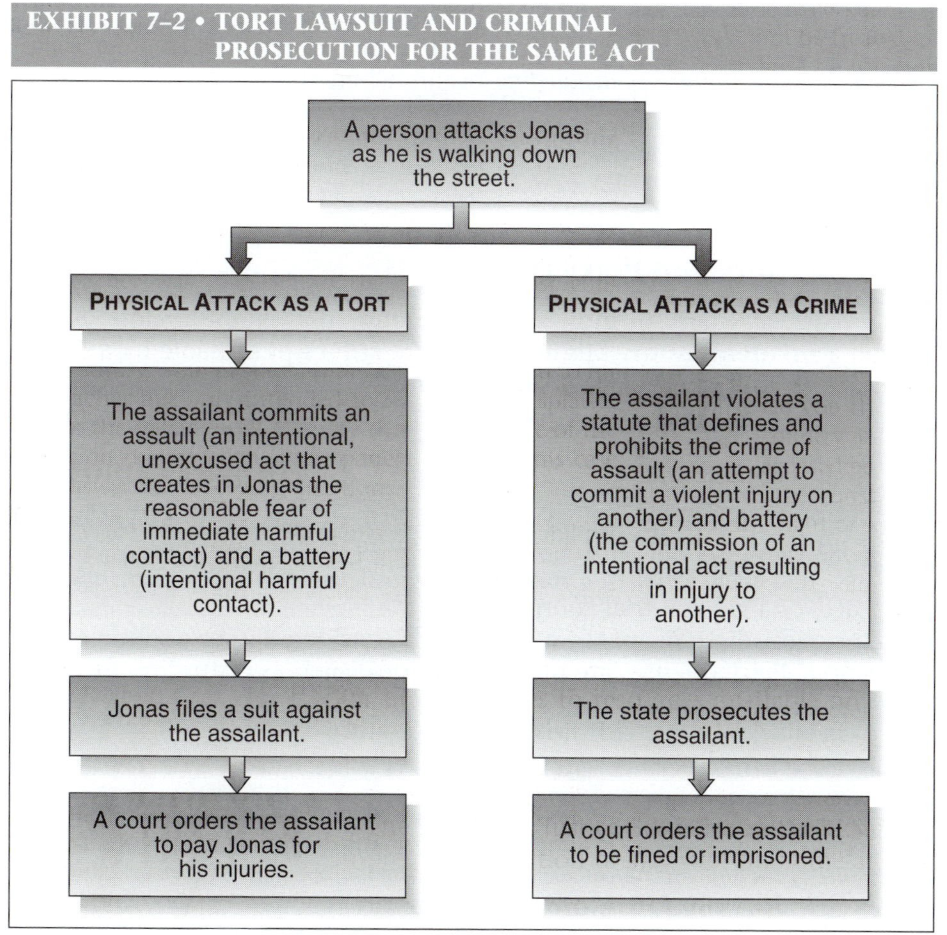

Felonies

Felony • A crime—such as arson, murder, rape, or robbery—that carries the most severe sanctions, usually ranging from one year in a state or federal prison to the forfeiture of one's life.

Felonies are serious crimes punishable by death or by imprisonment in a federal or state penitentiary for one year or longer.[1] The Model Penal Code[2] provides for four degrees of felony:

1. Capital offenses, for which the maximum penalty is death.
2. First degree felonies, punishable by a maximum penalty of life imprisonment.
3. Second degree felonies, punishable by up to ten years' imprisonment.
4. Third degree felonies, punishable by up to five years' imprisonment.

Although criminal laws vary from state to state, some general rules apply when grading crimes by degree. For example, most jurisdictions punish a burglary that involves a forced entry into a home at night more harshly than a burglary that takes place during the day and involves a nonresidential building or structure. A homicide—the taking of another's life—is classified according to the degree of intent involved.

For example, first degree murder requires that the homicide be premeditated and deliberate, as opposed to a spontaneous act of violence. When no premeditation or deliberation is present but the offender acts with *malice aforethought* (that is, with wanton disregard of the consequences of his or her actions for the victim), the homicide is classified as second degree murder. A homicide that is committed without malice toward the victim is known as *manslaughter. Voluntary manslaughter* occurs when the intent to kill may be present, as in a crime committed in the heat of passion, but malice is lacking. A homicide is classified as *involuntary manslaughter* when it results from an act of negligence, such as when a drunk driver causes the death of another person, and there is no intent to kill.

Misdemeanors and Petty Offenses

Misdemeanor • A lesser crime than a felony, punishable by a fine or imprisonment for up to one year in jail.

Under federal law and in most states, any crime that is not a felony is considered a **misdemeanor.** Misdemeanors are crimes punishable by a fine or by incarceration for up to one year. If confined, the guilty party goes to a local jail instead of a penitentiary. Disorderly conduct and trespass are common misdemeanors. Some states have several classes of misdemeanors. For example, in Illinois, misdemeanors are either Class A (confinement for up to a year), Class B (not more than six months), or Class C (not more than thirty days). Whether a crime is a felony or a misdemeanor can also determine whether the case is tried in a magistrate's court (for example, by a justice of the peace) or a general trial court.

Petty offense • In criminal law, the least serious kind of criminal offense, such as a traffic or building-code violation.

In most jurisdictions, **petty offenses** are considered to be a subset of misdemeanors. Petty offenses are minor violations, such as disturbing the peace

1. Some states, such as North Carolina, consider felonies to be punishable by incarceration for at least two years.
2. The American Law Institute issued the Official Draft of the Model Penal Code in 1962. The Model Penal Code contains four parts: (1) general provisions, (2) definitions of special crimes, (3) provisions concerning treatment and corrections, and (4) provisions on the organization of correction. The Model Penal Code is not a uniform code, however. Because of our federal structure of government, each state has developed its own set of laws governing criminal acts. Thus, types of crime and prescribed punishments may differ from one jurisdiction to another.

and violations of building codes. Even for petty offenses, however, a guilty party can be put in jail for a few days, fined, or both, depending on state law.

Probation and community service are often imposed on those who commit misdemeanors, especially juveniles. Also, most states have decriminalized all but the most serious traffic offenses. These infractions are treated as civil proceedings, and civil fines are imposed. In many states, "points" are assessed against the violator's driving record.

THE ESSENTIALS OF CRIMINAL LIABILITY

Two elements must exist for a person to be convicted of a crime: (1) the performance of a prohibited act and (2) a specified state of mind, or intent, on the part of the actor. Additionally, to establish criminal liability, there must be a *concurrence* between the act and the intent. In other words, these two elements must occur together.

For example, suppose that a woman plans to kill her husband by poisoning him. On the day she plans to do so, she is driving her husband home from work and swerves to avoid hitting a cat crossing the road. The car crashes into a tree as a result, killing her husband. Even though she had planned to murder her husband, the woman would not be guilty of murder in this situation because she had not planned to kill him by driving the car into a tree.

The Criminal Act

Every criminal statute prohibits certain behavior. Most crimes require an act of *commission;* that is, a person must *do* something in order to be accused of a crime. In criminal law, a prohibited act is referred to as the ***actus reus,***[3] or guilty act. In some cases, an act of omission can be a crime, but only when a person has a legal duty to perform the omitted act. Failure to file a tax return is an example of an act that is a crime by omission.

Actus reus • A guilty (prohibited) act. The commission of a prohibited act is one of the two essential elements required for criminal liability.

The *guilty act* requirement is based on one of the premises of criminal law—that a person should be punished for harm done to society. Thus, for a crime to exist, the guilty act must cause some harm to a person or to property. Thinking about killing someone or about stealing a car may be morally wrong, but the thoughts do no harm until they are translated into action. Of course, a person can be punished for *attempting* murder or robbery, but only if substantial steps toward the criminal objective have been taken. Additionally, the punishment for an attempt to commit a crime is normally less severe than it would be if the act had been completed.

State of Mind

A wrongful mental state **(*mens rea*)**[4] is as necessary as a wrongful act in establishing guilt. The mental state, or requisite intent, required to establish guilt of a crime is indicated in the applicable statute or law. Murder, for example, involves the guilty act of killing another human being, and the guilty mental state is the desire, or intent, to take another's life. For theft, the guilty act is the taking of another person's property, and the mental state involves

Mens rea • Mental state, or intent. A wrongful mental state is as necessary as a wrongful act to establish criminal liability.

3. Pronounced *ak*-tuhs *ray*-uhs.
4. Pronounced *mehns ray*-uh.

both the awareness that the property belongs to another and the desire to deprive the owner of it.

A guilty mental state can be attributed to persons who commit acts of negligence or recklessness as well. *Criminal negligence* involves the mental state in which the defendant deviates from the standard of care that a reasonable person would use under the same circumstances. The defendant is accused of taking an unjustified, substantial, and foreseeable risk that resulted in harm. Under the Model Penal Code, a defendant is negligent even if she or he was not actually aware of the risk but *should have been aware of it.*[5] The Model Penal Code defines *criminal recklessness* as "consciously disregard[ing] a substantial and unjustifiable risk."[6] In other words, a defendant is reckless if she or he is *actually aware* of the risk. A defendant who commits an act *recklessly* is more blameworthy than one who is criminally negligent.

Corporate Criminal Liability

A corporation is a legal entity created under the laws of a state. Both the corporation as an entity and the individual directors and officers of the corporation are potentially subject to liability for criminal acts.

Liability of the Corporate Entity

At one time, it was thought that a corporation could not incur criminal liability because, although a corporation is a legal person, it can act only through its agents (corporate directors, officers, and employees). Therefore, the corporate entity itself could not "intend" to commit a crime. Under modern criminal law, however, a corporation may be held liable for crimes. Obviously, corporations cannot be imprisoned, but they can be fined or denied certain legal privileges (such as a license).

The Model Penal Code provides that a corporation may be convicted of a crime in the following situations:

1. The criminal act by the corporation's agent or employee is within the scope of his or her employment, and the purpose of the statute defining the act as a crime is to impose liability on the corporation.
2. The crime consists of a failure to perform a specific affirmative duty imposed on corporations by law.
3. The crime was authorized, requested, commanded, committed, or recklessly tolerated by one of the corporation's high managerial agents.[7]

As implied by the first statement in the above list, corporate criminal liability is *vicarious,* or indirect—the corporation as an entity may be liable for the criminal acts of its employees when the acts are committed within the scope of employment. Thus, a corporation that is found to be criminally responsible for an act committed by an employee can be fined for that offense. Through the fine, stockholders and other employees suffer because of the vicarious liability of the corporation. For such criminal liability to be imposed, the prosecutor must show that the corporation could have pre-

5. Model Penal Code Section 2.02(2)(d).
6. Model Penal Code Section 2.02(2)(c).
7. Model Penal Code Section 2.07.

vented the act or that someone with authority in the corporation knew about or consented to the act.

Liability of Corporate Officers and Directors

Corporate directors and officers are personally liable for the crimes they commit, regardless of whether the crimes were committed for their private benefit or on the corporation's behalf. Additionally, corporate directors and officers may be held liable for the actions of employees under their supervision. Under what has become known as the *responsible corporate officer* doctrine, a court may impose criminal liability on a corporate officer regardless of whether he or she participated in, directed, or even knew about a given criminal violation.

For example, in *United States v. Park,*[8] the chief executive officer of a national supermarket chain was held personally liable for sanitation violations in corporate warehouses, where food was exposed to contamination by rodents. The United States Supreme Court imposed personal liability on the corporate officer not because he intended the crime or even knew about it, but rather because he was in a "responsible relationship" to the corporation and had the power to prevent the violation. Since the *Park* decision, courts have applied this "responsible corporate officer" doctrine on a number of occasions to hold corporate officers liable for their employees' statutory violations.

The following case illustrates that corporate officers and supervisors who oversee operations causing environmental harm may be held liable under the criminal provisions of environmental statutes. (The statute involved in this case—the federal Clean Water Act—will be discussed at some length in Chapter 16.)

8. 421 U.S. 658, 95 S.Ct. 1903, 44 L.Ed.2d 489 (1975).

CASE 7.1

United States Court of Appeals, Ninth Circuit, 1999.
176 F.3d 1116.
http://www.ca9.uscourts.gov[a]

UNITED STATES v. HANOUSEK

Edward Hanousek worked for Pacific & Arctic Railway and Navigation Company (P&A) as a roadmaster of the White Pass & Yukon Railroad in Alaska. Hanousek was responsible "for every detail of the safe and efficient maintenance and construction of track, structures and marine facilities of the entire railroad," including special projects. One project was a rock quarry, known as "6-mile," above the Skagway River. Next to the quarry, and just beneath the surface, ran a high-pressure oil pipeline owned by Pacific & Arctic Pipeline, Inc., P&A's sister company. When the quarry's backhoe operator punctured the pipeline, an estimated 1,000 to 5,000 gallons of oil were discharged into the river. Hanousek was charged with, among other things, negligently discharging a harmful quantity of oil into a navigable water of the United States in violation of the criminal provisions of the Clean Water Act (CWA). After a trial in a federal district court, a jury convicted Hanousek, and the court imposed a sentence of six

a. The U.S. Court of Appeals for the Ninth Circuit maintains this Web site. Click on the "Opinions" box. From that page, click on the "Opinions by date" section. On the next page, click on the "1999" icon, and when the menu opens, click on "March." Scroll down to "USA V HANOUSEK" and click on the case name to access the case.

months' imprisonment, six months in a halfway house, six months' supervised release, and a fine of $5,000. Hanousek appealed to the U.S. Court of Appeals for the Ninth Circuit, arguing in part that the statute under which he was convicted violated his right to due process because he was not aware of what the CWA required.

THOMPSON, J.

The criminal provisions of the CWA [Clean Water Act] constitute public welfare legislation. Public welfare legislation is designed to protect the public from potentially harmful or injurious items and may render criminal a type of conduct that a reasonable person should know is subject to stringent public regulation and may seriously threaten the community's health or safety.

It is well established that a public welfare statute may subject a person to criminal liability for his or her ordinary negligence without violating due process. [Emphasis added.]

* * * [W]here * * * dangerous or deleterious devices or products or obnoxious waste materials are involved, the probability of regulation is so great that anyone who is aware that he is in possession of them or dealing with them must be presumed to be aware of the regulation.

Hanousek argues that * * * he was simply the roadmaster of the White Pass & Yukon railroad charged with overseeing a rock-quarrying project and was not in a position to know what the law required under the CWA. * * * In the context of a public welfare statute, as long as a defendant knows he is dealing with a dangerous device of a character that places him in responsible relation to a public danger, he should be alerted to the probability of strict regulation. * * * Hanousek * * * does not dispute that he was aware that a high-pressure petroleum products pipeline owned by Pacific & Arctic's sister company ran close to the surface next to the railroad tracks at 6-mile, and does not argue that he was unaware of the dangers a break or puncture of the pipeline by a piece of heavy machinery would pose. Therefore, Hanousek should have been alerted to the probability of strict regulation.

In light of [the fact] that the criminal provisions of the CWA constitute public welfare legislation, and the fact that a public welfare statute may impose criminal penalties for ordinary negligent conduct without offending due process, we conclude that [the CWA] does not violate due process by permitting criminal penalties for ordinary negligent conduct.

The U.S. Court of Appeals for the Ninth Circuit affirmed Hanousek's conviction. A corporate manager who has responsibility for operations with the potential to cause harm can be held criminally liable for harm that results even if he or she does not actually know of the specific statute under which liability may be imposed.

QUESTIONS

1. Why did Hanousek appeal this case to the U.S. Court of Appeals for the Ninth Circuit?
2. What was the reasoning underlying the decision of the U.S. Court of Appeals for the Ninth Circuit in this case?
3. If corporate actors were able to avoid responsibility for violations of environmental statutes of which they were unaware, what might result?

TYPES OF CRIMES

The number of actions that are designated as criminal is nearly endless. Federal, state, and local laws provide for the classification and punishment of hundreds of thousands of different criminal acts. Generally, though, criminal acts can be grouped into five broad categories: violent crime (crimes against persons), property crime, public order crime, white-collar crime, and organized crime. Cyber crime—which consists of crimes committed in cyberspace with the use of computers—is, as mentioned earlier, less a category of crime than a new way to commit crime. We will examine cyber crime later in this chapter.

Violent Crime

Some types of crime are called *violent crimes,* or crimes against persons, because they cause others to suffer physical harm or death. Murder is a violent crime. So is sexual assault, or rape. Assault and battery are also classified as violent crimes. (Tort liability for assault and battery will be discussed in Chapter 12.) **Robbery**—defined as the taking of money, personal property, or any other article of value from a person by means of force or fear—is also a violent crime. Typically, states have more severe penalties for *aggravated robbery*—robbery with the use of a deadly weapon.

Robbery • The act of forcefully and unlawfully taking personal property of any value from another; force or intimidation is usually necessary for an act of theft to be considered a robbery.

Each of these violent crimes is further classified by degree, depending on the circumstances surrounding the criminal act. These circumstances include the intent of the person committing the crime, whether a weapon was used, and (in cases other than murder) the level of pain and suffering experienced by the victim.

Property Crime

The most common type of criminal activity is property crime, or those crimes in which the goal of the offender is some form of economic gain or the damaging of property. Robbery is a form of property crime, as well as a violent crime, because the offender seeks to gain the property of another. We look here at a number of other crimes that fall within the general category of property crime.

Burglary. At common law, **burglary** was defined as breaking and entering the dwelling of another at night with the intent to commit a felony. Originally, the definition was aimed at protecting an individual's home and its occupants. Most state statutes have eliminated some of the requirements found in the common law definition. The time at which the breaking and entering occurs, for example, is usually immaterial. State statutes frequently omit the element of breaking and often do not require that the building be a dwelling. *Aggravated burglary*—which is defined as burglary with the use of a deadly weapon, burglary of a dwelling, or both—incurs a greater penalty.

Burglary • The unlawful entry into a building with the intent to commit a felony. (Some state statutes expand this to include the intent to commit any crime.)

Larceny. Any person who wrongfully or fraudulently takes and carries away another person's personal property is guilty of **larceny.** Larceny includes the fraudulent intent to deprive an owner permanently of property. Many

Larceny • The wrongful taking and carrying away of another person's personal property with the intent to permanently deprive the owner of the property. Some states classify larceny as either grand or petit, depending on the property's value.

business-related larcenies entail fraudulent conduct. Whereas robbery involves force or fear, larceny does not. Therefore, picking pockets is larceny, not robbery.

In most states, the definition of property that is subject to larceny statutes has been expanded to cover relatively new forms of theft. For example, stealing computer programs may constitute larceny even though the "property" consists of magnetic impulses. Stealing computer time may also be considered larceny. So, too, may the theft of natural gas. Intercepting cellular phone calls to obtain another's phone-card number—and then using that number to place long-distance calls, often overseas—is a form of property theft. These types of larceny are covered by "theft of services" statutes in many jurisdictions.

The common law makes a distinction between grand and petit larceny based on the value of the property taken. Many states have abolished this distinction, but in those that have not, grand larceny (theft above a certain amount) is a felony and petit larceny, a misdemeanor.

Arson • The malicious burning of another's dwelling. Today, arson statutes have been extended to cover any real property regardless of ownership and the destruction of property by other means—for example, by explosion.

Arson. The willful and malicious burning of a building (and, in some states, personal property) owned by another is the crime of **arson.** At common law, arson applied only to burning down another person's house. The law was designed to protect human life. Today, arson statutes have been extended to cover the destruction of any building, regardless of ownership, by fire or explosion.

Every state has a special statute that covers the burning of a building for the purpose of collecting insurance. If Shaw owns an insured apartment building that is falling apart and sets fire to it himself or pays someone else to do so, he is guilty not only of arson but also of defrauding insurers, which is an attempted larceny. Of course, the insurer need not pay the claim when insurance fraud is proved.

Receiving Stolen Goods. It is a crime to receive stolen goods. The recipient of such goods need not know the true identity of the owner or the thief. All that is necessary is that the recipient knows or should know that the goods are stolen, which implies an intent to deprive the owner of those goods.

Forgery • The fraudulent making or altering of any writing in a way that changes the legal rights and liabilities of another.

Forgery. The fraudulent making or altering of any writing in a way that changes the legal rights and liabilities of another is **forgery.** If, without authorization, Severson signs Bennett's name to the back of a check made out to Bennett, Severson is committing forgery. Forgery also includes changing trademarks, falsifying public records, counterfeiting, and altering a legal document.

Obtaining Goods by False Pretenses. It is a criminal act to obtain goods by false pretenses—for example, to buy groceries with a check, knowing that one has insufficient funds to cover it. Using another's credit-card number to obtain goods is another example of obtaining goods by false pretenses. Statutes dealing with such illegal activities vary widely from state to state. For example, in some states an intent to defraud must be proved before a person is criminally liable for writing a bad check. Some states define the theft and use of another's credit card as a separate crime, while others consider credit-card crime to be a form of forgery.

Public Order Crime

Historically, societies have always outlawed activities that are considered contrary to public values and morals. Today, the most common public order crimes include prostitution, illegal gambling, and illegal drug use. These crimes are sometimes referred to as *victimless crimes* because they normally harm only the offender. From a broader perspective, however, they are deemed detrimental to society as a whole because they may create an environment that could give rise to property and violent crimes.

White-Collar Crime

Crimes occurring in the business context are popularly referred to as white-collar crimes. There is no official definition of **white-collar crime,** but the term is commonly used to mean an illegal act or a series of acts committed by an individual or business entity using some nonviolent means to obtain a personal or business advantage. Usually, this kind of crime takes place in the course of a legitimate business occupation. The crimes discussed next normally occur only in the business environment and thus fall into the category of white-collar crimes. Note, though, that certain property crimes, such as larceny and forgery, may also fall into this category if they occur within the business context.

White-collar crime • Nonviolent crime committed by individuals or corporations to obtain a personal or business advantage.

Embezzlement. When a person entrusted with another person's property or funds fraudulently appropriates that property or those funds, **embezzlement** occurs. Typically, embezzlement involves an employee who steals funds from her or his employer. Banks face this problem, and so do a number of businesses in which corporate officers or accountants "doctor" the books to cover up the fraudulent conversion of funds for their own benefit. Embezzlement is not larceny, because the wrongdoer does not *physically* take the property from the possession of another, and it is not robbery, because no force or fear is used.

Embezzlement • The fraudulent appropriation of money or other property by a person to whom the money or property has been entrusted.

It does not matter whether the accused takes the funds from the victim or from a third person. If, as the financial officer of a large corporation, Carlson pockets a certain number of checks from third parties that were given to her to deposit into the corporate account, she is embezzling.

Ordinarily, an embezzler who returns what has been taken will not be prosecuted because the owner usually will not bother to report the crime, thus avoiding having to give depositions and appear in court. That the accused intended eventually to return the embezzled property, however, does not constitute a sufficient defense to the crime of embezzlement.

Mail and Wire Fraud. One of the most potent weapons against white-collar criminals is the Mail Fraud Act of 1990.[9] Under this act, it is a federal crime to use the mails to defraud the public. Illegal use of the mails must involve (1) mailing or causing someone else to mail a writing—something written, printed, or photocopied—for the purpose of executing a scheme to defraud and (2) contemplating or organizing a scheme to defraud by false pretenses. If, for example, Johnson advertises by mail the sale of a cure for cancer that he knows to be fraudulent because it has no medical validity, he can be prosecuted for fraudulent use of the mails.

9. 18 U.S.C. Sections 1341–1342.

Federal law also makes it a crime (wire fraud) to use wire, radio, or television transmissions to defraud.[10] Violators may be fined up to $1,000, imprisoned for up to twenty years, or both. If the violation affects a financial institution, the violator may be fined up to $1 million, imprisoned for up to thirty years, or both.

Bribery. Basically, three types of bribery are considered crimes: commercial bribery, bribery of public officials, and bribery of foreign officials. As an element of the crime of bribery, intent must be present and proved. The bribe can be anything the recipient considers to be valuable. Realize that the *crime of bribery occurs when the bribe is offered.* It does not matter whether the person to whom the bribe is offered accepts the bribe or agrees to perform whatever action is desired by the person offering the bribe. *Accepting a bribe* is a separate crime.

Typically, people make commercial bribes to obtain proprietary information, cover up an inferior product, or secure new business. Industrial espionage sometimes involves commercial bribes. For example, a person in one firm may offer an employee in a competing firm some type of payoff in exchange for trade secrets or pricing schedules. So-called kickbacks, or payoffs for special favors or services, are a form of commercial bribery in some situations.

The attempt to influence a public official to act in a way that serves a private interest is also a crime. Bribing foreign officials to obtain favorable business contracts is a crime. This crime was discussed in detail in Chapter 4, along with the Foreign Corrupt Practices Act of 1977, which was passed to curb the use of bribery by American businesspersons in securing foreign contracts.

Bankruptcy Fraud. Today, federal bankruptcy law allows individuals and businesses to be relieved of oppressive debt through bankruptcy proceedings. Numerous white-collar crimes may be committed during the many phases of a bankruptcy action. A creditor, for example, may file a false claim against the debtor, which is a crime. Also, a debtor may fraudulently transfer assets to favored parties before or after the petition for bankruptcy is filed. For example, a company-owned automobile may be "sold" at a bargain price to a trusted friend or relative. Closely related to the crime of fraudulent transfer of property is the crime of fraudulent concealment of property, such as the hiding of gold coins.

Insider Trading. An individual who obtains "inside information" about the plans of publicly held corporations can often make stock-trading profits by using the information to guide decisions relating to the purchase or sale of corporate securities (corporate stocks and bonds). *Insider trading* is a violation of securities law and will be considered more fully in Chapter 18. At this point, it may be said that one who possesses inside information and who has a duty not to disclose it to outsiders may not profit from the purchase or sale of securities based on that information until the information is available to the public.

Trade secret • Information or a process that gives a business an advantage over competitors who do not know the information or process.

The Theft of Trade Secrets. **Trade secrets** constitute a form of intellectual property that for many businesses can be extremely valuable. The Economic Espionage Act of 1996[11] makes the theft of trade secrets a federal

10. 18 U.S.C. Section 1343.
11. 18 U.S.C. Sections 1831–1839.

crime. The act also makes it a federal crime to buy or possess another person's trade secrets, knowing that the trade secrets were stolen or otherwise acquired without the owner's authorization.

Violations of the act can result in steep penalties. The act provides that an individual who violates the act can be imprisoned for up to ten years and fined up to $500,000. If a corporation or other organization violates the act, it can be fined up to $5 million. Additionally, the law provides that any property acquired as a result of the violation or used in the commission of the violation is subject to criminal forfeiture—meaning that the government can take the property. A theft of trade secrets conducted via the Internet, for example, could result in the forfeiture of every computer, printer, or other device used to commit or facilitate the violation.

Organized Crime

White-collar crime takes place within the confines of the legitimate business world. Organized crime, in contrast, operates *illegitimately* by satisfying the public's demand for illegal goods and services. Traditionally, the preferred markets for organized crime have been gambling, prostitution, illegal narcotics, pornography, and loan sharking (lending money at higher than legal interest rates), along with more recent ventures into counterfeiting and credit-card scams.

Money Laundering. The profits from organized crime and other illegal activities amount to billions of dollars a year, particularly the profits from illegal drug transactions and, to a lesser extent, from racketeering, prostitution, and gambling. Under federal law, banks, savings and loan associations, and other financial institutions are required to report currency transactions of over $10,000. Consequently, those who engage in illegal activities face difficulties in depositing their cash profits from illegal transactions.

As an alternative to simply depositing cash from illegal transactions in bank accounts, wrongdoers and racketeers have invented ways to launder "dirty" money to make it "clean." This **money laundering** is done through legitimate businesses. For example, a successful drug dealer might become a partner with a restaurateur. Little by little, the restaurant shows an increasing profit. As a shareholder or partner in the restaurant, the wrongdoer is able to report the "profits" of the restaurant as legitimate income on which federal and state taxes are paid. The wrongdoer can then spend those monies without worrying about whether his or her lifestyle exceeds the level possible with his or her reported income.

Money laundering • Falsely reporting income that has been obtained through criminal activity as income obtained through a legitimate business enterprise—in effect, "laundering" the "dirty money."

The Federal Bureau of Investigation (FBI) estimates that organized crime alone has invested tens of billions of dollars in as many as a hundred thousand business establishments in the United States for the purpose of money laundering. Globally, it is estimated that $300 billion in illegal money moves through the world banking system every year.

RICO. In 1970, in an effort to curb the apparently increasing entry of organized crime into the legitimate business world, Congress passed the Racketeer Influenced and Corrupt Organizations Act (RICO).[12] The statute, which was

12. 18 U.S.C. Sections 1961–1968.

enacted as part of the Organized Crime Control Act, makes it a federal crime to (1) use income obtained from racketeering activity to purchase any interest in an enterprise, (2) acquire or maintain an interest in an enterprise through racketeering activity, (3) conduct or participate in the affairs of an enterprise through racketeering activity, or (4) conspire to do any of the preceding activities.

Racketeering activity is not a new type of substantive crime created by RICO; rather, RICO incorporates by reference twenty-six separate types of federal crimes and nine types of state felonies[13] and declares that a person who commits two of these offenses is guilty of "racketeering activity." The act provides for both civil and criminal liability.

To read the text of the Racketeer Influenced and Corrupt Organizations Act of 1970, go to the "Statutes" page of our Web site at **http://ele.westbuslaw.com**

Civil Liability under RICO. The penalties for violations of the RICO statute are harsh. In the event of a violation, the statute permits the government to seek civil penalties, including the divestiture of a defendant's interest in a business (called forfeiture) or the dissolution of the business. Perhaps the most controversial aspect of RICO is that in some cases, private individuals are allowed to recover three times their actual losses (treble damages), plus attorneys' fees, for business injuries caused by a violation of the statute.

The broad language of RICO has allowed it to be applied in cases that have little or nothing to do with organized crime, and an aggressive trial attorney may attempt to show that any business fraud constitutes "racketeering activity." In its 1985 decision in *Sedima, S.P.R.L. v. Imrex Co.,*[14] the United States Supreme Court interpreted RICO broadly and set a significant precedent for subsequent applications of the act. Plaintiffs have used the RICO statute in numerous commercial fraud cases because of the inviting prospect of being awarded treble damages if they win. The most frequent targets of civil RICO lawsuits are insurance companies, employment agencies, commercial banks, and stockbrokerage firms.

One of the requirements of RICO is that there be more than one offense—there must be a "pattern of racketeering activity." What constitutes a "pattern" has been the subject of much litigation. According to the interpretation of some courts, a pattern must involve, among other things, continued criminal activity. This is known as the "continuity" requirement. Part of this requirement is that the activity occur over a "substantial" period of time.

Criminal Liability under RICO. Many criminal RICO offenses, such as gambling, arson, and extortion, have little, if anything, to do with normal business activities. But securities fraud (involving the sale of stocks and bonds) and mail and wire fraud may also constitute criminal RICO violations, and RICO has become an effective tool in attacking these white-collar crimes in recent years. Under the criminal provisions of RICO, any individual found guilty of a violation is subject to a fine of up to $25,000 per violation, imprisonment for up to twenty years, or both.

---

13. See 18 U.S.C. Section 1961(1)(A). The crimes listed in this section relate to murder, kidnapping, gambling, arson, robbery, bribery, extortion, money laundering, securities fraud, counterfeiting, dealing in obscene matter, dealing in controlled substances, and a number of others.

14. 473 U.S. 479, 105 S.Ct. 3275, 87 L.Ed.2d 346 (1985).

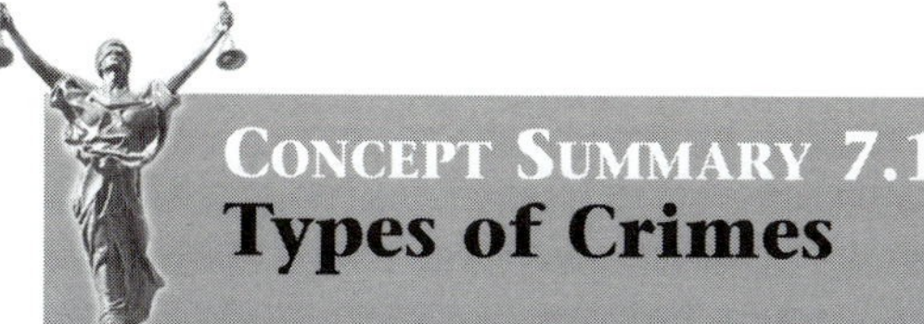

CONCEPT SUMMARY 7.1
Types of Crimes

CRIME CATEGORY	DEFINITION AND EXAMPLES
Violent Crime	① *Definition*—Crimes that cause others to suffer physical harm or death. ② *Examples*—Murder, assault and battery, sexual assault (rape), and robbery.
Property Crime	① *Definition*—Crimes in which the goal of the offender is some form of economic gain or the damaging of property; the most common form of crime. ② *Examples*—Burglary, larceny, arson, receiving stolen goods, forgery, and obtaining goods by false pretenses.
Public Order Crime	① *Definition*—Crimes contrary to public values and morals. ② *Examples*—Prostitution, illegal gambling, and illegal drug use.
White-Collar Crime	① *Definition*—An illegal act or series of acts committed by an individual or business entity using some nonviolent means to obtain a personal or business advantage; usually committed in the course of a legitimate occupation. ② *Examples*—Embezzlement, mail and wire fraud, bribery, bankruptcy fraud, insider trading, and the theft of trade secrets.
Organized Crime	① *Definition*—A form of crime conducted by groups operating illegitimately to satisfy the public's demand for illegal goods and services (such as narcotics or pornography). ② *Money laundering*—The establishment of legitimate enterprises through which "dirty" money (obtained through criminal activities, such as organized crime) can be "laundered" (made to appear as legitimate income). ③ *RICO*—The Racketeer Influenced and Corrupt Organizations Act (RICO) of 1970 makes it a federal crime to (a) use income obtained from racketeering activity to purchase any interest in an enterprise, (b) acquire or maintain an interest in an enterprise through racketeering activity, (c) conduct or participate in the affairs of an enterprise through racketeering activity, or (d) conspire to do any of the preceding activities. RICO provides for both civil and criminal liability.

DEFENSES TO CRIMINAL LIABILITY

In certain circumstances, the law may allow a person to be excused from criminal liability because she or he lacks the required mental state. Criminal defendants may also be relieved of criminal liability if they can show that their criminal actions were justified, given the circumstances. Other defenses to criminal liability are infancy, intoxication, insanity, mistake, consent, duress, justifiable use of force, necessity, entrapment, and the statute of limitations. Also, in some cases, defendants are given *immunity* from prosecution and thus relieved, at least in part, of criminal liability for their actions. We look next at each of these defenses.

Note that procedural violations (such as obtaining evidence without a valid search warrant) can operate as defenses also—because evidence obtained in violation of a defendant's constitutional rights may not be admitted in court. If the evidence is suppressed, then there may be no basis for prosecuting the defendant.

Infancy

The term *infant,* as used in the law, refers to any person who has not yet reached the age of majority. In all states, certain courts handle cases involving children who allegedly have violated the law. In some states, juvenile courts handle children's cases exclusively. In most states, however, courts that handle children's cases also have jurisdiction over other matters, such as traffic offenses.

Originally, juvenile court hearings were informal, and lawyers were rarely present. Since 1967, however, when the United States Supreme Court ordered that a child charged with delinquency must be allowed to consult with an attorney before being committed to a state institution,[15] juvenile court hearings have become more formal. In most states, the law allows juvenile court judges the discretion to decide whether a child should be treated as an adult and tried in a regular court if he or she is above a certain age (usually fourteen) and is accused of a felony, such as rape or murder.

Intoxication

The law recognizes two types of intoxication, whether from drugs or from alcohol: involuntary and voluntary. *Involuntary intoxication* occurs when a person either is physically forced to ingest or inject an intoxicating substance or is unaware that a substance contains drugs or alcohol. Involuntary intoxication is a defense to a crime if its effect was to make a person incapable of understanding that the act committed was wrong or incapable of obeying the law.

Using voluntary drug or alcohol intoxication as a defense is based on the theory that extreme levels of intoxication may negate the state of mind that a crime requires. Many courts are reluctant to allow *voluntary intoxication* as a defense to a crime, however. After all, the defendant, by definition, voluntarily chose to put herself or himself into an intoxicated state.

Insanity

Just as a child is often judged incapable of the state of mind required to commit a crime, so also may be someone suffering from a mental illness. Thus, insanity may be a defense to a criminal charge. The courts have had difficulty deciding what standards should be used to measure sanity for the purposes of a criminal trial. One of the oldest standards, or tests, for insanity is the *M'Naghten* test,[16] which is still used in about one-third of the states. Under this test, which is sometimes called the "right-wrong" test, a criminal defendant is not responsible if, at the time of the offense, he or she did not know the nature and quality of the act or did not know that the act was wrong.

Several other jurisdictions use the less restrictive irresistible-impulse test to determine sanity. Under this test, a person may be found insane even if the person was aware that a criminal act was wrong, providing that some "irresistible impulse" resulting from a mental deficiency drove her or him to commit the crime.

Today, almost all federal courts and about half of the states use the relatively liberal standard set forth in the Model Penal Code:

---

15. *In re Gault,* 387 U.S. 1, 87 S.Ct. 1428, 18 L.Ed.2d 527 (1967).
16. A rule derived from *M'Naghten's Case,* 8 Eng.Rep. 718 (1843).

> A person is not responsible for criminal conduct if at the time of such conduct as a result of mental disease or defect he lacks *substantial capacity* either to appreciate the wrongfulness of his conduct or to conform his conduct to the requirements of the law.[17] [Emphasis added.]

This "substantial-capacity" standard is considerably easier to meet than the *M'Naghten* test or the irresistible-impulse test.

Under any of these tests, it is extremely difficult to prove insanity. For this reason, the insanity defense is rarely used. It is raised in only about 1 percent of felony cases and is unsuccessful in about three-fourths of those cases.

Mistake

Everyone has heard the saying "Ignorance of the law is no excuse." Ordinarily, ignorance of the law or a mistaken idea about what the law requires is not a valid defense. In some states, however, that rule has been modified. People who claim that they honestly did not know that they were breaking a law may have a valid defense if (1) the law was not published or reasonably made known to the public or (2) the people relied on an official statement of the law that was erroneous.

A *mistake of fact,* as opposed to a *mistake of law,* operates as a defense if it negates the mental state necessary to commit a crime. If, for example, Oliver Wheaton mistakenly walks off with Julie Tyson's briefcase because he thinks it is his, there is no theft. Theft requires knowledge that the property belongs to another.

Consent

What if a victim consents to a crime or even encourages the person intending a criminal act to commit it? Ordinarily, **consent** does not operate as a bar to criminal liability. In some rare circumstances, however, the law may allow consent to be used as a defense. In each case, one question is whether the law forbids an act committed against the victim's will or forbids the act without regard to the victim's wish.

Consent • Voluntary agreement to a proposition or an act of another.

If consent is permitted as a defense, it normally only operates as a defense in cases involving crimes against property. The law forbids murder, prostitution, and drug use whether the victim consents or not. Also, if the act causes harm to a third person who has not consented, there is no escape from criminal liability. Consent or forgiveness given after a crime has been committed is not really a defense, although it can affect the likelihood of prosecution.

Duress

Duress exists when the *wrongful threat* of one person induces another person to perform an act that he or she would not otherwise have performed. In such a situation, duress is said to negate the mental state necessary to commit a crime. For duress to qualify as a defense, the following requirements must be met:

Duress • Unlawful pressure brought to bear on a person, causing the person to perform an act that he or she would not otherwise perform.

1. The threat must be of serious bodily harm or death.
2. The harm threatened must be greater than the harm caused by the crime.

---

17. Model Penal Code Section 4.01.

3. The threat must be immediate and inescapable.
4. The defendant must have been involved in the situation through no fault of his or her own.

One crime that cannot be excused by duress is murder. It is difficult to justify taking a life as a result of duress even if one's own life is threatened.

Justifiable Use of Force

Self-defense • The legally recognized privilege to protect one's self against injury by another. The privilege of self-defense protects only acts that are reasonably necessary to protect one's self.

Probably the most well-known defense to criminal liability is **self-defense**—the protection of one's self against injury by another. Other situations, however, also justify the use of force: the defense of one's dwelling, the defense of other property, and the prevention of a crime. In all of these situations, it is important to distinguish between deadly and nondeadly force. *Deadly force* is likely to result in death or serious bodily harm. *Nondeadly force* is force that reasonably appears necessary to prevent the imminent use of criminal force.

Generally speaking, people can use the amount of nondeadly force that seems necessary to protect themselves, their dwellings, or other property or to prevent the commission of a crime. Deadly force can be used in self-defense if there is a *reasonable belief* that imminent death or serious bodily harm will otherwise result, if the attacker is using unlawful force (an example of lawful force is that exerted by a police officer), and if the defender has not initiated or provoked the attack. Deadly force can be used to defend a dwelling only if the unlawful entry is violent and the person believes deadly force is necessary to prevent imminent death or great bodily harm or—in some jurisdictions—if the person believes deadly force is necessary to prevent the commission of a felony in the dwelling.

Necessity

Necessity • In criminal law, a defense against liability; under Section 3.02 of the Model Penal Code, this defense is justifiable if "the harm or evil sought to be avoided" by a given action "is greater than that sought to be prevented by the law defining the offense charged."

Sometimes criminal defendants can be relieved of liability by showing that a criminal act was necessary to prevent an even greater harm. According to the Model Penal Code, the defense of **necessity** is justifiable if "the harm or evil sought to be avoided by such conduct is greater than that sought to be prevented by the law defining the offense charged."[18] For example, in one case a convicted felon was threatened by an acquaintance with a gun. The felon grabbed the gun and fled the scene, but subsequently he was arrested under a statute that prohibits convicted felons from possessing firearms. In this situation, the necessity defense succeeded because the defendant's crime avoided a "greater evil."[19]

Entrapment

Entrapment • In criminal law, a defense in which the defendant claims that he or she was induced by a public official—usually an undercover agent or police officer—to commit a crime that he or she would otherwise not have committed.

Entrapment is a defense designed to prevent police officers or other government agents from encouraging crimes in order to apprehend persons wanted for criminal acts. In the typical entrapment case, an undercover agent *suggests* that a crime be committed and somehow pressures or induces an individual to commit it. The agent then arrests the individual for the crime. For entrapment to be considered a defense, both the suggestion and the inducement must take place. The defense is not intended to prevent law enforce-

18. Model Penal Code Section 3.02.
19. *United States v. Paolello,* 951 F.3d 537 (3d Cir. 1991).

ment agents from setting a trap for an unwary criminal; rather, the intent is to prevent them from pushing the individual into that trap. The crucial issue is whether a person who committed a crime was predisposed to commit the crime or did so because the agent induced it.

Statute of Limitations

With some exceptions, such as for the crime of murder, statutes of limitations apply to crimes, just as they do to civil wrongs. In other words, criminal cases must be prosecuted within a certain number of years. If a criminal action is brought after the statutory time period has expired, the accused person can raise the statute of limitations as a defense. The running of the time period in a statute of limitations may be tolled—that is, suspended or stopped temporarily—if the defendant is a minor or is not in the jurisdiction. When the defendant reaches the age of majority or returns to the jurisdiction, the statute revives—that is, its time period begins to run or to run again.

Immunity

At times, the state may wish to obtain information from a person accused of a crime. Accused persons are understandably reluctant to give information if it will be used to prosecute them, and they cannot be forced to do so. The privilege against self-incrimination is granted by the Fifth Amendment to the Constitution, which reads, in part, "nor shall [any person] be compelled in any criminal case to be a witness against himself." In cases in which the state wishes to obtain information from a person accused of a crime, the state can grant *immunity* from prosecution or agree to prosecute for a less serious offense in exchange for the information. Once immunity is given, the person has an absolute privilege against self-incrimination and therefore can no longer refuse to testify on Fifth Amendment grounds.

Often a grant of immunity from prosecution for a serious crime is part of a **plea bargain** between the defendant and the prosecuting attorney. The defendant may be convicted of a lesser offense, while the state uses the defendant's testimony to prosecute accomplices for serious crimes carrying heavy penalties.

Plea bargain • A negotiated agreement between a criminal defendant and the prosecutor in a criminal case that usually involves the defendant's pleading guilty to a lesser offense in return for a lighter sentence.

Criminal Procedures

Criminal law brings the force of the state, with all of its resources, to bear against the individual. Criminal procedures are designed to protect the constitutional rights of individuals and to prevent the arbitrary use of power on the part of the government.

The U.S. Constitution provides specific safeguards for those accused of crimes. The United States Supreme Court has ruled that most of these safeguards apply not only in federal but also in state courts by virtue of the due process clause of the Fourteenth Amendment. These safeguards include the following:

1. The Fourth Amendment protection from unreasonable searches and seizures.
2. The Fourth Amendment requirement that no warrant for a search or an arrest be issued without probable cause.

3. The Fifth Amendment requirement that no one be deprived of "life, liberty, or property without due process of law."
4. The Fifth Amendment prohibition against **double jeopardy** (being tried twice for the same criminal offense).[20]
5. The Fifth Amendment requirement that no person be required to be a witness against (incriminate) himself or herself.
6. The Sixth Amendment guarantees of a speedy trial, a trial by jury, a public trial, the right to confront witnesses, and the right to a lawyer at various stages in some proceedings.
7. The Eighth Amendment prohibitions against excessive bail and fines and cruel and unusual punishment.

Double jeopardy • Being tried twice for the same criminal offense; prohibited by the Fifth Amendment to the Constitution.

The Exclusionary Rule

Exclusionary rule • In criminal procedure, a rule under which any evidence that is obtained in violation of the accused's constitutional rights guaranteed by the Fourth, Fifth, and Sixth Amendments, as well as any evidence derived from illegally obtained evidence, will not be admissible in court.

Under what is known as the **exclusionary rule,** all evidence obtained in violation of the constitutional rights spelled out in the Fourth, Fifth, and Sixth Amendments normally is not admissible at trial. All evidence derived from the illegally obtained evidence is known as the "fruit of the poisonous tree," and such evidence normally must also be excluded from the trial proceedings. For example, if a confession is obtained after an illegal arrest, the arrest is the "poisonous tree," and the confession, if "tainted" by the arrest, is the "fruit." In the following case, the court considered whether certain evidence had been obtained improperly and should be excluded as "fruit of the poisonous tree."

20. The prohibition against double jeopardy means that once a criminal defendant is found not guilty of a particular crime, the government may not reindict the person and retry him or her for the same crime. The prohibition against double jeopardy does not preclude a *civil* suit's being brought against the same person by the crime victim to recover damages. For example, a person found not guilty of assault and battery in a criminal case may be sued by the victim in a civil tort case for damages. Additionally, a state's prosecution of a crime will not prevent a separate federal prosecution of the same crime, and vice versa. For example, a defendant found not guilty of violating a state law can be tried in federal court for the same act, if the act is also defined as a crime under federal law.

CASE 7.2

New York Supreme Court, 2002.[a]
191 Misc.2d 531,
744 N.Y.S.2d 287.

PEOPLE v. MCFARLAN

In 1999, the state of New York adopted the Electronic Signatures and Records Act (ESRA).[b] *ESRA concerns the use and legal admissibility in New York state courts of records that are stored by electronic means. Under rules issued pursuant to ESRA, an electronic record has the same force and effect as a record not produced or maintained by electronic means. Those rules state that ESRA's purpose is to "ensure that persons who voluntarily elect to use . . . electronic records can do so with confidence that they carry the same force and effect of nonelectronic . . . records." In May 2001, Lisa Kordes saw two men picking pockets on a Lexington Avenue bus in Manhattan, in New York City. Based on Kordes's description of the men, a police department computer produced a six-photo array of possible suspects. Kordes selected a photo of Kevin McFarlan as one of the men she had seen. Five days later, on a bus, Neal Ariano, a police officer, arrested*

a. In New York, a supreme court is a trial court.
b. New York Technology Law Sections 101–109.

McFarlan after seeing him bump an elderly woman while placing his hand near her pocketbook. At the police station, Kordes viewed a lineup including McFarlan and identified him as the man she had seen on the Lexington Avenue bus. McFarlan was charged in a New York state court with various crimes. The printout of the computer-generated photo array that Kordes had been shown was lost, but the "People" (the state of New York) introduced into evidence a second printout to show what Kordes had seen. McFarlan argued, among other things, that the first printout was the original photo array and that because that printout had been lost, the court should presume the photo-array procedure had been illegal. Thus, McFarlan's arrest and Kordes's identification of him in the lineup should be excluded as "fruit of the poisonous tree." The court considered the application of ESRA in this context.

STONE, J.

Since the advent of the computer and the growth of the electronic storage of information, there has been a growing appreciation of the need to rearticulate rules of law relating to what is a writing, and in such context, what is an original document. There now seems [to be] a consensus embodied in recent proposed and enacted legislation that *for the pre-computer concept of "writing" the term "record" should now be substituted to accommodate this new reality.* * * * [Emphasis added.]

Under this concept, the record is electronic information which is retrievable in usable form. As no reported New York decision has yet cited or construed ESRA * * * , this is generally a case of first impression [a case presenting a legal issue that has not been addressed by the court's jurisdiction], and especially as to whether such law applies in the context of a criminal proceeding or trial. ESRA itself makes no distinction between civil and criminal proceedings, and was designed to be generally applicable and to change prior ways of doing business, superseding all other statutes, cases and rules. The only reason that a criminal or civil context might lead to a different result is, if in some way, an important constitutional protection of a criminal defendant would be lost by applying ESRA in a criminal proceeding. Thus, the issue here is whether the maintenance of a record in electronic form, and the use of a manifestation of the record, either as a printout or as a screen or other display, in connection with the arrest, prosecution and possible conviction of a criminal defendant, could violate constitutional rules.

Here, as both printouts were generated in the same format, there can be no prejudice from the fact that the defendant was selected from the first printout and that a second identical printout was later [introduced into evidence]. Each is identical and conveys the full recoverable information. To decide * * * to the contrary * * * is absurd. Where, for example, a witness is shown only the screen display, what must the People [public prosecutor] keep? For on such an analysis the printout of the screen could not be the "original." The purpose of requiring the preservation of a record is clear. Concern for the integrity of information has always led the Courts to prefer the original, and have led to many rules to bar or limit the use of non-"original" material. Here the original array was in electronic form in the computer memory, the testimony was unequivocal that [both] printout[s] * * * were generated in the same manner. * * * [A]s a result, defendant's argument crumbles.

The New York state court held that the second printout of the photo array was not "fruit of the poisonous tree" and could be properly accepted into evidence. While acknowledging that the first printout was lost, the court reasoned that this did not indicate that the photo-array procedure had been illegal because the first printout was not the original photo array. The original photo array was the electronic record in the computer.

QUESTIONS

1. Who was the defendant in this case, and what did he or she argue about the evidence?
2. According to the state trial court, could the second printout of the photo array be admitted into evidence? Why or why not?
3. Are there any circumstances in which the use of a *record,* as that term is defined in this case, could violate constitutional principles?

Purpose of the Exclusionary Rule. The purpose of the exclusionary rule is to deter police from conducting warrantless searches and from engaging in other misconduct. The rule is sometimes criticized because it can lead to injustice. Many a defendant has "gotten off on a technicality" because law enforcement personnel failed to observe procedural requirements based on the above-mentioned constitutional amendments. Even though a defendant may be obviously guilty, if the evidence of that guilt is obtained improperly (without a valid search warrant, for example), it cannot be used against the defendant in court.

Exceptions to the Exclusionary Rule. Over the last several decades, however, the United States Supreme Court has diminished the scope of the exclusionary rule by creating some exceptions to its applicability. For example, in 1984 the Court held that if illegally obtained evidence would have been discovered "inevitably" and obtained by the police using lawful means, the evidence will be admissible at trial.[21] In another case decided in the same year, the Court held that a police officer who used a technically incorrect search warrant form to obtain evidence had acted in good faith and therefore the evidence was admissible. The Court thus created the "good faith" exception to the exclusionary rule.[22] Additionally, the courts can exercise a certain amount of discretion in determining whether evidence has been obtained improperly, thus somewhat balancing the scales.

The *Miranda* Rule

In regard to criminal procedure, one of the questions many courts faced in the 1950s and 1960s was not whether suspects had constitutional rights—that was not in doubt—but how and when those rights could be exercised. Could the right to be silent (under the Fifth Amendment's prohibition against self-incrimination) be exercised during pretrial interrogation proceedings, or only during the trial? Were confessions obtained from suspects admissible in court if the suspects had not been advised of their right to remain silent and other constitutional rights?

21. *Nix v. Williams,* 467 U.S. 431, 104 S.Ct. 2501, 81 L.Ed. 377 (1984).
22. *Massachusetts v. Sheppard,* 468 U.S. 981, 104 S.Ct. 3424, 82 L.Ed.2d 737 (1984).

To clarify these issues, the United States Supreme Court issued a landmark decision in 1966 in *Miranda v. Arizona,* which we present here. The procedural rights required by the Supreme Court in this case are familiar to virtually every American.

CASE 7.3

Supreme Court of the United States, 1966.
384 U.S. 436,
86 S.Ct. 1602,
16 L.Ed.2d 694.

MIRANDA v. ARIZONA

On March 13, 1963, Ernesto Miranda was arrested at his home for the kidnapping and rape of an eighteen-year-old woman. Miranda was taken to a Phoenix, Arizona, police station and questioned by two officers. Two hours later, the officers emerged from the interrogation room with a written confession signed by Miranda. A paragraph at the top of the confession stated that the confession had been made voluntarily, without threats or promises of immunity, and "with full knowledge of my legal rights, understanding any statement I make may be used against me." Miranda was at no time advised that he had a right to remain silent and a right to have a lawyer present. The confession was admitted into evidence at the trial, and Miranda was convicted and sentenced to prison for twenty to thirty years. Miranda appealed the decision, claiming that he had not been informed of his constitutional rights. The Supreme Court of Arizona held that Miranda's constitutional rights had not been violated and affirmed his conviction. The Miranda *case was subsequently consolidated with three other cases involving similar issues and reviewed by the United States Supreme Court.*

WARREN, J.

The cases before us raise questions which go to the roots of our concepts of American criminal jurisprudence; the restraints society must observe consistent with the Federal Constitution in prosecuting individuals for crime. * * *

* * * *

At the outset, if a person in custody is to be subjected to interrogation, he must first be informed in clear and unequivocal terms that he has the right to remain silent. * * *

* * * *

The warning of the right to remain silent must be accompanied by the explanation that anything said can and will be used against the individual in court. This warning is needed in order to make him aware not only of the privilege, *but also of the consequences of forgoing it.* * * * [Emphasis added.]

The circumstances surrounding in-custody interrogation can operate very quickly to overbear the will of one merely made aware of his privilege by his interrogators. Therefore the right to have counsel present at the interrogation is indispensable to the protection of the Fifth Amendment privilege under the system we delineate today.

* * * *

In order fully to apprise a person interrogated of the extent of his rights under this system then, it is necessary to warn him not only that he has the right to consult with an attorney, but also that if he is indigent [without funds] a lawyer will be appointed to represent him. * * * The warning of a right to counsel would be hollow if not couched in terms that would convey to the indigent—the person most often subjected to interrogation—the knowledge that he too has a right to have counsel present.

The Supreme Court held that Miranda could not be convicted of the crime on the basis of his confession because his confession was inadmissible as evidence. For any statement made by a defendant to be admissible, the defendant must be informed of certain constitutional rights prior to police interrogation. If the accused waives his or her rights to remain silent and to have counsel present, the government must demonstrate that the waiver was made knowingly, voluntarily, and intelligently.

QUESTIONS

1. What did the United States Supreme Court hold in Miranda's case, and why?
2. Why wasn't the paragraph at the top of Miranda's signed confession, stating that he had "full knowledge of [his] legal rights," sufficient to waive those rights?
3. Should defendants who have admitted that they are guilty be allowed to avoid criminal liability because of procedural violations?

Congress's Response to the *Miranda* Ruling. The Supreme Court's *Miranda* decision was controversial, and two years later Congress attempted to overrule it by enacting Section 3501 of the Omnibus Crime Control and Safe Streets Act[23] of 1968. Essentially, Section 3501 reinstated the rule that had been in effect for 180 years before *Miranda*—namely, that statements by defendants can be used against them as long as the statements are made voluntarily. The U.S. Justice Department immediately disavowed Section 3501 as unconstitutional, however, and the section has never been enforced. Although the U.S. Court of Appeals for the Fourth Circuit attempted to enforce the provision in 1999, the court's decision was reversed by the United States Supreme Court in 2000. The Supreme Court held that the *Miranda* rights enunciated by the Court in the 1966 case were constitutionally based and thus could not be overruled by a legislative act.[24]

Exceptions to the *Miranda* Rule. Over time, as part of a continuing attempt to balance the rights of accused persons against the rights of society, the Supreme Court has made a number of exceptions to the *Miranda* ruling. In 1984, for example, the Court recognized a "public-safety" exception to the *Miranda* rule. The need to protect the public warranted the admissibility of statements made by the defendant (in this case, indicating where he placed the gun) as evidence at trial, even though the defendant had not been informed of his *Miranda* rights.[25]

In 1986, the Court further held that a confession need not be excluded even though the police failed to inform a suspect in custody that his attorney had tried to reach him by telephone.[26] In an important 1991 decision, the Court stated that a suspect's conviction will not be overturned solely on the ground that the suspect was coerced by law enforcement personnel into making a confession. If the other evidence admitted at trial was strong enough to

23. 42 U.S.C. Section 3789d.
24. *Dickerson v. United States,* 530 U.S. 428, 120 S.Ct. 2326, 147 L.Ed.2d 405 (2000).
25. *New York v. Quarles,* 467 U.S. 649, 104 S.Ct. 2626, 81 L.Ed.2d 550 (1984).
26. *Moran v. Burbine,* 475 U.S. 412, 106 S.Ct. 1135, 89 L.Ed.2d 410 (1986).

justify the conviction without the confession, then the fact that the confession was obtained illegally can be, in effect, ignored.[27]

In yet another case, in 1994, the Supreme Court ruled that a suspect must unequivocally and assertively request to exercise his or her right to counsel in order to stop police questioning. Saying, "Maybe I should talk to a lawyer" during an interrogation after being taken into custody is not enough. The Court held that police officers are not required to decipher the suspect's intentions in such situations.[28] In sum, today juries are able to consider confessions in many cases, even when they are not unequivocally voluntary.

Videotaped Interrogations. There are no guarantees that *Miranda* will survive indefinitely—particularly in view of the numerous exceptions that are made to the rule. Additionally, law enforcement personnel are increasingly using digital cameras to record interrogations. According to some scholars, the taping of *all* custodial interrogations would satisfy the Fifth Amendment's prohibition against coercion and in the process render the *Miranda* warnings unnecessary.

Are there too many exceptions to the *Miranda* rule? As mentioned, the Supreme Court's decision in *Miranda* has always been controversial. Initially, many were concerned that the *Miranda* requirements would hamper efforts by law enforcement officials to bring criminals to justice. After all, even obviously guilty persons could "get off on a technicality" if their *Miranda* rights were violated. Over time, these criticisms lessened as the courts carved out various exceptions to the *Miranda* rule. As a result of these decisions, some legal scholars now contend that there are too many exceptions to the rule. David Steinberg, the director of the Thomas Jefferson School of Law's Center for Law and Social Justice in San Diego, argues that "the current patchwork of exceptions to *Miranda* is confusing and costly." Steinberg believes that the Supreme Court should either create a "standard rule," under which the *Miranda* rule would be strictly applied in all cases, or "deregulate confessions." Under the latter approach, it would be left to the courts to decide whether a confession had been coerced by the police and should be excluded.[29] As already mentioned, others have suggested abandoning *Miranda* entirely and requiring instead that all custodial interrogations be videotaped.

Criminal Process

As mentioned earlier in this chapter, a criminal prosecution differs significantly from a civil case in several respects. These differences reflect the desire to safeguard the rights of the individual against the state. Exhibit 7–3 on the next page summarizes the major steps in processing a criminal case. Here we discuss three phases of the criminal process—arrest, indictment or information, and trial—in more detail.

27. *Arizona v. Fulminante,* 499 U.S. 279, 111 S.Ct. 1246, 113 L.Ed.2d 302 (1991).
28. *Davis v. United States,* 512 U.S. 452, 114 S.Ct. 2350, 129 L.Ed.2d 362 (1994).
29. David Steinberg, "*Miranda* No Longer Works," *The National Law Journal,* August 14, 2000, p. A18.

EXHIBIT 7–3 • MAJOR STEPS IN PROCESSING A CRIMINAL CASE

ARREST

Police officer takes suspect into custody. Most arrests are made without a warrant. After the arrest, the officer searches the suspect, who is then taken to the police station.

BOOKING

At the police station, the suspect is searched again, photographed, fingerprinted, and allowed at least one telephone call. After the booking, charges are reviewed, and if they are not dropped, a complaint is filed and a magistrate reviews the case for probable cause.

INITIAL APPEARANCE

The suspect appears before the magistrate, who informs the suspect of the charges and of his or her rights. If the suspect requires a lawyer, one is appointed. The magistrate sets bail (conditions under which a suspect can obtain release pending disposition of the case).

GRAND JURY

A grand jury determines if there is probable cause to believe that the defendant committed the crime. The federal government and about half of the states require grand jury indictments for at least some felonies.

PRELIMINARY HEARING

In a court proceeding, a prosecutor presents evidence, and the judge determines if there is probable cause to hold the defendant over for trial.

INDICTMENT

An indictment is the charging instrument issued by the grand jury.

INFORMATION

An information is the charging instrument issued by the prosecutor.

ARRAIGNMENT

The suspect is brought before the trial court, informed of the charges, and asked to enter a plea.

PLEA BARGAIN

A plea bargain is a prosecutor's promise to make concessions (or promise to seek concessions) in return for a suspect's guilty plea. Concessions may include a reduced charge or a lesser sentence.

GUILTY PLEA

In many jurisdictions, most cases that reach the arraignment stage do not go to trial but are resolved by a guilty plea, often as a result of a plea bargain. The judge sets the case for sentencing.

TRIAL

Generally, most felony trials are jury trials, and most misdemeanor trials are bench trials (trials before judges). If the verdict is "guilty," the judge sets the case for sentencing. Everyone convicted of a crime has the right to an appeal.

Arrest. Before a warrant for arrest can be issued, there must be probable cause for believing that the individual in question has committed a crime. As discussed in Chapter 5, *probable cause* can be defined as a substantial likelihood that the person has committed or is about to commit a crime. Note that probable cause involves a likelihood, not just a possibility. Arrests are often made without a warrant if there is no time to get one, but the action of the arresting officer is still judged by the standard of probable cause.

Indictment or Information. Individuals must be formally charged with having committed specific crimes before they can be brought to trial. If issued by a grand jury, such a charge is called an **indictment.**[30] A **grand jury** does not determine the guilt or innocence of an accused party; rather, its function is to determine, after hearing the state's evidence, whether a reasonable basis (probable cause) exists for supposing that the suspect has committed a crime and should be held for trial.

Usually, grand juries are called in cases involving serious crimes, such as murder. For lesser crimes, an individual may be formally charged with a crime by an **information,** or criminal complaint. An information will be issued by a government prosecutor if the prosecutor determines that there is sufficient evidence to justify bringing the individual to trial.

Indictment • The formal written accusation of a crime, made by a grand jury and presented to a court for prosecution against the accused person.

Grand jury • A group of citizens called to decide, after hearing the state's evidence, whether a reasonable basis (probable cause) exists for believing that a crime has been committed and whether a trial ought to be held.

Information • A formal accusation or complaint made by a government prosecutor without a grand-jury indictment.

Trial. At a criminal trial, the accused person does not have to prove anything; the entire burden of proof is on the prosecutor (the state). As discussed at the beginning of this chapter, the burden of proof is higher in a criminal case than in a civil case. The prosecution must show that, based on all the evidence, the defendant's guilt is established *beyond a reasonable doubt.* If there is any reasonable doubt that a criminal defendant did not commit the crime with which she or he has been charged, then the verdict must be "*not* guilty." Note that giving a verdict of "not guilty" is not the same as stating that the defendant is innocent; it merely means that not enough evidence was properly presented to the court to prove guilt beyond a reasonable doubt.

Courts have complex rules about what types of evidence may be presented and how the evidence may be brought out in criminal cases, especially in jury trials. These rules are designed to ensure that evidence presented at trials is relevant, reliable, and not prejudicial against the defendant.

Federal Sentencing Guidelines

Traditionally, persons who committed the same crime might receive very different sentences, depending on the judge hearing the case, the jurisdiction in which it was heard, and many other factors. In 1984, however, Congress passed the Sentencing Reform Act. This act created the U.S. Sentencing Commission, which was charged with the task of standardizing sentences for federal crimes. The commission's guidelines, which became effective in 1987, established a range of possible penalties for each federal crime. When sentencing a criminal defendant, the judge must select a sentence from within this range, taking into consideration the defendant's criminal record, the seriousness of the offense, and other factors specified in the guidelines.

The commission also created specific guidelines for the punishment of crimes committed by corporate employees (white-collar crimes). These guidelines, which went into effect in 1991, established stiffer penalties for mail and

30. Pronounced in-*dyte*-ment.

wire fraud, commercial bribery and kickbacks, and money laundering, as well as for criminal violations of employment laws (see Chapters 14 and 15), securities laws (see Chapter 18), and antitrust laws (see Chapter 17).[31] The guidelines allow judges to take into consideration a number of factors when selecting from the range of possible penalties for a specified crime. These factors include the defendant company's history of past violations, the extent of management's cooperation with federal investigators, and the extent to which the firm has undertaken specific programs and procedures to prevent criminal activities by its employees.

In imposing a sentence, a judge may depart from the guidelines only if the defendant has some notice of this possibility and thus can prepare to argue against it. Does the same notice requirement apply to unusual conditions of supervised release, or probation? That was the question in the following case.

31. The Sarbanes-Oxley Act of 2002 directed the Sentencing Commission to revise the guidelines to reflect the stiffer penalties imposed by the act for corporate securities fraud.

CASE 7.4

United States Court of Appeals, Seventh Circuit, 2003. 316 F.3d 733.

UNITED STATES v. SCOTT

Todd Scott was charged in a federal district court with fraud and pleaded guilty. Based on his conduct and previous crimes, the court imposed the maximum sentence—twenty-four months' imprisonment followed by three years' supervised release. During the sentencing, the prosecutor suggested that because a police search of a computer in Scott's office turned up a few images of child pornography, Scott's access to the Internet should be limited as part of the supervised release. The court agreed, and ordered that Scott "shall be prohibited from access to any Internet Services without prior approval of the probation officer." Scott appealed this order to the U.S. Court of Appeals for the Seventh Circuit, contending in part that he should have received notice of this condition so that at the sentencing, he could have proposed an alternative.

EASTERBROOK, J.

Scott's lawyer opposed the condition at sentencing but did not offer any alternative. This omission does not forfeit his ability to advance alternatives on appeal; the surprise addition of the Internet-access condition made it impossible for Scott's lawyer to formulate proposals in time. And there were other possibilities. Scott obtained the pictures from a newsgroup on the Usenet, one of many services available on the Internet. The district judge might have prohibited Scott from accessing newsgroups, as opposed to the entire Internet. Or the judge might have required Scott to install filtering software that would block access to sexually oriented sites, and to permit the probation officer unannounced access to verify that the filtering software was functional. Filtering software is imperfect and may block access to some sites that lack the attributes sought to be put off limits * * * but is less restrictive than blocking the whole Internet—and reliance on software avoids any problem in giving discretion to a probation officer, whose errors may be greater.

Knowledge that a condition of this kind was in prospect would have enabled the parties to discuss such options intelligently. Notice also would have afforded defense counsel time to look up, and remind the district judge * * * that special conditions of supervised release must entail no greater deprivation of liberty than is reasonably necessary for the purposes of sentencing * * * . The judge did not explain how the no-Internet condition could be thought to entail no greater deprivation of liberty than is reasonably necessary. If Scott had used the Internet extensively to commit the crime of conviction, then perhaps a ban might be justified. But here the only justification was misbehavior that neither resulted in a conviction nor was treated as relevant conduct, making an outright ban difficult to justify. The sort of engagement that would have been facilitated by notice to Scott's lawyers could have averted this problem.

So was notice required? * * * Scott received the maximum sentence of imprisonment allowed by the Guidelines without a departure. *Making supervised release significantly more onerous than the norm adds to the severity of punishment and thus may be seen as a back-door form of departure.* If the Guidelines had permitted the judge to sentence Scott to 60 months in prison, then a combination of 24 months in jail plus 36 months of release under conditions no more severe than imprisonment (prisoners can't access the Internet from their cells) would not require special justification. Judges may choose middle grounds between imprisonment and complete freedom. But what happened here looks more like a departure, given that Scott received the maximum imprisonment in the prescribed range. [Emphasis added.]

* * * *An upward departure from the Guidelines is permissible only if the defendant has some notice * * * of this possibility, and thus can prepare to meet it.* Exactly the same may be said about unusual conditions of supervised release. * * * [This] requires notice of terms that are out of the ordinary, and thus unexpected—and the United States does not contend that Scott should have foreseen that Internet access would be a subject of discussion at sentencing. So Scott is entitled to a new proceeding, at which he can offer alternatives to a flat ban * * * . [Emphasis added.]

* * * *

Scott wants us to go further and say that limitations on Internet access cannot be justified at all * * * . That is not a tenable argument. Computers and the Internet may be used to commit crimes, of which child pornography and fraud are only two examples. Inveterate hackers who have used access to injure others may be ordered to give up the digital world. If full access posed an unacceptable risk of recidivism, yet all controls on access were forbidden, then a judge would have little alternative but to increase the term of imprisonment in order to incapacitate the offender. Few defendants would deem that a beneficial exchange; most would prefer the conditional freedom of supervised release, even with restrictions on using the Internet, to the more regimented life in prison.

This is not to gainsay the point that because the Internet is a medium of communication a total restriction rarely could be justified. The Internet is a vast repository, offering books, newspapers, magazines, and research tools along with smut. A judge who would not forbid Scott to enter a video rental store (which may have an adult-video section) also should not forbid Scott to enter the Internet, even though Disney's web site coexists with others offering filthy pictures or audio files circulated in violation of the copyright laws. A judge who would not forbid a defendant to send or receive postal mail or use the telephone should not forbid that person to send or receive e-mail or to order books at Amazon.com. Scott does not have a record of extensive abuse of digital communications that could justify an outright ban. * * * What conditions short of a ban may be appropriate in this case is a subject for the district judge to address in the first instance.

The U.S. Court of Appeals for the Seventh Circuit vacated the judgment of the lower court and remanded the case for a new sentencing proceeding at which the defendant could offer alternatives to a total ban on his postimprisonment access to the Internet.

QUESTIONS

1. Why did Scott argue that the court's order limiting his access to the Internet should be reversed?
2. What action did the U.S. Court of Appeals for the Seventh Circuit take in this case, and why?
3. Can limitations on a convicted criminal's access to the Internet ever be justified?

CYBER CRIME

Computer crime • Any wrongful act that is directed against computers and computer parts, or the wrongful use or abuse of computers or software.

Some years ago, the American Bar Association defined **computer crime** as any act that is directed against computers and computer parts, that uses computers as instruments of crime, or that involves computers and constitutes abuse. Today, because much of the crime committed with the use of computers occurs in cyberspace, many computer crimes fall under the broad label of *cyber crime.*

As we mentioned earlier, most cyber crimes are not "new" crimes. Rather, they are existing crimes in which the Internet is the instrument of wrongdoing. The challenge for law enforcement is to apply traditional laws—which were designed to protect persons from physical harm or to safeguard their physical property—to crimes committed in cyberspace. Here we look at several types of activity that constitute cyber crimes against persons or property. Additional cyber crimes will be discussed in later chapters as they relate to other topics.

Cyber Theft

In cyberspace, thieves are not subject to the physical limitations of the "real" world. A thief with dial-in access can steal data stored in a networked computer from anywhere on the globe. Only the speed of the connection and the thief's computer equipment limit the quantity of data that can be stolen.

Financial Crimes. Computer networks also provide opportunities for employees to commit crimes that can involve serious economic losses. For example, employees of a company's accounting department can transfer funds among accounts with little effort and often with less risk than would be involved in transactions evidenced by paperwork.

Generally, the dependence of businesses on computer operations has left firms vulnerable to sabotage, fraud, embezzlement, and the theft of proprietary data, such as trade secrets or other intellectual property. The piracy of intellectual property via the Internet is one of the most serious legal challenges facing lawmakers and the courts today.

Identity Theft. A form of cyber theft that has become particularly troublesome in recent years is **identity theft.** Identity theft occurs when the wrongdoer steals a form of identification—such as a name, date of birth, or Social Security number—and uses the information to access the victim's financial resources. This crime existed to a certain extent before the widespread use of the Internet. Thieves would "steal" calling-card numbers by watching people using public telephones, or they would rifle through garbage to find bank account or credit-card numbers. The identity thief would then use the calling-card or credit-card numbers or would withdraw funds from the victim's account.

Identity theft • A form of theft that occurs when a person steals another's identifying information—such as a name, date of birth, or Social Security number—and uses the information to access the victim's financial resources.

The Internet, however, has turned identity theft into perhaps the fastest-growing financial crime in the United States. From the identity thief's perspective, the Internet provides those who steal information offline with an easy medium for using items such as stolen credit-card numbers while protected by anonymity. An estimated 5 million Americans are victims of identity theft each year.

Cyber Stalking

California enacted the first stalking law in 1990, in response to the murders of six women—including Rebecca Schaeffer, a television star—by men who had harassed them. The law made it a crime to harass or follow a person while making a "credible threat" that puts that person in reasonable fear for his or her safety or the safety of the person's immediate family.[32] **Cyber stalkers** (stalkers who commit their crimes in cyberspace), however, find their victims through Internet chat rooms, newsgroups or other bulletin boards, or e-mail. To close this "loophole" in existing stalking laws, more than three-fourths of the states now have laws specifically designed to combat cyber stalking and other forms of online harassment.

Cyber stalker • A person who commits the crime of stalking in cyberspace. Generally, stalking consists of harassing a person and putting that person in reasonable fear for his or her safety or the safety of the person's immediate family.

Note that cyber stalking can be even more threatening than physical stalking in some respects. While it takes a great deal of effort to physically stalk someone, it is relatively easy to harass a victim with electronic messages. Furthermore, the possibility of personal confrontation may discourage a stalker from actually following a victim. This disincentive is removed in cyberspace. Finally, there is always the possibility that a cyber stalker will eventually pose a physical threat to her or his target.

Hacking

Persons who use one computer to break into another are sometimes referred to as **hackers.** Hackers who break into computers without authorization often commit cyber theft. Sometimes, however, their principal aim is to prove how smart they are by gaining access to others' password-protected computers and causing random data errors or making unpaid-for telephone calls.[33]

Hacker • A person who uses one computer to break into another.

It is difficult to know just how frequently hackers succeed in breaking into databases across the United States. The FBI estimates that only 25 percent of

32. Ca. Penal Code Section 646.9.

33. The total cost of crime on the Internet is estimated to be several billion dollars annually, but two-thirds of that total is said to consist of unpaid-for toll calls.

all corporations that suffer such security breaches report the incident to a law enforcement agency. For one thing, corporations do not want it to become publicly known that the security of their data has been breached. For another, admitting to a breach would be admitting to a certain degree of incompetence, which could damage their reputations.

Cyber Terrorism

Cyber terrorist • A hacker whose purpose is to exploit a target computer for a serious impact, such as the corruption of a program to sabotage a business.

Cyber terrorists are also hackers, but rather than trying to gain attention, they strive to remain undetected so that they can exploit computers for a serious impact. Just as a "real" terrorist might explode a bomb to shut down an embassy, a cyber terrorist might explode a "logic bomb" to shut down a central computer. Such activities can pose a danger to national security.

Businesses may also be targeted by cyber terrorists. A hacking operation might engage in a wholesale theft of data, such as a merchant's customer files, or monitor a computer to discover a business firm's plans and transactions. A cyber terrorist might also want to insert false codes or data. For example, by hacking into the processing control system of a food manufacturer, a cyber terrorist might alter the levels of ingredients so that consumers of the food would become ill. A cyber terrorist attack on a major financial institution such as the New York Stock Exchange or a large bank could leave securities or money markets in flux and seriously affect the daily lives of millions of citizens. Similarly, any prolonged disruption of computer, cable, satellite, or telecommunications systems due to the actions of expert hackers would have serious repercussions on business operations—and national security—on a global level.

Prosecuting Cyber Crimes

The "location" of cyber crime (cyberspace) has raised new issues in the investigation of crimes and the prosecution of offenders. A threshold issue is, of course, jurisdiction. A person who commits an act against a business in California, where the act is a cyber crime, might never have set foot in California but might instead reside in New York, or even in Canada, where the act may not be a crime. If the crime was committed via e-mail, the question arises as to whether the e-mail would constitute sufficient "minimum contacts" (see Chapter 2) for the victim's state to exercise jurisdiction over the perpetrator.

Identifying the wrongdoers can also be difficult. Cyber criminals do not leave physical traces, such as fingerprints or DNA samples, as evidence of their crimes. Even electronic "footprints" can be hard to find and follow. For example, e-mail may be sent through a remailer, an online service that guarantees that a message cannot be traced to its source.

For these reasons, laws written to protect physical property are difficult to apply in cyberspace. Nonetheless, governments at both the federal and state levels have taken significant steps toward controlling cyber crime, both by applying existing criminal statutes and by enacting new laws that specifically address wrongs committed in cyberspace.

The Computer Fraud and Abuse Act

Perhaps the most significant federal statute specifically addressing cyber crime is the Counterfeit Access Device and Computer Fraud and Abuse Act of 1984 (commonly known as the Computer Fraud and Abuse Act, or CFAA).

This act, as amended by the National Information Infrastructure Protection Act of 1996,[34] provides, among other things, that a person who accesses a computer online, without authority, to obtain classified, restricted, or protected data, or attempts to do so, is subject to criminal prosecution. Such data could include financial and credit records, medical records, legal files, military and national security files, and other confidential information in government or private computers. The crime has two elements: accessing a computer without authority and taking the data.

This theft is a felony if it is committed for a commercial purpose or for private financial gain, or if the value of the stolen data (or computer time) exceeds $5,000. Penalties include fines and imprisonment for up to twenty years. A victim of computer theft can also bring a civil suit against the violator to obtain damages, an injunction, or other relief.

34. 18 U.S.C. Section 1030.

KEY TERMS

actus reus 213
arson 218
beyond a reasonable doubt 210
burglary 217
computer crime 238
consent 225
crime 209
cyber crime 209
cyber stalker 239
cyber terrorist 240
double jeopardy 228
duress 225
embezzlement 219
entrapment 226
exclusionary rule 228
felony 212
forgery 218
grand jury 235
hacker 239
identity theft 239
indictment 235
information 235
larceny 217
mens rea 213
misdemeanor 212
money laundering 221
necessity 226
petty offense 212
plea bargain 227
robbery 217
self-defense 226
trade secrets 220
white-collar crime 219

FOR REVIEW

1. What two elements must exist before a person can be held liable for a crime? Can a corporation be liable for crimes?
2. What are the five broad categories of crimes? What is white-collar crime?
3. What defenses might be raised to avoid liability for criminal acts?
4. What constitutional safeguards protect persons accused of crimes? What are the basic steps in the criminal process?
5. What is cyber crime? How does cyber crime differ from traditional crime?

QUESTIONS AND CASE PROBOLEMS

7–1. The following situations are similar (in all of them, Juanita's television set is stolen), yet three different crimes are described. Identify the three crimes, noting the differences among them.

(a) While passing Juanita's house one night, Sarah sees a portable television set left unattended on Juanita's lawn. Sarah takes the television set, carries it home, and tells everyone she owns it.

(b) While passing Juanita's house one night, Sarah sees Juanita outside with a portable television set. Holding Juanita at gunpoint, Sarah forces her to give up the set. Then Sarah runs away with it.

(c) While passing Juanita's house one night, Sarah sees a portable television set in a window. Sarah breaks the front-door lock, enters, and leaves with the set.

7–2. Which, if any, of the following crimes necessarily involves illegal activity on the part of more than one person?

(a) Bribery.
(b) Forgery.
(c) Embezzlement.
(d) Larceny.
(e) Receiving stolen property.

7–3. Armington, while robbing a drugstore, shot and seriously injured a drugstore clerk, Jennings. Later, in a criminal trial, Armington was convicted of armed robbery and assault and battery. Jennings subsequently brought a civil tort suit against Armington for damages. Armington contended that he could not be tried again for the same act because as that would constitute double jeopardy, which is prohibited by the Fifth Amendment to the Constitution. Is Armington correct? Explain.

7–4. Rafael stops Laura on a busy street and offers to sell her an expensive wristwatch for a fraction of its value. After some questioning by Laura, Rafael admits that the watch is stolen property, although he says he was not the thief. Laura pays for and receives the wristwatch. Has Laura committed any crime? Has Rafael? Explain.

7–5. Suppose that in the hypothetical situation discussed in Problem 7–4, Rafael is an undercover police officer. As soon as Laura pays for and receives the wristwatch, Rafael arrests her for the crime of receiving stolen property. At trial, Laura contends that she was a victim of entrapment. What should be the result of the trial? Discuss fully.

CASE PROBLEM WITH SAMPLE ANSWER

7–6. Searches and Seizures. The city of Ferndale enacted an ordinance regulating massage parlors. Among other things, the ordinance provided for periodic inspections of the establishments by "[t]he chief of police or other authorized inspectors from the City." Operators and employees of massage parlors in Ferndale filed a suit in a Michigan state court against the city. The plaintiffs pointed out that the ordinance did not require a warrant to conduct a search and argued in part that this was a violation of the Fourth Amendment. On what ground might the court uphold the ordinance? Do massage parlors qualify on this ground? Why or why not? [*Gora v. City of Ferndale,* 456 Mich. 704, 576 N.W.2d 141 (1998)]

➧ *To view a sample answer for this case problem, go to this book's Web site at* **http://ele.westbuslaw.com** *and click on "Interactive Study Center."*

7–7. Fifth Amendment. The federal government was investigating a corporation and its employees. The alleged criminal wrongdoing, which included the falsification of corporate books and records, occurred between 1993 and 1996 in one division of the corporation. In 1999, the corporation pled guilty and agreed to cooperate in an investigation of the individuals who might have been involved in the improper corporate activities. "Doe I," "Doe II," and "Doe III" were officers of the corporation during the period in which the illegal activities occurred and worked in the division where the wrongdoing took place. They were no longer working for the corporation, however, when, as part of the subsequent investigation, the government asked them to provide specific corporate documents in their possession. All three asserted the Fifth Amendment privilege against self-incrimination. The government asked a federal district court to order the three to produce the records. Corporate employees can be compelled to produce corporate records in a criminal proceeding because they hold the records as representatives of the corporation, to which the Fifth Amendment privilege against self-incrimination does not apply. Should *former* employees also be compelled to produce corporate records in their possession? Why or why not? [*In re Three Grand Jury Subpoenas* Duces Tecum *Dated January 29, 1999,* 191 F.3d 173 (2d Cir. 1999)]

7–8. Computer Fraud. The District of Columbia Lottery Board licensed Soo Young Bae, a Washington, D.C., merchant, to operate a terminal that prints and dispenses lottery tickets for sale. Bae used the terminal to generate tickets with a face value of $525,586, for which he did not pay. The winning tickets among these had a total redemption value of $296,153, of which Bae successfully obtained all but $72,000. Bae pleaded guilty to computer fraud, and the court sentenced him to eighteen months in prison. In sentencing a defendant for fraud, a federal court must make a reasonable estimate of the victim's loss. The court determined that the value of the loss due to the fraud was $503,650—the market value of the tickets less the commission Bae would have received from the lottery board had he sold those tickets. Bae appealed, arguing that "[a]t the instant any lottery ticket is printed," it is worth whatever value the lottery drawing later assigns to it; that is, losing tickets have no value. Bae thus calculated the loss at $296,153, the value of his winning tickets. Should the U.S. Court of Appeals for the District of Columbia Circuit affirm or reverse Bae's sentence? Why? [*United States v. Bae,* 250 F.3d 774 (D.C. Cir. 2001)]

7–9. Theft of Trade Secrets. Four Pillars Enterprise Co. is a Taiwanese company owned by Pin Yen Yang. Avery Dennison, Inc., a U.S. corporation, is one of Four Pillars's chief competitors in the manufacture of adhesives. In 1989, Victor Lee, an Avery employee, met Yang and Yang's daughter Hwei Chen. They agreed to pay Lee $25,000 a year to serve as a consultant to Four Pillars. Over the next eight years, Lee supplied the Yangs with confidential Avery reports, including information that Four Pillars used to make a new adhesive that had been developed by Avery. The Federal Bureau of Investigation (FBI) confronted Lee, and he agreed to cooperate in an operation to catch the Yangs. When Lee next met the Yangs, he showed them documents provided by the FBI. The documents bore "confidential" stamps, and Lee said that they were Avery's confidential property. The FBI arrested the Yangs with the documents in their possession. The Yangs and Four Pillars were charged with, among other crimes, the attempted theft of trade secrets. The defendants argued in part that it was impossible for them to have committed this crime because the documents were not actually trade secrets. Should the court acquit them? Why or why not? [*United States v. Yang,* 281 F.3d 534 (6th Cir. 2002)]

7–10. IN YOUR COURT

Gavin, a fifteen-year-old student, was eating lunch on the grounds of a school. He threw a half-eaten apple toward the outside wall of a classroom some distance away. The apple sailed through a slowly closing door and struck a teacher who was in the room. The teacher was knocked to the floor and lost consciousness for a few minutes. Gavin was charged with assault by "any means of force likely to produce great bodily injury." Gavin stated that he did not intend to hit the teacher but only intended to see the apple splatter against the outside wall. Assume that you are one of the judges on the appellate court panel reviewing this case and answer the following questions:

(a) What are the two elements of criminal liability? Are both elements present in this case?
(b) The trial court convicted Gavin, among other things, to send a "message" to his classmates that his actions were wrong. Is this a sufficient reason, in itself, to convict a defendant such as Gavin? Why or why not?
(c) Would you affirm the trial court's decision in this case? Would you reverse the decision? Explain your reasoning.

7–11. A QUESTION OF ETHICS AND SOCIAL RESPONSIBILITY

A troublesome issue concerning the constitutional privilege against self-incrimination has to do with "jail plants"—that is, undercover police officers placed in cells with criminal suspects to gain information from the suspects. For example, in one case the police placed an undercover agent, Parisi, in a jail cell block with Lloyd Perkins, who had been imprisoned on charges unrelated to the murder that Parisi was investigating. When Parisi asked Perkins if he had ever killed anyone, Perkins made statements implicating himself in the murder. Perkins was then charged with the murder. [*Illinois v. Perkins,* 496 U.S. 292, 110 S.Ct. 2394, 110 L.Ed.2d 243 (1990)]

(a) Should Perkins's statements be suppressed—that is, not be treated as admissible evidence at trial—because he was not "read his rights," as required by the *Miranda* decision, prior to making his self-incriminating statements? Does *Miranda* apply to Perkins's situation?
(b) Do you think that it is fair for the police to resort to trickery and deception to bring those who have committed crimes to justice? Why or why not? What rights or public policies must be balanced in deciding this issue?

7–12. FOR CRITICAL ANALYSIS

Do you think that criminal procedure in this country is weighted too heavily in favor of accused persons? Can you think of a fairer way to balance the constitutional rights of accused persons against the right of society to be protected against criminal behavior? Should different criminal procedures be used when terrorism is involved? Explain.

For updated links to resources available on the Web, as well as a variety of other materials, visit this text's Web site at

http://ele.westbuslaw.com

The Bureau of Justice Statistics in the U.S. Department of Justice offers an impressive collection of statistics on crime at the following Web site:

http://www.ojp.usdoj.gov/bjs

For summaries of famous criminal cases and documents relating to these trials, go to Court TV's Web site at

http://www.courttv.com/index.html

If you would like to learn more about criminal procedures, the following site offers an "Anatomy of a Murder: A Trip through Our Nation's Legal Justice System":

http://library.thinkquest.org/2760/home.htm

At the above site, you can also find a glossary of terms used in criminal law, view actual forms that are filled out during the course of an arrest, and learn about some controversial issues in criminal law.

Many state criminal codes are now online. To find your state's code, go to

http://www.findlaw.com

and select "State" under the link to "Laws: Cases and Codes."

You can learn about some of the constitutional questions raised by various criminal laws and procedures by going to the Web site of the American Civil Liberties Union at

http://www.aclu.org

The following Web site, which is maintained by the U.S. Department of Justice, offers information ranging from the various types of cyber crime to a description of how computers and the Internet are being used to prosecute cyber crime:

http://www.cybercrime.gov

LEGAL RESEARCH EXERCISES ON THE WEB

Go to **http://ele.westbuslaw.com**, the Web site that accompanies this text. Select "Interactive Study Center," and then click on "Chapter 7." There you will find the following Internet research exercises that you can perform to learn more about topics covered in this chapter.

Activity 7–1: LEGAL PERSPECTIVE—Revisiting *Miranda*

Activity 7–2: MANAGEMENT PERSPECTIVE—Hackers

Activity 7–3: INTERNATIONAL PERSPECTIVE—Fighting Cyber Crime Worldwide

BEFORE THE TEST

Go to **http://ele.westbuslaw.com**, the Web site that accompanies this text. Select "Interactive Quizzes." You will find at least twenty interactive questions relating to this chapter.

WESTLAW® CAMPUS

If your textbook provided for a subscription to Westlaw® Campus, or if you have otherwise purchased access to the Westlaw Campus database, you can access any of the cases presented or cited in this chapter by using your Westlaw Campus account.

CHAPTER 8

International and Comparative Law

CONTENTS

CHAPTER OBJECTIVES

After reading this chapter, you should be able to answer the following questions:

1. What is the principle of comity, and when do courts deciding disputes involving a foreign law or judicial decree apply this principle?

2. What is the act of state doctrine? In what circumstances is this doctrine applied?

3. Under the Foreign Sovereign Immunities Act of 1976, on what basis might a foreign state be subject to the jurisdiction of U.S. courts?

4. How does the United States control imports?

5. Do U.S. laws prohibiting employment discrimination apply in all circumstances to U.S. employees working for U.S. employers abroad?

International business transactions are not unique to the modern world. Indeed, since ancient times independent peoples and nations have traded their goods and wares with one another. What is new in our day is the dramatic growth in world trade and the emergence of a global business community. Today, nearly every major business considers the potential of international markets for its products or services. It is no longer uncommon for a U.S. corporation to have investments or manufacturing plants in a foreign country or for a foreign corporation to have operations in the United States. Because the exchange of goods, services, and ideas on a worldwide level is now routine, students of business law should be familiar with the laws pertaining to international business transactions.

Laws affecting the international legal environment of business include both international law and national law. **International law** can be defined as a body of law—formed as a result of international customs, treaties, and organizations—that governs relations among or between nations. **National law** is the law of a particular nation, such as the United States, Japan, Germany, or Brazil. In this chapter, we examine how both international law and national law frame business operations in the international context.

International law • The law that governs relations among nations. International customs, treaties, and organizations are generally considered to be the most important sources of international law.

National law • Law that governs a particular nation (as opposed to international law).

INTERNATIONAL LAW

The major difference between international law and national law is that government authorities can enforce national law. What government, however, can enforce international law? By definition, a *nation* is a sovereign entity—which means that there is no higher authority to which that nation must submit. If a nation violates an international law and persuasive tactics fail, other countries or international organizations have no recourse except to take coercive actions—from severance of diplomatic relations and boycotts to, as a last resort, war—against the violating nation.

In essence, international law is the result of centuries-old attempts to reconcile the traditional need of each country to be the final authority over its own affairs with the desire of nations to benefit economically from trade and harmonious relations with one another. Sovereign nations can, and do, voluntarily agree to be governed in certain respects by international law for the purpose of facilitating international trade and commerce, as well as civilized discourse. As a result, a body of international law has evolved. In this section, we examine the primary sources and characteristics of that body of law, as well as some important legal principles and doctrines that have been developed over time to facilitate dealings among nations.

Sources of International Law

Basically, there are three sources of international law: international customs, treaties and international agreements, and international organizations and conferences. We look at each of these sources here.

International Customs. One important source of international law consists of the international customs that have evolved among nations in their relations with one another. Article 38(1) of the Statute of the International Court of Justice refers to an international custom as "evidence of a general practice accepted as law." The legal principles and doctrines that you will read about shortly are rooted in international customs and traditions that have evolved over time in the international arena.

Treaties and International Agreements. Treaties and other explicit agreements between or among foreign nations provide another important source of international law. A **treaty** is an agreement or contract between two or more nations that must be authorized and ratified by the supreme power of each nation. Under Article II, Section 2, of the U.S. Constitution, the president has the power, "by and with the Advice and Consent of the Senate, to make Treaties, provided two-thirds of the Senators present concur."

Treaty • An agreement formed between two or more independent nations.

A *bilateral* agreement, as the term implies, is an agreement formed by two nations to govern their commercial exchanges or other relations with one another. A *multilateral* agreement is formed by several nations. For example, regional trade associations such as the European Union (EU) and the trading unit established by the North American Free Trade Agreement (NAFTA), both of which are discussed later in this chapter, are the result of multilateral trade agreements. Other regional trade associations that have been created through multilateral agreements include the Association of Southeast Asian Nations (ASEAN) and the Andean Common Market (ANCOM).

International Organizations and Conferences. International organizations and conferences further contribute to international law. In international law, the term **international organization** generally refers to an organization composed mainly of nations and usually established by treaty.

International organization • In international law, a term that generally refers to an organization composed mainly of nations and usually established by treaty. The United States is a member of more than one hundred multilateral and bilateral organizations, including at least twenty through the United Nations.

The United States is a member of more than one hundred multilateral and bilateral organizations, including at least twenty through the United Nations (see Exhibit 8–1 on the next page). These organizations adopt resolutions, declarations, and other types of standards that often require nations to behave in a particular manner. The General Assembly of the United Nations, for example, has adopted numerous nonbinding resolutions and declarations that embody principles of international law. Disputes with respect to these resolutions and declarations may be brought before the International Court

EXHIBIT 8–1 • SELECTED MULTILATERAL INTERNATIONAL ORGANIZATIONS IN WHICH THE UNITED STATES PARTICIPATES

NAME	PURPOSE
Customs Cooperation Council	Established in 1950. Supervises the application and interpretation of an international code classifying goods and customs tariffs.
International Bank for Reconstruction and Development (World Bank)	Popularly known as the World Bank; a specialized agency of the United Nations since 1947. Promotes growth, trade, and balance of trade by facilitating and providing technical assistance, particularly in agriculture, energy, transportation, and telecommunications.
International Center for the Settlement of Investment Disputes	Established in 1966. Conciliates and arbitrates disputes between private investors and governments of other countries.
International Civil Aviation Organization	Established in 1947 and became a specialized agency of the United Nations seven months later. Develops international civil aviation by issuing rules and policies for safe and efficient airports and air navigation.
International Court of Justice (World Court)	Established in 1922 and became one of the principal organs of the United Nations in 1945. The World Court has jurisdiction over all cases that are referred to it and decides disputes in accordance with the rules of international law.
International Maritime Organization	Established in 1948. Promotes cooperation in the areas of government regulation, technical and other practices affecting shipping in international trade, the adoption of standards of maritime safety and efficiency, and the abolition of discrimination and unnecessary restrictions.
International Monetary Fund (IMF)	Created in 1944 at the United Nations Monetary and Financial Conference. Promotes economic stability by aiding the growth of international trade and the stability of currency exchange rates, as well as by providing for a system of international monetary assistance.
International Telecommunications Satellite Organization	Established in 1964. Operates an international public communications satellite system on a commercial, nondiscriminatory basis.
Permanent Court of Arbitration	Established in 1899 to facilitate the settlement of international disputes. The court has jurisdiction over all cases that it is requested to arbitrate.
United Nations (UN)	Established in 1945 to maintain international peace and security. Promotes international cooperation.
World Intellectual Property Organization	Established in 1967 and became a specialized agency of the United Nations in 1974. Promotes protection of intellectual property throughout the world.
World Trade Organization (WTO)	Established in 1994 during the final round of negotiations of the General Agreement on Tariffs and Trade (GATT). The GATT was created in 1947 and was the first global commercial agreement in history. It became the principal instrument for regulating international trade and limiting tariffs and other barriers to world trade on particular commodities and other items. GATT ceased to exist in 1995, when the WTO came into existence to regulate world trade.

of Justice. That court, however, normally has authority to settle legal disputes only when nations voluntarily submit to its jurisdiction.

The United Nations Commission on International Trade Law has made considerable progress in establishing uniformity in international law as it relates to trade and commerce. One of the commission's most significant creations to date is the 1980 Convention on Contracts for the International Sale of Goods (CISG). The CISG is similar to Article 2 of the Uniform Commercial Code (see Chapter 11) in that it is designed to settle disputes between parties to sales contracts. It spells out the duties of international buyers and sellers that will apply if the parties have not agreed otherwise in their contracts. The CISG only governs sales contracts between trading partners in nations that have ratified the CISG, however.

To read the text of the United Nations Convention on Contracts for the International Sale of Goods, go to the "Statutes" page of our Web site at **http://ele.westbuslaw.com**

Legal Principles and Doctrines

Over time, a number of legal principles and doctrines have evolved and have been employed—to a greater or lesser extent—by the courts of various nations to resolve or reduce conflicts that involve a foreign element. The three important legal principles discussed below are based primarily on courtesy and respect and are applied in the interests of maintaining harmonious relations among nations.

The Principle of Comity. Under what is known as the **principle of comity,** one nation will defer and give effect to the laws and judicial decrees of another country, as long as those laws and judicial decrees are consistent with the law and public policy of the accommodating nation. For example, assume that a Swedish seller and an American buyer have formed a contract, which the buyer breaches. The seller sues the buyer in a Swedish court, which awards damages. The buyer's assets, however, are in the United States and cannot be reached unless the judgment is enforced by a U.S. court of law. In this situation, if a U.S. court determines that the procedures and laws applied in the Swedish court are consistent with U.S. national law and policy, the U.S. court will likely defer to, and enforce, the foreign court's judgment.

Principle of comity • A principle under which one nation will defer and give effect to the laws and judicial decrees of another nation. This principle is based primarily on respect.

One way to understand the principle of comity (and the act of state doctrine, which will be discussed shortly) is to consider the relationships among the states in our federal form of government. Each state honors (gives "full faith and credit" to) the contracts, property deeds, wills, and other legal obligations formed in other states, as well as judicial decisions with respect to such obligations. On a worldwide basis, nations similarly attempt to honor judgments rendered in other countries when it is feasible to do so. Of course, a major difference between U.S. federalism and the relationships among nations is that the states within the United States are constitutionally bound to honor other states' actions (see the discussion of the full faith and credit clause in Chapter 5). There is no world constitution, so international doctrines rest primarily on courtesy.

The Act of State Doctrine. The **act of state doctrine** is a judicially created doctrine that provides that the judicial branch of one country will not examine the validity of public acts committed by a recognized foreign government within its own territory. This doctrine is premised on the theory that the judicial branch should not "pass upon the validity of foreign acts when to do so would vex the harmony of our international relations with that foreign nation."

Act of state doctrine • A doctrine that provides that the judicial branch of one country will not examine the validity of public acts committed by a recognized foreign government within its own territory.

The act of state doctrine can have important consequences for individuals and firms doing business with, and investing in, other countries. For example, this doctrine is frequently employed in cases involving **expropriation,** which occurs when a government seizes a privately owned business or privately

Expropriation • The seizure by a government of privately owned business or personal property for a proper public purpose and with just compensation.

Confiscation • A government's taking of privately owned business or personal property without a proper public purpose or an award of just compensation.

owned goods for a proper public purpose and awards just compensation. When a government seizes private property for an illegal purpose and without just compensation, the taking is referred to as a **confiscation.** The line between these two forms of taking is sometimes blurred because of differing interpretations of what is illegal and what constitutes just compensation. To illustrate: Tim Flaherty, an American businessperson, owns a mine in Brazil. The government of Brazil seizes the mine for public use and claims that the profits Tim has already realized from the mine constitute just compensation. Tim disagrees, but the act of state doctrine may prevent Tim's recovery in a U.S. court of law.

When applicable, both the act of state doctrine and the doctrine of *sovereign immunity*, which we discuss next, tend to shield foreign nations from the jurisdiction of U.S. courts. As a result, firms or individuals who own property overseas generally have little legal protection against government actions in the countries where they operate.

Sovereign immunity • A doctrine that immunizes foreign nations from the jurisdiction of U.S. courts when certain conditions are satisfied.

The Doctrine of Sovereign Immunity. When certain conditions are satisfied, the doctrine of **sovereign immunity** exempts foreign nations from the jurisdiction of the U.S. courts. In 1976, Congress codified this rule in the Foreign Sovereign Immunities Act (FSIA).[1] The FSIA also modified previous applications of the doctrine in certain respects by expanding the rights of plaintiff creditors against foreign nations.

The FSIA exclusively governs the circumstances in which an action may be brought in the United States against a foreign nation. Section 1605 of the FSIA sets forth the major exceptions to the jurisdictional immunity of a foreign state. A foreign state is not immune from the jurisdiction of U.S. courts when the state has "waived its immunity either explicitly or by implication" or when the state has engaged in actions that are taken "in connection with a commercial activity carried on in the United States by the foreign state" or that have "a direct effect in the United States."

Defining a Foreign State. Questions frequently arise as to whether particular entities fall within the category of foreign state. Under Section 1603 of the FSIA, a foreign state is defined to include both a political subdivision of a foreign state and an instrumentality of a foreign state (an agency or entity acting for the state).

Is a corporation an "instrumentality" of a foreign state if the state owns less than a majority of the corporation's stock? That was the question in the following case.

1. 28 U.S.C. Sections 1602–1611.

CASE 8.1

Supreme Court of the United States, 2003. __ U.S. __, 123 S.Ct. 1655, 155 L.Ed.2d 643. **http://supct.law.cornell.edu/supct**[a]

DOLE FOOD CO. v. PATRICKSON

In 1997, Gerardo Patrickson and other farm workers who worked in banana fields in Costa Rica, Ecuador, Guatemala, and Panama filed a suit in a Hawaii state court against Dole Food Company and others, seeking damages for injuries from exposure to dibromochloropropane, a chemical used as an agricultural pesticide. Dole

a. Enter the name of the case in the "Search" box and click on "submit." Select the case name to access the opinion.

impleaded[b] *two Israeli firms—Dead Sea Bromine Company and Bromine Compounds, Limited (the Dead Sea companies)—that allegedly made the pesticides. The Dead Sea companies asked a federal district court to hear the suit on the ground that they were instrumentalities of a foreign state as defined in the FSIA. The court denied this request but held that it had jurisdiction on other grounds and dismissed the suit. The workers appealed to the U.S. Court of Appeals for the Ninth Circuit, which reversed the dismissal but agreed that the Dead Sea companies were not instrumentalities of a foreign state as defined in the FSIA. The Dead Sea companies appealed to the United States Supreme Court.*

KENNEDY, J.

Foreign states may invoke certain rights and immunities in litigation under the Foreign Sovereign Immunities Act of 1976 (FSIA or Act). Some of the Act's provisions also may be invoked by a corporate entity that is an "instrumentality" of a foreign state as defined by the Act. The corporate entities in this action claim instrumentality status to invoke the Act's provisions allowing removal of state court actions to federal court. * * * The [question] is whether a corporate subsidiary can claim instrumentality status where the foreign state does not own a majority of its shares but does own a majority of the shares of a corporate parent one or more tiers above the subsidiary. * * *

* * * *

The State of Israel did not have direct ownership of shares in either of the Dead Sea Companies at any time pertinent to this suit. Rather, these companies were, at various times, separated from the State of Israel by one or more intermediate corporate tiers. For example, from 1984–1985, Israel wholly owned a company called Israeli Chemicals, Ltd.; which owned a majority of shares in another company called Dead Sea Works, Ltd.; which owned a majority of shares in Dead Sea Bromine Co., Ltd.; which owned a majority of shares in Bromine Compounds, Ltd.

* * * *

* * * The Dead Sea Companies urge us to ignore corporate formalities and use the colloquial sense of that term. They ask whether, in common parlance, Israel would be said to own the Dead Sea Companies. We reject this analysis. In issues of corporate law structure often matters. It is evident from the Act's text that Congress was aware of settled principles of corporate law and legislated within that context. *The language of [Section] 1603(b)(2) refers to ownership of "shares," showing that Congress intended statutory coverage to turn on formal corporate ownership.* Likewise, [Section] 1603(b)(1), another component of the definition of instrumentality, refers to a "separate legal person, corporate or otherwise." In light of these *indicia* [signs] that Congress had corporate formalities in mind, we assess whether Israel owned shares in the Dead Sea Companies as a matter of corporate law, irrespective of whether Israel could be said to have owned the Dead Sea Companies in everyday parlance. [Emphasis added.]

A basic tenet of American corporate law is that the corporation and its shareholders are distinct entities. An individual shareholder, by virtue of his ownership of shares, does not own the corporation's assets and, as a result, does not own subsidiary corporations in which the corporation holds an

---

b. In this context, *implead* means to bring a new party into an action on the ground that the new party is, or may be, liable to the party who brings him or her in, for all or part of the claim.

interest. A corporate parent which owns the shares of a subsidiary does not, for that reason alone, own or have legal title to the assets of the subsidiary; and, it follows with even greater force, the parent does not own or have legal title to the subsidiaries of the subsidiary. The fact that the shareholder is a foreign state does not change the analysis.

Applying these principles, it follows that *Israel did not own a majority of shares in the Dead Sea Companies.* The State of Israel owned a majority of shares, at various times, in companies one or more corporate tiers above the Dead Sea Companies, but at no time did Israel own a majority of shares in the Dead Sea Companies. Those companies were subsidiaries of other corporations. [Emphasis added.]

* * * *

The FSIA's definition of instrumentality refers to a foreign state's majority ownership of "shares or other ownership interest." The Dead Sea Companies would have us read "other ownership interest" to include a state's "interest" in its instrumentality's subsidiary. The better reading of the text, in our view, does not support this argument. The words "other ownership interest," when following the word "shares," should be interpreted to refer to a type of interest other than ownership of stock. The statute had to be written for the contingency of ownership forms in other countries, or even in this country, that depart from conventional corporate structures. The statutory phrase "other ownership interest" is best understood to accomplish this objective. Reading the term to refer to a state's interest in entities lower on the corporate ladder would make the specific reference to "shares" redundant. *Absent a statutory text or structure that requires us to depart from normal rules of construction, we should not construe the statute in a manner that is strained and, at the same time, would render a statutory term superfluous.* [Emphasis added.]

The Dead Sea Companies say that the State of Israel exercised considerable control over their operations, notwithstanding Israel's indirect relationship to those companies. They appear to think that, in determining instrumentality status under the Act, control may be substituted for an ownership interest. Control and ownership, however, are distinct concepts. The terms of [Section] 1603(b)(2) are explicit and straightforward. Majority ownership by a foreign state, not control, is the benchmark of instrumentality status.

The United States Supreme Court affirmed the lower court's ruling that a corporation is an instrumentality of a foreign state under the FSIA only if the foreign state itself—not an entity owned by the state—directly owns a majority of the corporation's shares.

QUESTIONS

1. How did this case come before the United States Supreme Court?
2. What was the United States Supreme Court's ruling in this case, and on what was it based?
3. Why did the United States Supreme Court conclude that "[m]ajority ownership by a foreign state, not control, is the benchmark of instrumentality status"?

Commercial Activity. The question of what constitutes a commercial activity has also been the subject of dispute because the FSIA does not spell out the particulars of what constitutes a commercial activity. Rather, it is left to the courts to decide whether a particular activity is governmental or commercial in nature.

In the following case, the court applied the "commercial activity" exception to circumstances that included a financial scam.

KELLER v. CENTRAL BANK OF NIGERIA

CASE 8.2

United States Court of Appeals, Sixth Circuit, 2002.
277 F.3d 811.
http://pacer.ca6.uscourts.gov/opinions/main.php[a]

Prince Arthur Ossai, a government official in Nigeria, entered into a contract with Henry Keller, a sales representative for H.K. Enterprises, Inc., a Michigan-based manufacturer of medical equipment. They agreed that among other things, Ossai would have exclusive distribution rights to sell H.K. products in Nigeria, which would buy $4.1 million of H.K. equipment for $6.63 million, plus a $7.65 million "licensing fee." Ossai said that, first, $25.5 million on deposit in the Central Bank of Nigeria (CBN) had to be transferred into an account set up by Keller. CBN employees charged Keller $28,950 in fees for the transaction, but the funds were never transferred. Keller and H.K. filed a suit in a federal district court against the CBN and others, asserting in part a claim under the Racketeer Influenced and Corrupt Organizations Act (RICO).[b] *The defendants filed a motion to dismiss under the Foreign Sovereign Immunities Act (FSIA). The court denied the motion, concluding that the claim fell within the FSIA's "commercial activity" exception. The defendants appealed to the U.S. Court of Appeals for the Sixth Circuit.*

NORRIS, J.

The commercial activity exception provides that a foreign state will not be immune in a case

> in which the action is based * * * upon an act outside the territory of the United States in connection with a commercial activity of the foreign state elsewhere and that act causes a direct effect in the United States. * * *

* * * *

* * * [The defendants] claim that the illegality of the deal alleged precludes a finding that it is a commercial activity. The FSIA defines "commercial activity" as "either a regular course of commercial conduct or a particular commercial transaction or act. *The commercial character of an activity shall be determined by reference to the nature of the course of conduct or particular transaction or act, rather than by reference to its purpose."* * * * [W]hen a foreign government acts, not as regulator of a market, but in the manner of a private player within it, the foreign sovereign's actions are commercial within the meaning of the FSIA. [Emphasis added.]

* * * *

In the instant case, the conduct was a deal to license and sell medical equipment, a type of activity done by private parties and not a "market regulator" function. The district court correctly concluded that this was a commercial activity, and that any fraud and bribery involved did not render the plan noncommercial.

* * * *

---

a. In the left-hand column, click on "Opinions Search." In the "Short Title contains" box, type "Keller" and click "Submit Query." In the "Opinion" box corresponding to the name of the case, click on the number to access the opinion.

b. RICO was discussed in Chapter 7.

Defendants claim that plaintiffs cannot establish another element of the commercial activity exception, namely, that there was a direct effect in the United States. * * * [A]n effect is "direct" if it follows as an immediate consequence of the defendant's * * * activity. * * *

* * * *

In this case, defendants agreed to pay but failed to transmit the promised funds to an account in a Cleveland bank. Other courts have found a direct effect when a defendant agrees to pay funds to an account in the United States and then fails to do so. * * * The district court in the instant case correctly concluded, in accord with the other [courts], that defendant's failure to pay promised funds to a Cleveland account constituted a direct effect in the United States.

The U.S. Court of Appeals for the Sixth Circuit affirmed the lower court's holding that the commercial activity exception applied. Keller could bring his action against the defendants in a U.S. court. A deal to license and sell medical equipment is a commercial activity, and the defendants' failure to pay the promised funds had a direct effect in the United States.

QUESTIONS

1. Who filed this suit, and why?
2. What was the defendants' claim in this case, and how did the U.S. Court of Appeals for the Sixth Circuit rule with respect to this argument?
3. What reasoning did the U.S. Court of Appeals for the Sixth Circuit use to rule in favor of the plaintiff?

Doing Business Internationally

A U.S. domestic firm can engage in international business transactions in a number of ways. Here, we look first at the ways in which businesspersons typically extend their business operations into the international arena and then at laws regulating business activities in the international context.

Types of International Business Operations

Most U.S. companies make the initial foray into international business through exporting, which we discuss next. There are other alternatives as well, including manufacturing goods abroad.

Export • To sell products to buyers located in other countries.

Exporting. The simplest way to engage in international business operations is to seek out foreign markets for domestically produced products. In other words, U.S. firms can **export** their goods and services to foreign markets. Exporting can take two forms: direct exporting and indirect exporting. In *direct exporting,* a U.S. company signs a sales contract with a foreign purchaser who provides for the conditions of shipment and payment for the goods. If business expands sufficiently in a foreign country, a U.S. company may develop a specialized marketing organization in that foreign market by appointing a foreign agent or a foreign distributor. This is called *indirect exporting.*

When a U.S. firm wishes to limit its involvement in an international market, it will typically establish an agency relationship with a foreign firm. In an agency relationship, one person (the agent) agrees to act on behalf of, or instead of, another (the principal). The foreign agent is thereby empowered to enter into contracts in the agent's country on behalf of the U.S. principal.

When a substantial market exists in a foreign country, a U.S. firm may wish to appoint a distributor located in that country. The U.S. firm and the distributor enter into a **distribution agreement,** which is a contract between the seller and the distributor setting out the terms and conditions of the distributorship—for example, price, currency of payment, guaranty of supply availability, and method of payment. The terms and conditions primarily involve contract law. Disputes concerning distribution agreements may involve jurisdictional or other issues, however.

Distribution agreement • A contract between a seller and a distributor of the seller's products setting out the terms and conditions of the distributorship.

Manufacturing Abroad. An alternative to direct or indirect exporting is the establishment of foreign manufacturing facilities. Typically, U.S. firms establish manufacturing plants abroad when they believe that by doing so they will reduce costs—particularly for labor, shipping, and raw materials—and thereby be able to compete more effectively in foreign markets. Apple Computer, IBM, General Motors, and Ford are some of the many U.S. companies that have established manufacturing facilities abroad. Foreign firms have done the same in the United States. Sony, Nissan, and other Japanese manufacturers have established U.S. plants to avoid import duties that the U.S. Congress may impose on Japanese products entering this country.

A U.S. firm can conduct manufacturing operations in other countries in several ways. They include licensing and franchising, as well as investing in a wholly owned subsidiary or a joint venture.

Licensing. A U.S. firm can obtain business from abroad by licensing a foreign manufacturing company to use its copyrighted, patented, or trademarked intellectual property or trade secrets. Like any other licensing agreement (see Chapter 13), a licensing agreement with a foreign-based firm calls for a payment of royalties on some basis—such as so many cents per unit produced or a certain percentage of profits from units sold in a particular geographic territory. For example, the Coca-Cola Bottling Company licenses firms worldwide to use (and keep confidential) its secret formula for the syrup used in its soft drink, in return for a percentage of the income gained from the sale of Coca-Cola by those firms.

The licensing of intellectual property rights benefits all parties to the transaction. The firm that receives the license can take advantage of an established reputation for quality. The firm that grants the license receives income from the foreign sales of its products and also establishes a global reputation. Additionally, once a firm's trademark is known worldwide, the demand for other products manufactured or sold by that firm may increase—obviously, an important consideration.

Franchising. Franchising is a well-known form of licensing. As will be explained in Chapter 9, a franchise is an arrangement in which the owner of a trademark, trade name, or copyright (the franchisor) licenses another (the franchisee) to use the trademark, trade name, or copyright, under certain conditions or limitations, in the selling of goods or services. In return, the franchisee pays a fee, which is usually based on a percentage of gross or net sales. Examples of international franchises include McDonald's, Holiday Inn, Avis, and Hertz.

Investing in a Wholly Owned Subsidiary or a Joint Venture. Another way to expand into a foreign market is to establish a wholly owned subsidiary firm in a foreign country. A European subsidiary would likely take the form of a *société anonyme (S.A.),* which is similar to a U.S. corporation. In German-speaking nations, it would be called an *Aktiengesellschaft (A.G.).* When a wholly owned subsidiary is established, the parent company, which remains in the United States, retains complete ownership of all the facilities in the foreign country, as well as total authority and control over all phases of the operation.

A U.S. firm can also expand into international markets through a joint venture. In a joint venture, the U.S. company owns only part of the operation; the rest is owned either by local owners in the foreign country or by another foreign entity. All of the firms involved in a joint venture share responsibilities, as well as profits and liabilities. (See Chapter 9 for a more detailed discussion of joint ventures.)

The Regulation of International Business Activities

International business transactions can affect the economies, foreign policies, domestic politics, and other national interests of the countries involved. For this reason, nations impose laws to restrict or facilitate international business. Controls may also be imposed by international agreements.

Investing. Firms that invest in foreign nations face the risk that the foreign government may expropriate or confiscate the investment property. As mentioned earlier in this chapter, expropriation occurs when property is taken and the owner is paid just compensation for what is taken. This does not violate generally observed principles of international law. Such principles are normally violated, however, when property is confiscated by a government without compensation (or without adequate compensation).

Few remedies are available when property is confiscated by a foreign government. Claims are often resolved by lump-sum settlements following negotiations between the United States and the taking nation. For example, investors whose claims arose out of confiscations following the Russian Revolution in 1917 were offered a lump-sum settlement by the Union of Soviet Socialist Republics in 1974. Still outstanding are $2 billion in claims against Cuba for confiscations that occurred in 1959 and 1960.

To counter the deterrent effect that the possibility of confiscation may have on potential investors, many countries guarantee compensation to foreign investors if property is taken. A guarantee can be in the form of national constitutional or statutory laws or provisions in international treaties. As further protection for foreign investments, some countries provide insurance for their citizens' investments abroad.

Export Control. The U.S. Constitution provides in Article I, Section 9, that "No Tax or Duty shall be laid on Articles exported from any State." Thus, Congress cannot impose any export taxes. Congress can, however, use a variety of other devices to restrict or encourage exports. Congress may set export quotas on various items, such as grain being sold abroad. Under the Export Administration Act of 1979,[2] restrictions can be imposed on the flow of technologically advanced products and technical data. A controversial control in recent years has been the U.S. Department of Commerce's attempt to restrict the export of encryption software.

Devices to stimulate exports and thereby aid domestic businesses include export incentives and subsidies. The Revenue Act of 1971, for example, gave tax benefits to firms marketing their products overseas through certain foreign sales corporations by exempting income produced by the exports.[3] Under the Export Trading Company Act of 1982,[4] U.S. banks are encouraged to invest in export trading companies, which are formed when exporting firms join together to export a line of goods. The Export-Import Bank provides financial assistance, consisting primarily of credit guaranties given to commercial banks that in turn loan funds to U.S. exporting companies.

Import Control. All nations have restrictions on imports, and the United States is no exception. Restrictions include strict prohibitions, quotas, and tariffs. Under the Trading with the Enemy Act of 1917,[5] for example, no goods may be imported from nations that have been designated enemies of the United States. Other laws prohibit the importation of illegal drugs, books that urge insurrection against the United States, and agricultural products that pose dangers to domestic crops or animals.

Quotas and Tariffs. Limits on the amounts of goods that can be imported are known as **quotas.** At one time, the United States had legal quotas on the number of automobiles that could be imported from Japan. Currently, Japan "voluntarily" restricts the number of automobiles exported to the United States. **Tariffs** are taxes on imports. A tariff is usually a percentage of the value of the import, but it can be a flat rate per unit (such as per barrel of oil). Tariffs raise the prices of goods, causing some consumers to purchase less expensive, domestically manufactured goods.

Quota • An assigned import limit on goods.

Tariff • A tax on imported goods.

In the following case, the United States Supreme Court considered a challenge to tariff classifications imposed on clothing assembled from U.S. components and then "permapressed" in Mexico.

2. 50 U.S.C. App. Sections 2401–2420.
3. 26 U.S.C. Sections 991–994.
4. 15 U.S.C. Sections 4001, 4003.
5. 12 U.S.C. Section 95a.

UNITED STATES v. HAGGAR APPAREL CO.

CASE 8.3

Supreme Court of the United States, 1999.
526 U.S. 380,
119 S.Ct. 1392,
143 L.Ed.2d 480.
http://supct.law.cornell.edu/supct[a]

Haggar Apparel Company buys fabric in the United States, has it treated with a chemical resin, has it cut, and then ships the fabric to Mexico with thread, buttons, and zippers to make pants. The trousers are then sewn, permapressed, and shipped back to

a. Enter the name of the case in the "Search" box and click on "submit." Then select the case name to access the opinion.

the United States. Permapressing is designed to maintain a garment's crease in the desired place and to avoid other creases or wrinkles that detract from its appearance. Permapressing is a baking process that activates the chemical resin to impart the permapress quality. Extra steps would be needed to obtain that quality if the baking were delayed until the garments were shipped back to the United States. Under a federal agency regulation, goods with U.S. components that are assembled abroad and reshipped to the United States are exempt from a duty that is charged against other incoming goods. The U.S. Customs Service levied a duty on Haggar's pants, however, under a regulation that deems all permapressing operations to be an additional step in manufacture, not part of or incidental to the assembly process. Haggar filed a suit in the U.S. Court of International Trade against the federal government, seeking a refund of the duty. Haggar argued that its permapressing was part of the assembly process. The court ruled in Haggar's favor, and the U.S. Court of Appeals for the Federal Circuit affirmed this ruling. The government appealed to the United States Supreme Court.

KENNEDY, J.

[Haggar] says the regulation binds Customs Service employees when they classify imported merchandise under the tariff schedules but does not bind the importers themselves. The statutory scheme does not support this limited view of the force and effect of the regulation. The Customs Service (which is within the Treasury Department) is charged [by statute] with the classification of imported goods under the proper provision of the tariff schedules in the first instance. * * * In addition, the Secretary [of the Treasury] is directed by statute to "establish and promulgate such rules and regulations not inconsistent with the law * * * as may be necessary to secure a just, impartial and uniform appraisement of imported merchandise and the classification and assessment of duties thereon at the various ports of entry." The Secretary, in turn, has delegated to the Commissioner of Customs the authority to issue generally applicable regulations, subject to the Secretary's approval.

Respondent [Haggar] relies on the specific direction to the Secretary to make rules of classification for "the various ports of entry" to argue that the statute authorizes promulgation of regulations that do nothing more than ensure that customs officers in field offices around the country classify goods according to a similar and consistent scheme. The regulations issued under the statute have no bearing, says respondent, on the rights of the importer. We disagree. The phrase in question is explained by the simple fact that *classification decisions must be made at the port where goods enter.* We shall not assume Congress was concerned only to ensure that customs officials at the various ports of entry make uniform decisions but that it had no concern for uniformity once the goods entered the country and judicial proceedings commenced. *The tariffs do not mean one thing for customs officers and another for importers.* * * * [Emphasis added.]

* * * *

* * * Particularly in light of the fact that the agency utilized the notice-and-comment rulemaking process[b] before issuing the regulations, the argument that they were not intended to be entitled to judicial deference implies a sufficient departure from conventional contemporary administrative prac-

b. Notice-and-comment rulemaking was discussed in Chapter 6.

tice that we ought not to adopt it absent a different statutory structure and more express language to this effect in the regulations themselves.

The Supreme Court vacated the judgment of the lower court and remanded the case for further proceedings. Congress authorized the Treasury Department and the Customs Service to administer the tariff regulations, which were the product of notice-and-comment rulemaking. The Court held that without language to the contrary in the enabling statutes or the regulations, the tariff classifications were entitled to "judicial deference."

QUESTIONS

1. What is the most likely reason that Haggar filed this suit against the federal government?
2. What was Haggar's principal argument on appeal, and how did the United States Supreme Court respond?
3. Why did the United States Supreme Court vacate the judgment of the lower court and remand the case for further proceedings?

Antidumping Duties. The United States has specific laws directed at what it sees as unfair international trade practices. **Dumping,** for example, is the sale of imported goods at "less than fair value." *Fair value* is usually determined by the price of those goods in the exporting country. Dumping is designed to undersell U.S. businesses and obtain a larger share of the U.S. market. To prevent this, an extra tariff—known as an *antidumping duty*—may be assessed on the imports.

Dumping • The selling of goods in a foreign country at a price below the price charged for the same goods in the domestic market.

The procedure for imposing antidumping duties involves two U.S. government agencies: the International Trade Commission (ITC) and the International Trade Administration (ITA). The ITC is an independent agency that assesses the effects of dumping on domestic businesses and then makes recommendations to the president concerning temporary import restrictions. The ITA, which is part of the Department of Commerce, decides whether imports were sold at less than fair value. The ITA's determination establishes the amount of antidumping duties, which are set to equal the difference between the price charged in the United States and the price charged in the exporting country. A duty may be retroactive to cover past dumping.

International and Regional Organizations. Over the last decade, countries competing for international trade have become more evenly matched competitors than in earlier years. In part, this is due to the increased use and success of international and regional organizations, such as the World Trade Organization, the European Union, and the North American Free Trade Agreement.

The World Trade Organization. The origins of the World Trade Organization (WTO) date to 1947, when the General Agreement on Tariffs and Trade (GATT) was formed for the purpose of minimizing trade barriers among nations. In subsequent decades, the GATT became the principal instrument for regulating international trade and, over time, negotiated tariff reductions on a broad range of products.

In 1994, in a final round of GATT negotiations, called the "Uruguay Round," representatives from over one hundred nations signed agreements relating to investment policies, dispute resolution, and other topics. One of these agreements, the Trade-Related Aspects of Intellectual Property Rights agreement (TRIPS), will be discussed in Chapter 13. The Uruguay Round also established the WTO, which replaced the GATT beginning in 1995. Each member country of the WTO agreed to grant **most-favored-nation status** (now known as Normal Trade Relations, or NTR) to other member countries. This means that each WTO member must treat other WTO members at least as well as it treats the country that receives its most favorable treatment with regard to imports or exports.

Most-favored-nation status • A status granted in an international treaty by a provision stating that the citizens of the contracting nations may enjoy the privileges accorded by either party to citizens of the most favored nations. Generally, most-favored-nation clauses are designed to establish equality of international treatment.

The European Union (EU). The European Union (EU) arose out of the 1957 Treaty of Rome, which created the Common Market, a free trade zone comprising the nations of Belgium, France, West Germany, Italy, the Netherlands, and Luxembourg. By 2004, the EU consisted of twenty-five countries.

The EU has its own governing authorities. These include the Council of Ministers, which coordinates economic policies and includes one representative from each nation; a commission, which proposes regulations to the council; and an elected assembly, which oversees the commission. The EU also has its own court, the European Court of Justice, which can review each nation's judicial decisions and is the ultimate authority on EU law.

The EU has gone far toward creating a new body of law to govern all of the member nations—although some of its efforts to create uniform laws have been confounded by nationalism. The council and the commission issue regulations, or directives, that define EU law in various areas, and these requirements normally are binding on all member countries. EU directives govern such issues as environmental law, product liability, anticompetitive practices, and laws governing corporations. The EU directive on product liability, for example, states that a "producer of an article shall be liable for damages caused by a defect in the article, whether or not he knew or could have known of the defect." Liability extends to anyone who puts a trademark or other identifying feature on an article, and liability may not be excluded, even by contract.

The North American Free Trade Agreement (NAFTA). The North American Free Trade Agreement (NAFTA), which was signed in 1993 and became effective on January 1, 1994, created a regional trading unit consisting of Mexico, the United States, and Canada. The primary goal of NAFTA is to eliminate tariffs among these three nations on substantially all goods over a period of fifteen to twenty years.

NAFTA gives the three countries a competitive advantage by retaining tariffs on goods imported from countries outside the NAFTA trading unit. Additionally, NAFTA provides for the elimination of barriers that traditionally have prevented the cross-border movement of services, such as financial and transportation services. For example, NAFTA provides that, with some exceptions, U.S. firms do not have to relocate in Mexico or Canada to provide services in those countries. NAFTA also attempts to eliminate citizenship requirements for the licensing of accountants, attorneys, physicians, and other professionals.

COMPARATIVE LAW

When doing business in a foreign nation, a company generally will be subject to the jurisdiction and laws of that nation. Therefore, businesspersons will find it helpful to become familiar with the legal systems and laws of foreign nations in which they conduct commercial transactions. We look at some similarities and differences in national legal systems, laws, and cultural and business traditions in this section on **comparative law,** which can be defined as the study and comparison of legal systems and laws across nations.

Comparative law • The study and comparison of legal systems and laws across nations.

Comparative Legal Systems

The legal systems of foreign nations differ, in widely varying degrees, from that of the United States. Additionally, a number of nations have specialized commercial law courts to deal with business disputes (in the United States, some jurisdictions are establishing similar courts). France instituted such courts in 1807, and most nations with commercial codes have done likewise. The United Kingdom also has special commercial courts overseen by judges with expertise in business law.

Common Law and Civil Law Systems. Legal systems around the globe generally are divided into *common law* and *civil law* systems.

Common Law Systems. As discussed in Chapter 1, in a common law system, the courts independently develop the rules governing certain areas of law, such as torts and contracts. These common law rules apply to all areas not covered by statutory law. Although the common law doctrine of *stare decisis* obligates judges to follow precedential decisions in their jurisdictions, courts may modify or even overturn precedents when deemed necessary. Additionally, if there is no case law to guide a court, the court may create a new rule of law. Common law systems exist today in countries that were once part of the British Empire (such as Australia, India, and the United States).

Civil Law Systems. In contrast to Great Britain and the other common law countries, most of the European nations base their legal systems on Roman civil law, or "code law." The term *civil law,* as used here, refers not to civil as opposed to criminal law but to *codified* law—an ordered grouping of legal principles enacted into law by a legislature or other governing body. In a **civil law system,** the only official source of law is a statutory code. Courts are required to interpret the code and apply the rules to individual cases, but courts may not depart from the code and develop their own laws. In theory, the law code will set forth all of the principles needed for the legal system.

Civil law system • A system of law derived from that of the Roman Empire and based on a code rather than case law; the predominant system of law in the nations of continental Europe and the nations that were once their colonies. In the United States, Louisiana is the only state that has a civil law system.

Countries Using Common Law or Civil Law Systems. Today, civil law systems are found in most of the continental European countries, as well as in those Latin American, African, and Asian countries that were once colonies of the continental European nations. Japan and South Africa also have civil law systems. The Islamic courts of predominantly Muslim countries also use elements of the civil law system. In the United States, the state of Louisiana, because of its historical ties to France, has, in part, a civil law system. Exhibit 8–2 on page 262 lists some of the nations that use common law and civil law systems.

EXHIBIT 8–2 • THE LEGAL SYSTEMS OF NATIONS

CIVIL LAW	COMMON LAW
Argentina	Australia
Austria	Bangladesh
Brazil	Canada
Chile	Ghana
China	India
Egypt	Israel
Finland	Jamaica
France	Kenya
Germany	Malaysia
Greece	New Zealand
Indonesia	Nigeria
Iran	Singapore
Italy	United Kingdom
Japan	United States
Mexico	Zambia
Poland	
South Korea	
Sweden	
Tunisia	
Venezuela	

Legal Systems Compared. Common law and civil law systems are not wholly distinct. For example, although the United States has a common law system, crimes are defined by statute as in civil law systems. Civil law systems may also allow considerable room for judges to develop law. There is also some variation within common law and civil law systems. The judges of different common law nations have produced differing common law principles. Although the United States and India both derived their legal traditions from England, for example, the common law principles governing contract law vary in some respects between the two countries.

Similarly, the laws of nations that have civil law systems differ considerably. For example, the French code tends to set forth general principles of law, while the German code is far more specific and runs to thousands of sections. In some Middle Eastern countries, codes are grounded in the religious law of Islam. The religious basis of these codes makes them far more difficult to alter.

Foreign laws may apply to international transactions of U.S. companies, even in those cases heard in U.S. courts, as the following case illustrates.

CASE 8.4

United States Court of Appeals, Ninth Circuit, 1999. 182 F.3d 1036. **http://www.ca9.uscourts.gov**[a]

UNIVERSE SALES CO., LTD. v. SILVER CASTLE, LTD.

Universe Sales Company, Ltd., sold sportswear and had been paying royalties on products to Offshore Sportswear, Inc. (Sportswear). After a general dispute, Universe

a. On the left side of the page, click on the "Opinions" box. When that page opens, click on "1999" to open the menu. Click on "June," then scroll down the list to the name of the case. Click on the case name to access the opinion.

claimed to have discovered that Sportswear did not own the trademarks on the products under Japanese law, which applied to the contract. Universe sued to recover the royalties as unjust enrichment. The parties presented evidence to a federal district court. Sportswear presented as evidence the declaration of a Japanese attorney, Mitsuhiro Kamiya, who specialized in trademark and contract law. Kamiya declared that Universe owed royalties under Japanese contract law regardless of the trademark's ownership at the time the license agreement was executed. The district court did not give credit to the affidavit and granted summary judgment for Universe. Sportswear appealed.

BRUNETTI, J.

We agree with Sportswear's arguments regarding the district court's failure properly to take the Kamiya declaration into account.

The Kamiya declaration states that Japanese contract law, not Japanese trademark law, is controlling in this situation. Under Japanese contract law, explains the declaration, the License Agreement is both valid and enforceable, and as such requires that Universe make royalty payments to Sportswear. According to the declaration, under Japanese contract law a "licensee will be unable to cancel the license agreement or refuse to pay royalties strictly on the grounds that the licensor was not the registered owner of the licensed trademark when the license agreement was executed. In other words, only if the licensor cannot acquire proper title from the registered owner of the licensed trademark * * * will the license agreement be terminable." Here, the declaration states, Sportswear can and has obtained proper title of the two trademarks at issue, and therefore is entitled to collect royalty payments from Universe.

The Kamiya declaration is admissible pursuant to Federal Rule of Civil Procedure Rule 44.1, which provides, in relevant part: *"The court, in determining foreign law, may consider any relevant material or source, including testimony, whether or not submitted by a party or admissible under the Federal Rules of Evidence."* * * * [Emphasis added.]

In this case, the expert testimony of Kamiya, in the form of a declaration with attached exhibits, was submitted by Sportswear. * * * [T]he declaration reasons that Japanese contract law applies, and under that body of law, Universe is obligated to pay royalties to Sportswear. Although Universe had numerous opportunities to present evidence that would rebut this portion of Kamiya's declaration regarding Japanese law, Universe introduced nothing. Also, the district court performed no independent research of Japanese law. The district court should have considered the fact that the Kamiya declaration states that Japanese contract law is controlling. The district court then could have instructed the parties to present further evidence regarding the interpretation of Japanese law on that point; or, the district court may have performed its own research. Because the Kamiya declaration stands as an unrebutted presentation and interpretation of Japanese law, the district court erred in granting summary judgment to Universe.

The Court of Appeals for the Ninth Circuit reversed the grant of summary judgment for Universe, granted summary judgment for Offshore Sportswear, and remanded the case to the district court to consider any remaining issues.

QUESTIONS

1. Who were the parties in this case, and what was their dispute?

2. Why did the U.S. Court of Appeals for the Ninth Circuit reverse the lower court's judgment?
3. According to Japanese law, as cited by the U.S. Court of Appeals for the Ninth Circuit, on what basis might Universe have successfully terminated its agreement with Sportswear?

Judges and Procedures. Judges play similar roles in virtually all countries: their primary function is the resolution of litigation. The characteristics and qualifications of judges, which are typically set forth in the nation's constitution, can vary widely, however. In the United States, the judge normally does not actively participate in a trial, but many foreign judges involve themselves closely in the proceedings, such as by questioning witnesses.

The procedures employed in resolving cases also vary substantially from country to country. A knowledge of a nation's legal procedures is important for a person conducting business transactions in that nation. For example, an American businessperson was on trial in Saudi Arabia for assaulting and slandering a coworker, an offense for which he might have been jailed or deported. He initially was required to present two witnesses to his version of events, but he had only one. Fortunately, he became aware that he could "demand the oath." In this procedure, he swore before God that he had neither kicked nor slandered the complainant. After taking the oath, he was promptly adjudged not guilty, as lying under oath is one of the most serious sins under Islamic law. Had he failed to demand the oath, he almost certainly would have been found guilty.

National Laws Compared

A businessperson engaging in business operations abroad would be wise to learn about the relevant national laws that may affect those operations. Virtually all nations have laws governing torts, contracts, employment, and other areas. Even when the basic principles are fundamentally similar (as in contract law), there are significant variations in the practical application and effect of these laws across countries. This section summarizes some of the similarities and differences among national laws relating to tort law, contracts, and employment relationships.

Tort Law. Tort law, which allows persons to recover damages for harms or injuries caused by the wrongful actions of others (see Chapter 12), may vary widely among nations. Common law nations have developed a body of judge-made law regarding what kinds of actions constitute negligence or some other tort that permits recovery. Civil law nations must authorize such recovery in their codes. Exhibit 8–3 shows how the civil law codes of several nations define what constitutes a tort.

Even when the statutory language is similar, the application of tort law varies among nations. For example, which party has the burden of proof in a tort lawsuit differs among countries. In the United States, the burden of proof is on the plaintiff. In Russia, the defendant has the burden of proving that he or she was not at fault. Statutes of limitations (deadlines for filing a lawsuit) in other countries also vary considerably. Generally, the limitations period is longer in other countries than it is in the United States. Additionally, national tort laws vary with respect to certain concepts, including failures to act and damages.

EXHIBIT 8–3 • CIVIL CODE TORT DEFINITIONS

Brazil: He who, by a voluntary act or omission, by negligence or carelessness, violates another's right, or causes him harm, is bound to compensate for the damage.

Egypt: Every culpable act that causes damage to another obliges the person who did it to compensate for it.

The Netherlands: Every unlawful act by which damage is caused to another obliges the person by whose fault the damage occurred to compensate for it.

Spain: He who by act or omission causes damage to another, either by fault or negligence, is obliged to compensate for the damage caused.

Tunisia: Every act a person does without lawful justification that causes willful and voluntary damage—material or moral—to another obliges the person who did it to compensate for the aforesaid damage, when it is shown that the act is the direct cause.

Uruguay: Every unlawful act a person does which causes damage to another imposes on the person whose malice, fault, or negligence brought it about the obligation to compensate for it. When the unlawful act was done maliciously, i.e., with the intention of causing harm—it amounts to a delict [an intentional tort, discussed in Chapter 12, or a crime]; when the intention to cause harm is not present, the unlawful act amounts to a quasi-delict [a tort or a crime caused by negligence]. In either case, the unlawful act can be negative or positive according to whether the breach of duty consists of an act or omission.

Source: Andre Tunc, *International Encyclopedia of Comparative Law,* Vol. XI, Chapter 2, pp. 5–6.

Failures to Act. National tort laws differ considerably with respect to liability for omissions, or failures to act. In some situations, a failure to act will not be regarded as a tort. For example, in the United States, tort law imposes no "duty to rescue," and a person normally is not liable for failing to rescue another person in distress. German law is basically similar. In some countries, though, the failure to rescue another in distress is regarded as negligence.

Damages. National tort laws also differ in the way in which damages in tort cases are calculated. For example, Swiss law and Turkish law permit a court to reduce damages if an award of full damages would cause undue hardship for the party who was found negligent. In some nations of northern Africa, the amount of damages awarded varies depending on the type of wrongful action committed and the degree of intent involved. In the United States, the calculation of actual (compensatory) damages does not depend on whether the tort was negligent or intentional.

Contract Law. Because international business transactions typically involve contracts, businesspersons should familiarize themselves with the contract law of the countries in which they do business. To a degree, the United Nations Convention on Contracts for the International Sale of Goods

(CISG) has simplified matters for parties to international sales contracts. For many transactions, however, the CISG may not be applicable.

The CISG applies only to transactions involving firms in countries that have signed the convention, or agreement, and parties (in nonsignatory nations) that have stipulated in their contracts that the CISG will govern any dispute. When a transaction involves firms in countries that are not signatory to the CISG, the contract parties need to determine which nation's law will govern any disputes that may arise under the contract. Additionally, even when the CISG would apply, it does so only if the parties have not agreed otherwise in their contract. For example, parties may agree in their contract that German law or U.S. law or some other nation's law will govern any contract dispute that arises. For these reasons, the contract laws of individual nations remain important to businesspersons involved in international contracts.

To read the text of Article 2 of the Uniform Commercial Code, go to the "Statutes" page of our Web site at **http://ele.westbuslaw.com**

The Importance of National Law. Generally, the laws of other nations governing contracts are similar to those in the United States. As you will read in Chapter 10, a *contract* is an agreement that can be enforced in court. In the United States, under the common law of contracts, several requirements must be met for a contract to be valid. The common law of contracts also applies to contracts for the sale of goods, except when the Uniform Commercial Code (UCC)—the statutory law governing sales and lease contracts—has modified common law requirements.

One requirement is *agreement,* which is commonly divided into two events: offer and acceptance. One party, the *offeror,* offers to enter into a contract with another party, the *offeree.* Once the offer is accepted by the offeree, a valid contract is created—provided that the other requirements for a contract are met. Another requirement is *consideration*—each party must give something of legally sufficient value (such as a monetary payment) to the other party, or the contract will fail. Other requirements include *legality* (the contract must not be contrary to the law or to public policy) and *capacity* (the parties must have the mental capacity to enter into a binding contract). Additionally, the parties' assent to the terms of the contract must be genuine (that is, not due to a mistake, fraud, or duress), and certain contracts must be in writing to be enforceable.

Many of these requirements exist under other nations' laws as well. There are some significant differences, however.

Agreement. The requirement of agreement (offer and acceptance) is common among countries, although what is considered an offer varies by jurisdiction. In the United States, an offer, once made, normally can be revoked (canceled, or taken back) by the offeror at any time prior to the offer's acceptance. Many nations, however, require that an offer remain open for some minimum period of time. For example, the German Civil Code, which has detailed provisions governing offer and acceptance, requires that a written contractual offer be held open for a reasonable time, unless the offer specifically states otherwise. Unlike in the United States, oral contractual offers (those made in person or by telephone) in Germany must be accepted immediately, or they terminate.

Mexico has some special rules for offer and acceptance. If an offer does not state a time for acceptance, the offer is deemed to be held open for three days, plus whatever time is necessary for the offer and acceptance to be sent through the mails. If acceptance is desired sooner, the offeror must state the time for acceptance in the offer.

In the United States, a contract's terms must be sufficiently definite that the parties (and a court) can determine whether a contract has been formed (see Chapter 10). For contracts for the sale of goods, however, the UCC has substantially relaxed the common law requirements in respect to definiteness of contract terms (see Chapter 11). Mexico also has adopted a commercial code, which, like the UCC, liberalizes the traditional requirements of definiteness in mercantile transactions. In some countries, such as Saudi Arabia, however, contract law sets out strict requirements about the definiteness of a contract's terms. If the terms of an offer are too vague or indefinite, acceptance of that offer normally will not create a valid contract.

Consideration. In contrast to contract law in the United States, contract law in most civil law countries does not require consideration in order for a contract to be legally binding on the parties. German law, for example, does not require the exchange of consideration. An agreement to make a gift may thus be enforceable by the donee (the gift's recipient). In the United States, because consideration is required for a valid contract, promises to make gifts normally are not enforceable (because the donee does not give consideration for the gift—see Chapter 10).

In other countries, such as Saudi Arabia, consideration is required. Similarly, in India, consideration normally is required, although some contracts may be lawful even when the consideration consists of "past consideration" (that is, consideration that consists of an action that occurred in the past). As will be noted in Chapter 10, in the United States past consideration is no consideration.

Remedies for Breach of Contract. The types of remedies available for breach of contract vary widely throughout the world. In many countries, as in the United States, the normal remedy is damages—money given to the nonbreaching party to compensate that party for the losses incurred owing to the breach (see Chapter 10). Like the calculation of damages under tort law, however, the calculation of damages resulting from a breach of contract may differ from one country to another.

National contract laws also differ as to whether and when equitable remedies, such as specific performance (discussed in Chapter 10), will be granted. Germany's typical remedy for a breach of contract is specific performance, which means that the party must go forward and perform the contract. Damages are available only after certain procedures have been employed to seek performance. In contrast, in the United States, the equitable remedy of specific performance will usually not be granted unless the remedy at law (money damages) is inadequate and the subject matter of the contract is unique.

Defenses. As in the United States, contract law in most nations allows parties to defend against contractual liability by claiming that certain requirements for contract enforceability are lacking. For example, many nations, including the United States, have laws stipulating that certain types of contracts must be in writing. If such contracts are not in writing, they will not be enforced. In Saudi Arabia, the law strongly encourages parties to put all contracts in writing, and any written contract should be formally witnessed by two males or a male and a female. In that country, it may be difficult to enforce an oral contract.

Another common defense is the assertion that a contract was entered into because of a mistake, fraud, or duress and, thus, that genuineness of assent to the contract's terms was lacking. In some countries, a party may claim that a contract was not formed because the consideration supporting the contract was inadequate—that is, not *enough* value or money was given in exchange for a contractual promise. Indian courts, for example, look to the adequacy of consideration when determining whether the parties' assent to the contract was truly genuine and, therefore, whether the contract should be enforced. In the United States, in contrast, courts rarely inquire into the adequacy of consideration. Normally, only in cases in which the consideration is so grossly inadequate as to "shock the conscience of the court" will a court refuse to enforce a contract on this basis.

Employment Law. Employment law is particularly important in many foreign nations. Traditionally, in the United States the details of the employment relationship were left to negotiations between the employer and the employee. Under the common law *employment-at-will doctrine,* employers are free to hire and fire employees "at will," meaning that an employee can be fired for any reason or no reason at all. Today, this common law doctrine is less applicable in the United States because the workplace is regulated extensively by federal and state statutory law. Employment relationships in other nations are also subject to government regulation.

Modifications to the At-Will Doctrine. Like the United States, many other countries have modified their traditional at-will employment rules. In France, for example, the concept of employment at will can be traced back to the original Napoleonic Code. Over the years, the French have modified this doctrine considerably. French courts developed the doctrine of ***abus de droit*** ("abuse of rights"), which prohibits employers from firing workers for illness, pregnancy, unionization, political beliefs, the exercise of certain rights, or even personal dislike. French courts also began requiring employers to follow customary procedures before terminating workers. French employee-discharge laws were codified in the Dismissal Law of 1973, which also established procedural requirements that employers must follow when discharging workers (to be discussed shortly).

Abus de droit • A doctrine developed in the French courts. The doctrine modified employment at will and protected workers exercising their rights from wrongful discharge and other employer abuses.

Under the Polish labor code, employment continues to be predominantly "at will." Either party may terminate the employment relationship at any time. Advance notice is generally required, however, and notice requirements vary, depending on the length of the worker's tenure with the employer. An employer may terminate an employee immediately and without notice if the worker has committed a criminal offense, lost a license or other employment qualification, seriously breached her or his duties, or failed to appear regularly at the job site. An employer cannot immediately discharge an employee for the last reason, however, if the employee's absence was due to child-care needs, infectious disease, or entitled sick leave.

Wages and Benefits. One of the reasons U.S. businesspersons may decide to establish business operations, such as factories, in other countries is to cut production costs by taking advantage of lower wage rates. Although workers' wages may be lower in some countries than in the United States, typically workers in other countries are entitled to many paid holidays, plus vacation time. In addition, employers in other countries may be subject to a variety of requirements not found in the United States.

In Mexico, for example, workers have a right to an annual bonus equal to fifteen days' salary and paid at the end of the year. Mexican law requires a minimum amount of paid vacation time (six days in the first year of employment) and also requires that companies give workers a 25 percent bonus above their ordinary pay rates during those vacations. For example, if a worker's ordinary pay is $200 per week, the vacation pay is $250 per week. Mexican employers also must periodically provide training courses for workers. In some countries, such as Egypt, fringe benefits for employees account for as much as 40 percent of an employer's payroll costs.

Equal Employment Opportunity. National laws around the globe vary widely with respect to equal employment opportunity. In the United States, as you will read in Chapter 15, employers are prohibited from discriminating against employees or job applicants on the basis of race, color, national origin, gender, religion, age, or disability. U.S. laws prohibiting discrimination on these bases also apply to all U.S. employees working for U.S. employers abroad. Generally, a U.S. employer must abide by U.S. laws prohibiting employment discrimination *unless* to do so would violate the laws of the country where the employer's workplace is located. This "foreign laws exception" usually allows U.S. employers abroad to avoid being subjected to conflicting laws.

Some other countries also prohibit discriminatory practices. For example, in Indonesia, the Ministry of Manpower, which implements employment laws and regulations, prohibits discrimination in the workplace. Mexican law forbids employers from discriminating against employees on the basis of race, religion, or gender. The Japanese constitution prohibits discrimination based on race, religion, nationality, or gender.

In contrast, some countries, such as Egypt and Turkey, have no laws requiring equal employment opportunity. In Argentina, racial, religious, or other discrimination is not prohibited by law. Similarly, in Brazil, equal opportunity is not a factor in employment relationships.

Generally, in those countries that do prohibit employment discrimination, employers retain some flexibility in hiring and firing managerial personnel. In Mexico, for example, employers traditionally have been allowed to hire and fire "confidential" employees—managerial employees—at their discretion. In Italy, workers classified as managers are also less protected by the law than rank-and-file employees are.

Employment Termination. In many countries, employers find it difficult, and often quite costly, to discharge employees. Employment laws may prohibit the firing of employees for discriminatory reasons, and other laws may also come into play. For example, in France, if an employment contract is for an indefinite term, the employer can fire the worker only for genuine and serious cause or for economic reasons. The law also establishes procedural requirements. Before terminating a worker for cause, the employer must undertake a conciliatory session with labor court mediators. The employer has the burden of proving to the labor court that the dismissal is for serious cause.

In Egypt, employers commonly use fixed-period employment contracts, which are automatically terminated at the end of the contract period. If an employee continues to work after the end of the contract period and no new contract is created, the employment contract becomes indefinite. It is very difficult to discharge an employee with an indefinite contract. The employee must first commit a serious offense, whereupon the employer must submit a proposal for termination to a committee consisting of representatives of the union, the employer, and the government. Employees may appeal adverse decisions of this committee.

Taiwanese law places clear restrictions on the termination of employment. An employer must provide a reason for discharging an employee. An employer may discharge an employee with advance notice and severance pay for a number of economic reasons or if the worker is incapable of performing the assigned work. Employers may fire employees without notice or severance pay only for certain reasons, such as violence, imprisonment, or extensive absenteeism.

Cultural and Business Traditions

Conducting business successfully in a foreign nation requires not only a knowledge of that nation's laws but also some familiarity with its cultural traditions, economy, and business climate. Here we look at some ways in which difficulties can arise due to cultural differences among nations.

Language Problems. One obvious cultural difference among nations is language. For example, Rolls-Royce changed the name of its "Silver Mist" line in Germany because in that country, *mist* translates as "manure." Esso had difficulty selling gasoline in Japan in part because *Esso* sounds like the Japanese word for stalled car. Pepsi's "Come Alive with Pepsi" campaign was translated in Taiwan as "Pepsi brings your ancestors back from the grave."

The meaning of nonverbal language (body movements, gestures, facial expressions, and the like) also varies from culture to culture. In the United States, for example, a nod of the head indicates "yes," but in some countries, such as Greece, the same gesture means "no."

Ethical Differences. There are also some important ethical differences among nations. In Islamic countries, for example, the consumption of alcohol and certain foods is forbidden. Thus, it would be thoughtless and imprudent to invite a Saudi Arabian business contact out for a drink. Additionally, in many foreign nations, gift giving is a common practice between contracting companies or between companies and government officials. To Americans, such gift giving may look suspiciously like an unethical (and possibly illegal) bribe. This has been an important source of friction in international business, particularly after the U.S. Congress passed the Foreign Corrupt Practices Act in 1977 (discussed in Chapter 4). This act prohibits U.S. business firms from offering certain side payments to foreign officials to secure favorable contracts.

The Role of Women. The role played by women in other countries may present some troublesome ethical problems for U.S. firms doing business internationally. Equal employment opportunity is a fundamental public policy in the United States, and Title VII of the Civil Rights Act of 1964 (discussed in Chapter 15) prohibits discrimination against women in the employment context. Some other countries, however, largely reject any professional role for women, which may cause difficulties for American women conducting business transactions in those countries. For example, when the World Bank sent a delegation including women to negotiate with the Central Bank of Korea, the Koreans were surprised and offended. They thought that the presence of women meant that the Koreans were not being taken seriously.

KEY TERMS

abus de droit 268
act of state doctrine 249
civil law system 261
comparative law 261
confiscation 250
distribution agreement 255
dumping 259
export 254
expropriation 249
international law 246
international organization 247
most-favored-nation status 260
national law 246
principle of comity 249
quota 257
sovereign immunity 250
tariff 257
treaty 247

FOR REVIEW

1. What is the principle of comity, and when do courts deciding disputes involving a foreign law or judicial decree apply this principle?
2. What is the act of state doctrine? In what circumstances is this doctrine applied?
3. Under the Foreign Sovereign Immunities Act of 1976, on what basis might a foreign state be subject to the jurisdiction of U.S. courts?
4. How does the United States control imports?
5. Do U.S. laws prohibiting employment discrimination apply in all circumstances to U.S. employees working for U.S. employers abroad?

QUESTIONS AND CASE PROBLEMS

8–1. Assume that you are the president of a manufacturing company that intends to expand overseas. Shipping costs and tariffs for your product are uniformly low. Your manufacturing process, however, is highly labor intensive. How would the employment laws of various nations influence your decision on where to situate a new manufacturing plant?

8–2. Joe Henderson is the president of an Asian branch of a U.S. bank. His top vice president is a woman, Betty Carter. He would like to take her with him to an important meeting at which he will undertake loan negotiations with a huge overseas company. He has been advised, however, that he will lose respect in the eyes of the foreign company—and perhaps the company's business—if she accompanies him. He talks with her, and she informs him that she does not mind deferring to men at social activities, if local customs demand such deference, but that at corporate meetings, she will expect business as usual and will not alter her behavior simply because she is a woman. What should Henderson do? Discuss.

8–3. In 1995, France implemented a law making the use of the French language mandatory in certain legal documents. Certain documents relating to securities offerings, for example, must be written in French. So must instruction manuals and warranties for goods and services offered for sale in France. Additionally, all agreements entered into with French state or local authorities, with entities controlled by state or local authorities, and with private entities carrying out a public service (such as providing utilities) must be written in French. What kinds of problems might this law pose for U.S. businesspersons who wish to form contracts with French persons or business firms?

8–4. As China and formerly Communist nations move toward free enterprise, they must develop a new set of business laws. If you could start from scratch, what kind of business law system would you adopt, a civil law system or a common law system? What kind of business regulations would you impose?

CASE PROBLEM WITH SAMPLE ANSWER

8–5. Act of State Doctrine. W. S. Kirkpatrick & Co. learned that the Republic of Nigeria was interested in contracting for the construction and equipping of a medical center in Nigeria. Kirkpatrick, with the aid of a Nigerian citizen, secured the contract as a result of bribing Nigerian officials. Nigerian law prohibits both the payment and the receipt of bribes in connection with the awarding of government contracts, and the U.S. Foreign Corrupt Practices Act of 1977 expressly prohibits U.S. firms and their agents from bribing foreign officials to secure favorable contracts. Environmental Tectonics Corp., International (ETC), an unsuccessful bidder for the contract, learned of the bribery and sued Kirkpatrick in a federal district court for damages. The district court granted summary judgment for Kirkpatrick on the ground that resolution of the case in favor of ETC would require imputing to foreign officials an unlawful motivation (the obtaining of bribes) and accordingly might embarrass the Nigerian government or interfere with the conduct of U.S. foreign policy. Was the district court correct in assuming that the act of state doctrine barred ETC's action against Kirkpatrick? What should happen on appeal? Discuss fully. [*W. S. Kirkpatrick & Co. v. Environmental Tectonics Corp., International,* 493 U.S. 400, 110 S.Ct. 701, 107 L.Ed.2d 816 (1990)]

➧ *To view a sample answer for this case problem, go to this book's Web site at* **http://ele.westbuslaw.com** *and click on "Interactive Study Center."*

8–6. Discrimination Claims. Radio Free Europe and Radio Liberty (RFE/RL), a U.S. corporation doing business in Germany, employs more than three hundred U.S. citizens at its principal place of business in Munich, Germany. The concept of mandatory retirement is deeply embedded in German labor policy, and a contract formed in 1982 between RFE/RL and a German labor union contained a clause that required workers to be retired when they reached the age of sixty-five. When William Mahoney and other U.S. employees (the plaintiffs) reached the age of sixty-five, RFE/RL terminated their employment as required under its contract with the labor union. The plaintiffs sued RFE/RL for discriminating against them on the basis of age, in violation of the U.S. Age Discrimination in Employment Act of 1967. Will the plaintiffs succeed in their suit? Discuss fully. [*Mahoney v. RFE/RL, Inc.,* 47 F.3d 447 (D.C. Cir. 1995)]

8–7. Dumping. In response to a petition filed on behalf of the U.S. pineapple industry, the U.S. Commerce Department initiated an investigation of canned pineapple fruit imported from Thailand. The investigation concerned Thai producers of the canned fruit, including The Thai Pineapple Public Co. The Thai producers also turned out products, such as pineapple juice and juice concentrate, outside the scope of the investigation. These products use separate parts of the same fresh pineapple, so they share raw material costs. The Commerce Department had to calculate the Thai producers' cost of production, for the purpose of determining fair value and antidumping duties, and in so doing, it had to allocate a portion of the shared fruit costs to the canned fruit. These allocations were based on the producers' own financial records, which were consistent with Thai generally accepted accounting principles. The result was a determination that more than 90 percent of the canned fruit sales were below the cost of production. The producers filed a suit in the U.S. Court of International Trade against the federal government, challenging this allocation. The producers argued that their records did not reflect actual production costs, which instead should be based on the weight of fresh fruit used to make the products. Did the Commerce Department act reasonably in determining the cost of production? Why or why not? [*The Thai Pineapple Public Co. v. United States,* 187 F.3d 1362 (Fed. Cir. 1999)]

8–8. Sovereign Immunity. Tonoga, Ltd., doing business as Taconic Plastics, Ltd., is a manufacturer incorporated in Ireland with its principal place of business in New York. In 1997, Taconic entered into a contract with a German construction company to supply special material for a tent project designed to shelter religious pilgrims visiting holy sites in Saudi Arabia. Most of the material was made in, and shipped from, New York. The company did not pay Taconic and eventually filed for bankruptcy. Another German firm, Werner Voss Architects and Engineers, acting as an agent for the government of Saudi Arabia, guaranteed the payments due Taconic to induce it to complete the project. When Taconic received all but the final payment, the firm filed a suit in a federal district court against the government of Saudi Arabia, claiming a breach of the guaranty and seeking to collect, in part, about $3 million. The defendant filed a motion to dismiss based, in part, on the doctrine of sovereign immunity. Under what circumstances does this doctrine apply? What are its exceptions? Should this suit be dismissed under the "commercial activity" exception? Explain. [*Tonoga, Ltd. v. Ministry of Public Works and Housing of Kingdom of Saudi Arabia,* 135 F.Supp.2d 350 (N.D.N.Y. 2001)]

8–9. Import Control. In 1996, the International Trade Administration (ITA) of the U.S. Department of Commerce assessed antidumping duties against Koyo Seiko Co., NTN Corp., and other companies, on certain tapered roller bearings and their components imported from Japan. In assessing these duties, the ITA requested information from the makers about their home market sales. NTN responded in part that its figures should not include many sample and small-quantity sales, which were made to enable customers to decide whether to buy the products. NTN provided no evidence to support this assertion, however. In calculating the fair market value of the bearings in Japan, the ITA determined, among other things, that sample and small-quantity sales were within the makers' ordinary course of trade. Koyo and others appealed these assessments to the U.S. Court of International Trade. NTN objected in part to the ITA's inclusion of sample and small-quantity sales. On what basis should the ITA make such determinations? Should the court order the ITA to recalculate its assessment on the basis of NTN's objection? Explain. [*Koyo Seiko Co. v. United States,* 186 F.Supp.2d 1332 (CIT [Court of International Trade] 2002)]

8–10. IN YOUR COURT

Texas Trading & Milling Corp. and other companies brought an action for breach of contract against the Republic of Nigeria and its central bank. Nigeria, a rapidly developing and oil-rich nation, had contracted to purchase more cement from Texas Trading than it could use. Unable to accept delivery of the cement, Nigeria repudiated the contract, claiming immunity under the Foreign Sovereign Immunities Act (FSIA) of 1976 because the buyer of the cement was the Nigerian government. Assume that you are the judge in the trial court hearing this case and answer the following questions:

(a) What section of the FSIA is particularly applicable to this dispute?
(b) Given the provisions of that section, should the doctrine of sovereign immunity remove the dispute from the jurisdiction of U.S. courts? Explain your reasoning.

8–11. A QUESTION OF ETHICS AND SOCIAL RESPONSIBILITY

Ronald Riley, a U.S. citizen, and Council of Lloyd's, a British insurance corporation with its principal place of business in London, entered into an agreement in 1980 that allowed Riley to underwrite insurance through Lloyd's. The agreement provided that if any dispute arose between Lloyd's and Riley, the courts of England would have exclusive jurisdiction, and the laws of England would apply. Over the next decade, some of the parties insured under policies that Riley underwrote experienced large losses, for which they filed claims. Instead of paying his share of the claims, Riley filed a lawsuit in a U.S. district court against Lloyd's and its managers and directors (all British citizens or entities), seeking, among other things, rescission of the 1980 agreement. Riley alleged that the defendants had violated U.S. securities laws (discussed in Chapter 18). The defendants asked the court to enforce the forum-selection clause in the agreement. Riley argued that if the clause was enforced, he would be deprived of his rights under the U.S. securities laws. The court held that the parties were to resolve their dispute in England. [*Riley v. Kingsley Underwriting Agencies, Ltd.,* 969 F.2d 953 (10th Cir. 1992)]

(a) Did the court's decision fairly balance the rights of the parties? How would you argue in support of the court's decision in this case? How would you argue against it?
(b) Should the fact that an international transaction may be subject to laws and remedies different from or less favorable than those of the United States be a valid basis for denying enforcement of forum-selection and choice-of-law clauses?
(c) All parties to this litigation other than Riley were British. Should the court consider this fact in deciding this case?

8–12. FOR CRITICAL ANALYSIS

You are the human resources director for a major American conglomerate. Your company decides that it wants to expand its international presence considerably and asks you to develop a training program for managers. The aim of this training program is to develop managers who can operate more effectively in foreign nations. What components would you include in such a program?

For updated links to resources available on the Web, as well as a variety of other materials, visit this text's Web site at

http://ele.westbuslaw.com

FindLaw, which is now a part of West Group, includes an extensive array of links to international doctrines and treaties, as well as to the laws of other nations, on its Web site. Go to

http://www.findlaw.com

and click on "International Law."

To learn more about what is involved in exporting goods to other countries, go to the state of New Mexico's Web page on "How to Export" at

http://www.edd.state.nm.us/TRADE/HOWTO/howto.htm

For information on the legal requirements of doing business in other nations, a good source is the Internet Law Library's collection of laws of other nations. You can access this source at

http://www.lawguru.com/ilawlib/index.html

LEGAL RESEARCH EXERCISES ON THE WEB

Go to **http://ele.westbuslaw.com**, the Web site that accompanies this text. Select "Interactive Study Center," and then click on "Chapter 8." There you will find the following Internet research exercises that you can perform to learn more about topics covered in this chapter.

Activity 8–1: LEGAL PERSPECTIVE—The World Trade Organization

Activity 8–2: MANAGEMENT PERSPECTIVE—Overseas Business Opportunities

BEFORE THE TEST

Go to **http://ele.westbuslaw.com**, the Web site that accompanies this text. Select "Interactive Quizzes." You will find at least twenty interactive questions relating to this chapter.

WESTLAW® CAMPUS

If your textbook provided for a subscription to Westlaw® Campus, or if you have otherwise purchased access to the Westlaw Campus database, you can access any of the cases presented or cited in this chapter by using your Westlaw Campus account.

FOCUS ON LEGAL REASONING
Kasky v. Nike, Inc.

INTRODUCTION

In Chapter 5, we discussed the principles governing commercial speech under the First Amendment to the Constitution. In this *Focus on Legal Reasoning,* we examine *Kasky v. Nike, Inc.,*[1] a case in which the California Supreme Court considered whether certain statements constituted commercial speech.

CASE BACKGROUND

Nike, Inc., makes and sells athletic shoes and apparel. Subcontractors in China, Vietnam, and Indonesia make most of Nike's products. In October 1996, the media began to publicize allegations that in the factories where Nike products are made, workers were paid less than the local minimum wage; were required to work overtime; were permitted and encouraged to work more hours than local laws permitted; were subjected to physical, verbal, and sexual abuse; and were exposed to toxic chemicals, noise, heat, and dust without adequate safety equipment, in violation of local health and safety regulations.

Nike responded that workers who make its products are protected from physical and sexual abuse, that they are paid in accordance with local laws governing wages, that they receive free meals and health care, and that their working conditions comply with local regulations. Nike made these statements in press releases; in full-page newspaper ads; and in letters to newspapers, university presidents, and athletic directors.

Marc Kasky, a California resident, filed a suit in a California state court against Nike, alleging in part that these statements were false and misleading in violation of state law. Kasky asked the court to order Nike to "disgorge all monies . . . acquired by means of any act found . . . to be an unlawful and/or unfair business practice" and to begin corrective advertising. Nike asserted in part that the relief Kasky sought "is absolutely barred by the First Amendment." The court dismissed the suit. On Kasky's appeal, a state intermediate appellate court affirmed the dismissal. Kasky petitioned the California Supreme Court for review, arguing in part that Nike's statements were entitled to less protection under the First Amendment because they constituted commercial speech.

1. 27 Cal.4th 939, 45 P.3d 243, 119 Cal.Rptr.2d 296 (2002). This case was appealed to the United States Supreme Court, which granted *cert.* After hearing oral arguments, however, the Court decided not to issue a ruling. *Nike, Inc. v. Kasky,* ___ U.S. ___, 123 S.Ct. 2554, ___ L.Ed.2d ___ (2003). In the fall of 2003, the parties settled the dispute out of court.

MAJORITY OPINION

KENNARD, J.

The United States Supreme Court has not adopted an all-purpose test to distinguish commercial from noncommercial speech under the First Amendment * * * . A close reading of the high court's commercial speech decisions [including *Bolger v. Young Drug Products Corp.,* 463 U.S. 60, 103 S.Ct. 2875, 77 L.Ed.2d 469 (1983)] suggests, however, that it is possible to formulate a limited-purpose test. We conclude, therefore, that when a court must decide whether particular speech may be subjected to laws aimed at preventing false advertising or other forms of commercial deception, *categorizing a particular statement as commercial or noncommercial speech requires consideration of three elements: the speaker, the intended audience, and the content of the message.* [Emphasis added.]

In typical commercial speech cases, the *speaker* is likely to be someone engaged in commerce—that is, generally, the production, distribution, or sale of goods or services—or someone acting on behalf of a person so engaged, and the *intended audience* is likely to be actual or potential buyers or customers of the speaker's goods or services, or persons acting for actual or potential buyers or customers, or persons (such as reporters or reviewers) likely to repeat the message to or otherwise influence actual or potential buyers or customers. * * *

* * * *

FOCUS ON LEGAL REASONING

Finally, the factual content of the message should be commercial in character. In the context of regulation of false or misleading advertising, this typically means that the speech consists of representations of fact about the business operations, products, or services of the speaker * * *, made for the purpose of promoting sales of, or other commercial transactions in, the speaker's products or services * * *.

* * * *

Here, the first element—a commercial speaker—is satisfied because the speakers—Nike and its officers and directors—are engaged in commerce. Specifically, they manufacture, import, distribute, and sell consumer goods in the form of athletic shoes and apparel.

The second element—an intended commercial audience—is also satisfied. Nike's letters to university presidents and directors of athletic departments were addressed directly to actual and potential purchasers of Nike's products, because college and university athletic departments are major purchasers of athletic shoes and apparel. * * *

The third element—representations of fact of a commercial nature—is also present. In describing its own labor policies, and the practices and working conditions in factories where its products are made, Nike was making factual representations about its own business operations. * * *

* * * *

The judgment of the Court of Appeals is reversed, and the matter is remanded to that court for further proceedings consistent with this opinion.

DISSENTING OPINION

BROWN, J.

[T]he majority's test for commercial speech contravenes long-standing principles of First Amendment law.

First, the test flouts the very essence of the distinction between commercial and noncommercial speech * * *. If commercial speech is to be distinguished, it must be distinguished by its content. * * * [T]he majority distinguishes commercial from noncommercial speech using two criteria wholly unrelated to the speech's content: the identity of the speaker and the intended audience. * * *

Second, the test contravenes a fundamental tenet of First Amendment jurisprudence by making the identity of the speaker potentially dispositive [decisive]. * * * [T]he identity of the speaker is not decisive in determining whether speech is protected, and speech does not lose its protection because of the corporate identity of the speaker. This is because corporations and other speakers engaged in commerce contribute to the discussion, debate, and the dissemination of information and ideas that the First Amendment seeks to foster. Thus, the inherent worth of the speech in terms of its capacity for informing the public does not depend upon the identity of its source, whether corporation, association, union, or individual. * * *

Third, the test violates the First Amendment by stifling the ability of speakers engaged in commerce, such as corporations, to participate in debates over public issues. * * * Speech on public issues occupies the highest rung of the hierarchy of First Amendment values, and is entitled to special protection because such speech is more than self-expression; it is the essence of self-government. The * * * [First] Amendment remove[s] governmental restraints from the arena of public discussion, putting the decision as to what views shall be voiced largely into the hands of each of us, in the hope that use of such freedom will ultimately produce a more capable citizenry and more perfect polity [nation or government] * * *.

LEGAL REASONING AND ANALYSIS

❶ **Legal Analysis.** Find the *Bolger v. Young Drug Products Corp.* case (see the *Law on the Web* feature at the end of Chapter 2 for instructions on how to access federal court opinions). Compare the facts and issues in that case to the facts and issues of the *Kasky* case. How are they similar? How are they different? Why did the court refer to this case in its opinion?

❷ **Legal Reasoning.** Contrast the conclusion of the majority with that of the dissent. What arguments did the dissent make to support its assertion that the majority's conclusion was incorrect? What legal sources did the dissent cite to justify its position?

❸ **Legal Reasoning.** Review the discussion of legal reasoning in Chapter 1. Which, if any, of the forms of legal reasoning described there did the majority use to reach its conclusion?

❹ **Implications for the Business Manager.** What effect might the holding in this case have on businesses that are, or may be, subject to negative allegations about their operations?

❺ **Case Briefing Assignment.** Using the guidelines for briefing cases given in the "Preface to the Student" at the beginning of this text, brief the *Kasky* case.

GOING ONLINE

This text's Web site, at **http://ele.westbuslaw.com**, offers links to West's Court Case Updates, as well as to other online research sources. You can also locate court cases at the Web sites listed in the *Law on the Web* section at the end of Chapter 2.

The United States Supreme Court commonly issues opinions in cases involving the Constitution, including disputes concerning commercial speech and the First Amendment. Supreme Court cases are online at a number of sites, including **http://www.findlaw.com**. FindLaw, Inc., which is now a part of West Group, maintains this Web site.

UNIT TWO

FOCUS ON ETHICS

The Public and International Environment

No other areas of law are as dynamic and engender as much controversy as those relating to the public and international environment. All areas of law touch on ethical considerations. But many laws have as their basis practical necessity or commercial need. The law of the public environment, however, concerns issues such as the protection of freedom of speech, the promotion of racial equality, and government regulation of behavior for the public welfare versus individual rights. The law of the international environment involves such questions as the influence of foreign and international laws, divergent cultures, and different legal, political, and economic systems on business activities.

Little guidance is provided by considerations of practicality in resolving these issues. Moreover, these issues are in large measure purely ethical in nature. In resolving them, one must rely on basic notions of fairness and justice. Yet conceptions of fairness, justice, and equality differ among individuals and change over time. Not surprisingly, at any moment in history, there is seldom a broad social consensus over legal issues in the public and international environment.

FREE SPEECH AND THE CORPORATION

Free speech is regarded as one of the basic rights of a democratic society. Yet it has never been considered an absolute right. The right of free speech must be balanced against other important rights and the advancement of

other important social goals. In that sense, the proper extent of freedom of speech, in its many forms, involves ethical considerations.

Because freedom of speech is not absolute, not all forms of expression are protected. Pornography, for example, is not protected by the First Amendment. Nor are utterances protected that would induce an immediate threat of violence or injury. Even within the context of protected speech, the Supreme Court has historically looked to the nature of the speech involved in determining the extent of the protection afforded.

Commercial speech, for example, is afforded less protection from government restriction than is noncommercial speech. The lesser degree of protection means in practical terms that it is easier for government to show that the interest it seeks to promote by regulating the speech is more important than protecting the right of speech. But in balancing such conflicting rights and goals, value judgments must be made.

Judging the Source

The nature of the speech involved may be a legitimate concern in assessing the extent of freedom of speech, but is it legitimate to consider the source of the speech? For example, should it make a difference that the speaker, through either a spokesperson or an advertisement, is a corporation? Most corporate "speech" has as its primary purpose the promotion of a product; that is, it is commercial in nature and, as just discussed, is afforded less protection than noncommercial speech. But what if the speech is political in nature? Should it matter that the speaker is a corporation? This issue was addressed by the United States Supreme Court in *First National Bank of Boston v. Bellotti*, a case referred to in Chapter 5. Although the justices deciding the case were applying their concepts of the free speech clause of the First Amendment, the case raises some ethical questions, which are implicit in the Court's decision and in the opinions of the dissenting justices.

First National Bank of Boston v. Bellotti concerned a Massachusetts law that forbade corporations from using their resources to try to influence public opinion on issues that were submitted to a referendum vote when those issues did not materially relate to the corporation's business. Controversy arose when five corporations announced their intentions to mount a campaign in opposition to a proposed state individual income tax, which was to be submitted to a referendum vote. The state threatened to fine the corporations and punish their executives if the corporations entered the political debate. The corporations sought protection by asking the courts to declare the Massachusetts law unconstitutional. Ultimately, the case was appealed to the United States Supreme Court.

A divided Court decided in favor of the corporations. The majority held that free speech protections extended to corporations and that the Massachusetts law violated those constitutional protections. In deciding the case, the majority recast the issue involved. For the majority, the issue was *not* whether corporations were protected by the free speech clause but, rather, whether the speech involved was protected. Because the speech was political in nature, the majority concluded that the speech could not be restricted in the manner employed by the state. To the majority, it did not matter that the speaker was a corporation. And indeed, as the majority viewed the case, it was not protecting the corporation. Instead, it believed that the political nature of the speech meant that it should be heard.

The Ethical Dimensions

The majority's reasoning has some strong points. After all, political debate is the fundamental ingredient of the democratic political process. There is virtually uniform agreement that the authors of the Constitution definitely had the public exchange of political views in mind when they constructed the free speech clause of the First Amendment. But there are other considerations, largely of an ethical nature, involved when a corporation uses its extensive resources to influence the political process.

Certainly, bribing officials is wrong both ethically and legally. But other forms of corporate spending that influence the political process also might be unethical. One concern is that a corporation can "leverage" political power through its economic skills. Corporations acquire resources through skilled marketing, management, and utilization of technology. Yet these skills, however beneficial to society's material well-being they may be, do not involve political ideas or necessarily indicate a concern for the public welfare. Should the resources garnered in the economic arena be redeployed in the political arena? Is it fair to allow economic skill to be translated into political power? These were concerns raised in dissent to the majority's opinion in the *Bellotti* case, but they are as much ethical issues as legal ones.

Notwithstanding these concerns, there are ethical as well as practical considerations that support the majority's view. Recall that the Massachusetts law challenged in *Bellotti* did not ban corporate expenditures on referendum issues that materially related to the corporation's business. The issue was a state *individual* income tax. The very fact that the corporations would not be materially affected by a state individual income tax might imply that their political participation was motivated solely by concern for the public welfare rather than their self-interest. Even if they were concerned that the proposed tax might affect the economy of the state and thus the profitability of their businesses, that does not in itself make their views less worthy to be heard. After all, on economic matters, the corporate view of the issues would seem to be extremely relevant. Possibly, the corporate view should be heard for that reason alone. And if the corporations choose to subsidize with their own resources the dissemination of important views, maybe they should be praised rather than condemned.

ETHICS AND THE ADMINISTRATIVE PROCESS

In Chapter 5 we noted some of the other constitutional protections that apply in the context of business. We looked in Chapter 6 at how some of those protections apply in the administrative process. As noted in Chapter 6, effective governmental regulation necessitates the gathering of relevant information. Often that information can be obtained only by an on-site inspection of business premises or a first-hand examination of business records. When regulatory needs conflict with constitutional principles, not only are legal issues raised, but ethical ones as well.

Recall that the Fourth Amendment protection from unreasonable searches and seizures applies in the context of business. Within the context of administrative law, this protection has been interpreted as requiring that information sought by a regulatory agency be relevant to the matter under scrutiny. Furthermore, any demand for information must be reasonably specific and not unduly burdensome to the business providing the information.

The Need to Know

The ideals embodied in the Fourth Amendment are deeply ingrained in America's political culture. The image of midnight raids in which

FOCUS ON ETHICS

innocent families watch helplessly as gruff, heavily armed officers ransack their homes is often invoked when one thinks of a "search and seizure." Protection against such abhorrent practices is fundamental to the American ideal of liberty.

But are the same ideals felt as strongly in other contexts? What about in the business context, especially with regard to agency regulation? Even though the first significant degree of federal economic regulation can be traced as far back as the first half of the nineteenth century, Americans continue to hold extremely ambivalent feelings toward the very idea of government regulation. Americans are prone to look to government to address every new ill society encounters, but then stridently resent, as governmental intrusion, the regulatory schemes designed to cure those ills.

Whatever the sentiments Americans hold regarding government regulation, most accept and many welcome it as an important part of modern society. In accepting such regulation, Americans also accept the fact that regulators must gather information. For example, the Securities and Exchange Commission desires information about proposed stock offerings. The Environmental Protection Agency may request to make an inspection of a chemical plant to ensure compliance with hazardous waste-disposal regulations.

Regulation and Privacy Rights

Despite acceptance of the need for regulators to gather information, an inherent conflict exists between the regulatory need for information and the individual's right of privacy. Specifically, how much latitude should be afforded to regulators in gathering information and overseeing private activities?

The United States Supreme Court has attempted to resolve the conflict by balancing the regulators' need to know against individual and corporate expectations of freedom from excessive government prying. An important consideration in resolving the conflict is the less intrusive nature of regulatory searches of businesses: most people simply do not have the same degree of concern about protecting places of business as they do about protecting the family dwelling. As a result, the standards for conducting regulatory investigations and searches are different from those that apply when ordinary police investigations and searches are conducted. For example, even though there may be no suspicion of a regulatory violation, an agency may conduct an investigation or search the premises of a business merely to be assured that no violation is occurring. Within industries subject to a history of extensive regulation, searches may be made even without a warrant. Still, though, as noted in Chapter 6 and earlier in this feature, the government is restricted in obtaining private information for regulatory purposes only.

The Ethics of Legal Avoidance

In the face of an agency investigation, a business may prevent or delay agency efforts by asserting legal challenges to the nature or manner of the investigation. There remains, however, the question of whether—in an ethical rather than legal sense—a business should challenge any such investigation. We would be expected to challenge an unreasonable search of our homes. We would owe it to our families to challenge such abuse. Arguably, it would be one's civic duty to challenge it to protect future abuse of other families in our communities as well. Regulatory investigations may be somehow different, though.

Most regulatory investigations have as their objective ensuring compliance with existing regulatory schemes or gathering information for future ones. Such schemes are designed to promote the public welfare. Though individuals may disagree about the effectiveness of the scheme or the individual motives of the regulators, society generally accepts the underlying purpose of the regulation—the promotion of public welfare. In such instances, businesses may have an ethical duty not to use legal means to avoid agency action. Indeed, they may have an ethical duty to aid in regulation by compliance, even though they may have a legal right to delay or avoid it.

ETHICS AND INTERNATIONAL LAW

Differences in the laws and customs of the various nations of the globe present unique ethical issues for firms engaged in international business transactions. Some of these issues were discussed in Chapter 8. Here, we look at a few other problems, focusing particularly on some ethical issues relating to international doctrines

FOCUS ON ETHICS

and to U.S. laws as they apply to international transactions.

Intellectual Property Rights

The licensing of technology allows U.S. owners of intellectual property (such as patents, trademarks, and copyrights) to benefit from sales of their products in other countries. Much intellectual property, however, is "pirated"—that is, unauthorized copies of the property (such as a software program) are made and sold. In 1994, to protect intellectual property rights on a worldwide basis, more than one hundred nations signed the international agreement on Trade-Related Aspects of Intellectual Property Rights (TRIPS), which is administered by the World Trade Organization. These nations pledged to pass and enforce laws protecting patents, copyrights, and trademarks (see the discussion of TRIPS in Chapter 13).

The attempted enforcement of intellectual property rights on a worldwide basis, however, raises some ethical concerns. For example, in a developing country, the welfare of small-business firms and consumers may be enhanced by the ability to purchase pirated (less expensive) copies of high-tech products. Although the owners of the pirated intellectual property lose out, they might have received nothing anyway, if no authorized copies (at higher prices) could have been sold in the less affluent nation. Therefore, if a developing country's government is somewhat slack in curbing the piracy of intellectual property, it may be because this laxity is in the developing country's interests.

Furthermore, laws governing intellectual property rights are necessarily somewhat arbitrary. For example, if the United States grants copyright protection for a longer period of time than Japan, does this mean that U.S. law is "right" and Japanese law is "wrong"?

Sovereign Immunity

Sometimes, the application of the doctrine of sovereign immunity may lead to seemingly inequitable results. The economy of the United States is primarily controlled by private interests, whereas the economies of many foreign countries, particularly developing nations, are extensively controlled by government. When a U.S. firm does business with a foreign firm in a developing country, therefore, the chances are that the U.S. firm will work closely with foreign government officials.

Should a dispute arise between the parties, the question then becomes whether the U.S. firm can bring a lawsuit against the foreign firm. If the foreign defendant raises the defense of sovereign immunity, alleging that it is a government-controlled operation, then it may be immune from liability. The ethical issue in these situations is whether it is fair that U.S. firms be left without any legal recourse when they suffer damages as a result of actions controlled by foreign governments.

The *Antares* Case. Consider, for example, the situation that arose in *Antares Aircraft, L.P. v. Federal Republic of Nigeria.*[1] In that case, Antares Aircraft, a New York limited partnership, had one asset—a DC-8-55 aircraft registered in Nigeria. Antares was required by the Nigerian government to leave the plane at the airport in Lagos, Nigeria, until certain fees (which had been incurred by a previous owner of the plane) were paid. Antares paid the $100,000 in fees, but the Nigerian government did not release the plane until five months later. In the meantime, the plane had been damaged by exposure to the elements.

Antares filed suit against the Nigerian government for the tort of conversion (this tort will be discussed in Chapter 12), alleging that the Nigerian government had wrongfully detained the plane. Antares argued that the Nigerian government's actions fell within the commercial activity exception to the Foreign Sovereign Immunities Act (FSIA) and therefore the Nigerian government was not immune from the jurisdiction of U.S. courts.

Although the court agreed with Antares that the fees collected by the Nigerian government were connected with a commercial activity, it found that the activity did not have a "direct effect" in the United States—in which case the commercial activity exception to the FSIA did not apply. The court therefore held that the Nigerian government was immune from liability. The court stated that "the detention of Antares's sole asset affected the financial well-being of the American partnership. However, the fact that an American individual or firm suffers some financial loss from a foreign tort cannot, standing alone, suffice to trigger the [commercial activity] exception."

1. 999 F.2d 33 (2d Cir. 1993).

FOCUS ON ETHICS

Different Interpretations of the FSIA. Because the FSIA does not define exactly what types of activities on the part of a foreign government fall under the commercial activity exception, the courts exercise considerable discretion in deciding such issues. Although the majority on the court hearing the *Antares* case concluded that the loss suffered by Antares was not sufficiently significant to constitute a "direct effect in the United States," other courts might have concluded differently. (See, for example, the court's decision in Case 8.2, which was presented in Chapter 8.)

Certainly, the dissenting judge in *Antares* believed that the detention of the plane did have a direct effect in the United States. The partners lived in the United States and lost money because of a foreign government's interference with their property. The dissent concluded that the partnership's loss should be sufficient to establish an exception to immunity under the FSIA.

DISCUSSION QUESTIONS

❶ You serve as chief executive officer of a large corporation. The state in which your company is headquartered has scheduled a statewide referendum on whether to allow casino gambling to be conducted within the state. Your company is in no way involved in gambling or in the sale of products used in the gaming industry, but you believe that evidence supports the inference that casino gambling, though potentially lucrative for those who operate the casinos, will hurt the state's economy. Some members of the board of directors have expressed similar concerns to you in casual conversation. Should you authorize the use of your company's resources to mount an opposition campaign to the proposal? Why or why not?

❷ What if, in the situation described in question 1, you knew of no conclusive evidence to support or refute the proposition that casino gambling will have an effect on the overall economy of the state? Suppose, though, that you have a strong moral conviction that gambling is wrong. How would that change the ethical dimensions of the question of whether you should authorize the use of corporate resources to oppose the gambling initiative?

❸ The United States banned the pesticide DDT, primarily because of its adverse effects on wildlife. In Asia, however, DDT has been a critical component of the mosquito control necessary to combat malaria. Should the ban in the United States prevent U.S. firms from manufacturing DDT and shipping it to an Asian country, where it could be used to save lives? Should the U.S. chemical manufacturer be required to produce the DDT in the same country that uses the chemical?

❹ What are some of the implications of the doctrine of sovereign immunity for businesspersons doing business internationally? Should the courts make more exceptions to this doctrine?

UNIT THREE

The Commercial Environment

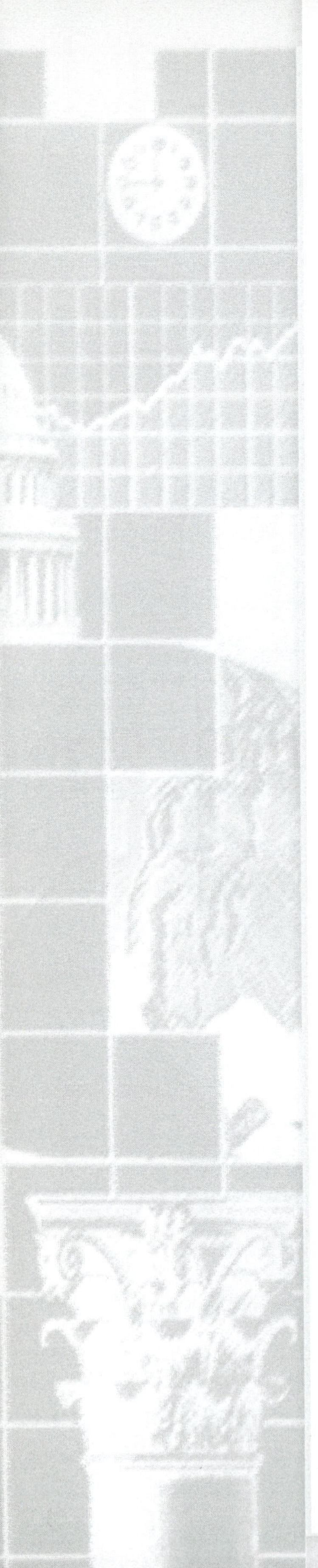

CHAPTER 9

Business Organizations

CONTENTS

CHAPTER OBJECTIVES

After reading this chapter, you should be able to answer the following questions:

1. What are the major traditional forms of business organization?
2. How do limited liability companies and limited liability partnerships fulfill needs not met by traditional forms of business organizations?
3. What are the major characteristics of other business organizational forms?
4. What law governs franchising relationships?
5. What are some of the methods used for raising financial capital?

A basic question facing anyone who wishes to start up a business is which of the several forms of business organization will be most appropriate for the business endeavor. In deciding this question, the **entrepreneur** (one who initiates and assumes the financial risk of a new enterprise) needs to consider a number of factors. Four important factors are (1) ease of creation, (2) the liability of the owners, (3) tax considerations, and (4) the need for capital. Keep these factors in mind as you read about the various business organizational forms available to entrepreneurs.

Entrepreneur • One who initiates and assumes the financial risks of a new enterprise and who undertakes to provide or control its management.

The three major traditional forms of business organization are the sole proprietorship, the partnership, and the corporation. Two relatively new forms of business enterprise—limited liability companies (LLCs) and limited liability partnerships (LLPs)—offer special advantages to businesspersons, particularly with respect to taxation and liability. There are also a number of other business forms, including joint ventures, syndicates, joint stock companies, business trusts, and cooperatives.

In this chapter, we look at all of these options for business organization. Additionally, we examine private franchises. Although a private franchise is not really a business organizational form, it is a popular way of doing business today.

MAJOR TRADITIONAL BUSINESS FORMS

Historically, entrepreneurs used the three major forms just mentioned—the sole proprietorship, the partnership, and the corporation—to structure their business enterprises.

Sole Proprietorships

The **sole proprietorship** is the simplest form of business. In this form, the owner is the business; thus, anyone who does business without creating a separate business organization has a sole proprietorship. Sole proprietorships constitute over two-thirds of all American businesses. They are also usually small enterprises—about 99 percent of the sole proprietorships existing in the

Sole proprietorship • The simplest form of business, in which the owner is the business; the owner reports business income on his or her personal income tax return and is legally responsible for all debts and obligations incurred by the business.

United States have revenues of less than $1 million per year. Sole proprietors can own and manage any type of business from an informal, home-office undertaking to a large restaurant or construction firm.

The Internet has expanded the ability of sole proprietorships to market their products nationwide without greatly increasing their costs. Does this mean that sole proprietorships should now, for some purposes, be considered the equivalent of corporations and other associational business forms? That was the question presented to the court in the following case.

CASE 9.1

United States District Court, Southern District of New York, 2000. 138 F.Supp.2d 449.

HSIN TEN ENTERPRISE USA, INC. v. CLARK ENTERPRISES

Clark Enterprises is a Kansas company with its only established offices in Salina, Kansas. Clark is a sole proprietorship owned and operated by Clifford Clark, who lives in Salina. Through representatives and trade shows, Clark sells "The Exercise Machine," an aerobic exercise device. The Exercise Machine can also be purchased through Clark's Web sites. Clark markets the Exercise Machine in direct competition with "The Chi Machine," another aerobic exercise product. The Chi Machine is manufactured and sold by Hsin Ten Enterprise USA, Inc., a corporation with its principal place of business in Farmingdale, New York. Hsin Ten also makes and sells other products under the "Chi" trademark, which it owns. One of Clark's Web sites uses the name "Chi Exerciser 2000" to promote Clark's Exercise Machine, and the term Chi *is frequently used on the Web sites to refer to the product. Hsin Ten filed a complaint in a federal district court in New York against Clark, asserting trademark infringement and other claims. Clark filed a motion to dismiss the trademark claim, in part on the ground that the court did not have venue under 28 U.S.C. Section 1391(c), the applicable statute.*[a] *That section provides, "For purposes of venue * * *, a defendant that is a corporation shall be deemed to reside in any judicial district in which it is subject to personal jurisdiction." Hsin Ten argued that although Clark is an unincorporated sole proprietorship with its principal offices in Kansas, it should be deemed a "corporation" for venue purposes.*

SCHEINDLIN, J.

On its face, Section 1391(c) applies only to corporations. However, the [United States] Supreme Court has held that it also applies to unincorporated associations. Since then, other courts have held that Section 1391(c) is applicable to partnerships and foreign trusts.

* * * [C]ourts have been unwilling to expand the definition of "corporation" beyond [these] general categories * * *. In fact, at least two other federal courts have declined to extend Section 1391(c) to include sole proprietorships such as Clark.

Hsin Ten argues that Clark is unlike other sole proprietorships because it does business in forty-seven states. Plaintiff [Hsin Ten] contends that Clark "resembles a national corporation in all respects except its choice of legal structure * * *. An entity such as Clark * * *, which obviously enjoys the benefits of doing business on a national scale, should not be granted preferential treatment in venue determinations simply because it chose not to incorporate." Plaintiff's argument is unconvincing.

---

a. As explained in Chapter 2, venue concerns the most appropriate location for a trial.

First, broad geographic distribution does not convert a small sole proprietorship into a corporation. With the advent of the Internet and e-commerce, a sole proprietorship can distribute its products throughout the United States with only a relatively minor investment of resources. Moreover, although Clark does business in forty-seven states, it still is not the type of unincorporated business entity that has been included in the definition of corporation. For instance, * * * [t]he defendant partnership in [one case] was one of only four snowmobile manufacturers in the world [and] had annual sales of over $240 million * * * . By contrast, between July 8, 1999 and October 17, 2000, Clark sold 1,855 Exercise Machines. Although this is impressive for a sole proprietorship, it is hardly remarkable. Nor does it convert Clark to the functional equivalent of a corporation.

Second, expanding the definition of "corporation" would greatly burden sole proprietors. Unlike corporations, partnerships and unincorporated associations— all of which are associations of two or more persons—a sole proprietorship is owned and controlled by a single person. *Venue is primarily a question of convenience for litigants and witnesses and venue provisions should be treated in practical terms.* In practical terms, expanding the definition of "corporation" to include sole proprietorships would be overly burdensome and inconvenient to sole proprietors, most of whom would be unable to afford the expense of litigating in distant states. [Emphasis added.]

The court agreed with Clark that Clark's enterprise should not be deemed a "corporation" for venue purposes. The court denied Clark's motion to dismiss other parts of Hsin Ten's complaint, however, and ordered the case to proceed to trial.

QUESTIONS

1. Who were the parties to this dispute, and how did their case come to this federal district court?
2. According to the court, should a sole proprietorship be deemed a "corporation" for venue purposes? Why or why not?
3. If federal district courts "heard" disputes online, what effect might that have had on the court's ruling and reasoning in this case?

Advantages of the Sole Proprietorship. A major advantage of the sole proprietorship is that the proprietor receives all of the profits (because he or she assumes all of the risk). In addition, it is often easier and less costly to start a sole proprietorship than to start any other kind of business, as few legal forms are involved. This type of business organization also provides more flexibility than does a partnership or a corporation. The sole proprietor is free to make all decisions concerning the business, including whom to hire, when to take a vacation, and what kind of business to pursue. A sole proprietor pays only personal income taxes on the business's profits, which are reported as personal income on the proprietor's personal income tax return. Sole proprietors are also allowed to establish tax-exempt retirement accounts in the form of Keogh plans.[1]

1. A *Keogh plan* is a retirement program designed for self-employed persons by which a certain percentage of their income can be contributed to the plan, and interest earnings will not be taxed until funds are withdrawn from the plan, usually after the age of fifty-nine and a half.

Disadvantages of the Sole Proprietorship. The major disadvantage of the sole proprietorship is that, as sole owner, the proprietor alone bears the burden of any losses or liabilities incurred by the business enterprise. In other words, the sole proprietor has unlimited liability, or legal responsibility, for all obligations that arise in doing business. This unlimited liability is a major factor to be considered in choosing a business form. The sole proprietorship also has the disadvantage of lacking continuity on the death of the proprietor. When the owner dies, so does the business—it is automatically dissolved. If the business is transferred to family members or other heirs, a new proprietorship is created.

Another disadvantage is that the proprietor's opportunity to raise capital is limited to personal funds and the funds of those who are willing to make loans to him or her. If the owner wishes to expand the business significantly, one way to raise more capital to finance the expansion is to join forces with another entrepreneur and establish a partnership or form a corporation.

Partnerships

Partnership • An agreement by two or more persons to carry on, as co-owners, a business for profit.

A **partnership** arises from an agreement, express or implied, between two or more persons to carry on a business for a profit. Partners are co-owners of a business and have joint control over its operation and the right to share in its profits. Generally, unless the partnership agreement provides otherwise, profits are to be shared equally and losses are to be shared in the same ratio as profits. No particular form of partnership agreement is necessary for the creation of a partnership, but for practical reasons, the agreement should be in writing. Basically, the partners may agree to almost any terms when establishing the partnership so long as they are not illegal or contrary to public policy.

Advantages of the Partnership. As with a sole proprietorship, one of the advantages of a partnership is that it can be organized fairly easily and inexpensively. Additionally, the partnership form of business offers important tax advantages. The partnership itself files only an informational tax return with the Internal Revenue Service. In other words, the firm itself pays no taxes. A partner's profit from the partnership (whether distributed or not) is taxed as individual income to the individual partner.

A partnership may also allow for greater capital contributions to the business than is possible in a sole proprietorship. Two or more persons can invest in the business, and lenders may be more willing to make loans to a partnership than they would be to a sole proprietorship.

Disadvantages of the Partnership. The main disadvantage of the partnership form of business is that the partners are subject to personal liability for partnership obligations. If the partnership cannot pay its debts, the personal assets of the partners are subject to creditors' claims. This disadvantage of the partnership is one of the major reasons that many entrepreneurs choose to form corporations. As will be discussed later in this chapter, in the corporate form of business the owners' liability is limited to the amount of their investments in the business. The limited liability companies and limited liability partnerships also discussed later in this chapter are additional business forms that allow business owners to limit their personal liability for business debts and obligations.

Limited Partnerships

A special form of partnership is the limited partnership. Limited partnerships consist of at least one **general partner** and one or more **limited partners.** A general partner assumes management responsibility for the partnership and so has full responsibility for the partnership and for all debts of the partnership. A limited partner contributes cash or other property and owns an interest in the firm but does not undertake any management duties and is not personally liable for partnership debts beyond the amount of his or her investment.

General partner • In a limited partnership, a partner who assumes responsibility for the management of the partnership and liability for all partnership debts.

Limited partner • In a limited partnership, a partner who contributes capital to the partnership but has no right to participate in the management and operation of the business. The limited partner assumes no liability for partnership debts beyond the capital contributed.

One of the major benefits of becoming a limited partner is this limitation on liability, with respect to both lawsuits brought against the partnership and the amount of money placed at risk. A limited partner can forfeit limited liability by taking part in the management of the business.

Compared with the informal, private, and voluntary agreement that usually suffices for a general partnership, the formation of a limited partnership is a public and formal proceeding that must follow statutory requirements. The partners must sign a **certificate of limited partnership.** The certificate must be filed with the designated state official, usually the secretary of state. The certificate is open to public inspection.

Certificate of limited partnership • The basic document filed with a designated state official by which a limited partnership is formed.

Limited Liability Limited Partnerships

A **limited liability limited partnership (LLLP)** is a type of limited partnership in which the liability of all partners is limited to the amount of their investments in the firm. The difference between a limited partnership and an LLLP is that the liability of a general partner in an LLLP is the same as the liability of a limited partner.

Limited liability limited partnership (LLLP) • A type of limited partnership in which the liability of all partners is limited to the amount of their investments in the firm. The difference between a limited partnership and an LLLP is that the liability of the general partner in an LLLP is the same as the liability of the limited partner.

A few states provide expressly for LLLPs.[2] In states that do not provide for LLLPs but do allow for limited partnerships and limited liability partnerships, a limited partnership should probably still be able to register with the state as an LLLP.

Corporations

A third and widely used business organizational form is the **corporation.** The corporation, like the limited partnership, is a creature of statute. The corporation's existence as a legal entity generally depends on state law. Today, it is possible to incorporate—and receive a **certificate of incorporation**—via online incorporation services.

Corporation • A legal entity formed in compliance with statutory requirements. The entity is distinct from its shareholders-owners.

Certificate of incorporation • The primary document that evidences corporate existence (referred to as articles of incorporation in some states).

Responsibility for the overall management of the corporation is entrusted to a board of directors, which is elected by the shareholders (those who have purchased ownership shares in the business). The board of directors hires corporate officers and other employees to run the daily business operations of the corporation. Corporate **bylaws** include the rules of management adopted and applied by the corporation.

Bylaws • A set of governing rules adopted by a corporation or other association.

One of the key advantages of the corporation is that the liability of its owners (shareholders) is limited to their investments. The shareholders usually are

2. See, for example, Colorado Revised Statutes Annotated Section 7-62-109. Other states that provide expressly for limited liability limited partnerships include Delaware, Florida, Missouri, Pennsylvania, Texas, and Virginia.

not personally liable for the obligations of the corporation. Another advantage is that a corporation can raise capital by selling shares of corporate stock to investors. A key disadvantage of the corporate form is that any distributed corporate income is taxed twice. The corporate entity pays taxes on the firm's income, and when income is distributed to shareholders, the shareholders again pay taxes on that income.

More than 50 percent of the publicly traded companies in the United States are incorporated under Delaware law.[3] Consequently, decisions of the Delaware courts on questions of corporate law have a wide impact. In the following case, a board increased the number of its members to diminish the effect that subsequently elected directors would have on the board's decisions. This may have been permissible according to the firm's bylaws, but was it legal under Delaware law?

3. *Publicly traded* means that the stock of a company can be bought and sold among members of the general public. In contrast, the shares of a *closely held*, or *close, corporation* are often owned by only a few individuals whose right to buy or sell those shares may be restricted, at least initially, to each other.

CASE 9.2

Delaware Supreme Court, 2003. 813 A.2d 1118.

MM COMPANIES, INC. v. LIQUID AUDIO, INC.

MM Companies, Inc., a Delaware corporation with its principal place of business in New York City, owned 7 percent of the stock of Liquid Audio, Inc., which provides software and services for the delivery of music over the Internet. In October 2001, MM sent a letter to Liquid Audio's board of directors offering to buy all of the company's stock for about $3 per share. The board rejected the offer. Liquid Audio's bylaws provide for a board of five directors divided into three classes. One class is elected each year. The next election, at which two directors would be chosen, was set for September 2002. By mid-August, it appeared that MM's nominees, Seymour Holtzman and James Mitarotonda, would win the election. The board amended the bylaws to increase the number of directors to seven and appointed Judith Frank and James Somes to fill the new positions. In September, MM's nominees were elected to the board, but their influence was diminished because there were now seven directors. MM filed a suit in a Delaware state court against Liquid Audio and others, challenging the board's actions. The court ruled in favor of the defendants. MM appealed to the Delaware Supreme Court.

HOLLAND, J.

The most fundamental principles of corporate governance are a function of the allocation of power within a corporation between its stockholders and its board of directors. The stockholders' power is the right to vote on specific matters, in particular, in an election of directors. The power of managing the corporate enterprise is vested in the shareholders' duly elected board representatives. Accordingly, while these fundamental tenets of Delaware corporate law provide for a separation of control and ownership, the stockholder franchise has been characterized as the ideological "underpinning" upon which the legitimacy of the director's managerial power rests. [Emphasis added.]

Maintaining a proper balance in the allocation of power between the stockholders' right to elect directors and the board of directors' right to manage the corporation is dependent upon the stockholders' unimpeded right to vote effectively in an election of directors. This Court has repeatedly stated that, *if the stockholders are not satisfied with the management or actions of their elected representatives on the board of directors, the power of corporate democracy is available to the stockholders to replace the incumbent directors when they stand for re-election.* * * * The Courts of this State will not allow the wrongful subversion of corporate democracy by manipulation of the corporate machinery or by machinations under the cloak of Delaware law. Accordingly, careful judicial scrutiny will be given a situation in which the right to vote for the election of successor directors has been *effectively frustrated* and denied. [Emphasis added.]

[Delaware's courts] have remained assiduous [diligent, attentive] in carefully reviewing any board actions designed to interfere with or impede the effective exercise of corporate democracy by shareholders, especially in an election of directors.

* * * *

When the *primary purpose* of a board of directors' [action] is to interfere with or impede the effective exercise of the shareholder franchise in a contested election for directors, the board must first demonstrate a compelling justification for such action as a condition precedent to any judicial consideration of reasonableness and proportionality. As this case illustrates, such defensive actions by a board need not actually prevent the shareholders from attaining any success in seating one or more nominees in a contested election for directors and the election contest need not involve a challenge for outright control of the board of directors. * * * [T]he defensive actions of the board only need to be taken for the primary purpose of interfering with or impeding the effectiveness of the stockholder vote in a contested election for directors.

* * * *

The record reflects that the primary purpose of the [directors'] action was to interfere with and impede the effective exercise of the stockholder franchise in a contested election for directors. The [lower court] concluded that the [directors] amended the bylaws to provide for a board of seven and appointed two additional members of the board for the primary purpose of diminishing the influence of MM's two nominees on a five-member board by eliminating either the possibility of a deadlock on the board or of MM controlling the board, if one or two [directors] resigned from the board. *That defensive action by the [directors] compromised the essential role of corporate democracy in maintaining the proper allocation of power between the shareholders and the board, because that action was taken in the context of a contested election for successor directors.* Since the * * * defendants did not demonstrate a compelling justification for that defensive action, the bylaw amendment that expanded the size of the Liquid Audio board, and permitted the appointment of two new members on the eve of a contested election, should have been invalidated by the [lower court]. [Emphasis added.]

One of the most venerable precepts of Delaware's common law corporate jurisprudence is the principle that *inequitable action does not become permissible simply because it is legally possible.* At issue in this case is not the validity generally of either a bylaw that permits a board of directors to expand the size of its membership or a board's power to appoint successor members to fill board vacancies. In this case, however, *the incumbent board timed its utilization of these otherwise valid powers to expand the size and composition of the Liquid Audio board for the primary purpose of impeding and interfering with the efforts of the stockholders' power to effectively exercise their voting rights in a contested election for directors.* * * * [T]hese are inequitable purposes, contrary to established principles of corporate democracy * * * and may not be permitted to stand. [Emphasis added.]

The Delaware Supreme Court reversed the judgment of the lower court and remanded the case for further proceedings. The state supreme court concluded that the board's amending the bylaws to increase the number of directors and filling the new positions with appointments was invalid, because the board acted primarily to impede the shareholders' right to vote in an impending election for successor directors.

QUESTIONS

1. Who were the parties in this case, and what was their dispute?
2. On what basis did the Delaware Supreme Court conclude that it was invalid for Liquid Audio's board to amend the corporate bylaws to increase the number of directors and fill the new positions with appointments?
3. How could MM's newly elected nominees, or any two directors, affect the decisions of a five-member board?

S Corporations

S corporation • A corporation that has met certain requirements as set out by the Internal Revenue Code and thus qualifies for special income tax treatment. Essentially, an S corporation is taxed the same as a partnership, but its owners enjoy the privilege of limited liability.

A corporation that meets the qualifying requirements specified in Subchapter S of the Internal Revenue Code can operate as an **S corporation.** If a corporation has S corporation status, it can avoid the imposition of income taxes at the corporate level while retaining many of the advantages of a corporation, particularly limited liability.

Qualification Requirements for S Corporations. Among the numerous requirements for S corporation status, the following are the most important:

1. The corporation must be a domestic corporation.
2. The corporation must not be a member of an affiliated group of corporations.
3. The shareholders of the corporation must be individuals, estates, or certain trusts. Nonqualifying trusts and partnerships cannot be shareholders. Corporations can be shareholders under certain circumstances.
4. The corporation must have seventy-five or fewer shareholders.
5. The corporation must have only one class of stock, although not all shareholders need have the same voting rights.
6. No shareholder of the corporation may be a nonresident alien.

Benefits of S Corporations. At times, it is beneficial for a regular corporation to elect S corporation status. Benefits include the following:

1. When the corporation has losses, the S election allows the shareholders to use the losses to offset other income.
2. When the shareholder's tax bracket is lower than the tax bracket for regular corporations, the S election causes the corporation's entire income to be taxed in the shareholder's bracket (because it is taxed as personal income), whether or not it is distributed. This is particularly attractive

when the corporation wants to accumulate earnings for some future business purpose.

Because of these tax benefits, many *close corporations* (corporations in which stockholders are limited to a small group of persons, usually family members) opted for S corporation status in the past. Today, however, the S corporation is losing some of its significance—because the limited liability company and the limited liability partnership (discussed in the next sections) offer similar advantages plus additional benefits, including increased flexibility in forming and operating a business.

LIMITED LIABILITY COMPANIES

The most common forms of business organization selected by two or more persons entering into business together are the partnership and the corporation. As explained previously, each form has distinct advantages and disadvantages. For partnerships, the advantage is that partnership income is taxed only once (all income is "passed through" the partnership entity to the partners themselves, who are taxed only as individuals); the disadvantage is the personal liability of the partners. For corporations, the advantage is the limited liability of shareholders; the disadvantage is the double taxation of corporate income. For many entrepreneurs and investors, the ideal business form would combine the tax advantages of the partnership form of business with the limited liability of the corporate enterprise.

A relatively new form of business organization called the **limited liability company (LLC)** is a hybrid form of business enterprise that meets these needs by offering the limited liability of the corporation and the tax advantages of a partnership. LLCs are becoming an increasingly popular organizational form among businesspersons.

Limited liability company (LLC) • A hybrid form of business enterprise that offers the limited liability of the corporation but the tax advantages of a partnership.

Internal Revenue Service (IRS) rules provide that any unincorporated business will automatically be taxed as a partnership unless it indicates otherwise on the tax form. The exceptions involve publicly traded firms, companies formed under a state incorporation statute, and certain foreign-owned enterprises. If a business chooses to be taxed as a corporation, it can indicate this choice by checking a box on the IRS form.

Part of the impetus behind creating LLCs in this country is that foreign investors are allowed to become LLC members. Generally, in an era increasingly characterized by global business efforts and investments, the LLC offers U.S. firms and potential investors from other countries flexibility and opportunities greater than those available through partnerships or corporations.

LLC Formation

Like the corporation, an LLC must be formed and operated in compliance with state law. About one-fourth of the states specifically require LLCs to have at least two owners, called **members.** In the rest of the states, although some LLC statutes are silent on this issue, one-member LLCs are usually permitted.

Member • The term used to designate a person who has an ownership interest in a limited liability company.

To form an LLC, **articles of organization** must be filed with a central state agency—usually the secretary of state's office. Typically, the articles are required to set forth such information as the name of the business, its principal address, the name and address of a registered agent, the names of the owners, and

Articles of organization • The document filed with a designated state official by which a limited liability company is formed.

information on how the LLC will be managed. The business's name must include the words "Limited Liability Company" or the initials "LLC." In addition to filing the articles of organization, a few states require that a notice of the intention to form an LLC be published in a local newspaper.

Note that although the LLC, like the corporation, is a legal entity apart from its owners, for federal jurisdictional purposes an LLC is treated differently than a corporation. The federal jurisdiction statute provides that a corporation is deemed to be a citizen of the state in which it is incorporated and in which it maintains its principal place of business. The statute does not mention the citizenship of partnerships and other unincorporated associations, but courts have tended to regard these entities as citizens of every state in which their members are citizens.

The following case illustrates some of the problems that can arise during the first years of a newly formed enterprise, including an LLC.

CASE 9.3

United States District Court, District of Maine, 2000. __ F.Supp.2d __.

SKYWIZARD.COM, LLC v. COMPUTER PERSONALITIES SYSTEMS, INC.

Gary Cubeta and Gail Ejdys founded Skywizard.com, LLC, as an Internet Service Provider (ISP). *In May 1999, they entered into an agreement with Computer Personalities Systems, Inc. (CPSI), a retailer of computer hardware and software whose principal, George Cappell, markets products through infomercials on cable television channels. CPSI agreed, among other things, that beginning September 1, it would run, one weekend per month, a "special promotion," according to which a customer who bought a specified computer would receive a year's Internet service through Skywizard.com to start whenever the customer wanted. For each computer sold under this promotion, CPSI agreed to pay Skywizard.com $79. Despite this fee, the ISP incurred a loss of about $44 per year for each "special promotion" subscriber. By March 2000, most of the ISP's subscribers were people who had bought computers through CPSI, including about a third of those who bought the "special promotion" computers. CPSI had failed to run the promotion on September 1, 1999, however, and for this reason, among others, Skywizard.com filed a suit in a federal district court against CPSI, alleging breach of contract. Skywizard.com estimated that 1,500 units would have been shipped if the September promotion had run and one-third of the buyers would have subscribed to Skywizard.com, representing lost profits of $67,500.*

COHEN, J.

Regardless of the number of computers that CPSI may have shipped to customers had a September 1999 Special Promotion aired, the evidence is insufficient to substantiate the amount of Skywizard's damages based on loss of the $79 fee with reasonable probability. As counsel for the defendant pointed out at trial, were all of CPSI's Special Promotion customers to take advantage of the offer of one year's free Internet service (as they theoretically could), the $79 per customer fee would be more than offset by the cost to Skywizard to service all of the new subscribers. Skywizard adduced evidence that as of March 2000 only one-third of CPSI's Special Promotion customers were Skywizard subscribers. If I could conclude with confidence that, had the September 1999 Special Promotion aired, only one-third of the resultant customers would have become Skywizard subscribers, Skywizard would have demonstrated that, by avoiding the cost of servicing the remaining two-thirds of the Special Promotion customers, it lost monies that would have been generated by the $79 fee. However, in view of the newness of the Skywizard enterprise, the fact that Skywizard imposed no deadline within which customers were obliged to accept the offer of one year's free Internet service and the fact that Skywizard's evidence at most amounted to a snapshot of its customer base as of one point in time, I am constrained to conclude that *the record is barren of sufficient historic company data from which a reliable projection of the composition of the customer base can be made.* In view of the clear breach of contract, an award of nominal damages [a small amount of damages to establish that the defendant acted wrongfully] nonetheless is appropriate. [Emphasis added.]

* * * In light of the foregoing, judgment shall enter in favor of Skywizard and against CPSI in the amount of $100.00.

The court held that CPSI breached the contract to run the September promotion, but that damages could not be determined because the life of Skywizard.com had been too short. For these reasons, the court entered a judgment in favor of Skywizard.com for $100 in nominal damages.

QUESTIONS

1. What were the plaintiff's chief complaint and the defendant's principal defense in this case?
2. Did the court rule that either party was entitled to damages for the other party's conduct? Why or why not?
3. How long should a company's "track record" be to enable it to recover lost profits for a breach of contract?

Advantages and Disadvantages of LLCs

A key advantage of the LLC is that the liability of members is limited to the amount of their investments. Another significant advantage is that an LLC with two or more members can choose whether to be taxed as a partnership or a corporation. LLCs that want to distribute profits to the members may prefer to be taxed as partnerships, to avoid the "double taxation" characteristic of the corporate entity. Remember that in the corporate form of business, the corporation as an entity pays income taxes on its profits, and the shareholders pay personal income taxes on profits distributed as dividends. Unless the LLC indicates that it wishes to be taxed as a corporation, it is automatically taxed as a partnership by the IRS. This means that the LLC as an entity pays no taxes; rather, as in a partnership, profits are "passed through" the LLC and taxes are paid personally by the members.

If LLC members want to reinvest profits in the business, however, rather than distribute the profits to members, they may prefer to be taxed as a corporation if corporate income tax rates are lower than personal tax rates. Part of the attractiveness of the LLC for businesspersons is this flexibility with respect to taxation options. For federal income tax purposes, one-member LLCs are automatically taxed as sole proprietorships unless they indicate that they wish to be taxed as corporations. With respect to state taxes, most states follow the IRS rules. Still another advantage of the LLC for businesspersons is the flexibility it offers in terms of business operations and management, as will be discussed shortly.

The disadvantages of the LLC are relatively few. Some of the initial drawbacks with respect to uncertainties over how LLCs would be taxed no longer exist. The only remaining disadvantage of the LLC is that state statutes covering LLCs are not uniform. In an attempt to promote some uniformity among the states with respect to LLC statutes, the National Conference of Commissioners on Uniform State Laws drafted a Uniform Limited Liability Company Act for submission to the states to consider for adoption. Until all of the states have adopted the uniform law, however, an LLC in one state will have to check the rules in the other states in which the firm does business to ensure that it retains its limited liability.

The LLC Operating Agreement

Operating agreement • In a limited liability company, an agreement in which the members set forth the details of how the business will be managed and operated.

In an LLC, the members themselves can decide how to operate the various aspects of the business by forming an **operating agreement.** Operating agreements typically contain provisions relating to management, how profits will be divided, the transfer of membership interests, whether the LLC will be dissolved on the death or departure of a member, and other important issues.

Operating agreements need not be in writing, and indeed they need not even be formed for an LLC to exist. Generally, though, LLC members should protect their interests by forming a written operating agreement.[4] As with any business arrangement, disputes may arise over a number of different issues. If there is no agreement covering the topic being disputed, such as how profits will be divided, the state LLC statute will govern the outcome. For example, most LLC statutes provide that if the members have not specified how profits will be divided among the members, they will be divided equally.

Generally, with respect to issues not covered by an operating agreement or an LLC statute, the principles of partnership law are applied. At issue in the following case was whether partnership law should pertain to a dispute between LLC members as to how business receipts were to be divided on the firm's dissolution.

4. Some experts suggest that even a one-member LLC should have an operating agreement. An operating agreement provides evidence that the LLC is a separate entity and thus strengthens the member-owner's protection against being held personally liable for a business obligation.

CASE 9.4

Court of Appeals of Minnesota, 1998. 581 N.W.2d 359. **http://www.lawlibrary.state.mn.us/archive/index.html**[a]

HURWITZ v. PADDEN

Thomas Hurwitz and Michael Padden formed a two-person law firm as a partnership without a written agreement. They shared all proceeds on a fifty-fifty basis and reported all income as partnership income. Less than eighteen months later, Hurwitz filed articles of organization with the state of Minnesota to establish the firm as an LLC. More than three years later, Padden told Hurwitz that he wanted to dissolve their professional relationship. They resolved all business issues between them except for a

a. This page includes a partial list of Minnesota Court of Appeals opinions available in the Minnesota State Law Library online database. In the "Court of Appeals Opinions" box, click on "Index by Case Name (First Party)." The last name of the parties in the cases on this page begins with the letter G, H, or I. Scroll down the list to the *Hurwitz* name and click on the link to read the case.

division of fees from several of the firm's cases. Hurwitz filed a suit in a Minnesota state court against Padden, seeking, among other things, a distribution of the fees on a fifty-fifty basis. The court applied the principles of partnership law, ruled that the fees should be divided equally, and entered a judgment in favor of Hurwitz for $101,750. Padden appealed, arguing in part that these principles of partnership law should not apply to an LLC.

SHORT, J.

[T]he Minnesota Limited Liability Company Act specifically incorporates the definition and use of the term "dissolution" from the Uniform Partnership Act [UPA]. Under both statutes, the entity is not terminated upon dissolution, but continues until all business issues are resolved. Thus, the UPA provides guidance when examining the end stages of either entity's life. * * *

It is undisputed: (1) the firm had no written or oral agreement regarding the division of * * * fees upon dissolution; (2) the firm existed for approximately five-and-a-half years before Padden requested dissolution; (3) a little over five months elapsed between the date of dissolution and the date the parties [filed a suit] to settle the firm's remaining issues; (4) the firm's [disputed] fee cases were acquired before the firm's dissolution; (5) prior to its dissolution, the firm divided fees equally between the parties; and (6) at the time the parties filed suit, the firm was in a winding-up phase. Under these circumstances, partnership principles * * * govern the division of fees obtained from pre-dissolution * * * files. Thus, the * * * fees obtained from pre-dissolution case files must be divided equally between the parties, which is consistent with the pre-dissolution method of allocation.

The state intermediate appellate court affirmed the decision of the lower court. The state intermediate appellate court concluded that the disputed fees should be divided equally, just as the receipts had been divided before the dissolution.

QUESTIONS

1. Do partnership principles apply to the dissolution, winding up, and distribution of business receipts of an LLC, under the ruling of the state intermediate appellate court in this case?
2. What facts influenced the court's application of the law to the circumstances in this case?
3. Should the principles of partnership law apply to other forms of business entities?

LLC Management

Basically, there are two options with respect to the management of an LLC. The members may decide in their operating agreement to be either a "member-managed" or a "manager-managed" LLC.

In a *member-managed* LLC, all of the members participate in management. In a *manager-managed* LLC, the members designate a group of persons to manage the firm. The management group may consist of only members, both members and nonmembers, or only nonmembers. Most LLC statutes provide that unless the members agree otherwise, all members of the LLC will participate in management.

The members of an LLC can also set forth in their operating agreement provisions governing decision-making procedures. For example, the agreement can indicate what procedures are to be followed for choosing or removing managers, an issue on which most LLC statutes are silent. The members are also free to include in the agreement provisions designating when and for what purposes formal members' meetings will be held. In contrast to state laws governing corporations, LLC statutes in most states have no provisions regarding members' meetings. Members may also specify in their agreement how voting rights will be apportioned. If they do not, LLC statutes in most states provide that voting rights are apportioned according to the capital contributions made by each member. Some states provide that, in the absence of an agreement to the contrary, each member has one vote.

Limited Liability Partnerships

Limited liability partnership (LLP) • A form of partnership that allows professionals to enjoy the tax benefits of a partnership while limiting their personal liability for the malpractice of other partners.

The **limited liability partnership (LLP)** is similar to the LLC. The difference between an LLP and an LLC is that the LLP is designed more for professionals who normally do business as partners in a partnership. The major advantage of the LLP is that it allows a partnership to continue as a pass-through entity for tax purposes but limits the personal liability of the partners.

The first state to enact an LLP statute was Texas, in 1991. Other states quickly followed suit, and by 1997, virtually all of the states had enacted LLP statutes. Like LLCs, LLPs must be formed and operated in compliance with state statutes. The appropriate form must be filed with a central state agency, usually the secretary of state's office, and the business's name must include either "Limited Liability Partnership" or "LLP."

In most states, it is relatively easy to convert a traditional partnership into an LLP because the firm's basic organizational structure remains the same. Additionally, all of the statutory and common law rules governing partnerships still apply (apart from those modified by the LLP statute). Normally, LLP statutes are simply amendments to a state's already existing partnership law.

The LLP is especially attractive for two categories of businesses: professional services and family businesses. Professional service companies include law firms and accounting firms. Family limited liability partnerships are basically business organizations in which all of the partners are related. Generally, the LLP allows professionals to avoid personal liability for the malpractice of other partners. Although LLP statutes vary from state to state, generally each state statute limits in some way the liability of partners. For example, Delaware law protects each innocent partner from the "debts and obligations of the partnership arising from negligence, wrongful acts, or misconduct." In North Carolina, Texas, and Washington, D.C., the statutes protect innocent partners from obligations arising from "errors, omissions, negligence, incompetence, or malfeasance." A partner who commits a wrongful act, such as negligence, however, is still liable for the results of the act. Also liable is the partner who supervises the party who commits a wrongful act.

Major Business Forms Compared

When deciding which form of business organization would be most appropriate, businesspersons normally take several factors into consideration. These factors include ease of creation, the liability of the owners, tax ramifications, and the need for capital. Each major form of business organization offers distinct advantages and disadvantages with respect to these and other factors.

Exhibit 9–1 on pages 300 and 301 summarizes the essential advantages and disadvantages of each of the major forms of business organization.

Special Business Forms

Besides the major business forms already discussed, several other forms can be used to organize a business. For the most part, these other business forms are hybrid organizations—that is, they have characteristics similar to those of partnerships or corporations, or combine features of both.

Joint Venture

A **joint venture,** which is sometimes referred to as a joint adventure, is a relationship in which two or more persons or business entities combine their efforts or their property for a single transaction or project or for a related series of transactions or projects. Joint ventures are taxed like partnerships, and unless otherwise agreed, joint venturers share profits and losses equally. For example, when several contractors combine their resources to build and sell houses in a single development, their relationship is a joint venture.

Joint venture • A joint undertaking of a specific commercial enterprise by an association of persons. A joint venture is normally not a legal entity and is treated like a partnership for federal income tax purposes.

Joint ventures range in size from very small activities to huge, multimillion-dollar projects undertaken by some of the world's biggest corporations. Large organizations often investigate new markets or new ideas by forming joint ventures with other enterprises. For instance, General Motors Corporation and Volvo Truck Corporation were involved in a joint venture—Volvo GM—to manufacture heavy-duty trucks and market them in the United States.

A joint venture resembles a partnership. The essential difference is that a joint venture typically involves the pursuit of a single project or series of transactions, and a partnership usually concerns an ongoing business. Of course, a partnership may be created to conduct a single transaction. For this reason, most courts apply the same principles to joint ventures as they apply to partnerships.

Syndicate

A group of individuals getting together to finance a particular project, such as the building of a shopping center or the purchase of a professional basketball franchise, is called a **syndicate,** or an *investment group.* The form of such groups varies considerably. A syndicate may exist as a corporation or as a general or limited partnership. In some cases, the members merely own property jointly and have no legally recognized business arrangement.

Syndicate • An investment group of persons or firms brought together for the purpose of financing a project that they would not or could not undertake independently.

Joint Stock Company

A **joint stock company** is a true hybrid of a partnership and a corporation. It has many characteristics of a corporation in that (1) its ownership is represented by transferable shares of stock, (2) it is usually managed by directors

Joint stock company • A hybrid form of business organization that combines characteristics of a corporation and a partnership. Usually, the joint stock company is regarded as a partnership for tax and other legally related purposes.

EXHIBIT 9–1 • MAJOR FORMS OF BUSINESS COMPARED

CHARACTERISTIC	SOLE PROPRIETORSHIP	PARTNERSHIP	CORPORATION
Method of Creation	Created at will by owner.	Created by agreement of the parties.	Charter issued by state—created by statutory authorization.
Legal Position	Not a separate entity; owner is the business.	Not a separate legal entity in many states.	Always a legal entity separate and distinct from its owners—a legal fiction for the purposes of owning property and being a party to litigation.
Liability	Unlimited liability.	Unlimited liability.	Limited liability of shareholders—shareholders are not liable for the debts of the corporation.
Duration	Determined by owner; automatically dissolved on owner's death.	Terminated by agreement of the partners, by the death of one or more of the partners, by withdrawal of a partner, by bankruptcy, and so on.	Can have perpetual existence.
Transferability of Interest	Interest can be transferred, but individual's proprietorship then ends.	Although partnership interest can be assigned, assignee does not have full rights of a partner.	Shares of stock can be transferred.
Management	Completely at owner's discretion.	Each general partner has a direct and equal voice in management unless expressly agreed otherwise in the partnership agreement.	Shareholders elect directors, who set policy and appoint officers.
Taxation	Owner pays personal taxes on business income.	Each partner pays pro rata share of income taxes on net profits, whether or not they are distributed.	Double taxation—corporation pays income tax on net profits, with no deduction for dividends, and shareholders pay income tax on disbursed dividends they receive.
Organizational Fees, Annual License Fees, and Annual Reports	None.	None.	All required.
Transaction of Business in Other States	Generally, no limitation.	Generally, no limitation.[a]	Normally must qualify to do business and obtain certificate of authority.

a. A few states have enacted statutes requiring that foreign (out-of-state) partnerships qualify to do business there.

EXHIBIT 9–1 • MAJOR FORMS OF BUSINESS COMPARED (CONTINUED)

CHARACTERISTIC	LIMITED PARTNERSHIP	LIMITED LIABILITY COMPANY	LIMITED LIABILITY PARTNERSHIP
Method of Creation	Created by agreement to carry on a business for a profit. Must have at least one general partner and one limited partner. Certificate of limited partnership is filed. Charter must be issued by the state.	Created by an agreement of the owner-members of the company. Articles of organization are filed. Charter must be issued by the state.	Created by agreement of the partners. Certificate of limited liability partnership is filed. Charter must be issued by the state.
Legal Position	Treated as a legal entity.	Treated as a legal entity.	Generally, treated same as a general partnership.
Liability	Unlimited liability of all general partners; limited partners are liable only to the extent of capital contributions.	Member-owners' liability is limited to the amount of their capital contributions or investments.	Varies from state to state but usually limits liability of a partner for certain acts committed by other partners.
Duration	By agreement in certificate, or by termination of the last general partner (withdrawal, death, and so on) or last limited partner.	Unless a single-member LLC, can have perpetual existence (same as a corporation).	Terminated by agreement of partners, by death or withdrawal of a partner, or by law (such as bankruptcy).
Transferability of Interest	Interest can be assigned (as in a general partnership), but if assignee becomes a member with consent of other partners, certificate must be amended.	Member interests are freely transferable.	Interest can be assigned, as in a general partnership.
Management	General partners have equal voice or by agreement. Limited partners may not retain limited liability if they actively participate in management.	Member-owners can fully participate in management, or member-owners can select managers to manage the firm on behalf of the members.	Same as a general partnership.
Taxation	Generally taxed as a partnership.	LLC is not taxed, and members are taxed personally on profits "passed through" the LLC.	Same as a general partnership.
Organizational Fees, Annual License Fees, and Annual Reports	Organizational fee required; usually not others.	Organizational fee required; others vary with states.	Organizational fee required (such as a set amount per partner); usually not others.
Transaction of Business in Other States	Generally, no limitation.	Generally, no limitation but may vary depending on state.	Generally, no limitation, but state laws vary as to formation and limitation of liability.

and officers of the company or association, and (3) it can have a perpetual existence. Most of its other features, however, are more characteristic of a partnership, and it is usually treated like a partnership. As with a partnership, it is formed by agreement (not statute), property is usually held in the names of the members, shareholders have personal liability, and generally the company is not treated as a legal entity for purposes of a lawsuit. In a joint stock company, however, shareholders are not considered to be agents of each other, as would be the case if the company were a true partnership.

Business Trust

Business trust • A voluntary form of business organization in which investors (trust beneficiaries) transfer cash or property to trustees in exchange for trust certificates that represent their investment shares. Management of the business and trust property is handled by the trustees for the use and benefit of the investors. The certificate holders have limited liability and share in the trust's profits.

A **business trust** is created by a written trust agreement that sets forth the interests of the beneficiaries (investors) and the obligations and powers of the trustees. With a business trust, legal ownership and management of the property of the business stay with one or more of the trustees, and the profits are distributed to the beneficiaries.

The business trust was started in Massachusetts in an attempt to obtain the limited liability advantage of corporate status while avoiding certain restrictions on a corporation's ownership and development of real property. The business trust resembles a corporation in many respects. Beneficiaries of the trust, for example, are not personally responsible for the trust's debts or obligations. In fact, in a number of states, business trusts must pay corporate taxes.

Cooperative

Cooperative • An association that is organized to provide an economic service to its members (or shareholders). An incorporated cooperative is subject to state laws governing nonprofit corporations.

A **cooperative** is an association, either incorporated or not, that is organized to provide an economic service, without profit, to its members (or shareholders). An incorporated cooperative is subject to state laws governing nonprofit corporations. It makes distributions of dividends, or profits, to its owners on the basis of their transactions with the cooperative rather than on the basis of the amount of capital they contribute. Cooperatives that are unincorporated are often treated like partnerships. The members have joint liability for the cooperative's acts.

The cooperative form of business is generally adopted by groups of individuals who wish to pool their resources to gain some advantage in the marketplace. Consumer purchasing co-ops are formed to obtain lower prices through quantity discounts. Seller marketing co-ops are formed to control the market and thereby obtain higher sales prices from consumers. Often, because of their special status, cooperatives are exempt from certain federal laws, such as antitrust laws (laws prohibiting anticompetitive practices—see Chapter 17).

Private Franchises

Franchise • Any arrangement in which the owner of a trademark, trade name, or copyright licenses another to use that trademark, trade name, or copyright, under specified conditions or limitations, in the selling of goods and services.

Franchisee • One receiving a license to use another's (the franchisor's) trademark, trade name, or copyright in the sale of goods and services.

Franchisor • One licensing another (the franchisee) to use his or her trademark, trade name, or copyright in the sale of goods or services.

A **franchise** is defined as any arrangement in which the owner of a trademark, a trade name, or a copyright licenses others to use the trademark, trade name, or copyright in the selling of goods or services. A **franchisee** (a purchaser of a franchise) is generally legally independent of the **franchisor** (the seller of the franchise). At the same time, the franchise is economically dependent on the franchisor's integrated business system. This means, in effect, that a franchisee can operate as an independent businessperson but still obtain the advantages of a regional or national organization.

Although the franchise is not really a business organizational form, the franchising arrangement has become widely used by those seeking to make profits. Well-known franchises include McDonald's, KFC, and Burger King.

Types of Franchises

Because the franchising industry is so extensive and so many different kinds of businesses sell franchises, it is difficult to summarize the many types of franchises that now exist. Generally, though, franchises fall into one of the following three classifications: distributorships, chain-style business operations, and manufacturing or processing-plant arrangements.

Distributorship. A *distributorship* arises when a manufacturing concern (franchisor) licenses a dealer (franchisee) to sell its product. Often, a distributorship covers an exclusive territory. An example is an automobile dealership.

Chain-Style Business Operation. A *chain-style business operation* exists when a franchise operates under a franchisor's trade name and is identified as a member of a select group of dealers that engage in the franchisor's business. The franchisee is generally required to follow standardized or prescribed methods of operation. Often, the franchisor demands that the franchisee maintain certain standards of operation. In addition, sometimes the franchisee is obligated to deal exclusively with the franchisor to obtain materials and supplies. Examples of this type of franchise are McDonald's and most other fast-food chains.

Manufacturing or Processing-Plant Arrangement. A *manufacturing* or *processing-plant arrangement* exists when the franchisor transmits to the franchisee the essential ingredients or formula to make a particular product. The franchisee then markets it either at wholesale or at retail in accordance with the franchisor's standards. Examples of this type of franchise are Coca-Cola and other soft-drink bottling companies.

Laws Governing Franchising

Because a franchise relationship is primarily a contractual relationship, it is governed by contract law. If the franchise exists primarily for the sale of products that are manufactured by the franchisor, the law governing sales contracts as expressed in Article 2 of the Uniform Commercial Code applies. Additionally, the federal government and most states have enacted laws governing certain aspects of franchising. Generally, these laws are designed to protect prospective franchisees from dishonest franchisors and to prohibit franchisors from terminating franchises without good cause.

To read the text of Article 2 of the Uniform Commercial Code, go to the "Statutes" page of our Web site at **http://ele.westbuslaw.com**

Federal Protection for Franchisees. Automobile dealership franchisees are protected from automobile manufacturers' bad faith termination of their franchises by the Automobile Dealers' Franchise Act[5]—also known as the Automobile Dealers' Day in Court Act—of 1965. If a manufacturer-franchisor terminates a franchise because of a dealer-franchisee's failure to comply with

5. 15 U.S.C. Sections 1221 *et seq.*

unreasonable demands (for example, failure to attain an unrealistically high sales quota), the manufacturer may be liable for damages.

Another federal statute is the Petroleum Marketing Practices Act (PMPA)[6] of 1979, which prescribes the grounds and conditions under which a franchisor may terminate or decline to renew a gasoline station franchise. Federal antitrust laws, which prohibit certain types of anticompetitive agreements (see Chapter 17), may also apply in certain circumstances.

Additionally, the Franchise Rule[7] of the Federal Trade Commission (FTC) requires franchisors to disclose certain material facts relating to the franchise so that a prospective franchisee can make an informed decision about whether to purchase the franchise. The rule was adopted largely to prevent deceptive and unfair practices in the sale of franchises.

ETHICAL ISSUE

Should traditional franchising rules apply to the Internet? When the FTC issued its Franchise Rule in 1978, the Internet as we know it today did not exist. Adapting the rule to the online environment has proved difficult. For example, suppose that a franchisor has a Web site with downloadable information for prospective franchisees. Is this the equivalent of an offer that requires compliance with the FTC's Franchise Rule? Further, does the franchisor have to comply with every different state's franchise regulations? Generally, how can the interests of franchisees be protected in the cyber environment? In view of these problems, the FTC has proposed several changes to its Franchise Rule. One proposed change would require that the franchisor provide a prospective franchisee with a proper disclosure document at least fourteen days before the signing of any franchise agreement or any payment to the franchisor. In addition, to give the franchisee more time to consider the franchise contract, the franchisor would have to provide the franchisee with a copy of the contract five calendar days before the agreement is to be signed. Another proposed rule would require online franchisors to state very clearly that franchisees would not be entitled to exclusive territorial rights (these rights will be discussed shortly). Notwithstanding these changes, however, one problem would remain: given the speed with which online franchises can be created, it may be difficult—if not impossible—for the FTC to effectively enforce these regulations.

State Protection for Franchisees. State legislation tends to be similar to federal statutes and the FTC regulations. For example, to protect franchisees, a state law might require the disclosure of facts that are material to making an informed decision regarding the purchase of a franchise. This could include such information as the actual costs of operation, recurring expenses, and profits earned, along with details substantiating these figures. State deceptive trade practices acts may also prohibit certain types of actions on the part of franchisors.

The Franchise Contract

The franchise relationship is defined by a contract between the franchisor and the franchisee. The franchise contract specifies the terms and conditions of the franchise and spells out the rights and duties of the franchisor

6. 15 U.S.C. Sections 2801 *et seq.*
7. 16 C.F.R. Part 436.

and the franchisee. If either party fails to perform its contractual duties, that party may be subject to a lawsuit for breach of contract. Furthermore, if a franchisee is induced to enter into a franchise contract by the franchisor's fraudulent misrepresentation, the franchisor may be liable for damages. Generally, the statutory and case law governing franchising tend to emphasize the importance of good faith and fair dealing in franchise relationships.

Because each type of franchise relationship has its own characteristics, it is difficult to describe the broad range of details a franchising contract may include. In the remaining pages of this chapter, we look at some of the major issues that typically are addressed in a franchise contract.

Payment for the Franchise. The franchisee ordinarily pays an initial fee or lump-sum price for the franchise license (the privilege of being granted a franchise). This fee is separate from the various products that the franchisee purchases from or through the franchisor. In some industries, the franchisor relies heavily on the initial sale of the franchise for realizing a profit. In other industries, the continued dealing between the parties brings profit to both. In most situations, the franchisor will receive a stated percentage of the annual sales or annual volume of business done by the franchisee. The franchise agreement may also require the franchisee to pay a percentage of the franchisor's advertising costs and certain administrative expenses.

Business Premises. The franchise agreement may specify whether the premises for the business must be leased or purchased outright. In some cases, construction of a building is necessary to meet the terms of the agreement. Certainly, the agreement will specify whether the franchisor supplies equipment and furnishings for the premises or whether this is the responsibility of the franchisee.

Location of the Franchise. Typically, the franchisor will determine the territory to be served. Some franchise contracts will give the franchisee exclusive rights, or "territorial rights," to a certain geographic area. Other franchise contracts, while they define the territory allotted to a particular franchise, either specifically state that the franchise is nonexclusive or are silent on the issue of territorial rights.

In today's online world, franchisees face a problem when franchisors attempt to sell their products themselves via their Web sites. For a discussion of this issue, see this chapter's *Contemporary Legal Debates* feature on page 306.

Business Organization and Quality Control. The business organization of the franchisee is of great concern to the franchisor. Depending on the terms of the franchise agreement, the franchisor may specify particular requirements for the form and capital structure of the business. The franchise agreement may also provide that standards of operation—relating to such aspects of the business as sales quotas, quality, and record keeping—be met by the franchisee. Furthermore, a franchisor may wish to retain stringent control over the training of personnel involved in the operation and over administrative aspects of the business.

When the franchise is a service operation, such as a motel, the contract often provides that the franchisor will establish certain standards for the facility in order to protect the franchise's name and reputation. Typically, the

CONTEMPORARY LEGAL DEBATES

Exclusive Territorial Rights and the Internet

Many franchise lawsuits involve disputes over territorial rights—an aspect of franchising that often involves an implied covenant of good faith and fair dealing. For example, suppose that the franchise contract does not give the franchisee exclusive territorial rights or is silent on the issue. If the franchisor allows a competing franchise to be established nearby, the franchisee may suffer a significant loss in profits. In this situation, a court may hold that the franchisor's actions breached an implied covenant of good faith and fair dealing.

If, in contrast, the franchisee has been given exclusive territorial rights to serve a specific area, then the matter is more straightforward. If the franchisor allows a competing franchise to be established in the vicinity, the contract has been breached. Yet how do these rules apply in a cyber age, when a franchisor may offer its products for sale via its Web site?

ENTER THE INTERNET

With the growth of inexpensive and easy online marketing, it was inevitable that cyberturf conflicts would eventually arise between franchisors and franchisees. Suppose, for example, that a franchise contract does grant to the franchisee exclusive rights to sell the franchised product within a certain territory. What happens if the franchisor then begins to sell the product from its Web site to anyone anywhere in the world, including in the franchisee's territory? Does this constitute a breach of the franchise contract?

This is a relatively new issue to come before the courts, and how the question is resolved has important implications for both franchisors and franchisees. From the franchisor's perspective, it would seem unfair to deprive it of the ability to market its goods, efficiently and inexpensively, from its Web site. From the franchisee's perspective, it would seem only fair (and consistent with the franchise contract's guarantee of exclusive territorial rights) to have the exclusive right to market the franchisor's product within its area.

DRUG EMPORIUM'S "ELECTRONIC ENCROACHMENT"

The issue of "electronic encroachment" came before a panel of arbitrators in an American Arbitration Association (AAA) proceeding. (As you learned in Chapter 3, the AAA is a leading provider of arbitration services.) The proceeding involved franchise contracts between the Drug Emporium, Inc., and several of its franchisees. The contracts provided that each franchisee had the exclusive right to conduct business in a specific geographic area. The franchisees claimed that the Drug Emporium had breached its contractual obligation to honor their territories by using its Web site to sell directly to customers within the franchisees' territories.

Ultimately, in what is believed to be the first ruling by a court or arbitrating panel on the issue of electronic encroachment, the arbitrating panel decided in favor of the franchisees. The panel ordered the Drug Emporium to cease marketing its goods from its Web site to potential customers who were physically located within the franchisees' territories.[a]

WHERE DO YOU STAND?

Although the AAA panel held in favor of the franchisees, there is no way to know how other arbitrating panels or courts will decide this issue. On the one hand, a valid contract that grants exclusive territorial rights to a franchisee deserves to be enforced, just as any contract does if the parties have voluntarily agreed to its terms. On the other hand, the Internet offers franchisors an inexpensive marketing vehicle, which, according to some, they should be able to utilize. If franchisors are prevented from any direct competition with their franchisees via the Web, franchisors may stop granting exclusive territorial rights to any of their franchisees—which, of course, could also be detrimental to franchisees. Where do you stand on this issue? Should a franchisor be able to market its goods on the Internet, even though customers in its franchisees' exclusive territories may purchase the goods directly from the Web site? Why or why not?

---

a. *Emporium Drug Mart, Inc. of Shreveport v. Drug Emporium, Inc.*, No. 71-114-0012600 (American Arbitration Association, September 2, 2000).

contract will state that the franchisor is permitted to make periodic inspections to ensure that the standards are being maintained.

Pricing Arrangements. Franchises provide the franchisor with an outlet for the firm's goods and services. Depending on the nature of the business, the franchisor may require the franchisee to purchase certain supplies from the franchisor at an established price.[8] A franchisor cannot, however, set the prices at which the franchisee will resell the goods, because this may be a violation of state or federal antitrust laws, or both. A franchisor can suggest retail prices but cannot mandate them.

Termination of the Franchise. The duration of the franchise is a matter to be determined between the parties. Generally, a franchise relationship starts with a short trial period, such as a year, so that the franchisee and the franchisor can determine whether they want to stay in business with one another. Usually, the franchise agreement specifies that termination must be "for cause," such as death or disability of the franchisee, insolvency of the franchisee, breach of the franchise agreement, or failure to meet specified sales quotas. Most franchise contracts provide that notice of termination must be given. If no set time for termination is specified, then a reasonable time, with notice, is implied. A franchisee must be given sufficient time to wind up the business—that is, to do the accounting and return relevant property to the franchisor.

Raising Financial Capital

Raising financial capital is critical to entrepreneurial success. In the early days of a business, sole proprietors or partners may be able to contribute only very limited amounts of capital. If the business becomes successful, the owner or owners may want to raise capital from external sources to expand the enterprise. There are several ways to do this. One way is to borrow funds. Another is to exchange equity (ownership rights) in the company in return for financial capital, either through private arrangements or through public stock offerings.

Loans

A business can raise capital through a bank loan, but this option may not be available for many entrepreneurs. Banks are usually reluctant to lend significant sums to unestablished businesses. Even if a bank is willing to make such a loan, it may require that an entrepreneur personally guarantee repayment.

If a bank loan is available, the entrepreneur may find it beneficial to obtain one, because raising capital in this way leaves the entrepreneur in full ownership and control of the business (though the loan itself may place some restrictions on future business decisions). Loans with desirable terms may be available from the federal Small Business Administration (SBA). One special

8. Although a franchisor can require franchisees to purchase supplies from it, requiring a franchisee to purchase exclusively from the franchisor may violate federal antitrust laws (laws prohibiting certain anticompetitive practices—see Chapter 17). For two landmark cases on this topic, see *United States v. Arnold, Schwinn & Co.*, 388 U.S. 365, 87 S.Ct. 1956, 18 L.Ed.2d 1249 (1967), and *Fortner Enterprises, Inc. v. U.S. Steel Corp.*, 394 U.S. 495, 89 S.Ct. 1252, 22 L.Ed.2d 495 (1969).

SBA program provides loans of up to $25,000 for women, low-income, and minority businesspersons. Some entrepreneurs have even used their credit cards to obtain initial capital.

The following case illustrates some of the problems that can occur in funding a new company.

CASE 9.5

Massachusetts Superior Court, 2000.
11 Mass.L.Rptr. 659.

MALIHI v. GHOLIZADEH

In January 1996, Ali Malihi, Dariush Gholizadeh, and Ali Kazeroonian founded Worldwide Broadcasting Network (WBN), a corporation, to provide video content over the Internet. WBN was to take material typically shown on television and make it available over the Internet through hundreds of thousands of customized video channels. Gholizadeh and Kazeroonian had technological expertise. Malihi had a financial background, having worked for fourteen years for an investment firm, with over $100 million in assets under his management. Malihi agreed to obtain $5 million in financing for WBN by June. In March, however, Malihi lowered the amount to $2 million and extended the date to October. Meanwhile, he used his own money to fund WBN, including $40,910 for which Malihi asked Gholizadeh to sign promissory notes.[a] *At Gholizadeh's insistence, each note provided that the repayment schedule depended on his WBN salary, which in turn depended on Malihi's obtaining financing. If Malihi did not obtain financing as agreed, the notes' payment schedule was to be renegotiated. By March 1997, Malihi had not met the $2 million goal and WBN faced a financial crisis. Gholizadeh found an investor willing to help in exchange for WBN stock. When WBN fired Malihi as an employee and discharged him as a director, he filed a suit in a Massachusetts state court against Gholizadeh, seeking payment on the notes.*

HINKLE, J.

Defendant [Gholizadeh] argues that, under the language of the promissory notes, he is not obligated to repay the monies loaned him by plaintiff [Malihi] because 1) plaintiff failed to secure the required funding and 2) the parties were unable to renegotiate a mutually acceptable repayment schedule. Defendant contends that unless he agrees to renegotiate the repayment schedule, he has no obligation to repay the money loaned him by plaintiff. That interpretation is not consistent with the express language of the promissory notes.

If the wording of a contract is unambiguous, the contract must be enforced according to its terms. Both promissory notes executed by defendant were subject to the condition that if WBN failed to obtain financing of at least $2,000,000 by October 30, 1996, the schedule of payments, *but not the underlying debt itself,* would be modified and adjusted by the mutual written agreement of the parties. [Emphasis added.]

This provision clearly reflected the parties' understanding that the timing of defendant's repayment, but not the fact of repayment, depended on his receiving a salary from WBN. The promissory notes suggest, although not with any degree of precision, that the repayment period and terms are to be renegotiated if WBN failed to raise $2 million by October 30, 1996. Thus, the

a. A *promissory note* is a written promise by one person to pay a fixed sum of money to another on demand or on a specified date.

express language of the notes enabled defendant to restructure the repayment schedule, but specifically did not excuse him from his obligation to pay the underlying debt.

It is undisputed that WBN failed to obtain $2 million in financing by October 30, 1996, but had secured that amount by early 1997. It is also undisputed that defendant never agreed to a revised payment schedule. Consequently, I find and rule that defendant is liable to plaintiff for payment of the full $40,910 * * * , as well as the interest provided in the notes.

As noted, under the terms of the notes, the parties are required to negotiate a new payment schedule. Because that has not occurred, although defendant is liable for payment of the notes * * * , he is not technically in default, because the parties failed to work out the new payment schedule.

Therefore, judgment will enter for plaintiff on the complaint in the amount of $40,910 plus interest. Defendant and plaintiff shall, within 30 days from the date of judgment, mutually agree in writing on a repayment schedule.

The court held that Gholizadeh was obligated to repay the notes, but that technically he was not yet in default. Because Malihi had not obtained the financing for WBN as he had agreed, the parties had to negotiate a new payment schedule.

QUESTIONS

1. What was the basis for Malihi's suit against Gholizadeh in this case?
2. Why did Gholizadeh argue that he was not obligated to repay the money loaned to him by Malihi?
3. What did the court decide in this dispute, and on what reasoning did the court base its decision?

Venture Capital

Many new businesses raise needed capital by exchanging certain ownership rights (equity) in the firm for **venture capital.** In other words, an outsider contributes money in exchange for an ownership interest in the company. **Venture capitalists** are those who seek out promising entrepreneurial ventures and fund them in exchange for an ownership share in the business. Akin to venture capitalists are individuals, known as "angels," who typically invest somewhat smaller sums in new businesses.

Venture capital • Funds that are invested in, or that are available for investment in, a new business enterprise.

Venture capitalist • A person or entity that seeks out promising entrepreneurial ventures and funds them in exchange for equity stakes.

Venture capitalists, in addition to making needed financing available, offer other advantages for entrepreneurs. Venture capitalists are often experienced managers who can provide invaluable assistance to entrepreneurs with respect to strategic business decisions, marketing, and making important business contacts. Obtaining this assistance may be crucial to a new company's success. The disadvantage is that the venture capitalist with a substantial equity stake will demand a corresponding degree of operational control over a company and proportion of future profits.

To attract outside venture capital, you will need a business plan. The plan should be relatively concise (less than fifty pages). It should describe the company, its products, and its anticipated future performance. You may present your plan to a venture capitalist who may then carefully investigate your venture. This may require you to disclose trade secrets, and you should insist that the potential investor sign a confidentiality agreement. If all goes well, you will then negotiate the terms of financing. A key point to be negotiated is how much ownership and control the venture capitalist will receive in exchange for the capital contribution. Exhibit 9–2 summarizes some key issues involved in venture capital negotiations.

Locating Potential Investors

Technology via the Internet has allowed promoters and others to access, easily and inexpensively, a large number of potential investors. Today, there are several online "matching services." These services specialize in matching potential investors with companies or future companies that are seeking investors. A corporate promoter or a small company seeking capital investment could pay a fee to one of these service companies, which would then include a description of the company in a list that it makes available to investors, also for a fee. Matching services are not new. For decades, several enterprises have provided such services by using computerized databases to match business firms' investment needs with potential investors. What is new is that many of these service providers are now online and have significantly expanded the geographic scope of their operations.

A number of companies specialize in matching entrepreneurs in specific industries with potential investors. Also, some companies include listings of companies or start-ups not only in the United States but in other countries as well. Other enterprises restrict their services to firms within a certain region, such as the Pacific Northwest in the United States.

EXHIBIT 9–2 • VENTURE CAPITAL ISSUES

Type and Quantity of Stock	The venture capitalists will negotiate the amount of stock (which will determine their ownership share of the enterprise) and the type of stock (which will usually be preferred stock).
Stock Preferences	If the venture capitalists receive preferred shares, the shares will generally (1) provide for an annual per-share dividend to be paid before common stockholders receive any dividends and (2) give the venture capitalists priority among shareholders in the event of the firm's liquidation.
Conversion and Antidilution Rights	The preferred shares will be convertible into common stock at the option of the venture capitalists, and the company will be restrained from issuing new stock in an amount that would materially dilute the venture capitalists' ownership interests.
Board of Directors	The venture capitalists will define their proportionate representation on the board of directors.
Registration Rights	Should the company conduct a public offering or register its shares at a later date, the venture capitalists will have the right to have their shares registered also ("piggy-backed"), making those shares more marketable.
Representations and Warranties	The entrepreneur will be required to make representations about the firm's capital structure, its possession of necessary government authorizations, its financial statements, and other material facts.

Online matching services allow entrepreneurs to reach a wide group of potential investors quickly and with relatively little effort. They also make it possible for a new or existing company to locate investors who are interested in the company's specific type of business venture. Several of these online matching services also offer other kinds of assistance, such as help with creating an effective business plan or tips on how to manage financial issues. Businesspersons, and especially entrepreneurs just starting up their enterprises, can benefit from this type of guidance.

Securities Regulation

Securities regulation is an area of significant concern to those raising capital. Many entrepreneurs do not use venture capitalists but raise money from friends or business acquaintances. Whatever method is used, the investor exchanges capital for an interest in the enterprise. If this interest consists of shares of stock (or otherwise qualifies as a security under federal or state law), the entrepreneur may become subject to extraordinarily detailed regulatory requirements. It may be necessary to register the securities with the Securities and Exchange Commission (SEC) or with the state in which the offering is made, unless the offering falls within an exemption to securities laws. These and other aspects of securities law are discussed in Chapter 18.

KEY TERMS

articles of organization 293
business trust 302
bylaws 289
certificate of incorporation 289
certificate of limited partnership 289
cooperative 302
corporation 289
entrepreneur 285
franchise 302
franchisee 302
franchisor 302
general partner 289
joint stock company 299
joint venture 299
limited liability company (LLC) 293
limited liability limited partnership (LLLP) 289
limited liability partnership (LLP) 298
limited partner 289
member 293
operating agreement 296
partnership 288
S corporation 292
sole proprietorship 285
syndicate 299
venture capital 309
venture capitalist 309

FOR REVIEW

1. What are the major traditional forms of business organization?
2. How do limited liability companies and limited liability partnerships fulfill needs not met by traditional forms of business organizations?
3. What are the major characteristics of other business organizational forms?
4. What law governs franchising relationships?
5. What are some of the methods used for raising financial capital?

QUESTIONS AND CASE PROBLEMS

9–1. In each of the following situations, determine whether Georgio's Fashions is a sole proprietorship, a partnership, a limited partnership, or a corporation.

(a) Georgio's defaults on a payment to supplier Dee Creations. Dee sues Georgio's and each of the owners of Georgio's personally for payment of the debt.
(b) Georgio's raises $200,000 through the sale of shares of its stock.
(c) At tax time, Georgio's files a tax return with the IRS and pays taxes on the firm's net profits.
(d) Georgio's is owned by three persons, two of whom are not allowed to participate in the firm's management.

9–2. Jorge, Marta, and Jocelyn are college graduates, and Jorge has come up with an idea for a new product that he believes could make the three of them very rich. His idea is to manufacture soft-drink dispensers for home use and market them to consumers throughout the Midwest. Jorge's personal experience qualifies him to be both first-line supervisor and general manager of the new firm. Marta is a born salesperson. Jocelyn has little interest in sales or management but would like to invest a large sum of money that she has inherited from her aunt. What factors should Jorge, Marta, and Jocelyn consider in deciding which form of business organization to adopt?

9–3. John, Lesa, and Trevor form an LLC. John contributes 60 percent of the capital, and Lesa and Trevor each contribute 20 percent. Nothing is decided about how profits will be divided. John assumes that he will be entitled to 60 percent of the profits, in accordance with his contribution. Lesa and Trevor, however, assume that the profits will be divided equally. A dispute over the issue arises, and ultimately a court has to decide the issue. What law will the court apply? In most states, what will result? How could this dispute have been avoided in the first place? Discuss fully.

9–4. Omega Computers, Inc., is a franchisor that grants exclusive physical territories to its franchisees with retail locations, including Pete's Digital Products. Omega sells over two hundred of the franchises before establishing an interactive Web site. On the site, a customer can order Omega's products directly from the franchisor. When Pete's sets up a Web site through which a customer can also order Omega's products, Omega and Pete file suits against each other, alleging that each is in violation of the franchise relationship. To decide this issue, what factors should the court consider? How might these parties have avoided this conflict? Discuss.

9–5. Indications of Partnership. Sandra Lerner was one of the original founders of Cisco Systems. When she sold her interest in Cisco, she received a substantial amount of money, which she invested, and she became extremely wealthy. Patricia Holmes met Lerner at Holmes's horse training facility, and they became friends. One evening in Lerner's mansion, while applying nail polish, Holmes layered a raspberry color over black to produce a new color, which Lerner liked. Later, the two created other colors with names like "Bruise," "Smog," and "Oil Slick," and titled their concept "Urban Decay." Lerner and Holmes started a firm to produce and market the polishes but never discussed the sharing of profits and losses. They agreed to build the business and then sell it. Together, they did market research, experimented with colors, worked on a logo and advertising, obtained capital from an investment firm, and hired employees. Then Lerner began working to edge Holmes out of the firm. Several months later, when Holmes was told not to attend meetings of the firm's officers, she filed a suit in a California state court against Lerner, claiming, among other things, a breach of their partnership agreement. Lerner responded in part that there was no partnership agreement because there was no agreement to divide profits. Was Lerner right? Why or why not? How should the court rule? [*Holmes v. Lerner,* 74 Cal.App.4th 442, 88 Cal.Rptr.2d 130 (1 Dist. 1999)]

9–6. Limited Liability Companies. Gloria Duchin, a Rhode Island resident, was the sole shareholder and chief executive officer of Gloria Duchin, Inc. (Duchin, Inc.), which manufactured metallic Christmas ornaments and other novelty items. The firm was incorporated in Rhode Island. Duchin Realty, Inc., also incorporated in Rhode Island, leased real estate to Duchin, Inc. The Duchin entities hired Gottesman Co. to sell Duchin, Inc., and to sign with the buyer a consulting agreement for Gloria Duchin and a lease for Duchin Realty's property. Gottesman negotiated a sale, a consulting agreement, and a lease with Somerset Capital Corp. James Mitchell, a resident of Massachusetts, was the chairman and president of Somerset, and Mary Mitchell, also a resident of Massachusetts, was the senior vice president. The parties agreed that to buy Duchin, Inc., Somerset would create a new limited liability company, JMTR Enterprises, L.L.C., in Rhode Island, with the Mitchells as its members. When the deal fell apart, JMTR filed a suit in a Massachusetts state court against the Duchin entities, alleging, among other things, breach of contract. When the defendants tried to remove the case to a federal district court, JMTR argued that the court did not have jurisdiction because there was no diversity of citizenship among the parties; all of the plaintiffs and defendants were citizens of Rhode Island. Is JMTR correct?

Why or why not? [*JMTR Enterprises, L.L.C. v. Duchin*, 42 F.Supp.2d 87 (D.Mass. 1999)]

CASE PROBLEM WITH SAMPLE ANSWER

9–7. Indications of Partnership. In August 1998, Jea Yu contacted Cameron Eppler, president of Design88, Ltd., to discuss developing a Web site that would cater to investors and provide services to its members for a fee. Yu and Patrick Connelly invited Eppler and Ha Tran, another member of Design88, to a meeting to discuss the site. The parties agreed that Design88 would perform certain Web design, implementation, and maintenance functions for 10 percent of the profits from the site, which would be called "The Underground Trader." They signed a "Master Partnership Agreement," which was later amended to include Power Uptik Productions, LLC (PUP). The parties often referred to themselves as partners. From Design88's offices in Virginia, Design88 designed and hosted the site, solicited members through Internet and national print campaigns, processed member applications, provided technical support, monitored access to the site, and negotiated and formed business alliances on the site's behalf. When relations among the parties soured, PUP withdrew. Design88 filed a suit against PUP and the others. Did a partnership exist among these parties? Why or why not? [*Design88, Ltd. v. Power Uptik Productions, LLC*, 133 F.Supp.2d 873 (W.D.Va. 2001)]

➧ *To view a sample answer for this case problem, go to this book's Web site at* **http://ele.westbuslaw.com** *and click on "Interactive Study Center."*

9–8. IN YOUR COURT

Excel Lodge entered into a contract with Host Inn, Inc., to operate a Host Inn franchise west of a major city's airport. Because another Host Inn, named "Host East," already served the market near the airport, the franchisor (Host Inn, Inc.) named Excel's facility "Host West." Three years later, the franchisor bought a Hyatt hotel in the vicinity of the same airport and called it "Host Gateway." The presence of three Host properties in the same market caused some customer confusion. Also, Host West and the new Host Gateway competed for the same customers, which caused Host West to suffer a decrease in the growth of its business. Host West sued the franchisor, alleging that by establishing Host Gateway, the franchisor had denied Host West the fruits of its contract in breach of the implied covenant of good faith and fair dealing. Assume that you are the judge in the trial court hearing this case, and answer the following questions:

(a) Assume that the franchisor has made a motion for summary judgment in its favor, claiming that its actions were perfectly legal because the franchise contract itself was silent as to whether, and where, the franchisor could authorize a franchise to compete with Host West. Would you grant this motion? Why or why not?

(b) Does a franchisor violate the implied covenant of good faith and fair dealing if it competes against one of its franchisees in the same geographic market, as Host West alleged? How will you rule on this issue, and why?

(c) Suppose that instead of purchasing a hotel in the area and operating it itself in direct competition with its franchisee, the franchisor instead contracted with another company to serve as a franchisee in the same area. Would this change in the factual situation affect your decision as to whether the franchisor had violated the implied covenant of good faith and fair dealing?

9–9. A QUESTION OF ETHICS AND SOCIAL RESPONSIBILITY

Graham Oil Co. (Graham) had been a distributor of ARCO gasoline in Coos Bay, Oregon, for nearly forty years under successive distributorship agreements. ARCO notified Graham that it intended to terminate the franchise because Graham had not been purchasing the minimum amount of gasoline required under their most recent agreement. Graham sought a preliminary injunction against ARCO, arguing that ARCO had violated the Petroleum Marketing Practices Act (PMPA) by deliberately raising its prices so that Graham would be unable to meet the minimum gasoline requirements; thus, ARCO should not be allowed to terminate the agreement. The court ordered Graham to submit the claim to arbitration, in accordance with an arbitration clause in the distributorship agreement. Graham refused to do so, and the court granted summary judgment for ARCO. On appeal, Graham claimed that the arbitration clause was invalid because it forced Graham to forfeit rights given to franchisees under the PMPA, including the right to punitive damages and attorneys' fees. The appellate court agreed with Graham and remanded the case for trial. In view of these facts, answer the following questions. [*Graham Oil Co. v. ARCO Products Co., A Division of Atlantic Richfield Co.*, 43 F.3d 1244 (9th Cir. 1994)]

(a) Do you agree with Graham and the appellate court that statutory rights cannot be forfeited contractually—for example, through an arbitration clause?

(b) Review the discussion of arbitration in Chapter 3. Does the decision in this case conflict with any established public policy concerning arbitration? Is the court's decision in the case consistent with other court decisions on arbitration discussed in Chapter 3, including decisions of the United States Supreme Court?

9–10. FOR CRITICAL ANALYSIS

The law permits individuals to organize business enterprises in many different forms. What policy interests are served by granting entrepreneurs so many options? Would it be better if the law required all businesspersons to organize their businesses in the same form? Discuss.

For updated links to resources available on the Web, as well as a variety of other materials, visit this text's Web site at

http://ele.westbuslaw.com

The Web site of the law firm of Reinhart *et al.* provides extensive information about business organizations. The URL for this site is

http://www.rbvdnr.com

To learn how the U.S. Small Business Administration assists in forming, financing, and operating businesses, go to

http://www.sbaonline.sba.gov

For information on the FTC regulations on franchising, as well as state laws regulating franchising, go to

http://www.ftc.gov/bcp/franchise/netfran.htm

A good source of information on the purchase and sale of franchises is Franchising.org, which is online at

http://www.franchising.org

LEGAL RESEARCH EXERCISES ON THE WEB

Go to **http://ele.westbuslaw.com**, the Web site that accompanies this text. Select "Interactive Study Center," and then click on "Chapter 9." There you will find the following Internet research exercises that you can perform to learn more about topics covered in this chapter.

Activity 9–1: LEGAL PERSPECTIVE—Starting a Business

Activity 9–2: MANAGEMENT PERSPECTIVE—Franchises

BEFORE THE TEST

Go to **http://ele.westbuslaw.com**, the Web site that accompanies this text. Select "Interactive Quizzes." You will find at least twenty interactive questions relating to this chapter.

WESTLAW® CAMPUS

If your textbook provided for a subscription to Westlaw® Campus, or if you have otherwise purchased access to the Westlaw Campus database, you can access any of the cases presented or cited in this chapter by using your Westlaw Campus account.

CHAPTER 10

Contract Law

CONTENTS

CHAPTER OBJECTIVES

After reading this chapter, you should be able to answer the following questions:

1. What is a contract? What is the objective theory of contracts?
2. What are the four basic requirements for the formation of a valid contract?
3. In what types of situations might genuineness of assent to a contract's terms be lacking?
4. How are most contracts discharged?
5. What is the difference between compensatory and consequential damages?

Promise • A declaration that something either will or will not happen in the future.

The noted legal scholar Roscoe Pound once said that "[t]he social order rests upon the stability and predictability of conduct, of which keeping promises is a large item."[1] A **promise** is a person's assurance that the person will or will not do something. As you will read shortly, a *contract* is essentially a promise or a set of promises.

Like other types of law, contract law reflects our social values, interests, and expectations at a given point in time. It shows, for example, to what extent our society allows people to make promises or commitments that are legally binding. It distinguishes between promises that create only *moral* obligations (such as a promise to take a friend to lunch) and promises that are legally binding (such as a promise to pay for merchandise purchased). Contract law also demonstrates what excuses our society accepts for breaking certain types of promises. In addition, it indicates what promises are considered to be contrary to public policy—against the interests of society as a whole—and therefore legally invalid. When a promise is made by a child or a mentally incompetent person, for example, a question will arise as to whether the promise should be enforced. Resolving such questions is the essence of contract law.

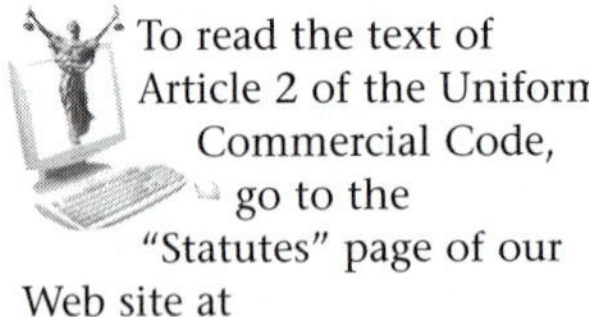

To read the text of Article 2 of the Uniform Commercial Code, go to the "Statutes" page of our Web site at **http://ele.westbuslaw.com**

The common law governs all contracts except when it has been modified or replaced by statutory law, such as the Uniform Commercial Code (UCC),[2] or by administrative agency regulations. Contracts relating to services, real estate, employment, insurance, and so on generally are governed by the common law of contracts. Contracts for the sale and lease of goods, however, are governed by the UCC—to the extent that the UCC has modified general contract law. The relationship between general contract law and the law governing sales and leases of goods will be explored in detail in Chapter 11. In the discussion of general contract law that follows, we indicate in footnotes the areas in which the UCC has significantly altered common law contract principles.

1. R. Pound, *Jurisprudence,* Vol. 3 (St. Paul: West Publishing Co., 1959), p. 162.
2. See Chapter 1 and Chapter 11 for further discussions of the significance and coverage of the Uniform Commercial Code.

THE FUNCTION OF CONTRACT LAW

The law encourages competent parties to form contracts for lawful objectives. Indeed, no aspect of modern life is entirely free of contractual relationships. Even the ordinary consumer in his or her daily activities acquires rights and obligations based on contract law. You acquire rights and obligations, for example, when you borrow funds to make a purchase or when you buy a DVD or a house. Contract law is designed to provide stability and predictability, as well as certainty, for both buyers and sellers in the marketplace.

Contract law deals with, among other things, the formation and enforcement of agreements between parties (in Latin, *pacta sunt servanda*—"agreements shall be kept"). By supplying procedures for enforcing private contractual agreements, contract law provides an essential condition for the existence of a market economy. Without a legal framework of reasonably assured expectations within which to plan and venture, businesspersons would be able to rely only on the good faith of others. Duty and good faith are usually sufficient to obtain compliance with a promise, but when price changes or adverse economic factors make compliance costly, these elements may not be enough. Contract law is necessary to ensure compliance with a promise or to entitle the innocent party to some form of relief.

DEFINITION OF A CONTRACT

A **contract** is "a promise or a set of promises for the breach of which the law gives a remedy, or the performance of which the law in some way recognizes as a duty."[3] Put simply, a contract is a legally binding agreement between two or more parties who agree to perform or to refrain from performing some act now or in the future. Generally, contract disputes arise when there is a promise of future performance. If the contractual promise is not fulfilled, the party who made it is subject to the sanctions of a court. That party may be required to pay money damages for failing to perform the contractual promise; in limited instances, the party may be required to perform the promised act.

Contract • An agreement that can be enforced in court; formed by two or more parties, each of whom agrees to perform or to refrain from performing some act now or in the future.

In determining whether a contract has been formed, the element of intent is of prime importance. In contract law, intent is determined by what is called the *objective theory of contracts,* not by the personal or subjective intent, or belief, of a party. The theory is that a party's intention to enter into a legally binding agreement, or contract, is judged by outward, objective facts as interpreted by a *reasonable* person, rather than by the party's own secret, subjective intentions. Objective facts include (1) what the party said when entering into the contract, (2) how the party acted or appeared (intent may be manifested by conduct as well as by oral or written words), and (3) the circumstances surrounding the transaction. We will look further at the objective theory of contracts later in this chapter in the context of the role of intention in contract formation.

---

3. *Restatement (Second) of Contracts.* The *Restatement of the Law of Contracts* is a nonstatutory, authoritative exposition of the common law of contracts compiled by the American Law Institute in 1932. The *Restatement,* which is now in its second edition (a third edition is being drafted), will be referred to throughout this chapter on contract law.

ELEMENTS OF A CONTRACT

The many topics that will be discussed in the following pages on the common law of contracts require an understanding of the basic elements of a valid contract and the way in which a contract is created. These topics also require an understanding of the types of circumstances in which even legally valid contracts will not be enforced.

Requirements of a Valid Contract

The following list briefly describes the four requirements that must be met before a valid contract exists. If any of these elements is lacking, no contract will have been formed. Each requirement will be explained more fully later in this chapter.

1. *Agreement.* An agreement to form a contract includes an *offer* and an *acceptance.* One party must offer to enter into a legal agreement, and another party must accept the terms of the offer.
2. *Consideration.* Any promises made by the parties to the contract must be supported by legally sufficient and bargained-for *consideration* (something of value received or promised, such as money, to convince a person to make a deal).
3. *Contractual capacity.* Both parties entering into the contract must have the contractual *capacity* to do so; the law must recognize them as possessing characteristics that qualify them as competent parties.
4. *Legality.* The contract's purpose must be to accomplish some goal that is legal and not against public policy.

Defenses to the Enforceability of a Contract

Even if all of the above-listed requirements are met, a contract may be unenforceable if the following requirements are not met. These requirements typically are considered to be *defenses* to the enforceability of an otherwise valid contract.

1. *Genuineness of assent.* The apparent consent of both parties must be genuine. For example, if a contract was formed as a result of fraud, undue influence, mistake, or duress, the contract may not be enforceable.
2. *Form.* The contract must be in whatever form the law requires; for example, some contracts must be in writing to be enforceable.

TYPES OF CONTRACTS

There are many types of contracts. The categories into which contracts are placed involve legal distinctions relating to formation, enforceability, and performance.

Bilateral versus Unilateral Contracts

Every contract involves at least two parties. The *offeror* is the party making the offer. The *offeree* is the party to whom the offer is made. Whether the contract is classified as *unilateral* or *bilateral* depends on what the offeree must do to accept the offer and to bind the offeror to a contract.

Bilateral Contracts. If to accept the offer the offeree must only *promise* to perform, the contract is a *bilateral contract.* Hence, a bilateral contract is a "promise for a promise." No performance, such as payment of money or delivery of goods, need take place for a bilateral contract to be formed. The contract comes into existence at the moment the promises are exchanged.

For example, Jeff offers to buy Ann's digital camera for $200. Jeff tells Ann that he will give her the money for the camera next Friday, when he gets paid. Ann accepts Jeff's offer and promises to give him the camera when Jeff pays her on Friday. Jeff and Ann have formed a bilateral contract.

Unilateral Contracts. In a *unilateral contract,* in contrast, the offer is phrased so that the offeree can accept the offer only by completing the contract performance. Hence, a unilateral contract is a "promise for an act."[4] A classic example of a unilateral contract is as follows: O'Malley says to Parker, "If you carry this package across the Brooklyn Bridge, I'll give you $10." Only on Parker's complete crossing with the package does she fully accept O'Malley's offer to pay $10. If she chooses not to undertake the walk, there are no legal consequences. Contests, lotteries, and other competitions involving prizes are examples of offers inviting unilateral contract formation. If a person complies with the rules of the contest—such as by submitting the right lottery number at the right place and time—a unilateral contract is formed, binding the organization offering the prize to a contract to perform as promised in the offer.

Can a school's, or an employer's, letter of tentative acceptance to a prospective student, or a possible employee, qualify as a unilateral contract? That was the issue in the following case.

4. Clearly, a contract cannot be "one sided," because, by definition, an agreement implies the existence of two or more parties. Therefore, the phrase *unilateral contract,* if read literally, is a contradiction in terms. As traditionally used in contract law, however, the phrase refers to the kind of contract that results when only one promise is being made (the promise made by the offeror in return for the offeree's performance).

ARDITO v. CITY OF PROVIDENCE

CASE 10.1

United States District Court, District of Rhode Island, 2003. 263 F.Supp.2d 358.

In 2001, the City of Providence, Rhode Island, decided to begin hiring police officers to fill vacancies in its police department. Because only individuals who graduated from the Providence Police Academy were eligible, the city also decided to conduct two training sessions, the "60th and 61st Police Academies." To be admitted, an applicant had to pass a series of tests and be deemed qualified by members of the department after an interview. The applicants deemed most qualified were sent a letter informing them that they had been selected to attend if they successfully completed a medical examination and a psychological examination. The letter to the applicants to the 61st Academy, dated October 15, stated that it was "a conditional offer of employment." Meanwhile, a new chief of police, Dean Esserman, decided to revise the selection process, which caused some of those who had received the letter to be rejected. Derek Ardito and thirteen other newly rejected applicants filed a suit in a federal district court against the city, seeking a halt to the 61st Academy unless they were allowed to attend. They alleged in part that the city was in breach of contract.

TORRES, J.

A contract arises when the parties manifest their mutual assent to its terms and consideration is given. Ordinarily, the expression of mutual assent takes the form of an offer by one party manifesting its willingness to enter into the proposed agreement and an acceptance of that offer by the other party. *In determining whether a contract exists, it is the words, conduct and other objective manifestations of intent that govern* * * *. [Emphasis added.]

In the case of a bilateral contract, acceptance consists of a promise by the offeree to render the bargained-for performance. In the case of a unilateral contract, on the other hand, the offer invites and is accepted by actual performance.

In this case, *the October 15 letter* * * * *is a classic example of an offer to enter into a unilateral contract.* The October 15 letter expressly stated that it was a "conditional offer of employment" and the message that it conveyed was that the recipient would be admitted into the 61st Academy if he or she successfully completed the medical and psychological examinations, requirements that the City could not lawfully impose unless it was making a conditional offer of employment. [Emphasis added.]

Moreover, the terms of that offer were perfectly consistent with what applicants had been told when they appeared [for their interviews]. At that time, [Police Major Dennis] Simoneau informed them that, if they "passed" the [interviews], they would be offered a place in the Academy provided that they also passed medical and psychological examinations.

The October 15 letter also was in marked contrast to notices sent to applicants by the City at earlier stages of the selection process. Those notices merely informed applicants that they had completed a step in the process and remained eligible to be considered for admission into the Academy. Unlike the October 15 letter, the prior notices did not purport to extend a "conditional offer" of admission.

The plaintiffs accepted the City's offer of admission into the Academy by satisfying the specified conditions. Each of the plaintiffs submitted to and passed lengthy and intrusive medical and psychological examinations. In addition, many of the plaintiffs, in reliance on the City's offer, jeopardized their standing with their existing employers by notifying the employers of their anticipated departure, and some plaintiffs passed up opportunities for other employment.

The City argues that the October 15 letter should not be construed as a conditional offer of admission to the Academy because the third paragraph stated that the number of qualified applicants exceeded the number of available slots and that an "actual offer of employment" would not be made until "all of the results are known." This Court rejects that argument * * *.

* * * [A]t most, that paragraph may make ambiguous what, otherwise, was the clear and unequivocal offer set forth in the first two paragraphs that the recipient would be accepted into the 61st Academy if the recipient passed medical and psychological examinations. Since the defendants drafted the October 15 letter, if the letter contains an ambiguity that makes it susceptible to more than one reasonable interpretation, the letter should be construed in the manner most favorable to the plaintiffs.

Here, the only ambiguity would be whether an applicant's admission to the Academy also was conditioned upon a final decision regarding the size of the class. Such an interpretation is, at least, debatable because, while an additional condition might be inferred from the statement that the number of qualified applicants exceeded the number of available slots, that inference appears to be inconsistent with the statement that an "actual offer of employment will not be made until all of the results are known". Since the only "results" not known when the October 15 letter was sent were the results of the medical and psychological examinations, the statement suggests that successful completion of those examinations were the only requirements on which the offer of admission was conditioned.

However, even assuming, *arguendo* [for the sake of argument], that the October 15 letter should be construed as making a decision fixing the size of the Academy class at forty an additional condition of admission, that condition was satisfied. A final decision has been made fixing the size of the Academy at forty recruits. Indeed, * * * the decision had been made before the October 15 letter was sent.

* * * *

The City [also] argues that there is no contract between the parties because the plaintiffs have no legally enforceable right to employment. The City correctly points out that, even if the plaintiffs graduate from the Academy and there are existing vacancies in the Department, they would be required to serve a one-year probationary period during which they could be terminated without cause * * *. That argument misses the point. The contract that the plaintiffs seek to enforce is not a contract that they will be appointed as permanent Providence police officers; rather, it is a contract that they would be admitted to the Academy if they passed the medical and psychological examinations.

The court issued an injunction to prohibit the city from conducting the 61st Police Academy unless the plaintiffs were included. The October 15 letter was a unilateral offer that the plaintiffs had accepted by passing the required medical and psychological examinations.

QUESTIONS

1. Why did fourteen rejected applicants to the Providence Police Academy file a suit in a federal district court against the City of Providence?
2. On the basis of what reasoning did the court order the city not to conduct the 61st Police Academy unless the plaintiffs were included?
3. How might the city have phrased the letter to avoid its being considered a unilateral contract?

Express versus Implied-in-Fact Contracts

Contracts may also be categorized as express or implied by the conduct of the parties. We look here at the differences between these two types of contracts.

Express Contracts. In an *express contract,* the terms of the agreement are fully and explicitly stated in words, oral or written. A signed lease for an apartment or a house is an express written contract. If a classmate calls you on the phone and agrees to buy your textbooks from last semester for $75, an express oral contract has been made.

Implied-in-Fact Contracts. A contract that is implied from the conduct of the parties is called an *implied-in-fact contract* or an implied contract. This type of contract differs from an express contract in that the *conduct* of the parties, rather than their words, creates and defines the terms of the contract. (Note that a contract may be a mixture of an express contract and an implied-in-fact contract. In other words, a contract may contain some express terms, while others are implied.)

Requirements for an Implied-in-Fact Contract. For an implied-in-fact contract to arise, certain requirements must be met. Normally, if the following conditions exist, a court will hold that an implied contract was formed:

1. The plaintiff furnished some service or property.
2. The plaintiff expected to be paid for that service or property, and the defendant knew or should have known that payment was expected.
3. The defendant had a chance to reject the services or property and did not.

For example, suppose that you need an accountant to complete your tax return this year. You look through the Yellow Pages and find an accountant at an office in your neighborhood, so you drop by to see her. You go into the accountant's office and explain your problem, and she tells you what her fees are. The next day you return and give her secretary all the necessary information and documents—canceled checks, W-2 forms, and the like. You then walk out the door without saying anything expressly to the secretary. In this situation, you have entered into an implied-in-fact contract to pay the accountant the usual and reasonable fees for her services. The contract is implied by your conduct and by hers. She expects to be paid for completing your tax return; and by bringing in the records she will need to do the work, you have implied an intent to pay her.

Quasi Contracts—Contracts Implied in Law

Quasi contract • A fictional contract imposed on parties by a court in the interests of fairness and justice; usually, quasi contracts are imposed to avoid the unjust enrichment of one party at the expense of another.

Quasi contracts, or contracts *implied in law,* are wholly different from actual contracts. Whereas express contracts and implied-in-fact contracts are actual contracts formed by the words or conduct of the parties, quasi contracts are fictional contracts created by courts and imposed on parties in the interests of fairness and justice. Quasi contracts are therefore equitable, rather than contractual, in nature. Usually, quasi contracts are imposed to avoid the *unjust enrichment* of one party at the expense of another. Under the doctrine of quasi contract, a plaintiff may recover in *quantum meruit,*[5] a Latin phrase meaning "as much as he deserves." *Quantum meruit* essentially describes the extent of compensation owed under a contract implied in law.

For example, suppose that a vacationing doctor is driving down the highway and encounters Potter lying unconscious on the side of the road. The doctor renders medical aid that saves Potter's life. Although the injured, unconscious Potter did not solicit the medical aid and was not aware that the aid had been rendered, Potter received a valuable benefit, and the requirements for a quasi contract were fulfilled. In such a situation, the law will impose a quasi contract, and Potter normally will have to pay the doctor for the reasonable value of the medical services rendered.

Because quasi contracts are fictional constructs designed to prevent injustice, judges weigh the facts of each individual case to determine whether to impose a contract. As the following *Featured Case* illustrates, judges often disagree on which factors they consider to be the most important.

---

5. Pronounced *kwahn*-tuhm *mehr*-oo-wit.

Superior Court of Pennsylvania, 2001. 787 A.2d 988.

AMERIPRO SEARCH, INC. v. FLEMING STEEL CO.

MAJORITY OPINION

DEL SOLE, J.

Fleming Steel Company ("Fleming") appeals from the judgment entered against it, and in favor of AmeriPro Search, Inc. ("AmeriPro"). Upon review, we reverse.

* * * AmeriPro is an employment referral firm that places professional employees with interested employers. Fleming is a steel fabricator. In May of 1993, Elaine Brauninger, an agent of AmeriPro, contacted Fleming and inquired about Fleming's need for professional employees. * * * Fleming was seeking an employee with an engineering background. * * * Ms. Brauninger was advised that [she] would have to speak to Seth Kohn, president of Fleming, who alone made all decisions relating to employment and salaries.

* * * Ms. Brauninger advised Mr. Kohn that if her services were accepted she would be entitled to a fee equal to 30% of the candidate's first year's salary. Mr. Kohn did not agree because he believed the fee to be too high. Mr. Kohn told Ms. Brauninger that the fee would be as determined by him and AmeriPro only after an agreement to hire a candidate was made. Ms. Brauninger agreed and told Mr. Kohn that she would work with him on the amount of the fee.

One of the candidates referred to Fleming was Dominic Barracchini. Ms. Brauninger had contacted Mr. Barracchini in November of 1993 to determine whether Mr. Barracchini would be interested in a position at Fleming. * * * Despite Mr. Barracchini's statement of interest, an interview could not be arranged with Fleming and Mr. Barracchini took employment with [another] company. In April of 1994, Ms. Brauninger again contacted Mr. Barracchini and informed him that she could arrange for an interview with Fleming. Mr. Kohn interviewed Mr. Barracchini on April 8, 1994. Fleming did not hire Mr. Barracchini because Mr. Barracchini's salary request was too high.

* * * [In February of 1995,] Mr. Barracchini called Ms. Brauninger to inquire whether Fleming was still trying to fill the position for which he had previously interviewed. Ms. Brauninger never got back to Mr. Barracchini regarding his inquiry. Mr. Barracchini then contacted Fleming on his own. * * * Fleming hired Mr. Barracchini as an engineer on June 19, 1995.

On September 6, 1995, AmeriPro sent an invoice to Fleming claiming entitlement to $14,400.00 for placement of Mr. Barracchini with Fleming. Fleming refused to pay * * *.

* * * *

The trial court determined that there was no express contract formed in this case. * * * The trial court did, however, find that there was a contract implied in law, or a quasi-contract, in this case. It was on this basis that the trial court ordered Fleming to pay AmeriPro the fee for placement of Barracchini.

* * * *

A quasi contract imposes a duty, not as a result of any agreement, whether express or implied, but in spite of the absence of an agreement, when one party receives unjust enrichment at the expense of another. In determining if the doctrine applies, we focus not on the intention of the parties, but rather on whether the defendant has been unjustly enriched. * * * *The most significant element of the doctrine is whether the enrichment of the defendant is unjust* * * *. [Emphasis added.]

We cannot find that Fleming was unjustly enriched in this case. Mr. Barracchini was referred to Fleming and the first interview was arranged by AmeriPro. Fleming did not hire Mr. Barracchini at that time because the candidate's salary requirements were too high. Approximately ten months after Mr. Barracchini's initial interview with Fleming, he was laid off from Montage. He contacted Ms. Brauninger to inquire about the job at Fleming and whether it was still open. Ms. Brauninger never responded to Mr. Barracchini's inquiry. As a result, Mr. Barracchini contacted Fleming directly to determine whether the position for which he had previously interviewed was still available. * * * After interviewing Mr. Barracchini in June of 1995, Fleming hired him.

The events leading to the hiring of Mr. Barracchini were separate from any actions taken by Ms. Brauninger and AmeriPro on his behalf. While it is true that AmeriPro and Brauninger first introduced Barracchini to Fleming and the available position, that connection was broken when Fleming refused to hire Barracchini after the interview in April of 1994. * * * Mr. Barracchini's subsequent independent interaction with Mr. Kohn, which led to his actual employment by Fleming, was removed from previous actions taken by AmeriPro on his behalf.

While it may be argued that Fleming received a benefit from AmeriPro because Barracchini would not have known about the position at Fleming without the initial interaction involving AmeriPro, *the doctrine of quasi contract does not apply simply because the defendant may have benefited as a result of the actions of the plaintiff.* Regardless of any benefit Fleming received by AmeriPro's action of first introducing Mr. Barracchini to Fleming, the enrichment of Fleming was not unjust. Mr. Barracchini approached Fleming the second time on his own and the two parties came to an agreement regarding Mr. Barracchini's employment without any involvement by AmeriPro. Fleming did nothing to wrongly secure the benefit of Mr. Barracchini's employment. * * * Because Fleming was not unjustly enriched, we find that there was no quasi contract, or contract implied in law. Thus, Fleming owes AmeriPro nothing in restitution. [Emphasis added.]

Judgment reversed.

DISSENTING OPINION

TAMILIA, J.

I agree with the majority that the efforts of AmeriPro were interrupted by the initial failure of the prospective employee * * * [and Fleming] to enter an employment agreement. I would find, however, that a quasi-contract to locate a suitable employee for Fleming existed and that despite the elapsed time and breakdown of negotiations in the intervening period, the contract was breached when the parties, introduced by AmeriPro, entered into an employment contract.

Because Barracchini and Fleming did not meet by happenstance but as a result of the efforts of AmeriPro, I would affirm the judgment of the trial court.

TEST YOUR COMPREHENSION: CASE DETAILS

1. Did Brauninger (the employment agent) and Kohn (the president of Fleming) agree on how much money AmeriPro would be paid if Fleming hired an engineer recommended by the agency?
2. How did Barracchini (the employee) originally find out about the job opportunity with Fleming Steel in 1993?
3. Who arranged the interview in April 1994, and why did Fleming not hire Barracchini at that time? What about the interview in 1995?
4. In your opinion, would the majority have ruled differently if Brauninger had returned the employee's call in 1995 and thereafter set up Barracchini's interview with Fleming?
5. Why did the dissenting judge feel that a quasi contract existed between Fleming and AmeriPro?

Executed versus Executory Contracts

Contracts are also classified according to the degree to which they have been performed. A contract that has been fully performed on both sides is called an *executed contract.* A contract that has not been fully performed on either side is called an *executory contract.* If one party has fully performed but the other has not, the contract is said to be executed on the one side and executory on the other, but the contract is still classified as executory.

For example, assume that you agree to buy ten tons of coal from the Northern Coal Company. Further assume that Northern has delivered the coal to your steel mill, where it is now being burned. At this point, the contract is executed on the part of Northern and executory on your part. After you pay Northern for the coal, the contract will be executed on both sides.

Valid, Void, Voidable, and Unenforceable Contracts

Contracts may also be classified as valid, void, voidable, or unenforceable. We look here at the meaning of each of these terms.

Valid Contracts. A *valid contract* has the elements necessary to entitle at least one of the parties to enforce it in court. Those elements, as mentioned earlier, consist of (1) an agreement made up of an offer and an acceptance of that offer, (2) supported by legally sufficient consideration, (3) made by parties who have the legal capacity to enter into the contract, and (4) made for a legal purpose.

Void and Voidable Contracts. A *void contract* is no contract at all. The terms *void* and *contract* are contradictory. A void contract produces no legal obligations on the part of any of the parties. For example, a contract can be void because the purpose of the contract was illegal.

A *voidable contract* is a valid contract but one that can be avoided at the option of one or both of the parties. The party having the option can elect either to avoid any duty to perform or to *ratify* (make valid) the contract. If the contract is avoided, both parties are released from it. If it is ratified, both parties must fully perform their respective legal obligations.

As a general rule, but subject to exceptions, contracts made by minors are voidable at the option of the minor. Contracts entered into under fraudulent conditions are voidable at the option of the defrauded party. In addition, contracts entered into under duress or undue influence are voidable.

Unenforceable Contracts. An *unenforceable contract* is one that cannot be enforced because of certain legal defenses against it. It is not unenforceable because a party failed to satisfy a legal requirement of the contract; rather, it is a valid contract rendered unenforceable by some statute or law. For example, certain contracts must be in writing, and if they are not, they will not be enforceable except in certain exceptional circumstances.

AGREEMENT

Agreement • A meeting of the minds in regard to the terms of a contract; usually broken down into two events—an offer by one party to form a contract, and an acceptance of the offer by the person to whom the offer is made.

Mutual assent • The element of agreement in the formation of a contract. The manifestation of contract parties' mutual assent to the same bargain is required to establish a contract.

An essential element for contract formation is **agreement**—the parties must agree on the terms of the contract and manifest to each other their **mutual assent** to the same bargain. Ordinarily, agreement is evidenced by two events: an *offer* and an *acceptance.* One party offers a certain bargain to another party, who then accepts that bargain. The agreement does not necessarily have to be in writing. Both parties, however, must manifest their assent to the same bargain. Once an agreement is reached, if the other elements of a contract are present (consideration, capacity, and legality—discussed later in this chapter), a valid contract is formed, generally creating enforceable rights and duties between the parties.

Note that not all agreements are contracts. John and Kevin may agree to play golf on a certain day, but a court would not hold that their agreement is an enforceable contract. A *contractual* agreement only arises when the terms of the agreement impose legally enforceable obligations on the parties.

In today's world, contracts are frequently formed via the Internet. For a discussion of some important factors to be considered in online offers and acceptances, see Chapter 11.

Requirements of the Offer

Offer • A promise or commitment to perform or refrain from performing some specified act in the future.

As mentioned earlier, the parties to a contract are the *offeror,* the one who makes an offer or proposal to another party, and the *offeree,* the one to whom the offer or proposal is made. An **offer** is a promise or commitment to do or refrain from doing some specified thing in the future. Under the common law, three elements are necessary for an offer to be effective:

1. The offeror must have a serious intention to become bound by the offer.
2. The terms of the offer must be reasonably certain, or definite, so that the parties and the court can ascertain the terms of the contract.
3. The offer must be communicated by the offeror to the offeree, resulting in the offeree's knowledge of the offer.

Once an effective offer has been made, the offeree has the power to accept the offer. If the offeree accepts, an agreement is formed (and thus a contract, if other essential elements of a contract are present).

Intention. The first requirement for an effective offer is a serious intent on the part of the offeror. Serious intent is not determined by the *subjective* intentions, beliefs, and assumptions of the offeror. As discussed earlier in this chapter, courts generally adhere to the *objective theory of contracts* in determining whether a contract has been formed.

Offers made in obvious anger, jest, or undue excitement do not meet the intent test, because a reasonable person would realize that a serious offer was not being made. Because these offers are not effective, an offeree's acceptance does not create an agreement. For example, suppose that you and three classmates ride to school each day in Davina's new automobile, which has a market value of $20,000. One cold morning, the four of you get into the car, but Davina cannot get the car started. She yells in anger, "I'll sell this car to anyone for $500!" You drop $500 in her lap. Given these facts, a reasonable person, taking into consideration Davina's frustration and the obvious difference in worth between the market value of the car and the proposed purchase price, would conclude that her offer was not made with serious intent and that you did not have an agreement.

The concept of intention can be further clarified through an examination of the types of expressions and statements that are *not* offers. We look at these expressions and statements in the subsections that follow.

Expressions of Opinion. An expression of opinion is not an offer. It does not evidence an intention to enter into a binding agreement. Consider a classic example. Hawkins took his son to McGee, a doctor, and asked McGee to operate on the son's hand. McGee said that the boy would be in the hospital three or four days and that the hand would *probably* heal a few days later. The son's hand did not heal for a month, but the father did not win a suit for breach of contract. The court held that McGee had not made an offer to heal the son's hand in a few days. He had merely expressed an opinion as to when the hand would heal.[6]

Statements of Intention. If Arif says, "I *plan* to sell my stock in Novation, Inc., for $150 per share," a contract is not created if John "accepts" and tenders the $150 per share for the stock. Arif has merely expressed his intention to enter into a future contract for the sale of the stock. If John accepts and tenders the $150 per share, no contract is formed, because a reasonable person would conclude that Arif was only *thinking about* selling his stock, not *promising* to sell it.

Preliminary Negotiations. A request or invitation to negotiate is not an offer. It only expresses a willingness to discuss the possibility of entering into a contract. Included are statements such as "Will you sell Blythe Estate?" or "I wouldn't sell my car for less than $1,000." A reasonable person in the offeree's position would not conclude that these statements evidenced an intention to enter into a binding obligation. Likewise, when construction work is done for the government and private firms, contractors are invited to submit bids. The *invitation* to submit bids is not an offer, and a contractor does not bind the government or private firm by submitting a bid. (The bids that the contractors submit are offers, however, and the government or private firm can bind the contractor by accepting the bid.)

---

6. *Hawkins v. McGee,* 84 N.H. 114, 146 A. 641 (1929).

Agreements to Agree. During preliminary negotiations, the parties may form an agreement to agree to a material term of a contract at some future date. Traditionally, such "agreements to agree" were not considered to be binding contracts. More modern cases illustrate the view that agreements to agree serve valid commercial purposes and can be enforced if the parties clearly intended to be bound by such agreements.

For example, suppose that Zahn Consulting leases office space from Leon Properties, Inc. Their lease agreement includes a clause permitting Zahn to extend the lease at an amount of rent to be agreed on when the lease is extended. Under the traditional rule, because the amount of rent is not specified in the lease clause itself, the clause would be too indefinite in its terms to enforce. Under the current view, a court could hold that the parties intended the future rent to be a *reasonable* amount and could enforce the clause.[7] In other words, under the current view, the emphasis is on the parties' intent rather than on form.

Advertisements. Advertisements—including representations made in mail-order catalogues, price lists, and circulars—are generally treated not as offers to contract but as invitations to negotiate. Suppose that Loeser advertises a used paving machine. The ad is mailed to hundreds of firms and reads, "Used Loeser Construction Co. paving machine. Builds curbs and finishes cement work all in one process. Price $42,350." If Star Paving calls Loeser and says, "We accept your offer," no contract is formed. Any reasonable person would conclude that Loeser was not promising to sell the paving machine but rather was soliciting offers to buy it. If such an ad were held to constitute a legal offer, and fifty people accepted the offer, there would be no way for Loeser to perform all fifty of the resulting contracts. He would have to breach forty-nine contracts. Obviously, the law seeks to avoid such unfairness.

Price lists are another form of invitation to negotiate or trade. A seller's price list is not an offer to sell at that price; it merely invites the buyer to offer to buy at that price. In fact, the seller usually puts "prices subject to change" on the price list. Only in rare circumstances will a price quotation be construed as an offer.

Although most advertisements are treated as invitations to negotiate, this does not mean that an advertisement can *never* be an offer. If the advertisement makes a promise so definite in character that it is apparent that the offeror is binding himself or herself to the conditions stated, the advertisement is treated as an offer.

Definiteness of Terms. The second requirement for an effective offer involves the definiteness of its terms. An offer must have terms that are reasonably definite so that, if a contract is formed, a court can determine if a breach has occurred and can provide an appropriate remedy. What specific terms are required depends, of course, on the type of contract. Generally, a contract must include the following terms, either expressed in the contract or capable of being reasonably inferred from it:

1. The identification of the parties.

---

7. *Restatement (Second) of Contracts,* Section 33. See also UCC 2–204, 2–305.

2. The identification of the object or subject matter of the contract (also the quantity, when appropriate), including the work to be performed, with specific identification of such items as goods, services, and land.
3. The consideration to be paid.
4. The time of payment, delivery, or performance.

Courts sometimes are willing to supply a missing term in a contract when the parties have clearly manifested an intent to form a contract. If, in contrast, the parties have attempted to deal with a particular term of the contract but their expression of intent is too vague or uncertain to be given any precise meaning, the court will not supply a "reasonable" term, because to do so might conflict with the intent of the parties. In other words, the court will not rewrite the contract.[8]

Communication. A third requirement for an effective offer is communication of the offer to the offeree, resulting in the offeree's knowledge of the offer. Ordinarily, one cannot agree to a bargain without knowing that it exists. Suppose that Estrich advertises a reward for the return of his lost dog. Hoban, not knowing of the reward, finds the dog and returns it to Estrich. Hoban cannot recover the reward, because she did not know that it had been offered.[9]

Termination of the Offer

The communication of an effective offer to an offeree gives the offeree the power to transform the offer into a binding, legal obligation (a contract) by an acceptance. This power of acceptance, however, does not continue forever. It can be terminated either by the action of the parties or by operation of law.

Termination by Action of the Parties. An offer can be terminated by the action of the parties in any of three ways: by revocation, by rejection, or by counteroffer.

Revocation of the Offer by the Offeror. The offeror's act of withdrawing (revoking) an offer is known as **revocation.** Unless an offer is irrevocable, the offeror usually can revoke the offer (even if he or she has promised to keep it open), as long as the revocation is communicated to the offeree before the offeree accepts. Revocation may be accomplished by express repudiation of the offer (for example, with a statement such as "I withdraw my previous offer of October 17") or by performance of acts inconsistent with the existence of the offer, which are made known to the offeree.

Revocation • In contract law, the withdrawal of an offer by an offeror. Unless an offer is irrevocable, it can be revoked at any time prior to acceptance without liability.

The general rule followed by most states is that a revocation becomes effective when the offeree or offeree's agent (a person acting on behalf of the offeree) actually receives it. Therefore, a letter of revocation mailed on April 1 and delivered at the offeree's residence or place of business on April 3 becomes effective on April 3.

---

8. See Chapter 11 and UCC 2–204. Article 2 of the UCC specifies different rules relating to the definiteness of terms used in a contract for the sale of goods. In essence, Article 2 modifies the common law of contracts by requiring less specificity.

9. A few states allow recovery of the reward, but not on contract principles. Because Estrich wanted his dog to be returned, and Hoban returned it, these few states would allow Hoban to recover on the basis that it would be unfair to deny her the reward just because she did not know it had been offered.

Irrevocable Offers. Although most offers are revocable, some can be made irrevocable—that is, they cannot be revoked, or canceled. One type of irrevocable offer involves the option contract. Increasingly, courts also refuse to allow an offeror to revoke an offer when the offeree has changed position because of justifiable reliance on the offer. (In some circumstances, an offer for the sale of goods made by a merchant may also be considered irrevocable—see the discussion of the "merchant's firm offer" in Chapter 11.)

An *option contract* is created when an offeror promises to hold an offer open for a specified period of time in return for a payment (consideration) given by the offeree. An option contract takes away the offeror's power to revoke the offer for the period of time specified in the option. If no time is specified, then a reasonable period of time is implied.

Promissory estoppel • A doctrine that applies when a promisor makes a clear and definite promise on which the promisee justifiably relies; such a promise is binding if justice will be better served by the enforcement of the promise.

When the offeree justifiably relies on an offer to his or her detriment, the court may hold that this *detrimental reliance* makes the offer irrevocable. In this situation, the doctrine of **promissory estoppel** comes into play. To *estop* means to bar, impede, or preclude someone from doing something. Thus, promissory estoppel means that the promisor (the offeror) is barred from revoking the offer because the offeree has already changed her actions in reliance on the offer. We look again at the doctrine of promissory estoppel later in this chapter, in the context of consideration.

Detrimental reliance on the part of the offeree can also involve partial performance by the offeree in response to an offer looking toward the formation of a unilateral contract. As discussed earlier in this chapter, the offer to form a unilateral contract invites acceptance only by full performance; merely promising to perform does not constitute acceptance. Injustice can result if an offeree expends time and money in partial performance, and then the offeror revokes the offer before performance can be completed. Many courts will not allow the offeror to revoke the offer after the offeree has performed some substantial part of his or her duties.[10] In effect, partial performance renders the offer irrevocable, giving the original offeree a reasonable time to complete performance. Of course, once the performance is complete, a unilateral contract exists.

Rejection of the Offer by the Offeree. The offer may be rejected by the offeree, in which case the offer is terminated. Any subsequent attempt by the offeree to accept will be construed as a new offer, giving the original offeror (now the offeree) the power of acceptance. A rejection is ordinarily accomplished by words or conduct evidencing an intent not to accept the offer. As with revocation, rejection of an offer is effective only when it is actually received by the offeror or the offeror's agent.

Merely inquiring about an offer does not constitute rejection. Suppose that a friend offers to buy your CD-ROM library for $300, and you respond, "Is that your best offer?" or "Will you pay me $375 for it?" A reasonable person would conclude that you had not rejected the offer but had merely made an inquiry for further consideration of the offer. You can still accept and bind your friend to the $300 purchase price. When the offeree merely inquires as to the firmness of the offer, there is no reason to presume that he or she intends to reject it.

Counteroffer • An offeree's response to an offer in which the offeree rejects the original offer and at the same time makes a new offer.

Counteroffer by the Offeree. A rejection of the original offer and the simultaneous making of a new offer is called a **counteroffer.** Suppose that Duffy

10. *Restatement (Second) of Contracts,* Section 45.

offers to sell her home to Wong for $170,000. Wong responds, "Your price is too high. I'll offer to purchase your house for $160,000." Wong's response is a counteroffer, because it terminates Duffy's offer to sell at $170,000 and creates a new offer by Wong to purchase at $160,000.

At common law, the **mirror image rule** requires the offeree's acceptance to match the offeror's offer exactly—to mirror the offer. Any material change in, or addition to, the terms of the original offer automatically terminates that offer and substitutes the counteroffer. The counteroffer, of course, need not be accepted; but if the original offeror does accept the terms of the counteroffer, a valid contract is created.[11]

Mirror image rule • A common law rule that requires, for a valid contractual agreement, that the terms of the offeree's acceptance adhere exactly to the terms of the offeror's offer.

Termination by Operation of Law. The power of the offeree to transform the offer into a binding, legal obligation can be terminated by operation of law through the occurrence of the following events:

1. Lapse of time.
2. Destruction of the specific subject matter of the offer.
3. Death or incompetence of the offeror or the offeree.
4. Supervening illegality of the proposed contract.

An offer terminates automatically by law when the period of time specified in the offer has passed. For example, suppose that Alejandro offers to sell his camper to Kelly if she accepts within twenty days. Kelly must accept within the twenty-day period, or the offer will lapse (terminate). The time period specified in an offer normally begins to run when the offer is actually received by the offeree, not when it is sent or drawn up. When the offer is delayed (through the misdelivery of mail, for example), the period begins to run from the date the offeree would have received the offer, but only if the offeree knows or should know that the offer has been delayed.[12]

If no time for acceptance is specified in the offer, the offer terminates at the end of a *reasonable* period of time. What constitutes a reasonable period of time depends on the subject matter of the contract, business and market conditions, and other relevant circumstances. An offer to sell farm produce, for example, will terminate sooner than an offer to sell farm equipment because farm produce is perishable and subject to greater fluctuations in market value.

Acceptance

Acceptance is a voluntary act (either words or conduct) by the offeree that shows assent (agreement) to the terms of an offer. The acceptance must be unequivocal and communicated to the offeror.

Acceptance • In contract law, the offeree's notification to the offeror that the offeree agrees to be bound by the terms of the offeror's proposal.

Unequivocal Acceptance. To exercise the power of acceptance effectively, the offeree must accept unequivocally. This is the *mirror image rule* previously discussed. If the acceptance is subject to new conditions or if the terms of the acceptance *materially* change the original offer, the acceptance may be

11. The mirror image rule has been greatly modified in regard to sales contracts. Section 2–207 of the UCC provides that a contract is formed if the offeree makes a definite expression of acceptance (such as signing the form in the appropriate location), even though the terms of the acceptance modify or add to the terms of the original offer (see Chapter 11).
12. *Restatement (Second) of Contracts,* Section 49.

deemed a counteroffer that implicitly rejects the original offer. An acceptance may be unequivocal even though the offeree expresses dissatisfaction with the contract. For example, "I accept the offer, but I wish I could have gotten a better price" is an effective acceptance. So, too, is "I accept, but can you shave the price?" In contrast, the statement "I accept the offer but only if I can pay on ninety days' credit" is not an unequivocal acceptance and operates as a counteroffer, rejecting the original offer.

Certain terms when added to an acceptance will not qualify the acceptance sufficiently to constitute rejection of the offer. Suppose that in response to an offer to sell a piano, the offeree replies, "I accept; please send a written contract." The offeree is requesting a written contract but is not making it a condition for acceptance. Therefore, the acceptance is effective without the written contract. If the offeree replies, "I accept if you send a written contract," however, the acceptance is expressly conditioned on the request for a writing, and the statement is not an acceptance but a counteroffer. (Notice how important each word is!)

Silence as Acceptance. Ordinarily, silence cannot constitute acceptance, even if the offeror states, "By your silence and inaction you will be deemed to have accepted this offer." This general rule applies because an offeree should not be obligated to act affirmatively to reject an offer when no consideration has passed to the offeree to impose such a duty.

In some instances, however, the offeree's silence or inaction will operate as an acceptance. For example, silence may be an acceptance when an offeree takes the benefit of offered services even though he or she had an opportunity to reject them and knew that they were offered with the expectation of compensation.

Silence can also operate as acceptance when the offeree has had prior dealings with the offeror. Suppose that a merchant routinely receives shipments from a certain supplier and always notifies the supplier when defective goods are rejected. In this situation, silence regarding a shipment will constitute acceptance. Additionally, if a person solicits an offer specifying that certain terms and conditions are acceptable, and the offeror makes the offer in response to the solicitation, the offeree has a duty to reject—that is, a duty to tell the offeror that the offer is not acceptable. In this situation, failure to reject (silence) operates as an acceptance.

Communication of Acceptance. Whether the offeror must be notified of the acceptance depends on the nature of the contract. In a bilateral contract, communication of acceptance is necessary because acceptance is in the form of a promise (not performance) and the contract is formed when the promise is made (rather than when the act is performed). The offeree must communicate the acceptance to the offeror. Communication of acceptance is not necessary, however, if the offer dispenses with the requirement. Additionally, if the offer can be accepted by silence, no communication is necessary.

Because a unilateral contract calls for the full performance of some act, acceptance is usually evident, and notification is therefore unnecessary. Exceptions do exist, however. When the offeror requests notice of acceptance or has no adequate means of determining whether the requested act has been performed, or when the law requires notice of acceptance, then notice is necessary.

Timeliness and Mode of Acceptance. Acceptance in bilateral contracts must be timely. The general rule is that acceptance in a bilateral contract is timely if it is made before the offer is terminated. Problems arise, however, when the parties involved are not dealing face to face. In such cases, acceptance takes effect, thus completing formation of the contract, at the time the acceptance is communicated via the mode expressly or impliedly authorized by the offeror.

The Mailbox Rule. This rule traditionally has been referred to as the **mailbox rule,** also called the "deposited acceptance rule," because once an acceptance has been deposited into a mailbox, it is "out of the offeree's possession." Under this rule, if the authorized mode of communication is the mail, then an acceptance becomes valid when it is dispatched by mail (even if it is never received by the offeror). Thus, whereas a revocation becomes effective only when it is received by the offeree, an acceptance becomes effective on *dispatch,* providing that *authorized* means of communication are used.

Mailbox rule • A rule providing that an acceptance of an offer becomes effective on dispatch (on being placed in a mailbox), if mail is, expressly or impliedly, an authorized means of communication of acceptance to the offeror.

Authorized Means of Acceptance. An authorized means of communication may be either expressly authorized—that is, expressly stipulated in the offer—or impliedly authorized by the facts and circumstances surrounding the situation or by law. When an offeror specifies how acceptance should be made (for example, by overnight delivery), *express authorization* is said to exist, and the contract is not formed unless the offeree uses that specified mode of acceptance. Moreover, both offeror and offeree are bound in contract the moment this means of acceptance is employed. If overnight delivery is expressly authorized as the only means of acceptance, a contract is created as soon as the offeree delivers the message to the express delivery company. The contract would still exist even if the delivery company failed to deliver the message.

Many offerors, for one reason or another, do not indicate their preferred method of acceptance. When the offeror does not specify expressly that the offeree is to accept by a certain means, or that the acceptance will be effective only when received, acceptance of an offer may be made by any medium that is *reasonable under the circumstances.*[13] Several factors determine whether the acceptance was reasonable: the nature of the circumstances as they existed at the time the offer was made, the means used by the offeror to transmit the offer to the offeree, and the reliability of the offer's delivery.

An acceptance sent by means not expressly or impliedly authorized is normally not effective until it is received by the offeror. If an acceptance is timely sent and timely received, however, despite the means by which it is transmitted, it is considered to have been effective on its dispatch.

Technology and Acceptance Rules. Clearly, some of the traditional rules governing acceptance do not seem to apply to an age in which acceptances are commonly delivered via electronic means, such as by e-mail or fax. For example, the mailbox rule does not apply to online acceptances, which typically are communicated instantaneously to the offeror. Nonetheless, the traditional rules—and the principles that underlie those rules—provide a basis for understanding what constitutes a valid acceptance in today's online environment. This is because, as in other areas of the law, much of the law governing online offers and acceptances has been adapted from traditional law to a new environment.

13. *Restatement (Second) of Contracts,* Section 30.

While online offers are not significantly different from traditional offers contained in paper documents, online acceptances have posed some unusual problems for the courts. These problems, as well as other aspects of e-contracting, will be discussed in detail in Chapter 11.

CONSIDERATION

Consideration • Generally, the value given in return for a promise or a performance. Consideration, which must be present to make a contract legally binding, must be something of legally sufficient value and bargained for.

The fact that a promise has been made does not mean the promise can or will be enforced. No promise is enforceable without consideration. **Consideration** is usually defined as the value (such as money) given in return for a promise (such as the promise to sell a stamp collection on receipt of payment).

Often, consideration is broken down into two parts: (1) something of *legal value* must be given in exchange for the promise, and (2) there must be a *bargained-for* exchange. The "something of legal value" may consist of a return promise that is bargained for. If it consists of performance, that performance may be (1) an act (other than a promise); (2) a forbearance (a refraining from action); or (3) the creation, modification, or destruction of a legal relation.[14]

The following case is one of the classics of contract law. The issue before the court was whether refraining from certain behavior at the request of another is sufficient consideration to support a promise to pay a sum of money.

14. *Restatement (Second) of Contracts,* Section 71.

CASE 10.3

Court of Appeals of New York, Second Division, 1891. 124 N.Y. 538, 27 N.E. 256.

HAMER v. SIDWAY

William E. Story, Sr., was the uncle of William E. Story II. In the presence of family members and guests invited to a family gathering, the elder Story promised to pay his nephew $5,000 ($72,000 in today's dollars) if he would refrain from drinking, using tobacco, swearing, and playing cards or billiards for money until he reached the age of twenty-one. (Note that in 1869, when this contract was formed, it was legal in New York to drink and play cards for money prior to age twenty-one.) The nephew agreed and fully performed his part of the bargain. When he reached the age of twenty-one, he wrote and told his uncle that he had kept his part of the agreement and was therefore entitled to $5,000. The uncle replied that he was pleased with his nephew's performance, writing, "I have no doubt but you have, for which you shall have five thousand dollars, as I promised you. I had the money in the bank the day you was twenty-one years old that I intend for you, and you shall have the money certain. . . . P.S. You can consider this money on interest." The nephew received his uncle's letter and thereafter consented that the money should remain with his uncle according to the terms and conditions of the letter. The uncle died about twelve years later without having paid his nephew any part of the $5,000 and interest. The executor of the uncle's estate (Sidway, the defendant in this action) claimed that there had been no valid consideration for the promise and therefore refused to pay the $5,000 (with interest) to Hamer, a third party to whom the nephew had transferred his rights in the note. The court reviewed the case to determine whether the nephew had given valid consideration under the law.

PARKER, J.

Courts will not ask whether the thing which forms the consideration * * * is of any substantial value to any one. It is enough that something is promised, done, forborne, or suffered by the party to whom the promise is made as consideration for the promise made to him. *In general a waiver of any legal right at the request of another party is a sufficient consideration for a promise.* Any damage, or suspension, or forbearance of a right will be sufficient to sustain a promise. * * * Now, applying this rule to the facts before us, the promisee used tobacco, occasionally drank liquor, and he had a legal right to do so. That right he abandoned for a period of years upon the strength of the promise of the testator [his uncle] that for such forbearance he would give him $5,000. We need not speculate on the effort which may have been required to give up the use of those stimulants. It is sufficient that he restricted his lawful freedom of action within certain prescribed limits upon the faith of his uncle's agreement * * *. [Emphasis added.]

The court ruled that the nephew had provided legally sufficient consideration by giving up smoking, drinking, swearing, and playing cards or billiards for money until he reached the age of twenty-one and was therefore entitled to the money.

QUESTIONS

1. On what legal ground did the defendant in this case base his refusal to pay money to the plaintiff?
2. What was the issue before the court? What did the court rule on this issue, and why?
3. Read the section on legality on pages 337 and 338, and then answer the following question: If Story had not had a legal right to engage in the behavior in which he agreed not to indulge, would the result in this case have been different?

Adequacy of Consideration

Adequacy of consideration involves "how much" consideration is given and relates to the fairness of the bargain. In general, a court will not question the adequacy of consideration if the consideration is legally sufficient. Under the doctrine of freedom of contract, parties are normally free to bargain as they wish. If people could sue merely because they had entered into an unwise contract, the courts would be overloaded with frivolous suits.

In extreme cases, a court may consider the adequacy of consideration in terms of its amount or worth because inadequate consideration may indicate that fraud, duress, or undue influence was involved or that the element of bargained-for exchange was lacking. Inadequate consideration may also reflect a party's incompetence (for example, an individual might have been too intoxicated or simply too young to make a contract). Suppose that Dylan has a house worth $100,000 and he sells it for $50,000. A $50,000 sale could indicate that the buyer unduly pressured Dylan into selling the house at that price or that Dylan was defrauded into selling the house at far below market value. (Of course, it might also indicate that

Dylan was in a hurry to sell, in which situation the amount would be legally sufficient.)

Agreements That Lack Consideration

Sometimes, one of the parties (or both parties) to an agreement may think that consideration has been exchanged when in fact it has not. Here, we look at some situations in which the parties' promises or actions do not qualify as contractual consideration.

Preexisting Duty. Under most circumstances, a promise to do what one already has a legal duty to do does not constitute legally sufficient consideration.[15] The preexisting legal duty may be imposed by law or may arise out of a previous contract. A sheriff, for example, cannot collect a reward for providing information leading to the capture of a criminal if the sheriff already has a legal duty to capture the criminal.

Likewise, if a party is already bound by contract to perform a certain duty, that duty cannot serve as consideration for a second contract. For example, suppose that Bauman-Bache, Inc., begins construction on a seven-story office building and after three months demands an extra $75,000 on its contract. If the extra $75,000 is not paid, it will stop working. The owner of the land, having no one else to complete construction, agrees to pay the extra $75,000. The agreement is not enforceable, because it is not supported by legally sufficient consideration; Bauman-Bache was under a preexisting contract to complete the building.

Past Consideration. Promises made in return for actions or events that have already taken place are unenforceable. These promises lack consideration in that the element of bargained-for exchange is missing. In short, you can bargain for something to take place now or in the future but not for something that has already taken place. Therefore, **past consideration** is no consideration.

Past consideration • An act done before the contract is made, which ordinarily, by itself, cannot be consideration for a later promise to pay for the act.

Suppose, for example, that Elsie, a real estate agent, does her friend Judy a favor by selling Judy's house and not charging any commission. Later, Judy says to Elsie, "In return for your generous act, I will pay you $3,000." This promise is made in return for past consideration and is thus unenforceable; in effect, Judy is stating her intention to give Elsie a gift.

Promissory Estoppel

As discussed previously, under the doctrine of *promissory estoppel,* a person who has reasonably and substantially relied on the promise of another may be able to obtain some measure of recovery. This doctrine is applied in a wide variety of contexts in which a promise is otherwise unenforceable, such as when a promise is not supported by consideration. Under this doctrine, a court may enforce an otherwise unenforceable promise to avoid the injustice that would result if the promise were not enforced. For the doctrine to be applied, the following elements are required:

15. See *Foakes v. Beer,* 9 App.Cas. 605 (1884).

1. There must be a clear and definite promise.
2. The promisee must justifiably rely on the promise.
3. The reliance normally must be of a substantial and definite character.
4. Justice will be better served by enforcement of the promise.

If these requirements are met, a promise may be enforced even though it is not supported by consideration. In essence, the promisor will be *estopped* (prevented) from asserting the lack of consideration as a defense. For example, suppose that your uncle tells you, "I'll pay you $150 a week so you won't have to work anymore." In reliance on your uncle's promise, you quit your job, but your uncle refuses to pay you. Under the doctrine of promissory estoppel, you may be able to enforce such a promise.[16] (See this chapter's *Contemporary Legal Debates* feature on pages 338 and 339 for a discussion of the applicability of promissory estoppel to promises of employment.)

CAPACITY

Although the parties to a contract must assume certain risks, the law indicates that neither party should be allowed to benefit from the other party's lack of *contractual capacity*—the legal ability to enter into a contractual relationship. Courts generally presume the existence of contractual capacity, but there are some situations in which capacity is lacking or may be questionable. In many situations, a party may have the capacity to enter into a valid contract but also have the right to avoid liability under it.

Minors usually are not legally bound by contracts. Subject to certain exceptions, the contracts entered into by a minor are voidable at the option of that minor. The minor has the option of *disaffirming* (renouncing) the contract and setting aside the contract and all legal obligations arising from it. An adult who enters into a contract with a minor, however, cannot avoid his or her contractual duties on the ground that the minor can do so. Unless the minor exercises the option to disaffirm the contract, the adult party is bound by it.

Intoxication is a condition in which a person's normal capacity to act or think is inhibited by alcohol or some other drug. If the person was sufficiently intoxicated to lack mental capacity, the transaction is voidable at the option of the intoxicated person even if the intoxication was purely voluntary.

If a person has been adjudged mentally incompetent by a court of law and a guardian has been appointed, any contract made by the mentally incompetent person is void—no contract exists. Only the guardian can enter into binding legal duties on the incompetent person's behalf.

LEGALITY

A contract to do something that is prohibited by federal or state statutory law is illegal and, as such, void from the outset and thus unenforceable. Also, a contract that calls for a tortious act or an action that is contrary to public policy is illegal and unenforceable. It is important to note that a contract or a clause in a contract may be illegal even in the absence of a specific statute prohibiting the action promised by the contract.

---

16. *Ricketts v. Scothorn,* 57 Neb. 51, 77 N.W. 365 (1898).

CONTEMPORARY LEGAL DEBATES

Promissory Estoppel and Employment Contracts

Today, approximately 85 percent of American workers have the legal status of "employees at will." Under this common law employment doctrine, which applies in all states but Montana, an employer may fire an employee for any reason or no reason. The at-will doctrine, however, does not apply to employees who have employment contracts or who fall under the protection of a state or federal statute—which add up, of course, to a large number of employees. Even when an employee is subject to the employment-at-will doctrine, the courts sometimes make exceptions to the doctrine based on tort theory or contract principles or on the ground that a termination violates an established public policy.

These exceptions to the at-will doctrine, however, apply only when a current employee's employment is *terminated.* Should they also apply when a company fails to *hire* a job candidate after promising to do so? Consider an example. Suppose that a job candidate, relying on a company's offer of employment, quits his or her existing job, moves to another city, and rents or buys housing in the new location. Then the company decides not to hire the candidate after all. Given the employee's detrimental reliance on the company's job offer, should the company be prevented from revoking its offer under the doctrine of promissory estoppel? This question has come before a number of courts. As yet, however, the courts have not reached a consensus on the issue. Some jurisdictions allow the doctrine of promissory estoppel to be applied; others do not.

PROMISSORY ESTOPPEL SHOULD NOT BE APPLIED

Many jurisdictions believe that reliance on a prospective employer's promise of at-will employment is unreasonable as a matter of law. Courts in these jurisdictions reason that an employee should know that, even if she or he is hired, the employer could terminate the employment at any time for any reason without liability. According to these courts, it would be contrary to reason to allow an employee who has not yet begun work to recover damages under a theory of promissory estoppel, given that the same employee's job could be terminated without liability one day after the employee begins work.

Consider a case example. Arlie Thompson had worked for nine years at a hospital as a technician assistant when she was laid off. A year later, the same hospital offered her a clerical position, which she accepted. She was measured for a new uniform, given a security badge, and provided with the password for the computer system. Thompson, who was then working at another job, quit the other job in reliance on the hospital's job offer. Shortly thereafter, the hospital asked her to take a test. When she failed the test, the hospital refused to hire her. Thompson sued, asking the court, among other things, to apply the doctrine of promissory estoppel to prevent the hospital from revoking its offer. The court, however, held that the hospital's promise of employment was not sufficiently "clear and definite" for that doctrine to be applied. According to the court, "The allegations, at most, amounted to an agreement

Although contracts involve private parties, some are not enforceable because of the negative impact they would have on society. Contracts in restraint of trade (anticompetitive agreements) usually adversely affect the public (which favors competition in the economy) and typically violate one or more federal or state statutes.[17] Many such contracts involve a type of restraint called a *covenant not to compete,* or a restrictive covenant. Basically, a restriction on competition must be reasonable—that is, not any greater than necessary to protect a legitimate business interest.

17. The federal statutes include the Sherman Act, the Clayton Act, and the Federal Trade Commission Act (see Chapter 17).

CONTEMPORARY LEGAL DEBATES

Promissory Estoppel and Employment Contracts

to enter into an at-will employment relationship and not a contract to employ the plaintiff for a specific term."[a]

PROMISSORY ESTOPPEL SHOULD BE APPLIED

A number of other jurisdictions have held that an employee can recover damages incurred as a result of resigning from a former job in reliance on an offer of at-will employment. These jurisdictions have determined that when a prospective employer knows or should know that a promise of employment will induce the future employee to leave his or her current job, the employer should be responsible for the prospective employee's damages. After all, without the offer from the prospective employer, the prospective employee would have continued to work in his or her prior employment.

This approach is reflected in a case involving Julie Goff-Hamel, who had worked for Hastings Family Planning for eleven years. Her job benefits included six weeks' paid maternity leave, six weeks' vacation time, twelve paid holidays, twelve paid sick days, educational reimbursement, and medical and dental insurance. Representatives of a women's health group asked Goff-Hamel to work for the group. Although the pay would be less than she was making at her current job, the offer included a retirement plan that would start at the end of the second year, retroactive to the end of the first year. Goff-Hamel quit her job with Hastings and accepted the job offer from the women's health group. The prospective employer gave her uniforms for her new job and a copy of her work schedule. The day before she was scheduled to start, however, a representative of the women's health group told her that she need not report to work because the wife of a part owner of that group opposed hiring her. Goff-Hamel filed suit, seeking damages, in part, on the basis of detrimental reliance.

The trial court concluded that because she was to be employed as an at-will employee, she could not seek damages. On appeal, however, the appellate court reversed the trial court's decision, holding that promissory estoppel could be asserted in connection with an offer of at-will employment. The court reasoned that "a cause of action for promissory estoppel is based upon a promise which the promisor should reasonably expect to induce action or forbearance on the part of the promisee [and] which does in fact induce such action or forbearance."[b]

WHERE DO YOU STAND?

Some jurisdictions maintain that it would be irrational to apply the doctrine of promissory estoppel to a promise of at-will employment, given that the employee could be fired after working for only one day on the job. Other jurisdictions, in contrast, conclude that the doctrine should apply because the employer should reasonably expect a job candidate in this situation to act in reliance on the promise. Does one of these two arguments have greater merit than the other? What is your position on this issue?

a. *Thompson v. Bridgeport Hospital,* 2001 WL 823130 (Conn.Super. 2001).

b. *Goff-Hamel v. Obstetricians & Gynecologists, P.C.,* 256 Neb. 19, 588 N.W.2d 798 (1999).

GENUINENESS OF ASSENT

A contract has been entered into by two parties, each with full legal capacity and for a legal purpose. The contract is also supported by consideration. Nonetheless, the contract may be unenforceable if the parties have not genuinely assented to its terms. Lack of **genuineness of assent** can be used as a defense to the contract's enforceability. Genuineness of assent may be lacking because of a mistake, misrepresentation, undue influence, or duress—in other words, because there is no true "meeting of the minds."

Genuineness of assent • Knowing and voluntary assent to the terms of a contract. If a contract is formed as a result of a mistake, misrepresentation, undue influence, or duress, genuineness of assent is lacking, and the contract will be voidable.

Mistakes

We all make mistakes, and it is therefore not surprising that mistakes are made when contracts are formed. It is important to distinguish between *mistakes of fact* and *mistakes of value or quality*. Only a mistake of fact may allow a contract to be avoided (unenforceable).

Mistakes of fact occur in two forms—*mutual (bilateral)* and *unilateral*. A mutual, or bilateral, mistake is made by both of the contracting parties. A unilateral mistake is made by only one of the parties.

Bilateral (Mutual) Mistakes of Fact. A bilateral, or mutual, mistake occurs when both parties are mistaken as to some *material fact*—that is, a fact important to the subject matter of the contract. When a bilateral mistake occurs, the contract can be rescinded, or canceled, by either party.[18] For example, Keeley buys a landscape painting from Umberto's art gallery. Both Umberto and Keeley believe that the painting is by the artist Van Gogh. Later, Keeley discovers that the painting is a very clever fake. Because neither Umberto nor Keeley was aware of this material fact when they made their deal, Keeley can rescind the contract and recover the purchase price of the painting.

A word or term in a contract may be subject to more than one reasonable interpretation. In that situation, if the parties to the contract attach materially different meanings to the term, their mutual mistake of fact may allow the contract to be rescinded because there has been no "meeting of the minds," or true assent, which is required for a contract to arise.

The classic case on bilateral mistake is *Raffles v. Wichelhaus*,[19] which was decided by an English court in 1864. The defendant, Wichelhaus, paid for a shipment of Surat cotton from the plaintiff, Raffles, "to arrive 'Peerless' from Bombay." Wichelhaus expected the goods to be shipped on the *Peerless*, a ship sailing from Bombay, India, in October. Raffles expected to ship the goods on a different *Peerless*, which sailed from Bombay in December. When the goods arrived and Raffles tried to deliver them, Wichelhaus refused to accept them. The court held for Wichelhaus, concluding that no mutual assent existed because the parties had attached materially different meanings to an essential term of the written contract (the ship that was to transport the goods).

Unilateral Mistakes of Fact. A unilateral mistake occurs when only one of the contracting parties makes a mistake as to some material fact. The general rule is that a unilateral mistake does not afford the mistaken party any right to relief from the contract. For example, DeVinck intends to sell his motor home for $17,500. When he learns that Benson is interested in buying a used motor home, DeVinck faxes Benson an offer to sell the vehicle to him. When typing the fax, however, DeVinck mistakenly keys in the price of $15,700. Benson immediately sends DeVinck a fax, accepting DeVinck's offer. Even though DeVinck intended to sell his motor home for $17,500, his unilateral mistake falls on him. He is bound in contract to sell the motor home to Benson for $15,700.

There are at least two exceptions to this general rule.[20] First, if the *other* party to the contract knows or should have known that a mistake of fact was made, the contract may not be enforceable. In the above example, if Benson

18. *Restatement (Second) of Contracts,* Section 152.

19. 159 Eng.Rep. 375 (1864).

20. The *Restatement (Second) of Contracts,* Section 153, liberalizes the general rule to take into account the modern trend of allowing avoidance even though only one party has been mistaken.

knew that DeVinck intended to sell his motor home for $17,500, then DeVinck's unilateral mistake (stating $15,700 in his offer) may render the resulting contract unenforceable. The second exception arises when a unilateral mistake of fact was due to a mathematical mistake in addition, subtraction, division, or multiplication and was made inadvertently and without gross (extreme) negligence. If a contractor's bid was significantly low because he or she made a mistake in addition when totaling the estimated costs, any contract resulting from the bid may be rescinded, or canceled. Of course, in both situations, the mistake must still involve some *material* fact.

Fraudulent Misrepresentation

As you will read in Chapter 12, **fraudulent misrepresentation (fraud)**—knowingly making a false or misleading statement with the intention of deceiving another—is a tort. In the context of contract law, fraud may affect the genuineness of the innocent party's consent to the contract. Thus, the transaction is not voluntary in the sense of involving "mutual assent." When an innocent party is fraudulently induced to enter into a contract, the contract normally can be avoided because that party has not *voluntarily* consented to its terms.[21] Normally, the innocent party can either rescind (cancel) the contract and be restored to his or her original position or enforce the contract and seek damages for any injuries resulting from the fraud.

Fraudulent misrepresentation (fraud) • Any misrepresentation, either by misstatement or omission of a material fact, knowingly made with the intention of deceiving another and on which a reasonable person would and does rely to his or her detriment.

The word *fraudulent* means many things in the law. Generally, fraudulent misrepresentation refers only to misrepresentation that is consciously false and is intended to mislead another. The perpetrator of the fraudulent misrepresentation knows or believes that the assertion is false or knows that he or she does not have a basis (stated or implied) for the assertion.[22] What is at issue is whether the defendant believed that the plaintiff was substantially certain to be misled as a result of the misrepresentation.

Typically, fraudulent misrepresentation consists of the following elements:

1. A misrepresentation of a material fact must occur.
2. There must be an intent to deceive.
3. The innocent party must justifiably rely on the misrepresentation.

To collect damages, a party must also have been injured. In most states, however, a party need not have suffered an injury to obtain rescission of a contract or to defend against the enforcement of a contract on the basis of fraudulent misrepresentation.

In the following case, a buyer claimed that he had relied on certain representations by the owner of a business in deciding whether to become a partner with the owner and ultimately buy the business. Were these representations sufficient to support a finding of fraud? That was one of the questions before the court.

21. *Restatement (Second) of Contracts,* Sections 163 and 164.
22. *Restatement (Second) of Contracts,* Section 162.

FOLEY v. PARLIER

Court of Appeals of Texas, Fort Worth, 2002. 68 S.W.3d 870.

Diane Foley owned Finishes, a commercial tile business in Dallas and Fort Worth, Texas. Rick Parlier operated a residential tile business in California. In 1999, Foley and Parlier negotiated the terms of a potential partnership and the purchase by Parlier of

Foley's business. Parlier said that he needed to make at least $6,000 a month to make it feasible to move to Texas. Foley assured Parlier that he would be able to make "well over [that] amount." She gave him a list of five purported contracts and represented that he would receive $8,500 per month under the contracts if he bought into the business. In a letter, she sent him photocopies of checks, claiming that they represented work done for customers. Parlier shut down his business and moved to Texas. They entered into a contract, under which Parlier was to become a partner with Foley, receive a share of the profits, be paid for certain expenses, and eventually buy the business. Parlier did not receive any money, however, and when he hired an accountant to review the firm's records, Foley terminated their relationship. Parlier filed a suit in a Texas state court against Foley, alleging in part fraud in misrepresenting what Parlier would receive. The jury ruled in Parlier's favor, and the court awarded him damages of $55,750. Foley appealed to a state intermediate appellate court, arguing in part that there was insufficient evidence to support the jury's finding.

GARDNER, J.

[In the trial court] Parlier testified that one of the factors he relied upon was Foley's representation that she had five contracts valued at a total gross revenue of $172,190. Parlier also testified that he relied upon copies of checks Foley furnished him as proof of the income of the business and that she misrepresented those checks. Parlier further testified that the checks in question were provided in order to prove to Parlier that Foley made a sufficient amount of money to make it profitable for him to buy the business. Foley insists that there was no evidence of fraud regarding her statements about the monthly income checks and relies upon a portion of Parlier's testimony to support her argument:

> "Q. And through the process of this litigation, have you discovered anything about these checks that was misrepresented to you?
> "A. The only thing I found out is that I haven't seen this kind of money since I arrived."

Additional testimony from Parlier provides evidence of Foley's fraudulent actions * * * :

> "Q. And did Ms. Foley ever tell you anything about these draws [checks] other than what was represented in the letter?
> "A. Pretty much this is the kind of money I could expect to be making when I came out. That's the reason why she sent these to me was to show me it was a good business to buy into."

Parlier's testimony reveals that Foley utilized the checks to misrepresent the company's monthly profit. Parlier testified that when he asked if he would make more than $6,000 per month, Foley assured him he would be able to make over $6,000 a month. * * * [A]sked about the checks and what they meant to him, Parlier responded, "Well, * * * those checks show large amounts of money. $15-, $30-, $40-, $65,000, one was for $80,000, and these were monthly income checks. So looking at that, I'm thinking, well this is a very, very good business."

In light of the above evidence, * * * we hold that there is more than a scintilla [tiny amount] of evidence to support the jury's fraud finding.

The state intermediate appellate court affirmed the judgment of the lower court. The appellate court concluded that there was sufficient evidence to support the jury's finding of fraud.

QUESTIONS

1. Who filed this suit, and why?
2. What was the defendant's principal contention in the appeal from the trial court's ruling?
3. On what reasoning did the state intermediate appellate court base its decision in this case?

Nonfraudulent Misrepresentation

If a plaintiff seeks to rescind a contract because of *fraudulent* misrepresentation, the plaintiff must prove that the defendant had the intent to deceive. Most courts also allow rescission in cases involving *nonfraudulent* misrepresentation—that is, innocent or negligent misrepresentation—if all of the other elements of misrepresentation exist.

Undue Influence

Undue influence arises from special kinds of relationships in which one party can greatly influence another party, thus overcoming that party's free will. A contract entered into under excessive or undue influence lacks genuine assent and is therefore voidable.[23]

Minors and elderly people, for example, are often under the influence of guardians. If the guardian induces a young or elderly ward to enter into a contract that benefits the guardian, undue influence may have been exerted. Undue influence can arise from a number of confidential or fiduciary relationships:[24] attorney-client, physician-patient, guardian-ward, parent-child, husband-wife, or trustee-beneficiary. The essential feature of undue influence is that the party being taken advantage of does not, in reality, exercise free will in entering into a contract.

Duress

Assent to the terms of a contract is not genuine if one of the parties is *forced* into the agreement. Forcing a party to do something, including entering into a contract, through fear created by threats is legally defined as *duress*. In addition, blackmail or extortion to induce consent to a contract constitutes duress. Duress is both a defense to the enforcement of a contract and a ground for the rescission of a contract.

The Threatened Act Must Be Illegal or Wrongful. Generally, the threatened act must be wrongful or illegal. Threatening to exercise a legal right, such as the right to sue someone, is not ordinarily illegal and usually does not constitute duress. Suppose that Donovan injures Jaworski in an auto accident. The police are not called. Donovan has no automobile insurance, but she has substantial assets. Jaworski is willing to settle the potential claim out of court for $3,000. Donovan refuses. After much arguing, Jaworski loses her patience and says, "If you don't pay me $3,000 right now, I'm going to sue you for $35,000." Donovan is frightened and gives Jaworski a check for $3,000. Later

---

23. *Restatement (Second) of Contracts,* Section 177.
24. A fiduciary relationship is one involving a high degree of trust and confidence.

in the day, she stops payment on the check. Jaworski comes back to sue her for the $3,000. Although Donovan argues that she was the victim of duress, the threat of a civil suit is normally not considered duress.

Economic Duress. Economic need is generally not sufficient to constitute duress, even when one party exacts a very high price for an item that the other party needs. If the party exacting the price also creates the need, however, *economic duress* may be found. For example, suppose that the Internal Revenue Service (IRS) assesses a large tax and penalty against Weller. Weller retains Eyman, the accountant who filed the tax returns on which the assessment was based, to contest the assessment. Two days before the deadline for filing a reply with the IRS, Eyman declines to represent Weller unless he signs a very high contingency-fee agreement for his services. This agreement would be unenforceable. Although Eyman has threatened only to withdraw his services, something that he is legally entitled to do, he is responsible for delaying the withdrawal until the last days. Because it would be impossible at that late date to obtain adequate representation elsewhere, Weller is forced either to sign the contract or to lose his right to challenge the IRS assessment.

Adhesion Contracts and Unconscionability

Questions concerning genuineness of assent may arise when the terms of a contract are dictated by a party with overwhelming bargaining power and the signer must agree to those terms or go without the commodity or service in question. Such contracts are often referred to as *adhesion contracts*. An adhesion contract is written exclusively by one party (the dominant party, usually the seller or the creditor) and presented to the other party (the adhering party, usually the buyer or the borrower) on a take-it-or-leave-it basis. In other words, the adhering party has no opportunity to negotiate the terms of the contract.

Standard-form contracts often contain fine-print provisions that shift a risk naturally borne by one party to the other. Such contracts are used by a variety of businesses and include life insurance policies, residential leases, loan agreements, and employment agency contracts. To avoid enforcement of the contract or of a particular clause, the aggrieved party must show that the parties had substantially unequal bargaining positions and that enforcement would be manifestly unfair or oppressive. If the required showing is made, the contract or particular term is deemed **unconscionable**[25]—that is, generally speaking, so one sided under the circumstances as to be unfair—and not enforced. Technically, unconscionability under Section 2–302 of the Uniform Commercial Code (UCC) applies only to contracts for the sale of goods. Many courts, however, have broadened the concept and applied it in other situations.

Unconscionable contract or clause • A contract or clause that is void on the basis of public policy because one party, as a result of his or her disproportionate bargaining power, is forced to accept terms that are unfairly burdensome and that unfairly benefit the dominating party.

Courts have been permitted a great degree of discretion to invalidate or strike down a contract or clause as being unconscionable, and this practice has sometimes met with resistance. As a result, some states have not adopted Section 2–302 of the UCC. In those states, the legislature and the courts prefer to rely on traditional notions of fraud, undue influence, and duress. On the one hand, this gives certainty to contractual relationships, because parties know they will be held to the exact terms of their contracts. On the other hand, public policy does require that there be some limit on the power of individuals and businesses to dictate the terms of contracts.

25. Pronounced un-*kon*-shun-uh-bul.

THE STATUTE OF FRAUDS

At early common law, parties to a contract were not allowed to testify. This led to the practice of hiring third party witnesses. As early as the seventeenth century, the English recognized the many problems presented by this practice and enacted a statute to help deal with it. The statute, passed by the English Parliament in 1677, was known as "An Act for the Prevention of Frauds and Perjuries." The act established that certain types of contracts, to be enforceable, had to be evidenced by a writing and signed by the party against whom enforcement was sought.

The Statute of Frauds Today

Today, almost every state has a statute, modeled after the English act, that stipulates what types of contracts must be in writing. Although the statutes vary slightly from state to state, all states require certain types of contracts to be in writing or evidenced by a written memorandum signed by the party against whom enforcement is sought, unless certain exceptions apply. In this text, we refer to these statutes collectively as the **Statute of Frauds.** The actual name of the Statute of Frauds is misleading because it neither applies to fraud nor invalidates any type of contract. Rather, it denies *enforceability* to certain contracts that do not comply with its requirements. The following types of contracts are said to fall "within" or "under" the Statute of Frauds and therefore require a writing:

Statute of Frauds • A state statute under which certain types of contracts must be in writing to be enforceable.

1. Contracts involving interests in land.
2. Contracts that cannot by their terms be performed within one year from the day after the date of contract formation.
3. Collateral, or secondary, contracts, such as promises to answer for the debt or duty of another and promises by the administrator or executor of an estate to pay a debt of the estate personally—that is, out of his or her own pocket.
4. Promises made in consideration of marriage.
5. Under the UCC, contracts for the sale of goods priced at $500 or more. (Note that under the 2003 Amendments to Article 2 of the UCC—see Chapter 11—this amount has been raised to $5,000.)

Promissory Estoppel and the Statute of Frauds

In some states, an oral contract that would otherwise be unenforceable under the Statute of Frauds may be enforced under the doctrine of promissory estoppel, based on detrimental reliance. Section 139 of the *Restatement (Second) of Contracts* provides that in these circumstances, an oral promise can be enforceable notwithstanding the Statute of Frauds if the reliance was foreseeable to the person making the promise and if injustice can be avoided only by enforcing the promise.

THIRD PARTY RIGHTS

Once it has been determined that a valid and legally enforceable contract exists, attention can turn to the rights and duties of the parties to the contract. A contract is a private agreement between the parties who have entered into it, and traditionally these parties alone have rights and liabilities under the contract. This principle is referred to as *privity of contract.* A *third party*—one who is not a direct party to a particular contract—normally does not have rights under that contract.

There are exceptions to the rule of privity of contract. One exception allows a party to a contract to transfer the rights or duties arising from the contract to another person through an *assignment* (of rights) or a *delegation* (of duties). Another exception involves a *third party beneficiary contract*—a contract in which the parties to the contract intend at the time of contracting that the contract performance directly benefit a third person.

Assignments

In a bilateral contract, the two parties have corresponding rights and duties. One party has a *right* to require the other to perform some task, and the other has a *duty* to perform it. The transfer of contractual *rights* to a third party is known as an **assignment.** When rights under a contract are assigned unconditionally, the rights of the *assignor* (the party making the assignment) are extinguished. The third party (the *assignee,* or party receiving the assignment) has a right to demand performance from the other original party to the contract. The assignee takes only those rights that the assignor originally had.

Assignment • The act of transferring to another all or part of one's rights arising under a contract.

As a general rule, all rights can be assigned. Exceptions are made, however, in some circumstances. If a statute expressly prohibits assignment of a particular right, that right cannot be assigned. When a contract calls for personal services (such as tutoring children), the rights under the contract cannot be assigned unless all that remains is a money payment.[26] A right cannot be assigned if assignment will materially increase or alter the risk or duties of the obligor (the other original party owing performance under the contract).[27] If a contract stipulates that a right cannot be assigned, then ordinarily the right cannot be assigned.

There are several exceptions to the rule that a contract can, by its terms, prohibit any assignment of the contract. These exceptions are as follows:

1. A contract cannot prevent an assignment of the right to receive money. This exception exists to encourage the free flow of money and credit in modern business settings.
2. The assignment of rights in real estate often cannot be prohibited, because such a prohibition is contrary to public policy. Prohibitions of this kind are called restraints against **alienation** (transfer of land ownership).
3. The assignment of *negotiable instruments* (which include checks and promissory notes) cannot be prohibited.
4. In a contract for the sale of goods, the right to receive damages for breach of contract or for payment of an account owed may be assigned even though the sales contract prohibits such assignment.

Alienation • In real property law, the voluntary transfer of property from one person to another (as opposed to a transfer by operation of law).

Delegations

Just as a party can transfer rights through an assignment, a party can also transfer duties. The transfer of contractual *duties* to a third party is known as a **delegation.** Normally, a delegation of duties does not relieve the party

Delegation • The transfer of a contractual duty to a third party. The party delegating the duty (the delegator) to the third party (the delegatee) is still obliged to perform on the contract should the delegatee fail to perform.

26. *Restatement (Second) of Contracts,* Sections 317 and 318.
27. UCC 2–210(2).

making the delegation (the *delegator*) of the obligation to perform in the event that the party to whom the duty has been delegated (the *delegatee*) fails to perform. No special form is required to create a valid delegation of duties. As long as the delegator expresses an intention to make the delegation, it is effective; the delegator need not even use the word *delegate.*

As a general rule, any duty can be delegated. Delegation is prohibited, however, in the following circumstances:

1. When special trust has been placed in the *obligor* (the person contractually obligated to perform).
2. When performance depends on the personal skill or talents of the obligor.
3. When performance by a third party will vary materially from that expected by the *obligee* (the one to whom performance is owed) under the contract.
4. When the contract expressly prohibits delegation.

If a delegation of duties is enforceable, the obligee (the one to whom performance is owed) must accept performance from the delegatee (the one to whom the duties have been delegated). The obligee can legally refuse performance from the delegatee only if the duty is one that cannot be delegated.

A valid delegation of duties does not relieve the delegator of obligations under the contract. Thus, if the delegatee fails to perform, the delegator is still liable to the obligee.

Third Party Beneficiaries

Another exception to the doctrine of privity of contract exists when the original parties to the contract intend at the time of contracting that the contract performance is to directly benefit a third person. In this situation, the third person becomes a **third party beneficiary** of the contract. As an **intended beneficiary** of the contract, the third party has legal rights and can sue the promisor (the person who made the promise benefiting the third party) directly for breach of the contract.

The benefit that an **incidental beneficiary** receives from a contract between two parties is *unintentional.* Because the benefit is unintentional, an incidental beneficiary cannot sue to enforce the contract. For example, suppose that Bollow contracts with Coolidge to build a recreational facility on Coolidge's land. Once the facility is constructed, it will greatly enhance the property values in the neighborhood. If Bollow subsequently refuses to build the facility, Tran, Coolidge's neighbor, cannot enforce the contract against Bollow, because Tran is an incidental beneficiary.

Third party beneficiary • One for whose benefit a promise is made in a contract but who is not a party to the contract.

Intended beneficiary • A third party for whose benefit a contract is formed; an intended beneficiary can sue the promisor if such a contract is breached.

Incidental beneficiary • A third party who incidentally benefits from a contract but whose benefit was not the reason the contract was formed; an incidental beneficiary has no rights in a contract and cannot sue to have the contract enforced.

Performance and Discharge

The most common way to **discharge,** or terminate, one's contractual duties is by the **performance** of those duties. For example, a buyer and seller have a contract for the sale of a 2004 Buick for $34,000. This contract will be discharged on the performance by the parties of their obligations under the contract—the buyer's payment of $34,000 to the seller and the seller's transfer of possession of the Buick to the buyer.

The duty to perform under a contract may be *conditioned* on the occurrence or nonoccurrence of a certain event, or the duty may be *absolute.* In the first part of this section, we look at conditions of performance and the degree of performance required. We then examine some other ways in which a contract can

Discharge • The termination of an obligation. In contract law, discharge occurs when the parties have fully performed their contractual obligations or when events, conduct of the parties, or operation of the law releases the parties from performance.

Performance • In contract law, the fulfillment of one's duties arising under a contract with another; the normal way of discharging one's contractual obligations.

be discharged, including discharge by agreement of the parties and discharge by operation of law.

Conditions

In most contracts, promises of performance are not expressly conditioned or qualified. Instead, they are *absolute promises*. They must be performed, or the parties promising the acts will be in breach of contract. For example, Jerome contracts to sell Alfonso a painting for $3,000. The parties' promises—Jerome's transfer of the painting to Alfonso and Alfonso's payment of $3,000 to Jerome—are unconditional. The payment does not have to be made if the painting is not transferred.

Condition • A qualification, provision, or clause in a contractual agreement, the occurrence of which creates, suspends, or terminates the obligations of the contracting parties.

In some situations, however, performance is contingent on the occurrence or nonoccurrence of a certain event. A **condition** is a possible future event, the occurrence or nonoccurrence of which will trigger the performance of a legal obligation or terminate an existing obligation under a contract.[28] If this condition is not satisfied, the obligations of the parties are discharged. Suppose that Alfonso, in the previous example, offers to purchase Jerome's painting only if an independent appraisal indicates that it is worth at least $3,000. Jerome accepts Alfonso's offer. Their obligations (promises) are conditioned on the outcome of the appraisal. Should the condition not be satisfied (for example, if the appraiser deems the value of the painting to be only $1,500), the parties' obligations to each other are discharged and cannot be enforced.

Discharge by Performance

Tender • An unconditional offer to perform an obligation by a person who is ready, willing, and able to do so.

The great majority of contracts are discharged by performance. The contract comes to an end when both parties fulfill their respective duties by performing the acts they have promised. Performance can also be accomplished by **tender.** Therefore, a seller who places goods at the disposal of a buyer has tendered delivery and can demand payment. A buyer who offers to pay for goods has tendered payment and can demand delivery of the goods. Once performance has been tendered, the party making the tender has done everything possible to carry out the terms of the contract. If the other party then refuses to perform, the party making the tender can sue for breach of contract.

There are two basic types of performance—*complete performance* and *substantial performance.* A contract may stipulate that performance must meet the personal satisfaction of either the contracting party or a third party. Such a provision must be considered in determining whether the performance rendered satisfies the contract.

Complete Performance. When a party performs exactly as agreed, there is no question as to whether the contract has been performed. When a party's performance is perfect, it is said to be complete.

Conditions expressly stated in a contract must be fully satisfied for complete performance to take place. For example, most construction contracts require the builder to meet certain specifications. If the specifications are conditions,

28. The *Restatement (Second) of Contracts,* Section 224, defines a condition as "an event, not certain to occur, which must occur, unless its nonoccurrence is excused, before performance under a contract becomes due."

complete performance is required to avoid material breach. (Material breach will be discussed shortly.) If the conditions are met, the other party to the contract must then fulfill his or her obligation to pay the builder. If the specifications are not conditions and if the builder, without the other party's permission, fails to comply with the standards, performance is not complete. What effect does such a failure have on the other party's obligation to pay? The answer is part of the doctrine of substantial performance.

Substantial Performance. A party who in good faith performs substantially all of the terms of a contract can enforce the contract against the other party under the doctrine of substantial performance. Note that good faith is required, which means that the failure to fully perform must not be willful. Willfully failing to comply with the terms is a breach of the contract. Generally, performance that provides a party with the important and essential benefits of a contract, in spite of any omission or deviation from the terms, is substantial performance.

Determining whether performance has provided the "important and essential benefits" of a contract requires taking into consideration all of the facts. For example, in a construction contract, these facts would include the intended purpose of the structure and the expense required to bring the structure into compliance with the contract. Thus, the exact point at which performance is considered substantial varies from case to case.

Because substantial performance is not perfect, the other party is entitled to damages to compensate for the failure to comply with the contract. The measure of the damages is the cost to bring the object of the contract into compliance with its terms, if that cost is reasonable under the circumstances. If the cost is unreasonable, the measure of damages is the difference in value between the performance that was rendered and the performance that would have been rendered if the contract had been performed completely.

Performance to the Satisfaction of One of the Parties. Contracts often state that completed work must personally satisfy one of the parties. The question then arises whether this satisfaction becomes a *condition* of the contract, requiring actual personal satisfaction or approval for discharge, or whether the test of satisfaction is an absolute promise requiring such performance as would satisfy a "reasonable person" (substantial performance).

When the subject matter of the contract is personal, a contract to be performed to the satisfaction of one of the parties is conditioned, and performance must actually satisfy that party. For example, contracts for portraits, works of art, medical or dental work, and tailoring are considered personal. Therefore, only the personal satisfaction of the party will be sufficient to fulfill the condition. To illustrate: Suppose that Williams agrees to paint a portrait of Hirshon's daughter for $750. The contract provides that Hirshon must be satisfied with the portrait. If Hirshon is not, she will not be required to pay for it. The only requirement imposed on Hirshon is that she act honestly and in good faith. If Hirshon expresses dissatisfaction only to avoid paying for the portrait, the condition of satisfaction is excused, and her duty to pay becomes absolute. (Of course, the jury, or the judge acting as a jury, will have to decide whether she is acting honestly.)[29]

29. For a classic case illustrating this principle, see *Gibson v. Cranage*, 39 Mich. 49 (1878).

Contracts that involve mechanical fitness, utility, or marketability need only be performed to the satisfaction of a reasonable person. For example, construction contracts and manufacturing contracts are usually not considered to be personal, so the party's personal satisfaction is normally irrelevant. As long as the performance will satisfy a reasonable person, the contract is fulfilled.[30]

Performance to the Satisfaction of a Third Party. At times, contracts may require performance to the satisfaction of a third party (not a party to the contract). To illustrate: Assume that you contract to pave several city streets. The contract provides that the work will be done "to the satisfaction of Phil Hopper, the supervising engineer." In this situation, the courts are divided.

A few courts require the personal satisfaction of the third party—in this example, Phil Hopper. If Hopper is not satisfied, you will not be paid, even if a reasonable person would be satisfied. Again, the personal judgment must be made honestly, or the condition will be excused.

A majority of courts, however, require the work to be satisfactory to a *reasonable* person. Thus, even if Hopper is dissatisfied with the paving work, you will be paid, as long as a qualified supervising engineer would have been satisfied. All of the above examples demonstrate the necessity for *clear, specific wording in contracts.*

Breach of contract • The failure, without legal excuse, of a promisor to perform the obligations of a contract.

Material Breach of Contract. A **breach of contract** is the nonperformance of a contractual duty. The breach is *material*[31] when performance is not at least substantial—in other words, when there has been a failure of consideration. In such cases, the nonbreaching party is excused from the performance of contractual duties and has a cause of action to sue for damages caused by the breach.

If the breach is *minor* (not material), the nonbreaching party's duty to perform can sometimes be suspended until the breach has been remedied, but the duty to perform is not entirely excused. Once the minor breach has been cured, the nonbreaching party must resume performance of the contractual obligations undertaken. Any breach entitles the nonbreaching party to sue for damages, but only a material breach discharges the nonbreaching party from the contract. The policy underlying these rules allows contracts to go forward when only minor problems occur but permits them to be terminated if major difficulties arise.

Time for Performance. If no time for performance is stated in the contract, a *reasonable time* is implied.[32] If a specific time is stated, the parties must usually perform by that time. Unless time is expressly stated to be vital, however, a delay in performance will not destroy the performing party's right to payment. When time is expressly stated to be vital, or when it is construed to be "of the essence," the parties normally must perform within the stated time period. The time element becomes a condition.

The court in the following case explained the reasoning behind the requirement that payment be made within a reasonable time.

---

30. If, however, the contract specifically states that it is to be fulfilled to the "personal" satisfaction of one or more of the parties, and the parties so intended, the outcome will probably be different.

31. *Restatement (Second) of Contracts,* Section 241.

32. See UCC 2–204.

CASE 10.5

United States District Court, District of Columbia, 2002. 193 F.Supp.2d 88.

MANGANARO CORP. v. HITT CONTRACTING, INC.

Lucent Technologies, Inc., engaged HITT Contracting, Inc., to act as the general contractor for a construction project at Metropolitan Square in Washington, D.C. In July 1999, HITT hired Manganaro Corporation to perform dry wall and ceiling work and to install two specialty ceilings. As the project progressed, Manganaro submitted invoices to HITT for payment to cover finished contract work. On average, HITT paid Manganaro within thirty-six days of each of these invoices. Manganaro was also expected to perform "change order" work, or work in excess of its contract, for which it could seek additional payment. By December 23, after completing all of the work except for the two specialty ceilings and certain punch list items,[a] *Manganaro was owed more than $22,000 for unpaid contract work (the most recent invoice had been submitted on November 19) and $64,000 for unpaid change order work. Manganaro notified HITT that it was suspending performance until it was paid. HITT claimed that Manganaro was abandoning the project. HITT therefore terminated their contract and hired another subcontractor to finish the job. Manganaro filed a suit in a federal district court against HITT for breach of contract.*

FACCIOLA, J.

The first question is * * * when was payment due, since the contract did not specify a date certain.

* * * On an average, Manganaro was being paid within 36 days for its contract work; the median was 34.5 days.

HITT seizes on this fact and asserts that the November 19, 1999, requisition was not past due when Manganaro ceased performance on December 23, 1999. That is, at best, half true. HITT paid for the contract work in a reasonably timely manner. But, HITT *never* paid for the change order work in a timely manner. * * *

Perhaps more significant is the amount outstanding when viewed absolutely or in relation to the total change order work billed. * * * By December 23, 1999, Manganaro had billed $108,301.28 in change order work * * * but had been paid $34,485.07. That is as unfair as it is unreasonable.

Since HITT's failure to pay the outstanding change order invoices by December 23, 1999, was unreasonable, Manganaro was entitled to suspend performance. * * * *[A] subcontractor who is unreasonably denied payment as he progresses towards completion is justified in suspending performance until he is paid.* * * * There is a special factor to be considered in the case of a building contract, or any other contract the financing of which requires a progressive expenditure in the course of performance. In these cases, one reason for providing for installment payments as construction proceeds is to supply the funds necessary for the agreed performance; and failure to pay one or more installments is more likely to cause inconvenience and difficulty to the building contractor. Therefore, a failure to make one of the progress payments, even though the contract is not divisible into pairs of separate equivalents and the installment unpaid is only a small part of the whole consideration, is more likely to justify suspension of performance by the builder, or even total renunciation of further duty. [Emphasis added.]

a. After a contractor finishes work, the architect or another party inspects it and can demand that the contractor make the repairs that the party details on a *punch list.*

> * * * [A] subcontractor cannot and should not be expected to finance the project until such time that the prime contractor * * * decides to pay the amount due. If the subcontractor is ordered to perform the work or even required to do so, then the obligation in the absence of an express contract provision falls upon the party so ordering the work to be done to pay a reasonable amount for that work within a reasonable time. To hold otherwise would cast a burden upon the subcontractor which in many cases would be impossible to carry as the subcontractors are usually smaller in size than the prime contractors.

The court held that Manganaro was justified in suspending its performance on its contract with HITT until payment was made after HITT had failed to pay the outstanding invoices for change order work during the customary time period.

QUESTIONS

1. What "special factor" did the court consider in this case, and why?
2. Why did the court hold that Manganaro was justified in suspending its performance on its contract with HITT until payment was made?
3. Suppose that the contract with Manganaro contained a clause that required the subcontractor to wait for HITT to be paid before the subcontractor was paid. If HITT had difficulties obtaining payment from Lucent, how would that have affected the outcome in this case?

Discharge by Agreement

Any contract can be discharged by agreement of the parties. The agreement can be contained in the original contract, or the parties can form a new contract for the express purpose of discharging the original contract.

Discharge by Rescission. *Rescission* is the process by which a contract is canceled or terminated and the parties are returned to the positions they occupied prior to forming it. For **mutual rescission** to take place, the parties have to make another agreement, which must also satisfy the legal requirements for a contract. There must be an *offer*, an *acceptance,* and *consideration.*

Mutual rescission • An agreement between the parties to cancel their contract, releasing the parties from further obligations under the contract. The object of the agreement is to restore the parties to the positions they would have occupied had no contract ever been formed.

Ordinarily, in an executory contract in which neither party has yet performed, if the parties agree to rescind the original contract, their promises not to perform the acts stipulated in the original contract will be legal consideration for the second contract. The rescission agreement is generally enforceable even if made orally. An exception applies under the UCC to agreements rescinding a contract for the sale of goods regardless of price when the contract requires written rescission.[33]

When one party has fully performed, an agreement to call off the original contract normally will not be enforceable. Because the performing party has received no consideration for the promise to call off the original bargain, additional consideration will be necessary.

33. UCC 2–209(2), (4).

In sum, contracts that are *executory on both sides* (contracts on which neither party has performed) can be rescinded solely by agreement.[34] But contracts that are *executed on one side* (contracts on which one party has performed) can be rescinded only if the party who has performed receives consideration for the promise to call off the deal.

Discharge by Novation. A contractual obligation may also be discharged through novation. A **novation** occurs when both of the parties to a contract agree to substitute a third party for one of the original parties. The requirements of a novation are as follows:

Novation • The substitution, by agreement, of a new contract for an old one, with the rights under the old one being terminated. Typically, there is a substitution of a new person who is responsible for the contract and the removal of an original party's rights and duties under the contract.

1. A previous valid obligation.
2. An agreement of all the parties to a new contract.
3. The extinguishment of the old obligation (discharge of the prior party).
4. A new contract that is valid.

For example, suppose that Union Corporation contracts to sell its pharmaceutical division to British Pharmaceuticals, Ltd. Before the transfer is completed, Union, British Pharmaceuticals, and a third company, Otis Chemicals, execute a new agreement to transfer all of British Pharmaceuticals's rights and duties in the transaction to Otis Chemicals. As long as the new contract is supported by consideration, the novation will discharge the original contract (between Union and British Pharmaceuticals) and replace it with the new contract (between Union and Otis Chemicals).

A novation expressly or impliedly revokes and discharges a prior contract.[35] The parties involved may expressly state in the new contract that the old contract is now discharged. If the parties do not expressly discharge the old contract, it will be impliedly discharged because of the change or because of the new contract's different terms, which are inconsistent with the old contract's terms.

Discharge by Substituted Agreement. A *compromise,* or settlement agreement, that arises out of a genuine dispute over the obligations under an existing contract will be recognized at law. Such an agreement will be substituted as a new contract, and it will either expressly or impliedly revoke and discharge the obligations under any prior contract. In contrast to a novation, a substituted agreement does not involve a third party. Rather, the two original parties to the contract form a different agreement to substitute for the original one.

Discharge by Accord and Satisfaction. For a contract to be discharged by accord and satisfaction, the parties must agree to accept performance that is different from the performance originally promised. An *accord* is defined as an

---

34. Certain sales made to a consumer at home can be rescinded by the consumer within three days for no reason at all. This three-day "cooling-off" period is designed to aid consumers who are susceptible to high-pressure door-to-door sales tactics. See 15 U.S.C. Section 1635(a).

35. It is this immediate discharge of the prior contract that distinguishes a novation from both an accord and satisfaction, to be discussed shortly, and an assignment, discussed earlier in this chapter. In an assignment, the original party to the contract (the assignor) remains liable under the original contract if the assignee fails to perform the contractual obligations. In contrast, in a novation, the original party's obligations are completely discharged.

executory contract to perform some act to satisfy an existing contractual duty.[36] The duty has not yet been discharged. A *satisfaction* is the performance of the accord agreement. An accord and its satisfaction discharge the original contractual obligation.

Once the accord has been made, the original obligation is merely suspended. The obligor (the one owing the obligation) can discharge the obligation by performing the obligation agreed to in the accord or the original obligation. If the obligor refuses to perform the accord, the obligee (the one to whom performance is owed) can bring action on the original obligation or seek a decree compelling specific performance on the accord.

Discharge by Operation of Law

Under certain circumstances, contractual duties may be discharged by operation of law. These circumstances include material alteration of the contract, the running of the statute of limitations, bankruptcy, and the impossibility or impracticability of performance.

Alteration of the Contract. To discourage parties from altering written contracts, the law operates to allow an innocent party to be discharged when the other party has materially altered a written contract without consent. For example, contract terms such as quantity or price might be changed without the knowledge or consent of all parties. If so, the party who was unaware of the alteration can treat the contract as discharged or terminated.[37]

Statutes of Limitations. As mentioned earlier in this text, statutes of limitations restrict the period during which a party can sue on a particular cause of action. After the applicable limitations period has passed, a suit can no longer be brought. For example, the limitations period for bringing suits for breach of oral contracts is usually two to three years; for written contracts, four to five years; and for recovery of amounts awarded in judgments, ten to twenty years, depending on state law.

Section 2–725 of the UCC deals with the statute of limitations applicable to contracts for the sale of goods. For purposes of applying this section, the UCC does not distinguish between oral and written contracts. Section 2–725 provides that an action for the breach of any contract for sale must be commenced within four years after the cause of that action has accrued. The cause of action accrues when the breach occurs, regardless of the aggrieved party's lack of knowledge of the breach. By original agreement, the parties can reduce this four-year period to one year. They cannot, however, extend it beyond the four-year limitation period.

Technically, the running of a statute of limitations bars access only to *judicial* remedies; it does not extinguish the debt or the underlying obligation. The statute precludes access to the courts for collection. If, however, the party who owes the debt or obligation agrees to perform (that is, makes a new promise to perform), the cause of action barred by the statute of limitations

36. *Restatement (Second) of Contracts,* Section 281.

37. The contract is voidable, and the innocent party can also treat the contract as in effect, either on the original terms or on the terms as altered. For example, a buyer who discovers that a seller altered the quantity of goods in a sales contract from 100 to 1,000 by secretly inserting a zero can purchase either 100 or 1,000 of the items.

will be revived. For the old agreement to be restored by a new promise in this manner, many states require that the promise be in writing or that there be evidence of partial performance.

Bankruptcy. A proceeding in bankruptcy attempts to allocate the assets the debtor owns to the creditors in a fair and equitable fashion. Once the assets have been allocated, the debtor receives a discharge in bankruptcy. A discharge in bankruptcy will ordinarily bar enforcement of most of a debtor's contracts by the creditors. Partial payment of a debt *after* discharge in bankruptcy will not revive the debt.

Impossibility or Impracticability of Performance. After a contract has been made, performance may become impossible in an objective sense. This is known as **impossibility of performance** and may discharge a contract.[38]

Impossibility of performance • A doctrine under which a party to a contract is relieved of his or her duty to perform when performance becomes impossible or totally impracticable (through no fault of either party).

Objective Impossibility of Performance. *Objective impossibility* ("It can't be done") must be distinguished from *subjective impossibility* ("I'm sorry, I simply can't do it"). Examples of subjective impossibility include cases in which goods cannot be delivered on time because of freight car shortages and cases in which money cannot be paid on time because the bank is closed. In effect, the party in each of these cases is saying, "It is impossible for me to perform," not "It is impossible for anyone to perform." Accordingly, such excuses do not discharge a contract, and the nonperforming party is normally held in breach of contract. Three basic types of situations, however, generally qualify as grounds for the discharge of contractual obligations based on impossibility of performance:[39]

1. *When one of the parties to a personal contract dies or becomes incapacitated prior to performance.* For example, Fred, a famous dancer, contracts with Ethereal Dancing Guild to play a leading role in its new ballet. Before the ballet can be performed, Fred becomes ill and dies. His personal performance was essential to the completion of the contract. Thus, his death discharges the contract and his estate's liability for his nonperformance.
2. *When the specific subject matter of the contract is destroyed.* For example, A-1 Farm Equipment agrees to sell Gudgel the green tractor on its lot and promises to have it ready for Gudgel to pick up on Saturday. On Friday night, however, a truck veers off the nearby highway and smashes into the tractor, destroying it beyond repair. Because the contract was for this specific tractor, A-1's performance is rendered impossible owing to the accident.
3. *When a change in law renders performance illegal.* An example is a contract to build an apartment building, when the zoning laws are changed to prohibit the construction of residential rental property at this location. This change renders the contract impossible to perform.

Commercial Impracticability. Courts may excuse parties from their performance obligations when the performance becomes much more difficult or expensive than originally contemplated at the time the contract was

38. *Restatement (Second) of Contracts,* Section 261.
39. *Restatement (Second) of Contracts,* Sections 262–266; UCC 2–615.

Commercial impracticability • A doctrine under which parties may be excused from their performance obligations when performance becomes extremely difficult or costly as a result of circumstances that could not have been foreseen when the contract was formed.

formed. For someone to invoke successfully the doctrine of **commercial impracticability,** however, the anticipated performance must become *extremely* difficult or costly.[40] More important, the added burden of performing *must not have been foreseeable by the parties when the contract was made.* Thus, caution should be used in invoking commercial impracticability.

ETHICAL ISSUE

Should the courts allow the defense of impossibility of performance to be used more often? The doctrine of impossibility is applied only when the parties could not have reasonably foreseen, at the time the contract was formed, the event or events that rendered performance impossible. In some cases, the courts may seem to go too far in holding that certain events or conditions should have been foreseen by the parties, thus precluding parties from avoiding contractual obligations under the doctrine of impossibility of performance. Yet even though the courts rarely excuse parties from performance under the doctrine of impossibility, they allow parties to raise this defense more often than they once did. Indeed, until the latter part of the nineteenth century, courts were reluctant to discharge a contract even when it appeared that performance was literally impossible. Generally, the courts must balance the freedom of parties to contract as they will (and assume the risks involved) against the injustice that may result when certain contractual obligations are enforced. If the courts allowed parties to raise impossibility of performance as a defense to contractual obligations more often, freedom of contract would suffer.

Frustration of purpose • A doctrine under which a party to a contract will be relieved of his or her duty to perform when the objective purpose for performance no longer exists (due to reasons beyond that party's control).

Frustration of Purpose. A theory closely allied with the doctrine of commercial impracticability is the doctrine of **frustration of purpose.** In principle, a contract will be discharged if supervening circumstances make it impossible to attain the purpose both parties had in mind when making the contract. The origins of the doctrine lie in the old English "coronation cases." A coronation procession was planned for Edward VII when he became king of England following the death of his mother, Queen Victoria. Hotel rooms along the coronation route were rented at exorbitant prices for that day. When the king became ill and the procession was canceled, a flurry of lawsuits resulted. Hotel and building owners sought to enforce the room-rent bills against would-be parade observers, and would-be parade observers sought to be reimbursed for rental monies paid in advance on the rooms. Would-be parade observers were excused from their duty of payment because the purpose of the room contracts had been "frustrated."

Temporary Impossibility. An occurrence or event that makes performance temporarily impossible operates to suspend performance until the impossibility ceases. Then, ordinarily, the parties must perform the contract as originally planned. If, however, the lapse of time and the change in circumstances surrounding the contract make it substantially more burdensome for the parties to perform the promised acts, the contract is discharged.

40. *Restatement (Second) of Contracts,* Section 264.

The leading case on the subject, *Autry v. Republic Productions,*[41] involved an actor who was drafted into the army in 1942. Being drafted rendered the actor's contract temporarily impossible to perform, and it was suspended until the end of the war. When the actor got out of the army, the value of the dollar had so changed that performance of the contract would have been substantially burdensome to the actor. Therefore, the contract was discharged.

BREACH OF CONTRACT AND REMEDIES

When one party breaches a contract, the other party—the nonbreaching party—can choose one or more of several remedies. A *remedy* is the relief provided for an innocent party when the other party has breached the contract. It is the means employed to enforce a right or to redress an injury.

The most common remedies available to a nonbreaching party include damages, rescission and restitution, specific performance, and reformation. As discussed in Chapter 1, a distinction is made between *remedies at law* and *remedies in equity.* Today, the remedy at law is normally money damages, which are discussed next. Equitable remedies include rescission and restitution, specific performance, and reformation. Usually, a court will not award an equitable remedy unless the remedy at law is inadequate.

Damages

A breach of contract entitles the nonbreaching party to sue for money (damages). Damages are designed to compensate a party for harm suffered as a result of another's wrongful act. In the context of contract law, damages compensate the nonbreaching party for the loss of the bargain.[42]

Often, courts say that innocent parties are to be placed in the position they would have occupied had the contract been fully performed.[43] For example, in the famous case of the "hairy hand," a doctor promised to make a boy's scarred hand "a hundred percent perfect." Skin was taken from the boy's chest and grafted onto his thumb and fingers. The hand became infected, and the boy was hospitalized for three months. Use of the hand was greatly restricted, and hair grew out of the grafted skin. In a suit against the doctor, the court explained that the amount of damages was to be determined by the difference between the value to the boy of the "perfect" hand that the doctor had promised and the value of the hand in its condition after the operation.[44]

Types of Damages. There are basically four broad categories of damages:

1. Compensatory (to cover direct losses and costs).
2. Consequential (to cover indirect and foreseeable losses).

41. 30 Cal.2d 144, 180 P.2d 888 (1947).
42. Bear in mind that although a nonbreaching party may succeed in obtaining damages in court from the breaching party, the court's judgment may be difficult to enforce. As discussed in Chapter 2, the breaching party may not have sufficient funds or assets to pay the damages awarded.
43. *Restatement (Second) of Contracts,* Section 347; UCC 1–106(1).
44. *Hawkins v. McGee,* 84 N.H. 114, 146 A. 641 (1929).

3. Punitive (to punish and deter wrongdoing).
4. Nominal (to recognize wrongdoing when no monetary loss is shown).

We look here at compensatory and consequential damages.

Compensatory damages • In contract law, a money award to compensate a nonbreaching party for damages actually sustained as a result of the breach of a contract.

Compensatory Damages. Damages compensating the nonbreaching party for the *loss of the bargain* are known as **compensatory damages.** These damages compensate the injured party only for damages actually sustained and proved to have arisen directly from the loss of the bargain caused by the breach of contract. They simply replace what was lost because of the wrong or damage.

To illustrate: Wilcox contracts to perform certain services exclusively for Hernandez during the month of March for $3,000. Hernandez cancels the contract and is in breach. Wilcox is able to find another job during the month of March but can earn only $2,000. He can sue Hernandez for breach and recover $1,000 as compensatory damages. Wilcox can also recover from Hernandez the amount that he spent to find the other job. Expenses that are caused directly by a breach of contract—such as those incurred to obtain performance from another source—are known as *incidental damages.*

Contracts for the Sale of Goods. The measurement of compensatory damages varies by type of contract. In a contract for the sale of goods, the usual measure of compensatory damages is an amount equal to the difference between the contract price and the market price.[45] For example, suppose that Chrysler Corporation contracts to buy ten model UTS 400 network servers from an XEXO Corporation dealer for $8,000 each. The dealer, however, fails to deliver the ten servers to Chrysler. The market price of the servers at the time the buyer learns of the breach is $8,150. Chrysler's measure of damages is therefore $1,500 (10 × $150) plus any incidental damages (expenses) caused by the breach. In a situation in which the buyer breaches and the seller has not yet produced the goods, compensatory damages normally equal lost profits on the sale, not the difference between the contract price and the market price.

Contracts for the Sale of Land. Ordinarily, because each parcel of land is unique, the remedy for a seller's breach of a contract for a sale of real estate is specific performance—that is, the buyer is awarded the parcel of property for which he or she bargained (specific performance is discussed more fully later in this chapter). When this remedy is unavailable (for example, when the seller has sold the property to someone else), or when the breach is on the part of the buyer, the measure of damages is ordinarily the same as in contracts for the sale of goods—that is, the difference between the contract price and the market price of the land. The majority of states follow this rule.

A minority of states follow a different rule when the seller breaches the contract and the breach is not deliberate.[46] In this situation, these states allow the prospective purchaser to recover any down payment plus any expenses incurred

45. That is, the amount is the difference between the contract price and the market price at the time and place at which the goods were to be delivered or tendered. See UCC 2–708 and UCC 2–713.

46. "Deliberate" breaches include the seller's failure to transfer the land because the market price has gone up. "Nondeliberate" breaches include the seller's failure to transfer the land because an unknown easement (another's right of use over the property) has rendered title unmarketable.

(such as fees for title searches, attorneys, and escrows). This minority rule effectively places purchasers in the position they occupied prior to the sale.

Consequential Damages. Foreseeable damages that result from a party's breach of contract are called **consequential damages,** or *special damages.* They differ from compensatory damages in that they are caused by special circumstances beyond the contract itself. They flow from the consequences, or results, of a breach.

Consequential damages • Special damages that result from the consequences of a breach of contract (for example, lost profits). To recover consequential damages, the breaching party must know, or have reason to know, that special circumstances will cause the nonbreaching party to suffer an additional loss.

For example, if a seller fails to deliver goods, and the seller knows that a buyer is planning to resell these goods immediately, consequential damages will be awarded for the loss of profit from the planned resale. The buyer will also recover compensatory damages for the difference between the contract price and the market price of the goods.

To recover consequential damages, the breaching party must know (or have reason to know) that special circumstances will cause the nonbreaching party to suffer an additional loss. Compensation is given only for those injuries that the defendant could *reasonably have foreseen* as a probable result of the usual course of events following a breach.

Mitigation of Damages. In most situations, when a breach of contract occurs, the innocent injured party has a duty to mitigate, or reduce, the damages that he or she suffers. Under this doctrine of **mitigation of damages,** the duty owed depends on the nature of the contract.

Mitigation of damages • A rule requiring a plaintiff to have done whatever was reasonable to minimize the damages caused by the defendant.

For example, some states require a landlord to use reasonable means to find a new tenant if a tenant abandons the premises and fails to pay rent. If an acceptable tenant becomes available, the landlord is required to lease the premises to this tenant to mitigate the damages recoverable from the former tenant. The former tenant is still liable for the difference between the amount of the rent under the original lease and the rent received from the new tenant. If the landlord has not used the reasonable means necessary to find a new tenant, presumably a court can reduce the award made by the amount of rent he or she could have received had such reasonable means been used.

In the majority of states, persons whose employment has been wrongfully terminated owe a duty to mitigate damages suffered because of their employers' breach of the employment contract. The damages they receive are their salaries less the incomes they would have received in similar jobs that they could have obtained by reasonable means. The employer must prove both that such a job existed and that the employee could have been hired. Normally, however, the employee is under no duty to take a job of a different type and rank.

Liquidated damages • An amount, stipulated in the contract, that the parties to a contract believe to be a reasonable estimation of the damages that will occur in the event of a breach.

Penalty • A sum inserted into a contract, not as a measure of compensation for its breach but rather as punishment for a default. The agreement as to the amount will not be enforced, and recovery will be limited to actual damages.

Liquidated Damages versus Penalties. Unliquidated damages are damages that have not been calculated or determined. **Liquidated damages,** in contrast, are damages that are certain in amount. A liquidated damages provision in a contract specifies a certain amount to be paid in the event of a *future* default or breach of contract. For example, a provision requiring a construction contractor to pay $300 for every day he or she is late in completing the construction is a liquidated damages provision.

Liquidated damages differ from penalties. **Penalties** specify a certain amount to be paid in the event of a default or breach of contract and are designed to *penalize* the breaching party. Liquidated damages provisions are enforceable; penalty provisions are not.

To determine if a particular provision is for liquidated damages or for a penalty, two questions must be answered:

1. When the contract was entered into, was it apparent that damages would be difficult to estimate in the event of a breach?
2. Was the amount set as damages a reasonable estimate and not excessive?[47]

If the answers to both questions are yes, the provision normally is enforced. If either answer is no, the provision normally is not enforced. Section 2–718(1) of the UCC specifically permits the inclusion of liquidated damages clauses in contracts for the sale of goods as long as both of these tests are met. In construction contracts, it is difficult to estimate the amount of damages that would be caused by a delay in completing construction, so liquidated damages clauses are often used.

Rescission and Restitution

As discussed earlier in this chapter, *rescission* is essentially an action to undo, or terminate, a contract—to return the contracting parties to the positions they occupied prior to the transaction. When fraud, a mistake, duress, undue influence, misrepresentation, or lack of capacity to contract is present, unilateral rescission is available.[48] Rescission may also be available by statute.[49] In addition, the failure of one party to perform entitles the other party to rescind the contract. The rescinding party must give prompt notice to the breaching party.

Restitution • An equitable remedy under which a person is restored to his or her original position prior to loss or injury, or placed in the position he or she would have been in had the breach not occurred.

Restitution. Generally, to rescind a contract, both parties must make **restitution** to each other by returning goods, property, or money previously conveyed.[50] If the goods or property received can be restored *in specie*—that is, if the *actual* goods or property can be returned—they must be. If the goods or property have been consumed, restitution must be made in an equivalent amount of money.

Essentially, *restitution* refers to the plaintiff's recapture of a benefit conferred on the defendant through which the defendant has been unjustly enriched. For example, Katie pays $10,000 to Bob in return for Bob's promise to design a house for her. The next day Bob calls Katie and tells her that he has taken a position with a large architectural firm in another state and cannot design the house. Katie decides to hire another architect that afternoon. Katie can obtain restitution of the $10,000.

Restitution Is Not Limited to Rescission Cases. Restitution may be appropriate when a contract is rescinded, but the right to restitution is not limited to rescission cases. Restitution may be sought in actions for breach of contract, tort actions, and other actions at law or in equity. Usually, restitution of

---

47. *Restatement (Second) of Contracts,* Section 356(1).

48. In *unilateral* rescission, only one party wants to undo the contract. In *mutual* rescission, both parties agree to undo the contract. Mutual rescission discharges the contract; unilateral rescission is generally available as a remedy for breach of contract.

49. The Federal Trade Commission and many states have rules or statutes allowing consumers to unilaterally rescind contracts made at home with door-to-door salespersons. Rescission is allowed within three days for any reason or for no reason at all. See, for example, California Civil Code Section 1689.5.

50. *Restatement (Second) of Contracts,* Section 370.

money or property transferred by mistake or because of fraud can be awarded. An award in a case may include restitution of money or property obtained through embezzlement, conversion, theft, copyright infringement, or misconduct by a party in a confidential or other special relationship.

Specific Performance

The equitable remedy of **specific performance** calls for the performance of the act promised in the contract. This remedy is quite attractive to the nonbreaching party for three reasons:

Specific performance • An equitable remedy requiring the breaching party to perform as promised under the contract; usually granted only when money damages would be an inadequate remedy and the subject matter of the contract is unique (for example, real property).

1. The nonbreaching party need not worry about collecting the money damages awarded by a court (see the discussion in Chapter 2 of some of the difficulties that may arise when trying to enforce court judgments).
2. The nonbreaching party need not spend time seeking an alternative contract.
3. The performance is more valuable than the money damages.

Normally, however, specific performance will not be granted unless the party's legal remedy (money damages) is inadequate.[51] For this reason, contracts for the sale of goods rarely qualify for specific performance. The legal remedy, money damages, is ordinarily adequate in such situations because substantially identical goods can be bought or sold in the market. If the goods are unique, however, a court of equity will grant specific performance. For example, paintings, sculptures, or rare books or coins are so unique that money damages will not enable a buyer to obtain substantially identical substitutes in the market.

Sale of Land. Specific performance is granted to a buyer in a contract for the sale of land. The legal remedy for breach of a land sales contract is inadequate, because every parcel of land is considered to be unique. Money damages will not compensate a buyer adequately, because the same land in the same location obviously cannot be obtained elsewhere. Only when specific performance is unavailable (for example, when the seller has sold the property to someone else) will money damages be awarded instead.

Contracts for Personal Services. Personal-service contracts require one party to work personally for another party. Courts of equity normally refuse to grant specific performance of personal-service contracts. If a contract is not deemed personal, the remedy at law may be adequate if substantially identical service (for example, lawn mowing) is available from other persons.

In individually tailored personal-service contracts, courts will not order specific performance by the party who was to be employed because public policy strongly discourages involuntary servitude.[52] Moreover, the courts do not want to have to monitor a continuing service contract if supervision would be difficult—as it would be if the contract required the exercise of personal judgment or talent. For example, if you contracted with a brain surgeon

51. *Restatement (Second) of Contracts,* Section 359.

52. The Thirteenth Amendment to the U.S. Constitution prohibits involuntary servitude, and thus a court will not order a person to perform under a personal-service contract. A court may grant an order (injunction) prohibiting that person from engaging in similar contracts in the future for a period of time, however.

to perform brain surgery on you and the surgeon refused to perform, the court would not compel (and you certainly would not want) the surgeon to perform under those circumstances. A court cannot assure meaningful performance in such a situation.[53]

Reformation

Reformation • A court-ordered correction of a written contract so that it reflects the true intentions of the parties.

Reformation is an equitable remedy used when the parties have *imperfectly* expressed their agreement in writing. Reformation allows the contract to be rewritten to reflect the parties' true intentions. It applies most often when fraud or mutual mistake (for example, a clerical error) is present.

Reformation is almost always sought so that some other remedy may then be pursued. For example, if Gregory contracts to buy a certain parcel of land from Cavendish but their contract mistakenly refers to a parcel of land different from the one being sold, the contract does not reflect the parties' intentions. Accordingly, a court can reform the contract so that it conforms to the parties' intentions and accurately refers to the parcel of land being sold. Gregory can then, if necessary, show that Cavendish has breached the contract as reformed. She can at that time request an order for specific performance.

Two other examples deserve mention. The first involves two parties who have made a binding oral contract. They further agree to put the oral contract in writing, but in doing so, they make an error in stating the terms. Normally, the courts will allow into evidence the correct terms of the oral contract, thereby reforming the written contract. The second example deals with written agreements (covenants) not to compete. If the covenant is for a valid and legitimate purpose (such as the sale of a business) but the area or time restraints of the covenant are unreasonable, some courts will reform the restraints by making them reasonable and will enforce the entire contract as reformed. Other courts, however, will throw out the entire restrictive covenant as illegal.

Recovery Based on Quasi Contract

As stated earlier in this chapter, quasi contract is a legal theory under which an obligation is imposed in the absence of an agreement. The courts use this theory to prevent unjust enrichment.

The Nature of Quasi-Contractual Recovery. A quasi contract provides a basis for relief when no enforceable contract exists. The legal obligation arises because the law considers that a promise to pay for benefits received is implied by the party accepting the benefits. Generally, when one party has conferred a benefit on another party, justice requires the party receiving the benefit to pay the reasonable value for it. As discussed earlier in this chapter, the party conferring the benefit can recover in *quantum meruit,* which means "as much as he deserves."

Quasi-contractual recovery is useful when one party has partially performed under a contract that is unenforceable. It can be used as an alternative to a suit for damages and will allow the party to recover the reasonable value of the partial performance, measured in some cases according to the benefit received and in others according to the detriment suffered.

53. Similarly, courts often refuse to order specific performance of construction contracts because courts are not set up to operate as construction supervisors or engineers.

Requirements for Quasi-Contractual Recovery. To recover on a quasi contract, the party seeking recovery must show the following:

1. The party conferred a benefit on the other party.
2. The party conferred the benefit with the reasonable expectation of receiving payment.
3. The party did not act as a volunteer in conferring the benefit.
4. The other party (the party receiving the benefit) would be unjustly enriched by retaining the benefit without making payment.

For example, suppose that Watson contracts to build two oil derricks for Energy Industries. The derricks are to be built over a period of three years, but the parties do not make a written contract. Enforcement of the contract will therefore be barred by the Statute of Frauds.[54] Watson completes one derrick, and then Energy Industries informs him that it will not pay for the derrick. Watson can sue in quasi contract because he conferred a benefit on Energy Industries with the expectation of being paid, and allowing Energy Industries to retain the derrick without paying would enrich the company unjustly. Therefore, Watson should be able to recover in *quantum meruit* the reasonable value of the oil derrick. The reasonable value is ordinarily equal to the fair market value.

Election of Remedies

In many cases, a nonbreaching party has several remedies available. When the remedies are inconsistent with one another, the common law of contracts requires a party to choose which remedy to pursue.

The Purpose of the Doctrine. The purpose of the doctrine of *election of remedies* is to prevent double recovery. Suppose, for example, that McCarthy agrees in writing to sell his land to Tally. Then McCarthy changes his mind and repudiates the contract. Tally can sue for compensatory damages or for specific performance. If Tally could seek compensatory damages in addition to specific performance, she would recover twice for the same breach of contract. The doctrine of election of remedies requires Tally to choose the remedy she wants, and it eliminates any possibility of double recovery. In other words, the election doctrine represents the legal embodiment of the adage "You can't have your cake and eat it, too."

The doctrine has often been applied in a rigid and technical manner, leading to some harsh results. For example, suppose that Wilson is fraudulently induced to buy a parcel of land for $150,000. He spends an additional $10,000 moving onto the land and then discovers the fraud. Instead of suing for damages, Wilson sues to rescind the contract. The court allows Wilson to recover only the purchase price of $150,000. The court denies recovery of the additional $10,000 because the seller, Martin, did not receive the $10,000 and is therefore not required to reimburse Wilson for his moving expenses. So Wilson suffers a net loss of $10,000 on the transaction. If Wilson had elected to sue for damages instead of seeking the remedy of rescission and restitution, he could have recovered the $10,000 as well as the $150,000.

---

54. Contracts that by their terms cannot be performed within one year must be in writing to be enforceable.

The UCC's Rejection of the Doctrine. Because of its many problems, the UCC expressly rejects the doctrine of election of remedies.[55] Remedies under the UCC are not exclusive but cumulative in nature and include all the available remedies for breach of contract.

55. See UCC 2–703 and UCC 2–711.

KEY TERMS

acceptance 331
agreement 326
alienation 346
assignment 346
breach of contract 350
commercial impracticability 356
compensatory damages 358
condition 348
consequential damages 359
consideration 334
contract 317
counteroffer 330
delegation 346
discharge 347
fraudulent misrepresentation (fraud) 341
frustration of purpose 356
genuineness of assent 339
impossibility of performance 355
incidental beneficiary 347
intended beneficiary 347
liquidated damages 359
mailbox rule 333
mirror image rule 331
mitigation of damages 359
mutual assent 326
mutual rescission 352
novation 353
offer 326
past consideration 336
penalty 359
performance 347
promise 316
promissory estoppel 330
quasi contract 322
reformation 362
restitution 360
revocation 329
specific performance 361
Statute of Frauds 345
tender 348
third party beneficiary 347
unconscionable 344

FOR REVIEW

1. What is a contract? What is the objective theory of contracts?
2. What are the four basic requirements for the formation of a valid contract?
3. In what types of situations might genuineness of assent to a contract's terms be lacking?
4. How are most contracts discharged?
5. What is the difference between compensatory and consequential damages?

QUESTIONS AND CASE PROBLEMS

10–1. Ball writes Sullivan and inquires how much Sullivan is asking for a specific forty-acre tract of land Sullivan owns. In a letter received by Ball, Sullivan states, "I will not take less than $60,000 for the forty-acre tract as specified." Ball immediately sends Sullivan a telegram stating, "I accept your offer for $60,000 for the forty-acre tract as specified." Discuss whether Ball can hold Sullivan to a contract for sale of the land.

10–2. Discuss whether either of the following contracts will be unenforceable on the ground that genuineness of assent is lacking.

(a) Simmons finds a stone in his pasture that he believes to be quartz. Jenson, who also believes that the stone is quartz, contracts to purchase it for $10. Just before delivery, the stone is discovered to be a diamond worth $1,000.

(b) Jacoby's barn is burned to the ground. He accuses Goldman's son of arson and threatens to bring a criminal action unless Goldman agrees to pay him $5,000. Goldman agrees to pay.

10–3. Marsala is a student attending college. He signs a one-year lease agreement that runs from September 1 to August 31. The lease agreement specifies that the lease cannot be assigned without the landlord's consent. In late May, Marsala decides not to go to summer school and assigns the balance of the lease (three months) to a close friend, Fred. The landlord objects to the assignment and denies Fred access to the apartment. Marsala claims Fred is financially sound and should be allowed the full rights and privileges of an assignee. Discuss fully whether the landlord or Marsala is correct.

10–4. In which of the following situations would specific performance be an appropriate remedy? Discuss fully.

(a) Thompson contracts to sell her house and lot to Cousteau. Then, on finding another buyer willing to pay a higher purchase price, she refuses to deed the property to Cousteau.
(b) Amy contracts to sing and dance in Fred's nightclub for one month, beginning May 1. She then refuses to perform.
(c) Hoffman contracts to purchase a rare coin owned by Erikson, who is breaking up his coin collection. At the last minute, Erikson decides to keep his coin collection intact and refuses to deliver the coin to Hoffman.
(d) ABC Corp. has three shareholders: Panozzo, who owns 48 percent of the stock; Chang, who owns another 48 percent; and Ryan, who owns 4 percent. Ryan contracts to sell her 4 percent to Chang. Later, Ryan refuses to transfer the shares to Chang.

10–5. Performance. In May 1996, O'Brien-Shiepe Funeral Home, Inc., in Hempstead, New York, hired Teramo & Co. to build an addition to O'Brien's funeral home. The parties' contract did not specify a date for the completion of the work. The city of Hempstead issued a building permit for the project on June 14, and Teramo began work about two weeks later. There was some delay in construction because O'Brien asked that no work be done during funeral services, but by the end of March 1997, the work was substantially complete. The city of Hempstead issued a "Certificate of Completion" on April 15. During the construction, O'Brien made periodic payments to Teramo, but there was a balance due of $17,950, which O'Brien did not pay. To recover this amount, Teramo filed a suit in a New York state court against O'Brien. O'Brien filed a counterclaim to recover lost profits for business allegedly lost due to the time Teramo took to build the addition and for $6,180 spent to correct problems caused by poor work. Which, if either, party is entitled to an award in this case? Explain. [*Teramo & Co. v. O'Brien-Shiepe Funeral Home, Inc.,* 725 N.Y.S.2d 87 (A.D. 2 Dept. 2001)]

CASE PROBLEM WITH SAMPLE ANSWER

10–6. Bilateral versus Unilateral Contracts. D.L. Peoples Group (D.L.) placed an ad in a Missouri newspaper to recruit admissions representatives, who were hired to recruit Missouri residents to attend D.L.'s college in Florida. Donald Hawley responded to the ad, his interviewer recommended him for the job, and he signed, in Missouri, an "Admissions Representative Agreement." The agreement was mailed to D.L.'s president, who signed it in his office in Florida. The agreement provided in part that Hawley would devote exclusive time and effort to the business in his assigned territory in Missouri and that D.L. would pay Hawley a commission if he successfully recruited students for the school. While attempting to make one of his first calls on his new job, Hawley was accidentally shot and killed. On the basis of his death, a claim was filed in Florida for workers' compensation. (Under Florida law, when an accident occurs outside Florida, workers' compensation benefits are payable only if the employment contract was made in Florida.) Is this admissions representative agreement a bilateral or a unilateral contract? What are the consequences of the distinction in this case? Explain. [*D.L. Peoples Group, Inc. v. Hawley,* 804 So.2d 561 (Fla.App. 1 Dist. 2002)]

To view a sample answer for this case problem, go to this book's Web site at **http://ele.westbuslaw.com** *and click on "Interactive Study Center."*

10–7. Unconscionability. Frank Rodziewicz was driving a Volvo tractor-trailer on Interstate 90 in Lake County, Indiana, when he struck a concrete barrier. His tractor-trailer became stuck on the barrier, and the Indiana State Police contacted Waffco Heavy Duty Towing, Inc., to assist in the recovery of the truck. Before beginning work, Waffco told Rodziewicz that it would cost $275 to tow the truck. There was no discussion of labor or any other costs. Rodziewicz told Waffco to take the truck to a local Volvo dealership. Within a few minutes, Waffco pulled the truck off the barrier and towed it to Waffco's nearby towing yard. Rodziewicz was soon notified that, in addition to the $275 towing fee, he would have to pay $4,070 in labor costs and that Waffco would not release the truck until payment was made. Rodziewicz paid the total amount. Disputing the labor charge, however, he filed a suit in an Indiana state court against Waffco, alleging in part breach of contract. Was the towing contract unconscionable? Would it make a difference if the parties had discussed the labor charge before the tow? Explain. [*Rodziewicz v. Waffco Heavy Duty Towing, Inc.,* 763 N.E.2d 491 (Ind.App. 2002)]

10–8. Substantial Performance. Adolf and Ida Krueger contracted with Pisani Construction, Inc., to erect a metal building as an addition to an existing structure.

The two structures were to share a common wall, and the frames and panel heights of the new building were to match those of the existing structure. Shortly before completion of the project, however, it was apparent that the roof line of the new building was approximately three inches higher than that of the existing structure. Pisani modified the ridge caps of the buildings to blend the roof lines. The discrepancy had other consequences, however, including misalignment of the gutters and windows of the two buildings, which resulted in an icing problem in the winter. The Kruegers occupied the new structure but refused to make the last payment under the contract. Pisani filed a suit in a Connecticut state court to collect. Did Pisani substantially perform its obligations? Should the Kruegers be ordered to pay? Why or why not? [*Pisani Construction, Inc. v. Krueger,* 68 Conn.App. 361, 791 A.2d 634 (2002)]

10–9. Mitigation of Damages. William West, an engineer, worked for Bechtel Corp., an organization of about 150 engineering and construction companies, which is headquartered in San Francisco, California, and operates worldwide. Except for a two-month period in 1985, Bechtel employed West on long-term assignments or short-term projects for thirty years. In October 1997, West was offered a position on a project with Saudi Arabian Bechtel Co. (SABCO), which West understood would be for two years. In November, however, West was terminated for what he believed was his "age and lack of display of energy." After his return to California, West received numerous offers from Bechtel for work that suited his abilities and met his salary expectations, but he did not accept any of them and did not look for other work. Three months later, he filed a suit in a California state court against Bechtel, alleging in part breach of contract and seeking the salary he would have earned during two years with SABCO. Bechtel responded in part that, even if there had been a breach, West had failed to mitigate his damages. Is Bechtel correct? Discuss. [*West v. Bechtel Corp.,* 96 Cal.App.4th 966, 117 Cal.Rptr.2d 647 (1 Dist. 2002)]

10–10. IN YOUR COURT

Charles Kloss had worked for Honeywell, Inc., for over fifteen years when Honeywell decided to transfer the employees at its Ballard facility to its Harbour Pointe facility. Honeywell planned to hire a medical person at the Harbour Pointe facility and promised Kloss that if he completed a nursing program and became a registered nurse (RN), the company would hire him for the medical position. When Kloss graduated from his RN program, however, Honeywell did not assign him to a nursing or medical position. Instead, the company gave Kloss a job in its maintenance department. Shortly thereafter, Kloss left the company and eventually sued Honeywell for damages (lost wages) resulting from Honeywell's breach of the employment contract. Assume that you are the judge in the trial court hearing this case and answer the following questions:

(a) One of the issues you will need to decide in this case is whether Kloss, by voluntarily leaving the maintenance job at Honeywell, had failed to mitigate his damages. How will you rule on this issue? Explain your reasoning.
(b) Assume that Honeywell's promise to hire Kloss after he completed his nursing program was made orally. Is there any legal theory under which you can enforce the promise?

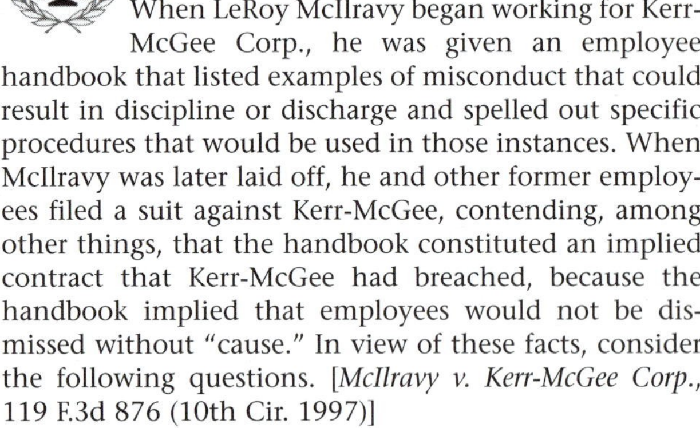

10–11. A QUESTION OF ETHICS AND SOCIAL RESPONSIBILITY

When LeRoy McIlravy began working for Kerr-McGee Corp., he was given an employee handbook that listed examples of misconduct that could result in discipline or discharge and spelled out specific procedures that would be used in those instances. When McIlravy was later laid off, he and other former employees filed a suit against Kerr-McGee, contending, among other things, that the handbook constituted an implied contract that Kerr-McGee had breached, because the handbook implied that employees would not be dismissed without "cause." In view of these facts, consider the following questions. [*McIlravy v. Kerr-McGee Corp.,* 119 F.3d 876 (10th Cir. 1997)]

(a) Would it be fair to the employer for the court to hold that an implied contract had been created in this case, given that the employer did not *intend* to create a contract? Would it be fair to the employees to hold that no contract was created? If the decision were up to you, how would you decide this issue?
(b) Suppose that the handbook contained a disclaimer stating that the handbook was not to be construed as a contract. How would this affect your answers to the above questions? From an ethical perspective, would it ever be fair to hold that an implied contract exists *notwithstanding* such a disclaimer?

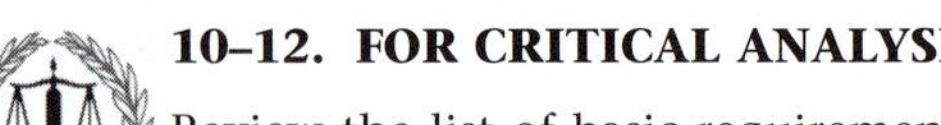

10–12. FOR CRITICAL ANALYSIS

Review the list of basic requirements for contract formation given at the beginning of this chapter. In view of those requirements, analyze the relationship entered into when a student enrolls in a college or university. Has a contract been formed? If so, is it a bilateral contract or a unilateral contract? Discuss.

For updated links to resources available on the Web, as well as a variety of other materials, visit this text's Web site at

http://ele.westbuslaw.com

The 'Lectric Law Library provides information on contract law, including a definition of *contract,* the elements required for a contract, and so on. Go to

http://www.lectlaw.com

Click on "The Library's Rotunda" and then go to the Laypeople's Law Lounge and scroll down to "Contracts."

To learn what kinds of clauses are included in typical contracts for certain goods and services, you can explore the collection of contract forms made available by FindLaw (now a part of West Group) at

http://forms.lp.findlaw.com

For a summary of how contracts may be discharged and other information on contract law, go to

http://www.lawyers.com/lawyers-com/content/aboutlaw/about_contr.html

When you access this site, select "Business Needs," and then click on "Contracts" under the "General Business" category.

The following sites offer information on contract law, including breach of contract and remedies:

http://www.nolo.com

http://www.law.cornell.edu/topics/contracts.html

LEGAL RESEARCH EXERCISES ON THE WEB

Go to **http://ele.westbuslaw.com**, the Web site that accompanies this text. Select "Interactive Study Center," and then click on "Chapter 10." There you will find the following Internet research exercises that you can perform to learn more about topics covered in this chapter.

Activity 10–1: LEGAL PERSPECTIVE—Contract Damages and Contract Theory

Activity 10–2: MANAGEMENT PERSPECTIVE—Commercial Impracticability

Activity 10–3: HISTORICAL PERSPECTIVE—Contracts in Ancient Mesopotamia

BEFORE THE TEST

Go to **http://ele.westbuslaw.com**, the Web site that accompanies this text. Select "Interactive Quizzes." You will find at least twenty interactive questions relating to this chapter.

WESTLAW® CAMPUS

If your textbook provided for a subscription to Westlaw® Campus, or if you have otherwise purchased access to the Westlaw Campus database, you can access any of the cases presented or cited in this chapter by using your Westlaw Campus account.

CHAPTER 11

Sales, Leases, and E-Contracts

CONTENTS

CHAPTER OBJECTIVES

After reading this chapter, you should be able to answer the following questions:

1

How do Article 2 and Article 2A of the UCC differ? What types of transactions does each article cover?

2

What is the significance of identifying goods to a contract?

3

If the parties to a contract do not specify when the risk of loss passes and the goods are to be delivered without their movement by the seller, when does risk of loss pass?

What are the respective obligations of the parties under a contract for a sale or lease of goods?

What are some of the clauses that offerors should include when making offers to form e-contracts?

When we turn to contracts for the sale and lease of goods, we move away from common law principles and into the area of statutory law. State statutory law governing sales and lease transactions is based on the Uniform Commercial Code (UCC), which, as mentioned in Chapter 1, has been adopted as law by all states.[1] Relevant sections of the UCC are noted in the following discussion of sales and lease contracts. As you will read shortly, in 2003 the National Conference of Commissioners on Uniform State Laws and the American Law Institute approved amendments to the UCC's Article 2 (on sales) and Article 2A (on leases).

To read the text of Article 2 of the Uniform Commercial Code, go to the "Statutes" page of our Web site at **http://ele.westbuslaw.com**

We open this chapter with a look at the scope of Article 2 and Article 2A. Article 2 of the UCC sets out the requirements of sales contracts and how they are formed. It also addresses the sometimes sticky concept of when title passes and who bears the risk of loss for goods in the process of being sold—for example, goods en route from the seller to the buyer—along with the concept of insurable interest. Article 2 regulates performance and obligations required under sales contracts. It also delineates when a breach by either the buyer or the seller occurs and what remedies normally may be sought. A sale of goods usually carries with it at least one type of warranty; sales warranties, likewise are governed by the UCC. Article 2A covers similar issues for lease contracts.

In the final section of this chapter, we look at how traditional laws are being applied to contracts formed online. We also examine some new laws that have been created to apply in situations in which traditional laws governing contracts have sometimes been thought inadequate. For example, traditional laws governing signature and writing requirements are not easily adapted to contracts formed in the online environment. Thus, new laws have been created to address these issues.

1. Louisiana has not adopted Articles 2 and 2A, however.

THE SCOPE OF ARTICLE 2—THE SALE OF GOODS

Sales contract • A contract for the sale of goods under which the ownership of goods is transferred from a seller to a buyer for a price.

Article 2 of the UCC governs **sales contracts,** or contracts for the sale of goods. To facilitate commercial transactions, Article 2 modifies some of the common law contract requirements that were discussed in Chapter 10. To the extent that it has not been modified by the UCC, however, the common law of contracts also applies to sales contracts. For example, the common law requirements for a valid contract—agreement (offer and acceptance), consideration, capacity, and legality—that were discussed in Chapter 10 are also applicable to sales contracts. Thus, you may want to reexamine these common law principles when studying the law of sales.

In general, the rule is that whenever there is a conflict between a common law contract rule and the UCC, the UCC controls. In other words, when a UCC provision addresses a certain issue, the UCC governs; when the UCC is silent, the common law governs.

In regard to Article 2, you should keep in mind two things. First, Article 2 deals with the sale of *goods;* it does not deal with real property (real estate), services, or intangible property such as stocks and bonds. Thus, if the subject matter of a dispute is goods, the UCC governs. If it is real estate or services, the common law applies. Second, in some cases, the rules may vary quite a bit, depending on whether the buyer or the seller is a *merchant.* We look now at how the UCC defines a *sale, goods,* and *merchant status.*

What Is a Sale?

Section 2–102 of the UCC states that Article 2 "applies to transactions in goods." This implies a broad scope—covering gifts, bailments (temporary deliveries of personal property), and purchases of goods. In this chapter, however, we treat Article 2 as being applicable only to an actual sale (as would most authorities and courts). The UCC defines a **sale** as "the passing of title from the seller to the buyer for a price," where *title* refers to the formal right of ownership of property [UCC 2–106(1)]. The price may be payable in money or in other goods, services, or realty (real estate).

Sale • The passing of title from the seller to the buyer for a price.

What Are Goods?

To be characterized as a *good,* an item of property must be *tangible,* and it must be *movable.* **Tangible property** has physical existence—it can be touched or seen. Intangible property—such as corporate stocks and bonds, patents and copyrights, and ordinary contract rights—have only conceptual existence and thus do not come under Article 2.[2] A *movable* item can be carried from place to place. Hence, real estate is excluded from Article 2.

Tangible property • Property that has physical existence and can be distinguished by the senses of touch, sight, and so on. A car is tangible property; a patent right is intangible property.

Who Is a Merchant?

Article 2 governs the sale of goods in general. It applies to sales transactions between all buyers and sellers. In a limited number of instances, however, the UCC presumes that in certain phases of sales transactions involving mer-

2. Also specifically excluded under the 2003 amendments to UCC Article 2 is "information," which may mean data, text, images, sounds, computer programs, software, databases, or the like, and "computer information" [Amended UCC 2–103(1)(k)].

chants, special business standards ought to be imposed because of the merchants' relatively high degree of commercial expertise.[3] Such standards do not apply to the casual or inexperienced seller or buyer ("consumer").

In general, a person is a **merchant** when he or she, acting in a mercantile capacity, possesses or uses an expertise specifically related to the goods being sold. This basic distinction is not always clear-cut. For example, courts in some states have determined that farmers may be merchants, while courts in other states have determined that the drafters of the UCC did not intend to include farmers as merchants.

Merchant • A person who deals in goods of the kind involved in the sales contract; see UCC 2–104.

THE SCOPE OF ARTICLE 2A—LEASES

In the past few decades, leases of personal property (goods) have become increasingly common. Consumers and business firms lease automobiles, industrial equipment, items for use in the home (such as floor polishers), and many other types of goods. Until Article 2A was added to the UCC, no specific body of law addressed the legal problems that arose when goods were leased, rather than sold. In cases involving leased goods, the courts generally applied a combination of common law rules, real estate law, and principles expressed in Article 2 of the UCC.

Article 2A of the UCC was created to fill the need for uniform guidelines in this area. Article 2A covers any transaction that creates a lease of goods, as well as subleases of goods [UCC 2A–102, 2A–103(k)].[4] Article 2A is essentially a repetition of Article 2, except that it applies to leases of goods, rather than sales of goods, and thus varies to reflect differences between sales and lease transactions.

Article 2A defines a **lease agreement** as the bargain of the lessor and lessee, as found in their language and as implied by other circumstances [UCC 2A–103(k)]. A **lessor** is one who sells the right to the possession and use of goods under a lease [UCC 2A–103(p)]. A **lessee** is one who acquires the right to the possession and use of goods under a lease [UCC 2A–103(o)]. Article 2A applies to all types of leases of goods, including commercial leases and consumer leases.

Lease agreement • In regard to the lease of goods, an agreement in which one person (the lessor) agrees to transfer the right to the possession and use of property to another person (the lessee) in exchange for rental payments.

Lessor • A person who sells the right to the possession and use of property to another in exchange for rental payments.

Lessee • A person who acquires the right to the possession and use of another's property in exchange for rental payments.

THE AMENDMENTS TO ARTICLES 2 AND 2A

For the most part, the 2003 amendments to Articles 2 and 2A mark an attempt by the National Conference of Commissioners on Uniform State Laws and the American Law Institute to update the UCC to accommodate electronic commerce. Among other things, the amendments include revised definitions of various terms to make the definitions consistent with those given in the Uniform Electronic Transactions Act (UETA) and the federal Electronic Signatures in Global and National Commerce Act (E-SIGN Act) of

3. The provisions that apply only to merchants deal principally with the Statute of Frauds, firm offers, confirmatory memoranda, warranties, and contract modification. These special rules reflect expedient business practices commonly known to merchants in the commercial setting. They will be discussed later in this chapter.

4. The 2003 amendments to UCC Article 2A, like those to UCC Article 2, expressly exclude "information" from the definition of "goods" [Amended UCC 2A–103(1)(n) and (p)].

2000—discussed later in this chapter. Throughout the amendments, for example, the word *writing* has been replaced by *record,* and the term *sign* has been amended to include electronic signatures. Provisions governing electronic contracts have also been included.

In addition, the amendments include a number of new protections for buyers, some of which apply only to buyers who are consumers. Other new or revised provisions relate to contract formation (offer and acceptance), the Statute of Frauds, warranties, and other topics. In this chapter, we refer to the amendments, often in footnotes, whenever the amendments significantly change the law currently in effect under Articles 2 and 2A.

The Formation of Sales and Lease Contracts

In regard to the formation of sales and lease contracts, the UCC modifies the common law of contracts in several ways. We look here at how Article 2 and Article 2A of the UCC modify common law contract rules. Realize that parties to sales contracts are free to establish whatever terms they wish. The UCC comes into play when the parties have not, in their contract, provided for a contingency that later gives rise to a dispute. The UCC makes this very clear time and again by its use of such phrases as "unless the parties otherwise agree" and "absent a contrary agreement by the parties."

Offer

In general contract law, the moment a definite offer is met by an unqualified acceptance, a binding contract is formed. In commercial sales transactions, the verbal exchanges, the correspondence, and the actions of the parties may not reveal exactly when a binding contractual obligation arises. The UCC states that an agreement sufficient to constitute a contract can exist even if the moment of its making is undetermined [UCC 2–204(2), 2A–204(2)].

Open Terms. According to contract law, an offer must be definite enough for the parties (and the courts) to ascertain its essential terms when it is accepted. The UCC states that a sales or lease contract will not fail for indefiniteness even if one or more terms are left open as long as (1) the parties intended to make a contract, and (2) there is a reasonably certain basis for the court to grant an appropriate remedy [UCC 2–204(3), 2A–204(3)].

Although the UCC has radically lessened the requirement of definiteness of terms, keep in mind that if too many terms are left open, a court may find that the parties did not intend to form a contract.

Open Price Term. If the parties have not agreed on a price, the court will determine a "reasonable price at the time for delivery" [UCC 2–305(1)]. If either the buyer or the seller is to determine the price, the price is to be fixed in good faith [UCC 2–305(2)].

Sometimes the price fails to be fixed through the fault of one of the parties. In that case, the other party can treat the contract as canceled or fix a reasonable price. For example, Johnson and Merrick enter into a contract for the sale of goods and agree that Johnson will fix the price. Johnson refuses to fix the price. Merrick can either treat the contract as canceled or set a reasonable price [UCC 2–305(3)].

ETHICAL ISSUE

Should merchants be required to act in good faith? This question was one of many facing the drafters of the UCC. Their answer was a resounding "Yes." UCC 1–203 states, "Every contract or duty within this act imposes an obligation of good faith in its performance or enforcement." The difficulty, of course, was in defining *good faith* in a meaningful way. The UCC resolved the problem by stating that good faith in the case of a merchant means honesty in fact and the observance of reasonable commercial standards of fair dealing in the trade [UCC 2–103(1)(b)]. Indeed, the concepts of *good faith* and *commercial reasonableness* permeate the UCC. As you just read, if the buyer or the seller is to determine the price, the UCC requires that the price be determined in good faith. This is but one of many UCC provisions requiring good faith in the formation and performance of sales contracts. The concept of commercial reasonableness also underlies numerous UCC provisions. A merchant is expected to act in a reasonable manner according to reasonable commercial customs. The importance of commercial reasonableness as a component of good faith is underscored by the fact that the word *reasonable* appears about ninety times in Article 2.

Open Payment Term. When parties do not specify payment terms, payment is due at the time and place at which the buyer is to receive the goods [UCC 2–310(a)]. The buyer can tender payment using any commercially normal or acceptable means, such as a check or credit card. If the seller demands payment in cash, however, the buyer must be given a reasonable time to obtain it [UCC 2–511(2)]. This is especially important when the contract states a definite and final time for performance.

Open Delivery Term. When no delivery terms are specified, the buyer normally takes delivery at the seller's place of business [UCC 2–308(a)]. If the seller has no place of business, the seller's residence is used. When goods are located in some other place and both parties know it, delivery is made there. If the time for shipment or delivery is not clearly specified in the sales contract, the court will infer a "reasonable" time for performance [UCC 2–309(1)].

Open Quantity Term. Normally, if the parties do not specify a quantity, a court will have no basis for determining a remedy. The UCC recognizes two exceptions in requirements and output contracts [UCC 2–306(1)].

In a **requirements contract,** the buyer agrees to purchase and the seller agrees to sell all or up to a stated amount of what the buyer *needs* or *requires.* There is implicit consideration in a requirements contract, for the buyer gives up the right to buy from any other seller, and this forfeited right constitutes implicit consideration. Requirements contracts are common in the business world and are normally enforceable. If, however, the buyer promises to purchase only if the buyer *wishes* to do so, or if the buyer reserves the right to buy the goods from someone other than the seller, the promise is *illusory* (without consideration) and unenforceable by either party.

Requirements contract • An agreement in which a buyer agrees to purchase and the seller agrees to sell all or up to a stated amount of what the buyer needs or requires.

Output contract • An agreement in which a seller agrees to sell and a buyer agrees to buy all or up to a stated amount of what the seller produces.

In an **output contract,** the seller agrees to sell and the buyer agrees to buy all or up to a stated amount of what the seller *produces*. Again, because the seller essentially forfeits the right to sell goods to another buyer, there is implicit consideration in an output contract.

The UCC imposes a *good faith limitation* on requirements and output contracts. The quantity under such contracts is the amount of requirements or the amount of output that occurs during a *normal* production year. The actual quantity purchased or sold cannot be unreasonably disproportionate to normal or comparable prior requirements or output [UCC 2–306].

Merchant's Firm Offer. Under regular contract principles, an offer can be revoked at any time before acceptance. The major common law exception is an *option contract,* in which the offeree pays consideration for the offeror's irrevocable promise to keep the offer open for a stated period. The UCC creates a second exception, which applies only to firm offers for the sale or lease of goods made by a merchant (regardless of whether or not the offeree is a merchant). A **firm offer** arises when a merchant-offeror gives assurances *in a signed writing* that the offer will remain open. The merchant's firm offer is irrevocable without the necessity of consideration[5] for the stated period or, if no definite period is stated, a reasonable period (neither to exceed three months) [UCC 2–205, 2A–205].

Firm offer • An offer (by a merchant) that is irrevocable without consideration for a period of time (not longer than three months). A firm offer by a merchant must be in writing and must be signed by the offeror.

Acceptance

Acceptance of an offer to buy, sell, or lease goods generally may be made in any reasonable manner and by any reasonable means. The UCC generally takes the position that if the offeree's response indicates a *definite* acceptance of the offer, a contract is formed, even if the acceptance includes terms additional to or different from those contained in the offer [UCC 2–207(1)].

Promise to Ship or Prompt Shipment. The UCC permits acceptance of an offer to buy goods "either by a prompt promise to ship or by the prompt or current shipment of conforming or nonconforming goods" [UCC 2–206(1)(b)]. *Conforming* goods accord with the contract's terms; *nonconforming* goods do not. The prompt shipment of *nonconforming* goods constitutes both an *acceptance,* which creates a contract, and a *breach* of that contract. This rule does not apply if the seller seasonably (within a reasonable amount of time) notifies the buyer that the nonconforming shipment is offered only as an *accommodation,* or as a favor. The notice of accommodation must clearly indicate to the buyer that the shipment does not constitute an acceptance and that, therefore, no contract has been formed.

Communication of Acceptance. Under the common law of contracts, because a unilateral offer invites acceptance by a performance, the offeree need not notify the offeror of performance unless the offeror would not otherwise know about it. The UCC is more stringent than the common law, stating that when the beginning of the requested performance is a reasonable mode of acceptance, an offeror who is not notified of acceptance within a reasonable

5. If the offeree pays consideration, then an option contract (not a merchant's firm offer) is formed.

time may treat the offer as having lapsed before acceptance [UCC 2–206(2), 2A–206(2)].

Additional Terms. If the acceptance includes terms additional to or different from those contained in the offer and one (or both) of the parties is a *nonmerchant,* the contract is formed according to the terms of the original offer submitted by the original offeror and not according to the additional terms of the acceptance [UCC 2–207(2)]. In contracts *between merchants,* the additional terms automatically become part of the contract *unless* (1) the original offer expressly limits acceptance to its terms, (2) the new or changed terms materially alter the contract, or (3) the offeror objects to the new or changed terms within a reasonable period of time [UCC 2–207(2)].[6]

CONSIDERATION

The common law rule that a contract requires consideration also applies to sales and lease contracts. Unlike the common law, however, the UCC does not require a contract modification to be supported by new consideration. The UCC states that an agreement modifying a contract for the sale or lease of goods "needs no consideration to be binding" [UCC 2–209(1), 2A–208(1)].

Of course, any contract modification must be made in good faith [UCC 1–203]. For example, Jim agrees to lease certain goods to Louise for a stated price. Subsequently, a sudden shift in the market makes it difficult for Jim to lease the items to Louise at the given price without suffering a loss. Jim tells Louise of the situation, and Louise agrees to pay an additional sum for the goods. Later, Louise reconsiders and refuses to pay more than the original price. Under the UCC, Louise's promise to modify the contract needs no consideration to be binding. Hence, Louise is bound by the modified contract.

In this example, a shift in the market is a *good faith* reason for contract modification. What if there really was no shift in the market, however, and Jim knew that Louise needed the goods immediately but refused to deliver them unless Louise agreed to pay an additional sum of money? This sort of extortion of a modification without a legitimate commercial reason would be ineffective, because it would violate the duty of good faith. Jim would not be permitted to enforce the higher price.

THE STATUTE OF FRAUDS

As discussed in Chapter 10, the Statute of Frauds requires that certain types of contracts, to be enforceable, must be in writing or evidenced by a writing. The UCC contains Statute of Frauds provisions covering sales and lease contracts. Under these provisions, sales contracts for goods priced at $500 or more and

6. The 2003 amendments to UCC Article 2 do not distinguish between merchants and others in setting out rules for the effect of additional terms in contracts for sale, nor do they give a preference to the first or the last terms to be stated. Instead, a court is directed to determine whether (1) the terms appear in the records of both parties, (2) both parties agree to the terms even if they are not in a record, or (3) the terms are supplied or incorporated under another provision of Article 2 [Amended UCC 2–207]. The amendments give the courts more discretion to include or exclude certain terms.

lease contracts requiring total payments of $1,000 or more must be in writing to be enforceable [UCC 2–201(1), 2A–201(1)].[7]

Sufficiency of the Writing

The UCC has greatly relaxed the requirements for the sufficiency of a writing to satisfy the Statute of Frauds. A writing or a memorandum will be sufficient as long as it indicates that the parties intended to form a contract and as long as it is signed by the party (or agent of the party) against whom enforcement is sought. The contract normally will not be enforceable beyond the quantity of goods shown in the writing, however. All other terms can be proved in court by oral testimony. For leases, the writing must reasonably identify and describe the goods leased and the lease term.

Special Rules for Contracts between Merchants

Once again, the UCC provides a special rule for merchants. The rule, however, applies only to sales (under Article 2); there is no corresponding rule that applies to leases (under Article 2A).[8] Merchants can satisfy the requirements of a writing for the Statute of Frauds if, after the parties have agreed orally, one of the merchants sends a signed written confirmation to the other merchant. The communication must indicate the terms of the agreement, and the merchant receiving the confirmation must have reason to know of its contents. Unless the merchant who receives the confirmation gives written notice of objection to its contents within ten days after receipt, the writing is sufficient against the receiving merchant, even though he or she has not signed anything [UCC 2–201(2)].

Exceptions

The UCC defines three exceptions to the writing requirements of the Statute of Frauds. An oral contract for the sale of goods priced at $500 or more or the lease of goods involving total payments of $1,000 or more will be enforceable despite the absence of a writing in the circumstances described in the following subsections [UCC 2–201(3), 2A–201(4)].

Specially Manufactured Goods. An oral contract is enforceable if (1) it is for goods that are specially manufactured for a particular buyer or specially manufactured or obtained for a particular lessee, (2) these goods are not suitable for resale or lease to others in the ordinary course of the seller's or lessor's business, and (3) the seller or lessor has substantially started to manufacture the goods or has made commitments for the manufacture or procurement of the goods. In these situations, once the seller or lessor has taken action, the buyer or lessee cannot repudiate the agreement claiming the Statute of Frauds as a defense.

---

7. Under the 2003 amendments to UCC 2–201(1), a contract for a sale of goods must involve goods priced at $5,000 or more to be subject to the record (writing) requirement.
8. According to the comments accompanying UCC 2A–201 (Article 2A's Statute of Frauds), the "between merchants" provision was not included because "the number of such transactions involving leases, as opposed to sales, was thought to be modest."

Admissions. An oral contract for the sale or lease of goods is enforceable if the party against whom enforcement is sought admits in pleadings, testimony, or other court proceedings that a sales or lease contract was made.[9] In this situation, the contract will be enforceable even though it was oral, but enforceability will be limited to the quantity of goods admitted.

Partial Performance. An oral contract for the sale or lease of goods is enforceable if payment has been made and accepted or goods have been received and accepted. This is the "partial performance" exception. The oral contract will be enforced at least to the extent that performance *actually* took place.

TITLE, RISK, AND INSURABLE INTEREST

Before the creation of the UCC, *title*—the right of ownership—was the central concept in sales law, controlling all issues of rights and remedies of the parties to a sales contract. There were numerous problems with this concept. For example, frequently it was difficult to determine when title actually passed from seller to buyer, and therefore it was also difficult to predict which party a court would decide had title at the time of a loss. Because of such problems, the UCC divorced the question of title as completely as possible from the question of the rights and obligations of buyers, sellers, and third parties (such as subsequent purchasers, creditors, or the tax collector).

In some situations, title is still relevant under the UCC, and the UCC has special rules for locating title. In most situations, however, the UCC has replaced the concept of title with three other concepts: (1) identification, (2) risk of loss, and (3) insurable interest.

In lease contracts, of course, title to the goods is retained by the lessor-owner of the goods. Hence, the UCC's provisions relating to passage of title do not apply to leased goods. Other concepts discussed in this chapter, though, including identification, risk of loss, and insurable interest, relate to lease contracts as well as to sales contracts.

Identification

Before any interest in specific goods can pass from the seller or lessor to the buyer or lessee, two conditions must prevail:

1. The goods must be in existence.
2. They must be identified as the specific goods designated in the contract.

The Significance of Identification. **Identification** is a designation of goods as the subject matter of a sales or lease contract. Title and risk of loss cannot pass to the buyer from the seller unless the goods are identified to the contract [UCC 2–105(2)]. (As mentioned, title to leased goods remains with the lessor—or, if the owner is a third party, with that party. The lessee does not acquire title to leased goods.) Identification is significant because it gives the buyer or lessee the right to insure (or obtain an insurable interest in) the goods and the right to recover from third parties who damage the goods.

Identification • In a sale or lease of goods, the express designation of the specific goods provided for in the contract.

9. Any admission under oath, including one *not* made in a court, satisfies UCC 2–201(3)(b) and 2A–201(4)(b) under the 2003 amendments to Article 2 and 2A.

When Identification Takes Place. Once the goods are in existence, the parties can agree in their contract on when identification will take place. If they do not so specify, however, and if the contract calls for the sale or lease of specific and ascertained goods that are already in existence, identification takes place at the time the contract is made.

If a sale involves unborn animals to be born within twelve months after contracting, identification takes place when the animals are conceived. If a lease involves any unborn animals, identification also occurs when the animals are conceived. If a sale involves crops that are to be harvested within twelve months (or the next harvest season occurring after contracting, whichever is longer), identification takes place when the crops are planted or begin to grow. In a sale or lease of any other future goods, identification occurs when the goods are shipped, marked, or otherwise designated by the seller or lessor as the goods to which the contract refers. Goods that are part of a larger mass are identified when the goods are marked, shipped, or somehow designated by the seller or lessor as the particular goods to pass under the contract.

When Title Passes

Once goods exist and are identified, the provisions of UCC 2–401 apply to the passage of title. Unless an agreement is explicitly made,[10] title passes to the buyer at the time and the place the seller performs the *physical delivery* of the goods [UCC 2–401(2)]. The following case illustrates the significance of this event.

10. In many sections of the UCC, the words "unless otherwise explicitly agreed" appear, meaning that any explicit agreement between the buyer and the seller determines the rights, duties, and liabilities of the parties, including when title passes.

CASE 11.1

United States Bankruptcy Court, Western District of Arkansas, 2002. 274 Bankr. 503.

In re STEWART

In July 1997, Gary Stewart began to buy, and occasionally sell, cattle through Barry County Livestock Auction, Inc., in Exeter, Missouri. On January 29 and February 19, 2000, Stewart bought $46,749.55 worth of cattle through Barry County, but the checks he gave in payment were returned by the bank because his account did not have sufficient funds. By March 4, Stewart had given cashier's checks to Barry County to pay for the cattle.[a] *Less than forty days later, on April 11, Stewart filed for bankruptcy in a federal bankruptcy court. Some payments made to creditors within ninety days of the filing of a petition in bankruptcy can be recovered so that their amounts can be distributed more equitably among a debtor's creditors. Stewart asked the court to recover his payments to Barry County. Barry County claimed that the payments were "contemporaneous exchanges for new value," which cannot be recovered. The question on which the outcome of this case turned was whether the transfer of title to the cattle occurred on the day of the sale or on the day of the payment.*

FUSSELL, J.

In this case, Barry County Livestock Auction printed on the face of each bill of sale language dealing with the transfer of title:

a. A cashier's check is considered nearly the equivalent of cash because the bank assumes responsibility for paying it.

ALL SALES ARE MADE, AND TITLE IS TRANSFERRED, SUBJECT TO FINAL PAYMENT * * *. IF ANY CHECK * * * TENDERED IN PAYMENT IS NOT PAID PROMPTLY ON PRESENTATION, THIS BILL OF SALE DOES NOT TRANSFER TITLE AND SHALL BE NULL AND VOID, AND OF NO EFFECT.

The first sentence states that the sale is voidable—all sales are made subject to final payment. Based on this sentence, the transfer occurred on the date of the sale. The second sentence states that the sale is void if a check is not paid upon [its presentation to the bank for payment]. Based on this sentence, it appears that Barry County Livestock Auction was attempting to retain title to the cattle in the event the debtor's personal checks were not honored [paid]. According to the UCC, any attempt to retain title to the cattle pending the debtor's personal checks being honored by the bank is ineffective. * * * [UCC] 2–401(2) states the time at which title to the goods passes to the buyer: *"Unless otherwise explicitly agreed title passes to the buyer at the time and place at which the seller completes his performance with reference to the physical delivery of the goods* * * *." Although [UCC] 2–401(2) begins with the phrase "[u]nless otherwise explicitly agreed," the prior subsection places limits on the parties' contractual freedom. Specifically, [UCC] 2–401(1) *negates any attempt to forestall passage of title beyond the moment of final delivery* * * *. Similarly, [UCC] 2–401(1) prohibits the passage of title prior to the identification of the goods in question to the contract. In between these extremes, however, the parties may by contract specify the point at which title passes. * * * Under subsection (1), by agreement of the parties, title to goods can pass from the time the goods are identified in the contract up to the time the goods are delivered. Subsection (2) deals with fact patterns in the absence of an agreement to the contrary pursuant to subsection (1). The Court finds that under the UCC, title to the cattle passed upon delivery of the cattle on the day of the respective sales. [Emphasis added.]

The court held that the transfer of title to the cattle occurred on the dates of the sales when the cattle were physically delivered. Thus, Stewart's payments with the cashier's checks were not part of a "contemporaneous exchange"—the payments occurred after the bank returned his personal checks for insufficient funds, more than two weeks after the transfer of title.

QUESTIONS

1. What was the central issue in this case, and who brought this issue to the attention of the court?
2. What were the parties' respective claims with regard to this issue?
3. What was the question on which the outcome of this case turned, and how did the court answer this question?

Shipment contract • A contract for the sale of goods in which the seller is required or authorized to ship the goods by carrier. The buyer assumes liability for any losses or damage to the goods after they are delivered to the carrier.

Shipment and Destination Contracts. In the absence of agreement, delivery arrangements can determine when title passes from the seller to the buyer. In a **shipment contract,** the seller is required or authorized to ship goods by carrier, such as a trucking company. Under a shipment contract, the seller is required only to deliver the goods into the hands of a carrier, and title passes to the buyer at the time and place of shipment [UCC 2–401(2)(a)].

Generally, all contracts are assumed to be shipment contracts if nothing to the contrary is stated in the contract.

Destination contract • A contract in which the seller is required or authorized to ship the goods by carrier and deliver them at a particular destination. The seller assumes liability for any losses or damage to the goods until they are tendered at the destination specified in the contract.

In a **destination contract,** the seller is required to deliver the goods to a particular destination, usually directly to the buyer, although sometimes the buyer designates that the goods should be delivered to another party. Title passes to the buyer when the goods are *tendered* at that destination [UCC 2–401(2)(b)]. As you will read later in this chapter, a *tender of delivery* is the seller's placing or holding of conforming goods at the buyer's disposition (with any necessary notice), enabling the buyer to take delivery [UCC 2–503(1)].

Delivery without Movement of the Goods. When the contract of sale does not call for the seller's shipment or delivery of the goods (when the buyer is to pick up the goods), the passage of title depends on whether the seller must deliver a *document of title,* such as a bill of lading or a warehouse receipt, to the buyer. A *bill of lading* is a receipt for goods that is signed by a carrier and that serves as a contract for the transportation of the goods. A *warehouse receipt* is a receipt issued by a warehouser for goods stored in a warehouse.

When a document of title is required, title passes to the buyer *when and where the document is delivered.* Thus, if the goods are stored in a warehouse, title passes to the buyer when the appropriate documents are delivered to the buyer. The goods never move. In fact, the buyer can choose to leave the goods at the same warehouse for a period of time, and the buyer's title to those goods will be unaffected.

When no documents of title are required, and delivery is made without moving the goods, title passes at the time and place the sales contract is made, if the goods have already been identified. If the goods have not been identified, title does not pass until identification occurs. Consider an example. Rogers sells lumber to Bodan. It is agreed that Bodan will pick up the lumber at the yard. If the lumber has been identified (segregated, marked, or in any other way distinguished from all other lumber), title passes to Bodan when the contract is signed. If the lumber is still in storage bins at the mill, title does not pass to Bodan until the particular pieces of lumber to be sold under this contract are identified [UCC 2–401(3)].

Risk of Loss

Under the UCC, risk of loss does not necessarily pass with title. When risk of loss passes from a seller or lessor to a buyer or lessee is generally determined by the contract between the parties. Sometimes, the contract states expressly when the risk of loss passes. At other times, it does not, and a court must interpret the existing terms to ascertain whether the risk has passed.

Delivery with Movement of the Goods. When there is no specification in the agreement, the following rules apply to cases involving movement of the goods (so-called carrier cases). If the seller or lessor is required or authorized to ship goods by carrier but not required to deliver them to a particular destination, risk of loss passes to the buyer or lessee when the goods are duly delivered to the carrier [UCC 2–509(1)(a), 2A–219(2)(a)]. In a destination contract, the risk of loss passes to the buyer or lessee when the goods are tendered to the buyer or lessee at the specified destination [UCC 2–509(1)(b), 2A–219(2)(b)].

Specific terms in the contract help determine when risk of loss passes to the buyer. These terms, which are listed and defined in Exhibit 11–1, relate generally to the determination of which party will bear the costs of delivery, as well as which party will bear the risk of loss. The 2003 amendments to UCC Article 2 omit these terms because they are "inconsistent with modern commercial practice." Until most states adopt the amended version of Article 2, however, these terms will remain in use.

Delivery without Movement of the Goods. The UCC also addresses situations in which the seller or lessor is required neither to ship nor to deliver the goods. Frequently, the buyer or lessee is to pick up the goods from the seller or lessor, or the goods are to be held by a bailee. A *bailment* is a temporary delivery of personal property, without passage of title, into the care of another, called a *bailee*. Under the UCC, a bailee is a party who, by a bill of lading, warehouse receipt, or other document of title, acknowledges possession of goods and contracts to deliver them. A warehousing company, for example, or a trucking company that normally issues documents of title for the goods it receives is a bailee.

Goods Held by the Seller. If the goods are held by the seller, a document of title is usually not used. If the seller is a merchant, risk of loss to goods held by the seller passes to the buyer when the buyer *actually takes physical possession of the goods* [UCC 2–509(3)]. If the seller is not a merchant, the risk of loss to goods held by the seller passes to the buyer on tender of delivery [UCC 2–509(3)].

In respect to leases, the risk of loss passes to the lessee on the lessee's receipt of the goods if the lessor is a merchant. Otherwise, the risk passes to the lessee on tender of delivery [UCC 2A–219(c)].[11]

11. Under the 2003 amendments to UCC 2–509(3) and 2A–219(c), the risk of loss passes to the buyer or the lessee on that party's receipt of the goods whether or not the seller or the lessor is a merchant.

EXHIBIT 11–1 • CONTRACT TERMS—DEFINITIONS

The contract terms listed and defined in this exhibit help to determine which party will bear the costs of delivery and when risk of loss will pass from the seller to the buyer.

F.O.B. (free on board)—Indicates that the selling price of goods includes transportation costs to the specific F.O.B. place named in the contract. The seller pays the expenses and carries the risk of loss to the F.O.B. place named [UCC 2–319(1)]. If the named place is the place from which the goods are shipped (for example, the seller's city or place of business), the contract is a shipment contract. If the named place is the place to which the goods are to be shipped (for example, the buyer's city or place of business), the contract is a destination contract.

F.A.S. (free alongside)—Requires that the seller, at his or her own expense and risk, deliver the goods alongside the ship before risk passes to the buyer [UCC 2–319(2)].

C.I.F. or **C.&F.** (cost, insurance, and freight or just cost and freight)—Requires, among other things, that the seller "put the goods in possession of a carrier" before risk passes to the buyer [UCC 2–320(2)]. (These are basically pricing terms, and the contracts remain shipment contracts, not destination contracts.)

Delivery ex-ship (delivery from the carrying vessel)—Means that risk of loss does not pass to the buyer until the goods leave the ship or are otherwise properly unloaded [UCC 2–322].

Goods Held by a Bailee. When a bailee is holding goods for a person who has contracted to sell them and the goods are to be delivered without being moved, the goods are usually represented by a negotiable or nonnegotiable document of title (a bill of lading or a warehouse receipt). Risk of loss passes to the buyer when (1) the buyer receives a negotiable document of title for the goods, (2) the bailee acknowledges the buyer's right to possess the goods, or (3) the buyer receives a nonnegotiable document of title *and* has had a *reasonable time* to present the document to the bailee and demand the goods. Obviously, if the bailee refuses to honor the document, the risk of loss remains with the seller [UCC 2–503(4)(b), 2–509(2)].

With respect to leases, if goods held by a bailee are to be delivered without being moved, the risk of loss passes to the lessee on acknowledgment by the bailee of the lessee's right to possession of the goods [UCC 2A–219(2)(b)].

Conditional Sales. Buyers and sellers sometimes form sales contracts that are conditioned either on the buyer's approval of the goods or on the buyer's resale of the goods. Under such contracts, the buyer is in possession of the goods. Sometimes, however, problems arise as to whether the buyer or seller should bear the loss if, for example, the goods are damaged or stolen while in the possession of the buyer.

Sale or return • A type of conditional sale in which title and possession pass from the seller to the buyer; however, the buyer retains the option to return the goods during a specified period even though the goods conform to the contract.

Sale or Return. A **sale or return** (sometimes called a *sale and return*) is a type of contract by which the buyer purchases the goods but has a conditional right to return the goods (undo the sale) within a specified time period. When the buyer receives possession at the time of sale, title and risk of loss pass to the buyer. Title and risk of loss remain with the buyer until the buyer returns the goods to the seller within the time period specified. If the buyer fails to return the goods within this time period, the sale is finalized. The return of the goods is made at the buyer's risk and expense. Goods held under a sale-or-return contract are subject to the claims of the buyer's creditors while they are in the buyer's possession.

Consignment • A transaction in which an owner of goods (the consignor) delivers the goods to another (the consignee) for the consignee to sell. The consignee pays the consignor for the goods when they are sold by the consignee.

The UCC treats a consignment as a sale or return. Under a **consignment,** the owner of goods (the *consignor*) delivers them to another (the *consignee*) for the consignee to sell or to keep. If the consignee sells the goods, the consignee must pay the consignor for them. If the consignee does not sell or keep the goods, they may simply be returned to the consignor. While the goods are in the possession of the consignee, the consignee holds title to them, and creditors of the consignee will prevail over the consignor in any action to repossess the goods [UCC 2–326(3)].[12]

Sale on approval • A type of conditional sale in which the buyer may take the goods on a trial basis. The sale becomes absolute only when the buyer approves of (or is satisfied with) the goods being sold.

Sale on Approval. Usually, when a seller offers to sell goods to a buyer and permits the buyer to take the goods on a trial basis, a **sale on approval** is made. The term *sale* here is a misnomer, as only an *offer* to sell has been made, along with a bailment created by the buyer's possession.

Therefore, title and risk of loss (from causes beyond the buyer's control) remain with the seller until the buyer accepts (approves) the offer. Acceptance can be made expressly, by any act inconsistent with the *trial* purpose or the

12. This provision on consignments is omitted from the 2003 amendments to UCC Article 2. Consignments are to be covered by UCC Article 9. See, for example, UCC 9–103(d), 9–109(a)(4), and 9–319.

seller's ownership, or by the buyer's election not to return the goods within the trial period. If the buyer does not wish to accept, the buyer may notify the seller of that fact within the trial period, and the return is made at the seller's expense and risk [UCC 2–327(1)]. Goods held on approval are not subject to the claims of the buyer's creditors until acceptance.

Risk of Loss When a Sales or Lease Contract Is Breached. There are many ways to breach a sales or lease contract, and the transfer of risk operates differently depending on which party breaches. Generally, the party in breach bears the risk of loss.

When the Seller or Lessor Breaches. If the goods are so nonconforming that the buyer has the right to reject them, the risk of loss does not pass to the buyer until the defects are *cured* (that is, until the goods are repaired, replaced, or discounted in price by the seller) or until the buyer accepts the goods in spite of their defects (thus waiving the right to reject). For example, a buyer orders blue file cabinets from a seller, F.O.B. seller's plant. The seller ships black file cabinets instead. The black cabinets (nonconforming goods) are damaged in transit. The risk of loss falls on the seller. Had the seller shipped blue cabinets (conforming goods) instead, the risk would have fallen on the buyer [UCC 2–510(2)].

If a buyer accepts a shipment of goods and later discovers a defect, acceptance can be revoked. Revocation allows the buyer to pass the risk of loss back to the seller, at least to the extent that the buyer's insurance does not cover the loss [UCC 2–510(2)].

In regard to leases, Article 2A states a similar rule. If the lessor or supplier tenders goods that are so nonconforming that the lessee has the right to reject them, the risk of loss remains with the lessor or the supplier until cure or acceptance [UCC 2A–220(1)(a)]. If the lessee, after acceptance, revokes his or her acceptance of nonconforming goods, the risk of loss passes back to the seller or supplier to the extent that the lessee's insurance does not cover the loss [UCC 2A–220(1)(b)].

When the Buyer or Lessee Breaches. The general rule is that when a buyer or lessee breaches a contract, the risk of loss *immediately* shifts to the buyer or lessee. There are three important limitations to this rule [UCC 2–510(3), 2A–220(2)]:

1. The seller or lessor must already have identified the contract goods.
2. The buyer or lessee bears the risk for only a *commercially reasonable time* after the seller or lessor has learned of the breach.
3. The buyer or lessee is liable only to the extent of any deficiency in the seller's or lessor's insurance coverage.

Insurable Interest

Parties to sales and lease contracts often obtain insurance coverage to protect against damage, loss, or destruction of goods. Any party purchasing insurance, however, must have a sufficient interest in the insured item to obtain a valid policy. Insurance laws—not the UCC—determine sufficiency. The UCC is helpful, however, because it contains certain rules regarding insurable interests in goods.

Insurable interest • An interest either in a person's life or well-being or in property that is sufficiently substantial that insuring against injury to (or the death of) the person or against damage to the property does not amount to a mere wagering (betting) contract.

A buyer or lessee has an **insurable interest** in identified goods. The moment the contract goods are *identified* by the seller or lessor, the buyer or lessee has a special property interest that allows the buyer or lessee to obtain necessary insurance coverage for those goods even before the risk of loss has passed [UCC 2–501(1), 2A–218(1)].

A seller has an insurable interest in goods as long as he or she retains title to the goods. Even after title passes to a buyer, however, a seller who has a security interest in the goods, which is a legal right to secure payment, still has an insurable interest and can insure the goods [UCC 2–501(2)]. Hence, both a buyer and a seller can have an insurable interest in identical goods at the same time. Of course, the buyer or seller must sustain an actual loss to have the right to recover from an insurance company. In regard to leases, the lessor retains an insurable interest in leased goods until an option to buy has been exercised by the lessee and the risk of loss has passed to the lessee [UCC 2A–218(3)].

Performance of Sales and Lease Contracts

To understand the obligations of the parties under a sales or lease contract, it is necessary to know the duties and obligations that each party has assumed under the terms of the contract. Keep in mind that "duties and obligations" under the terms of the contract include those specified by the agreement, by custom, and by the UCC.

In the performance of a sales or lease contract, the basic obligation of the seller or lessor is to *transfer and deliver conforming goods.* The basic obligation of the buyer or lessee is to *accept and pay for conforming goods* in accordance with the contract [UCC 2–301, 2A–516(1)]. Overall performance of a sales or lease contract is controlled by the agreement between the parties. When the contract is unclear and disputes arise, the courts look to the UCC.

The Good Faith Requirement

The obligations of good faith and commercial reasonableness underlie every sales and lease contract within the UCC. These obligations can form the basis for a suit for breach of contract later on. As discussed earlier in this chapter, the UCC's good faith provision, which can never be disclaimed, reads as follows: "Every contract or duty within this Act imposes an obligation of good faith in its performance or enforcement" [UCC 1–203]. Good faith means honesty in fact. In the case of a merchant, it means honesty in fact and the observance of reasonable commercial standards of fair dealing in the trade [UCC 2–103(1)(b)]. In other words, merchants are held to a higher standard of performance or duty than nonmerchants. Note, though, that the 2003 amendments to UCC Article 2 apply the same high standard to all parties, regardless of merchant status.

Tender of delivery • Under the UCC, a seller's or lessor's act of placing conforming goods at the disposal of the buyer or lessee and giving the buyer or lessee whatever notification is reasonably necessary to enable the buyer or lessee to take delivery.

Obligations of the Seller or Lessor

The major obligation of the seller or lessor under a sales or lease contract is to tender conforming goods to the buyer or lessee. **Tender of delivery** requires that the seller or lessor have and hold *conforming* goods at the disposal of the buyer or lessee and give the buyer or lessee whatever notification is reasonably necessary to enable the buyer or lessee to take delivery [UCC 2–503(1), 2A–508(1)]. **Conforming goods** are goods that conform exactly to the description of the goods in the contract.

Conforming goods • Goods that conform to contract specifications.

Tender must occur at a *reasonable hour* and in a *reasonable manner.* For example, a seller cannot call the buyer at 2:00 A.M. and say, "The goods are ready. I'll give you twenty minutes to get them." Unless the parties have agreed otherwise, the goods must be tendered for delivery at a reasonable hour and kept available for a reasonable period of time to enable the buyer to take possession of them [UCC 2–503(1)(a)].

All goods called for by a contract must be tendered in a single delivery unless the parties agree otherwise [UCC 2–612, 2A–510] or the circumstances are such that either party can rightfully request delivery in lots [UCC 2–307].

Place of Delivery. As noted earlier, if the contract does not designate the place of delivery for the goods, and the buyer is expected to pick them up, the place of delivery is the *seller's place of business* or, if the seller has none, the *seller's residence* [UCC 2–308]. If the contract involves the sale of *identified goods,* and the parties know when they enter into the contract that these goods are located somewhere other than at the seller's place of business (such as at a warehouse), then the *location of the goods* is the place for their delivery [UCC 2–308].

The Perfect Tender Rule. As previously noted, the seller or lessor has an obligation to ship or tender *conforming goods,* and this entitles the buyer or lessee to accept and pay for the goods according to the terms of the contract. Under the common law, the seller was obligated to deliver goods in conformity with the terms of the contract in every detail. This was called the **perfect tender rule.** The UCC preserves the perfect tender doctrine by stating that if goods or tender of delivery fail in *any respect* to conform to the contract, the buyer or lessee has the right to accept the goods, reject the entire shipment, or accept part and reject part [UCC 2–601, 2A–509].

Perfect tender rule • A common law rule under which a seller was required to deliver to the buyer goods that conformed perfectly to the requirements stipulated in the sales contract. A tender of nonconforming goods would automatically constitute a breach of contract. Under the UCC, the rule has been greatly modified.

Exceptions to the Perfect Tender Rule. Because of the rigidity of the perfect tender rule, several exceptions to the rule have been created, some of which we discuss here.

Agreement of the Parties. Exceptions to the perfect tender rule may be established by agreement. If the parties have agreed, for example, that defective goods or parts will not be rejected if the seller or lessor is able to repair or replace them within a reasonable period of time, the perfect tender rule does not apply.

Cure. The UCC does not specifically define the term **cure,** but it refers to the right of the seller or lessor to repair, adjust, or replace defective or nonconforming goods [UCC 2–508, 2A–513]. When any tender of delivery is rejected because of nonconforming goods and the time for performance has not yet expired, the seller or lessor can promptly notify the buyer or lessee of the intention to cure and can then do so *within the contract time for performance* [UCC 2–508(1), 2A–513(1)]. Once the time for performance under the contract has expired, the seller or lessor can still exercise the

Cure • Under the UCC, the right of a party who tenders nonconforming performance to correct his or her performance within the contract period.

right to cure if he or she had *reasonable grounds to believe that the nonconforming tender would be acceptable to the buyer or lessee* [UCC 2–508(2), 2A–513(2)].[13]

The right to cure substantially restricts the right of the buyer or lessee to reject goods. For example, if a lessee refuses a tender of goods as nonconforming but does not disclose the nature of the defect to the lessor, the lessee cannot later assert the defect as a defense if the defect is one that the lessor could have cured. Generally, buyers and lessees must act in good faith and state specific reasons for refusing to accept goods [UCC 2–605, 2A–514].

Substitution of Carriers. When an agreed-on manner of delivery (such as the use of a particular carrier to transport the goods) becomes impracticable or unavailable through no fault of either party, but a commercially reasonable substitute is available, this substitute performance is sufficient tender to the buyer and must be used [UCC 2–614(1)].

Commercial Impracticability. Occurrences unforeseen by either party when a contract was made may make performance commercially impracticable. When this occurs, the rule of perfect tender no longer holds. According to UCC 2–615(a) and 2A–405(a), delay in delivery or nondelivery in whole or in part is not a breach when performance has been made impracticable "by the occurrence of a contingency the nonoccurrence of which was a basic assumption on which the contract was made." The seller or lessor must, however, notify the buyer or lessee as soon as practicable that there will be a delay or nondelivery.

An increase in cost resulting from inflation does not in and of itself excuse performance, as this kind of risk is ordinarily assumed by a seller or lessor conducting business. The unforeseen contingency must be one that would have been impossible to contemplate in a given business situation.

Destruction of Identified Goods. Sometimes, an unexpected event, such as a fire, totally destroys goods through no fault of either party and before risk passes to the buyer or lessee. In such a situation, if the *goods were identified at the time the contract was formed,* the parties are excused from performance [UCC 2–613, 2A–221]. If the goods are only partially destroyed, however, the buyer or lessee can inspect them and either treat the contract as void or accept the damaged goods with a reduction of the contract price.

Cooperation and Assurance. Two other exceptions to the perfect tender doctrine apply equally to parties to sales and lease contracts: the duty of cooperation and the right of assurance.

Sometimes the performance of one party depends on the cooperation of the other. The UCC provides that when such cooperation is not forthcoming,

---

13. The 2003 amendments to UCC Articles 2 and 2A expressly exempt "consumer contracts" and "consumer leases" from these provisions [Amended UCC 2–508, 2A–508]. A consumer is an individual who acquires goods to be used primarily for personal, family, or household purposes [Amended UCC 2–103(1)(c), 2A–103(1)(f)]. Although the "reasonable grounds to believe" test has been abandoned in the new provisions, the requirement that the initial tender be made in good faith helps to prevent a seller or lessor from deliberately tendering goods that the seller or lessor knows would not be acceptable to the buyer or lessee.

the other party can either suspend his or her own performance without liability and hold the uncooperative party in breach or proceed to perform the contract in any reasonable manner [see UCC 2–311(3)(b)].

The UCC provides that if one of the parties to a contract has "reasonable grounds" to believe that the other party will not perform as contracted, he or she may *in writing* "demand adequate assurance of due performance" from the other party. Until such assurance is received, he or she may "suspend" further performance without liability. What constitutes "reasonable grounds" is determined by commercial standards. If such assurances are not forthcoming within a reasonable time (not to exceed thirty days), the failure to respond may be treated as a *repudiation* of the contract [UCC 2–609, 2A–401]. The following case illustrates this principle.

KOCH MATERIALS CO. v. SHORE SLURRY SEAL, INC.

CASE 11.2

United States District Court, District of New Jersey, 2002. 205 F.Supp.2d 324.

http://lawlibrary.rutgers.edu/fed/search.html[a]

Koch Materials Company is a manufacturer of road surfacing materials. In February 1998, Koch agreed to pay $5 million, payable in three installments, to Shore Slurry Seal, Inc., for an asphalt plant in New Jersey and the rights to license a specialty road surfacing substance known as Novachip. Shore also agreed that for seven years following the sale, it would buy all of its asphalt requirements from Koch, or at least 2 million gallons of asphalt per year (the Exclusive Supply Agreement). Shore promised to use at least 2.5 million square yards of Novachip annually and to pay royalties to Koch accordingly (the Sublicense Agreement). Midway through the term of the contract, Shore told Koch that it planned to sell its assets to Asphalt Paving Systems, Inc. Koch sought assurances that Asphalt Paving would continue the original deal. Shore refused to provide any more information. Koch filed a suit in a federal district court against Shore, asking in part for the right to treat Shore's failure to give assurances as a repudiation of their contract. Koch filed a motion for summary judgment on this issue.

ORLOFSKY, J.

Koch had a commercially reasonable basis for demanding assurances on both the Exclusive Supply and Sublicense Agreements. The Sublicense Agreement analysis is straightforward. Shore reported that it planned to sell all of its " * * * assets," but retain * * * the Sublicense Agreement. Even assuming that historically, Shore had met most of its Novachip obligations by selling sublicenses to third parties, rather than laying its own road surfacing, any reasonable person would wonder how Shore planned to sell *anything* with no telephones, no computers, and no office furniture. That Shore might well have leased these items only prompts further questions: Would Shore have had the financial capacity to obtain leases and hire a sales staff? Or were the proceeds of the sale going directly to [Shore's president]?

The Exclusive Supply Agreement [ESA] is a bit more complex, but no less certain. * * * Shore promised Koch not only a minimum annual purchase, but also all of the potential upside of Shore's requirements over and above the

a. In the "Find Decisions by Docket Number" section, select "Civil Case," type "01-2059" in the "Enter Docket Number" box, and click on "Submit Form." From the results, click on "ca01-2059-1.html" to access the opinion. Rutgers University School of Law in Camden, New Jersey, maintains this Web site.

minimum should Shore's demand for asphalt grow over time. Thus, the identity of the purchaser, its future business plans, and its anticipated need for Koch's product could all affect significantly the amount of money that Koch would realize under the ESA, not only from the two million gallon minimum, but also from the potential upside. [Shore], it is true, promised that Shore's contracts, presumably including the ESA, would be assigned to the purchaser. *Start-up construction businesses, however, begin unbonded, [are] unable to win any bid for their first year and unable to secure sufficient bonding for large construction bids for several years.*[b] Koch had no way of knowing whether Asphalt was already a going business, and, if not, whether it would be able to win sufficient sub-contracting bids even to meet the minimum requirements, let alone approach the potential upside of an established enterprise like Shore. [Emphasis added.]

* * * *

The remaining question, then, is whether [Shore provided those assurances]. * * * Far from assuring Koch that Shore would secure Koch's permission before assigning the ESA, [Shore's president] asserted that "I am not aware of provisions within our agreements requiring me to notify Koch of any business negotiations that I may be involved in." This evasive answer not only failed to give Koch any information about the potential successor party to the contract, but also raised a new inference that Shore might be actively planning to evade the exclusive supply aspects of the ESA. It was, furthermore, close to a vow to breach * * * the ESA. Nor did Shore give any indication about its ability to meet the Sublicense Agreement volume requirements.

The court issued a summary judgment in Koch's favor. The court concluded that Shore's failure to provide assurances to Koch constituted a repudiation of their contract, authorizing Koch to terminate the contract and seek damages.

QUESTIONS

1. Who filed the complaint that formed the basis for the suit in this case, and why?
2. What were the two questions before the court, and how did the court rule on them?
3. On what reasoning did the court base its final judgment in this case?

b. In this context, a *bond* is a guaranty to complete or to pay the cost of a construction contract if the contractor defaults.

Obligations of the Buyer or Lessee

Once the seller or lessor has adequately tendered delivery, the buyer or lessee is obligated to accept the goods and pay for them according to the terms of the contract.

Payment. In the absence of any specific agreements, the buyer or lessee must make payment at the time and place the buyer or lessee *receives* the goods [UCC 2–310(a), 2A–516(1)]. When a sale is made on credit, the buyer is obliged to pay according to the specified credit terms (for example, 60, 90, or

120 days), not when the goods are received. The credit period usually begins on the *date of shipment* [UCC 2–310(d)]. Under a lease contract, a lessee must make the lease payment specified in the contract [UCC 2A–516(1)].

Payment can be made by any means agreed on between the parties—cash or any other method generally acceptable in the commercial world. If the seller demands cash when the buyer offers a check, credit card, or the like, the seller must permit the buyer reasonable time to obtain legal tender [UCC 2–511].

Acceptance. A buyer or lessee can manifest assent to the delivered goods in the following ways, each of which constitutes acceptance:

1. There is an acceptance if the buyer or lessee, after having had a reasonable opportunity to inspect the goods, signifies agreement to the seller or lessor either that the goods are conforming or that the goods are acceptable in spite of their nonconformity [UCC 2–606(1)(a), 2A–515(1)(a)].
2. Acceptance is presumed if the buyer or lessee has had a reasonable opportunity to inspect the goods and has failed to reject them within a reasonable period of time [UCC 2–602(1), 2–606(1)(b), 2A–515(1)(b)].
3. In sales contracts, the buyer will be deemed to have accepted the goods if he or she performs any act inconsistent with the seller's ownership. For example, any use or resale of the goods generally constitutes an acceptance. Limited use for the sole purpose of testing or inspecting the goods is not an acceptance, however [UCC 2–606(1)(c)].

If some of the goods delivered do not conform to the contract and the seller or lessor has failed to cure, the buyer or lessee can make a *partial* acceptance [UCC 2–601(c), 2A–509(1)]. The same is true if the nonconformity was not reasonably discoverable before acceptance. A buyer or lessee cannot accept less than a single commercial unit, however. A *commercial unit* is defined by the UCC as a unit of goods that, by commercial usage, is viewed as a "single whole" for purposes of sale, division of which would materially impair the character of the unit, its market value, or its use [UCC 2–105(6), 2A–103(c)]. A commercial unit can be a single article (such as a machine), a set of articles (such as a suite of furniture or an assortment of sizes), a quantity (such as a bale, a gross, or a carload), or any other unit treated in the trade as a single whole.

Anticipatory Repudiation

What if, before the time for contract performance, one party clearly communicates to the other the intention not to perform? Such an action is a breach of the contract by *anticipatory repudiation.* When anticipatory repudiation occurs, the nonbreaching party has a choice of two responses. One option is to treat the repudiation as a final breach by pursuing a remedy; the other is to wait and hope that the repudiating party will decide to honor the obligations required by the contract despite the avowed intention to renege [UCC 2–610, 2A–402]. (In either situation, the nonbreaching party may suspend performance.)

Should the second option be pursued, the UCC permits the breaching party (subject to some limitations) to "retract" his or her repudiation. This can be done by any method that clearly indicates an intent to perform. Once retraction is made, the rights of the repudiating party under the contract are reinstated [UCC 2–611, 2A–403].

Remedies for Breach of Sales and Lease Contracts

Sometimes, circumstances make it difficult for a person to carry out the performance promised in a contract. In this situation, the contract may be breached. When breach occurs, the aggrieved party looks for remedies. These remedies range from retaining the goods to requiring the breaching party's performance under the contract. The general purpose of these remedies is to put the aggrieved party "in as good a position as if the other party had fully performed." Remedies under the UCC are *cumulative* in nature. In other words, an innocent party to a breached sales or lease contract is not limited to one, exclusive remedy. (Of course, a party still may not recover twice for the same harm.)

Remedies of the Seller or Lessor

A buyer or lessee breaches a sales or lease contract by any of the following actions: (1) wrongfully rejecting tender of the goods, (2) wrongfully revoking acceptance of the goods, (3) failing to make payment on or before delivery of the goods, or (4) repudiating the contract. On the buyer's or lessee's breach, the seller or lessor is afforded several distinct remedies under the UCC, including those discussed here.

The Right to Withhold Delivery. In general, sellers and lessors can withhold or discontinue performance of their obligations under sales or lease contracts when the buyers or lessees are in breach. If a buyer or lessee has wrongfully rejected or revoked acceptance of contract goods (rejection and revocation of acceptance will be discussed shortly), failed to make proper and timely payment, or repudiated a part of the contract, the seller or lessor can withhold delivery of the goods in question [UCC 2–703(a), 2A–523(1)(c)]. If the breach results from the buyer's or lessee's insolvency (inability to pay debts as they become due), the seller or lessor can refuse to deliver the goods unless the buyer or lessee pays in cash [UCC 2–702(1), 2A–525(1)].

The Right to Resell or Dispose of the Goods. When a buyer or lessee breaches or repudiates the contract while the seller or lessor is still in possession of the goods, the seller or lessor can resell or dispose of the goods, holding the buyer or lessee liable for any loss [UCC 2–703(d), 2–706(1), 2A–523(1)(e), 2A–527(1)].[14]

14. Under the 2003 amendments to UCC Articles 2 and 2A, this loss includes consequential damages, except that a seller or lessor cannot recover consequential damages from a consumer under a consumer contract or lease [Amended UCC 2–706(1), 2–710, 2A–527(2), 2A–530]. Consequential damages may also be recovered, except from a consumer under a consumer contract or lease, when a seller or lessor has a right to recover the purchase price or lease payments due or to recover other damages [Amended UCC 2–708(1), 2–709(1), 2–710, 2A–528(1), 2A–529(1), 2A–530]. Subtracted from these amounts, of course, would be any expenses saved as a consequence of the buyer's or lessee's breach.

The Right to Recover the Purchase Price or Lease Payments Due. Under the UCC, an unpaid seller or lessor who is unable to resell or dispose of the goods can bring an action to recover the purchase price or the payments due under the lease contract, plus incidental damages, but only under one of the following circumstances:

1. When the buyer or lessee has accepted the goods and has not revoked acceptance.
2. When conforming goods have been lost or damaged after the risk of loss has passed to the buyer or lessee.
3. When the buyer or lessee has breached after the goods have been identified to the contract and the seller or lessor is unable to resell or otherwise dispose of the goods [UCC 2–709(1), 2A–529(1)].

If a seller or lessor sues under these circumstances, the goods must be held for the buyer or lessee. The seller or lessor can resell or dispose of the goods at any time prior to collection of the judgment from the buyer or lessee, but in that situation the net proceeds from the sale must be credited to the buyer or lessee. This is an example of the duty to mitigate damages.

The Right to Recover Damages. If a buyer or lessee repudiates a contract or wrongfully refuses to accept the goods, a seller or lessor can maintain an action to recover the damages sustained. Ordinarily, the amount of damages equals the difference between the contract price (or lease payments) and the market price (or lease payments that could be obtained for the goods) at the time and place of tender of the goods, plus incidental damages [UCC 2–708(1), 2A–528(1)]. The time and place of tender are frequently given by such terms as F.O.B., F.A.S., C.I.F., and the like (see Exhibit 11–1 on page 381), which determine whether there is a shipment or destination contract.

If the difference between the contract price (or payments due under the lease contract) and the market price (or payments due under the lease contract) is too small to place the seller or lessor in the position that he or she would have been in if the buyer or lessee had fully performed, the proper measure of damages is the lost profits of the seller or lessor, including a reasonable allowance for overhead and other expenses [UCC 2–708(2), 2A–528(2)].

In the following case, the court considered the amount of damages to which a seller was entitled for a buyer's wrongful rejection of conforming goods.

BRANDEIS MACHINERY & SUPPLY CO. v. CAPITOL CRANE RENTAL, INC.

CASE 11.3

Court of Appeals of Indiana, 2002.
765 N.E.2d 173.
http://www.in.gov/judiciary/opinions/search.html[a]

Brandeis Machinery & Supply Company and Capitol Crane Rental, Inc., entered into a lease agreement in June 1998, under which Capitol rented a thirty-five-ton rough-terrain crane from Brandeis for six months. The lease included an option to buy the crane. When the term expired, Capitol continued to rent the crane on a month-to-

a. In the "Select one or more opinion groups to search" section, select "Appeals Court," type "Brandeis Machinery" in the search terms box, and click on "Search." From the results, click on "Converted file nhv" above the name of the case to access the opinion. The state of Indiana maintains this Web site.

month basis. On June 22, 1999, Capitol's owner, Steve Dotlich, signed a contract under which Capitol agreed to buy the crane for $291,773.46, and on June 29, Brandeis sent Capitol an invoice for the price. The same week, Maxim Crane Works approached Dotlich about buying Capitol. Dotlich returned the crane to Brandeis, saying that he "did not want to buy [the crane] any more." Brandeis then spent $9,794.86 to inspect repairs that Capitol had made to the crane. Brandeis filed a suit in an Indiana state court against Capitol to recover damages for breach of contract. The court awarded Brandeis $29,067—the difference between the contract price and the market price of the crane at the time of delivery, plus the cost of the inspection. Brandeis appealed to a state intermediate appellate court, contending that the award should include, among other things, the purchase price of the crane.

VAIDIK, J.

An action for the price is sustainable only if the buyer has accepted the goods. Acceptance is defined under [Indiana Code Section 26-1-2-606 (Indiana's version of UCC 2–606)] as "failure to make an effective rejection." * * * Therefore, an action for the price is a remedy for an ineffective rejection * * *.

Rejection of goods by the buyer may be effective, but nonetheless wrongful. *A wrongful rejection is a rejection of a conforming tender. Put differently, a rejection may be timely made and thus, effective, but wrongful in that conforming goods are rejected.* [Emphasis added.]

* * * [Under Indiana Code Section 26-1-2-708] damages for a wrongful rejection are limited to the difference between the market value of the goods and the unpaid contract price together with any incidental damages.

* * * *

* * * [T]he trial court could have concluded that Capitol made a wrongful, but effective rejection of the Crane. Capitol's rejection was wrongful because it was not based on any nonconformity. The trial court could, however, have concluded that Capitol made an effective rejection by meeting the requirements of [Indiana Code Section 26-1-2-602, under which] "[r]ejection of goods must be within a reasonable time after their delivery or tender. It is ineffective unless the buyer seasonably [in a timely fashion] notifies the seller." The giving of seasonable notice is to permit the seller to take protective action such as withdrawing the goods, proposing a cure, or beginning negotiations to settle the dispute. What constitutes a reasonable time for notification of rejection is dependent upon the nature, purpose, and circumstances of the situation.

In this case, the trial court could have justifiably concluded that Capitol returned the Crane within a reasonable time and provided seasonable notification of its rejection of the Crane. * * *

* * * *

Because the trial court could have concluded that Capitol made a wrongful, yet effective rejection, Brandeis's action for the price must fail. Instead, the appropriate calculation of damages is the difference between the contract price and the market price at the time of delivery plus incidental damages. Therefore, we find that the trial court did not err when it declined to include the contract price in the damage award.

The state intermediate appellate court affirmed the judgment of the lower court, upholding its conclusions that Capitol wrongfully, but effectively, rejected the crane and that Brandeis could not then maintain an action for the contract price. The appropriate measure of damages was the difference between the contract price and the market price at the time of delivery, plus incidental damages.

QUESTIONS

1. Why did Brandeis file this suit, and what did Brandeis contend on appeal?
2. According to the Indiana Court of Appeals, how can a rejection of goods by a buyer be both wrongful and effective?
3. If Capitol's rejection of the conforming goods in this case had been ineffective, what would have been the measure of Brandeis's damages?

Remedies of the Buyer or Lessee

A seller or lessor breaches a sales or lease contract by failing to deliver conforming goods or repudiating the contract prior to delivery. On the breach, the buyer or lessee has a choice of several remedies under the UCC, in addition to recovery of as much of the price as has been paid.

The Right of Cover. In certain situations, buyers and lessees can protect themselves by obtaining **cover**—that is, by buying or leasing substitute goods for those that were due under the contract. This option is available when the seller or lessor repudiates the contract or fails to deliver the goods. It is also available to a buyer or lessee who has rightfully rejected goods or revoked acceptance. Rejection and revocation of acceptance will be discussed shortly.

Cover • Under the UCC, a remedy of the buyer or lessee that allows the buyer or lessee, on the seller's or lessor's breach, to purchase the goods from another seller or lessor and substitute them for the goods due under the contract. If the cost of cover exceeds the cost of the contract goods, the breaching seller or lessor will be liable to the buyer or lessee for the difference.

In obtaining cover, the buyer or lessee must act in good faith and without unreasonable delay [UCC 2–712, 2A–518]. After purchasing or leasing substitute goods, the buyer or lessee can recover from the seller or lessor the difference between the cost of cover and the contract price (or lease payments), plus incidental and consequential damages, less the expenses (such as delivery costs) that were saved as a result of the breach [UCC 2–712, 2–715, 2A–518]. Consequential damages are any losses suffered by the buyer or lessee that the seller or lessor could have foreseen (had reason to know about) at the time of the contract and any injury to the buyer's or lessee's person or property proximately resulting from the contract's breach [UCC 2–715(2), 2A–520(2)].

Buyers and lessees are not required to cover, and failure to do so will not bar them from using any other remedies available under the UCC. A buyer or lessee who fails to cover, however, risks not being able to collect consequential damages—a situation that could have been avoided had he or she purchased or leased substitute goods.

The Right to Obtain Specific Performance. A buyer or lessee can obtain specific performance when the goods are unique or when the remedy at law is inadequate [UCC 2–716(1), 2A–521(1)]. Ordinarily, an award of money damages is sufficient to place a buyer or lessee in the position he or she would have occupied if the seller or lessor had fully performed. When the contract is for the purchase of a particular work of art or a similarly unique item, however, money damages may not be sufficient. Under these circumstances, equity will require that the seller or lessor perform exactly by delivering the particular goods identified to the contract (a remedy of specific performance).

The Right to Recover Damages. If a seller or lessor repudiates the sales contract or fails to deliver the goods, or if the buyer is justified in rejecting goods that the seller or lessor tenders, then the buyer or lessee has several options under the UCC. The buyer or lessee may cancel the contract and recover as much of the price as has been paid to the seller or lessor. Following cancellation, the buyer or lessee may either (1) cover by obtaining goods from another seller or lessor and seeking reimbursement for the extra costs incurred or (2) recover damages for breach of the contract.

If the buyer or lessee elects to sue for damages, the measure of recovery is the difference between the contract price (or lease payments) and the market price of the goods (or lease payments that could be obtained for the goods) at the time the buyer (or lessee) *learned* of the breach.[15] The market price or market lease payments are determined at the place where the seller or lessor was supposed to deliver the goods. The buyer or lessee can also recover incidental and consequential damages, less the expenses that were saved as a result of the breach [UCC 2–713, 2A–519].

The Right to Reject the Goods. If either the goods or the tender of the goods by the seller or lessor fails to conform to the contract in any respect, the buyer or lessee can reject the goods. If some of the goods conform to the contract, the buyer or lessee can keep the conforming goods and reject the rest [UCC 2–601, 2A–509]. The buyer or lessee must reject the goods within a reasonable amount of time after delivery or tender of delivery, and the seller or lessor must be notified *seasonably*—that is, in a timely fashion or at the proper time [UCC 2–602(1), 2A–509(2)].

If a *merchant buyer* or *lessee* rightfully rejects goods, and the seller or lessor has no agent or business at the place of rejection, the buyer or lessee is required to follow any reasonable instructions received from the seller or lessor with respect to the goods controlled by the buyer or lessee. The buyer or lessee is entitled to reimbursement for the care and cost entailed in following the instructions [UCC 2–603, 2A–511]. The same requirements hold if the buyer or lessee rightfully revokes his or her acceptance of the goods at some later time [UCC 2–608(3), 2A–517(5)].

If no instructions are forthcoming and the goods are perishable or threaten to decline in value quickly, the buyer or lessee can resell the goods in good faith, taking appropriate reimbursement and a selling commission (not to exceed 10 percent of the gross proceeds) from the proceeds [UCC 2–603(1), (2); 2A–511(1)]. If the goods are not perishable, the buyer or lessee may store them for the seller or lessor or reship them to the seller or lessor [UCC 2–604, 2A–512].

The Right to Recover Damages for Accepted Goods. A buyer or lessee who has accepted nonconforming goods may also keep the goods and recover for any loss "resulting in the ordinary course of events . . . as determined in

15. The 2003 amendments to UCC Article 2 provide that, in a case not involving repudiation, the buyer's damages are based on the market price at the time for tender [Amended UCC 2–713(1)(a)]. In a case involving repudiation, the buyer's damages are based on the difference between the contract price and the market price at the expiration of a commercially reasonable time after the buyer learned of the breach [Amended UCC2–713(1)(b)].

any manner which is reasonable" [UCC 2–714(1), 2A–519(3)]. The buyer or lessee, however, must notify the seller or lessor of the breach within a reasonable time after the defect was or should have been discovered.

When the goods delivered are not as warranted, the measure of damages equals the difference between the value of the goods as accepted and their value if they had been delivered as warranted, unless special circumstances show proximately caused damages of a different amount, plus incidental and consequential damages [UCC 2–714, 2A–519].

Revocation of Acceptance. Acceptance of the goods precludes the buyer or lessee from exercising the right of rejection, but it does not necessarily preclude the buyer or lessee from pursuing other remedies. Additionally, in certain circumstances, a buyer or lessee is permitted to *revoke* his or her acceptance of the goods. Acceptance of a lot or a commercial unit can be revoked if the nonconformity *substantially* impairs the value of the lot or unit and if one of the following factors is present:

1. Acceptance was predicated on the reasonable assumption that the nonconformity would be cured, and it has not been cured within a reasonable period of time [UCC 2–608(1)(a), 2A–517(1)(a)].[16]
2. The buyer or lessee did not discover the nonconformity before acceptance, either because it was difficult to discover before acceptance or because assurances made by the seller or lessor that the goods were conforming kept the buyer or lessee from inspecting the goods [UCC 2–608(1)(b), 2A–517(1)(b)].

Revocation of acceptance is not effective until notice is given to the seller or lessor. Notice must occur within a reasonable time after the buyer or lessee either discovers or *should have discovered* the grounds for revocation. In addition, revocation must occur before the goods have undergone any substantial change (such as spoilage) not caused by their own defects [UCC 2–608(2), 2A–517(4)]. Once acceptance is revoked, the buyer or lessee can pursue remedies, just as if the goods had been rejected.

Contractual Provisions Affecting Remedies

The parties to a sales or lease contract can vary their respective rights and obligations by contractual agreement. For example, a seller and buyer can expressly provide for remedies in addition to those provided in the UCC. They can also specify remedies in lieu of those provided in the UCC, or they can change the measure of damages. The seller can stipulate that the buyer's only remedy on the seller's breach be repair or replacement of the item, or the seller can limit the buyer's remedy to return of the goods and refund of the purchase price. In sales and lease contracts, an agreed-on remedy is in addition to those provided in the UCC unless the parties expressly agree that the remedy is exclusive of all others [UCC 2–719(1), 2A–503(1)].

If the parties state that a remedy is exclusive, then it is the sole remedy. When circumstances cause an exclusive remedy to fail in its essential purpose, however, it is no longer exclusive [UCC 2–719(2), 2A–503(2)]. For example, a

16. Under the 2003 amendments to UCC 2–508 and 2A–513, cure after a justifiable revocation of acceptance is not available as a matter of right in a consumer contract or lease.

sales contract that limits the buyer's remedy to repair or replacement fails in its essential purpose if the item cannot be repaired and no replacements are available.

Sales and Lease Warranties

Warranty • An assurance by one party of the existence of a fact on which the other party can rely.

Warranty is an age-old concept. In sales and lease law, a **warranty** is an assurance by one party of the existence of a fact on which the other party can rely. Article 2 and Article 2A of the UCC designate several types of warranties that can arise in a sales or lease contract. These warranties include warranties of title, express warranties, and implied warranties.

Because a warranty imposes a duty on the seller or lessor, a breach of warranty is a breach of the seller's or lessor's promise. If the parties have not agreed to limit or modify the remedies available to the buyer or lessee and if the seller or lessor breaches a warranty, the buyer or lessee can sue to recover damages from the seller or lessor. Under some circumstances, a breach can allow the buyer or lessee to rescind (cancel) the agreement.[17]

Warranty of Title

Title warranty arises automatically in most sales contracts. Section 2–312 of the UCC imposes three types of warranties of title. First, in most cases, sellers warrant that they have good and valid title to the goods sold and that transfer of the title is rightful [UCC 2–312(1)(a)].

A second warranty of title provided by the UCC protects buyers who are *unaware* of any encumbrances (claims, charges, or liabilities—usually called *liens*[18]) against goods at the time the contract is made [UCC 2–312(1)(b)]. This warranty protects buyers who, for example, unknowingly purchase goods that are subject to a creditor's *security interest*—a creditor's interest in goods that serve as collateral to secure payment or performance of an obligation. If a creditor legally repossesses the goods from a buyer *who had no actual knowledge of the security interest,* the buyer can recover from the seller for breach of warranty. (The buyer who has *actual knowledge of a security interest* has no recourse against a seller.) Article 2A affords similar protection for lessees. Section 2A–211(1) provides that during the term of the lease, no claim of any third party will interfere with the lessee's enjoyment of the leasehold interest.

Finally, a merchant seller is also deemed to warrant that the goods delivered are free from any copyright, trademark, or patent claims of a third person [UCC 2–312(3), 2A–211(2)].

Disclaimer of Title Warranty. In an ordinary sales transaction, the title warranty can be disclaimed or modified only by *specific language* in a contract. For example, sellers may assert that they are transferring only such rights, title, and interest as they have in the goods. In a lease transaction, the disclaimer must "be specific, be by a writing, and be conspicuous" [UCC 2A–214(4)]. In certain cases, the circumstances surrounding the sale are sufficient to indicate

17. Rescission restores the parties to the positions they were in before the contract was made.
18. Pronounced *leens*.

clearly to a buyer that no assurances as to title are being made. The classic example is a sheriff's sale, when buyers know that the goods have been seized to satisfy debts and that the sheriff cannot guarantee title [UCC 2–312(2)].

Express Warranties

A seller or lessor can create an **express warranty** by making representations concerning the quality, condition, description, or performance potential of the goods. Under UCC 2–313 and 2A–210, express warranties arise when a seller or lessor indicates any of the following:

Express warranty • A seller's or lessor's oral or written promise, ancillary to an underlying sales or lease agreement, as to the quality, description, or performance of the goods being sold or leased.

1. That the goods conform to any *affirmation or promise of fact* that the seller or lessor makes to the buyer or lessee about the goods. Such affirmations or promises are usually made during the bargaining process. Statements such as "these drill bits will *easily* penetrate stainless steel—and without dulling" are express warranties.[19]
2. That the goods conform to any *description* of them. For example, a label that reads "Crate contains one 150-horsepower diesel engine" or a contract that calls for the delivery of a "wool coat" creates an express warranty that the content of the goods sold conforms to the description.
3. That the goods conform to any *sample* or *model* of the goods shown to the buyer or lessee.

Express warranties can be found in a seller's or lessor's advertisement, brochure, or promotional materials, in addition to being made orally or in an express warranty provision in a sales or lease contract. To create an express warranty, a seller or lessor does not have to use formal words such as *warrant* or *guarantee.* It is only necessary that a reasonable buyer or lessee would regard the representation as part of the basis of the bargain [UCC 2–313(2), 2A–210(2)].[20]

Basis of the Bargain. The UCC requires that for an express warranty to be created, the affirmation, promise, description, or sample must become part of the "basis of the bargain" [UCC 2–313(1), 2A–210(1)]. Just what constitutes the basis of the bargain is hard to say. The UCC does not define the concept, and it is a question of fact in each case whether a representation was made at such a time and in such a way that it induced the buyer or lessee to enter into the contract. Therefore, if an express warranty is not intended, the marketing agent or salesperson should not promise too much.

---

19. The 2003 amendments to UCC Article 2 introduce the term *remedial promise,* which is a promise by the seller to repair or replace the goods or to refund all or part of the price of the goods on the happening of a specified event [Amended UCC 2–103(1)(n), 2–313(4)]. A remedial promise is not an express warranty, so a right of action for its breach accrues not at the time of tender, as with warranties, but if the promise is not performed when due [Amended UCC 2–725(2)(c)].

20. The 2003 amendments to the UCC distinguish between immediate buyers (those who enter into contracts with sellers) and remote purchasers (those who buy or lease goods from immediate buyers) and extend sellers' obligations regarding new goods to remote purchasers. For example, a manufacturer sells packaged goods to a retailer, who resells the goods to a consumer. If a reasonable person in the position of the consumer would believe that a description on the package creates an obligation, the manufacturer is liable for its breach. [See Amended UCC 2–313, 2–313A, and 2–313B.]

Statements of Opinion and Value. If the seller or lessor merely makes a statement that relates to the value or worth of the goods, or makes a statement of opinion or recommendation about the goods, the seller or lessor is not creating an express warranty [UCC 2–313(2), 2A–210(2)].

For example, a seller claims that "this is the best used car to come along in years; it has four new tires and a 150-horsepower engine just rebuilt this year." The seller has made several *affirmations of fact* that can create a warranty: the automobile has an engine; it has a 150-horsepower engine; the engine was rebuilt this year; there are four tires on the automobile; and the tires are new. The seller's *opinion* that the vehicle is "the best used car to come along in years," however, is known as **puffery** and creates no warranty. (*Puffing* is an expression of opinion by a seller or lessor that is not made as a representation of fact.) A statement relating to the value of the goods, such as "it's worth a fortune" or "anywhere else you'd pay $10,000 for it," usually does not create a warranty.

Puffery • A salesperson's exaggerated claims concerning the quality of items offered for sale. Such claims involve opinions rather than facts and are not considered to be legally binding promises or warranties.

An Exception—Statements of Opinion by Experts. Although an ordinary seller or lessor can give an opinion that is not a warranty, if the seller or lessor is an expert and gives an opinion as an expert to a layperson, then a warranty may be created. For example, Saul is an art dealer and an expert in seventeenth-century paintings. If Saul states to Lauren, a purchaser, that in his opinion a particular painting is a Rembrandt, Saul has warranted the accuracy of his opinion.

Puffing versus Express Warranties. It is not always easy to determine what constitutes an express warranty and what constitutes puffing. The reasonableness of the buyer's or lessee's reliance appears to be the controlling criterion in many cases. For example, a salesperson's statements that a ladder will "never break" and will "last a lifetime" are so clearly improbable that no reasonable buyer should rely on them. Additionally, the context in which a statement is made may be relevant in determining the reasonableness of a buyer's or lessee's reliance. For example, a reasonable person is more likely to rely on a written statement made in an advertisement than on a statement made orally by a salesperson.

Implied warranty • A warranty that the law derives by implication or inference from the nature of the transaction or the relative situation or circumstances of the parties.

Implied warranty of merchantability • A warranty that goods being sold or leased are reasonably fit for the ordinary purpose for which they are sold or leased, are properly packaged and labeled, and are of fair quality. The warranty automatically arises in every sale or lease of goods made by a merchant who deals in goods of the kind sold or leased.

Implied Warranties

An **implied warranty** is one that *the law derives* by inference from the nature of the transaction or the relative situations or circumstances of the parties. Under the UCC, merchants impliedly warrant that the goods they sell or lease are merchantable and, in certain circumstances, fit for a particular purpose. In addition, an implied warranty may arise from a course of dealing or usage of trade. We examine these three types of implied warranties in the following subsections.

Implied Warranty of Merchantability. The **implied warranty of merchantability** automatically arises in every sale or lease of goods made *by a merchant* who deals in goods of the kind sold or leased [UCC 2–314, 2A–212]. Thus, a merchant who is in the business of selling ski equipment makes an implied warranty of merchantability every time the merchant sells a pair of skis, but a neighbor selling his or her skis at a garage sale does not.

To be *merchantable,* goods must be "reasonably fit for the ordinary purposes for which such goods are used." They must be of at least average, fair, or medium-grade quality. The quality must be comparable to quality that will pass without objection in the trade or market for goods of the same description. To be merchantable, the goods must also be adequately packaged and labeled as provided by the agreement, and they must conform to the promises or affirmations of fact made on the container or label, if any.

It makes no difference whether the merchant knew of or could have discovered that a product was defective (not merchantable). Of course, merchants are not absolute insurers against *all* accidents arising in connection with the goods. For example, a bar of soap is not unmerchantable merely because a user could slip and fall by stepping on it.

Implied Warranty of Fitness for a Particular Purpose. The **implied warranty of fitness for a particular purpose** arises when any *seller or lessor* (merchant or nonmerchant) knows the particular purpose for which a buyer or lessee will use the goods *and* knows that the buyer or lessee is relying on the skill and judgment of the seller or lessor to select suitable goods [UCC 2–315, 2A–213].

Implied warranty of fitness for a particular purpose • A warranty that goods sold or leased are fit for a particular purpose. The warranty arises when any seller or lessor knows the particular purpose for which a buyer or lessee will use the goods and knows that the buyer or lessee is relying on the skill and judgment of the seller or lessor to select suitable goods.

A "particular purpose" of the buyer or lessee differs from the "ordinary purpose for which goods are used" (merchantability). Goods can be merchantable but unfit for a particular purpose. For example, suppose that you need a gallon of paint to match the color of your living room walls—a light shade somewhere between coral and peach. You take a sample to your local hardware store and request a gallon of paint of that color. Instead, you are given a gallon of bright blue paint. Here, the salesperson has not breached any warranty of implied merchantability—the bright blue paint is of high quality and suitable for interior walls—but he or she has breached an implied warranty of fitness for a particular purpose.

A seller or lessor does not need to have actual knowledge of the buyer's or lessee's particular purpose. It is sufficient if a seller or lessor "has reason to know" the purpose. The buyer or lessee, however, must have *relied* on the skill or judgment of the seller or lessor in selecting or furnishing suitable goods for an implied warranty to be created.

For example, Bloomberg leases a computer from Future Tech, a lessor of technical business equipment. Bloomberg tells the clerk that she wants a computer that will run a complicated new engineering graphics program at a realistic speed. Future Tech leases Bloomberg an Architex One computer with a CPU speed of only 1.8 gigahertz, even though a speed of at least 3.2 gigahertz would be required to run Bloomberg's graphics program at a "realistic speed." Bloomberg, after realizing that it takes her forever to run her program, wants her money back. Here, because Future Tech has breached the implied warranty of fitness for a particular purpose, Bloomberg normally will be able to recover. The clerk knew specifically that Bloomberg wanted a computer with enough speed to run certain software. Furthermore, Bloomberg relied on the clerk to furnish a computer that would fulfill this purpose. Because Future Tech did not do so, the warranty was breached.

Implied Warranty Arising from Course of Dealing or Trade Usage. Implied warranties can also arise (or be excluded or modified) as a result of a course of dealing or usage of trade [UCC 2–314(3), 2A–212(3)]. In the absence of evidence to the contrary, when both parties to a sales or lease contract have knowledge of a well-recognized trade custom, the courts will infer that both parties intended for that custom to apply to their contract. For example, if it is an industry-wide custom to lubricate a new car before it is delivered and a dealer fails to do so, the dealer can be held liable to a buyer for damages resulting from the breach of an implied warranty. (This, of course, would also be negligence on the part of the dealer.)

Warranty Disclaimers

Because each type of warranty is created in a special way, the manner in which warranties can be disclaimed or qualified by a seller or lessor varies with the type of warranty.

Express Warranties. As already stated, any affirmation of fact or promise, description of the goods, or use of samples or models by a seller or lessor creates an express warranty. Obviously, then, express warranties can be excluded if the seller or lessor carefully refrains from making any promise or affirmation of fact relating to the goods, describing the goods, or using a sample or model.

The UCC does permit express warranties to be negated or limited by specific and unambiguous language, provided that this is done in a manner that protects the buyer or lessee from surprise. Therefore, a written disclaimer in language that is clear and conspicuous, and called to a buyer's or lessee's attention, could negate all oral express warranties not included in the written sales or lease contract [UCC 2–316(1), 2A–214(1)]. This allows the seller or lessor to avoid false allegations that oral warranties were made, and it ensures that only representations made by properly authorized individuals are included in the bargain.

Implied Warranties. Generally speaking, unless circumstances indicate otherwise, the implied warranties of merchantability and fitness are disclaimed by the expressions "as is," "with all faults," and other similar expressions that in common understanding for *both* parties call the buyer's or lessee's attention to the fact that no implied warranties are being made [UCC 2–316(3)(a), 2A–214(3)(a)].

The UCC also permits a seller or lessor to specifically disclaim an implied warranty either of fitness or of merchantability [UCC 2–316(2), 2A–214(2)].[21] To disclaim an implied warranty of fitness for a particular purpose, the disclaimer must be in writing and be conspicuous. The word *fitness* does not have to be mentioned in the writing; it is sufficient if, for example, the disclaimer states, "THERE ARE NO WARRANTIES THAT EXTEND BEYOND THE DESCRIPTION ON THE FACE HEREOF."

A merchantability disclaimer must be more specific; it must mention *merchantability*. It need not be written; but if it is, the writing must be conspicuous [UCC 2–316(2), 2A–214(4)].[22]

---

21. The 2003 amendments to the UCC require more informative language for disclaimers of implied warranties [Amended UCC 2–316(2), 2A–214(2)].

22. Under the 2003 amendments to UCC Articles 2 and 2A, if a consumer contract or lease is set forth in a record (writing), the implied warranty of merchantability can be disclaimed only by language also set forth conspicuously in the record [Amended UCC 2–316(3) and 2A–214(3)].

At the center of the dispute in the following case was a disclaimer, in a lease, of all warranties. In defense against a suit for amounts due under the lease, the lessee contended that the leased goods were defective when delivered and not fit for the purpose intended and that, for this reason, the consideration for the contract failed. What was the effect of the disclaimer in this situation?

INTERNATIONAL TURBINE SERVICES, INC. v. VASP BRAZILIAN AIRLINES

CASE 11.4

United States Court of Appeals, Fifth Circuit, 2002.
278 F.3d 494.
http://www.ca5.uscourts.gov/Opinions/OpinHome.cfm[a]

On October 1, 1997, International Turbine Services, Inc. (ITS) leased an aircraft turbine engine to VASP Brazilian Airlines. The lease required ITS to deliver the engine with a tag indicating that the Federal Aviation Administration (FAA) approved its return to service. VASP otherwise leased the engine in "'AS IS, WHERE IS' condition and with all faults." VASP bore "the risk of loss and damage to the Engine and all component parts from any and every cause whatsoever" with one exception: ITS agreed to overhaul and repair "time-controlled" and "on-condition" parts.[b] *At the end of the term—which the parties extended through August 18, 1998—VASP was to return the engine in operable condition to ITS's facility in Dallas. On June 15, the pilot of a VASP plane on which the engine was mounted aborted takeoff because of strong vibrations in the engine. VASP discovered that a high-pressure turbine (HPT) blade had failed, causing severe damage to the engine. VASP disputed responsibility for the repair cost and stopped making payments under the lease. ITS filed a suit against VASP, alleging breach of contract. A federal district court awarded ITS $8,825,000 in damages, including the cost to repair the engine and the past-due lease payments. On appeal to the U.S. Court of Appeals for the Fifth Circuit, VASP argued, in part, that it had not bargained for a defective engine.*

BALDOCK, J.

VASP * * * asserts a genuine issue of material fact exists as to whether VASP received the bargained-for consideration. * * * The Texas Business and Commercial Code [Texas's version of the Uniform Commercial Code] expressly authorizes the exclusion of warranties in lease agreements where the requisite language is present. The Code also provides that all implied warranties are excluded by the language "as is" or "with all faults."

The Lease provides:

> On the Delivery Date, Lessor will ensure that each Engine will have a Federal Aviation Administration ("FAA") approved return to service tag affixed to it. * * * [Aside from the FAA tag], the Equipment is leased and accepted by Lessee in "AS IS, WHERE IS" condition and with all faults. Lessor makes no warranties whatsoever with respect to any Equipment, express or implied, except [the warranty of title].

a. Click on the "Search opinions by Docket Number or Party Name" box. When the page opens, type "00-11231" in the "Seven-digit Docket Number" box and select "Get Opinions." From the results, scroll to the name of the case, and click on the docket number to access the opinion. The Clerk's Office of the U.S. Court of Appeals for the Fifth Circuit maintains this Web site.

b. A time-controlled part must be replaced or repaired after a specified number of hours or cycles. An on-condition part must be replaced or repaired whenever, on inspection, it does not comply with relevant FAA specifications.

The Lease also expressly excludes any implied warranties of merchantability or fitness for a particular purpose. The language of these provisions tracks the language authorized by the Code. *The Lease validly excludes all warranties with the exception of title and requires only delivery of an engine with an FAA approved return to service tag.* [Emphasis added.]

VASP acknowledges the engine arrived with the appropriate FAA tag. According to VASP, however, the FAA tag constitutes an implied representation that all applicable maintenance regulations and manufacturers' recommendations have been followed, including the manufacturer's recommendations regarding HPT blades. Yet, this is precisely the type of implied representation or warranty the Lease expressly excludes. Under the express terms of the Lease, VASP waived the right to complain about the condition of the engine upon receipt.

VASP's failure of consideration claim also wants for lack of any competent * * * proof. VASP representatives signed an Equipment Delivery Receipt acknowledging the engine's compliance with the terms and conditions of the Lease. VASP also was sufficiently satisfied with the engine's performance to execute a series of extensions and amendments to the original two-month lease term.

The U.S. Court of Appeals for the Fifth Circuit affirmed the judgment of the lower court. The appellate court held that VASP could not successfully assert the defense of a failure of consideration because the lease excluded all warranties (except the warranty of title and the FAA return-to-service approval tag), which meant that VASP could not legitimately complain about the condition of the leased goods.

QUESTIONS

1. What did VASP contend on appeal in this case, and what did the court rule on this point?
2. Why did the U.S. Court of Appeals for the Fifth Circuit hold that VASP could not successfully assert the defense of failure of consideration?
3. If there had been no disclaimer in this case and the HPT blade had been defective on the engine's receipt (which would have been discovered on a reasonable inspection), but VASP declined to examine the engine, would the outcome have been different?

E-CONTRACTS

E-contract • A contract that is entered into in cyberspace and is evidenced only by electronic impulses (such as those that make up a computer's memory), rather than, for example, a typewritten form.

The fundamental principles of contract law evolved over a long period of time. Certainly, they were formed long before cyberspace and electronic contracting became realities. Therefore, new legal theories, new adaptations of existing laws, and new laws were needed to govern **e-contracts,** or contracts entered into electronically. To date, however, most courts have adapted traditional contract law principles and, when applicable, provisions of the UCC to cases involving e-contract disputes.

Online Contract Formation

Today, numerous contracts are being formed online. Although the medium through which these contracts are generated has changed, the age-old problems attending contract formation have not. Disputes concerning contracts formed online continue to center around contract terms and whether the parties voluntarily assented to those terms.

Note that online contracts may be formed not only for the sale of goods and services but also for the purpose of *licensing*. For example, the "sale" of software generally involves a license, or a right to use the software, rather than the passage of title (ownership rights) from the seller to the buyer. As you read through the following pages, keep in mind that although we typically refer to the offeror and offeree as a *seller* and a *buyer,* in many transactions these parties would be more accurately described as a *licensor* and a *licensee.*

Online Offers. Sellers doing business via the Internet can protect themselves against contract disputes and legal liability by creating offers that clearly spell out the terms that will govern their transactions if the offers are accepted. All important terms should be conspicuous and easily viewed by potential buyers.

An important rule for a seller to keep in mind is that the offeror controls the offer, and thus the resulting contract. Therefore, the seller should anticipate the terms that he or she wants to include in a contract and provide for them in the offer. At a minimum, an online offer should include the following provisions:

1. A provision specifying the remedies available to the buyer if the goods turn out to be defective or if the contract is otherwise breached. Any limitation of remedies should be clearly spelled out.
2. A clause that clearly indicates what will constitute the buyer's agreement to the terms of the offer.
3. A provision specifying how payment for the goods or services and for any applicable taxes must be made.
4. A statement of the seller's refund and return policies.
5. Disclaimers of liability for certain uses of the goods. For example, an online seller of business forms may add a disclaimer that the seller does not accept responsibility for the buyer's reliance on the forms rather than on an attorney's advice.
6. A statement explaining how the seller will use the information gathered about the buyer.

Dispute-Settlement Provisions. In addition to the above provisions, many online offers include provisions relating to dispute settlement. For example, an arbitration clause might be included, indicating that any dispute arising under the contract will be arbitrated in a specified forum.

Many online contracts also contain a **forum-selection clause**—a clause indicating the forum, or location, for the resolution of any dispute arising under the contract. For a further discussion of forum-selection clauses in online contracts, see this chapter's *Contemporary Legal Debates* feature on page 404.

Forum-selection clause • A provision in a contract designating the court or jurisdiction that will decide any dispute arising under the contract.

Displaying the Offer. The seller's Web site should include a hypertext link to a page containing the full contract so that potential buyers are made aware of the terms to which they are assenting. The contract generally must be displayed online in a readable format such as a twelve-point typeface. All provisions should be reasonably clear. For example, if a seller is offering certain

CONTEMPORARY LEGAL DEBATES

The Enforceability of Forum-Selection Clauses

Parties to contracts frequently include clauses in their contracts indicating how any disputes that arise may be resolved. For example, contracts often contain arbitration clauses stipulating that any dispute will be resolved through arbitration proceedings rather than through litigation. A contract may also include a *forum-selection clause,* specifying the forum (such as the court or jurisdiction) in which the dispute will be resolved.

Forum-selection clauses are routinely included in contracts for the international sale of goods because the parties to such contracts are often quite distant from one another geographically. Determining the forum where any dispute arising under a contract will be settled is thus normally part of the bargaining process when the contract is being formed.

FORUM SELECTION AND ONLINE CONTRACTS

Because parties to contracts formed online may be located in physically distant sites, online sellers of goods and services normally include forum-selection clauses in their contracts. These clauses can help online sellers avoid having to appear in court in many distant jurisdictions when customers are dissatisfied with their purchases. (Recall from Chapter 2 that under a state long arm statute, a state court may exercise jurisdiction over an out-of-state defendant if the defendant has "minimum contacts" with the state.)

For example, suppose that a California buyer purchases defective goods sold online by a company located in New York. Unable to obtain a refund or adequate replacement goods from the seller, the California buyer files suit against the seller in a California state court. If the New York seller meets the "minimum-contacts" requirement for the California court to exercise jurisdiction over the dispute, the New York seller will need to travel to California to defend against the lawsuit. Forum-selection clauses in online contracts offer a way for sellers to avoid this problem.

ARE FORUM-SELECTION CLAUSES FAIR TO ONLINE PURCHASERS?

Clearly, those who market goods and services online benefit from including forum-selection clauses in their contracts. Yet what about the purchasers of these goods and services? Continuing with the above example, suppose that the seller's contract includes a forum-selection clause specifying New York as the forum where any disputes under the contract must be resolved. An individual in California may not have the resources to travel to New York to initiate proceedings against the seller in a New York court. In effect, the clause deprives the buyer of the ability to easily sue the seller in the buyer's home state.

Nonetheless, normally the courts will enforce clauses or contracts to which parties have voluntarily agreed, and this principle extends to forum-selection clauses in online contracts as well. As one court held (in a case challenging the enforceability of the forum-selection clause in Microsoft Network's online agreement), "If a forum-selection clause is clear in its

goods priced according to a complex price schedule, that schedule must be fully provided and explained.

Indicating How the Offer Can Be Accepted. An online offer should also include some mechanism by which the customer can accept the offer. Typically, online sellers include boxes containing the words "I agree" or "I accept the terms of the offer" that offerees can click on to indicate acceptance.

Online Acceptances. Section 2–204 of the UCC, the law governing sales contracts, provides that any contract for the sale of goods "may be made in any manner sufficient to show agreement, including conduct by both parties

CONTEMPORARY LEGAL DEBATES

The Enforceability of Forum-Selection Clauses

purport and has been presented to the party to be bound in a fair and forthright fashion, no . . . policies or principles have been violated."[a]

FORUM-SELECTION CLAUSES ARE NOT ALWAYS ENFORCED

Depending on the jurisdiction, however, a court may make an exception to the rule that forum-selection clauses in online contracts should be enforced. Consider a case decided by a California appellate court in 2001. The case was brought against America Online, Inc. (AOL), by Al Mendoza and other former AOL subscribers living in California. The plaintiffs, who sought compensatory and punitive damages, claimed that AOL had continued to debit their credit cards for monthly service fees, without authorization, for some time after they had terminated their subscriptions. AOL moved to dismiss the action on the basis of the forum-selection clause in its "Terms of Service" agreement with subscribers. That clause required all lawsuits under the agreement to be brought in Virginia, AOL's home state. At issue in the case was whether the clause was enforceable.

A California trial court held that it was not. The court based its conclusion on the finding that the clause, among other things, was contained in a standard form and was not readily identifiable by subscribers because of its small type and location at the end of the agreement. According to the court, the clause was "unfair and unreasonable," and public policy was best served by denying enforceability to the clause. A California appellate court affirmed the lower court's ruling and also gave another reason why the clause should not be enforced. The appellate court noted that Virginia law provides "significantly less" consumer protection than California law, and therefore enforcing the forum-selection clause would violate the "strong California public policy" expressed in the state's consumer protection statutes.[b]

WHERE DO YOU STAND?

The case just discussed may mark an exception to the rule that forum-selection clauses in online contracts are generally enforceable. Yet different courts have reached different conclusions on this issue, which continues to elicit debate. On the one hand, online sellers do need to protect themselves from the possibility of having to travel to distant states time and again to resolve disputes. Also, it is a general principle of contract law that clauses voluntarily entered into by the parties should be enforced. On the other hand, in some instances forum-selection clauses clearly impose an unfair burden on those who purchase goods or services from online vendors. What is your position on this issue? Can you think of a solution that is fair to all parties and consistent with contract law principles?

a. *Caspi v. MSN, Inc.,* 323 N.J.Super. 118, 732 A.2d 528 (1999).

b. *America Online, Inc. v. Superior Court,* 90 Cal.App.4th 1, 108 Cal.Rptr.2d 699 (2001).

which recognizes the existence of such a contract." The *Restatement (Second) of Contracts,* a compilation of common law contract principles, has a similar provision. It states that parties may agree to a contract "by written or spoken words or by other action or by failure to act."[23]

Click-On Agreements. The courts have used the provisions just discussed to conclude that a binding contract can be created by conduct, including conduct accepting an online offer by clicking on a box indicating "I agree" or

23. *Restatement (Second) of Contracts,* Section 19.

Click-on agreement • An agreement that arises when a buyer, engaging in a transaction on a computer, indicates his or her assent to be bound by the terms of an offer by clicking on a button that says, for example, "I agree."

"I accept." The agreement resulting from such an acceptance is often called a **click-on agreement.**

Generally, the law governing contracts, including sales and lease contracts under the UCC, does not require that all of the terms in a contract must actually have been read by all of the parties to be effective. Therefore, clicking on a button or box that states "I agree" to certain terms can be enough.[24]

In many ways, click-on agreements are the Internet equivalents of *shrink-wrap agreements* (or *shrink-wrap licenses,* as they are sometimes called). A shrink-wrap agreement is an agreement the terms of which are expressed inside a box in which the goods are packaged. (The term *shrink-wrap* refers to the plastic that covers the box.) Usually, the party who opens the box is told that he or she agrees to the terms by keeping whatever is in the box. When the purchaser opens the software package, he or she agrees to abide by the terms of the limited license agreement.

Even when a click-on or shrink-wrap agreement would be enforceable in principle, a court may refuse to enforce certain terms for any of the reasons that would render the terms of other contracts unenforceable. The following case illustrates this point.

24. See, for example, *i.LANSystems, Inc. v. NetScout Service Level Corp.*, 183 F.Supp.2d 838 (D.Mass. 2002).

CASE 11.5

New York Supreme Court, 2003.
195 Misc.2d 384,
758 N.Y.S.2d 466.

PEOPLE v. NETWORK ASSOCIATES, INC.

Network Associates, Inc., markets Gauntlet, a software firewall product, via the Internet and at retail locations. Network Associates included on the face of many of its disks, and on its download page on the Internet, a restrictive clause that provided:

> *Installing this software constitutes acceptance of the terms and conditions of the license agreement in the box. Please read the license agreement before installation. Other rules and regulations of installing the software are: * * * The customer shall not disclose the result of any benchmark test to any third party without Network Associates' prior written approval. * * * The customer will not publish reviews of this product without prior consent from Network Associates.*

In July 1999, Network World Fusion, *an online magazine, published a comparative review of firewall software products, including Network Associates's Gauntlet, without the maker's permission. Network Associates protested. Eliot Spitzer, the attorney general of the state of New York, filed a suit in a New York state court on behalf of "The People of the State of New York" against Network Associates, alleging, among other things, that the restrictive clause constituted fraud.*

SHAFER, J.

Petitioner argues that respondent's acts of including the reference to "rules and regulations" in the Restrictive Clause are deceptive. * * *

Petitioner argues that the use of words "rules and regulations" in the Restrictive Clause is designed to mislead consumers by leading them to believe that some rules and regulations * * * exist under state or federal law prohibiting consumers from publishing reviews and the results of benchmark tests. Petitioner also maintains that the language is deceptive because it may mislead consumers to believe that such clause is enforceable under the lease agreement, when in fact it is not enforceable under the terms of the lease. Petitioner argues that as a result consumers may be deceived into abandoning their right to publish reviews and results of benchmark tests.

* * * *

Respondent argues that there is no evidence that consumers were misled by the language of the Restrictive Clause or that it deterred them from publishing their reviews and results of tests. The Attorney General need not first receive consumer complaints in order to commence a proceeding, but may proceed on his own initiative. *The standard to be used to determine whether a representation is false and deceptive is not whether the actual practice is deceptive, but whether it has the capacity to deceive consumers.* The following are examples of conduct which New York courts have found to represent deceptive practices * * * : misleading authors into believing that their work has been selected for referral to an editing company because of its commercial potential, where instead authors were referred to the editing company only so that the editing company and agents could derive profits; mailing to prospective customers a card that creates an impression that it is from some type of a parcel delivery service, when the card, which does not identify the sender, is a solicitation for a free gift to be delivered by a salesperson devised to lure prospective customers into admitting the salesperson into their house; [and] representations by an employment agency that it had access to [a] "hidden job market" and job orders for positions around the world, and that the agency arranged interviews for clients and had successfully placed hundreds of top-level executives and professionals, when in fact the agency received only one job order and utilized only readily available public information. [Emphasis added.]

Respondent is correct in contending that the plain meaning of the language of the Restrictive Clause indicates that the rules and regulations referred to are the three rules listed immediately thereafter. Petitioner, however, argues that the clause clearly distinguishes between the license agreement containing contractual provisions, and listed rules and regulations. The language of the Restrictive Clause specifically directs consumers to read the license agreement. Because the license agreement contains a * * * clause which states that all of the rights and duties of the parties are contained within that agreement, and does not contain any of the restrictions on publishing reviews and results of benchmark testing, consumers may conclude that those restrictions are not contractual restrictions. Therefore, following respondent's instructions, after reading the license agreement and the Restrictive Clause, consumers may reasonably interpret that the rules and regulations enumerated in the Restrictive Clause exist independent of the license contract and are made and enforced by an entity other than the corporation itself. This language implies that limitations on the publication of reviews do not reflect the policy of Network Associates, but result from some binding law or other rules and regulations imposed by an entity other than Network Associates. Thus, *the Attorney General has made a showing that the language at issue may be deceptive, and as such, the language is not merely unenforceable, but warrants an injunction and the imposition of civil sanctions.* [Emphasis added.]

* * * *

Even though the attorney general requests the imposition of a penalty in the amount of $.50 for each instance of violation, as the number of violations is yet to be determined, the amount of penalties cannot be determined at this time. Similarly, no costs may be awarded at this time.

* * * *

Respondents * * * argue in conclusory fashion that it would be very costly and complicated to require respondent to remove the Restrictive Clause, which contains the deceptive language referring to "rules and regulations" that limit consumers' rights to publish reviews and results of benchmark tests, that may be contained in embedded files available for download from Network Associates' web-site. As respondent gives no details as to the cost or the difficulty in removing the Restrictive Clause, this relief is granted.

The court ordered Network Associates to stop including the restrictive clause on its software. The court also directed the defendant to reveal "the number of instances in which software was sold on disks or through the Internet containing the above-mentioned language in order for the court to determine what, if any, penalties and costs should be ordered."

QUESTIONS

1. Is there an important difference between reading a disputed clause as part of a shrink-wrap agreement and accessing it through a link as part of a click-on agreement?
2. Why did the court order the defendant in this case to stop including the restrictive clause on its software?
3. Can you think of some unique aspects of e-contracting that would not be covered by traditional laws, such as the UCC?

Browse-wrap terms • Terms and conditions of use that are presented to an Internet user at the time certain products, such as software, are being downloaded but that need not be agreed to (by clicking "I agree," for example) before being able to install or use the product.

Browse-Wrap Terms. Like the terms of a click-on agreement, **browse-wrap terms** can occur in a transaction conducted over the Internet. Unlike a click-on agreement, however, browse-wrap terms do not require an Internet user to assent to the terms before, say, downloading or using certain software. In other words, a person can install the software without clicking "I agree" to the terms of a license. Offerors of browse-wrap terms generally assert that the terms are binding without the user's active consent.

Critics contend that browse-wrap terms are not enforceable because they do not satisfy the basic elements of contract formation. It has been suggested that to form a valid contract online, a user must at least be presented with the terms before indicating assent.[25] With a browse-wrap term, this would require that a user navigate past it and agree to it before being able to obtain whatever is being granted.

E-Signatures

E-signature • As defined by the Uniform Electronic Transactions Act, "an electronic sound, symbol, or process attached to or logically associated with a record and executed or adopted by a person with the intent to sign the record."

In many instances, a contract cannot be enforced unless it is signed by the party against whom enforcement is sought. A significant issue in the context of e-commerce has to do with how electronic signatures, or **e-signatures,** can be created and veritifed on e-contracts.

---

25. American Bar Association Committee on the Law of Cyberspace, "Click-Through Agreements: Strategies for Avoiding Disputes on the Validity of Assent" (document presented at the annual American Bar Association meeting in August 2001).

E-Signature Technologies. Today, numerous technologies allow electronic documents to be signed. The most prevalent e-signature technology is the *asymmetric cryptosystem,* which creates a digital signature using two different (asymmetric) cryptographic "keys," one private and one public. With this system, a person attaches a digital signature to a document using a private key, or code. The key has a publicly available counterpart. Anyone with the appropriate software can use the public key to verify that the digital signature was made using the private key. A *cybernotary,* or legally recognized certification authority, issues the key pair, identifies the owner of the keys, and certifies the validity of the public key. The cybernotary also serves as a repository for public keys. Cybernotaries already are available.

State Laws Governing E-Signatures. Most states have laws governing e-signatures. The problem is that state e-signature laws are not uniform. Some states—California is a notable example—prohibit many types of documents from being signed with e-signatures, whereas other states are more permissive.

In an attempt to create more uniformity among the states, in 1999 the National Conference of Commissioners on Uniform State Laws and the American Law Institute promulgated the Uniform Electronic Transactions Act (UETA). To date, the UETA has been adopted, at least in part, by more than forty states. Among other things, the UETA states that a signature may not be denied legal effect or enforceability solely because it is in electronic form.[26] (We will look more closely at the UETA shortly.)

Federal Law on E-Signatures and E-Documents. In 2000, Congress enacted the Electronic Signatures in Global and National Commerce Act (E-SIGN Act),[27] which provides that no contract, record, or signature may be "denied legal effect" solely because it is in an electronic form. In other words, under this law, an e-signature is as valid as a signature on paper, and an e-document can be as enforceable as a paper one.

To read excerpts from the Electronic Signatures in Global and National Commerce Act of 2000, go to the "Statutes" page of our Web site at **http://ele.westbuslaw.com**

For an e-signature to be enforceable, the contracting parties must have agreed to use electronic signatures. For an electronic document to be valid, it must be in a form that can be retained and accurately reproduced.

The E-SIGN Act does not apply to all types of documents, however. Contracts and documents that are exempt include court papers, divorce decrees, evictions, foreclosures, health-insurance terminations, prenuptial agreements, and wills. Also, the only agreements governed by the UCC that fall under this law are those covered by Articles 2 and 2A and UCC 1–107 and 1–206.

The E-SIGN Act refers explicitly to the UETA and provides that if a state has enacted the uniform version of the UETA, that law is not preempted by the E-SIGN Act. In other words, if the state has enacted the UETA without modification, state law will govern. The problem is that many states have enacted nonuniform (modified) versions of the UETA, largely for the purpose of excluding other areas of state law from the UETA's terms. The E-SIGN Act specifies that those exclusions will be preempted to the extent that they are inconsistent with the E-SIGN Act's provisions.

26. The 2003 amendments to UCC Article 2 include a similar provision in Amended UCC 2–211.
27. 15 U.S.C. Sections 7001 *et seq.*

The Uniform Electronic Transactions Act

To read excerpts from the Uniform Electronic Transactions Act, go to the "Statutes" page of our Web site at **http://ele.westbuslaw.com**

The UETA, promulgated in 1999, represents one of the first comprehensive efforts to create uniformity and introduce certainty in state laws pertaining to e-commerce. The primary purpose of the UETA is to remove barriers to e-commerce by giving the same legal effect to electronic records and signatures as is currently given to paper documents and signatures. The UETA broadly defines an *e-signature* as "an electronic sound, symbol, or process attached to or logically associated with a record and executed or adopted by a person with the intent to sign the record."[28] A *record* is defined as "information that is inscribed on a tangible medium or that is stored in an electronic or other medium and is retrievable in perceivable form."[29]

The UETA does not apply to all writings and signatures but only to electronic records and electronic signatures *relating to a transaction.* A *transaction* is defined as an interaction between two or more people relating to business, commercial, or governmental activities.[30] The act specifically does not apply to laws governing wills or testamentary trusts, the UCC (other than Articles 2 and 2A), or the Uniform Computer Information Transactions Act (discussed next).[31] In addition, the provisions of the UETA allow the states to exclude its application to other areas of law.

The Uniform Computer Information Transactions Act

To read excerpts from the Uniform Computer Information Transactions Act, go to the "Statutes" page of our Web site at **http://ele.westbuslaw.com**

The National Conference of Commissioners on Uniform State Laws (NCCUSL) promulgated the Uniform Computer Information Transactions Act (UCITA) in 1999. The primary purpose of the UCITA is to validate e-contracts to license or purchase software, or contracts that give access to—or allow the distribution of—computer information.[32] The UCITA is controversial, and only two states (Maryland and Virginia) have adopted it; four states (Iowa, North Carolina, Vermont, and West Virginia) have passed anti–UCITA provisions. In 2003, the NCCUSL withdrew its support of the UCITA. Because the NCCUSL is no longer recommending that states adopt the UCITA, its significance will likely diminish in future years.

---

28. UETA 2(8).
29. UETA 2(13).
30. UETA 2(12) and 3.
31. UETA 3(b).
32. *Computer information* is "information in an electronic form obtained from or through use of a computer, or that is in digital or an equivalent form capable of being processed by a computer" [UCITA 102(10)].

KEY TERMS

insurable interest 384
lease agreement 371
lessee 371
lessor 371
merchant 371
output contract 374
perfect tender rule 385
requirements contract 373
sale 370
sale on approval 382
sale or return 382
sales contract 370
shipment contract 379
tangible property 370
tender of delivery 384
warranty 396

FOR REVIEW

1. How do Article 2 and Article 2A of the UCC differ? What types of transactions does each article cover?
2. What is the significance of identifying goods to a contract?
3. If the parties to a contract do not specify when the risk of loss passes and the goods are to be delivered without their movement by the seller, when does risk of loss pass?
4. What are the respective obligations of the parties under a contract for a sale or lease of goods?
5. What are some of the clauses that offerors should include when making offers to form e-contracts?

QUESTIONS AND CASE PROBLEMS

11–1. A. B. Zook, Inc., is a manufacturer of washing machines. Over the telephone, Zook offers to sell Radar Appliances one hundred model Z washers at a price of $150 per unit. Zook agrees to keep this offer open for ninety days. Radar tells Zook that the offer appears to be a good one and that it will let Zook know of its acceptance within the next two to three weeks. One week later, Zook sends and Radar receives notice that Zook has withdrawn its offer. Radar immediately thereafter telephones Zook and accepts the $150-per-unit offer. Zook claims, first, that no sales contract was ever formed between it and Radar and, second, that if there is a contract, the contract is unenforceable. Discuss Zook's contentions.

11–2. Flint, a retail seller of television sets, orders one hundred Color-X sets from manufacturer Martin. The order specifies the price and that the television sets are to be shipped by Humming Bird Express on or before October 30. The order is received by Martin on October 5. On October 8, Martin writes Flint a letter indicating that the order was received and that the sets will be shipped as directed, at the specified price. This letter is received by Flint on October 10. On October 28, Martin, in preparing the shipment, discovers it has only ninety Color-X sets in stock. Martin ships the ninety Color-X sets and ten television sets of a different model, stating clearly on the invoice that the ten are being shipped only as an accommodation. Flint claims that Martin is in breach of contract. Martin claims that the shipment was not an acceptance, and therefore no contract was formed. Explain who is correct, and why.

11–3. On May 1, Sikora goes into Carson's retail clothing store to purchase a suit. Sikora finds a suit he likes for $190 and buys it. The suit needs alteration. Sikora is to pick up the altered suit at Carson's store on May 10. Consider the following separate sets of circumstances:

(a) One of Carson's major creditors obtains a judgment on the debt Carson owes and has the court issue a writ of execution (a court order to seize a debtor's property to satisfy a debt) to collect on that judgment all clothing in Carson's possession. Discuss Sikora's rights in the suit under these circumstances.
(b) On May 9, through no fault of Carson's, the store burns down, and all contents are a total loss. Between Carson and Sikora, who suffers the loss of the suit destroyed by fire? Explain.

11–4. McDonald has contracted to purchase five hundred pairs of shoes from Vetter. Vetter manufactures the shoes and tenders delivery to McDonald. McDonald accepts the shipment. Later, on inspection, McDonald discovers that ten pairs of the shoes are poorly made and will have to be sold to customers as seconds. If McDonald decides to keep all five hundred pairs of shoes, what remedies are available to her? Discuss.

11–5. Kirk has contracted to deliver to Doolittle one thousand cases of Wonder brand beans on or before October 1. Doolittle is to specify the means of transportation twenty days prior to the date of shipment. Payment for the beans is to be made by Doolittle on tender of delivery. On September 10, Kirk prepares the one thousand cases for shipment. Kirk asks Doolittle how he would like the goods to be shipped, but Doolittle does not respond. On September 21, Kirk, in writing, demands assurance that Doolittle will be able to pay on tender of the beans. Kirk asks that the money be placed in escrow prior to October 1 in a bank in Doolittle's city named by Kirk. Doolittle does not respond to any of Kirk's requests, but on October 5 he wants to file suit against Kirk for breach of contract for failure to deliver the beans as agreed. Discuss Kirk's liability for failure to tender delivery on October 1.

CASE PROBLEM WITH SAMPLE ANSWER

11–6. Risk of Loss. H.S.A. II, Inc., made parts for motor vehicles. Under an agreement with Ford Motor Co., Ford provided steel to H.S.A. to make Ford parts. Ford's purchase orders for the parts contained the term "FOB Carrier Supplier's [Plant]." GMAC Business Credit, L.L.C., loaned money to H.S.A. under terms that guaranteed payment would be made, if the funds were not otherwise available, from H.S.A.'s inventory, raw materials, and finished goods. H.S.A. filed for bankruptcy on February 2, 2000, and ceased operations on June 20, when it had in its plant more than $1 million in finished goods for Ford. Ford sent six trucks to H.S.A. to pick up the goods. GMAC halted the removal. The parties asked the bankruptcy court to determine whose interest had priority. GMAC contended in part that Ford did not have an interest in the goods because there had not yet been a sale. Ford responded that under its purchase orders, title and risk of loss transferred on completion of the parts. In whose favor should the court rule, and why? [*In re H.S.A. II, Inc.,* 271 Bankr. 534 (E.D.Mich. 2002)]

➧ *To view a sample answer for this case problem, go to this book's Web site at* **http://ele.westbuslaw.com** *and click on "Interactive Study Center."*

11–7. Acceptance. In April 1996, Excalibur Oil Group, Inc., applied for credit and opened an account with Standard Distributors, Inc., to obtain snack foods and other items for Excalibur's convenience stores. For three months, Standard delivered the goods, and Excalibur paid the invoices. In July, Standard was dissolved, and its assets were distributed to J. F. Walker Co. Walker continued to deliver the goods to Excalibur, which continued to pay the invoices until November, when the firm began to experience financial difficulties. By January 1997, Excalibur owed Walker $54,241.77. Walker then dealt with Excalibur only on a collect-on-delivery basis until Excalibur's stores closed in 1998. Walker filed a suit in a Pennsylvania state court against Excalibur and its owner to recover amounts due on unpaid invoices. To successfully plead its case, Walker had to show that there was a contract between the parties. One question was whether Excalibur had manifested acceptance of the goods delivered by Walker. How does a buyer manifest acceptance? Was there an acceptance in this case? In whose favor should the court rule, and why? [*J. F. Walker Co. v. Excalibur Oil Group, Inc.,* 792 A.2d 1269 (Pa.Super. 2002)]

11–8. Click-On Agreements. America Online, Inc. (AOL), provided e-mail service to Walter Hughes and other members under a click-on agreement titled "Terms of Service." This agreement consisted of three parts: a "Member Agreement," "Community Guidelines," and a "Privacy Policy." The "Member Agreement" included a forum-selection clause that read, "You expressly agree that exclusive jurisdiction for any claim or dispute with AOL or relating in any way to your membership or your use of AOL resides in the courts of Virginia." When Officer Thomas McMenamon of the Methuen, Massachusetts, Police Department received threatening e-mail sent from an AOL account, he requested and obtained from AOL Hughes's name and other personal information. Hughes filed a suit in a federal district court against AOL, which filed a motion to dismiss on the basis of the forum-selection clause. Considering that the clause was a click-on provision, is it enforceable? Explain. [*Hughes v. McMenamon,* 204 F.Supp.2d 178 (D.Mass. 2002)].

11–9. Implied Warranties. Shalom Malul contracted with Capital Cabinets, Inc., in August 1999 for new kitchen cabinets for $1,600. Burger finished the job in March 2000, and Malul contracted for more cabinets at a price of $2,300, which Burger installed in April. Within a couple of weeks, the doors on several of the cabinets began to "melt"—the laminate (surface covering) began to pull away from the substrate (the material underneath the surface). Capital replaced several of the doors, but the problem occurred again, involving a total of six of thirty doors. A Holiday Kitchens representative inspected the cabinets and concluded that the melting was due to excessive heat, the result of placing the doors too close to the stove. Malul filed a suit in a New York state court against Capital, alleging, among other things, a breach of the implied warranty of merchantability. Were these goods "merchantable"? Why or why not? [*Malul v. Capital Cabinets, Inc.,* 191 Misc.2d 399, 740 N.Y.S.2d 828 (N.Y.City Civ.Ct. 2002)]

11–10. IN YOUR COURT

PopCo, Inc., which is in the business of bottling and distributing soft drinks, purchased bottle-labeling equipment from Gemini

Industries Co. The contract stated that in the event of a breach of contract, PopCo's remedy was limited to repair, replacement, or refund. When the equipment was installed in PopCo's plant, problems arose immediately. Gemini attempted to repair the equipment, but when it still did not work properly several months later, Gemini refunded the purchase price, and PopCo returned the equipment. PopCo then asked Gemini to pay PopCo for the losses it had incurred due to the equipment's failure and the delay in obtaining alternative machinery. Gemini claimed that it owed nothing to PopCo because its remedy for breach was limited to repair, replacement, or refund. PopCo asserted that the limited remedy had failed of its essential purpose. In the lawsuit that followed, the court granted summary judgment in Gemini's favor, and PopCo appealed. Assume that you are a judge on the appellate court reviewing the case, and answer the following questions:

(a) PopCo argued that Gemini had eliminated the remedy of "refund" by electing to pursue repair or replacement; thus, the remedy had failed in its essential purpose. Do you find PopCo's argument persuasive?
(b) In whose favor will you rule in this case, and why?
(c) Suppose that PopCo had argued that Gemini's limitation of its remedies was unconscionable. How would you respond to this argument?

11–11. A QUESTION OF ETHICS AND SOCIAL RESPONSIBILITY

Over the phone, Rich and Enza Hill ordered a computer from Gateway 2000, Inc. Inside the box were the computer and a list of contract terms, which provided that the terms governed the transaction unless the customers returned the computer within thirty days. Among those terms was a clause that required any claims to be submitted to arbitration. The Hills kept the computer for more than thirty days before complaining to Gateway about the computer's components and its performance. When the matter was not resolved to their satisfaction, the Hills filed a suit in a federal district court against Gateway, arguing, among other things, that the computer was defective. Gateway asked the court to enforce the arbitration clause. The Hills claimed that this term was not part of a contract to buy the computer because the list on which it appeared had been in the box and they did not see the list until after the computer was delivered. In view of these facts, consider the following questions. [*Hill v. Gateway 2000, Inc.*, 105 F.3d 1147 (7th Cir. 1997)]

(a) Should the court enforce the arbitration clause in this case? If you were the judge, how would you rule on this issue?
(b) In your opinion, do shrink-wrap agreements impose too great a burden on purchasers? Why or why not?
(c) An ongoing complaint about shrink-wrap and click-wrap agreements is that all too often the terms of these agreements go unread. Should purchasers be bound in contract by terms that they have not even read? Why or why not?

11–12. FOR CRITICAL ANALYSIS

Would you say that, on balance, most of the legal issues presented by e-commerce and e-contracting are unique to the cyber age or just simply old legal issues in a new form?

For updated links to resources available on the Web, as well as a variety of other materials, visit this text's Web site at

http://ele.westbuslaw.com

For information about the National Conference of Commissioners on Uniform State Laws (NCCUSL) and links to online uniform acts, go to

http://www.nccusl.org

The NCCUSL, in association with the University of Pennsylvania Law School, now offers an official site for in-process and final drafts of uniform and model acts. For an index of in-process drafts, go to

http://www.law.upenn.edu/bll/ulc/ulc.htm

For an index of final drafts, go to

http://www.law.upenn.edu/bll/ulc/ulc_final.htm

Cornell University's Legal Information Institute offers online access to the UCC, as well as to UCC articles as enacted by particular states and proposed revisions to articles, at

http://www.law.cornell.edu/ucc/ucc.table.html

Information on current commercial law topics, including some of the topics discussed in this chapter, is available at the Web site of the law firm of Hale and Dorr. Go to

http://www.haledorr.com

LEGAL RESEARCH EXERCISES ON THE WEB

Go to **http://ele.westbuslaw.com**, the Web site that accompanies this text. Select "Interactive Study Center," and then click on "Chapter 11." There you will find the following Internet research exercises that you can perform to learn more about topics covered in this chapter.

Activity 11–1: LEGAL PERSPECTIVE—E-Contract Formation

Activity 11–2: MANAGEMENT PERSPECTIVE—A Checklist for Sales Contracts

BEFORE THE TEST

Go to **http://ele.westbuslaw.com**, the Web site that accompanies this text. Select "Interactive Quizzes." You will find at least twenty interactive questions relating to this chapter.

WESTLAW® CAMPUS

If your textbook provided for a subscription to Westlaw® Campus, or if you have otherwise purchased access to the Westlaw Campus database, you can access any of the cases presented or cited in this chapter by using your Westlaw Campus account.

CHAPTER 12

Torts and Product Liability

CONTENTS

CHAPTER OBJECTIVES

After reading this chapter, you should be able to answer the following questions:

1. What is the purpose of tort law? What are two basic categories of torts?
2. What are the four elements of a cause of action for negligence?
3. What is a cyber tort, and how are tort theories being applied in cyberspace?
4. What are the elements of a cause of action in strict product liability?
5. What defenses can be raised in a product liability suit?

Part of doing business today—and, indeed, part of everyday life—is the risk of being involved in a lawsuit. The list of circumstances in which businesspersons can be sued is long and varied. An employee injured on the job may attempt to sue the employer because of an unsafe working environment. A consumer who is injured while using a product may attempt to sue the manufacturer because of a defect in the product. At issue in these examples is alleged wrongful conduct by one person that causes injury to another. Such wrongful conduct is covered by the law of **torts** (the word *tort* is French for "wrong").

Tort • A civil wrong not arising from a breach of a legal duty that proximately causes harm or injury to another.

Of course, a tort is not the only type of wrong that exists in the law. Crimes also involve wrongs. A crime, however, is an act so reprehensible that it is considered a wrong against the state or against society as a whole, as well as against the individual victim. Therefore, the *state* prosecutes and punishes (through fines and/or imprisonment—and possibly death) persons who commit criminal acts. A tort action, in contrast, is a civil action in which one party brings a suit against another to obtain compensation (money damages—a remedy at law discussed in Chapter 1) or other relief for the harm suffered. Some torts, however, provide a basis for both a criminal prosecution and a tort action—see Chapter 7.

Some of the torts examined in this chapter can occur in any context, including the business environment. Others traditionally have been referred to as **business torts,** which are defined as wrongful interferences with the business rights of others. Included in business torts are such vaguely worded concepts as *unfair competition* and *wrongfully interfering with the business relations of others*. Torts committed via the Internet are sometimes referred to as **cyber torts.** Later in this chapter, we look at how the courts have applied traditional tort law to wrongful actions in the online environment. Tort theories also come into play in the context of product liability (liability for defective products), which we discuss in the concluding pages of this chapter.

Business tort • The wrongful interference with the business rights of another.

Cyber tort • A tort committed in cyberspace.

THE BASIS OF TORT LAW

The basic purpose of tort law is to provide remedies for the invasion of various *protected interests*. Society recognizes an interest in personal physical safety, and tort law provides remedies for acts that cause physical injury or that interfere with physical security and freedom of movement. Society recognizes an interest in protecting property, and tort law provides remedies for acts that cause destruction or damage to property. Society also recognizes an interest in protecting certain intangible interests, such as personal privacy, family relations, reputation, and dignity, and tort law provides remedies for invasions of these interests.

There are two broad classifications of torts: *intentional torts* and *unintentional torts* (torts involving negligence). The classification of a particular tort depends largely on how the tort occurs (intentionally or negligently) and the surrounding circumstances.

Intentional Torts against Persons and Business Relationships

An **intentional tort,** as the term implies, requires *intent.* The **tortfeasor** (the one committing the tort) must intend to commit an act, the consequences of which interfere with the personal or business interests of another in a way not permitted by law. An evil or harmful motive is not required—in fact, the actor may even have a beneficial motive for committing what turns out to be a tortious act. In tort law, intent means only that the actor intended the consequences of his or her act or knew with substantial certainty that specific consequences would result from the act. The law generally assumes that individuals intend the *normal* consequences of their actions. Thus, forcefully pushing another—even if done in jest and without any evil motive—is an intentional tort (if injury results), because the object of a strong push can ordinarily be expected to go flying.

Intentional tort • A wrongful act knowingly committed.

Tortfeasor • One who commits a tort.

Intentional torts against persons and business relationships include assault and battery, false imprisonment, infliction of emotional distress, defamation, invasion of the right to privacy, appropriation, misrepresentation, and wrongful interference. We discuss these torts in the following subsections.

Assault and Battery

Any intentional, unexcused act that creates in another person a reasonable apprehension or fear of immediate harmful or offensive contact constitutes an **assault.** Note that apprehension is not the same as fear. If a contact is such that a reasonable person would want to avoid it, and if there is a reasonable basis for believing that the contact will occur, then the plaintiff suffers apprehension whether or not she or he is afraid. The interest protected by tort law concerning assault is the freedom from having to expect harmful or offensive contact. The arousal of apprehension is enough to justify compensation.

Assault • Any word or action intended to make another person fearful of immediate physical harm; a reasonably believable threat.

The *completion* of the act that caused the apprehension, if it results in harm to the plaintiff, is a **battery,** which is defined as an unexcused and harmful or offensive physical contact *intentionally* performed. For example, Ivan threatens Jean with a gun, then shoots her. The pointing of the gun at Jean is an assault; the firing of the gun (if the bullet hits Jean) is a battery. The interest protected by tort law concerning battery is the right to personal security and safety.

Battery • The unprivileged, intentional touching of another.

Essentially, any unpermitted, offensive contact, whether harmful or not, is a battery. The contact may be merely an unwelcome kiss or smoke intentionally blown in one's face. The contact can involve any part of the body or anything attached to it—for example, a hat or other item of clothing, a purse, or a chair or an automobile in which one is sitting. Whether the contact is offensive is determined by the *reasonable person standard.*[1] The contact can be made by the defendant or by some force the defendant sets in motion—for example, a rock thrown, food poisoned, or a stick swung. If the plaintiff shows there was contact, and the jury agrees that the contact was offensive, the plaintiff has a right to compensation. There is no need to establish that the defendant acted out of malice; in fact, proving a motive is never necessary.

A number of legally recognized defenses can be raised by a defendant who is sued for assault, battery, or both:

1. *Consent.* When a person consents to the act that damages her or him, there is generally no liability for the damage done.
2. *Self-defense.* An individual who is defending his or her life or physical well-being can claim self-defense. In a situation of either *real* or *apparent* danger, a person may normally use whatever force is *reasonably* necessary to prevent harmful contact (see Chapter 7 for a more detailed discussion of self-defense).
3. *Defense of others.* An individual can act in a reasonable manner to protect others who are in real or apparent danger.
4. *Defense of property.* Reasonable force may be used in attempting to remove intruders from one's home, although force that is likely to cause death or great bodily injury normally cannot be used just to protect property.

False Imprisonment

False imprisonment is defined as the intentional confinement or restraint of another person's activities without justification. It involves interference with the freedom to move without restriction. The confinement can be accomplished through the use of physical barriers, physical restraint, or threats of physical force. Moral pressure does not constitute false imprisonment. Furthermore, it is essential that the person being restrained not comply with the restraint willingly. In other words, the person being restrained must not agree to the restraint.

Businesspersons are often confronted with suits for false imprisonment after they have attempted to confine a suspected shoplifter for questioning. Under the privilege to detain granted to merchants in some states, a merchant can use the defense of *probable cause* to justify delaying a suspected shoplifter. Probable cause exists when the evidence to support the belief that a person is guilty outweighs the evidence against that belief. The detention, however, must be conducted in a *reasonable* manner and for only a *reasonable* length of time.

Intentional Infliction of Emotional Distress

The tort of *intentional infliction of emotional distress* can be defined as an intentional act that amounts to extreme and outrageous conduct resulting in severe emotional distress to another. For example, a prankster telephones an individual and says that the individual's spouse has just been in a horrible accident.

---

1. The *reasonable person standard* is an objective test of how a reasonable person would have acted under the same circumstances. See the subsection entitled "The Duty of Care and Its Breach" later in this chapter.

As a result, the individual suffers intense mental pain or anxiety. The caller's behavior is deemed to be extreme and outrageous conduct that exceeds the bounds of decency accepted by society and is therefore **actionable** (capable of serving as the ground for a lawsuit).

Actionable • Capable of serving as the basis of a lawsuit.

Emotional distress claims pose several problems. One major problem is that such claims must be subject to some limitation, or the courts could be flooded with lawsuits alleging emotional distress. A society in which individuals are rewarded if they are unable to endure the normal emotional stresses of day-to-day living is obviously undesirable. Therefore, the law usually focuses on the nature of the acts that fall under this tort. Indignity or annoyance alone is usually not sufficient to support a lawsuit based on intentional infliction of emotional distress.

Many times, however, repeated annoyances (such as those experienced by a person who is being stalked), coupled with threats, are enough. In a business context, for example, the repeated use of extreme methods to collect an overdue debt may be actionable. Also, an event causing an unusually severe emotional reaction, such as the severe distress of a woman incorrectly informed that her husband and two sons have been killed, may be actionable. Because it is difficult to prove the existence of emotional suffering, many courts require that the emotional distress be evidenced by some physical symptom or illness or a specific emotional disturbance that can be documented by a psychiatric consultant or other medical professional.

Defamation

As discussed in Chapter 5, the freedom of speech guaranteed by the First Amendment is not absolute. In interpreting the First Amendment, the courts must balance the vital guarantee of free speech against other pervasive and strong social interests, including society's interest in preventing and redressing attacks on reputation.

Defamation of character involves wrongfully hurting a person's good reputation. The law imposes a general duty on all persons to refrain from making false, defamatory *statements of fact* about others. Breaching this duty orally involves the tort of **slander;** breaching it in writing (or other permanent medium) involves the tort of **libel.** The tort of defamation also arises when a false statement of fact is made about a person's product, business, or title to property. We deal with these torts later in this chapter.

Defamation • Any published or publicly spoken false statement that causes injury to another's good name, reputation, or character.

Slander • Defamation in oral form.

Libel • Defamation in writing or other permanent medium (such as in a videotape).

If a false statement constitutes "slander *per se,*" no proof of special damages is required for it to be actionable. The following four types of utterances are considered to be slander *per se:*

1. A statement that another has a loathsome communicable disease.
2. A statement that another has committed improprieties while engaging in a profession or trade.
3. A statement that another has committed or has been imprisoned for a serious crime.
4. A statement that a woman is unchaste.

The Publication Requirement. The basis of the tort of defamation is the publication of a statement or statements that hold an individual up to contempt, ridicule, or hatred. *Publication* here means that the defamatory statements are communicated to persons other than the defamed party. If Thompson writes

Andrews a private letter falsely accusing him of embezzling funds, the action does not constitute libel. If Peters falsely states that Gordon is dishonest and incompetent when no one else is around, the action does not constitute slander. In neither case was the message communicated to a third party.

The courts have generally held that even dictating a letter to a secretary constitutes publication, although the publication may be privileged (a concept that will be explained shortly). Moreover, if a third party overhears defamatory statements by chance, the courts usually hold that this also constitutes publication. Defamatory statements made via the Internet are actionable as well. Note also that any individual who repeats, or republishes, defamatory statements normally is liable even if that person reveals the source of the statements.

Defenses to Defamation. Truth is almost always a defense against a defamation charge. In other words, if a defendant in a defamation case can prove that the allegedly defamatory statement of fact was actually true, normally no tort has been committed. Other defenses to defamation may exist if the speech is privileged or concerns a public figure.

Privilege • In tort law, the ability to act contrary to another person's right without that person's having legal redress for such acts. Privilege may be raised as a defense to defamation.

Privileged Speech. In some circumstances, a person will not be liable for defamatory statements because she or he enjoys a **privilege,** or immunity. With respect to defamation, privileged communications are of two types: absolute and qualified.[2] Only in limited circumstances, such as in judicial and legislative proceedings, is *absolute* privilege granted. For example, statements made by attorneys and judges in the courtroom during a trial are absolutely privileged. So are statements made by legislators during congressional floor debate, even if the legislators make such statements maliciously—that is, knowing them to be untrue. An absolute privilege is granted in these situations because judicial and legislative personnel deal with matters that are so much in the public interest that the parties involved should be able to speak out fully and freely and without restriction.

Public figures • Individuals who are thrust into the public limelight. Public figures include government officials and politicians, movie stars, well-known businesspersons, and generally anybody who becomes known to the public because of his or her position or activities.

Actual malice • Real and demonstrable evil intent. In a defamation suit, a statement made about a public figure normally must be made with actual malice (with either knowledge of its falsity or a reckless disregard of the truth) for liability to be incurred.

Public Figures. In general, false and defamatory statements that are made about **public figures** (public officials who exercise substantial governmental power and any persons in the public limelight) and published in the press are privileged if they are made without "actual malice." To be made with **actual malice,** a statement must be made *with either knowledge of its falsity or a reckless disregard of the truth.*[3]

Statements made about public figures, especially when they are communicated via a public medium, are usually related to matters of general public interest; they refer to people who substantially affect all of us. Furthermore, public figures generally have some access to a public medium for answering disparaging falsehoods about themselves; private individuals do not. For these reasons, public figures have a greater burden of proof in defamation cases (they must prove actual malice) than do private individuals.

2. Note that the term *privileged communication* in this context is not the same as privileged communication between a professional, such as an attorney, and his or her client.
3. *New York Times Co. v. Sullivan,* 376 U.S. 254, 84 S.Ct. 710, 11 L.Ed.2d 686 (1964).

Invasion of Privacy

A person has a right to solitude and freedom from prying public eyes—in other words, to privacy. As mentioned in Chapter 5, the courts have held that certain amendments to the U.S. Constitution imply a right to privacy. Some state constitutions explicitly provide for privacy rights. Additionally, a number of federal and state statutes have been enacted to protect individual privacy rights in specific areas. Tort law also safeguards these rights through the tort of *invasion of privacy.* Four acts qualify as invasions of privacy:

1. *The use of a person's name, picture, or other likeness for commercial purposes without permission.* For example, using without permission someone's picture to advertise a product or someone's name to enhance a company's reputation invades the person's privacy. (This tort, which is usually referred to as the tort of *appropriation,* will be examined shortly.)
2. *Intrusion on an individual's affairs or seclusion.* For example, invading someone's home or illegally searching someone's briefcase is an invasion of privacy. This tort has been held to extend to eavesdropping by wiretap, unauthorized scanning of a bank account, compulsory blood testing, and window peeping.
3. *Publication of information that places a person in a false light.* This could be a story attributing to someone ideas not held or actions not taken by that person. (The publication of such a story could involve the tort of defamation as well.)
4. *Public disclosure of private facts about an individual that an ordinary person would find objectionable.* A newspaper account of a private citizen's sex life or financial affairs could be an actionable invasion of privacy.

Appropriation

The use of another person's name, likeness, or other identifying characteristic, without permission and for the benefit of the user, constitutes the tort of **appropriation.** Under the law, normally an individual's right to privacy includes the right to the exclusive use of his or her identity. For example, in a case involving a Ford Motor Company television commercial in which a Bette Midler "sound-alike" sang a song that Midler had made famous, the court held that Ford "for their own profit in selling their product did appropriate part of her identity."[4]

Appropriation • In tort law, the use by one person of another person's name, likeness, or other identifying characteristic without permission and for the benefit of the user.

A court ruled similarly in a case brought by Vanna White, the hostess of the popular television game show *Wheel of Fortune,* against Samsung Electronics America, Inc. Without White's permission, Samsung included in an advertisement for Samsung videocassette recorders a depiction of a robot dressed in a wig, gown, and jewelry, posed in a setting that resembled the *Wheel of Fortune* set, in a stance for which White is famous. The court ruled in White's favor, holding that the tort of appropriation does not require the use of a celebrity's name or likeness. The court stated that Samsung's robot ad left "little doubt" as to the identity of the celebrity that the ad was meant to depict.[5]

---

4. *Midler v. Ford Motor Co.,* 849 F.2d 460 (9th Cir. 1988).
5. *White v. Samsung Electronics America, Inc.,* 971 F.2d 1395 (9th Cir. 1992).

Cases of wrongful appropriation, or misappropriation, may also involve the rights of those who invest time and money in the creation of a special system, such as a method of broadcasting sports events. Commercial misappropriation may occur as well when a person takes and uses the property of another for the sole purpose of capitalizing unfairly on the goodwill or reputation of the property owner.

Fraudulent Misrepresentation

A misrepresentation leads another to believe in a condition that is different from the condition that actually exists. This is often accomplished through a false or an incorrect statement. As noted in Chapter 10, misrepresentation may be a basis for rescinding, or canceling, a contract. Although misrepresentations may be innocently made by someone who is unaware of the facts, the tort of *fraudulent misrepresentation,* or *fraud,* involves intentional deceit for personal gain.

Elements of Fraud. The tort of fraudulent misrepresentation includes several elements:

1. A misrepresentation of material facts or conditions with knowledge that they are false or with reckless disregard for the truth.
2. An intent to induce another party to rely on the misrepresentation.
3. A justifiable reliance on the misrepresentation by the deceived party.
4. Damages suffered as a result of that reliance.
5. A causal connection between the misrepresentation and the injury suffered.

Fact versus Opinion. For fraud to occur, more than mere *puffery,* or *seller's talk,* must be involved. Fraud exists only when a person represents as a fact something he or she knows is untrue. For example, it is fraud to claim that the roof of a building does not leak when one knows it does. Facts are objectively ascertainable, whereas seller's talk is not. "I am the best architect in town" is seller's talk. The speaker is not trying to represent something as fact because the term best is a subjective, not an objective, term.

Normally, the tort of fraudulent misrepresentation occurs only when there is reliance on a *statement of fact.* Sometimes, however, reliance on a *statement of opinion* may involve the tort of fraudulent misrepresentation if the individual making the statement of opinion has a superior knowledge of the subject matter. For example, when a lawyer, in a state in which she or he is licensed to practice, makes a statement of opinion about the law, a court would construe reliance on such a statement to be equivalent to reliance on a statement of fact.

Wrongful Interference

Torts involving wrongful interference with another's business rights generally fall into two categories—interference with a contractual relationship and interference with a business relationship.

Wrongful Interference with a Contractual Relationship. The body of tort law relating to *wrongful interference with a contractual relationship* has increased greatly in recent years. A landmark case in this area involved an opera singer, Joanna Wagner, who was under contract to sing for a man named Lumley for a specified period of years. Another man, Gye, who knew of this contract, nonetheless "enticed" Wagner to refuse to carry out the agreement, and Wagner began to sing for Gye. Gye's action constituted a tort because it interfered with the contractual relationship between Wagner and Lumley. (Of course, Wagner's refusal to carry out the agreement also entitled Lumley to sue Wagner for breach of contract.)[6]

Three elements are necessary for wrongful interference with a contractual relationship to occur:

1. A valid, enforceable contract must exist between two parties.
2. A third party must know that this contract exists.
3. This third party must *intentionally* cause one of the two parties to the contract to breach the contract, and the interference must be for the purpose of advancing the economic interest of the third party.

The contract may be between a firm and its employees or a firm and its customers, suppliers, competitors, or other parties. Sometimes, a competitor of a firm draws away a key employee. If the original employer can show that the competitor induced the breach of the employment contract—that is, that the employee normally would not otherwise have broken the contract—damages can be recovered.

The following case illustrates the elements of the tort of wrongful interference with a contractual relationship in the context of a contract between an independent sales representative and his agent. The case was complicated by the existence of a second contract between the sales representative and the third party.

6. *Lumley v. Gye,* 118 Eng.Rep. 749 (1853).

MATHIS v. LIU

CASE 12.1

United States Court of Appeals, Eighth Circuit, 2002. 276 F.3d 1027.

Ching and Alex Liu own Pacific Cornetta, Inc. In 1997, Pacific Cornetta entered into a contract with Lawrence Mathis, under which Mathis agreed to solicit orders for Pacific Cornetta's products from Kmart Corporation for a commission of 5 percent on net sales. Under the terms, either party could terminate the contract at any time. The next year, Mathis entered into a one-year contract with John Evans, under which Evans agreed to serve as Mathis's agent to solicit orders from Kmart for the product lines that Mathis represented, including Pacific Cornetta, for a commission of 1 percent on net sales. Under the terms of this contract, either party could terminate it only on written notice of six months. A few months later, Pacific Cornetta persuaded Evans to break his contract with Mathis and enter into a contract with Pacific Cornetta to be its sales representative to Kmart. Evans terminated his contract with Mathis without notice. Two days later, Pacific Cornetta terminated its contract with Mathis. Mathis filed a suit in a federal district court against the Lius and Pacific Cornetta, alleging in part wrongful interference with a contractual relationship. The court issued a judgment that included a ruling in Mathis's favor on this claim, but Mathis appealed the amount of damages to the U.S. Court of Appeals for the Eighth Circuit.

ARNOLD, J.

[A] defendant is liable for tortious interference only if the defendant's interference with some relevant advantage was improper. [The] courts [look at a number of

considerations] to determine whether a defendant's interference is improper. These considerations include the nature of the actor's conduct[,] * * * the actor's motive[,] * * * the interests of the other with which the actor's conduct interferes[,] * * * the interests sought to be advanced by the actor[,] * * * the social interests in protecting the freedom of action of the actor and the contractual interests of the other[,] * * * the proximity or remoteness of the actor's conduct to the interference[,] and * * * the relations between the parties. [Emphasis added.]

We conclude that Mr. Mathis made out a * * * case on this element of his claim. If Mr. Evans's agency arrangement with Mr. Mathis had been purely at-will [a legal doctrine under which a contractual relationship can be terminated at any time by either party for any or no reason], we do not believe that Pacific Cornetta's successful effort to hire Mr. Evans * * * would have risen to the level of impropriety necessary to make out a case for tortious interference. That is because a party's interference with an at-will contract is primarily an interference with the future relation between the parties, and *when an at-will contract is terminated there is no breach of it.* In such circumstances, the interfering party is free for its own competitive advantage, to obtain the future benefits for itself by causing the termination, provided it uses suitable means. [Emphasis added.]

Mr. Evans's contract with Mr. Mathis, however, did not create a simple at-will arrangement because Mr. Evans could terminate it only after giving Mr. Mathis six months' notice of his intention to do so. In these circumstances, we think that the jury was entitled to conclude that Pacific Cornetta's blandishments [flattering statements] were improper, especially since *inducing a breach of contract absent compelling justification is, in and of itself, improper.* [Emphasis added.]

* * * *

Mr. Mathis asked for damages for the loss of anticipatory profits on his tortious interference claim. He argues that the damages that the jury awarded were supported by Mr. Evans's sales of * * * Pacific Cornetta products to Kmart [after Pacific Cornetta terminated the firm's contract with Mathis].

* * * *

We reject this theory * * * . Mr. Mathis's losses on these sales were a result of Pacific Cornetta exercising its right to terminate its contract with him at will, not Pacific Cornetta's tortious interference, and the losses were therefore not recoverable under a theory of tortious interference.

The U.S. Court of Appeals for the Eighth Circuit affirmed the judgment of the lower court. The appellate court concluded that the defendants had committed wrongful interference with Mathis's contract with Evans. Evans's sales of Pacific Cornetta products after Pacific Cornetta terminated its contract with Mathis could not furnish a basis for an award of damages on this claim, however, because the firm's contract with Mathis was terminable at will.

QUESTIONS

1. Why did Mathis appeal this case to the U.S. Court of Appeals for the Eighth Circuit, and how did the court rule on this claim?
2. On what basis did the U.S. Court of Appeals for the Eighth Circuit hold Pacific Cornetta liable for wrongful interference with a contractual relationship?

❸ What might be the result for society if there were no cause of action for wrongful interference with a contractual relationship?

Wrongful Interference with a Business Relationship. Individuals devise countless schemes to attract customers, but they are forbidden by the courts to interfere unreasonably with another's business in their attempts to gain a share of the market. There is a difference between *competitive practices* and *predatory behavior.* The distinction usually depends on whether a business is attempting to attract prospects in general or to solicit only those customers who have already shown an interest in the similar product or service of a specific competitor.

For example, if a shopping center contains two shoe stores, an employee of Store A cannot be positioned at the entrance of Store B for the purpose of diverting customers to Store A. This type of activity constitutes the tort of wrongful interference with a business relationship, often referred to as interference with a prospective (economic) advantage, and it is commonly considered to be an unfair trade practice. If this type of activity were permitted, Store A would reap the benefits of Store B's advertising.

Defenses to Wrongful Interference. A person will not be liable for the tort of wrongful interference with a contractual or business relationship if it can be shown that the interference was justified, or permissible. Bona fide competitive behavior is a permissible interference even if it results in the breaking of a contract.

For example, if Jerrod's Meats advertises so effectively that it induces Sam's Restaurant to break its contract with Burke's Meat Company, Burke's Meat Company will be unable to recover against Jerrod's Meats on a wrongful interference theory. After all, the public policy that favors free competition in advertising definitely outweighs any possible instability that such competitive activity might cause in contractual relations. Therefore, although luring customers away from a competitor through aggressive marketing and advertising strategies obviously interferes with the competitor's relationship with its customers, such activity is permitted by the courts.

Intentional Torts against Property

Intentional torts against property include trespass to land, trespass to personal property, conversion, and disparagement of property. These torts are wrongful actions that interfere with individuals' legally recognized rights with regard to their land or personal property. The law distinguishes real property from personal property. *Real property* is land and things permanently attached to the land. *Personal property* consists of all other items, which are basically movable. Thus, a house and lot are real property, whereas the furniture inside a house is personal property. Cash and securities (stocks and bonds) are also personal property.

Trespass to Land

Trespass to land • The entry onto, above, or below the surface of land owned by another without the owner's permission or legal authorization.

The tort of **trespass to land** occurs anytime a person, without permission, enters onto, above, or below the surface of land that is owned by another; causes anything to enter onto the land; or remains on the land or permits anything to remain on it. Note that actual harm to the land is not an essential element of this tort because the tort is designed to protect the right of an owner to exclusive possession. Common types of trespass to land include walking or driving on another's land; shooting a gun over another's land; throwing rocks at or spraying water on a building that belongs to someone else; building a dam across a river, thus causing water to back up on someone else's land; and constructing one's building so that it extends onto an adjoining landowner's property.

Trespass Criteria, Rights, and Duties. Before a person can be a trespasser, the real property owner (or other person in actual and exclusive possession of the property) must establish that person as a trespasser. For example, "posted" trespass signs expressly establish as a trespasser a person who ignores these signs and enters onto the property. Any person who enters onto another's property to commit an illegal act (such as a thief entering a lumberyard at night to steal lumber) is established impliedly as a trespasser, without posted signs.

A guest in one's home is not a trespasser—unless he or she has been asked to leave but refuses. A *licensee* (a person who has a revocable right to come onto another person's land) who is asked to leave and refuses to do so is also a trespasser. For example, one who purchases a ticket to a play has a right to enter the theater, but the theater manager may revoke (take back) that right—if the playgoer becomes rowdy during the play's performance, for instance.

At common law, a trespasser is liable for damages caused to the property and generally cannot hold the owner liable for injuries that the trespasser sustains on the premises. This common law rule is being abandoned in many jurisdictions, however, in favor of a "reasonable duty" rule that varies depending on the status of the parties. For example, a landowner may have a duty to post a notice that the property is patrolled by guard dogs. Also, under the "attractive nuisance" doctrine, a landowner may be held liable for injuries sustained by young children on the landowner's property if the children were attracted to the premises by some object, such as a swimming pool or an abandoned building. Finally, an owner can remove a trespasser from the premises—or detain a trespasser on the premises for a reasonable time—through the use of reasonable force without being liable for assault and battery or false imprisonment.

Defenses against Trespass to Land. Trespass to land involves wrongful interference with another person's real property rights. If it can be shown that the trespass was warranted, however, as when a trespasser enters to assist someone in danger, a defense exists.

Trespass to Personal Property

Trespass to personal property • The unlawful taking or harming of another's personal property; interference with another's right to the exclusive possession of his or her personal property.

Whenever any individual, without consent, harms the personal property of another or otherwise interferes with the personal property owner's right to exclusive possession and enjoyment of that property, **trespass to personal property**—also called *trespass to personalty*—occurs. Trespass to personal property involves intentional meddling. If Kelly takes Ryan's business law book as a practical joke and hides it so that Ryan is unable to find it for several days prior to the final examination, Kelly has engaged in a trespass to personal property.

If it can be shown that trespass to personal property was warranted, then a complete defense exists. Most states, for example, allow automobile repair shops to hold a customer's car when the customer refuses to pay for repairs already completed.

Conversion

Conversion • The wrongful taking, using, or retaining possession of personal property that belongs to another.

Conversion is defined as any act that deprives an owner of personal property without that owner's permission and without just cause. Conversion is the civil side of crimes related to theft. A store clerk who steals merchandise from the store commits a crime and engages in the tort of conversion at the same time. When conversion occurs, the lesser offense of trespass to personal property usually occurs as well. If the initial taking of the property was a trespass, retention of that property is conversion. If the initial taking of the property was permitted by the owner or for some other reason is not a trespass, failure to return it may still be conversion.

Even if a person mistakenly believed that she or he was entitled to the goods, a tort of conversion may still have occurred. In other words, good intentions are not a defense against conversion; in fact, conversion can be an entirely innocent act. Someone who buys stolen goods, for example, has committed the tort of conversion even if he or she did not know the goods were stolen.

A successful defense against the charge of conversion is that the purported owner does not in fact own the property or does not have a right to possess it that is superior to the right of the holder. Necessity is another possible defense against conversion. If Abrams takes Mendoza's cat, Abrams is guilty of conversion. If Mendoza sues Abrams, Abrams must return the cat or pay damages. If, however, the cat had rabies and Abrams took the cat to protect the public, Abrams has a valid defense—necessity.

Conversion was one of the claims in the following case.

PEARL INVESTMENTS, LLC v. STANDARD I/O, INC.

CASE 12.2

United States District Court, District of Maine, 2003.
257 F.Supp.2d 326.

Pearl Investments, LLC, operates automated stock-trading computer systems (ATSs) in Portland, Maine. Standard I/O, Inc., provides custom software-programming services. Jesse Chunn owns Standard. In April 2000, Pearl hired Standard to develop software for Pearl's ATS. Standard installed the software on several of Pearl's servers, including one Pionex server, at a computer facility maintained by On-Site Trading, Inc., in New York. In March 2001, with Pearl's consent, Chunn opened an account with On-Site. Chunn bought and delivered a Pionex server to On-Site and told On-Site to maintain the server apart from Pearl's equipment. In November, On-Site sold its assets to A. B. Watley, Inc. (ABW). Pearl asked ABW to install a new Linux operating system on Pearl's Pionex server, but ABW mistakenly installed the system on Chunn's server, which ABW found connected to Pearl's network. Dennis Daudelin, Pearl's chief executive officer, took the server from ABW's facility. After repeated demands, Daudelin returned the server in January 2002 and its hard disk drive in October. Pearl filed a suit in a federal district court against Standard and Chunn, alleging, among other things, misappropriation of trade secrets. Chunn filed a counterclaim against Pearl, alleging conversion.

HORNBY, J.

After consulting with legal counsel, and with the sole intent of preserving the suspect server for legal proceedings, Daudelin drove to ABW's premises on November 15, 2001, took pictures of [Chunn's] server (which was unplugged and shut down before he arrived) and the networking hardware to which it was connected, removed the server and returned to his home in Harvard, Massachusetts. As it turned out, the Linux software was installed on Chunn's server, overwriting his hard drive and obliterating his programming code. Pearl had not authorized Standard or Chunn to use any element of Pearl's network or server, to view any Pearl data or to develop or operate an automated trading system. After discovering that the server was owned by Chunn, Pearl's legal counsel tried over the ensuing several weeks to reach agreement with Chunn's legal counsel on the best manner to preserve any evidence contained on the hard disk drive ("HDD") within the server.

Counsel for Chunn provided proof of Chunn's ownership and demanded the return of his server beginning on December 14, 2001. In early January 2002, Daudelin delivered the server to Pearl's counsel. Prior to doing so, Daudelin removed the HDD from the server and delivered it to Pearl's counsel at the same time he delivered the server. Counsel for Pearl placed the HDD in a secure location and informed counsel for Standard and Chunn that it could pick up the server (without the HDD) while the parties attempted to agree on the best manner to preserve any evidence contained on the HDD. In early January 2002, Pearl purchased a replacement hard disk drive and delivered it to counsel for Standard and Chunn. On January 9, 2002 counsel for Pearl delivered the server (without the HDD) to counsel for Standard and Chunn.

On February 4, 2002 counsel for Pearl sent the HDD that was removed from Chunn's server to Pearl's expert for imaging, with explicit instructions that no information on the drive was to be accessed or viewed in any way. Pearl's expert made a duplicate copy of the HDD, and the original HDD was returned to counsel for Pearl, who retained the drive in a secure location until a protective order[a] was agreed to by the parties. Only after Pearl's expert executed a protective order on September 24, 2002 was the expert instructed to perform any forensic analysis of the drive.

The original HDD was returned to the Defendants' counsel on October 24, 2002 in response to a discovery request by the Defendants. At no point did any employee of Pearl turn on, boot up or in any way access the server or the HDD or view the contents of the HDD.

* * * *

In * * * his counterclaim, Chunn asserts that Daudelin, acting on behalf of and in concert with Pearl, wrongfully converted to his own use property owned by Chunn without Chunn's knowledge or consent. Chunn, Daudelin and Pearl [filed motions] for summary judgment as to this [counterclaim].

* * * *The necessary elements to make out a claim for conversion are: (1) a showing that the person claiming that his property was converted has a property interest in the property; (2) that he had the right to possession at the time of the alleged conversion; and (3) that the party with the right to possession made a demand for its return that was denied by the holder.* * * * [C]onversion is

a. In the circumstances of this case, a *protective order* describes an order of a court to protect against one party's destroying any evidence relevant to the litigation.

defined as the unauthorized assumption and exercise of the right of ownership over goods belonging to another to the exclusion of the owner's rights. [Emphasis added.]

It is undisputed that Daudelin seized Chunn's server from ABW without Chunn's knowledge or permission and that Daudelin and Pearl were unwilling to return the server, despite demand, without certain conditions that evidently were unacceptable to Chunn. Daudelin and Pearl emphasize that the server was discovered to have been connected to Pearl's [network] without its authorization and that Daudelin's intent was solely to preserve evidence for any later claim against whomever owned the server.

As Chunn observes, *wrongful intent is not a necessary element of a claim of conversion* (and, conversely, good faith is not a defense). [Emphasis added.]

To the extent that Pearl and Daudelin suggest that, rather than having been "mistaken," they were privileged to act as they did (for example, to prevent spoliation [destruction] of evidence), they fail to develop the argument, citing no authority for any claimed privilege. They thereby effectively waive the point.

Nor is summary judgment staved off by Pearl's and Daudelin's contention that Chunn fails to show damages—an assertion that Chunn disputes.

Chunn accordingly is entitled to summary judgment as to liability with respect to * * * his counterclaim, with damages to be determined by a trier of fact.

The court denied the plaintiffs' motions for summary judgment and granted a summary judgment to Chunn on his counterclaim for conversion against Pearl. The court ordered a trial for a determination as to the amount of damages. The court also ordered that other issues, including some of the plaintiffs' claims, be submitted for trial, adding, however, that Pearl could not base any claim on the contents of Chunn's server.

QUESTIONS

1. Who filed this suit, and why?
2. What was the ground on which the court issued a summary judgment in this case?
3. On what basis might Daudelin and Pearl successfully assert necessity as a defense to Chunn's charge?

Disparagement of Property

Disparagement of property occurs when economically injurious false statements are made not about another's reputation but about another's product or property. *Disparagement of property* is a general term for torts that can be more specifically referred to as *slander of quality* or *slander of title.*

Disparagement of property • An economically injurious false statement made about another's product or property. A general term for torts that are more specifically referred to as slander of quality or slander of title.

Slander of Quality. Publishing false information about another's product, alleging it is not what its seller claims, constitutes the tort of **slander of quality.** This tort has also been given the name **trade libel.** The plaintiff must prove that actual damages proximately resulted from the slander of quality; that is, the plaintiff must show not only that a third person refrained from dealing with the plaintiff because of the improper publication but also

Slander of quality (trade libel) • The publication of false information about another's product, alleging that it is not what its seller claims.

that the plaintiff suffered damages because the third person refrained from dealing with him or her. The economic calculation of such damages—they are, after all, conjectural—is often extremely difficult.

It is possible for an improper publication to be both a slander of quality and a defamation. For example, a statement that disparages the quality of a product may also, by implication, disparage the character of a person who would sell such a product.

Slander of title • The publication of a statement that denies or casts doubt on another's legal ownership of any property, causing financial loss to that property's owner.

Slander of Title. When a publication falsely denies or casts doubt on another's legal ownership of property, and when this results in financial loss to the property's owner, the tort of **slander of title** occurs. Usually, this tort arises in situations in which someone knowingly publishes an untrue statement about another's ownership of certain property with the intent of discouraging a third person from dealing with the person slandered. For example, it would be difficult for a car dealer to attract customers after competitors published a notice that the dealer's stock consisted of stolen autos.

NEGLIGENCE

Negligence • The failure to exercise the standard of care that a reasonable person would exercise in similar circumstances.

In contrast to intentional torts, in torts involving **negligence,** the tortfeasor neither wishes to bring about the consequences of the act nor believes that they will occur. The actor's conduct merely creates a risk of such consequences. If no risk is created, there is no negligence. Moreover, the risk must be foreseeable; that is, it must be such that a reasonable person engaging in the same activity would anticipate the risk and guard against it. In determining what is reasonable conduct, courts consider the nature of the possible harm. A very slight risk of a dangerous explosion might be unreasonable, whereas a distinct possibility of someone's burning his or her fingers on a stove might be reasonable.

To succeed in a negligence action, the plaintiff must prove the following:

1. That the defendant owed a duty of care to the plaintiff.
2. That the defendant breached that duty.
3. That the plaintiff suffered a legally recognizable injury.
4. That the defendant's breach caused the plaintiff's injury.

We discuss here each of these four elements of negligence.

Duty of care • The duty of all persons, as established by tort law, to exercise a reasonable amount of care in their dealings with others. Failure to exercise due care, which is normally determined by the "reasonable person standard," constitutes the tort of negligence.

Reasonable person standard • The standard of behavior expected of a hypothetical "reasonable person." The standard against which negligence is measured and that must be observed to avoid liability for negligence.

The Duty of Care and Its Breach

Central to the tort of negligence is the concept of a **duty of care.** This concept arises from the notion that if we are to live in society with other people, some actions can be tolerated, and some cannot; some actions are right, and some are wrong; and some actions are reasonable, and some are not. The basic principle underlying the duty of care is that people are free to act as they please so long as their actions do not infringe on the interests of others.

The law of torts defines and measures the duty of care by the **reasonable person standard.** In determining whether a duty of care has been breached, for example, the courts ask how a reasonable person would have acted in the same circumstances. The reasonable person standard is said to be (though in an absolute sense it cannot be) objective. It is not necessarily how a particular person would act. It is society's judgment of how an ordinarily prudent

CONCEPT SUMMARY 12.1
Intentional Torts

CATEGORY	NAME OF TORT
Intentional Torts against Persons and Business Relationships	① *Assault and battery*—Any unexcused and intentional act that causes another person to be apprehensive of immediate harm is an assault. An assault resulting in physical contact is battery. ② *False imprisonment*—An intentional confinement or restraint of another person's movement without justification. ③ *Intentional infliction of emotional distress*—An intentional act that amounts to extreme and outrageous conduct resulting in severe emotional distress to another. ④ *Defamation (libel or slander)*—A false statement of fact, not made under privilege, that is communicated to a third person and that causes damage to a person's reputation. For public figures, the plaintiff must also prove that the statement was made with actual malice. ⑤ *Invasion of privacy*—Publishing or otherwise making known or using information relating to a person's private life and affairs, with which the public had no legitimate concern, without that person's permission or approval. ⑥ *Appropriation*—The use of another person's name, likeness, or other identifying characteristic, without permission and for the benefit of the user. ⑦ *Fraudulent misrepresentation (fraud)*—A false representation made by one party, through the misstatement or omission of material facts, with the intention of deceiving another and on which the other reasonably relies to his or her detriment. ⑧ *Wrongful interference with a contractual or a business relationship*—The knowing, intentional interference by a third party with an enforceable contractual relationship or an established business relationship between other parties for the purpose of advancing the economic interests of the third party.
Intentional Torts against Property	① *Trespass to land*—The invasion of another's real property without consent or privilege. Specific rights and duties apply once a person is expressly or impliedly established as a trespasser. ② *Trespass to personal property*—The intentional interference with an owner's right to use, possess, or enjoy his or her personal property without the owner's consent. ③ *Conversion*—The wrongful taking, use, or retention of another's personal property for the benefit of the tortfeasor or someone else. ④ *Disparagement of property*—Any economically injurious false statement that is made about another's product or property; an inclusive term for the torts of *slander of quality* and *slander of title*.

person *should* act. If the so-called reasonable person existed, he or she would be careful, conscientious, prudent, even tempered, and honest. That individuals are required to exercise a reasonable standard of care in their activities is a pervasive concept in business law.

In negligence cases, the degree of care to be exercised varies depending on the defendant's occupation or profession, her or his relationship with the plaintiff, and other factors. Generally, whether an action constitutes a breach of the duty of care is determined on a case-by-case basis. The outcome depends on how the judge (or jury, if it is a jury trial) decides a reasonable person in the position of the defendant would act in the particular circumstances of the case. In the following subsections, we examine the degree of care typically expected of landowners and professionals.

Duty of Landowners. Landowners are expected to exercise reasonable care to protect individuals coming onto their property from harm. As mentioned earlier in this chapter, in some jurisdictions, landowners are held to have a duty to protect even trespassers against certain risks. Landowners who rent or lease premises to tenants are expected to exercise reasonable care to ensure that the tenants and their guests are not harmed in common areas, such as stairways, entryways, and laundry rooms.

Retailers and other firms that explicitly or implicitly invite persons to come onto their premises are usually charged with a duty to exercise reasonable care to protect these **business invitees.** For example, if you entered a supermarket, slipped on a wet floor, and sustained injuries as a result, the owner of the supermarket would be liable for damages if, when you slipped, there was no sign warning that the floor was wet. A court would hold that the business owner was negligent because the owner failed to exercise a reasonable degree of care in protecting the store's customers against foreseeable risks about which the owner knew or *should have known.* That a patron might slip on the wet floor and be injured as a result was a foreseeable risk, and the owner should have taken care to avoid this risk or warn the customer of it.[7]

Business invitees • Those people, such as customers or clients, who are invited onto business premises by the owner of those premises for business purposes.

Some risks, of course, are so obvious that an owner need not warn of them. For example, a business owner does not need to warn customers to open a door before attempting to walk through it. Other risks, however, even though they may seem obvious to a business owner, may not be so in the eyes of another, such as a child. For example, a hardware store proprietor may not think it is necessary to warn customers that, if climbed, a stepladder leaning against the back wall of the store could fall down and harm them. It is possible, though, that a child could tip the ladder over while climbing it and be hurt as a result.

Duty of Professionals. If an individual has knowledge, skill, or intelligence superior to that of an ordinary person, the individual's conduct must be consistent with that status. Professionals—including physicians, dentists, psychiatrists, architects, engineers, accountants, and lawyers, among others—are required to have a standard minimum level of special knowledge and ability. Therefore, in determining what constitutes reasonable care in the case of professionals, the court takes their training and expertise into account. In other words, an accountant cannot defend against a lawsuit for negligence by stating, "But I was not familiar with that general principle of accounting."

If a professional violates his or her duty of care toward a client, the client may bring a **malpractice** suit against the professional. For example, a patient might sue a physician for *medical malpractice.* A client might sue an attorney for *legal malpractice.*

Malpractice • Professional misconduct or the failure to exercise the requisite degree of skill as a professional. Negligence on the part of a professional, such as a physician or an attorney, is commonly referred to as malpractice.

7. A business owner can warn of a risk in a number of ways—for example, by placing a sign, traffic cone, sawhorse, board, or the like near a hole in the business's parking lot. See *Hartman v. Walkertown Shopping Center, Inc.,* 113 N.C.App. 632, 439 S.E.2d 787 (1994).

The Injury Requirement and Damages

To recover damages (receive compensation), the plaintiff in a tort lawsuit must prove that she or he suffered a *legally recognizable* injury. That is, the plaintiff must have suffered some loss, harm, wrong, or invasion of a protected interest. This is true in lawsuits for intentional torts as well as lawsuits for negligence. Essentially, the purpose of tort law is to compensate for legally recognized harms and injuries resulting from wrongful acts. If no harm or injury results from a given negligent action, there is nothing to compensate—and no tort exists.

For example, if you carelessly bump into a passerby, who stumbles and falls as a result, you may be liable in tort if the passerby is injured in the fall. If the person is unharmed, however, there normally can be no suit for damages because no injury was suffered. Although the passerby might be angry and suffer emotional distress, few courts recognize negligently inflicted emotional distress as a tort unless it results in some physical disturbance or dysfunction.

As already mentioned, the purpose of tort law is not to punish people for tortious acts but to compensate the injured parties for damages suffered. As you learned in Chapter 10, *compensatory damages* are intended to compensate, or reimburse, a plaintiff for actual losses. Occasionally, however, punitive damages are also awarded in tort lawsuits. **Punitive damages,** or *exemplary damages,* are intended to punish the wrongdoer and deter others from similar wrongdoing. Punitive damages are rarely awarded in lawsuits for ordinary negligence and usually are given only in cases involving intentional torts. They may be awarded, however, in suits involving *gross negligence,* which can be defined as an intentional failure to perform a manifest duty in reckless disregard of the consequences of such a failure for the life or property of another.

Punitive damages • Money damages that may be awarded to a plaintiff to punish the defendant and to deter future similar conduct.

Causation

Another element necessary to a tort is *causation.* If a person breaches a duty of care and someone suffers injury, the wrongful activity must have caused the harm for a tort to have been committed.

Causation in Fact and Proximate Cause. In deciding whether the requirement of causation is met, the court must address two questions:

1. *Is there causation in fact?* Did the injury occur because of the defendant's act, or would it have occurred anyway? If an injury would not have occurred without the defendant's act, then there is causation in fact. **Causation in fact** can usually be determined by use of the *but for* test: "but for" the wrongful act, the injury would not have occurred.
2. *Was the act the proximate cause of the injury?* In theory, causation in fact is limitless. One could claim, for example, that "but for" the creation of the world, a particular injury would not have occurred. Thus, as a practical matter, the law has to establish limits, and it does so through the concept of proximate cause. **Proximate cause,** or *legal cause,* exists when the connection between an act and an injury is strong enough to justify imposing liability. Consider an example. Ackerman carelessly leaves a campfire burning. The fire not only burns down the forest but also sets off an explosion in a nearby chemical plant that spills chemicals into a river, killing all the fish for a hundred miles downstream and ruining the

Causation in fact • An act or omission without ("but for") which an event would not have occurred.

Proximate cause • Legal cause; exists when the connection between an act and an injury is strong enough to justify imposing liability.

economy of a tourist resort. Should Ackerman be liable to the resort owners? To the tourists whose vacations were ruined? These are questions of proximate cause that a court must decide.

Both questions must be answered in the affirmative for liability in tort to arise. If a defendant's action constitutes causation in fact but a court decides that the action is not the proximate cause of the plaintiff's injury, the causation requirement has not been met—and the defendant normally will not be liable to the plaintiff.

Foreseeability. Questions of proximate cause are linked to the concept of foreseeability because it would be unfair to impose liability on a defendant unless the defendant's actions created a foreseeable risk of injury. Probably the most cited case on the concept of foreseeability as a requirement for proximate cause—and as a measure of the extent of the duty of care generally—is the *Palsgraf* case, which we present next. The question before the court was as follows: Does the defendant's duty of care extend only to those who may be injured as a result of a foreseeable risk, or does it extend also to persons whose injuries could not reasonably be foreseen?

CASE 12.3

Court of Appeals of New York, 1928. 248 N.Y. 339, 162 N.E. 99.

PALSGRAF v. LONG ISLAND RAILROAD CO.

The plaintiff, Palsgraf, was waiting for a train on a station platform. A man carrying a package was rushing to catch a train that was moving away from a platform across the tracks from Palsgraf. As the man attempted to jump aboard the moving train, he seemed unsteady and about to fall. A railroad guard on the car reached forward to grab him, and another guard on the platform pushed him from behind to help him board the train. In the process, the man's package, which (unknown to the railroad guards) contained fireworks, fell on the railroad tracks and exploded. There was nothing about the package to indicate its contents. The repercussions of the explosion caused scales at the other end of the train platform to fall on Palsgraf, causing injuries for which she sued the railroad company. At the trial, the jury found that the railroad guards had been negligent in their conduct. The railroad company appealed. The appellate court affirmed the trial court's judgment, and the railroad company appealed to New York's highest state court.

CARDOZO, C.J.

The conduct of the defendant's guard, if a wrong in its relation to the holder of the package, was not a wrong in its relation to the plaintiff, standing far away. Relatively to her it was not negligence at all. * * *

* * * *

* * * What the plaintiff must show is "a wrong" to herself; i.e., a violation of her own right, and not merely a wrong to someone else[.] * * * *The risk reasonably to be perceived defines the duty to be obeyed[.]* * * * Here, by concession, there was nothing in the situation to suggest to the most cautious mind that the parcel wrapped in newspaper would spread wreckage through the station. If the guard had thrown it down knowingly and willfully, he would not have threatened the plaintiff's safety, so far as appearances could warn him. His conduct would not have involved, even then, an unreasonable probability of invasion of her bodily security. Liability can be no greater where the act is inadvertent. [Emphasis added.]

* * * One who seeks redress at law does not make out a cause of action by showing without more that there has been damage to his person. If the harm was not willful, he must show that the act as to him had possibilities of danger so many and apparent as to entitle him to be protected against the doing of it though the harm was unintended. * * * The victim does not sue * * * to vindicate an interest invaded in the person of another. * * * He sues for breach of a duty owing to himself.

* * * [To rule otherwise] would entail liability for any and all consequences, however novel or extraordinary.

Palsgraf's complaint was dismissed. The railroad had not been negligent toward her because injury to her was not foreseeable. Had the owner of the fireworks been harmed, and had he filed suit, there could well have been a different result.

QUESTIONS

1. Why did the railroad appeal this case to the New York Court of Appeals?
2. What was the question before the New York Court of Appeals in this case?
3. According to the court, on what did the determination of whether the guards were negligent with respect to Palsgraf depend?

Defenses to Negligence

The basic defenses to liability in negligence cases are (1) assumption of risk, (2) superseding cause, (3) contributory negligence, and (4) comparative negligence.

Assumption of Risk. A plaintiff who voluntarily enters into a risky situation, knowing the risk involved, will not be allowed to recover. This is the defense of **assumption of risk.** For example, a driver entering an automobile race knows there is a risk of being injured or killed in a crash. The driver has assumed the risk of injury. The requirements of this defense are (1) knowledge of the risk and (2) voluntary assumption of the risk.

Assumption of risk • A defense against negligence that can be used when the plaintiff is aware of a danger and voluntarily assumes the risk of injury from that danger.

The risk can be assumed by express agreement, or the assumption of risk can be implied by the plaintiff's knowledge of the risk and subsequent conduct. Of course, the plaintiff does not assume a risk different from or greater than the risk normally carried by the activity. In our example, the race driver assumes the risk of being injured in the race but not the risk that the banking in the curves of the racetrack will give way during the race because of a construction defect.

Risks are not deemed to be assumed in situations involving emergencies. Neither are they assumed when a statute protects a class of people from harm and a member of the class is injured by the harm. For example, courts have generally held that an employee cannot assume the risk of an employer's violation of safety statutes passed for the benefit of employees.

Superseding Cause. An unforeseeable intervening event may break the causal connection between a wrongful act and an injury to another. If so, the intervening event acts as a *superseding cause*—that is, it relieves a defendant of liability for injuries caused by that event. For example, suppose that Derrick, while riding his bicycle, negligently hits Julie, who is walking on the sidewalk.

As a result of the impact, Julie falls and fractures her hip. While she is waiting for help to arrive, a small aircraft crashes nearby and explodes, and some of the fiery debris hits her, causing her to sustain severe burns. Derrick will be liable for the damages caused by Julie's fractured hip, but normally he will not be liable for the wounds caused by the plane crash—because the risk of a plane crashing nearby and injuring Julie was not foreseeable.

Contributory negligence • A theory in tort law under which a complaining party's own negligence contributed to or caused his or her injuries. Contributory negligence is an absolute bar to recovery in a minority of jurisdictions.

Contributory Negligence. Traditionally, under the common law, if a plaintiff's own negligence contributed to her or his injury, the defendant could raise the defense of **contributory negligence.** Contributory negligence on the part of the plaintiff was a complete defense to liability for negligence. Today, contributory negligence can be used as a defense in only a very few states.

In those jurisdictions that do allow the defense of contributory negligence, the *last clear chance* doctrine can excuse the effect of a plaintiff's negligence. The last clear chance doctrine allows the plaintiff to recover full damages despite his or her failure to exercise care. This rule operates when, through his or her own negligence, the plaintiff is endangered (or his or her property is endangered) by a defendant who has an opportunity to avoid causing damage but fails to take advantage of that opportunity. For example, if Murphy walks across the street against the light, and Lewis, a motorist, sees her in time to avoid hitting her but hits her anyway, Lewis (the defendant) is not permitted to use Murphy's (the plaintiff's) prior negligence as a defense. The defendant negligently missed the opportunity to avoid injuring the plaintiff.

Comparative negligence • A theory in tort law under which the liability for injuries resulting from negligent acts is shared by all parties who were negligent (including the injured party), on the basis of each person's proportionate negligence.

Comparative Negligence. Neither the complete defense of contributory negligence nor the last clear chance doctrine applies in states that have adopted a **comparative negligence** standard, as the majority of states have done. Under this standard, both the plaintiff's negligence and the defendant's negligence are considered, and damages are awarded accordingly. Some jurisdictions have adopted a "pure" form of comparative negligence that allows the plaintiff to recover damages even if her or his fault is greater than that of the defendant. Many states' comparative negligence statutes, however, contain a "50 percent" rule, under which the plaintiff recovers nothing if she or he was more than 50 percent at fault. Under this rule, a plaintiff who is 35 percent at fault could recover 65 percent of his or her damages, but a plaintiff who is 65 percent (over 50 percent) at fault would recover nothing.

Special Negligence Doctrines and Statutes

A number of special doctrines and statutes relating to negligence are also important. We examine a few of them here.

Res ipsa loquitur • A doctrine under which negligence may be inferred simply because an event occurred, if it is the type of event that would not occur in the absence of negligence. Literally, the term means "the facts speak for themselves."

Res Ipsa Loquitur. Generally, in lawsuits involving negligence, the plaintiff has the burden of proving that the defendant was negligent. In certain situations, however, the courts may presume that negligence has occurred, in which case the burden of proof rests on the defendant—that is, the defendant must prove that he or she was *not* negligent. The presumption of the defendant's negligence is known as the doctrine of ***res ipsa loquitur,***[8] which translates as "the facts speak for themselves."

---

8. Pronounced *rehz ihp*-suh *low*-kwuh-duhr.

This doctrine is applied only when the event creating the damage or injury is one that ordinarily does not occur in the absence of negligence. For example, if a person undergoes knee surgery and following the surgery has a severed nerve in the knee area, that person can sue the surgeon under a theory of *res ipsa loquitur.* In this case, the injury would not have occurred but for the surgeon's negligence.[9] For the doctrine of *res ipsa loquitur* to apply, the event must have been within the defendant's power to control, and it must not have been due to any voluntary action or contribution on the part of the plaintiff.

Negligence *Per Se.* Certain conduct, whether it consists of an action or a failure to act, may be treated as **negligence *per se*** ("in or of itself"). Negligence *per se* may occur if an individual violates a statute or an ordinance providing for a criminal penalty and that violation causes another to be injured. The injured person must prove (1) that the statute clearly sets out what standard of conduct is expected, when and where it is expected, and of whom it is expected; (2) that he or she is in the class intended to be protected by the statute; and (3) that the statute was designed to prevent the type of injury that he or she suffered. The standard of conduct required by the statute is the duty that the defendant owes to the plaintiff, and a violation of the statute is the breach of that duty.

Negligence *per se* • An act (or failure to act) in violation of a statutory requirement.

For example, a statute may require a landowner to keep a building in safe condition and may also subject the landowner to a criminal penalty, such as a fine, if the building is not kept safe. The statute is meant to protect those who are rightfully in the building. Thus, if the owner, without a sufficient excuse, violates the statute and a tenant is thereby injured, a majority of courts will hold that the owner's unexcused violation of the statute conclusively establishes a breach of a duty of care—that is, that the owner's violation is negligence *per se.*

"Danger Invites Rescue" Doctrine. Under the "danger invites rescue" doctrine, if a person commits an act that endangers another, the person committing the act will be liable not only for any injuries the other party suffers but also for any injuries suffered by a third person in an attempt to rescue the endangered party. For example, suppose that Ludlam, while driving down a street, fails to see a stop sign because he is trying to stop a squabble between his two young children in the car's back seat. Salter, on the curb near the stop sign, realizes that Ludlam is about to hit a pedestrian walking across the street at the intersection. Salter runs into the street to push the pedestrian out of the way, and Ludlam's vehicle hits Salter instead. In this situation, Ludlam will be liable for Salter's injury, as well as for any injuries the other pedestrian sustained. Rescuers can injure themselves, or the persons rescued, or even bystanders, but the original wrongdoers will still be liable.

Special Negligence Statutes. A number of states have enacted statutes prescribing duties and responsibilities in certain circumstances. For example, most states now have what are called **Good Samaritan statutes.**[10] Under these

Good Samaritan statute • A state statute that provides that persons who rescue or provide emergency services to others in peril—unless they do so recklessly and thus cause further harm—cannot be sued for negligence.

9. *Edwards v. Boland,* 41 Mass.App.Ct. 375, 670 N.E.2d 404 (1996).

10. These laws derive their name from the Good Samaritan story in the Bible. In the story, a traveler who had been robbed and beaten lay along the roadside, ignored by those passing by. Eventually, a man from the country of Samaria (the "Good Samaritan") stopped to render assistance to the injured person.

statutes, persons whom others aid voluntarily cannot turn around and sue the "Good Samaritans" for negligence. These laws were passed largely to protect physicians and medical personnel who voluntarily render their services in emergency situations to those in need, such as individuals hurt in car accidents.

Dram shop act • A state statute that imposes liability on tavern owners and bartenders who serve alcoholic drinks to the public for injuries resulting from accidents caused by intoxicated persons when the sellers or servers of alcoholic drinks contributed to the intoxication.

Many states have also passed **dram shop acts,** under which a tavern owner or bartender may be held liable for injuries caused by a person who became intoxicated while drinking at the bar or who was already intoxicated when served by the bartender. Some states have statutes that impose liability on *social hosts* (persons hosting parties) for injuries caused by guests who became intoxicated at the hosts' homes. Under these statutes, it is unnecessary to prove that the tavern owner, bartender, or social host was negligent. Sometimes, the definition of a "social host" is fashioned broadly. For example, in a New York case, the court held that the father of a minor who hosted a "bring your own keg" party could be held liable for injuries caused by an intoxicated guest.[11]

CYBER TORTS

In recent years, the courts have had to consider the question of who should be held liable for *cyber torts,* or torts committed in cyberspace. For example, who should be held liable when someone posts a defamatory message online? Should an Internet service provider (ISP)—a company that provides access to the Internet through a local phone line, cable, or DSL connection—be held liable for the remark if the ISP was unaware that it was being made? How can the identity of the person who made the remark be discovered? Can an ISP be forced to reveal the source of an anonymous comment? We explore some of these questions in this section, as well as a number of legal issues that have arisen with respect to bulk e-mail advertising. In the *Ethical Issue* that follows, we look at yet another topic: the legal questions raised by computer viruses.

ETHICAL ISSUE

Who should be held liable for computer viruses? As everybody knows, viruses sent into cyberspace can cause significant damage to the computer systems they "infect." To date, adapting tort law to virus-caused damages has been difficult because it is not all that clear who should be held liable for these damages. For example, who should be held liable for damages caused by the "ILOVEYOU" virus that spread around the globe in 2000 and caused an estimated $10 billion in damage? Of course, the person who wrote the virus is responsible. But what about the producer of the e-mail software that the virus utilized to spread itself so rapidly? What about the antivirus software companies? Were they negligent in failing to market products that were capable of identifying and disabling the virus before damage occurred? Should the users themselves share part of the blame? After all, even after the virus had received widespread publicity, users continued to open e-mail attachments containing the virus.

Generally, determining what tort duties apply in cyberspace and the point at which one of those duties is breached continues to be a pressing issue for today's courts.

11. *Rust v. Reyer,* 693 N.E.2d 1074, 670 N.Y.S.2d 822 (1998).

Defamation Online

Online forums allow anyone—customers, employees, or crackpots—to complain about a business firm's personnel, policies, practices, or products. Regardless of whether the complaint is justified and whether it is true, it might have an impact on the firm's business. One of the early questions in the online legal arena was whether the providers of such forums could be held liable for defamatory statements made in those forums.

Liability of Internet Service Providers. Newspapers, magazines, and television and radio stations may be held liable for defamatory remarks that they disseminate, even if those remarks are prepared or created by others. Under the Communications Decency Act of 1996, however, Internet service providers (ISPs), or "interactive computer service providers," are not liable for such material.[12] An ISP typically provides access to the Internet through a local phone number and may provide other services, including access to databases available only to the ISP's subscribers. (See this chapter's *Emerging Trends* feature on the next two pages for a further discussion of the immunity of ISPs.)

Piercing the Veil of Anonymity. A threshold barrier to anyone who seeks to bring an action for online defamation is discovering the identity of the person who posted the defamatory message online. ISPs can disclose personal information about their customers only when ordered to do so by a court. Consequently, businesses and individuals are increasingly resorting to lawsuits against "John Does," a fictitious name that is used when the names of the particular persons are not known. Then, using the authority of the courts, they can obtain from the ISPs the identities of the persons responsible for the messages.

In one case, for example, Eric Hvide, a former chief executive of a company called Hvide Marine, sued a number of John Does who had posted allegedly defamatory statements about his company on various online message boards. Hvide, who eventually lost his job, sued the John Does for libel in a Florida court. The court ruled that the ISPs, Yahoo and AOL, had to reveal the identities of the defendant Does.[13]

In some other cases, however, the rights of plaintiffs in such situations have been balanced against the defendants' rights to free speech. For example, some courts refuse to compel disclosure because, in their view, more than a bare allegation of defamation is required to outweigh an individual's competing right of anonymity in the exercise of the right of free speech.

Spam

Bulk, unsolicited e-mail ("junk" e-mail) sent to all of the users on a particular e-mailing list is often called **spam.** Typical spam consists of a product ad sent to all of the users on an e-mailing list or all of the members of a newsgroup.

Spam • Bulk, unsolicited ("junk") e-mail.

Spam as a Form of Trespass to Personal Property. Spam can waste user time and network bandwidth (the amount of data that can be transmitted within a certain time). It can also impose a burden on an ISP's equipment. As a result, some courts have held that spam is a trespass to personal property.

12. 47 U.S.C. Section 230.
13. *Does v. Hvide,* 770 So.2d 1237 (Fla.App.3d 2000).

EMERGING TRENDS

Internet Service Providers' Immunity from Liability

In the world of print publications, if you write an article falsely accusing an individual of being, say, a stalker, then both you and the newspaper can be sued for defamation. The equivalent of a newspaper in the online world is an Internet service provider (ISP) or a Web-hosting service. If this same article is published on the Internet, you may still be sued for defamation, but the ISP or Web-hosting service is now normally immune from liability.

THE COMMUNICATIONS DECENCY ACT OF 1996

In 1995, a New York court held that an ISP could be held liable for defamation as a publisher.[a] Congress responded with Section 230 of the Communications Decency Act of 1996 (CDA). That section states that "no provider or user of an interactive computer service shall be treated as the publisher or speaker of any information provided by another information content provider."[b]

a. *Stratton Oakmont, Inc. v. Prodigy Services Co.*, 1995 WL 323710 (N.Y.Sup.Ct. 1995).
b. 47 U.S.C. Section 230(c)(1).

In a number of key cases, Section 230 of the CDA has been invoked to shield ISPs from liability for defamatory postings on their bulletin boards. In one leading case, America Online, Inc. (AOL), avoided liability for defamation even though it did not promptly remove defamatory messages of which it had been made aware. In upholding a district court's ruling in AOL's favor, a federal appellate court stated that the CDA "plainly immunizes computer service providers like AOL from liability for information that originates with third parties." The court went on to explain that the purpose of the statute is "to maintain the robust nature of Internet communications and, accordingly, to keep government interference in the medium to a minimum." The court added that "none of this means, of course, that the original culpable [guilty] party who posts defamatory messages would escape accountability."[c]

c. *Zeran v. America Online, Inc.*, 129 F.3d 327 (4th Cir. 1997); *cert.* denied, 524 U.S. 937, 118 S.Ct. 2341, 141 L.Ed.2d 712 (1998).

IMMUNITY FOR DESTRUCTIVE COMPUTER PROGRAMS

The courts have extended the liability-immunity provision of Section 230 of the CDA to destructive computer programs downloaded from Web sites. In another case against AOL, the plaintiff alleged that AOL should be held liable for $400 of damages to the plaintiff's computer because of a destructive computer program sent through AOL. The plaintiff failed at trial, because the court applied Section 230 of the CDA.[d]

Another court applied Section 230 of the CDA in a suit against a company that was hosting Web sites. One of the sites offered for sale photographs and videos of major college athletes that had been taken illegally while they were undressing. The court held that Web-hosting services could not be held liable for materials

d. *Green v. America Online, Inc.* (D.N.J., December 20, 2000). For a discussion of this unpublished decision, see Laurin H. Mills, "ISP Immunity Provision Is Broadly Interpreted," *The National Law Journal*, April 13, 2002, p. C19.

In one case, for example, Cyber Promotions, Inc., sent bulk e-mail to subscribers of CompuServe, Inc., an ISP. CompuServe subscribers complained to the service about the ads, and many canceled their subscriptions. Handling the ads also placed a tremendous burden on CompuServe's equipment. CompuServe told Cyber Promotions to stop using CompuServe's equipment to process and store the ads—in effect, to stop sending the ads to CompuServe subscribers. Ignoring the demand, Cyber Promotions stepped up the volume of its ads. After CompuServe attempted unsuccessfully to block the flow with screening software, it filed a suit against Cyber Promotions in a federal district court, seeking an injunction on the ground that the ads constituted trespass

EMERGING TRENDS

Internet Service Providers' Immunity from Liability

posted on their sites by their customers.[e]

In essence, then, the trend is toward extending defamation immunity to the entire range of ISP services, provided that the ISPs themselves are not directly involved in creating the content.

THE TREND TOWARD EXTENDING CDA IMMUNITY TO ONLINE AUCTION SERVICES

In 2000, a California state court extended the immunity provision of Section 230 of the CDA to the realm of e-commerce when it ruled that eBay, one of the world's major online auction sites, could not be held liable for the sale of pirated sound recordings on its Web site. In *Stoner v. eBay, Inc.*,[f] the plaintiff alleged that eBay had knowingly reaped "massive profits" from the sale of pirated sound recordings in violation of a California statute. The court reasoned otherwise, concluding that there was nothing to indicate that eBay's function should be transformed from that of an interactive service provider to that of a seller responsible for items sold on the site. The court noted that "a principal objective of the immunity provision [of the CDA] is to encourage commerce over the Internet by ensuring that interactive computer service providers are not held responsible for how third parties use their services."

e. *Doe v. Franco Productions*, 2000 WL 16779 (N.D.Ill. 2000).

f. For a discussion of this unpublished decision, see "California Judge Grants E-Bay Immunity under CDA," *e-commerce Law & Strategy*, November 2000, p. 9.

IMPLICATIONS FOR THE BUSINESSPERSON

1. It appears relatively certain that as Internet technology evolves, the courts will increasingly utilize Section 230 of the CDA to immunize virtually all third party providers of Web content from defamation liability.
2. Given that it is increasingly possible to hide one's identity when posting messages and Web pages, businesspersons should be aware that there may be no one to hold responsible if they are victims of defamation on the Internet. Reputations have already been ruined by anecdotal comments posted online by anonymous persons. Public figures in particular have been anonymously accused of rape and murder. Well-known business figures have seen their names dragged through the mud. But no ISP has been held responsible.

FOR CRITICAL ANALYSIS

1. In your opinion, did Congress grant too broad an immunity to ISPs when it limited their liability for defamation? Do you agree with the courts that ISP immunity should be extended to Web hosts, Internet auctions, and the like by categorizing these providers as ISPs?
2. What might be the result if ISPs were held liable for defamatory content posted by those who use their services?

RELEVANT WEB SITES

To locate information on the Web concerning the issues discussed in this feature, go to this text's Web site at **http://ele.westbuslaw.com** and click on "Interactive Study Center."

to personal property. The court agreed and ordered Cyber Promotions to stop sending its ads to e-mail addresses maintained by CompuServe.[14]

Statutory Regulation of Spam. Because of the problems associated with spam, some states have taken steps to prohibit or regulate its use. For example, a few states, such as Washington, prohibit unsolicited e-mail that is promoting goods, services, or real estate for sale or lease. In California, an unsolicited e-mail ad must state in its subject line that it is an ad ("ADV"). The ad must

14. *CompuServe, Inc. v. Cyber Promotions, Inc.*, 962 F.Supp.2d 1015 (S.D.Ohio 1997).

also include a toll-free phone number or return e-mail address through which the recipient can contact the sender to request that no more ads be e-mailed.[15] An ISP can bring a successful suit in a California state court against a spammer who violates the ISP's policy prohibiting or restricting unsolicited e-mail ads. The court can award damages of up to $25,000 per day.[16]

Some of these statutes have raised constitutional issues, however. Because the Internet is a public forum, free speech rights may also be involved (see Chapter 5). In at least one case, the issue concerned the commerce clause. When the state of Washington sued an Oregon resident for violating Washington's anti-spam statute, the Oregon resident argued that the statute violated the commerce clause. (Recall from Chapter 5 that the commerce clause, as interpreted by the United States Supreme Court, allows only the national government to regulate interstate commerce. If a state law substantially burdens interstate commerce, the law may be held to violate the commerce clause.) Although a Washington state trial court agreed with the Oregon resident's argument, the Washington State Supreme Court reversed the ruling, holding that the law did not unconstitutionally burden interstate commerce.[17]

Strict Liability

Strict liability • Liability regardless of fault. In tort law, strict liability may be imposed on defendants in cases involving abnormally dangerous activities, dangerous animals, or defective products.

Another category of torts is called **strict liability,** or *liability without fault.* Intentional torts and torts of negligence involve acts that depart from a reasonable standard of care and cause injuries. Under the doctrine of strict liability, liability for injury is imposed for reasons other than fault. Strict liability for damages proximately caused by an abnormally dangerous or exceptional activity is one application of this doctrine. Courts apply the doctrine of strict liability in such cases because of the extreme risk of the activity. Even if blasting with dynamite is performed with all reasonable care, for example, there is still a risk of injury. Balancing that risk against the potential for harm, it seems reasonable to ask the person engaged in the activity to pay for injuries caused by that activity. Although there is no fault, there is still responsibility because of the dangerous nature of the undertaking.

There are other applications of the strict liability principle. Persons who keep dangerous animals, for example, are strictly liable for any harm inflicted by the animals. A significant application of strict liability is in the area of *product liability,* which we discuss next.

Product Liability

Product liability • The legal liability of manufacturers, sellers, and lessors of goods to consumers, users, and bystanders for injuries or damages that are caused by the goods.

Bystander • A spectator, witness, or person standing nearby when an event occurred and who did not engage in the business or act leading to the event.

Product liability refers to the liability incurred by manufacturers and sellers of products when product defects cause injury or property damage to consumers, users, or **bystanders** (people in the vicinity of the product).

Product liability encompasses the tort theories of negligence and misrepresentation, which were discussed earlier in this chapter, as well as strict liabil-

15. Ca. Bus. & Prof. Code Section 17538.4.
16. Ca. Bus. & Prof. Code Section 17538.45.
17. *State v. Heckel,* 143 Wash.2d 824, 24 P.3d 404 (2001).

ity. Product liability can also be based on warranty theory, a topic we treated in Chapter 11.

Product Liability Based on Negligence

Earlier in this chapter, *negligence* was defined as the failure to exercise the degree of care that a reasonable, prudent person would have exercised under the circumstances. If a manufacturer fails to exercise "due care" to make a product safe, a person who is injured by the product may sue the manufacturer for negligence.

Due care must be exercised in designing the product, in selecting the materials, in using the appropriate production process, in assembling and testing the product, and in placing adequate warnings on the label informing the user of dangers of which an ordinary person might not be aware. The duty of care also extends to the inspection and testing of any purchased components that are used in the product sold by the manufacturer.

A product liability action based on negligence does not require the injured plaintiff and the negligent defendant-manufacturer to be in *privity of contract*. That is, the plaintiff and the defendant need not be directly involved in a contractual relationship. A manufacturer is liable for its failure to exercise due care to *any person* who sustains an injury proximately caused by a negligently made (defective) product. Relative to the long history of the common law, this exception to the privity requirement is a fairly recent development, dating to the early part of the twentieth century.[18]

Product Liability Based on Misrepresentation

When a fraudulent misrepresentation has been made to a user or consumer and that misrepresentation ultimately results in an injury, the basis of liability may be the tort of fraud. In this situation, the misrepresentation must have been made knowingly or with reckless disregard for the facts.

An example is the intentional concealment of a product's defects. In contrast to actions based on negligence and strict liability, in a suit based on fraudulent misrepresentation, the plaintiff does not have to show that the product was defective or that it malfunctioned in any way.

Strict Product Liability

As explained previously, under the doctrine of strict liability people may be liable for the results of their acts regardless of their intentions or their exercise of reasonable care. In the 1960s, courts applied the doctrine of strict liability in several landmark cases involving manufactured goods, and it has since become a common method of holding manufacturers liable. Some states, however, including Massachusetts and Virginia, have refused to recognize strict product liability. Additionally, some courts limit the application of the doctrine only to cases involving personal injuries, not property damage. Until recently, recovery for economic loss was not available in an action based on strict liability; even today, it is rarely available.

18. A landmark case in this respect is *MacPherson v. Buick Motor Co.,* 217 N.Y. 382, 111 N.E. 1050 (1916).

Strict Product Liability and Public Policy

Strict product liability is imposed by law as a matter of public policy. This public policy rests on the threefold assumption that (1) consumers should be protected against unsafe products; (2) manufacturers and distributors should not escape liability for faulty products simply because they are not in privity of contract with the ultimate user of those products; and (3) manufacturers, sellers, and lessors of products are in a better position to bear the costs associated with injuries caused by their products—costs that they can ultimately pass on to all consumers in the form of higher prices.

California was the first state to impose strict product liability in tort on manufacturers. In the landmark decision that follows, the California Supreme Court sets out the reason for applying tort law, rather than contract law (including laws governing warranties), to cases involving consumers who were injured by defective products.

CASE 12.4

Supreme Court of California, 1962.
59 Cal.2d 57,
377 P.2d 897,
27 Cal.Rptr. 697.
http://www2.newpaltz.edu/~zuckerpr/cases/green1.htm[a]

GREENMAN v. YUBA POWER PRODUCTS, INC.

The plaintiff, Greenman, wanted a Shopsmith—a combination power tool that could be used as a saw, drill, and wood lathe—after seeing a Shopsmith demonstrated by a retailer and studying a brochure prepared by the manufacturer. The plaintiff's wife gave him one for Christmas. More than a year later, a piece of wood flew out of the lathe attachment of the Shopsmith while the plaintiff was using it, inflicting serious injuries on him. About ten and a half months later, the plaintiff filed suit in a California state court against both the retailer and the manufacturer for breach of warranties and negligence. The trial court jury found for the plaintiff. The case was ultimately appealed to the Supreme Court of California.

TRAYNOR, J.

Plaintiff introduced substantial evidence that his injuries were caused by defective design and construction of the Shopsmith. * * * The jury could therefore reasonably have concluded that the manufacturer negligently constructed the Shopsmith. The jury could also reasonably have concluded that statements in the manufacturer's brochure were untrue, that they constituted express warranties, and that plaintiff's injuries were caused by their breach.

* * * *

[But] to impose strict liability on the manufacturer under the circumstances of this case, it was not necessary for plaintiff to establish an express warranty * * * . *A manufacturer is strictly liable in tort when an article he places on the market, knowing that it is to be used without inspection for defects, proves to have a defect that causes injury to a human being.* * * * [Emphasis added.]

* * * *

* * * The purpose of such liability is to insure that the costs of injuries resulting from defective products are borne by the manufacturers * * * rather than by the injured persons who are powerless to protect themselves.

---

a. This case is included within the Web site for an "Introduction to Law" course taught by Paul Zuckerman, a professor with the State University of New York at New Paltz.

The Supreme Court of California upheld the jury verdict for the plaintiff. The manufacturer was held strictly liable in tort for the harm caused by its unsafe product.

QUESTIONS

1. On what reasoning did the California Supreme Court base its decision in this case?
2. If the plaintiff's injury in this case had been due to his own negligence, would the California Supreme Court have held the defendant liable?
3. Should a manufacturer be held liable to *any* person who suffers an injury proximately caused by the manufacturer's product?

The Requirements for Strict Product Liability

As mentioned in Chapter 1, the courts often look to the *Restatements of the Law* for guidance, even though the *Restatements* are not binding authorities. Section 402A of the *Restatement (Second) of Torts* indicates how its drafters believed that the doctrine of strict product liability should be applied. This *Restatement* was issued in 1964, and during the decade following its release, it became a widely accepted statement of the liabilities of sellers of goods (including manufacturers, processors, assemblers, packagers, bottlers, wholesalers, distributors, retailers, and lessors). Section 402A reads as follows:

> (1) One who sells any product in a defective condition unreasonably dangerous to the user or consumer or to his property is subject to liability for physical harm thereby caused to the ultimate user or consumer or to his property, if
> (a) the seller is engaged in the business of selling such a product, and
> (b) it is expected to and does reach the user or consumer without substantial change in the condition in which it is sold.
>
> (2) The rule stated in Subsection (1) applies although
> (a) the seller has exercised all possible care in the preparation and sale of his product, and
> (b) the user or consumer has not bought the product from or entered into any contractual relation with the seller.

The Six Requirements for Strict Liability. The bases for an action in strict liability as set forth in Section 402A of the *Restatement (Second) of Torts,* and as the doctrine came to be commonly applied, can be summarized as a series of six requirements:

1. The product must be in a defective condition when the defendant sells it.
2. The defendant must normally be engaged in the business of selling (or otherwise distributing) that product.
3. The product must be unreasonably dangerous to the user or consumer because of its defective condition (in most states).
4. The plaintiff must incur physical harm to self or property by use or consumption of the product.
5. The defective condition must be the proximate cause of the injury or damage.
6. The goods must not have been substantially changed from the time the product was sold to the time the injury was sustained.

Depending on the jurisdiction, if these requirements were met, a manufacturer's liability to an injured party could be virtually unlimited.[19]

Unreasonably Dangerous Products. Under these requirements, in any action against a manufacturer, seller, or lessor, the plaintiff does not have to show why or in what manner the product became defective. To recover damages, however, the plaintiff must show that the product was so "defective" as to be "unreasonably dangerous"; that the product caused the plaintiff's injury; and that, at the time the injury was sustained, the condition of the product was essentially the same as when it left the hands of the defendant manufacturer, seller, or lessor.

Unreasonably dangerous product • A product that is defective to the point of threatening a consumer's health and safety. A product will be considered unreasonably dangerous if it is dangerous beyond the expectation of the ordinary consumer or if a less dangerous alternative was economically feasible for the manufacturer, but the manufacturer failed to produce it.

A court could consider a product so defective as to be an **unreasonably dangerous product** if either (1) the product was dangerous beyond the expectation of the ordinary consumer or (2) a less dangerous alternative was *economically* feasible for the manufacturer, but the manufacturer failed to produce it. As will be discussed next, a product may be unreasonably dangerous due to a flaw in the manufacturing process, a design defect, or an inadequate warning.

Product Defects

Because Section 402A of the *Restatement (Second) of Torts* did not clearly define such terms as "defective" and "unreasonably dangerous," these terms have been subject to different interpretations by different courts. In 1997, to address these concerns, the American Law Institute (ALI) issued the *Restatement (Third) of Torts: Products Liability.* The *Restatement* defines the three types of product defects that have traditionally been recognized in product liability law—manufacturing defects, design defects, and warning defects.

Manufacturing Defects. According to Section 2(a) of the *Restatement,* a product "contains a manufacturing defect when the product departs from its intended design even though all possible care was exercised in the preparation and marketing of the product." This statement imposes liability on the manufacturer (and on the wholesaler and retailer) regardless of whether the manufacturer acted "reasonably." This is strict liability, or liability without fault.

Design Defects. A determination that a product has a design defect (or a warning defect, to be discussed shortly) can affect all of the units of a product. A product "is defective in design when the foreseeable risks of harm posed by the product could have been reduced or avoided by the adoption of a reasonable alternative design by the seller or other distributor, or a predecessor in the commercial chain of distribution, and the omission of the alternative design renders the product not reasonably safe."[20]

To succeed in a product liability suit alleging a design defect, a plaintiff has to show that there is a reasonable alternative design. In other words, a manufacturer or other defendant is liable only when the harm was *reasonably* preventable. According to the Official Comments accompanying the *Restatement*

19. In a number of states, *statutes of repose* (discussed later in this chapter) place a limit on the time period within which product liability actions may be brought.

20. *Restatement (Third) of Torts: Products Liability,* Section 2(b).

(Third) of Torts: Products Liability, factors that a court may consider on this point include

> the magnitude and probability of the foreseeable risks of harm, the instructions and warnings accompanying the product, and the nature and strength of consumer expectations regarding the product, including expectations arising from product portrayal and marketing. The relative advantages and disadvantages of the product as designed and as it alternatively could have been designed may also be considered. Thus, the likely effects of the alternative design on production costs; the effects of the alternative design on product longevity, maintenance, repair, and esthetics; and the range of consumer choice among products are factors that may be taken into account.

Warning Defects. A product may also be deemed defective because of inadequate instructions or warnings. A product "is defective because of inadequate instructions or warnings when the foreseeable risks of harm posed by the product could have been reduced or avoided by the provision of reasonable instructions or warnings by the seller or other distributor, or a predecessor in the commercial chain of distribution, and the omission of the instructions or warnings renders the product not reasonably safe."[21]

Important factors for a court to consider under the *Restatement (Third) of Torts: Products Liability* include the risks of a product, the "content and comprehensibility" and "intensity of expression" of warnings and instructions, and the "characteristics of expected user groups."[22] For example, children would likely respond readily to bright, bold, simple warning labels, whereas educated adults might need more detailed information.

Obvious Risks. There is no duty to warn about risks that are obvious or commonly known. Warnings about such risks do not add to the safety of a product and could even detract from it by making other warnings seem less significant. The obviousness of a risk and a user's decision to proceed in the face of that risk may be a defense in a product liability suit based on a warning defect. (Defenses to product liability will be discussed shortly.)

Foreseeable Misuses. Generally, a seller must warn those who purchase its product of the harm that can result from the foreseeable misuse of the product as well. The key is the foreseeability of the misuse. According to the Official Comments accompanying the *Restatement (Third) of Torts: Products Liability,* sellers "are not required to foresee and take precautions against every conceivable mode of use and abuse to which their products might be put."

Market-Share Liability

Generally, in cases involving product liability, a plaintiff must prove that the defective product that caused his or her injury was the product of a specific defendant. In recent decades, however, when plaintiffs could not prove which of many distributors of a harmful product supplied the particular product that caused their injuries, courts have dropped this requirement.

---

21. *Restatement (Third) of Torts: Products Liability,* Section 2(c).
22. *Restatement (Third) of Torts: Products Liability,* Section 2, Comment h.

This has occurred, for example, in several product liability cases involving DES (diethylstilbestrol), a drug administered in the past to prevent miscarriages. DES's harmful character was not realized until, a generation later, daughters of the women who had taken DES developed health problems, including vaginal carcinomas, that were linked to the drug. Partly because of the passage of time, a plaintiff-daughter often could not prove which pharmaceutical company—out of as many as three hundred—had marketed the DES her mother had ingested. In these cases, some courts applied **market-share liability,** holding that all firms that manufactured and distributed DES during the period in question were liable for the plaintiffs' injuries in proportion to the firms' respective shares of the market.[23]

Market-share liability • A method of sharing liability among several firms that manufactured or marketed a particular product that may have caused a plaintiff's injury. This form of liability sharing is used when the true source of the product is unidentifiable. Each firm's liability is proportionate to its respective share of the relevant market for the product.

Market-share liability has also been applied in a few other situations.[24] In one case, the New York Court of Appeals (that state's highest court) held that even if a firm can prove that it did not manufacture the particular product that caused injuries to the plaintiff, the firm can be held liable based on its share of the national market.[25]

Other Applications of Strict Product Liability

Strict product liability also applies to suppliers of component parts. For example, suppose that General Motors buys brake pads from a subcontractor and puts them in Chevrolets without changing their composition. If those pads are defective, both the supplier of the brake pads and General Motors will be held strictly liable for the damages caused by the defective parts. Under the *Restatement (Third) of Torts: Products Liability*, a component supplier may be liable if the component is defective "at the time of sale or distribution." A supplier may also be liable if it "substantially participates in the integration of the component into the design of the product," the "integration" causes the product to be defective, and the defect causes harm.[26]

Although the drafters of Section 402A of the *Restatement (Second) of Torts* did not take a position on bystanders, all courts extend the strict liability of manufacturers and other sellers to injured bystanders. For example, in one case, an automobile manufacturer was held liable for injuries caused by the explosion of a car's motor. A cloud of steam resulting from the explosion caused multiple collisions because other drivers could not see well.[27]

Defenses to Product Liability

Defendants in product liability suits can raise a number of defenses. One defense, of course, is to show that there is no basis for the plaintiff's claim. For example, in a product liability case based on negligence, if a defendant can show that the plaintiff has *not* met the requirements (such as causation) for an action in negligence, generally the defendant will not be liable. In regard to strict product liability, a defendant can claim that the plaintiff failed to meet one of the requirements for an action in strict liability. For example, if

23. See, for example, *Martin v. Abbott Laboratories,* 102 Wash.2d 581, 689 P.2d 368 (1984).
24. See, for example, *Smith v. Cutter Biological, Inc.,* 72 Haw. 416, 823 P.2d 717 (1991).
25. *Hymowitz v. Eli Lilly and Co.,* 73 N.Y.2d 487, 539 N.E.2d 1069, 541 N.Y.S.2d 941 (1989).
26. *Restatement (Third) of Torts: Products Liability,* Section 5.
27. *Giberson v. Ford Motor Co.,* 504 S.W.2d 8 (Mo. 1974).

the defendant establishes that the goods have been subsequently altered, normally the defendant will not be held liable.[28] Defendants may also assert the defenses discussed next.

Assumption of Risk

Assumption of risk, which we discussed earlier in this chapter, can sometimes be used as a defense in a product liability action. To establish such a defense, the defendant must show that (1) the plaintiff knew and appreciated the risk created by the product defect, and (2) the plaintiff voluntarily assumed the risk, even though it was unreasonable to do so. For example, if a buyer failed to heed a seller's product recall, the buyer may be deemed to have assumed the risk of the product defect that the seller offered to cure.

Product Misuse

Similar to the defense of voluntary assumption of risk is that of **product misuse.** Here, the injured party *does not know that the product is dangerous for a particular use* (contrast this with assumption of risk), but the use is not the one for which the product was designed. The courts have severely limited this defense. Even if the injured party does not know about the inherent danger of using the product in a wrong way, if the misuse is reasonably foreseeable, the seller must take measures to guard against it.

Product misuse • A defense against product liability that may be raised if the plaintiff used a product in a manner not intended by the manufacturer. If the misuse is reasonably foreseeable, the seller will not escape liability unless measures were taken to guard against the misuse.

For example, in one case two men were using a crane to retrieve drilling pipe from beneath power lines when the crane cable touched one of the lines. The cable did not have an insulated link and thus conducted electricity from the line to the pipe, electrocuting one of the men. The man's widow sued the crane manufacturer, alleging that the crane—without the insulated link—was defectively designed and unreasonably dangerous. The manufacturer argued that the men had been using the crane to sideload (a practice that causes the crane's cable to extend its slack in unpredictable ways) and that sideloading was an unreasonable misuse of the product. The court held that although sideloading was a misuse, the misuse was reasonably foreseeable. Because the manufacturer had failed to guard against this foreseeable misuse, it was liable to the widow for damages.[29]

Comparative Negligence (Fault)

Developments in the area of comparative negligence, or fault (discussed earlier in this chapter), have affected the doctrine of strict liability—the most extreme theory of product liability. Whereas previously the plaintiff's conduct was not a defense to strict liability, today many jurisdictions, when apportioning liability and damages, consider the negligent or intentional actions of both the plaintiff and the defendant. This means that even if the plaintiff misused the product, she or he may nonetheless be able to recover at least some damages for injuries caused by the defendant's defective product.

28. Under some state laws, the failure to properly maintain a product may constitute a subsequent alteration. See, for example, *LaPlante v. American Honda Motor Co.,* 27 F.3d 731 (1st Cir. 1994).
29. *Lutz v. National Crane Corp.,* 884 P.2d 455 (Mont. 1994).

Commonly Known Dangers

The dangers associated with certain products (such as matches and sharp knives) are so commonly known that, as already mentioned, manufacturers need not warn users of those dangers. If a defendant succeeds in convincing the court that a plaintiff's injury resulted from a *commonly known danger,* the defendant will not be liable.

A classic case on this issue involved a plaintiff who was injured when an elastic exercise rope she had purchased slipped off her foot and struck her in the eye, causing a detachment of the retina. The plaintiff claimed that the manufacturer should be liable because it had failed to warn users that the exerciser might slip off a foot in such a manner. The court stated that to hold the manufacturer liable in these circumstances "would go beyond the reasonable dictates of justice in fixing the liabilities of manufacturers." After all, stated the court, "[a]lmost every physical object can be inherently dangerous or potentially dangerous in a sense. . . . A manufacturer cannot manufacture a knife that will not cut or a hammer that will not mash a thumb or a stove that will not burn a finger. The law does not require [manufacturers] to warn of such common dangers."[30]

A related defense is the *knowledgeable user* defense. If a particular danger is or should be commonly known by particular users of a product, the manufacturer need not warn these users of the danger.

The following case was the first of its kind. As the defendants argued, and the court acknowledged, the outcome of the case "could spawn thousands of similar 'McLawsuits' against restaurants. Even if limited to that ilk of fare dubbed 'fast food,' the potential for lawsuits is great."

30. *Jamieson v. Woodward & Lothrop,* 247 F.2d 23 (D.C. 1957).

CASE 12.5

United States District Court, Southern District of New York, 2003. 237 F.Supp.2d 512.

PELMAN v. McDONALD'S CORP.

McDonald's Corporation has its main corporate office in Oak Brook, Illinois, but does business throughout the world, serving nearly 46 million customers each day. McDonald's, with about 13,000 restaurants in the United States, has a 43 percent share of the U.S. fast-food market. McDonald's of New York has its principal place of business in Albany, New York, but owns and operates fast-food outlets throughout the state. Ashley Pelman, a New York resident, and other teenagers who often ate at the McDonald's outlets, became overweight and developed adverse health effects. Their parents filed a suit in a New York state court against McDonald's and others, alleging in part that the defendants failed to warn of the quantities, qualities, and levels of cholesterol, fat, salt, sugar, and other ingredients in their products, and that a diet high in fat, salt, sugar, and cholesterol could lead to obesity and health problems. The suit was transferred to a federal district court. The defendants filed a motion to dismiss the complaint.

SWEET, J.

This action presents unique and challenging issues. The plaintiffs have alleged that the practices of McDonald's in making and selling their products are deceptive and that this deception has caused the minors who have consumed McDonald's products to injure their health by becoming obese. Questions of personal responsibility, common knowledge and public health are presented * * *.

* * * *

This opinion is guided by the principle that *legal consequences should not attach to the consumption of hamburgers and other fast food fare unless consumers are unaware of the dangers of eating such food.* * * * [K]nowledge is power. Following from this aphorism, one important principle in assigning legal responsibility is the common knowledge of consumers. If consumers know (or reasonably should know) the potential ill health effects of eating at McDonald's, they cannot blame McDonald's if they, nonetheless, choose to satiate their appetite with a surfeit of supersized McDonald's products. On the other hand, consumers cannot be expected to protect against a danger that was solely within McDonald's knowledge. Thus, one necessary element of any potentially viable claim must be that McDonald's products involve a danger that is not within the common knowledge of consumers. * * * [Emphasis added.]

* * * Americans now spend more than $110 billion on fast food each year, and on any given day in the United States, almost one in four adults visits a fast food restaurant. * * *

* * * *

Today there are nearly twice as many overweight children and almost three times as many overweight adolescents as there were in 1980. In 1999, an estimated 61 percent of U.S. adults were overweight or obese and 13 percent of children aged 6 to 11 years and 14 percent of adolescents aged 12 to 19 years were overweight. In 1980, those figures for children were 7 percent for children aged 6 to 11 years and 5 percent for adolescents aged 12 to 19 years.

Obese individuals have a 50 to 100 percent increased risk of premature death from all causes. Approximately 300,000 deaths a year in the United States are currently associated with overweight and obesity * * *. [L]eft unabated, overweight and obesity may soon cause as much preventable disease and death as cigarette smoking.

* * * *

[Among other things, the plaintiffs assert] that McDonald's failed to post nutritional labeling on the products and at points of purchase. * * *

* * * *

* * * Plaintiffs admit that McDonald's has made its nutritional information available online and do not contest that such information is available upon request. Unless McDonald's has specifically promised to provide nutritional information on all its products and at all points of purchase, plaintiffs do not state a claim.

* * * *

[Or] in order to state a claim, the Complaint must allege either that the attributes of McDonald's products are so extraordinarily unhealthy that they are outside the reasonable contemplation of the consuming public or that the products are so extraordinarily unhealthy as to be dangerous in their intended use. The Complaint—which merely alleges that the foods contain high levels of cholesterol, fat, salt and sugar, and that the foods are therefore unhealthy—fails to reach this bar. It is well known that fast food in general, and McDonald's products in particular, contain high levels of cholesterol, fat, salt, and sugar, and that such attributes are bad for one.

* * * If a person knows or should know that eating copious orders of supersized McDonald's products is unhealthy and may result in weight gain (and its concomitant problems) because of the high levels of cholesterol, fat, salt and sugar, it is not the place of the law to protect them from their own excesses. Nobody is forced to eat at McDonald's. (Except, perhaps, parents of small children who desire McDonald's food, toy promotions or playgrounds and demand their parents' accompaniment.) Even more pertinent, nobody is forced to supersize their meal or choose less healthy options on the menu.

*As long as a consumer exercises free choice with appropriate knowledge, liability * * * will not attach to a manufacturer.* It is only when that free choice becomes but a chimera [fantasy]—for instance, by the masking of information necessary to make the choice, such as the knowledge that eating at McDonald's with a certain frequency would irrefragably [indisputably] cause harm—that manufacturers should be held accountable. Plaintiffs have failed to allege in the Complaint that their decisions to eat at McDonald's several times a week were anything but a choice freely made and which now may not be pinned on McDonald's. [Emphasis added.]

The court dismissed the plaintiffs' complaint, which failed to allege, among other things, that the products consumed by the plaintiffs were dangerous in any way other than that which was open and obvious to a reasonable consumer.

QUESTIONS

1. On what reasoning did the court base its dismissal of the plaintiffs' complaint?
2. What might the plaintiffs have alleged (and substantiated with proof) to succeed in their suit?
3. Where should the line be drawn between an individual's responsibility to take care of himself or herself and society's responsibility to protect that individual?

Statutes of Limitations and Repose

As discussed in Chapter 1, *statutes of limitations* restrict the time within which an action may be brought. A typical statute of limitations provides that an action must be brought within a specified period of time after the cause of action accrues. Generally, a cause of action is held to accrue when some damage occurs. Sometimes, the running of the prescribed period is *tolled* (that is, suspended) until the party suffering an injury has discovered it or should have discovered it.

Statute of repose • Basically, a statute of limitations that is not dependent on the happening of a cause of action. Statutes of repose generally begin to run at an earlier date and run for a longer period of time than statutes of limitations.

Many states have passed laws, called **statutes of repose,** placing outer time limits on some claims so that the defendant will not be left vulnerable to lawsuits indefinitely. These statutes may limit the time within which a plaintiff can file a product liability suit. Typically, a statute of repose begins to run at an earlier date and runs for a longer time than a statute of limitations. For example, a statute of repose may require that claims must be brought within twelve years from the date of sale or manufacture of the defective product. It is immaterial that the product is defective or causes an injury if the injury occurs *after* this statutory period has lapsed. In addition, some of these legislative enactments have limited the application of the doctrine of strict liability to new goods only.

KEY TERMS

actionable 419
actual malice 420
appropriation 421
assault 417
assumption of risk 435
battery 417
business invitee 432
business tort 416
bystander 442
causation in fact 433
comparative negligence 436
contributory negligence 436
conversion 427
cyber tort 416
defamation 419
disparagement of property 429
dram shop act 438
duty of care 430
Good Samaritan statute 437
intentional tort 417
libel 419
malpractice 432
market-share liability 448
negligence 430
negligence *per se* 437
privilege 420
product liability 442
product misuse 449
proximate cause 433
public figure 420
punitive damages 433
reasonable person standard 430
***res ipsa loquitur* 436**
slander 419
slander of quality 429
slander of title 430
spam 439
statute of repose 452
strict liability 442
tort 416
tortfeasor 417
trade libel 429
trespass to land 425
trespass to personal property 426
unreasonably dangerous product 446

FOR REVIEW

❶ What is the purpose of tort law? What are two basic categories of torts?

❷ What are the four elements of a cause of action for negligence?

❸ What is a cyber tort, and how are tort theories being applied in cyberspace?

❹ What are the elements of a cause of action in strict product liability?

❺ What defenses can be raised in a product liability suit?

QUESTIONS AND CASE PROBLEMS

12–1. In which of the following situations will the acting party be liable for the tort of negligence? Explain fully.

(a) Shannon goes to the golf course on Sunday morning, eager to try out a new set of golf clubs she has just purchased. As she tees off on the first hole, the head of her club flies off and injures a nearby golfer.

(b) Shannon goes to the golf course on Sunday morning. While she is teeing off at the eleventh hole, her golf ball veers off toward a roadway next to the golf course and shatters the windshield of a car.

(c) Shannon's physician gives her some pain medication and tells her not to drive after she takes it, as the medication induces drowsiness. In spite of the doctor's warning, Shannon decides to drive to the store while on the medication. Owing to her lack of alertness, she fails to stop at a traffic light and crashes into another vehicle, causing a passenger in that vehicle to be injured.

12–2. Ruth carelessly parks her car on a steep hill, leaving the car in neutral and failing to engage the parking brake. The car rolls down the hill and knocks down an electric line. The sparks from the broken line ignite a grass fire. The fire spreads until it reaches a barn one mile away. The barn houses dynamite, and the burning barn explodes, causing part of the roof to fall on and injure a passing motorist, Jim. Can Jim recover damages from Ruth? Why or why not?

12–3. Lothar owns a bakery. He has been trying to obtain a long-term contract with the owner of Martha's Tea Salons for some time. Lothar starts a local advertising campaign on radio and television and in the newspaper. This advertising campaign is so persuasive that Martha decides to break the contract she has had with Harley's Bakery so that she can patronize Lothar's bakery. Is Lothar liable to Harley's Bakery for the tort of wrongful interference with a contractual relationship? Is Martha liable for this tort? For anything?

12–4. Gina is standing on a street corner waiting for a ride to work. Gomez has just purchased a new car manufactured by Optimal Motors. He is driving down the street when suddenly the steering mechanism breaks, causing him to run over Gina. Gina suffers permanent injuries. Gomez's total income per year has never exceeded $15,000. Thus, instead of suing Gomez, Gina files suit against Optimal under the theory of strict liability in tort. Optimal claims that it is not liable because (1) due care was used in the manufacture of the car, (2) Optimal is not the manufacturer of the steering mechanism (Smith is), and (3) strict product liability applies only to users or consumers, and Gina is neither. Discuss the validity of the defenses claimed by Optimal.

CASE PROBLEM WITH SAMPLE ANSWER

12–5. Duty of Care. As pedestrians exited at the close of an arts and crafts show, Jason Davis, an employee of the show's producer, stood near the exit. Suddenly and without warning, Davis turned around and collided with Yvonne Esposito, an eighty-year-old woman. Esposito was knocked to the ground, fracturing her hip. After hip-replacement surgery, she was left with a permanent physical impairment. Esposito filed a suit in a federal district court against Davis and others, alleging negligence. What are the factors that indicate whether Davis owed Esposito a duty of care? What do those factors indicate in these circumstances? [*Esposito v. Davis,* 47 F.3d 164 (5th Cir. 1995)]

➧ *To view a sample answer for this case problem, go to this book's Web site at* **http://ele.westbuslaw.com** *and click on "Interactive Study Center."*

12–6. Trespass to Property. America Online, Inc. (AOL), provides services to its customers (members), including the transmission of e-mail to and from other members and across the Internet. To become a member, a person must agree not to use AOL's computers to send bulk, unsolicited, commercial e-mail (spam). AOL uses filters to block spam, but bulk e-mailers sometimes use other software to thwart the filters. National Health Care Discount, Inc. (NHCD), sells discount optical and dental service plans. To generate leads for NHCD's products, sales representatives, who included AOL members, sent more than 300 million pieces of spam through AOL's computer system. Each item cost AOL an estimated $.00078 in equipment expenses. Some of the spam used false headers and other methods to hide the source. After receiving more than 150,000 complaints, AOL asked NHCD to stop. When the spam continued, AOL filed a suit in a federal district court against NHCD, alleging in part trespass to chattels—an unlawful interference with another's rights to possess personal property. AOL asked the court for a summary judgment on this claim. Did the spamming constitute trespass to chattels? Explain. [*America Online, Inc. v. National Health Care Discount, Inc.,* 121 F.Supp.2d 1255 (N.D.Iowa 2000)]

12–7. Invasion of Privacy. During the spring and summer of 1999, Edward and Geneva Irvine received numerous "hang-up" phone calls, including three calls in the middle of the night. With the help of their local phone company, the Irvines learned that many of the calls were from the telemarketing department of the *Akron Beacon Journal* in Akron, Ohio. The *Beacon's* sales force was equipped with an automatic dialing machine. During business hours, the dialer was used to maximize productivity by calling multiple phone numbers at once and connecting a call to a sales representative only after it was answered. After business hours, the dialer was used to dial a list of disconnected numbers to determine whether they had been reconnected. If the dialer detected a ring, it recorded the information and dropped the call. If the automated dialing system crashed, which it did frequently, it redialed the entire list. The Irvines filed a suit in an Ohio state court against the *Beacon* and others, alleging in part an invasion of privacy. In whose favor should the court rule, and why? [*Irvine v. Akron Beacon Journal,* 147 Ohio App.3d 428, 770 N.E.2d 1105 (9 Dist. 2002)]

12–8. Design Defect. In May 1995, Ms. McCathern and her daughter, together with McCathern's cousin, Ms. Sanders, and her daughter, were riding in Sanders's 1994 Toyota 4Runner. Sanders was driving, McCathern was in the front passenger seat, and the children were in the back seat. Everyone was wearing a seat belt. While the group was traveling south on Oregon State Highway 395 at a speed of approximately fifty miles per hour, an oncoming vehicle veered into Sanders's lane of travel. When Sanders tried to steer clear, the 4Runner rolled over and landed upright on its four wheels. During the rollover, the roof over the front passenger seat collapsed, and as a result, McCathern sustained serious, permanent injuries. McCathern filed a suit in an Oregon state court against Toyota Motor Corp. and others, alleging in part that the 1994 4Runner "was dangerously defective and unreasonably dangerous in that the vehicle, as designed and sold, was unstable and prone to rollover." What is the test for product liability based on a design defect? What would McCathern have to prove to succeed under that test? [*McCathern v. Toyota Motor Corp.*, 332 Or. 59, 23 P.3d 320 (2001)]

12–9. Liability to Third Parties. Lee Stegemoller was a union member who insulated large machinery between 1947 and 1988. During his career, he worked for a number of different companies, including ACandS, Inc. Stegemoller primarily worked with asbestos insulation, which was used on industrial boilers, engines, furnaces, and turbines. After he left a work site, some of the asbestos dust always remained on his clothing. His wife Ramona, who laundered his work clothes, was also exposed to the dust on a daily basis. Allegedly as a result of this contact, she was diagnosed with colon cancer, pulmonary fibrosis, and pleural thickening in April 1998. The Stegemollers filed a suit in an Indiana state court against ACandS and thirty-three others, contending, among other things, that the asbestos originated from products attributable to some of the defendants and from the premises of other defendants. Several defendants filed a motion to dismiss the complaint, asserting that Ramona was not a "user or consumer" of asbestos because she was not in the vicinity of the product when it was used. Should the court dismiss the suit on this basis? Explain. [*Stegemoller v. ACandS, Inc.*, 767 N.E.2d 974 (Ind. 2002)]

12–10. IN YOUR COURT

Judy Dunne weighed more than 450 pounds. For a birthday present, her children bought her an exercise bike from Wal-Mart Stores, Inc. When Dunne received the bike, she rode it for only a moment. Later, she mounted the bike for a second time and pedaled for three or four rotations. The bike then collapsed, and Dunne fell off, sustaining numerous injuries. The bike was designed for use by people who weigh under 250 pounds (which is 99 percent of the population) and had been tested up to 440 pounds. The manufacturer did not specify any weight limit in marketing the bike, however, and there was no way that Dunne could have known of this weight limit. Assume that you are the judge in this case and answer the following questions:

(a) Was it reasonably foreseeable that a person who weighed over 450 pounds would use the exercise bike?
(b) Why is the question of foreseeability relevant to this case?
(c) Was the bike "unreasonably dangerous" because an adequate warning was not provided?
(d) Suppose that Wal-Mart argues that the risk of the bike collapsing under a weight of more than 450 pounds was "open and obvious." Would you allow Wal-Mart to avoid liability based on this defense?

12–11. A QUESTION OF ETHICS AND SOCIAL RESPONSIBILITY

On July 1, 1993, Gian Luigi Ferri entered the offices of a law firm against which he had a grudge. Using two semiautomatic assault weapons (TEC-9 and TEC-DC9) manufactured and distributed by Navegar, Inc., he killed eight persons and wounded six others before killing himself. The survivors and the families of some of those who had died sued Navegar, based in part on negligence. They claimed that Navegar had a duty not to create risks to the public beyond those inherent in the lawful use of firearms. They offered evidence that Navegar knew or should have known that the assault guns had "no legitimate sporting or self-defense purpose" and that the guns were "particularly well adapted to military-style assault on large numbers of people." They also claimed that the TEC-DC9 advertising "targets a criminal clientele," further increasing the risk of harm. A California trial court granted summary judgment in Navegar's favor. The appellate court reversed, ruling that the case should go to trial. The court stated that "the likelihood that a third person would make use of the TEC-DC9 in the kind of criminal rampage Ferri perpetrated is precisely the hazard that would support a determination that Navegar's conduct was negligent." Navegar appealed the decision to the California Supreme Court. In view of these facts, consider the following questions. [*Merrill v. Navegar, Inc.*, 26 Cal.4th 465, 28 P.3d 116, 110 Cal.Rptr.2d 370 (2001)]

(a) Do you agree with the appellate court that Navegar could be held negligent in marketing the TEC-DC9? What should the California Supreme Court decide?
(b) Should gun manufacturers ever be held liable for deaths caused by nondefective guns? Why or why not?
(c) Generally, do you believe that policy decisions regarding the liability of gun manufacturers should be made by the courts, whose job is to interpret the law, or by Congress and state legislatures, whose job is to make the law?
(d) In your opinion, have Congress and state legislatures gone far enough in regulating the use of firearms, or have they gone too far? Explain.

12–12. FOR CRITICAL ANALYSIS

What general principle underlies the common law doctrine that business owners have a duty of care toward their customers? Does the duty of care unfairly burden business owners? Why or why not?

For updated links to resources available on the Web, as well as a variety of other materials, visit this text's Web site at

http://ele.westbuslaw.com

You can find cases and articles on torts in the tort law library at the Internet Law Library's Web site. Go to

http://www.lawguru.com/ilawlib

For information on the *Restatements of the Law,* including the *Restatement (Second) of Torts* and the *Restatement (Third) of Torts: Products Liability,* go to the Web site of the American Law Institute at

http://www.ali.org

The law firm of Horvitz & Levy offers a review of recent judicial decisions in the area of product liability at

http://www.horvitzlevy.com/practoxi.html

You can find articles, cases, and other information on litigation in the area of product liability by going to the following Web site and selecting "products liability" on the pull-down menu titled "Choose a Practice Area":

http://www.law.com/jsp/pc/litlaw.jsp

LEGAL RESEARCH EXERCISES ON THE WEB

Go to **http://ele.westbuslaw.com**, the Web site that accompanies this text. Select "Interactive Study Center," and then click on "Chapter 12." There you will find the following Internet research exercises that you can perform to learn more about topics covered in this chapter.

Activity 12–1: LEGAL PERSPECTIVE—Product Liability Litigation

Activity 12–2: MANAGEMENT PERSPECTIVE—Legal and Illegal Uses of Spam

Activity 12–3: ECONOMIC PERSPECTIVE—Class-Action Lawsuits

BEFORE THE TEST

Go to **http://ele.westbuslaw.com**, the Web site that accompanies this text. Select "Interactive Quizzes." You will find at least twenty interactive questions relating to this chapter.

WESTLAW® CAMPUS

If your textbook provided for a subscription to Westlaw® Campus, or if you have otherwise purchased access to the Westlaw Campus database, you can access any of the cases presented or cited in this chapter by using your Westlaw Campus account.

CHAPTER 13

Intellectual Property and Internet Law

CONTENTS

CHAPTER OBJECTIVES

After reading this chapter, you should be able to answer the following questions:

1. What is intellectual property?
2. Why does the law protect trademarks and patents?
3. What laws protect authors' copyrights in the works they generate?
4. What are trade secrets, and what laws offer protection for this form of intellectual property?
5. What steps have been taken to protect intellectual property rights in today's digital age?

Intellectual property • Property resulting from intellectual, creative processes. Patents, trademarks, and copyrights are examples of intellectual property.

Most people think of wealth in terms of houses, land, cars, stocks, and bonds. Wealth, however, also includes **intellectual property**, which consists of the products that result from intellectual, creative processes. Although it is an abstract term for an abstract concept, intellectual property is nonetheless wholly familiar to virtually everyone. *Trademarks, service marks, copyrights,* and *patents* are all forms of intellectual property. The book you are reading is copyrighted. Undoubtedly, the personal computer you use at home is trademarked. The software you utilize, the movies you see, and the music you listen to are all forms of intellectual property. Exhibit 13–1 on the next two pages offers a comprehensive summary of these forms of intellectual property, as well as intellectual property that consists of *trade secrets*. In this chapter, we examine each of these forms in some detail.

The study of intellectual property law is important because intellectual property has taken on increasing significance, not only within the United States but globally as well. Today, the value of the world's intellectual property exceeds the value of physical property, such as machines and houses. For U.S. companies, ownership rights in intangible intellectual property are more important to their prosperity than are their tangible assets. As you will read in this chapter, a pressing issue for businesspersons today is how to protect these valuable rights in the online world.

CONSTITUTIONAL PROTECTION

The need to protect creative works was voiced by the framers of the U.S. Constitution over two hundred years ago: Article I, Section 8, of the U.S. Constitution authorized Congress "[t]o promote the Progress of Science and useful Arts, by securing for limited Times to Authors and Inventors the exclusive Right to their respective Writings and Discoveries." Laws protecting patents, trademarks, and copyrights are explicitly designed to protect and reward inventive and artistic creativity. Although intellectual property law

EXHIBIT 13–1 • FORMS OF INTELLECTUAL PROPERTY

	PATENT	COPYRIGHT	TRADEMARKS (SERVICE MARKS AND TRADE DRESS)	TRADE SECRETS
Definition	A grant from the government that gives an inventor exclusive rights to an invention.	An intangible property right granted to authors and originators of a literary work or artistic production that falls within specified categories.	Any distinctive word, name, symbol, or device (image or appearance), or combination thereof, that an entity uses to identify and distinguish its goods or services from those of others.	Any information (including formulas, patterns, programs, devices, techniques, and processes) that a business possesses and that gives the business an advantage over competitors who do not know the information or processes.
Requirements	An invention must be: 1. Novel. 2. Not obvious. 3. Useful.	Literary or artistic works must be: 1. Original. 2. Fixed in a durable medium that can be perceived, reproduced, or communicated. 3. Within a copyrightable category.	Trademarks, service marks, and trade dresses must be sufficiently distinctive (or must have acquired a secondary meaning) to enable consumers and others to distinguish the manufacturer's, seller's, or business user's products or services from those of competitors.	Information and processes that have commercial value, that are not known or easily ascertainable by the general public or others, and that are reasonably protected from disclosure.
Types or Categories	1. Utility (general). 2. Design. 3. Plant (flowers, vegetables, and so on).	1. Literary works (including computer programs). 2. Musical works. 3. Dramatic works. 4. Pantomime and choreographic works. 5. Pictorial, graphic, and sculptural works. 6. Films and audiovisual works. 7. Sound recordings.	1. Strong, distinctive marks (such as fanciful, arbitrary, or suggestive marks). 2. Marks that have acquired a secondary meaning by use. 3. Other types of marks, including certification marks and collective marks. 4. Trade dress (such as a distinctive decor, menu, or style or type of service).	1. Customer lists. 2. Research and development. 3. Plans and programs. 4. Pricing information. 5. Production techniques. 6. Marketing techniques. 7. Formulas. 8. Compilations.
How Acquired	By filing a patent application with the U.S. Patent and Trademark Office and receiving that office's approval.	Automatic (once in tangible form); to recover for infringement, the copyright must be registered with the U.S. Copyright Office.	1. At common law, ownership is created by use of mark. 2. Registration (either with the U.S. Patent and Trademark Office or with the appropriate state office) gives constructive notice of date of use.	Through the originality and development of information and processes that are unique to a business, that are unknown by others, and that would be valuable to

(Continued on next page)

EXHIBIT 13–1 • FORMS OF INTELLECTUAL PROPERTY (CONTINUED)

	PATENT	COPYRIGHT	TRADEMARKS (SERVICE MARKS AND TRADE DRESS)	TRADE SECRETS
How Acquired (continued)			3. Federal registration is permitted if the mark is currently in use *or* if the applicant intends use within six months (period can be extended to three years). 4. Federal registration can be renewed between the fifth and sixth years and, thereafter, every ten years.	competitors if they knew of the information and processes.
Rights	An inventor has the right to make, use, sell, assign, or license the invention during the duration of the patent's term. The first to invent has patent rights.	The author or originator has the exclusive right to reproduce, distribute, display, license, or transfer a copyrighted work.	The owner has the right to use the mark or trade dress and to exclude others from using it. The right of use can be licensed or sold (assigned) to another.	The owner has the right to sole and exclusive use of the trade secrets and the right to use legal means to protect against misappropriation of the trade secrets by others. The owner can license or assign a trade secret.
Duration	Twenty years from the date of application; for design patents, fourteen years.	1. For authors: the life of the author, plus 70 years. 2. For publishers: 95 years after the date of publication or 120 years after creation.	Unlimited, as long as it is in use. To continue notice by registration, the registration must be renewed by filing between the fifth and sixth years after the initial registration and every ten years thereafter.	Unlimited, as long as not revealed to others.
Civil Remedies for Infringement	Monetary damages, which include reasonable royalties and lost profits, *plus* attorneys' fees. (Treble [triple] damages are available for intentional infringement.)	Actual damages, plus profits received by the infringer; *or* statutory damages of not less than $500 and not more than $20,000 ($150,000, if infringement is willful); *plus* costs and attorneys' fees in either case.	1. Injunction prohibiting future use of mark. 2. Actual damages, plus profits received by the infringer (can be increased to three times the actual damages under the Lanham Act). 3. Impoundment and destruction of infringing articles. 4. *Plus* costs and attorneys' fees.	Monetary damages for misappropriation (the Uniform Trade Secrets Act permits punitive damages up to twice the amount of actual damages for willful and malicious misappropriation); *plus* costs and attorneys' fees.

limits the economic freedom of some individuals, it does so to protect the freedom of others to enjoy the fruits of their labors—in the form of profits.

TRADEMARKS AND RELATED PROPERTY

A **trademark** is a distinctive mark, motto, device, or implement that a manufacturer stamps, prints, or otherwise affixes to the goods it produces so that they may be identified on the market and their origin vouched for. At common law, the person who used a symbol or mark to identify a business or product was protected in the use of that trademark. Clearly, by using another's trademark, a person could lead consumers to believe that his or her goods were made by the other person. The law seeks to avoid this kind of confusion. We examine in this section various aspects of the law governing trademarks.

Trademark • A distinctive mark, motto, device, or implement that a manufacturer stamps, prints, or otherwise affixes to the goods it produces so that they may be identified on the market and their origins made known. Once a trademark is established (under the common law or through registration), the owner is entitled to its exclusive use.

In the following famous case concerning Coca-Cola, the defendants argued that the Coca-Cola trademark was entitled to no protection under the law because the term did not accurately represent the product.

CASE 13.1

Supreme Court of the United States, 1920.
254 U.S. 143,
41 S.Ct. 113,
65 L.Ed. 189.
http://www.findlaw.com/casecode/supreme.html[a]

THE COCA-COLA CO. v. THE KOKE CO. OF AMERICA

The Coca-Cola Company sought to enjoin (prevent) the Koke Company of America and other beverage companies from, among other things, using the word Koke *for their products. The Koke Company of America and other beverage companies contended that the Coca-Cola trademark was a fraudulent representation and that Coca-Cola was therefore not entitled to any help from the courts. The Koke Company and the other defendants alleged that the Coca-Cola Company, by its use of the Coca-Cola name, represented that the beverage contained cocaine (from coca leaves), which it no longer did. The trial court granted the injunction against the Koke Company, but the appellate court reversed the lower court's ruling. Coca-Cola then appealed to the United States Supreme Court.*

HOLMES, J.

Before 1900 the beginning of [Coca-Cola's] good will was more or less helped by the presence of cocaine, a drug that, like alcohol or caffeine or opium, may be described as a deadly poison or as a valuable item [pharmaceutical, depending on the speaker's purposes]. The amount seems to have been very small,[b] but it may have been enough to begin a bad habit and after the Food and Drug Act of June 30, 1906, if not earlier, long before this suit was brought, it was eliminated from the plaintiff's compound. * * *

* * * Since 1900 the sales have increased at a very great rate corresponding to a like increase in advertising. The name now characterizes a beverage to be had at almost any soda fountain. It means a single thing coming from a single source, and well known to the community. It hardly would be too much to say

a. In the "Citation Search" section, enter "254" in the left box and "143" in the right box, and click on "Get It" to access the opinion.

b. In reality, until 1903 the amount of active cocaine in each bottle of Coke was equivalent to one "line" of cocaine.

that the drink characterizes the name as much as the name the drink. In other words *Coca-Cola probably means to most persons the plaintiff's familiar product to be had everywhere rather than a compound of particular substances.* * * * [B]efore this suit was brought the plaintiff had advertised to the public that it must not expect and would not find cocaine, and had eliminated everything tending to suggest cocaine effects except the name and the picture of [coca] leaves and nuts, which probably conveyed little or nothing to most who saw it. It appears to us that it would be going too far to deny the plaintiff relief against a palpable [readily evident] fraud because possibly here and there an ignorant person might call for the drink with the hope for incipient cocaine intoxication. The plaintiff's position must be judged by the facts as they were when the suit was begun, not by the facts of a different condition and an earlier time. [Emphasis added.]

The district court's injunction was allowed to stand. The competing beverage companies were enjoined from calling their products Koke.

QUESTIONS

1. Why did Coca-Cola appeal this case to the United States Supreme Court?
2. What was the reasoning underlying the decision of the United States Supreme Court in this case?
3. If Coca-Cola had been trying to make the public believe that its product contained cocaine, would the result in this case likely have been different?

Statutory Protection of Trademarks

Statutory protection of trademarks and related property is provided at the federal level by the Lanham Act of 1946.[1] The Lanham Act was enacted in part to protect manufacturers from losing business to rival companies that used confusingly similar trademarks. The Lanham Act incorporates the common law of trademarks and provides remedies for owners of trademarks who wish to enforce their claims in federal court. Many states also have trademark statutes.

Trademark Dilution. In 1995, Congress amended the Lanham Act by passing the Federal Trademark Dilution Act,[2] which extended the protection available to trademark owners by creating a federal cause of action for trademark **dilution.** Until the passage of this amendment, federal trademark law prohibited the unauthorized use of the same mark on competing—or on noncompeting but "related"—goods or services only when such use would likely confuse consumers as to the origin of those goods and services. Trademark dilution laws, which have also been enacted by about half of the states, protect "distinctive" or "famous" trademarks (such as Jergens, McDonald's, RCA, and Macintosh) from certain unauthorized uses of the marks *regardless* of a showing of competition or a likelihood of confusion.

Dilution • With respect to trademarks, a doctrine under which distinctive or famous trademarks are protected from certain unauthorized uses of the marks regardless of a showing of competition or a likelihood of confusion.

1. 15 U.S.C. Sections 1051–1128.
2. 15 U.S.C. Section 1125.

Use of a Similar Mark May Constitute Trademark Dilution. In one of the first cases to be decided under the 1995 act's provisions, a federal court held that a famous mark may be diluted not only by the use of an *identical* mark but also by the use of a *similar* mark. The lawsuit was brought by Ringling Bros.—Barnum & Bailey, Combined Shows, Inc., against the state of Utah. Ringling Bros. claimed that Utah's use of the slogan "The Greatest Snow on Earth"—to attract visitors to the state's recreational and scenic resorts—diluted the distinctiveness of the circus's famous trademark, "The Greatest Show on Earth." Utah moved to dismiss the suit, arguing that the 1995 provisions protect owners of famous trademarks only against the unauthorized use of identical marks. The court disagreed and refused to grant Utah's motion to dismiss the case.[3]

Trademark Registration

Trademarks may be registered with the state or with the federal government. To register for protection under federal trademark law, a person must file an application with the U.S. Patent and Trademark Office in Washington, D.C. Under current law, a mark can be registered (1) if it is currently in commerce or (2) if the applicant intends to put it into commerce within six months.

In special circumstances, the six-month period can be extended by thirty months, giving the applicant a total of three years from the date of notice of trademark approval to make use of the mark and file the required use statement. Registration is postponed until the mark is actually used. Nonetheless, during this waiting period, any applicant can legally protect his or her trademark against a third party who previously has neither used the mark nor filed an application for it. Registration is renewable between the fifth and sixth years after the initial registration and every ten years thereafter (every twenty years for those trademarks registered before 1990).

Trademark Infringement

Registration of a trademark with the U.S. Patent and Trademark Office gives notice on a nationwide basis that the trademark belongs exclusively to the registrant. The registrant is also allowed to use the symbol ® to indicate that the mark has been registered. Whenever that trademark is copied to a substantial degree or used in its entirety by another, intentionally or unintentionally, the trademark has been *infringed* (used without authorization). When a trademark has been infringed, the owner of the mark has a cause of action against the infringer. A person need not have registered a trademark in order to sue for trademark infringement, but registration does furnish proof of the date of inception of the trademark's use.

A central objective of the Lanham Act is to reduce the likelihood that consumers will be confused by similar marks. For that reason, only those trademarks that are deemed sufficiently distinctive from all competing trademarks will be protected.

---

3. *Ringling Bros.—Barnum & Bailey, Combined Shows, Inc. v. Utah Division of Travel Development*, 935 F.Supp. 763 (E.D.Va. 1996).

Distinctiveness of Mark

A trademark must be sufficiently distinct to enable consumers to identify the manufacturer of the goods easily and to distinguish between those goods and competing products.

Strong Marks. Fanciful, arbitrary, or suggestive trademarks are generally considered to be the most distinctive (strongest) trademarks. This is because these types of marks are normally taken from outside the context of the particular product and thus provide the best means of distinguishing one product from another.

Fanciful trademarks include invented words, such as "Xerox" for one manufacturer's copiers and "Kodak" for another company's photographic products. Arbitrary trademarks include actual words used with products that have no literal connection to the words, such as "English Leather" used as a name for an after-shave lotion (and not for leather processed in England). Suggestive trademarks are those that suggest something about a product without describing the product directly. For example, the trademark "Dairy Queen" suggests an association between the products and milk, but it does not directly describe ice cream.

Secondary Meaning. Descriptive terms, geographic terms, and personal names are not inherently distinctive and do not receive protection under the law until they acquire a secondary meaning. A secondary meaning may arise when customers begin to associate a specific term or phrase (such as "London Fog") with specific trademarked items (coats with London Fog labels). Whether a secondary meaning becomes attached to a term or name usually depends on how extensively the product is advertised, the market for the product, the number of sales, and other factors. Once a secondary meaning is attached to a term or name, a trademark is considered distinctive and is protected. The United States Supreme Court has held that even a shade of color can qualify for trademark protection, once customers associate the color with the product.[4]

Generic Terms. Generic terms, such as *bicycle* and *computer,* receive no protection, even if they acquire secondary meanings. A particularly thorny problem arises when a trademark acquires generic use. For example, *aspirin* and *thermos* were originally the names of trademarked products, but today the words are used generically. Other examples are *escalator, trampoline, raisin bran, dry ice, lanolin, linoleum, nylon,* and *corn flakes.*

As noted, a generic term will not be protected under trademark law even if the term has acquired a secondary meaning. In one case, for example, America Online, Inc. (AOL), sued AT&T Corporation, claiming that AT&T's use of "You Have Mail" on its WorldNet Service infringed AOL's trademark rights in the same phrase. The court ruled, however, that because each of the three words in the phrase was a generic term, the phrase as a whole was generic. Although the phrase had become widely associated with AOL's

4. *Qualitex Co. v. Jacobson Products Co.,* 514 U.S. 159, 115 S.Ct. 1300, 131 L.Ed.2d 248 (1995).

e-mail notification service, and thus may have acquired a secondary meaning, this issue was of no significance in the case. The court stated that it would not consider whether the mark had acquired any secondary meaning because "generic marks with secondary meaning are still not entitled to protection."[5]

Trade Dress

The term **trade dress** refers to the image and overall appearance of a product—for example, the distinctive decor, menu, layout, and style of service of a particular restaurant. Basically, trade dress is subject to the same protection as trademarks. In cases involving trade dress infringement, as in trademark infringement cases, a major consideration is whether consumers are likely to be confused by the allegedly infringing use.

Trade dress • The image and overall appearance of a product—for example, the distinctive decor, menu, layout, and style of service of a particular restaurant. Basically, trade dress is subject to the same protection as trademarks.

Service, Certification, and Collective Marks

A **service mark** is similar to a trademark but is used to distinguish the services of one person or company from those of another. For example, each airline has a particular mark or symbol associated with its name. Titles and character names used in radio and television are frequently registered as service marks.

Service mark • A mark used in the sale or the advertising of services to distinguish the services of one person from the services of others.

Other marks protected by law include certification marks and collective marks. A **certification mark** is used by one or more persons, other than the owner, to certify the region, materials, mode of manufacture, quality, or accuracy of the owner's goods or services. When used by members of a cooperative, association, or other organization, it is referred to as a **collective mark.** Examples of certification marks are the phrases "Good Housekeeping Seal of Approval" and "UL Tested." Collective marks appear at the ends of motion picture credits to indicate the various associations and organizations that participated in the making of the films. The union marks found on the tags of certain products are also collective marks.

Certification mark • A mark used by one or more persons, other than the owner, to certify the region, materials, mode of manufacture, quality, or accuracy of the owner's goods or services.

Collective mark • A mark used by members of a cooperative, association, or other organization to certify the region, materials, mode of manufacture, quality, or accuracy of the specific goods or services.

Trade Names

Trademarks apply to *products*. The term **trade name** is used to indicate part or all of a business's name, whether the business is a sole proprietorship, a partnership, or a corporation. Generally, a trade name is directly related to a business and its goodwill. A trade name may be protected as a trademark if the trade name is the same as the name of the company's trademarked product—for example, Coca-Cola. Unless also used as a trademark or service mark, a trade name cannot be registered with the federal government. Trade names are protected under the common law, however. As with trademarks, words must be unusual or fancifully used if they are to be protected as trade names. The word *Safeway*, for example, was held by the courts to be sufficiently fanciful to obtain protection as a trade name for a supermarket chain.[6]

Trade name • A term that is used to indicate part or all of a business's name and that is directly related to the business's reputation and goodwill. Trade names are protected under the common law (and under trademark law, if the name is the same as the firm's trademarked property).

---

5. *America Online, Inc. v. AT&T Corp.,* 243 F.3d 812 (4th Cir. 2001).
6. *Safeway Stores v. Suburban Foods,* 130 F.Supp. 249 (E.D.Va. 1955).

CYBER MARKS

Cyber mark • A trademark in cyberspace.

In cyberspace, trademarks are sometimes referred to as **cyber marks.** We turn now to a discussion of issues in cyberspace relating to trademarks and how new laws and the courts are addressing these issues. One concern relates to the rights of a trademark's owner to use the mark as part of a domain name (Internet address). Other issues have to do with domain names and cybersquatting, meta tags, and trademark dilution on the Web. The use of licensing as a way to avoid liability for infringing on another's intellectual property rights in cyberspace will be discussed later in this chapter.

Domain Names

In the real world, one business can often use the same name as another without causing any conflict, particularly if the businesses are small, their goods or services are different, and the geographic areas in which they do business are distinctly separate. In the online world, however, there is only one geographic area of business—cyberspace. Thus, disputes between parties over which one has the right to use a particular domain name have become common.

Domain name • The series of letters and symbols used to identify site operators on the Internet; Internet "addresses."

A **domain name** is the core part of an Internet address—for example, "westlaw.com." It includes at least two parts. The top level domain (TLD) is the part of the name to the right of the period, such as *com* or *gov*. The second level (the part of the name to the left of the period) is chosen by the business entity or individual registering the domain name.

Conflicts over Domain Names. Conflicts over rights to domain names emerged during the 1990s as e-commerce expanded on a worldwide scale. As e-commerce expanded, the *.com* TLD came to be widely used by businesses on the Web. Competition among firms with identical or similar names and products for the second level domains preceding the *.com* TLD led, understandably, to numerous disputes over domain name rights. By using the same, or a similar, domain name, parties have attempted to profit from the goodwill of a competitor, to sell pornography, to offer for sale another party's domain name, and to otherwise infringe on others' trademarks.

To read the text of ICANN's Uniform Domain Name Dispute Resolution Policy, go to the "Statutes" page of our Web site at

http://ele.westbuslaw.com

Dispute Resolution through Online Arbitration. The federal government set up the Internet Corporation for Assigned Names and Numbers (ICANN), a nonprofit corporation, to oversee the distribution of domain names. ICANN has also played a leading role in facilitating the settlement of domain name disputes worldwide. Since January 2000, ICANN has been operating an online arbitration system to resolve domain name disputes. Now, if trademark infringement involves a domain name, a party may submit a complaint to an ICANN–approved dispute-resolution provider instead of—or in addition to—filing a lawsuit. By 2003, ICANN–approved online arbitration providers were handling over one thousand disputes annually.

Cybersquatting • An act that occurs when a person registers a domain name that is the same as, or confusingly similar to, the trademark of another and offers to sell the domain name to the trademark owner.

Anticybersquatting Legislation

Cybersquatting occurs when a person registers a domain name that is the same as, or confusingly similar to, the trademark of another and then offers to sell the domain name back to the trademark owner. During the 1990s, cybersquatting became a contentious subject and led to much litigation. Often at issue in these cases was whether cybersquatting constituted a commercial use of the mark so as to violate federal trademark law. In 1999, Congress addressed this problem by passing the Anticybersquatting Consumer Protection Act (ACPA), which amended the Lanham Act—the federal law protecting trademarks discussed earlier in this chapter.

Provisions of the ACPA. The ACPA makes it illegal for a person to "register, traffic in, or use" a domain name (1) if the name is identical or confusingly similar to the trademark of another and (2) if the one registering, trafficking in, or using the domain name has a "bad faith intent" to profit from that trademark. The act lists several factors that courts can consider in deciding whether bad faith exists, including the trademark rights of the other person, whether there is an intent to divert consumers in a way that could harm the goodwill represented by the trademark, whether there is an offer to transfer or sell the domain name to the trademark owner, and whether there is an intent to use the domain name to offer goods and services.

Applicability of the ACPA and Sanctions under the Act. The ACPA applies to all domain name registrations of trademarks, even domain names registered before the passage of the act. Successful plaintiffs in suits brought under the act can collect actual damages and profits, or they can elect to receive statutory damages ranging from $1,000 to $100,000.

The question in the following case—which was an appeal from the first decision on the issue—was whether the ACPA applied to reregistrations of domain names containing family names that were initially registered before the effective date of the act.

SCHMIDHEINY v. WEBER

CASE 13.2

United States Court of Appeals, Third Circuit, 2003.
319 F.3d 581.

In February 1999, Steven Weber registered the domain name schmidheiny.com. *The ACPA took effect nine months later, on November 29. Weber reregistered the name on behalf of Famology.com, Inc., in June 2000, with a different registrar. Weber is the president and treasurer of Famology.com and the administrative and technical contact person for the schmidheiny.com domain. The following November, Weber sent an e-mail to Stephan Schmidheiny, offering to sell him the name. With a net worth of $3.1 billion, Schmidheiny is among the wealthiest individuals in the world. Schmidheiny filed a suit in a federal district court against Weber and Famology.com, alleging violations of the ACPA. The court granted a summary judgment to the defendants. Schmidheiny appealed to the U.S. Court of Appeals for the Third Circuit.*

NYGAARD, J.

Domain name registrars are organizations that keep track of Internet domain names and ensure that only one party controls a specific domain name during any given period. To register a domain name, the party interested in the exclusive use of the domain name, the registrant, must contact a registrar, and enter into a contractual agreement with the registrar. In exchange for the right to use the domain name for a fixed period of time, the registrant pays a certain sum of money and agrees to certain other conditions.

According to the Anti-cybersquatting Act, "[a]ny person who registers a domain name that consists of the name of another living person, or a name substantially and confusingly similar thereto, without that person's consent, with the specific intent to profit from such name by selling the domain name for financial gain to that person or any third party, shall be liable in a civil action by such person." The purpose of the Anti-cybersquatting Act is to curtail one form of "cybersquatting"—the act of registering someone else's name as a domain name for the purpose of demanding remuneration from the person in exchange for the domain name.

The Anti-cybersquatting Act provision at issue applies to "[a]ny person who registers a domain name that consists of the name of another living person * * * with the specific intent to profit from such name by selling the domain name for financial gain to that person or any third party." The provision does not define what a "person who registers" must do to fall within the scope of the statute, and the legislative history does not provide an explanation.

The District Court decided that the registration of *schmidheiny.com* was not covered by the Anti-cybersquatting Act because the domain name was *first* registered several months before the date when the statute became effective, and "the statute references only 'registrations,' not 're-registrations.'" The District Court stressed that "Congress made a clear legislative choice that [the Anti-cybersquatting Act] is not to be applied retroactively," and focused on the "creation date" of *schmidheiny.com*—the date when the domain name was initially created. "[T]o consider a re-registration to be a registration," the District Court stated, "would enfog the bright line [clear-cut] date established by the Act * * * ." According to the District Court, "the plain meaning of the word 'registration' as used by Congress imparts to us no other meaning but the initial registration of the domain name."

We disagree. *We do not consider the "creation date" of a domain name to control whether a registration is subject to the Anti-cybersquatting Act, and we believe that the plain meaning of the word "registration" is not limited to "creation registration."* [Emphasis added.]

The words "initial" and "creation" appear nowhere in [the ACPA], and Congress did not add an exception for "non-creation registrations" * * * . The District Court's rationale that "if Congress chose to treat re-registrations as registrations, it could have used words appropriate to impart that definition," is not a sufficient reason for courts to infer the word "initial." Instead, we conclude that the language of the statute does not limit the word "registration" to the narrow concept of "creation registration."

Here, in March 2000, the named registrant for *schmidheiny.com* was "Weber Net" and the domain name registrar was Network Solutions, Inc. In June 2000, a new registrant, Famology.com, contractually bound itself in a new registration agreement with a new registrar, Internet Names Worldwide, to secure the *schmidheiny.com* domain name for a new one-year period. *We hold that the word "registration" includes a new contract at a different registrar and to a different registrant.* In this case, with respect to Famology.com—that occurs after the effective date of the Anti-cybersquatting Act. [Emphasis added.]

To conclude otherwise would permit the domain names of living persons to be sold and purchased without the living persons' consent, *ad infinitum,* so long as the name was first registered before the effective date of the Act. We do not believe that this is the correct construction of the Anti-cybersquatting Act. We are therefore satisfied that Famology.com, Inc. engaged in a "registration" that is covered by the Anti-cybersquatting Act.

The U.S. Court of Appeals for the Third Circuit concluded that a domain name's "re-registration" qualifies as a "registration" for purposes of the ACPA. The court reversed the judgment of the lower court and remanded the case for further proceedings consistent with this opinion.

QUESTIONS

1. Who were the defendants in this case, and what did the lower court rule with respect to those parties?
2. Did the U.S. Court of Appeals for the Third Circuit agree or disagree with the lower court, and why?
3. Should all legislation be presumed to apply retroactively?

Meta Tags

Search engines compile their results by looking through a Web site's key-words field. **Meta tags,** or key words, may be inserted into this field to increase the frequency of a site's inclusion in search engine results, even though the site has nothing to do with the inserted words. Using this same technique, one site may appropriate the key words of other sites with more frequent hits so that the appropriating site will be included in the same search engine results as the more popular sites. Using another's trademark in a meta tag without the owner's permission, however, constitutes trademark infringement. One use of meta tags was at issue in the following case.

Meta tags • Words inserted into a Web site's key-words field to increase the site's inclusion in search engine results.

CASE 13.3

United States Court of Appeals, Ninth Circuit, 2002.
279 F.3d 796.

PLAYBOY ENTERPRISES, INC. v. WELLES

Playboy Enterprises, Inc. (PEI), maintains Web sites to promote Playboy *magazine and PEI models. PEI's trademarks include the terms* Playboy, Playmate, *and* Playmate of the Year. *PEI encourages its models to identify themselves and to use their titles for their self-promotion and the promotion of its magazines and other goods and services. Terri Welles is a self-employed model and spokesperson, who was featured as the "Playmate of the Year" in June 1981. Welles maintains a Web site titled "Terri Welles—Playmate of the Year 1981." As meta tags, Welles's site uses the terms* Playboy *and* Playmate, *among others. PEI asked Welles to stop using these terms, but she refused. PEI filed a suit in a federal district court against Welles, asking the court to order her to, among other things, stop using those terms as meta tags. On this issue, the court granted a summary judgment in Welles's favor. PEI appealed to the U.S. Court of Appeals for the Ninth Circuit.*

NELSON, J.

[The] test for nominative use [of a trademark is]:[a]

> First, the product or service in question must be one not readily identifiable without use of the trademark; second, only so much of the mark or marks may be used as is reasonably necessary to identify the product or service; and third, the user must do nothing that would, in conjunction with the mark, suggest sponsorship or endorsement by the trademark holder. * * *

* * * *

A large portion of Welles' website discusses her association with Playboy over the years. Thus, the trademarked terms accurately describe the contents of Welles' website, in addition to describing Welles. Forcing Welles and others to use absurd turns of phrase in their metatags, such as those necessary to identify Welles, would be particularly damaging in the Internet search context. *Searchers would have a much more difficult time locating relevant websites if they could do so only by correctly guessing the long phrases necessary to substitute for trademarks.* We can hardly expect someone searching for Welles' site to imagine [a] phrase * * * to describe Welles without referring to Playboy—"the nude model selected by Mr. Hefner's organization * * * ." Yet if someone could not remember her name, that is what they would have to do. Similarly, someone searching for critiques of Playboy on the Internet would have a difficult time if Internet sites could not list the object of their critique in their metatags. [Emphasis added.]

There is simply no descriptive substitute for the trademarks used in Welles' metatags. Precluding their use would have the unwanted effect of hindering the free flow of information on the Internet, something which is certainly not a goal of trademark law. Accordingly, the use of trademarked terms in the metatags meets the first part of the test for nominative use.

We conclude that the metatags satisfy the second and third elements of the test as well. The metatags use only so much of the marks as reasonably necessary and nothing is done in conjunction with them to suggest sponsorship or endorsement by the trademark holder. We note that our decision might differ if the metatags listed the trademarked term so repeatedly that Welles' site would regularly appear above PEI's in searches for one of the trademarked terms.

The U.S. Court of Appeals for the Ninth Circuit concluded that Welles's use of PEI's trademarks as meta tags was a permissible, nominative use. The use implied no current sponsorship or endorsement by PEI. Instead, the meta tags identified Welles as a past PEI "Playmate of the Year."

QUESTIONS

1. What was the plaintiff's principal complaint against the defendant in this case?
2. On what basis did the U.S. Court of Appeals for the Ninth Circuit justify its ruling in this case?
3. Why would PEI encourage its models to use its marks outside cyberspace but attempt to block such uses within cyberspace?

a. A *nominative use* of a trademark is one that does not imply sponsorship or endorsement of a product because the product's mark is used only to describe the thing, rather than to identify its source. See *New Kids on the Block v. News America Publishing, Inc.*, 971 F.2d 302 (9th Cir. 1992).

Dilution in the Online World

As discussed earlier, trademark *dilution* occurs when a trademark is used, without authorization, in a way that diminishes the distinctive quality of the mark. Unlike trademark infringement, a dilution cause of action does not require proof that consumers are likely to be confused by a connection between the unauthorized use and the mark. For this reason, the products involved do not have to be similar.

In the first case alleging dilution on the Web, a court precluded the use of "candyland.com" as the URL for an adult site. The suit was brought by the maker of the "Candyland" children's game and owner of the "Candyland" mark.[7] In another case, a court issued an injunction on the ground that spamming under another's logo is trademark dilution. In that case, Hotmail Corporation provided e-mail services and worked to dissociate itself from spam. Van$ Money Pie, Inc., and others spammed thousands of e-mail customers, using the free e-mail Hotmail as a return address. The court ordered the defendants to stop.[8]

PATENTS

A **patent** is a grant from the government that gives an inventor the exclusive right to make, use, and sell an invention for a period of twenty years from the date of filing the application for a patent. Patents for designs, as opposed to inventions, are given for a fourteen-year period. For either a regular patent or a design patent, the applicant must demonstrate to the satisfaction of the U.S. Patent and Trademark Office that the invention, discovery, process, or design is genuine, novel, useful, and not obvious in light of current technology. A patent holder gives notice to all that an article or design is patented by placing on it the word *Patent* or *Pat.* plus the patent number. In contrast to patent law in other countries, in the United States patent protection is given to the first person to invent a product or process, even though someone else may have been the first to file for a patent on that product or process.

Patent • A government grant that gives an inventor the exclusive right or privilege to make, use, or sell his or her invention for a limited time period. The word *patent* usually refers to some invention and designates either the instrument by which patent rights are evidenced or the patent itself.

A significant development relating to patents is the availability online of the world's patent databases. The Web site of the U.S. Patent and Trademark Office (see the *Law on the Web* section at the end of this chapter for its URL) provides searchable databases covering U.S. patents granted since 1976. The Web site of the European Patent Office maintains databases covering all patent documents in sixty-five nations and the legal status of patents in twenty-two of those countries.

Patent Infringement

If a firm makes, uses, or sells another's patented design, product, or process without the patent owner's permission, the tort of patent infringement occurs. Patent infringement may arise even though the patent owner has not put the patented product in commerce. Patent infringement may also occur even though not all features or parts of an invention are copied. (With respect to a patented process, however, all steps or their equivalents must be copied for infringement to occur.)

7. *Hasbro, Inc. v. Internet Entertainment Group, Ltd.*, 1996 WL 84853 (W.D.Wash. 1996).
8. *Hotmail Corp. v. Van$ Money Pie, Inc.*, 1998 WL 388389 (N.D.Cal. 1998).

Often, litigation for patent infringement is so costly that the patent holder will instead offer to sell to the infringer a license to use the patented design, product, or process (licensing will be discussed later in this chapter). Indeed, in many cases, the costs of detection, prosecution, and monitoring are so high that patents have little value to their owners because the owners cannot afford to protect them.

Patents for Software

At one time, it was difficult for developers and manufacturers of software to obtain patent protection because many software products simply automate procedures that can be performed manually. In other words, the computer programs do not meet the "novel" and "not obvious" requirements previously mentioned. Also, the basis for software is often a mathematical equation or formula, which is not patentable. In 1981, however, the United States Supreme Court held that it is possible to obtain a patent for a process that incorporates a computer program—providing, of course, that the process itself is patentable.[9] Subsequently, many patents have been issued for software-related inventions.

Patents for Business Processes

In a landmark 1998 case, *State Street Bank & Trust Co. v. Signature Financial Group, Inc.,*[10] the U.S. Court of Appeals for the Federal Circuit ruled that only three categories of subject matter will always remain *un*patentable: (1) the laws of nature, (2) natural phenomena, and (3) abstract ideas.

After this decision, numerous technology firms applied for business process patents. Walker Digital applied for a business process patent for its "Dutch auction" system, which allowed consumers to make offers for airline tickets on the Internet and led to the creation of Priceline.com. About.com obtained a patent for its "Elaborative Internet Data Mining System," which creates and pulls together the Web content of a large range of topics onto a single Web site. Amazon.com obtained a business process patent for its "one-click" ordering system, a method of processing credit-card orders securely without asking for the customer's card number or other personal information, such as the customer's name and address, more than once. Indeed, since the *State Street* decision, the number of Internet-related patents issued by the U.S. Patent and Trademark Office has increased by more than 800 percent.

ETHICAL ISSUE

Will business process patents have a chilling effect on e-commerce? Business process patents have raised some troublesome legal and ethical questions with respect to Internet commerce. Some argue that venture capitalists are more inclined to invest in Internet and high-tech companies if they believe that such start-ups can obtain patents for their business processes. Others believe that business process patents will have a chilling effect on Internet enterprises. This group points out that Internet firms have obtained business process patents for processes that are neither new nor nonobvious. For example,

9. *Diamond v. Diehr,* 450 U.S. 175, 101 S.Ct. 1048, 67 L.Ed.2d 155 (1981).
10. 149 F.3d 1368 (Fed. Cir. 1998).

the Dutch auction system, which Walker Digital patented for use by Priceline.com, is simply the electronic version of a procedure that has been around for centuries. Some argue that the more patents are granted for some of the building blocks of e-commerce, the more those involved in e-commerce will have to pay licensing fees to use those building blocks. Consider an analogy: had a business process patent been obtained for the granting of frequent flyer miles, then all airlines would have to pay a license fee for such programs.

COPYRIGHTS

A **copyright** is an intangible property right granted by federal statute to the author or originator of a literary or artistic production of a specified type. Currently, copyrights are governed by the Copyright Act of 1976,[11] as amended. Works created after January 1, 1978, are automatically given statutory copyright protection for the life of the author plus 70 years. For copyrights owned by publishing houses, the copyright expires 95 years from the date of publication or 120 years from the date of creation, whichever is first. For works by more than one author, the copyright expires 70 years after the death of the last surviving author.

Copyright • The exclusive right of authors to publish, print, or sell an intellectual production for a statutory period of time. A copyright differs from a patent or a trademark in that it applies exclusively to works of art, literature, and other works of authorship, including computer programs.

Copyrights can be registered with the U.S. Copyright Office in Washington, D.C. A copyright owner no longer needs to place the symbol © or the term *Copr.* or *Copyright* on the work, however, to have the work protected against infringement. Chances are that if somebody created it, somebody owns it.

What Is Protected Expression?

Works that are copyrightable include books, records, films, artworks, architectural plans, menus, music videos, product packaging, and computer software. To obtain protection under the Copyright Act, a work must be original and fall into one of the following categories: (1) literary works; (2) musical works; (3) dramatic works; (4) pantomimes and choreographic works; (5) pictorial, graphic, and sculptural works; (6) films and other audiovisual works; and (7) sound recordings. To be protected, a work must be "fixed in a durable medium" from which it can be perceived, reproduced, or communicated. Protection is automatic. Registration is not required.

Section 102 Exclusions. Section 102 of the Copyright Act specifically excludes copyright protection for any "idea, procedure, process, system, method of operation, concept, principle, or discovery, regardless of the form in which it is described, explained, illustrated, or embodied." Note that it is not possible to copyright an *idea*. The underlying ideas embodied in a work may be freely used by others. What *is* copyrightable is the particular way in which an idea is expressed. Whenever an idea and an expression are inseparable, the expression cannot be copyrighted. Generally, anything that is not an original expression will not qualify for copyright protection. Facts widely known to the public are not copyrightable. Page numbers are not copyrightable because they follow a sequence known to everyone. Mathematical calculations are not copyrightable.

11. 17 U.S.C. Sections 101 *et seq.*

Compilations of Facts. *Compilations* of facts are copyrightable. Section 103 of the Copyright Act defines a compilation as "a work formed by the collection and assembling of preexisting materials or data that are selected, coordinated, or arranged in such a way that the resulting work as a whole constitutes an original work of authorship." The key requirement in the copyrightability of a compilation is originality. Therefore, the White Pages of a telephone directory do not qualify for copyright protection when the information that makes up the directory (names, addresses, and telephone numbers) is not selected, coordinated, or arranged in an original way.[12] In one case, even the Yellow Pages of a telephone directory did not qualify for copyright protection.[13]

Copyright Infringement

Whenever the form or expression of an idea is copied, an infringement of copyright has occurred. The reproduction does not have to be exactly the same as the original, nor does it have to reproduce the original in its entirety. If a substantial part of the original is reproduced, there is copyright infringement.

Damages for Copyright Infringement. Those who infringe copyrights may be liable for damages or criminal penalties. These range from actual damages or statutory damages, imposed at the court's discretion, to criminal proceedings for willful violations. Actual damages are based on the harm caused to the copyright holder by the infringement, while statutory damages, not to exceed $150,000, are provided for under the Copyright Act. Criminal proceedings may result in fines and/or imprisonment.

The "Fair Use" Exception. An exception to liability for copyright infringement is made under the "fair use" doctrine. In certain circumstances, a person or organization can reproduce copyrighted material without paying royalties (fees paid to the copyright holder for the privilege of reproducing the copyrighted material). Section 107 of the Copyright Act provides as follows:

> [T]he fair use of a copyrighted work, including such use by reproduction in copies or phonorecords or by any other means specified by [Section 106 of the Copyright Act], for purposes such as criticism, comment, news reporting, teaching (including multiple copies for classroom use), scholarship, or research, is not an infringement of copyright. In determining whether the use made of a work in any particular case is a fair use the factors to be considered shall include—
>
> (1) the purpose and character of the use, including whether such use is of a commercial nature or is for nonprofit educational purposes;
> (2) the nature of the copyrighted work;
> (3) the amount and substantiality of the portion used in relation to the copyrighted work as a whole; and
> (4) the effect of the use upon the potential market for or value of the copyrighted work.

---

12. *Feist Publications, Inc. v. Rural Telephone Service Co.*, 499 U.S. 340, 111 S.Ct. 1282, 113 L.Ed.2d 358 (1991).

13. *Bellsouth Advertising & Publishing Corp. v. Donnelley Information Publishing, Inc.*, 999 F.2d 1436 (11th Cir. 1993).

Because these guidelines are very broad, the courts determine whether a particular use is fair on a case-by-case basis. Thus, anyone reproducing copyrighted material may still be committing a violation. In determining whether a use is fair, courts have often considered the fourth factor to be the most important.

Copyright Protection for Software

In 1980, Congress passed the Computer Software Copyright Act, which amended the Copyright Act of 1976 to include computer programs in the list of creative works protected by federal copyright law. The 1980 statute, which classifies computer programs as "literary works," defines a computer program as a "set of statements or instructions to be used directly or indirectly in a computer in order to bring about a certain result."

The unique nature of computer programs, however, has created many problems for the courts in applying and interpreting the 1980 act. Generally, though, the courts have held that copyright protection extends not only to those parts of a computer program that can be read by humans, such as the "high-level" language of a source code, but also to the binary-language object code, which is readable only by the computer.[14] Additionally, such elements as the overall structure, sequence, and organization of a program have been deemed copyrightable.[15] The courts have disagreed on the issue of whether the "look and feel"—the general appearance, command structure, video images, menus, windows, and other screen displays—of computer programs should also be protected by copyright. The courts have tended, however, not to extend copyright protection to look-and-feel aspects of computer programs.

Copyrights in Digital Information

Copyright law is probably the most significant form of intellectual property protection on the Internet. This is because much of the material on the Internet consists of works of authorship (including multimedia presentations, software, and database information), which are the traditional focus of copyright law. Copyright law is also important because the nature of the Internet requires that data be "copied" to be transferred online. Copies are a significant part of the traditional controversies arising in this area of the law.

The Copyright Act of 1976

When Congress drafted the principal U.S. law governing copyrights, the Copyright Act of 1976, cyberspace did not exist for most of us. At that time, the rights of copyright owners were threatened not by computer technology but by unauthorized tangible copies of works and the sale of rights to movies, television, and other media.

Some of the issues that were unimagined when the Copyright Act was drafted have posed thorny questions for the courts. For example, to sell a copy of a work, permission of the copyright holder is necessary. Because of the nature of cyberspace, however, one of the early controversies involved

14. See *Stern Electronics, Inc. v. Kaufman*, 669 F.2d 852 (2d Cir. 1982); and *Apple Computer, Inc. v. Franklin Computer Corp.*, 714 F.2d 1240 (3d Cir. 1983).

15. *Whelan Associates, Inc. v. Jaslow Dental Laboratory, Inc.*, 797 F.2d 1222 (3d Cir. 1986).

determining at what point an intangible, electronic "copy" of a work has been made. The courts have held that loading a file or program into a computer's random access memory, or RAM, constitutes the making of a "copy" for purposes of copyright law.[16] RAM is a portion of a computer's memory into which a file, for example, is loaded so that it can be accessed (read or written over). Thus, a copyright is infringed when a party downloads software into RAM without owning the software or otherwise having a right to download it.[17]

Other rights, including those relating to the revision of "collective works" such as magazines, were acknowledged thirty years ago but were considered to have only limited economic value. Today, technology has made some of those rights vastly more significant. How does the old law apply to these rights? That was one of the questions in the following case.

16. *MAI Systems Corp. v. Peak Computer, Inc.*, 991 F.2d 511 (9th Cir. 1993).

17. *DSC Communications Corp. v. Pulse Communications, Inc.*, 170 F.3d 1354 (Fed. Cir. 1999).

CASE 13.4

Supreme Court of the United States, 2001. 533 U.S. 483, 121 S.Ct. 2381, 150 L.Ed.2d 500.
http://www.findlaw.com/casecode/supreme.html[a]

NEW YORK TIMES CO. v. TASINI

Magazines and newspapers, including the New York Times, *buy and publish articles written by freelance writers. Besides circulating hard copies of their periodicals, these publishers sell the contents to e-publishers for inclusion in online, and other electronic, databases. Jonathan Tasini and other freelance writers filed a suit in a federal district court against the New York Times Company and other publishers, including the e-publishers, contending that the e-publication of the articles violated the Copyright Act. The publishers claimed, among other things, that the Copyright Act gave them a right to produce "revisions" of their publications. The writers argued that the Copyright Act did not cover electronic "revisions." The court granted a summary judgment in the publishers' favor, which was reversed on the writers' appeal to the U.S. Court of Appeals for the Second Circuit. The publishers appealed to the United States Supreme Court.*

GINSBURG, J.

[Under the Copyright Act, a] newspaper or magazine publisher is * * * privileged to reproduce or distribute an article contributed by a freelance author, absent a contract otherwise providing, only "as part of" any (or all) of three categories of collective works: (a) "that collective work" to which the author contributed her work, (b) "any revision of that collective work," or (c) "any later collective work in the same series." *In accord with Congress' prescription, a publishing company could reprint a contribution from one issue in a later issue of its magazine, and could reprint an article from a 1980 edition of an encyclopedia in a 1990 revision of it; the publisher could not revise the contribution itself or include it in a new anthology or an entirely different magazine or other collective work.* [Emphasis added.]

* * * *

In determining whether the Articles have been reproduced and distributed "as part of" a "revision" of the collective works in issue, we focus on the Articles as presented to, and perceptible by, the user of the Databases. In this case, the three Databases [GPO, NEXIS, and NYTO] present articles to users

a. In the "Citation Search" section, enter "533" in the left box and "483" in the right box, and click on "Get It" to access the opinion.

clear of the context provided either by the original periodical editions or by any revision of those editions. The Databases first prompt users to search the universe of their contents: thousands or millions of files containing individual articles from thousands of collective works (*i.e.,* editions), either in one series (the *Times,* in NYTO) or in scores of series (the sundry titles in NEXIS and GPO). When the user conducts a search, each article appears as a separate item within the search result. In NEXIS and NYTO, an article appears to a user without the graphics, formatting, or other articles with which the article was initially published. In GPO, the article appears with the other materials published on the same page or pages, but without any material published on other pages of the original periodical. In either circumstance, we cannot see how the Database perceptibly reproduces and distributes the article "as part of" either the original edition or a "revision" of that edition.

One might view the articles as parts of a new compendium—namely, the entirety of works in the Database. In that compendium, each edition of each periodical represents only a minuscule fraction of the ever-expanding Database. The Database no more constitutes a "revision" of each constituent edition than a 400-page novel quoting a sonnet in passing would represent a "revision" of that poem.

The United States Supreme Court held that, to put the contents of periodicals into e-databases and onto CD-ROMs, publishers must obtain the permission of the writers whose contributions are included in the periodicals. The Court affirmed the appellate court's judgment but remanded the case for a determination as to how the writers should be compensated.

QUESTIONS

1. What was at the center of the dispute between the parties involved in this case?
2. According to the United States Supreme Court, do publishers who want to put the contents of periodicals into e-databases and onto CD-ROMs need to obtain the permission of the writers whose contributions are included in the periodicals?
3. When technology creates a situation in which rights such as those involved in this case become more valuable, should the law be changed to redistribute the economic benefit of those rights?

Further Developments in Copyright Law

In the last several years, Congress has enacted legislation designed specifically to protect copyright holders in a digital age. Particularly significant are the No Electronic Theft Act of 1997 and the Digital Millennium Copyright Act of 1998.

The No Electronic Theft Act. Prior to 1997, criminal penalties could be imposed under copyright law only if unauthorized copies were exchanged for financial gain. Yet much piracy of copyrighted materials was "altruistic" in nature; that is, unauthorized copies were made and distributed not for financial gain but simply for reasons of generosity—to share the copies with others. To combat altruistic piracy and for other reasons, Congress passed the No Electronic Theft (NET) Act of 1997.

NET extends criminal liability for the piracy of copyrighted materials to persons who exchange unauthorized copies of copyrighted works, such as software, even though they realize no profit from the exchange. The act also imposes penalties on those who make unauthorized electronic copies of books, magazines, movies, or music for personal use, thus altering the traditional "fair use" doctrine. The criminal penalties for violating the act are relatively severe; they include fines as high as $250,000 and incarceration for up to five years.

The Digital Millennium Copyright Act of 1998. The passage of the Digital Millennium Copyright Act (DMCA) of 1998[18] gave significant protection to owners of copyrights in digital information. Among other things, the act established civil and criminal penalties for anyone who circumvents (bypasses, or gets around—by using a special decryption program, for example) encryption software or other technological antipiracy protection. Also prohibited are the manufacture, import, sale, and distribution of devices or services for circumvention.

To read the text of the Digital Millennium Copyright Act of 1998, go to the "Statutes" page of our Web site at

http://ele.westbuslaw.com

One of the questions raised by the DMCA is whether prohibiting the use of decryption technology violates the freedom of speech guaranteed by the First Amendment to the Constitution. See this chapter's *Contemporary Legal Debates* feature for a discussion of this issue.

"Fair Use" Exceptions. The DMCA provides for exceptions to fit the needs of libraries, scientists, universities, and others. In general, the law does not restrict the "fair use" of circumvention methods for educational and other noncommercial purposes. For example, circumvention is allowed to test computer security, to conduct encryption research, to protect personal privacy, and to enable parents to monitor their children's use of the Internet. The exceptions are to be reconsidered every three years.

Limited Liability for ISPs. The DMCA also limits the liability of Internet service providers (ISPs). Under the act, an ISP is not liable for any copyright infringement by its customer *unless* the ISP is aware of the subscriber's violation. An ISP may be held liable only if it fails to take action to shut the subscriber down after learning of the violation. A copyright holder has to act promptly, however, by pursuing a claim in court, or the subscriber has the right to be restored to online access.

MP3 and File-Sharing Technology

Soon after the Internet became popular, a few enterprising programmers created software to compress large data files, particularly those associated with music. The reduced file sizes make transmitting music over the Internet feasible. The most widely known compression and decompression system is MP3, which enables music fans to download songs or entire CDs onto their computers or onto portable listening devices, such as Rio. The MP3 system also made it possible for music fans to access other music fans' files by engaging in file-sharing via the Internet. (A new format, called MP4, is becoming popular. It provides CD–quality audio.)

18. This act implemented the World Intellectual Property Organization Copyright Treaty of 1996, which will be discussed later in this chapter.

CONTEMPORARY LEGAL DEBATES

Copyright Law versus Free Speech

Since the ratification of the First Amendment to the U.S. Constitution in 1791, Congress has been prohibited from making any law "abridging the freedom of speech." Clearly, at that time the framers did not anticipate radio, television, the movies, computers, computer programs, or the Internet. As radio, television, and the movies became important at the beginning and middle of the twentieth century, they gave rise to free speech issues. As the Internet moves into virtually everyone's home and place of work in the twenty-first century, First Amendment issues have arisen and will continue to do so.

A major contemporary legal debate today concerns free speech rights in the context of intellectual property in digital form that is encrypted to prevent its unauthorized copying and use. More specifically, the courts are now addressing the tension between movie studios, which are encrypting their DVDs, and "hackers" who have posted code-cracking programs on the Internet so that DVDs can be copied numerous times.

APPLYING THE DIGITAL MILLENNIUM COPYRIGHT ACT OF 1998

Almost as soon as encryption technology was used to safeguard the contents of DVDs, the code was cracked by a group of hackers, including nineteen-year-old Norwegian John Johansen. His decryption program, called DeCCS, was quickly made available at various sites on the Internet including 2600.com, owned by Ed Corley. Almost immediately after DeCCS was posted, a group of movie companies, including Disney and Twentieth Century-Fox, filed suit.

In what was seen as a victory for the motion picture industry, a federal district court ruled, in *Universal City Studios, Inc. v. Reimerdes,*[a] that DeCCS violated the Digital Millennium Copyright Act (DMCA) of 1998. As noted elsewhere, among other things the DMCA prohibits the circumvention (by decryption programs, for example) of encryption systems that are embedded in intellectual property to protect the property from piracy, or unauthorized use. The court noted that since the posting of DeCCS, along with a separate video-compression program known as Divx, the pirating of movies had become increasingly common on the Internet.

a. 111 F.Supp.2d 294 (S.D.N.Y. 2000).

The defendants argued that software programs designed to break encryption schemes were a form of constitutionally protected speech. The court, however, rejected the free speech argument. "Computer code is not purely expressive any more than assassination of a political figure is purely a political statement . . . . The Constitution, after all, is a framework for building a just and democratic society. It is not a suicide pact," stated the court. A federal appellate court affirmed the trial court's decision.[b]

CONFLICTING APPROACHES IN CALIFORNIA

In August 2003, the California Supreme Court reviewed a case brought by a trade association of movie industry businesses against Internet Web site operators who made DeCCS programs available from their Web sites. The trade association asked the court to enjoin the defendants from copying, distributing, publishing, or otherwise marketing the DeCCS program because, by doing so, the defendants were, by necessity, disclosing or using the trade secrets contained in the encryption programs.

A California appellate court weighed in on the side of free speech and refused to grant the injunction. In contrast to the *Universal City Studios* decision, the court reasoned that the DeCCS program was a form of "pure speech." Furthermore, stated the court, the "scope of protection of trade secrets does not override the protection offered by the First Amendment." The court labeled any attempt at blocking the future use of computer programs "an impermissible prior restraint" on Web site operators' First Amendment rights. The California Supreme Court, however, reversed this ruling, holding that the injunction did not violate the Web site operators' free speech rights.[c]

THE DEBATE CONTINUES

If you buy a book, you can read it, throw it away, give it to someone else, or sell it to a used bookstore.

b. *Universal City Studios, Inc. v. Corley,* 273 F.3d 429 (2d Cir. 2001).
c. *DVD Copy Control Association v. Bunner,* 31 Cal.4th 864, 75 P.3d 1, 4 Cal.Rptr.3d 69 (2003).

(Continued on next page)

CONTEMPORARY LEGAL DEBATES

Copyright Law versus Free Speech

Once you have bought it, you can legally do just about anything with it except make copies for resale. There is no way that the owner of the intellectual property contained in that book can insert an encryption system to prevent you from letting someone else read it. In contrast, any form of digitized intellectual property can contain an encryption system.

In principle, the 1998 DMCA protects all such encryption systems from being circumvented by "code cracking." Understandably, the movie industry is urging the courts to interpret the DMCA's provisions against circumvention narrowly. Yet some argue that several passages in the act would seem to allow for a broader interpretation—one that would allow constitutional challenges to succeed. Ultimately, the controversy may have to be decided by the United States Supreme Court.

WHERE DO YOU STAND?

At issue in the twenty-first century is the trade-off between the necessity of writers, musicians, artists, and movie studios to profit from their work and the free flow of ideas for the public's benefit. Movie (and music) industry participants claim that encryption programs are necessary to prevent piracy. Others, however, including the defendants in cases such as those discussed in this feature, argue that the law should at least allow purchasers of movies, music, and books in digital form to make limited copies for fair use. Which side of this debate do you support? Is it possible to strike an appropriate balance between the rights of both groups on this issue?

Peer-to-peer (P2P) networking • The sharing of resources (such as files, hard drives, and processing cycles) among multiple computers that does not necessarily require a central network server.

Peer-to-Peer (P2P) Networking. File-sharing via the Internet is accomplished through what is called **peer-to-peer (P2P) networking.** The concept is simple. Rather than going through a central Web server, P2P uses numerous personal computers (PCs) that are connected to the Internet. Files stored on one PC can be accessed by others who are members of the same network. File-sharing offers an unlimited number of uses for distributed networks. Currently, for example, many researchers allow their home computers' computing power to be accessed through file-sharing software so that very large mathematical problems can be solved quickly. Additionally, persons scattered throughout the country or the world can work together on the same project by using file-sharing programs.

Sharing Stored Music Files. File-sharing clearly offers many advantages. When file-sharing is used to download others' stored music files, however, copyright issues arise. Recording artists and their labels stand to lose large amounts of royalties and revenues if relatively few CDs are purchased and then made available on distributed networks, from which everyone can get them for free. In the following widely publicized case, several firms in the recording industry sued Napster, Inc., the owner of the then-popular Napster Web site. The firms alleged that Napster was contributing to copyright infringement by those who downloaded CDs from other computers in the Napster file-sharing system. At issue was whether Napster could be held vicariously liable for the infringement.[19]

19. Vicarious (substitute) liability exists when one person is subject to liability for another's actions. A common example occurs in the employment context, when an employer is held vicariously liable by third parties for torts committed by employees in the course of their employment.

CASE 13.5

United States Court of Appeals, Ninth Circuit, 2001.
239 F.3d 1004.
http://guide.lp.findlaw.com/casecode/courts/9th.html[a]

A&M RECORDS, INC. v. NAPSTER, INC.

*Napster, Inc. (**http://www.napster.com**), facilitated the transmission of MP3 files among the users of its Web site through P2P file-sharing. This was made possible by Napster's MusicShare software, available free of charge from Napster's site, and Napster's network servers and server-side software. Napster also provided technical support. A&M Records, Inc., and others engaged in the commercial recording, distribution, and sale of copyrighted musical compositions and sound recordings, filed a suit in a federal district court against Napster, alleging copyright infringement. The court issued a preliminary injunction ordering Napster to stop "facilitating others in copying, downloading, uploading, transmitting, or distributing plaintiffs' copyrighted musical compositions and sound recordings, * * * without express permission of the rights owner." Napster appealed to the U.S. Court of Appeals for the Ninth Circuit.*

BEEZER, J.

In the context of copyright law, vicarious liability extends * * * to cases in which a defendant has the right and ability to supervise the infringing activity and also has a direct financial interest in such activities.

* * * *

The ability to block infringers' access to a particular environment for any reason whatsoever is evidence of the right and ability to supervise. Here, plaintiffs have demonstrated that Napster retains the right to control access to its system. Napster has an express reservation of rights policy, stating on its website that it expressly reserves the "right to refuse service and terminate accounts in [its] discretion, including, but not limited to, if Napster believes that user conduct violates applicable law * * * or for any reason in Napster's sole discretion, with or without cause."

To escape imposition of vicarious liability, the reserved right to police must be exercised to its fullest extent. *Turning a blind eye to detectable acts of infringement for the sake of profit gives rise to liability*. [Emphasis added.]

The district court correctly determined that Napster had the right and ability to police its system and failed to exercise that right to prevent the exchange of copyrighted material. * * *

Napster, however, has the ability to locate infringing material listed on its search indices, and the right to terminate users' access to the system. The file name indices, therefore, are within the "premises" that Napster has the ability to police. We recognize that the files are user-named and may not match copyrighted material exactly (for example, the artist or song could be spelled wrong). For Napster to function effectively, however, file names must reasonably or roughly correspond to the material contained in the files, otherwise no user could ever locate any desired music. As a practical matter, Napster, its users and the record company plaintiffs have equal access to infringing material by employing Napster's "search function."

Our review of the record requires us to accept the district court's conclusion that plaintiffs have demonstrated a likelihood of success on the merits of the

a. This URL will take you to a Web site maintained by FindLaw, which is now a part of West Group. When you access the site, enter "Napster" in the "Party Name Search" box and then click on "Search." Select the *Napster* case dated "02/12/2001" from the list on the page that opens.

vicarious copyright infringement claim. Napster's failure to police the system's "premises," combined with a showing that Napster financially benefits from the continuing availability of infringing files on its system, leads to the imposition of vicarious liability.

The U.S. Court of Appeals for the Ninth Circuit affirmed the lower court's decision that Napster was obligated to police its own system and had likely infringed the plaintiffs' copyrights. Holding that the injunction was "overbroad," however, the appellate court remanded the case for a clarification of Napster's responsibility to determine whether music on its Web site was copyrighted.[b]

QUESTIONS

1. Who were the plaintiffs in this case, and what did they allege with respect to the defendant?
2. Did Napster's failure to obtain permission before facilitating the transmission of copyrighted material via its Web site constitute copyright infringement, according to the U.S. Court of Appeals for the Ninth Circuit?
3. How might the Napster system be put to commercially significant but noninfringing uses?

b. Napster later filed for bankruptcy. Bertelsmann sought to purchase Napster's assets, but the bankruptcy court denied Bertelsmann's bid. Note that there are numerous sites on the Web today that offer similar services.

TRADE SECRETS

Some business processes and information that are not, or cannot be, patented, copyrighted, or trademarked are nevertheless protected against appropriation by competitors as trade secrets. As discussed in Chapter 7, *trade secrets* consist of customer lists, plans, research and development, pricing information, marketing techniques, production techniques, and generally anything that makes an individual company unique and that would have value to a competitor.

Unlike copyright and trademark protection, protection of trade secrets extends both to ideas and to their expression. (For this reason, and because a trade secret involves no registration or filing requirements, trade secret protection may be well suited for software.) Of course, the secret formula, method, or other information must be disclosed to some persons, particularly to key employees. Businesses generally attempt to protect their trade secrets by having all employees who use the process or information agree in their contracts, or in confidentiality agreements, never to divulge it.

State and Federal Law on Trade Secrets

Under Section 757 of the *Restatement of Torts,* "One who discloses or uses another's trade secret, without a privilege to do so, is liable to the other if (1) he discovered the secret by improper means, or (2) his disclosure or use constitutes a breach of confidence reposed in him by the other in disclosing the secret to him." The theft of confidential business data by industrial espionage, as when a business taps into a competitor's computer, is a theft of trade secrets without any contractual violation and is actionable in itself.

Until recently, virtually all law with respect to trade secrets was common law. In an effort to reduce the unpredictability of the common law in this area, a model act, the Uniform Trade Secrets Act, was presented to the states for adoption in 1979. Parts of the act have been adopted in more than twenty states. Typically, a state that has adopted parts of the act has adopted only those parts that encompass its own existing common law. Additionally, in 1996 Congress passed the Economic Espionage Act,[20] which made the theft of trade secrets a federal crime. We examined the provisions and significance of this act in Chapter 7, in the context of crimes related to business.

Trade Secrets in Cyberspace

New computer technology is undercutting a business firm's ability to protect its confidential information, including trade secrets.[21] For example, a dishonest employee could e-mail trade secrets in a company's computer to a competitor or a future employer. If e-mail is not an option, the employee might walk out with the information on a computer disk.

LICENSING

One way to make use of another's trademark, copyright, patent, or trade secret, while avoiding litigation, is to obtain a license to do so. A license in this context is essentially an agreement permitting the use of a trademark, copyright, patent, or trade secret for certain purposes. For example, a licensee (the party obtaining the license) might be allowed to use the trademark of the licensor (the party issuing the license) as part of the name of its company, or as part of its domain name, without otherwise using the mark on any products or services.

INTERNATIONAL PROTECTION FOR INTELLECTUAL PROPERTY

For many years, the United States has been a party to various international agreements relating to intellectual property rights. For example, the Paris Convention of 1883, to which about ninety countries are signatory, allows parties in one country to file for patent and trademark protection in any of the other member countries. Other international agreements in this area include the Berne Convention and the TRIPS agreement.

The Berne Convention

Under the Berne Convention of 1886, as amended, an international copyright agreement, if an American writes a book, her or his copyright in the book must be recognized by every country that has signed the convention. Also, if a citizen of a country that has not signed the convention first publishes a

20. 18 U.S.C. Sections 1831–1839.

21. Note that in at least one case, a court has held that customers' e-mail addresses may constitute trade secrets. See *T-N-T Motorsports, Inc. v. Hennessey Motorsports, Inc.*, 965 S.W.2d 18 (Tex.App.—Hous. [1 Dist.] 1998); rehearing overruled (1998); petition dismissed (1998).

book in a country that has signed, all other countries that have signed the convention must recognize that author's copyright. Copyright notice is not needed to gain protection under the Berne Convention for works published after March 1, 1989.

Currently, the laws of many countries, as well as international laws, are being updated to reflect changes in technology and the expansion of the Internet. Copyright holders and other owners of intellectual property generally agree that changes in the law are needed to stop the increasing international piracy of their property. The World Intellectual Property Organization (WIPO) Copyright Treaty of 1996, a special agreement under the Berne Convention, attempts to update international law governing copyright protection to include more safeguards against copyright infringement via the Internet. The United States signed the WIPO treaty in 1996 and implemented its terms in the Digital Millennium Copyright Act of 1998, which was discussed earlier in this chapter.

The Berne Convention and other international agreements have given some protection to intellectual property on a global level. Another significant worldwide agreement to increase such protection is the Trade-Related Aspects of Intellectual Property Rights agreement—or, more simply, the TRIPS agreement.

The TRIPS Agreement

The TRIPS agreement was signed by representatives from over one hundred nations in 1994. It was one of several documents that were annexed to the agreement that created the World Trade Organization, or WTO, in 1995. The TRIPS agreement established, for the first time, standards for the international protection of intellectual property rights, including patents, trademarks, and copyrights for movies, computer programs, books, and music.

Important Provisions of the Agreement. Prior to the TRIPS agreement, one of the difficulties faced by U.S. sellers of intellectual property in the international market was that another country might either lack laws to protect intellectual property rights or fail to enforce what laws it had. To address this problem, the TRIPS agreement provides that each member country must include in its domestic laws broad intellectual property rights and effective remedies (including civil and criminal penalties) for violations of those rights.

Generally, the TRIPS agreement provides that member nations must not discriminate (in terms of the administration, regulation, or adjudication of intellectual property rights) against foreign owners of such rights. In other words, a member nation cannot give its own nationals (citizens) favorable treatment without offering the same treatment to nationals of all member countries. For example, if a U.S. software manufacturer brings a suit for the infringement of intellectual property rights under Japan's national laws, the U.S. manufacturer is entitled to receive the same treatment as a Japanese domestic manufacturer. Each member nation must also ensure that legal procedures are available for parties who wish to bring actions for infringement of intellectual property rights. Additionally, as part of the agreement creating the WTO, a mechanism for settling disputes among member nations was established.

Type of Intellectual Property Covered by the Agreement. Particular provisions of the TRIPS agreement refer to patent, trademark, and copyright protection for intellectual property. The agreement specifically provides copyright protection for computer programs by stating that compilations of data, databases, and other materials are "intellectual creations" and are to be protected as copyrightable works. Other provisions relate to trade secrets and the rental of computer programs and cinematographic works.

KEY TERMS

certification mark 465
collective mark 465
copyright 473
cyber mark 466
cybersquatting 466
dilution 462
domain name 466
intellectual property 458
meta tag 469
patent 471
peer-to-peer (P2P) networking 480
service mark 465
trade dress 465
trade name 465
trademark 461

FOR REVIEW

1. What is intellectual property?
2. Why does the law protect trademarks and patents?
3. What laws protect authors' copyrights in the works they generate?
4. What are trade secrets, and what laws offer protection for this form of intellectual property?
5. What steps have been taken to protect intellectual property rights in today's digital age?

QUESTIONS AND CASE PROBLEMS

13–1. Professor Wise is teaching a summer seminar in business torts at State University. Several times during the course, he makes copies of relevant sections from business law texts and distributes them to his students. Wise does not realize that the daughter of one of the textbook authors is a member of his seminar. She tells her father about Wise's copying activities, which have taken place without her father's or his publisher's permission. Her father sues Wise for copyright infringement. Wise claims protection under the fair use doctrine. Who will prevail? Explain.

13–2. In which of the following situations would a court likely hold Ursula liable for copyright infringement?

(a) From a scholarly journal at the library, Ursula photocopies ten pages relating to a topic on which she is writing a term paper.
(b) Ursula makes blouses, dresses, and other clothes and sells them in her small shop. She advertises some of the outfits as Guest items, hoping that customers might mistakenly assume that they were made by Guess, the well-known clothing manufacturer.
(c) Ursula teaches Latin American history at a small university. She has a VCR and frequently tapes television programs relating to Latin America. She then takes the videos to her classroom so that her students can watch them.

13–3. One day during algebra class, Diedra, an enterprising fourteen-year-old student, began drawing designs on her shoelaces. By the end of the class, Diedra had decorated her shoelaces with the name of the school, Broadson Junior High, written in blue and red (the school colors) and with pictures of bears, the school's mascot. After class, she showed the designs to her teacher, Mrs. Laxton. When Diedra got home that night, she wrote about her idea in her diary, in which she also drew her shoelace design. Mrs. Laxton had been trying to think of a way to build school spirit. She thought about Diedra's shoelaces and decided to go into business for herself. She called her business Spirited Shoelaces and designed shoelaces for each of the local schools, decorating the shoelaces in each case with the school's name, mascot, and colors. The business became tremendously profitable. Even though Diedra never registered her idea with the U.S. Patent and Trademark Office or the U.S. Copyright Office, does she nonetheless have intellectual property rights in the shoelace design? Will her diary account be sufficient proof that she created the idea? Discuss.

CASE PROBLEM WITH SAMPLE ANSWER

13–4. Copyright Infringement. The owner of Michigan Document Services, Inc. (MDS), James Smith, concluded that it was unnecessary to obtain the copyright owners' permission to reproduce copyrighted materials in course packs. Smith publicized his conclusion, claiming that professors would not have to worry about any delay in production at his shop. MDS then compiled, bound, and sold course packs to students at the University of Michigan without obtaining the permission of copyright owners. Princeton University Press and two other publishers filed a suit in a federal district court against MDS, alleging copyright infringement. MDS claimed that its course packs were covered under the fair use doctrine. Were they? Explain. [*Princeton University Press v. Michigan Document Services, Inc.*, 99 F.3d 1381 (6th Cir. 1996)]

➧ *To view a sample answer for this case problem, go to this book's Web site at* **http://ele.westbuslaw.com** *and click on "Interactive Study Center."*

13–5. Trademark Infringement. Elvis Presley Enterprises, Inc. (EPE), owns all of the trademarks of the Elvis Presley estate. None of these marks is registered for use in the restaurant business. Barry Capece registered "The Velvet Elvis" as a service mark for a restaurant and tavern with the U.S. Patent and Trademark Office. Capece opened a nightclub called "The Velvet Elvis" with a menu, decor, advertising, and promotional events that evoked Elvis Presley and his music. EPE filed a suit in a federal district court against Capece and others, claiming, among other things, that "The Velvet Elvis" service mark infringed on EPE's trademarks. During the trial, witnesses testified that they thought the bar was associated with Elvis Presley. Should Capece be ordered to stop using the mark "The Velvet Elvis"? Why or why not? [*Elvis Presley Enterprises, Inc. v. Capece*, 141 F.3d 188 (5th Cir. 1998)]

13–6. Trademark Infringment. A&H Sportswear Co., a swimsuit maker, obtained a trademark for its MIRACLESUIT in 1992. The MIRACLESUIT design makes the wearer appear slimmer. The MIRACLESUIT, which was widely advertised and discussed in the media, was also sold for a brief time in the Victoria's Secret (VS) catalogue, which is published by Victoria's Secret Catalogue, Inc. In 1993, Victoria's Secret Stores, Inc., began selling a cleavage-enhancing bra, which was named THE MIRACLE BRA and for which a trademark was obtained. The next year, THE MIRACLE BRA swimwear debuted in the VS catalogue and stores. A&H filed a suit in a federal district court against VS Stores and VS Catalogue, alleging in part that the mark THE MIRACLE BRA, when applied to swimwear, infringed on the MIRACLESUIT mark. A&H argued that there was a "possibility of confusion" between the marks. The VS entities contended that the appropriate standard was "likelihood of confusion" and that, in this case, there was no likelihood of confusion. In whose favor will the court rule, and why? [*A&H Sportswear, Inc. v. Victoria's Secret Stores, Inc.*, 166 F.3d 197 (3d Cir. 1999)]

13–7. Domain Name Disputes. In 1999, Steve and Pierce Thumann and their father, Fred, created Spider Webs, Ltd., a partnership, to, according to Steve, "develop Internet address names." Spider Webs registered nearly two thousand Internet domain names at an average cost of $70 each, including the names of cities, the names of buildings, names related to a business or trade (such as air conditioning or plumbing), and the names of famous companies. It offered many of the names for sale on its Web site and through eBay.com. Spider Webs registered the domain name "ERNESTANDJULIOGALLO.COM" in Spider Webs's name. E. and J. Gallo Winery filed a suit against Spider Webs, alleging, in part, violations of the Anticybersquatting Consumer Protection Act (ACPA). Gallo asked the court for, among other things, statutory damages. Gallo also sought to have the domain name at issue transferred to Gallo. During the suit, Spider Webs published anticorporate articles and opinions against Gallo, as well as discussions of the suit and of the risks associated with alcohol use, at the URL ERNESTANDJULIOGALLO.COM. Should the court rule in Gallo's favor? Why or why not? [*E. & J. Gallo Winery v. Spider Webs, Ltd.*, 129 F.Supp.2d 1033 (S.D.Tex. 2001)]

13–8. Fair Use Doctrine. Leslie Kelly is a professional photographer who has copyrighted many of his images of the American West. Some of the images can be seen on Kelly's Web site or other sites with which Kelly has a contract. Arriba Soft Corp. operates an Internet search engine that displays its results in the form of small pictures (thumbnails) rather than text. The thumbnails consist of images copied from other sites and reduced in size. By clicking on one of the thumbnails, a user can view a large version of the picture within the context of an Arriba Web page. Arriba displays the large picture by inline linking (importing the image from the other site without copying it onto Arriba's site). When Kelly discovered that his photos were displayed through Arriba's site without his permission, he filed a suit in a federal district court against Arriba, alleging copyright infringement. Arriba claimed that its use of Kelly's images was a "fair use." Considering the factors courts take into account to determine whether a use is fair, do Arriba's thumbnails qualify? Does Arriba's use of the larger images infringe on Kelly's copyright? Explain. [*Kelly v. Arriba Soft Corp.*, 280 F.3d 934 (9th Cir. 2002)]

13–9. IN YOUR COURT

Over an approximately forty-year time span, several well-known authors gave Random House, Inc., an exclusive license to "print, publish and sell" their specific works "in book form." The authors later individually contracted with Rosetta Books, giving Rosetta Books a license to print exactly the same text as electronic books, or e-books. The e-books would have different online covers, title pages, and forewords, along with various other features unique to the electronic format. When the e-books came out in 2001, Random House filed suit against Rosetta Books, alleging copyright infringement and asking for an injunction to prohibit Rosetta from offering these works in digital form. Assume that you are the judge in the federal court hearing this case and answer the following questions:

(a) Compare this case with Case 13.4, *New York Times Co. v. Tasini*. How are the two cases similar? How are they different? Is the legal reasoning employed in the *Tasini* case applicable to the case now before your court?
(b) A central issue in this case has to do with how to interpret the language of the contract (license) between the parties, particularly with respect to the phrase "in book form." Should the phrase be interpreted to include electronic books? Why or why not?
(c) What will your ruling be in this case? How will your interpretation of the phrase "in book form" affect your ruling?
(d) Some of the contracts were signed long before electronic books became an option for publishers. Should this fact affect your interpretation of the phrase "in book form"?

13–10. A QUESTION OF ETHICS AND SOCIAL RESPONSIBILITY

Storm Impact, Inc., produces software, including the games TaskMaker and MacSki. To market upgraded versions of the games, Storm distributed them as shareware with locks built into the programs. A user could sample the unlocked portions at no charge and then buy a key, in the form of a floppy disk and registration number, to access the entire program. A legend expressly encouraged users to give unaltered copies to others but prohibited charging for the shareware. Software of the Month Club (SOMC) provides collections of new shareware to its members for a fee of $24.95 per month. When Storm's games were included in one of SOMC's collections, Storm filed a suit in a federal district court against SOMC, alleging, among other things, copyright infringement. SOMC argued that its copying and distribution of the games was a "fair use." The court held that SOMC had infringed Storm's copyrights and awarded Storm $20,000 in damages. [*Storm Impact, Inc. v. Software of the Month Club*, 13 F.Supp.2d 782 (N.D.Ill. 1998)]

(a) SOMC claimed that by endorsing and distributing shareware, it was performing a service for the creators, much as a book reviewer does for a book. Do you agree? Why or why not? How might SOMC have avoided this suit?
(b) Should the fact that SOMC was charging for something that was otherwise free on the Internet affect the outcome in this suit? Should Storm's restriction on charging for its shareware affect the result? Why or why not? What are the implications of the holding in this case for other shareware distributors?

13–11. FOR CRITICAL ANALYSIS

Can copyright law effectively regulate the distribution of copyrighted materials via the Internet? Should it?

For updated links to resources available on the Web, as well as a variety of other materials, visit this text's Web site at

http://ele.westbuslaw.com

An excellent overview of the laws governing various forms of intellectual property is available at FindLaw's Web site. Go to

http://profs.lp.findlaw.com

You can find answers to frequently asked questions (FAQs) about trademark and patent law—and links to registration forms, statutes, international patent and trademark offices, and numerous other related materials—at the Web site of the U.S. Patent and Trademark Office. Go to

http://www.uspto.gov

To perform patent searches and to access information on the patenting process, go to

http://www.bustpatents.com

You can also access information on patent law at the following Internet site:

http://www.patents.com

For information on copyrights, go to the U.S. Copyright Office at

http://www.loc.gov/copyright

You can find extensive information on copyright law—including United States Supreme Court decisions in this area and the texts of the Berne Convention and other international treaties on copyright issues—at the Web site of the Legal Information Institute at Cornell University's School of Law. Go to

http://www.law.cornell.edu/topics/copyright.html

Law.com's Web site offers articles, case decisions, and other information concerning intellectual property at

http://www.law.com/jsp/pc/iplaw.jsp

LEGAL RESEARCH EXERCISES ON THE WEB

Go to **http://ele.westbuslaw.com**, the Web site that accompanies this text. Select "Interactive Study Center," and then click on "Chapter 13." There you will find the following Internet research exercises that you can perform to learn more about topics covered in this chapter.

Activity 13–1: LEGAL PERSPECTIVE—Unwarranted Legal Threats

Activity 13–2: MANAGEMENT PERSPECTIVE—Protecting Intellectual Property across Borders

Activity 13–3: TECHNOLOGICAL PERSPECTIVE—File-Sharing

BEFORE THE TEST

Go to **http://ele.westbuslaw.com**, the Web site that accompanies this text. Select "Interactive Quizzes." You will find at least twenty interactive questions relating to this chapter.

WESTLAW® CAMPUS

If your textbook provided for a subscription to Westlaw® Campus, or if you have otherwise purchased access to the Westlaw Campus database, you can access any of the cases presented or cited in this chapter by using your Westlaw Campus account.

FOCUS ON LEGAL REASONING
Ford v. Trendwest Resorts, Inc.

INTRODUCTION

In Chapter 10, we outlined the remedies for a breach of contract. In this *Focus on Legal Reasoning,* we examine *Ford v. Trendwest Resorts, Inc.,*[1] a decision in which the court considered the appropriate measure for an award of damages for an employer's breach of an agreement to rehire a former employee.

CASE BACKGROUND

Trendwest Resorts, Inc., sells vacation time at a network of resorts in North America. Bobby Ford began working for Trendwest in 1991. By April 1997, Ford held a highly paid position in Trendwest's "Upgrades" department. On April 30, the department's assistant manager fired Ford for arriving at work a second time smelling of alcohol. The sales director, however, told Ford that if he completed an alcohol-counseling program, the company would rehire him in "a position equal to that which [he] held." Ford agreed to participate in the program, and the parties signed an employee-assistance agreement.

After establishing a treatment schedule, Ford called Trendwest to arrange a new work schedule. The Upgrades department manager told Ford that he could not return to Upgrades but that he could work in the "Discovery Program" as a telemarketer, a far less lucrative position than Ford had held. Ford declined. Trendwest terminated his employment.

Ford filed a suit in a Washington state court against Trendwest, alleging, among other things, breach of contract. A jury found that Trendwest had breached its promise to rehire Ford in a specific position and awarded him $235,000 in damages based on his anticipated lost earnings. A state intermediate appellate court affirmed the award, and Trendwest appealed to the Washington Supreme Court. The question was whether lost earnings are the measure of damages for a breach of an agreement to hire a person for employment at will.[2]

1. 146 Wash.2d 146, 43 P.3d 1223 (2002).

2. Under the employment-at-will doctrine, either party may terminate the relationship at any time for any reason, unless a contract or statute specifies otherwise.

MAJORITY OPINION

JOHNSON, J.

To the extent possible, the law of contracts seeks to protect an injured party's reasonably expected benefit of the bargain * * * . Contract damages are ordinarily based on the injured party's expectation[s] * * * and are intended to give that party the benefit of the bargain by awarding him or her a sum of money that will, to the extent possible, put the injured party in as good a position as that party would have been in had the contract been performed. *The central objective behind the system of contract remedies is compensatory, not punitive. Punishment of a promisor for having broken his promise has no justification on either economic or other grounds* * * * . [Emphasis added.]

Employment contracts are governed by the same rules as other contracts. Thus, Ford argues, once the breach of contract was established, Ford's damages were limited only by their foreseeability.

But a contract confers no greater rights on a party than it bargains for. In other words, *a party to a contract has a contractual right only to that which it bargained for—its reasonable expectation.* The parties do not dispute Ford bargained for at-will employment, nor does Ford dispute Trendwest could have hired him as an at-will employee and then immediately fired him without fear of liability. An employee's expectations under an employment at-will contract are no different from the employment itself. Although Ford presents compelling facts that suggest he was treated unfairly by Trendwest, we are unwilling to abandon the long-standing distinction between at-will employment and for-cause employment [an employment contract providing that the employee can only be fired for cause]. Since we are dealing with an at-will employment contract for hire and not a for-cause employment contract for hire, the question is whether we should treat the breach of one different from the breach of the other. The answer is yes, and the reason is because if we treat them the same (i.e., if the breach of either gives rise to expectation damages), there will be no difference between at-will or for-cause employment. [Emphasis added.]

FOCUS ON LEGAL REASONING

When the parties contracted for at-will employment, Ford had no greater expectations than an at-will employee, and Trendwest had no fewer rights than an at-will employer. * * * Although Ford entered into a contract with Trendwest, neither party bargained for something other than employment at-will. Nothing in this contract changed the at-will employment relationship.

The Court of Appeals in *Bakotich v. Swanson,* 91 Wash.App. 311, 957 P.2d 275 (1998), reached the right result but for the wrong reasons. The court held that in a breach of an employment at-will contract case, anticipated lost earnings evidence is "highly speculative and [therefore] properly excluded by the trial court." But to simply characterize lost earnings as speculative does not fairly explain why they are [not] available to remedy * * * a breach of contract. We hold *lost earnings cannot measure damages for the breach of an employment at-will contract because the parties to such a contract do not bargain for future earnings.* By its very nature, at-will employment precludes an expectation of future earnings. Because Ford did not bargain for future earnings, he cannot claim they measure the harm he sustained by Trendwest's breach. * * * [Emphasis added.]

* * * *

* * * We reverse the Court of Appeals as to the damages award and remand this case for entry of nominal damages on Ford's breach of contract claim.

DISSENTING OPINION

CHAMBERS, J.

[I]f an employer, for whatever reason, creates an atmosphere of job security and fair treatment with promises of specific treatment in specific situations and an employee is induced thereby to remain on the job and not actively seek other employment, those promises are enforceable components of the employment relationship. * * *

* * * *

* * * Once breach of [an employment at-will] contract is established, the mere fact an employer could have fired the employee without liability the next day or under some other circumstance not amounting to breach of contract does not render the actual breach of contract null or render a claim for lost wages speculative.

* * * The majority cites only one Washington case for support, a Court of Appeals opinion, *Bakotich v. Swanson,* which the majority acknowledges was decided for the wrong reasons. The *Bakotich* court grounded its decision on the theory that lost wages, as an element of damages in an at-will employment relationship, is too speculative—an analysis that the majority concedes is simply wrong.

* * * I therefore propose a different analytical approach to Ford's claim against Trendwest. First, the [judge or jury] should determine whether a contract was created modifying the at-will employment relationship; second, if a contract was created, whether it was breached; and third, the measure of any damages. * * *

* * * *

* * * Bobby Ford pleaded and proved a violation of a contract. His damages should properly be entrusted to the jury to determine. Therefore, I would affirm the Court of Appeals.

LEGAL REASONING AND ANALYSIS

❶ **Legal Analysis.** Find the *Bakotich v. Swanson* case (see the appendix following Chapter 1 for instructions on how to find state court opinions). Did the court's reasoning in the *Bakotich* case affect the majority's opinion or the dissent's opinion in this case? If so, how? If not, why was the case cited?

❷ **Legal Reasoning.** What reasons do the majority and the dissent provide to support their conclusions?

❸ **Legal Application.** Damages recoverable for a breach of contract are those which may fairly and reasonably be considered as either arising naturally (that is, according to the usual course of things) from the breach of contract itself, or such as may reasonably be supposed to have been in the contemplation of both parties, at the time they made the contract, as the probable result of the breach of it. How does the majority apply this principle in this case? What is the dissent's position?

FOCUS ON LEGAL REASONING

❹ **Implications for the Employer.** Does the decision in this case indicate that damages are never recoverable for a breach of an agreement to hire for employment at will? Explain.

❺ **Case Briefing Assignment.** Using the guidelines for briefing cases given in the "Preface to the Student" at the beginning of this text, brief the *Ford* case.

GOING ONLINE

This text's Web site, at **http://ele.westbuslaw.com**, offers links to West's Court Case Updates, as well as to other online research sources. You can also locate court cases at the Web sites listed in the *Law on the Web* section at the end of Chapter 2.

Additionally, you can find cases on contract law by going to the Hieros Gamos Web site at **http://www.hg.org/index.html**. On Hieros Gamos's home page, in the "Law Practice Center" section, click on "70 Areas of Practice." On the next page, in the "C" section, click on "Contract Law." HGE.org, Inc., in Houston, Texas, maintains this Web site.

FOCUS ON ETHICS
The Commercial Environment

Many aspects of the commercial environment lend themselves to ethical analysis. Businesspersons certainly face ethical questions when they deal with the application of black-letter law to contracts. (*Black-letter law* is an informal term for the principles of law that courts generally accept or that are embodied in statutes.) Courts, for example, generally will not inquire into the adequacy of the consideration given in a contract. In other words, a court will not reevaluate a contract to determine whether what each party gave is equivalent to what that party received.

Ethical questions are also at the core of many principles of the law of sales. Many of the provisions of the Uniform Commercial Code (UCC), such as good faith and commercial reasonableness, though designed to meet the practical needs of business dealings, express ethical standards as well. Product liability also involves ethics. Many of the tenets of product liability are based on principles designed to aid individuals injured, without extensive inquiry into issues of fault.

The areas of law covered in the previous unit constitute an important part of the legal environment of business. In each of these areas, new legal (and ethical) challenges have emerged as a result of developments in technology. Today, we are witnessing some of the challenges posed by the use of new communications networks, particularly the Internet. In this *Focus on Ethics,* we look at the ethical dimensions of selected topics discussed in the preceding chapters, including some issues that are unique to the cyber age.

ETHICS AND FREEDOM OF CONTRACT

In Chapter 4, we pointed out the importance of ethical business behavior. But what does acting ethically mean in the area of contracts? If an individual with whom you enter into a contract fails to look after his or her own interests, is that your fault, and should you therefore be doing something about it? If the contract happens to be to your advantage and therefore to the other party's detriment, do you have a responsibility to correct the situation?

The answer to this question is not simple. On the one hand, a common ethical assumption in our society is that individuals should be held responsible for the consequences of their own actions, including their contractual promises. This principle is expressed in the legal concept of freedom of contract.

On the other hand, there are times when courts will hold that the principle of freedom *of* contract should give way to the principle of freedom *from* contract, a principle based on the assumption that people should not be harmed by the actions of others. We look below at some examples of how parties to contracts may be excused from performance under their contracts if that is the only way injustice can be prevented.

UNCONSCIONABILITY

The doctrine of unconscionability represents a good example of how the law attempts to enforce ethical behavior. Under this doctrine, a contract may be deemed to be so unfair to one party as to be unenforceable—even though that party voluntarily agreed to the contract's terms. Unconscionable action, like unethical action, is incapable of precise definition. Information about the particular facts and specific circumstances surrounding the contract is essential. For example, a contract with a marginally literate consumer might be seen as unfair and unenforceable, whereas the same contract with a major business firm would be upheld by the courts.

Section 2–302 of the UCC, which incorporates the common law concept of unconscionability, similarly does not define the concept with any precision. Rather, it leaves it to the courts to determine when a contract is so one sided and unfair to one party as to be unconscionable and thus unenforceable.

Usually, courts will do all they can to save contracts rather than render them unenforceable. Thus, only in extreme situations, as when a contract or clause is so one sided as to "shock the conscience" of the court, will a court hold that a contract or contractual clause is unconscionable.

ETHICS AND SALES: GOOD FAITH AND COMMERCIAL REASONABLENESS

Good faith and commercial reasonableness are two key concepts that permeate the UCC and help to prevent unethical behavior by businesspersons. These two concepts are read into every contract and impose certain duties on all parties. Section 2–311(1) of the UCC indicates that when parties leave the particulars of performance to be specified by one of the parties, "[a]ny such specification must be made in good faith and within limits set by commercial reasonableness."

Commercial Reasonableness

The requirement of commercial reasonableness means that the term subsequently supplied by one party should not come as a surprise to the other. The party filling in the missing term may not take advantage of the opportunity to add a contractual term that will be beneficial to himself or herself (and detrimental to the other party) and then demand contractual performance of the other party that was totally unanticipated. Under the UCC, the party filling in the missing term may not deviate from what is commercially reasonable in the context of the transaction. Courts frequently look to course of dealing, usage of trade, and the surrounding circumstances in determining what is commercially reasonable in a given situation.

Good Faith in Output and Requirements Contracts

The obligation of good faith is particularly important in so-called output and requirements contracts. UCC 2–306 states that "quantity" in these contracts "means such actual output or requirements as may occur in good faith." In many situations, parties may find it advantageous (profitable) to avoid a legal obligation. Without the counter-obligation of good faith, there would be greater potential for abuse in the area of sales and lease contracts.

Suppose, for example, that the market price of the goods subject to a requirements contract rises rapidly and dramatically because of a shortage of materials necessary to their production. The buyer could claim that his or her needs are equivalent to the entire output of the seller. Then, after buying all of the seller's output at the contract price, which is substantially below the market price, the buyer could turn around and sell the goods that he or she does not need at the higher market price. Under the UCC, this type of unethical behavior is prohibited—even though the buyer in this instance has not technically breached the contract.

TORT LAW AND GUN MANUFACTURERS

One of the issues facing today's courts is how tort law and strict liability principles apply to harms caused by guns. Many lawsuits against gun manufacturers include allegations that gun makers have a duty to warn users of their products of the dangers associated with gun use. Would it be fair to impose such a requirement on gun manufacturers? Some say no, because such dangers are "open and obvious." (Recall from Chapter 12 that manufacturers and sellers do not have a duty to warn of open and obvious dangers.) Others contend that warnings could prevent numerous gun accidents.

In one of the first appellate court decisions addressing this issue, an Ohio appellate court ruled in favor of the gun manufacturer. Said the court, "Knives are sharp, bowling balls are heavy, bullets cause puncture wounds in flesh. The law has long recognized that obvious dangers are an excluded class." "Were we to decide otherwise," concluded the court, "we would open a Pandora's box."[1] Some other appellate courts are helping to make sure that "Pandora's box" stays closed. New York's highest court, for example, has held that a gun manufacturer's duty of care does not extend to those who are injured by the illegal use of handguns.[2]

Another controversial issue is whether gun manufacturers have a duty to incorporate safety measures to protect gun users. In one of the few appellate court cases involving this issue, a New Mexico court has held that they do. The court held that "existing principles of product liability under New Mexico law" should apply to manufacturers of guns, just as they apply to other "products that pose an unreasonable risk of injury."[3]

1. *City of Cincinnati v. Beretta U.S.A. Corp.*, 2000 WL 1133078 (Ohio.App. 1st Dist. 2000).
2. *Hamilton v. Beretta U.S.A. Corp.*, 96 N.Y.2d 222, 750 N.E.2d 1055, 727 N.Y.S.2d 7 (2001).
3. *Smith v. Bryco Arms*, 131 N.M. 87, 33 P.3d 638 (2001).

FOCUS ON ETHICS

HOW LONG SHOULD COPYRIGHT PROTECTION LAST?

An ongoing issue with respect to intellectual property has to do with balancing the rights of intellectual property owners against the rights of the public—to free speech, for example, or to the fair use of copyrighted materials. We touched on one aspect of this issue in the *Contemporary Legal Debates* feature in Chapter 13, which looked at the debate over the use of code-breaking programs to make unauthorized copies of DVDs. Here, we look at another issue involving the protection afforded to copyright owners.

As noted in Chapter 13, the U.S. Constitution, in Article I, Section 8, gives Congress the power to "promote the Progress of Science and useful Arts, by securing for limited times to Authors and Inventors the exclusive Right to their respective Writings and Discoveries." Once these limited times have expired, copyrighted works enter the public domain—that is, anyone can use them without having to obtain permission from the original copyright owners. A question at issue in recent years has concerned what Congress meant by the phrase *for limited times*. Just how long should these "limited times" be? In other words, how long must the public wait before copyrighted works enter the public domain and are freely available for use by anyone?

Extensions of the Copyright Term over Time

Congress began establishing the framework for copyright law in 1790, when it fixed the term of copyright protection at 14 years. This term could be extended for another 14 years, so the maximum term of copyright protection was 28 years. Since then, Congress has extended this term numerous times. The most recent extension occurred in 1998, when Congress passed the Sonny Bono Copyright Term Extension Act. This act, which amended the Copyright Act of 1976, extended copyright protection by another 20 years. Thus, as pointed out in Chapter 13, works created after January 1, 1978, are now protected for the life of the author plus 70 years. For copyrights owned by publishing houses, the copyright expires 95 years from the date of publication or 120 years from the date of creation, whichever is first.

As one scholar noted, the maximum term of copyright protection could be even longer than 120 years. After all, if a person creates a copyrighted work at the age of 20 and lives for another 60 years, the work will be protected for that 60-year period plus an additional 70 years—or 130 years in all.

A Constitutional Issue

The major criticisms of the 1998 act were outlined in a case that came before the United States Supreme Court in 2003. The plaintiffs—operators of Internet libraries, commercial publishers, and other groups and individuals that rely on the public domain for their livelihood—challenged the constitutionality of the act. They argued that copyright protection for 120 years exceeds the "for limited times" language set forth by the framers of the Constitution. Furthermore, the 1998 act's extension of the term does not serve the purpose of copyright law—to encourage creativity (by promoting "the Progress of Science and useful Arts"). How does extending copyright protection for works that have already been created, some as early as 1978, promote creativity?

In response to these arguments, the government claimed that to grant copyright protection for as long as 120 years is within the scope of the "limited times" stated in the Constitution. Moreover, one of the reasons the 1998 act was passed was to bring the United States into line with the European Union's treatment of copyright duration. Ultimately, the Supreme Court agreed with the government and rejected the plaintiffs' challenge to the 1998 act. According to the Court, the 1998 act did not violate the "limited times" requirement of the Constitution.[4]

The Stakes Were High

As with many constitutional cases, the stakes in this case were high. If the plaintiffs had prevailed, publishers, the movie industry, record companies, and other groups would have benefited significantly as works were swept into the public domain. These works would have included many that were created in the 1920s, including novels such as *The Great Gatsby,* movies such as *The Jazz Singer,* and cartoon characters such as Mickey Mouse and Pluto. At the same time, copyright owners would have seen their protection diminished. The Supreme Court's

4. *Eldred v. Ashcroft,* 537 U.S. 186, 123 S.Ct. 769, 154 L.Ed.2d 683 (2003).

FOCUS ON ETHICS

ruling, however, maintained this protection for copyright owners. Additionally, the outcome of the case determined that U.S. copyright law will remain in line with that of the European Union—an important consideration given the global nature of today's communications networks.

TRADEMARK PROTECTION VERSUS FREE SPEECH RIGHTS

Another legal issue involving questions of fairness pits the rights of trademark owners against the right to free speech. The issue—so-called cybergriping—is unique to the cyber age.

Cybergriping

Cybergripers are individuals who complain in cyberspace about corporate products, services, or activities. For trademark owners, the issue becomes particularly thorny when cybergriping sites add the word *sucks* or *stinks* or some other disparaging term to the domain name of the mark's owners. These sites, sometimes referred to collectively as "sucks" sites, are established solely for the purpose of criticizing the products or services sold by the owners of the marks.

The Question of Trademark Infringement

A number of companies have sued the owners of such sites for trademark infringement in the hope that a court or an arbitrating panel will order the site owner to cease using the domain name. Generally, however, the courts have been reluctant to hold that the use of a business's domain name in a "sucks" site infringes on the trademark owner's rights. After all, one of the primary reasons trademarks are protected under U.S. law is to prevent customers from becoming confused over the origins of the goods for sale—and a cybergriping site would certainly not create such confusion. Furthermore, American courts give extensive protection to free speech rights, including the right to express opinions about companies and their products.[5]

5. Many businesses have concluded that while they cannot control what people say about them, they can make it more difficult for it to be said. Today, businesses commonly register such insulting domain names before the cybergripers themselves can register them.

DISCUSSION QUESTIONS

❶ Suppose that you contract to purchase steel at a fixed price per ton. A lengthy steelworkers' strike causes the price of steel to triple from the price specified in the contract. If you demand that the supplier fulfill the contract, the supplier will go out of business. What are your ethical obligations in this situation? What are your legal rights?

❷ How can a court objectively measure good faith and commercial reasonableness?

❸ In your opinion, should guns be considered unreasonably dangerous products? Should gun manufacturers ever be held liable for harms caused by guns? Should they be held liable for failing to include safety features in their designs?

❹ Do you think that Congress has gone too far in protecting the rights of copyright owners? In other words, notwithstanding the Supreme Court's ruling on this issue, do you believe that the current maximum length of copyright protection (120 years) is so long that it exceeds the "limited times" language of the Constitution?

UNIT FOUR

The Employment Environment

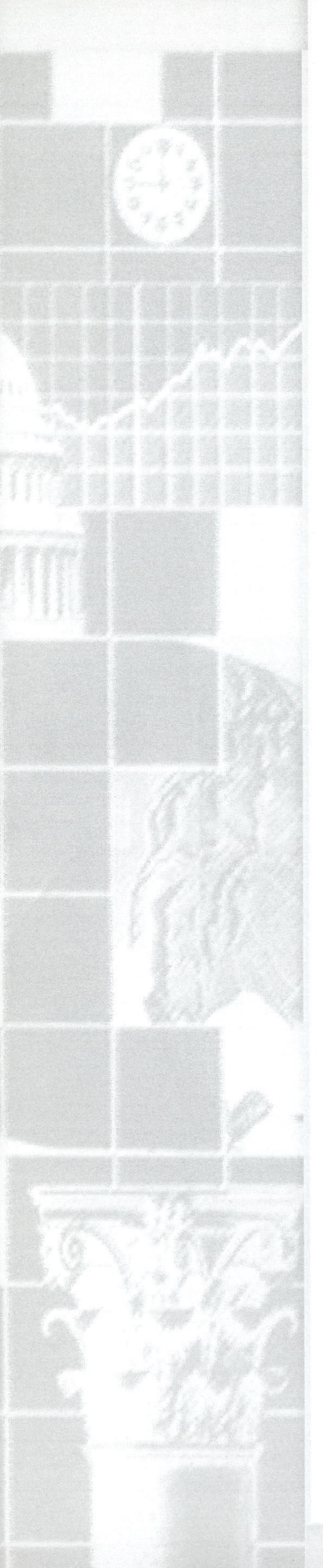

CHAPTER 14

Employment Relationships

CONTENTS

CHAPTER OBJECTIVES

After reading this chapter, you should be able to answer the following questions:

1. What is the difference between an employee and an independent contractor? How do agency relationships arise?

2. What duties do agents and principals owe to each other?

3. When is a principal liable for an agent's actions with respect to third parties? When is the agent liable?

4. What federal statute governs working hours and wages? What federal act protects the health and safety of employees? What are state workers' compensation laws?

5. Does electronic performance monitoring violate employees' privacy rights? What other types of activities undertaken by employers might violate the privacy rights of employees?

Employment relationships are agency relationships. In fact, one of the most common, important, and pervasive legal relationships is that of **agency.** In an agency relationship between two parties, one of the parties, called the *agent,* agrees to represent or act for the other, called the *principal.* The principal has the right to control the agent's conduct in matters entrusted to the agent. By using agents, a principal can conduct multiple business operations simultaneously in various locations. Thus, for example, contracts that bind the principal can be made at different places with different persons at the same time.

Agency • A relationship between two parties in which one party (the agent) agrees to represent or act for the other (the principal).

Generally, agency relationships permeate the business world. For that reason, an understanding of the law of agency is crucial to understanding business law.

Also essential to the framework of the legal environment are statutes relating to employment. For most of the last century, the relationship between employer and employee has been the subject of federal and state legislation. Many of these statutes are discussed in this chapter.

AGENCY RELATIONSHIPS

Section 1(1) of the *Restatement (Second) of Agency*[1] defines *agency* as "the fiduciary relation [that] results from the manifestation of consent by one person to another that the other shall act in his behalf and subject to his control, and consent by the other so to act." The term **fiduciary** is at the heart of agency law. The term can be used both as a noun and as an adjective. When used as a noun, it refers to a person having a duty to act primarily for another's

Fiduciary • As a noun, a person having a duty to act primarily for another's benefit concerning matters within the scope of the relationship. As an adjective, a relationship founded on trust and confidence.

1. The *Restatement (Second) of Agency* is an authoritative summary of the law of agency and is often referred to by jurists in their decisions and opinions.

benefit concerning matters within the scope of the relationship. When used as an adjective, as in the phrase "fiduciary relationship," it means that the relationship involves trust and confidence.

Agency relationships commonly exist between employers and employees. Agency relationships may sometimes also exist between employers and independent contractors who are hired to perform special tasks or services.

Employer-Employee Relationships

Normally, all employees who deal with third parties are deemed to be agents. All employment laws (state and federal) apply only to the employer-employee relationship. Statutes governing Social Security, withholding taxes, workers' compensation, unemployment compensation, workplace safety laws, employment discrimination, and other aspects of employment are applicable only when an employer-employee relationship exists. *These laws do not apply to the independent contractor.*

Because employees may be deemed agents of their employers, agency law and employment law overlap considerably. Agency relationships, though, as will become apparent, can exist outside an employer-employee relationship and thus have a broader reach than employment laws do.

Employer–Independent Contractor Relationships

Independent contractors are not employees, because by definition, those who hire them have no control over the details of their work performance. Section 2 of the *Restatement (Second) of Agency* defines an **independent contractor** as follows:

Independent contractor • One who works for, and receives payment from, an employer but whose working conditions and methods are not controlled by the employer. An independent contractor is not an employee but may be an agent.

> [An independent contractor is] a person who contracts with another to do something for him [or her] but who is not controlled by the other nor subject to the other's right to control with respect to his [or her] physical conduct in the performance of the undertaking. He [or she] may or may not be an agent.

Building contractors and subcontractors are independent contractors, and a property owner does not control the acts of either of these professionals. Truck drivers who own their equipment and hire out on a per-job basis are independent contractors, but truck drivers who drive company trucks on a regular basis are usually employees.

The relationship between a principal and an independent contractor may or may not involve an agency relationship. To illustrate: An owner of real estate who hires a real estate broker to negotiate a sale of her or his property not only has contracted with an independent contractor (the real estate broker) but also has established an agency relationship for the specific purpose of assisting in the sale of the property. Another example is an insurance agent, who is both an independent contractor and an agent of the insurance company for which she or he sells policies.

Determining Employee Status

A question that frequently comes before the courts is whether a worker should be deemed an employee or an independent contractor. How a court decides this issue can have a significant effect on the rights and liabilities of the parties. For example, employers normally are held liable as principals for the actions of their employee-agents if those actions are carried out within the scope of employment.

Criteria Used by the Courts. In deciding whether a worker is categorized as an employee or an independent contractor, courts often consider the following questions:

1. How much control can the employer exercise over the details of the work? (If an employer can exercise considerable control over the details of the work and the day-to-day activities of the worker, this indicates employee status. This is perhaps the most important factor weighed by the courts in determining employee status.)
2. Is the worker engaged in an occupation or business distinct from that of the employer? (If so, this points to independent-contractor status, not employee status.)
3. Is the work usually done under the employer's direction or by a specialist without supervision? (If the work is usually done under the employer's direction, this indicates employee status.)
4. Does the employer supply the tools at the place of work? (If so, this indicates employee status.)
5. For how long is the person employed? (If the person is employed for a long period of time, this indicates employee status.)
6. What is the method of payment—by time period or at the completion of the job? (Payment by time period, such as once every two weeks or once a month, indicates employee status.)
7. What degree of skill is required of the worker? (If a great degree of skill is required, this may indicate that the person is an independent contractor hired for a specialized job and not an employee.)

Sometimes, it is advantageous for a worker to have employee status—to take advantage of laws protecting employees, for example. At other times, it may be advantageous to have independent-contractor status, such as for tax purposes.

Criteria Used by the IRS. Often, the criteria for determining employee status are established by a statute or an administrative agency regulation. The Internal Revenue Service (IRS), for example, has guidelines for its auditors to follow in determining whether a worker is an independent contractor or an employee. In the past, auditors were to consider twenty factors in making this decision. Guidelines effective in 1997, however, encouraged IRS examiners to look closely at just one of those factors—the degree of control the business exercises over the worker.

The IRS tends to scrutinize closely a firm's classification of a worker as an independent contractor rather than an employee because employers can avoid certain tax liabilities by hiring independent contractors instead of employees. Even when the firm has classified a worker as an independent contractor, if the IRS decides that the worker is actually an employee, the employer will be responsible for paying any applicable Social Security, withholding, and unemployment taxes.

For example, in the widely publicized case of *Vizcaino v. U.S. District Court for the Western District of Washington,*[2] a court ordered Microsoft Corporation

2. 173 F.3d 713 (9th Cir. 1999).

to pay back payroll taxes for hundreds of temporary workers who had contractually agreed to work for Microsoft as independent contractors. (The alternative, for the most part, was not to work for Microsoft at all.) The IRS concluded that the independent contractors were actually employees of the company for tax purposes, largely because of the significant control that Microsoft exercised over the workers' performance.

Employee Status and "Works for Hire." Under the Copyright Act of 1976, any copyrighted work created by an employee within the scope of her or his employment at the request of the employer is a "work for hire," and the employer owns the copyright to the work. In contrast, when an employer hires an independent contractor—a freelance artist, writer, or computer programmer, for example—the independent contractor normally owns the copyright. In this situation, the employer can own the copyright only if the parties agree in writing that the work is a "work for hire" and the work falls into one of nine specific categories, including audiovisual and other works.

The following case involved a dispute over ownership rights in a computer program. The outcome of the case hinged on whether the creator of the program, at the time it was created, was an employee or an independent contractor.

CASE 14.1

United States Court of Appeals, Second Circuit, 1998. 144 F.3d 229. **http://guide.lp.findlaw.com/casecode/courts/2nd.html**[a]

GRAHAM v. JAMES

Richard Graham marketed CD-ROM discs containing compilations of shareware, freeware, and public domain software.[b] *With five to ten thousand programs per disc, Graham needed a file-retrieval program to enable users to access the software on the discs. Larry James agreed to create the program in exchange for, among other things, credit on the final product. James built into the final version of the program a notice attributing authorship and copyright to himself. Graham removed the notice, claiming that the program was a work for hire and that the copyright was his. Graham used the program on several subsequent releases. James sold the program to another CD-ROM publisher. Graham filed a suit in a federal district court against James, alleging, among other things, copyright infringement. The court ruled that James was an independent contractor and that he owned the copyright. Graham appealed the ruling.*

JACOBS, J.

The Copyright Act provides, *inter alia* [among other things], that "a work prepared by an employee within the scope of his or her employment" is a work for hire. "[T]he employer or other person for whom the work [for hire] was prepared is considered the author" and the employer owns the copyright * * * .

* * * *

a. This page, which is part of the FindLaw Web site, has links to some of the opinions of the U.S. Court of Appeals for the Second Circuit. In the "Docket Number Search" box, type in "969224" and click "get it."

b. *Shareware* is software released to the public to sample, with the understanding that anyone using it will register with the author and pay a fee. *Freeware* is software available for use at no charge. *Public domain software* is software unprotected by copyright.

* * * [In determining whether a hired party is an employee, the important factors are:] (i) the hiring party's right to control the manner and means of creation; (ii) the skill required; (iii) the provision of employee benefits; (iv) the tax treatment of the hired party; and (v) whether the hiring party had the right to assign additional projects to the hired party. * * *

We are persuaded by the district court's conclusion that James was an independent contractor. Almost all of the * * * factors line up in favor of that conclusion: James is a skilled computer programmer, he was paid no benefits, no payroll taxes were withheld, and his engagement by Graham was project-by-project. The only * * * factor arguably favoring Graham is his general control over the work; but the district court has found, plausibly, that Graham's participation in the development of the [file-retrieval program] was minimal and that his instructions to James were very general.

The U.S. Court of Appeals for the Second Circuit affirmed the lower court's judgment on this issue. The court agreed that James owned the copyright because he was an independent contractor when he developed the program.

QUESTIONS

1. Is a skilled person who controls the manner and method of his or her work, who is paid no employee benefits and has no payroll taxes withheld, and who is engaged on a project-by-project basis an independent contractor, according to the U.S. Court of Appeals for the Second Circuit in this case?
2. If Graham had provided James benefits such as health insurance, withheld payroll taxes from his pay, and employed him on a continual basis, would the conclusion of the U.S. Court of Appeals for the Second Circuit have been different?
3. What are some of the advantages and disadvantages of being an independent contractor?

FORMATION OF THE AGENCY RELATIONSHIP

Agency relationships are *consensual;* that is, they come about by voluntary consent and agreement between the parties. Generally, the agreement need not be in writing, and consideration is not required. A principal must have contractual capacity. A person who cannot legally enter into contracts directly should not be allowed to do so indirectly through an agent.

An agency relationship can be created for any legal purpose. An agency relationship created for a purpose that is illegal or contrary to public policy is unenforceable. If LaSalle (as principal) contracts with Burke (as agent) to sell illegal narcotics, the agency relationship is unenforceable, because selling illegal narcotics is a felony and is contrary to public policy. It is also illegal for medical doctors and other licensed professionals to employ unlicensed agents to perform professional actions.

Generally, an agency relationship can arise in four ways: by agreement of the parties, by ratification, by estoppel, and by operation of law. We look here at each of these possibilities.

Agency by Agreement

Because an agency relationship is, by definition, consensual, normally it must be based on an express or implied agreement that the agent will act for the principal and the principal agrees to have the agent so act. An agency agreement can take the form of an express written or oral contract.

An agency relationship can also be implied by conduct. For example, a hotel expressly allows only Hans Cooper to park cars, but Hans has no employment contract there. The hotel's manager tells Hans when to work, as well as where and how to park the cars. The hotel's conduct amounts to a manifestation of its willingness to have Hans park its customers' cars, and Hans can infer from the hotel's conduct that he has authority to act as a parking valet. It can be inferred that Hans is an agent for the hotel, his purpose being to provide valet parking services for hotel guests.

In the following case, the court considered whether an agency relationship could be inferred from the conduct of the parties.

CASE 14.2

Supreme Court of Virginia, 2002.
263 Va. 377,
560 S.E.2d 246.
http://www.courts.state.va.us/opin.htm[b]

ACORDIA OF VIRGINIA INSURANCE AGENCY, INC. v. GENITO GLENN, L.P.[a]

Genito Glenn, Limited Partnership, was the owner of a proposed apartment complex project in Chesterfield County, Virginia. Rather than searching out the best insurance policy itself, Genito arranged with National Housing Corporation (NHC) to procure insurance coverage for the project. NHC contracted with Acordia of Virginia Insurance Agency, Inc., to obtain a policy. The project's builder used, as ground fill, fly ash, which was defective, resulting in cracks in the buildings' foundations. This compromised the structural integrity of the buildings, which had to be demolished and rebuilt. Genito filed a claim for its loss under what it believed to be its insurance policy. Coverage was denied, however, because Genito had not been named as the insured party. Genito filed a suit in a Virginia state court against Acordia, alleging, in part, negligence in the performance of contractual obligations. Acordia argued that it and Genito were not in privity of contract (were not involved in a direct contractual relationship), a required element of Genito's cause of action. The court ruled that Acordia and Genito were in privity and awarded Genito $1,825,136.54, plus interest. Acordia appealed to the Virginia Supreme Court.

KINSER, J.

In the absence of privity, a person cannot be held liable for economic loss damages caused by the negligent performance of a contract.

Genito asserts that when NHC contracted with Acordia to procure a builders risk insurance policy to cover Genito, * * * NHC was acting as Genito's agent, thus creating privity between Genito and Acordia. * * * Acordia argues that evidence of an element necessary to establish a principal-agent relationship, specifically, the right to control, is absent * * *.

---

a. *L.P.* is an abbreviation for the term *limited partnership,* a type of business organization. Limited partnerships were discussed in detail in Chapter 9.

b. In the "Supreme Court of Virginia Opinions" section, click on one of the links to access a list of the case names. Scroll down the list to the name of the case and click on the record number to access the opinion. Virginia's Judicial System maintains this Web site.

* * * [A]gency [is] a fiduciary relationship resulting from one person's manifestation of consent to another person that the other shall act on his behalf and subject to his control, and the other person's manifestation of consent so to act. *While the power of control is an important factor to consider in determining whether an agency relationship exists, agency may be inferred from the conduct of the parties and from the surrounding facts and circumstances.* [Emphasis added.]

* * * *

Applying these principles, we conclude that the facts and circumstances in this case, as well as the parties' conduct, demonstrate that an agency relationship existed between Genito and NHC. Russell W. Johnson, who previously worked as a financial manager at NHC, stated that he contacted Acordia for the purpose of obtaining insurance coverage for several limited partnerships and their respective apartment complex building projects, including the Genito project. Continuing, Johnson testified that he told J. Scott Eckmann, a property casualty insurance broker who was formerly a senior vice president at Acordia, about the various limited partnerships, explained that these partnerships would own the projects, and stressed the necessity that every partnership be protected under the insurance policy. * * *

Eckmann acknowledged that he knew that NHC was acting on behalf of all of the limited partnerships to procure insurance coverage * * *. Eckmann also stated that he delivered the builders risk insurance policy purportedly issued to cover Genito and its apartment complex project to Johnson at NHC. NHC's responsibility for procuring insurance, the manner in which it set about to do so, and the information disclosed by Johnson to Eckmann were consistent with the existence of an agency relationship between NHC and Genito. An agent commonly represents the principal in the creation and performance of contracts with third parties.

The Virginia Supreme Court affirmed the lower court's ruling in Genito's favor. NHC acted as Genito's agent in procuring the insurance policy through Acordia, thus establishing the element of privity, which was needed to allow Genito to recover damages for its economic loss resulting from Acordia's negligent performance of its contractual obligations.

QUESTIONS

1. Who filed this suit, and why?
2. Why was it necessary for the court to determine whether NHC acted as Genito's agent in this case?
3. What did the Virginia Supreme Court rule in this case with respect to whether NHC acted as Genito's agent, and why?

Agency by Ratification

On occasion, a person who is in fact not an agent may make a contract on behalf of another (a principal). If the principal approves or affirms that contract by word or by action, an agency relationship is created by ratification. Ratification involves a question of intent, and intent can be expressed by either words or conduct.

Agency by Estoppel

When a principal causes a third person to believe that another person is the principal's agent, and the third person acts to his or her detriment in reasonable reliance on that belief, the principal is "estopped to deny" the agency relationship. In such a situation, the principal's actions have created the *appearance* of an agency that does not in fact exist. The third person must prove that he or she *reasonably* believed that an agency relationship existed, however.[3]

Suppose that Jerry accompanies Grant, a seed sales representative, to call on a customer, Palko, the proprietor of the Neighborhood Seed Store. Jerry has performed independent sales work but has never signed an employment agreement with Grant. Grant boasts to Palko that he wishes he had three more assistants "just like Jerry." Palko has reason to believe from Grant's statements that Jerry is an agent for Grant, because Grant's representation to Palko created the impression that Jerry was Grant's agent and had authority to solicit orders. Palko then places seed orders with Jerry.

If Grant does not correct the impression that Jerry is an agent, Grant will be bound to fill the orders just as if Jerry were really Grant's agent. The acts or declarations of a purported agent in and of themselves do not create an agency by estoppel. Rather, it is the deeds or statements *of the principal* that create an agency by estoppel. If Jerry walked into Palko's store and claimed to be Grant's agent, when in fact he was not, and Grant had no knowledge of Jerry's representations, Grant would not be bound to any deal struck by Jerry and Palko.

Agency by Operation of Law

There are also other situations in which the courts will find an agency relationship in the absence of a formal agreement. This may occur in family relationships. For example, suppose that one spouse purchases certain basic necessaries (such as food or clothing) and charges them to the other spouse's charge account. The courts will often rule that the latter is liable for payment of the necessaries, either because of a social policy of promoting the general welfare of the spouse or because of a legal duty to supply necessaries to family members.

Agency by operation of law may also occur in emergency situations, when the agent's failure to act outside the scope of his or her authority would cause the principal substantial loss. If the agent is unable to contact the principal, the courts will often grant this emergency power. For example, a railroad engineer may contract on behalf of his or her employer for medical care for an injured motorist hit by the train.

Duties of Agents and Principals

Once the principal-agent relationship has been created, both parties have duties that govern their conduct. As discussed previously, the principal-agent relationship is *fiduciary*—one of trust. In a fiduciary relationship, each party

3. These concepts also apply when a person who is in fact an agent undertakes an action that is beyond the scope of his or her authority, as will be discussed later in this chapter.

CONCEPT SUMMARY 14.1
Formation of the Agency Relationship

METHOD OF FORMATION	DESCRIPTION
By Agreement	Agency relationship is formed through express consent (oral or written) or implied by conduct.
By Ratification	Principal either by act or by agreement ratifies conduct of a person who is not in fact an agent.
By Estoppel	Principal causes a third person to believe that another person is the principal's agent, and the third person acts to his or her detriment in reasonable reliance on that belief.
By Operation of Law	Agency relationship is based on a social duty (such as the need to support family members) or formed in emergency situations when the agent is unable to contact the principal.

owes the other the duty to act with the utmost good faith. In this section, we examine the various duties of agents and principals.

Agent's Duties to the Principal

Generally, the agent owes the principal five duties—performance, notification, loyalty, obedience, and accounting.

Performance. An implied condition in every agency contract is the agent's agreement to use reasonable diligence and skill in performing the work. When an agent fails to perform his or her duties, liability for breach of contract may result. The degree of skill or care required of an agent is usually that expected of a reasonable person under similar circumstances. Generally, this is interpreted to mean ordinary care. An agent may, however, have represented himself or herself as possessing special skills or, by virtue of his or her profession, be expected to exercise certain skills (such as those that an accountant or attorney possesses). In these situations, the agent is expected to exercise the skill or skills claimed. Failure to do so constitutes a breach of the agent's duty.

Notification. An agent is required to notify the principal of all matters that come to his or her attention concerning the subject matter of the agency. This is the duty of notification, or the duty to inform. For example, suppose that Lang, an artist, is about to negotiate a contract to sell a series of paintings to Barber's Art Gallery for $15,000. Lang's agent learns that Barber is insolvent and will be unable to pay for the paintings. Lang's agent has a duty to inform Lang of this knowledge because it is relevant to the subject matter of the agency—the sale of Lang's paintings. Generally, the law assumes that the principal knows of any information acquired by the agent that is relevant to the agency—regardless of whether the agent actually passes on this information to the principal.

Loyalty. Loyalty is one of the most fundamental duties in a fiduciary relationship. Basically stated, the agent has the duty to act *solely for the benefit of his or her principal* and not in the interest of the agent or a third party.

For example, an agent cannot represent two principals in the same transaction unless both know of the dual capacity and consent to it. The duty of loyalty also means that any information or knowledge acquired through the agency relationship is confidential. It would be a breach of loyalty to disclose such information either during the agency relationship or after its termination. Typical examples of confidential information are trade secrets and customer lists compiled by the employer-principal (see Chapter 13).

In short, the agent's loyalty must be undivided. The agent's actions must be strictly for the benefit of the principal and must not result in any secret profit for the agent. For example, suppose that Remington contracts with Averly, a real estate agent, to sell Remington's property. Averly knows that he can find a buyer who will pay substantially more for the property than Remington is asking. If Averly secretly purchased Remington's property, however, and then sold it at a profit to another buyer, Averly would breach his duty of loyalty as Remington's agent. Averly has a duty to act in Remington's best interests and can only become the purchaser in this situation with Remington's knowledge and approval.

Obedience. When an agent is acting on behalf of the principal, a duty is imposed on that agent to follow all lawful and clearly stated instructions of the principal. Any deviation from such instructions is a violation of this duty. During emergency situations, however, when the principal cannot be consulted, the agent may deviate from the instructions without violating this duty. Whenever instructions are not clearly stated, the agent can fulfill the duty of obedience by acting in good faith and in a manner reasonable under the circumstances.

Accounting. Unless an agent and a principal agree otherwise, the agent has the duty to keep and make available to the principal an account of all property and funds received and paid out on behalf of the principal. The agent has a duty to maintain separate accounts for the principal's funds and the agent's personal funds, and no intermingling of these accounts is allowed. Whenever a licensed professional (such as an attorney) violates this duty to account, he or she may be subject to disciplinary proceedings carried out by the appropriate regulatory institution (such as the state bar association) in addition to being liable to the principal (the professional's client) for failure to account.

Principal's Duties to the Agent

The principal also has certain duties to the agent. These duties relate to compensation, reimbursement and indemnification, cooperation, and safe working conditions.

Compensation. In general, when a principal requests certain services from an agent, the agent reasonably expects payment. The principal therefore has a duty to pay the agent for services rendered. For example, when an accountant or an attorney is asked to act as an agent, an agreement to compensate the agent for this service is implied. The principal also has a duty to pay that compensation in a timely manner. Except in a gratuitous agency relationship, in which the agent does not act for money, the principal must pay the agreed-on value for the agent's services. If no amount has been expressly agreed on, the principal owes the agent the customary compensation for such services.

Reimbursement and Indemnification. Whenever an agent disburses sums of money to fulfill the request of the principal or to pay for necessary expenses in the course of a reasonable performance of his or her agency duties, the principal has the duty to reimburse the agent for these payments.[4] Agents cannot recover for expenses incurred by their own misconduct or negligence, however.

Subject to the terms of the agency agreement, the principal has the duty to *indemnify* (compensate) an agent for liabilities incurred because of authorized and lawful acts and transactions. For example, if the agent, on the principal's behalf, forms a contract with a third party, and the principal fails to perform the contract, the third party may sue the agent for damages. In this situation, the principal is obligated to compensate the agent for any costs incurred by the agent as a result of the principal's failure to perform the contract. Additionally, the principal must indemnify (pay) the agent for the value of benefits that the agent confers on the principal. The amount of indemnification is usually specified in the agency contract. If it is not, the courts will look to the nature of the business and the type of loss to determine the amount.

Cooperation. A principal has a duty to cooperate with the agent and to assist the agent in performing his or her duties. The principal must do nothing to prevent such performance. For example, when a principal grants an agent an exclusive territory, creating an *exclusive agency,* the principal cannot compete with the agent or appoint or allow another agent to so compete in violation of the exclusive agency. If the principal did so, he or she would be exposed to liability for the agent's lost sales or profits.

Safe Working Conditions. The common law requires the principal to provide safe working premises, equipment, and conditions for all agents and employees. The principal has a duty to inspect working areas and to warn agents and employees about any unsafe situations. When the agency is one of employment, the employer's liability is frequently covered by state workers' compensation insurance, which is the primary remedy for an employee's injury on the job.

AGENT'S AUTHORITY

An agent's authority to act can be either *actual* (express or implied) or *apparent. Express authority* is authority declared in clear, direct, and definite terms. Express authority can be given orally or in writing. *Implied authority* can be (1) conferred by custom, (2) inferred from the position the agent occupies,

---

4. This rule applies to acts by gratuitous agents as well. If a finder of a dog that becomes sick takes the dog to a veterinarian and pays the required fees for the veterinarian's services, the agent is entitled to be reimbursed by the owner of the dog for those fees.

or (3) inferred as being reasonably necessary to carry out express authority. For example, Al's Supermarket employs Mueller to manage one of its stores. Al's has not expressly stated that Mueller has authority to contract with third persons. In this situation, however, authority to manage a business implies authority to do what is reasonably required (as is customary or can be inferred from a manager's position) to operate the business. Reasonably required actions include creating contracts to hire employees, to buy merchandise and equipment, and to arrange for advertising the products sold in the store.

Actual authority arises from what the principal manifests *to the agent. Apparent authority* exists when the principal, by either words or actions, causes a *third party* reasonably to believe that an agent has authority to act, even though the agent has no express or implied authority. If the third party changes his or her position in reliance on the principal's representations, the principal may be *estopped* from denying that the agent had authority. Note that here, in contrast to agency formation by estoppel, the issue has to do with the apparent authority of an *agent,* not the apparent authority of a person who is in fact not an agent.

ETHICAL ISSUE

Does an agent's breach of loyalty terminate the agent's authority? Suppose that an employee-agent who is authorized to access company trade secrets contained in computer files e-mails those secrets to a competitor for whom the employee is about to begin working. Clearly, in this situation the employee has violated the ethical—and legal—duty of loyalty to his or her employer. Does this breach of loyalty mean that the employee's act of accessing the trade secrets was unauthorized? The question has significant implications because if the act was unauthorized, the employee would be subject to laws prohibiting unauthorized access to computer information and data. If the act was authorized, the employee would not be subject to such laws. When this unusual question came before a federal district court in 2000, the court held that the moment the employee accessed trade secrets for the purpose of divulging them to a competitor, the employee's authority as an agent was terminated. Thus, the employee could be subject to both criminal and civil sanctions under a federal law prohibiting unauthorized access to protected computer information. In reaching its decision, the court cited Section 112 of the *Restatement (Second) of Agency.* That section reads, in part, "Unless otherwise agreed, the authority of an agent terminates if, without knowledge of the principal, he acquires adverse interests or if he is otherwise guilty of a serious breach of loyalty to the principal."[5]

Liability in Agency Relationships

Frequently, the issue arises as to which party, the principal or the agent, should be held liable for the contracts formed by the agent or for the torts or crimes committed by the agent. We look here at these aspects of agency law.

5. *Shurgard Storage Centers, Inc. v. Safeguard Self Storage, Inc.,* 119 F.Supp.2d 1121 (W.D.Wash. 2000).

Liability for Contracts

An important consideration in determining liability for a contract formed by an agent is whether the third party knew the identity of the principal at the time the contract was made. Principals are classified as disclosed, partially disclosed, or undisclosed.[6]

Disclosed or Partially Disclosed Principal. A principal whose identity is known to the third party at the time the agent makes the contract is a **disclosed principal.** For example, Martha Evans, president of Comquant Computing, Inc., purchases ten new copiers for the business from ABC Copiers. She signs the purchase order, "Comquant Computing, Inc., by Martha Evans, President." In this situation, the principal (Comquant Computing, Inc.) is clearly disclosed to the third party (ABC Copiers).

Disclosed principal • A principal whose identity is known to a third party at the time the agent makes a contract with the third party.

The identity of a **partially disclosed principal** is not known by the third party, but the third party knows that the agent is or may be acting for a principal at the time the contract is made. For example, Sarah contracts with a real estate agent to sell certain property. She wishes to keep her identity a secret, but the agent can make it perfectly clear to a purchaser of the real estate that the agent is acting in an agency capacity for a principal. In this situation, Sarah is a partially disclosed principal.

Partially disclosed principal • A principal whose identity is unknown by a third person, but the third person knows that the agent is or may be acting for a principal at the time the agent and the third person form a contract.

A disclosed or partially disclosed principal is liable to a third party for a contract made by an agent who is acting within the scope of his or her authority. If the principal is disclosed, the agent has no contractual liability if the principal or the third party does not perform. If the principal is partially disclosed, in most states the agent is treated as a party to the contract, and the third party can hold the agent liable.[7] If the agent *exceeds* the scope of his or her authority and the principal fails to ratify the contract, however, the third party cannot hold the principal liable for nonperformance. In such situations, the agent is generally liable unless the third party knew of the agent's lack of authority.

The following case illustrates the rules that apply to contracts signed by agents on behalf of fully disclosed principals.

6. *Restatement (Second) of Agency,* Section 4.
7. *Restatement (Second) of Agency,* Section 321.

MCBRIDE v. TAXMAN CORP.

CASE 14.3

Appellate Court of Illinois, First District, 2002. 327 Ill.App.3d 992, 765 N.E.2d 51, 262 Ill.Dec. 225. **http://state.il.us/court/default.htm**[a]

Walgreens Company entered into a lease with Taxman Corporation to operate a drugstore in Kedzie Plaza, a shopping center in Chicago, Illinois, owned by Kedzie Plaza Associates; Taxman was the center's property manager. The lease required the "Landlord" to promptly remove snow and ice from the center's sidewalks. Taxman also signed, on behalf of Kedzie Associates, an agreement with Arctic Snow and Ice Control, Inc., to remove ice and snow from the sidewalks surrounding the Walgreens store. On

a. On this page, click on "Appellate Court of Illinois." On the next page, in the "Appellate Court Documents" section, click on "Appellate Court Opinions." In the result, in the "Appellate Court" section, click on "2002." On the next page, in the "First District" section, click on "January." Finally, scroll to the bottom of the chart and click on the case name to access the opinion. The state of Illinois maintains this Web site.

January 27, 1996, Grace McBride, a Walgreens employee, slipped and fell on snow and ice outside the entrance to the store. McBride filed a suit in an Illinois state court against Taxman and others, alleging, among other things, that Taxman had negligently failed to remove the accumulation of ice and snow.[b] *Taxman filed a motion for summary judgment in its favor, which the court granted. McBride appealed to a state intermediate appellate court.*

CERDA, J.

On October 10, 1995, Taxman signed, on behalf of the owner, Arctic's one-page "Snow Removal Proposal & Contract" (although dated August 7, 1995), for the term November 15, 1995, through April 15, 1996, for the shopping center where this Walgreens store was located. * * *

Also on October 10, 1995, Arctic and Taxman signed a multi-page document dated October 3, 1995, that was apparently drafted by Taxman. The document was not given a title but contained several pages of terms concerning snow removal "per contract(s) attached." * * *

* * * *

Plaintiff argues that the contract between Taxman and Arctic created a duty of Taxman to remove ice and snow for the benefit of plaintiff. * * *

* * * *

The Arctic proposal and contract was signed "Kedzie Associates by the Taxman." The Taxman-drafted portion of the contract contained a line above the signature of Taxman's director of property management stating "The Taxman Corporation, agent for per contracts attached." The latter document specifically stated that the contract was not an obligation of Taxman and that all liabilities were those of the owner and not Taxman. We conclude that Taxman was the management company for the property owner and entered into the two contracts for snow and ice removal only as the owner's agent.

Taxman did not assume a contractual obligation to remove snow or ice; it merely retained Arctic as a contractor on behalf of the owner.

The state intermediate appellate court affirmed the judgment of the lower court. The appellate court held that Taxman entered into the snow removal contracts only as the agent of the owner, whose identity was fully disclosed. As agent for a disclosed principal, Taxman had no liability for the nonperformance of the principal or the third party to the contract.

QUESTIONS

1. On what basis did the state intermediate appellate court hold in this case that Taxman acted only as the owner's agent?
2. What were the reasons for the state intermediate appellate court's ruling regarding the parties' liability for the nonperformance of their contract?
3. If the Arctic contract had not identified Kedzie as the principal, could the court's decision in this case have been different?

b. McBride included in her suit complaints against Walgreens and Kedzie Associates but settled these complaints before trial.

Undisclosed Principal. The identity of an **undisclosed principal** is totally unknown to the third party. Furthermore, the third party has no knowledge that the agent is acting in an agency capacity at the time the contract is made.

Undisclosed principal • A principal whose identity is unknown by a third person, and the third person has no knowledge that the agent is acting for a principal at the time the agent and the third person form a contract.

When neither the fact of agency nor the identity of the principal is disclosed, a third party is deemed to be dealing with the agent personally, and the agent is liable as a party to the contract. If an agent has acted within the scope of his or her authority, the undisclosed principal is also liable as a party to the contract, just as if the principal had been fully disclosed at the time the contract was made. Conversely, with some exceptions, the undisclosed principal can hold the third party to the contract.

Liability for Torts and Crimes

Obviously, any person, including an agent, is liable for his or her own torts and crimes. Whether a principal can also be held liable for an agent's torts and crimes depends on several factors. A principal may also be liable for an agent's torts under the doctrine of ***respondeat superior,***[8] a Latin term meaning "let the master respond." This doctrine is similar to the theory of strict liability discussed in Chapter 12. The doctrine imposes vicarious (substitute) liability on the employer without regard to the personal fault of the employer for torts committed by an employee in the course or scope of employment.

Respondeat superior • In Latin, "Let the master respond." A doctrine under which a principal or an employer is held liable for the wrongful acts committed by agents or employees while acting within the course and scope of their agency or employment.

Liability for Agent's Torts. The key to determining whether a principal may be liable for the torts of the agent under the doctrine of *respondeat superior* is whether the torts are committed within the scope of the agency or employment. The *Restatement (Second) of Agency,* Section 229, indicates the factors that courts will consider in determining whether a particular act occurred within the course and scope of employment. These factors are as follows:

1. Whether the act was authorized by the employer.
2. The time, place, and purpose of the act.
3. Whether the act was one commonly performed by employees on behalf of their employers.
4. The extent to which the employer's interest was advanced by the act.
5. The extent to which the private interests of the employee were involved.
6. Whether the employer furnished the means or instrumentality (for example, a truck or a machine) by which the injury was inflicted.
7. Whether the employer had reason to know that the employee would perform the act in question and whether the employee had ever done it before.
8. Whether the act involved the commission of a serious crime.

A principal is exposed to tort liability whenever a third person sustains a loss due to the agent's misrepresentation. The principal's liability depends on whether the agent was actually or apparently authorized to make representations and whether such representations were made within the scope of the agency. The principal is always directly responsible for an agent's misrepresentation made within the scope of the agent's authority, whether the misrepresentation was made fraudulently or simply by the agent's mistake or oversight.

---

8. Pronounced ree-*spahn*-dee-uht soo-*peer*-ee-your.

Liability for Independent Contractor's Torts. Generally, the principal is not liable for physical harm caused to a third person by the negligent act of an independent contractor in the performance of the contract. This is because the employer does not have the *right to control* the details of an independent contractor's performance. Exceptions to this rule are made in certain situations, however, as when extremely hazardous activities are involved. Such activities include, for example, blasting operations, the transportation of highly volatile chemicals, and the use of poisonous gases. In these situations, a principal cannot be shielded from liability merely by using an independent contractor. Strict liability is imposed on the principal as a matter of law and, in some states, by statute.

Liability for Agent's Crimes. An agent is liable for his or her own crimes. A principal or employer is not liable for an agent's crime even if the crime was committed within the scope of authority or employment—unless the principal participated by conspiracy or other action. In some jurisdictions, under specific statutes, a principal may be liable for an agent's violation, in the course and scope of employment, of such regulations as those governing sanitation, prices, weights, and the sale of liquor.

WAGE-HOUR LAWS

In the 1930s, to protect employees against some of the adverse effects of the employment-at-will doctrine, Congress enacted several laws regulating the wages and working hours of employees. In 1931, Congress passed the Davis-Bacon Act,[9] which requires the payment of "prevailing wages" to employees of contractors and subcontractors working on government construction projects. In 1936, the Walsh-Healey Act[10] was passed. This act requires that a minimum wage, as well as overtime pay of time and a half, be paid to employees of manufacturers or suppliers entering into contracts with agencies of the federal government.

In 1938, with the passage of the Fair Labor Standards Act[11] (FLSA), wage-hour requirements were extended to cover all employers engaged in interstate commerce or engaged in the production of goods for interstate commerce. We examine here the FLSA's provisions in regard to child labor, maximum hours, and minimum wages.

Child Labor

The FLSA prohibits oppressive child labor. Children under fourteen years of age are allowed to do certain types of work, such as deliver newspapers, work for their parents, and be employed in the entertainment and (with some exceptions) agricultural areas. Children who are fourteen or fifteen years of age are allowed to work, but not in hazardous occupations. There are also numerous restrictions on how many hours per day and per week they can work. For example, they cannot work during school hours, for more than three hours on a school day (or eight hours on a nonschool day), for more

9. 40 U.S.C. Sections 276a–276a-5.
10. 41 U.S.C. Sections 35–45.
11. 29 U.S.C. Sections 201–260.

than eighteen hours during a school week (or forty hours during a nonschool week), or before 7 A.M. or after 7 P.M. (9 P.M. during the summer). Most states require persons under sixteen years of age to obtain work permits.

Persons between the ages of sixteen and eighteen do not face such restrictions on working times and hours, but they cannot be employed in hazardous jobs or in jobs detrimental to their health and well-being. Persons over the age of eighteen are not affected by any of the above-mentioned restrictions.

Hours and Wages

Under the FLSA, any employee who agrees to work more than forty hours per week must be paid no less than one and a half times his or her regular pay for all hours over forty. Certain employees are exempt from the overtime provisions of the act. Exempt employees fall into four categories: executives, administrative employees, professional employees, and outside salespersons. Generally, to fall into one of these categories, an employee must earn more than a specified amount of income per week and devote a certain percentage of work time to the performance of specific types of duties, as determined by the FLSA. To qualify as an outside salesperson, the employee must regularly engage in sales work away from the office and spend no more than 20 percent of work time per week performing duties other than sales.

The FLSA provides that a **minimum wage** of a specified amount (currently, $5.15 per hour) must be paid to employees in covered industries. Congress periodically revises the amount of the minimum wage. Under the FLSA, the term *wages* includes the reasonable costs of the employer in furnishing employees with board, lodging, and other facilities if they are customarily furnished by that employer.

Minimum wage • The lowest wage, either by government regulation or union contract, that an employer may pay an hourly worker.

Do the FLSA's provisions apply to "telecommuters" and others in the work force who do not perform their jobs in the employer's workplace? For a discussion of this issue and others relating to the "virtual workplace," see this chapter's *Emerging Trends* feature on pages 516 and 517.

Worker Health and Safety

Under the common law, employees injured on the job had to rely on tort law or contract law theories in suits they brought against their employers. Additionally, workers had some recourse under the common law governing agency relationships, which imposes a duty on an employer to provide a safe workplace for his or her agent-employee. Today, numerous state and federal statutes protect employees from the risk of accidental injury, death, or disease resulting from their employment. This section discusses the primary federal statute governing health and safety in the workplace, along with state workers' compensation acts.

The Occupational Safety and Health Act

At the federal level, the primary legislation for employee health and safety protection is the Occupational Safety and Health Act of 1970.[12] Congress passed this act in an attempt to ensure safe and healthful working conditions

---

12. 29 U.S.C. Sections 553, 651–678.

EMERGING TRENDS

Employment Issues in the Virtual Workplace

Over thirty million workers in the United States telecommute, up from fewer than twenty million at the end of the last decade. Between eight and ten million U.S. workers now telecommute full-time and never lay eyes on, or feet in, a physical office building. As often happens, though, a spurt in technology—mainly due to the growth in Internet use—has caused real-world conditions to leap ahead of the law. After all, virtually all state and federal statutes governing employment were drafted when the only workplace was the traditional workplace.

In this feature, we examine the application of overtime and minimum-wage laws to the virtual work force. We then look at the thorny issue of safety regulation of home-based work sites, particularly with respect to the workplace safety regulations of the Occupational Safety and Health Administration.

DO OVERTIME AND MINIMUM-WAGE LAWS APPLY TO THE VIRTUAL WORK FORCE?

Not until the early 1990s did the U.S. Department of Labor issue regulations defining exemptions to the overtime-pay requirements for employees in computer-related occupations. Under the regulations, these employees can qualify as "professionals" and thus be exempt from the overtime-pay requirements. When an employee falls within this (or any other) exemption to the overtime-pay requirements of the Fair Labor Standards Act, the employee is not entitled to be paid time and a half for overtime hours.

For employees in computer-related occupations to qualify for this exemption, they must meet certain requirements. They must be (1) highly skilled in computer analysis, programming, or related work; (2) involved in the application of systems analysis, techniques, and procedures or in the design, development, creation, or testing of computer programs; or (3) involved in the modification, creation, or testing of machine operating systems.

Just because employees work in a remote location—telecommute—does not mean that they are automatically exempt from the overtime-pay requirements or the minimum-wage laws. Any employer who misclassifies employees as exempt from these regulations may be subject to both criminal and civil penalties.

Under all circumstances, employers are required to monitor the hours worked by nonexempt telecommuting employees, even if doing so presents a challenge. Today, software programs are available that will monitor hours of work for a telecommuting employee.

NONEXEMPT EMPLOYEES IN COMPUTER-RELATED OCCUPATIONS

The professional exemption does not apply to trainees or to entry-level employees in computer specialties, such as programming and analysis. Individuals operating computers or manufacturing, repairing, or maintaining computer hardware are also not included in the professional exemption for overtime pay. Moreover, the mere fact that an employee relies heavily on computers or computer software in his or her work does not qualify that person for a professional exemption.

Under most circumstances, junior programmers, programmer trainees, keypunch operators, and computer operators are considered not to have sufficient discretion and independence to qualify as administrative

for practically every employee in the country. The act provides for specific standards that employers must meet, plus a general duty to keep workplaces safe.

Enforcement Agencies. Three federal agencies develop and enforce the standards set by the Occupational Safety and Health Act. The Occupational Safety and Health Administration (OSHA) is part of the Department of Labor and has the authority to promulgate standards, make inspections, and enforce the act. OSHA has safety standards governing many workplace details, such as

EMERGING TRENDS

Employment Issues in the Virtual Workplace

employees. They are, consequently, subject to federal overtime regulations.

REGULATING THE SAFETY OF AT-HOME WORK SITES

The Occupational Safety and Health Administration (OSHA) did not issue a formal directive on home-office safety until 2000. At that time, OSHA stated that it would not conduct home-office inspections and would not hold employers liable for their employees' home offices. It also stated that it did not expect employers to inspect the home offices of their telecommuting employees.

Nonetheless, OSHA holds employers responsible for any situation in which hazardous materials or work processes are provided or required to be used in an employee's home office. Additionally, employers are required to keep OSHA injury and illness records for any work-related injuries and illnesses that occur in home work environments (these records will be discussed further elsewhere in this chapter). In contrast, OSHA has not applied these record-keeping requirements to virtual workers working out of their cars, hotel rooms, and airports, for example. At some point in the future, OSHA may audit remote work sites and increase record-keeping requirements.

IMPLICATIONS FOR THE BUSINESSPERSON

❶ Simply designating an employee as a telecommuting employee does not change the employee's status with respect to the overtime-pay requirements of state and federal laws. If an employee did not fall under a professional or management exemption prior to her or his switch to the virtual work force, then once that switch is made, overtime requirements will still apply.

❷ Because OSHA may in the future change its audit requirements for remote work sites, businesses are well advised to take reasonable preventive measures; that is, businesses should encourage remote employees to maintain safe and healthful work environments away from the office.

FOR CRITICAL ANALYSIS

❶ Why might telecommuting employees sometimes accept being wrongly classified (and not being paid overtime)?

❷ Under what scenario might a home-based employee sue his or her employer for injuries in the home office?

RELEVANT WEB SITES

To locate information on the Web concerning the issues discussed in this feature, go to this text's Web site at **http://ele.westbuslaw.com** and click on "Interactive Study Center."

the structural stability of ladders and the requirements for railings. OSHA also establishes standards that protect employees against exposure to substances that may be harmful to their health.

The National Institute for Occupational Safety and Health is part of the Department of Health and Human Services. Its main duty is to conduct research on safety and health problems and to recommend standards for OSHA to adopt. Finally, the Occupational Safety and Health Review Commission is an independent agency set up to handle appeals from actions taken by OSHA administrators.

Procedures and Violations. OSHA compliance officers may enter and inspect facilities of any establishment covered by the Occupational Safety and Health Act.[13] Employees may also file complaints of violations. Under the act, an employer cannot discharge an employee who files a complaint or who, in good faith, refuses to work in a high-risk area if bodily harm or death might result.

Employers with eleven or more employees are required to keep occupational injury and illness records for each employee. Each record must be made available for inspection when requested by an OSHA inspector. Whenever a work-related injury or disease occurs, employers must make reports directly to OSHA. Whenever an employee is killed in a work-related accident or when five or more employees are hospitalized in one accident, the employer must notify the Department of Labor within forty-eight hours. If the company fails to do so, it will be fined. Following the accident, a complete inspection of the premises is mandatory.

Criminal penalties for willful violation of the Occupational Safety and Health Act are limited. Employers may be prosecuted under state laws, however. In other words, the act does not preempt state and local criminal laws.[14]

State Workers' Compensation Laws

Workers' compensation laws • State statutes establishing an administrative procedure for compensating workers' injuries that arise out of—or in the course of—their employment, regardless of fault.

State **workers' compensation laws** establish an administrative procedure for compensating workers injured on the job. Instead of suing, an injured worker files a claim with the administrative agency or board that administers the local workers' compensation claims.

Employees Covered by Workers' Compensation. Most workers' compensation statutes are similar. No state covers all employees. Typically excluded are domestic workers, agricultural workers, temporary employees, and employees of common carriers (companies that provide shipping and transportation services to the public). Generally, the statutes cover minors. Usually, the statutes allow employers to purchase insurance from a private insurer or a state fund to pay workers' compensation benefits in the event of a claim. Most states also allow employers to be *self-insured*—that is, employers who show an ability to pay claims do not need to buy insurance.

Requirements for Receiving Workers' Compensation. In general, the right to recover benefits is predicated wholly on the existence of an employment relationship and the fact that the worker's injury was *accidental* and *occurred on the job or in the course of employment,* regardless of fault. Intentionally inflicted self-injury, for example, would not be considered accidental and hence would not be covered. If an injury occurs while an employee is commuting to or from work, it usually will not be considered to have occurred on the job or in the course of employment and hence will not be covered.

---

13. In the past, warrantless inspections were conducted. In 1978, however, the United States Supreme Court held that warrantless inspections violated the warrant clause of the Fourth Amendment to the Constitution. See *Marshall v. Barlow's, Inc.,* 436 U.S. 307, 98 S.Ct. 1816, 56 L.Ed.2d 305 (1978).

14. *Pedraza v. Shell Oil Co.,* 942 F.2d 48 (1st Cir. 1991); *cert.* denied, *Shell Oil Co. v. Pedraza,* 502 U.S. 1082, 112 S.Ct. 993, 117 L.Ed.2d 154 (1992).

An employee must notify his or her employer of an injury promptly (usually within thirty days of the injury's occurrence). Generally, an employee also must file a workers' compensation claim with the appropriate state agency or board within a certain period (sixty days to two years) from the time the injury is first noticed, rather than from the time of the accident.

Workers' Compensation versus Litigation. An employee's acceptance of workers' compensation benefits bars the employee from suing for injuries caused by the employer's negligence. By barring lawsuits for negligence, workers' compensation laws also bar employers from raising common law defenses to negligence, such as contributory negligence. For example, an employer can no longer raise such defenses as contributory negligence or assumption of risk to avoid liability for negligence. A worker may sue an employer who *intentionally* injures the worker, however.

INCOME SECURITY

Federal and state governments participate in insurance programs designed to protect employees and their families by covering the financial impact of retirement, disability, death, hospitalization, and unemployment. The key federal law on this subject is the Social Security Act of 1935.[15]

Social Security

The Social Security Act of 1935 provides for old-age (retirement), survivors, and disability insurance. The act is therefore often referred to as OASDI. Both employers and employees must "contribute" under the Federal Insurance Contributions Act (FICA)[16] to help pay for the employees' loss of income on retirement.

The basis for the employee's and the employer's contribution is the employee's annual wage base—the maximum amount of the employee's wages that are subject to the tax. The employer withholds the employee's FICA contribution from the employee's wages and then matches this contribution.

The annual wage base increases each year to take into account increases in the cost of living. In 2003, employers were required to withhold 6.2 percent of each employee's wages, up to a maximum amount of $87,000, and to match this contribution.

Retired workers are eligible to receive monthly payments from the Social Security Administration, which administers the Social Security Act. Social Security benefits are fixed by statute but increase automatically with increases in the cost of living.

One issue that has arisen under FICA and the Federal Unemployment Tax Act (FUTA) (discussed later in this chapter) is whether wages should be taxed according to the rates in effect when the wages are owed or the rates in effect when the wages are actually paid. The amounts in dispute can be large, as the following case illustrates.

15. 42 U.S.C. Sections 301–1397e.
16. 26 U.S.C. Sections 3101–3125.

CASE 14.4

Supreme Court of the United States, 2001.
532 U.S. 200,
121 S.Ct. 1433,
149 L.Ed.2d 401.
http://supct.law.cornell.edu/supct/cases/historic.htm[a]

UNITED STATES v. CLEVELAND INDIANS BASEBALL CO.

In any given year, the amount of FICA and FUTA tax owed depends on two factors: the tax rate and the ceiling on taxable wages (also called the wage base), which limits the amount of wages subject to tax. The rates and the ceilings increase over time. For example, in 1986, the FICA tax on employees and employers was 5.7 percent on wages up to $42,000; in 1987, it was 5.7 percent on wages up to $43,800; and in 1994, 6.2 percent on wages up to $60,600. The Medicare tax on employees and employers remained constant at 1.45 percent each from 1986 to 1994, but the wage base rose from $42,000 in 1986 to $43,800 in 1987, and by 1994, Congress had abolished the ceiling, subjecting all wages to the Medicare tax. In 1986 and 1987, the FUTA tax was 6.0 percent on wages up to $7,000; in 1994, it was 6.2 percent on wages up to $7,000. In 1994, the Major League Baseball Players Association settled a grievance with twenty-six major league baseball teams for conspiring to stop the steep escalation of salaries for free agent players. Several teams agreed to pay a total of $280 million to the players. Under the agreement, the Cleveland Indians Baseball Company owed eight players a total of $610,000 in salary for 1986 and fourteen players a total of $1,457,848 for 1987. The company paid the amounts in 1994. The company also paid taxes on the amounts according to the 1994 rates and ceilings and then applied for a refund of more than $100,000, claiming that the taxes should have been computed according to the 1986 and 1987 rates and ceilings.[b] *The Internal Revenue Service denied the claim, and the company filed a suit in a federal district court against the federal government. The court ordered a refund of the FICA and FUTA taxes. The government appealed to the U.S. Court of Appeals for the Sixth Circuit, which affirmed the lower court's order. The government appealed to the United States Supreme Court.*

GINSBURG, J.

The Internal Revenue Service has long maintained regulations interpreting the FICA and FUTA tax provisions. In their current form, the regulations specify that the employer tax "attaches *at the time that the wages are paid* by the employer" and "is computed by applying to the wages paid by the employer the rate in effect *at the time such wages are paid.*" Echoing the language in [FICA] and [FUTA], these regulations have continued unchanged in their basic substance since 1940.

Although the regulations, like the statute, do not specifically address backpay, the Internal Revenue Service has consistently interpreted them to require taxation of back wages according to the year the wages are actually paid, regardless of when those wages were earned or should have been paid. We

a. In the "Search" box, type "Cleveland Indians." Select "all current and historic decisions," and click on "submit." In the result, scroll to the name of the case and click on it to access the opinion. The Legal Information Institute of Cornell Law School in Ithaca, New York, maintains this Web site.

b. All but one of the players had collected wages from the company exceeding the ceilings in 1986 and 1987. Because those players, and the company, paid the maximum amount of employment taxes in 1986 and 1987, allocating the 1994 payments back to those years would mean that no taxes would be owed on the amounts. Treating the back wages as taxable in 1994, however, would create significant tax liability, partly because the company did not pay any of the players any other wages in 1994.

need not decide whether the Revenue Rulings themselves are entitled to deference [high regard]. In this case, the Rulings simply reflect the agency's longstanding interpretation of its own regulations. Because that interpretation is reasonable, it attracts substantial judicial deference. We do not resist according such deference in reviewing an agency's steady interpretation of its own 61-year-old regulation implementing a 62-year-old statute. *Treasury regulations and interpretations long continued without substantial change, applying to unamended or substantially reenacted statutes, are deemed to have received congressional approval and have the effect of law.* [Emphasis added.]

* * * *

In line with the text and administrative history of the relevant taxation provisions, we hold that, for FICA and FUTA tax purposes, back wages should be attributed to the year in which they are actually paid.

The United States Supreme Court held that taxes on wages should be computed using the rates and ceilings that apply in the year when the wages are actually paid, not those in effect in the year when the wages should have been paid. The Court reversed the decision of the lower court.

QUESTIONS

1. Who appealed this case to the United States Supreme Court, and why?
2. Should wages be taxed by reference to the year that they are actually paid, according to the United States Supreme Court in this case?
3. The rule applied by the Court in this case disadvantaged the taxpayer, while in other cases it has disadvantaged the government. With that in mind, what was Congress's likely intent regarding the FICA and FUTA tax provisions?

Medicare

Medicare, a federal government health-insurance program, is administered by the Social Security Administration for people sixty-five years of age and older and for some under age sixty-five who are disabled. It has two parts, one pertaining to hospital costs and the other to nonhospital medical costs, such as visits to physicians' offices. People who have Medicare hospital insurance can obtain additional federal medical insurance if they pay small monthly premiums, which increase as the cost of medical care increases.

As with Social Security contributions, both the employer and the employee contribute to Medicare. Currently, 1.45 percent of the amount of all wages and salaries paid to employees, plus a matching amount paid by the employer, go toward financing Medicare. There is no cap on the amount of wages subject to the Medicare tax.

Private Pension Plans

There has been significant legislation to regulate employee retirement plans set up by employers to supplement Social Security benefits. The major federal act covering these retirement plans is the Employee Retirement Income Security

Act (ERISA) of 1974.[17] This statute empowers the Labor Management Services Administration of the Department of Labor to enforce its provisions governing employers who have private pension funds for their employees. ERISA does not require an employer to establish a pension plan. When a plan exists, however, ERISA establishes standards for its management.

Vesting • The creation of an absolute or unconditional right or power. A pension plan becomes vested when an employee has a legal right to the benefits provided.

A key provision of ERISA concerns vesting. **Vesting** gives an employee a legal right to receive pension benefits at some future date when he or she stops working. Before ERISA was enacted, some employees who had worked for companies for as long as thirty years received no pension benefits when their employment terminated, because those benefits had not vested. ERISA establishes complex vesting rules. Generally, however, all employee contributions to pension plans vest immediately, and employee rights to employer pension-plan contributions vest after five years of employment.

In an attempt to prevent mismanagement of pension funds, ERISA has established rules on how they must be invested. Pension managers must be cautious in their investments and refrain from investing more than 10 percent of the fund in securities (stocks and bonds) of the employer. ERISA also contains detailed record-keeping and reporting requirements.

Unemployment Compensation

The United States has a system of unemployment insurance in which employers pay into a fund, the proceeds of which are paid out to qualified unemployed workers. The Federal Unemployment Tax Act (FUTA) of 1935[18] created a state-administered system that provides unemployment compensation to eligible individuals. The FUTA and state laws require employers that fall under the provisions of the act to pay unemployment taxes at regular intervals.

COBRA

Federal legislation also addresses the issue of health insurance for workers whose jobs have been terminated and who are thus no longer eligible for group health-insurance plans. The Consolidated Omnibus Budget Reconciliation Act (COBRA) of 1985[19] prohibits the elimination of a worker's medical, optical, or dental insurance coverage on the voluntary or involuntary termination of the worker's employment. The act applies to most workers who have either lost their jobs or had their hours decreased so that they are no longer eligible for coverage under the employer's health plan. Only workers fired for gross misconduct are excluded from protection.

Application of COBRA

The worker has sixty days (beginning with the date that the group coverage would stop) to decide whether to continue with the employer's group insurance plan. If the worker chooses to discontinue the coverage, then the employer has no further obligation. If the worker chooses to continue coverage, however, the employer is obligated to keep the policy active for up to eighteen months. If the worker is disabled, the employer must extend coverage up to twenty-nine

17. 29 U.S.C. Sections 1001 *et seq.*
18. 26 U.S.C. Sections 3301–3310.
19. 29 U.S.C. Sections 1161–1169.

months. The coverage provided must be the same as that enjoyed by the worker prior to the termination or reduction of employment. If family members were originally included, for example, COBRA would prohibit their exclusion. This is not a free ride for the worker, however. To receive continued benefits, he or she may be required to pay all of the premium, as well as a 2 percent administrative charge.

Employers' Obligations under COBRA

Employers, with some exceptions, must comply with COBRA if they employ twenty or more workers and provide a benefit plan to those workers. An employer must inform an employee of COBRA's provisions when that worker faces termination or a reduction of hours that would affect his or her eligibility for coverage under the plan.

An employer is relieved of the responsibility to provide benefit coverage if it completely eliminates its group benefit plan. An employer is also relieved of responsibility when the worker becomes eligible for Medicare, falls under a spouse's health plan, becomes insured under a different plan (with a new employer, for example), or fails to pay the premium.

An employer that fails to comply with COBRA risks substantial penalties. These penalties include a tax of up to 10 percent of the annual cost of the group plan or $500,000, whichever is less.

Family and Medical Leave

In 1993, Congress passed the Family and Medical Leave Act (FMLA)[20] to protect employees who need time off work for family or medical reasons. A majority of the states also have legislation allowing for a leave from employment for family or medical reasons, and many employers maintain private family-leave plans for their workers.

Coverage and Application of the FMLA

The FMLA requires employers who have fifty or more employees to provide employees with up to twelve weeks of family or medical leave during any twelve-month period. During the employee's leave, the employer must continue the worker's health-care coverage and guarantee employment in the same or a comparable position when the employee returns to work. An important exception to the FMLA, however, allows the employer to avoid reinstatement of a *key employee*—defined as an employee whose pay falls within the top 10 percent of the firm's work force. Additionally, the act does not apply to employees who have worked less than one year or less than twenty-five hours a week during the previous twelve months.

The FMLA expressly covers private and public (government) employees. Some states argued, and some courts agreed, however, that public employees could not sue their state employers in federal courts to enforce their FMLA rights unless the states consented to be sued.[21] This argument was presented to the United States Supreme Court in the following case.

20. 29 U.S.C. Sections 2601, 2611–2619, 2651–2654.

21. Under the U.S. Constitution's Eleventh Amendment, a state is immune from suit in a federal court unless the state agrees to be sued.

CASE 14.5

Supreme Court of the United States, 2003.
__ U.S. __,
123 S.Ct. 1972,
155 L.Ed.2d 953.
http://supct.law.cornell.edu/supct[a]

NEVADA DEPARTMENT OF HUMAN RESOURCES v. HIBBS

William Hibbs worked for the Nevada Department of Human Resources. In April 1997, Hibbs asked for time off under the FMLA to care for his sick wife, who was recovering from a car accident and neck surgery. The department granted Hibbs's request, allowing him to use the leave intermittently, as needed, beginning in May. Hibbs did this until August 5, after which he did not return to work. In October, the department told Hibbs that he had exhausted his FMLA leave, that no further leave would be granted, and that he must return to work by November 12. When he did not return, he was discharged. Hibbs filed a suit in a federal district court against the department. The court held that the U.S. Constitution's Eleventh Amendment barred the suit. On Hibbs's appeal, the U.S. Court of Appeals for the Ninth Circuit reversed this holding. The department appealed to the United States Supreme Court.

REHNQUIST, J.

The history of the many state laws limiting women's employment opportunities is chronicled in—and, until relatively recently, was sanctioned by—this Court's own opinions. For example, in [previous cases] the Court upheld state laws prohibiting women from practicing law and tending bar * * * . State laws frequently subjected women to distinctive restrictions, terms, conditions, and benefits for those jobs they could take. In [one case] for example, this Court approved a state law limiting the hours that women could work for wages, and observed that 19 States had such laws at the time. Such laws were based on the related beliefs that (1) woman is, and should remain, the center of home and family life, and (2) a proper discharge of a woman's maternal functions—having in view not merely her own health, but the well-being of the race—justifies legislation to protect her from the greed as well as the passion of man. Until [1971] it remained the prevailing doctrine that government, both federal and state, could withhold from women opportunities accorded men so long as any basis in reason—such as the above beliefs—could be conceived for the discrimination.

Congress responded to this history of discrimination by abrogating States' sovereign immunity in Title VII of the Civil Rights Act of 1964 * * * .[b] But state gender discrimination did not cease. It can hardly be doubted that * * * women still face[d] pervasive, although at times more subtle, discrimination * * * in the job market. According to evidence that was before Congress when it enacted the FMLA, States continue[d] to rely on invalid gender stereotypes in the employment context, specifically in the administration of leave benefits. Reliance on such stereotypes cannot justify the States' gender discrimination in this area. *The long and extensive history of sex discrimination prompted us to hold that measures that differentiate on the basis of gender warrant heightened scrutiny;* here, the persistence of such unconstitutional discrimination by the States justifie[d] Congress' passage of prophylactic [preventive] * * * legislation. [Emphasis added.]

* * * *

Congress * * * heard testimony that parental leave for fathers * * * is rare. Even * * * where child-care leave policies do exist, men, *both in the*

---

a. In the "Search" box, type in the name of the case. Select "all current and historic decisions," and then click on "submit." In the result, scroll to the name of the case and click on it to access the opinion.

b. This statute, and employment discrimination generally, will be discussed in detail in Chapter 15.

public and private sectors, receive notoriously discriminatory treatment in their requests for such leave. Many States offered women extended "maternity" leave that far exceeded the typical 4- to 8-week period of physical disability due to pregnancy and childbirth, but very few States granted men a parallel benefit: Fifteen States provided women up to one year of extended maternity leave, while only four provided men with the same. This and other differential leave policies were not attributable to any differential physical needs of men and women, but rather to the pervasive sex-role stereotype that caring for family members is women's work.

Evidence pertaining to parenting leave is relevant here because state discrimination in the provision of both types of benefits is based on the same gender stereotype: that women's family duties trump those of the workplace. [Emphasis added.] * * *

* * * *

* * * Because employers continued to regard the family as the woman's domain, they often denied men similar accommodations or discouraged them from taking leave. These mutually reinforcing stereotypes created a self-fulfilling cycle of discrimination that forced women to continue to assume the role of primary family caregiver, and fostered employers' stereotypical views about women's commitment to work and their value as employees. Those perceptions * * * lead to subtle discrimination that may be difficult to detect on a case-by-case basis.

* * * *

By creating an across-the-board, routine employment benefit for all eligible employees, Congress sought to ensure that family-care leave would no longer be stigmatized as an inordinate drain on the workplace caused by female employees, and that employers could not evade leave obligations simply by hiring men. By setting a minimum standard of family leave for *all* eligible employees, irrespective of gender, the FMLA attacks the formerly state-sanctioned stereotype that only women are responsible for family caregiving, thereby reducing employers' incentives to engage in discrimination by basing hiring and promotion decisions on stereotypes. [Emphasis added.]

* * * *

* * * [T]he FMLA is narrowly targeted at the fault line between work and family—precisely where sex-based overgeneralization has been and remains strongest—and affects only one aspect of the employment relationship.

* * * *

For the above reasons, we conclude that [the FMLA] is congruent [corresponds to] and [is] proportional to its remedial object, and can be understood as responsive to, or designed to prevent, unconstitutional behavior.

The United States Supreme Court affirmed the lower court's decision, concluding that the FMLA is "congruent and proportional" to the discrimination that Congress intended the FMLA to address. Thus, the FMLA, which expressly covers public employees, can serve as the basis for a suit against a state employer regardless of whether the state consents to the suit.

QUESTIONS

1. Who appealed this case to the United States Supreme Court, and why?
2. What was the primary issue before the Court in this case, and what did the Court hold with respect to that issue?

3. Can a law foster discrimination even when the law itself is not obviously discriminatory?

Requirements for Family or Medical Leave

Generally, an employee may take family leave when he or she wishes to care for a newborn baby, a newly adopted child, or a foster child just placed in the employee's care.[22] An employee may take medical leave when the employee or the employee's spouse, child, or parent has a "serious health condition" requiring care. For most absences, the employee must demonstrate that the health condition requires continued treatment by a health-care provider and includes a period of incapacity of more than three days.

Under regulations issued by the Department of Labor (DOL) in 1995, employees suffering from certain chronic health conditions may take FMLA leave for their own incapacities that require absences of less than three days. For example, an employee who has asthma or diabetes may have periodic occurrences of illness, rather than episodes continuing over an extended period of time. Similarly, pregnancy may involve periodic visits to a health-care provider and bouts of morning sickness. According to the DOL's regulations, employees with such conditions are covered by the FMLA.

Remedies for Violations of the FMLA

Remedies for violations of the FMLA include (1) damages for unpaid wages (or salary), lost benefits, denied compensation, and actual monetary losses (such as the cost of providing for care) up to an amount equivalent to the employee's wages for twelve weeks; (2) job reinstatement; and (3) promotion. The successful plaintiff is entitled to court costs, attorneys' fees, and—in cases involving bad faith on the part of the employer—double damages.

EMPLOYEE PRIVACY RIGHTS

In the last twenty-five years, concerns about the privacy rights of employees have arisen in response to the sometimes invasive tactics used by employers to monitor and screen workers. Perhaps the greatest privacy concern in today's employment arena has to do with electronic performance monitoring. Clearly, employers need to protect themselves from liability for their employees' online activities. They also have a legitimate interest in monitoring the productivity of their workers. At the same time, employees expect to have a certain zone of privacy in the workplace. Indeed, many lawsuits have involved allegations that employers' intrusive monitoring practices violate employees' privacy rights.

Electronic Monitoring in the Workplace

According to a survey by the American Management Association, more than two-thirds of employers engage in some form of electronic monitoring of their employees. Types of monitoring include reviewing employees' e-mail

---

22. The foster care must be state sanctioned for such an arrangement to fall within the coverage of the FMLA.

and computer files, video recording employees' job performance, and recording and reviewing telephone conversations and voice mail.

Another type of monitoring involves employees' use of the Internet. Specially designed software products have made it easier for an employer to track employees' Internet use. For example, software is now available that allows an employer to track virtually every move made using the Internet, including the specific Web sites visited and the time spent surfing the Web.

Often, employer security measures involve the use of filtering software as well. As discussed in Chapter 5, filtering software prevents access to specified Web sites, such as sites containing pornographic or sexually explicit images. Other filtering software may be used to screen incoming e-mail and block mail that consists of spam or that may contain a virus.

The use of filtering software by public employers (government agencies) has led to charges that blocking access to Web sites violates employees' rights to free speech, which are guaranteed by the First Amendment to the U.S. Constitution. Although the use of filtering software by government institutions has been controversial, this issue does not arise in private businesses because the First Amendment's protection of free speech applies only to *government* restraints on speech, not restraints imposed in the private sector.

Laws Protecting Employee Privacy Rights. A number of laws protect privacy rights. We look here at laws that apply in the employment context, particularly with respect to electronic monitoring.

Protection under Constitutional and Tort Law. Recall from Chapter 5 that the U.S. Constitution does not contain a provision that explicitly guarantees a right to privacy. A personal right to privacy, however, has been inferred from other constitutional guarantees provided by the First, Third, Fourth, Fifth, and Ninth Amendments to the Constitution. Tort law (see Chapter 12), state constitutions, and a number of state and federal statutes also provide for privacy rights.

The Electronic Communications Privacy Act. The major statute with which employers must comply is the Electronic Communications Privacy Act (ECPA) of 1986.[23] This act amended existing federal wiretapping law to cover electronic forms of communications, such as communications via cellular telephones or e-mail. The ECPA prohibits the intentional interception of any wire or electronic communication or the intentional disclosure or use of the information obtained by the interception. Excluded from coverage, however, are any electronic communications through devices that are furnished to the subscriber or user by a provider of wire or electronic communication service and that are being used by the subscriber or user, or by the provider of the service, "in the ordinary course of its business."

This "business-extension exception" to the ECPA permits an employer to monitor employee electronic communications in the ordinary course of business. It does not permit an employer to monitor employees' personal communications. Under another exception to the ECPA, however, an employer may avoid liability under the act if the employees consent to having their electronic communications intercepted by the employer. Thus, an employer

23. 18 U.S.C. Sections 2510–2521.

may be able to avoid liability under the ECPA by simply requiring employees to sign forms indicating that they consent to such monitoring.

Clearly, the law allows employers to engage in electronic monitoring in the workplace. In fact, cases in which courts have held that an employer's monitoring of electronic communications in the workplace violated employees' privacy rights are rare. Yet there are some limits on how far an employer can go in monitoring employee communications.

Factors Considered by the Courts in Employee Privacy Cases. When determining whether an employer should be held liable for violating an employee's privacy rights, the courts generally weigh the employer's interests against the employee's reasonable expectation of privacy. Generally, if employees are informed that their communications are being monitored, they cannot reasonably expect those communications to be private. If employees are not informed that certain communications are being monitored, however, the employer may be held liable for invading their privacy.

In one case, for example, an employer secretly recorded conversations among his four employees by placing a tape recorder in their common office. The conversations were of a highly personal nature and included harsh criticisms of the employer. The employer immediately fired two of the employees, informing them that their termination was due to their comments on the tape. In the ensuing suit, one of the issues was whether the employees, in these circumstances, had a reasonable expectation of privacy. The court held that they did and granted summary judgment in their favor. The employees clearly would not have criticized their boss if they had not assumed that their conversations were private. Furthermore, the office was small, and the employees were careful that no third parties ever overheard their comments.[24]

Privacy Expectations and E-Mail Systems. In cases brought by employees alleging that their privacy has been invaded by e-mail monitoring, the courts have tended to hold for the employers. This is true even when employees were not informed that their e-mail would be monitored. In a leading case on this issue, the Pillsbury Company promised its employees that it would not read their e-mail or terminate or discipline them based on the content of their e-mail. Despite this promise, Pillsbury intercepted employee Michael Smyth's e-mail, decided that it was unprofessional and inappropriate, and fired him. In Smyth's suit against the company, he claimed that his termination was a violation of the public policy protecting employee privacy rights. The court, however, found no "reasonable expectation of privacy in e-mail communications voluntarily made by an employee to his supervisor over the company e-mail system."[25]

Courts are reluctant to hold that employees' privacy interests have been violated even if employers access employees' password-protected files. In one case, for example, Microsoft Corporation had suspended an employee pending an investigation into accusations of sexual harassment and other misconduct. During the suspension, Microsoft read his e-mail, which was stored in "personal folders" and protected by a password. After Microsoft fired the employee, he sued the company for invasion of privacy, claiming that the e-mail was his personal property. The court reasoned that because the com-

---

24. *Dorris v. Abscher,* 179 F.3d 420 (6th Cir. 1999).

25. *Smyth v. Pillsbury Co.,* 914 F.Supp. 97 (E.D.Pa. 1996).

pany gave the employee the computer to enable him to do his job and provided him with the e-mail application, the e-mail on his computer was "merely an inherent part of the office environment."[26]

Other Types of Monitoring

In addition to monitoring their employees' online activities, employers also engage in other types of employee screening and monitoring practices. These practices, which have included lie-detector tests, drug tests, AIDS (acquired immune deficiency syndrome) tests, and screening procedures, have often been subject to challenge as violations of employee privacy rights.

Lie-Detector Tests. At one time, many employers required employees or job applicants to take polygraph examinations (lie-detector tests) in connection with their employment. To protect the privacy interests of employees and job applicants, in 1988 Congress passed the Employee Polygraph Protection Act.[27] The act prohibits employers from (1) requiring or causing employees or job applicants to take lie-detector tests or suggesting or requesting that they do so; (2) using, accepting, referring to, or asking about the results of lie-detector tests taken by employees or applicants; and (3) taking or threatening negative employment-related action against employees or applicants based on results of lie-detector tests or on refusal to take the tests.

Employers excepted from these prohibitions include federal, state, and local government employers; certain security service firms; and companies manufacturing and distributing controlled substances. Other employers may use polygraph tests when investigating losses attributable to theft, including embezzlement and the theft of trade secrets.

Drug Testing. In the interests of public safety and to reduce unnecessary costs, many employers, including the government, require their employees to submit to drug testing. State laws relating to the privacy rights of private-sector employees vary from state to state. Some state constitutions may prohibit private employers from testing for drugs, and state statutes may restrict drug testing by private employers in any number of ways. A collective bargaining agreement may also provide protection against drug testing. In some instances, employees have brought an action against the employer for the tort of invasion of privacy (discussed in Chapter 12).

Constitutional limitations apply to the testing of government employees. The Fourth Amendment provides that individuals have the right to be "secure in their persons" against "unreasonable searches and seizures" conducted by government agents. Drug tests have been held constitutional, however, when there was a reasonable basis for suspecting government employees of using drugs. Additionally, when drug use in a particular government job could threaten public safety, testing has been upheld. For example, a Department of Transportation rule that requires employees engaged in oil and gas pipeline operations to submit to random drug testing was upheld, even though the rule did not require that before being tested the individual must have been suspected of drug use.[28] The court

26. *McLaren v. Microsoft Corp.,* 1999 WL 339015 (Tex.App.—Dallas 1999).

27. 29 U.S.C. Sections 2001 *et seq.*

28. *Electrical Workers Local 1245 v. Skinner,* 913 F.2d 1454 (9th Cir. 1990).

held that the government's interest in promoting public safety in the pipeline industry outweighed the employees' privacy interests.

AIDS Testing. A number of employers test their workers for acquired immune deficiency syndrome (AIDS). Some state laws restrict or ban AIDS testing, and federal statutes offer some protection to employees or job applicants who have AIDS or have tested positive for the AIDS virus. The federal Americans with Disabilities Act of 1990[29] (discussed in Chapter 15), for example, prohibits discrimination against persons with disabilities, and the term *disability* has been broadly defined to include individuals with diseases such as AIDS. The law also requires employers to reasonably accommodate the needs of persons with disabilities. As a rule, although the law may not prohibit AIDS testing, it may prohibit the *discharge* of employees based on the results of those tests.

Genetic Testing. A serious privacy issue arose when some employers began conducting genetic testing of employees or prospective employees in an effort to identify individuals who might develop significant health problems in the future. To date, however, only a few cases have come before the courts on this issue. In one case, the Lawrence Berkeley Laboratory screened prospective employees for the gene that causes sickle cell anemia, although the applicants were not informed of this. In a lawsuit subsequently brought by the prospective employees, a federal appellate court held that they had a cause of action for violation of their privacy rights.[30] The parties later settled the case for $2.2 million.

In another case, the Equal Employment Opportunity Commission (EEOC), the federal agency in charge of administering laws prohibiting employment discrimination, brought an action against a railroad company that had genetically tested its employees. The EEOC contended that the genetic testing violated the Americans with Disabilities Act of 1990. In 2002, this case was settled out of court, also for $2.2 million.[31]

Screening Procedures. Preemployment screening procedures are another area of concern to potential employees. What kinds of questions are permissible on an employment application or a preemployment test? What kinds of questions go too far in invading the potential employee's privacy? Is it an invasion of privacy, for example, to ask questions about the potential employee's sexual orientation or religious convictions? Although an employer may believe that such information is relevant to the job for which the individual has applied, the applicant may feel differently about the matter. Generally, questions on an employment application must have a reasonable nexus, or connection, with the job for which an applicant is applying.[32]

---

29. 42 U.S.C. Sections 12102–12118.

30. *Norman-Bloodsaw v. Lawrence Berkeley Laboratory,* 135 F.3d 1260 (9th Cir. 1998).

31. For a discussion of this settlement, see David Hechler, "Railroad to Pay $2.2 Million over Genetic Testing," *The National Law Journal,* May 13, 2002, p. A22.

32. See, for example, *Soroka v. Dayton Hudson Corp.,* 7 Cal.App.4th 203, 1 Cal.Rptr.2d 77 (1991).

KEY TERMS

agency 499
disclosed principal 511
fiduciary 499
independent contractor 500
minimum wage 515
partially disclosed principal 511
***respondeat superior* 513**
undisclosed principal 513
vesting 522
workers' compensation laws 518

FOR REVIEW

❶ What is the difference between an employee and an independent contractor? How do agency relationships arise?

❷ What duties do agents and principals owe to each other?

❸ When is a principal liable for the agent's actions with respect to third parties? When is the agent liable?

❹ What federal statute governs working hours and wages? What federal act protects the health and safety of employees? What are state workers' compensation laws?

❺ Does electronic performance monitoring violate employees' privacy rights? What other types of activities undertaken by employers might violate the privacy rights of employees?

QUESTIONS AND CASE PROBLEMS

14–1. John Paul Corp. made the following contracts:

(a) A contract with Able Construction to build an addition to the corporate office building.
(b) A contract with a certified public accountant (CPA), a recent college graduate, to head the cost-accounting section.
(c) A contract with a salesperson to travel a designated area to solicit orders (contracts) for the corporation.

Able contracts with Apex for materials for the addition; the CPA hires an experienced accountant to advise her on certain accounting procedures; and the salesperson contracts to sell a large order to Green, agreeing to deliver the goods in person within twenty days. Later, Able refuses to pick up the materials, the CPA is in default in paying the hired consultant, and the salesperson does not deliver on time. Apex, the accountant, and Green claim John Paul Corp. is liable under agency law. Discuss fully whether an agency relationship was created by John Paul with Able, the CPA, or the salesperson.

14–2. Ankir is hired by Potter as a traveling salesperson. Ankir not only solicits orders but also delivers the goods and collects payments from his customers. Ankir places all payments in his private checking account and at the end of each month draws sufficient cash from his bank to cover the payments made. Potter is totally unaware of this procedure. Because of a slowdown in the economy, Potter tells all of his salespeople to offer 20 percent discounts on orders. Ankir solicits orders, but he offers only 15 percent discounts, pocketing the extra 5 percent paid by customers. Ankir has not lost any orders by this practice, and he is rated one of Potter's top salespersons. Potter learns of Ankir's actions. Discuss fully Potter's rights in this matter.

14–3. Denton and Carlo were employed at an appliance plant. Their job required them to do occasional maintenance work while standing on a wire mesh platform twenty feet above the plant floor. Other employees had fallen through the mesh, and one of them had been killed by the fall. When Denton and Carlo were asked by their supervisor to do work that would likely require them to walk on the mesh, they refused because of their fear of bodily harm or death. Because of their refusal to do the requested work, the two employees were fired from their jobs. Was their discharge wrongful? If so, under what federal employment law? To what federal agency or department should they turn for assistance?

14–4. Galvin Strang worked for a tractor company in one of its factories. Near his work station was a conveyor belt that ran through a large industrial oven. Sometimes, the workers would use the oven to heat their meals. Thirty-inch-high flasks containing molds were fixed at regular intervals on the conveyor and were transported into the oven. Strang had to walk between the flasks to get to his work station. One day, the conveyor was not moving, and Strang used the oven to cook a frozen pot pie. As he was removing the pot pie from the oven, the conveyor came on. One of the flasks struck Strang and seriously injured him. Strang sought recovery under the state workers' compensation law. Should he recover? Why or why not?

CASE PROBLEM WITH SAMPLE ANSWER

14–5. Agent's Duties to Principal. Ana Barreto and Flavia Gugliuzzi asked Ruth Bennett, a real estate salesperson who worked for Smith Bell Real Estate, to list for sale their house in the Pleasant Valley area of Underhill, Vermont. Diana Carter, a California resident, visited the house as a potential buyer. Bennett worked under the supervision of David Crane, an officer of Smith Bell. Crane knew, but did not disclose to Bennett or Carter, that the house was subject to frequent and severe winds, that a window had blown in years earlier, and that other houses in the area had suffered wind damage. Crane knew of this because he lived in the Pleasant Valley area, had sold a number of nearby properties, and had been Underhill's zoning officer. Many valley residents, including Crane, had wind gauges on their homes to measure and compare wind speeds with their neighbors. Carter bought the house, and several months later, high winds blew in a number of windows and otherwise damaged the property. Carter filed a suit in a Vermont state court against Smith Bell and others, alleging fraud. She argued in part that Crane's knowledge of the winds was imputable to Smith Bell. Smith Bell responded that Crane's knowledge was obtained outside the scope of employment. What is the rule regarding how much of an agent's knowledge a principal is assumed to know? How should the court rule in this case? Why? [*Carter v. Gugliuzzi,* 716 A.2d 17 (Vt. 1998)]

➧ *To view a sample answer for this case problem, go to this book's Web site at* **http://ele.westbuslaw.com** *and click on "Interactive Study Center."*

14–6. Performance Monitoring. Patience Oyoyo worked as a claims analyst in the claims management department of Baylor Healthcare Network, Inc. When questions arose about Oyoyo's performance on several occasions, department manager Debbie Outlaw met with Oyoyo to discuss, among other things, Oyoyo's personal use of a business phone. Outlaw reminded Oyoyo that company policy prohibited excessive personal calls and that these would result in the termination of her employment. Outlaw began to monitor Oyoyo's phone usage, noting lengthy outgoing calls on several occasions, including some long-distance calls. Eventually, Outlaw terminated Oyoyo's employment, and Oyoyo filed a suit in a federal district court against Baylor. Oyoyo asserted in part that in monitoring her phone calls, the employer had invaded her privacy. Baylor asked the court to dismiss this claim. In whose favor should the court rule, and why? [*Oyoyo v. Baylor Healthcare Network, Inc.,* __ F.Supp.2d __ (N.D.Tex. 2000)]

14–7. Agency Formation. Ford Motor Credit Co. is a subsidiary of Ford Motor Co. with its own offices, officers, and directors. Ford Credit buys contracts and leases of automobiles entered into by dealers and consumers. Ford Credit also provides inventory financing for dealers' purchases of Ford and non-Ford vehicles and makes loans to Ford and non-Ford dealers. Dealers and consumers are not required to finance their purchases or leases of Ford vehicles through Ford Credit. Ford Motor is not a party to the agreements between Ford Credit and its customers and does not directly receive any payments under those agreements. Also, Ford Credit is not subject to any agreement with Ford Motor "restricting or conditioning" its ability to finance the dealers' inventories or the consumers' purchases or leases of vehicles. A number of plaintiffs filed a product liability suit in a Missouri state court against Ford Motor. Ford Motor claimed that the court did not have venue. The plaintiffs asserted that Ford Credit, which had an office in the jurisdiction, acted as Ford's "agent for the transaction of its usual and customary business" there. Is Ford Credit an agent of Ford Motor? Discuss. [*State ex rel. Ford Motor Co. v. Bacon,* 63 S.W.3d 641 (Mo. 2002)]

14–8. Liability for Independent Contractor's Torts. Greif Brothers Corp., a steel drum manufacturer, owned and operated a manufacturing plant in Youngstown, Ohio. In 1987, Lowell Wilson, the plant superintendent, hired Youngstown Security Patrol, Inc. (YSP), a security company, to guard Greif property and "deter thieves and vandals." Some YSP security guards, as Wilson knew, carried firearms. Eric Bator, a YSP security guard, was not certified as an armed guard but nevertheless took his gun, in a briefcase, to work. While working at the Greif plant on August 12, 1991, Bator fired his gun at Derrell Pusey, in the belief that Pusey was an intruder. The bullet struck and killed Pusey. Pusey's mother filed a suit in an Ohio state court against Greif and others, alleging in part that her son's death was the result of YSP's negligence, for which Greif was responsible. Greif filed a motion for a directed verdict. What is the plaintiff's best argument that Greif is responsible for YSP's actions? What is Greif's best defense? Explain. [*Pusey v. Bator,* 94 Ohio St.3d 275, 762 N.E.2d 968 (2002)]

14–9. Hours and Wages. Tradesmen International, Inc., leases skilled tradespersons (field employees) to construction contractors. To receive a job offer through Tradesmen, applicants must either complete an Occupational Safety and Health Administration (OSHA) ten-hour general construction safety course or commit to registering for the course within sixty days and completing it within a reasonable time. The class instruction has no effect on the trade skills of any field employee. The classes are held outside of regular working hours. Employees perform no work in the class and are not compensated for the time spent in the class. Elaine Chao, the U.S. secretary of labor, filed a suit in a federal district court against Tradesmen for failing to pay overtime compensation to those who attend the class. Does Tradesmen's practice—requiring the class as a prerequisite to employment but not paying applicants to attend it—violate the Fair Labor Standards Act? Explain. [*Chao v. Tradesmen International, Inc.*, 310 F.3d 904 (6th Cir. 2002)]

14–10. IN YOUR COURT

Lynne Meyer, on her way to a business meeting and in a hurry, stopped by a Wal-Mart store for a new pair of pantyhose to wear to the meeting. There was a long line at one of the checkout counters, but a cashier, Valerie Watts, opened another counter and began loading the cash drawer. Meyer told Watts that she was in a hurry and asked Watts to work faster. Watts, however, only slowed her pace. At this point, Meyer hit Watts. It is not clear from the record whether Meyer hit Watts intentionally or, in an attempt to retrieve the pantyhose, hit her inadvertently. In response, Watts grabbed Meyer by the hair and hit her repeatedly in the back of the head, while Meyer screamed for help. Management personnel separated the two women and questioned them about the incident. Watts was immediately fired for violating the store's no-fighting policy. Meyer subsequently sued Wal-Mart, alleging that the store was liable for the tort (assault and battery) committed by its employee. Assume that you are the judge in the trial court hearing this case and answer the following questions:

(a) Meyer sued Wal-Mart but not Watts. Why didn't she sue Watts instead, or as well, given that it was Watts who committed the tort?
(b) Did Watts's behavior constitute an intentional tort or a tort of negligence? Is this distinction relevant in this case? Why or why not?
(c) Under what doctrine discussed in this chapter might Wal-Mart be held liable for the tort committed by its employee? What is the underlying rationale for this doctrine? What is the key factor that you must consider in deciding whether Wal-Mart can be held liable under this doctrine?
(d) Generally, how will you rule in this case, and why?

14–11. A QUESTION OF ETHICS AND SOCIAL RESPONSIBILITY

Keith Cline worked for Wal-Mart Stores, Inc., as a night maintenance supervisor. When he suffered a recurrence of a brain tumor, he took a leave from work, which was covered by the Family Medical and Leave Act (FMLA) of 1993 and authorized by his employer. When he returned to work, his employer refused to allow him to continue his supervisory job and demoted him to the status of a regular maintenance worker. A few weeks later, the company fired him, ostensibly because he "stole" company time by clocking in thirteen minutes early for a company meeting. Cline sued Wal-Mart, alleging, among other things, that Wal-Mart had violated the FMLA by refusing to return him to his prior position when he returned to work. In view of these facts, answer the following questions. [*Cline v. Wal-Mart Stores, Inc.*, 144 F.3d 294 (4th Cir. 1998)]

(a) Did Wal-Mart violate the FMLA by refusing to return Cline to his prior position when he returned to work?
(b) From an ethical perspective, the FMLA has been viewed as a choice on the part of society to shift to the employer family burdens caused by changing economic and social needs. What "changing" needs does the act meet? In other words, why did Congress feel that workers should have the right to family and medical leave in 1993 but not in 1983, or 1973, or earlier?
(c) "Congress should amend the FMLA, which currently applies to employers with fifty or more employees, so that it applies to employers with twenty-five or more employees." Do you agree with this statement? Why or why not?

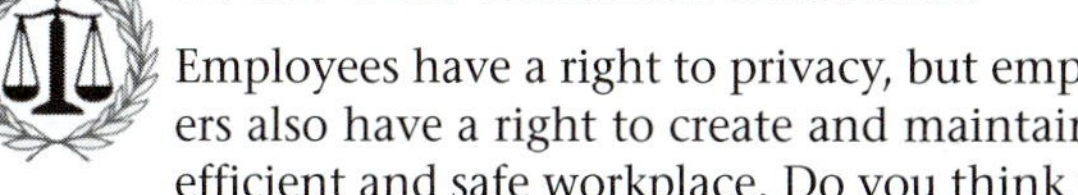

14–12. FOR CRITICAL ANALYSIS

Employees have a right to privacy, but employers also have a right to create and maintain an efficient and safe workplace. Do you think that existing laws strike an appropriate balance between the rights of employers and those of employees?

For updated links to resources available on the Web, as well as a variety of other materials, visit this text's Web site at

http://ele.westbuslaw.com

An excellent source for information on agency law, including court cases involving agency concepts, is the Legal Information Institute (LII) at Cornell University. You can access the LII's Web page on this topic at

http://www.law.cornell.edu/topics/agency.html

The 'Lectric Law Library's Lawcopedia contains a summary of agency laws at

http://www.lectlaw.com/d-a.htm

Scroll down through the A's and select the link to Agent for useful information on this area of the law.

An excellent Web site for information on employee benefits, including the FMLA, COBRA, other relevant statutes, case law, and current articles, is BenefitsLink. Go to

http://www.benefitslink.com/index.shtml

The Occupational Safety and Health Administration (OSHA) offers information related to workplace health and safety at

http://www.osha.gov

The Bureau of Labor Statistics provides a wide variety of data on employment, including data on employment compensation, working conditions, and productivity. Go to

http://www.bls.gov

The American Civil Liberties Union has a section on its Web site devoted to employee privacy rights with respect to electronic monitoring, as well as other employment issues. Go to

http://www.aclu.org

and click on "Workplace Rights" on the right-hand side of the screen.

LEGAL RESEARCH EXERCISES ON THE WEB

Go to **http://ele.westbuslaw.com**, the Web site that accompanies this text. Select "Interactive Study Center," and then click on "Chapter 14." There you will find the following Internet research exercises that you can perform to learn more about topics covered in this chapter.

Activity 14–1: LEGAL PERSPECTIVE—Employees or Independent Contractors?

Activity 14–2: MANAGEMENT PERSPECTIVE—Workplace Monitoring and Surveillance

BEFORE THE TEST

Go to **http://ele.westbuslaw.com**, the Web site that accompanies this text. Select "Interactive Quizzes." You will find at least twenty interactive questions relating to this chapter.

WESTLAW® CAMPUS

If your textbook provided for a subscription to Westlaw® Campus, or if you have otherwise purchased access to the Westlaw Campus database, you can access any of the cases presented or cited in this chapter by using your Westlaw Campus account.

CHAPTER 15

Employment Discrimination

CONTENTS

TITLE VII OF THE CIVIL RIGHTS ACT OF 1964
Procedures under Title VII
Intentional and Unintentional Discrimination
Discrimination Based on Race, Color, and National Origin
Discrimination Based on Religion
Discrimination Based on Gender
Sexual Harassment
Online Harassment
Remedies under Title VII

EQUAL PAY ACT OF 1963

DISCRIMINATION BASED ON AGE
Procedures under the ADEA
A Special Case—State Employees

DISCRIMINATION BASED ON DISABILITY
Procedures under the ADA
What Is a Disability?
Reasonable Accommodation
Hostile-Environment Claims under the ADA

DEFENSES TO EMPLOYMENT DISCRIMINATION
Business Necessity
Bona Fide Occupational Qualification
Seniority Systems
After-Acquired Evidence of Employee Misconduct

AFFIRMATIVE ACTION
Challenges to Affirmative Action
State Actions

STATE LAWS PROHIBITING DISCRIMINATION

CHAPTER OBJECTIVES

After reading this chapter, you should be able to answer the following questions:

1. Generally, what kind of conduct does Title VII of the Civil Rights Act of 1964 prohibit?

2. What is the difference between disparate-treatment discrimination and disparate-impact discrimination?

3. What remedies are available under Title VII of the 1964 Civil Rights Act?

4. Which federal acts prohibit discrimination based on age and discrimination based on disability?

5. What are three defenses to claims of employment discrimination?

Out of the 1960s civil rights movement to end racial and other forms of discrimination grew a body of law protecting employees against discrimination in the workplace. In the past several decades, judicial decisions, administrative agency actions, and legislation have restricted the ability of employers, as well as unions, to discriminate against workers on the basis of race, color, religion, national origin, gender, age, or disability. A class of persons defined by one or more of these criteria is known as a **protected class.**

Protected class • A class of persons with identifiable characteristics who historically have been victimized by discriminatory treatment for certain purposes. Depending on the context, these characteristics include age, color, gender, national origin, race, religion, and disability.

Employment discrimination • Treating employees or job applicants unequally on the basis of race, color, national origin, religion, gender, age, or disability; prohibited by federal statutes.

Several federal statutes prohibit **employment discrimination** against members of protected classes. The most important statute is Title VII of the Civil Rights Act of 1964.[1] Title VII prohibits employment discrimination on the basis of race, color, religion, national origin, and gender. The Age Discrimination in Employment Act of 1967[2] and the Americans with Disabilities Act of 1990[3] prohibit discrimination on the basis of age and disability, respectively. The protections afforded under these laws extend to U.S. citizens who are working abroad for U.S. firms or for companies that are controlled by U.S. firms—*unless* to do so would violate the laws of the countries in which their workplaces are located. This "foreign laws exception" allows employers to avoid being subjected to conflicting laws.

This chapter focuses on the kinds of discrimination prohibited by these federal statutes. Note, however, that discrimination against employees on the basis of any of the above-mentioned criteria may also violate state human rights statutes or other state laws prohibiting discrimination.

TITLE VII OF THE CIVIL RIGHTS ACT OF 1964

Title VII of the Civil Rights Act of 1964 and its amendments prohibit job discrimination against employees, applicants, and union members on the basis of race, color, national origin, religion, and gender at any stage of employ-

1. 42 U.S.C. Sections 2000e–2000e-17.
2. 29 U.S.C. Sections 621–634.
3. 42 U.S.C. Sections 12102–12118.

ment. Title VII applies to employers affecting interstate commerce with fifteen or more employees, labor unions with fifteen or more members, labor unions that operate hiring halls (to which members go regularly to be rationed jobs as they become available), employment agencies, and state and local governing units or agencies. A special section of the act prohibits discrimination in most federal government employment.

Procedures under Title VII

Compliance with Title VII is monitored by the Equal Employment Opportunity Commission (EEOC). A victim of alleged discrimination, before bringing a suit against the employer, must first file a claim with the EEOC. The EEOC may investigate the dispute and attempt to obtain the parties' voluntary consent to an out-of-court settlement. If voluntary agreement cannot be reached, the EEOC may then file a suit against the employer on the employee's behalf. If the EEOC decides not to investigate the claim, the victim may bring his or her own lawsuit against the employer.

The EEOC does not investigate every claim of employment discrimination; rather, it investigates only "priority cases." Generally, priority cases are cases that affect many workers, cases involving retaliatory discharge (firing an employee in retaliation for submitting a claim with the EEOC), and cases involving types of discrimination that are of particular concern to the EEOC.

Intentional and Unintentional Discrimination

Title VII of the Civil Rights Act of 1964 prohibits both intentional and unintentional discrimination.

Intentional Discrimination. Intentional discrimination by an employer against an employee is known as **disparate-treatment discrimination.** Because intent may sometimes be difficult to prove, courts have established certain procedures for resolving disparate-treatment cases. Suppose that a woman applies for employment with a construction firm and is rejected. If she sues on the basis of disparate-treatment discrimination in hiring, she must show that (1) she is a member of a protected class, (2) she applied and was qualified for the job in question, (3) she was rejected by the employer, and (4) the employer continued to seek applicants for the position or filled the position with a person not in a protected class.

Disparate-treatment discrimination • A form of employment discrimination that results when an employer intentionally discriminates against employees who are members of protected classes.

If the woman can meet these relatively easy requirements, she makes out a ***prima facie* case** of illegal discrimination. Making out a *prima facie* case of discrimination means that the plaintiff has met her initial burden of proof and will win in the absence of a legally acceptable employer defense (defenses to claims of employment discrimination will be discussed later in this chapter). The burden then shifts to the employer-defendant, who must articulate a legal reason for not hiring the plaintiff. For example, the employer might say that the plaintiff was not hired because she lacked sufficient experience or training. To prevail, the plaintiff must then show that the employer's reason is a *pretext* (not the true reason) and that discriminatory intent actually motivated the employer's decision.

***Prima facie* case** • A case in which the plaintiff has produced sufficient evidence of his or her claim that the case can go to a jury; a case in which the evidence compels the plaintiff's conclusion if the defendant produces no evidence to disprove it.

Disparate-Impact Discrimination. Employers often find it necessary to use interviews and testing procedures to choose from among a large number of applicants for job openings. Minimum educational requirements are also

Disparate-impact discrimination • A form of employment discrimination that results from certain employer practices or procedures that, although not discriminatory on their face, have a discriminatory effect. Intent is irrelevant in a disparate-impact claim.

common. Employer practices, such as those involving educational requirements, may have an unintended discriminatory impact on a protected class. **Disparate-impact discrimination** occurs when, as a result of educational or other job requirements or hiring procedures, an employer's work force does not reflect the percentage of nonwhites, women, or members of other protected classes that characterizes the pool of qualified individuals in the local labor market. If a person challenging an employment practice having a discriminatory effect can show a connection between the practice and the disparity, she or he makes out a *prima facie* case and does not need to provide evidence of discriminatory intent.

Disparate-impact discrimination can also occur when an educational or other job requirement or hiring procedure excludes members of a protected class from an employer's work force at a substantially higher rate than nonmembers, regardless of the racial balance in the employer's work force. The EEOC has devised a test, called the "four-fifths rule," to determine whether an employment examination is discriminatory on its face. Under this rule, a selection rate for protected classes that is less than four-fifths, or 80 percent, of the rate for the group with the highest rate will generally be regarded as evidence of disparate impact. To illustrate: One hundred majority applicants take an employment test, and fifty pass the test and are hired. One hundred minority applicants take the test, and twenty pass the test and are hired. Because twenty is less than four-fifths (80 percent) of fifty, the test would be considered discriminatory under the EEOC guidelines.

Discrimination Based on Race, Color, and National Origin

Title VII prohibits employers from discriminating against employees or job applicants on the basis of race, color, or national origin. National origin can refer to the country of a person's ancestors as well as to cultural characteristics.

This prohibition extends to both intentional (disparate-treatment) and unintentional (disparate-impact) discrimination. If a company's standards or policies for selecting or promoting employees have the effect of discriminating against employees or job applicants on the basis of race, color, or national origin, they are illegal—unless (except for race) they have a substantial, demonstrable relationship to realistic qualifications for the job in question. Discrimination against these protected classes in regard to employment conditions and benefits is also illegal.

Note that victims of racial or ethnic discrimination may also have a cause of action under 42 U.S.C. Section 1981. This section, which was enacted as part of the Civil Rights Act of 1866, prohibits discrimination on the basis of race or ethnicity in the formation or enforcement of contracts. Although Section 1981 remained a "dead letter" on the books for over a century, since the 1970s many plaintiffs have succeeded in Section 1981 cases against their employers. Unlike Title VII, Section 1981 does not place a cap on damages (see the discussion of Title VII remedies later in this chapter). Thus, if an employee can prove that he or she was discriminated against in the formation or enforcement of a contract, the employee may be able to obtain a greater amount in damages under Section 1981 than under Title VII.

Discrimination Based on Religion

Title VII of the Civil Rights Act of 1964 also prohibits government employers, private employers, and unions from discriminating against persons because of their religion. An employer must "reasonably accommodate" the religious practices of its employees, unless to do so would cause undue hardship to the employer's business. For example, if an employee's religion prohibits him from working on a certain day of the week or at a certain type of job, the employer must make a reasonable attempt to accommodate these religious requirements. Employers must reasonably accommodate an employee's religious belief even if the belief is not based on the tenets or dogma of a particular church, sect, or denomination. The only requirement is that the belief be sincerely held by the employee.[4]

Discrimination Based on Gender

Under Title VII, as well as other federal acts, employers are forbidden to discriminate against employees on the basis of gender. Employers are prohibited from classifying jobs as male or female and from advertising in help-wanted columns that are designated male or female unless the employer can prove that the gender of the applicant is essential to the job. Furthermore, employers cannot have separate male and female seniority lists. Generally, to succeed in a suit for gender discrimination, a plaintiff must demonstrate that gender was a determining factor in the employer's decision to hire, fire, or promote him or her. Typically, this involves looking at all of the surrounding circumstances.

The Pregnancy Discrimination Act of 1978,[5] which amended Title VII, expanded the definition of gender discrimination to include discrimination based on pregnancy. Women affected by pregnancy, childbirth, or related medical conditions must be treated—for all employment-related purposes, including the conferring of benefits under employee benefit programs—the same as other persons not so affected but similar in ability to work.

In the following case, the plaintiff (a male) charged the defendant (a female) with gender discrimination. The plaintiff made out a *prima facie* case, and the defendant presented a nondiscriminatory reason as a defense. Was the defendant's reason a pretext covering a discriminatory motive? That was the question before the court.

4. *Frazee v. Illinois Department of Employment Security,* 489 U.S. 829, 109 S.Ct. 1514, 103 L.Ed.2d 914 (1989).

5. 42 U.S.C. Section 2000e(k).

CAREY v. MOUNT DESERT ISLAND HOSPITAL

CASE 15.1

United States Court of Appeals, First Circuit, 1998. 156 F.3d 31. **http://www.law.emory.edu/1circuit/aug98**[a]

Michael Carey was a vice president in charge of the finance department for Mount Desert Island Hospital (MDI) in Bar Harbor, Maine. When the position of chief executive officer (CEO) opened up, Carey applied, and his application was endorsed by Dan

a. This page contains links to opinions of the U.S. Court of Appeals for the First Circuit issued in August 1998. Click on the *Carey* case name to access the opinion. This Web site is maintained by Emory University School of Law in Atlanta, Georgia.

Hobbs, the acting CEO. At the time, an audit of the finance department revealed some deficiencies, but the auditor concluded that the department was "already attacking the problem." MDI's board offered the CEO post to Leslie Hawkins, a woman, who accepted. Less than a year later, Hawkins terminated Carey, giving as reasons the problems cited in the audit and "lack of confidence" in Carey. Carey filed a suit in a federal district court against MDI for gender discrimination in violation of Title VII and other laws. Evidence introduced during the trial included a statement by one female executive that "we have different standards for men and women," with regard to discipline and termination; and a statement by another female executive that "it's about time that we get a woman for this [CEO] position." The court awarded Carey more than $300,000 in damages. MDI appealed to the U.S. Court of Appeals for the First Circuit.

COFFIN, J.

[T]his was a case with much to say on either side, involving the always difficult question of probing the wellsprings of human motivation. * * *

* * * *

In a case such as this, where a plaintiff must rely on circumstantial as opposed to direct evidence of gender discrimination, the evidence will necessarily be composed of bits and pieces, which may or may not point to an atmosphere of gender discrimination. While an employer should not find itself in jeopardy by reason of occasional stray remarks by ordinary employees, *circumstantial evidence of a discriminatory atmosphere at a plaintiff's place of employment is relevant to the question of motive in considering a discrimination claim* * * *. [Emphasis added.]

* * * *

* * * [Based on the record, we] hold that there was sufficient evidence to support a finding that deficiencies in Carey's handling of financial controls were not the real reason for his discharge but instead covered an action stemming from gender discrimination.

The U.S. Court of Appeals for the First Circuit affirmed the lower court's judgment. The court held that that there was sufficient evidence to support a finding that the reason for Carey's discharge was gender discrimination.

QUESTIONS

1. Who initially filed this suit? Who appealed the court's award, and why?
2. According to the court, was there enough evidence for a jury to find that MDI's board had discriminated against Carey on the basis of gender?
3. Is it possible for jurors and judges to overcome their own prejudices in deciding cases in which gender plays a key role?

Sexual Harassment

Sexual harassment • In the employment context, the granting of job promotions or other benefits in return for sexual favors, or language or conduct that is so sexually offensive that it creates a hostile working environment.

Title VII also protects employees against **sexual harassment** in the workplace. Sexual harassment can take two forms: *quid pro quo* harassment and hostile-environment harassment. *Quid pro quo* is a Latin phrase that is often translated to mean "something in exchange for something else." *Quid pro quo* harassment occurs when job opportunities, promotions, salary increases, and the like are given in return for sexual favors. According to the United States

Supreme Court, hostile-environment harassment occurs when "the workplace is permeated with discriminatory intimidation, ridicule, and insult, that is sufficiently severe or pervasive to alter the conditions of the victim's employment and create an abusive working environment."[6]

Generally, the courts apply this Supreme Court guideline on a case-by-case basis. Some courts have held that just one incident of sexually offensive conduct—such as a sexist remark by a co-worker or a photo on an employer's desk of his bikini-clad wife—can create a hostile environment.[7] At least one court has held that a worker may recover damages under Title VII because *other* persons were sexually harassed in the workplace.[8] According to some employment specialists, employers should assume that hostile-environment harassment has occurred if an employee claims that it has.

Harassment by Supervisors. What if an employee is harassed by a manager or supervisor of a large firm, and the firm itself (the "employer") is not aware of the harassment? Should the employer be held liable for the harassment nonetheless? For some time, the courts were in disagreement on this issue. Typically, employers were held liable for Title VII violations by the firm's managerial or supervisory personnel in *quid pro quo* harassment cases regardless of whether the employer knew about the harassment. In hostile-environment cases, in contrast, the majority of courts tended to hold employers liable only if the employer knew or should have known of the harassment and failed to take prompt remedial action.

Tangible Employment Action. For an employer to be held liable for a supervisor's sexual harassment, the supervisor must have taken a tangible employment action against the employee. A *tangible employment action* is a significant change in employment status, such as firing or failing to promote an employee, reassigning the employee to a position with significantly different responsibilities, or effecting a significant change in employment benefits.

Only a supervisor, or another person acting with the authority of the employer, can cause this sort of injury. A co-worker can sexually harass another employee, and anyone who has regular contact with an employee can inflict psychological injuries by offensive conduct. A co-worker cannot dock another's pay, demote her or him, or set conditions for continued employment, however.

The elements of the definition of *tangible employment* action were at issue in the following case.

6. *Harris v. Forklift Systems,* 510 U.S. 17, 114 S.Ct. 367, 126 L.Ed.2d 295 (1993).
7. For other examples, see *Radtke v. Everett,* 442 Mich. 368, 501 N.W.2d 155 (1993); and *Nadeau v. Rainbow Rugs, Inc.,* 675 A.2d 973 (Me. 1996).
8. *Leibovitz v. New York City Transit Authority,* 4 F.Supp.2d 144 (E.D.N.Y. 1998).

JIN v. METROPOLITAN LIFE INSURANCE CO.

CASE 15.2

United States Court of Appeals, Second Circuit, 2002.
310 F.3d 84.
http://www.tourolaw.edu/2ndCircuit[a]

In 1989, Min Jin began working for Metropolitan Life Insurance Company (MetLife) as a sales agent at the company's "Broadway branch" in Manhattan, New York. In May 1993, Gregory Morabito assumed supervisory duties at the Broadway branch. At the

a. In the left-hand column, click on "Reported Decisions." From the menu, click on "2002 Decisions." In the list, click on "June." Scroll to the name of the case and click on it to access the opinion.

same time, Morabito began to engage in a pattern of conduct toward Jin that included making sexual remarks to her in the office and calling her at home; offensively touching her buttocks, breasts, and legs at the office when she was making sales calls from her desk and when she was walking clients to the elevator; requiring her to attend weekly private meetings in his locked office during which he would threaten her and force her to engage in sexual acts; and threatening to fire her and physically harm her if she did not accede to his demands. Her later request for disability benefits for the harassment was denied, and MetLife fired her in 1995. Jin filed a suit in a federal district court against MetLife, alleging sexual harassment in violation of Title VII. The court instructed the jury to determine whether Jin was subject to a tangible employment action. When the jury found that she was not, the court ruled in MetLife's favor. Jin appealed to the U.S. Court of Appeals for the Second Circuit.

FEINBERG, J.

In its instructions, the district court utilized what appeared to be an exclusive list of three economic-based harms to define a tangible employment action: "One, unjustifiably refusing to process policies sold by [Jin], or two, unjustifiably causing her disability claim to be denied, or three, unjustifiably firing her." * * * By leading the jury to believe it could consider *only* the three enumerated harms, * * * the district court improperly narrowed the scope of possible tangible employment actions considered by the jury.

* * * *

Jin argues that the jury should have been allowed to consider as a tangible employment action Morabito's use of his supervisory authority to require Jin to submit to weekly sexual abuse.

* * * *

Requiring an employee to engage in unwanted sex acts is one of the most pernicious and oppressive forms of sexual harassment that can occur in the workplace. * * * *It is hardly surprising that this type of conduct* * * * *fits squarely within the definition of "tangible employment action"* * * * . [Emphasis added.]

Here, Jin presented evidence that Morabito ordered her to submit to demeaning sexual acts, explicitly threatened to fire her if she did not submit, and then allowed her to keep her job after she submitted. Essentially, according to Jin, he used his authority to impose on her the added job requirement that she submit to weekly sexual abuse in order to retain her employment.

* * * It was Morabito's empowerment by MetLife as an agent who could make economic decisions affecting employees under his control that enabled him to force Jin to submit to his weekly sexual abuse. * * * Also, that Morabito as a supervisor could require Jin to report to his private office where he could make his threats and carry on his abuses further supports the claim that his empowerment was as the company's agent.

* * * *

* * * When a supervisor makes decisions affecting the terms and conditions of [a] plaintiff's employment based upon her submission to his sexual advances, he uses his authority to effect * * * a significant change in employment status.

The U.S. Court of Appeals for the Second Circuit vacated the order of the lower court and remanded the case for a new trial. Because Morabito, as Jin's supervisor, threatened to fire her if she did not submit to sexual acts and then allowed her to keep her job after she submitted, the jury should have been instructed to consider the conditioning of her continued employment on her submission as a possible tangible employment action.

QUESTIONS

1. What was the plaintiff's principal argument in the appeal of this case?
2. What was the judgment of the U.S. Court of Appeals for the Second Circuit in this case, and what was the reasoning underlying this decision?
3. If the roles in this case had been reversed so that a woman had made sexual demands of a man, would the result have been different?

Supreme Court Guidelines. In 1998, in two separate cases, the United States Supreme Court issued some significant guidelines relating to the liability of employers for their supervisors' harassment of employees in the workplace. In *Faragher v. City of Boca Raton,*[9] the Court held that an employer (a city) could be held liable for a supervisor's harassment of employees even though the employer was unaware of the behavior. The Court reached this conclusion primarily because, although the city had a written policy against sexual harassment, the policy had not been distributed to city employees. Additionally, the city had not established any procedures that could be followed by employees who felt that they were victims of sexual harassment. In *Burlington Industries, Inc. v. Ellerth,*[10] the Court ruled that a company could be held liable for the harassment of an employee by one of its vice presidents even though the employee suffered no adverse job consequences.

In these two cases, the Court set forth some common-sense guidelines on liability for harassment in the workplace that are helpful to employers and employees alike. On the one hand, employees benefit by the ruling that employers may be held liable for their supervisors' harassment even though the employers were unaware of the actions and even though the employees suffered no adverse job consequences. On the other hand, the Court made it clear in both decisions that employers have an affirmative defense against liability for their supervisors' harassment of employees if the employers can show the following:

1. That they have taken "reasonable care to prevent and correct promptly any sexually harassing behavior" (by establishing effective harassment policies and complaint procedures, for example).
2. That the employee suing for harassment failed to follow these policies and procedures.

Harassment by Co-Workers and Nonemployees. Often, employees alleging harassment complain that the actions of co-workers, not supervisors, are responsible for creating a hostile working environment. In such cases, the employee still has a cause of action against the employer. Generally, though, the employer will be held liable only if it knew or should have known about the harassment and failed to take immediate remedial action.

9. 524 U.S. 775, 118 S.Ct. 2275, 141 L.Ed.2d 662 (1998).
10. 524 U.S. 742, 118 S.Ct. 2257, 141 L.Ed.2d 633 (1998).

Employers may also be liable for harassment by *nonemployees* under certain conditions. For example, if a restaurant owner or manager knows that a particular customer repeatedly harasses a waitress and permits the harassment to continue, the restaurant owner may be liable under Title VII even though the customer is not an employee of the restaurant. The issue turns on the control that the employer exerts over a nonemployee. In one case, the owner of a Pizza Hut franchise was held liable for the harassment of a waitress by two male customers because no steps were taken to prevent the harassment.[11]

Same-Gender Harassment. The courts have also had to address the issue of whether men who are harassed by other men, or women who are harassed by other women, are also protected by laws that prohibit gender-based discrimination in the workplace. For example, what if the male president of a firm demands sexual favors from a male employee? Does this action qualify as sexual harassment? For some time, the courts were widely split on this question. In 1998, in *Oncale v. Sundowner Offshore Services, Inc.*,[12] the United States Supreme Court resolved the issue by holding that Title VII protection extends to same-gender harassment.

Online Harassment

Employees' online activities can create a hostile working environment in many ways. Racial jokes, ethnic slurs, or other comments contained in e-mail may become the basis for a claim of hostile-environment harassment or other forms of discrimination. A worker who sees sexually explicit images on a co-worker's computer screen and finds the images offensive may claim that they create a hostile working environment.

Avoiding Liability through Prompt Remedial Action. Generally, employers may be able to avoid liability for online harassment if they take prompt remedial action. For example, in *Daniels v. WorldCom, Inc.*,[13] Angela Daniels, an employee of Robert Half International under contract to WorldCom, Inc., received racially harassing e-mailed jokes from another employee. After receiving the jokes, Daniels complained to WorldCom managers. Shortly afterward, the company issued a warning to the offending employee about the proper use of the e-mail system and held two meetings to discuss company policy on the use of the system. In Daniels's suit against WorldCom for racial discrimination, a federal district court concluded that the employer was not liable for its employee's racially harassing e-mails because the employer took prompt remedial action.

An Ongoing Challenge. Employers who have taken steps to avoid online harassment in the workplace continue to face challenging problems. Clearly, if they do not take effective steps to curb such harassment, they may face liability for violating Title VII. At the same time, if they monitor their employees' communications, they may face liability under other laws—for invading their employees' privacy, for example.

---

11. *Lockard v. Pizza Hut, Inc.*, 162 F.3d 1062 (10th Cir. 1998).
12. 523 U.S. 75, 118 S.Ct. 998, 140 L.Ed.2d 207 (1998).
13. 1998 WL 91261 (N.D.Tex. 1998).

Additionally, an employee who is fired for misusing the employer's computer system to, say, e-mail pornographic images to co-workers or others may claim that he or she was wrongfully discharged for one reason or another. In one case, an employer discovered that two employees had, on numerous occasions, sent messages to co-workers containing jokes, photos, and short videos that were sexually explicit and clearly offensive in nature. When the employees were fired, they claimed that they had not been fired for just cause. Furthermore, they argued, they had not knowingly engaged in any misconduct, and if the employer concluded that they were, the employer should have warned them. Interestingly, in this case, a state appellate court ultimately held for the employer, concluding that the employees' conduct constituted "a flagrant violation of a universal standard of behavior."[14]

Finally, there are constitutional rights to be considered. In one case, a court held that religious speech that unintentionally creates a hostile environment is constitutionally protected.[15]

Remedies under Title VII

Employer liability under Title VII may be extensive. If the plaintiff successfully proves that unlawful discrimination occurred, he or she may be awarded reinstatement, back pay, retroactive promotions, and damages.[16] Compensatory damages are available only in cases of intentional discrimination. Punitive damages may be recovered against a private employer only if the employer acted with malice or reckless indifference to an individual's rights. The sum of the amount of compensatory and punitive damages is limited by the statute to specific amounts against specific employers—ranging from $50,000 against employers with one hundred or fewer employees to $300,000 against employers with more than five hundred employees.

Equal Pay Act of 1963

The Equal Pay Act of 1963 was enacted as an amendment to the Fair Labor Standards Act of 1938. Basically, the act prohibits gender-based discrimination in the wages paid for similar work. For the equal pay requirements to apply, the male and female employees must be employed at the same establishment.

A person alleging wage discrimination in violation of the Equal Pay Act may sue her or his employer. To determine whether the act has been violated, a court will look to the primary duties of the two jobs—it is job content rather than job description that controls in all cases. The jobs of a barber and a beautician, for example, are considered essentially equal. So, too, are those of a tailor and a seamstress. Small differences in job content do not legally justify higher pay for one gender. An employer will *not* be found liable for violating the act if it can show that the wage differential for equal work was based on

14. *Autoliv ASP, Inc. v. Department of Workforce Services,* 29 P.3d 7 (Utah Ct. App. 2001).

15. *Meltebeke v. B.O.L.I.,* 322 Or. 122, 903 P.2d 351 (Or. 1995).

16. Damages were not available under Title VII until 1991. The Civil Rights Act of that year amended Title VII to provide for both compensatory and punitive damages, as well as jury trials.

(1) a seniority system, (2) a merit system, (3) a system that pays according to quality or quantity of production, or (4) any factor other than gender.

ETHICAL ISSUE

Should market forces be considered a "factor other than gender" in wage-discrimination cases? Traditionally, one of the defenses employers have raised in discrimination cases brought under the Equal Pay Act has been that their pay determinations were based on the market forces of supply and demand. In other words, if, say, more women than men were available for a particular job at a lower pay rate, the employer could argue that this characteristic of the marketplace was a factor other than gender. Employers have not always succeeded in this defense, and guidelines on wage discrimination issued by the Equal Employment Opportunity Commission (EEOC) in 2000 have made it even more difficult to do so. Among other things, the guidelines state that "payment of lower wages to women based on an assumption that women are available . . . at lower compensation rates does not qualify as a factor other than sex." The guidelines then state that an employer may cite market factors as a reason for compensation discrimination "only if the employer proves that any compensation disparity is not based on sex." Critics of the guidelines point out that the EEOC's somewhat circular reasoning makes it extremely difficult for employers to cite market factors as a defense at all. Although EEOC compliance guidelines are not legal requirements in themselves, they do influence case outcomes because the courts normally give deference to the EEOC's interpretations of the law.[17]

Discrimination Based on Age

Age discrimination is potentially the most widespread form of discrimination, because anyone—regardless of race, color, national origin, or gender—could be a victim at some point in life. The Age Discrimination in Employment Act (ADEA) of 1967, as amended, prohibits employment discrimination on the basis of age against individuals forty years of age or older. The act also prohibits mandatory retirement for nonmanagerial workers. For the act to apply, an employer must have twenty or more employees, and the employer's business activities must affect interstate commerce. The EEOC administers the ADEA, but the act also permits private causes of action against employers for age discrimination.

Procedures under the ADEA

The burden-shifting procedure under the ADEA is similar to that under Title VII. If a plaintiff can establish that he or she (1) was a member of the protected age group, (2) was qualified for the position from which he or she was discharged, and (3) was discharged under circumstances that give rise to an inference of discrimination, the plaintiff has established a *prima facie* case of

17. You can access the section of the EEOC's Compliance Manual that contains these guidelines at the EEOC's Web site at **http://www.eeoc.gov**. The Web site also contains an "Equal Pay" page that includes information on compensation-discrimination laws, as well as descriptions of recent EEOC equal-pay cases.

unlawful age discrimination. The burden then shifts to the employer, who must articulate a legitimate reason for the discrimination. If the plaintiff can prove that the employer's reason is only a pretext and that the plaintiff's age was a determining factor in the employer's decision, the employer will be held liable under the ADEA.

Numerous cases of alleged age discrimination have been brought against employers who, to cut costs, replaced older, higher-salaried employees with younger, lower-salaried workers. Whether a firing is discriminatory or simply part of a rational business decision to prune the company's ranks is not always clear. Companies generally defend a decision to discharge a worker by asserting that the worker could no longer perform her or his duties or that the worker's skills were no longer needed. The employee must prove that the discharge was motivated, at least in part, by age bias. Proof that qualified older employees are generally discharged before employees who are younger or that co-workers continually made unflattering age-related comments about the discharged worker may be enough. The plaintiff need not prove that she or he was replaced by a person outside the protected class—that is, by a person under the age of forty years.[18] Rather, the issue in all ADEA cases turns on whether age discrimination has, in fact, occurred, regardless of the age of the replacement worker.

A Special Case—State Employees

The Eleventh Amendment to the U.S. Constitution, as that amendment has been interpreted by the United States Supreme Court, provides that states are immune from lawsuits brought by private individuals in federal court, unless the state consents to the suit. In a number of age-discrimination cases brought in the late 1990s, state agencies that were sued by state employees for age discrimination sought to have the suits dismissed on this ground.

For example, in two Florida cases, professors and librarians contended that their employers—two Florida state universities—denied them salary increases and other benefits because they were getting old and their successors could be hired at lower cost. The universities claimed that as agencies of a sovereign state, they could not be sued without the state's consent. Because the courts were rendering conflicting opinions in these cases, the United States Supreme Court agreed to address the issue. In *Kimel v. Florida Board of Regents*,[19] decided in 2000, the Court held that the sovereign immunity granted the states by the Eleventh Amendment precluded suits against them by private parties alleging violations of the ADEA. According to the Court, Congress had exceeded its constitutional authority when it included in the ADEA a provision stating that "all employers," including state employers, were subject to the act.

DISCRIMINATION BASED ON DISABILITY

The Americans with Disabilities Act (ADA) of 1990 is designed to eliminate discriminatory employment practices that prevent otherwise qualified workers with disabilities from fully participating in the national labor force. Prior

18. *O'Connor v. Consolidated Coin Caterers Corp.*, 517 U.S. 308, 116 S.Ct. 1307, 134 L.Ed.2d 433 (1996).
19. 528 U.S. 62, 120 S.Ct. 631, 145 L.Ed.2d 522 (2000).

to 1990, the major federal law providing protection to those with disabilities was the Rehabilitation Act of 1973. That act covered only federal government employees and those employed under federally funded programs. The ADA extends federal protection against disability-based discrimination to all workplaces with fifteen or more workers. Note, though, that the United States Supreme Court has held, as it did with respect to the ADEA, that lawsuits under the ADA cannot be brought against state government employers.[20]

The ADA does not apply to very small businesses. Under the ADA an "employer" is not covered unless its work force includes "15 or more employees for each working day in each of 20 or more calendar weeks in the current or preceding calendar year." The question in the following case was whether the shareholders and directors of a corporation should be counted as "employees" of the corporation.

20. *Board of Trustees of the University of Alabama v. Garrett,* 531 U.S. 356, 121 S.Ct. 955, 148 L.Ed.2d 866 (2001).

Supreme Court of the United States, 2003.
__ U.S. __,
123 S.Ct. 1673,
155 L.Ed.2d 615.
http://supct.law.cornell.edu/supct[a]

CLACKAMAS GASTROENTEROLOGY ASSOCIATES, P.C. v. WELLS

Clackamas Gastroenterology Associates, P.C., a medical clinic in Oregon, employed Deborah Anne Wells as a bookkeeper from 1986 until 1997. After the clinic terminated Wells's employment, she filed a suit in a federal district court against the clinic, alleging discrimination on the basis of disability in violation of the ADA. The clinic asserted that it was not covered by the ADA because it did not have fifteen employees and filed a motion for summary judgment. The court granted the motion, and Wells appealed to the U.S. Court of Appeals for the Ninth Circuit, which reversed the judgment. The clinic appealed to the United States Supreme Court. The question was whether the four physician-shareholders who owned the corporation and constituted its board of directors counted as employees.

STEVENS, J.

We have often been asked to construe the meaning of "employee" where the statute containing the term does not helpfully define it. The definition of the term in the ADA simply states that an "employee" is "an individual employed by an employer." That surely qualifies as a mere nominal [insignificant, in name only] definition that is completely circular and explains nothing. * * *

* * * [In a previous case] we explained that when Congress has used the term "employee" without defining it, we have concluded that Congress intended to describe the conventional master-servant [employer-employee] relationship as understood by common law agency doctrine.[b]

Rather than looking to the common law, petitioner argues that courts should determine whether a shareholder-director of a professional corporation is an "employee" by asking whether the shareholder-director is, in real-

a. In the "Search" box, type in the name of the case. Select "all current and historic decisions" and click on "submit." On the page that opens, click on the name of the case to access the opinion.
b. See Chapter 14 for a discussion of the characteristics of employer-employee relationships, which have traditionally been called "master-servant" relationships.

ity, a "partner." The question whether a shareholder-director is an employee, however, cannot be answered by asking whether the shareholder-director appears to be the functional equivalent of a partner. Today there are partnerships that include hundreds of members, some of whom may well qualify as "employees" because control is concentrated in a small number of managing partners. * * *

Nor does the approach adopted by the Court of Appeals in this case fare any better. The majority's approach, which paid particular attention to "the broad purpose of the ADA," is consistent with the statutory purpose of ridding the Nation of the evil of discrimination. Nevertheless, two countervailing considerations must be weighed in the balance. First, * * * the congressional decision to limit the coverage of the legislation to firms with 15 or more employees has its own justification that must be respected—namely, easing entry into the market and preserving the competitive position of smaller firms. Second, * * * *congressional silence often reflects an expectation that courts will look to the common law to fill gaps in statutory text, particularly when an undefined term has a settled meaning at common law.* * * * [Emphasis added.]

* * * *

* * * [T]he common law's definition of the master-servant relationship does provide helpful guidance. *At common law the relevant factors defining the master-servant relationship focus on the master's control over the servant.* * * * *We think that the common law element of control is the principal guidepost that should be followed in this case.* [Emphasis added.]

This is the position that is advocated by the Equal Employment Opportunity Commission (EEOC), the agency that has special enforcement responsibilities under the ADA and other federal statutes containing similar threshold issues for determining coverage. It argues that a court should examine "whether shareholder-directors operate independently and manage the business or instead are subject to the firm's control." According to the EEOC's view, *"[i]f the shareholder-directors operate independently and manage the business, they are proprietors and not employees; if they are subject to the firm's control, they are employees."* [Emphasis added.]

* * * *

We are persuaded by the EEOC's focus on the common-law touchstone of control, and specifically by its submission that each of the following six factors is relevant to the inquiry [of] whether a shareholder-director is an employee:

> "Whether the organization can hire or fire the individual or set the rules and regulations of the individual's work
> "Whether and, if so, to what extent the organization supervises the individual's work
> "Whether the individual reports to someone higher in the organization
> "Whether and, if so, to what extent the individual is able to influence the organization
> "Whether the parties intended that the individual be an employee, as expressed in written agreements or contracts
> "Whether the individual shares in the profits, losses, and liabilities of the organization."

As the EEOC's standard reflects, an employer is the person, or group of persons, who owns and manages the enterprise. The employer can hire and fire employees, can assign tasks to employees and supervise their performance, and can decide how the profits and losses of the business are to be distributed. The mere fact that a person has a particular title—such as partner, director, or vice president—should not necessarily be used to determine whether he or she is an employee or a proprietor. Nor should the mere existence of a document styled "employment agreement" lead inexorably to the conclusion that either party is an employee. Rather * * * the answer to whether a shareholder-director is an employee depends on all of the incidents of the relationship * * * with no one factor being decisive.

The United States Supreme Court reversed the lower court's decision and remanded the case to that court to determine whether the four director-shareholder physicians were employees of the clinic. The Supreme Court endorsed a standard that used "the common-law element of control" as "the principal guidepost" for making that determination.

QUESTIONS

1. According to the United States Supreme Court, why is the ADA limited in its application to workplaces with fifteen or more employees?
2. Can shareholders who own a corporation and constitute its board of directors count as employees for purposes of the ADA and other federal discrimination laws, according to the United States Supreme Court?
3. What factors might be relevant to determining whether an individual controls a business organization or is controlled by it?

Procedures under the ADA

To prevail on a claim under the ADA, a plaintiff must show that he or she (1) has a disability, (2) is otherwise qualified for the employment in question, and (3) was excluded from the employment solely because of the disability. As in Title VII cases, a claim alleging violation of the ADA may be commenced only after the plaintiff has pursued the claim through the EEOC, which administers the provisions of the act relating to disability-based discrimination in the employment context. The EEOC may decide to investigate and perhaps even sue the employer on behalf of the employee. If the EEOC decides not to sue, then the employee is entitled to sue.

Significantly, the United States Supreme Court held in 2002 that the EEOC could bring a suit against an employer for disability-based discrimination even though the employee had agreed to submit any job-related disputes to arbitration (see Chapter 3). The Court reasoned that because the EEOC was not a party to the arbitration agreement, the agreement was not binding on the EEOC.[21]

Plaintiffs in lawsuits brought under the ADA may seek many of the same remedies available under Title VII. These include reinstatement, back pay, a limited amount of compensatory and punitive damages (for intentional discrimination), and certain other forms of relief. Repeat violators may be ordered to pay fines of up to $100,000.

---

21. *EEOC v. Waffle House, Inc.*, 534 U.S. 279, 122 S.Ct. 754, 151 L.Ed.2d 75 (2002).

What Is a Disability?

The ADA is broadly drafted to define persons with disabilities as persons with physical or mental impairments that "substantially limit" their everyday activities. More specifically, the ADA defines a *disability* as "(1) a physical or mental impairment that substantially limits one or more of the major life activities of such individuals; (2) a record of such impairment; or (3) being regarded as having such an impairment."

Health conditions that have been considered disabilities under federal law include blindness, alcoholism, heart disease, cancer, muscular dystrophy, cerebral palsy, paraplegia, diabetes, acquired immune deficiency syndrome (AIDS), and morbid obesity (defined as existing when an individual's weight is two times that of a normal person).[22] In 1998, the United States Supreme Court held that a person who is infected with the human immunodeficiency virus (HIV) but who has no symptoms of AIDS is protected under the ADA.[23] The ADA excludes from coverage certain conditions, such as kleptomania.

In a series of cases decided in the last several years, the courts have been significantly narrowing the scope of the ADA through their interpretation of what constitutes a disability under the act. For a discussion of these cases, see this chapter's *Emerging Trends* feature found on pages 556 and 557.

A question that frequently arises in ADA cases is whether a person whose disability is controlled or corrected by medication still qualifies for protection under the ADA. That issue arose in the following *Featured Case.*

---

22. *Cook v. Rhode Island Department of Mental Health,* 10 F.3d 17 (1st Cir. 1993).
23. *Bragdon v. Abbott,* 524 U.S. 624, 118 S.Ct. 2196, 141 L.Ed.2d 540 (1998).

Supreme Court of the United States, 1999.
527 U.S. 471,
119 S.Ct. 2139,
144 L.Ed.2d 450.

SUTTON v. UNITED AIRLINES, INC.

MAJORITY OPINION

O'CONNOR, J.

Petitioners [Karen and Kimberly Sutton] are twin sisters, both of whom have severe myopia [nearsightedness]. Each petitioner's uncorrected visual acuity is 20/200 or worse in her right eye and 20/400 or worse in her left eye, but with the use of corrective lenses, each * * * has vision that is 20/20 or better. Consequently, without corrective lenses, each effectively cannot see to conduct numerous activities such as driving a vehicle, watching television or shopping in public stores, but with corrective measures, such as glasses or contact lenses, both function identically to individuals without a similar impairment.

In 1992, petitioners applied to respondent [United Airlines, Inc.] for employment as commercial airline pilots. They met respondent's basic age, education, experience, and Federal Aviation Administration certification qualifications. After submitting their applications for employment, both petitioners were invited by respondent to an interview and to flight simulator tests. Both were told during their interviews, however, that a mistake had been made in inviting them to interview because petitioners did not meet respondent's minimum vision requirement, which was uncorrected visual acuity of 20/100 or better. Due to their failure to meet this requirement, petitioners' interviews were terminated, and neither was offered a pilot position.

In light of respondent's proffered [offered] reason for rejecting them, petitioners filed a charge of disability discrimination under the [Americans with Disabilities Act of 1990 (ADA)] with the Equal Employment Opportunity Commission (EEOC). After receiving a right to sue letter, petitioners filed suit in the United States District Court for the District of Colorado, alleging that respondent had discriminated against them "on the basis of their disability, or because [respondent] regarded [petitioners] as having a disability" in violation of the ADA. Specifically, petitioners alleged that due to their severe myopia they actually have a substantially limiting impairment or are regarded as having such an impairment and are thus disabled under the Act.

The District Court dismissed petitioners' complaint for failure to state a claim upon which relief could be granted. * * * [T]he Court of Appeals for the Tenth Circuit affirmed the District Court's judgment. * * * We granted *certiorari* * * * .

* * * *

* * * The Act defines a "disability" as "a physical or mental impairment that *substantially limits* one or more of the major life activities" of an individual. Because the phrase "substantially limits" appears in the Act in the present indicative verb form, we think the language is properly read as requiring that a person be presently—not potentially or hypothetically—substantially limited in order to demonstrate a disability. A "disability" exists only where an impairment "substantially limits" a major life activity, not where it "might," "could," or "would" be substantially limiting if mitigating measures were not taken. A person whose physical or mental impairment is corrected by medication or other measures does not have an impairment that presently "substantially limits" a major life activity. To be sure, *a person whose physical or mental impairment is corrected by mitigating measures still has an impairment, but if the impairment is corrected it does not "substantially limi[t]" a major life activity.* [Emphasis added.]

* * * *

* * * The use of a corrective device does not, by itself, relieve one's disability. Rather, one has a disability under [the ADA] if, notwithstanding the use of a corrective device, that individual is substantially limited in a major life activity. For example, individuals who use prosthetic limbs or wheelchairs may be mobile and capable of functioning in society but still be disabled because of a substantial limitation on their ability to walk or run. The same may be true of individuals who take medicine to lessen the symptoms of an impairment so that they can function but nevertheless remain substantially limited. Alternatively, one whose high blood pressure is "cured" by medication may be regarded as disabled by a covered entity, and thus disabled under [the ADA]. *The use or nonuse of a corrective device does not determine whether an individual is disabled; that determination depends on whether the limitations an individual with an impairment actually faces are in fact substantially limiting.* [Emphasis added.]

Applying this reading of the Act to the case at hand, we conclude that the Court of Appeals correctly resolved the issue of disability in respondent's favor. As noted above, petitioners allege that with corrective measures, their visual acuity is 20/20 and that they "function identically to individuals without a similar impairment." In addition, petitioners concede that they "do not argue that the use of corrective lenses in itself demonstrates a substantially limiting impairment." Accordingly, because we decide that disability under the Act is to be determined with reference to corrective measures, we agree with the [lower] courts * * * that petitioners have not stated a claim that they are substantially limited in any major life activity.

* * * *

Our conclusion that petitioners have failed to state a claim that they are actually disabled under [the ADA's] disability definition does not end our inquiry. * * * [The ADA] provides that having a disability includes "being regarded as having a physical or mental impairment that substantially limits one or more of the major life activities of such individual." There are two apparent ways in which individuals may fall within this statutory definition: (1) a covered entity mistakenly believes that a person has a physical impairment that substantially limits one or more major life activities, or (2) a covered entity mistakenly believes that an actual, non-limiting impairment substantially limits one or more major life activities. In both cases, it is necessary that a covered entity entertain misperceptions about the individual—it must believe either that one has a substantially limiting impairment that one does not have or that one has a substantially limiting impairment when, in fact, the impairment is not so limiting. These misperceptions often result from stereotypic assumptions not truly indicative of * * * individual ability.

* * * *

* * * By its terms, the ADA allows employers to prefer some physical attributes over others and to establish physical criteria. *An employer runs afoul of the ADA when it makes an employment decision based on a physical or mental impairment, real or imagined, that is regarded as substantially limiting a major life activity.* * * * [Emphasis added.]

* * * The EEOC has codified regulations interpreting the term "substantially limits" * * * to mean "[u]nable to perform" or "[s]ignificantly restricted." When the major life activity under consideration is that of working, the statutory phrase "substantially limits" requires, at a minimum, that plaintiffs allege they are unable to work in a broad class of jobs. * * * The inability to perform a single, particular job does not constitute a substantial limitation in the major life activity of working.

* * * *

* * * [P]etitioners have failed to allege adequately that their poor eyesight is regarded as an impairment that substantially limits them in the major life activity of working. They allege only that respondent regards their poor vision as precluding them from holding positions as a "global airline pilot." Because the position of global airline pilot is a single job, this allegation does not support the claim that respondent regards petitioners as having a *substantially limiting* impairment. Indeed, there are a number of other positions utilizing petitioners' skills, such as regional pilot and pilot instructor to name a few, that are available to them. * * *

* * * *

For these reasons, the judgment of the Court of Appeals for the Tenth Circuit is affirmed.

It is so ordered.

DISSENTING OPINION

STEVENS, J.

[I]f we apply customary tools of statutory construction, it is quite clear that the threshold question whether an individual is "disabled" within the meaning of the Act * * * focuses on her past or present physical condition without regard to mitigation that has resulted from rehabilitation, self-improvement, prosthetic devices, or medication. One might reasonably argue that the general rule should not apply to an impairment that merely requires a nearsighted person to wear glasses. But I believe that, in order to be faithful to the remedial purpose of the Act, we should give it a generous, rather than a miserly, construction.

* * * *

* * * [E]ach of the three Executive agencies charged with implementing the Act has consistently interpreted the Act as mandating that the presence of disability turns on an individual's uncorrected state. * * *

* * * *

* * * In my judgment * * * [t]he Act generally protects individuals who have "correctable" substantially limiting impairments from unjustified employment discrimination on the basis of those impairments. * * *

* * * *

* * * [V]isual impairments should be judged by the same standard as hearing impairments or any other medically controllable condition.

* * * *

* * * Only two percent of the population suffers from such myopia. Such acuity precludes a person from driving, shopping in a public store, or viewing a computer screen from a reasonable distance. Uncorrected vision, therefore, can be "substantially limiting" in the same way that unmedicated epilepsy or diabetes can be. Because Congress obviously intended to include individuals with the latter impairments in the Act's protected class, we should give petitioners the same protection.

* * * *

Accordingly * * * I am persuaded that [the petitioners] have a disability covered by the ADA. I therefore respectfully dissent.

TEST YOUR COMPREHENSION: CASE DETAILS

1. What job were the plaintiffs applying for, and what disability did the plaintiffs claim they had?
2. Did United Airlines refuse to interview the plaintiffs? Did United reject all applicants with less than perfect vision?
3. What did the lower court hold regarding the plaintiffs' disability discrimination claim?
4. Did the majority of the United States Supreme Court justices conclude that the plaintiffs were not disabled under the terms of the ADA? Why or why not?
5. Did the dissenting justices think that these plaintiffs were substantially impaired as defined by the ADA? What reasons do the dissenting justices give to support their conclusion?

Reasonable Accommodation

If a job applicant or an employee with a disability can perform essential job functions with reasonable accommodation, the employer must make the accommodation. Required modifications may include installing ramps for a wheelchair, establishing flexible working hours, creating or modifying job assignments, and creating or improving training materials and procedures.

Considering Employees' Preferences. Generally, employers should give primary consideration to employees' preferences in deciding what accommodations should be made. If an applicant or employee fails to let the employer know how his or her disability can be accommodated, the employer may avoid liability for failing to hire or retain the individual on the ground that the individual has failed to meet the "otherwise qualified" requirement.[24]

Employers should be cautious in making this assumption in situations involving mental illness, though. For example, in one case, an employee was held to have a cause of action against his employer under the ADA even though the employee never explicitly told the employer how his disability could be accommodated.[25]

Undue Hardship. Employers need not accommodate the needs of persons with disabilities if they can demonstrate that the accommodations would cause *undue hardship.* Generally, the law offers no uniform standards for identifying what is an undue hardship other than the imposition of a "significant difficulty or expense" on the employer.

Usually, the courts decide whether an accommodation constitutes an undue hardship on a case-by-case basis. In one case, the court decided that paying for a parking space near the office for an employee with a disability was not an undue hardship.[26] In another case, the court held that accommodating the request of an employee with diabetes for indefinite leave until his disease was under control would create an undue hardship for the employer, because the employer would not know when the employee was returning to work. The court stated that reasonable accommodation under the ADA means accommodation so that the employee can perform the job now or "in the immediate future" rather than at some unspecified distant time.[27]

Job Applications and Preemployment Physical Exams. Employers must modify their job-application process so that those with disabilities can compete for jobs with those who do not have disabilities. A job announcement that has only a phone number, for example, would discriminate against potential job applicants with hearing impairments. Thus, the job announcement must also provide an address.

Employers are restricted in the kinds of questions they may ask on job-application forms and during preemployment interviews. Furthermore, employers cannot require persons with disabilities to submit to preemployment physicals unless such exams are required of all other applicants. Employers can condition an offer of employment on the applicant's successfully passing a medical examination, but disqualification must result from the discovery of problems that render the applicant unable to perform the job for which she or he is to be hired.

---

24. See, for example, *Beck v. University of Wisconsin Board of Regents,* 75 F.3d 1130 (7th Cir. 1996); and *White v. York International Corp.,* 45 F.3d 357 (10th Cir. 1995).
25. *Bultemeyer v. Fort Wayne Community Schools,* 100 F.3d 1281 (7th Cir. 1996).
26. *Lyons v. Legal Aid Society,* 68 F.3d 1512 (2d Cir. 1995).
27. *Myers v. Hase,* 50 F.3d 278 (4th Cir. 1995).

EMERGING TRENDS

Narrowing the Definition of "Disability"

The Americans with Disabilities Act (ADA) does not precisely define what constitutes a disability under the act. Thus, deciding which disabilities qualify under the ADA has largely been left to the courts. Clearly, how the courts interpret the act has significant implications for both employers and employees. When a court holds that a person's impairment does not "substantially limit" a major life activity, that person will not be considered to have a disability under the ADA. Employers benefit from such a holding because they will not be required to accommodate persons with similar disabilities. In contrast, of course, individuals suffering from similar disabilities will not be able to obtain the protections afforded by the ADA.

Starting in 1999, the United States Supreme Court has issued a series of decisions narrowing the definition of what constitutes a disability under the act. As mentioned elsewhere in this chapter, one way that the courts have limited the applicability of the ADA is by holding that conditions that can be corrected with medication or special devices do not qualify as disabilities under the act. Here, we look at some other cases that are furthering this trend toward limiting the scope of the ADA.

THE *TOYOTA* CASE

In 2002, the Supreme Court further limited the scope of the ADA by its broad interpretation of what constitutes a substantially limiting impairment of a major life activity. The case before the Court involved Ella Williams, an employee of Toyota Motor Manufacturing in Kentucky. Williams's use of tools on an engine fabrication assembly line eventually caused pain in her hands, wrists, and arms. For the following two years, she held modified-duty jobs to avoid repetitive physical activity. Nonetheless, she started to experience pain in her neck and shoulders and was finally placed on a no-work-of-any-kind restriction. Toyota then terminated her employment.

The Supreme Court had to decide whether her condition, commonly referred to as carpal tunnel syndrome, constituted a disability under the ADA. The Court unanimously held that it did not. The Court stated that although the employee could not perform the manual tasks associated with her job, the condition did not constitute a disability under the ADA because it did not "substantially limit" the major life activity of performing manual tasks. For the fired worker, Williams, to prevail, her carpal tunnel syndrome would have had to be so severe that it prevented or severely restricted activities that were of central importance to her

Dangerous Workers. Employers are not required to hire or retain workers who, because of their disabilities, pose a "direct threat to the health or safety" of their co-workers. (In contrast, as noted in this chapter's *Emerging Trends* feature, employers may refuse to hire persons with disabilities if the job would pose a threat to their own health.)

In the wake of the AIDS epidemic, many employers became concerned about hiring or continuing to employ workers who have AIDS under the assumption that they might pose a direct threat to the health or safety of others in the workplace. Courts have generally held, however, that AIDS is not so contagious as to disqualify employees from most jobs. Therefore, employers must reasonably accommodate job applicants or employees who have AIDS or who test positive for HIV, the virus that causes AIDS.

Substance Abusers. Drug addiction is a disability under the ADA because drug addiction is a substantially limiting impairment. Those who are currently using illegal drugs are not protected by the act, however. The ADA only protects persons with *former* drug addictions—those who have completed a supervised drug-rehabilitation program or who are currently in a supervised

EMERGING TRENDS

Narrowing the Definition of "Disability"

daily life, not just work-related activities.[a]

FURTHER LIMITING THE SCOPE OF THE ADA

As noted elsewhere, the Supreme Court has also limited the applicability of the ADA by holding that lawsuits under the ADA cannot be brought against state government employers. The Court concluded that states, as sovereigns, are immune from lawsuits brought against them by private parties under the federal ADA.[b]

The Court has also further limited the scope of the ADA by supporting Equal Employment Opportunity Commission regulations that permit an employer to refuse to hire a person when the job would pose a threat to that person's health.[c]

IMPLICATIONS FOR THE BUSINESSPERSON

1. If this emerging trend continues, employers will more easily be able to refuse to hire job candidates who suffer from certain impairments that might make it difficult for them to work effectively at a particular task. In other words, if the trend continues, the burden of accommodating persons with disabilities may be lessened.
2. Even though recent decisions have limited the protections available under the ADA, employers must still strive to reasonably accommodate persons with disabilities.

FOR CRITICAL ANALYSIS

1. Prior to 1999, the Supreme Court and other federal courts had tended to interpret the ADA's definition of disability expansively, thus enlarging the scope of the act's coverage. Why do you think that the courts have reversed this trend in the last few years?
2. What are the costs and benefits of the ADA?

RELEVANT WEB SITES

To locate information on the Web concerning the issues discussed in this feature, go to this text's Web site at **http://ele.westbuslaw.com** and click on "Interactive Study Center."

a. *Toyota Motor Manufacturing, Kentucky, Inc. v. Williams,* 534 U.S. 184, 122 S.Ct. 681, 151 L.Ed.2d 615 (2002).

b. *Board of Trustees of the University of Alabama v. Garrett,* 531 U.S. 356, 121 S.Ct. 955, 148 L.Ed.2d 866 (2001).

c. *Chevron USA, Inc. v. Echazabal,* 536 U.S. 73, 122 S.Ct. 2045, 153 L.Ed.2d 82 (2002).

rehabilitation program. Individuals who have used drugs casually in the past are not protected under the act. They are not considered addicts and therefore do not have a disability (addiction).

People suffering from alcoholism are protected by the ADA. Employers cannot legally discriminate against employees simply because they are living with alcoholism and must treat them the same way other employees are treated. For example, an employee with alcoholism who comes to work late because she was drinking the night before cannot be disciplined any differently than an employee who comes to work late for another reason. Of course, employers have the right to prohibit the use of alcohol in the workplace and can require that employees not be under the influence of alcohol while they are working. Employers can also fire or refuse to hire a person with alcoholism if he or she poses a substantial risk of harm either to himself or herself or to others and the risk cannot be reduced by reasonable accommodation.

Health-Insurance Plans. Workers with disabilities must be given equal access to any health insurance provided to other employees. Employers can exclude from coverage preexisting health conditions and certain types of diagnostic or surgical procedures, however. An employer can also put a limit, or cap, on health-care payments under its particular group health policy as long as the cap is "applied equally to all insured employees" and does not "discriminate on the basis of disability." Whenever a group health-care plan makes a disability-based distinction in its benefits, the plan violates the ADA. The employer must then be able to justify the distinction by proving one of the following:

1. That limiting coverage of certain ailments is required to keep the plan financially sound.
2. That coverage of certain ailments would cause a significant increase in premium payments or their equivalent, making the plan unappealing to a significant number of employees.
3. That the disparate treatment is justified by the risks and costs associated with a particular disability.

Hostile-Environment Claims under the ADA

As discussed earlier in this chapter, under Title VII of the Civil Rights Act of 1964, an employee may base certain types of employment discrimination causes of action on a hostile-environment theory. Using this theory, a worker may successfully sue her or his employer, even if the worker was not fired or otherwise discriminated against. Typically, hostile-environment lawsuits brought under Title VII involve claims of sexual harassment. Suits have also been brought for hostile-environment harassment based on race, ethnic origin, or age.

Can a worker file a suit founded on a hostile-environment claim under the ADA? The ADA does not expressly provide for such suits, but some courts have allowed them. Others have assumed that the claim was possible without deciding whether the ADA allowed it.[28] To succeed, such a claim would likely have to be based on conduct that a reasonable person would find so offensive that it would change the conditions of the person's employment.

Whether a worker with a disability who was harassed by her co-workers could successfully sue her employer for a hostile environment was the issue in the following case.

28. See, for example, *Steele v. Thiokol Corp.*, 241 F.3d 1248 (10th Cir. 2001).

CASE 15.5

United States Court of Appeals, Fifth Circuit, 2001. 247 F.3d 229. **http://www.ca5.uscourts.gov/oparchdt.cfm**[a]

FLOWERS v. SOUTHERN REGIONAL PHYSICIAN SERVICES, INC.

From September 1993, Sandra Flowers worked for Southern Regional Physician Services, Inc., as a medical assistant to Dr. James Osterberger. In March 1995, Margaret Hallmark, Flowers's immediate supervisor, discovered that Flowers was infected with the human immunodeficiency virus (HIV). Suddenly, Flowers, who had received only excellent performance reviews, was the subject of several negative disci-

a. This is the "Opinion Archive by Date Released" page within the Web site of the U.S. Court of Appeals for the Fifth Circuit. Click on "2001." When the link opens, click on "May." When that link opens, click on "May 4." From the list that appears, click on the docket number next to the name of the case to access the opinion.

plinary reports. Also, in one week, she was required to take four drug tests. Previously, she had been asked to take only one. Hallmark stopped socializing with Flowers, her co-workers began avoiding her, and the president of the hospital refused to shake her hand. In November 1995, after being put on probation twice, Flowers was fired. She filed a suit in a federal district court against Southern Regional under the ADA, arguing in part that she had been subjected to a hostile environment on the basis of her disability. The court entered a judgment in her favor and awarded her $100,000. Southern Regional appealed to the U.S. Court of Appeals for the Fifth Circuit.

KING, J.

The ADA provides that no employer covered by the Act "shall discriminate against a qualified individual with a disability because of the disability of such individual in regard to * * * *terms, conditions, and privileges of employment.*" In almost identical fashion, Title VII provides that it is unlawful for an employer "to fail or refuse to hire or to discharge any individual, or otherwise to discriminate against any individual with respect to his compensation, *terms, conditions, or privileges of employment,* because of such individual's race, color, religion, sex, or national origin[.]"

It is evident, after a review of the ADA's language, purpose, and remedial framework, that Congress's intent in enacting the ADA was, *inter alia* [among other things], to eradicate disability-based harassment in the workplace. First, as a matter of statutory interpretation, * * * the [United States] Supreme Court interpreted Title VII, which contains language similar to that in the ADA, to provide a cause of action for harassment which is sufficiently severe or pervasive to alter the conditions of the victim's employment and create an abusive working environment * * * because it affects a term, condition, or privilege of employment. We conclude that the language of Title VII and [of] the ADA dictates a consistent reading of the two statutes. Therefore, following the Supreme Court's interpretation of the language contained in Title VII, we interpret the phrase "terms, conditions, and privileges of employment," as it is used in the ADA, to strike at harassment in the workplace.

Not only are Title VII and the ADA similar in their language, they are also alike in their purposes and remedial structures. *Both Title VII and the ADA are aimed at the same evil—employment discrimination against individuals of certain classes.* Moreover, this court has recognized that the ADA is part of the same broad remedial framework as * * * Title VII, and that all the antidiscrimination acts have been subjected to similar analysis. Furthermore, other courts of appeals have noted the correlation between the two statutes. We conclude, therefore, that the purposes and remedial frameworks of the two statutes also command our conclusion that the ADA provides a cause of action for disability-based harassment. [Emphasis added.]

The U.S. Court of Appeals for the Fifth Circuit held that the right to bring a hostile-environment claim can be inferred because the ADA is similar in language, purpose, and "remedial structure" to Title VII. (The court added that Flowers was entitled only to nominal damages, however, because she did not prove that she actually suffered emotional injury.)

QUESTIONS

1. What circumstances formed the basis of the plaintiff's complaint against her employer in this case?

❷ Can a hostile-environment claim be brought under the ADA under the reasoning of the U.S. Court of Appeals for the Fifth Circuit in this case? Why or why not?

❸ What might an employer do to avoid hostile-environment claims under the ADA?

Defenses to Employment Discrimination

The first line of defense for an employer charged with employment discrimination is, of course, to assert that the plaintiff has failed to meet his or her initial burden of proof—proving that discrimination in fact occurred. As noted, plaintiffs bringing cases under the ADA may find it difficult to meet this initial burden because they must prove that their alleged disabilities are disabilities covered by the ADA. Furthermore, plaintiffs in ADA cases must prove that they were otherwise qualified for the job.

Once a plaintiff succeeds in proving that discrimination occurred, the burden shifts to the employer to justify the discriminatory practice. Often, employers attempt to justify the discrimination by claiming that it was the result of a business necessity, a bona fide occupational qualification, a seniority system, or employee misconduct.

Business Necessity

Business necessity • A defense to allegations of employment discrimination in which the employer demonstrates that an employment practice that discriminates against members of a protected class is related to job performance.

An employer may defend against a claim of disparate-impact discrimination by asserting that a practice that has a discriminatory effect is a **business necessity.** If requiring a high school diploma, for example, is shown to have a discriminatory effect, an employer might argue that a high school education is required for workers to perform the job at a required level of competence. If the employer can demonstrate to the court's satisfaction that a definite connection exists between a high school education and job performance, then the employer will succeed in this business necessity defense. This defense cannot be asserted to avoid liability for *intentional* discrimination, however.

Bona Fide Occupational Qualification

Bona fide occupational qualification (BFOQ) • Identifiable characteristics reasonably necessary to the normal operation of a particular business. These characteristics can include gender, national origin, and religion, but not race or color.

Another defense applies when discrimination against a protected class is essential to a job—that is, when a particular trait is a **bona fide occupational qualification (BFOQ).** For example, a women's clothing boutique might legitimately hire only female attendants if part of an attendant's job involves assisting clients in the boutique's dressing rooms. Similarly, the Federal Aviation Administration can legitimately impose age limits for airline pilots. Race or color, however, can never be a BFOQ. Generally, courts have restricted the BFOQ defense to instances in which the employee's gender or religion is essential to the job.

Seniority Systems

An employer with a history of discrimination may have no members of protected classes in upper-level positions. Even if the employer now seeks to be unbiased, it may face a lawsuit seeking an order that members of protected classes be promoted ahead of schedule to compensate for past discrimination.

If no present intent to discriminate is shown, however, and if promotions or other job benefits are distributed according to a fair **seniority system** (in which workers with more years of service are promoted first or laid off last), the employer has a good defense against the suit.

Seniority system • In regard to employment relationships, a system in which those who have worked longest for the company are first in line for promotions, salary increases, and other benefits; they are also the last to be laid off if the work force must be reduced.

According to the United States Supreme Court, this defense may also apply to alleged discrimination under the ADA. According to the Court, if an employee's requested accommodation conflicts with an employer's seniority system, the accommodation will generally not be considered "reasonable" under the act.[29] In other words, if an employee with a disability requests that she or he be assigned to a particular position and another employee is entitled to that position under the employer's seniority system, the employer normally need not accommodate the request.

After-Acquired Evidence of Employee Misconduct

In some situations, employers have attempted to avoid liability for employment discrimination on the basis of "after-acquired evidence" of an employee's misconduct. For example, suppose that an employer fires a worker, who then sues the employer for employment discrimination. During pretrial investigation, the employer learns that the employee made material misrepresentations on his employment application—misrepresentations that, had the employer known about them, would have served as a ground to fire the individual. Can this after-acquired evidence be used as a defense?

According to the United States Supreme Court, after-acquired evidence of wrongdoing should not operate, "in every instance, to bar all relief for an earlier violation" of a federal law prohibiting discrimination.[30] Since this decision, the courts have generally held that after-acquired evidence, at best, can only serve to limit liability. Although such evidence cannot shield an employer entirely from liability for employment discrimination, it may serve to limit the amount of damages for which the employer is liable.

Affirmative Action

The laws discussed in this chapter were designed to reduce or eliminate discriminatory practices with respect to hiring, retaining, and promoting employees. **Affirmative action** programs go a step further and attempt to "make up" for past patterns of discrimination by giving members of protected classes preferential treatment in hiring or promotion.

Affirmative action • Job-hiring and admissions policies that give special consideration to members of protected classes in an effort to overcome present effects of past discrimination.

Affirmative action policies were first mandated by an executive order issued by President Lyndon Johnson in 1965. All government agencies, including those of state and local governments, were required to implement such policies. Affirmative action requirements were also imposed on companies that contract to do business with the federal government and on institutions that receive federal funds. Because a significant percentage of the nation's employees work for government agencies or for firms that do business with the government, this presidential executive order has had a profound impact on the American workplace.

29. *U.S. Airways, Inc. v. Barnett,* 535 U.S. 391, 122 S.Ct. 1516, 152 L.Ed.2d 589 (2002).
30. *McKennon v. Nashville Banner Publishing Co.,* 513 U.S. 352, 115 S.Ct. 879, 130 L.Ed.2d 852 (1995).

Title VII of the Civil Rights Act of 1964 neither requires nor prohibits affirmative action, and thus private companies and organizations that do not do business with the government or receive federal funds have not been required to implement such policies—although many have done so voluntarily. Note, though, that the courts and the Equal Employment Opportunity Commission have sometimes ordered private companies to undertake affirmative action when they found evidence of past discrimination. Labor unions that have been found to discriminate against women or minorities in the past have also been required to establish and follow affirmative action plans.

Affirmative action programs have caused much controversy, particularly when they result in what is called "reverse discrimination"—discrimination against "majority" workers, such as white males (or discrimination against other minority groups that are not given preferential treatment under a particular affirmative action program). At issue is whether affirmative action programs, because of their inherently discriminatory nature, violate employee rights or the equal protection clause of the Fourteenth Amendment to the U.S. Constitution.

Challenges to Affirmative Action

When an affirmative action plan undertaken by a private employer (one that does not do business with the government) is challenged on the basis of reverse discrimination, the court decides the issue under Title VII. Generally, the courts have held that an affirmative action plan is valid if the employer can show that minorities and women have been notably underrepresented in the workplace in the past and that the plan does not unnecessarily restrict the rights of male or nonminority employees. More controversial today is the issue of whether affirmative action plans required by the government (that is, plans undertaken by employers that receive government funds or that do business with the government) violate the equal protection clause of the Fourteenth Amendment to the Constitution.

The *Bakke* Case. An early nonemployment-related case addressing this issue, *Regents of the University of California v. Bakke,*[31] involved an affirmative action program implemented by the University of California at Davis. Allan Bakke, who had been turned down for medical school at the Davis campus, sued the university for reverse discrimination after he discovered that his academic record was better than the records of some of the minority applicants who had been admitted to the program.

The United States Supreme Court held that affirmative action programs were subject to intermediate scrutiny. Recall from the discussion of the equal protection clause in Chapter 5 that any law or action evaluated under a standard of intermediate scrutiny, to be constitutionally valid, must be substantially related to important government objectives. Applying this standard, the Court held that the university could give favorable weight to minority applicants as part of a plan to increase minority enrollment so as to achieve a more culturally diverse student body. The Court stated, however, that the use of a quota system, in which a certain number of places are explicitly reserved for minority applicants, violated the equal protection clause of the Fourteenth Amendment.

31. 438 U.S. 265, 98 S.Ct. 2733, 57 L.Ed.2d 750 (1978).

The *Adarand* Case. Although the *Bakke* case and later court decisions alleviated the harshness of the quota system, today's courts are going even further in questioning the constitutional validity of affirmative action programs. In 1995, in its landmark decision in *Adarand Constructors, Inc. v. Peña,*[32] the United States Supreme Court held that any federal, state, or local affirmative action program that uses racial or ethnic classifications as the basis for making decisions is subject to strict scrutiny by the courts.

In effect, the Court's ruling in *Adarand* means that an affirmative action program is constitutional only if it attempts to remedy past discrimination and does not make use of quotas or preferences. Furthermore, once such a program has succeeded in the goal of remedying past discrimination, it must be changed or dropped.

Subsequent Court Decisions. In 1996, in *Hopwood v. State of Texas,*[33] the Court of Appeals for the Fifth Circuit went beyond the Supreme Court's *Adarand* decision. In the *Hopwood* case, two white law school applicants sued the University of Texas School of Law in Austin, alleging that they were denied admission because of the school's affirmative action program. The program allowed admitting officials to take racial and other factors into consideration when determining which students would be admitted. The court held that the program violated the equal protection clause because it discriminated in favor of minority applicants. In its decision, the court directly challenged the *Bakke* decision by stating that the use of race even as a means of achieving diversity on college campuses "undercuts the Fourteenth Amendment."

In 2003, the United States Supreme Court reviewed two cases involving issues similar to that in the *Hopwood* case. Both cases involved admissions programs at the University of Michigan. In *Gratz v. Bollinger,*[34] two white applicants who were denied undergraduate admission to the university alleged reverse discrimination. The school's policy gave each applicant a score based on a number of factors, including grade point average, standardized test scores, and personal achievements. The system *automatically* awarded every "underrepresented" minority (African American, Hispanic, and Native American) applicant twenty points—one-fifth of the points needed to guarantee admission. The Court held that this policy violated the equal protection clause.

In contrast, in *Grutter v. Bollinger,*[35] the Court held that the University of Michigan Law School's admission policy was constitutional. In that case, the Court concluded that "[u]niversities can, however, consider race or ethnicity more flexibly as a 'plus' factor in the context of individualized consideration of each and every applicant." The significant difference between the two admissions policies, in the Court's view, was that the law school's approach did not apply a mechanical formula giving "diversity bonuses" based on race or ethnicity.

State Actions

In the meantime, some state governments have been taking action. California and Washington, by voter initiatives in 1996 and 1998, respectively, ended state-government–sponsored affirmative action in those states. Similar movements

---

32. 575 U.S. 200, 115 S.Ct. 2097, 132 L.Ed.2d 158 (1995).
33. 84 F.3d 720 (5th Cir. 1996).
34. __U.S.__, 123 S.Ct. 2411, 156 L.Ed.2d 257(2003).
35. __U.S.__, 123 S.Ct. 2325, 156 L.Ed.2d 304 (2003).

are currently under way in other state and local areas as well. Additionally, a number of universities have modified their admissions policies to increase opportunities for minority students without directly considering racial or ethnic factors. For example, California has put into effect a "top 4 percent plan." Under this plan, the top 4 percent of students from certain low-performing and predominantly minority high schools are automatically accepted at the Berkeley and Los Angeles campuses of the University of California. Since 1996, Texas has had a similar plan that uses a much higher percentage.

State Laws Prohibiting Discrimination

Although the focus of this chapter is on federal legislation, most states also have statutes that prohibit employment discrimination. Generally, the kinds of discrimination forbidden under federal legislation are also forbidden by state laws. In addition, state statutes often provide protection for certain individuals who are not protected under federal laws. For example, a New Jersey appellate court held that anyone over the age of eighteen was entitled to sue for age discrimination under the state law, which specified no threshold age limit.[36]

Furthermore, state laws prohibiting discrimination may apply to firms with fewer employees than the threshold number required under federal statutes, thus offering protection to a greater number of workers. Even when companies are too small to be covered by state statutes, state courts may uphold employees' rights against discrimination in the workplace for public-policy reasons.[37] Finally, state laws may provide for additional damages, such as damages for emotional distress, that are not provided for under federal statutes.

36. *Bergen Commercial Bank v. Sisler,* 307 N.J.Super. 333, 704 A.2d 1017 (1998).
37. See, for example, *Roberts v. Dudley,* 92 Wash.App. 652, 966 P.2d 377 (1998); and *Insignia Residential Corp. v. Ashton,* 359 Md. 560, 755 A.2d 1080 (2000).

KEY TERMS

affirmative action 561
bona fide occupational qualification (BFOQ) 560
business necessity 560
disparate-impact discrimination 538
disparate-treatment discrimination 537
employment discrimination 536
***prima facie* case 537**
protected class 536
seniority system 561
sexual harassment 540

FOR REVIEW

1. Generally, what kind of conduct does Title VII of the Civil Rights Act of 1964 prohibit?
2. What is the difference between disparate-treatment discrimination and disparate-impact discrimination?
3. What remedies are available under Title VII of the 1964 Civil Rights Act?
4. Which federal acts prohibit discrimination based on age and discrimination based on disability?
5. What are three defenses to claims of employment discrimination?

QUESTIONS AND CASE PROBLEMS

15–1. Discuss fully whether any of the following actions would constitute a violation of Title VII of the 1964 Civil Rights Act, as amended.

(a) Tennington, Inc., is a consulting firm and has ten employees. These employees travel on consulting jobs in seven states. Tennington has an employment record of hiring only white males.

(b) Novo Films is making a movie about Africa and needs to employ approximately one hundred extras for this picture. Novo advertises in all major newspapers in southern California for the hiring of these extras. The ad states that only African Americans need apply.

15–2. Tavo Jones had worked since 1974 for Westshore Resort, where he maintained golf carts. During the first decade, he received positive job evaluations and numerous merit pay raises. He was promoted to the position of supervisor of golf-cart maintenance at three courses. Then a new employee, Ben Olery, was placed in charge of the golf courses. He demoted Jones, who was over the age of forty, to running one of the three cart facilities, and he froze Jones's salary indefinitely. Olery also demoted five other men over the age of forty. Another cart facility was placed under the supervision of Blake Blair. Later, the cart facilities for the three courses were again consolidated, but Blair—not Jones—was put in charge. At the time, Blair was in his twenties. Jones overheard Blair say that "we are going to have to do away with these . . . old and senile" men. Jones quit and sued Westshore for employment discrimination. Should he prevail? Explain.

15–3. Ananda is a hearing-impaired repairperson currently employed with the Southwestern Telephone Co. Her job requires her to drive the company truck to remote rural areas in all kinds of weather, to climb telephone poles, to make general repairs to telephone lines, and so on. She has held this position for five years, a full year longer than any other employee, and she is quite competent. Ananda recently applied for a promotion to the position of repair crew coordinator, a position that would require her to be in constant communication with all repairpersons in the field. Southwestern rejected Ananda's application, stating that the company "needs someone in this critical position who can speak and hear clearly, someone who does not suffer from any hearing disability." Ananda says she could easily perform the essentials of the job if Southwestern would provide her with a sign interpreter. Although Southwestern agrees that Ananda is otherwise qualified for the coordinator position, the company has concluded that the cost of hiring an interpreter would be prohibitive, and therefore it should not be required to accommodate her disability under the Americans with Disabilities Act. Who is correct? Discuss.

CASE PROBLEM WITH SAMPLE ANSWER

15–4. Defenses to Employment Discrimination. Dorothea O'Driscoll had worked as a quality control inspector for Hercules, Inc., for six years when her employment was terminated in 1986. O'Driscoll, who was over forty years of age, sued Hercules for age discrimination in violation of the Age Discrimination in Employment Act of 1967. While preparing for trial, Hercules learned that O'Driscoll had made several misrepresentations when she applied for the job. Among other things, she misrepresented her age, did not disclose a previous employer, falsely represented that she had never applied for work with Hercules before, and untruthfully stated that she had completed two quarters of study at a technical college. Additionally, on her application for group insurance coverage, she misrepresented the age of her son, who would otherwise have been ineligible for coverage as her dependent. Hercules defended against O'Driscoll's claim of age discrimination by stating that had it known of this misconduct, it would have terminated her employment anyway. What should the court decide? Discuss fully. [*O'Driscoll v. Hercules, Inc.,* 12 F.3d 176 (10th Cir. 1994)]

➧ *To view a sample answer for this case problem, go to this book's Web site at* **http://ele.westbuslaw.com** *and click on "Interactive Study Center."*

15–5. Discrimination Based on Disability. When the University of Maryland Medical System Corp. learned that one of its surgeons was HIV positive, the university offered him transfers to positions that did not involve surgery. The surgeon refused, and the university terminated him. The surgeon filed a suit in a federal district court against the university, alleging in part a violation of the Americans with Disabilities Act. The surgeon claimed that he was "otherwise qualified" for his former position. What does he have to prove to win his case? Should he be reinstated? [*Doe v. University of Maryland Medical System Corp.,* 50 F.3d 1261 (4th Cir. 1995)]

15–6. Religious Discrimination. Mary Tiano, a devout Roman Catholic, worked for Dillard Department Stores, Inc. (Dillard's), in Phoenix, Arizona. Dillard's considered Tiano a productive employee because her sales exceeded \$200,000 a year. At the time, the store gave its managers the discretion to grant unpaid leave to employees but prohibited vacations or leave during the holiday season—October through December. Tiano felt that she had a "calling" to go on a "pilgrimage" in October 1988 to Medjugorje, Yugoslavia, where some persons claimed to have had visions of the Virgin Mary. The Catholic Church had not designated the site an official pilgrimage site, the visions were not expected to be stronger in October, and tours were available at other times. The store managers denied Tiano's request for leave, but she had a nonrefundable ticket and left anyway. Dillard's terminated her employment. For a year, Tiano searched for a new job and did not attain the level of her Dillard's salary for four years. She filed a suit in a federal district court against Dillard's, alleging religious discrimination in violation of Title VII. Can Tiano establish a *prima facie* case of religious discrimination? Explain. [*Tiano v. Dillard Department Stores, Inc.,* 139 F.3d 679 (9th Cir. 1998)]

15–7. Discrimination Based on Disability. Vaughn Murphy was first diagnosed with hypertension (high blood pressure) when he was ten years old. Unmedicated, his blood pressure is approximately 250/160. With medication, however, he can function normally and engage in the same activities as anyone else. In 1994, United Parcel Service, Inc. (UPS), hired Murphy to be a mechanic, a position that required him to drive commercial motor vehicles. To get the job, Murphy had to meet a U.S. Department of Transportation (DOT) regulation that a driver have "no current clinical diagnosis of high blood pressure likely to interfere with his/her ability to operate a commercial vehicle safely." At the time, Murphy's blood pressure was measured at 186/124, but he was erroneously certified and started work. Within a month, the error was discovered and he was fired. Murphy obtained another mechanic's job—one that did not require DOT certification—and filed a suit in a federal district court against UPS, claiming discrimination under the Americans with Disabilities Act. UPS filed a motion for summary judgment. Should the court grant UPS's motion? Explain. [*Murphy v. United Parcel Service, Inc.,* 527 U.S. 516, 119 S.Ct. 2133, 144 L.Ed.2d 484 (1999)]

15–8. Discrimination Based on Disability. PGA Tour, Inc., sponsors professional golf tournaments. A player may enter in several ways, but the most common method is to compete successfully in a three-stage qualifying tournament known as the "Q-School." Anyone may enter the Q-School by submitting two letters of recommendation and paying $3,000 to cover greens fees and the cost of a golf cart, which is permitted during the first two stages, but is prohibited during the third stage. The rules governing the events include the "Rules of Golf," which apply at all levels of amateur and professional golf and do not prohibit the use of golf carts, and the "hard card," which applies specifically to the PGA tour and requires the players to walk the course during most of a tournament. Casey Martin is a talented golfer with a degenerative circulatory disorder that prevents him from extensive walking. Martin entered the Q-School and asked for permission to use a cart during the third stage. PGA refused. Martin filed a suit in a federal district court against PGA, alleging a violation of the Americans with Disabilities Act. Is a golf cart in these circumstances a "reasonable accommodation" under the ADA? Why or why not? [*PGA Tour, Inc. v. Martin,* 532 U.S. 661, 121 S.Ct. 1879, 149 L.Ed.2d 904 (2001)]

15–9. Discrimination Based on Race. The hiring policy of Phillips Community College of the University of Arkansas (PCCUA) is to conduct an internal search for qualified applicants before advertising outside the college. Steven Jones, the university's chancellor, can determine the application and appointment process for vacant positions, however, and is the ultimate authority in hiring decisions. Howard Lockridge, an African American, was the chair of PCCUA's Technical and Industrial Department. Between 1988 and 1998, Lockridge applied for several different positions, some of which were unadvertised, some of which were unfilled for years, and some of which were filled with less qualified persons from outside the college. In 1998, when Jones advertised an opening for the position of dean of Industrial Technology and Workforce Development, Lockridge did not apply for the job. Jones hired Tracy McGraw, a white male. Lockridge filed a suit in a federal district court against the university under Title VII. The university filed a motion for summary judgment in its favor. What are the elements of a *prima facie* case of disparate-treatment discrimination? Can Lockridge pass this test, or should the court issue a judgment in the university's favor? Explain. [*Lockridge v. Board of Trustees of the University of Arkansas,* 294 F.3d 1010 (8th Cir. 2002)]

15–10. IN YOUR COURT

Calvin Rhodes sold oil-field equipment for Anson Oil Tools. When he was discharged in 1986 at age fifty-six, he was told that the discharge was part of a reduction in the work force (RIF) and that he would be considered for reemployment. Within six weeks, Anson hired a forty-two-year-old person to do the same job. Rhodes brought a suit against Anson in a federal district court, claiming that the real reason he was discharged was age discrimination. At the trial, Anson offered as a defense Rhodes's "poor work performance" but did not present any company sales records or goals. Rhodes countered with customers' testimony about his expertise and diligence. The jury found that Rhodes was discharged because of his age. Anson appealed the decision. Assume that you are a judge on the federal appellate court reviewing this case and answer the following questions:

(a) Remember that as an appellate court judge, you should defer to the trial court's findings of fact—unless you conclude that there is no justification for the trial court's findings. Thus, the question you need to decide is whether a reasonable jury could have found that Rhodes was a victim of age discrimination in violation of the Age Discrimination in Employment Act (ADEA). How will you answer this question? Why?

(b) Does it matter that Rhodes's replacement was also a member of the class of persons protected by the ADEA? Will your answer to this question affect your answer to question (a) above?

15–11. A QUESTION OF ETHICS AND SOCIAL RESPONSIBILITY

Luz Long and three other Hispanic employees (the plaintiffs) worked as bank tellers for the Culmore branch of the First Union Corp. of Virginia. The plaintiffs often conversed with one another in Spanish, their native language. In 1992, the Culmore branch manager adopted an "English-only" policy, which required all employees to speak English during working hours unless they had to speak another language to assist customers. The plaintiffs refused to cooperate with the new policy and were eventually fired. In a suit against the bank, the plaintiffs alleged that the English-only policy discriminated against them on the basis of their national origin. The court granted the bank's motion for summary judgment, concluding that "[t]here is nothing in Title VII which . . . provides that an employee has a right to speak his or her native tongue while on the job." [*Long v. First Union Corp. of Virginia,* 894 F.Supp. 933 (E.D.Va. 1995)]

(a) The bank argued that the policy was implemented in response to complaints made by fellow workers that the Spanish-speaking employees were creating a hostile environment by speaking Spanish among themselves in the presence of other employees. From an ethical perspective, is this a sufficient reason to institute an English-only policy?

(b) Is it ever ethically justifiable for employers to deny bilingual employees the opportunity to speak their native language while on the job?

(c) Might there be situations in which English-only policies are necessary to promote worker health and safety?

(d) Generally, what are the pros and cons of English-only policies in the workplace?

15–12. FOR CRITICAL ANALYSIS

Why has the federal government limited the application of the statutes discussed in this chapter only to firms with a specified number of employees, such as fifteen or twenty? Should these laws apply to *all* employers, regardless of size?

For updated links to resources available on the Web, as well as a variety of other materials, visit this text's Web site at

http://ele.westbuslaw.com

The law firm of Arent Fox posts articles on current issues in the area of employment law, including sexual harassment, on its Web site at

http://www.arentfox.com/home.html

An abundance of helpful information on disability-based discrimination, including the text of the Americans with Disabilities Act of 1990, can be found at the following Web site:

http://jan.wvu.edu/links/adalinks.htm

An excellent source for information on various forms of employment discrimination is the Equal Employment Opportunity Commission's Web site at

http://www.eeoc.gov

LEGAL RESEARCH EXERCISES ON THE WEB

Go to **http://ele.westbuslaw.com**, the Web site that accompanies this text. Select "Interactive Study Center," and then click on "Chapter 15." There you will find the following Internet research exercises that you can perform to learn more about topics covered in this chapter.

Activity 15–1: LEGAL PERSPECTIVE—Americans with Disabilities

Activity 15–2: MANAGEMENT PERSPECTIVE—Equal Employment Opportunity

Activity 15–3: SOCIAL PERSPECTIVE—Religious and National-Origin Discrimination

BEFORE THE TEST

Go to **http://ele.westbuslaw.com**, the Web site that accompanies this text. Select "Interactive Quizzes." You will find at least twenty interactive questions relating to this chapter.

WESTLAW® CAMPUS

If your textbook provided for a subscription to Westlaw® Campus, or if you have otherwise purchased access to the Westlaw Campus database, you can access any of the cases presented or cited in this chapter by using your Westlaw Campus account.

FOCUS ON LEGAL REASONING
Redi-Floors, Inc. v. Sonenberg Co.

INTRODUCTION

In Chapter 14, we outlined the liability of principals and agents for contracts formed by agents. In this *Focus on Legal Reasoning,* we look at *Redi-Floors, Inc. v. Sonenberg Co.,*[1] a decision in which the court set out these principles.

CASE BACKGROUND

Sonenberg Company was the manager of Westchester Manor Apartments in Atlanta, Georgia. Manor Associates Limited Partnership owned the complex.[2] Manor's partners included Westchester Manor, Limited. The entry sign to the property disclosed only that Sonenberg managed it.

1. 254 Ga.App. 615, 563 S.E.2d 505 (2002).
2. A *limited partnership* is a form of business organization that was discussed in Chapter 9.

Sonenberg's on-site property manager contacted Redi-Floors, Inc., and requested a proposal for installing carpet in several apartments. In preparing the proposal, Redi-Floors confirmed that Sonenberg was the managing company. The property manager ordered, and Redi-Floors installed, the carpet as per the proposal. Redi-Floors sent invoices to the complex and received checks from "Westchester Manor Apartments." Believing that Sonenberg owned the complex, Redi-Floors did not learn the true owner's identity until a dispute arose concerning payment for some of the invoices.

To recover on the outstanding invoices, Redi-Floors filed a suit in a Georgia state court against Sonenberg, Manor Associates, and Westchester Manor. The court granted Sonenberg's motion for a directed verdict[3] on the ground that Redi-Floors knew Sonenberg was only an agent. Against the other parties, Redi-Floors obtained a verdict exceeding $20,000. Unable to collect on this judgment, Redi-Floors appealed to a state intermediate appellate court.

3. Recall from Chapter 2 that a *motion for a directed verdict* is a motion for the judge to take the decision out of the hands of the jury and direct a verdict for the party who filed the motion on the ground that the other party has not produced sufficient evidence to support his or her claim.

MAJORITY OPINION

BLACKBURN, J.

An agent who makes a contract without identifying his principal becomes personally liable on the contract. *If the agent wishes to avoid personal liability, the duty is on him to disclose his agency, and not on the party with whom he deals to discover it.* The agent's disclosure of a trade name and the plaintiff's awareness of that name are not necessarily sufficient so as to protect the agent from liability. *The disclosure of an agency is not complete for the purpose of relieving the agent from personal liability unless it embraces the name of the principal.* [Emphasis added.]

Based on these principles, *Reed v. Burns International Security Services,* 215 Ga.App. 60, 449 S.E.2d 888 (1994), upheld a judgment in favor of a security company and against the apartment management company that contracted for security services at the apartment complex but failed to identify to the security company the name of the limited partnership owning the complex. * * * Here, at least some evidence showed that Sonenberg never disclosed the name of Manor Associates Limited Partnership to Redi-Floors. Accordingly, the trial court erred in entering a directed verdict in favor of Sonenberg.

* * * *

With respect to an undisclosed principal, the rule in Georgia is that if the buyer is in fact merely an agent and acts with the authority of an undisclosed principal, either he or such principal may be held liable at the election of the opposite party; but the contractual liability of such agent and principal is not joint, and, after an election to proceed against one, the other cannot be held. Thus, if an agent buys in his own name, without disclosing his principal, and the seller subsequently discovers that the purchase was, in fact, made for another, he may, at his choice, look for payment either to the agent or the principal * * * . On the other hand, if, at the time of the sale, the seller knows not only the person, who is nominally dealing with him, is not principal, but agent, and also knows who the principal really is, and notwithstanding all the knowledge, chooses to make the agent his debtor—

dealing with him and him alone—the seller must be taken to have abandoned his recourse against the principal, and cannot afterwards, upon the failure of the agent, turn round and charge the principal, having once made his election at the time when he had the power of choosing between the one and the other. An election deliberately made, with knowledge of facts and absence of fraud, is conclusive; and the party who has once elected, can claim no right to make a second choice. Thus, while it is true that a judgment against both the agent and the principal cannot stand, it is the plaintiff who is entitled to elect against which of the defendants, principal or agent, to take the judgment. * * *

* * * In the present case the trial court's erroneous granting of a directed verdict deprived the plaintiff of its right to elect which defendant it would proceed against. * * *

* * * *

This case must be remanded to the trial court with instructions to allow Redi-Floors to make an election as to which defendant it wishes to proceed against, thus restoring to Redi-Floors the right to make such election. Should Redi-Floors elect to hold Manor Associates liable, nothing further is required as the existing judgment would stand against this defendant. On the other hand, should Redi-Floors seek to proceed against Sonenberg, the existing judgment is vacated and a new trial will be necessary.

DISSENTING OPINION

MILLER, J.

I dissent * * * because I believe that Redi-Floors's decision to obtain a judgment against Manor Associates Limited Partnership has rendered the error harmless. Redi-Floors had the right, as do all plaintiffs, to pursue mutually exclusive remedies prior to the verdict; but once Redi-Floors procured a judgment order which was reduced to writing against Manor Associates, that constituted an election of alternative remedies that precluded plaintiff from pursuing the excluded remedy against Sonenberg.

A corollary to the principle that a nondisclosing agent is personally liable is that the contract liability of a principal and his agent is not joint, and after election to proceed against one, the other cannot be held. As the plaintiff may not obtain judgment against both, he must make an election *prior to judgment* as to whether he wants a judgment against the agent or against the principal. If the plaintiff does not expressly announce an election, his taking a judgment against the principal constitutes an election and precludes any further action against the agent. Here, after the court entered a directed verdict in favor of Sonenberg, Redi-Floors (1) had every opportunity to reevaluate its case and to obtain court permission to dismiss its case * * * against Manor Associates instead of proceeding further or (2) could have had the court withhold entry of judgment (once the verdict against Manor Associates was obtained) until an appeal of the directed verdict was decided. In either case, Redi-Floors could have then brought this issue here as an appeal from the directed verdict *without* electing to obtain a *judgment* against Manor Associates. Redi-Floor's decision to obtain a judgment against the principal, however, was an election and precludes it from pursuing Sonenberg further.

LEGAL REASONING AND ANALYSIS

❶ **Legal Analysis.** The majority cites, in its opinion, *Reed v. Burns International Security Services,* 215 Ga.App. 60, 449 S.E.2d 888 (1994) (see the appendix to Chapter 1 for instructions on how to access state court opinions). How do the facts, issues, and holdings of the *Redi-Floors* and *Reed* cases compare? Why does the majority in the *Redi-Floors* case cite the *Reed* case?

❷ **Legal Reasoning.** What reasons does the majority provide to justify its conclusion? How do those reasons contrast with the dissent's reasoning? With whom do you agree? Why?

❸ **Social Considerations.** Do agents owe to those with whom they deal on behalf of their principals any obligations besides a public duty to obey the law? If so, what is the nature of those obligations?

❹ **Implications for Creditors.** What does the outcome in this case indicate to those who do business with others' agents on a credit basis?

❺ **Case Briefing Assignment.** Using the guidelines for briefing cases given in the "Preface to the Student" at the beginning of this text, brief the *Redi-Floors* case.

UNIT FOUR

FOCUS ON LEGAL REASONING

GOING ONLINE

This text's Web site, at **http://ele.westbuslaw.com**, offers links to West's Court Case Updates, as well as to other online research sources. You can also locate court cases at the Web sites listed in the *Law on the Web* section at the end of Chapter 2.

The Legal Information Institute (LII) offers links to state court decisions on agency principles at **http://www.law.cornell.edu/topics/agency.html**, a page within the LII Web site. LII is affiliated with Cornell Law School in Ithaca, New York.

UNIT FOUR

FOCUS ON ETHICS

The Employment Environment

Ethical principles—and challenging ethical issues—pervade the employment environment. In part, this is because employment relationships often involve intricate duties of agency. As you read in Chapter 14, when one person agrees to act on behalf of another, as an agent does in an agency relationship, that person assumes certain ethical responsibilities. Similarly, the principal also assumes certain ethical duties. In essence, agency law gives legal force to the ethical duties arising in an agency relationship. Although agency law also focuses on the rights of agents and principals, those rights are framed by the concept of duty—that is, an agent's duty becomes a right for the principal and vice versa.

Employees who deal with third parties are also deemed to be agents and thus share the ethical (and legal) duties imposed under agency law. In the employment context, however, it is not always possible for an employee to negotiate favorable employment terms. Often, an employee who is offered a job either accepts the job on the employer's terms or looks elsewhere for a position. Although numerous federal and state statutes protect employees, in some situations employees still have little recourse against their employers. At the same time, employers complain that statutes regulating employment relationships impose so many requirements that they find it hard to exercise a reasonable amount of control over their workplaces.

In the following pages, we focus on the ethical dimensions of

selected issues in agency and employment law.

THE AGENT'S DUTY TO THE PRINCIPAL

The very nature of the principal-agent relationship is one of trust, which we call a fiduciary relationship. Because of the nature of this relationship, an agent is considered to owe certain duties to the principal. These duties include being loyal and obedient, informing the principal of important facts concerning the agency, accounting to the principal for property or money received, and performing with reasonable diligence and skill.

Thus, ethical conduct would prevent an agent from representing two principals in the same transaction, making a secret profit from the agency relationship, or failing to disclose the interest of the agent in property the principal was purchasing. The expected ethical conduct of the agent has evolved into rules that, if breached, cause the agent to be held legally liable.

But does an agent's obligation extend beyond the duty to the principal and include a duty to society as well? Consider, for example, the situation faced by an employee who knows that her employer is engaging in an unethical—or even illegal—practice, such as marketing an unsafe product. Does the employee's duty to the principal include keeping silent about this practice, which may harm users of the product? Does the employee have a duty to protect consumers by disclosing this information to the public, even if she loses her job as a result? Some scholars have argued that many of the greatest evils in the past thirty years have been accomplished in the name of duty to the principal.

THE PRINCIPAL'S DUTY TO THE AGENT

Just as agents owe certain fiduciary duties to their principals, so do principals owe ethical duties to their agents, such as compensation and job-related expenses. If an agent incurs expenses or liability while acting on the principal's behalf, for example, it is only fair that the principal should assume responsibility for those expenses or that liability.

Principals also owe their agents a duty of cooperation. One might expect most principals to cooperate with their agents out of self-interest, but this is not universally the case. Suppose that a principal hires an agent on commission to sell a building, and the agent puts considerable time and expense into the process. If the principal changes his mind and decides to retain the building, he might want to prevent the agent from completing a sale. Is such action ethical? Does it violate the principal's duty of cooperation?

FOCUS ON ETHICS

What alternatives would the principal have?

Although a principal is legally obligated to fulfill certain duties to the agent, these duties do not include any specific duty of loyalty. Some argue that the lack of employer loyalty to employees has resulted in a reduction in employee loyalty to employers. After all, they maintain, why should an employee be loyal to an employer's interests over the years when the employee knows that the employer has no corresponding legal duty to be loyal to the employee's interests? Employers who do show a sense of loyalty to employees—for example, by not laying off long-time, faithful employees when business is slow or when those employees could be replaced by younger workers at lower cost—base that sense of loyalty primarily on ethical, not legal, considerations.

RESPONDEAT SUPERIOR

Agency law is designed to enforce the ethical or fiduciary duties that arise once an agency relationship is established. To perhaps an even greater extent, agency law is designed to protect third parties—people outside the agency relationship.

One legal concept that addresses the effect of agency relationships on third parties is the doctrine of *respondeat superior*. The doctrine raises a significant ethical question: Why should innocent employers be required to assume responsibility for the tortious, or wrongful, actions of their agent-employees? The answer has to do with the courts' perception that when one of two innocent parties must suffer a loss, the party in the best position to prevent that loss should bear the burden. In an employment relationship, for example, the employer has more control over the employee's behavior than a third party to the relationship does.

Another reason for retaining the doctrine of *respondeat superior* in our laws is based on the employer's assumed ability to pay any damages that are incurred by a third party. Our collection of shared beliefs suggests that an injured party should be afforded the most effective relief possible. Thus, even though an employer may be absolutely innocent, the employer has "deeper pockets" than the employee and will be more likely to have the funds necessary to make the injured party whole.

EMPLOYEE VERSUS INDEPENDENT CONTRACTOR

An aspect of agency law that has troubled employers and employees alike on numerous occasions has to do with a worker's declared status as an independent contractor. Not surprisingly, many employers prefer to designate certain workers as independent contractors rather than as employees. Yet, increasingly, the courts are holding that some workers who are designated as independent contractors are, in fact, employees if the employer exercises a significant degree of control over their performance. It does not matter whether the parties had specified, in written contracts, that the workers were independent contractors.

For example, in one case a group of drivers for a delivery service agreed to work as independent contractors and to use their own cars to make deliveries. Each driver signed a contract explicitly agreeing to work as an independent contractor. Nonetheless, a court held that the workers qualified as employees because they were dependent for their business on the employer. The delivery service "procured the customers, set the delivery prices, made the delivery assignments, billed the customers, set the commission rate, and paid the drivers."[1]

Why Should the Courts Intervene?

If a worker agrees to be classified as an independent contractor, why should a court interfere with this decision? The answer is, at least in part, that issues of fairness may be involved. The common law of agency, as developed and applied by the courts, implicitly recognizes these issues.

After all, if a worker is an independent contractor, the worker must pay all Social Security taxes, instead of sharing them with his or her employer. Additionally, the worker will not be entitled to employer-provided benefits—such as group health insurance, pension plans, and stock options—that are available to employees. Furthermore, the worker will not receive the legal protections afforded to employees under such laws as those prohibiting employment discrimination. For example, in one case an independent contractor who worked for a nursing home was

1. *AFM Messenger Service, Inc. v. The Department of Employment Security,* 198 Ill.2d 380, 763 N.E.2d 272, 261 Ill.Dec. 302 (2001).

FOCUS ON ETHICS

fired from her job after she submitted a complaint about the facility to the state inspection department. She sued the employer, contending that she had been fired in retaliation for submitting the complaint. The court, however, held for the nursing home. Because the worker was an independent contractor, she was free to negotiate the terms of her employment, which diminished the need for court-based remedies.[2]

The Disparity in Bargaining Power

For some types of work, especially work that requires great expertise, the worker may have sufficient bargaining power to negotiate favorable contract terms with the employer. Often, however, workers lack such power. If an employer states that a worker is being hired as an independent contractor, what can the worker do? Generally, in this situation the worker has only two options—accept the arrangement or forfeit the job. Certainly, that was the choice faced by many workers at Microsoft Corporation when that company, to save costs, required employees to agree to become independent contractors if they wished to continue to work for Microsoft (see the discussion of this case in Chapter 14).

FAMILY AND MEDICAL LEAVE

The Family and Medical Leave Act (FMLA) of 1993 provides a clear example of a law that was necessitated by changing practices and values in our society. By 1993, nearly two-thirds of women with children worked outside the home, by choice or necessity. Additionally, about a fourth of all adults provided care for elderly relatives or anticipated the need to provide this care within the next five years. With both spouses working in many families, there was often no caretaker available to attend to medical emergencies or other family needs in the home. By allowing employees to take a leave from work for family or medical reasons, the FMLA recognized the changing circumstances faced by the U.S. work force.

The FMLA has now been in effect for over a decade, and both employers and employees say that they have benefited from the act. Indeed, many have concluded that the FMLA does not go far enough. As it is, the act applies only to employers with fifty or more employees. Consequently, more than half of the work force in the private sector does not fall under the act's protection. Should the government drop this threshold number to twenty-five or even fifteen? Many believe that it should. Indeed, Congress is currently considering legislation that would broaden the scope of the FMLA to cover employers with twenty-five or more employees and to provide leave for education-related purposes.

AGE DISCRIMINATION

Today, some older employees face discrimination in the form of age-based harassment. In other words, they are subjected to offensive comments and conduct from their supervisors or co-workers simply because of their age.

An employee who experiences a hostile work environment because of racial or gender discrimination may file a claim against his or her employer under Title VII of the Civil Rights Act of 1964. In contrast, an employee who alleges a hostile work environment based on age has no such recourse—at least, according to many courts—under the Age Discrimination in Employment Act (ADEA) of 1967. Some argue that age-based hostile-environment claims should be recognized under the ADEA because the types of protections offered by the ADEA are so similar to those offered by Title VII. To date, however, only one federal appellate court—the U.S. Court of Appeals for the Sixth Circuit—has squarely addressed the question and concluded that the ADEA extends to hostile-environment age-based discrimination.[3] The other federal appellate courts either have not addressed the question or have dismissed such claims with no real analysis of the issue.

DISCUSSION QUESTIONS

1. How much obedience and loyalty does an agent-employee owe an employer? What if the employer engages in an activity—or requests that the employee engage in an activity—that violates the employee's ethical standards but does not necessarily violate any public policy or law? In such a situation, does an employee's duty to abide by her or his own ethical standards override the employee's duty of loyalty to the employer?

2. *Harvey v. Care Initiatives, Inc.*, 634 N.W.2d 681 (Iowa 2001). Note that some courts might have held that a worker's discharge in these circumstances was contrary to public policy.

3. *Crawford v. Medina General Hospital*, 96 F.3d 830 (6th Cir. 1996).

FOCUS ON ETHICS

❷ If an agent injures a third party during the course of employment, under the doctrine of *respondeat superior,* the employer may be held liable for the agent's actions even though the employer did not authorize the action and was not even aware of it. Do you think that it is fair to hold employers liable in such situations? Do you think that it would be more equitable to hold that the employee alone should bear the responsibility for his or her tortious (legally wrongful) actions to third parties, even when the actions are committed within the scope of employment?

❸ Suppose that a company, as part of its job-benefits package for employees, provides free tuition for those employees who want to continue their education. The company, however, refuses to provide this educational benefit to workers over the age of fifty. Would this be a violation of the ADEA? May a company legally refuse to provide older workers with the same benefits as younger workers?

UNIT FIVE

The Regulatory Environment

CHAPTER 16

Environmental Law

CONTENTS

CHAPTER OBJECTIVES

After reading this chapter, you should be able to answer the following questions:

1. Under what common law theories may polluters be held liable?
2. What is an environmental impact statement, and who must file one?
3. What does the Environmental Protection Agency do?
4. Which major federal statutes regulate air and water pollution?
5. What is Superfund? Which categories of persons may be liable under Superfund?

Concerns over the degradation of the environment have increased over time in response to the environmental effects of population growth, urbanization, and industrialization. Environmental protection is not without a price, however. For many businesses, the costs of complying with environmental regulations are high, and for some they are too high. A constant tension exists between the desire to increase profits and productivity and the need to protect the environment.

In this chapter, we discuss laws and regulations designed to protect and preserve our environmental resources. To a great extent, **environmental law** consists of statutes passed by federal, state, or local governments and regulations issued by administrative agencies. Before examining statutory and regulatory environmental laws, however, we look at the remedies against environmental pollution available under the common law.

Environmental law • The body of statutory, regulatory, and common law relating to the protection of the environment.

COMMON LAW ACTIONS

Common law remedies against environmental pollution originated centuries ago in England. Those responsible for operations that created dirt, smoke, noxious odors, noise, or toxic substances were sometimes held liable under common law theories of nuisance or negligence. Today, injured individuals continue to rely on the common law to obtain damages and injunctions against business polluters.

Nuisance

Under the common law doctrine of **nuisance,** persons may be held liable if they use their property in a manner that unreasonably interferes with others' rights to use or enjoy their own property. In these situations, courts commonly balance the equities between the harm caused by the pollution and the costs of stopping it.

Nuisance • A common law doctrine under which persons may be held liable for using their property in a manner that unreasonably interferes with others' rights to use or enjoy their own property.

Courts have often denied injunctive relief on the ground that the hardships that would be imposed on the polluter and on the community are greater than the hardships suffered by the plaintiff. For example, a factory that causes neighboring landowners to suffer from smoke, dirt, and vibrations may be left in operation if it is the core of a local economy. The injured parties may be awarded only money damages. These damages may include compensation for the decline in the value of their property as a result of the factory's operation.

A property owner may be given relief from pollution if he or she can identify a distinct harm separate from that affecting the general public. This harm is referred to as a "private" nuisance. Under the common law, citizens were denied standing (access to the courts—see Chapter 2) unless they suffered a harm distinct from the harm suffered by the public at large. Some states still require this. Therefore, a group of citizens who wishes to stop a new development that would cause significant water pollution may be denied access to the courts on the ground that the harm to them does not differ from the harm to the general public.[1] A public authority (such as a state's attorney general), however, can sue to abate a "public" nuisance.

Negligence and Strict Liability

An injured party may sue a business polluter in tort under the negligence and strict liability theories discussed in Chapter 12. The basis for a negligence action is a business's alleged failure to use reasonable care toward a party whose injury was foreseeable and was caused by the lack of reasonable care. For example, employees might sue an employer whose failure to use proper pollution controls contaminated the air, causing the employees to suffer respiratory illnesses. A developing area of tort law involves **toxic torts**—actions against toxic polluters.

Toxic tort • Failure to properly use or clean up toxic chemicals that cause harm to a person or society.

Businesses that engage in ultrahazardous activities—such as the transportation of radioactive materials—are strictly liable for whatever injuries the activities cause. In a strict liability action, the injured party does not need to prove that the business failed to exercise reasonable care.

State and Local Regulation

Many states regulate the degree to which the environment may be polluted. Thus, for example, even when state zoning laws permit a business's proposed development, the proposal may have to be altered to lessen the development's impact on the environment. State laws may restrict a business's discharge of chemicals into the air or water or regulate its disposal of toxic wastes. States may also regulate the disposal or recycling of other wastes, including glass, metal, and plastic containers and paper. Additionally, states may restrict the emissions from motor vehicles.

City, county, and other local governments control some aspects of the environment. For instance, local zoning laws control some land use. These laws may be designed to inhibit or direct the growth of cities and suburbs or to protect the natural environment. In the interest of protecting the environment, these laws may prohibit certain land uses. One of the issues subject to ongoing debate is whether landowners should be compensated when restric-

1. See, for example, *Save the Bay Committee, Inc. v. Mayor of City of Savannah,* 227 Ga. 436, 181 S.E.2d 351 (1971).

tions are placed on the use of their property. For a discussion of this issue, see this chapter's *Contemporary Legal Debates* feature on pages 586 and 587.

Other aspects of the environment may also be subject to local regulation. Methods of waste and garbage removal and disposal, for example, can have a substantial impact on a community. The appearance of buildings and other structures, including advertising signs and billboards, may affect traffic safety, property values, or local aesthetics. Noise generated by a business or its customers may be annoying, disruptive, or damaging to its neighbors. The location and condition of parks, streets, and other public uses of land subject to local control affect the environment and can also affect business.

FEDERAL REGULATION

Congress has passed a number of statutes to control the impact of human activities on the environment. Exhibit 16–1 on the following page lists and summarizes the major federal environmental statutes, most of which are discussed in this chapter. Some of these statutes were passed in an attempt to improve air and water quality. Others specifically regulate toxic chemicals, including pesticides, herbicides, and hazardous wastes.

Environmental Regulatory Agencies

The most well known of the federal agencies regulating environmental law is the Environmental Protection Agency (EPA), which was created in 1970 to coordinate federal environmental responsibilities. Other federal agencies with authority for regulating specific environmental matters include the Department of the Interior, the Department of Defense, the Department of Labor, the Food and Drug Administration, and the Nuclear Regulatory Commission. These regulatory agencies—and all other agencies of the federal government—must take environmental factors into consideration when making significant decisions.

Most federal environmental laws provide that citizens can sue to enforce environmental regulations if government agencies fail to do so—or can sue to protest agency enforcement actions if they believe that these actions go too far. Typically, a threshold hurdle in such suits is meeting the requirements for standing to sue (see Chapter 2).

State and local regulatory agencies also play a significant role in carrying out federal environmental legislation. Typically, the federal government relies on state and local governments to implement federal environmental statutes and regulations, such as those regulating air quality.

Environmental Impact Statements

The National Environmental Policy Act (NEPA) of 1969[2] requires that an **environmental impact statement (EIS)** be prepared for every major federal action that significantly affects the quality of the environment. An EIS must analyze (1) the impact on the environment that the action will have, (2) any adverse effects on the environment and alternative actions that might be taken, and (3) irreversible effects the action might generate.

Environmental impact statement (EIS) • A document required by the National Environmental Policy Act for any major federal action that will significantly affect the quality of the environment. The document must analyze the action's impact on the environment and explore alternative actions that might be taken.

2. 42 U.S.C. Sections 4321–4370d.

EXHIBIT 16–1 • MAJOR FEDERAL ENVIRONMENTAL STATUTES

POPULAR NAME	PURPOSE	STATUTE REFERENCE
Rivers and Harbors Appropriations Act (1899)	To prohibit ships and manufacturers from discharging and depositing refuse in navigable waterways.	33 U.S.C. Sections 401–418.
Federal Insecticide, Fungicide, and Rodenticide Act (1947)	To control the use of pesticides and herbicides.	7 U.S.C. Sections 136–136y.
Federal Water Pollution Control Act (1948)	To eliminate the discharge of pollutants from major sources into navigable waters.	33 U.S.C. Sections 1251–1387.
Atomic Energy Act (1954)	To limit environmental harm from the private nuclear industry.	42 U.S.C. Sections 2011 to 2297g-4.
Clean Air Act (1963)	To control air pollution from mobile and stationary sources.	42 U.S.C. Sections 7401–7671q.
National Environmental Policy Act (1969)	To limit environmental harm from federal government activities.	42 U.S.C. Sections 4321–4370d.
Marine Protection, Research, and Sanctuaries Act, or Ocean Dumping Act (1972)	To regulate the transporting and dumping of material into ocean waters.	16 U.S.C. Sections 1401–1445.
Noise Control Act (1972)	To regulate noise pollution from transportation and nontransportation sources.	42 U.S.C. Sections 4901–4918.
Endangered Species Act (1973)	To protect species that are threatened with extinction.	16 U.S.C. Sections 1531–1544.
Safe Drinking Water Act (1974)	To regulate pollutants in public drinking water systems.	42 U.S.C. Sections 300f to 300j-25.
Resource Conservation and Recovery Act (1976)	To establish standards for hazardous waste disposal.	42 U.S.C. Sections 6901–6986.
Toxic Substances Control Act (1976)	To regulate toxic chemicals and chemical compounds.	15 U.S.C. Sections 2601–2692.
Comprehensive Environmental Response, Compensation, and Liability Act (1980)	To regulate the clean-up of hazardous waste–disposal sites.	42 U.S.C. Sections 9601–9675.
Low Level Radioactive Waste Policy Act (1980)	To assign to the states responsibility for nuclear power plants' low-level radioactive waste.	42 U.S.C. Sections 2021b–2021j.
Nuclear Waste Policy Act (1982)	To provide for the designation of a permanent radioactive waste–disposal site.	42 U.S.C. Sections 10101–10270.
Oil Pollution Act (1990)	To establish liability for the clean-up of navigable waters after oil-spill disasters.	33 U.S.C. Sections 2701–2761.
Small Business Liability Relief and Brownfields Revitalization Act (2002)	To allow developers who comply with state voluntary clean-up programs to avoid federal liability for the properties that they decontaminate and develop.	42 U.S.C. Section 9628.

An action qualifies as "major" if it involves a substantial commitment of resources (monetary or otherwise). An action is "federal" if a federal agency has the power to control it. Construction by a private developer of a ski resort on federal land, for example, may require an EIS. Building or operating a nuclear plant, which requires a federal permit, or constructing a dam as part of a federal project requires an EIS. If an agency decides that an EIS is unnecessary, it must issue a statement supporting this conclusion. EISs have become instruments for private citizens, consumer interest groups, businesses, and others to challenge federal agency actions on the basis that the actions improperly threaten the environment.

The question in the following case was whether the U.S. Department of Transportation (DOT) acted "arbitrarily and capriciously" in failing to prepare an EIS before issuing final regulations that permitted Mexico-based "motor carriers" to operate within the United States. The regulations were important to U.S. compliance with its treaty obligations under the North American Free Trade Agreement (NAFTA). Labor unions representing U.S. truck drivers, and other organizations, challenged the DOT's action.

PUBLIC CITIZEN v. DEPARTMENT OF TRANSPORTATION

CASE 16.1

United States Court of Appeals, Ninth Circuit, 2003.
316 F.3d 1002.

In 1992, the United States, Canada, and Mexico signed the NAFTA to establish a free trade zone encompassing those nations. All parties expected an expansion of international trade, which would be facilitated at least in part by increased truck traffic. Foreign trucks are permitted to enter the United States only if they are authorized to do so. The DOT is generally required to grant permission to any carrier that is willing and able to comply with certain statutes and regulations. In 2002, the Federal Motor Carrier Safety Administration (FMCSA), an agency within the DOT, proposed "Application and Safety Rules" to permit complying trucks based in Mexico to operate in the United States beyond specified border zones. After soliciting public comments on the proposed rules, the DOT determined that an EIS was not required. The DOT concluded that the rules would not significantly affect the quality of the environment, and issued a statement—an "Environmental Assessment" (EA)—to support this conclusion and an order to implement the rules. Various unions and environmental groups, including Public Citizen, petitioned the U.S. Court of Appeals for the Ninth Circuit for a review of this order, asserting that the agency failed to examine adequately its environmental consequences.

WARDLAW, J.

The Council on Environmental Quality ("CEQ"), a body established by NEPA, has issued regulations implementing NEPA. We rely on these regulations to guide our review of an agency's compliance with NEPA * * *. The relevant CEQ regulations implementing NEPA define "major Federal action[s]" as "actions with effects that may be major and which are potentially subject to Federal control and responsibility," including "[a]doption of official policy, such as rules, regulations, and interpretations." * * * [Emphasis added.]

* * * *

As for the requirement that the federal action be "major," the CEQ regulations tell us that "[m]ajor * * * does not have a meaning independent of significantly," meaning that *a federal action is "major" whenever it has "significant" environmental effects.* [Emphasis added.]

* * * *

The CEQ regulations also define the crucial term "significantly," to clarify the situations in which an agency must prepare an EIS:

> "Significantly" as used in NEPA requires considerations of * * * context * * * [.] This means that the significance of an action must be analyzed in several contexts such as society as a whole (human, national), the affected region, the affected interests, and the locality. Significance varies with the setting of the proposed action. For instance, in the case of a site-specific action, significance would usually depend upon the effects in the locale rather than in the world as a whole. Both short- and long-term effects are relevant. * * *

* * * *

The CEQ regulations explain that the proposed federal action must be analyzed with regard to several contexts—national, regional, and local—as well as by looking at the short- and long-term effects of the proposed action. Measured against this standard, DOT's EA is woefully inadequate. The EA calculates likely emissions increases if the Application and Safety Rules are implemented. It dismisses those increases as insignificant, however, because they are "very small relative to national levels of emissions." It does not conduct any analysis regarding whether these increases may be localized in certain areas near the Mexican border, including such likely destinations as Southern California or Texas. [Emphasis added.]

[The defense] considers it "unreasonable" that DOT should have to "make a determination of the expected routes of 34,000 hypothetical [Mexican trucks]." Regardless of the law's "reasonableness" (a question properly addressed by Congress—not us), this is precisely what NEPA and the CEQ regulations require. The law requires DOT to consider the most likely localities to be affected by increased Mexican truck traffic and to perform more localized analyses for these areas. Indeed, comments submitted to FMCSA * * * analyzed publicly available government data to predict, not surprisingly, that major cities near the Mexican border would likely suffer the greatest environmental impact as a result of the regulations. The fact that commenters performed such an analysis does not indicate that their analysis was correct, but rather that it was possible to conduct such an analysis. DOT's failure to do so indicates that it did not take a sufficiently "hard look" at the environmental effects of its actions or at the public comments it received.

Furthermore, DOT failed to address adequately the long-term effects of its actions. In conducting its EA, DOT limited its analysis to the environmental impact of Mexican trucks in the year 2002. This is anomalous in itself, considering that the regulations were scheduled to become effective only as of May 3, 2002. More significantly, the EA offered no projections of the increase (or decrease) in Mexican truck traffic after 2002, though the regulations were certainly expected to continue in effect beyond the end of [2002]; indeed they would be in effect now absent this action.

[The defense] contends that increases in Mexican truck traffic in years subsequent to 2002 would be attributable to the "success of NAFTA," rather than to the regulations themselves. This argument is beside the point, as it is impossible to separate increases in truck traffic due to the opening of the border from increases in truck traffic due to successful international trade; it is precisely this desired increase in international trade that prompted DOT to issue regulations facilitating cross-border truck traffic in the first place.

Once again, DOT received this very criticism in public comments during its rulemaking process. The commenters used available government data to estimate future increases in Mexican truck traffic after 2002. This alone should have prompted DOT to conduct a long-term analysis, as required by the CEQ regulations, or at the very least, to convincingly * * * explain its absence.

The U.S. Court of Appeals for the Ninth Circuit found that the "Application and Safety Rules" were major federal actions that could significantly affect the environment, and held that the DOT acted arbitrarily and capriciously in concluding that it did not need to prepare an EIS for the regulations. The court remanded the matter to the DOT for the agency to prepare an EIS.

QUESTIONS

1. Why did the DOT argue that an EIS was not required in this case?
2. Why did the U.S. Court of Appeals for the Ninth Circuit remand this matter to the DOT for the agency to prepare an EIS?
3. When state environmental regulations are stricter than those of the federal government, should a federal agency consider whether its proposed action might violate the state rules? Why or why not?

Agency Decision Making and Wildlife Preservation

Other federal laws also require that environmental values be considered in agency decision making. Among the most important of these laws are those that have been enacted to protect fish and wildlife. Under the Fish and Wildlife Coordination Act of 1958,[3] federal agencies proposing to approve the impounding or diversion of a stream's waters must consult with the Fish and Wildlife Service with a view to preventing the loss of fish and wildlife resources.

Also important is the Endangered Species Act of 1973.[4] This act requires all federal agencies to take steps to ensure that their actions "do not jeopardize the continued existence of endangered species" or the habitat of an endangered species. An action may jeopardize the continued existence of a species if it sets in motion a chain of events that reduces the chances that the species will survive.

AIR POLLUTION

Federal involvement with air pollution goes back to the 1950s, when Congress authorized funds for air-pollution research. In 1963, the federal government passed the Clean Air Act,[5] which focused on multistate air pollution and provided assistance to the states. Various amendments, particularly in

3. 16 U.S.C. Sections 661–666c.
4. 16 U.S.C. Sections 1531–1544.
5. 42 U.S.C. Sections 7401–7671q.

CONTEMPORARY LEGAL DEBATES

Environmental Takings

Environmental regulations and other legislation to control land use are prevalent throughout the United States. Generally, these laws reflect the public's interest in preserving natural resources and habitats for wildlife. At times, their goal is to enable the public to have access to and enjoy limited natural resources, such as coastal areas. Although few would disagree with the rationale underlying these laws, the owners of the private property directly affected by the laws often feel that they should be compensated for the limitation imposed on their right to do as they wish with their land.

The Fifth Amendment to the U.S. Constitution gives the government the power to "take" private property for public use. The Fifth Amendment attaches an important condition to this power, however: when private land is taken for public use, the landowner must be given "just compensation." An ongoing legal debate has to do with whether environmental regulations that limit private property owners' uses of their property constitute a "taking" of private property in the public interest. If so, the property owners should receive the just compensation guaranteed under the Fifth Amendment.

In some cases, the courts have held for the property owners on this issue. In others, however, the courts have sided with government regulators. We consider here two significant cases concerning this issue, both of which ultimately came before the United States Supreme Court.

THE *DEL MONTE DUNES* CASE

One case involved an owner of ocean-front property in Monterey, California. The owner had applied to the city of Monterey on several occasions for a permit to build a residential development. Each time, the city denied the use of more of the property until none of it remained available for any use. In effect, the entire property had to be left in its natural state. The city claimed that it was seeking to protect various forms of wildlife that inhabit the coastal sand dunes, particularly the endangered Smith's blue butterfly. Eventually, the property owner sold the property to the city and then sued the city, claiming that the restrictions on use amounted to an unconstitutional taking without just compensation. The jury agreed and awarded the owner nearly $1.45 million in damages. The award was affirmed on appeal.[a]

The city then appealed to the United States Supreme Court, arguing that the question of whether a taking had occurred should have been decided by a judge, not a jury. The Supreme Court, however, held that whether a taking has occurred is a predominantly factual question and, thus, was a question for a jury to decide.[b]

The *Del Monte Dunes* case was regarded as a victory for property rights advocates. For state and

a. *Del Monte Dunes at Monterey, Ltd. v. City of Monterey,* 95 F.3d 1422 (9th Cir. 1996).

b. *City of Monterey v. Del Monte Dunes at Monterey, Ltd.,* 526 U.S. 687, 119 S.Ct. 1624, 143 L.Ed.2d 882 (1999).

1970, 1977, and 1990, strengthened the government's authority to regulate air quality. These laws provide the basis for issuing regulations to control pollution coming primarily from mobile sources (such as automobiles) and stationary sources (such as industrial and power plants).

Mobile Sources

Automobiles and other vehicles are referred to as mobile sources of pollution. The EPA has issued regulations specifying standards for mobile sources of pollution, as well as service stations. The agency periodically updates these standards in light of new developments and data.

Motor Vehicles. Regulations governing air pollution from automobiles and other mobile sources specify pollution standards and time schedules for meeting these standards. For example, the 1990 amendments to the Clean Air Act

CONTEMPORARY LEGAL DEBATES

Environmental Takings

local governments, however, the decision meant that they would find it more costly to preserve natural resources in their communities.

THE *TAHOE* CASE

In a 2002 case, *Tahoe-Sierra Preservation Council v. Tahoe Regional Planning Agency,*[c] the United States Supreme Court reviewed another case involving a takings claim. This time, however, the Court supported the local regulators. Essentially, the case revolved around an attempt to curb pollution and the growth of algae in Lake Tahoe, on the California-Nevada border. In 1981, the Tahoe Regional Planning Agency issued a temporary moratorium (suspension) on the construction of residential housing in areas around the lake that were the most susceptible to further environmental damage. The moratorium was extended over the next several years until 1987 when it was replaced by a "revised plan," which is still in effect.

Most of the affected property owners were older couples who had purchased their lots decades earlier and had planned to build their retirement homes along the lake. The moratorium, however, allowed no exceptions and forbade any land use whatsoever. The regulations were so stringent that some owners were even forbidden to enter their own land without the agency's permission. Ultimately, the owners sued the agency, claiming that a regulatory taking had occurred. Even if the taking was only temporary, the regulations had forced the owners to give up all reasonable use of their land, economically and personally, for a period of time, and they deserved to be compensated for this deprivation.

The United States Supreme Court sided with the regulators. The Court held that the agency's actions had not deprived the owners of their property for too long a time, and thus no taking had occurred. How long is too long? The Court said no categorical rule could be stated; the answer always depends on "the facts presented."

c. 535 U.S.302, 122 S.Ct. 1465, 152 L.Ed.2d 517 (2002).

WHERE DO YOU STAND?

Even though the Supreme Court sided with the regulators in the *Tahoe* case, the debate over environmental takings continues. On the one hand, states, cities, and other local governments want to preserve their natural resources and need some authority to regulate land use to achieve this goal. On the other hand, private property owners complain that they alone should not have to bear the costs of environmental preservation, given that all members of the public reap the benefits. Where do you stand on this issue? Should private landowners be compensated when their land is essentially "taken" for public use by environmental regulations? Should landowners be compensated even when a taking is temporary?

required automobile manufacturers to cut new automobiles' exhaust emissions of nitrogen oxide by 60 percent and emissions of other pollutants by 35 percent. By 1998, all new automobiles had to meet this standard. Regulations that became effective beginning with 2004 model cars called for nitrogen oxide tail pipe emissions to be cut by nearly 10 percent by 2007. For the first time, sport utility vehicles (SUVs) and light trucks were required to meet the same emission standards as automobiles.

Service Stations. Service stations are also subject to environmental regulations. The 1990 amendments require service stations to sell gasoline with a higher oxygen content in forty-one cities that experience carbon monoxide pollution in the winter. Service stations are required to sell even cleaner burning gasoline in the most polluted urban areas, including Los Angeles and eight other cities.

Updating Pollution-Control Standards. The Environmental Protection Agency (EPA) attempts to update pollution-control standards when new scientific information becomes available. For example, some studies conducted in the 1990s showed that very small particles (2.5 microns, or millionths of a meter) of soot affect our health as significantly as larger particles. Based on this evidence, the EPA issued new particulate standards for motor vehicle exhaust systems and other sources of pollution in 1996. The EPA also set a more rigorous acceptable standard for ozone, which is formed when sunlight combines with pollutants from cars and other sources. Ozone is the basic ingredient of smog.

ETHICAL ISSUE

Should the costs of EPA regulations be weighed against their prospective benefits? In setting standards governing air quality, traditionally the EPA has not been required to take costs into account. Rather, the emphasis has been on the benefits. For example, when the EPA issued its new rules on particulate matter and ozone, the head of the EPA claimed that the new standards would save 15,000 lives a year. Given that the EPA values a human life at $5 million, the agency calculated that the lives saved and medical expenses avoided by the strict standards would amount to $100 billion a year in benefits. Nothing was said about the costs of implementing these rules, however. Environmental groups tend to downplay these costs and to value potential lives saved very highly. In contrast, business groups, particularly those affected adversely by strict air standards, think that the EPA should factor in these costs. In 2000, the debate over this issue was resolved by the United States Supreme Court. In the case, a number of business groups had challenged the EPA's stricter air-quality standards, claiming that the EPA had exceeded its authority under the Clean Air Act by issuing the regulations. The groups also claimed that the EPA had to take economic costs into account when developing new regulations. The Court, however, held that the EPA had not exceeded its authority under the Clean Air Act and confirmed that the EPA did not have to take economic costs into account when creating new rules.[6]

Stationary Sources

The Clean Air Act also authorizes the EPA to establish air-quality standards for stationary sources (such as manufacturing plants) but recognizes that the primary responsibility for implementing these standards rests with state and local governments. The EPA sets primary and secondary levels of ambient standards—that is, the maximum levels of certain pollutants—and the states formulate plans to achieve those standards. The plans are to provide for the attainment of primary standards within three years and secondary standards within a reasonable time. For economic, political, and technological reasons, however, the deadlines are often subject to change.

Different Standards May Apply. Different standards apply to sources of pollution in clean areas and those in polluted areas. Different standards also apply to existing sources of pollution and major new sources. Major new sources include existing sources modified by a change in a method of operation that increases emissions. Performance standards for major sources require

6. *Whitman v. American Trucking Associations*, 531 U.S. 457, 121 S.Ct. 903, 149 L.Ed.2d 1 (2000).

use of the *maximum achievable control technology*, or *MACT*, to reduce emissions from the combustion of fossil fuels (coal and oil). As mentioned, the EPA issues guidelines as to what equipment meets this standard.

Curbing Acid Rain and Ground-Level Pollution. Under the 1990 amendments to the Clean Air Act, 110 of the oldest coal-burning power plants in the United States had to cut their emissions by 40 percent by the year 2001 to reduce acid rain. Utilities were granted "credits" to emit certain amounts of sulfur dioxide, and those that emit less than the allowed amounts can sell their credits to other polluters. Controls on other factories and businesses are intended to reduce ground-level ozone pollution in ninety-six cities to healthful levels by 2005 (except Los Angeles, which has until 2010). The amendments also required an end to the production of chlorofluorocarbons, carbon tetrachloride, and methyl chloroform, which are used in air-conditioning, refrigeration, and insulation and have been linked to depletion of the ozone layer.

The relationship between the Clean Air Act's 1990 amendments and a New York state law was at issue in the following case.

CLEAN AIR MARKETS GROUP v. PATAKI

CASE 16.2

United States District Court, Northern District of New York, 2002. 194 F.Supp.2d 147.

Acid rain consists of atmospheric sulfates and nitrates, which are formed from sulfur dioxide (SO_2) and nitrogen oxides (NOx). These substances are emitted as by-products of the combustion of fossil fuels, most notably during the generation of electricity. Emissions originating in fourteen midwestern, eastern, and southern states contribute significantly to acid rain in New York. These high-contributing states are referred to as "Upwind States." By 1999, it was clear to some scientists that SO_2 emissions at the rates permitted by the Clean Air Act would not permit the environmental restoration of parts of the state of New York. Additional reductions in SO_2 emissions would be required. George Pataki, the governor of New York, ordered New York utilities to cut SO_2 emissions to half of the amount permitted by the Clean Air Act by January 2, 2007. By doing this, the New York utilities would have additional SO_2 credits to sell. In May 2000, the New York state legislature enacted the Air Pollution Mitigation Law (APML), which stipulated that most sums received for the sale or trade of SO_2 allowances to a polluter in an Upwind State would be forfeited to the New York Public Service Commission (PSC), which regulates New York utilities. This effectively lowered the market value of credits originating with New York utilities. Clean Air Markets Group (CAMG) filed a suit in a federal district court against Pataki and others, claiming in part that the APML was preempted under the U.S. Constitution's supremacy clause.[a] *All parties filed motions for summary judgment.*

HURD, J.

[The APML] creates an obstacle to the accomplishment and execution of the full purposes and objectives of Congress. [The Clean Air Act] provides

a. As explained in Chapter 5, if federal law has not supplanted a whole field of state law, state law is preempted to the extent that it actually conflicts with federal law. A conflict between state and federal law occurs when compliance with both is physically impossible or when the state law is an obstacle to accomplishing the objective of federal law.

that SO_2 allowances "may be transferred among designated representatives of the owners or operators of [covered units (utilities)] and *any* other person who holds such allowances." [The APML's] restrictions on transferring allowances to units in the Upwind States is contrary to the federal provision that allowances be tradeable to *any* other person. Additionally, Congress considered geographically restricted allowance transfers and rejected it. The EPA, in setting regulations to implement [the Clean Air Act], also considered geographically restricted allowance trading and rejected it * * * . *The rejection of a regionally restricted allowance trading system illustrates the Congressional objective of having a nationwide trading market for SO_2 allowances. New York's regional restrictions on SO_2 allowance trading by New York units are an obstacle to the execution of that objective.* [Emphasis added.]

Pataki argues that the Air Pollution Mitigation Law * * * imposes a more stringent requirement for air pollution control or abatement, as expressly permitted. However, * * * the Air Pollution Mitigation Law sets no emissions requirements. It sets no requirements for air pollution control or abatement at all. Rather, the New York law is a state regulation of federally allocated SO_2 allowances. Further, it is a restriction on the nationwide trading system for which the Clean Air Act provides. It is insufficient to merely say that it imposes requirements for air pollution control, or that the goal is air pollution control or abatement. New York's Air Pollution Mitigation Law is preempted because it interferes with the Clean Air Act's method for achieving the goal of air pollution control: a cap and nationwide SO_2 allowance trading system.

In addition to interfering with the nationwide trading of SO_2 allowances, the Air Pollution Mitigation Law would result in decreased availability of SO_2 allowances in the Upwind States. Restricted availability of SO_2 allowances could indirectly reduce emissions in the Upwind States. No doubt * * * the New York legislators had this in mind when the Air Pollution Mitigation Law was enacted. However, the Clean Air Act permits restrictions on emissions by a state in that state, but it does not permit one state to control emissions in another state. Thus, the inevitable result of laws such as New York's Air Pollution Mitigation Law would be the indirect regulation of allowance trading and emissions in other states, which could not be done directly.

The court granted the CAMG's motion for summary judgment, holding that New York's Air Pollution Mitigation Law is preempted, under the supremacy clause, by the Clean Air Act because it interferes with that law's methods for achieving air-pollution control. The court enjoined the enforcement of the state law.

QUESTIONS

1. Who filed this suit, and why?
2. On what reasoning did the court base the holding that the Clean Air Act preempts New York's Air Pollution Mitigation Law (APML)?
3. If the APML also provided for a subsidy to those who claimed that the value of their pollution credits had been reduced, would the outcome of the case have been different?

Hazardous Air Pollutants

Hazardous air pollutants are those likely to cause an increase in mortality or in serious irreversible or incapacitating illness. In all, there are 189 of these pollutants, including asbestos, benzene, beryllium, cadmium, mercury, and vinyl chloride. These pollutants may cause cancer as well as neurological and reproductive damage. They are emitted from stationary sources by a variety of business activities, including smelting, dry cleaning, house painting, and commercial baking. Instead of establishing specific emissions standards for each hazardous air pollutant, the 1990 amendments to the Clean Air Act require industries to use pollution-control equipment that represents the maximum achievable control technology, or MACT, to limit emissions. The EPA issues guidelines as to what equipment meets this standard.

In 1996, the EPA issued a rule to regulate hazardous air pollutants emitted by landfills. The rule requires landfills constructed after May 30, 1991, that emit more than a specified amount of pollutants to install landfill gas collection and control systems. The rule also requires the states to impose the same requirements on landfills constructed before May 30, 1991, if they accepted waste after November 8, 1987.[7]

Violations of the Clean Air Act

For violations of emission limits under the Clean Air Act, the EPA can assess civil penalties of up to $25,000 per day. Additional fines of up to $5,000 per day can be assessed for other violations, such as failing to maintain the required records. To penalize those who find it more cost-effective to violate the act than to comply with it, the EPA is authorized to impose a penalty equal to the violator's economic benefits from noncompliance. Persons who provide information about violators may be paid up to $10,000. Private citizens can also sue violators.

Those who knowingly violate the act may be subject to criminal penalties, including fines of up to $1 million and imprisonment for up to two years (for false statements or failures to report violations). Corporate officers are among those who may be subject to these penalties.

Water Pollution

Water pollution stems mostly from industrial, municipal, and agricultural sources. Pollutants entering streams, lakes, and oceans include organic wastes, heated water, sediments from soil run-off, nutrients (including detergents, fertilizers, and human and animal wastes), and toxic chemicals and other hazardous substances. We look here at laws and regulations governing water pollution.

Navigable Waters

Federal regulations governing water pollution can be traced back to the Rivers and Harbors Appropriations Act of 1899.[8] These regulations prohibited ships and manufacturers from discharging or depositing refuse in navigable waters.

---

7. 40 C.F.R. Sections 60.750–759.
8. 33 U.S.C. Sections 401–418.

Once limited to waters actually used for navigation, the term *navigable waters* is today interpreted to include intrastate lakes and streams used by interstate travelers and industries, as well as coastal and freshwater wetlands (wetlands will be defined shortly).

The Clean Water Act and Its Amendments. In 1948, Congress passed the Federal Water Pollution Control Act (FWPCA),[9] but its regulatory system and enforcement powers proved to be inadequate. In 1972, amendments to the FWPCA—known as the Clean Water Act—established the following goals: (1) make waters safe for swimming, (2) protect fish and wildlife, and (3) eliminate the discharge of pollutants into the water. The amendments required that municipal and industrial polluters apply for permits before discharging wastes into navigable waters. The Clean Water Act also set specific schedules, which were extended by amendment in 1977 and by the Water Quality Act of 1987.[10] Under these schedules, the EPA establishes limitations for discharges of various types of pollutants based on the technology available for controlling them.

Standards for Equipment. Regulations, for the most part, specify that the *best available control technology,* or *BACT,* be installed. The EPA issues guidelines as to what equipment meets this standard; essentially, the guidelines require the most effective pollution-control equipment available. New sources must install BACT equipment before beginning operations. Existing sources are subject to timetables for the installation of BACT equipment. These sources must immediately install equipment that utilizes the best *practical control technology,* or *BPCT.* The EPA also issues guidelines as to what equipment meets this standard.

Wetlands • Areas of land designated by government agencies (such as the Army Corps of Engineers or the Environmental Protection Agency) as protected areas that support wildlife and that therefore cannot be filled in or dredged by private contractors or parties.

Wetlands. The Clean Water Act prohibits the filling or dredging of **wetlands** unless a permit is obtained from the Army Corps of Engineers. The EPA defines *wetlands* as "those areas that are inundated or saturated by surface or ground water at a frequency and duration sufficient to support, and that under normal circumstances do support, a prevalence of vegetation typically adapted for life in saturated soil conditions." In recent years, the broad interpretation of what constitutes a wetland subject to the regulatory authority of the federal government has generated substantial controversy.

Perhaps one of the most controversial regulations was the "migratory-bird rule" issued by the Army Corps of Engineers. Under this rule, any bodies of water that could affect interstate commerce, including seasonal ponds or waters "used or suitable for use by migratory birds" that fly over state borders, were "navigable waters" subject to federal regulation under the Clean Water Act as wetlands. The rule was challenged in a case brought by a group of communities in the Chicago suburbs that wanted to build a landfill in a tract of land northwest of Chicago that had once been used as a strip mine. Over time, areas that were once pits in the mine became ponds used by a variety of migratory birds. The Army Corps of Engineers, claiming that the shallow ponds formed a habitat for migratory birds, refused to grant a permit for the landfill.

9. 33 U.S.C. Sections 1251–1387.
10. This act amended 33 U.S.C. Section 1251.

Ultimately, the United States Supreme Court held that the Army Corps of Engineers had exceeded its authority under the Clean Water Act. The Court stated that it was not prepared to hold that isolated and seasonable ponds, puddles, and "prairie potholes" become "navigable waters of the United States" simply because they serve as a habitat for migratory birds.[11]

Violations of the Clean Water Act. Under the Clean Water Act, violators are subject to a variety of civil and criminal penalties. Depending on the violation, civil penalties range from a maximum of $10,000 per day, and not more than $25,000 per violation, to as much as $25,000 per day. Criminal penalties range from a fine of $2,500 per day and imprisonment for up to one year to a fine of $1 million and fifteen years' imprisonment. Injunctive relief and damages can also be imposed. The polluting party can be required to clean up the pollution or pay for the cost of doing so. Criminal penalties apply only if a violation was intentional.

Drinking Water

Another statute governing water pollution is the Safe Drinking Water Act.[12] Passed in 1974, this act requires the EPA to set maximum levels for pollutants in public water systems. Operators of public water supply systems must come as close as possible to meeting the EPA's standards by using the best available technology that is economically and technologically feasible. The EPA is particularly concerned with contamination from underground sources. Pesticides and wastes leaked from landfills or disposed of in underground injection wells are among the more than two hundred pollutants known to exist in groundwater used for drinking in at least thirty-four states. Many of these substances are associated with cancer and damage to the central nervous system, liver, and kidneys.

The act was amended in 1996 to give the EPA greater flexibility in setting regulatory standards governing drinking water. Prior to the 1996 amendments, the EPA had to set standards for twenty-five different drinking water contaminants every three years, which it had largely failed to do. Under the 1996 amendments, the EPA can move at whatever rate it deems necessary to control contaminants that are of greatest concern to the public health. The 1996 amendments also imposed new requirements on suppliers of drinking water. Each supplier must send to every household it supplies with water an annual statement describing the source of its water, the level of any contaminants contained in the water, and any possible health concerns associated with the contaminants.

Ocean Dumping

The Marine Protection, Research, and Sanctuaries Act of 1972[13] (known popularly as the Ocean Dumping Act) regulates the transportation and dumping of material into ocean waters. (The term *material* is synonymous with the

11. *Solid Waste Agency of Northern Cook County v. U.S. Army Corps of Engineers,* 531 U.S. 159, 121 S.Ct. 675, 148 L.Ed.2d 576 (2001).
12. 42 U.S.C. Sections 300f to 300j-25.
13. 16 U.S.C. Sections 1401–1445.

term *pollutant* as used in the Federal Water Pollution Control Act.) The Ocean Dumping Act prohibits entirely the ocean dumping of radiological, chemical, and biological warfare agents and high-level radioactive waste.

The act establishes a permit program for transporting and dumping other materials. There are specific exemptions—materials subject to the permit provisions of other pollution legislation, wastes from structures regulated by other laws (for example, offshore oil exploration and drilling platforms), sewage, and other wastes. The Ocean Dumping Act also authorizes the designation of marine sanctuaries for "preserving or restoring such areas for their conservation, recreational, ecological, or esthetic values."

Each violation of any provision or permit may result in a civil penalty of not more than $50,000 or revocation or suspension of the permit. A knowing violation is a criminal offense that may result in a $50,000 fine, imprisonment for not more than a year, or both. An injunction may also be imposed.

Oil Pollution

The Oil Pollution Act of 1990[14] provides that any onshore or offshore oil facility, oil shipper, vessel owner, or vessel operator that discharges oil into navigable waters or onto an adjoining shore may be liable for clean-up costs, as well as damages. The act created a $1 billion oil clean-up and economic compensation fund and decreed that by the year 2011, oil tankers using U.S. ports must be double hulled to limit the severity of accidental spills.

Under the act, damage to natural resources, private property, and the local economy, including the increased cost of providing public services, is compensable. The act provides for civil penalties of $1,000 per barrel spilled or $25,000 for each day of the violation. The party held responsible for the clean-up costs can bring a civil suit for contribution from other potentially liable parties.

Noise Pollution

Regulations concerning noise pollution include the Noise Control Act of 1972.[15] This act requires the EPA to establish noise emission standards (maximum noise levels below which no harmful effects occur from interference with speech or other activity)—for example, for railroad noise emissions. The standards must be achievable by the best available technology, and they must be economically within reason.

The act prohibits, among other things, distributing products manufactured in violation of the noise emission standards and tampering with noise-control devices. Either of these activities can result in an injunction or whatever other remedy "is necessary to protect the public health and welfare." Illegal product distribution can also result in a fine and imprisonment. Violations of the Noise Control Act can result in penalties of not more than $50,000 per day and imprisonment for not more than two years.

---

14. 33 U.S.C. Sections 2701–2761.
15. 42 U.S.C. Sections 4901–4918.

Toxic Chemicals

Originally, most environmental clean-up efforts were directed toward reducing smog and making water safe for fishing and swimming. Over time, however, control of toxic chemicals became an important part of environmental law.

Pesticides and Herbicides

The federal statute regulating pesticides and herbicides is the Federal Insecticide, Fungicide, and Rodenticide Act (FIFRA) of 1947.[16] Under the FIFRA, pesticides and herbicides must be (1) registered before they can be sold, (2) certified and used only for approved applications, and (3) used in limited quantities when applied to food crops. If a substance is identified as harmful, the EPA can cancel its registration after a hearing. If the harm is imminent, the EPA can suspend registration pending the hearing. The EPA, as well as state officers or employees, may also inspect factories where these chemicals are manufactured.

Under 1996 amendments to the Federal Food, Drug and Cosmetic Act, for a pesticide to remain on the market, there must be a "reasonable certainty of no harm" to people from exposure to the pesticide.[17] This means that there must be no more than a one-in-a-million risk to people of developing cancer from exposure in any way, including eating food that contains residues from the pesticide. Nearly all fruits and vegetables and processed foods contain some pesticide residues. Under the 1996 amendments, the EPA must distribute to grocery stores brochures on high-risk pesticides that are in food, and the stores must display these brochures for consumers.

Violations of the FIFRA. It is a violation of the FIFRA to sell a pesticide or herbicide that is unregistered, a pesticide or herbicide with a registration that has been canceled or suspended, or a pesticide or herbicide with a false or misleading label. For example, it is an offense to sell a substance that is adulterated (that has a chemical strength different from the concentration declared on the label). It is also an offense to destroy or deface any labeling required under the act. The act's labeling requirements include directions for the use of the pesticide or herbicide, warnings to protect human health and the environment, a statement of treatment in the case of poisoning, and a list of the ingredients.

A private party can petition the EPA to suspend or cancel the registration of a pesticide or herbicide. If the EPA fails to act, the private party can petition a federal court to review the EPA's lack of action.

Penalties for Violations. Penalties for registrants and producers for violating the FIFRA include imprisonment for up to one year and a fine of no more than $50,000. Penalties for commercial dealers include imprisonment for up to one year and a fine of no more than $25,000. Farmers and other private

16. 7 U.S.C. Sections 136–136y.
17. 21 U.S.C. Section 346a.

users of pesticides or herbicides who violate the act are subject to a $1,000 fine and imprisonment for up to thirty days.

Toxic Substances

The Toxic Substances Control Act of 1976[18] was the first comprehensive law covering toxic substances. The act was passed to regulate chemicals and chemical compounds that are known to be toxic—such as asbestos and polychlorinated biphenyls, popularly known as PCBs—and to institute investigation of any possible harmful effects from new chemical compounds. The regulations authorize the EPA to require that manufacturers, processors, and other organizations planning to use chemicals first determine their effects on human health and the environment. The EPA can regulate substances that may pose an imminent hazard or an unreasonable risk of injury to health or the environment. The EPA may require special labeling, limit the use of a substance, set production quotas, or prohibit the use of a substance altogether.

HAZARDOUS WASTES

Some industrial, agricultural, and household wastes pose more serious threats than others. If not properly disposed of, these toxic chemicals may present a substantial danger to human health and the environment. If released into the environment, they may contaminate public drinking water resources.

Resource Conservation and Recovery Act

In 1976, Congress passed the Resource Conservation and Recovery Act (RCRA)[19] in reaction to an ever-increasing concern about the effects of hazardous waste materials on the environment. The RCRA required the EPA to establish regulations to monitor and control hazardous waste disposal and to determine which forms of solid waste should be considered hazardous and thus subject to regulation. The act authorized the EPA to promulgate various technical requirements for certain facilities that store and treat hazardous waste. The act also requires all producers of hazardous waste materials to properly label and package any hazardous waste to be transported.

Amendments to the RCRA. The RCRA was amended in 1984 and 1986 to decrease the use of land containment in the disposal of hazardous waste. The amendments also require compliance with the act by some generators of hazardous waste—such as those generating less than 1,000 kilograms (2,200 pounds) a month—that had previously been excluded from regulation under the RCRA.

Penalties under the RCRA. Under the RCRA, a company may be assessed a civil penalty based on the seriousness of the violation, the probability of harm, and the extent to which the violation deviates from RCRA requirements. The assessment may be up to $25,000 for each violation. Criminal penalties include fines up to $50,000 for each day of violation, imprisonment

18. 15 U.S.C. Sections 2601–2692.
19. 42 U.S.C. Sections 6901–6986.

for up to two years (in most instances), or both. In addition, if a person knowingly violates the RCRA requirements and endangers the life of another, he or she may be imprisoned for up to fifteen years and fined up to $250,000. Criminal fines and the time of imprisonment can also be doubled for certain repeat offenders.

The following case involved a conviction under the criminal provisions of the RCRA. The defendant questioned whether the federal government retains the authority to enforce those provisions, considering that the EPA has authorized the states to manage hazardous waste programs under the RCRA.

CASE 16.3

United States Court of Appeals, Ninth Circuit, 2001. 269 F.3d 1003.

UNITED STATES v. ELIAS

Allen Elias was the owner of Evergreen Resources, Inc., a fertilizer company in Idaho, when he decided to transfer sulfuric acid from two railroad cars into a stationary 25,000-gallon tank. Elias had used the tank in his previous business to store by-products of a cyanide leaching process. At the bottom of the thirty-six-foot-long, eleven-foot-high tank were one to two tons of cyanide-laced sludge, hardened and more than a foot deep. Elias ordered four employees, including Scott Dominguez, to enter the tank and wash the sludge out. Elias did not provide any safety equipment. Forty-five minutes after entering the tank, wearing only his regular work clothes, Dominguez collapsed. The treating physician concluded that the cause was cyanide poisoning. A federal grand jury charged Elias with, among other things, storing or disposing of hazardous waste without a permit while knowingly placing others in imminent danger of death or serious bodily injury in violation of the RCRA. Elias was convicted, sentenced to 204 months (17 years) in prison, and ordered to pay $6.3 million in restitution to Dominguez.[a] *Elias appealed to the U.S. Court of Appeals for the Ninth Circuit, arguing in part that Idaho's EPA–authorized hazardous waste program had displaced the federal program, leaving no federal crimes and no federal jurisdiction.*

NELSON, J.

[42 U.S.C. Section 6926 of the RCRA], which governs "Authorized State hazardous waste programs," provides in relevant part:

> Any State which seeks to administer and enforce a hazardous waste program pursuant to this subchapter may * * * submit to the [EPA] an application * * * . [If the EPA approves the program,] [s]uch State is authorized to carry out such program in lieu of the Federal program * * * .

* * * *

* * * The linchpin [central element] of [Elias's] argument * * * is that the term "program" in Section 6926 incorporates the exclusive responsibility to enforce criminal provisions penalizing the disposal of hazardous wastes. * * *

* * * [T]he EPA [does] not interpret RCRA to cede [give] exclusive enforcement authority to states and * * * if the EPA's interpretation of

---

a. When this case was decided, the prison term was the harshest ever imposed for an environmental crime in the United States.

Section 6926's "in lieu of" provision is reasonable, we must defer to the agency's interpretation even if the agency could also have reached another reasonable interpretation, or even if we would have reached a different result had we construed the statute initially. * * * *[T]he EPA's interpretation [is] reasonable because we [can] discern no clear congressional intent that Section 6926 be read to disable the EPA from issuing orders* * * *wherever an authorized state hazardous waste program operates "in lieu of the Federal program" and because the EPA's conclusion that its power to issue orders* * * *survives in those states where an authorized state program is operating is plainly consistent with a straightforward reading of the [RCRA].* [Emphasis added.]

* * * *

Legislative history also supports the EPA's contention that RCRA's criminal enforcement provisions are meant to apply within states having authorized programs * * * : Prior to the 1984 RCRA Amendments—when, as today, RCRA provided for state programs which, when federally approved, would be carried out "in lieu" of the federal program, and which authorized the state to issue and enforce permits—the [criminal provision] was worded so as to apply in so many words to violations both of federal and state permitting programs. * * *

The 1984 amendments increased the applicable criminal penalties and simply substituted "under this subchapter" for the references to the specific subsections under which permits, federal and state, may be granted. * * * [This language] did not, therefore, in any way narrow the scope of federal criminal jurisdiction. Nor did the legislative record hint at any intention by Congress to narrow the scope of federal criminal jurisdiction. To the contrary, Congress manifested its desire to retain a strong federal presence. Had Congress intended to impose a hitherto unknown limitation upon the scope of its laws criminalizing permit violations, its intentions would surely have been manifested * * * .

For these reasons, we conclude that, under RCRA, the federal government retains * * * its criminal * * * enforcement powers.

The U.S. Court of Appeals for the Ninth Circuit affirmed the judgment of the lower court. The appellate court held that the EPA's authorization of Idaho's hazardous waste program did not deprive the federal government of its enforcement authority under the RCRA. The court also upheld Elias's prison sentence. It remanded the case to strike the restitution order, however, because Elias's offense "is one of the few for which Congress has not sanctioned the imposition of restitution."

QUESTIONS

1. Why did Elias argue on appeal that Idaho's hazardous waste program displaced the federal program, leaving no federal crimes and no federal jurisdiction?
2. Why did the U.S. Court of Appeals for the Ninth Circuit hold that the EPA's authorization of Idaho's hazardous waste program did not deprive the federal government of its RCRA enforcement authority?
3. In light of the court's reasoning in this case, what authority do states with federally approved hazardous waste programs have under the RCRA?

Superfund

In 1980, Congress passed the Comprehensive Environmental Response, Compensation, and Liability Act (CERCLA),[20] commonly known as Superfund. The basic purpose of Superfund is to attempt to regulate the clean-up of disposal sites in which hazardous waste is leaking into the environment. A special federal fund was created for that purpose.

Potentially responsible party (PRP) • A potentially liable party under the Comprehensive Environmental Response, Compensation and Liability Act (CERCLA). Any person who generated the hazardous waste, transported the hazardous waste, owned or operated a waste site at the time of disposal, or currently owns or operates a site may be responsible for some or all of the clean-up costs involved in removing the hazardous chemicals.

Potentially Responsible Parties. Superfund provides that when a release or a threatened release of hazardous chemicals from a site occurs, the EPA can clean up the site and recover the cost of the clean-up from the following persons: (1) the person who generated the wastes disposed of at the site, (2) the person who transported the wastes to the site, (3) the person who owned or operated the site at the time of the disposal, or (4) the current owner or operator. A person falling within one of these categories is referred to as a **potentially responsible party (PRP).** In the following case, the issue was the meaning of *disposal* as that term is used in the provision of CERCLA that lists PRPs.

20. 42 U.S.C. Sections 9601–9675.

CARSON HARBOR VILLAGE, LTD. v. UNOCAL CORP.

United States Court of Appeals, Ninth Circuit, 2001.
270 F.3d 863.

Beginning in 1945, Unocal Corporation leased property in Carson, California, and used it for petroleum production, operating oil wells, pipelines, aboveground storage tanks, and production facilities. Carson Harbor Village Mobile Home Park, a general partnership controlled by Richard Braley and Walker Smith, owned a mobile home park on seventy acres of the property from 1977 until 1983, when Carson Harbor Village, Ltd., took over the park. An undeveloped wetlands area covered nearly seventeen acres of the site. In 1993, Carson Harbor discovered hazardous substances in the wetlands area. An investigation revealed that the materials were by-products of petroleum production and had been on the property for several decades before its development as a mobile home park. The materials and surrounding soils contained elevated levels of total petroleum hydrocarbons (TPH) and lead. Carson Harbor paid $285,000 for their removal and then filed a suit in a federal district court against the partnership and others under CERCLA, seeking in part to recover the removal cost plus damages. The partnership filed a motion for summary judgment, which the court granted. Carson Harbor appealed to the U.S. Court of Appeals for the Ninth Circuit.

McKEOWN, J.

CERCLA defines "disposal" * * * with reference to the definition of "disposal" in RCRA, which in turn defines "disposal" as follows:

> The term "disposal" means the discharge, deposit, injection, dumping, spilling, leaking, or placing of any solid waste or hazardous waste into or on any land or water so that such solid waste or hazardous waste or any constituent thereof may enter the environment or be emitted into the air or discharged into any waters, including ground waters.

Under this definition, for the Partnership Defendants to be PRPs, there must have been a "discharge, deposit, injection, dumping, spilling, leaking, or placing" of contaminants on the property during their ownership.

* * * *

Examining the facts of this case, we hold that the gradual passive migration of contamination through the soil that allegedly took place during the Partnership Defendants' ownership was not a "discharge, deposit, injection, dumping, spilling, leaking, or placing" and, therefore, was not a "disposal" within the meaning of [CERCLA]. The contamination on the property included tar-like and slag materials. The tar-like material was highly viscous and uniform, without any breaks or stratification. The slag material had a vesicular structure and was more porous and rigid than the tar-like material. There was some evidence that the tar-like material moved through the soil and that lead and/or TPH may have moved from that material into the soil. If we try to characterize this passive soil migration in plain English, a number of words come to mind, including gradual "spreading," "migration," "seeping," "oozing," and possibly "leaching." But certainly none of those words fits within the plain and common meaning of "discharge, * * * injection, dumping, * * * or placing." *Although these words generally connote active conduct, even if we were to infuse passive meanings, these words simply do not describe the passive migration that occurred here.* Nor can the gradual spread here be characterized as a "deposit," because there was neither a deposit by someone, nor does the term deposit encompass the gradual spread of contaminants. The term "spilling" is likewise inapposite. Nothing spilled out of or over anything. Unlike the spilling of a barrel or the spilling over of a holding pond, movement of the tar-like and slag materials was not a spill. [Emphasis added.]

Of the terms defining "disposal," the only one that might remotely describe the passive soil migration here is "leaking." But under the plain and common meaning of the word, we conclude that there was no "leaking." The circumstances here are not like that of the leaking barrel or underground storage tank envisioned by Congress, or a vessel or some other container that would connote "leaking." Therefore, there was no "disposal," and the Partnership Defendants are not PRPs. On this basis, we affirm the district court's grant of summary judgment to the Partnership Defendants on the CERCLA claim.

The U.S. Court of Appeals for the Ninth Circuit affirmed the judgment of the lower court. The appellate court held that the partnership was not liable as a PRP. The passive migration of the contaminants through the soil during the partnership's ownership of the site was not a disposal as that term is used in CERCLA.

QUESTIONS

1. What was the reasoning underlying the judgment of the U.S. Court of Appeals for the Ninth Circuit that the partnership was not liable as a PRP?
2. Why not interpret the term *disposal* to include all subsoil passive migration of hazardous substances, and thus hold any owner of contaminated property liable for the cost of its clean-up?
3. Is it possible to objectively determine how clean-up costs for hazardous waste sites should be apportioned among the responsible parties?

Joint and Several Liability. Normally, liability under Superfund is joint and several—that is, a PRP who generated only a fraction of the hazardous waste disposed of at the site may nevertheless be liable for *all* of the clean-up costs. Under CERCLA, a party who has incurred clean-up costs is authorized to bring a "contribution action" against any other person who is liable or potentially liable for a percentage of the costs.

Global Environmental Issues

Pollution does not respect geographic borders. Indeed, one of the reasons that the federal government became involved in environmental protection was that state regulation alone could not solve the problem of air or water pollution. Pollutants generated in one state moved in the air and water to other states. Neither does pollution respect national borders. Environmental issues, perhaps more than any others, bring home to everyone the fact that the world today is truly a global community. What one country does or does not do with respect to environmental preservation may be felt by citizens in countries thousands of miles distant.

Cross-Border Pollution

One issue that has come to the fore in recent years is **cross-border pollution.** On numerous occasions, beaches in San Diego, California, have been closed because of pollution originating in Mexico. Canada has complained for years about air pollution in that nation caused by sulfuric acid generated by coal-burning power plants in the United States. Examples similar to these can be found everywhere in the world. Countries have made various attempts to reduce cross-border pollution, through treaties or other agreements, but it remains a challenging issue for virtually all nations.

Cross-border pollution • Pollution across national boundaries; air and water degradation in one nation resulting from pollution-causing activities in a neighboring country.

Global Warming

Another challenging—and controversial—issue is potential global warming. The fear is that emissions, largely from combustion of fossil fuels, will remain in the atmosphere and create a "greenhouse effect" by preventing heat from radiating outward. Concerns over this issue have led to many attempts to force all world polluters to "clean up their acts." For example, leaders of 160 nations have already agreed to reduce greenhouse emissions in their respective countries. They did this when they ratified the Kyoto Protocol, which was drawn up at a world summit meeting held in Kyoto, Japan, in 1997. The Kyoto Protocol, which is often referred to as the global warming treaty, established different rates of reduction in greenhouse emissions for different countries or regions. Most nations, however, including the United States, will not meet the treaty's objectives. Indeed, the Bush administration told the world in early 2001 that the treaty was a dead letter because it did not address the problem of curbing greenhouse gases from most of the developing world.

Is Economic Development the Answer?

Economists have shown that economic development is the quickest way to reduce pollution worldwide; that is, after a nation reaches a certain per capita income level, the more economic growth the nation experiences, the lower its pollution output. This occurs because richer nations have the resources to pay for pollution reduction. For example, the United States pollutes much less per unit of output than do developing nations—because we are willing to pay for pollution abatement.

KEY TERMS

cross-border pollution 601
environmental impact statement (EIS) 581
environmental law 579
nuisance 579
potentially responsible party (PRP) 599
toxic tort 580
wetland 592

FOR REVIEW

1. Under what common law theories may polluters be held liable?
2. What is an environmental impact statement, and who must file one?
3. What does the Environmental Protection Agency do?
4. Which major federal statutes regulate air and water pollution?
5. What is Superfund? Which categories of persons may be liable under Superfund?

QUESTIONS AND CASE PROBLEMS

16–1. Some scientific knowledge indicates that there is no safe level of exposure to a cancer-causing agent. In theory, even one molecule of such a substance has the potential for causing cancer. Section 112 of the Clean Air Act requires that all cancer-causing substances be regulated to ensure a margin of safety. Some environmental groups have argued that all emissions of such substances must be eliminated to reach such a margin of safety. Total elimination would likely shut down many major U.S. industries. Should the Environmental Protection Agency totally eliminate all emissions of cancer-causing chemicals? Discuss.

16–2. Fruitade, Inc., is a processor of a soft drink called Freshen Up. Fruitade uses returnable bottles, which it cleans with a special acid to allow for further beverage processing. The acid is diluted with water and then allowed to pass into a navigable stream. Fruitade crushes its broken bottles and throws the crushed glass into the stream. Discuss fully any environmental laws that Fruitade has violated.

16–3. Moonbay is a home-building corporation that primarily develops retirement communities. Farmtex owns a number of feedlots in Sunny Valley. Moonbay purchased 20,000 acres of farmland in the same area and began building and selling homes on this acreage. In the meantime, Farmtex continued to expand its feedlot business, and eventually only 500 feet separated the two operations. Because of the odor and flies from the feedlots, Moonbay found it difficult to sell the homes in its development. Moonbay wants to enjoin Farmtex from operating its feedlot in the vicinity of the retirement home development. Under what common law theory could Moonbay file this action? Has Farmtex violated any federal environmental laws? Discuss.

CASE PROBLEM WITH SAMPLE ANSWER

16–4. Toxic Chemicals. The Environmental Protection Agency canceled the registration of the pesticide diazinon for use on golf courses and sod farms because of concerns over the effects of diazinon on birds. The Federal Insecticide, Fungicide, and Rodenticide Act authorizes cancellation of the registration of products that "generally cause unreasonable adverse effects on the environment." The statute further defines "unreasonable adverse effects on the environment" to mean "any unreasonable risk to man or the environment, taking into account the . . . costs and benefits." Thus, in determining whether a pesticide should continue to be used, it is necessary to balance the risks and benefits of the use of the pesticide. Does this mean that, to prohibit the pesticide's use, a judge must find that the pesticide kills birds more often than not, or is it sufficient to find that the use of the pesticide results in recurrent bird kills? [*Ciba-Geigy Corp. v. Environmental Protection Agency,* 874 F.2d 277 (5th Cir. 1989)]

➧ *To view a sample answer for this case problem, go to this book's Web site at* **http://ele.westbuslaw.com** *and click on "Interactive Study Center."*

16–5. Water Pollution. Taylor Bay Protective Association is a nonprofit corporation established for the purpose of restoring and improving the water quality of Taylor Bay. Local water districts began operating a flood-control project in the area. As part of the project, a pumping station was developed. Testimony at trial revealed that the pumps were operated contrary to the instructions provided in the operation and maintenance manual. The pumps acted as vacuums, sucking up silt and depositing the silt in Taylor Bay. Thus, the project resulted in sedimentation and turbidity (a condition of having dense, stirred-up particles) problems in the downstream watercourse of Taylor Bay. The association sued the local water districts, alleging that the pumping operations created a nuisance. Do the pumping operations qualify as a common law nuisance? Who should be responsible for the clean-up costs? Discuss both questions fully. [*Taylor Bay Protective Association v. Environmental Protection Agency,* 884 F.2d 1073 (8th Cir. 1989)]

16–6. Environmental Impact Statement. Greers Ferry Lake is in Arkansas, and its shoreline is under the management of the U.S. Army Corps of Engineers, which is part of the U.S. Department of Defense (DOD). The Corps's 2000 Shoreline Management Plan (SMP) rezoned numerous areas along the lake, authorized the Corps to issue permits for the construction of new boat docks in the rezoned areas, increased by 300 percent the area around habitable structures that could be cleared of vegetation, and instituted a Wildlife Enhancement Permit to allow limited modifications of the shoreline. In relation to the SMP's adoption, the Corps issued a Finding of No Significant Impact, which declared that no environmental impact statement (EIS) was necessary. The Corps issued thirty-two boat dock construction permits under the SMP before Save Greers Ferry Lake, Inc., filed a suit in a federal district court against the DOD, asking the court to, among other things, stop the Corps from acting under the SMP and order it to prepare an EIS. What are the requirements for an EIS? Is an EIS needed in this case? Explain. [*Save Greers Ferry Lake, Inc. v. Department of Defense,* 255 F.3d 498 (8th Cir. 2001)]

16–7. CERCLA. Beginning in 1926, Marietta Dyestuffs Co. operated an industrial facility in Marietta, Ohio, to make dyes and other chemicals. In 1944, Dyestuffs became part of American Home Products Corp. (AHP), which sold the Marietta facility to American Cyanamid Co. in 1946. In 1950, AHP sold the rest of the Dyestuffs's assets and all of its stock to Goodrich Co., which immediately liquidated the acquired corporation. Goodrich continued to operate the dissolved corporation's business, however. Cyanamid continued to make chemicals at the Marietta facility, and in 1993, it created Cytec Industries, Inc., which expressly assumed all environmental liabilities associated with Cyanamid's ownership and operation of the facility. Cytec spent nearly $25 million on clean-up and filed a suit in a federal district court against Goodrich to recover, under CERCLA, a portion of the costs attributable to the clean-up of hazardous wastes that may have been discarded at the site between 1926 and 1946. Cytec filed a motion for summary judgment in its favor. Should the court grant Cytec's motion? Explain. [*Cytec Industries, Inc. v. B. F. Goodrich Co.,* 196 F.Supp.2d 644 (S.D. Ohio 2002)]

16–8. IN YOUR COURT

The Endangered Species Act of 1973 makes it unlawful for any person to "take" endangered or threatened species. The act defines *take* to mean "harass, harm, pursue," "wound," or "kill." The Secretary of the Interior issued a regulation that further defined *harm* to include "significant habitat modification or degradation where it actually kills or injures wildlife." A group of businesses and individuals involved in the timber industry brought an action against the Secretary of the Interior and others. The group complained that the application of the "harm" regulation to the red-cockaded woodpecker and the northern spotted owl had injured the group economically by preventing logging operations (habitat modification) in the Pacific Northwest forests containing these species. The group challenged the regulation's validity, contending that Congress had not intended the word *take* to include habitat modification. Assume that you are a judge in the trial court hearing this case and answer the following questions:

(a) Traditionally, the term *take* has been used to refer to the capture or killing of wildlife, usually for private gain. Is the secretary's regulation prohibiting habitat modification consistent with this definition?
(b) How will you respond to the group's complaint that the application of the "harm" regulation injured the group economically? Should the economic effect of the regulation on the group be taken into consideration when deciding whether the regulation is valid?
(c) Generally, how will you rule in this case, and why?

16–9. A QUESTION OF ETHICS AND SOCIAL RESPONSIBILITY

Attique Ahmad owned the Spin-N-Market, a convenience store and gas station. The gas pumps were fed by underground tanks, one of which had a leak at its top that allowed water to enter the tank. Ahmad emptied the tank by pumping its contents into a storm drain and sewer system. Through the storm drain, gasoline flowed into a creek, forcing the city to clean the water. Through the sewer system, gasoline flowed into a sewage treatment plant, forcing the city to evacuate the plant and two nearby schools. Ahmad was charged with discharging a pollutant without a permit, which is a criminal violation of the Clean Water Act. The act provides that a person who "knowingly violates" the act commits a felony. Given these facts, discuss the following questions. [*United States v. Ahmad,* 101 F.3d 386 (5th Cir. 1996)]

(a) Ahmad claimed that he believed that he was discharging only water from the tank, not gasoline. How should this claim affect the court's decision?

(b) Suppose that Ahmad knew that he was discharging gasoline into the storm drain and sewer system, but told the court that he was not aware that he was doing so. Assuming that no evidence was presented to demonstrate that Ahmad had knowledge of the tank's contents, should the court take Ahmad's word for it and hold that he was not guilty of violating the act? Why or why not?

(c) If the court held that Ahmad had "knowingly violated" the act despite the lack of any evidence proving that he had done so, how might this decision affect innocent parties in the future who find themselves in similar situations?

16–10. FOR CRITICAL ANALYSIS

It has been estimated that for every dollar spent cleaning up hazardous waste sites, administrative agencies spend seven dollars in overhead. Can you think of any way to reduce the administrative costs associated with the clean-up of contaminated sites?

For updated links to resources available on the Web, as well as a variety of other materials, visit this text's Web site at

http://ele.westbuslaw.com

For information on the EPA's standards, guidelines, and regulations, go to the EPA's Web site at

http://www.epa.gov

To learn about the RCRA's "buy-recycled" requirements and other steps that the federal government has taken toward "greening the environment," go to

http://www.epa.gov/cpg

LEGAL RESEARCH EXERCISES ON THE WEB

Go to **http://ele.westbuslaw.com**, the Web site that accompanies this text. Select "Interactive Study Center," and then click on "Chapter 16." There you will find the following Internet research exercises that you can perform to learn more about topics covered in this chapter.

Activity 16–1: LEGAL PERSPECTIVE—Nuisance Law

Activity 16–2: MANAGEMENT PERSPECTIVE—Complying with Environmental Regulations

Activity 16–3: ETHICAL PERSPECTIVE—Environmental Justice

BEFORE THE TEST

Go to **http://ele.westbuslaw.com**, the Web site that accompanies this text. Select "Interactive Quizzes." You will find at least twenty interactive questions relating to this chapter.

WESTLAW® CAMPUS

If your textbook provided for a subscription to Westlaw® Campus, or if you have otherwise purchased access to the Westlaw Campus database, you can access any of the cases presented or cited in this chapter by using your Westlaw Campus account.

CHAPTER 17

Antitrust Law

CONTENTS

CHAPTER OBJECTIVES

After reading this chapter, you should be able to answer the following questions:

What do the terms *monopoly* and *market power* mean? What is the relationship between these terms?

What types of activities are prohibited by Section 1 and Section 2 of the Sherman Act?

What types of activities are prohibited by the Clayton Act?

What federal agencies enforce the federal antitrust laws?

What are four activities that are exempt from the antitrust laws?

Restraint on trade • Any contract or combination that tends to eliminate or reduce competition or otherwise hamper the course of trade and commerce as it would be carried on if left to the control of natural economic forces.

Antitrust law • The body of federal and state laws that regulate competition by protecting trade and commerce from unlawful restraints.

Today's antitrust laws are the direct descendants of common law actions intended to limit **restraints on trade** (agreements between firms that have the effect of reducing competition in the marketplace). Concern over anticompetitive practices arose following the Civil War with the growth of large corporate enterprises and their attempts to reduce or eliminate competition. They did this by legally tying themselves together in a *business trust,* a type of business entity in which investors transfer cash or property to trustees in exchange for trust certificates that represent their investment shares. The participants in the most famous trust—the Standard Oil trust in the late 1800s—transferred their stock to a trustee and received trust certificates in exchange. The trustee then made decisions fixing prices, controlling production, and determining the control of exclusive geographic markets for all of the oil companies that were in the Standard Oil trust. It became apparent that the trust wielded so much economic power that corporations outside the trust could not compete effectively.

Many states attempted to control such anticompetitive behavior by enacting statutes outlawing the use of trusts. That is why all of the laws that regulate economic competition today are referred to as **antitrust laws.** At the national level, the government recognized the problem in 1887 and passed the Interstate Commerce Act,[1] followed by the Sherman Antitrust Act in 1890.[2] In 1914, Congress passed the Clayton Act[3] and the Federal Trade Commission Act[4] to further curb anticompetitive or unfair business practices. Since their passage, the 1914 acts have been amended by Congress to broaden and strengthen their coverage, and they continue to be an important element in the legal environment in which businesses operate.

1. 49 U.S.C. Sections 501–526.
2. 15 U.S.C. Sections 1–7.
3. 15 U.S.C. Sections 12–26a.
4. 15 U.S.C. Sections 45–48a.

This chapter examines these major antitrust statutes, focusing particularly on the Sherman Act and the Clayton Act, as amended, and the types of activities prohibited by those acts. Remember in reading this chapter that the basis of antitrust legislation is the desire to foster competition. Antitrust legislation was initially created—and continues to be enforced—because of our belief that competition leads to lower prices, more product information, and a better distribution of wealth between consumers and producers.

THE SHERMAN ANTITRUST ACT

The author of the Sherman Antitrust Act of 1890, Senator John Sherman, was the brother of the famed Civil War general and a recognized financial authority. He had been concerned for years about the diminishing competition within U.S. industry. He told Congress that the Sherman Act "does not announce a new principle of law, but applies old and well-recognized principles of the common law."[5]

To read the text of the Sherman Antitrust Act of 1890, go to the "Statutes" page of our Web site at **http://ele.westbuslaw.com**

The common law regarding trade regulation was not always consistent. Certainly, it was not very familiar to the legislators of the Fifty-first Congress of the United States in 1890. The public concern over large business integrations and trusts was familiar, however, and in 1890 Congress passed "An Act to Protect Trade and Commerce against Unlawful Restraints and Monopolies"—more commonly referred to as the Sherman Antitrust Act, or simply the Sherman Act.

Major Provisions of the Sherman Act

Sections 1 and 2 contain the main provisions of the Sherman Act:

> 1: Every contract, combination in the form of trust or otherwise, or conspiracy, in restraint of trade or commerce among the several States, or with foreign nations, is hereby declared to be illegal [and is a felony punishable by fine and/or imprisonment].
>
> 2: Every person who shall monopolize, or attempt to monopolize, or combine or conspire with any other person or persons, to monopolize any part of the trade or commerce among the several States, or with foreign nations, shall be deemed guilty of a felony [and is similarly punishable].

Differences between Section 1 and Section 2

These two sections of the Sherman Act are quite different. Section 1 requires two or more persons, as a person cannot contract, combine, or conspire alone. Thus, the essence of the illegal activity is *the act of joining together.* Section 2 applies both to an individual person and to several people, because it refers to "[e]very person." Thus, unilateral conduct can result in a violation of Section 2.

The cases brought to the courts under Section 1 of the Sherman Act differ from those brought under Section 2. Section 1 cases are often concerned with finding an agreement (written or oral) that leads to a restraint of trade. Section 2 cases deal with the structure of a **monopoly** that exists in

Monopoly • A term generally used to describe a market in which there is a single seller or a limited number of sellers.

5. 21 Congressional Record 2456 (1890).

the marketplace. The term *monopoly* is generally used to describe a market in which there is a single seller. Whereas Section 1 focuses on agreements that are restrictive—that is, agreements that have a wrongful purpose—Section 2 looks at the so-called misuse of **monopoly power** in the marketplace.

Monopoly power • The ability of a monopoly to dictate what takes place in a given market.

Market power • The power of a firm to control the market price of its product. A monopoly has the greatest degree of market power.

Monopoly power exists when a firm has an extreme amount of **market power**—the power to affect the market price of its product. Both Section 1 and Section 2 seek to curtail market industrial practices that result in undesired monopoly pricing and output behavior. For a case to be brought under Section 2, however, the "threshold" or "necessary" amount of monopoly power must already exist. We will return to a discussion of these two sections of the Sherman Act after we look at the act's jurisdictional requirements.

Jurisdictional Requirements

The Sherman Act applies only to restraints that have a significant impact on interstate commerce. As will be discussed later in this chapter, the Sherman Act also extends to U.S. nationals abroad who are engaged in activities that have an effect on U.S. foreign commerce. State regulation of anticompetitive practices addresses purely local restraints on competition.

Courts have generally held that any activity that substantially affects interstate commerce falls within the scope of the Sherman Act. As discussed in Chapter 5, courts have construed the meaning of *interstate commerce* more and more broadly over the years, bringing even local activities within the regulatory power of the national government.

Section 1 of the Sherman Act

The underlying assumption of Section 1 of the Sherman Act is that society's welfare is harmed if rival firms are permitted to join in an agreement that consolidates their market power or otherwise restrains competition. To prevent such harm, Section 1 prohibits two broad categories of restraints on trade: *horizontal restraints* and *vertical restraints,* both of which will be discussed shortly. First, though, we look at the rules that the courts may apply when assessing the anticompetitive impact of alleged restraints on trade.

***Per se* violation** • A type of anticompetitive agreement that is considered to be so injurious to the public that there is no need to determine whether it actually injures market competition; rather, it is in itself *(per se)* a violation of the Sherman Act.

Rule of reason • A test by which a court balances the positive effects (such as economic efficiency) of an agreement against its potentially anticompetitive effects. In antitrust litigation, many practices are analyzed under the rule of reason.

Per Se Violations versus the Rule of Reason

Some restraints are so blatantly and substantially anticompetitive that they are deemed ***per se* violations**—illegal *per se* (on their face, or inherently)—under Section 1. Other agreements, however, even though they result in enhanced market power, do not *unreasonably* restrain trade. Under what is called the **rule of reason,** anticompetitive agreements that allegedly violate Section 1 of the Sherman Act are analyzed with the view that they may, in fact, constitute reasonable restraints on trade.

The need for a rule-of-reason analysis of some agreements in restraint of trade is obvious—if the rule of reason had not been developed, virtually any business agreement could conceivably be held to violate the Sherman Act. Justice Louis Brandeis effectively phrased this sentiment in *Chicago Board of Trade v. United States,*[6] a case decided in 1918:

> Every agreement concerning trade, every regulation of trade, restrains. To bind, to restrain, is of their very essence. The true test of legality is whether the restraint imposed is such as merely regulates and perhaps thereby promotes competition or whether it is such as may suppress or even destroy competition.

When analyzing an alleged Section 1 violation under the rule of reason, a court will consider several factors including the purpose of the agreement, the parties' power to implement the agreement to achieve that purpose, and the effect or potential effect of the agreement on competition. The court might also consider whether the parties could have relied on less restrictive means to achieve their purpose.

Horizontal Restraints

The term **horizontal restraint** is encountered frequently in antitrust law. A horizontal restraint is any agreement that in some way restrains competition between rival firms competing in the same market.

Horizontal restraint • Any agreement that in some way restrains competition between rival firms competing in the same market.

Price-fixing agreement • An agreement between competitors in which the competitors agree to fix the prices of products or services at a certain level; prohibited by the Sherman Act.

Price Fixing. Any agreement among competitors to fix prices, or **price-fixing agreement,** constitutes a *per se* violation of Section 1 of the Sherman Act. Perhaps the definitive case regarding price-fixing agreements remains the 1940 case of *United States v. Socony-Vacuum Oil Co.*[7] In that case, a group of independent oil producers in Texas and Louisiana were caught between falling demand due to the Great Depression of the 1930s and increasing supply from newly discovered oil fields in the region. In response to these conditions, a group of the major refining companies agreed to buy "distress" gasoline (excess supplies) from the independents so as to dispose of it in an "orderly manner." Although there was no explicit agreement as to price, it was clear that the purpose of the agreement was to limit the supply of gasoline on the market and thereby raise prices.

There may have been good reasons for the agreement. Nonetheless, the United States Supreme Court recognized the dangerous effects that such an agreement could have on open and free competition. The Court held that the reasonableness of a price-fixing agreement is never a defense; any agreement that restricts output or artificially fixes price is a *per se* violation of Section 1. The rationale of the *per se* rule was best stated in what is now the most famous portion of the Court's opinion. In footnote 59, Justice William O. Douglas compared a freely functioning price system to a body's central nervous system, condemning price-fixing agreements as threats to "the central nervous system of the economy."

Competitors' pooling of market data can make a market more efficient and benefit consumers. Fixing the price that the "pooler" pays for that data, however, may make the market less competitive and innovative. Whether this is a violation of antitrust law was the question in the following case.

6. 246 U.S. 231, 38 S.Ct. 242, 62 L.Ed. 683 (1918).
7. 310 U.S. 150, 60 S.Ct. 811, 84 L.E.2d 1129 (1940).

CASE 17.1

United States Court of Appeals, Ninth Circuit, 2003. 322 F.3d 1133.

FREEMAN v. SAN DIEGO ASSOCIATION OF REALTORS

Real estate professionals (agents) share information about properties on the market with the help of a computerized database known as a multiple listing service (MLS). At one time, twelve MLSs served San Diego County, California. Different real estate trade associations, including the San Diego Association of Realtors (SDAR), operated the MLSs to cover different regions of the county. Individual associations' costs varied widely, depending on the support services and the number of subscribers, but each association set its prices independently. In 1992, the associations formed Sandicor, a new corporation, to maintain a single MLS covering the entire county. Each association agreed to provide support services for a fixed price and to charge uniform subscription fees. For the smaller associations whose costs exceeded the agreed price, Sandicor returned a portion of the fees to cover the difference. Arleen Freeman, and other agents who subscribed to Sandicor's MLS, filed a suit in a federal district court against SDAR and others, claiming that by fixing support prices, the defendants violated Section 1 of the Sherman Act. The court issued a summary judgment in the defendants' favor. Both sides appealed to the U.S. Court of Appeals for the Ninth Circuit.

KOZINSKI, J.

Competition is the mainspring of a capitalist economy. Sometimes, however, cooperation can make markets more efficient; setting industry standards and pooling market data are two examples of arrangements that often benefit consumers. Antitrust laws acknowledge these benefits, but still treat the arrangements with skepticism, for seemingly benign agreements may conceal highly anticompetitive schemes. * * *

* * * *

* * * *No antitrust violation is more abominated than the agreement to fix prices. With few exceptions, price-fixing agreements are unlawful* per se *under the Sherman Act* and * * * no showing of so-called competitive abuses or evils which those agreements were designed to eliminate or alleviate may be interposed as a defense. The dispositive [decisive] question generally is not whether any price fixing was justified, but simply whether it occurred. [Emphasis added.]

* * * Prior to 1992, the associations made independent decisions about how to price their support services, even though many of them shared common databases. When they decided to form a countywide database, they debated whether to continue that system of independent pricing or to set a fixed, uniform fee that they would receive for providing support services. They opted for the latter arrangement and selected a fee that was more than double the cost of the most efficient association. They admit that they fixed the fee in order to ensure that financially weaker associations would make more money than under a competitive regime, and thus concede by implication that they intentionally fixed the fee at a supracompetitive level.

* * * *

[The defendants] claim that price fixing was justified to convince the smaller associations [with the higher costs] to join the countywide MLS. This theory at least attempts to explain why the restraint itself was necessary to the joint venture. Nonetheless, it fails to state a valid defense.

* * * *

* * * [T]he associations here seek to justify not only fixing prices, but intentionally fixing prices at a supracompetitive level. * * * Sandicor and the associations * * * fixed prices precisely in order to keep them above competitive levels. Their ultimate purpose may have been to entice the smaller associations to join the countywide MLS, but the fee had this effect only because it was supracompetitive, not because it was fixed. Defendants seek to justify not only the forbidden practice (price fixing) but its forbidden effect (supracompetitive prices), and this they may not do. Firms cannot fix prices as a mere *quid pro quo* [something in return for something else] for providing consumers with better products. Antitrust law presumes that competitive markets offer sufficient incentives and resources for innovation, and that cartel pricing [pricing by an anticompetitive business combination or group] leads not to a dedication of newfound wealth to the public good but to complacency and stagnation.

The presumption that higher prices are bad for consumers is, in any case, amply borne out by the record. The associations' scheme bore no reasonable relation to its asserted goal. Fallbrook and Valley Center [two of the smallest associations] served about 400 subscribers, less than 3% of the San Diego County total. By fixing support fees, Fallbrook and Valley Center together may have made an additional $6000 per month (on top of their cash subsidy of $3000 [from Sandicor]). Here's the catch: The support fee was fixed at $25 not just for those 400 subscribers, but for all 14,000 subscribers in San Diego County. And, other than the trivial $3000 per month cash subsidy, only 3% of the countywide overcharge actually went to Fallbrook and Valley Center. The other 97% went into the coffers of the other associations. In the case of SDAR alone, this could have amounted to more than $1.2 million per year. Defendants are thus trying to justify overcharging consumers millions by the need to provide an implicit subsidy worth less than one-twentieth that amount. If the other associations believed it was essential to involve Fallbrook and Valley Center in the MLS, they could have allowed price competition for support services and increased the subsidies to these two associations. Instead, they adopted an anticompetitive scheme that was completely out of proportion to its asserted purpose.

Moreover, defendants assume that, without Fallbrook and Valley Center, there couldn't be a true countywide MLS. But Sandicor could have formed without them and then competed for their 400 subscribers. An MLS's listings come from its subscribers, so its coverage is simply a function of who subscribes. * * * [N]othing prevented subscribers in Fallbrook or Valley Center from choosing Sandicor's MLS over their local service. The competitive option at a minimum was not so plainly unworkable that price fixing was necessary as a matter of law.

Stripped to its essentials, defendants' argument is that some of the firms they wanted to include in the joint venture were so inefficient that they could survive only under cartel pricing. Defendants' concern for the weakest among them has a quaint * * * charm to it, but we find it hard to square with the competitive philosophy of our antitrust laws. Inefficiency is precisely what the market aims to weed out. The Sherman Act, to put it bluntly, contemplates some roadkill on the turnpike to Efficiencyville.

The U.S. Court of Appeals for the Ninth Circuit concluded that the defendants violated Section 1 of the Sherman Act by fixing support fees. The court reversed the lower court's judgment on this issue and remanded the case for the entry of a summary judgment in favor of the plaintiffs.

QUESTIONS

1. How did the defendants in this case violate Section 1 of the Sherman Act?
2. What reasoning underlies the conclusion of the U.S. Court of Appeals for the Ninth Circuit in this case?
3. Could the defendants have maintained a comprehensive MLS without fixing prices?

Group boycott • An agreement by two or more parties to refuse to deal with (boycott) a particular person or firm; prohibited by the Sherman Act.

Group Boycotts. A **group boycott** is an agreement by two or more sellers to refuse to deal with (boycott) a particular person or firm. Such group boycotts have been held to constitute *per se* violations of Section 1 of the Sherman Act. Section 1 has been violated if it can be demonstrated that the boycott or joint refusal to deal was undertaken with the intention of eliminating competition or preventing entry into a given market. Some boycotts, such as group boycotts against a supplier for political reasons, may be protected under the First Amendment right to freedom of expression.

Horizontal Market Division. It is a *per se* violation of Section 1 of the Sherman Act for competitors to divide up territories or customers. For example, manufacturers A, B, and C compete against one another in the states of Kansas, Nebraska, and Iowa. They agree that A will sell products only in Kansas, B only in Nebraska, and C only in Iowa. This concerted action reduces costs and allows each of the three (assuming there is no other competition) to raise the price of the goods sold in its own state. The same violation would take place if A, B, and C simply agreed that A would sell only to institutional purchasers (such as school districts, universities, state agencies and departments, and cities) in the three states, B only to wholesalers, and C only to retailers.

Trade Associations. Businesses in the same general industry or profession frequently organize trade associations to pursue common interests. Their joint activities may provide for exchanges of information, representation of the members' business interests before governmental bodies, advertising campaigns, and the setting of regulatory standards to govern their industry or profession. Generally, the rule of reason is applied to many of these horizontal actions. For example, if a court finds that a trade association practice or agreement that restrains trade is nonetheless sufficiently beneficial both to the association and to the public, it may deem the restraint reasonable.

Other trade association agreements may have such substantially anticompetitive effects that the court will consider them to be in violation of Section 1 of the Sherman Act. For example, in one case a group of chiropractors sued the American Medical Association (AMA), alleging that the AMA had violated Section 1 of the Sherman Act by conducting an illegal boycott in restraint of trade. The boycott stemmed from a 1966 resolution passed by the AMA that labeled chiropractic an unscientific cult. In effect, this label prevented physicians from associating with chiropractors because one of the principles of the AMA's code of ethical conduct provided that a "physician should practice a method of healing founded on a scientific basis, and should not voluntarily associate with anyone who violates this principle." The court held that the

AMA had violated Section 1 of the Sherman Act because the boycott was intended, at least in part, to destroy a competitor—chiropractors.[8]

Joint Ventures. Joint ventures undertaken by competitors are also subject to antitrust laws. A *joint venture* is an undertaking by two or more individuals or firms for a specific purpose. If a joint venture does not involve price fixing or market divisions, the agreement will be analyzed under the rule of reason. Whether the venture will then be upheld under Section 1 depends on an overall assessment of the purposes of the venture, a strict analysis of the potential benefits relative to the likely harms, and, in some cases, an assessment of whether there are less restrictive alternatives for achieving the same goals.[9]

Vertical Restraints

A **vertical restraint** of trade results from an agreement between firms at different levels in the manufacturing and distribution process. In contrast to horizontal relationships, which occur at the same level of operation, vertical relationships encompass the entire chain of production: the purchase of inputs, basic manufacturing, distribution to wholesalers, and eventual sale of a product at the retail level. For some products, these distinct phases are carried on by different firms. In other instances, a single firm carries out two or more of the separate functional phases. Such enterprises are considered to be **vertically integrated firms.**

Vertical restraint • Any restraint on trade created by agreements between firms at different levels in the manufacturing and distribution process.

Vertically integrated firm • A firm that carries out two or more functional phases (such as manufacture, distribution, and retailing) of a product.

Even though firms operating at different functional levels are not in direct competition with one another, they are in competition with other firms operating at their own respective levels of operation. Thus, agreements between firms standing in a vertical relationship may affect competition. Some vertical restraints are *per se* violations of Section 1; others are judged under the rule of reason.

Territorial or Customer Restrictions. In arranging for the distribution of its products, a manufacturer often wishes to insulate dealers from direct competition with other dealers selling its products. In this endeavor, the manufacturer may institute territorial restrictions or attempt to prohibit wholesalers or retailers from reselling the products to certain classes of buyers, such as competing retailers.

There may be legitimate, procompetitive reasons for imposing such territorial or customer restrictions. For example, a computer manufacturer may wish to prevent a dealer from reducing costs and undercutting rivals by offering computers without promotion or customer service, while relying on a nearby dealer to provide these services. In this situation, the cost-cutting dealer reaps the benefits (sales of the product) paid for by other dealers who undertake promotion and arrange for customer service. This is an example of the "free rider" problem.[10] By not providing customer service, the cost-cutting dealer may also harm the manufacturer's reputation.

---

8. *Wilk v. American Medical Association,* 895 F.2d 352 (7th Cir. 1990).

9. See, for example, *United States v. Morgan,* 118 F.Supp. 621 (S.D.N.Y. 1953). This case is often cited as a classic example of how to judge joint ventures under the rule of reason.

10. For a discussion of the free rider problem in the context of sports telecasting, see *Chicago Professional Sports Limited Partnership v. National Basketball Association,* 961 F.2d 667 (7th Cir. 1993).

Territorial and customer restrictions are judged under a rule of reason. In the following case, *Continental T.V., Inc. v. GTE Sylvania, Inc.,* the United States Supreme Court overturned its earlier stance, which had been set out in *United States v. Arnold, Schwinn & Co.*[11] In *Schwinn,* the Court had held territorial and customer restrictions to be *per se* violations of Section 1 of the Sherman Act. The *Continental* case has been heralded as one of the most important antitrust cases since the 1940s. It marked a definite shift from rigid characterization of these kinds of vertical restraints to a more flexible, economic analysis of the restraints under the rule of reason.

11. 388 U.S. 365, 87 S.Ct. 1856, 18 L.Ed.2d 1249 (1967).

CASE 17.2

Supreme Court of the United States, 1977.
433 U.S. 36,
97 S.Ct. 2549,
53 L.Ed.2d 568.
http://www.findlaw.com/casecode/supreme.html[a]

CONTINENTAL T.V., INC. v. GTE SYLVANIA, INC.

GTE Sylvania, Inc., a manufacturer of television sets, adopted a franchise plan that limited the number of franchises granted in any given geographic area and that required each franchise to sell only Sylvania products from the location or locations at which it was franchised. Sylvania retained sole discretion to increase the number of retailers in an area, depending on the success or failure of existing retailers in developing their markets. Continental T.V., Inc., was a retailer under Sylvania's franchise plan. Shortly after Sylvania proposed a new franchise that would compete with Continental, Sylvania terminated Continental's franchise, and a suit was brought in a federal district court for money owed. Continental claimed that Sylvania's vertically restrictive franchise system violated Section 1 of the Sherman Act. The district court held for Continental, and Sylvania appealed. The appellate court reversed the trial court's decision. Continental appealed to the United States Supreme Court.

POWELL, J.

Vertical restrictions reduce intrabrand competition by limiting the number of sellers of a particular product competing for the business of a given group of buyers. * * *

Vertical restrictions promote interbrand competition by allowing the manufacturer to achieve certain efficiencies in the distribution of his products. * * * Established manufacturers can use them to induce retailers to engage in promotional activities or to provide service and repair facilities necessary to the efficient marketing of their products. * * * The availability and quality of such services affect a manufacturer's goodwill and the competitiveness of his product. * * * [Emphasis added.]

* * * *

* * * When anticompetitive effects are shown to result from particular vertical restrictions they can be adequately policed under the rule of reason * * *.

The United States Supreme Court upheld the appellate court's reversal of the district court's decision. Sylvania's vertical system, which was not price restrictive, did not constitute a per se *violation of Section 1 of the Sherman Act.*

a. In the "Citation Search" section, type "433" in the first box, type "36" in the second box, and click on "Get It" to access the case.

QUESTIONS

1. Who were the parties to this suit, and what was their dispute?
2. What were the decisions of the various courts in this dispute?
3. What did the United States Supreme Court rule in this case with respect to future cases, and why?

Resale Price Maintenance Agreements. An agreement between a manufacturer and a distributor or retailer in which the manufacturer specifies what the retail prices of its products must be is known as a **resale price maintenance agreement.** This type of agreement may violate Section 1 of the Sherman Act.

Resale price maintenance agreement • An agreement between a manufacturer and a retailer in which the manufacturer specifies the minimum retail price of its products.

In a 1968 case, *Albrecht v. Herald Co.*,[12] the United States Supreme Court held that these vertical price-fixing agreements constituted *per se* violations of Section 1 of the Sherman Act. In the following case, which involved an agreement that set a maximum price for the resale of products supplied by a wholesaler to a dealer, the Supreme Court reevaluated its approach in *Albrecht.* At issue was whether such price-fixing arrangements should continue to be deemed *per se* violations of Section 1 of the Sherman Act or whether the rule of reason should be applied.

12. 390 U.S. 145, 88 S.Ct. 869, 19 L.Ed.2d 998 (1968).

STATE OIL CO. v. KHAN

CASE 17.3

Supreme Court of the United States, 1997.
522 U.S. 3,
118 S.Ct. 275,
139 L.Ed.2d 199.
http://www.findlaw.com/casecode/supreme.html[a]

Barkat Khan leased a gas station under a contract with State Oil Company, which also agreed to supply gas to Khan for resale. Under the contract, State Oil would set a suggested retail price and sell gas to Khan for 3.25 cents per gallon less than that price. Khan could sell the gas at a higher price, but he would then be required to pay State Oil the difference (which would equal the entire profit Khan realized from raising the price). Khan failed to pay some of the rent due under the lease, and State Oil terminated the contract. Khan filed a suit in a federal district court against State Oil, alleging, among other things, price fixing in violation of the Sherman Act. The court granted summary judgment for State Oil. Khan appealed. The U.S. Court of Appeals for the Seventh Circuit reversed this judgment, and State Oil appealed to the United States Supreme Court.

O'CONNOR, J.

Our analysis is * * * guided by our general view that the primary purpose of the antitrust laws is to protect interbrand competition. * * * [C]ondemnation of practices resulting in lower prices to consumers is especially costly because cutting prices in order to increase business often is the very essence of competition.

a. This page, which is part of a Web site maintained by FindLaw (now a part of West Group), contains links to opinions of the United States Supreme Court. In the "Party Name Search" box, type "Khan" and click on "search." When the results appear, click on the case name to access the opinion.

* * * *[W]e find it difficult to maintain that vertically imposed maximum prices could harm consumers or competition to the extent necessary to justify their* per se *invalidation.* * * * [Emphasis added.]

* * * *

* * * [T]he *per se* rule * * * could in fact exacerbate [make worse] problems related to the unrestrained exercise of market power by monopolist-dealers. Indeed, *both courts and antitrust scholars have noted that [the* per se*] rule may actually harm consumers and manufacturers.* * * * [Emphasis added.]

* * * *

* * * [V]ertical maximum price fixing, like the majority of commercial arrangements subject to the antitrust laws, should be evaluated under the rule of reason. In our view, rule-of-reason analysis can effectively identify those situations in which vertical maximum price fixing amounts to anticompetitive conduct.

The United States Supreme Court vacated the decision of the appellate court and remanded the case. The Supreme Court held that vertical price fixing is not a per se *violation of the Sherman Act but should be evaluated under the rule of reason.*

QUESTIONS

1. What was the circumstance in this case that the plaintiff claimed constituted price fixing in violation of the Sherman Act?
2. According to the United States Supreme Court in this case, does an agreement that sets a maximum price for the resale of products supplied by a supplier to a distributor constitute price fixing in violation of Section 1 of the Sherman Act?
3. Should all "commercial arrangements subject to the antitrust laws" be evaluated under the rule of reason?

Refusals to Deal. As discussed previously, joint refusals to deal (group boycotts) are prohibited under Section 1 of the Sherman Act. A single manufacturer, however, is generally free to deal, or not deal, with whomever it wishes. A manufacturer can refuse to deal with retailers or dealers that cut prices to levels substantially below the manufacturer's suggested retail prices. For example, in *United States v. Colgate & Co.,*[13] the United States Supreme Court held that a manufacturer's advance announcement that it would not sell to price cutters was not a violation of the Sherman Act.

In some instances, however, a unilateral refusal to deal violates antitrust laws. These instances involve offenses proscribed under Section 2 of the Sherman Act and occur only if (1) the firm refusing to deal has—or is likely to acquire—monopoly power and (2) the refusal is likely to have an anticompetitive effect on a particular market.

---

13. 250 U.S. 300, 39 S.Ct. 465, 63 L.Ed. 992 (1919).

SECTION 2 OF THE SHERMAN ACT

Section 1 of the Sherman Act proscribes certain concerted, or joint, activities that restrain trade. In contrast, Section 2 condemns "every person who shall monopolize, or attempt to monopolize." Thus, two distinct types of behavior are subject to sanction under Section 2: *monopolization* and *attempts to monopolize.* A tactic that may be involved in either offense is **predatory pricing.** Predatory pricing occurs when one firm attempts to drive its competitors from the market by selling its product at prices substantially *below* the normal costs of production; once the competitors are eliminated, the firm will attempt to recapture its losses and go on to earn very high profits by driving up prices far above their competitive levels.

Predatory pricing • The pricing of a product below cost with the intent to drive competitors out of the market.

Monopolization

In *United States v. Grinnell Corp.,*[14] the United States Supreme Court defined **monopolization** as involving the following two elements: "(1) the possession of monopoly power in the relevant market and (2) the willful acquisition or maintenance of the power as distinguished from growth or development as a consequence of a superior product, business acumen, or historic accident." A violation of Section 2 requires that both these elements—monopoly power and an intent to monopolize—be established.

Monopolization • The possession of monopoly power in the relevant market and the willful acquisition or maintenance of that power, as distinguished from growth or development as a consequence of a superior product, business acumen, or historic accident.

Monopoly Power. The Sherman Act does not define *monopoly.* In economic parlance, monopoly refers to control of an entire market by a single entity. It is well established in antitrust law, however, that a firm may be a monopolist even though it is not the sole seller in a market. Additionally, size alone does not determine whether a firm is a monopoly. For example, a "mom and pop" grocery located in an isolated desert town is a monopolist if it is the only grocery serving that particular market. Size in relation to the market is what matters, because monopoly involves the power to affect prices and output.

Market Power. *Monopoly power,* as mentioned earlier in this chapter, exists when a firm has sufficient market power to control prices and exclude competition. As difficult as it is to define market power precisely, it is even more difficult to measure it. Courts often use the so-called **market-share test**[15]—a firm's percentage share of the "relevant market"—in determining the extent of the firm's market power. A firm generally is considered to have monopoly power if its share of the relevant market is 70 percent or more. This is merely a rule of thumb, however; it is not a binding principle of law. In some cases, a smaller share may be held to constitute monopoly power.[16]

Market-share test • The primary measure of monopoly power. A firm's market share is the percentage of a market that the firm controls.

14. 384 U.S. 563, 86 S.Ct. 1698, 16 L.Ed.2d 778 (1966).

15. Other measures of market power have been devised, but the market-share test is the most widely used.

16. This standard was first articulated by Judge Learned Hand in *United States v. Aluminum Co. of America,* 148 F.2d 416 (2d Cir. 1945). A 90 percent share was held to be clear evidence of monopoly power. Anything less than 64 percent, said Judge Hand, made monopoly power doubtful, and anything less than 30 percent was clearly not monopoly power.

Relevant Market. The relevant market consists of two elements: (1) a relevant product market and (2) a relevant geographic market. What should the relevant product market include? No doubt, it must include all products that, although produced by different firms, have identical attributes, such as sugar. Products that are not identical, however, may sometimes be substituted for one another. Coffee may be substituted for tea, for example. In defining the relevant product market, the key issue is the degree of interchangeability between products. If one product is a sufficient substitute for another, the two products are considered to be part of the same product market.

The second component of the relevant market is the geographic boundaries of the market. For products that are sold nationwide, the geographic boundaries of the market encompass the entire United States. If a producer and its competitors sell in only a limited area (one in which customers have no access to other sources of the product), then the geographic market is limited to that area. A national firm may thus compete in several distinct areas and have monopoly power in one area but not in another.

The Intent Requirement. Monopoly power, in and of itself, does not constitute the offense of monopolization under Section 2 of the Sherman Act. The offense also requires an *intent* to monopolize. A dominant market share may be the result of business acumen or the development of a superior product. It may simply be the result of historical accident. In these situations, the acquisition of monopoly power is not an antitrust violation. Indeed, it would be counter to society's interest to condemn every firm that acquired a position of power because it was well managed and efficient, and marketed a product desired by consumers.

If, however, a firm possesses market power as a result of carrying out some purposeful act to acquire or maintain that power through anticompetitive means, it is in violation of Section 2. In most monopolization cases, intent may be inferred from evidence that the firm had monopoly power and engaged in anticompetitive behavior.

The following case included an allegation of a violation of Section 2 of the Sherman Act.

CASE 17.4

United States Court of Appeals, District of Columbia Circuit, 2001.
253 F.3d 34.
http://www.cadc.uscourts.gov[a]

UNITED STATES v. MICROSOFT CORP.

In 1981, Microsoft Corporation released the first version of its Microsoft Disk Operating System (MS-DOS). When International Business Machines Corporation (IBM) selected MS-DOS for preinstallation on its first generation of personal computers (PCs), Microsoft's product became the dominant operating system for Intel-compatible PCs.[b] *In 1985, Microsoft began shipping a software package called Windows. Although originally a user interface on top of MS-DOS, Windows took on more operating-system*

a. On this page, in the left column, click on "Opinions." In the section headed "Please select from the following menu to find opinions by date of issue," choose "June" from the "Month" menu, select "2001" from the "Year" menu, and click on "Go!" From the result, scroll to the name of the case and click on the docket number to access the opinion. The U.S. Court of Appeals for the District of Columbia Circuit maintains this Web site.

b. An *Intel-compatible PC* is designed to function with Intel Corporation's 80×86/Pentium families of microprocessors or with compatible microprocessors.

functionality over time. Throughout the 1990s, Microsoft's share of the market for Intel-compatible operating systems was more than 90 percent. In 1994, Netscape Communications Corporation began marketing Navigator, the first popular graphical Internet browser. Navigator worked with Java, a technology developed by Sun Microsystems, Inc. Java enabled applications to run on a variety of platforms, which meant that users did not need Windows. Microsoft perceived a threat to its dominance of the operating-system market and developed a competing browser, Internet Explorer (Explorer). Microsoft then began to require computer makers that wanted to install Windows also to install Explorer and exclude Navigator. Meanwhile, Microsoft commingled browser code and other code in Windows so that deleting files containing Explorer would cripple the operating system. Microsoft offered to promote and pay Internet service providers (ISPs) to distribute Explorer and exclude Navigator. Microsoft also developed its own Java code and deceived many independent software sellers into believing that this code would help in designing cross-platform applications when, in fact, it would run only on Windows. The U.S. Department of Justice and a number of state attorneys general filed a suit in a federal district court against Microsoft, alleging, in part, monopolization in violation of Section 2 of the Sherman Act. The court ruled against Microsoft.[c] *Microsoft appealed to the U.S. Court of Appeals for the District of Columbia Circuit.*

PER CURIAM [by the whole court].

Claiming that software competition is uniquely "dynamic," [Microsoft] suggests * * * that monopoly power in the software industry should be proven directly, that is, by examining a company's actual behavior to determine if it reveals the existence of monopoly power. * * *

* * * *

* * * *Microsoft's pattern of exclusionary conduct could only be rational if the firm knew that it possessed monopoly power.* It is to that conduct that we now turn. [Emphasis added.]

* * * *

* * * [P]rovisions in Microsoft's agreements licensing Windows to [computer makers] * * * reduce usage share of Netscape's browser and, hence, protect Microsoft's operating system monopoly. * * *

* * * *

Therefore, Microsoft's efforts to gain market share in one market (browsers) served to meet the threat to Microsoft's monopoly in another market (operating systems) by keeping rival browsers from gaining the critical mass of users necessary to attract developer attention away from Windows as the platform for software development. * * *

* * * *

* * * [W]e conclude that [Microsoft's] commingling [of browser and non-browser code] has an anticompetitive effect; * * * the commingling deters [computer makers] from pre-installing rival browsers, thereby reducing the rivals' usage share and, hence, developers' interest in rivals' [Application Programming Interfaces (APIs)] as an alternative to the API set exposed by Microsoft's operating system.

* * * *

---

c. The district court ordered, among other things, a structural reorganization of Microsoft, including a separation of its operating-system and applications businesses. See *United States v. Microsoft,* 97 F.Supp.2d 59 (D.D.C. 2000).

> * * * By ensuring that the majority of all [ISP] subscribers are offered [Internet Explorer] either as the default browser or as the only browser, Microsoft's deals with the [ISPs] clearly have a significant effect in preserving its monopoly * * *.
>
> * * * *
>
> * * * Microsoft's exclusive deals with the [independent software vendors] had a substantial effect in further foreclosing rival browsers from the market * * *.

The U.S. Court of Appeals for the District of Columbia Circuit affirmed the part of the lower court's opinion holding that Microsoft did possess and maintain monopoly power in the market for Intel-compatible operating systems. The appellate court reversed other holdings of the lower court, however, and remanded the case for a reconsideration of the appropriate remedy. Since then, the Department of Justice and nine of the state attorneys general who brought the suit agreed with Microsoft to settle the case. On November 1, 2002, a federal trial court judge approved the settlement. Generally, the settlement gives consumers more choices and allows Microsoft's rivals more flexibility to offer competing software features on computers running Windows.

QUESTIONS

1. Who filed the suit in this case, and why?
2. Did Microsoft possess and maintain monopoly power in the market for Intel-compatible operating systems, according to the U.S Court of Appeals for the District of Columbia Circuit in this opinion?
3. What effect does the passage of time between certain conduct and the outcome of litigation have on judicial rulings that apply to technological product markets?

Attempts to Monopolize

Attempted monopolization • Any action by a firm that is specifically intended to eliminate competition and gain monopoly power.

Section 2 also prohibits **attempted monopolization** of a market. Any action challenged as an attempt to monopolize must have been specifically intended to exclude competitors and garner monopoly power. In addition, the attempt must have had a "dangerous" probability of success—only *serious* threats of monopolization are condemned as violations. The probability cannot be dangerous unless the alleged offender possesses some degree of market power.

ETHICAL ISSUE

Are we destined for more monopolies in the future? Knowledge and information form the building blocks of the so-called new economy. Some observers believe that the nature of this new economy means that we will see an increasing number of monopolies similar to Microsoft. Consider that the basis for all antitrust law is that monopoly leads to restricted output and hence higher prices for consumers; that is how a monopolist maximizes profits relative to a competitive firm. In a knowledge-based sector, however, increasing output often leads to reduced prices (because the long-run average costs decrease when output is increased). This is exactly what Microsoft has done over the years—increased its output, which has led to lower prices for operating systems and applications, especially when corrected for inflation.

This may mean that antitrust authorities will have to have a greater tolerance for knowledge-based monopolies to allow them to benefit from economies of scale. After all, the ultimate beneficiary of such economies of scale is the consumer. In the early 1900s, economist Joseph Schumpeter argued in favor of allowing monopolies. According to his theory of "creative destruction," monopolies stimulate innovation and economic growth because firms that capture monopoly profits have a greater incentive to innovate. Those that do not survive—the firms that are "destroyed"—leave room for more efficient firms, ones that will survive.

THE CLAYTON ACT

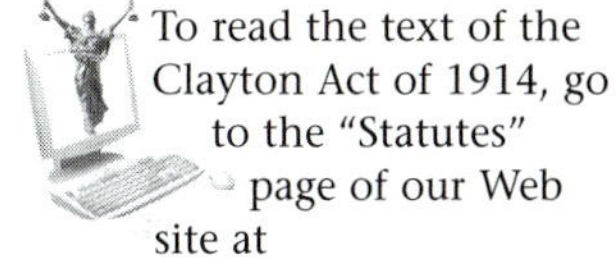

To read the text of the Clayton Act of 1914, go to the "Statutes" page of our Web site at

http://ele.westbuslaw.com

In 1914, Congress attempted to strengthen federal antitrust laws by enacting the Clayton Act. The Clayton Act was aimed at specific anticompetitive or monopolistic practices that the Sherman Act did not cover. The substantive provisions of the act deal with four distinct forms of business behavior, which are declared illegal but not criminal. With regard to each of the four provisions, the act's prohibitions are qualified by the general condition that the behavior is illegal only if it tends to substantially lessen competition or to create monopoly power. The major offenses under the Clayton Act are set out in Sections 2, 3, 7, and 8 of the act.

Price Discrimination

Price discrimination • Setting prices in such a way that two competing buyers pay two different prices for an identical product or service.

Price discrimination, which occurs when a seller charges different prices to competing buyers for identical goods, is prohibited by Section 2 of the Clayton Act. Because businesses frequently circumvented Section 2 of the act, Congress strengthened this section by amending it with the passage of the Robinson-Patman Act in 1936.

As amended, Section 2 prohibits price discrimination that cannot be justified by differences in production costs, transportation costs, or cost differences due to other reasons. To violate Section 2, the seller must be engaged in interstate commerce, and the effect of the price discrimination must be to lessen substantially competition or to create a competitive injury.

In other words, a seller is prohibited from reducing a price to one buyer below the price charged to that buyer's competitor. An exception is made if the seller can justify the price reduction by demonstrating (1) that the seller charged the lower price temporarily and in good faith to meet another seller's equally low price to the buyer's competitor or (2) that a particular buyer's purchases saved the seller costs in producing and selling the goods (called *cost justification*). To violate the Clayton Act, a seller's pricing policies must also include a reasonable prospect of the seller's recouping its losses.[17]

17. See, for example, *Brooke Group, Ltd. v. Brown & Williamson Tobacco Corp.*, 509 U.S. 209, 113 S.Ct. 2578, 125 L.Ed.2d 168 (1993), in which the Supreme Court held that a seller's price-cutting policies could not be predatory "[g]iven the market's realities"—the size of the seller's market share, expanding output by other sellers, and other factors.

Exclusionary Practices

Under Section 3 of the Clayton Act, sellers or lessors cannot sell or lease goods "on the condition, agreement or understanding that the . . . purchaser or lessee thereof shall not use or deal in the goods . . . of a competitor or competitors of the seller." In effect, this section prohibits two types of vertical agreements involving exclusionary practices—exclusive-dealing contracts and tying arrangements.

Exclusive-dealing contract • An agreement under which a seller forbids a buyer to purchase products from the seller's competitors.

Exclusive-Dealing Contracts. Under an **exclusive-dealing contract,** a seller forbids a buyer to purchase products from the seller's competitors. A seller is prohibited from making an exclusive-dealing contract under Section 3 if the effect of the contract is "to substantially lessen competition or tend to create a monopoly."

The leading exclusive-dealing decision was made by the United States Supreme Court in the case of *Standard Oil Co. of California v. United States.*[18] In this case, the then-largest gasoline seller in the nation made exclusive-dealing contracts with independent stations in seven western states. The contracts involved 16 percent of all retail outlets, whose sales were approximately 7 percent of all retail sales in that market. The Court noted that the market was substantially concentrated because the seven largest gasoline suppliers all used exclusive-dealing contracts with their independent retailers and together controlled 65 percent of the market. Looking at market conditions after the arrangements were instituted, the Court found that market shares were extremely stable, and entry into the market was apparently restricted. Thus, the Court held that Section 3 of the Clayton Act had been violated because competition was "foreclosed in a substantial share" of the relevant market.

Tying arrangement • An agreement between a buyer and a seller in which the buyer of a specific product or service becomes obligated to purchase additional products or services from the seller.

Tying Arrangements. In a **tying arrangement,** or *tie-in sales agreement,* a seller conditions the sale of a product (the tying product) on the buyer's agreement to purchase another product (the tied product) produced or distributed by the same seller. The legality of a tie-in agreement depends on many factors, particularly the purpose of the agreement and the agreement's likely effect on competition in the relevant markets (the market for the tying product and the market for the tied product).

In 1936, for example, the United States Supreme Court held that International Business Machines and Remington Rand had violated Section 3 of the Clayton Act by requiring the purchase of their own machine cards (the tied product) as a condition to the leasing of their tabulation machines (the tying product). Because only these two firms sold completely automated tabulation machines, the Court concluded that each possessed market power sufficient to "substantially lessen competition" through the tying arrangements.[19]

Section 3 of the Clayton Act has been held to apply only to commodities, not to services. Tying arrangements, however, can also be considered agreements that restrain trade in violation of Section 1 of the Sherman Act. Thus, cases involving tying arrangements of services have been brought under Section 1 of the Sherman Act. Traditionally, the courts have held tying

18. 357 U.S. 293, 69 S.Ct. 1051, 93 L.Ed. 1371 (1949).

19. *International Business Machines Corp. v. United States,* 298 U.S. 131, 56 S.Ct. 701, 80 L.Ed. 1085 (1936).

arrangements brought under the Sherman Act to be illegal *per se.* In recent years, however, courts have shown a willingness to look at factors that are important in a rule-of-reason analysis.

Mergers

Under Section 7 of the Clayton Act, a person or business organization cannot hold stock or assets in more than one business when "the effect . . . may be to substantially lessen competition." Section 7 is the statutory authority for preventing mergers that could result in monopoly power or a substantial lessening of competition in the marketplace. Section 7 applies to three types of mergers: horizontal mergers, vertical mergers, and conglomerate mergers. We discuss each type of merger in the following subsections.

A crucial consideration in most merger cases is **market concentration.** Determining market concentration involves allocating percentage market shares among the various companies in the relevant market. When a small number of companies share a large part of the market, the market is concentrated. For example, if the four largest grocery stores in Chicago accounted for 80 percent of all retail food sales, the market clearly would be concentrated in those four firms. Competition, however, is not necessarily diminished solely as a result of market concentration, and other factors must be considered in determining whether a merger will violate Section 7. Another concept of particular importance in evaluating the effects of a merger is whether the merger will make it more difficult for *potential* competitors to enter the relevant market.

Market concentration • A situation that exists when a small number of firms share the market for a particular good or service.

Horizontal Mergers. Mergers between firms that compete with each other in the same market are called **horizontal mergers.** If a horizontal merger creates an entity with a resulting significant market share, the merger may be presumed illegal. This is because of the United States Supreme Court's interpretation that Congress, in amending Section 7 of the Clayton Act in 1950, intended to prevent mergers that increase market concentration.[20] Three other factors that the courts also consider in analyzing the legality of a horizontal merger are the overall concentration of the relevant market, the relevant market's history of tending toward concentration, and whether the merger is apparently designed to establish market power or restrict competition.

Horizontal merger • A merger between two firms that are competing in the same market.

The Federal Trade Commission (FTC) and the U.S. Department of Justice (DOJ) have established guidelines indicating which mergers will be challenged. Under the guidelines, the first factor to be considered in determining whether a merger will be challenged is the degree of concentration in the relevant market. This is done by comparing the premerger market concentration with the anticipated postmerger market concentration. The FTC and the DOJ will also consider other factors, including the ease of entry into the relevant market, economic efficiency, the financial condition of the merging firms, and the nature and price of the product or products involved. In the situation of a leading firm—one having a market share that is at least 35 percent and is twice that of the next leading firm—any merger with another firm will be closely scrutinized.

Vertical Mergers. A **vertical merger** occurs when a company at one stage of production acquires a company at a higher or lower stage of production. An

Vertical merger • The acquisition by a company at one stage of production of a company at a higher or lower stage of production (such as its supplier or retailer).

20. *Brown Shoe v. United States,* 370 U.S. 294, 82 S.Ct. 1502, 8 L.Ed.2d 510 (1962).

example of a vertical merger is a company merging with one of its suppliers or retailers. Courts in the past have almost exclusively focused on "foreclosure" in assessing vertical mergers. Foreclosure occurs when competitors of the merging firms lose opportunities either to sell products to or buy products from the merging firms.

For example, in *United States v. E. I. du Pont de Nemours & Co.*,[21] du Pont was challenged for acquiring a considerable amount of General Motors (GM) stock. In holding that the transaction was illegal, the United States Supreme Court noted that the stock acquisition would enable du Pont to foreclose other sellers of fabrics and finishes from selling to GM, which then accounted for 50 percent of all auto fabric and finishes purchases.

Today, whether a vertical merger will be deemed illegal generally depends on several factors, including market concentration, barriers to entry into the market, and the apparent intent of the merging parties. Mergers that do not prevent competitors of either of the merging firms from competing in a segment of the market will not be condemned as foreclosing competition and are legal.

Conglomerate merger • A merger between firms that do not compete with each other because they are in different markets (as opposed to horizontal and vertical mergers).

Conglomerate Mergers. There are three general types of **conglomerate mergers:** market-extension, product-extension, and diversification mergers. A market-extension merger occurs when a firm seeks to sell its product in a new market by merging with a firm already established in that market. A product-extension merger occurs when a firm seeks to add a closely related product to its existing line by merging with a firm already producing that product. For example, a manufacturer might seek to extend its line of household products to include floor wax by acquiring a leading manufacturer of floor wax. Diversification occurs when a firm merges with another firm that offers a product or service wholly unrelated to the first firm's existing activities. An example of a diversification merger is an automobile manufacturer's acquisition of a motel chain.

Interlocking Directorates

Section 8 of the Clayton Act deals with *interlocking directorates*—that is, the practice of having individuals serve as directors on the boards of two or more competing companies simultaneously. Specifically, no person may be a director in two or more competing corporations at the same time if either of the corporations has capital, surplus, or undivided profits aggregating more than $18,919,000 or competitive sales of $1,891,900 or more. The threshold amounts are adjusted each year by the Federal Trade Commission. (The amounts given here are those announced by the commission in 2003.)

Enforcement of Antitrust Laws

To read the text of the Federal Trade Commission Act of 1914, go to the "Statutes" page of our Web site at **http://ele.westbuslaw.com**

The federal agencies that enforce the federal antitrust laws are the U.S. Department of Justice (DOJ) and the Federal Trade Commission (FTC). The FTC was established by the Federal Trade Commission Act of 1914. Section 5 of that act is its sole substantive provision. Section 5 provides, in part, as follows: "Unfair methods of competition in or affecting commerce, and unfair or deceptive acts or practices in or affecting commerce are hereby declared

21. 353 U.S. 586, 77 S.Ct. 872, 1 L.Ed.2d 1057 (1957).

illegal." Section 5 condemns all forms of anticompetitive behavior that are not covered under other federal antitrust laws.

Only the DOJ can prosecute violations of the Sherman Act as either criminal or civil violations. Violations of the Clayton Act are not crimes, and either the DOJ or the FTC can enforce that statute through civil proceedings. The DOJ or the FTC may ask the courts to impose various remedies, including **divestiture** (making a company give up one or more of its operating functions) and dissolution. A group of meat packers, for example, might be forced to divest itself of control or ownership of butcher shops.

Divestiture • The act of selling one or more of a company's parts, such as a subsidiary or plant; often mandated by the courts in merger or monopolization cases.

The FTC has sole authority to enforce violations of Section 5 of the Federal Trade Commission Act. FTC actions are effected through administrative orders, but if a firm violates an FTC order, the FTC can seek court sanctions for the violation.

Private Actions

A private party who has been injured as a result of a violation of the Sherman Act or the Clayton Act can sue for damages and attorneys' fees. In some instances, private parties may also seek injunctive relief to prevent antitrust violations. The courts have determined that the ability to sue depends on the directness of the injury suffered by the would-be plaintiff. Thus, a person wishing to sue under the Sherman Act must prove (1) that the antitrust violation either caused or was a substantial factor in causing the injury that was suffered and (2) that the unlawful actions of the accused party affected business activities of the plaintiff that were protected by the antitrust laws.

Treble Damages

In recent years, more than 90 percent of all antitrust actions have been brought by private plaintiffs. One reason for this is that successful plaintiffs may recover treble damages—three times the damages that they have suffered as a result of the violation. Such recoveries by private plaintiffs for antitrust violations have been rationalized as encouraging people to act as "private attorneys general" who will vigorously pursue antitrust violators on their own initiative.

In a situation involving a price-fixing agreement, normally each competitor is jointly and severally liable for the total amount of any damages, including treble damages if they are imposed. Should the presence of multiple wholesalers, retailers, and other intermediaries affect this assessment of damages? That was the question before the court in the following case.

PAPER SYSTEMS, INC. v. NIPPON PAPER INDUSTRIES CO.

CASE 17.5

United States Court of Appeals, Seventh Circuit, 2002.
281 F.3d 629.
http://www.ca7.uscourts.gov[a]

In 1993, two Japanese paper companies merged to form Nippon Paper Industries Company. At the time, the five major producers of thermal fax paper used different distribution systems. Kanzaki Specialty Papers, Inc., and Appleton Papers, Inc., sold directly to firms such as Paper Systems, Inc., which resold the paper to its own

a. In the left column, click on "CASE INFORMATION," and then, at the bottom of the page on the right, select "Opinions." On the next page, in the "Last Name or Corporation" box, enter "Nippon," select "Begins," and click on "Search for Person." Click on the number next to the name of the case in the result to access the opinion.

customers. Two other manufacturers, Oji Paper Company and Mitsubishi Paper Mills Limited, sold exclusively to distributors that resold the paper to firms such as Paper Systems. Nippon's predecessor, the fifth manufacturer, sold its output in Japan to Japanese firms, which resold through subsidiaries around the world. Paper Systems and two other buyers filed a suit in a federal district court against Nippon and the other paper producers, alleging violations of the antitrust laws. Four of the defendants reached a settlement with the plaintiffs, and the court dismissed the claim against Nippon. The plaintiffs appealed this dismissal to the U.S. Court of Appeals for the Seventh Circuit. Nippon argued that even if it was liable, the presence of so many wholesalers, retailers, and others in the chain of distribution created complications, including possible double recovery, too great to impose joint liability.

EASTERBROOK, J.

*[Under] the rule of joint and several liability * * * each member of a conspiracy is liable for all damages caused by the conspiracy's entire output.* * * * If Nippon Paper was among those conspirators, then it is responsible for the *entire* overcharge of *all five manufacturers*—and any direct purchaser from any conspirator can collect its own portion of damages (that is, the damages attributable to its direct purchases) from any conspirator. This makes it impossible to dismiss Nippon Paper outright. [Emphasis added.]

* * * *

* * * The difficulty of tracing overcharges through the chain of distribution * * * is unimportant; duplicative recovery has been blocked at the outset. * * *

A simple example makes the point. Suppose that five vertically integrated manufacturers sell directly to consumers at $12 per unit, and that this price is an overcharge attributable to a cartel [anticompetitive business combination or group]; the competitive price would have been $10 per unit. Each manufacturer sells 100 units per year, so the total overcharge is $1,000 ($2 on each of 500 units) and treble damages under the Sherman Act are $3,000. Given joint and several liability, each of the five conspirators is liable to pay the whole $3,000—though no consumer can recover more than $6 per unit purchased. Now suppose further that one of the five manufacturers gets out of the distribution business and sells its output to a wholesaler for $10 per unit; the wholesaler resells the product for $12 per unit. It is hard to see why this should change the *total* damages any conspirator must pay under the antitrust laws. * * * [I]t changes *who* may collect damages (the wholesaler, as direct purchaser, owns the right to collect damages on 100 units each year) but not how much each [member of the cartel] owes in the aggregate. Yet Nippon Paper's position is that the use of a wholesaler has a profound effect; it reduces that manufacturer's total exposure from $3,000 to $600 (treble the $2 overcharge on 100 units sold to the wholesaler)—and then only if the wholesaler sues. * * * [The courts reject] just such a proposal. * * * [I]f one direct purchaser wholesaler declines to sue, then the total damages the five example manufacturers owe jointly and severally cannot exceed what is recoverable by direct purchasers that do litigate (in our example, for $2,400). Every participant in the conspiracy remains liable for damages on every sale to every direct purchaser from any of the manufacturers.

The U.S. Court of Appeals for the Seventh Circuit reversed the lower court's decision and remanded the case for a determination as to whether Nippon had been a mem-

ber of the cartel. The appellate court held that if Nippon was a member, it was jointly and severally liable for the cartel's entire overcharge to any direct purchaser from any conspirator, to the extent of the damages attributable to that buyer's direct purchases.

QUESTIONS

1. What was the defendant's argument against liability in this case?
2. Could Nippon be held jointly and severally liable for the cartel's entire overcharge to any direct purchaser, in the view of the U.S. Court of Appeals for the Seventh Circuit?
3. If there had been no wholesalers, retailers, or other intermediaries between the alleged conspirators and the direct purchasers in this case, would the result have been the same?

EXEMPTIONS FROM ANTITRUST LAWS

There are many legislative and constitutional limitations on antitrust enforcement. Most statutory and judicially created exemptions to the antitrust laws apply to the following areas or activities:

1. *Labor.* Section 6 of the Clayton Act generally permits labor unions to organize and bargain without violating antitrust laws. Section 20 of the Clayton Act specifies that strikes and other labor activities are not violations of any law of the United States. A union can lose its exemption, however, if it combines with a nonlabor group rather than acting simply in its own self-interest.
2. *Agricultural associations and fisheries.* Section 6 of the Clayton Act (along with the Cooperative Marketing Associations Act of 1922[22]) exempts agricultural cooperatives from the antitrust laws. The Fisheries Cooperative Marketing Act of 1976 exempts from antitrust legislation individuals in the fishing industry who collectively catch, produce, and prepare their products for market. Both exemptions allow members of such co-ops to combine and set prices for a particular product but do not allow them to engage in exclusionary practices or restraints of trade directed at competitors.
3. *Insurance.* The McCarran-Ferguson Act of 1945[23] exempts the insurance business from the antitrust laws whenever state regulation exists. This exemption does not cover boycotts, coercion, or intimidation on the part of insurance companies.
4. *Foreign trade.* Under the provisions of the 1918 Webb-Pomerene Act,[24] U.S. exporters may engage in cooperative activity to compete with similar foreign associations. This type of cooperative activity may not, however, restrain trade within the United States or injure other U.S. exporters. The Export Trading Company Act of 1982[25] broadened the Webb-Pomerene Act by permitting the Department of Justice to certify properly qualified

22. 7 U.S.C. Sections 291–292.
23. 15 U.S.C. Sections 1011–1015.
24. 15 U.S.C. Sections 61–66.
25. 15 U.S.C. Sections 4001–4003.

export trading companies. Any activity within the scope described by the certificate is exempt from public prosecution under the antitrust laws.

5. *Professional baseball.* In 1922, the United States Supreme Court held that professional baseball was not within the reach of federal antitrust laws because it did not involve "interstate commerce."[26] Some of the effects of this decision, however, were modified by the Curt Flood Act of 1998. Essentially, the act allows players the option of suing team owners for anticompetitive practices if, for example, the owners collude to "blacklist" players, hold down players' salaries, or force players to play for specific teams.
6. *Oil marketing.* The 1935 Interstate Oil Compact allows states to determine quotas on oil that will be marketed in interstate commerce.
7. *Cooperative research and production.* Cooperative research among small-business firms is exempt under the Small Business Act of 1958.[27] Research or production of a product, process, or service by joint ventures consisting of competitors is exempt under special federal legislation, including the National Cooperative Research Act of 1984,[28] as amended by the National Cooperative Research and Production Act of 1993.
8. *Joint efforts by businesspersons to obtain legislative or executive action.* This is often referred to as the Noerr-Pennington doctrine.[29] For example, DVD producers might jointly lobby Congress to change the copyright laws without being held liable for attempting to restrain trade. Though selfish rather than purely public-minded conduct is permitted, there is an exception: an action will not be protected if it is clear that the action is "objectively baseless in the sense that no reasonable [person] could reasonably expect success on the merits" and it is an attempt to make anticompetitive use of government processes.[30]
9. *Other exemptions.* Other activities exempt from antitrust laws include activities approved by the president in furtherance of the defense of our nation (under the Defense Production Act of 1950[31]); state actions, when the state policy is clearly articulated and the policy is actively supervised by the state; and activities of regulated industries (such as the transportation, communication, and banking industries) when federal agencies (such as the Federal Communications Commission) have primary regulatory authority.

U.S. Antitrust Laws in the Global Context

U.S. antitrust laws have a broad application. Not only may persons in foreign nations be subject to their provisions, but they may also be applied to protect foreign consumers and competitors from violations committed by U.S. business firms. Consequently, *foreign persons,* a term that by definition includes foreign governments, may sue under U.S. antitrust laws in U.S. courts.

---

26. *Federal Baseball Club of Baltimore, Inc. v. National League of Professional Baseball Clubs,* 259 U.S. 200, 42 S.Ct. 465, 66 L.Ed. 898 (1922).
27. 15 U.S.C. Sections 631–657.
28. 15 U.S.C. Sections 4301–4306.
29. See *United Mine Workers of America v. Pennington,* 381 U.S. 657, 89 S.Ct. 1585, 14 L.Ed.2d 626 (1965); and *Eastern Railroad Presidents Conference v. Noerr Motor Freight, Inc.,* 365 U.S. 127, 81 S.Ct. 523, 5 L.Ed.2d 464 (1961).
30. *Professional Real Estate Investors, Inc. v. Columbia Pictures Industries, Inc.,* 508 U.S. 49, 113 S.Ct. 1920, 123 L.Ed.2d 611 (1993).
31. 50 App.U.S.C. Sections 2061–2171.

Section 1 of the Sherman Act of 1890 provides for the extraterritorial effect of the U.S. antitrust laws. The United States is a major proponent of free competition in the global economy, and thus any conspiracy that has a *substantial effect* on U.S. commerce is within the reach of the Sherman Act. The violation may even occur outside the United States, and foreign governments as well as persons can be sued for violation of U.S. antitrust laws. Before U.S. courts will exercise jurisdiction and apply antitrust laws, it must be shown that the alleged violation had a substantial effect on U.S. commerce. U.S. jurisdiction is automatically invoked, however, when a *per se* violation occurs.

If a domestic firm, for example, joins a foreign cartel to control the production, price, or distribution of goods, and this cartel has a *substantial effect* on U.S. commerce, a *per se* violation may exist. Hence, both the domestic firm and the foreign cartel could be sued for violation of the U.S. antitrust laws. Likewise, if a foreign firm doing business in the United States enters into a price-fixing or other anticompetitive agreement to control a portion of U.S. markets, a *per se* violation may exist.

KEY TERMS

antitrust law 606
attempted monopolization 620
conglomerate merger 624
divestiture 625
exclusive-dealing contract 622
group boycott 612
horizontal merger 623
horizontal restraint 609
market concentration 623
market power 608
market-share test 617
monopolization 617
monopoly 607
monopoly power 608
***per se* violation 608**
predatory pricing 617
price discrimination 621
price-fixing agreement 609
resale price maintenance agreement 615
restraint on trade 606
rule of reason 608
tying arrangement 622
vertical merger 623
vertical restraint 613
vertically integrated firm 613

FOR REVIEW

1. What do the terms *monopoly* and *market power* mean? What is the relationship between these terms?
2. What types of activities are prohibited by Section 1 and Section 2 of the Sherman Act?
3. What types of activities are prohibited by the Clayton Act?
4. What federal agencies enforce the federal antitrust laws?
5. What are four activities that are exempt from the antitrust laws?

QUESTIONS AND CASE PROBLEMS

17–1. Allitron, Inc., and Donovan, Ltd., are interstate competitors selling similar appliances, principally in the states of Indiana, Kentucky, Illinois, and Ohio. Allitron and Donovan agree that Allitron will no longer sell in Ohio and Indiana and that Donovan will no longer sell in Kentucky and Illinois. Have Allitron and Donovan violated any antitrust law? If so, which law? Explain.

17–2. The partnership of Alvaredo and Parish is engaged in the oil-wellhead service industry in the states of New

Mexico and Colorado. The firm currently has about 40 percent of the market for this service. Webb Corp. competes with the Alvaredo-Parish partnership in the same states. Webb has approximately 35 percent of the market. Alvaredo and Parish acquire the stock and assets of Webb Corp. Do the antitrust laws prohibit the type of action undertaken by Alvaredo and Parish? Discuss fully.

17–3. Jorge's Appliance Corp. was a new retail seller of appliances in Sunrise City. Because of its innovative sales techniques and financing, Jorge's caused the appliance department of No-Glow Department Store, a large chain store with a great deal of buying power, to lose a substantial amount of sales. No-Glow told a number of appliance manufacturers from whom it made large-volume purchases that if they continued to sell to Jorge's, No-Glow would stop purchasing from them. The manufacturers immediately stopped selling appliances to Jorge's. Jorge's filed suit against No-Glow and the manufacturers, claiming that their actions constituted an antitrust violation. No-Glow and the manufacturers were able to prove that Jorge's was a small retailer with a small market share. They claimed that because the relevant market was not substantially affected, they were not guilty of restraint of trade. Discuss fully whether there was an antitrust violation.

17–4. Instant Foto Corp. is a manufacturer of photography film. At the present time, Instant Foto has approximately 50 percent of the market. Instant Foto advertises that the purchase price for Instant Foto film includes photo processing by Instant Foto Corp. Instant Foto claims that its film processing is specially designed to improve the quality of photos taken with Instant Foto film. Is Instant Foto's combination of film purchase and film processing an antitrust violation? Explain.

CASE PROBLEM WITH SAMPLE ANSWER

17–5. Antitrust Laws. Great Western Directories, Inc. (GW), is an independent publisher of telephone directory Yellow Pages. GW buys information for its listings from Southwestern Bell Telephone Co. (SBT). Southwestern Bell Corp. owns SBT, as well as Southwestern Bell Yellow Pages (SBYP), which publishes a directory in competition with GW. In June 1988, in some markets, SBT raised the price for its listing information, and SBYP lowered the price for advertising in its Yellow Pages. GW feared that these companies would do the same thing in other local markets, making it too expensive for GW to compete in those markets. Because of this fear, GW left one market and declined to compete in another. Consequently, SBYP had a monopoly in those markets. GW and another independent publisher filed a suit in a federal district court against Southwestern Bell Corp. What antitrust law, if any, did Southwestern Bell Corp. violate? Should the independent companies be entitled to damages? [*Great Western Directories, Inc. v. Southwestern Bell Telephone Co.*, 74 F.3d 613 (5th Cir. 1996)]

To view a sample answer for this case problem, go to this book's Web site at **http://ele.westbuslaw.com** *and click on "Interactive Study Center."*

17–6. Restraint of Trade. The National Collegiate Athletic Association (NCAA) coordinates the intercollegiate athletic programs of its members by issuing rules and setting standards governing, among other things, the coaching staffs. The NCAA set up a "Cost Reduction Committee" to consider ways to cut the costs of intercollegiate athletics while maintaining competition. The committee included financial aid personnel, intercollegiate athletic administrators, college presidents, university faculty members, and a university chancellor. It was felt that "only a collaborative effort could reduce costs while maintaining a level playing field." The committee proposed a rule to restrict the annual compensation of certain coaches to $16,000. The NCAA adopted the rule. Basketball coaches affected by the rule filed a suit in a federal district court against the NCAA, alleging a violation of Section 1 of the Sherman Antitrust Act. Is the rule a *per se* violation of the Sherman Act, or should it be evaluated under the rule of reason? If it is subject to the rule of reason, is it an illegal restraint of trade? Discuss fully. [*Law v. National Collegiate Athletic Association,* 134 F.3d 1010 (10th Cir. 1998)]

17–7. Tying Arrangement. Public Interest Corp. (PIC) owned and operated television station WTMV-TV in Lakeland, Florida. MCA Television, Ltd., owns and licenses syndicated television programs. The parties entered into a licensing contract with respect to several television shows. MCA conditioned the license on PIC's agreeing to take another show, *Harry and the Hendersons.* PIC agreed to this arrangement, although it would not have chosen to license *Harry* if it had not had to do so to secure the licenses for the other shows. More than two years into the contract, a dispute arose over PIC's payments, and negotiations failed to resolve the dispute. In a letter, MCA suspended PIC's broadcast rights for all of its shows and stated that "[a]ny telecasts of MCA programming by WTMV-TV . . . will be deemed unauthorized and shall constitute an infringement of MCA's copyrights." PIC nonetheless continued broadcasting MCA's programs, with the exception of *Harry.* MCA filed a suit in a federal district court against PIC, alleging breach of contract and copyright infringement. PIC filed a counterclaim, contending in part that MCA's deal was an illegal tying arrangement. Is PIC correct? Explain.

[*MCA Television, Ltd. v. Public Interest Corp.,* 171 F.3d 1265 (11th Cir. 1999)]

17–8. Attempted Monopolization. In 1995, to make personal computers (PCs) easier to use, Intel Corp. and other companies developed a standard, called the Universal Serial Bus (USB) specification, to enable the easy attachment of peripherals (printers and other hardware) to PCs. Intel and others formed the Universal Serial Bus Implementers Forum (USB-IF) to promote USB technology and products. Intel, however, makes relatively few USB products and does not make any USB interconnect devices. Multivideo Labs, Inc. (MVL), designed and distributed Active Extension Cables (AECs) to connect peripheral devices to each other or to a PC. The AECs were not USB compliant, a fact that Intel employees told other USB-IF members. Asserting that this caused a "general cooling of the market" for AECs, MVL filed a suit in a federal district court against Intel, claiming in part attempted monopolization in violation of the Sherman Act. Intel filed a motion for summary judgment. How should the court rule, and why? [*Multivideo Labs, Inc. v. Intel Corp.,* __ F.Supp.2d __ (S.D.N.Y. 2000)]

17–9. Monopolization. Moist snuff is a smokeless tobacco product sold in small round cans from racks, which include point-of-sale (POS) ads. POS ads are critical because tobacco advertising is restricted and the number of people who use smokeless tobacco products is relatively small. In the moist snuff market in the United States, there are only four competitors, including U.S. Tobacco Co. and its affiliates (USTC) and Conwood Co. In 1990, USTC, which held 87 percent of the market, began to convince major retailers, including Wal-Mart Stores, Inc., to use USTC's "exclusive racks" to display its products and those of all other snuff makers. USTC agents would then destroy competitors' racks. USTC also began to provide retailers with false sales data to convince them to maintain its poor-selling items and drop competitors' less expensive products. Conwood's Wal-Mart market share fell from 12 percent to 6.5 percent. In stores in which USTC did not have rack exclusivity, however, Conwood's market share increased to 25 percent. Conwood filed a suit in a federal district court against USTC, alleging in part that USTC used its monopoly power to exclude competitors from the moist snuff market. Should the court rule in Conwood's favor? What is USTC's best defense? Discuss. [*Conwood Co., L.P. v. U.S. Tobacco Co.,* 290 F.3d 768 (6th Cir. 2002)]

17–10. IN YOUR COURT

Timothy Lane purchased feed from Fur Breeders Agricultural Cooperative (the co-op) for use in his fur-breeding business. All members of the co-op, including Lane, were charged the same price for the feed. The co-op, however, offered free delivery services to all of its members except Lane, who had to pick up the feed. Lane sued the co-op, alleging that the co-op's actions constituted price discrimination in violation of Section 2 of the Clayton Act, as amended. Lane argued that the added cost he had to incur in picking up the feed (about $16,000 per year) effectively raised the "price" he paid for the feed relative to the price paid by other members. As a result, contended Lane, it was difficult for him to make significant profits in this highly competitive industry. The co-op moved to dismiss the case on the ground that all members were charged the same "price," and thus there could be no "price" discrimination. Assume that you are the judge in the trial court hearing this case and answer the following questions:

(a) Should the cost of picking up the feed be included in the "price" Lane paid for the feed? How will you answer this question?
(b) Generally, what factors should be considered when determining whether to grant a motion to dismiss a case?
(c) In the case now before your court, should you grant the defendant's motion to dismiss? Why or why not?

17–11. A QUESTIONS OF ETHICS AND SOCIAL RESPONSIBILITY

A group of lawyers in the District of Columbia regularly acted as court-appointed attorneys for indigent defendants in District of Columbia criminal cases. At a meeting of the Superior Court Trial Lawyers Association (SCTLA), the attorneys agreed to stop providing this representation until the district increased their compensation. Their subsequent boycott had a severe impact on the district's criminal justice system, and the District of Columbia gave in to the lawyers' demands for higher pay. After the lawyers had returned to work, the Federal Trade Commission filed a complaint against the SCTLA and four of its officers and, after an investigation, ruled that the SCTLA's activities constituted an illegal group boycott in violation of antitrust laws. [*Federal Trade Commission v. Superior Court Trial Lawyers Association,* 493 U.S. 411, 110 S.Ct. 768, 107 L.Ed.2d 851 (1990)]

(a) The SCTLA obviously was aware of the negative impact its decision would have on the district's criminal justice system. Given this fact, do you think the lawyers behaved ethically?
(b) On appeal, the SCTLA claimed that its boycott was undertaken to publicize the fact that the attorneys were underpaid and that the boycott thus constituted an expression protected by the First Amendment. Do you agree with this argument?

(c) Labor unions have the right to strike when negotiations between labor and management fail to result in agreement. Is it fair to prohibit members of the SCTLA from "striking" against their employer, the District of Columbia, simply because the SCTLA is a professional organization and not a labor union?

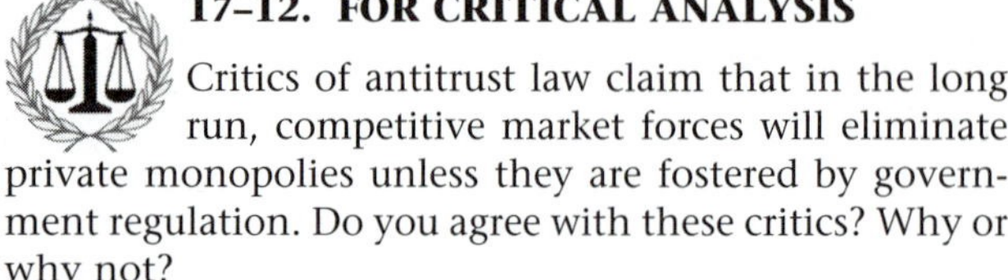

17–12. FOR CRITICAL ANALYSIS

Critics of antitrust law claim that in the long run, competitive market forces will eliminate private monopolies unless they are fostered by government regulation. Do you agree with these critics? Why or why not?

For updated links to resources available on the Web, as well as a variety of other materials, visit this text's Web site at

http://ele.westbuslaw.com

You can access the Antitrust Division of the U.S. Department of Justice online at

http://www.usdoj.gov

To see the American Bar Association's Web page on antitrust law, go to

http://www.abanet.org/antitrust

The Federal Trade Commission offers an abundance of information on antitrust law, including "A Plain English Guide to Antitrust Laws," at

http://www.ftc.gov/ftc/antitrust.htm

LEGAL RESEARCH EXERCISES ON THE WEB

Go to **http://ele.westbuslaw.com**, the Web site that accompanies this text. Select "Interactive Study Center," and then click on "Chapter 17." There you will find the following Internet research exercises that you can perform to learn more about topics covered in this chapter.

Activity 17–1: LEGAL PERSPECTIVE—The Standard Oil Trust

Activity 17–2: MANAGEMENT PERSPECTIVE—Avoiding Antitrust Problems

BEFORE THE TEST

Go to **http://ele.westbuslaw.com**, the Web site that accompanies this text. Select "Interactive Quizzes." You will find at least twenty interactive questions relating to this chapter.

WESTLAW® CAMPUS

If your textbook provided for a subscription to Westlaw® Campus, or if you have otherwise purchased access to the Westlaw Campus database, you can access any of the cases presented or cited in this chapter by using your Westlaw Campus account.

CHAPTER 18

Investor Protection and Online Securities Offerings

CONTENTS

CHAPTER OBJECTIVES

After reading this chapter, you should be able to answer the following questions:

1. What are securities?

2. What two major statutes regulate the securities industry? When was the Securities and Exchange Commission created, and what are its major purposes and functions?

3. Which federal laws regulate investment companies?

4. What are some of the features of state securities laws?

5. How do securities laws apply in the online environment?

The stock market crash of October 29, 1929, and the ensuing economic depression caused the public to focus on the importance of securities markets for the economic well-being of the nation. Congress was pressured to regulate securities trading, and the result was the Securities Act of 1933[1] and the Securities Exchange Act of 1934.[2] Both acts were designed to provide investors with more information to help them make buying and selling decisions about *securities*—generally defined as any documents evidencing corporate ownership (stock) or debts (bonds)—and to prohibit deceptive, unfair, and manipulative practices in the purchase and sale of securities.

This chapter discusses the nature of federal securities regulation and its effect on the business world. We begin by looking at the federal administrative agency that regulates securities transactions, the Securities and Exchange Commission. Next, we discuss the Sarbanes-Oxley Act, which was passed by Congress in 2002 and which will have a significant impact on certain types of securities transactions. We then examine the major traditional laws governing securities offerings and trading. The online world has brought some dramatic changes to securities offerings and regulation. In the concluding pages of this chapter, we look at how securities laws are being adapted to the online environment.

THE SECURITIES AND EXCHANGE COMMISSION

The 1934 act created the Securities and Exchange Commission (SEC) as an independent regulatory agency whose function was to administer the 1933 and 1934 acts. The SEC plays a key role in interpreting the provisions of these acts (and their amendments) and in creating regulations governing the purchase and sale of securities.

1. 15 U.S.C. Sections 77a–77aa.
2. 15 U.S.C. Sections 78a–78mm.

The Basic Functions of the SEC

The SEC regulates the securities industry by undertaking the following:

1. Requiring disclosure of facts concerning offerings of securities listed on national securities exchanges and offerings of certain securities traded over the counter (OTC).
2. Regulating the trade in securities on the national and regional securities exchanges and in the OTC markets.
3. Investigating securities fraud.
4. Requiring the registration of securities brokers, dealers, and investment advisers and regulating their activities.
5. Supervising activities conducted by mutual funds companies.
6. Recommending administrative sanctions, injunctive remedies, and criminal prosecution in cases involving violations of securities laws. (The Fraud Section of the Criminal Division of the U.S. Department of Justice prosecutes violations of federal securities laws.)

The Expanding Regulatory Powers of the SEC

Since its creation, the SEC's regulatory functions have gradually been increased by legislation granting it authority in different areas. A number of amendments during the 1990s significantly enlarged the regulatory powers of the SEC. In the 2002 legislation mentioned earlier, Congress again expanded the regulatory scope of the SEC. In all, since the early 1990s Congress has passed five acts that have significantly expanded the SEC's powers:

1. *The Penny Stock Reform Act of 1990.*[3] This act amended existing securities laws to allow SEC administrative law judges to hear many more types of securities violation cases and to greatly expand the SEC's enforcement options. The act also provides that courts can prevent persons who have engaged in securities fraud from serving as officers and directors of publicly held corporations. (Note that the Sarbanes-Oxley Act of 2002 also has provisions to this effect.)
2. *The Securities Acts Amendments of 1990.*[4] These amendments authorized the SEC to seek sanctions against those who violate foreign securities laws.
3. *The Market Reform Act of 1990.*[5] Under this act, the SEC can suspend trading in securities in the event that prices rise and fall excessively in a short period of time.
4. *The National Securities Markets Improvement Act of 1996.*[6] This act expanded the power of the SEC to exempt persons, securities, and transactions from the requirements of the securities laws. (This part of the act is also known as the Capital Markets Efficiency Act.) The act also limited the authority of the states to regulate certain securities transactions, as well as particular investment advisory firms.[7]

---

3. 15 U.S.C. Section 77g.
4. 15 U.S.C. Section 78a.
5. 15 U.S.C. Section 78i(h).
6. 15 U.S.C. Sections 77z-3, 78mm.
7. 15 U.S.C. Section 80b-3a.

5. *The Sarbanes-Oxley Act of 2002.*[8] As will be discussed shortly, this act represents a sweeping revision of federal securities laws. Among other things, this act further expanded the authority of the SEC by directing the agency to issue new rules relating to corporate disclosure requirements and by creating an SEC oversight board.

Streamlining the Regulatory Process

For years, Congress and the SEC have been attempting to streamline the regulatory process generally. The goal is to make the process more efficient and more relevant to today's securities trading practices, including those occurring in the online environment. Another goal is to create more oversight over securities transactions and accounting practices. Additionally, as the number and types of online securities frauds increase, the SEC is trying to keep pace by expanding its online fraud division.

THE SARBANES-OXLEY ACT OF 2002

Following a series of corporate scandals in the early 2000s, Congress passed the Sarbanes-Oxley Act of 2002, which some regard as one of the most significant modifications of securities regulation since the 1930s. Generally, the act attempts to increase corporate accountability by imposing stricter disclosure requirements and harsher penalties for violations of securities laws. Among other things, the act requires chief corporate executives to take responsibility for the accuracy of financial statements and reports that are filed with the SEC. Chief executive officers and chief financial officers personally must certify that the statements and reports are accurate and complete.

Additionally, the new rules require that certain financial and stock-transaction reports must be filed with the SEC earlier than was required under the previous rules. The act also mandates SEC oversight over a new entity, called the Public Company Accounting Oversight Board, that will regulate and oversee public accounting firms. Other provisions of the act create new private civil actions and expand the SEC's remedies in administrative and civil actions.

Because of the importance of this act for corporate leaders and for those dealing with securities transactions, we present some of the act's key provisions relating to corporate accountability in Exhibit 18–1. There are also provisions in the act that relate to public accounting firms and accounting practices.

THE SECURITIES ACT OF 1933

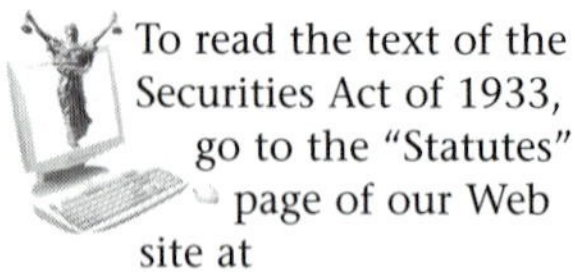

To read the text of the Securities Act of 1933, go to the "Statutes" page of our Web site at

http://ele.westbuslaw.com

The Securities Act of 1933 governs initial sales of stock by businesses. The act was designed to prohibit various forms of fraud and to stabilize the securities industry by requiring that all essential information concerning the issuance of securities be made available to the investing public.

8. H.R. 3762. This act was signed by President George W. Bush on July 30, 2002, and became effective on August 29, 2002.

EXHIBIT 18–1 • SOME KEY PROVISIONS OF THE SARBANES-OXLEY ACT OF 2002 RELATING TO CORPORATE ACCOUNTABILITY

Certification Requirements—Under Section 906 of the Sarbanes-Oxley Act, the chief executive officers (CEOs) and chief financial officers (CFOs) of most major companies listed on public stock exchanges must now certify financial statements that are filed with the SEC. For virtually all filed financial reports, CEOs and CFOs have to certify that such reports "fully comply" with SEC requirements and that all of the information reported "fairly represents in all material respects, the financial conditions and results of operations of the issuer." Under Section 302 of the act, CEOs and CFOs of reporting companies are required to certify, for each quarterly and annual filing with the SEC, the following:

- That a signing officer reviewed the report.
- That to the best of the signing officer's knowledge, the report contains no untrue statements of material fact and does not omit statements of material fact.
- That the signing officer or officers have established an internal control system designed to ensure discovery of material information that should be in the report.
- That the signing officer disclosed to the auditors any significant deficiencies in the internal control system.

Loans to Directors and Officers—To prevent companies from making loans to corporate officers and later forgiving those loans (to the detriment of shareholders), the Sarbanes-Oxley Act included a provision targeting this practice. Section 402 of the act prohibits any reporting company, as well as any private company that is filing an initial public offering, from extending, renewing, arranging, or maintaining personal loans to directors and executive officers. There are some exceptions under the act for certain consumer and housing loans.

Protection for Whistleblowers—The Sarbanes-Oxley Act also offers protection for "whistleblowers"—those employees who report ("blow the whistle" on) wrongdoing by their employers. Section 806 of the act prohibits publicly traded companies from discharging, demoting, suspending, threatening, harassing, or otherwise discriminating against an employee who provides information to the government or assists in any government investigation regarding conduct that the employee reasonably believes constitutes a violation of securities laws.

Blackout Periods—Rules established under Section 306 of the act prohibit certain types of securities transactions during "blackout periods"—periods during which the issuer's ability to purchase, sell, or otherwise transfer funds in individual account plans (such as pension funds) is suspended.

Enhanced Penalties—

- *Violations of Section 906 Certification Requirements*—A CEO or CFO who certifies a financial report or statement to be filed with the SEC knowing that the report or statement does not fulfill all of the requirements of Section 906 will be subject to criminal penalties up to $1 million in fines, up to ten years in prison, or both. Moreover, if a CEO or CFO "willfully" certifies a report knowing that it does not comport with all of the requirements of Section 906, the penalty can extend to up to $5 million in fines, twenty years in prison, or both.
- *Violations of the Securities Exchange Act of 1934*—Penalties for securities fraud under the Securities Exchange Act of 1934 were also increased (see the discussion of these penalties later in this chapter).
- *Destruction or Alteration of Documents*—The act provides that anyone who alters, destroys, or conceals documents or otherwise obstructs or impedes any official proceeding will be subject to fines, imprisonment for up to twenty years, or both.
- *Other Forms of White-Collar Crime*—The act also stiffened the criminal penalties for violations of federal mail and wire fraud laws (see Chapter 7) and the Employment Retirement Income Security Act of 1974 (see Chapter 14). The act orders the U.S. Sentencing Commission (discussed in Chapter 7) to revise the sentencing guidelines for white-collar crimes to conform with the provisions of the Sarbanes-Oxley Act.

Statute of Limitations for Securities Fraud—Section 804 of the act provides that a private right of action for securities fraud may be brought no later than two years after the discovery of the violation or five years after the violation, whichever is earlier.

The courts have interpreted the act's definition of what constitutes a security[9] to include investment contracts. An investment contract is any transaction in which a person (1) invests (2) in a common enterprise (3) reasonably expecting profits (4) derived *primarily* or *substantially* from others' managerial or entrepreneurial efforts.[10]

For our purposes, it is probably most convenient to think of securities in their most common form—stocks and bonds issued by corporations. Bear in mind, though, that securities can take many forms and have been held to include interests in whiskey, cosmetics, worms, beavers, boats, vacuum cleaners, muskrats, and cemetery lots, as well as investment contracts in condominiums, franchises, limited partnerships, oil or gas or other mineral rights, and farm animals accompanied by care agreements.

In the following *Featured Case,* the question was whether an "investment unit" in a limited liability company (LLC) falls within the definition of a security. (LLCs were discussed in Chapter 9.)

9. See 15 U.S.C. Section 77b(a)(1).

10. *SEC v. W. J. Howey Co.,* 328 U.S. 293, 66 S.Ct. 1100, 90 L.Ed. 1244 (1946).

FEATURED CASE

CASE 18.1

South Dakota Supreme Court, 2001. 2001 SD 11, 621 N.W.2d 372.

TSCHETTER v. BERVEN

MAJORITY OPINION

SABERS, J.

In 1994, [Venerts Investment, Inc., James Berven, and William Folkerts (collectively, Venerts)] entered into an agreement with Country Hospitality Corporation (CHC) to develop several Country Kitchen restaurants over a period of years. Venerts contacted Marvie and Kim Tschetter after learning from the architect retained by Country Kitchen that [Marvie, Kim, Clarence, and Goldie Tschetter (collectively, Tschetters)] were interested in the investment. Venerts contacted Clarence and Goldie, Marvie's parents, after learning from Marvie that they were also interested. Venerts met with Tschetters and provided them a business plan which described the project.

After additional meetings with Venerts, Tschetters eventually invested in [Huron Kitchen LLC, a limited liability company (Huron LLC), which was to construct and own a Country Kitchen restaurant]. Marvie and Kim purchased 6.750 units for $33,750.00, representing one ownership share of a total of eleven in Huron LLC. Clarence and Goldie purchased 13.5 units for $67,500, making them owners of two shares in Huron LLC. An operating agreement was entered into on April 4, 1995 and the Country Kitchen in Huron was opened in the fall of 1995.

Several months later, financing difficulties caused Tschetters and others to personally guarantee loans from First Madison Bank to Huron LLC. Nevertheless, the Country Kitchen continued to experience financial difficulties and closed November 1996. After the restaurant closed, First Madison Bank commenced an action against the personal guarantors, including

Tschetters, to recover the monies loaned. Tschetters responded with cross-claims against Venerts * * *.

Tschetters moved for summary judgment asserting that: 1) the units in the Huron LLC are "securities" * * * and 2) Venerts owed a duty to determine the suitability of Tschetters to invest in Huron LLC. The trial court denied both motions. Tschetters appeal. * * *

* * * *

* * * *[A]n "investment contract" is a "security" when a person 1) invests money 2) in a common enterprise and 3) is led to expect profits solely from the efforts of the promotor or a third party.* [Emphasis added.]

The critical inquiry is the third prong of the * * * test—whether Tschetters were led to expect profits solely from the efforts of the promotor or a third party. * * * [T]he use of the term "solely" is not to be taken literally. Rather, the third prong is satisfied if the efforts made by those other than the investor are the undeniably significant ones, those essential managerial efforts which effect the failure or success of the enterprise. * * * *[T]he definition of a security embodies a flexible rather than a static principle, one that is capable of adaptation to meet the countless and variable schemes devised by those who seek the use of the money of others in the promise of profits.* * * * [T]hree factors * * * aid in this determination: [Emphasis added.]

1. [A]n agreement among the parties leaves so little power in the hands of the partner or venturer that the arrangement in fact distributes power as would a limited partnership; or
2. [T]he partner or venturer is so inexperienced and unknowledgeable in business affairs that he is incapable of intelligently exercising his partnership or venture powers; or
3. [T]he partner or venturer is so dependent on some unique entrepreneurial or managerial ability of the promoter or manager that he cannot replace the manager or the enterprise or otherwise exercise meaningful partnership or venture powers.

* * *

* * * Tschetters had substantial rights and powers. South Dakota law vests the members of an LLC with management powers in proportion to their contribution of capital. The members have the power to elect the managers of the LLC and set their responsibilities.

In addition, the Operating Agreement vested management powers of the Huron LLC in its members, which included Tschetters. These members were given notice of meetings and any member could call a meeting. The day-to-day decisions were made by two managers who were required to be members of the Huron LLC, and selected by the other members. The Huron LLC maintained and provided access to all records of actions taken by its members. Members could authorize loans on behalf of the company by agreement. The members had the authority to select an attorney to review the legal affairs of the Huron LLC. The members had the right to receive profits and distributions when warranted. The members could authorize incidental expenses within an aggregate of $12,500. The members were empowered to make any other routine actions incidental to the day-to-day activity of Huron LLC. The members were allowed to select officers for the Huron LLC and could remove the accountant with or without cause.

The Huron LLC's operating agreement establishes that substantial power and responsibility was vested in its members. The record also establishes that Marvie, acting for all the Tschetters, exercised substantial control over the affairs of Huron LLC. Apparently, Clarence and Goldie acquiesced in relying on Marvie and Kim for information and action. The minutes kept by the Huron LLC show that Tschetters were informed and active in this entity. Tschetters actions on behalf of Huron LLC after the restaurant began to fail shows they were aware of and capable of exercising the powers which they held as members.

* * * *

We hold that the third prong of the * * * test * * * has not been met. In other words:

1. This agreement did not leave so little power in the hands of the partner as a limited partnership would;
2. The partner or venturer was not so inexperienced and unknowledgeable in the business affairs as to be incapable of intelligently exercising his partnership or venture powers; or
3. The partner was not so dependent on some unique entrepreneurial or managerial ability of the promoter or manager that he cannot replace [him] or otherwise exercise meaningful partnership or venture powers.

If an interest in a limited liability company constitutes a "security," then that entity must comply with our securities law or exempt themselves from the application of those laws. This question can only be addressed on a case-by-case basis. Here, Tschetters did not sustain their burden. These "units" were not "securities" under this law * * *.

* * * *

We conclude that the trial court correctly granted summary judgment in favor of Venerts.

DISSENTING OPINION

GILBERTSON, J.

I respectfully dissent * * *. I would hold there is a question of fact as to whether the investment made by the Tschetters constituted a security * * *. I would reverse and remand for trial on this cause of action.

* * * *

The timeline of the events involved in this case is critical when examining the rights held by Tschetters in Huron LLC. * * * By the time the Tschetters received their interests in Huron LLC, their hands had effectively been tied by Venerts through the management agreement with [Country Kitchen]. * * *

While Huron LLC was a separate legal entity, the sole asset of the LLC was the restaurant, which was subject to the management agreement negotiated by Venerts. * * * The economic realities of this situation suggest that the restaurant and Huron LLC were one investment. Without the restaurant, Tschetters would not have invested in Huron LLC. * * * While the terms of the LLC agreement on paper would indicate that Tschetters, as members, were given an opportunity to participate in management decisions, in reality, they were already locked out by the previously signed 15-year management agreement with [Country Kitchen] at the time of their investment. * * *

Furthermore, the applicable test is whether the efforts made by those other than the investor are the undeniably significant ones, those essential managerial efforts which affect the failure or success of the enterprise. Under the terms of the management contract, Tschetters were precluded from exercising any managerial efforts over the enterprise, namely the restaurant.

When the owners of a limited liability company are not expected to exercise control over the day-to-day business operations * * * interests in limited liability companies should be classified as investment contracts, except in those instances in which the investor will be playing a substantial role in the management of the business.

TEST YOUR COMPREHENSION: CASE DETAILS

1. What was the plaintiffs' argument regarding control of the LLC? What did the majority conclude on this issue, and why?
2. What was the dissent's major point concerning the control issue? What was the dissent's reasoning on this point?
3. On what basis might the investors have maintained an action against Country Kitchen?
4. Should there be any effect on the liability of investors in a limited liability entity if the investors have the power to control the enterprise but choose to remain passive?
5. Does the holding in this case indicate legal steps that an investor might take when considering a particular investment?

Registration Statement

Section 5 of the Securities Act of 1933 broadly provides that if a security does not qualify for an exemption, that security must be *registered* before it is offered to the public either through the mails or through any facility of interstate commerce, including securities exchanges. Issuing corporations must file a *registration statement* with the SEC. Investors must be provided with a *prospectus* that describes the security being sold, the issuing corporation, and the risk attaching to the security. In principle, the registration statement and the prospectus supply sufficient information to enable unsophisticated investors to evaluate the financial risk involved.

Contents of the Registration Statement. The registration statement must include the following:

1. A description of the significant provisions of the security offered for sale, including the relationship between that security and the other capital securities of the registrant. Also, the corporation must disclose how it intends to use the proceeds of the sale.
2. A description of the registrant's properties and business.
3. A description of the management of the registrant; its security holdings; and its remuneration (compensation) and other benefits, including pensions and stock options. Any interests of directors or officers in any material transactions with the corporation must be disclosed.

4. A financial statement certified by an independent public accounting firm.
5. A description of pending lawsuits.

Other Requirements. Before filing the registration statement and the prospectus with the SEC, the corporation is allowed to obtain an underwriter who will monitor the distribution of the new issue. There is a twenty-day waiting period (which can be accelerated by the SEC) after registration before the sale can take place. During this period, oral offers between interested investors and the issuing corporation concerning the purchase and sale of the proposed securities may take place, and very limited written advertising is allowed. At this time, what is known as a **red herring** prospectus may be distributed. The name comes from the red legend printed across the prospectus stating that the registration statement has been filed but has not yet become effective.

Red herring • A preliminary prospectus that can be distributed to potential investors after the registration statement (for a securities offering) has been filed with the Securities and Exchange Commission.

Tombstone ad • An advertisement, historically in a format resembling a tombstone, of a securities offering. The ad informs potential investors of where and how they may obtain a prospectus.

After the waiting period, the SEC allows the registration statement to become "effective." The registered securities can then be legally bought and sold. Written advertising is initially allowed in the form of a **tombstone ad,** so named because historically the format resembled a tombstone. Such ads simply tell the investor where and how to obtain a prospectus. Once the registration statement has become effective, other forms of written advertising, called "free writing," are allowed, as long as the advertising is preceded or accompanied by a final prospectus.

Exempt Securities

A number of specific securities are exempt from the registration requirements of the Securities Act of 1933. These securities—which can also generally be resold without being registered—include the following:[11]

1. All bank securities sold prior to July 27, 1933.
2. Commercial paper, if the maturity date does not exceed nine months.
3. Securities of charitable organizations.
4. Securities resulting from a corporate reorganization issued for exchange with the issuer's existing security holders and certificates issued by trustees, receivers, or debtors in possession under the bankruptcy laws.
5. Securities issued exclusively for exchange with the issuer's existing security holders, provided no commission is paid (for example, stock dividends and stock splits).
6. Securities issued to finance the acquisition of railroad equipment.
7. Any insurance, endowment, or annuity contract issued by a state-regulated insurance company.
8. Government-issued securities.
9. Securities issued by banks, savings and loan associations, farmers' cooperatives, and similar institutions subject to supervision by governmental authorities.
10. In consideration of the "small amount involved,"[12] an issuer's offer of up to $5 million in securities in any twelve-month period.

For the last exemption, under Regulation A,[13] the issuer must file with the SEC a notice of the issue and an offering circular, which must also be provided

11. 15 U.S.C. Section 77c.
12. 15 U.S.C. Section 77c(b).
13. 17 C.F.R. Sections 230.251–230.263.

to investors before the sale. This is a much simpler and less expensive process than the procedures associated with full registration. Companies are allowed to "test the waters" for potential interest before preparing the offering circular. (To *test the waters* means to determine potential interest without actually selling any securities or requiring any commitment on the part of those who are interested.) Small-business issuers (companies with less than $25 million in annual revenues and less than $25 million in outstanding voting stock) can also utilize an integrated registration and reporting system that uses simpler forms than the full registration system.

Exhibit 18–2 summarizes the securities (and transactions—discussed next) that are exempt from the registration requirements under the Securities Act of 1933 and SEC regulations.

Exempt Transactions

An issuer of securities that are not exempt under any of the categories listed above can avoid the high cost and complicated procedures associated with registration by taking advantage of certain *exempt transactions*. These exemptions are very broad, and thus many sales occur without registration. Because the exemptions overlap somewhat, an offering may qualify for more than one.

EXHIBIT 18–2 • EXEMPTIONS UNDER THE 1933 ACT FOR SECURITIES OFFERINGS BY BUSINESSES

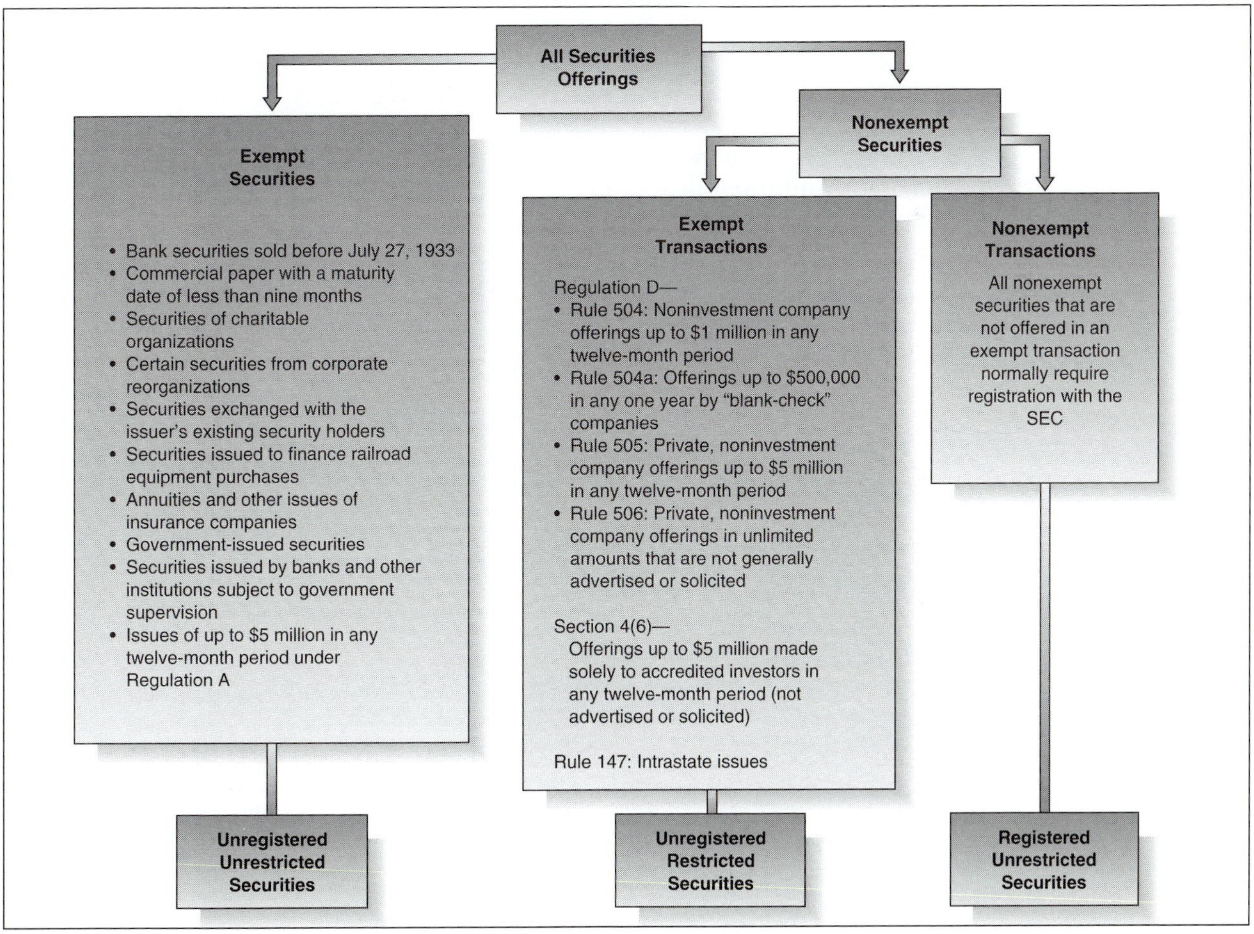

All Securities Offerings

Exempt Securities

- Bank securities sold before July 27, 1933
- Commercial paper with a maturity date of less than nine months
- Securities of charitable organizations
- Certain securities from corporate reorganizations
- Securities exchanged with the issuer's existing security holders
- Securities issued to finance railroad equipment purchases
- Annuities and other issues of insurance companies
- Government-issued securities
- Securities issued by banks and other institutions subject to government supervision
- Issues of up to $5 million in any twelve-month period under Regulation A

→ **Unregistered Unrestricted Securities**

Nonexempt Securities

Exempt Transactions

Regulation D—

- Rule 504: Noninvestment company offerings up to $1 million in any twelve-month period
- Rule 504a: Offerings up to $500,000 in any one year by "blank-check" companies
- Rule 505: Private, noninvestment company offerings up to $5 million in any twelve-month period
- Rule 506: Private, noninvestment company offerings in unlimited amounts that are not generally advertised or solicited

Section 4(6)—
Offerings up to $5 million made solely to accredited investors in any twelve-month period (not advertised or solicited)

Rule 147: Intrastate issues

→ **Unregistered Restricted Securities**

Nonexempt Transactions

All nonexempt securities that are not offered in an exempt transaction normally require registration with the SEC

→ **Registered Unrestricted Securities**

Small Offerings—Regulation D. Regulation D of the SEC contains four separate exemptions from registration requirements for limited offers (offers that either involve a small amount of money or are made in a limited manner). Regulation D provides that any of these offerings made during any twelve-month period are exempt from the registration requirements.

Rule 504. Noninvestment company offerings up to $1 million in any twelve-month period are exempt.[14] In contrast to investment companies (discussed later in this chapter), noninvestment companies are firms that are not engaged primarily in the business of investing or trading in securities.

Rule 504a. Offerings up to $500,000 in any one year by so-called blank-check companies—companies with no specific business plans except to locate and acquire currently unknown businesses or opportunities—are exempt if no general solicitation or advertising is used; the SEC is notified of the sales; and precaution is taken against nonexempt, unregistered resales.[15] The limits on advertising and unregistered resales do not apply if the offering is made solely in states that provide for registration and disclosure and the securities are sold in compliance with those provisions.[16]

Accredited investors • In the context of securities offerings, "sophisticated" investors, such as banks, insurance companies, investment companies, the issuer's executive officers and directors, and persons whose income or net worth exceeds certain limits.

Rule 505. Private, noninvestment company offerings up to $5 million in any twelve-month period are exempt, regardless of the number of **accredited investors** (banks, insurance companies, investment companies, the issuer's executive officers and directors, and persons whose income or net worth exceeds certain limits), so long as there are no more than thirty-five unaccredited investors; no general solicitation or advertising is used; the SEC is notified of the sales; and precaution is taken against nonexempt, unregistered resales. If the sale involves *any* unaccredited investors, *all* investors must be given material information about the offering company, its business, and the securities before the sale. Unlike Rule 506 (discussed next), Rule 505 includes no requirement that the issuer believe each unaccredited investor "has such knowledge and experience in financial and business matters that he is capable of evaluating the merits and the risks of the prospective investment."[17]

Rule 506. Private offerings in unlimited amounts that are not generally solicited or advertised are exempt if the SEC is notified of the sales; precaution is taken against nonexempt, unregistered resales; and the issuer believes that each unaccredited investor has sufficient knowledge or experience in financial matters to be capable of evaluating the investment's merits and risks. There may be no more than thirty-five unaccredited investors, although

---

14. 17 C.F.R. Section 230.504. Rule 504 is the exemption used by most small businesses, but that could change under new SEC Rule 1001. This rule permits, under certain circumstances, "testing the waters" for offerings of up to $5 million *per transaction*. These offerings, however, can be made only to "qualified purchasers" (knowledgeable, sophisticated investors).
15. Precautions to be taken against nonexempt, unregistered resales include asking the investor whether he or she is buying the securities for others; before the sale, disclosing to each purchaser in writing that the securities are unregistered and thus cannot be resold, except in an exempt transaction, without first being registered; and indicating on the certificates that the securities are unregistered and restricted.
16. 17 C.F.R. Section 230.504a.
17. 17 C.F.R. Section 230.505.

there may be an unlimited number of accredited investors. If there are any unaccredited investors, the issuer must provide to all purchasers material information about itself, its business, and the securities before the sale.[18]

This exemption is perhaps the most important one for those firms that want to raise funds through the sale of securities without registering them. It is often referred to as the *private placement* exemption because it exempts "transactions not involving any public offering."[19] This provision applies to private offerings to a limited number of persons who are sufficiently sophisticated and in a sufficiently strong bargaining position to be able to assume the risk of the investment (and who thus have no need for federal registration protection), as well as to private offerings to similarly situated institutional investors.

Small Offerings—Section 4(6). Under Section 4(6) of the Securities Act of 1933, an offer made *solely* to accredited investors is exempt if its amount is not more than $5 million. Any number of accredited investors may participate, but no unaccredited investors may do so. No general solicitation or advertising may be used; the SEC must be notified of all sales; and precaution must be taken against nonexempt, unregistered resales. Precaution is necessary because these are *restricted* securities and may be resold only by registration or in an exempt transaction.[20] (The securities purchased and sold by most people who deal in stock are called, in contrast, *unrestricted* securities.)

Intrastate Issues—Rule 147. Also exempt are intrastate transactions involving purely local offerings.[21] This exemption applies to most offerings that are restricted to residents of the state in which the issuing company is organized and doing business. For nine months after the last sale, virtually no resales may be made to nonresidents, and precautions must be taken against this possibility. These offerings remain subject to applicable laws in the state of issue.

Resales. Most securities can be resold without registration (although some resales may be subject to restrictions, as discussed above in connection with specific exemptions). The Securities Act of 1933 provides exemptions for resales by most persons other than issuers or underwriters. The average investor who sells shares of stock does not have to file a registration statement with the SEC. Resales of restricted securities acquired under Rule 504a, Rule 505, Rule 506, or Section 4(6), however, trigger the registration requirements unless the party selling them complies with Rule 144 or Rule 144A. These rules are sometimes referred to as "safe harbors."

Rule 144. Rule 144 exempts restricted securities from registration on resale if there is adequate current public information about the issuer, the person selling the securities has owned them for at least one year, they are sold in certain limited amounts in unsolicited brokers' transactions, and the SEC is

18. 17 C.F.R. Section 230.506.
19. 15 U.S.C. Section 77d(2).
20. 15 U.S.C. Section 77d(6).
21. 15 U.S.C. Section 77c(a)(11); 17 C.F.R. Section 230.147.

given notice of the resale.[22] "Adequate current public information" consists of the reports that certain companies are required to file under the Securities Exchange Act of 1934. A person who has owned the securities for at least two years is subject to none of these requirements, unless the person is an affiliate. An *affiliate* is one who controls, is controlled by, or is in common control with the issuer. Sales of *nonrestricted* securities by an affiliate are also subject to the requirements for an exemption under Rule 144 (except that the affiliate need not have owned the securities for at least two years).

Rule 144A. Securities that at the time of issue are not of the same class as securities listed on a national securities exchange or quoted in a U.S. automated interdealer quotation system may be resold under Rule 144A.[23] They may be sold only to a qualified institutional buyer (an institution, such as an insurance company, an investment company, or a bank, that owns and invests at least $100 million in securities). The seller must take reasonable steps to ensure that the buyer knows that the seller is relying on the exemption under Rule 144A. A sample restricted stock certificate is shown in Exhibit 18–3.

Violations of the 1933 Act

It is a violation of the Securities Act of 1933 to intentionally defraud investors by misrepresenting or omitting facts in a registration statement or prospectus. Liability is also imposed on those who are negligent for not discovering the fraud. Selling securities before the effective date of the registration statement or under an exemption for which the securities do not qualify results in liability.

Defenses. There are three basic defenses to charges of violations under the 1933 act. Even if a statement was not true or a fact was left out of the registration statement, a defendant can avoid liability if he or she can prove that the statement or omission was not material. A defendant can also avoid liability by proving that the plaintiff knew about the misrepresentation and bought the stock anyway.

Any defendant, except the issuer of the stock, can also assert what is called the *due diligence* defense. To make this defense, a person must prove that she or he reasonably believed, at the time the registration statement became effective, that the statements in it were true and there were no omissions of material facts.

Criminal Penalties. The U.S. Department of Justice brings criminal actions against those who willfully violate the 1933 act. Violators may be penalized by fines up to $10,000, imprisonment up to five years, or both.

Civil Sanctions. The SEC is authorized to seek an injunction against those who willfully violate the 1933 act to prevent further sales of the securities involved. The SEC can also ask the court to grant other relief, such as an order to a violator to refund profits.

Those who purchase the securities and suffer harm as a result of false or omitted statements, or other violations, may bring a suit in a federal court to

22. 17 C.F.R. Section 230.144.
23. 17 C.F.R. Section 230.144A.

EXHIBIT 18–3 • A SAMPLE RESTRICTED STOCK CERTIFICATE

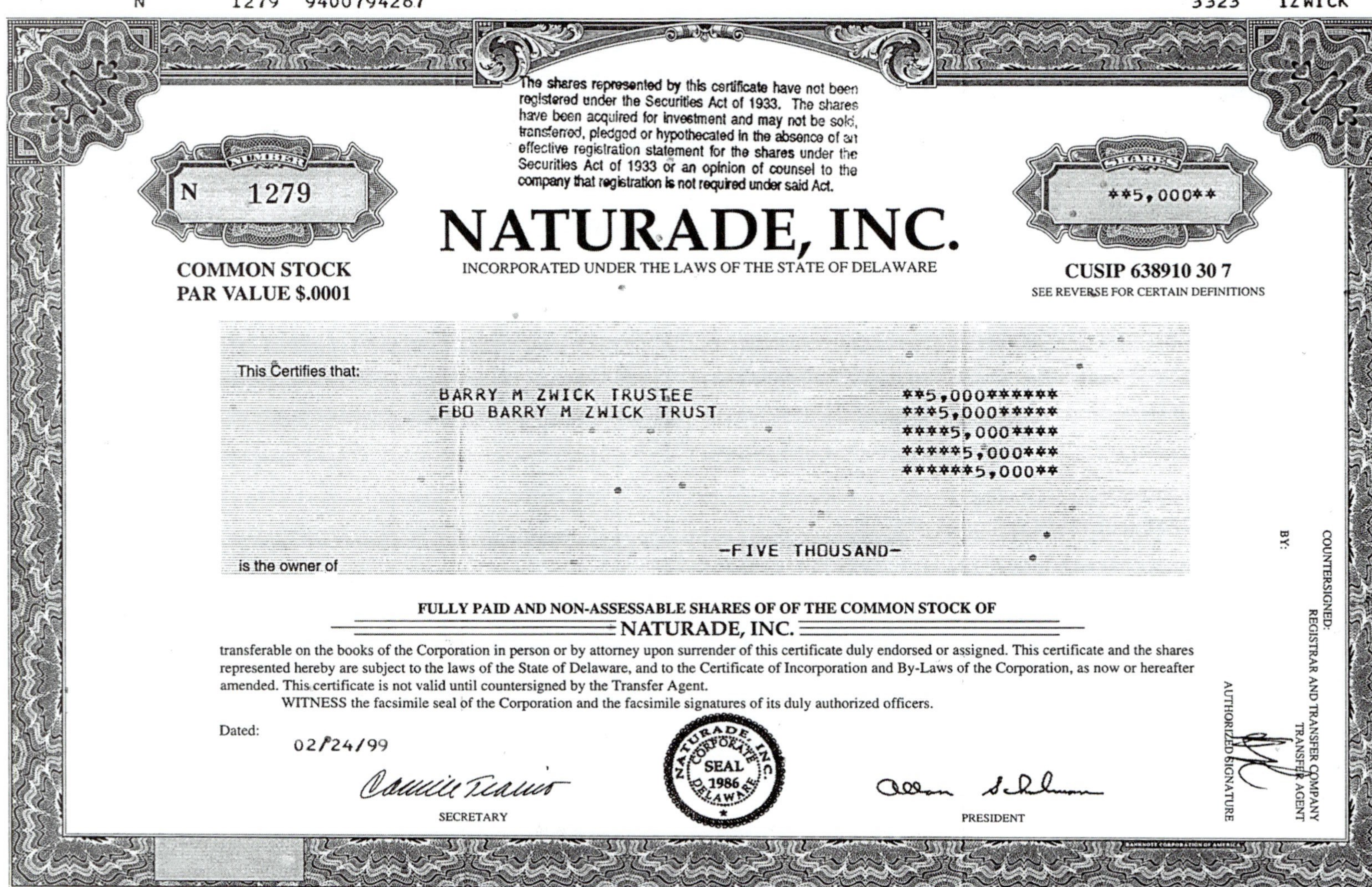

N 1279 9400794267 3323 1ZWICK

NUMBER N 1279

SHARES **5,000**

The shares represented by this certificate have not been registered under the Securities Act of 1933. The shares have been acquired for investment and may not be sold, transferred, pledged or hypothecated in the absence of an effective registration statement for the shares under the Securities Act of 1933 or an opinion of counsel to the company that registration is not required under said Act.

NATURADE, INC.

INCORPORATED UNDER THE LAWS OF THE STATE OF DELAWARE

COMMON STOCK
PAR VALUE $.0001

CUSIP 638910 30 7
SEE REVERSE FOR CERTAIN DEFINITIONS

This Certifies that:

BARRY M ZWICK TRUSTEE
FBO BARRY M ZWICK TRUST

5,000****
5,000**
****5,000****
*****5,000***
******5,000**

is the owner of

-FIVE THOUSAND-

FULLY PAID AND NON-ASSESSABLE SHARES OF OF THE COMMON STOCK OF

NATURADE, INC.

transferable on the books of the Corporation in person or by attorney upon surrender of this certificate duly endorsed or assigned. This certificate and the shares represented hereby are subject to the laws of the State of Delaware, and to the Certificate of Incorporation and By-Laws of the Corporation, as now or hereafter amended. This certificate is not valid until countersigned by the Transfer Agent.

WITNESS the facsimile seal of the Corporation and the facsimile signatures of its duly authorized officers.

Dated: 02/24/99

NATURADE, INC. CORPORATE SEAL 1986 DELAWARE

SECRETARY

PRESIDENT

COUNTERSIGNED:
REGISTRAR AND TRANSFER COMPANY
TRANSFER AGENT

BY:

AUTHORIZED SIGNATURE

recover their losses and other damages. If a registration statement or a prospectus contains false statements or omissions that are material, for example, damages may be imposed on those who signed the statement or those who provided information used in preparing the statement (such as accountants and other experts).

THE SECURITIES EXCHANGE ACT OF 1934

To read the text of the Securities Exchange Act of 1934, go to the "Statutes" page of our Web site at **http://ele.westbuslaw.com**

The Securities Exchange Act of 1934 provides for the regulation and registration of securities exchanges, brokers, dealers, and national securities associations, such as the National Association of Securities Dealers. The SEC regulates the markets in which securities are traded by maintaining a continuous disclosure system for all corporations with securities on the securities exchanges and for those companies that have assets in excess of $10 million and five hundred or more shareholders. These corporations are referred to as Section 12 companies, as they are required to file a registration application with the SEC for their securities under Section 12 of the 1934 act.

The act regulates proxy solicitation for voting, and it allows the SEC to engage in market surveillance to regulate undesirable market practices such as fraud, market manipulation, misrepresentation, and stabilization. (*Stabilization* is a market-manipulating technique in which securities underwriters bid for securities to stabilize their prices during their issuance.)

Section 10(b) and SEC Rule 10b-5

Section 10(b) is one of the most important sections of the Securities Exchange Act of 1934. This section prohibits the use of any manipulative or deceptive device in violation of SEC rules and regulations.

SEC Rule 10b-5 • A rule of the Securities and Exchange Commission that makes it unlawful, in connection with the purchase or sale of any security, to make any untrue statement of a material fact or to omit a material fact if such omission causes the statement to be misleading.

SEC Rule 10b-5. Among the rules prescribed by the SEC is **SEC Rule 10b-5,** which prohibits the commission of fraud in connection with the purchase or sale of any security. Rule 10b-5 states as follows:

> It shall be unlawful for any person, directly or indirectly, by the use of any means or instrumentality of interstate commerce, or of the mails or of any facility of any national securities exchange,
>
> (a) To employ any device, scheme, or artifice to defraud,
>
> (b) To make any untrue statement of a material fact or to omit to state a material fact necessary in order to make the statements made, in the light of the circumstances under which they were made, not misleading, or
>
> (c) To engage in any act, practice, or course of business which operates or would operate as a fraud or deceit upon any person, in connection with the purchase or sale of any security.[24]

Applicability of SEC Rule 10b-5. SEC Rule 10b-5 applies in virtually all situations involving the trading of securities, whether on organized exchanges, in over-the-counter markets, or in private transactions. The rule covers notes, bonds, certificates of interest and participation in any profit-sharing agreement, agreements to form a corporation, and joint-venture agreements; in

24. 17 C.F.R. Section 240.10b-5.

short, the rule covers just about any form of security. It is immaterial whether a firm has securities registered under the 1933 act for the 1934 act to apply.

SEC Rule 10b-5 is applicable only when the requisites of federal jurisdiction (such as the use of the mails, of stock exchange facilities, or of any instrumentality of interstate commerce) are present. Virtually no commercial transaction, however, can be completed without such contact. In addition, the states have corporate securities laws, many of which include provisions similar to SEC Rule 10b-5.

Disclosure Requirements under SEC Rule 10b-5. Any material omission or misrepresentation of material facts in connection with the purchase or sale of a security may violate Section 10(b) and SEC Rule 10b-5. The key to liability (which can be civil or criminal) under this rule is whether the information omitted or misrepresented is *material.*

Examples of Material Facts Calling for Disclosure. The following are some examples of material facts calling for disclosure under the rule:

1. Fraudulent trading in the company stock by a broker-dealer.
2. A dividend change (whether up or down).
3. A contract for the sale of corporate assets.
4. A new discovery, a new process, or a new product.
5. A significant change in the financial condition of the firm.
6. Potential litigation against the company.

Note that none of these facts, in itself, is *automatically* a material fact. Rather, it will be regarded as a material fact if it is significant enough that it will likely affect an investor's decision as to whether to purchase or sell certain securities.

The following case is a landmark decision interpreting SEC Rule 10b-5. The SEC sued several of Texas Gulf Sulphur Company's directors, officers, and employees under SEC Rule 10b-5 after they purchased large amounts of the corporate stock prior to the announcement of a rich ore discovery by the corporation. At issue was whether the ore discovery was a material fact that had to be disclosed under SEC Rule 10b-5.

SEC v. TEXAS GULF SULPHUR CO.

CASE 18.2

United States Court of Appeals, Second Circuit, 1968.
401 F.2d 833.

Texas Gulf Sulphur Company (TGS) conducted aerial geophysical surveys over more than 15,000 square miles of eastern Canada. The operations indicated concentrations of commercially exploitable minerals. At one site near Timmins, Ontario, TGS drilled a hole that appeared to yield a core with an exceedingly high mineral content. TGS kept secret the results of the core sample. Officers and employees of the company made substantial purchases of TGS's stock or accepted stock options after learning of the ore discovery, even though further drilling was necessary to establish whether there was enough ore to be mined commercially. Several months later, TGS announced that the strike was expected to yield at least 25 million tons of ore. Subsequently, the price of TGS stock rose substantially. The Securities and Exchange Commission (SEC) brought suit against the officers and employees of TGS for violating SEC Rule 10b-5. The officers and employees argued that the information on which they had traded had not been material at the time of their trades because the mine had not then been commercially proved. The trial court held that most of the defendants had not violated SEC Rule 10b-5, and the SEC appealed.

WATERMAN, J.

[W]hether facts are material within Rule 10b-5 when the facts relate to a particular event and are undisclosed by those persons who are knowledgeable thereof *will depend at any given time upon a balancing of both the indicated probability that the event will occur and the anticipated magnitude of the event in light of the totality of the company activity.* Here, * * * knowledge of the possibility, which surely was more than marginal, of the existence of a mine of the vast magnitude indicated by the remarkably rich drill core located rather close to the surface (suggesting mineability by the less expensive openpit method) within the confines of a large anomaly (suggesting an extensive region of mineralization) might well have affected the price of TGS stock and would certainly have been an important fact to a reasonable, if speculative, investor in deciding whether he should buy, sell, or hold. [Emphasis added.]

* * * *

* * * [A] major factor in determining whether the * * * discovery was a material fact is the importance attached to the drilling results by those who knew about it. * * * [T]he timing by those who knew of it of their stock purchases * * *—purchases in some cases by individuals who had never before purchased * * * TGS stock—virtually compels the inference that the insiders were influenced by the drilling results.

The appellate court ruled in favor of the SEC. All of the trading by insiders who knew of the mineral find before its true extent had been publicly announced violated SEC Rule 10b-5.

QUESTIONS

1. When the officers and employees of TGS bought their company's stock, did they violate SEC Rule 10b-5, in the opinion of the U.S. Court of Appeals for the Second Circuit?
2. Why did the U.S. Court of Appeals for the Second Circuit reverse the trial court's decision in this case?
3. Suppose that further drilling had revealed that there was not enough ore at this site to be mined commercially. Would the defendants still have been held liable for violating SEC Rule 10b-5?

The Private Securities Litigation Reform Act of 1995. Ironically, one of the effects of SEC Rule 10b-5 was to deter disclosure of forward-looking information. To understand why, consider an example. A company announces that its projected earnings in a certain time period will be X amount. It turns out that the forecast is wrong. The earnings are in fact much lower, and the price of the company's stock is affected—negatively. The shareholders then bring a class-action suit against the company, alleging that the directors violated SEC Rule 10b-5 by disclosing misleading financial information.

In an attempt to rectify this problem and promote disclosure, Congress passed the Private Securities Litigation Reform Act of 1995. Among other things, the act provides a "safe harbor" for publicly held companies that make forward-looking statements, such as financial forecasts. Those who make such statements are protected against federal liability for securities fraud as long as the statements are accompanied by "meaningful cautionary statements identifying important factors that could cause actual results to differ materially from those in the forward-looking statement."[25]

After the 1995 act was passed, a number of securities class-action suits were filed in state courts to skirt the requirements of the 1995 federal act. In response to this problem, Congress passed the Securities Litigation Uniform Standards Act of 1998. This act placed stringent limits on the ability of plaintiffs to bring class-action suits in state courts against firms whose securities are traded on national stock exchanges. Exceptions were made to preserve certain suits brought under state law affecting the conduct of corporate officers with respect to specific corporate actions, including tender offers.

Insider Trading. One of the most important purposes of Section 10(b) and SEC Rule 10b-5 is to prevent **insider trading.** Because of their positions, corporate directors and officers often obtain advance inside information that can affect the future market value of the corporate stock. Obviously, their positions can give them a trading advantage over the general public and shareholders. The 1934 Securities Exchange Act defines inside information and extends liability to officers and directors in their personal transactions for taking advantage of such information when they know that it is unavailable to the person with whom they are dealing.

Insider trading • The purchase or sale of securities on the basis of "inside information" (information that has not been made available to the public) in violation of a duty owed to the company whose stock is being traded.

Section 10(b) and SEC Rule 10b-5 cover not only corporate officers, directors, and majority shareholders but also any persons having access to or receiving information of a nonpublic nature on which trading is based.

ETHICAL ISSUE

Should liability under SEC Rule 10b-5 arise from the mere possession of inside information by a person trading in securities? Suppose that an investor has a plan to trade certain stocks but then, before the trade is actually carried out, comes into possession of inside information relating to that stock. If the investor goes ahead with the trading strategy, should he or she be held liable for violating SEC Rule 10b-5? After all, the investor did not plan to defraud or deceive anyone; he or she simply intended to implement a preexisting financial strategy. For some time, the courts differed in their approach to this question, which clearly has both ethical and legal implications. Some courts concluded that for liability under SEC Rule 10b-5 to arise, an investor had to *use* the inside information in his or her possession.[26] Other courts held that merely *possessing* inside information about certain stocks, while trading in those stocks, was enough to establish liability under SEC Rule 10b-5.[27] To clarify this issue, the SEC adopted a new rule in 2000, Rule 10b5-1.[28] Generally, the rule allows corporate insiders to engage in prearranged or certain other securities transactions without being subject to liability under SEC Rule 10b-5. In other words, a corporate insider is now permitted to buy or sell stock without having

25. 15 U.S.C. Sections 77z-2, 78u-5.
26. See, for example, *United States v. Smith,* 155 F.3d 1051 (9th Cir. 1998).
27. See, for example, *United States v. Teicher,* 987 F.2d 112 (2d Cir. 1993).
28. 65 F.R. 51716 (August 24, 2000).

to worry about liability if she or he, *after* deciding to buy or sell a stock, learns inside information relating to that stock.

Outsiders and SEC Rule 10b-5. The traditional insider-trading case involves true insiders—corporate officers, directors, and majority shareholders who have access to (and trade on) inside information. Increasingly, however, liability under Section 10(b) of the 1934 act and SEC Rule 10b-5 has been extended to include certain "outsiders"—those who trade on inside information acquired indirectly. Two theories have been developed under which outsiders may be held liable for insider trading: the *tipper/tippee theory* and the *misappropriation theory*.

Tippee • A person who receives inside information.

Tipper/Tippee Theory. Anyone who acquires inside information as a result of a corporate insider's breach of his or her fiduciary duty can be liable under SEC Rule 10b-5. This liability extends to **tippees** (those who receive "tips" from insiders) and even remote tippees (tippees of tippees).

The key to liability under this theory is that the inside information must be obtained as a result of someone's breach of a fiduciary duty to the corporation whose shares are traded. Unless there is a breach of a duty not to disclose inside information, the disclosure is made in exchange for personal benefit, and the tippee knows of this breach (or should know of it) and benefits from it, there is no liability under this theory.[29]

Misappropriation Theory. Liability for insider trading may also be established under the misappropriation theory. This theory holds that if an individual wrongfully obtains (misappropriates) inside information and trades on it for her or his personal gain, then the individual should be held liable because, in essence, the individual stole information rightfully belonging to another.

The misappropriation theory has been controversial because it significantly extends the reach of SEC Rule 10b-5 to outsiders who ordinarily would not be deemed fiduciaries of the corporations in whose stock they trade. In the following case, the United States Supreme Court addressed the issue of whether liability under SEC Rule 10b-5 can be based on the misappropriation theory.

29. See, for example, *Chiarella v. United States,* 445 U.S. 222, 100 S.Ct. 1108, 63 L.Ed.2d 348 (1980); and *Dirks v. SEC,* 463 U.S. 646, 103 S.Ct. 3255, 77 L.Ed.2d 911 (1983).

CASE 18.3

Supreme Court of the United States, 1997.
521 U.S. 642,
117 S.Ct. 2199,
138 L.Ed.2d 724.
http://supct.law.cornell.edu/supct/cases/disk.htm[a]

UNITED STATES v. O'HAGAN

James O'Hagan was a partner in the law firm of Dorsey & Whitney. Grand Metropolitan PLC (Grand Met) hired Dorsey & Whitney to assist in a takeover of the Pillsbury Company. Before Grand Met made its tender offer, O'Hagan bought shares of Pillsbury stock. When the tender offer was announced, the price of Pillsbury stock

a. This page provides access to some of the published opinions of the United States Supreme Court. In the "Search" box, type in the *O'Hagan* case name and click on "Submit" to access the Court's opinion.

increased more than 35 percent. O'Hagan sold his shares for a profit of more than $4 million. The Securities and Exchange Commission (SEC) prosecuted O'Hagan for, among other things, securities fraud in violation of Rule 10b-5 under the misappropriation theory. The SEC contended that O'Hagan breached fiduciary duties he owed to his law firm and Grand Met. When O'Hagan was convicted, he appealed to the U.S. Court of Appeals for the Eighth Circuit, which reversed the conviction. The SEC appealed to the United States Supreme Court.

GINSBURG, J.

[M]isappropriation * * * satisfies [Section] 10(b)'s requirement that chargeable conduct involve a "deceptive device or contrivance" used "in connection with" the purchase or sale of securities. * * * [M]isappropriators * * * deal in deception. A fiduciary who pretends loyalty to the principal while secretly converting the principal's information for personal gain dupes or defrauds the principal.

* * * *

* * * [T]he fiduciary's fraud is consummated [brought to fruition, fulfilled] * * * when, without disclosure to his principal, he uses the information to purchase or sell securities. * * *

* * * *

* * * An investor's informational disadvantage vis-à-vis a misappropriator with material, nonpublic information stems from contrivance, not luck; it is a disadvantage that cannot be overcome with research or skill.

The United States Supreme Court held that liability under Rule 10b-5 can be based on the misappropriation theory, reversed the lower court's judgment, and remanded the case.

QUESTIONS

1. Who was the plaintiff in this case, and what was the plaintiff's contention?
2. According to the judgment of the United States Supreme Court, can liability under SEC Rule 10b-5 be based on the misappropriation theory?
3. What were the reasons for the decision of the United States Supreme Court in this case?

Insider Reporting and Trading—Section 16(b)

Officers, directors, and certain large stockholders of Section 12 corporations (stockholders owning 10 percent of the class of equity securities registered under Section 12 of the 1934 act) are required to file reports with the SEC concerning their ownership and trading of the corporation's securities.[30] To discourage such insiders from using nonpublic information about their companies to their personal benefit in the stock market, Section 16(b) of the 1934 act provides for the recapture by the corporation of all profits realized

30. 15 U.S.C. Section 78l. Note that Section 403 of the Sarbanes-Oxley Act of 2002 speeds up the reporting deadlines specified in Section 16(b).

by the insider on any purchase and sale or sale and purchase of the corporation's stock within any six-month period. It is irrelevant whether the insider actually uses inside information; *all such short-swing profits must be returned to the corporation.*

Section 16(b) applies not only to stock but also to warrants, options, and securities convertible into stock. In addition, the courts have fashioned complex rules for determining profits. The SEC exempts a number of transactions under Rule 16b-3.[31] For all of these reasons, corporate insiders are wise to seek competent counsel prior to trading in the corporation's stock. Exhibit 18–4 compares the effects of SEC Rule 10b-5 and Section 16(b).

Proxy Statements

Section 14(a) of the Securities Exchange Act of 1934 regulates the solicitation of proxies from shareholders of Section 12 companies. The SEC regulates the content of proxy statements, which are statements sent to shareholders by corporate managers and others who are requesting authority to vote on behalf of the shareholders in a particular election on specified issues.

Whoever solicits a proxy must fully and accurately disclose in the proxy statement all of the facts that are pertinent to the matter on which the shareholders are to vote. SEC Rule 14a-9 is similar to the antifraud provisions of SEC Rule 10b-5. Remedies for violations are extensive, ranging from injunctions to prevent a vote from being taken to monetary damages.

31. 17 C.F.R. Section 240.16b-3.

EXHIBIT 18–4 • COMPARISON OF COVERAGE, APPLICATION, AND LIABILITY UNDER SEC RULE 10b-5 AND SECTION 16(b)

	RULE 10b-5	SECTION 16(b)
Subject matter of transaction	Any security (does not have to be registered).	Any security (does not have to be registered).
Transactions covered	Purchase or sale.	Short-swing purchase and sale or short-swing sale and purchase.
Who is subject to liability?	Virtually anyone with inside information under a duty to disclose—including officers, directors, controlling stockholders, and tippees.	Officers, directors, and certain holders of large amounts of stock.
Is omission or misrepresentation necessary for liability?	Yes.	No.
Any exempt transactions?	No.	Yes, a variety of exemptions.
Is direct dealing with the party necessary?	No.	No.
Who may bring an action?	A person transacting with an insider, the SEC, or a purchaser or seller damaged by a wrongful act.	Corporation and shareholder by derivative action.

Violations of the 1934 Act

As mentioned earlier, violations of Section 10(b) and Rule 10b-5 of the Securities Exchange Act of 1934 include insider trading. This is a criminal offense, with criminal penalties. Violators of these laws may also be subject to civil liability. For any sanctions to be imposed, however, there must be ***scienter***[32]—the violator must have had an intent to defraud or knowledge of his or her misconduct. *Scienter* can be proved by showing that a defendant made false statements or wrongfully failed to disclose material facts.

Scienter • Knowledge by the misrepresenting party that material facts have been falsely presented or omitted with an intent to deceive.

Violations of Section 16(b) include the sale by insiders of stock acquired less than six months before the sale. These violations are subject to civil sanctions. Liability under Section 16(b) is strict liability. Neither *scienter* nor negligence is required.

In the following case, investors charged a corporation with violating Section 10(b) and SEC Rule 10b-5. The question before the court was whether the investors alleged sufficient facts to indicate *scienter.*

32. Pronounced sy-*en*-ter.

In re MCI WORLDCOM, INC., SECURITIES LITIGATION

CASE 18.4

United States District Court, Eastern District of New York, 2000. 93 F.Supp.2d 276.

In early 1999, MCI WorldCom, Inc., began negotiating to buy SkyTel Communications, Inc., then a leading provider of wireless messaging services. When investors heard rumors of the deal, the price of SkyTel stock rose 12 percent. On the morning of May 25, an Internet news service, the Company Sleuth, reported that MCI had registered "skytelworldcom.com" as an Internet domain name.[a] *SkyTel's stock price rose 16 percent before noon. At noon, Barbara Gibson, an MCI spokesperson and senior manager of corporate communication, told the media that the name registration was done by an employee acting alone and "is not an indication of official company intention." Immediately following Gibson's statement, SkyTel's stock price fell to less than the previous day's price. On May 28, MCI announced that it would buy all of SkyTel's stock for $1.3 billion. Paul Curnin and other investors who sold the stock between May 25 and 28 filed a suit in a federal district court against MCI, alleging violations of Section 10(b) and SEC Rule 10b-5. MCI filed a motion to dismiss.*

GLASSER, J.

[A] plaintiff can plead [*scienter*] in one of two ways: (1) by identifying circumstances indicating conscious or reckless behavior by the defendant, or (2) by alleging facts showing a motive to commit fraud and a clear opportunity to do so. * * *

* * * *

To show motive, plaintiffs must show concrete benefits to a defendant that could be realized by one or more of the false statements and wrongful nondisclosures alleged. * * * Plaintiffs assert that MCI was motivated to artificially deflate the price of SkyTel stock in order to help ensure that the acquisition price would not have to be increased. It also did so to make the intended takeover [of SkyTel] more attractive and at a higher premium than if SkyTel's stock price had remained higher because of the merger rumors reignited by the

a. It is common for business firms to register domain names before their actual use to protect them from cybersquatters—see Chapter 13.

news stories reporting on the registration of the skytelworldcom.com domain name. [Emphasis added.]

* * * *

In response, defendant asserts that plaintiffs fail to allege that Gibson had any knowledge of the confidential merger negotiations, and that such knowledge cannot be assumed or conclusorily [positively] asserted. MCI argues that if Gibson is not alleged to have had any knowledge of the confidential merger negotiations, opportunity has not been sufficiently alleged. * * * [I]t is reasonable to assume the official MCI spokesperson, the Senior Manager of Corporation Communications at MCI, did know of an impending merger which was announced three days later.

* * * *

* * * Defendant argues that its alleged motive is insufficient as a matter of law because the alleged fraud did not entail any "concrete" economic benefit to MCI and, therefore, it was not in MCI's economic interests to deflate the price of SkyTel shares.

* * * [B]eing able to acquire a company for a significantly reduced price is a sufficient economic benefit to satisfy the motive requirement for *scienter.* * * *

* * * *

Plaintiffs have also alleged facts that constitute strong circumstantial evidence of conscious misbehavior or recklessness by MCI. * * * [T]hree days prior to the announcement of the merger, MCI's official corporate spokesperson falsely denied any "official company intention" regarding the registration of a domain name that was an obvious combination of MCI's and SkyTel's names. The [investors] understood the denial to mean there would be no takeover, as evidenced by the drop in SkyTel's price. * * * [I]t was MCI itself that registered the domain name, and not, as Ms. Gibson suggested, an MCI employee acting alone.

The court denied the motion to dismiss. The investors successfully alleged scienter *through motive and opportunity, as well as facts from which an inference of conscious misbehavior or recklessness could be drawn.*

QUESTIONS

1. Did the shareholders properly allege *scienter* in this case, in the opinion of the court?
2. If, instead of implying a lack of intent to buy SkyTel, MCI's spokesperson had made public the information about the firm's negotiations with SkyTel, would the outcome of the litigation have been affected?
3. What effect has the Internet had on the opportunity to commit violations of the securities laws, as well as to avoid such violations?

Criminal Penalties. For violations of Section 10(b) and Rule 10b-5, an individual may be fined up to $5 million, imprisoned for up to twenty years, or both.[33] A partnership or a corporation may be fined up to $25 million. Under

33. These numbers reflect the increased penalties imposed by the Sarbanes-Oxley Act of 2002.

Section 807 of the Sarbanes-Oxley Act of 2002, for a willful violation of the 1934 act the violator may, in addition to being subject to a fine, be imprisoned for up to twenty-five years.

Civil Sanctions. Both the SEC and private parties can bring actions to seek civil sanctions against violators of the 1934 act.

SEC Actions against Violators. The Insider Trading Sanctions Act of 1984 permits the SEC to bring suit in a federal district court against anyone violating, or aiding in a violation of, the 1934 act or SEC rules by purchasing or selling a security while in the possession of material nonpublic information.[34] The violation must occur on or through the facilities of a national securities exchange or from or through a broker or dealer. Transactions pursuant to a public offering by an issuer of securities are excepted. The court may assess as a penalty as much as triple the profits gained or the loss avoided by the guilty party. Profit or loss is defined as "the difference between the purchase or sale price of the security and the value of that security as measured by the trading price of the security at a reasonable period of time after public dissemination of the nonpublic information."[35]

The Insider Trading and Securities Fraud Enforcement Act of 1988 enlarged the class of persons who may be subject to civil liability for insider-trading violations. This act also gave the SEC authority to award **bounty payments** (rewards given by government officials for acts beneficial to the state) to persons providing information leading to the prosecution of insider-trading violations.[36]

Bounty payment • A reward (payment) given to a person or persons who perform a certain service—such as informing government authorities of illegal actions.

Private Actions against Violators. Private parties may also sue violators of Section 10(b) and Rule 10b-5. A private party may obtain rescission of a contract to buy securities or damages to the extent of the violator's illegal profits. Those found liable have a right to seek contribution from those who share responsibility for the violations, including accountants, attorneys, and corporations.[37] For violations of Section 16(b), a corporation can bring an action to recover the short-swing profits.

Regulation of Investment Companies

Investment companies, and mutual funds in particular, grew rapidly after World War II. **Investment companies** act on behalf of many smaller shareholders/owners by buying a large portfolio of securities and managing that portfolio professionally. A **mutual fund** is a specific type of investment company that continually buys or sells to investors shares of ownership in a portfolio. Such companies are regulated by the Investment Company Act of 1940,[38] which provides for SEC regulation of their activities. The 1940 act was

Investment company • A company that acts on behalf of many smaller shareholders/owners by buying a large portfolio of securities and professionally managing that portfolio.

Mutual fund • A specific type of investment company that continually buys or sells to investors shares of ownership in a portfolio.

34. 15 U.S.C. Section 78u(d)(2)(A).
35. 15 U.S.C. Section 78u(d)(2)(C).
36. 15 U.S.C. Section 78u-1.
37. Note that a private cause of action under Section 10(b) and SEC Rule 10b-5 cannot be brought against accountants, attorneys, and others who "aid and abet" violations of the act. Only the SEC can bring actions against so-called aiders and abettors. See *SEC v. Fehn,* 97 F.3d 1276 (9th Cir. 1996).
38. 15 U.S.C. Sections 80a-1 to 80a-64.

expanded by the Investment Company Act Amendments of 1970. Further minor changes were made in the Securities Acts Amendments of 1975. The National Securities Markets Improvement Act of 1996 increased the SEC's authority to regulate investment companies by limiting virtually all of the authority of the states to regulate these enterprises.

Definition of an Investment Company

For the purposes of the act, an *investment company* is defined as any entity that (1) "is . . . engaged primarily . . . in the business of investing, reinvesting, or trading in securities" or (2) is engaged in such business and more than 40 percent of the company's assets consist of investment securities. Excluded from coverage by the act are banks, insurance companies, savings and loan associations, finance companies, oil and gas drilling firms, charitable foundations, tax-exempt pension funds, and other special types of institutions, such as closely held corporations.

Registration and Reporting Requirements

The 1940 act requires that every investment company register with the SEC by filing a notification of registration. Each year, registered investment companies must file reports with the SEC. To safeguard company assets, all securities must be held in the custody of a bank or stock exchange member, and that bank or stock exchange member must follow strict procedures established by the SEC.

Restrictions on Investment Companies

The 1940 act also imposes restrictions on the activities of investment companies and persons connected with them. For example, investment companies are not allowed to purchase securities on the margin (pay only part of the total price, borrowing the rest), sell short (sell shares not yet owned), or participate in joint trading accounts. Additionally, no dividends may be paid from any source other than accumulated, undistributed net income.

State Securities Laws

Blue sky laws • State laws that regulate the offer and sale of securities.

Today, all states have their own corporate securities laws, or **blue sky laws,** that regulate the offer and sale of securities within individual state borders. (The phrase *blue sky laws* dates to a 1917 United States Supreme Court decision in which the Court declared that the purpose of such laws was to prevent "speculative schemes which have no more basis than so many feet of 'blue sky.'"[39]) Article 8 of the Uniform Commercial Code, which has been adopted by all of the states, also imposes various requirements relating to the purchase and sale of securities.

Requirements under State Securities Laws

Despite some differences in philosophy, all state blue sky laws have certain common features. Typically, state laws have disclosure requirements and antifraud provisions, many of which are patterned after Section 10(b) of the Securities Exchange Act of 1934 and SEC Rule 10b-5. State laws also provide

39. *Hall v. Geiger-Jones Co.,* 242 U.S. 539, 37 S.Ct. 217, 61 L.Ed. 480 (1917).

for the registration or qualification of securities offered or issued for sale within the state and impose disclosure requirements. Unless an exemption from registration is applicable, issuers must register or qualify their stock with the appropriate state official, often called a *corporations commissioner.* Most state securities laws also regulate securities brokers and dealers. The Uniform Securities Act, which has been adopted in part by several states, was drafted to be acceptable to states with differing regulatory philosophies.

Concurrent Regulation

State securities laws apply mainly to intrastate transactions. Since the adoption of the 1933 and 1934 federal securities acts, the state and federal governments have regulated securities concurrently. Issuers must comply with both federal and state securities laws, and exemptions from federal law are not necessarily exemptions from state laws.

The dual federal and state system has not always worked well, particularly during the early 1990s, when there was considerable expansion of the securities markets. The National Securities Markets Improvement Act of 1996 eliminated some of the duplicate regulations. While the states still regulate local and regional matters, the SEC exclusively regulates most national securities activities.

Online Securities Offerings and Disclosures

The Spring Street Brewing Company, headquartered in New York, made history when it became the first company to attempt to sell securities via the Internet. Through its online *initial public offering (IPO),* which ended in early 1996, Spring Street raised about $1.6 million—without having to pay any commissions to brokers or underwriters. The offering was made pursuant to Regulation A, which, as mentioned earlier in this chapter, allows small-business issuers to use a simplified registration procedure.

Such online IPOs are particularly attractive to small companies and start-up ventures that may find it difficult to raise capital from institutional investors or through underwriters. By making the offering online under Regulation A, the company can avoid both commissions and the costly and time-consuming filings required for a traditional IPO under federal and state law.

Clearly, technological advances have affected the securities industry—and securities law—just as they have affected other areas of the law. Corporations are now using the Internet to communicate information to the SEC, shareholders, potential investors, and others. Indeed, as you will read shortly, the SEC has changed or modified a number of its rules to encourage online filings of securities documents, including prospectuses.

Investors, in turn, can now use the Internet to access information that can help them make informed decisions. The SEC's EDGAR (Electronic Data Gathering, Analysis, and Retrieval) database includes IPOs, proxy statements, annual corporate reports, registration statements, and other documents that have been filed with the commission. (See this chapter's *Law on the Web* section for instructions on how to access the EDGAR database.) These and other developments have brought about what one scholar called a "near-revolution" in the way securities are issued and traded.[40]

---

40. Robert A. Prentice, "The Future of Corporate Disclosure: The Internet, Securities Fraud, and Rule 10b-5," 47 *Emory Law Journal* 1 (Winter 1998).

Suppose there is a discrepancy between a graph in a printed prospectus and the description of that graph in the electronic version of the prospectus filed with the SEC via the EDGAR database. Is the accompanying registration statement invalid? That was the question in the following case.

CASE 18.5

United States Court of Appeals, Second Circuit, 2003. 318 F.3d 170. **http://laws.lp.findlaw.com/2nd/017505.html**[a]

DeMARIA v. ANDERSEN

Bankrate, Inc., produces, syndicates, and publishes financial information on the Internet. In March 1999, in anticipation of an IPO, Bankrate, which was then known as ILife.com, Inc., filed a registration statement and a prospectus with the SEC via the EDGAR database. ILife.com also distributed a printed version of the prospectus to the public. Due to an apparently inadvertent error, the EDGAR prospectus inaccurately summarized a bar graph that appeared in the printed prospectus. The graph reported online publishing revenue and losses, but the summary incorrectly identified the losses as revenue and did not mention losses. The SEC declared the statement effective for an IPO of 3.5 million shares at $13 per share. Three days later, the stock closed at $10.50 per share. By August, the stock was trading at about $0.67 per share. Brian DeMaria and other investors filed a suit in a federal district court against William Andersen, an ILife.com officer, and others, arguing that because of the inaccurate summary, the securities in the IPO were "unregistered" and thus were sold in violation of the Securities Act of 1933. The court dismissed this claim. The plaintiffs appealed to the U.S. Court of Appeals for the Second Circuit.

WALKER, C.J.

Because of the novelty and importance of the issues raised in this appeal, we requested and received briefing from the SEC as *amicus curiae*[b] on a number of discrete questions after oral argument [by the plaintiffs' and defendants' attorneys].

* * * *

On appeal, plaintiffs argue that the district court erred * * * in dismissing their Section 12 * * * claim * * * .

* * * *

Section 12 of the 1933 [Securities] Act provides that "[a]ny person who * * * offers or sells a security in violation of [Section 5] * * * shall be liable * * * to the person purchasing such security from him." Section 5, in turn, states that "[u]nless a registration statement is in effect as to a security, it shall be unlawful" to sell or carry such security through interstate commerce or the mails.

* * * In this case, plaintiffs' [Section 12] claim is based on the theory that due to the error in the EDGAR Prospectus, the shares sold in the ILife IPO were unregistered, in violation of [Section] 5. * * * Plaintiffs contend that "[t]here is no compliance with Section 5 when the prospectus which is distributed to the public is not the same prospectus which has been declared

a. This is a page within the FindLaw Web site. FindLaw is now a part of West Group.

b. The Latin word *amicus* means "friend," and the phrase *amicus curiae* means "friend of the court." In the context of an appeal, a party who has a strong interest in the case, but who is not a party to the action, may file an *amicus* brief to suggest a rationale consistent with its own views. *Amicus* briefs are commonly filed in appeals of cases that concern matters of broad public interest. Sometimes, as in this case, the court requests *amicus* filings.

effective by the SEC." Arguing that the shares sold in the ILife IPO were sold pursuant to the Printed Prospectus, rather than the EDGAR Prospectus declared effective by the SEC, plaintiffs claim a violation of [Section] 5 and seek * * * damages under [Section 12].

We reject plaintiffs' argument because it rests on an erroneous interpretation of the regulations pertaining to SEC filings. [SEC] Rule 304[c] provides the rules and regulations for preparing EDGAR filings that include graphic, image or audio material as follows:

> (a) If a filer includes graphic, image or audio material in a document delivered to investors and others that cannot be reproduced in an electronic filing, the electronically filed version of that document shall include a fair and accurate narrative description, tabular representation or transcript of the omitted material * * *.
> (b)(1) The graphic, image and audio material in the version of a document delivered to investors and others shall be deemed part of the electronic filing and subject to the liability and anti-fraud provisions of the federal securities laws. * * *
> (2) Narrative descriptions, tabular representations or transcripts of graphic, image and audio material included in an electronic filing or appendix thereto also shall be deemed part of the filing. However, to the extent such descriptions, representations or transcripts represent a good faith effort to fairly and accurately describe omitted graphic, image or audio material, they shall not be subject to the liability and anti-fraud provisions of the federal securities laws.

* * * Plaintiffs contend that * * * subsection (b) of Rule 304 is applicable only "*if* and *when* Rule 304(a) has been satisfied."

In its *amicus* brief, the SEC asserts that

> [t]he "fair and accurate" requirement of Section 304(a) is not a precondition to a Printed Prospectus being "deemed part of" the EDGAR registration statement under Rule 304(b)(1). The two subsections operate independently, and nothing in the rule makes compliance with Section 304(a) a predicate condition to Section 304(b)(1).

Subsection (b) not only provides that the graphic, image and audio material is "deemed part of the electronic filing," but also establishes that these materials are "subject to the liability and antifraud provisions of the federal securities laws." Accordingly, as the SEC explains, *the purpose of Rule 304(b) is simply "to assure that the graphic material is subject to civil liability that relates to false or misleading statements in the registration statement."* In light of this purpose, plaintiffs' assertion that Rule 304(b) liability is contingent upon satisfaction of Rule 304(a)'s "fair and accurate" requirement makes no sense. [Emphasis added.]

*We are bound by the SEC's interpretations of its regulations * * * unless they are plainly erroneous or inconsistent with the regulations.* Because that deferential standard is easily met here, we adopt the SEC's position, which is dispositive of [decisive in relation to] plaintiffs' [Section 12] claim. Accordingly, we hold that the district court was correct in considering the graphic material contained in the Printed Prospectus to be part of the EDGAR Prospectus and registration statement in determining whether the ILife securities were unregistered and sold in violation of the 1933 Act. In a case such as this one, where the only claimed error in an electronically filed prospectus is an inaccurate summary of the graphic, audio, or visual material contained in the

c. 17 C.F.R. Section 232.304.

Printed Prospectus, the printed prospectus conforms to the registration statement * * *, and its distribution to investors cannot form the basis for a claim under Section 12 * * *. We thus affirm the district court's dismissal of plaintiffs' [Section 12] claim. [Emphasis added.]

The U.S. Court of Appeals for the Second Circuit affirmed the lower court's dismissal of the plaintiffs' claim. Under the SEC's rules, the graph in the printed prospectus was considered part of the EDGAR prospectus and registration statement. Because the printed prospectus conformed to the statement, the sale of the securities was not "unregistered."

QUESTIONS

1. What was the basis for the plaintiffs' claim in this case that the defendants violated Section 12 of the Securities Act of 1933?
2. For what reasons did the U.S. Court of Appeals for the Second Circuit affirm the lower court's ruling in this case?
3. Does deeming a printed prospectus to be part of a registration statement completely absolve those who sign the statement from any liability under the securities laws?

Regulations Governing Online Securities Offerings

One of the early questions posed by online offerings was whether the delivery of securities *information* via the Internet met the requirements of the 1933 Securities Act, which traditionally were applied to the delivery of paper documents. In an interpretative release issued in 1995, the SEC stated that "[t]he use of electronic media should be at least an equal alternative to the use of paper-based media" and that anything that can be delivered in paper form under the current securities laws might also be delivered in electronic form.[41] For example, a prospectus in downloadable form will meet SEC requirements.

Basically, there has been no change in the substantive law of disclosure; only the delivery vehicle has changed. When the Internet is used for delivery of a prospectus, the same rules apply as for the delivery of a paper prospectus. These rules are as follows:

1. *Timely and adequate notice of the delivery of information is required.* Hosting a prospectus on a Web site does not constitute adequate notice, but separate e-mails or even postcards will satisfy the SEC's notice requirements.
2. *The online communication system must be easily accessible.* This is very simple to do today because virtually anyone interested in purchasing securities has access to the Web.
3. *Some evidence of delivery must be created.* This requirement is relatively easy to satisfy. Those making online offerings can require an e-mail return receipt verification of any materials sent electronically.

---

41. "Use of Electronic Media for Delivery Purposes," Securities Act Release No. 33-7233 (October 6, 1995). The rules governing the use of electronic transmissions for delivery purposes were subsequently confirmed in Securities Act Release No. 33-7289 (May 9, 1996) and expanded in Securities Act Release No. 33-7856 (April 28, 2000).

Once these three requirements have been satisfied, the prospectus has been successfully delivered.

Potential Liability Created by Online Offering Materials

All printed prospectuses indicate that only the information given in the prospectuses can be used in making an investment decision in the securities offered. The same wording, of course, appears on Web-based offerings. Those who create such Web-based offerings may be tempted, however, to go one step further. They may include hyperlinks to other sites that have analyzed the future prospects of the company, the products and services sold by the company, or the offering itself. To avoid potential liability, however, online offerors (the entities making the offerings) need to exercise caution when including such hyperlinks.

Suppose that a hyperlink goes to an analyst's Web page on which the company making the offering is heavily touted. Further suppose that after the IPO, the stock price falls. By including the hyperlink on its Web site, the offering company is impliedly supporting the information presented on the linked page. In such a situation, the company may be liable under federal securities laws.[42]

Potential problems may also occur with some Regulation D offerings, if the offeror places the offering circular on its Web site for general consumption by anybody on the Internet. Because Regulation D offerings are private placements, general solicitation is restricted. If anyone can have access to the offering circular on the Web, the Regulation D exemption may be disqualified.

Online Securities Offerings by Foreign Companies

Online securities offerings by foreign companies may also present problems. Traditionally, foreign companies have not been able to offer new shares to the U.S. public without first registering them with the SEC. Today, however, anybody in the world can offer shares of stock worldwide via the Web.

The SEC asks that foreign issuers on the Internet implement measures to warn U.S. investors. For example, a foreign company offering shares of stock on the Internet must include a disclaimer on its Web site stating that it has not gone through the registration procedure in the United States. If the SEC believes that a Web site's offering of foreign securities has been targeted at U.S. residents, it will pursue that company in an attempt to require it to register in the United States.[43]

Online Securities Fraud

The Internet, of course, has also been used to commit fraud. A major problem facing the SEC today is how to enforce the antifraud provisions of the securities laws in the online environment. In 1999, in the first cases involving illegal online securities offerings, the SEC filed suit against three individuals for illegally offering securities on an Internet auction site.[44] In essence, all three

42. See, for example, *In re Syntex Corp. Securities Litigation,* 95 F.3d 922 (9th Cir. 1996).

43. International Series Release No. 1125 (March 23, 1998).

44. *In re Davis,* SEC Administrative File No. 3-10080 (October 20, 1999); *In re Haas,* SEC Administrative File No. 3-10081 (October 20, 1999); *In re Sitaras,* SEC Administrative File No. 3-10082 (October 20, 1999).

indicated that their companies would go public soon and attempted to sell unregistered securities via the Web auction site. All of these actions were in violation of Sections 5, 17(a)(1), and 17(a)(3) of the 1933 Securities Act. Since then, the SEC has brought a variety of Internet-related fraud cases, including cases involving investment scams and the manipulation of stock prices in Internet chat rooms.

Investment Scams

An ongoing problem for the SEC is how to curb investment scams. One fraudulent investment scheme involved twenty thousand investors, who lost, in all, more than $3 million. Some cases have involved false claims about the earnings potential of home-business programs, such as the claim that one could "earn $4,000 or more each month." Others have concerned claims of "guaranteed credit repair."

Using Chat Rooms to Manipulate Stock Prices

"Pumping and dumping" occurs when a person who has purchased a particular stock heavily promotes ("pumps up") that stock—thereby creating a great demand for it and driving up its price—and then sells ("dumps") it. The practice of pumping up a stock and then dumping it is quite old. In the online world, however, the process can occur much more quickly and efficiently.

The most famous case in this area involved Jonathan Lebed, a fifteen-year-old stock trader and Internet user from New Jersey. Lebed was the first minor ever charged with securities fraud by the SEC, but he is unlikely to be the last. The SEC charged that Lebed bought thinly traded stocks. After purchasing a stock, he would flood stock-related chat rooms, particularly at Yahoo!'s finance boards, with messages touting the stock's virtues. He used numerous false names so that no one would know that a single person was posting the messages. He would say that the stock was the most "undervalued stock in history" and that its price would jump by 1,000 percent "very soon." When other investors would buy the stock, the price would go up quickly, and Lebed would sell out. The SEC forced the teenager to repay almost $300,000 in gains plus interest. He was allowed, however, to keep about $500,000 of the profits he made trading small-company stocks that he also touted on the Internet.

The SEC has been bringing an increasing number of cases against those who manipulate stock prices in this way. Consider that in 1995, such fraud resulted in only six SEC cases. By 2004, the SEC had brought an estimated two hundred actions against online perpetrators of fraudulent stock-price manipulation.

KEY TERMS

accredited investor 644
blue sky laws 658
bounty payment 657
insider trading 651
investment company 657
mutual fund 657
red herring 642
***scienter* 655**
SEC Rule 10b-5 648
tippee 652
tombstone ad 642

FOR REVIEW

1. What are securities?
2. What two major statutes regulate the securities industry? When was the Securities and Exchange Commission created, and what are its major purposes and functions?
3. Which federal laws regulate investment companies?
4. What are some of the features of state securities laws?
5. How do securities laws apply in the online environment?

QUESTIONS AND CASE PROBLEMS

18–1. A corporation incorporated and doing business in Florida, Estrada Hermanos, Inc., decides to sell $1 million worth of its no-par-value common stock to the public. The stock will be sold only within the state of Florida. José Estrada, the chairman of the board, says the offering need not be registered with the Securities and Exchange Commission. His brother, Gustavo, disagrees. Who is right? Explain.

18–2. Huron Corp. has 300,000 common shares outstanding. The owners of these outstanding shares live in several different states. Huron has decided to split the 300,000 shares two for one. Will Huron Corp. have to file a registration statement and prospectus on the 300,000 new shares to be issued as a result of the split? Explain.

CASE PROBLEM WITH SAMPLE ANSWER

18–3. Investor Protection. In 1962, U.S. News & World Report, Inc., set up a profit-sharing plan that allotted to certain employees specially issued stock known as bonus or anniversary stock. The stock was given to the employees for past services and could not be traded or sold to anyone other than the corporate issuer, U.S. News. This special stock was issued only to employees and for no other purpose than as bonuses. Because there was no market for the stock, U.S. News hired an independent appraiser to estimate the fair value of the stock so that the employees could redeem the shares. Charles Foltz and several other employees held stock through this plan and sought to redeem the shares with U.S. News, but Foltz disputed the value set by the appraisers. Foltz sued U.S. News for violation of securities regulations. What defense would allow U.S. News to resist Foltz's claim successfully? [*Foltz v. U.S. News & World Report, Inc.,* 627 F.Supp. 1143 (D.D.C. 1986)]

➧ *To view a sample answer for this case problem, go to this book's Web site at* **http://ele.westbuslaw.com** *and click on "Interactive Study Center."*

18–4. SEC Rule 10b-5. Louis Ferraro was the chairman and president of Anacomp, Inc. In June 1988, Ferraro told his good friend Michael Maio that Anacomp was negotiating a tender offer for stock in Xidex Corp. Maio passed on the information to Patricia Ladavac, a friend of both Ferraro and Maio. Maio and Ladavac immediately purchased shares in Xidex stock. On the day that the tender offer was announced—an announcement that caused the price of Xidex shares to increase—Maio and Ladavac sold their Xidex stock and made substantial profits (Maio made $211,000 from the transactions, and Ladavac gained $78,750). The Securities and Exchange Commission (SEC) brought an action against the three individuals, alleging that they had violated, among other laws, SEC Rule 10b-5. Maio and Ladavac claimed that they had done nothing illegal. They argued that they had no fiduciary duty either to Anacomp or to Xidex, and therefore they had no duty to disclose or abstain from trading in the stock of those corporations. Had Maio and Ladavac violated SEC Rule 10b-5? Discuss fully. [*SEC v. Maio,* 51 F.3d 623 (7th Cir. 1995)]

18–5. Section 10(b). Joseph Jett worked for Kidder, Peabody & Co., a financial services firm owned by General Electric Co. (GE). Over a three-year period, Jett allegedly engaged in a scheme to generate false profits at Kidder, Peabody to increase his performance-based bonuses. When the scheme was discovered, Daniel Chill and other GE shareholders who had bought stock in the previous year filed a suit in a federal district court against GE. The shareholders alleged that GE had engaged in securities fraud in violation of Section 10(b). They claimed that GE's interest in justifying its investment in Kidder, Peabody gave GE "a motive to willfully blind itself to facts casting doubt on Kidder's purported profitability." On what basis might the court dismiss the shareholders' complaint? Discuss fully. [*Chill v. General Electric Co.,* 101 F.3d 263 (2d Cir. 1996)]

18–6. SEC Rule 10b-5. Grand Metropolitan PLC (Grand Met) planned to make a tender offer as part of an attempted takeover of the Pillsbury Company. Grand

Met hired Robert Falbo, an independent contractor, to complete electrical work as part of security renovations to its offices to prevent leaks of information concerning the planned tender offer. Falbo was given a master key to access the executive offices. When an executive secretary told Falbo that a takeover was brewing, he used his key to access the offices and eavesdrop on conversations to learn that Pillsbury was the target. Falbo bought thousands of shares of Pillsbury stock for less than $40 per share. Within two months, Grand Met made an offer for all outstanding Pillsbury stock at $60 per share and ultimately paid up to $66 per share. Falbo made over $165,000 in profit. The Securities and Exchange Commission (SEC) filed a suit in a federal district court against Falbo and others for alleged violations of, among other things, SEC Rule 10b-5. Under what theory might Falbo be liable? Do the circumstances of this case meet all of the requirements for liability under that theory? Explain. [*SEC v. Falbo,* 14 F.Supp.2d 508 (S.D.N.Y. 1998)]

18–7. Definition of a Security. In 1997, Scott and Sabrina Levine formed Friendly Power Co. (FPC) and Friendly Power Franchise Co. (FPCFranchise). FPC obtained a license to operate as a utility company in California. FPC granted FPCFranchise the right to pay commissions to "operators" who converted residential customers to FPC. Each operator paid for a "franchise"—a geographic area, determined by such factors as the number of households and competition from other utilities. In exchange for 50 percent of FPC's net profits on sales to residential customers in its territory, each franchise was required to maintain a 5 percent market share of power customers in that territory. Franchises were sold to telemarketing firms, which solicited customers. The telemarketers sold interests in each franchise to between fifty and ninety-four "partners," each of whom invested money. FPC began supplying electricity to its customers in May 1998. Less than three months later, the Securities and Exchange Commission (SEC) filed a suit in a federal district court against the Levines and others, alleging that the "franchises" were unregistered securities offered for sale to the public in violation of the Securities Act of 1933. What is the definition of a *security*? Should the court rule in favor of the SEC? Why or why not? [*SEC v. Friendly Power Co., LLC,* 49 F.Supp.2d 1363 (S.D.Fla. 1999)]

18–8. Violations of the 1934 Act. 2TheMart.com, Inc., was conceived in January 1999 to launch an auction Web site to compete with eBay, Inc. On January 19, 2TheMart announced that its Web site was in its "final development" stages and expected to be active by the end of July as a "preeminent" auction site, and that the company had "retained the services of leading Web site design and architecture consultants to design and construct" the site. Based on the announcement, investors rushed to buy 2TheMart's stock, causing a rapid increase in the price. On February 3, 2TheMart entered into an agreement with IBM to take preliminary steps to plan the site. Three weeks later, 2TheMart announced that the site was "currently in final development." On June 1, 2TheMart signed a contract with IBM to design, build, and test the site, with a target delivery date of October 8. When 2TheMart's site did not debut as announced, Mary Harrington and others who had bought the stock filed a suit in a federal district court against the firm's officers, alleging violations of the Securities Exchange Act of 1934. The defendants responded, in part, that any alleged misrepresentations were not material and asked the court to dismiss the suit. How should the court rule, and why? [*In re 2TheMart.com, Inc. Securities Litigation,* 114 F.Supp.2d 955 (C.D.Ca. 2000)]

18–9. Insider Reporting and Trading. Ronald Bleakney, an officer at Natural Microsystems Corp. (NMC), a Section 12 corporation, directed NMC sales in North America, South America, and Europe. In November 1998, Bleakney sold more than 7,500 shares of NMC stock. The following March, Bleakney resigned from the firm, and the next month, he bought more than 20,000 shares of its stock. NMC provided some guidance to employees concerning the rules of insider trading, and with regard to Bleakney's transactions, the corporation said nothing about potential liability. Richard Morales, an NMC shareholder, filed a suit against NMC and Bleakney to compel recovery, under Section 16(b) of the Securities Exchange Act of 1934, of Bleakney's profits from the purchase and sale of his shares. (When Morales died, his executor Deborah Donoghue became the plaintiff.) Bleakney argued that he should not be liable because he relied on NMC's advice. Should the court order Bleakney to disgorge his profits? Explain. [*Donoghue v. Natural Microsystems Corp.,* 198 F.Supp.2d 487 (S.D.N.Y. 2002)]

18–10. IN YOUR COURT

Emerson Electric Co. purchased 13.2 percent of Dodge Manufacturing Co.'s stock. Less than six months later, when Dodge merged with Reliance Electric Co., Emerson decided to sell its shares. To avoid being subject to the short-swing profit restrictions of Section 16(b) of the Securities Exchange Act of 1934, which pertain to any purchase and sale by any owner of 10 percent or more of a corporation's stock, Emerson decided on a two-step selling plan. First, it sold off sufficient shares to reduce its holdings to 9.96 percent, and then it sold the remaining stock—all within a six-month period. Reliance demanded that Emerson return the profits made on both sales. Emerson sought a declaratory judgment from the court that it was not liable, arguing that Section 16 did not apply because at the time of the second sale it had not owned 10 percent of Dodge stock. Assume that you are the judge in the trial court hearing this case and answer the following questions:

(a) Does Section 16(b) of the Securities Exchange Act of 1934 apply to Emerson's transactions? Why or why not?
(b) Is Emerson liable to Reliance for its profits? How will you rule on this issue? Why?
(c) Should Emerson's deliberate attempt to avoid the restrictions of Section 16(b) influence your decision? Why or why not?

18–11. A QUESTION OF ETHICS AND SOCIAL RESPONSIBILITY

Susan Waldbaum was a niece of the president and controlling shareholder of Waldbaum, Inc. Susan's mother (the president's sister) told Susan that the company was going to be sold at a favorable price and that a tender offer was soon to be made. She told Susan not to tell anyone except her husband, Keith Loeb, about the sale. (Loeb did not work for the company and was never brought into the family's inner circle, in which family members discussed confidential business information.) The next day, Susan told her husband of the sale and cautioned him not to tell anyone, because "it could possibly ruin the sale." The day after he learned of the sale, Loeb told Robert Chestman, his broker, about the sale, and Chestman purchased shares of the company for both Loeb and himself. Chestman was later convicted by a jury of, among other things, trading on misappropriated inside information in violation of SEC Rule 10b-5. [*United States v. Chestman,* 947 F.2d 551 (2d Cir. 1991)]

(a) On appeal, the central question was whether Chestman had acquired the inside information about the tender offer as a result of an insider's breach of a fiduciary duty. Could Loeb—the "tipper" in this case—be considered an insider?
(b) If Loeb was not an insider, did he owe any fiduciary (legal) duty to his wife or his wife's family to keep the information confidential? Would it be fair of the court to impose such a legal duty on Loeb?

18–12. FOR CRITICAL ANALYSIS

Do you think that the tipper/tippee and misappropriation theories extend liability under SEC Rule 10b-5 too far? Why or why not?

For updated links to resources available on the Web, as well as a variety of other materials, visit this text's Web site at

http://ele.westbuslaw.com

To access the SEC's EDGAR database, go to

http://www.sec.gov/index.htm

To access a user-friendly version of the EDGAR database, go to

http://www.freeedgar.com

The Center for Corporate Law at the University of Cincinnati College of Law examines all of the acts discussed in this chapter. Go to

http://www.law.uc.edu/CCL

To find the Securities Act of 1933, go to

http://www.law.uc.edu/CCL/33Act/index.html

To examine the Securities Exchange Act of 1934, go to

http://www.law.uc.edu/CCL/34Act/index.html

For information on investor protection and securities fraud, including answers to frequently asked questions on the topic of securities fraud, go to

http://www.securitieslaw.com

LEGAL RESEARCH EXERCISES ON THE WEB

Go to **http://ele.westbuslaw.com**, the Web site that accompanies this text. Select "Interactive Study Center," and then click on "Chapter 18." There you will find the following Internet research exercises that you can perform to learn more about topics covered in this chapter.

Activity 18–1: LEGAL PERSPECTIVE—Electronic Delivery

Activity 18–2: MANAGEMENT PERSPECTIVE—The SEC's Role

BEFORE THE TEST

Go to **http://ele.westbuslaw.com**, the Web site that accompanies this text. Select "Interactive Quizzes." You will find at least twenty interactive questions relating to this chapter.

WESTLAW® CAMPUS

If your textbook provided for a subscription to Westlaw® Campus, or if you have otherwise purchased access to the Westlaw Campus database, you can access any of the cases presented or cited in this chapter by using your Westlaw Campus account.

FOCUS ON LEGAL REASONING
In re Miller

INTRODUCTION

Section 10(b) of the Securities Exchange Act of 1934 and Rule 10b-5 issued by the Securities and Exchange Commission pursuant to the act were discussed in Chapter 18. In this *Focus on Legal Reasoning,* we look at *In re Miller,*[1] a decision in which the court considered whether a broker's violation of those laws could be imputed to his superiors under Section 20 of the 1934 act, which is known as the "control person" provision.[2]

CASE BACKGROUND

When Ronald Owens, Nicola Angelicola, and Ernest Waterman retired from their work at a steel mill in Utica, New York, they received large lump-sum

distributions from the mill's retirement plan. All of them wanted secure, income-producing investments to supplement their retirement income. They took their money to Gary Bohling, a vice president of Andover Securities, Inc.

Ignoring the retirees' desires, Bohling invested their funds in speculative, high-risk investments, including private placement offerings of a catfish farm, a medical office complex, and a credit company. Bohling told them that the investments were safe ("even better than Social Security") and falsified various documents. Ultimately, the investments failed.

At the time, Kent Miller was chairman of Andover, and Terry McGavern was president. Miller, who was responsible for reviewing Bohling's documents, later admitted that he "missed some inconsistencies and red flags." McGavern further admitted that "he may have conveyed the impression to his brokers that it was permissible to sell unaccredited investors 'a little bit' of the higher risk investments." Bohling quit Andover in 1993 and filed for bankruptcy.

The retirees settled their claims with Bohling for $12,000 and filed a complaint with the National Association of Securities Dealers (NASD) against Andover, Miller, and McGavern. NASD arbitrators found Andover and the officers jointly and severally liable for $226,000, plus interest. A federal district court affirmed the award. Miller and McGavern filed for bankruptcy, seeking to discharge this liability. When the court ruled against them, Miller and McGavern appealed to the U.S. Court of Appeals for the Eighth Circuit.

1. 276 F.3d 424 (8th Cir. 2002).
2. Section 20—15 U.S.C. Section 78t(a)—provides that "[e]very person who, directly or indirectly, controls any person liable under any provision of this [portion of the act] or of any rule or regulation thereunder shall also be liable jointly and severally with and to the same extent as such controlled person."

MAJORITY OPINION

WOLLMAN, J.

[The bankruptcy court] concluded * * * that Bohling's conduct violated [Section] 10b of the Securities Exchange Act of 1934 and Rule 10b-5 * * * [and] that pursuant to [Section] 20 of the Act, Miller and McGavern, as controlling persons, were jointly and severally liable for Bohling's fraud to the same extent that Bohling was liable * * * . In short, the bankruptcy court concluded that [Section] 20(a) created an "agency-like relationship" sufficient to impute Bohling's fraud to Miller and McGavern and therefore concluded that the debt in question was nondischargeable under [the Bankruptcy Code].

* * * *

The United States Supreme Court has recognized that a debt may be nondischargeable when the debtor personally commits fraud or when actual fraud is imputed to the debtor under agency principles. *Strang v. Bradner,* 114 U.S. 555, 5 S.Ct. 1038, 29 L.Ed. 248 (1885). *Strang* specifically relied on the common law of agency and partnership to impute the fraud of an innocent debtor's business partner to that debtor and so render his debt nondischargeable. The bankruptcy court determined that, like common law agency principles, [Section] 20(a) of the Securities Exchange Act of 1934 renders an innocent person's debt nondischargeable when a person over whom the innocent person exercised control committed actual fraud.

* * * *

FOCUS ON LEGAL REASONING

We see nothing in the Bankruptcy Code or the securities laws indicating that these two separate provisions of law should be combined in the manner the bankruptcy court did. * * * *[T]he Bankruptcy Code prevents persons from committing actual fraud and then wiping away their resulting debt. It also provides other specific exceptions to discharge, which do not include an exception for liability under the securities laws.* Section 20(a) of the Securities Exchange Act of 1934, on the other hand, is designed to ensure that securities brokers act properly and supervise their employees, and, therefore, it imposes liability in those cases in which the supervisor did not directly participate in the bad acts. Section 20(a) extends liability well beyond traditional doctrines, providing expansive remedies in a highly regulated industry. * * * [T]he Bankruptcy Code addresses actual, traditional fraud, and we are not persuaded that it should be read in such a way as to encompass the nontraditional liability imposed under [Section] 20(a). * * * [Emphasis added.]

The judgment is reversed, and the case is remanded to the district court for further proceedings not inconsistent with this opinion.

DISSENTING OPINION

BEAM, J.

I conclude that the bankruptcy court did not err by imputing Bohling's fraud to Miller and McGavern by way of [Section] 20(a) of the Securities Exchange Act. The court's determination that Bohling's conduct constituted fraud within the meaning of both [the Bankruptcy Code] and Rule 10b-5 is well supported. Thus, there is no question but that Bohling's individual debt to the appellees would be nondischargeable. The bankruptcy court also correctly held that Miller and McGavern were "control persons" and therefore, pursuant to [Section] 20(a), were jointly and severally liable to the same extent as Bohling. Accordingly, the bankruptcy court did not err in concluding that the debts in question are nondischargeable * * * .

* * * Miller and McGavern * * * argue that an agency-principal relationship is necessary to impute fraud for the purposes of dischargeability.

* * * The fact that Miller and McGavern cannot be liable under common law agency principles does not necessarily mean that they may not be liable under [Section] 20(a). The bankruptcy court applied [Section] 20(a) to supplement common law agency principles * * * . Thus, I respectfully disagree with the [majority] * * * because [their opinion does] not take [Section] 20(a) on its own terms, independent of agency law. Strang, decided nearly a half-century before the enactment of the Securities Exchange Act, should not be read to control the reach of the Act. * * * The statute's language is straightforward: control persons are liable to the same extent as the persons they control. Here, an aspect of Bohling's liability is that his debt to the appellees would be nondischargeable. Section 20(a) extends that aspect of Bohling's liability to Miller and McGavern as control persons, along with all other features of his liability.

LEGAL REASONING AND ANALYSIS

❶ **Legal Analysis.** The majority cites, in its opinion, *Strang v. Bradner,* 114 U.S. 555, 5 S.Ct. 1038, 29 L.Ed. 248 (1885) (see the *Law on the Web* feature at the end of Chapter 2 for instructions on how to access federal court opinions). How do the facts and issues in that case compare with the facts and issues of the *Miller* case? How do the applicable legal principles and holdings compare? Is the majority correct in applying the *Strang* case in the *Miller* case, or is the dissent correct in asserting that *Strang* "should not be read to control"?

❷ **Legal Reasoning.** What reasons does the majority provide to justify its conclusion? Do you agree? Why or why not?

❸ **Ethical Considerations.** What ethical obligations do officers in the positions of Miller and McGavern have to their subordinates and to their subordinates' clients?

❹ **Implications for Investors.** What are the implications of the decision in this case for those who invest through brokers?

❺ **Case Briefing Assignment.** Using the guidelines for briefing cases given in the "Preface to the Student" at the beginning of this text, brief the *Miller* case.

UNIT FIVE

FOCUS ON LEGAL REASONING

GOING ONLINE

This text's Web site, at **http://ele.westbuslaw.com**, offers links to West's Court Case Updates, as well as to other online research sources. You can also locate court cases at the Web sites listed in the *Law on the Web* section at the end of Chapter 2.

Sec Law.com, a Web site at **http://www.seclaw.com/Welcome.shtml**, is "an online guide to securities law." The site provides links to a variety of securities law resources, including its own monthly "Securities Law Letter," which covers recent developments in securities law. New York securities attorney Mark Astarita maintains this Web site.

FOCUS ON ETHICS
The Regulatory Environment

If this text had been written a hundred years ago, it would have had little to say about federal government regulation. To be sure, by the 1890s, the beginnings of federal antitrust law had been manifested in the form of the Interstate Commerce Act and the Sherman Act, but little or no legislation had been enacted to protect other areas, such as the environment. Today, in contrast, virtually every area of economic activity is regulated by the government.

From a very broad perspective, ethical issues in government regulation arise because regulation, by its very nature, means that some traditional rights and freedoms have to be given up to ensure that other rights and freedoms are protected. Essentially, government regulation brings two ethical principles into conflict. On the one hand, deeply embedded in American culture is the idea that the government should play a limited role in directing our lives. Indeed, this nation was founded so that Americans could be free from the "heavy hand of government" experienced by the colonists under British rule. On the other hand, one of the basic functions of government is to protect the welfare of individuals and the environment in which they live.

Ultimately, virtually every law or rule regulating business represents a decision to give up certain rights in order to protect other perceived rights. In this *Focus on Ethics,* we look at some of the ethical aspects of government regulation.

ENVIRONMENTAL LAW

Questions of fairness inevitably arise in regard to environmental law. Has the government gone too far in regulating businesses in the interest of protecting the environment? Has the government gone far enough? At what point do the costs of environmental regulations become too burdensome for society to bear? These are broad questions, but they are ethical in nature because they ultimately relate to society's notions of what is right, just, or good.

If the United States ceased all industrial production and returned to the rural economy of earlier times, the environment would certainly benefit. Obviously, we do not want to pay that high a cost. Certainly, we want to enjoy the fruits of our advanced economy, and economic productivity has always been a policy goal of the U.S. government. But environmental protection means that some sacrifices will have to be made. How much are we willing to sacrifice today to ensure that future generations will continue to have a healthful world in which to live?

Economic Productivity versus Environmental Protection

This tension between the two goals of economic productivity and environmental protection was highlighted in a case brought by two Oregon farmers, Marsha and Alvin Seiber, against the government. The Seibers claimed that the government had "taken" their property by denying them a permit to cut timber on forty acres of their land. The permit was denied to protect a pair of northern spotted owls known as Little Wiley and his mate. The owls were seen for two days in 1994 but were never found again. When the Oregon Department of Forestry learned about the owls, the department declared seventy acres surrounding the sighting as a northern spotted owl nesting site. Forty of the acres were on the Seibers' land. When the Seibers subsequently applied for a permit to cut the timber on those acres, the U.S. Fish and Wildlife Service (FWS) denied the permit for the forty acres that were designated as a northern spotted owl nesting site.

The Seibers were in the timber business, and it had taken them decades to grow the timber at issue. Yet they were required to leave the timber on the land for the sole purpose of providing a habitat for spotted owls that apparently did not return to the property. Repeated applications and negotiations with the FWS resulted only in further permit denials. Finally, in mid-2002, the FWS conceded that a permit was no longer required to log the property. Nonetheless, the Seibers had been deprived for eight years of the economic profits that they might have gained from the sale of the timber. Surely, thought the Seibers, this was a regulatory "taking" for which they should be compensated. To date, however, the courts have not come to their aid.[1]

Superfund and Toxic Waste

Although everybody is in favor of cleaning up toxic waste dumps, nobody has the slightest idea what this task will ultimately cost. Much of the problem in determining the eventual costs of the Comprehensive Environmental Response, Compensation, and Liability Act (CERCLA), commonly known as Superfund (see Chapter 16), stems from the difficulty of estimating the costs of cleaning up a site. Until the clean-up is actually undertaken, it is often difficult to assess the extent of contamination.

Moreover, there is no agreed-on standard as to how clean a site needs to be before it no longer poses any threat. Must *all* of the contamination be removed, or would removal of some lesser amount achieve a reasonable degree of environmental quality? On the cost side of the picture, another question arises: If, say, 90 percent of the waste at a given site can be removed for $50,000, but removing the last 10 percent will cost $2 million, is it reasonable to require that the last 10 percent of the waste be removed?

Another aspect of Superfund that raises questions of fairness is the joint and several liability imposed by the act. Thus, a party may be liable for the total costs of cleaning up a hazardous waste site even though that party was responsible for only a small fraction of the toxic waste dumped at the site.

For some time, Congress has been under pressure to overhaul the Superfund legislation for these and other reasons. Proposed changes to the law would, among other things, allow the Environmental Protection Agency to consider how the land is likely to be used in the future when determining how clean a site must be. Another proposed change would eliminate joint and several liability at most sites and exempt certain small businesses from liability.

ANTITRUST LAW—THE BASEBALL EXEMPTION

The fact that, until relatively recently, baseball remained totally exempt from antitrust laws not only seemed unfair to many but also defied logic: Why was an exemption made for baseball but not for other professional sports? The answer to this perfectly reasonable question has always been the same: baseball was exempt because the United States Supreme Court, in 1922, said that it was. The Court held that baseball was a sport played only locally by local players. Because the activity purportedly did not involve interstate commerce, it did not meet the requirements for federal jurisdiction.

The exemption was challenged in the early 1970s, but the Supreme Court ruled that it was up to Congress, not the Court, to overturn the exemption. In 1998, Congress did address the issue and passed the Curt Flood Act—named for the St. Louis Cardinals' star outfielder who challenged the exemption in the early 1970s. The act, however, did not invalidate the 1922 Supreme Court decision but only limited some of the effects of baseball's exempt status. Essentially, the act allows players the option of suing team owners for anticompetitive practices if, for example, the owners collude to "blacklist" players, hold down players' salaries, or force players to play for specific teams.

Baseball is still not subject to antitrust laws to the extent that football, basketball, and other professional sports are. Critics of the exemption argue that it should be completely abolished because it makes no sense to continue to treat an enterprise generating revenues of $3 billion a year as a "local" activity.

ONLINE CHAT ROOMS AND SECURITIES FRAUD

The Securities and Exchange Commission (SEC) typically claims that fraud occurs when a false statement of fact is made. Many statements about stock, however, such as "this stock is headed for $20," are simply opinions. Opinions can never be labeled true or false at the time they are made; otherwise, they would not be opinions. As long as a person has a "genuine belief" that an opinion is true, then, presumably, no fraud is

1. For the most recent decision in this case, see *Seiber v. United States,* 53 Fed.Cl. [Court of Federal Claims] 570 (2002).

FOCUS ON ETHICS

involved. Yet what if negative "opinions" about a certain company cause the price of its stock to drop? Does the company have any legal recourse against those giving the opinions?

The Problem Facing GTMI

Consider the problem facing Global Telemedia International, Inc. (GTMI). In March 2000, GTMI's stock was trading at $4.70 per share. That month, persons using various aliases began to post messages in the GTMI chat room on the Raging Bull Web site. (Raging Bull is a financial service Web site that organizes chat rooms dedicated to publicly traded companies.) The messages were critical of GTMI and its officers. Over the next six months, GTMI's stock price declined significantly—by October, the stock was closing at $0.25 a share. In an attempt to recoup damages, GTMI sued the "John Does" for defamation (see Chapter 12).

Had Defamation Occurred?

The court noted that defamation of a publicly traded company requires a "false statement of fact made with malice that caused damage." The defendants (those who posted the messages) asserted that their online statements were not actionable because they were statements of opinion, not statements of fact. Ultimately, the court agreed with the defendants.

In reaching its decision, the court looked at the "totality of the circumstances," including the context and format of the statements, as well as the expectations of the audience in that particular situation. Here, said the court, the context and format of the statements—anonymous postings "in the general cacophony of an Internet chat room in which about 1,000 messages a week are posted about GTMI"— strongly suggested that the postings constituted opinion, not fact.[2]

INSIDER TRADING

As you learned in Chapter 18, SEC Rule 10b-5 has broad applicability. The rule covers not only corporate insiders but even "outsiders" who trade on tips received from insiders. Investigating and prosecuting violations of SEC Rule 10b-5 is costly, both for the government and for those accused of insider trading. Some people doubt that such extensive regulation is necessary and even contend that insider trading should be legal. Would there be any benefit from the legalization of insider trading?

To evaluate this question, review the facts in *SEC v. Texas Gulf Sulphur Co.* (Case 18.2 in Chapter 18). If insider trading were legal, the discovery of the ore sample would probably have caused many more company insiders to purchase stock. Consequently, the price of Texas Gulf's stock would have increased fairly quickly. These increases presumably would have attracted the attention of outside investors, who would have realized sooner that something positive had happened to the company and would thus have purchased the stock. The higher demand for the stock would have more quickly translated into higher prices for the stock and hence, perhaps, a more efficient capital market.

2. *Global Telemedia International, Inc. v. Does*, 132 F.Supp.2d 1261 (C.D.Cal. 2001).

Nonetheless, the SEC and the courts have routinely upheld the rule that insider trading is illegal.

DISCUSSION QUESTIONS

1. The discussion of Superfund in this *Focus on Ethics* raised the following question: "If, say, 90 percent of the waste at a given site can be removed for $50,000, but removing the last 10 percent will cost $2 million, is it reasonable to require that the last 10 percent of the waste be removed?" How would you answer this question?

2. Both environmental and occupational safety laws strive to protect the public from hazardous substances. Should standards in these two contexts be the same? Or should employees be allowed to voluntarily accept some greater risk in return for higher wages?

3. Assume that removing all asbestos from all public buildings in the nation would save ten lives per year and that the cost of the asbestos removal would be $250 billion. Thus, in effect, Americans would be paying $25 billion per life saved. Is this too high a price to pay? Should cost ever be a consideration when human lives are at stake?

4. Some people contend that SEC Rule 10b-5 against insider trading is being applied too broadly when it is used to prosecute "outsiders"—those who are not corporate insiders but trade securities based on tips from insiders or misappropriated information. Others argue that insider trading should be made legal. Does liability under SEC Rule 10b-5 extend too far? Would there be any benefit from legalizing insider trading?

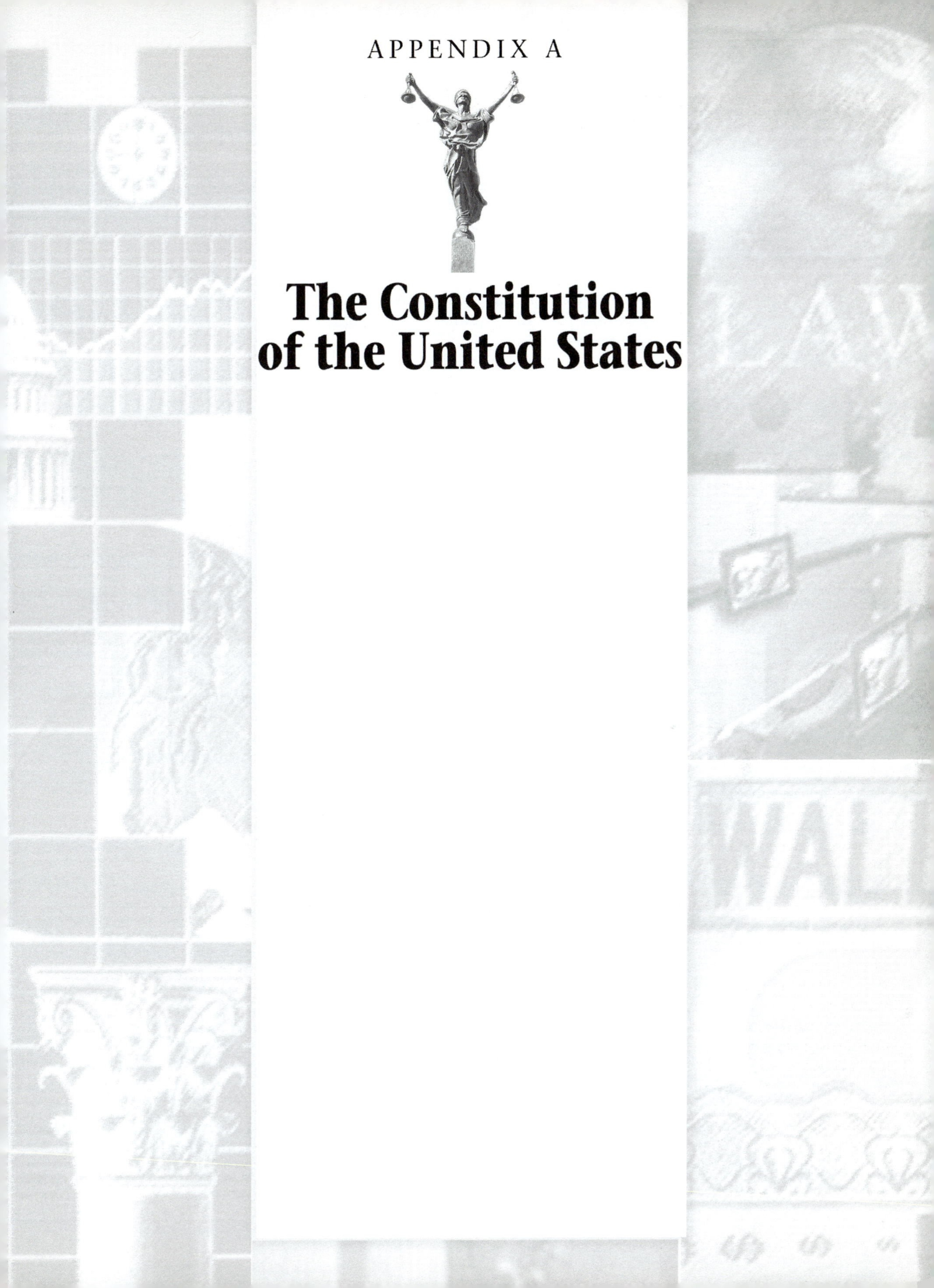

APPENDIX A

The Constitution of the United States

Preamble

We the People of the United States, in Order to form a more perfect Union, establish Justice, insure domestic Tranquility, provide for the common defence, promote the general Welfare, and secure the Blessings of Liberty to ourselves and our Posterity, do ordain and establish this Constitution for the United States of America.

Article I

Section 1. All legislative Powers herein granted shall be vested in a Congress of the United States, which shall consist of a Senate and House of Representatives.

Section 2. The House of Representatives shall be composed of Members chosen every second Year by the People of the several States, and the Electors in each State shall have the Qualifications requisite for Electors of the most numerous Branch of the State Legislature.

No Person shall be a Representative who shall not have attained to the Age of twenty five Years, and been seven Years a Citizen of the United States, and who shall not, when elected, be an Inhabitant of that State in which he shall be chosen.

Representatives and direct Taxes shall be apportioned among the several States which may be included within this Union, according to their respective Numbers, which shall be determined by adding to the whole Number of free Persons, including those bound to Service for a Term of Years, and excluding Indians not taxed, three fifths of all other Persons. The actual Enumeration shall be made within three Years after the first Meeting of the Congress of the United States, and within every subsequent Term of ten Years, in such Manner as they shall by Law direct. The Number of Representatives shall not exceed one for every thirty Thousand, but each State shall have at Least one Representative; and until such enumeration shall be made, the State of New Hampshire shall be entitled to chuse three, Massachusetts eight, Rhode Island and Providence Plantations one, Connecticut five, New York six, New Jersey four, Pennsylvania eight, Delaware one, Maryland six, Virginia ten, North Carolina five, South Carolina five, and Georgia three.

When vacancies happen in the Representation from any State, the Executive Authority thereof shall issue Writs of Election to fill such Vacancies.

The House of Representatives shall chuse their Speaker and other Officers; and shall have the sole Power of Impeachment.

Section 3. The Senate of the United States shall be composed of two Senators from each State, chosen by the Legislature thereof, for six Years; and each Senator shall have one Vote.

Immediately after they shall be assembled in Consequence of the first Election, they shall be divided as equally as may be into three Classes. The Seats of the Senators of the first Class shall be vacated at the Expiration of the second Year, of the second Class at the Expiration of the fourth Year, and of the third Class at the Expiration of the sixth Year, so that one third may be chosen every second Year; and if Vacancies happen by Resignation, or otherwise, during the Recess of the Legislature of any State, the Executive thereof may make temporary Appointments until the next Meeting of the Legislature, which shall then fill such Vacancies.

No Person shall be a Senator who shall not have attained to the Age of thirty Years, and been nine Years a Citizen of the United States, and who shall not, when elected, be an Inhabitant of that State for which he shall be chosen.

The Vice President of the United States shall be President of the Senate, but shall have no Vote, unless they be equally divided.

The Senate shall chuse their other Officers, and also a President pro tempore, in the Absence of the Vice President, or when he shall exercise the Office of President of the United States.

The Senate shall have the sole Power to try all Impeachments. When sitting for that Purpose, they shall be on Oath or Affirmation. When the President of the United States is tried, the Chief Justice shall preside: And no Person shall be convicted without the Concurrence of two thirds of the Members present.

Judgment in Cases of Impeachment shall not extend further than to removal from Office, and disqualification to hold and enjoy any Office of honor, Trust, or Profit under the United States: but the Party convicted shall nevertheless be liable and subject to Indictment, Trial, Judgment, and Punishment, according to Law.

Section 4. The Times, Places and Manner of holding Elections for Senators and Representatives, shall be prescribed in each State by the Legislature thereof; but the Congress may at any time by Law make or alter such Regulations, except as to the Places of chusing Senators.

The Congress shall assemble at least once in every Year, and such Meeting shall be on the first Monday in December, unless they shall by Law appoint a different Day.

Section 5. Each House shall be the Judge of the Elections, Returns, and Qualifications of its own Members, and a Majority of each shall constitute a Quorum to do Business; but a smaller Number may adjourn from day to day, and may be authorized to compel the Attendance of absent Members, in such Manner, and under such Penalties as each House may provide.

Each House may determine the Rules of its Proceedings, punish its Members for disorderly Behavior, and, with the Concurrence of two thirds, expel a Member.

Each House shall keep a Journal of its Proceedings, and from time to time publish the same, excepting such Parts as may in their Judgment require Secrecy; and the Yeas and Nays of the Members of either House on any question shall, at the Desire of one fifth of those Present, be entered on the Journal.

Neither House, during the Session of Congress, shall, without the Consent of the other, adjourn for more than three days, nor to any other Place than that in which the two Houses shall be sitting.

Section 6. The Senators and Representatives shall receive a Compensation for their Services, to be ascertained by Law, and paid out of the Treasury of the United States. They shall in all Cases, except Treason, Felony and Breach of the Peace, be privileged from Arrest during their Attendance at the Session of their respective Houses, and in going to and returning from the same; and for any Speech or Debate in either House, they shall not be questioned in any other Place.

No Senator or Representative shall, during the Time for which he was elected, be appointed to any civil Office under the Authority of the United States, which shall have been created, or the Emoluments whereof shall have been increased during such time; and no Person holding any Office under the United States, shall be a Member of either House during his Continuance in Office.

Section 7. All Bills for raising Revenue shall originate in the House of Representatives; but the Senate may propose or concur with Amendments as on other Bills.

Every Bill which shall have passed the House of Representatives and the Senate, shall, before it become a Law, be presented to the President of the United States; If he approve he shall sign it, but if not he shall return it, with his Objections to the House in which it shall have originated, who shall enter the Objections at large on their Journal, and proceed to reconsider it. If after such Reconsideration two thirds of that House shall agree to pass the Bill, it shall be sent together with the Objections, to the other House, by which it shall likewise be reconsidered, and if approved by two thirds of that House, it shall become a Law. But in all such Cases the Votes of both Houses shall be determined by Yeas and Nays, and the Names of the Persons voting for and against the Bill shall be entered on the Journal of each House respectively. If any Bill shall not be returned by the President within ten Days (Sundays excepted) after it shall have been presented to him, the Same shall be a Law, in like Manner as if he had signed it, unless the Congress by their Adjournment prevent its Return in which Case it shall not be a Law.

Every Order, Resolution, or Vote, to which the Concurrence of the Senate and House of Representatives may be necessary (except on a question of Adjournment) shall be presented to the President of the United States; and before the Same shall take Effect, shall be approved by him, or being disapproved by him, shall be repassed by two thirds of the Senate and House of Representatives, according to the Rules and Limitations prescribed in the Case of a Bill.

Section 8. The Congress shall have Power To lay and collect Taxes, Duties, Imposts and Excises, to pay the Debts and provide for the common Defence and general Welfare of the United States; but all Duties, Imposts and Excises shall be uniform throughout the United States;

To borrow Money on the credit of the United States;

To regulate Commerce with foreign Nations, and among the several States, and with the Indian Tribes;

To establish an uniform Rule of Naturalization, and uniform Laws on the subject of Bankruptcies throughout the United States;

To coin Money, regulate the Value thereof, and of foreign Coin, and fix the Standard of Weights and Measures;

To provide for the Punishment of counterfeiting the Securities and current Coin of the United States;

To establish Post Offices and post Roads;

To promote the Progress of Science and useful Arts, by securing for limited Times to Authors and Inventors the exclusive Right to their respective Writings and Discoveries;

To constitute Tribunals inferior to the supreme Court;

To define and punish Piracies and Felonies committed on the high Seas, and Offenses against the Law of Nations;

To declare War, grant Letters of Marque and Reprisal, and make Rules concerning Captures on Land and Water;

To raise and support Armies, but no Appropriation of Money to that Use shall be for a longer Term than two Years;

To provide and maintain a Navy;

To make Rules for the Government and Regulation of the land and naval Forces;

To provide for calling forth the Militia to execute the Laws of the Union, suppress Insurrections and repel Invasions;

To provide for organizing, arming, and disciplining, the Militia, and for governing such Part of them as may be employed in the Service of the United States, reserving to the States respectively, the Appointment of the Officers, and the Authority of training the Militia according to the discipline prescribed by Congress;

To exercise exclusive Legislation in all Cases whatsoever, over such District (not exceeding ten Miles square) as may, by Cession of particular States, and the Acceptance of Congress, become the Seat of the Government of the United States, and to exercise like Authority over all Places purchased by the Consent of the Legislature of the State in which the Same shall be, for the Erection of Forts, Magazines, Arsenals, dock-Yards, and other needful Buildings;—And

To make all Laws which shall be necessary and proper for carrying into Execution the foregoing Powers, and all other Powers vested by this Constitution in the Government of the United States, or in any Department or Officer thereof.

Section 9. The Migration or Importation of such Persons as any of the States now existing shall think proper to admit, shall not be prohibited by the Congress prior to the Year one thousand eight hundred and eight, but a Tax or duty may be imposed on such Importation, not exceeding ten dollars for each Person.

The privilege of the Writ of Habeas Corpus shall not be suspended, unless when in Cases of Rebellion or Invasion the public Safety may require it.

No Bill of Attainder or ex post facto Law shall be passed.

No Capitation, or other direct, Tax shall be laid, unless in Proportion to the Census or Enumeration herein before directed to be taken.

No Tax or Duty shall be laid on Articles exported from any State.

No Preference shall be given by any Regulation of Commerce or Revenue to the Ports of one State over those of another: nor shall Vessels bound to, or from, one State be obliged to enter, clear, or pay Duties in another.

No Money shall be drawn from the Treasury, but in Consequence of Appropriations made by Law; and a regular Statement and Account of the Receipts and Expenditures of all public Money shall be published from time to time.

No Title of Nobility shall be granted by the United States: And no Person holding any Office of Profit or Trust under them, shall, without the Consent of the Congress, accept of any present, Emolument, Office, or Title, of any kind whatever, from any King, Prince, or foreign State.

Section 10. No State shall enter into any Treaty, Alliance, or Confederation; grant Letters of Marque and Reprisal; coin Money; emit Bills of Credit; make any Thing but gold and silver Coin a Tender in Payment of Debts; pass any Bill of Attainder, ex post facto Law, or Law impairing the Obligation of Contracts, or grant any Title of Nobility.

No State shall, without the Consent of the Congress, lay any Imposts or Duties on Imports or Exports, except what may be absolutely necessary for executing its inspection Laws: and the net Produce of all Duties and Imposts, laid by any State on Imports or Exports, shall be for the Use of the Treasury of the United States; and all such Laws shall be subject to the Revision and Controul of the Congress.

No State shall, without the Consent of Congress, lay any Duty of Tonnage, keep Troops, or Ships of War in time of Peace, enter into any Agreement or Compact with another State, or with a foreign Power, or engage in War, unless actually invaded, or in such imminent Danger as will not admit of delay.

Article II

Section 1. The executive Power shall be vested in a President of the United States of America. He shall hold his Office during the Term of four Years, and, together with the Vice President, chosen for the same Term, be elected, as follows:

Each State shall appoint, in such Manner as the Legislature thereof may direct, a Number of Electors, equal to the whole Number of Senators and Representatives to which the State may be entitled in the Congress; but no Senator or Representative, or Person holding an Office of Trust or Profit under the United States, shall be appointed an Elector.

The Electors shall meet in their respective States, and vote by Ballot for two Persons, of whom one at least shall not be an Inhabitant of the same State with themselves. And they shall make a List of all the Persons voted for, and of the Number of Votes for each; which List they shall sign and certify, and transmit sealed to the Seat of the Government of the United States, directed to the President of the Senate. The President of the Senate shall, in the Presence of the Senate and House of Representatives, open all the Certificates, and the Votes shall then be counted. The Person having the greatest Number of Votes shall be the President, if such Number be a Majority of the whole Number of Electors appointed; and if there be more than one who have such Majority, and have an equal Number of Votes, then the House of Representatives shall immediately chuse by Ballot one of them for President; and if no Person have a Majority, then from the five highest on the List the said House shall in like Manner chuse the President. But in chusing the President, the Votes shall be taken by States, the Representation from each State having one Vote; A quorum for this Purpose shall consist of a Member or Members from two thirds of the States, and a Majority of all the States shall be necessary to a Choice. In every Case, after the Choice of the President, the Person having the greater Number of Votes of the Electors shall be the Vice President. But if there should remain two or more who have equal Votes, the Senate shall chuse from them by Ballot the Vice President.

The Congress may determine the Time of chusing the Electors, and the Day on which they shall give their Votes; which Day shall be the same throughout the United States.

No person except a natural born Citizen, or a Citizen of the United States, at the time of the Adoption of this Constitution, shall be eligible to the Office of President; neither shall any Person be eligible to that Office who shall not have attained to the Age of thirty five Years, and been fourteen Years a Resident within the United States.

In Case of the Removal of the President from Office, or of his Death, Resignation or Inability to discharge the Powers and Duties of the said Office, the same shall devolve on the Vice President, and the Congress may by Law provide for the Case of Removal, Death, Resignation or Inability, both of the President and Vice President, declaring what Officer shall then act as President, and such Officer shall act accordingly, until the Disability be removed, or a President shall be elected.

The President shall, at stated Times, receive for his Services, a Compensation, which shall neither be increased nor diminished during the Period for which he shall have been elected, and he shall not receive within that Period any other Emolument from the United States, or any of them.

Before he enter on the Execution of his Office, he shall take the following Oath or Affirmation: "I do solemnly swear (or affirm) that I will faithfully execute the Office of President of the United States, and will to the best of my Ability, preserve, protect and defend the Constitution of the United States."

Section 2. The President shall be Commander in Chief of the Army and Navy of the United States, and of the Militia of the several States, when called into the actual Service of the United States; he may require the Opinion, in writing, of the principal Officer in each of the executive Departments, upon any Subject relating to the Duties of their respective Offices, and he shall have Power to grant Reprieves and Pardons for Offenses against the United States, except in Cases of Impeachment.

He shall have Power, by and with the Advice and Consent of the Senate to make Treaties, provided two thirds of the Senators present concur; and he shall nominate, and by and with the Advice and Consent of the Senate, shall appoint Ambassadors, other public Ministers and Consuls, Judges of the supreme Court, and all other Officers of the United States, whose Appointments are not herein otherwise provided for, and which shall be established by Law; but the Congress may by Law vest the Appointment of such inferior Officers, as they think proper, in the President alone, in the Courts of Law, or in the Heads of Departments.

The President shall have Power to fill up all Vacancies that may happen during the Recess of the Senate, by granting Commissions which shall expire at the End of their next Session.

Section 3. He shall from time to time give to the Congress Information of the State of the Union, and recommend to their Consideration such Measures as he shall judge necessary and expedient; he may, on extraordinary Occasions, convene both Houses, or either of them, and in Case of Disagreement between them, with Respect to the Time of Adjournment, he may adjourn them to such Time as he shall think proper; he shall receive Ambassadors and other public Ministers; he shall take Care that the Laws be faithfully executed, and shall Commission all the Officers of the United States.

Section 4. The President, Vice President and all civil Officers of the United States, shall be removed from Office on Impeachment for, and Conviction of, Treason, Bribery, or other high Crimes and Misdemeanors.

Article III

Section 1. The judicial Power of the United States, shall be vested in one supreme Court, and in such inferior Courts as the Congress may from time to time ordain and establish. The Judges, both of the supreme and inferior Courts, shall hold their Offices during good Behaviour, and shall, at stated Times, receive for their Services a Compensation, which shall not be diminished during their Continuance in Office.

Section 2. The judicial Power shall extend to all Cases, in Law and Equity, arising under this Constitution, the Laws of the United States, and Treaties made, or which shall be made, under their Authority;—to all Cases affecting Ambassadors, other public Ministers and Consuls;—to all Cases of admiralty and maritime Jurisdiction;—to Controversies to which the United States shall be a Party;—to Controversies between two or more States;—between a State and Citizens of another State;—between Citizens of different States;—between Citizens of the same State claiming Lands under Grants of different States, and between a State, or the Citizens thereof, and foreign States, Citizens or Subjects.

In all Cases affecting Ambassadors, other public Ministers and Consuls, and those in which a State shall be a Party, the supreme Court shall have original Jurisdiction. In all the other Cases before mentioned, the supreme Court shall have appellate Jurisdiction, both as to Law and Fact, with such Exceptions, and under such Regulations as the Congress shall make.

The Trial of all Crimes, except in Cases of Impeachment, shall be by Jury; and such Trial shall be held in the State where the said Crimes shall have been committed; but when not committed within any State, the Trial shall be at such Place or Places as the Congress may by Law have directed.

Section 3. Treason against the United States, shall consist only in levying War against them, or, in adhering to their Enemies, giving them Aid and Comfort. No Person shall be convicted of Treason unless on the Testimony of two Witnesses to the same overt Act, or on Confession in open Court.

The Congress shall have Power to declare the Punishment of Treason, but no Attainder of Treason shall work Corruption of Blood, or Forfeiture except during the Life of the Person attainted.

Article IV

Section 1. Full Faith and Credit shall be given in each State to the public Acts, Records, and judicial Proceedings of every other State. And the Congress may by general Laws prescribe the Manner in which such Acts, Records and Proceedings shall be proved, and the Effect thereof.

Section 2. The Citizens of each State shall be entitled to all Privileges and Immunities of Citizens in the several States.

A Person charged in any State with Treason, Felony, or other Crime, who shall flee from Justice, and be found in another State, shall on Demand of the executive Authority of the State from which he fled, be delivered up, to be removed to the State having Jurisdiction of the Crime.

No Person held to Service or Labour in one State, under the Laws thereof, escaping into another, shall, in Consequence of any Law or Regulation therein, be discharged from such Service or Labour, but shall be delivered up on Claim of the Party to whom such Service or Labour may be due.

Section 3. New States may be admitted by the Congress into this Union; but no new State shall be formed or erected within the Jurisdiction of any other State; nor any State be formed by the Junction of two or more States, or Parts of States, without the Consent of the Legislatures of the States concerned as well as of the Congress.

The Congress shall have Power to dispose of and make all needful Rules and Regulations respecting the Territory or other Property belonging to the United States; and nothing in this Constitution shall be so construed as to Prejudice any Claims of the United States, or of any particular State.

Section 4. The United States shall guarantee to every State in this Union a Republican Form of Government, and shall protect each of them against Invasion; and on Application of the Legislature, or of the Executive (when the Legislature cannot be convened) against domestic Violence.

Article V

The Congress, whenever two thirds of both Houses shall deem it necessary, shall propose Amendments to this Constitution, or, on the Application of the Legislatures of two thirds of the several States, shall call a Convention for proposing Amendments, which, in either Case, shall be valid to all Intents and Purposes, as part of this Constitution, when ratified by the Legislatures of three fourths of the several States, or by Conventions in three fourths thereof, as the one or the other Mode of Ratification may be proposed by the Congress; Provided that no Amendment which may be made prior to the Year One thousand eight hundred and eight shall in any Manner affect the first and fourth Clauses in the Ninth Section of the first Article; and that no State, without its Consent, shall be deprived of its equal Suffrage in the Senate.

Article VI

All Debts contracted and Engagements entered into, before the Adoption of this Constitution shall be as valid against the United States under this Constitution, as under the Confederation.

This Constitution, and the Laws of the United States which shall be made in Pursuance thereof; and all Treaties made, or which shall be made, under the Authority of the United States, shall be the supreme Law of the Land; and the Judges in every State shall be bound thereby, any Thing in the Constitution or Laws of any State to the Contrary notwithstanding.

The Senators and Representatives before mentioned, and the Members of the several State Legislatures, and all executive and judicial Officers, both of the United States and of the several States, shall be bound by Oath or Affirmation, to support this Constitution; but no religious Test shall ever be required as a Qualification to any Office or public Trust under the United States.

Article VII

The Ratification of the Conventions of nine States shall be sufficient for the Establishment of this Constitution between the States so ratifying the Same.

Amendment I [1791]

Congress shall make no law respecting an establishment of religion, or prohibiting the free exercise thereof; or abridging the freedom of speech, or of the press; or the right of the people peaceably to assembly, and to petition the Government for a redress of grievances.

Amendment II [1791]

A well regulated Militia, being necessary to the security of a free State, the right of the people to keep and bear Arms, shall not be infringed.

Amendment III [1791]

No Soldier shall, in time of peace be quartered in any house, without the consent of the Owner, nor in time of war, but in a manner to be prescribed by law.

Amendment IV [1791]

The right of the people to be secure in their persons, houses, papers, and effects, against unreasonable searches and seizures, shall not be violated, and no Warrants shall issue, but upon probable cause, supported by Oath or affirmation, and particularly describing the place to be searched, and the persons or things to be seized.

Amendment V [1791]

No person shall be held to answer for a capital, or otherwise infamous crime, unless on a presentment or indictment of a Grand Jury, except in cases arising in the land or naval forces, or in the Militia, when in actual service in time of War or public danger; nor shall any person be subject for the same offence to be twice put in jeopardy of life or limb; nor shall be compelled in any criminal case to be a witness against himself, nor be deprived of life, liberty, or property, without due process of law; nor shall private property be taken for public use, without just compensation.

Amendment VI [1791]

In all criminal prosecutions, the accused shall enjoy the right to a speedy and public trial, by an impartial jury of the State and district wherein the crime shall have been committed, which district shall have been previously ascertained by law, and to be informed of the nature and cause of the accusation; to be confronted with the witnesses against him; to have compulsory process for obtaining witnesses in his favor, and to have the Assistance of Counsel for his defence.

Amendment VII [1791]

In Suits at common law, where the value in controversy shall exceed twenty dollars, the right of trial by jury shall be preserved, and no fact tried by jury, shall be otherwise re-examined in any Court of the United States, than according to the rules of the common law.

Amendment VIII [1791]

Excessive bail shall not be required, nor excessive fines imposed, nor cruel and unusual punishments inflicted.

Amendment IX [1791]

The enumeration in the Constitution, of certain rights, shall not be construed to deny or disparage others retained by the people.

Amendment X [1791]

The powers not delegated to the United States by the Constitution, nor prohibited by it to the States, are reserved to the States respectively, or to the people.

Amendment XI [1798]

The Judicial power of the United States shall not be construed to extend to any suit in law or equity, commenced or prosecuted against one of the United States by Citizens of another State, or by Citizens or Subjects of any Foreign State.

Amendment XII [1804]

The Electors shall meet in their respective states, and vote by ballot for President and Vice-President, one of whom, at least, shall not be an inhabitant of the same state with themselves; they shall name in their ballots the person voted for as President, and in distinct ballots the person voted for as Vice-President, and they shall make distinct lists of all persons voted for as President, and of all persons voted for as Vice-President, and of the number of votes for each, which lists they shall sign and certify, and transmit sealed to the seat of the government of the United States, directed to the President of the Senate;—The President of the Senate shall, in the presence of the Senate and House of Representatives, open all the certificates and the votes shall then be counted;—The person having the greatest number of votes for President, shall be the President, if such number be a majority of the whole number of Electors appointed; and if no person have such majority, then from the persons having the highest numbers not exceeding three on the list of those voted for as President, the House of Representatives shall choose immediately, by ballot, the President. But in choosing the President, the votes shall be taken by states, the representation from each state having one vote; a quorum for this purpose shall consist of a member or members from two-thirds of the states, and a majority of all states shall be necessary to a choice. And if the House of Representatives shall not choose a President whenever the right of choice shall devolve upon them, before the fourth day of March next following, then the Vice-President shall act as President, as in the case of the death or other constitutional disability of the President.—The person having the greatest number of votes as Vice-President, shall be the Vice-President, if such number be a majority of the whole number of Electors appointed, and if no person have a majority, then from the two highest numbers on the list, the Senate shall choose the Vice-President; a quorum for the purpose shall consist of two-thirds of the whole number of Senators, and a majority of the whole number shall be necessary to a choice. But no person constitutionally ineligible to the office of President shall be eligible to that of Vice-President of the United States.

Amendment XIII [1865]

Section 1. Neither slavery nor involuntary servitude, except as a punishment for crime whereof the party shall have been duly convicted, shall exist within the United States, or any place subject to their jurisdiction.

Section 2. Congress shall have power to enforce this article by appropriate legislation.

Amendment XIV [1868]

Section 1. All persons born or naturalized in the United States, and subject to the jurisdiction thereof, are citizens of the United States and of the State wherein they reside. No State shall make or enforce any law which shall abridge the privileges or immunities of citizens of the United States; nor shall any State deprive any person of life, liberty, or property, without due process of law; nor deny to any person within its jurisdiction the equal protection of the laws.

Section 2. Representatives shall be apportioned among the several States according to their respective numbers, counting the whole number of persons in each State, excluding Indians not taxed. But when the right to vote at any election for the choice of electors for President and Vice President of the United States, Representatives in Congress, the Executive and Judicial officers of a State, or the members of the Legislature thereof, is denied to any of the male inhabitants of such State, being twenty-one years of age, and citizens of the United States, or in any way abridged, except for participation in rebellion, or other crime, the basis of representation therein shall be reduced in the proportion which the number of such male citizens shall bear to the whole number of male citizens twenty-one years of age in such State.

Section 3. No person shall be a Senator or Representative in Congress, or elector of President and Vice President, or hold any office, civil or military, under the United States, or under any State, who having previously taken an oath, as a member of Congress, or as an officer of the United States, or as a member of any State legislature, or as an executive or judicial officer of any State, to support the Constitution of the United States, shall have engaged in insurrection or rebellion against the same, or given aid or comfort to the enemies thereof. But Congress may by a vote of two-thirds of each House, remove such disability.

Section 4. The validity of the public debt of the United States, authorized by law, including debts incurred for payment of pensions and bounties for services in suppressing insurrection or rebellion, shall not be questioned. But neither the United States nor any State shall assume or pay any debt or obligation incurred in aid of insurrection or rebellion against the United States, or any claim for the loss or emancipation of any slave; but all such debts, obligations and claims shall be held illegal and void.

Section 5. The Congress shall have power to enforce, by appropriate legislation, the provisions of this article.

Amendment XV [1870]

Section 1. The right of citizens of the United States to vote shall not be denied or abridged by the United States or by any State on account of race, color, or previous condition of servitude.

Section 2. The Congress shall have power to enforce this article by appropriate legislation.

Amendment XVI [1913]

The Congress shall have power to lay and collect taxes on incomes, from whatever source derived, without apportionment among the several States, and without regard to any census or enumeration.

Amendment XVII [1913]

Section 1. The Senate of the United States shall be composed of two Senators from each State, elected by the people thereof, for six years; and each Senator shall have one vote. The electors in each State shall have the qualifications requisite for electors of the most numerous branch of the State legislatures.

Section 2. When vacancies happen in the representation of any State in the Senate, the executive authority of such State shall issue writs of election to fill such vacancies: *Provided,* That the legislature of any State may empower the executive thereof to make temporary appointments until the people fill the vacancies by election as the legislature may direct.

Section 3. This amendment shall not be so construed as to affect the election or term of any Senator chosen before it becomes valid as part of the Constitution.

Amendment XVIII [1919]

Section 1. After one year from the ratification of this article the manufacture, sale, or transportation of intoxicating liquors within, the importation thereof into, or the exportation thereof from the United States and all territory subject to the jurisdiction thereof for beverage purposes is hereby prohibited.

Section 2. The Congress and the several States shall have concurrent power to enforce this article by appropriate legislation.

Section 3. This article shall be inoperative unless it shall have been ratified as an amendment to the Constitution by the legislatures of the several States, as provided in the Constitution, within seven years from the date of the submission hereof to the States by the Congress.

Amendment XIX [1920]

Section 1. The right of citizens of the United States to vote shall not be denied or abridged by the United States or by any State on account of sex.

Section 2. Congress shall have power to enforce this article by appropriate legislation.

Amendment XX [1933]

Section 1. The terms of the President and Vice President shall end at noon on the 20th day of January, and the terms of Senators and Representatives at noon on the 3d day of January, of the years in which such terms would have ended if this article had not been ratified; and the terms of their successors shall then begin.

Section 2. The Congress shall assemble at least once in every year, and such meeting shall begin at noon on the 3d day of January, unless they shall by law appoint a different day.

Section 3. If, at the time fixed for the beginning of the term of the President, the President elect shall have died, the Vice President elect shall become President. If the President shall not have been chosen before the time fixed for the beginning of his term, or if the President elect shall have failed to qualify, then the Vice President elect shall act as President until a President shall have qualified; and the Congress may by law provide for the case wherein neither a President elect nor a Vice President elect shall have qualified, declaring who shall then act as President, or the manner in which one who is to act shall be selected, and such person shall act accordingly until a President or Vice President shall have qualified.

Section 4. The Congress may by law provide for the case of the death of any of the persons from whom the House of Representatives may choose a

President whenever the right of choice shall have devolved upon them, and for the case of the death of any of the persons from whom the Senate may choose a Vice President whenever the right of choice shall have devolved upon them.

Section 5. Sections 1 and 2 shall take effect on the 15th day of October following the ratification of this article.

Section 6. This article shall be inoperative unless it shall have been ratified as an amendment to the Constitution by the legislatures of three-fourths of the several States within seven years from the date of its submission.

Amendment XXI [1933]

Section 1. The eighteenth article of amendment to the Constitution of the United States is hereby repealed.

Section 2. The transportation or importation into any State, Territory, or possession of the United States for delivery or use therein of intoxicating liquors, in violation of the laws thereof, is hereby prohibited.

Section 3. This article shall be inoperative unless it shall have been ratified as an amendment to the Constitution by conventions in the several States, as provided in the Constitution, within seven years from the date of the submission hereof to the States by the Congress.

Amendment XXII [1951]

Section 1. No person shall be elected to the office of the President more than twice, and no person who has held the office of President, or acted as President, for more than two years of a term to which some other person was elected President shall be elected to the office of President more than once. But this Article shall not apply to any person holding the office of President when this Article was proposed by the Congress, and shall not prevent any person who may be holding the office of President, or acting as President, during the term within which this Article becomes operative from holding the office of President or acting as President during the remainder of such term.

Section 2. This article shall be inoperative unless it shall have been ratified as an amendment to the Constitution by the legislatures of three-fourths of the several States within seven years from the date of its submission to the States by the Congress.

Amendment XXIII [1961]

Section 1. The District constituting the seat of Government of the United States shall appoint in such manner as the Congress may direct:

A number of electors of President and Vice President equal to the whole number of Senators and Representatives in Congress to which the District would be entitled if it were a State, but in no event more than the least populous state; they shall be in addition to those appointed by the states, but they shall be considered, for the purposes of the election of President and Vice President, to be electors appointed by a state; and they shall meet in the District and perform such duties as provided by the twelfth article of amendment.

Section 2. The Congress shall have power to enforce this article by appropriate legislation.

Amendment XXIV [1964]

Section 1. The right of citizens of the United States to vote in any primary or other election for President or Vice President, for electors for President or Vice President, or for Senator or Representative in Congress, shall not be denied or abridged by the United States, or any State by reason of failure to pay any poll tax or other tax.

Section 2. The Congress shall have power to enforce this article by appropriate legislation.

Amendment XXV [1967]

Section 1. In case of the removal of the President from office or of his death or resignation, the Vice President shall become President.

Section 2. Whenever there is a vacancy in the office of the Vice President, the President shall nominate a Vice President who shall take office upon confirmation by a majority vote of both Houses of Congress.

Section 3. Whenever the President transmits to the President pro tempore of the Senate and the Speaker of the House of Representatives his written declaration that he is unable to discharge the powers and duties of his office, and until he transmits to them a written declaration to the contrary, such powers and duties shall be discharged by the Vice President as Acting President.

Section 4. Whenever the Vice President and a majority of either the principal officers of the executive departments or of such other body as Congress may by law provide, transmit to the President pro tempore of the Senate and the Speaker of the House of Representatives their written declaration that the President is unable to discharge the powers and duties of his office, the Vice President shall immediately assume the powers and duties of the office as Acting President.

Thereafter, when the President transmits to the President pro tempore of the Senate and the Speaker of the House of Representatives his written declaration that no inability exists, he shall resume the powers and duties of his office unless the Vice President and a majority of either the principal officers of the executive department or of such other body as Congress may by law provide, transmit within four days to the President pro tempore of the Senate and the Speaker of the House of Representatives their written declaration that the President is unable to discharge the powers and duties of his office. Thereupon Congress shall decide the issue, assembling within forty-eight hours for that purpose if not in session. If the Congress, within twenty-one days after receipt of the latter written declaration, or, if Congress is not in session, within twenty-one days after Congress is required to assemble, determines by two-thirds vote of both Houses that the President is unable to discharge the powers and duties of his office, the Vice President shall continue to discharge the same as Acting President; otherwise, the President shall resume the powers and duties of his office.

Amendment XXVI [1971]

Section 1. The right of citizens of the United States, who are eighteen years of age or older, to vote shall not be denied or abridged by the United States or by any State on account of age.

Section 2. The Congress shall have power to enforce this article by appropriate legislation.

Amendment XXVII [1992]

No law, varying the compensation for the services of the Senators and Representatives, shall take effect, until an election of Representatives shall have intervened.

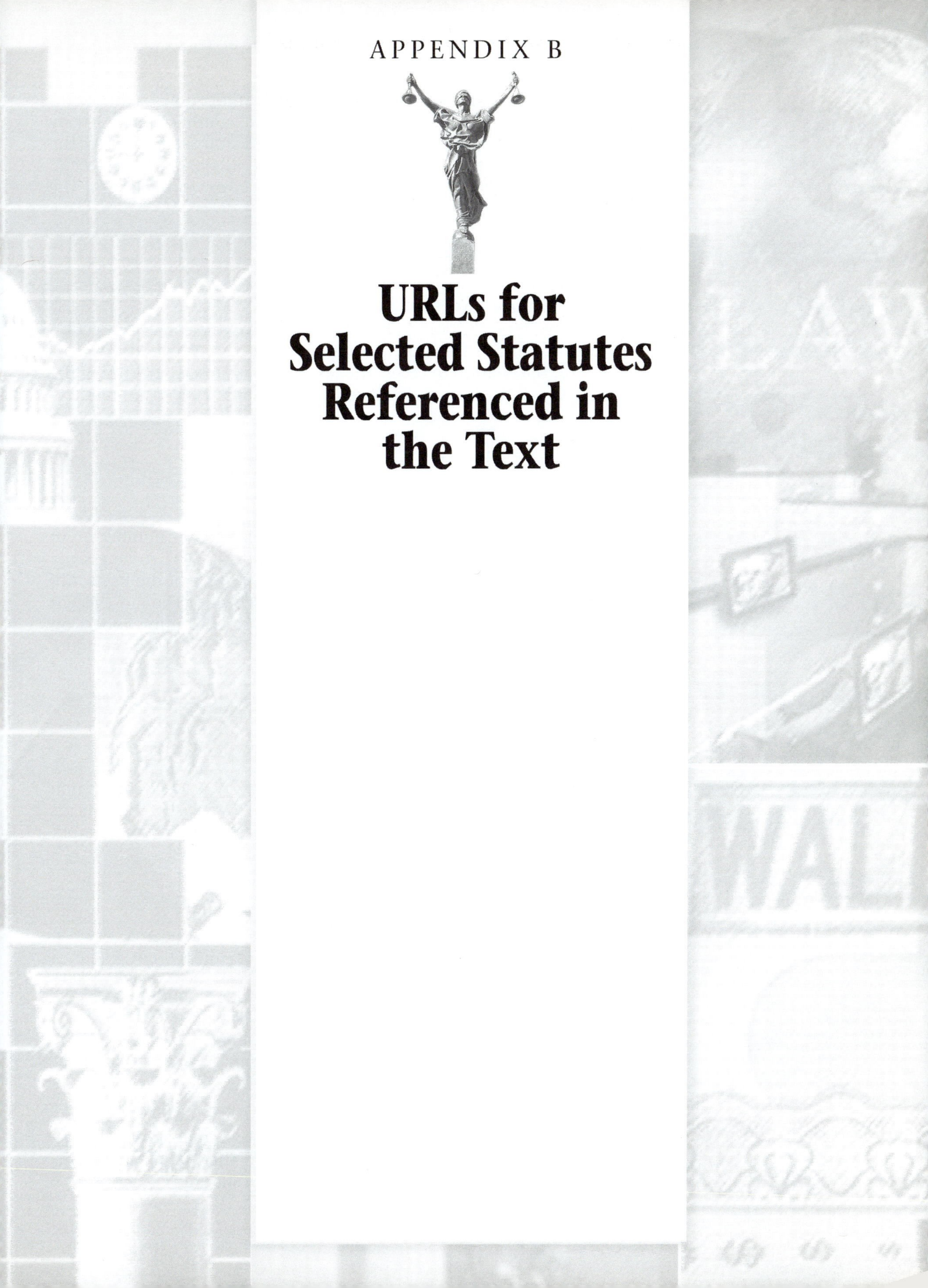

APPENDIX B

URLs for Selected Statutes Referenced in the Text

This appendix lists Uniform Resource Locators (URLs) for some of the significant laws or policies discussed in the text. The URLs are accompanied by explanations for accessing the items using those URLs. You can also access the statutes listed in this appendix by going to the *Essentials of the Legal Environment* Web site at **http://ele.westbuslaw.com** and selecting the "Statutes" page.

Administrative Procedure Act of 1946

5 U.S.C. Sections 551–706.
http://uscode.house.gov/usc.htm
In the "Title" box, type "5," and in the "Section" box, type a relevant section number (such as "551"). Click on "Search," and in the list of "documents found," click on the citation to access the text of the statute. The Office of the Law Revision Council of the U.S. House of Representatives maintains this Web site.

Article 2 of the Uniform Commercial Code

UCC 2–101 through 2–725.
http://www.leg.state.mn.us/leg/statutes.asp
In the "Retrieve a section:" box, type "336" and the section number of an appropriate UCC provision (such as "2-101"). Click on "GO" to access the text, which is Minnesota's version of the statute. The Office of the Revisor of Statutes of the State of Minnesota maintains this Web site. (The most recent draft of UCC Article 2 that the National Conference of Commissioners on Uniform State Laws and the American Law Institute proposed for the adoption of the states is not yet available on the Web.)

Clayton Act of 1914

15 U.S.C. Sections 12–27.
http://uscode.house.gov/usc.htm
In the "Title" box, type "15," and in the "Section" box, type a relevant section number (such as, for example, "12"). Click on "Search." In the list of "documents found," click on the citation with the appropriate title (such as, in this example, "Sec. 12. Definitions; short title") to access the text of the statute.

Constitution of the United States

Preamble through Article VII.
http://memory.loc.gov/const/const.html
This is a page within the THOMAS Web site, which the U.S. Library of Congress maintains. To read the Bill of Rights or other amendments to the U.S. Constitution, click on the link at the top of the page.

Digital Millennium Copyright Act of 1998

17 U.S.C. Sections 1201–1205, 1301–1332.
http://uscode.house.gov/usc.htm
In the "Title" box, type "17," and in the "Section" box, type a relevant section number (such as "1201"). Click on "Search." In the list of "documents found," click on the citation to access the text of the statute.

Electronic Signatures in Global and National Commerce Act of 2000

15 U.S.C. Sections 7001–7006.
http://uscode.house.gov/usc.htm
In the "Title" box, type "15," and in the "Section" box, type a relevant section number (such as "7001"). Click on "Search." In the list of "documents found," click on the citation to access the text of the statute.

Federal Arbitration Act of 1925

9 U.S.C. Sections 1–15.
http://uscode.house.gov/usc.htm
In the "Title" box, type "9," and in the "Section" box, type a relevant section number (such as, for example, "1"). In the list of "documents found," click on the citation to access the text of the statute.

Federal Trade Commission Act of 1914

15 U.S.C. Sections 41–58.
http://uscode.house.gov/usc.htm
In the "Title" box, type "15," and in the "Section" box, type a relevant section number (such as, for example, "45"). Click on "Search." In the list of "documents found," click on the citation to access the text of the statute.

Foreign Corrupt Practices Act of 1977

15 U.S.C. Sections 78dd-1 through 78dd-3.
http://uscode.house.gov/usc.htm
In the "Title" box, type "15," and in the "Section" box, type a relevant section number (such as, for example, "78dd-2"). In the list of "documents found," click on the citation to access the text of the statute.

ICANN's Uniform Domain Name Dispute Resolution Policy

UDRP Paragraphs 1–9.
http://www.icann.org/dndr/udrp/policy.htm
This is a page within the Web site of the Internet Corporation for Assigned Names and Numbers.

Racketeer Influenced and Corrupt Organizations Act of 1970

18 U.S.C. Sections 1961–1968.
http://uscode.house.gov/usc.htm
In the "Title" box, type "18," and in the "Section" box, type a relevant section number (such as, for example, "1961"). In the list of "documents found," click on the citation to access the text of the statute.

Securities Act of 1933

15 U.S.C. Sections 77a–77aa.
http://uscode.house.gov/usc.htm

In the "Title" box, type "15," and in the "Section" box, type a relevant section number (such as, for example, "77b"). Click on "Search." In the list of "documents found," click on the citation to access the text of the statute.

Securities Exchange Act of 1934

15 U.S.C. Sections 78a–78mm.
http://uscode.house.gov/usc.htm
In the "Title" box, type "15," and in the "Section" box, type a relevant section number (such as, for example, "78b"). Click on "Search." In the list of "documents found," click on the citation to access the text of the statute.

Sherman Act of 1890

15 U.S.C. Sections 1–7.
http://uscode.house.gov/usc.htm
In the "Title" box, type "15," and in the "Section" box, type a relevant section number (such as, for example, "1"). Click on "Search." In the list of "documents found," scroll to the citation with the appropriate title (such as, in this example, "Sec. 1. Trusts, etc., in restraint of trade illegal; penalty"). Click on the citation to access the text of the statute.

Uniform Computer Information Transactions Act

UCITA 101–905.
http://www.law.upenn.edu/bll/ulc/ucita/2002final.htm
This is a page within the Web site of the University of Pennsylvania Law School.

Uniform Electronic Transactions Act

UETA 1–21.
http://www.law.upenn.edu/bll/ulc/fnact99/1990s/ueta99.htm
This is a page within the Web site of the University of Pennsylvania Law School, which provides drafts of uniform and model acts in association with the National Conference of Commissioners on Uniform State Laws.

United Nations Convention on Contracts for the International Sale of Goods

CISG Articles 1–101.
http://untreaty.un.org/ENGLISH/series/simpleunts.asp
In the "Title/Key word:" box, type "Convention on Contracts for the International Sale of Goods," select "Match this phrase," and click on "Search UNTS." In the "Search Results," click on the link accompanying the appropriate title. On the "Document Display" page, in the "View Text" section, click on "English" to access the text of the treaty. This is a page within the Web site of the United Nations.

Glossary

A

Abus de droit A doctrine developed in the French courts. The doctrine modified employment at will and protected workers exercising their rights from wrongful discharge and other employer abuses.

Acceptance In contract law, the offeree's notification to the offeror that the offeree agrees to be bound by the terms of the offeror's proposal.

Accredited investors In the context of securities offerings, "sophisticated" investors, such as banks, insurance companies, investment companies, the issuer's executive officers and directors, and persons whose income or net worth exceeds certain limits.

Act of state doctrine A doctrine that provides that the judicial branch of one country will not examine the validity of public acts committed by a recognized foreign government within its own territory.

Actionable Capable of serving as the basis of a lawsuit.

Actual malice Real and demonstrable evil intent. In a defamation suit, a statement made about a public figure normally must be made with actual malice (with either knowledge of its falsity or a reckless disregard of the truth) for liability to be incurred.

Actus reus A guilty (prohibited) act. The commission of a prohibited act is one of the two essential elements required for criminal liability.

Adjudication The process of adjudicating, or formally resolving, a dispute.

Administrative agency A federal, state, or local government agency established to perform a specific function. Administrative agencies are authorized by legislative acts to make and enforce rules to administer and enforce the acts.

Administrative law The body of law created by administrative agencies (in the form of rules, regulations, orders, and decisions) in order to carry out their duties and responsibilities.

Administrative law judge (ALJ) One who presides over an administrative agency hearing and who has the power to administer oaths, take testimony, rule on questions of evidence, and make determinations of fact.

Administrative process The procedure used by administrative agencies in the administration of law.

Affidavit A written or printed voluntary statement of facts, confirmed by the oath or affirmation of the party making it and made before a person having the authority to administer the oath or affirmation.

Affirmative action Job-hiring and admissions policies that give special consideration to members of protected classes in an effort to overcome present effects of past discrimination.

Affirmative defense A response to a plaintiff's claim that does not deny the plaintiff's facts but attacks the plaintiff's legal right to bring an action.

Agency A relationship between two parties in which one party (the agent) agrees to represent or act for the other (the principal).

Agreement A meeting of the minds in regard to the terms of a contract; usually broken down into two events—an offer by one party to form a contract, and an acceptance of the offer by the person to whom the offer is made.

Alienation In real property law, the voluntary transfer of property from one person to another (as opposed to a transfer by operation of law).

Allege To state, claim, assert, or charge.

Alternative dispute resolution (ADR) The resolution of disputes in ways other than those involved in the traditional judicial process. Negotiation, mediation, and arbitration are forms of ADR.

Amend To change and improve through a formal procedure.

Analogy In logical reasoning, an assumption that if two things are similar in some respects, they will be similar in other respects also.

Answer Procedurally, a defendant's response to the plaintiff's complaint.

Antitrust law The body of federal and state laws that regulate competition by protecting trade and commerce from unlawful restraints.

Appropriation In tort law, the use by one person of another person's name, likeness, or other identifying characteristic without permission and for the benefit of the user.

Arbitration The settling of a dispute by submitting it to a disinterested third party (other than a court), who renders a decision. The decision may or may not be legally binding.

Arson The malicious burning of another's dwelling. Today, arson statutes have been extended to cover any real property regardless of ownership and the destruction of property by other means—for example, by explosion.

Articles of organization The document filed with a designated state official by which a limited liability company is formed.

Assault Any word or action intended to make another person fearful of immediate physical harm; a reasonably believable threat.

Assignment The act of transferring to another all or part of one's rights arising under a contract.

Assumption of risk A defense against negligence that can be used when the plaintiff is aware of a danger and voluntarily assumes the risk of injury from that danger.

Attempted monopolization Any action by a firm that is specifically intended to eliminate competition and gain monopoly power.

Award In the context of arbitration, the arbitrator's decision.

B

Bankruptcy court A federal court of limited jurisdiction that handles only bankruptcy proceedings. Bankruptcy proceedings are governed by federal bankruptcy law.

Battery The unprivileged, intentional touching of another.

Beyond a reasonable doubt The standard used to determine the guilt or innocence of a person who has been charged with a crime. To be guilty of a crime, one must be proved guilty "beyond and to the exclusion of every reasonable doubt." A reasonable doubt is one that would cause a prudent person to hesitate before acting in matters important to him or her.

Bill of Rights The first ten amendments to the U.S. Constitution.

Binding authority Any source of law that a court must follow when deciding a case. Binding authorities include constitutions, statutes, and regulations that govern the issue being decided, as well as court decisions that are controlling precedents within the jurisdiction.

Blue sky laws State laws that regulate the offer and sale of securities.

Bona fide occupational qualification (BFOQ) Identifiable characteristics reasonably necessary to the normal operation of a particular business. These characteristics can include gender, national origin, and religion, but not race or color.

Bounty payment A reward (payment) given to a person or persons who perform a certain service—such as informing government authorities of illegal actions.
Breach To violate a law, by an act or an omission, or to break a legal obligation that one owes to another person or to society.
Breach of contract The failure, without legal excuse, of a promisor to perform the obligations of a contract.
Brief A formal legal document submitted by the attorney for the appellant—or the appellee (in answer to the appellant's brief)—to an appellate court when a case is appealed. The appellant's brief outlines the facts and issues of the case, the trial court's rulings that should be reversed or modified, the applicable law, and the arguments on the client's behalf.
Browse-wrap terms Terms and conditions of use that are presented to an Internet user at the time certain products, such as software, are being downloaded but that need not be agreed to (by clicking "I agree," for example) before being able to install or use the product.
Bureaucracy A large organization that is structured hierarchically to carry out specific functions.
Burglary The unlawful entry into a building with the intent to commit a felony. (Some state statutes expand this to include the intent to commit any crime.)
Business ethics Ethics in a business context; a consensus of what constitutes right or wrong behavior in the world of business and the application of moral principles to situations that arise in a business setting.
Business invitees Those people, such as customers or clients, who are invited onto business premises by the owner of those premises for business purposes.
Business necessity A defense to allegations of employment discrimination in which the employer demonstrates that an employment practice that discriminates against members of a protected class is related to job performance.
Business tort The wrongful interference with the business rights of another.
Business trust A voluntary form of business organization in which investors (trust beneficiaries) transfer cash or property to trustees in exchange for trust certificates that represent their investment shares. Management of the business and trust property is handled by the trustees for the use and benefit of the investors. The certificate holders have limited liability and share in the trust's profits.
Bylaws A set of governing rules adopted by a corporation or other association.
Bystander A spectator, witness, or person standing nearby when an event occurred and who did not engage in the business or act leading to the event.

C

Case law The rules of law announced in court decisions. Case law includes the aggregate of reported cases that interpret statutes, regulations, and constitutional provisions.
Case on point A previous case involving factual circumstances and issues that are as similar as possible to the case before the court.
Categorical imperative A concept developed by the philosopher Immanuel Kant as an ethical guideline for behavior. In deciding whether an action is right or wrong, or desirable or undesirable, a person should evaluate the action in terms of what would happen if everybody else in the same situation, or category, acted the same way.
Causation in fact An act or omission without ("but for") which an event would not have occurred.
Certificate of incorporation The primary document that evidences corporate existence (referred to as articles of incorporation in some states).
Certificate of limited partnership The basic document filed with a designated state official by which a limited partnership is formed.
Certification mark A mark used by one or more persons, other than the owner, to certify the region, materials, mode of manufacture, quality, or accuracy of the owner's goods or services.
Chancellor An adviser to the king at the time of the early king's courts of England. Individuals petitioned the king for relief when they could not obtain an adequate remedy in a court of law, and these petitions were decided by the chancellor.
Checks and balances The national government is composed of three separate branches: the executive, the legislative, and the judicial branches. Each branch of the government exercises a check on the actions of the others.
Civil law The branch of law dealing with the duties that exist between persons or between citizens and their government, *excluding* the duty not to commit crimes.
Civil law system A system of law derived from that of the Roman Empire and based on a code rather than case law; the predominant system of law in the nations of continental Europe and the nations that were once their colonies. In the United States, Louisiana is the only state that has a civil law system.
Click-on agreement An agreement that arises when a buyer, engaging in a transaction on a computer, indicates his or her assent to be bound by the terms of an offer by clicking on a button that says, for example, "I agree."
Closing argument An argument made after the plaintiff and defendant have rested their cases. Closing arguments are made prior to the jury charges.
Collective mark A mark used by members of a cooperative, association, or other organization to certify the region, materials, mode of manufacture, quality, or accuracy of the specific goods or services.
Commerce clause The provision in Article I, Section 8, of the U.S. Constitution that gives Congress the power to regulate interstate commerce.
Commercial impracticability A doctrine under which parties may be excused from their performance obligations when performance becomes extremely difficult or costly as a result of circumstances that could not have been foreseen when the contract was formed.
Common law That body of law developed from custom or judicial decisions in English and U.S. courts, not attributable to a legislature.
Comparative law The study and comparison of legal systems and laws across nations.
Comparative negligence A theory in tort law under which the liability for injuries resulting from negligent acts is shared by all parties who were negligent (including the injured party), on the basis of each person's proportionate negligence.
Compensatory damages In contract law, a money award to compensate a nonbreaching party for damages actually sustained as a result of the breach of a contract.
Complaint The pleading made by a plaintiff alleging wrongdoing on the part of the defendant; the document that, when filed with a court, initiates a lawsuit.
Computer crime Any wrongful act that is directed against computers and computer parts, or the wrongful use or abuse of computers or software.
Conciliation A form of alternative dispute resolution in which the parties reach an agreement themselves with the help of a neutral third party, called a conciliator, who facilitates the negotiations.
Concurrent jurisdiction Jurisdiction that exists when two different courts have the power to hear a case. For example, some cases can be heard in either a federal or a state court.
Condition A qualification, provision, or clause in a contractual agreement, the occurrence of which creates, suspends, or terminates the obligations of the contracting parties.
Confiscation A government's taking of privately owned business or personal property without a proper public purpose or an award of just compensation.
Conforming goods Goods that conform to contract specifications.
Conglomerate merger A merger between firms that do not compete with each other because they are in different markets (as opposed to horizontal and vertical mergers).
Consent Voluntary agreement to a proposition or an act of another.
Consequential damages Special damages that result from the consequences of a breach of contract (for example, lost profits). To

recover consequential damages, the breaching party must know, or have reason to know, that special circumstances will cause the non-breaching party to suffer an additional loss.
Consideration Generally, the value given in return for a promise or a performance. Consideration, which must be present to make a contract legally binding, must be something of legally sufficient value and bargained for.
Consignment A transaction in which an owner of goods (the consignor) delivers the goods to another (the consignee) for the consignee to sell. The consignee pays the consignor for the goods when they are sold by the consignee.
Constitutional law Law that is based on the U.S. Constitution and the constitutions of the various states.
Contract An agreement that can be enforced in court; formed by two or more parties, each of whom agrees to perform or to refrain from performing some act now or in the future.
Contributory negligence A theory in tort law under which a complaining party's own negligence contributed to or caused his or her injuries. Contributory negligence is an absolute bar to recovery in a minority of jurisdictions.
Conversion The wrongful taking, using, or retaining possession of personal property that belongs to another.
Cooperative An association that is organized to provide an economic service to its members (or shareholders). An incorporated cooperative is subject to state laws governing nonprofit corporations.
Copyright The exclusive right of authors to publish, print, or sell an intellectual production for a statutory period of time. A copyright differs from a patent or a trademark in that it applies exclusively to works of art, literature, and other works of authorship, including computer programs.
Corporation A legal entity formed in compliance with statutory requirements. The entity is distinct from its shareholders-owners.
Cost-benefit analysis A decision-making technique that involves weighing the costs of a given action against the benefits of the action.
Counterclaim A claim made by a defendant in a civil lawsuit that in effect sues the plaintiff.
Counteroffer An offeree's response to an offer in which the offeree rejects the original offer and at the same time makes a new offer.
Court of equity A court that decides controversies and administers justice according to principles of equity.
Court of law A court in which the only remedies that could be granted were things of value, such as money damages. In the early English king's courts, courts of law were distinct from courts of equity.
Cover Under the UCC, a remedy of the buyer or lessee that allows the buyer or lessee, on the seller's or lessor's breach, to purchase the goods from another seller or lessor and substitute them for the goods due under the contract. If the cost of cover exceeds the cost of the contract goods, the breaching seller or lessor will be liable to the buyer or lessee for the difference.
Crime A wrong against society proclaimed in a statute and, if committed, punishable by society through fines and/or imprisonment—and, in some cases, death.
Criminal law Law that defines and governs actions that constitute crimes. Generally, criminal law has to do with wrongful actions committed against society as a whole for which society demands redress.
Cross-border pollution Pollution across national boundaries; air and water degradation in one nation resulting from pollution-causing activities in a neighboring country.
Cross-examination The questioning of an opposing witness during the trial.
Cure Under the UCC, the right of a party who tenders nonconforming performance to correct his or her performance within the contract period.
Cyber crime A crime that occurs online, in the virtual community of the Internet, as opposed to the physical world.
Cyber mark A trademark in cyberspace.
Cyber stalker A person who commits the crime of stalking in cyberspace. Generally, stalking consists of harassing a person and putting that person in reasonable fear for his or her safety or the safety of the person's immediate family.
Cyber terrorist A hacker whose purpose is to exploit a target computer for a serious impact, such as the corruption of a program to sabotage a business.
Cyber tort A tort committed in cyberspace.
Cybersquatting An act that occurs when a person registers a domain name that is the same as, or confusingly similar to, the trademark of another and offers to sell the domain name to the trademark owner.

D

Damages Money given to a party whose legal interests have been injured.
Defamation Any published or publicly spoken false statement that causes injury to another's good name, reputation, or character.
Default judgment A judgment entered by a court against a defendant who has failed to appear in court to answer or defend against the plaintiff's claim.
Defendant One against whom a lawsuit is brought; the accused person in a criminal proceeding.
Defense That which a defendant offers and alleges in an action or suit as a reason why the plaintiff should not recover or establish what he or she seeks.
Delegation The transfer of a contractual duty to a third party. The party delegating the duty (the delegator) to the third party (the delegatee) is still obliged to perform on the contract should the delegatee fail to perform.
Delegation doctrine A doctrine based on Article I, Sections 1 and 8, of the U.S. Constitution, which have been construed to allow Congress to delegate some of its power to make and implement laws to administrative agencies. The delegation is considered to be proper as long as Congress sets standards outlining the scope of the agency's authority.
Deposition The testimony of a party to a lawsuit or a witness taken under oath before a trial.
Destination contract A contract in which the seller is required or authorized to ship the goods by carrier and deliver them at a particular destination. The seller assumes liability for any losses or damage to the goods until they are tendered at the destination specified in the contract.
Dilution With respect to trademarks, a doctrine under which distinctive or famous trademarks are protected from certain unauthorized uses of the marks regardless of a showing of competition or a likelihood of confusion.
Direct examination The examination of a witness by the attorney who calls the witness to the stand to testify on behalf of the attorney's client.
Discharge The termination of an obligation. In contract law, discharge occurs when the parties have fully performed their contractual obligations or when events, conduct of the parties, or operation of the law releases the parties from performance.
Disclosed principal A principal whose identity is known to a third party at the time the agent makes a contract with the third party.
Discovery A phase in the litigation process during which the opposing parties may obtain information from each other and from third parties prior to trial.
Disparagement of property An economically injurious false statement made about another's product or property. A general term for torts that are more specifically referred to as slander of quality or slander of title.
Disparate-impact discrimination A form of employment discrimination that results from certain employer practices or procedures that, although not discriminatory on their face, have a discriminatory effect. Intent is irrelevant in a disparate-impact claim.
Disparate-treatment discrimination A form of employment discrimination that results when an employer intentionally discriminates against employees who are members of protected classes.
Distribution agreement A contract between a seller and a distributor of the seller's products setting out the terms and conditions of the distributorship.

Diversity of citizenship Under Article III, Section 2, of the Constitution, a basis for federal court jurisdiction over a lawsuit between (1) citizens of different states, (2) a foreign country and citizens of a state or of different states, or (3) citizens of a state and citizens or subjects of a foreign country. The amount in controversy must be more than $75,000 before a federal court can take jurisdiction in such cases.
Divestiture The act of selling one or more of a company's parts, such as a subsidiary or plant; often mandated by the courts in merger or monopolization cases.
Docket The list of cases entered on a court's calendar and thus scheduled to be heard by the court.
Domain name The series of letters and symbols used to identify site operators on the Internet; Internet "addresses."
Double jeopardy Being tried twice for the same criminal offense; prohibited by the Fifth Amendment to the Constitution.
Dram shop act A state statute that imposes liability on tavern owners and bartenders who serve alcoholic drinks to the public for injuries resulting from accidents caused by intoxicated persons when the sellers or servers of alcoholic drinks contributed to the intoxication.
Due process clause The provisions of the Fifth and Fourteenth Amendments to the Constitution that guarantee that no person shall be deprived of life, liberty, or property without due process of law. Similar clauses are found in most state constitutions.
Dumping The selling of goods in a foreign country at a price below the price charged for the same goods in the domestic market.
Duress Unlawful pressure brought to bear on a person, causing the person to perform an act that he or she would not otherwise perform.
Duty of care The duty of all persons, as established by tort law, to exercise a reasonable amount of care in their dealings with others. Failure to exercise due care, which is normally determined by the "reasonable person standard," constitutes the tort of negligence.

E

Early neutral case evaluation A form of alternative dispute resolution in which a neutral third party evaluates the strengths and weaknesses of the disputing parties' positions; the evaluator's opinion forms the basis for negotiating a settlement.
E-contract A contract that is entered into in cyberspace and is evidenced only by electronic impulses (such as those that make up a computer's memory), rather than, for example, a typewritten form.
Embezzlement The fraudulent appropriation of money or other property by a person to whom the money or property has been entrusted.
Employment discrimination Treating employees or job applicants unequally on the basis of race, color, national origin, religion, gender, age, or disability; prohibited by federal statutes.
Enabling legislation A statute enacted by Congress that authorizes the creation of an administrative agency and specifies the name, composition, purpose, functions, and powers of the agency being created.
Entrapment In criminal law, a defense in which the defendant claims that he or she was induced by a public official—usually an undercover agent or police officer—to commit a crime that he or she would otherwise not have committed.
Entrepreneur One who initiates and assumes the financial risks of a new enterprise and who undertakes to provide or control its management.
Environmental impact statement (EIS) A document required by the National Environmental Policy Act for any major federal action that will significantly affect the quality of the environment. The document must analyze the action's impact on the environment and explore alternative actions that might be taken.
Environmental law The body of statutory, regulatory, and common law relating to the protection of the environment.
Equal protection clause The provision in the Fourteenth Amendment to the Constitution that guarantees that no state will "deny to any person within its jurisdiction the equal protection of the laws." This clause mandates that state governments treat similarly situated individuals in a similar manner.
Equitable maxim A general proposition or principle of law that has to do with fairness (equity).
E-signature As defined by the Uniform Electronic Transactions Act, "an electronic sound, symbol, or process attached to or logically associated with a record and executed or adopted by a person with the intent to sign the record."
Establishment clause The provision in the First Amendment to the U.S. Constitution that prohibits Congress from creating any law "respecting an establishment of religion."
Ethical reasoning A reasoning process in which an individual links her or his moral convictions or ethical standards to the particular situation at hand.
Ethics Moral principles and values applied to social behavior.
Exclusionary rule In criminal procedure, a rule under which any evidence that is obtained in violation of the accused's constitutional rights guaranteed by the Fourth, Fifth, and Sixth Amendments, as well as any evidence derived from illegally obtained evidence, will not be admissible in court.
Exclusive jurisdiction Jurisdiction that exists when a case can be heard only in a particular court or type of court, such as a federal court or a state court.
Exclusive-dealing contract An agreement under which a seller forbids a buyer to purchase products from the seller's competitors.
Executive agency An administrative agency within the executive branch of government. At the federal level, executive agencies are those within the cabinet departments.
Export To sell products to buyers located in other countries.
Express warranty A seller's or lessor's oral or written promise, ancillary to an underlying sales or lease agreement, as to the quality, description, or performance of the goods being sold or leased.
Expropriation The seizure by a government of privately owned business or personal property for a proper public purpose and with just compensation.

F

Federal form of government A system of government in which the states form a union and the sovereign power is divided between a central government and the member states.
Federal question A question that pertains to the U.S. Constitution, acts of Congress, or treaties. A federal question provides a basis for federal jurisdiction.
Federal Rules of Civil Procedure (FRCP) The rules controlling procedural matters in civil trials brought before the federal district courts.
Felony A crime—such as arson, murder, rape, or robbery—that carries the most severe sanctions, usually ranging from one year in a state or federal prison to the forfeiture of one's life.
Fiduciary As a noun, a person having a duty to act primarily for another's benefit concerning matters within the scope of the relationship. As an adjective, a relationship founded on trust and confidence.
Filtering software A computer program that includes a pattern through which data are passed. When designed to block access to certain Web sites, the pattern blocks the retrieval of a site whose URL or key words are on a list within the program.
Final order The final decision of an administrative agency on an issue. If no appeal is taken, or if the case is not reviewed or considered anew by the agency commission, the administrative law judge's initial order becomes the final order of the agency.
Firm offer An offer (by a merchant) that is irrevocable without consideration for a period of time (not longer than three months). A firm offer by a merchant must be in writing and must be signed by the offeror.
Forgery The fraudulent making or altering of any writing in a way that changes the legal rights and liabilities of another.
Forum-selection clause A provision in a contract designating the court or jurisdiction that will decide any dispute arising under the contract.
Franchise Any arrangement in which the owner of a trademark, trade name, or copyright licenses another to use that trademark, trade name, or copyright, under specified conditions or limitations, in the selling of goods and services.

Franchisee One receiving a license to use another's (the franchisor's) trademark, trade name, or copyright in the sale of goods and services.
Franchisor One licensing another (the franchisee) to use his or her trademark, trade name, or copyright in the sale of goods or services.
Fraudulent misrepresentation (fraud) Any misrepresentation, either by misstatement or omission of a material fact, knowingly made with the intention of deceiving another and on which a reasonable person would and does rely to his or her detriment.
Free exercise clause The provision in the First Amendment to the U.S. Constitution that prohibits Congress from making any law "prohibiting the free exercise" of religion.
Frustration of purpose A doctrine under which a party to a contract will be relieved of his or her duty to perform when the objective purpose for performance no longer exists (due to reasons beyond that party's control).
Full faith and credit clause A clause in Article IV, Section 1, of the Constitution that provides that rights established under deeds, wills, contracts, and the like in one state will be honored by the other states and that any judicial decision with respect to such property rights will be honored and enforced in all states.

G

General partner In a limited partnership, a partner who assumes responsibility for the management of the partnership and liability for all partnership debts.
Genuineness of assent Knowing and voluntary assent to the terms of a contract. If a contract is formed as a result of a mistake, misrepresentation, undue influence, or duress, genuineness of assent is lacking, and the contract will be voidable.
Good Samaritan statute A state statute that provides that persons who rescue or provide emergency services to others in peril—unless they do so recklessly and thus cause further harm—cannot be sued for negligence.
Grand jury A group of citizens called to decide, after hearing the state's evidence, whether a reasonable basis (probable cause) exists for believing that a crime has been committed and whether a trial ought to be held.
Group boycott An agreement by two or more parties to refuse to deal with (boycott) a particular person or firm; prohibited by the Sherman Act.

H

Hacker A person who uses one computer to break into another.
Hearsay An oral or written statement made out of court that is later offered in court by a witness (not the person who made the statement) to prove the truth of the matter asserted in the statement. Hearsay is generally inadmissible as evidence.
Horizontal merger A merger between two firms that are competing in the same market.
Horizontal restraint Any agreement that in some way restrains competition between rival firms competing in the same market.

I

Identification In a sale or lease of goods, the express designation of the specific goods provided for in the contract.
Identity theft A form of theft that occurs when a person steals another's identifying information—such as a name, date of birth, or Social Security number—and uses the information to access the victim's financial resources.
Implied warranty A warranty that the law derives by implication or inference from the nature of the transaction or the relative situation or circumstances of the parties.
Implied warranty of fitness for a particular purpose A warranty that goods sold or leased are fit for a particular purpose. The warranty arises when any seller or lessor knows the particular purpose for which a buyer or lessee will use the goods and knows that the buyer or lessee is relying on the skill and judgment of the seller or lessor to select suitable goods.
Implied warranty of merchantability A warranty that goods being sold or leased are reasonably fit for the ordinary purpose for which they are sold or leased, are properly packaged and labeled, and are of fair quality. The warranty automatically arises in every sale or lease of goods made by a merchant who deals in goods of the kind sold or leased.
Impossibility of performance A doctrine under which a party to a contract is relieved of his or her duty to perform when performance becomes impossible or totally impracticable (through no fault of either party).
***In personam* jurisdiction** Court jurisdiction over the "person" involved in a legal action; personal jurisdiction.
***In rem* jurisdiction** Court jurisdiction over a defendant's property.
Incidental beneficiary A third party who incidentally benefits from a contract but whose benefit was not the reason the contract was formed; an incidental beneficiary has no rights in a contract and cannot sue to have the contract enforced.
Independent contractor One who works for, and receives payment from, an employer but whose working conditions and methods are not controlled by the employer. An independent contractor is not an employee but may be an agent.
Independent regulatory agency An administrative agency that is not considered part of the government's executive branch. Independent agency officials cannot be removed without cause.
Indictment The formal written accusation of a crime, made by a grand jury and presented to a court for prosecution against the accused person.
Information A formal accusation or complaint made by a government prosecutor without a grand-jury indictment.
Initial order In the context of administrative law, an administrative law judge's order. The order becomes final unless it is appealed.
Insider trading The purchase or sale of securities on the basis of "inside information" (information that has not been made available to the public) in violation of a duty owed to the company whose stock is being traded.
Insurable interest An interest either in a person's life or well-being or in property that is sufficiently substantial that insuring against injury to (or the death of) the person or against damage to the property does not amount to a mere wagering (betting) contract.
Intellectual property Property resulting from intellectual, creative processes. Patents, trademarks, and copyrights are examples of intellectual property.
Intended beneficiary A third party for whose benefit a contract is formed; an intended beneficiary can sue the promisor if such a contract is breached.
Intentional tort A wrongful act knowingly committed.
International law The law that governs relations among nations. International customs, treaties, and organizations are generally considered to be the most important sources of international law.
International organization In international law, a term that generally refers to an organization composed mainly of nations and usually established by treaty. The United States is a member of more than one hundred multilateral and bilateral organizations, including at least twenty through the United Nations.
Interrogatories A series of written questions for which written answers are prepared and then signed under oath by a party to a lawsuit, usually with the assistance of the party's attorney.
Investment company A company that acts on behalf of many smaller shareholders/owners by buying a large portfolio of securities and professionally managing that portfolio.

J

Joint stock company A hybrid form of business organization that combines characteristics of a corporation and a partnership. Usually, the joint stock company is regarded as a partnership for tax and other legally related purposes.
Joint venture A joint undertaking of a specific commercial enterprise by an association of persons. A joint venture is normally

not a legal entity and is treated like a partnership for federal income tax purposes.

Judicial process The procedures relating to, or connected with, the administration of justice through the judicial system.

Judicial review The process by which courts decide on the constitutionality of legislative enactments and actions of the executive branch.

Jurisdiction The authority of a court to hear and decide a specific action.

Jurisprudence The science or philosophy of law.

Justiciable controversy A controversy that is not hypothetical or academic but real and substantial; a requirement that must be satisfied before a court will hear a case.

L

Laches The equitable doctrine that bars a party's right to legal action if the party has neglected for an unreasonable length of time to act on his or her rights.

Larceny The wrongful taking and carrying away of another person's personal property with the intent to permanently deprive the owner of the property. Some states classify larceny as either grand or petit, depending on the property's value.

Law A body of enforceable rules governing relationships among individuals and between individuals and their society.

Lease agreement In regard to the lease of goods, an agreement in which one person (the lessor) agrees to transfer the right to the possession and use of goods to another person (the lessee) in exchange for rental payments.

Legal realism A school of legal thought that was popular in the 1920s and 1930s and that challenged many existing jurisprudential assumptions, particularly the assumption that subjective elements and social forces play no part in judicial reasoning.

Legal reasoning The process of reasoning by which a judge harmonizes his or her decision with the judicial decisions of previous cases.

Legislative rule An administrative agency rule that carries the same weight as a congressionally enacted statute.

Lessee A person who acquires the right to the possession and use of another's property in exchange for rental payments.

Lessor A person who sells the right to the possession and use of property to another in exchange for rental payments.

Libel Defamation in writing or other permanent medium (such as in a videotape).

Limited liability company (LLC) A hybrid form of business enterprise that offers the limited liability of the corporation but the tax advantages of a partnership.

Limited liability limited partnership (LLLP) A type of limited partnership in which the liability of all partners is limited to the amount of their investments in the firm. The difference between a limited partnership and an LLLP is that the liability of the general partner in an LLLP is the same as the liability of the limited partner.

Limited liability partnership (LLP) A form of partnership that allows professionals to enjoy the tax benefits of a partnership while limiting their personal liability for the malpractice of other partners.

Limited partner In a limited partnership, a partner who contributes capital to the partnership but has no right to participate in the management and operation of the business. The limited partner assumes no liability for partnership debts beyond the capital contributed.

Liquidated damages An amount, stipulated in the contract, that the parties to a contract believe to be a reasonable estimation of the damages that will occur in the event of a breach.

Long arm statute A state statute that permits a state to obtain personal jurisdiction over nonresident defendants. A defendant must have "minimum contacts" with that state for the statute to apply.

M

Mailbox rule A rule providing that an acceptance of an offer becomes effective on dispatch (on being placed in a mailbox), if mail is, expressly or impliedly, an authorized means of communication of acceptance to the offeror.

Malpractice Professional misconduct or the failure to exercise the requisite degree of skill as a professional. Negligence on the part of a professional, such as a physician or an attorney, is commonly referred to as malpractice.

Market concentration A situation that exists when a small number of firms share the market for a particular good or service.

Market power The power of a firm to control the market price of its product. A monopoly has the greatest degree of market power.

Market-share liability A method of sharing liability among several firms that manufactured or marketed a particular product that may have caused a plaintiff's injury. This form of liability sharing is used when the true source of the product is unidentifiable. Each firm's liability is proportionate to its respective share of the relevant market for the product.

Market-share test The primary measure of monopoly power. A firm's market share is the percentage of a market that the firm controls.

Mediation A method of settling disputes outside of court by using the services of a neutral third party, called a mediator. The mediator acts as a communicating agent between the parties and suggests ways in which the parties can resolve their dispute.

Member The term used to designate a person who has an ownership interest in a limited liability company.

Mens rea Mental state, or intent. A wrongful mental state is as necessary as a wrongful act to establish criminal liability.

Merchant A person who deals in goods of the kind involved in the sales contract; see UCC 2–104.

Meta tags Words inserted into a Web site's key-words field to increase the site's appearance in search engine results.

Minimum wage The lowest wage, either by government regulation or union contract, that an employer may pay an hourly worker.

Mini-trial A private proceeding in which each party to a dispute argues its position before the other side and vice versa. A neutral third party may be present and act as an adviser if the parties fail to reach an agreement.

Mirror image rule A common law rule that requires, for a valid contractual agreement, that the terms of the offeree's acceptance adhere exactly to the terms of the offeror's offer.

Misdemeanor A lesser crime than a felony, punishable by a fine or incarceration for up to one year in jail.

Mitigation of damages A rule requiring a plaintiff to have done whatever was reasonable to minimize the damages caused by the defendant.

Money laundering Falsely reporting income that has been obtained through criminal activity as income obtained through a legitimate business enterprise—in effect, "laundering" the "dirty money."

Monopolization The possession of monopoly power in the relevant market and the willful acquisition or maintenance of that power, as distinguished from growth or development as a consequence of a superior product, business acumen, or historic accident.

Monopoly A term generally used to describe a market in which there is a single seller or a limited number of sellers.

Monopoly power The ability of a monopoly to dictate what takes place in a given market.

Moral minimum The minimum degree of ethical behavior expected of a business firm, which is usually defined as compliance with the law.

Most-favored-nation status A status granted in an international treaty by a provision stating that the citizens of the contracting nations may enjoy the privileges accorded by either party to citizens of the most favored nations. Generally, most-favored-nation clauses are designed to establish equality of international treatment.

Motion A procedural request or application presented by an attorney to the court on behalf of a client.

Motion for a directed verdict In a jury trial, a motion for the judge to take the decision out of the hands of the jury and direct a

verdict for the party making the motion on the ground that the other party has not produced sufficient evidence to support his or her claim; referred to as a motion for judgment as a matter of law in the federal courts.
Motion for a new trial A motion asserting that the trial was so fundamentally flawed (because of error, newly discovered evidence, prejudice, or other reason) that a new trial is necessary to prevent a miscarriage of justice.
Motion for judgment *n.o.v.* A motion requesting the court to grant judgment in favor of the party making the motion on the ground that the jury verdict against him or her was unreasonable and erroneous.
Motion for judgment on the pleadings A motion by either party to a lawsuit at the close of the pleadings requesting the court to decide the issue solely on the pleadings without proceeding to trial. The motion will be granted only if no facts are in dispute.
Motion for summary judgment A motion requesting the court to enter a judgment without proceeding to trial. The motion can be based on evidence outside the pleadings and will be granted only if no facts are in dispute.
Motion to dismiss A pleading in which a defendant asserts that the plaintiff's claim fails to state a cause of action (that is, has no basis in law) or that there are other grounds on which a suit should be dismissed.
Mutual assent The element of agreement in the formation of a contract. The manifestation of contract parties' mutual assent to the same bargain is required to establish a contract.
Mutual fund A specific type of investment company that continually buys or sells to investors shares of ownership in a portfolio.
Mutual rescission An agreement between the parties to cancel their contract, releasing the parties from further obligations under the contract. The object of the agreement is to restore the parties to the positions they would have occupied had no contract ever been formed.

N

National law Law that governs a particular nation (as opposed to international law).
Natural law The belief that there are universal moral and ethical principles that are inherent in human nature. The natural law school is the oldest and one of the most significant schools of legal thought.
Necessity In criminal law, a defense against liability; under Section 3.02 of the Model Penal Code, this defense is justifiable if "the harm or evil sought to be avoided" by a given action "is greater than that sought to be prevented by the law defining the offense charged."
Negligence The failure to exercise the standard of care that a reasonable person would exercise in similar circumstances.
Negligence *per se* An act (or failure to act) in violation of a statutory requirement.
Negotiation In regard to dispute settlement, a process in which parties attempt to settle their dispute without going to court, with or without attorneys to represent them.
Notice-and-comment rulemaking An administrative rulemaking procedure that involves the publication of a notice of a proposed rulemaking in the *Federal Register*, a comment period for interested parties to express their views on the proposed rule, and the publication of the agency's final rule in the *Federal Register*.
Novation The substitution, by agreement, of a new contract for an old one, with the rights under the old one being terminated. Typically, there is a substitution of a new person who is responsible for the contract and the removal of an original party's rights and duties under the contract.
Nuisance A common law doctrine under which persons may be held liable for using their property in a manner that unreasonably interferes with others' rights to use or enjoy their own property.

O

Offer A promise or commitment to perform or refrain from performing some specified act in the future.
Online dispute resolution (ODR) The resolution of disputes with the assistance of organizations that offer dispute-resolution services via the Internet.
Opening statement A statement made to the jury at the beginning of a trial by a party's attorney, prior to the presentation of evidence. The attorney briefly outlines the evidence that will be offered and the legal theory that will be pursued.
Operating agreement In a limited liability company, an agreement in which the members set forth the details of how the business will be managed and operated.
Ordinance A law passed by a local governing unit, such as a municipality or a county.
Output contract An agreement in which a seller agrees to sell and a buyer agrees to buy all or up to a stated amount of what the seller produces.

P

Partially disclosed principal A principal whose identity is unknown by a third person, but the third person knows that the agent is or may be acting for a principal at the time the agent and the third person form a contract.
Partnership An agreement by two or more persons to carry on, as co-owners, a business for profit.
Past consideration An act done before the contract is made, which ordinarily, by itself, cannot be consideration for a later promise to pay for the act.
Patent A government grant that gives an inventor the exclusive right or privilege to make, use, or sell his or her invention for a limited time period. The word *patent* usually refers to some invention and designates either the instrument by which patent rights are evidenced or the patent itself.
Peer-to-peer (P2P) networking The sharing of resources (such as files, hard drives, and processing cycles) among multiple computers that does not necessarily require a central network server.
Penalty A sum inserted into a contract, not as a measure of compensation for its breach but rather as punishment for a default. The agreement as to the amount will not be enforced, and recovery will be limited to actual damages.
***Per se* violation** A type of anticompetitive agreement that is considered to be so injurious to the public that there is no need to determine whether it actually injures market competition; rather, it is in itself *(per se)* a violation of the Sherman Act.
Perfect tender rule A common law rule under which a seller was required to deliver to the buyer goods that conformed perfectly to the requirements stipulated in the sales contract. A tender of nonconforming goods would automatically constitute a breach of contract. Under the UCC, the rule has been greatly modified.
Performance In contract law, the fulfillment of one's duties arising under a contract with another; the normal way of discharging one's contractual obligations.
Petitioner In equity practice, a party that initiates a lawsuit.
Petty offense In criminal law, the least serious kind of criminal offense, such as a traffic or building-code violation.
Plaintiff One who initiates a lawsuit.
Plea bargain A negotiated agreement between a criminal defendant and the prosecutor in a criminal case that usually involves the defendant's pleading guilty to a lesser offense in return for a lighter sentence.
Pleadings Statements made by the plaintiff and the defendant in a lawsuit that detail the facts, charges, and defenses involved in the litigation; the complaint and answer are part of the pleadings.
Police powers Powers possessed by states as part of their inherent sovereignty. These powers may be exercised to protect or promote the public order, health, safety, morals, and general welfare.
Positive law The body of conventional, or written, law of a particular society at a particular point in time.
Positivist school A school of legal thought whose adherents believe that there can be no higher law than a nation's positive law—the body of conventional, or written, law of a particular society at a particular time.
Potentially responsible party (PRP) A potentially liable party under the Comprehensive Environmental Response, Compensation

and Liability Act (CERCLA). Any person who generated the hazardous waste, transported the hazardous waste, owned or operated a waste site at the time of disposal, or currently owns or operates a site may be responsible for some or all of the clean-up costs involved in removing the hazardous chemicals.

Precedent A court decision that furnishes an example or authority for deciding subsequent cases involving identical or similar facts.

Predatory pricing The pricing of a product below cost with the intent to drive competitors out of the market.

Preemption A doctrine under which certain federal laws preempt, or take precedence over, conflicting state or local laws.

Pretrial conference A conference, scheduled before the trial begins, between the judge and the attorneys litigating the suit. The parties may settle the dispute, clarify the issues, and so on during the conference.

Pretrial motion A written or oral application to a court for a ruling or order, made before trial.

Price discrimination Setting prices in such a way that two competing buyers pay two different prices for an identical product or service.

Price-fixing agreement An agreement between competitors in which the competitors agree to fix the prices of products or services at a certain level; prohibited by the Sherman Act.

***Prima facie* case** A case in which the plaintiff has produced sufficient evidence of his or her claim that the case can go to a jury; a case in which the evidence compels the plaintiff's conclusion if the defendant produces no evidence to disprove it.

Principle of comity A principle under which one nation will defer and give effect to the laws and judicial decrees of another nation. This principle is based primarily on respect.

Principle of rights The principle that human beings have certain fundamental rights (to life, freedom, and the pursuit of happiness, for example). Those who adhere to this "rights theory" believe that a key factor in determining whether a business decision is ethical is how that decision affects the rights of others.

Privilege In tort law, the ability to act contrary to another person's right without that person's having legal redress for such acts. Privilege may be raised as a defense to defamation.

Privileges and immunities clause A provision found in Article IV, Section 2, of the Constitution that requires states not to discriminate against one another's citizens. A resident of one state cannot be treated as an alien when in another state; he or she may not be denied such privileges and immunities as legal protection, access to courts, travel rights, or property rights.

Probable cause Reasonable grounds to believe the existence of facts warranting certain actions, such as the search or arrest of a person.

Probate court A state court of limited jurisdiction that conducts proceedings relating to the settlement of a deceased person's estate.

Procedural law Rules that define the manner in which the rights and duties established by substantive law may be enforced.

Product liability The legal liability of manufacturers, sellers, and lessors of goods to consumers, users, and bystanders for injuries or damages that are caused by the goods.

Product misuse A defense against product liability that may be raised if the plaintiff used a product in a manner not intended by the manufacturer. If the misuse is reasonably foreseeable, the seller will not escape liability unless measures were taken to guard against the misuse.

Promise A declaration that something either will or will not happen in the future.

Promissory estoppel A doctrine that applies when a promisor makes a clear and definite promise on which the promisee justifiably relies; such a promise is binding if justice will be better served by the enforcement of the promise.

Protected class A class of persons with identifiable characteristics who historically have been victimized by discriminatory treatment for certain purposes. Depending on the context, these characteristics include age, color, gender, national origin, race, religion, and disability.

Proximate cause Legal cause; exists when the connection between an act and an injury is strong enough to justify imposing liability.

Public figures Individuals who are thrust into the public limelight. Public figures include government officials and politicians, movie stars, well-known businesspersons, and generally anybody who becomes known to the public because of his or her position or activities.

Public policy A government policy based on widely held societal values and (usually) expressed or implied in laws or regulations.

Puffery A salesperson's exaggerated claims concerning the quality of items offered for sale. Such claims involve opinions rather than facts and are not considered to be legally binding promises or warranties.

Punitive damages Money damages that may be awarded to a plaintiff to punish the defendant and to deter future similar conduct.

Q

Quasi contract A fictional contract imposed on parties by a court in the interests of fairness and justice; usually, quasi contracts are imposed to avoid the unjust enrichment of one party at the expense of another.

Question of fact In a lawsuit, an issue involving a factual dispute that is decided by a trial court judge (or, in a jury trial, a jury).

Question of law In a lawsuit, an issue involving the application or interpretation of a law; therefore, the judge, and not the jury, decides the issue.

Quota An assigned import limit on goods.

R

Reasonable person standard The standard of behavior expected of a hypothetical "reasonable person." The standard against which negligence is measured and that must be observed to avoid liability for negligence.

Rebuttal The refutation by the plaintiff's attorney of evidence introduced by the defendant's attorney.

Red herring A preliminary prospectus that can be distributed to potential investors after the registration statement (for a securities offering) has been filed with the Securities and Exchange Commission.

Reformation A court-ordered correction of a written contract so that it reflects the true intentions of the parties.

Rejoinder The defendant's answer to the plaintiff's rebuttal.

Relevant evidence Evidence tending to make a fact at issue in the case more or less probable than it would be without the evidence. Only relevant evidence is admissible in court.

Remedy The relief given to an innocent party to enforce a right or compensate for the violation of a right.

Remedy at law A remedy available in a court of law. Money damages are awarded as a remedy at law.

Remedy in equity A remedy allowed by courts in situations in which remedies at law are not appropriate. Remedies in equity include injunction, specific performance, and rescission.

Reporter A publication in which court cases are published, or reported.

Requirements contract An agreement in which a buyer agrees to purchase and the seller agrees to sell all or up to a stated amount of what the buyer needs or requires.

Res ipsa loquitur A doctrine under which negligence may be inferred simply because an event occurred, if it is the type of event that would not occur in the absence of negligence. Literally, the term means "the facts speak for themselves."

Resale price maintenance agreement An agreement between a manufacturer and a retailer in which the manufacturer specifies the minimum retail price of its products.

Respondeat superior In Latin, "Let the master respond." A doctrine under which a principal or an employer is held liable for the wrongful acts committed by agents or employees while acting within the course and scope of their agency or employment.

Respondent In equity practice, the party against whom an action is taken.

Restitution An equitable remedy under which a person is restored to his or her original position prior to loss or injury, or placed in the position he or she would have been in had the breach not occurred.

Restraint on trade Any contract or combination that tends to eliminate or reduce competition or otherwise hamper the course of trade and commerce as it would be carried on if left to the control of natural economic forces.

Revocation In contract law, the withdrawal of an offer by an offeror. Unless an offer is irrevocable, it can be revoked at any time prior to acceptance without liability.

Robbery The act of forcefully and unlawfully taking personal property of any value from another; force or intimidation is usually necessary for an act of theft to be considered a robbery.

Rule of four A rule of the United States Supreme Court under which the Court will not issue a writ of *certiorari* unless at least four justices approve of the decision to issue the writ.

Rule of reason A test by which a court balances the positive effects (such as economic efficiency) of an agreement against its potentially anticompetitive effects. In antitrust litigation, many practices are analyzed under the rule of reason.

Rulemaking The process undertaken by an administrative agency when formally adopting a new regulation or amending an old one. Rulemaking involves notifying the public of a proposed rule or change and receiving and considering the public's comments.

Rules of evidence Rules governing the admissibility of evidence in trial courts.

S

S corporation A corporation that has met certain requirements as set out by the Internal Revenue Code and thus qualifies for special income tax treatment. Essentially, an S corporation is taxed the same as a partnership, but its owners enjoy the privilege of limited liability.

Sale The passing of title from the seller to the buyer for a price.

Sale on approval A type of conditional sale in which the buyer may take the goods on a trial basis. The sale becomes absolute only when the buyer approves of (or is satisfied with) the goods being sold.

Sale or return A type of conditional sale in which title and possession pass from the seller to the buyer; however, the buyer retains the option to return the goods during a specified period even though the goods conform to the contract.

Sales contract A contract for the sale of goods under which the ownership of goods is transferred from a seller to a buyer for a price.

Scienter Knowledge by the misrepresenting party that material facts have been falsely presented or omitted with an intent to deceive.

Search warrant An order granted by a public authority, such as a judge, that authorizes law enforcement personnel to search particular premises or property.

SEC Rule 10b-5 A rule of the Securities and Exchange Commission that makes it unlawful, in connection with the purchase or sale of any security, to make any untrue statement of a material fact or to omit a material fact if such omission causes the statement to be misleading.

Self-defense The legally recognized privilege to protect one's self against injury by another. The privilege of self-defense protects only acts that are reasonably necessary to protect one's self.

Seniority system In regard to employment relationships, a system in which those who have worked longest for the company are first in line for promotions, salary increases, and other benefits; they are also the last to be laid off if the work force must be reduced.

Service mark A mark used in the sale or the advertising of services to distinguish the services of one person from the services of others.

Service of process The delivery of the complaint and summons to a defendant.

Sexual harassment In the employment context, the granting of job promotions or other benefits in return for sexual favors, or language or conduct that is so sexually offensive that it creates a hostile working environment.

Shipment contract A contract for the sale of goods in which the seller is required or authorized to ship the goods by carrier. The buyer assumes liability for any losses or damage to the goods after they are delivered to the carrier.

Slander Defamation in oral form.

Slander of quality (trade libel) The publication of false information about another's product, alleging that it is not what its seller claims.

Slander of title The publication of a statement that denies or casts doubt on another's legal ownership of any property, causing financial loss to that property's owner.

Small claims courts Special courts in which parties may litigate small claims (usually, claims involving $5,000 or less). Attorneys are not required in small claims courts, and in many states attorneys are not allowed to represent the parties.

Sociological school A school of legal thought that views the law as a tool for promoting justice in society.

Sole proprietorship The simplest form of business, in which the owner is the business; the owner reports business income on his or her personal income tax return and is legally responsible for all debts and obligations incurred by the business.

Sovereign immunity A doctrine that immunizes foreign nations from the jurisdiction of U.S. courts when certain conditions are satisfied.

Spam Bulk, unsolicited ("junk") e-mail.

Specific performance An equitable remedy requiring the breaching party to perform as promised under the contract; usually granted only when money damages would be an inadequate remedy and the subject matter of the contract is unique (for example, real property).

Standing to sue The requirement that an individual must have a sufficient stake in a controversy before he or she can bring a lawsuit. The plaintiff must demonstrate that he or she either has been injured or threatened with injury.

Stare decisis A common law doctrine under which judges are obligated to follow the precedents established in prior decisions within their jurisdictions.

Statute of Frauds A state statute under which certain types of contracts must be in writing to be enforceable.

Statute of limitations A federal or state statute setting the maximum time period during which a certain action can be brought or certain rights enforced.

Statute of repose Basically, a statute of limitations that is not dependent on the happening of a cause of action. Statutes of repose generally begin to run at an earlier date and run for a longer period of time than statutes of limitations.

Statutory law The body of law enacted by legislative bodies (as opposed to constitutional law, administrative law, or case law).

Strict liability Liability regardless of fault. In tort law, strict liability may be imposed on defendants in cases involving abnormally dangerous activities, dangerous animals, or defective products.

Substantive law Law that creates and defines legal rights and obligations.

Summary jury trial A method of settling disputes in which a trial is held, but the jury's verdict is not binding. The verdict acts only as a guide to both sides in reaching an agreement during negotiations following the trial.

Summons A document informing a defendant that a legal action has been commenced against him or her and that the defendant must appear in court on a certain date to answer the plaintiff's complaint. The document is delivered by a sheriff or any other person so authorized.

Supremacy clause The provision in Article VI of the Constitution that provides that the Constitution, laws, and treaties of the United States are "the supreme Law of the Land." Under this clause, state and local laws that directly conflict with federal laws will be rendered invalid.

Syllogism A form of deductive reasoning consisting of a major premise, a minor premise, and a conclusion.

Symbolic speech Nonverbal conduct that expresses opinions or thoughts about a subject. Symbolic speech is protected under the First Amendment's guarantee of freedom of speech.

Syndicate An investment group of persons or firms brought together for the purpose of financing a project that they would not or could not undertake independently.

T

Tangible property Property that has physical existence and can be distinguished by the senses of touch, sight, and so on. A car is tangible property; a patent right is intangible property.

Tariff A tax on imported goods.

Tender An unconditional offer to perform an obligation by a person who is ready, willing, and able to do so.

Tender of delivery Under the UCC, a seller's or lessor's act of placing conforming goods at the disposal of the buyer or lessee and giving the buyer or lessee whatever notification is reasonably necessary to enable the buyer or lessee to take delivery.

Third party beneficiary One for whose benefit a promise is made in a contract but who is not a party to the contract.

Tippee A person who receives inside information.

Tombstone ad An advertisement, historically in a format resembling a tombstone, of a securities offering. The ad informs potential investors of where and how they may obtain a prospectus.

Tort A civil wrong not arising from a breach of a legal duty that proximately causes harm or injury to another.

Tortfeasor One who commits a tort.

Toxic tort Failure to use or properly clean up toxic chemicals that cause harm to a person or society.

Trade dress The image and overall appearance of a product—for example, the distinctive decor, menu, layout, and style of service of a particular restaurant. Basically, trade dress is subject to the same protection as trademarks.

Trade name A term that is used to indicate part or all of a business's name and that is directly related to the business's reputation and goodwill. Trade names are protected under the common law (and under trademark law, if the name is the same as the firm's trademarked property).

Trade secret Information or a process that gives a business an advantage over competitors who do not know the information or process.

Trademark A distinctive mark, motto, device, or implement that a manufacturer stamps, prints, or otherwise affixes to the goods it produces so that they may be identified on the market and their origins made known. Once a trademark is established (under the common law or through registration), the owner is entitled to its exclusive use.

Treaty An agreement formed between two or more independent nations.

Trespass to land The entry onto, above, or below the surface of land owned by another without the owner's permission or legal authorization.

Trespass to personal property The unlawful taking or harming of another's personal property; interference with another's right to the exclusive possession of his or her personal property.

Tying arrangement An agreement between a buyer and a seller in which the buyer of a specific product or service becomes obligated to purchase additional products or services from the seller.

U

Unconscionable contract or clause A contract or clause that is void on the basis of public policy because one party, as a result of his or her disproportionate bargaining power, is forced to accept terms that are unfairly burdensome and that unfairly benefit the dominating party.

Undisclosed principal A principal whose identity is unknown by a third person, and the third person has no knowledge that the agent is acting for a principal at the time the agent and the third person form a contract.

Uniform law A model law created by the National Conference of Commissioners on Uniform State Laws and/or the American Law Institute for the states to consider adopting. If the state adopts the law, it becomes statutory law in that state. Each state has the option of adopting or rejecting all or part of a uniform law.

Unreasonably dangerous product A product that is defective to the point of threatening a consumer's health and safety. A product will be considered unreasonably dangerous if it is dangerous beyond the expectation of the ordinary consumer or if a less dangerous alternative was economically feasible for the manufacturer, but the manufacturer failed to produce it.

Utilitarianism An approach to ethical reasoning in which ethically correct behavior is not related to any absolute ethical or moral values but to an evaluation of the consequences of a given action on those who will be affected by it. In utilitarian reasoning, a "good" decision is one that results in the greatest good for the greatest number of people affected by the decision.

V

Venture capital Funds that are invested in, or that are available for investment in, a new business enterprise.

Venture capitalist A person or entity that seeks out promising entrepreneurial ventures and funds them in exchange for equity stakes.

Venue The geographical district in which an action is tried and from which the jury is selected.

Verdict A formal decision made by a jury.

Vertical merger The acquisition by a company at one stage of production of a company at a higher or lower stage of production (such as its supplier or retailer).

Vertical restraint Any restraint on trade created by agreements between firms at different levels in the manufacturing and distribution process.

Vertically integrated firm A firm that carries out two or more functional phases (such as manufacture, distribution, and retailing) of a product.

Vesting The creation of an absolute or unconditional right or power. A pension plan becomes vested when an employee has a legal right to the benefits provided.

Voir dire Old French verbs meaning "to speak the truth." In jury trials, the phrase refers to the process in which the attorneys question prospective jurors to determine whether they are biased or have any connection with a party to the action or with a prospective witness.

W

Warranty An assurance by one party of the existence of a fact on which the other party can rely.

Wetlands Areas of land designated by government agencies (such as the Army Corps of Engineers or the Environmental Protection Agency) as protected areas that support wildlife and that therefore cannot be filled in or dredged by private contractors or parties.

White-collar crime Nonviolent crime committed by individuals or corporations to obtain a personal or business advantage.

Workers' compensation laws State statutes establishing an administrative procedure for compensating workers' injuries that arise out of—or in the course of—their employment, regardless of fault.

Writ of *certiorari* A writ from a higher court asking the lower court for the record of a case.

TABLE OF CASES

E

F

G

H

I

J

K

L

M

N

O

P

Q

R

S

T

U

V

W

Y

Z

INDEX

A

C

D

E

F

J

K

L

N

O

P

T

U

V

W

Z

CHAPTER-ENDING PEDAGOGY

- **Key Terms**
- **For Review**
- **Questions and Case Problems**
  Case Problem with Sample Answer
  In Your Court
  A Question of Ethics and Social Responsibility
  For Critical Analysis
- **Law on the Web**
  Legal Research Exercises on the Web
  Before the Test
  Westlaw® Campus

UNIT-ENDING PEDAGOGY